Ming Ch
Courts a
1400–145

Edited by
Craig Clunas,
Jessica Harrison-Hall
and Luk Yu-ping

The British Museum

Part 3: Objects, Images and Sites of Belief

13. The New Idea of Ritual Vessels in the Early Ming Dynasty: A Third System? 113
Shih Ching-fei

14. Gifts of Good Fortune and Praise-Songs for Peace: Images of Auspicious Portents and Panegyrics from the Yongle Period 122
Lina Lin

15. Enshrining the Dark Troops: The Printing of Daoist Books in the Early Ming Dynasty 134
Maggie Chui Ki Wan

16. Faces of Transnational Buddhism at the Early Ming Court 143
Marsha Haufler

17. The Early Ming Imperial Atelier on the Tibetan Frontier 152
Karl Debreczeny

18. Religious Consciousness and Beliefs in the Ming Tombs of Princes and Royal Family Members in Hubei Province 163
Yuan Wenqing

Part 4: Rules, Regulations and Material Culture

19. Paper Money of the Ming Dynasty: Examining the Material Evidence 170
Caroline R. Cartwright, Christina M. Duffy and Helen Wang

20. The Porcelain Pagoda: A Persisting Enigma 178
Clarence Eng

21. Architecture of the Early Ming Court: A Preliminary Look 189
Aurelia Campbell

22. Investigating Zheng He's Ships: What is Known and Knowable? 197
Sally K. Church

Part 5: Global Ming

23. 'Trees and Stones Are Only What They Are': Translating Ming Empire in the Fifteenth Century 206
Carla Nappi

24. Building Cultural Authority in Early Joseon Korea (1400–1450) 211
Lee Soomi

25. The *Book of the Five Relationships*: Thoughts on Mid-Fifteenth-Century Court Confucianism 219
Sarah Schneewind

26. Looking East, Looking West: The Artistic Connections of Ming China and Timurid Iran 228
Priscilla Soucek

27. Precious Stones and Ming Culture, 1400–1450 236
Craig Clunas

28. Ming Ceramics Discovered in Kenya and Some Related Issues 245
Qin Dashu

29. Traces of the Zheng He Voyages in Late Ming Navigational Materials 253
Timothy Brook

Bibliography 260

Contributors 280

Illustration Credits 284

Index 288

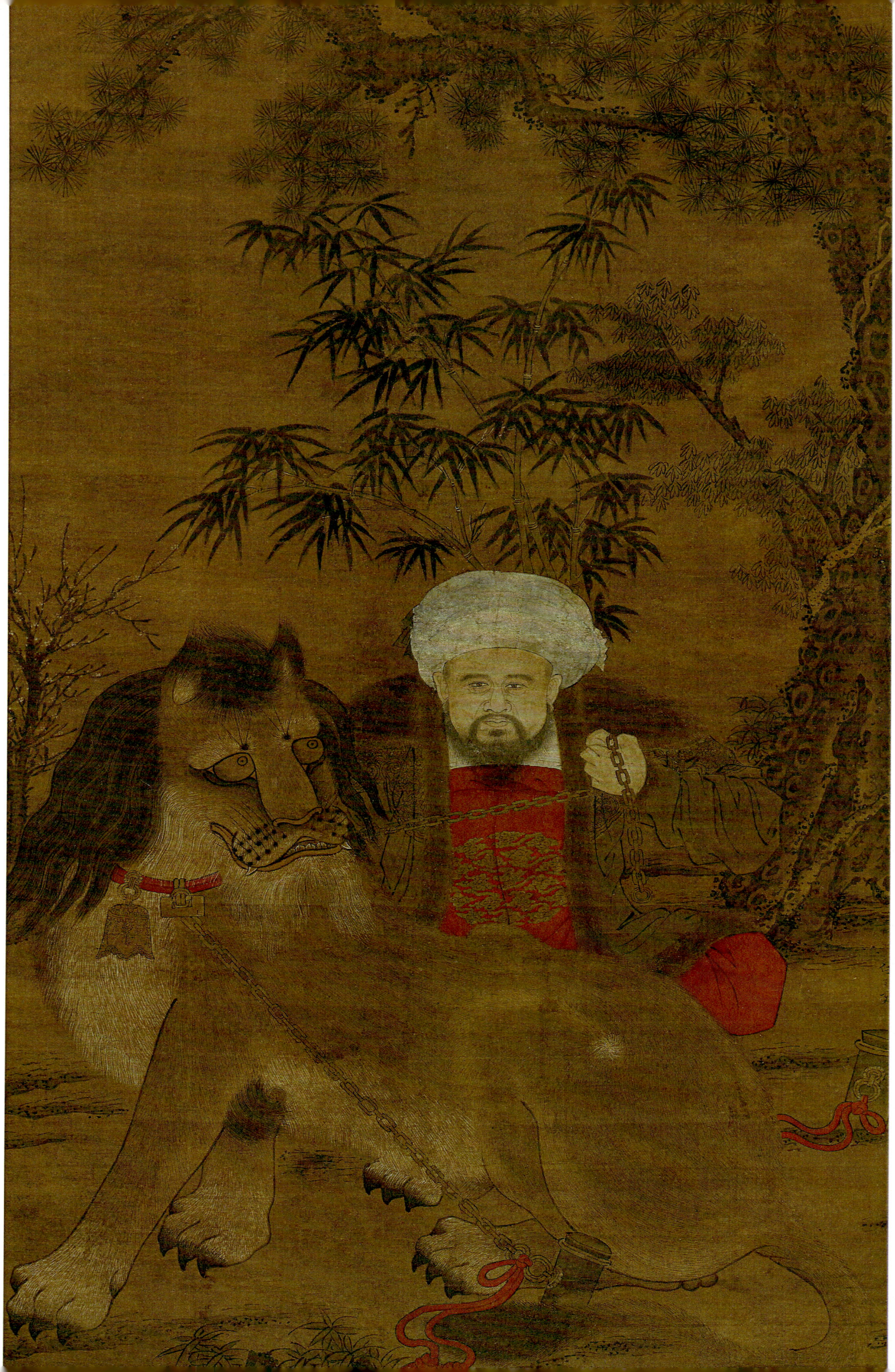

Acknowledgements

The editors would first like to thank the Arts and Humanities Research Council (AHRC) of Great Britain for supporting the research project into early Ming courts and their global connections which was the starting point for this volume. Their support has not only enabled us to work together, but to bring together this august group of scholars of Ming China's culture and history. The AHRC has also supported the project by making a film promoting the BP exhibition *Ming: 50 years that changed China*, publicising the research at other conferences and on their website and using it as an example of bringing together an international team of museum professionals, academics and researchers. The generous sponsorship of the James P. Geiss Foundation, Sir Percival David Foundation, the John Fell Fund, Giuseppe Eskenazi and Xining Group is equally reflected in the quality of production of this volume.

Grateful thanks are due to Wenyuan Xin who has worked so hard on the picture research for the 350 images in this volume, and who has been thoroughly involved with the production of this book from its inception to realisation. Her accurate credit lines may be relied on for a whole generation of researchers to come. Nina Shandloff and Sarah Faulks are to be thanked for the sensitive copyediting, design and production of the essays. Maps were made by Paul Goodhead and Craig Williams.

We would like to thank our three peer reviewers, Professor Shane McCausland, Professor Anne Gerritsen and Dr Elizabeth Lambourn. Their comments produced many useful insights into the texts and raised new questions for all the authors.

There are many people at the Museum to thank, and we are grateful to everyone involved, especially Jonathan Ould for the 3D design and Paul Goodhead for the graphic design of the exhibition.

Jessica Harrison-Hall would particularly like to thank the team that keeps all of these projects afloat, especially Martin Keady and Helen Valuks.

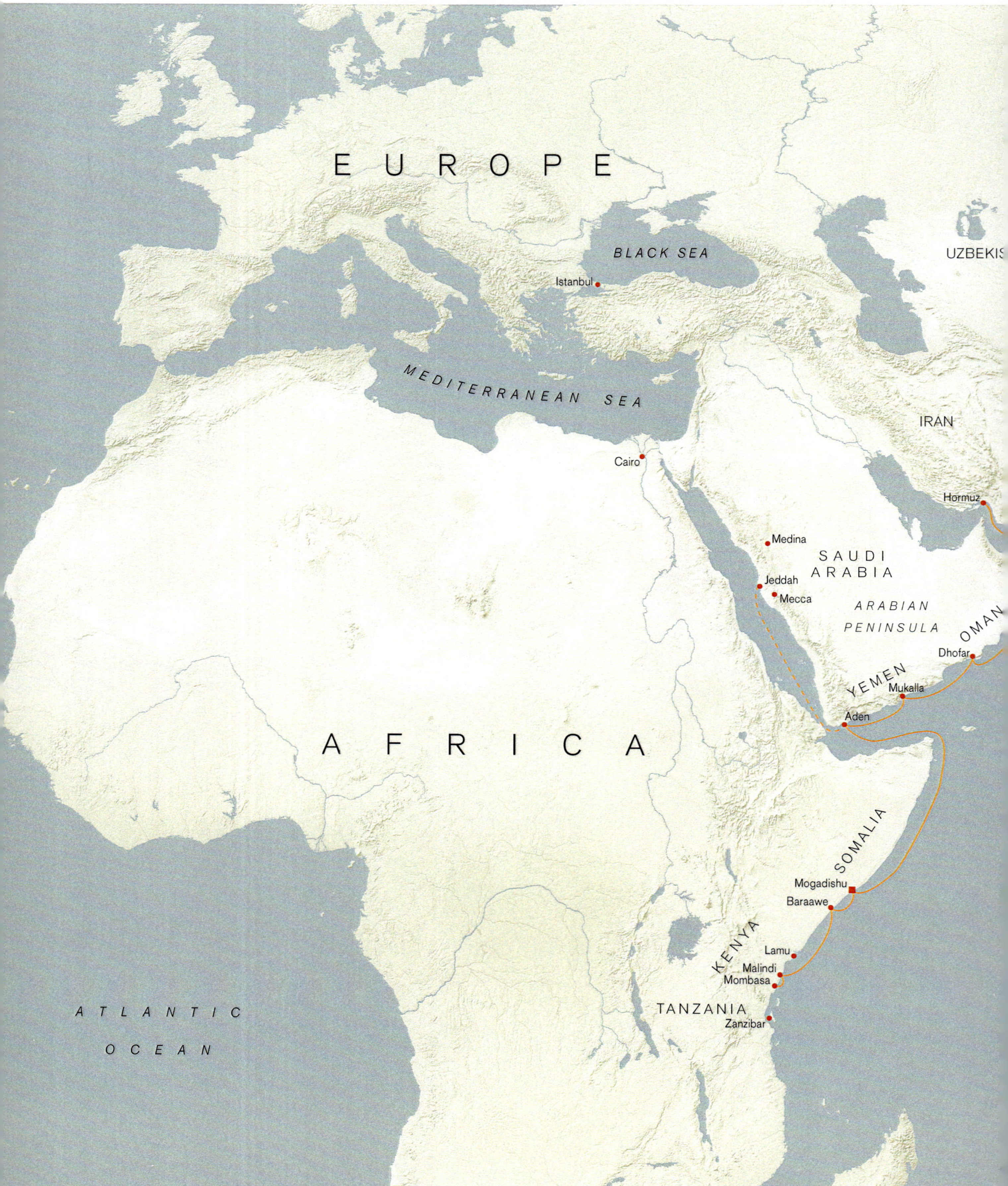
EUROPE
BLACK SEA
UZBEKIS
Istanbul
MEDITERRANEAN SEA
IRAN
Cairo
Hormuz
Medina
SAUDI ARABIA
Jeddah
Mecca
ARABIAN PENINSULA
OMAN
Dhofar
YEMEN
Mukalla
Aden
AFRICA
SOMALIA
Mogadishu
Baraawe
KENYA
Lamu
Malindi
Mombasa
TANZANIA
Zanzibar
ATLANTIC OCEAN

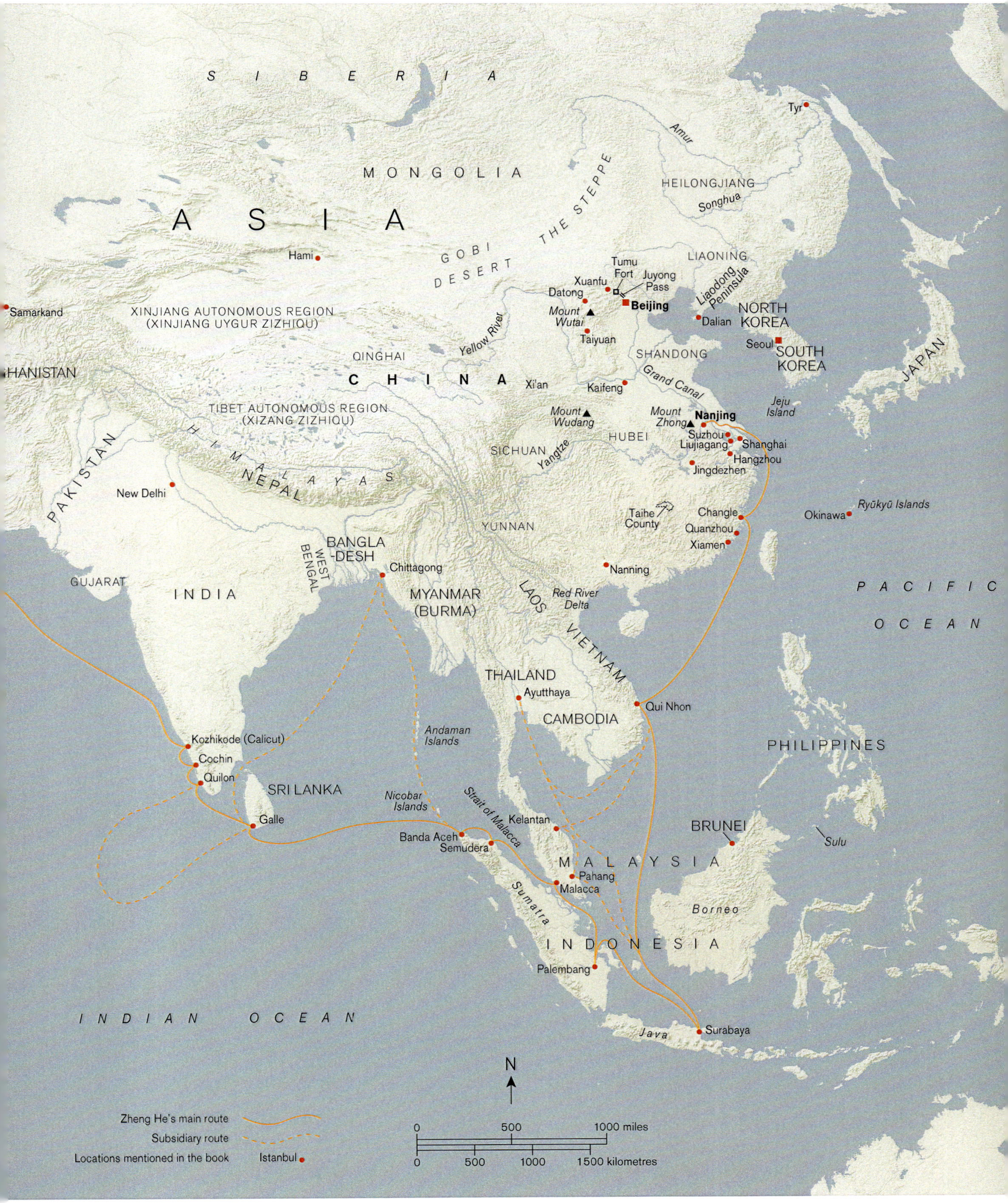
SIBERIA
MONGOLIA
ASIA
Hami
GOBI DESERT
THE STEPPE
Amur
HEILONGJIANG
Songhua
Tyr
LIAONING
Tumu Fort
Juyong Pass
Xuanfu
Datong
Beijing
Liaodong Peninsula
NORTH KOREA
Dalian
Samarkand
XINJIANG AUTONOMOUS REGION (XINJIANG UYGUR ZIZHIQU)
Mount Wutai
Taiyuan
Yellow River
Seoul
SOUTH KOREA
JAPAN
QINGHAI
SHANDONG
HANISTAN
CHINA
Xi'an
Kaifeng
Grand Canal
TIBET AUTONOMOUS REGION (XIZANG ZIZHIQU)
Mount Wudang
Mount Zhong
Nanjing
Jeju Island
HIMALAYAS
SICHUAN
HUBEI
Suzhou
Liujiagang
Shanghai
Hangzhou
Jingdezhen
PAKISTAN
Yangtze
New Delhi
NEPAL
Taihe County
Changle
Okinawa
Ryūkyū Islands
Quanzhou
Xiamen
YUNNAN
BANGLA-DESH
WEST BENGAL
Chittagong
Nanning
GUJARAT
INDIA
MYANMAR (BURMA)
LAOS
Red River Delta
PACIFIC OCEAN
VIETNAM
THAILAND
Ayutthaya
Qui Nhon
CAMBODIA
Andaman Islands
Kozhikode (Calicut)
PHILIPPINES
Cochin
Quilon
SRI LANKA
Nicobar Islands
Strait of Malacca
Kelantan
BRUNEI
Galle
Sulu
Banda Aceh
Semudera
MALAYSIA
Pahang
Malacca
Sumatra
Borneo
INDONESIA
Palembang
INDIAN OCEAN
Java
Surabaya
N
Zheng He's main route
Subsidiary route
Locations mentioned in the book
Istanbul
0 500 1000 miles
0 500 1000 1500 kilometres

CHRONOLOGY OF THE MING DYNASTY

Reign title	Reign period	Family name	Temple name
Hongwu 洪武	1368–98	Zhu Yuanzhang 朱元璋	Taizu 太祖
Jianwen 建文	1399–1402	Zhu Yunwen 朱允炆	Huidi 惠帝
Yongle 永樂	1403–24	Zhu Di 朱棣	Chengzu 成祖 or Taizong 太宗
Hongxi 洪熙	1425	Zhu Gaochi 朱高熾	Renzong 仁宗
Xuande 宣德	1426–35	Zhu Zhanji 朱瞻基	Xuanzong宣宗
Zhengtong 正統	1436–49	Zhu Qizhen 朱祁鎮	Yingzong 英宗
Jingtai 景泰	1450–56	Zhu Qiyu 朱祁鈺	Daizong 代宗
Tianshun 天順	1457–64	Zhu Qizhen	Yingzong 英宗
Chenghua 成化	1465–87	Zhu Jianshen 朱見深	Xianzong 憲宗
Hongzhi 弘治	1488–1505	Zhu Youtang 朱祐樘	Xiaozong 孝宗
Zhengde 正德	1506–21	Zhu Haozhao 朱厚照	Wuzong 武宗
Jiajing 嘉靖	1522–66	Zhu Houcong 朱厚熜	Shizong 世宗
Longqing 隆慶	1567–72	Zhu Zaihou 朱載垕	Muzong 穆宗
Wanli 萬曆	1573–1620	Zhu Yijun 朱翊鈞	Shenzong 神宗
Taichang 泰昌	1620	Zhu Changluo 朱常洛	Guangzong 光宗
Tianqi 天啟	1621–7	Zhu Youxiao 朱由校	Xizong 熹宗
Chongzhen 崇禎	1628–44	Zhu Youjian 朱由檢	Sizong 思宗

Introduction

Craig Clunas

The exhibition held at the British Museum from 18 September 2014 to 5 January 2015, and entitled *Ming: 50 years that changed China*, had as one of its central aims that of bringing before a wide public some elements of the recent revolution in scholarly perception of the early Ming dynasty (1368–1644). This has moved away from the tendency in older scholarship of viewing the period essentially as a nativist reaction to the Mongol conquest and the years of Yuan rule, and one which saw China pulling down the shutters on the outside world, in a 'turning away from the outside world [which] was accompanied by a growing introspection within Chinese life'.[1] Although the emerging new paradigm still requires further work (which this volume is a contribution to), many scholars now see the early Ming as a distinctive example among a group of states across Eurasia which descended from the era of Chinggis Khan, with its courtly culture in particular captured by the cosmopolitan glamour of Mongol styles of rulership. Almost all now see it as an age of unprecedented engagement, in both peaceful and violent forms, with the world beyond the borders of the Ming empire, the first period when (as in the Tang dynasty), Chinese power was projected deep into Central Asia, while at the same time (as in the Song dynasty) the possibilities of a maritime hegemony were also explored.

The conference which was held at the British Museum on 9–11 October 2014 under the title 'Ming: courts and contacts 1400–1450', sought in its turn to bring together a body of scholars working on the period from a range of disciplinary perspectives, to examine in particular the ways in which the material culture, visual culture and art of the (loosely defined) half century from around 1400 to around 1450 might help in advancing an understanding of the changes taking place in China at this time. The period chosen for investigation here requires a degree of justification. At one point in the study of Chinese history, both in China and beyond its borders, the prestige of the long historiographical tradition of taking the dynasty as a unit of analysis led to a 'history of the Ming' (or at most the early Ming, mid-Ming, late Ming) seeming like a natural, indeed an inevitable task. It was possible to write histories of more than one dynasty, and while earlier scholarship preferred Ming–Qing (1368–1911) as a unit, the most recent account by the Western doyen of Ming historians prefers to take Yuan–Ming (1271–1644) as its framework, perhaps thus implicitly endorsing the view of the continuities between Yuan and Ming as being at least as important as the many ruptures.[2] More recently too scholars have been willing to disregard dynastic boundaries in constructing frameworks of analysis; so for example Paul Jakov Smith and Richard von Glahn have assembled a body of studies on the period 1300–1550 (one they describe as 'a historiographical black hole'), with a view to understanding what they term the 'Song–Yuan–Ming transition' as a whole.[3] It seems evident that we need both these large-scale accounts *and* the more focused look at a briefer period presented by this volume and the research project/exhibition which it accompanied, if we are to deepen understanding of China's history beyond the large generalisations which were deemed sufficient in the past.

The decision to build the exhibition (and so by extension this volume of essays) around the reigns of the Yongle,

Hongxi, Xuande and Zhengtong emperors, covering the years from 1403 to 1449, was based on the argument that these initial and terminal years represent important turning points in China's history, and that the years between them have a distinctive character. In the first turning point, the Yongle emperor overthrew his nephew following a major war, and began the ultimately decisive process of moving the political (if not the economic) centre of gravity of the realm back to his own power base in the north. Described at the time as a 'second founding' of the Ming dynasty, the relocation of the capital accompanied a forward military policy in the steppe, which paralleled the famous voyages of Zheng He discussed in several chapters in this volume (see Chapters 2–3, 12, 20, 22, 26–9). In the latter year of 1449, the disastrous military adventure of Tumu, with the imperial person lost to the Mongols as a helpless captive, marked an era in which the 'residual interpenetration of China and the steppe came to an end', and served as a 'symbolic terminus for the transitional era that began in 1127 with the Jurchen conquest of North China'.[4]

The exhibition *Ming: 50 years that changed China*, and even more perhaps this volume of essays, took very seriously the importance of 'integrative' or 'connective' history, through which more and more historians have seen the period 1500–1800 (whether it is classified as 'early modern' or not), as one of parallel developments without a single point of origin occurring in different parts of the globe.[5] These 'connective' developments of course themselves have a history which in some aspects goes back beyond the centuries 1500–1800, as many writers here demonstrate. The historian Janet Abu-Lughod some 25 years ago saw 1250–1350 as the century in which a 'world system' came into being, although whether it went out of existence with the end of Mongol hegemony is something explicitly challenged by many contributors in this volume, as well as by others.[6] Thus the huge spike in the price of pepper on European markets between 1410 and 1414 (which for instance saw the price of pepper in England increase eightfold from 1410 to 1411), has recently been attributed by economic historians to the huge amounts of the South Indian spice purchased (or extorted) by the fleets of the Ming admiral Zheng He at precisely this time. It has been argued that: 'Thus, any impact of Zheng He in deflecting pepper and other spices away from the Levant and Europe would have taken place mainly between 1411 and 1422. It is only a correlation, of course, but this exogenous Asian supply-side shock seems to offer the most likely explanations for the European pepper price spike in the early fifteenth century'.[7]

The idea of parallel developments happening in different parts of the globe at the same time also has itself a long history, ranging back well before the modern era. The reign of the Yongle emperor (1403–24) was explicitly set up as a parallel to the Italian Renaissance as long ago as the second half of the 18th century, when the Anglo-Irish novelist, playwright and poet Oliver Goldsmith (1728–74) in his tract, *The Citizen of the World,* wrote:

> In succeeding ages Confucius and Pythagoras seem born nearly together, and a train of philosophers then sprung up as well in Greece as in China. The period of renewed barbarity began to have a universal spread much about the same time, and continued for several centuries, till, in the years of the Christian era 1400, the Emperor Yonglo [sic.] arose to revive the learning of the East; while about the same time the Medicean family laboured to raise infant genius from the cradle. Thus we see politeness spreading over every part of the world in one age, and barbarity succeeding in another; at one period a blaze of light diffusing itself over the whole world, and at another all mankind wrapped up in the profoundest ignorance.[8]

While there might be no doubt that the Yongle emperor certainly saw himself and his reign as 'a blaze of light diffusing itself over the whole world', he might have been less willing to share the honours with a family of Italian bankers. More recently the work of the late Jack Goody, in his volume *Renaissances: The One or the Many*, draws on Arnold Toynbee's 1954 *Study of History* in preferring to see the Song period (960–1279) as 'China's Renaissance'.[9] Building on the idea that a rebirth of an ancient culture is a recurring phenomenon in human history, Goody nevertheless might be criticised for working with a very old-fashioned notion of 'Renaissance' (developed in the 19th century by Jacob Burckhardt, and seen as characterised above all by the rise of secularism and individualism), which is now considered problematical by scholars working on this era of Europe's past. And parallelisms which see one local phenomenon replicated in another place, surely do more to reinforce than to challenge the view of some local histories (in this case that of Europe) as being the global norm (the same argument has been made in regard to the term 'early modern').

However equally powerful to those analyses which see parallels in historical developments, are those which assert the *Sonderweg*, the 'special way', of China's history. One of the most recent and most forceful statements of this position was made on 14 October 2014, coincidentally during the course of the British Museum Ming exhibition, by China's President Xi Jinping, who said in a widely reported speech:

> Several thousand years ago, the Chinese nation trod a path that was different from other nations' culture and development…It is not a coincidence that we started up 'socialism with Chinese characteristics'. It was decided by our country's historical inheritance and cultural traditions…History is created by the people and so is civilisation. We should be more respectful and mindful of 5,000 years of continuous Chinese culture.[10]

Arguably Xi Jinping's claim of China's 'different path' is itself an artefact of a common path which led in the 19th century to the creation of the idea of nations and of cultures as bounded entities, in opposition to Goldsmith's Enlightenment era notion of a universal 'politeness'. It is worth considering the extent to which comparative histories, if soundly based on a firm footing of specialist studies, can help us to look not only at connections and contacts between polities, but at the similarities and differences which both link and separate them.[11]

Comparative history will be both conceptually and empirically weak if it restricts itself to the search for laudable traits in one part of the globe, which are then identified as existing (and usually existing earlier) in another. There are certainly *un*attractive aspects of the history of Europe in the years 1400–50 which appear to be absent in China: the list might be headed by judicial murder on account of religious beliefs, and the initiation of a large-scale, long-distance coercive and racialised trade in slaves. This should not necessarily be read as meaning that early Ming China was therefore a nicer or a more civilised place (as a number of chapters in this volume show in graphic detail).

The years from the Yongle to Zhengtong reigns were ones in which China was only beginning to recover from centuries of devastation, centuries in which it has been argued that the years from 1200–1400 see the population decline in every major region of the empire *except* Jiangnan, the delta of the lower Yangtze River.[12] However, it has also been argued that in the very early Ming, and in particular in the reign of its founder, government policies still:

> had a devastating impact on the market towns of the Yangzi Delta. Not until the late fifteenth century did the market towns of the Yangzi Delta, reinvigorated by expanding national markets for cotton and silk textiles, begin to emerge from the torpor into which they had sunk in the early Ming.[13]

In addition to moving the capital of the empire, another of his father's policies which the Yongle emperor immediately reversed was the prohibition on having more than one Buddhist and one Daoist temple in each county, yet many temples never recovered their pre-Ming vitality.[14] Historians continue to hold very differing interpretations of the activist power of the Yuan and early Ming states; were they essentially effective or were they in fact rather feeble apparatuses for the enforcement of imperial policies and will?[15] 'Heaven is high and the emperor far away', is the still-proverbial piece of folk wisdom cited in one early Ming account of the Yuan dynasty as being essentially a weak government, one which Zhu Yuanzhang's activist goal of a more tightly controlled society was designed to replace. But it has been argued that in the decades following the reign of the Ming founder, 'succession crises and princely usurpations quickly drained the luster from imperial authority'.[16] There is much further work to be done to ascertain the degree to which this interpretation is in fact correct, given that the 'lustre of imperial authority' is the central concern of so many of the written sources on which we must depend. The material culture, with its ability to indicate lines of enquiry independent of the textual record, has great possibilities here.

This then is the background against which it is necessary to examine both early Ming connected histories, and shared histories, which are not exactly the same thing. The rubric of connected histories, as well as accounting for the many examples covered in this book, might also explain one piece of evidence of a continued inflow of Islamic intellectual and technical ideas after the fall of the Yuan. In 1450 the mathematician Wu Jing 吳敬 from Hangzhou published his 'Complete Book on the Classification of the Mathematical Arts in Nine Sections' (*Jiu zhang xiang zhu suan fa bi lei da quan* 九章詳注算法比類大全). This contains the first known description in Chinese of lattice (or 'gelosia') multiplication, in which a grid is used to multiply two multi-digit numbers; Wu calls this novel technique *xie suan* 寫算, 'written arithmetic'.[17] This technique, like so many mathematical ideas, was developed in the Arab world, where its earliest documented use is by the Moroccan writer Ibn al-Bannā' in the late 13th century.[18] It was in Europe by about 1300, but is not attested in China until Wu Jing's volume of 1450. This would seem to indicate that it was not just lions, fine stallions and courtly trinkets which made their way from the Islamicate world to China in the early Ming, and here we might want to think further about the actual mechanisms of connectedness, through such poorly documented activities as the involvement of Ming subjects in the Hajj pilgrimage, and any periods of study they may have undertaken in the learned institutions of the Arab and Persian-speaking worlds.

Consideration of shared rather than connected histories would require attention to the shared ecological history across Eurasia at the relevant period, an area of scholarship opened up by William Atwell, Mark Elvin and Timothy Brook. This would see the deep recession across Eurasia in the middle of the 15th century, certainly from the late 1440s to mid-1460s, and the extremely cool summers in 1446, 1448 and 1453, coupled with possible volcanic activity, as potential underlying causes of the bullion famine and social unrest which affected not only the Ming but a number of other states as well.[19] Major rebellion which convulsed large parts of Fujian, Jiangxi and Zhejiang provinces in the years 1448–9 certainly originated with silver miners, always at the abject base of the Ming social heap. The recent monumental work of Geoffrey Parker has reinvigorated debate about a global 17th-century crisis by focusing on environmental factors which were no respecter of political or cultural boundaries.[20] While the documentation for the 15th century may not be sufficiently fine grained to allow an account of this complexity, it is certain that any future accounts of large-scale historical movements in Eurasia will omit this aspect of the planet's history only at the cost of reduced effectiveness and a loss of analytical force.

This present volume does not seek to present a totally comprehensive account of all facets of early Ming culture, and there are many aspects of the period that require further study. The growing field of environmental history just referred to will no doubt continue to want to examine early Ming landscape management practices, for example at the major drainage project completed in 1403 which, by taking water from the Wusong river into the Yangtze, coped with the fluctuating level of Lake Tai and thus 'reduced the incidence of floods in the region'.[21] Major figures of the dynasty like Xia Yuanji (1366–1430) worked on such water-control projects, which absorbed huge amounts of state revenue, but have been little studied by comparison with the more glamorous voyages of Zheng He, or diplomatic contacts with Timurid West Asia. In casting aside an older model of an isolated and hermetic Ming dynasty, it is important that we do not overcompensate by coming to see *only* those parts of its history which are 'connected', as being worthy of intensive study.

Even within histories of connections, this one volume, standing as the record of a single scholarly gathering, cannot attain comprehensiveness. The broad themes under which the 29 chapters are organised – 'Rulership and war', 'Sites, images and objects of power', 'Objects, images and sites of belief', 'Rules, regulations and material culture', and 'Global Ming' – are to be read here as neither mutually exclusive, nor as attaining coverage of all facets of the theme. The all-important visual and material practice of calligraphy is

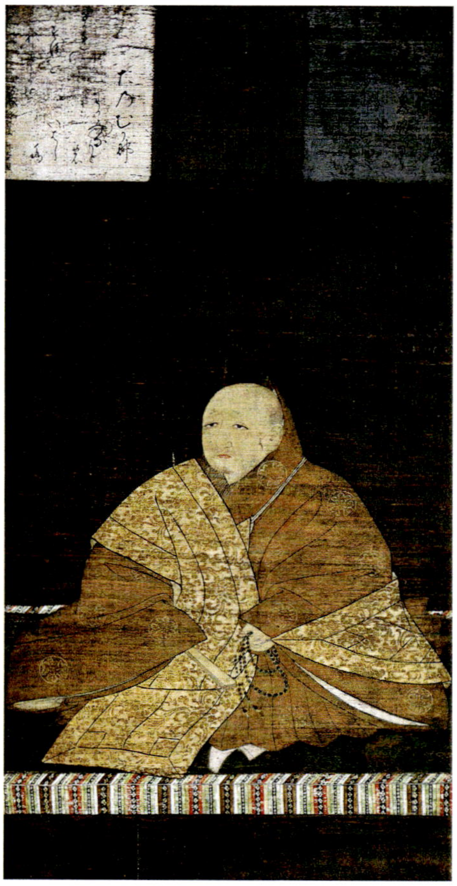

Plate 0.1 Anonymous, *Portrait of Ashikaga Yoshimitsu*, early 15th century. Colours on silk, height 80.5cm, width 39.5cm. Roku'on-ji Temple, Kyoto

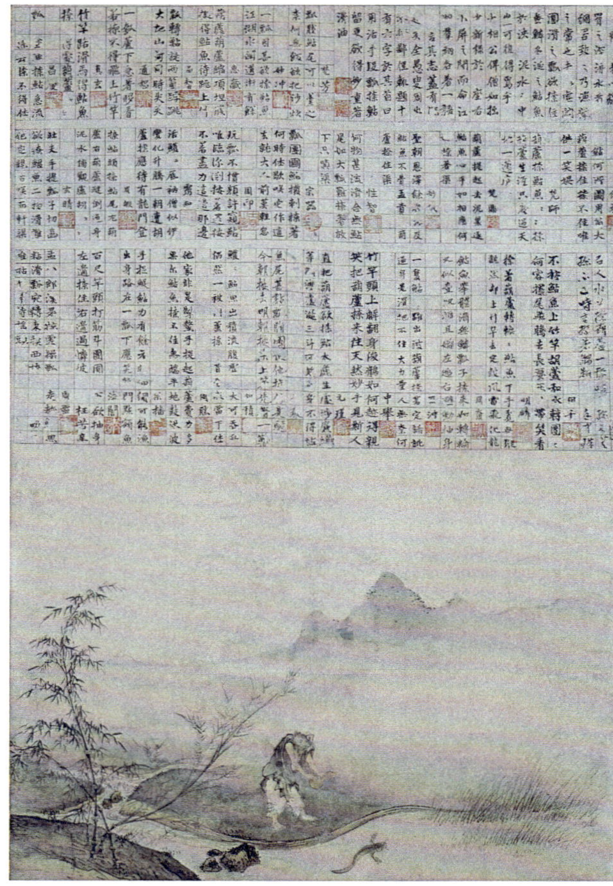

Plate 0.2 Josetsu 如拙, *Gourd and Catfish* (*Hyōnen zu* 瓢鮎図), c. 1413. Ink on paper, height 111.5cm, width 75.8cm. Taizo-in, Kyoto

unfortunately (as so often in Anglophone scholarship) given no sustained treatment here. It is also regretted that it has not been possible to include more work here on the important ties of culture, commerce and conflict which, as with Korea, bound early Ming China to its near neighbour, Japan. A paper entitled 'Sino-Japanese ink: Ashikaga envoys to the Ming and Muromachi ink painters' by Yukio Lippit of Harvard University was presented at the conference, but it has not in the end been possible to include this important contribution here. However, its absence is at least partially compensated for by the illustration of several of the key works of the period most telling of the cultural relations between Ming China and Japan in the early 15th century. The paper dealt with the increase in the sophistication of Japanese picture-making after about 1400, based on the shift towards direct patronage of monk-painters by the Ashikaga shoguns (**Pl. 0.1**), whose rich collections of Ming and pre-Ming Chinese works provided the inspiration for new directions in Japanese ink painting. *Gourd and Catfish* (**Pl. 0.2**), painted around 1413 by Josetsu 如拙 (fl. early 1400s–early 15th century), was shown to be explicitly described as being in this 'new manner', and it was demonstrated how it is possible to trace direct appropriation from specific Chinese treasures in the shogunal holdings in later 15th-century Japanese works like *Scholar Viewing a Waterfall* (**Pl. 0.3**) by Shingei Gei'ami 真芸芸阿弥 (1431–85) or *Mountain and River* (**Pl. 0.4**) by Kenkō Shōkei 賢江祥啓 (active *c.* 1478–after 1523). It was the subsequent prestige of another monk-painter (**Pl. 0.5**), the great Sesshū Tōyō 雪舟等楊 (1420–1506), prestige which was partly based on his own travels to Ming China itself, which made the 15th-century moment of Chinese-Japanese pictorial interaction so decisive in the history of Japanese art (**Pls 0.6–0.7**).

The essays which do appear here are designed to stand alone (hence a certain amount of repetition has been left in place), but also cumulatively to open up a number of areas of current work in the period, with the inevitable result that the gaps in our present understanding only become more visible. Although contiguous chapters may deal with cognate themes, such as the Ming intervention in Southeast Asia, the important exchange of images and ideas between the Ming and Joseon Korea, or the imperial patronage of religious institutions, the reader is above all invited to choose for themselves which themes speak most eloquently to them.

Other directions for future research might also be noted in passing. A number of contributors to this volume treat the theme of eunuch agency and eunuch patronage, and the role of eunuchs in both the politics and the culture of the early Ming is certainly ripe for a comprehensive reassessment, moving beyond the moralistic discourses which see them as the natural enemies of 'literati' officials.[22] Greater weight needs to be given in future to the evidence of cordial relations between these two bodies of imperial servants, as when the high official Wang Zhi 王直 (1379–1462), one of the scholarly participants in the *Elegant Gathering in the Apricot Garden* (on which see Chapter 11 in this volume), provided in

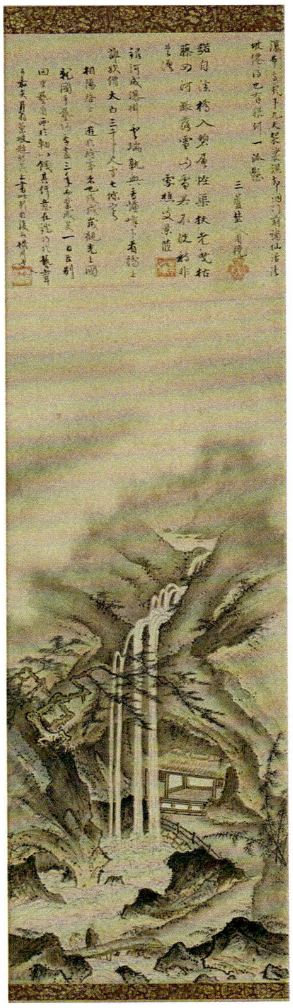

Plate 0.3 Shingei Gei'ami 真芸芸阿弥, *Scholar Viewing a Waterfall*, 15th century. Hanging scroll, ink and colour on paper, height 106cm, width 30.3cm. Nezu Museum, Tokyo

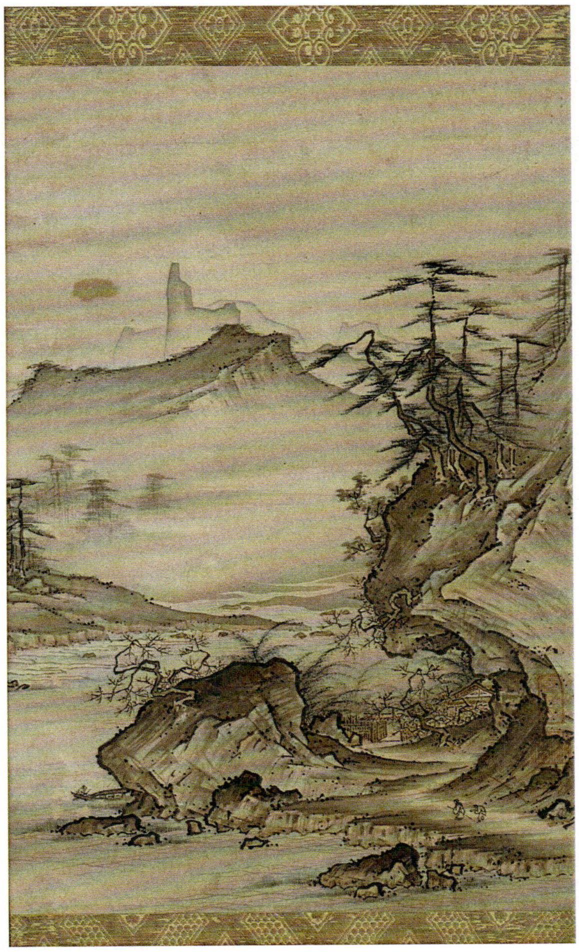

Plate 0.4 Kenkō Shōkei 賢江祥啓, *Mountain and River*, 15th–16th century. Ink and light colour on paper, height 51cm, width 33.5cm. Nezu Museum, Tokyo

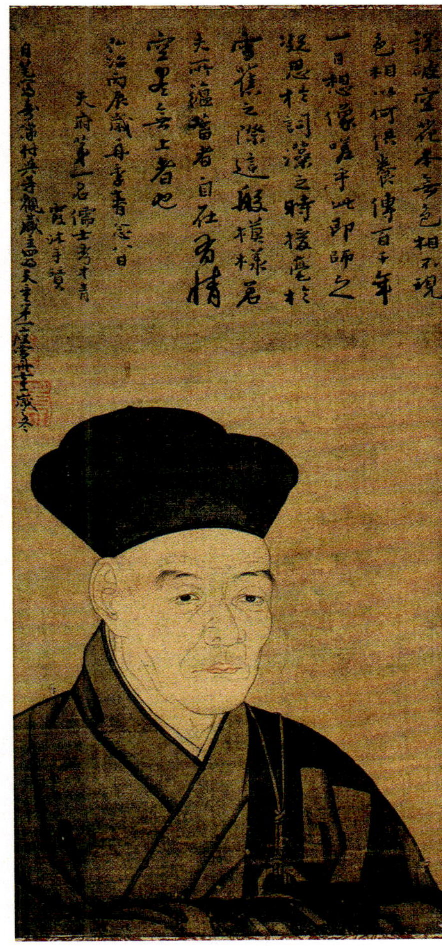

Plate 0.5 Anonymous, copy of 1491 self-portrait of Sesshū Tōyō 雪舟等楊, 16th century. Hanging scroll, ink and colour on paper, height 59.4cm, width 28.5cm. Fujita Art Museum, Osaka

1443 the text celebrating the construction of the Fahai si, the lavish Buddhist burial temple erected in the outskirts of Beijing by the high eunuch Li Tong 李童 (*c.* 1390–1453).[23] Like so many of the highest officials of the Yongle, Xuande and Zhengtong reigns, Li Tong was from the province of Jiangxi, and this association may well have trumped the schematic hostility between 'inner' and 'outer' courts which has so entranced many later historians. Here again a more comparative history might help to move beyond unwarranted perceptions of Chinese exceptionalism, since eunuchs were a common feature of a number of Eurasian courts of the period, and a less judgemental approach to their abject status can be shown to be a product of deeper understanding of their various roles.[24]

Despite the best efforts of its curators, the exhibition *Ming: 50 years that changed China* failed through the lack of surviving material evidence to reflect adequately the lives of the vast majority of China's population in the early Ming (as at any premodern period): its peasantry. Their tools, their clothes, their homes, all are materially lost to us, even if their appearance in images such as the painting sets showing the 'Water and Land' ritual (see **Pl. 6.20**) give some information concerning the clothing and equipment of carpenters, actors and performers, foot soldiers etc. Yet this was a period of momentous change for 'the people' too, as new forms of fertiliser made possible 'the start of a new era in Jiangnan rice cultivation' in the early Ming; this was mainly due to the development of new fertilising techniques, and the coming into use of oil cake fertilisers (bean cakes, cottonseed cakes, rapeseed cakes), described by one specialist as 'one of the most significant innovations in pre-modern Chinese agricultural history'.[25] Other aspects of everyday life not treated here include changes in the status of women, where the period saw on the one hand the abolition of the practice of aristocratic widow-suicide (forced or otherwise), but on the other changes to women's property rights which were to prevail to the end of the imperial system and beyond. Although Ming law was consciously based on Tang codes, it followed Yuan precedent (a novelty in the Chinese context) in inheritance law, which largely cut women out of earlier rights to inherit property from male relatives, and thus reduced their economic independence.[26]

Given the focus of this volume on courts, there is arguably too little attention paid here to literature, particularly given the perception of the courts of premodern rulers which, in many contexts around the globe, have served as the incubators of 'literary newness', of new forms and new genres of writing as well as of new uses of

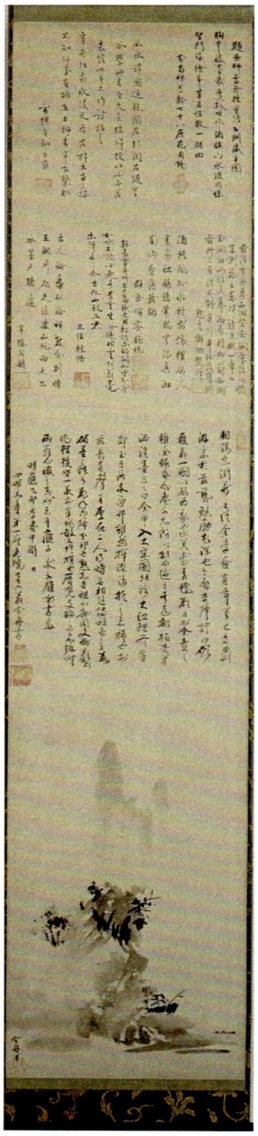

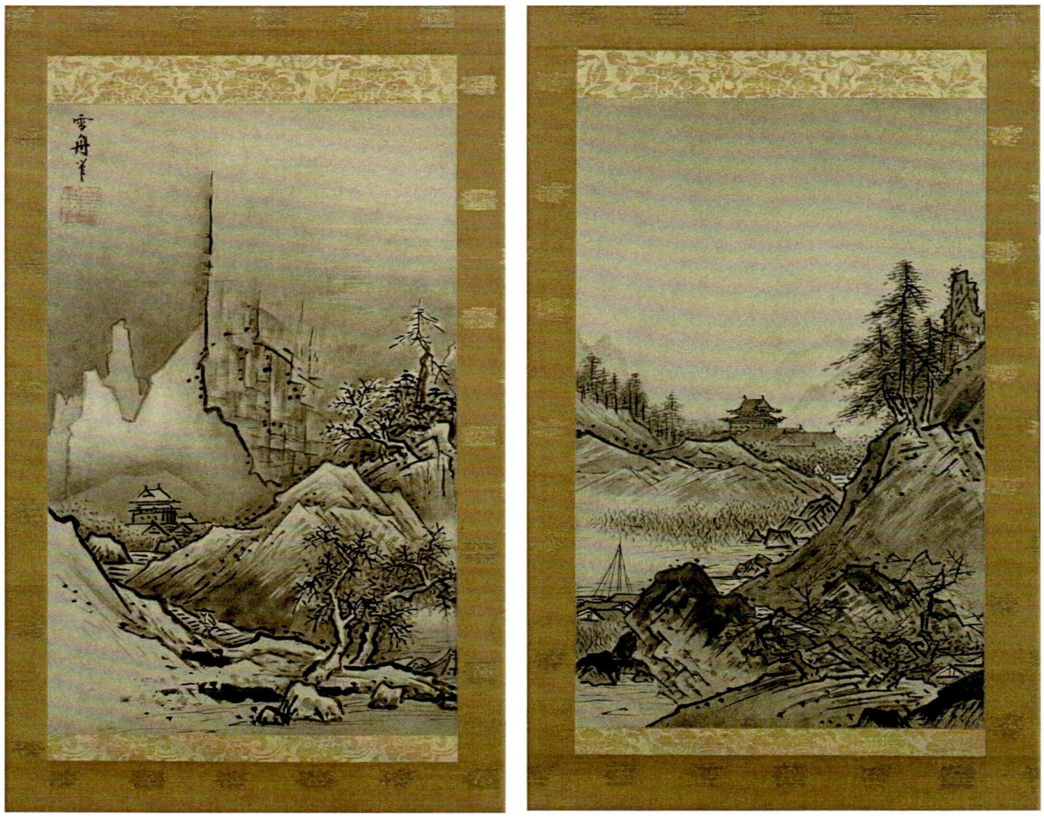

Plate 0.6 (left) Sesshū Tōyō 雪舟等楊, splashed-ink style landscape, Muromachi Period, 1495. Hanging scroll, ink on paper, height 148.6cm, width 32.7cm. Tokyo National Museum

Plate 0.7 (above) Sesshū Tōyō 雪舟等楊, *Landscapes of Autumn and Winter*, 15th–16th century. Hanging scrolls, ink on paper, height of each 47.7cm, width of each 30.2cm. Tokyo National Museum

language.[27] Scholars of Chinese literature have in general been disdainful of the period 1400–50, seeing it as one distinguished by a literature (particularly in poetry) devoted to servile fawning on the imperial project. Certainly literature was constrained in a number of ways. A law of Yongle 9 [1411] banned *zaju* 雜劇 dramas which had emperors in lead roles, lest rulers should be presented in a less than flattering light. So sensitive was early Ming court censorship to historical parallels that a number of drama texts were banned, rewritten or amended. In one case it can be demonstrated that the sensitive phrase 'kingly aura' (*wangqi* 王氣), much used in the justificatory propaganda for the Yongle emperor's usurpation of the throne, is written out of one text.[28] And yet, it is almost entirely due to the activities of early Ming editors, some of them of royal birth themselves, that we know anything at all about what the textbooks still call 'Yuan drama', an important part of the new and vernacularly inclined canon of 'Chinese literature' developed since the New Culture movement of the early 20th century. Only a small minority of surviving 'Yuan' dramas actually date from that era, and the earliest printed editions we have are those done by the Ming prince Zhu Youdun (1379–1439), in his collections *Chengzhai yuefu* 誠齋樂府 and *Chengzhai zaju* 誠齋雜劇. These have been described as, 'not only the earliest dramas but also the first *zaju* in which all the elements are presented in complete form'.[29] While it is very unlikely that the court poetry of the era will ever come to achieve comparable esteem, its success in its own terms surely makes it worthy of more serious investigation than it has hitherto received. In particular, the literary cultures of the numerous princely courts have received very little sustained attention to date, and there is surely further work to be done in this area, as we move towards seeing the Ming regional aristocracy as significant cultural and social actors in the vast majority of the empire which lay beyond the Jiangnan heartland of 'literati' culture.

In his afterword for this volume (Chapter 29), Timothy Brook looks at one of the ways in which events of the years between the Yongle and Zhengtong reigns were remembered, half-remembered and sometimes deliberately forgotten, through the rest of the Ming dynasty's course to its drawn-out collapse in the 17th century. And in fact the afterlife of the early Ming would in itself be a significant topic for further investigation, whether it is the ways in which the Zheng He voyages were used in the 'present-day' fiction of the late Ming, or the 'pervasive nostalgia' for the strong hand of the Hongwu and Yongle emperors shared by many intellectuals in the 16th century.[30] The role that the Zheng He voyages have played in modern Chinese understandings has also been enormous, starting perhaps with the 1905 essay by Liang Qichao (1873–1929) on 'Our Motherland's Great Navigator Zheng He' (*Zuguo da hanghaijia Zheng He zhuan* 祖國大航海家鄭和傳), and carrying through to his role as a popular cultural presence in television historical dramas, science fiction and even computer games.[31] If arguably any period of Chinese history saw developments which would benefit from close examination (and surely no era seems eventless to those who live their lives in it) it may well be true that 1403 to 1449 saw 'forty-six years that changed China', even if no public exhibition could be so titled. What those changes were, and how they will continue to play out into the future, are topics which go beyond the scope of the essays assembled here. It is hoped however that this collection goes some way to indicating what we now know, and what lines of enquiry might prove most productive for further study.

Notes

1 The quote is from Fairbank, Reischauer and Craig 1973, 178. For an expression of more recent views see Robinson 2008.
2 Brook 2010.
3 Smith 2003a, 1.
4 Smith 2003b, 73, 85.
5 Von Glahn 2003a, 64.
6 Abu-Lughod 1991.
7 O'Rourke and Williamson, 2009, 663; T'ien Ju-kang, 1981 (discussed by Tansen Sen in Chapter 3 of this volume).
8 Goldsmith 1769, II, 5–6, also cited in Clunas 2008, 8–9.
9 Goody 2010.
10 Didi Kirsten Tatlow 2014, http://sinosphere.blogs.nytimes.com/2014/10/14/xi-jinping-on-exceptionalism-with-chinese-characteristics/?_r=0 [accessed 20 November 2015].
11 For a recent example which includes consideration of the Ming in its framework see Duindam 2016.
12 Smith 2003a, 10.
13 Von Glahn 2003b, 210.
14 Von Glahn 2003b, 209–10.
15 Smith 2003a, 22.
16 Smith 2003b, 97.
17 Ho 1985, 106.
18 Ben Cheneb and Suter 2015.
19 Atwell 2002; Elvin 2004; Brook 2010, 270.
20 Parker 2013.
21 Li Bozhong 2003, 151.
22 A promised forthcoming volume on 'Art, Politics, and Palace Eunuchs in Ming China' by Professor Scarlett Jang of Williams College will be an important contribution to this topic, see http://art.williams.edu/profile/jjang/.
23 Toyka 2014, 108–18.
24 Duindam 2016, 214–18.
25 Li Bozhong 2003, 159.
26 Birge 2003, 220.
27 Pollock 2006, 283.
28 West 2003, 358–60.
29 West 2003, 331, 347.
30 Gregory 2014; Ditmanson 2015, 31.
31 https://en.wikipedia.org/wiki/Zheng_He [accessed 21 November 2015].

Chapter 1
Justifying Ming Rulership on a Eurasian Stage

David M. Robinson

Once upon a time, it was believed that under Ming rule, China had a pronounced xenophobic streak. Such a characterisation grew in part from the early Ming government's effort to limit contact with the outside world through restrictions on private trade and unauthorised travel abroad on the one hand, and a political rhetoric that highlighted a revival of pure Chinese values from antiquity on the other. One suspects that such an image took root because it seemed to confirm long-standing stereotypes about how the Chinese looked upon neighbours near and far as uncouth barbarians. Rather than standing in splendid isolation or smug self-complacency, however, the Ming court actively engaged the peoples and polities of eastern Eurasia. Through moral suasion, military coercion, economic incentives and lavish display, the Ming court sought the obedience and allegiance of its subjects and the cooperation of its neighbours.[1] Neglect of the Ming court's efforts to justify its rulership and to secure allegiance handicaps our understanding of Ming China in a global perspective and obscures the critical point that the Ming resembled other courts and empires in the world at that time, thus unnecessarily perpetuating the enduring myth of Chinese exceptionalism and hindering the incorporation of the Chinese experience into wider historical narratives.

Although they are recurring features of empires and polities, political rhetoric and display must be historicised since they change over time and are highly contingent. The 14th and 15th centuries, the focus of this chapter, were a time of unusual commensurability in Eurasia. During the 13th and 14th centuries, most of Eurasia had come under Mongol rule (**Pl. 1.1**); even polities such as the Mamluk Sultanate centred on Cairo or imperial Japan (to name two examples) that maintained independence through force of arms remained deeply tied to the Mongol empire through

Plate 1.1 Map of 13th-century Mongolian empire in Eurasia

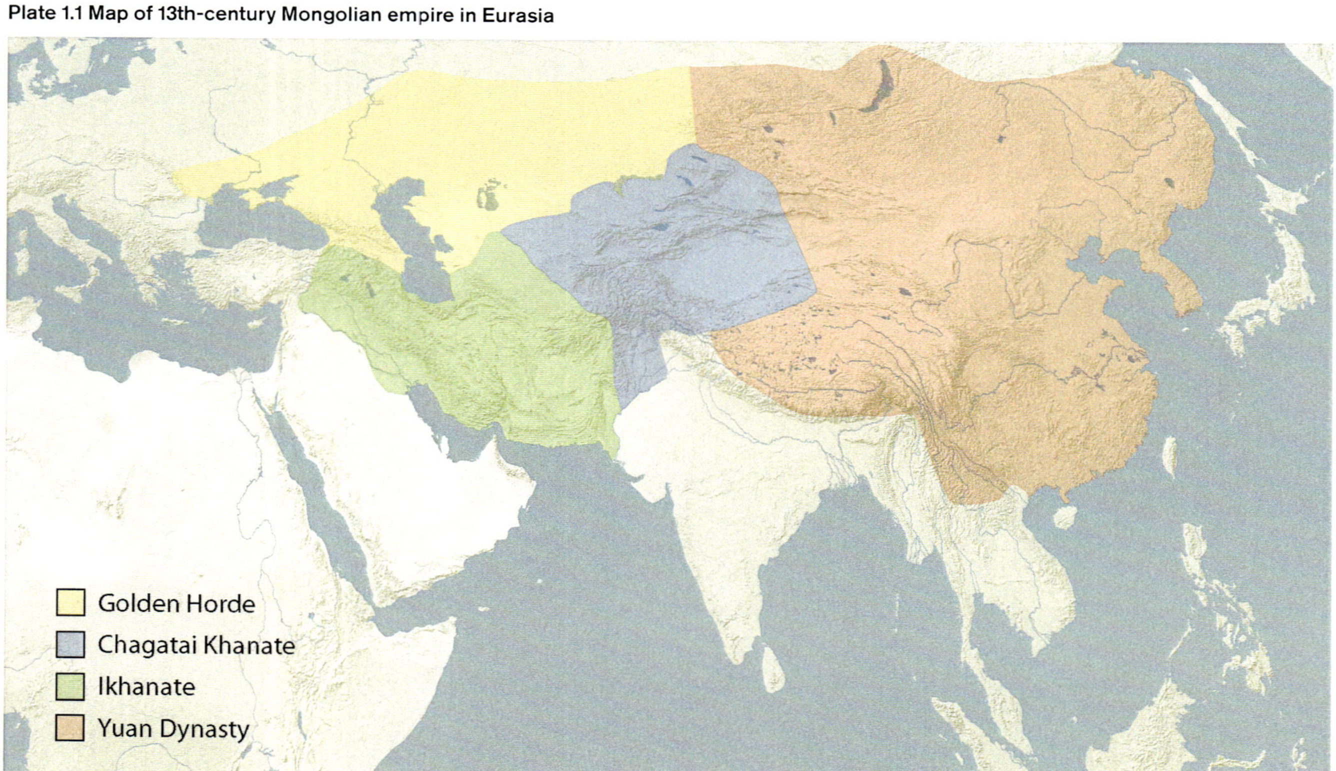

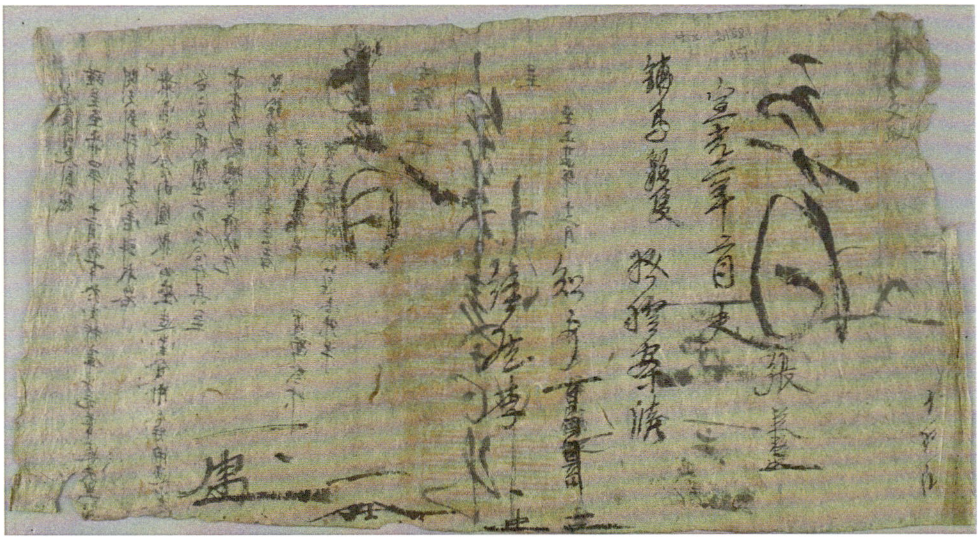

Plate 1.2 Document fragment from Qara-qoto, dated 1372 (second year of Xuanguang reign). Ink and red seal on paper, height 20.9/22.2cm, width 37/40.7cm. The Institute of Oriental Manuscripts, Russian Academy of Sciences, St Petersburg, дx2158V

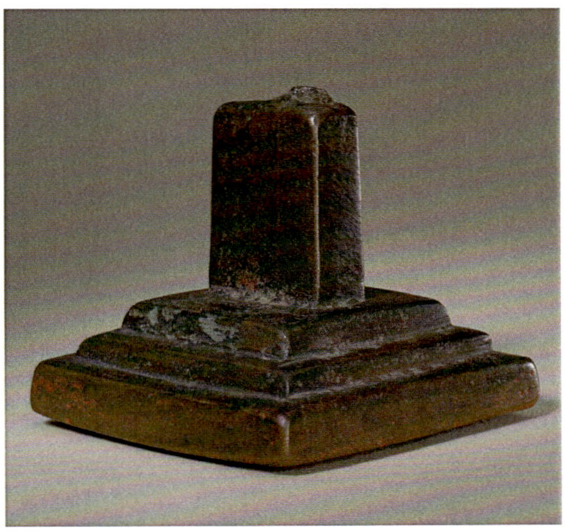

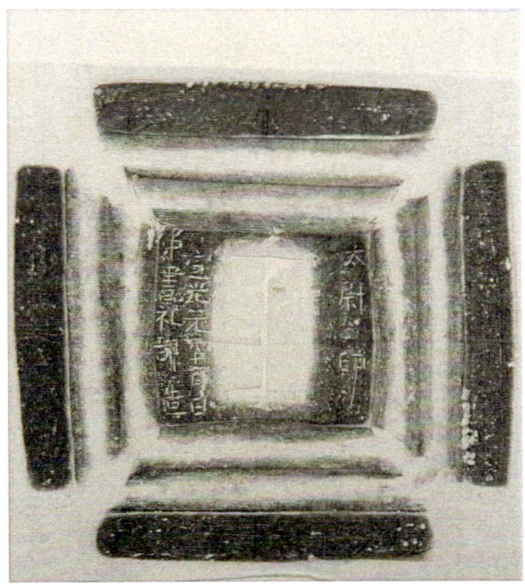

Plate 1.3 Seal with 'Phag-spa inscription, from Qara-qoto, dated 1371 (Xuanguang reign). Inscribed: 'Seal of the Minister of Defence, made by Ministry of Rites. First year of Xuanguan' ('太尉之印。宣光元年十一月 日，中書禮部造'). Bronze, height 9.5cm; depth 5cm. The Palace Museum, Beijing

diplomacy, trade and/or religion.[2] As Chinggisid power collapsed over the course of the 14th and 15th centuries, courts throughout Eurasia (including those in the Mongolian steppe) wrestled with how best to turn the legacy of the Mongol empire, along with its institutions, its personnel and its place in public memory, to their advantage (**Pls 1.2–1.3**). The Mongol empire and the Chinggisids became a shared reference point for much of Eurasia at that time. For this reason, the Ming court often invoked the Chinggisids in its efforts to justify its rulership and enhance its standing among rulers and subjects both at home and abroad. Finally, the prominence of the Chinggisids in imperial proclamations is further evidence of the Ming court's myriad ties to eastern Eurasia and its desire to influence the thinking and behaviour of its neighbours.

In his father's footsteps

The views which the Yongle 永樂 emperor (r. 1403–24) held of the steppe and the Mongol empire are sometimes contrasted with those of his father, the dynastic founder, the Hongwu 洪武 emperor (r. 1368–98). The founder often claimed he sought the restoration of Chinese social values and rituals which had been debased by a century of Mongol rule.[3] In contrast, the Yongle emperor is thought to have been far more comfortable with Mongolians and a vision of the Ming dynasty that closely approximated the scale and ambitions of the Mongol empire.[4] Despite such apparent differences, the two emperors believed the Chinggisids to be both a key audience and an essential reference point in their efforts to justify Ming rulership.

One way to think about Ming efforts to justify rulership is to ask on what fronts the Ming emperor and his advisors felt most vulnerable to attack.[5] The Ming court vehemently denied any betrayal of the Yuan dynasty (as the Mongol polity was known in East Asia) in general and of the last of Chinggis Khan's descendants to rule from Dadu 大都 (today's Beijing), Toghan-Temür (r. 1333–70), in particular. Efforts to explain away the Ming founder's armed revolt against the Yuan throne and the military drive towards the Mongols' capital at Dadu in the north began before he took power early in 1368 and continued until the end of his reign. Their basic argument was simple. When the Song dynasty (960–1279) grew corrupt, Heaven shifted its support to Chinggis Khan (1162?–1227), who then took control of China. Chinggis' successors, and in particular Qubilai Khan (1215–94), had brought peace and prosperity to the people of China. However, later emperors, most especially Toghan-Temür, had ignored Chinggis' injunctions, indulged in sex and drink, and neglected matters of state. The result was the collapse of governance and spiraling chaos. Into this political vacuum sprang warlords, who were concerned only with narrow self-interest. In other words, Toghan-Temür had forfeited control over the people and territory of China. Pitying the people's abject suffering, Heaven then chose the Ming founder as the vehicle through which to restore order and establish a new polity capable of saving the people. Thus, the Ming founder had not betrayed his sovereign or rebelled against the reigning dynasty. In such a view, although the Mongols may have still physically occupied Chinese territory when the Ming founder began to consolidate power, they had already lost possession of the Mandate of Heaven, rendering them illegitimate. The Ming founder and his court repeated this justification in official proclamations for domestic audiences, communications with neighbouring rulers and in letters to the Chinggisid court and its allies for decades.[6]

This was part of a wider narrative about the Chinggisids that the Hongwu emperor and his advisors developed to explain the rise, the glory and the irreversible fall of that house in terms that were advantageous to the Ming court. All such discussions of the Chinggisid past were explicitly tied to the Ming court's narrative of the Chinggisid present. The Ming court acknowledged the Chinggisids on the steppe as biological descendants of Chinggis, Qubilai and Toghan-Temür but categorically denied their status as political successors.[7]

The early fifteenth century

Before turning to the Yongle emperor and his successors in the early 15th century, a few words about developments on the Mongolian steppe are in order. By the late 14th century, the power and authority of the Yuan Mongol court on the steppe was in steep decline. Violent competition among different branches of the Chinggisid family intensified, and influential Mongol leaders outside of the Chinggisid family began to seize power, although most continued to use Chinggisid figureheads to legitimate their rule. At the same time, the Oirats (Qalmaqs/Kalmyks), based in present-day northwestern Xinjiang, began to rival the Eastern Mongols, occasionally even abandoning the Chinggisid principle, that is only Chinggis Khan's descendants were qualified to serve as the khan of khans, to rule in their own name.[8] To legitimise political ambitions, men and women on the steppe began crafting their own Chinggisid narratives.[9] The contested and contingent nature of such developing narratives, combined with the open rivalry between the Yuan and Ming courts during the late 14th and early 15th centuries, may have allowed the Ming court to exercise greater influence over recent memories of Chinggis, Qubilai, Toghan-Temür and their successors at this point than would be true later on, after the mid-15th century.

The Yongle emperor and his court in the early 15th century maintained key elements of the Ming founder's narrative of Chinggisid rule. They continued to insist that the Chinggisids' allotted span of rule or fortune (*yun* 運) had run its course; the biological descendants of Qubilai and Toghan-Temür might still populate the steppe, but they would never revive the Mongol empire. In an imperially commissioned poem celebrating one of the Yongle emperor's victorious campaigns against the Mongols, the official Zeng Qi 曾棨 (1372–1432) wrote:

> The Hu fortune is forever over, 胡運永終
>
> [Yet] there are these traitorous remnants. 有此遺孽[10]

The appellation *hu* 胡 referred in general to horse-riding nomadic pastoralists from the steppe and here in particular to the Chinggisid rulers of the Yuan dynasty. Zeng Qi's choice of Hu created a sense of distance and difference, suggesting a contrast between Hu with China on the one hand and between the Hu, a contemporary steppe polity without any transcendent basis of authority, and the Great Yuan, a historical dynasty that ruled China and that was acknowledged to have held the Mandate of Heaven. Zeng Qi's proud declaration that the fortunes of the Hu or Mongols were a thing of the past belied the Ming court's continuing unease about the imperial ambitions of these 'traitorous remnants', the Chinggisids, who retained considerable status in the present as successors to Chinggis and Qubilai. In a poem entitled 'Pacification of the Hu' (*Ping hu song* 平胡頌), one of the Yongle emperor's officials dismissed the Chinggisids in the following terms:

> Only they, the remnant Hu, 唯彼殘胡
>
> Those Hu did not know. 彼胡罔知
>
> The Mandate of Heaven is not usurped. 天命不饗
>
> The fortune of the Yuan is already ended. 元祚既終
>
> How can a taper blaze? 爝火何焰[11]

The official bemoans the Chinggisids and their allies who failed to acknowledge that their allotted span of rule had run its course. He seeks to minimise the Chinggisids' importance by contrasting the light given off by a single taper with the blazing illumination generated by the sun and moon, a reference to the Ming dynasty.

The Yongle emperor's court continued the founder's strategy of marginalising the Chinggisids by casting them as the aberration that failed to recognise the transfer of the Mandate of Heaven:

> Whosoever has teeth in his mouth and hair on his head, whosoever has blood and breath, none does not come in submission. Only the traitor remnants of the northern caitiffs located on the distant border gather like clouds and assemble like crows, moving without constancy. They are stubborn, conniving and arrogant.
>
> 凡含齒戴髮有血氣者罔不率服。獨北虜遺孽處於荒裔。雲聚烏合，遷徙無常，倔強黠驕。[12]

Although such rhetoric might suggest a blanket condemnation of all Mongols, the Ming court never pursued genocidal campaigns against the entire steppe. The Yongle emperor famously led his armies into the steppe five times, but the objective was always two-fold, namely to destroy a particular Mongolian polity and to secure Mongolian (and Jurchen) allies.[13] In the preface to a 'Poem of the Pacification of the Hu' (*Ping hu shi* 平胡詩), penned on the occasion of the Yongle emperor's first campaign in 1410, the senior court official Yang Shiqi 楊士奇 (1365–1444) wrote:

> As for the great mass of those with braided hair, felts and leather clothing from the steppe, each led his subordinates, surrendering in earnest and responding to righteousness. They prostrated themselves at the foot of the palace. Those who

> received posts and awards are beyond counting. Only Bunyashiri did not lead [his subordinates in submission], stubbornly remaining outside transformation.
>
> 至與朔漠氈裘辮髮之眾，合率其屬，歸誠慕義，拜俯闕下，蒙荷官賞者不可勝計。惟本雅失里弗率倔強化外。[14]

Bunyashiri (d. 1412) was a Chinggisid noble who reigned briefly (1408–11) as khan of khans. Yang Shiqi's effort to marginalise Bunyashiri was part of a wider attempt to justify the Yongle emperor's momentous decision to lead the imperial host in person. After taking the throne in 1368, the Ming founder had no longer commanded armies in the field. In fact, neither had any Chinese emperor in recent centuries. Thus, although at first glance the following imperial proclamation might seem no more than bombastic propaganda, it is actually an effort to rewrite history and justify the Yongle emperor's innovative actions:

> We have received the Mandate of Heaven and succeeded to the vast foundation of the Grand Progenitor the Lofty Emperor to rule the myriad regions and succour the multitudinous kinds. Barbarians of the four quarters and distant lands, there is none that has not come in submission. Only the remnants of the northern caitiffs located in the desolate wastelands brazenly perpetrate brutality. [We] have repeatedly dispatched envoys with messages [but] they have detained and murdered them. Recently their people raided the border. Border generals apprehended them. [We] again dispatched envoys to return them. Again they were detained and murdered. [Our] kindness has already been betrayed several times; how can we harbour virtue? Furthermore the jackals and wolves are avaricious and grasping. The duplicitous villains gnaw on their people, who crane their necks in search of respite. Investigating [such circumstances] by the Heavenly Path, their fortunes have already expired. Examining [them] in human affairs, their peoples are all divided. We now personally lead the Six Armies to go and chastise them. [We] inspire fear [through] martial awe and make manifest Heavenly punishment.
>
> 朕受天命，承太祖高皇帝洪基，統馭萬方，撫輯庶類。凡四夷僻遠靡不從，化獨北 虜殘孽處于荒裔，肆逞兇暴，屡遣使申諭輒拘留殺之。乃者其人鈔邊，邊將獲之，再遣使護還使者復被拘殺。恩既数背，德豈可懷。况豺狼野心貪悍，猾賊虐噬。其衆引領傒蘇，稽于天道則其運已絕，驗于人事則彼衆皆離。朕今親率六師往征之，肅振武威用彰天討。[15]

Space precludes a thorough analysis of the passage, but immediately in the opening lines, Yongle's usurpation of the throne from the founder's chosen successor in a four-year bloody civil war is transformed into a smooth transfer of power directly from the founder to the Yongle emperor. The proclamation justifies the emperor's decision to lead troops into the field in several ways. Bunyashiri, here left unnamed, is marginalised politically and physically, and his people reduced to desperate straits. The emperor asserts that the Ming court's repeated attempts at diplomatic negotiations have met only with vile betrayal, its envoys killed again and again. Bunyashiri is cast as a cruel ruler who abuses his people, who look to the Ming for help. To use terms familiar to us today, the Ming court is justifying its actions through an appeal for regime change.

One gets a clearer sense of why the Ming court felt compelled to explain its decisions when considering the wider geopolitical field. Let us begin with the neighbouring Joseon 朝鮮 court of Korea, ostensibly a devoted tributary ally of the Ming, led by King Taejong 太宗 (r. 1400–18), another man who had come to power through a bloody coup.[16] In mid-November 1409, King Taejong received the following brief secret report from one of his officials:

> The Tatar Emperor has stationed a powerful army outside the passes of Guanzhong. Regional Commander and Duke of Yiguo [i.e. Qiu Fu 丘福] and the Marquis of Wucheng [i.e. Wang Cong 王聰] clashed with them but suffered defeat. Their entire army was taken captive. The Emperor is mobilising troops from all routes; he will campaign against the north in the second month of next year.
>
> 韃靼皇帝將重兵屯關中口子外，總兵官沂國公武城侯禦之敗績，全師被擄，皇帝徵兵諸路, 將以明年二月北征。[17]

Within a few short lines, the report explicitly mentions two emperors, both of whom command considerable military forces. The document as preserved in the *Veritable Records of Joseon* (*Joseon sillok* 朝鮮實錄), a Korean royal chronicle, qualifies the reference to Bunyashiri as the Tatar Emperor, whereas the Yongle emperor requires no such qualification, but otherwise the Chinggisid and Ming rulers are treated as roughly analogous. Reading such reports, the Joseon king and his advisors could not have been sanguine about the Ming's military prospects. In initial clashes, the Ming army had been routed and now the Yongle emperor was forced to mobilise troops from throughout the empire. Given that the Ming founder had coerced the Joseon's predecessor, the Goryeo 高麗 dynasty (918–1392), into selling him some 50,000 horses for his wars with the Chinggisids, and that the Yongle emperor had similarly pressed the Joseon into selling him tens of thousands of horses during his civil war, King Taejong no doubt viewed the upcoming conflict with some concern.[18]

Perhaps this explains why the Yongle emperor felt the need to send a note to the Joseon king explaining in explicit terms the reason for his campaign into the steppe:

> Among the descendants of the Yuan emperors, some have submitted and some have not submitted. We intend to pacify those who have not submitted.
>
> 元帝子孫，有順附者，有不順者，其不順者，朕欲平之。[19]

We have no evidence for King Taejong's reaction, but the letter makes clear that the Yongle emperor understood the campaign in the context of the Mongol Yuan empire and its Chinggisid descendants rather than merely as another clash with nameless steppe nomads.

In fact, the early Ming imperial court understood that the Chinggisid world continued to span much of Eurasia. Ming records refer to the Timurid ruler of western Eurasia, Shah Rukh (1377–1447) as the fourth son of the 'Yuan/Chinggisid royal son-in-law Temür' (*Yuan fuma Tiemuer* 元駙馬帖木兒). Temür was the Mongolian version of Timūr, perhaps better known in Western language sources as Tamerlane (d. 1405), founder in 1370 of the Timurid dynasty. 'Royal son-in-law' or *gerügen* was a key political status under the Mongols and a description Timūr and his immediate successors adopted as an official title, and it appeared in proclamations and on coins (**Pl. 1.4**) as well as on objects made at their courts (**Pl. 1.5**). Likewise, late 14th- and early

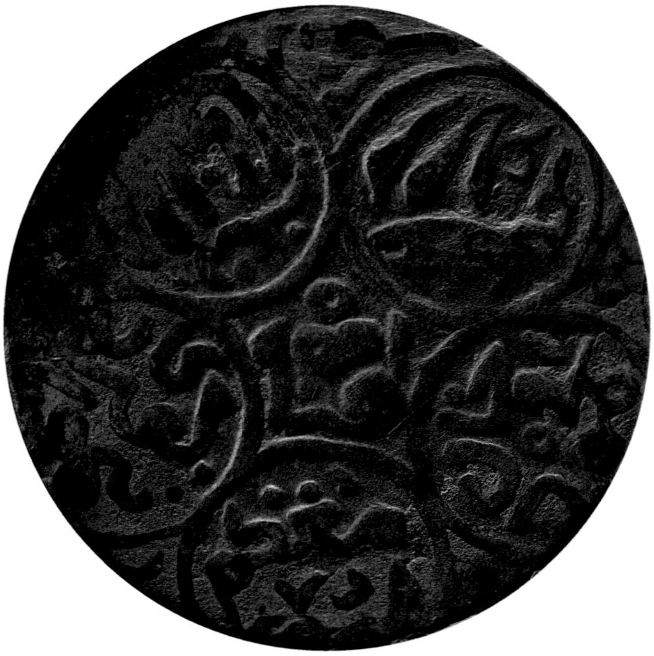

Plate 1.4 Coin, Timurid dynasty, 1393. Inscribed: (obverse) There is no god but God, Muhammad is the Messenger of God Abu bakr; 'Omar; 'Uthman; 'Ali; (reverse) Herat, The Supreme Sultan, Mahmud Khan, the Mighty Amir, Timur Gurkan. Silver, weight 6.96g; diameter 2.5cm. British Museum, London, 1887,1201.11

15th-century Ming imperial sources such as the *Veritable Records* refer to the rulers of Moghulistan in present-day Xinjiang as part of the Chinggisid oecumene, that is the wider Mongolian world centred on descendants of Chinggis Khan, with close ties to the Timurids, who in turn were directly tied to the Eastern Mongols. Officials at the Ming court knew that at one point Timūr had offered refuge to Bunyashiri at his capital in Samarqand. Finally, early Ming rulers and their advisors knew full well that members of the ruling house of the Goryeo dynasty in Korea had also been Chinggisid son-in-laws for nearly a century.[20]

Performing rulership

Winning the allegiance of subordinates of Chinggisid rulers was valuable evidence on the wider Eurasian stage of the superiority of Ming rulership. The Ming founder had initiated this strategy, offering economic incentives, providing positions of security and prestige within the Ming military, and supplying intellectual or emotional justifications for transferring allegiance from the Chinggisids to the Ming throne.[21] Early in the Yongle emperor's reign, a group of Mongols from the northwest offered gifts to the emperor. After the banquet, the Minister of Rites complimented the emperor on his skill in handling the Mongols. Yongle responded:

> People often speak of governing the Yi and Di without governing them. To cherish good and detest evil is common to human emotion. How can [we] distinguish this in regard to the Yi and Di? If you comfort them properly, it is not certain that they will not come [in submission]. Tigers are extremely violent. If you soothe them, you can cause them to become tame. How much more so with the caitiffs who [like us] eat when hungry and drink when thirsty. For those with a human heart, how would it be impossible to tame [them]? It is just a matter of treating those who come [in submission] with sincerity.
>
> 人恆言以不治治夷狄。夫好善惡惡，人情所同者。豈間於夷狄。撫之有道，未必不來。虎至暴，擾之能使馴帖。況虜亦飢食渴飲。有人心者何不可馴哉。但有來者推誠待之耳。[22]

Here the emperor uses the occasion to pontificate about an element of rulership considered essential in (if not unique to) Confucian ideology, the ability to win the allegiance of men by dealing with them with confidence and in good faith, regardless of apparent differences or backgrounds. Although the emperor chose the generic language of *Yi* 夷 and *Di* 狄, generalised terms to denote foreigners who do not necessarily share the cultural values and practices of China, to describe these men from afar, he was extending his rulership over Mongols who almost certainly had either direct experience or recent memory of being Chinggisid subjects.

The best-known example of the Yongle emperor winning the allegiance of a Mongol leader who had formerly fought for the Chinggisids occurred in 1423. The emperor had been on his fourth campaign to the steppe, this time against Arugtai (d. 1434), a powerful Mongol ostensibly wielding power on behalf of a Chinggisid. The emperor was keen to find a face-saving end to a long, inconclusive and increasingly demoralising campaign, and so when a former lieutenant of Arugtai, Esen-Tughal (d. 1431), signalled an interest in transferring his allegiance, the Yongle emperor and his advisors quickly agreed. The presentation of events in Ming records highlights the emperor's generosity and wisdom: 'To now have the good fortune to meet His Majesty', exclaimed Esen-Tughal, 'is Heaven granting Your Servant a day of rebirth' 今幸見陛下是天賜臣再生之日也.[23] The emperor responded warmly: 'The Chinese and Yi are one family. We received the Mandate of Heaven to be the Son of Heaven. All those who Heaven covers, all those who the earth carries are Our children' 華夷本一家。朕奉天命為天子，天之所覆地之所載皆朕赤子.[24] Here, through the incorporation of a Mongol leader, the emperor can claim universal rulership and evidence that he possesses the Mandate of Heaven.

Later, in an ostensibly unguarded moment with his family and close followers, Esen-Tughal is said to have declared: 'The emperor of the Great Ming truly is my lord' 大明皇帝真吾主也.[25] The term 'true lord' (*zhen zhu* 真主) had figured prominently in early Ming narratives of the Hongwu emperor's rise, distinguishing him from other ambitious Chinese warlords who sought regional domination prior to 1368. Here 'truly is my lord' suggests an implicit comparison with Esen-Tughal's former lord, Arugtai, and perhaps by extension even Bunyashiri, who at one point had been Arugtai's lord. In other words, although we have little way to know what if anything Esen-Tughal said about the Yongle emperor truly being his lord, Ming observers (who compiled the account we have today) contextualised rulership and patronage in a wider competitive and comparative field. Winning the allegiance of men from afar proved the superiority of Ming rulership.

In return the Yongle emperor is seen in the *Veritable Records* praising Esen-Tughal, in large part because it confirms his status as a superior ruler:

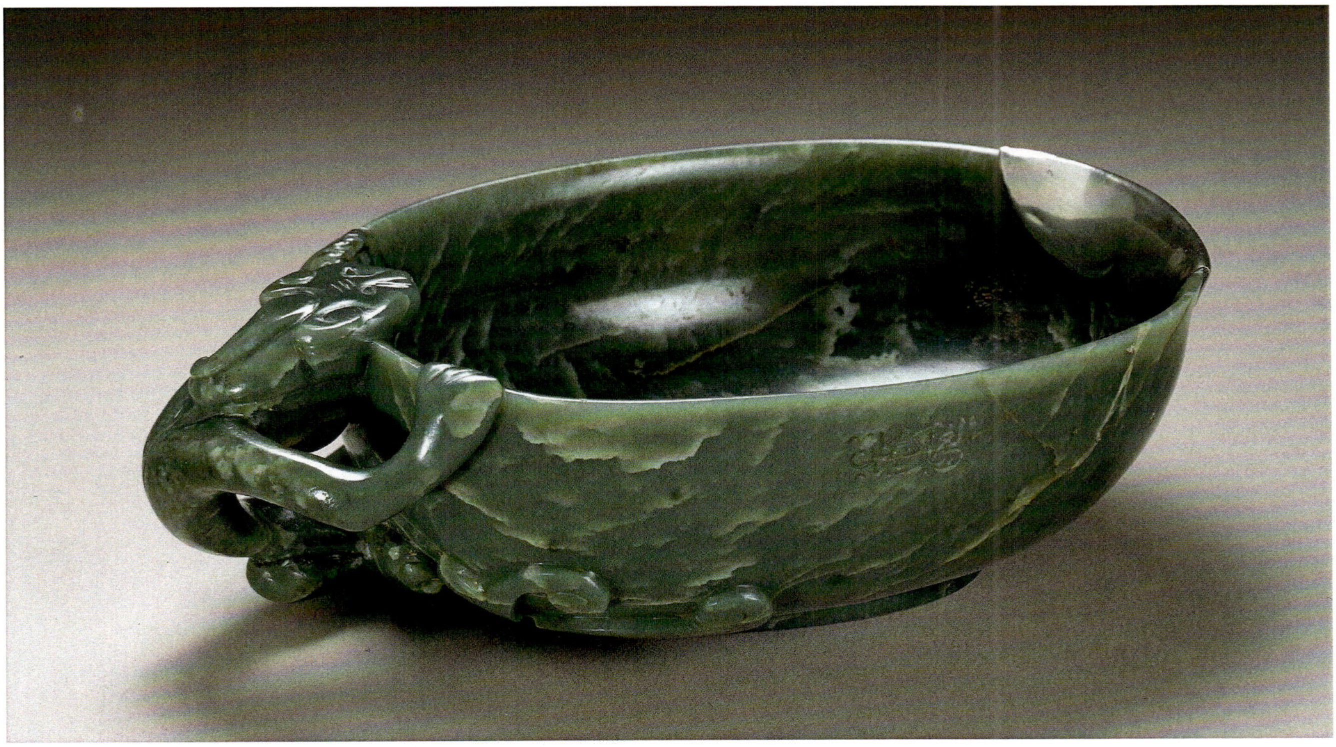

Plate 1.5 Jade cup, 1420–49; Ottoman silver repair, 1600–1800, Samarqand. A Turkish inscription at the rim of this jade cup reads 'Ulugh Beg Kuragan'. Ulugh Beg, Shah Rukh's son, was the ruler of Samarqand at the heart of the Silk Road from 1407 to 1447. Kuragan means 'royal son-in-law', a reference to Ulugh Beg's family connection to Chinggis Khan, the great leader of the Mongols. Height 6.4cm, width 19.4cm. British Museum, London, purchased through the Brooke Sewell Permanent Fund, 1959,1120.1

> Fierce and bold; he is the most treacherous among the Hu caitiffs. The caitiff soldiers fear and respect him. Now he has already bowed his head at Our camp and demonstrated good faith. Believing that the Mandate of Heaven resides with Us, he does not dare to violate [Our will] and has respectfully led his followers to follow the Heavenly path. He has personally come in submission to court where he has been received with kindness.
>
> 慓悍勇猛，乃胡虜中之最狡黠者，虜兵畏服，今既稽首軍門，敷陳誠悃，以為天命在朕，不敢違越，敬率部落上順天道，親來朝見眷。[26]

At the same time, the emperor was fully aware that he needed to demonstrate his superior rulership and patronage for broader audiences. He made a point of appointing Esen-Tughal and his nephew to senior military positions, giving them a real voice in strategic decisions such as the target of the next major campaign, defending them against jealous Chinese officials and granting them privileged economic and political status within the capital.[27]

In the following decades, the Yongle emperor's successors continued to justify their rulership through control of the story of the rise and irreversible fall of Chinggisid power and through displays of patronage intended to win the allegiance of men from afar. During the 1440s and 1450s, the most dangerous military and diplomatic challenge to face the Ming court was the rise of a newly powerful Mongol polity under the ambitious Oirat leader Esen (r. 1438–53/4) and his Chinggisid ruler (Toqto'a-Buqa, r. 1433–52). Through military strikes, coercion and the strategic use of marriage alliances, Esen sought to extend his control over regions that had formerly been within the Ming dynasty's sphere of interest.[28] In addition, Esen invoked the legacy of the Mongol empire to win the support of Jurchen groups, the Joseon throne, Eastern Mongols and polities in Central Asia, arguing that he was the true heir to the mantle of Chinggis and Qubilai. Each time Esen made such a claim, the Ming court responded in direct and explicit terms, because it saw that Chinggisid charisma retained appeal in Eurasia. Furthermore, Ming emperors understood the need to persuade multiple audiences that they, rather than their Chinggisid contemporaries, were the rightful successors to the Yuan dynasty. Finally, the Ming court believed that active engagement in Eurasia could persuade neighbours of the legitimacy, even superiority, of Ming rulership.

Notes

My deepest thanks to Sarah Schneewind, Anne Gerritsen and Craig Clunas for their comments and suggestions on drafts of this chapter.

1 Robinson 2013b.
2 Saeki 2009; Murai 2009; Ayalon 1951; Ayalon 1988; Amitai 1995; Amitai 2008; Broadbridge 2008.
3 Dardess 1983; Farmer 1995; Jiang 2011.
4 Dreyer 1982; Okada 1999; Robinson 2008.
5 Sharpe 2009 makes this point in reference to the Tudor monarchy.
6 Robinson forthcoming.
7 Robinson 2014.
8 Veit 2009.
9 Post-Yuan Mongols sought to exploit Chinggisid charisma for their own purposes. See Elverskog 2004; Elverskog 2006. For how one Christian Turkic people revised the account of its origins in response to shifting fortunes under the Chinggisids, see Atwood 2014.
10 *Ying zhi fu ping hu yue* 應制賦平胡樂 in Zeng Qi 1995–7, *ji* 30, 158.
11 Gao Deyang 1995–7, *ji* 29, 247.
12 *Ping hu zhi bei* 平胡之碑 in Hu Guang 1995–7, *ji* 28, 618.

13 Twitchett and Mote 1998, 226–9.
14 Yang Shiqi 1998, *juan* 23, 342.
15 *MSL Taizong shilu*, 101.2a–b (8/2/辛丑).
16 In 1398, he seized power in a coup that is often called the 'First Strife of the Princes'.
17 *JWS Taejong sillok* 18 (9/10/庚戌). Both men were killed in the fighting or shortly thereafter. Although the *Joseon Veritable Records* gives Qiu Fu's title incorrectly as Marquis of Yiguo, it should be Marquis of Qiguo 淇國.
18 Robinson 2016; Pak 1991, 231, 236–8, 243; Pak 2002, 141–5; Kitajima 1995, 200–2.
19 *JWS Taejong sillok* 18 (9/10/己未).
20 Morihira 2013; Robinson 2009.
21 Serruys 1959a, b. For citations to Chinese language scholarship, see Robinson 2012, 127, n. 23.
22 *MSL Taizong shilu*, 36.4a (2/1/庚戌).
23 *MSL Taizong shilu*, 264.2a (21/1/己巳).
24 *MSL Taizong shilu*, 264.2a (21/1/己巳).
25 *MSL Taizong shilu*, 264.2b (21/10/己巳).
26 *JWS Sejong sillok* 22 (5/11/壬午). For a slightly different version of the edict, see *MSL Taizong shilu*, 264.3a (21/10/庚午).
27 Robinson forthcoming.
28 Im 2011; Kawachi 1992; Mote 1974; Rossabi 1970.

Chapter 2
Domination in Four Keys: Ming China and its Southern Neighbours 1400–1450

Geoffrey Wade

In any discussion of imperial development, in any part of the globe, issues of political domination and attendant violence must inevitably be invoked. The half century of the Ming dynasty examined in this volume certainly constitutes no exception. This period witnessed state violence often on a massive scale domestically (as in the wars waged during Zhu Di's usurpation of the throne) as well as violence against neighbouring polities on all borders (as in the Tumu campaign of 1449). This chapter examines the manner in which the Ming state dominated polities to its south, and will suggest four different forms of domination of those polities: two forms of overland domination, comprising either indirect colonialism through the native office system (*tusi* 土司), whereby traditional rulers were retained under threat of military coercion and subject to corvée and tax demands, or formal colonialism, such as the incorporation of Đại Việt 大越 during the Yongle reign, and two forms of overseas domination, the first involving the establishment of a broad *pax* Ming in the East Asian oceanic realm through the Zheng He voyages, and the second comprising formal declaration of suzerainty through the erection of stelae in four maritime polities. Together these forms constituted the 'four keys' in which early Ming China pursued domination of its southern neighbours (**Pl. 2.1**).

Overland domination I: Ming military actions against Yunnan

In 1369, only a year after Zhu Yuanzhang had formally founded the Ming dynasty, he sent proclamations for the instruction of 'the countries of Yunnan and Japan'.[1] This early recognition of Yunnan as a 'country' (*guo* 國) which lay

Plate 2.1 The three prongs of southern expansion during the Yongle reign. The map is after Ma Huan 馬歡, *Ying yai shenglan* 瀛涯勝覽 (*Overall Survey of the Ocean's Shores*) (Mills 1970), with arrows added by author

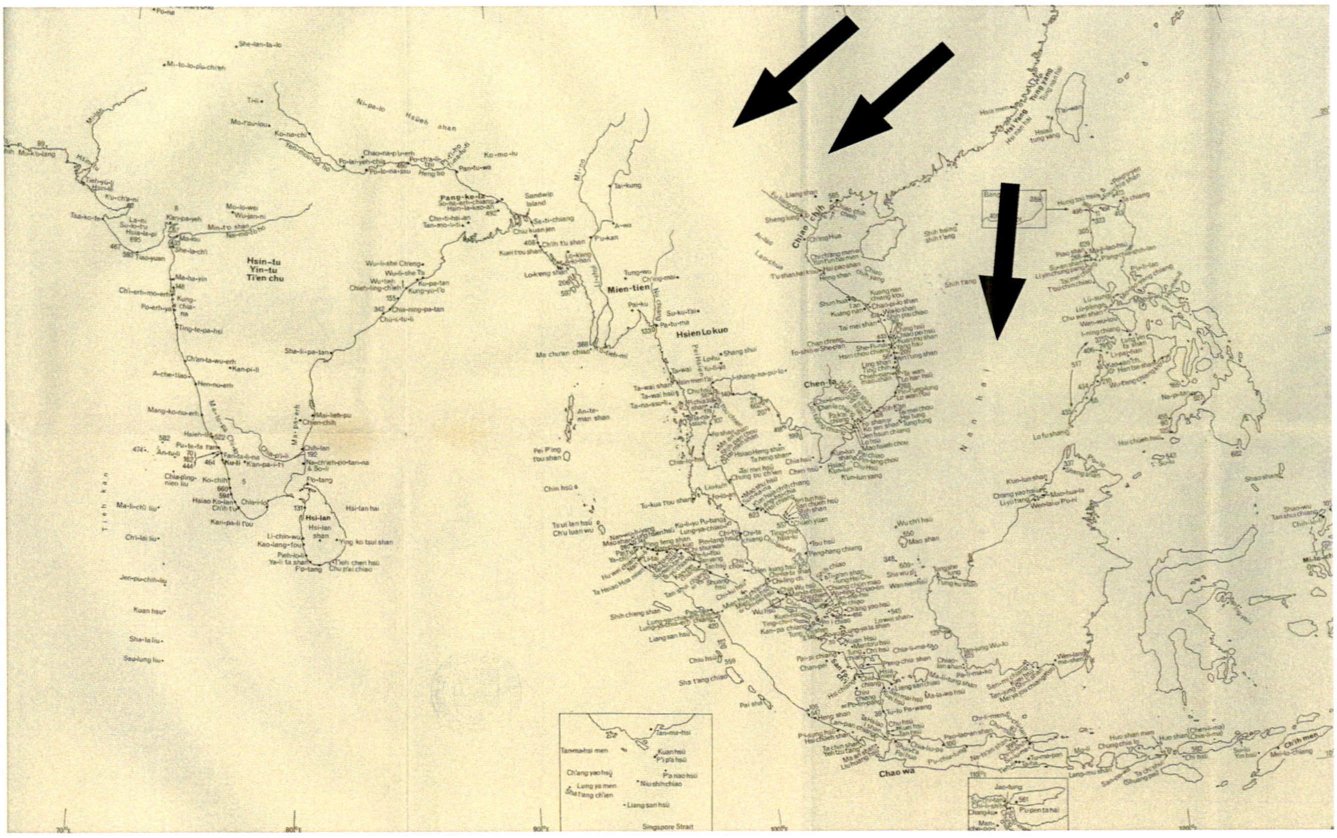

beyond the Ming was to change very soon thereafter. By 1380, Yunnan was considered to have 'been China's territory since the Han dynasty',[2] providing a moral basis for the invasion of the region. About 250,000 troops were then deployed in an attack on the polities of the region, taking Dali, Lijiang and Jinchi in 1382. The Ming founder thereby took control of the major urban centres of the northwestern part of what is today Yunnan, including several Tai areas. These colonies were the first to be absorbed into Ming 'Yunnan'.[3]

By 1387, the Ming founder had set his sights further and, in preparation for an attack on the Baiyi 百夷 (Möng Mao) polity to the south of his earlier conquests, a military officer was sent to Sichuan to buy 10,000 ploughing cattle. These were to be used to plough the fields necessary to feed the troops on a likely long-term expedition. When the invasion did occur, under the commander Mu Ying 沐英 (1345–92), the Ming forces attacked the Baiyi with firearms, reportedly taking 30,000 heads.[4] Si Lunfa 思倫發, the ruler of Möng Mao, a polity with a Tai-speaking elite which extended over much of what is today Northern Myanmar and south-western Yunnan, was subsequently made to pay for all the costs of the military expedition against him, as a quid pro quo for the Ming court recognising him as ruler of the Baiyi.[5] When a minister rebelled against Si Lunfa in 1397, the Chinese state gave sanctuary to the fleeing ruler, sent troops against the rebel and restored Si Lunfa to his position, extracting vast tracts of land from him in exchange for this assistance.[6] The Ming state also broke down his huge former territory into the polities of Luchuan 麓川, Mengyang 孟養, Mubang 木邦, Mengding 孟定, Lujiang 潞江, Ganyai 干崖, Dahou 大候 and Wan Dian 灣甸, all under separate rulers.[7]

In addition, when engaged in military activities, the Ming administration in Yunnan could call upon the military forces of the 'native offices' (*tusi* 土司). The new polities which were 'created' (or recognised) in Yunnan under the first Ming ruler by the breaking down of larger polities were known to the Ming as 'native offices', as they were controlled by non-Chinese persons. Initially they were usually left under the control of the hereditary rulers of the respective polities, and it was through this means that the Ming exerted control and engaged in economic expropriation through tribute demands and other levies. This was the beginning of a policy which was to be pursued throughout the Ming, which had such profound effects on the upland Tai polities, and which resulted in Yunnan becoming part of China.

In the process by which they were gradually absorbed by the Ming, these polities were subjected to a wide range of tribute demands, labour levies and other levies, including troop provision. As an example, in the case of the Tai Mao polity of Luchuan (also called Luchuan-Pingmian 麓川平緬), the Ming court demanded 15,000 horses, 500 elephants and 30,000 cattle from the ruler Si Lunfa in 1397.[8] Subsequently, large silver demands (silver in lieu of labour) were levied on this polity. The annual amount of 6,900 *liang*[9] of silver was initially set and then it was almost tripled to 18,000 *liang*. When it was realised that this was impossible to meet, the levy was reduced to the original amount.[10] Diverse other levies were applied to the other polities and enforced through the use or threat of military force. Again, we see the role of the Chinese colonial armies as providing the military 'muscle' necessary to ensure that economic expropriation could be carried out effectively.

The reign of the Yongle emperor was to see a major advance in the Ming colonisation of Yunnan, prior to his invasion of the Vietnamese polity in 1406. The Ming colonisation of the Tai areas of Yunnan during the 15th century was attained and maintained either by the actual use or the threat of military force. As such, the Ming established guards throughout the region to maintain security and political dominance. Independent battalions directly under the Regional Military Commission were established in Tengchong 騰衝[11] and Yongchang 永昌[12] in Yunnan in 1403,[13] and these were to be the major control centres for Chinese colonisation of the Tai polities over the following century.

In the same year, new Chief's Offices were 'established' in Yunnan, at Zhele Dian 者樂甸, Dahou, Ganyai, Wan Dian and Lujiang,[14] and in 1406 a further four Chief's Offices were established under Ningyuan 寧遠 Guard in what is today Sip Song Chau Tai in Vietnam.[15] Mubang (Hsenwi) and Mengyang were made Military and Civilian Pacification Superintendencies in 1404.[16] The recognition of these polities by the Ming court came at a cost to their independence and when they did not accord with what the new Ming emperor required, military actions were launched against them. In 1405, for example, the senior Chinese representative in Yunnan, Mu Sheng 沐晟 (1368–1439), launched an attack on Babai (Lanna).[17] The attempts at domination extended even to what is today Assam in India, with envoys carrying threats being dispatched to Da-gu-la, the Uttarakula which lay on the northern bank of the Brahmaputra River.[18]

After some sort of recognition or acceptance of the superior position of the Ming court, gained through military action or threat, Chinese clerks or registry managers were appointed to the 'native offices' to 'assist' the traditional ruler, and ensure that Ming interests were served. Chinese clerks were appointed to carry out Chinese language duties in the 'native offices' of Yunnan in 1404,[19] while similar circulating official clerk positions (to be filled by Chinese persons) were established in seven Chief's Offices in Yunnan in 1406.[20] Gradually, formal members of the Chinese bureaucracy were appointed to assist these rulers, much like the advisers appointed to the Malay States by the British in the 19th century. Here, then, we see the beginnings of the process by which formerly Southeast Asian polities were gradually absorbed into the Chinese polity through a process of colonisation.

The 'native office' polities were then subject to demands in terms of gold/silver in lieu of labour, administered by the Ministry of Revenue,[21] and also required to provide troops to assist in further Ming campaigns. Mubang, for example, was required to send its troops against Babai (Lanna) in the 1405 expedition mentioned above.[22] This employment of 'native troops' by the Ming colonisers reflected what was being done in Đại Việt and what was to be done by later colonial armies in Southeast Asia.

It was in the 1430s and 1440s that major Ming military invasions of the Tai polities of Yunnan again took place. The three major attacks against the Tai Mao polity in modern-day western Yunnan and northern Burma known to the Chinese as Luchuan – extending from 1438 to 1445 – have essentially been neglected in the studies of Southeast Asian history, and thus so has this aspect of Ming colonialism. However, they were some of the most important events in the history of 15th-century Southeast Asia, resulting in the fragmentation and colonisation of one of its largest polities. The Tai Mao political leader Si Renfa 思任發 (fl. 1400–44) had, during the 1430s, made attempts to recover territory formerly subject to his father Si Lunfa, but which had been atomised by earlier Ming policies. He had gained control over Ganyai, Nan Dian, Tengchong, Lujiang and Jinchi 金齒 by 1438, when the Ming court sent generals to assist the local commander Mu Sheng against him.[23] While the Chinese forces claimed initial success, a further 50,000 troops from all over southern China were mobilised in 1439 for the first major Luchuan expedition.[24] Further missions were dispatched in the 1440s and the year 1444 saw the destruction of Luchuan (the power base of Si Renfa), the killing of Si Renfa and the establishment by the Ming of Longchuan 隴川 Pacification Commission (apparently the first use of the term Pacification Commission *Xuan fu si* 宣撫司 in Chinese history) to partially replace Luchuan. A former Luchuan chieftain, Gong Xiang 恭項, who had gone over to the Ming, was then appointed as Pacification Commissioner.[25]

A further major Ming military expedition which was to greatly affect the upland Southeast Asian polities was that launched in 1448 to capture Si Jifa 思機發, a son of Si Renfa. At a date equivalent to April/May 1448, imperial instructions were issued to Wang Ji 王驥 (1378–1460) requiring him to capture Si Jifa and the chieftains of Mengyang.[26] The surrounding polities of Ava-Burma, Mubang, Nan Dian, Ganyai and Longchuan were also required to provide troops for deployment against Si Jifa.[27] The imperial orders sent to Wang Ji presaged the disruption which such an expedition would have wrought in the region. 'He [Si Jifa] may flee into Ava-Burma's territory and be concealed by the people there. If so, capture persons as the situation demands, so that the *yi* people[28] will know fear and the Great Army will not have been sent in vain.'[29] While Wang Ji reported success in his attack on Si Jifa's stockade,[30] later accounts tell of how Wang Ji had sought personal advantages from the 'native officials' and how in fact he had been defeated by Si Jifa.[31] Again in 1454, Chinese forces were dispatched, this time against Si Kenfa 思揹法 and others in Mengyang, who had established their own regime in competition with the Ming appointee.[32]

Achieving a balance between economically exploiting the newly conquered areas in Yunnan and trying to maintain social stability (and thereby control) in those areas was something the Ming and its agents constantly debated. Despite claims that social stability was at risk in Yunnan in the 1440s due to the levies, the Ministry of Revenue refused to reduce any of the gold and silver payments required, claiming that 'they are an old system dating from the Hongwu reign, and it is difficult to abolish them'.[33] The gold, silver and horse demands which the Ming state imposed on the Tai polities of Yunnan and beyond not only depleted their resources, but also left them open to imposition of other demands by the Ming. In the 1440s, for example, Mubang (Hsenwi/Theinni) deployed its forces to assist the Chinese forces arrayed against Si Renfa in exchange for the cancelling of an outstanding debt to the Chinese state (which had been unilaterally imposed by the Ming) of 14,000 *liang* of silver. In 1448, the gold, silver, rice, paper money, cowries and horses owed in lieu of labour by eight prefectures in Yunnan, plus Jinchi, Tengchong, Ganyai, Nan Dian, Longchuan, Cheli 車里, Mengyang, Mubang, Mengding, Menggen 孟艮, Weiyuan 威遠, Wan Dian, Zhenkang 鎮康 and Dahou, being mainly Tai polities stretching right across Indochina, were all cancelled in reward for their military assistance in destroying the power of the Möng Mao polity of Luchuan.[34]

Another of the essential policies of the Ming state in pursuing its colonial aims in the Tai regions of Yunnan, and in fact in all its colonial endeavours, was its efforts to keep colonised polities as divided from each other as possible. This had the dual role of firstly reducing the threat any single polity could pose to China, and secondly facilitating the manipulation of these polities. In this manner, China pursued an active policy of 'divide and rule' colonialism, and in this the military forces in Yunnan played an important role.

In 1404 there were efforts to divide Babai/Dadian (Lanna) into Babai/Dadian and Babai/Zhennai (Chiang Rai). This was eventually unsuccessful, despite a Chinese-sponsored military attack on Lanna.[35] A similar attempt by the Ming state to split the polity of Cheli (Chiang Hung) into Cheli and Cheli/Jingan was made in 1421, so as to reduce its power and allow the appointment of a Chinese registrar and military commissioner in the latter.[36] One hundred and fifty years later, when the power of Ava-Burma was expanding, the Ministry of War also urged in respect of Yunnan that 'special instructions should be sent to the various *yi* noting that they are not permitted to have communication or form links with each other'.[37] At the end of the 16th century, the Ministry of Rites urged that Ava-Burma only be given recognition by the court on condition that it 'not seek alliances with other tribes'.[38] And, all along, it was the power of the Ming colonial forces in this area and the local forces of other polities controlled by the Ming that provided the threat or actual power which allowed them to pursue these policies of divide and rule, which have marked all colonial regimes.

Overland domination II: Formal colonialism involving the incorporation of Đại Việt/Đại Ngu by the Yongle emperor

In 1406, in an effort to increase Ming influence and power in the Vietnamese polity of Đại Việt, known to the Ming as Annan 安南, the Yongle emperor attempted to send a puppet ruler named Chen Tianping 陳天平 (Trần Thiên Bình, d. 1406) into that polity.[39] Trần Thiên Bình was killed as he proceeded into the country. This killing by the Vietnamese became the immediate pretext for the Yongle emperor to launch a huge invasion, a move obviously planned well before the event. He appointed senior generals, sea-crossing commanders, firearms commanders, rapid

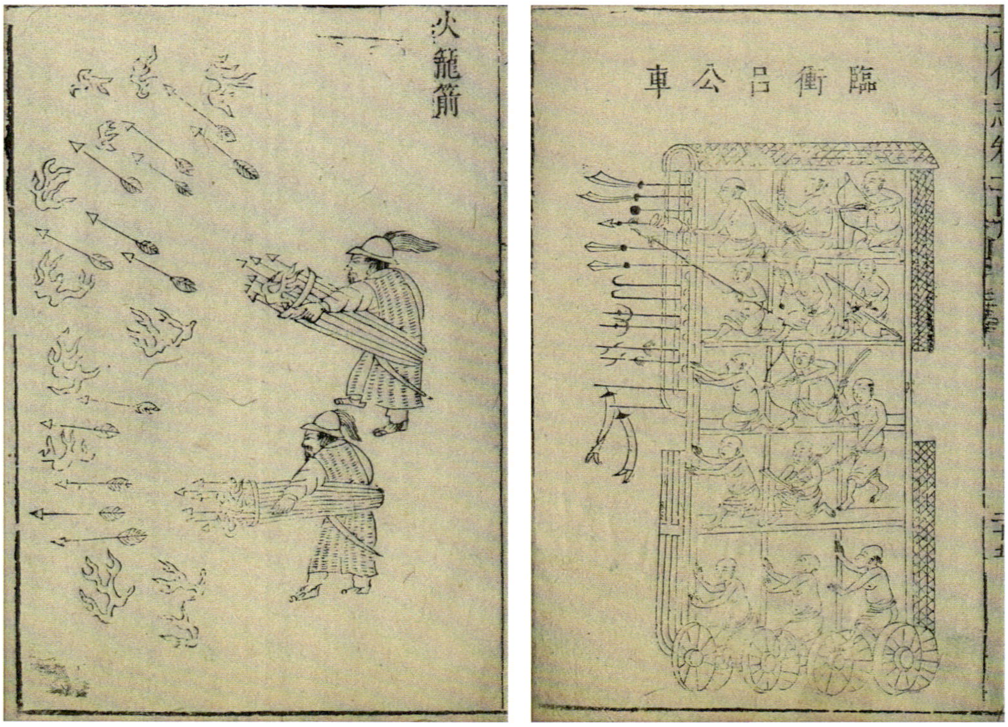

Plate 2.2a–b ***Treatise on Military Preparedness*** **(*Wubei zhi* 武備志); a) page from *Wubei zhi* showing firearms; b) page from *Wubei zhi* showing siege machine. Tianqi period edition, 1621–7. Woodblock printed, ink on paper. National Library of China**

attack commanders and cavalry commanders. On 30 July 1406, the boat-borne forces set sail from Nanjing. They landed in southern China and joined with other forces in the border province of Guangxi, comprising 95,000 troops from the provinces of Zhejiang, Jiangxi, Guangdong, Guangxi and Huguang, a further 10,000 cavalry and infantry troops from various other guards, and 30,000 'native troops'[40] from Guangxi. An additional 75,000 cavalry and troops were deployed from Yunnan, Guizhou and Sichuan. Sun Laichen has examined the use of firearms by the Ming armies in their invasion of Vietnam.[41] The Ming forces also built boats in Vietnam to continue their assault, and in January 1407 achieved one of the most significant victories of the campaign when they took Đa-bang City. Evocative descriptions of the Chinese forces disguising their horses with images of lions in order to frighten the elephants which led the Vietnamese forces, and advancing with firearms which shot fire-arrows, have been left to us (**Pl. 2.2a–b**).[42] In subsequent weeks, the Vietnamese Eastern Capital collapsed and the Western Capital was abandoned to the Chinese. Then, in the middle of 1407, the Vietnamese ruler Hồ Quý Ly and his son were captured, and the short-lived Hồ dynasty of Đại Ngu came to an end. The Chinese forces declared victory amid claims of seven million Vietnamese killed in this initial campaign.[43] In late 1407, Jiaozhi 交趾 (the occupied Đại Việt) became Ming China's 14th province and remained so until 1428, when the Ming formally withdrew provincial status.

The colonisation of the country began in earnest immediately, with the invading forces beginning to employ local forces to assist them. The Ming regional commander Zhang Fu 張輔 (1375–1449) memorialised to the court, 'Due to the circumstances, the expeditionary forces from Yunnan, Guangdong and Guangxi now have depleted ranks. They wish to select men from the Annan [Viet] native forces to make up their deficiencies.'[44] The request was approved and the conscription of the local arm of the colonial army commenced. New administrative boundaries were drawn, new tax offices, salt offices, Confucian schools, Buddhist registries and other offices were established, while 7,600 tradesmen and artisans (including gun founders) captured in Đại Việt were sent to the Ming capital at modern-day Nanjing.[45] By 1408, the Chinese had established 472 military and civilian offices in Jiaozhi,[46] all being administered in a Chinese mode but many staffed by Vietnamese. Within two years, three Maritime Trade Supervisorates (*Shi bo ti ju si* 市舶提舉司) had been created in this new province, the same number as existed in the rest of China. This was a clear indication of the desire of the Ming to control maritime trade to the south and exploit the economic advantage of such control.[47] Other economic exploitation involved grain taxes, annual levies of lacquer, sapan wood, kingfisher feathers, fans and aromatics and the imposition of monopolies on gold, silver, salt, iron and fish. In addition, eunuchs were sent to Jiaozhi with the task of collecting treasure for the emperor, but an equal amount of treasure collection appears to have been done for themselves.

New military guards were established in Jiaozhi: the Jiaozhou 交州 Left, Right and Central Guards within the capital, and the Jiaozhou Forward Guard to the north of the Fuliang 富良 River, and appointments of Vietnamese persons who had allied themselves to the Chinese were made. These were especially valuable in places where the Chinese troops could not be employed. For example, in a memorial to the court in 1408, we read:

> The Jiaozhi Provincial Administration Commission has memorialised that the three areas of Polei 坡壘, Qiuwen 丘溫 and Ailiu 隘留 are narrow passes into Jiaozhi and are affected by miasmic vapours. The official troops find it difficult to dwell in these places. It is proposed raising native forces and establishing guards in nearby Si Subprefecture 思州, Taiping 太平 Prefecture and Tian Subprefecture 田州.[48]

The proposal was accepted and implemented. Where there were insufficient troops available for a military guard, police offices were established.[49] Senior Chinese military figures would also command roving forces of up to 2,000 Vietnamese troops to be sent wherever there was military service to perform.

In an attempt to eliminate the cultural basis of the polity, the Ming emperor ordered the destruction of Vietnamese books. Some of the secret correspondence contains specific sets of orders that Ming commanders and troops were required to abide by during the military campaign. One of these letters contains instructions related to the handling of Vietnamese written works. Issued on 17 August 1406, they read in part:

> With the exception of Buddhist and Taoist texts, all written and printed materials within Annan are to be burnt. These include anything that promotes Vietnamese rites and customs as well as texts used by children, such as those containing the phrase *shang da ren Qiu Ji Yi*. In addition, all stelae from ancient times that are of Chinese origin are to be preserved, but those erected by Vietnamese should all be destroyed. Not even a single character [from the Vietnamese works] is to be preserved.[50]
>
> 兵入, 除釋道經板經文不燬外, 一切書板文字, 以至禮俗、童蒙所習, 如'上大人丘乙己'之類片紙隻字, 悉皆燬之。其境內, 凡有古昔中國所立碑刻,則存之。但是安南所立者, 悉壞之, 一字勿存。

Ong Eng Ann further cites 15th-century Vietnamese sources concerning the Ming destruction and confiscation of texts. Hồ Nguyên Trừng (Lê Trừng), eldest son of Hồ Quý Ly, commented: 'As for the burning of Vietnamese books during the war [with the Ming], which reduced most of them to ashes causing them to vanish without a single trace, I can only express deep regret!' In a draft memorial on the completion of the official chronicle Đại Việt Sử Ký Toàn Thư 大越史記全書, presented to the Lê emperor Thánh-tông (r. 1460–97) in 1479, the famous historian Ngô Sĩ Liên wrote: 'No [event can be compared to] the invasion of the fanatical Ming (狂明), [during which] one country's [Vietnam's] books and maps [were] reduced to ashes [as a consequence of this] catastrophe'.[51]

In order to try to inculcate some loyalty to China, senior Vietnamese military commanders who gave their allegiance to the Chinese were sent to the Chinese capital at Nanjing for an audience with the emperor and to receive rewards, and then sent back to serve their masters in Jiaozhi as members of the colonial army.[52] The appointment of such people to senior posts was also used as a propaganda weapon by the colonial authorities.[53]

While reinforcements were dispatched from China to meet a renewed military threat from the Vietnamese, the frequency and intensity of the uprisings grew, grain supplies continued to be scant and, in 1422, the Chinese supreme military commander Li Bin 李彬 died. The death of the Yongle emperor two years later also reduced Chinese enthusiasm for maintaining the troublesome colony. The growing power and momentum of Lê Lợi's opposition in 1425 also presaged the end of the colonial administration. The inefficiency of the Ming military at this time appears to have derived from the fact that most military units they deployed were Vietnamese, albeit sometimes under Chinese commanders.[54] A late attempt at reinforcing the colonial forces in Jiaozhi was made in 1426, when a further 20,000 troops were dispatched there from various provinces,[55] a further 1,000 tally slips were sent to Jiaozhi for appointing Vietnamese to military and civil posts, new commanders were dispatched with the orders to recruit 30,000 more Vietnamese for the military, new firearms were supplied, and the senior Chinese military commanders already in Vietnam were stripped of their ranks and titles and required to 'realise achievements'.[56] But by May 1427 the major Chinese citadels in Jiaozhi were under attack, and the arriving Chinese reinforcements had been put to flight. By the end of 1427, Lê Lợi had sent envoys to the Chinese court seeking the Chinese withdrawal,[57] and the Ming had recognised the benefits of withdrawal, albeit disguised in claims of benevolence by the Ming court. A process of decolonisation was thus set in train, inevitably involving the colonial forces. The imperial orders, after requiring that the Vietnamese find themselves a ruler, read:

> The Chengshan Marquis and Regional Commander Wang Tong and so on are to immediately lead the government troops back to their original guards and battalions. All of the civil and military officials and clerks, commanders and troops of the Jiaozhi Regional Military Commission, Provincial Administration Commission and provincial Surveillance Commission as well as of all guards, battalions, prefectures, subprefectures and counties, are all to return home together with their family members. Also, all of the grand defenders and eunuch and palace officials who have been sent on official duties are to return to the capital.[58]

The flood of people and materials northwards out of the former colony must have made the first few months of 1428 a hugely dislocated period for both Đại Việt and southern China, and at the speed at which this occurred it was more a flight rather than an organised withdrawal. After some pretence that a descendant of the Trần dynasty would be installed as ruler of the polity, Lê Lợi formally assumed the position in 1428, sending a proxy human figure in gold to the Chinese court.[59]

The unsuccessful attempt by Ming China at colonising Đại Việt thus extended over a period of 21 years from 1406 to 1428. During this period, a colonial administration was established in Đại Việt and economic exploitation of the region was pursued with vigour. The role of the colonial army, comprising both Chinese and locally recruited persons, was to ensure the security of the colonial administrative apparatus. The use of a large number of Vietnamese soldiers in the colonial army was eventually to prove a major flaw in the system, as it was they who eventually rebelled and drove out the Ming colonialists.

The policies pursued by the Ming in Đại Việt and some areas of Yunnan over the 15th century suggest that the process by which the Ming state expanded into new areas can be summarised as follows: 1) Validation of a military action was sought out or created; 2) A military expedition was launched; 3) Assistance of some local leaders was gained; 4) Intimidation by slaughter was conducted;[60] 5) The existing leaders were killed or removed elsewise; 6) Orders were issued locally proclaiming the moral rectitude of the military action and noting that it was conducted to free the

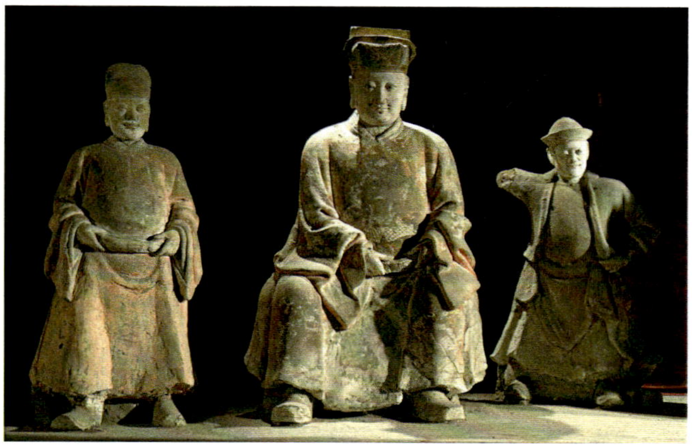

Plate 2.3 Statues of Zheng He and his attendants, *c.* 1573–1620. Earthenware and painted, central figure height: 100cm. Excavated from Xianying Temple, Changle, Fujian province, in 1992

people from their evil rulers or other predicament; 7) Chinese bureaucrats were appointed as either registry managers or more broadly in the larger polities; 8) Military guards and civil administrative offices were established; 9) Grain and labour levies were instituted, and monopolies over salt, gold and silver were instituted, or else it was demanded that such be provided to the state in lieu of labour; 10) Useful human resources were stripped;[61] 11) Further opportunities for territorial gain were sought out.

Overseas domination I: the voyages led by Zheng He and other eunuchs

The dispatch of various eunuch-led maritime missions to the 'Western Ocean' (*Xiyang* 西洋, or maritime Southeast Asia west of Borneo extending into the Indian Ocean), as well as other lesser-known missions to the Eastern Ocean (*Dongyang* 東洋, today's Philippines, Borneo and eastern Indonesia), was the third of the three prongs of southern expansion pursued by the Yongle emperor. The most widely known of these envoys was Zheng He 鄭和 (1371–1433), otherwise known as *Sanbao* 三寶, or 'Three Treasures' (**Pl. 2.3**), and it is around this eunuch that many of the legends relating to the voyages are centred. Other eunuch commanders included Wang Guitong 王貴通 (active *c.* 1407) and Hou Xian 侯顯 (active 1403–27). Eunuch envoys such as Zhang Qian 張謙 (active 1408–20) were responsible for voyages to the polities in the Eastern Ocean including Boni, Pangasinan, Sulu and Luzon, and for bringing their envoys and rulers to China.

The eunuch-led missions were, like Yongle's expansions into Yunnan and occupation of Đại Việt, intended to create legitimacy for the usurping emperor, display the might of the Ming, bring known polities to demonstrate submission to the Ming and collect treasures for the court.[62] To achieve these aims, the maritime forces needed to be both huge and powerful. Shipbuilding began almost as soon as the Yongle emperor assumed power. In 1405, just after Zheng He departed on his first expedition, Zhejiang and other regional military commissions were ordered to build 1,180 ocean-going ships.[63] By 1408, the task was assigned to a central ministry and the Ministry of Works was ordered to build 48 'treasure-ships' (*baochuan* 寶船).[64]

To enable these great fleets to maintain the *pax* Ming in the immediate region and sail through the Indian Ocean to Africa (**Pl. 2.4**), it was necessary to create staging posts in what is today Southeast Asia. These depots (*guanchang* 官場) were established at Melaka and at the northern end of the Straits of Melaka (old spelling Malacca) near the polity of Samudera. These can be seen on the *Wubei zhi* 武備志 maps which date in original from the first half of the 15th century. The Straits of Melaka were probably more vital in the 15th

Plate 2.4 Map of Zheng He's voyages

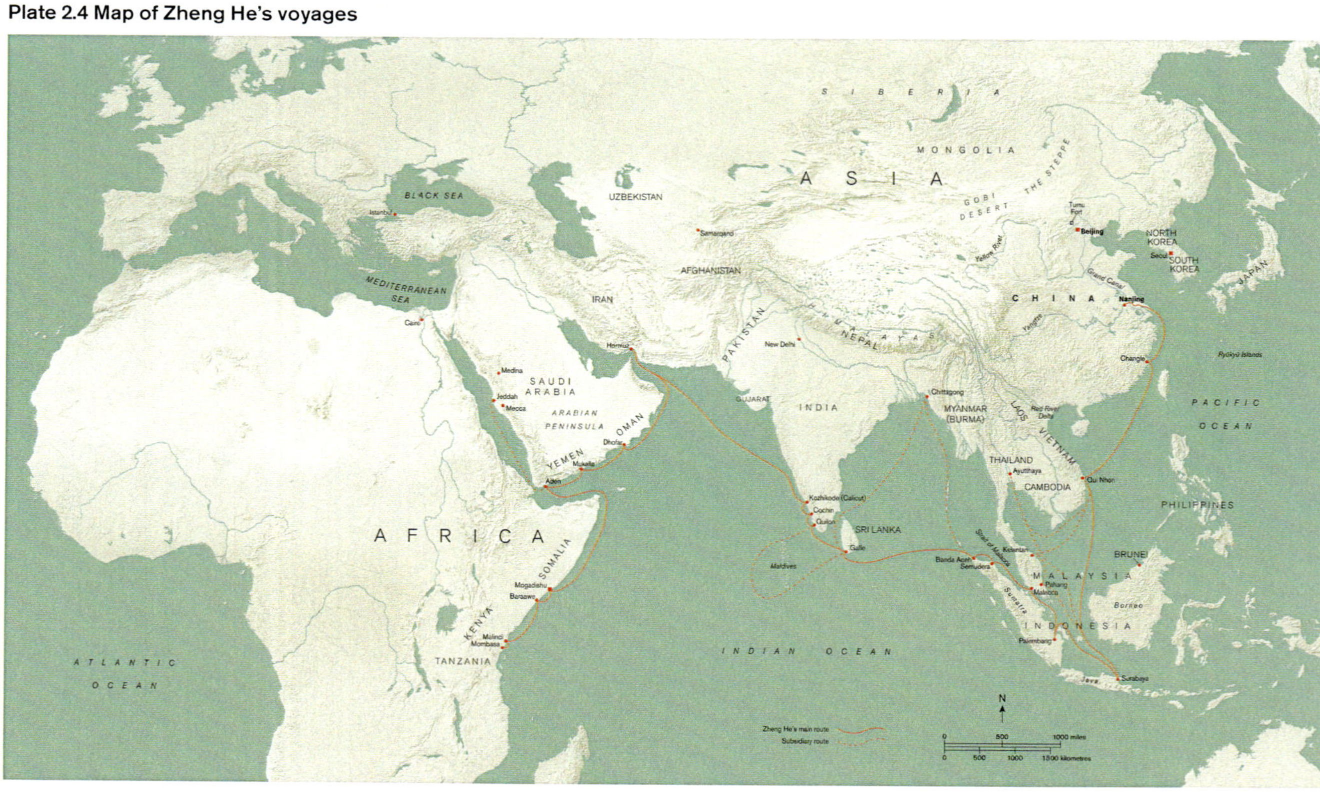

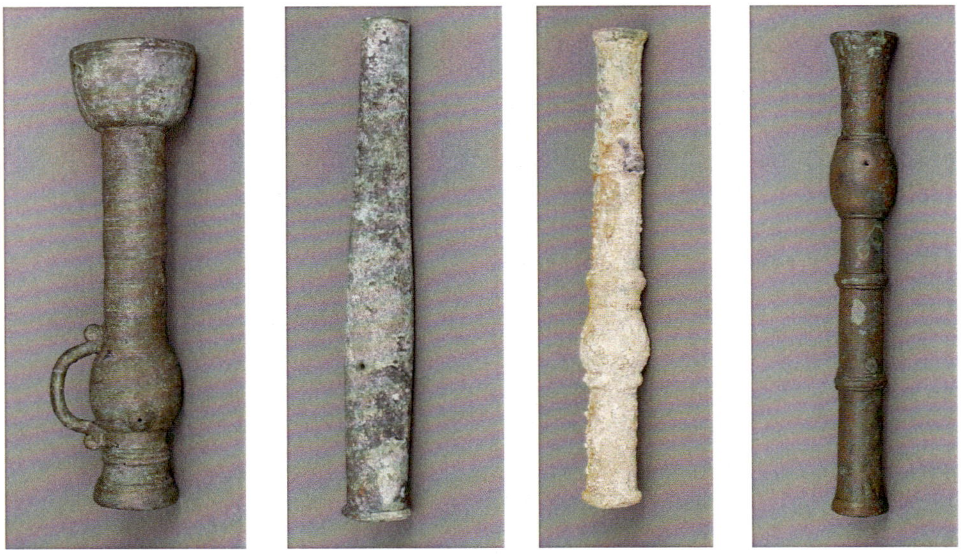

a) Dimensions: length 407mm x width 111mm

b) Dimensions: length 235mm x width 46mm

c) Dimensions: length 355mm x width 51mm

d) Dimensions: length 347mm x width 571mm

Plate 2.5a–d Guns from Bakau shipwreck, early 15th century. The Maritime Experiential Museum, Resorts World Sentosa Singapore

century, when international linkages were entirely dependent on shipping, than they are today, and managing this waterway was an essential first step in controlling the region. It was also thus that the Ming assisted the growth of the new polity of Melaka, around the Ming maritime base at that place. The links between Melaka and the Ming thereby remained intimate for much of the 15th century. The degree to which the development of the port city of Melaka and the northern port polities of Sumatra was a product of Ming policies in Southeast Asia at this period, needs to be further investigated.

The military aspect of these voyages (**Pl. 2.5a–d**) needs underlining, in part because of the stress placed on these missions in current scholarship in the People's Republic of China as 'voyages of friendship'.[65] A large proportion of the members of the missions were military personnel, and in a *Ming shilu* reference of 1427, there is reference to '10,000 crack troops who had formerly been sent to the Western Ocean',[66] suggesting that a great number were highly trained military men. It is obvious that such a force would have played a major threatening role, useful in encouraging recalcitrant foreign rulers to travel to the Ming court. However, there were other times when more than military threat was required, and the history of the Zheng He voyages is replete with violence as the eunuch commanders tried to implement the Ming emperor's demands. Major military actions included the following: attack on the Old Port Pacification Superintendency in Sumatra (1407); deployment of troops in Java (1407); threats against Burma (1409); attack on Sri Lanka (1411); attack on and capture of Suganla in Samudera (1415); and attack on and razing of Ayudhya (1400s, precise date unknown).[67]

These examples suggest that the maritime forces sent abroad in the first third of the 15th century were intended to achieve the recognition of Ming preeminence among all the polities of the known maritime world. Those who would not recognise this supremacy of the Ming were subjected to military force. This is not to say that all polities needed military coercion. The existence of economic benefits flowing from 'tribute missions' suggests that some would likely have gladly sent tribute and personally travelled to the Ming court. However, the number of Southeast Asian rulers travelling to China with the Zheng He missions suggests that coercion must have been an important element. There are very few other examples of rulers visiting other polities within Southeast Asia in this period, suggesting that some great pressure must have been imposed on them to encourage them to journey to the Ming court and thereby demonstrate their subordinate status before the Chinese emperor.

These were missions intended to coerce and obtain control of ports and shipping lanes. It was not control of territory which was sought, an element which came with later imperialism, but rather political and economic control across space, control of economic lifelines, nodal points and networks. By controlling ports and trade routes, one controlled trade, an essential element for the missions' treasure-collecting tasks. The colonial armies which manned these ships were the tools necessary to ensure that the control was maintained. In their methods, the Ming, through these maritime missions, was engaged in what might be called proto-colonialism. That is, they were engaged in that early form of colonialism by which a dominant maritime power took control (either through force or the threat thereof) of the main port polities along the major east–west maritime trade network, as well as the seas between, thereby gaining economic and political benefits.

Overseas domination II: formal declaration of suzerainty abroad

The actions which Ming emperors pursued in respect of offshore lands and polities differed with time and place. The topos of the emperor as supreme and virtuous mediator of all relations in *tianxia* 天下 (the known world) was stressed in the rhetoric of Chinese accounts. Thus the emperor was responsible for 'enfeoffing' rulers beyond the formal limits of the Ming empire, and charging them to look after their people. The removal of unworthy rulers was also inherent in

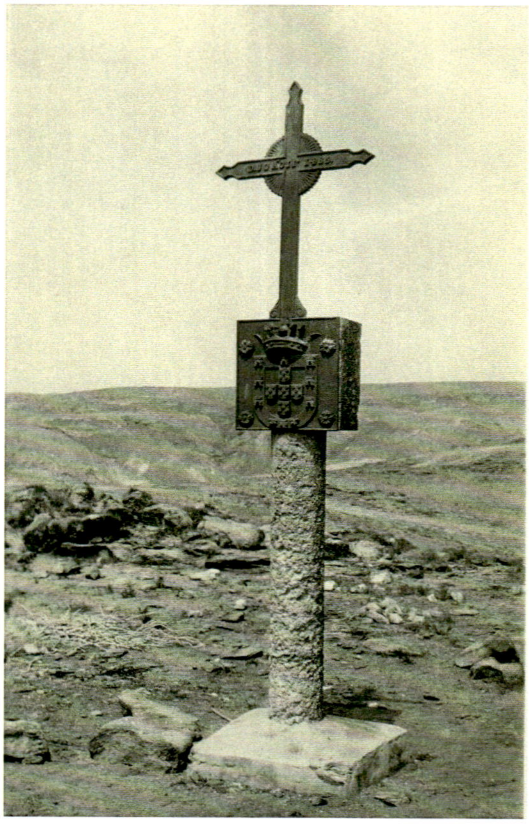

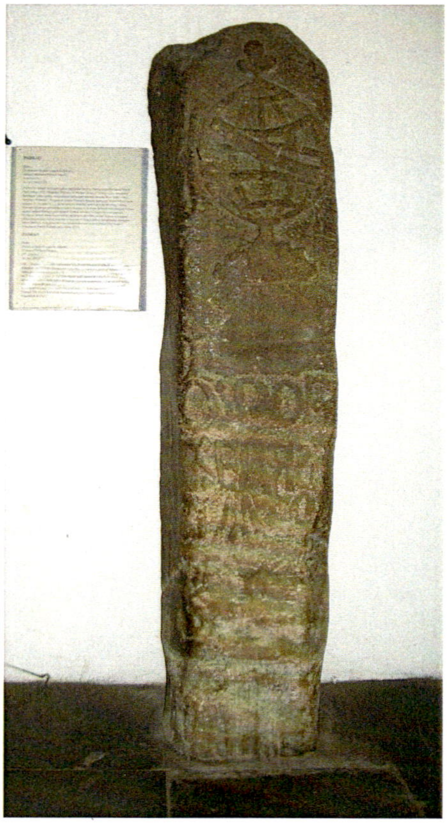

Plate 2.6a–b a) A *padrão* planted by Diogo Cão in Angola; b) Luso-Sundanese *padrão*, erected in 1522. Height 165cm. Indonesian National Museum, Jakarta

the emperor's responsibilities. As such, a certain suzerainty over maritime lands was asserted, at least within the scope of Chinese rhetoric.

However, on occasions, a more forceful assertion of suzerainty was made. In 1407, for example, Zheng He returned from his first major mission abroad, bringing with him the 'pirate' Chen Zuyi 陳祖義 (d. 1407), captured at Old Port (*Jiugang* 舊港) in Sumatra, for reportedly having 'feigned surrender but secretly plotted to attack the Imperial army'.[68] The Ming representative reported 5,000 persons killed, with ten ships burnt and seven captured in the battle. Later in the same year, the Ming formally recognised the existence of the polity of Old Port. However, because of the large numbers of Chinese from Guangdong and Fujian, both ex-military personnel and civilians, who lived there, it was deemed not to be a country (*guo* 國). Rather, it was recognised as a 'Pacification Superintendency' (*Xuan wei shi si* 宣慰使司), a term which was commonly used to refer to polities on the Chinese borders. The new superintendent, a Chinese person named Shi Jinqing 施進卿 (d. 1423), was appointed as the local ruler to represent the Ming state.[69] This gave the Ming state – again at least within its rhetorical bounds – a more direct power over Old Port.

Other formal declarations of suzerainty over overseas polities can be seen in Ming texts during the first half of the 15th century. These involved the erection of inscribed stone stelae in various lands, carrying forward the Chinese practice of establishing inscriptions in newly conquered areas. This also provides an interesting comparative practice vis-à-vis the Portuguese establishment of *padrão* – memorials usually comprising stone crosses inscribed with the coat of arms of Portugal – erected by the Portuguese as they claimed new overseas lands from the 15th century (**Pl. 2.6a–b**).

The Chinese inscriptions recorded as being erected abroad were established in at least five polities:

Melaka: The *Ming shilu*, or *Ming Veritable Records*, contains an entry dated to 11 November 1405. It refers to a mission commanded by Zheng He being sent to Melaka, a port polity which controlled the Straits of Melaka. In part the entry reads:

> A stele inscription for Mount Zhenguo 鎮國山 ['Mountain that Protects the Country'] was conferred upon the country of Melaka. At this time, the envoy of this country had said that his king admired righteousness, wished that Melaka, like the administrative divisions of China [*Zhongguo shu jun* 中國屬郡], could annually show its loyalty through offering tribute, and requested that their mountain be enfeoffed as protector of the whole country ...[70]

Here, while the stele itself asserted Ming suzerainty over this port polity, within the Chinese record this arrangement was depicted as not only acceptable to the ruler of Melaka, but actually desired.

Brunei: The origins of the Brunei Ming inscription are recorded in a *Ming shilu* entry dated to 20 December 1408. The entry reads in part:

> The eunuch Zhang Qian and the Messenger Zhou Hang 周航 were sent to escort Xiawang 遐旺, successor to the post of king of the country of Boni [Brunei], and others back to their country ... Previously, the former king of Boni, Ma-na-re-jia-na-nai 麻那惹加那乃, had said: '... Behind the country there is a mountain and it is humbly requested that it be enfeoffed as the protector of the country (*yi guo zhi zhen* 一國之鎮).' At this time, his son Xiawang repeated the request and thus the mountain was enfeoffed as the 'Mountain Which Will Ever Peacefully

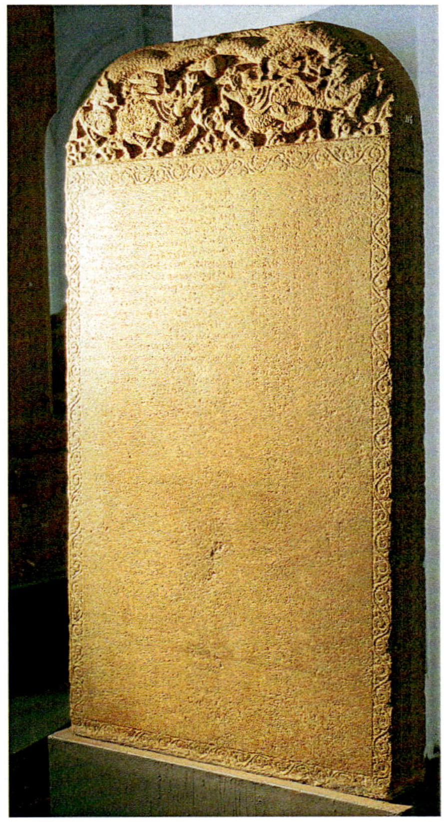

Plate 2.7 (left) Rubbing of the trilingual 1409 Galle stone stele from 1920–50. Ink on paper, height 144.8cm, width 76.2cm. Institute for Research in Humanities, Kyoto University

Plate 2.8 (right) Galle stele with the inscription written in Chinese, Tamil and Persian, erected in 1409 in Galle, Sri Lanka, 'to announce our mandate to foreign nations and to commemorate the sending of offerings from the Chinese emperor [Yongle] through the envoys Zheng He and Wang Qinglian'. Height 144.78cm, width 76.2cm, depth 12.7cm. National Museum of Colombo, Sri Lanka

> Protect the Country' (*Chang ning zhen guo zhi shan* 長寧鎮國之山). It was ordered that when they arrived at that place, Qian and so on should erect a tablet. The Emperor personally composed a text for it.[71]

Both the stele entry itself and the imperially conferred text underlined the degree to which this was an assertion of Ming protective suzerainty over this polity.

Sri Lanka: This stele (**Pls 2.7–2.8**), the only one extant, was taken to Sri Lanka by Zheng He in 1409 and erected in Galle in 1411. The inscription is in three languages – Chinese, Tamil and Persian – and much of the inscription refers to respect for the Buddha, Allah and the Tamil deity Tenavarai Nayanar. The Chinese inscription has been studied by Eva Nagel.[72] The assertion of Chinese suzerainty is implicit in the imperial decoration of the stele, the claims of the Ming heavenly mandate and the dating system employed, as well as in the Tamil inscription where the Ming ruler is entitled 'The great king of Cina, the supreme overlord of kings'. Suzerainty was also separately asserted through Zheng He's military engagement on the island, capturing the ruler and carrying him back to China.

Cochin: The reference to the Cochin inscription can be found in the standard *Ming History* or *Ming shi*, produced in the early 18th century. In the account of Cochin (*Kezhi* 柯枝) contained within this work, we read:

> In the tenth year of the Yongle reign [1412], Zheng He was again sent as an envoy to this country. They offered tribute for two successive years. Their envoy requested the conferral of a seal and the granting of a title, and that the mountain within their country be formally enfeoffed. The Emperor sent Zheng He carrying orders and a seal to confer upon their king. The Emperor also wrote a stele inscription and ordered that it be inscribed upon the stone on top of the mountain.[73]

This account closely reflects those of the Melaka and Brunei stelae and its function appears to have been similar, to assert Ming suzerainty over this port polity.

Japan: Another stele with an imperial inscription was erected on a mountain (Mount Aso) in Japan, which was given the title 'Mountain which will Ever Peacefully Guard the Country' (*shouan zhenguo zhi shan* 壽安鎮國之山).[74] Again this reflected the Yongle emperor's aspiration to assert his legitimacy by claiming to protect polities beyond China.

It is worthy of note that these stelae asserting Ming suzerainty were established in maritime polities which were either weak or new and were competing against established power centres. Melaka was a new polity rivalling Samudera on the Sumatran coast in the north of the Straits of Melaka, Cochin was a port rivalling the established centre of Calicut, while Brunei was attempting to stave off the demands of the Majapahit empire on the island of Java. The Japanese stele was erected on Kyushu where local polities were having to deal with the powerful Muromachi shogunate to the north. As such these assertions of Chinese attachment for these polities also likely worked in their own favour as much as in that of the Ming.

As has been noted above, early Ming China pursued domination of polities to its south through four modes: indirect overland colonialism, direct overland colonialism, assertion of maritime hegemony and claims of suzerainty over maritime polities. The importance of Ming state violence in pursuing this domination needs to be underlined, given that Chinese texts often obscure the mechanisms of domination and expansion through a range of rhetorical devices. Benevolent rulers punished 'bandits' (*tao zei* 討賊), pacified (*ping ding* 平定) areas, soothed (*fu* 撫) polities and instructed (*yu* 諭) recalcitrants, all manifestly desirable actions in maintaining social order. However, Chinese emperors have never been able to engage in 'aggression' (*qinlüe* 侵略) because Chinese rhetorical structures precisely preclude such actions by imperial rulers. It is these devices which have resulted in Chinese people, until today, often being unable to conceive of a Chinese polity as constituting a potential aggressor, or having latently violent or dangerous intentions towards neighbouring polities. It is also these devices that require Chinese historical maps to be redrawn in order to reflect more accurate portrayals of historical China.[75] It is thus that we need to unmask the tyranny of Chinese historiography and begin to recognise the differences between civilisational rhetoric and civilisational practice.

By explicitly highlighting Ming China's aim to dominate polities to the south and the attendant violence which occurred over the first 50 years of the 15th century, it is hoped that others will be able to examine other periods of Chinese history and, by deconstructing the rhetoric of traditional texts, more fully explore the political relations between China and its neighbours.

Notes

1 *MSL Taizu shilu* 39.1b (2/2/丙寅), Wade 2005b, http://epress.nus.edu.sg/msl/entry/298. Another reference to Yunnan as a country can be found at *MSL Taizu shilu* 53.9a–b (3/6/戊寅), Wade 2005b, http://epress.nus.edu.sg/msl/entry/499.

2 *MSL Taizu shilu* 138.5a–b (14/8/癸丑), Wade 2005b, http://epress.nus.edu.sg/msl/entry/2320.

3 For much of the Ming, in addition to being a provincial designation, 'Yunnan' was a generic term for areas to the southwest, extending as far as knowledge extended. In this respect, Yunnan was somewhat like the term 'the West' in the European movement across the North American continent in the 18th and 19th centuries.

4 *MSL Taizu shilu* 189.14b–16a (21/3/甲辰), Wade 2005b, http://epress.nus.edu.sg/msl/entry/2876.

5 *MSL Taizu shilu* 198.2a–b (22/11/乙亥), Wade 2005b, http://epress.nus.edu.sg/msl/entry/2922. This practice of claiming reparations from the polity one attacks became an integral part of many later colonialisms.

6 *MSL Taizu shilu* 255.2a–b (30/9/戊辰), Wade 2005b, http://epress.nus.edu.sg/msl/entry/3104 and *MSL Taizu shilu* 255.8a–b (30/12/乙巳), Wade 2005b, http://epress.nus.edu.sg/msl/entry/3107.

7 *MSL Taizong shilu* 15.2a (35/12/丙辰), Wade 2005b, http://epress.nus.edu.sg/msl/entry/3156 and *MSL Taizong shilu* 16.3a (1/1/戊子), Wade 2005b, http://epress.nus.edu.sg/msl/entry/15.

8 *MSL Taizu shilu* 190.3b (21/4/癸亥), Wade 2005b, http://epress.nus.edu.sg/msl/entry/2878.

9 A Chinese unit of weight, often referred to as a 'Chinese ounce'. During the Ming, it averaged 37g.

10 *MSL Taizong shilu* 17.6a (1/2/丁卯), Wade 2005b, http://epress.nus.edu.sg/msl/entry/19.

11 Located in Tengyue subprefecture, west of Baoshan in what is today Tengchong. Approximately 160km north of Bhamo and 150km southeast of Myitkyina. See Liew Foon Ming 1998, II, 94–5.

12 Previously known as the Jinchi (Golden Teeth) Guard. Located in what is today Baoshan. Liew Foon Ming 1998, II, 91–2.

13 *MSL Taizong shilu* 23.4b (1/9/甲戌), Wade 2005b, http://epress.nus.edu.sg/msl/entry/9.

14 *MSL Taizong shilu* 16.3a (1/1/戊子), Wade 2005b, http://epress.nus.edu.sg/msl/entry/15. These polities lay in the southwest of the modern province of Yunnan.

15 *MSL Taizong shilu* 53.2b (4/4/甲戌), Wade 2005b, http://epress.nus.edu.sg/msl/entry/882 .

16 *MSL Taizong shilu* 32.1a (2/6/癸酉), Wade 2005b, http://epress.nus.edu.sg/msl/entry/332 .

17 *MSL Taizong shilu* 49.1a–b (3/12/戊辰), Wade 2005b, http://epress.nus.edu.sg/msl/entry/524.

18 *MSL Taizong shilu* 82.1a–b (6/8/丙子), Wade 2005b, http://epress.nus.edu.sg/msl/entry/1274 .

19 *MSL Taizong shilu* 35.2b (2/10/辛未), Wade 2005b, http://epress.nus.edu.sg/msl/entry/317 .

20 *MSL Taizong shilu* 55.1b (4/6/癸亥), Wade 2005b, http://epress.nus.edu.sg/msl/entry/895 .

21 See for example *MSL Taizong shilu* 17.6a (1/2/丁卯), Wade 2005b, http://epress.nus.edu.sg/msl/entry/19.

22 *MSL Taizong shilu* 57.2a–b (4/inter 7/己巳), Wade 2005b, http://epress.nus.edu.sg/msl/entry/917.

23 *MSL Yingzong shilu* 44.7b (3/7/丁未), Wade 2005b, http://epress.nus.edu.sg/msl/entry/721.

24 *MSL Yingzong shilu* 51.7a–b (4/2/辛未), Wade 2005b, http://epress.nus.edu.sg/msl/entry/567.

25 *MSL Yingzong shilu* 127.1b (10/3/庚子), Wade 2005b, http://epress.nus.edu.sg/msl/entry/1945; Liew Foon Ming 1996.

26 The polity known in Shan as Möng Yang or Möng Kawng and in Burmese as Mohnyin or Mogaung.

27 *MSL Yingzong shilu* 164.5a–6a.

28 A generic term for persons outside Chinese culture.

29 *MSL Yingzong shilu* 164.5a–6a (13/3/壬寅), Wade 2005b, http://epress.nus.edu.sg/msl/entry/2276.

30 *MSL Yingzong shilu* 175.8b (14/2/辛未), Wade 2005b, http://epress.nus.edu.sg/msl/entry/2360.

31 *MSL Yingzong shilu* 179.7b–8a (14/9/癸巳), Wade 2005b, http://epress.nus.edu.sg/msl/entry/2366 .

32 *MSL Yingzong shilu* 241.4b–5a (5/5/庚申), Wade 2005b, http://epress.nus.edu.sg/msl/entry/1184.

33 *MSL Yingzong shilu* 156.1a (12/7/壬辰), Wade 2005b, http://epress.nus.edu.sg/msl/entry/2159.

34 *MSL Yingzong shilu* 189.3b (1/2/庚辰), Wade 2005b, http://epress.nus.edu.sg/msl/entry/226.

35 *MSL Taizong shilu* 31.5a–b (2/5/己巳), Wade 2005b, http://epress.nus.edu.sg/msl/entry/337.

36 Wade 2005b, http://epress.nus.edu.sg/msl/place/227.

37 *MSL Shizong shilu* 482.8b–9a (39/3/甲午) Wade 2005b, http://epress.nus.edu.sg/msl/entry/3207.

38 *MSL Shenzong shilu* 261.4b (21/6/丙申) Wade 2005b, http://epress.nus.edu.sg/msl/entry/2913.

39 *MSL Taizong shilu* 52.6a–7a.

40 These were non-Chinese troops under the 'native offices' of Guangxi, probably peoples who are today called Zhuang and Yao.

41 Sun 2003.

42 *MSL Taizong shilu* 52.6a–7a (4/3/丙午), Wade 2005b, http://epress.nus.edu.sg/msl/entry/875. See also Whitmore 1985, 91–2.

43 *MSL Taizong shilu* 68.3b–7a (5/6/癸未), Wade 2005b, http://epress.nus.edu.sg/msl/entry/1105.

44 *MSL Taizong shilu* 67.3b–4a (5/5/甲戌), Wade 2005b, http://epress.nus.edu.sg/msl/entry/1096, dated to the equivalent of 26 June 1407.

45 *MSL Taizong shilu* 71.6a (5/9/癸酉), Wade 2005b, http://epress.nus.edu.sg/msl/entry/1049.

46 *MSL Taizong shilu* 80.3b–4a (6/6/己丑), Wade 2005b, http://epress.nus.edu.sg/msl/entry/1268.

47 The importance of Vietnamese maritime trade in this period is underlined in Momoki 1998.

48 *MSL Taizong shilu* 77.3b (6/3/壬戌), Wade 2005b, http://epress.nus.edu.sg/msl/entry/1250.

49 *MSL Taizong shilu* 84.4b–5a (6/10/庚子), Wade 2005b, http://epress.nus.edu.sg/msl/entry/611.

50 Ong Eng Ann 2010, 157.

51 Ong Eng Ann 2010, 158.

52 For example, see *MSL Taizong shilu* 73.5a (5/11/己巳), Wade 2005b, http://epress.nus.edu.sg/msl/entry/1077.

53 *MSL Taizong shilu* 145.2b (11/11/乙未), Wade 2005b, http://epress.nus.edu.sg/msl/entry/2021 and *MSL Taizong shilu* 163.1b (13/4/丁丑), Wade 2005b, http://epress.nus.edu.sg/msl/entry/2249.

54 *MSL Xuanzong shilu* 15.1b–2a (1/3/丁酉), Wade 2005b, http://epress.nus.edu.sg/msl/entry/129 .

55 *MSL Xuanzong shilu* 15.8a–b (1/3/丙午), Wade 2005b, http://epress.nus.edu.sg/msl/entry/136.

56 *MSL Xuanzong shilu* 16.1a–b (1/4/丙寅), Wade 2005b, http://epress.nus.edu.sg/msl/entry/146.

57 *MSL Xuanzong shilu* 32.9b–10a (2/10/癸未), Wade 2005b, http://epress.nus.edu.sg/msl/entry/393.

58 *MSL Xuanzong shilu* 33.1a–b (2/11/乙酉), Wade 2005b, http://epress.nus.edu.sg/msl/entry/394.

59 *MSL Xuanzong shilu* 51.3b–4a (4/2/丁亥), Wade 2005b, http://epress.nus.edu.sg/msl/entry/935.

60 In their victory memorial to the throne, the Ming commanders who had captured Đại Việt claimed that seven million of the Vietnamese forces had been killed. See *MSL Taizong shilu* 60.5a–b (4/10/庚子), Wade 2005b, http://epress.nus.edu.sg/msl/entry/861. Even allowing for the rhetoric, other reports of the Ming invasion suggest huge mortality on both sides.

61 In 1407, 7,700 tradesmen and artisans, including gun founders, were forcibly transported from Annam to the Ming capital at modern Nanjing; *MSL Taizong shilu* 71.6a (5/9/癸酉), Wade 2005b, http://epress.nus.edu.sg/msl/entry/1049.

62 The eunuchs sent to Jiaozhi (the occupied Đại Việt) and to Yunnan by the Ming emperors were also engaged in collection of precious stones, gold and pearls. A later reference from 1459 suggests that the obtaining of gold was a major task of the eunuch-led voyages. See *MSL Yingzong shilu* 307.3b (3/9/癸巳), Wade 2005b, http://epress.nus.edu.sg/msl/entry/760.

63 *MSL Taizong shilu* 233.4b (19/1/甲申), Wade 2005b, http://epress.nus.edu.sg/msl/entry/2765 and *MSL Taizong shilu* 235.1b–2a (19/3/丙戌), Wade 2005b, http://epress.nus.edu.sg/msl/entry/2769.

64 *MSL Taizong shilu* 75.2b (6/1/丁卯), Wade 2005b, http://epress.nus.edu.sg/msl/entry/1239.

65 See for example Wang Mintong 2003.

66 *MSL Xuanzong shilu* 26.2a (2/3/庚寅), Wade 2005b, http://epress.nus.edu.sg/msl/entry/357.

67 For detailed accounts of the violence pursued by Ming forces during these various episodes, see Wade 2005a.

68 *MSL Taizong shilu* 75.2b (6/1/丁卯), Wade 2005b, http://epress.nus.edu.sg/msl/entry/1239.

69 *MSL Taizong shilu* 71.5a (5/9/戊午), Wade 2005b, http://epress.nus.edu.sg/msl/entry/1065.

70 The full entry can be accessed at Wade 2005b, http://epress.nus.edu.sg/msl/entry/516.

71 Wade 2005b, http://epress.nus.edu.sg/msl/entry/1230.

72 Nagel 2001.

73 *MS* 1984, 8441.

74 *MS* 1984, 8345.

75 Compare the borders of the Ming empire shown in Mote and Twitchett 1988, xxiv, the English edition of *The Cambridge History of China*, with those in Mou and Cui 1992, its Chinese translation.

Chapter 3
Diplomacy, Trade and the Quest for the Buddha's Tooth: The Yongle Emperor and Ming China's South Asian Frontier

Tansen Sen

Chinese courts and merchants rarely undertook diplomatic or commercial activities in the Indian Ocean region prior to the 11th century. In the first millennium AD, coastal China was connected to the maritime world of the Indian Ocean through the shipping and trading networks of people from Southeast Asia, the Persian Gulf and Sri Lanka (formerly Ceylon). China's engagement with the Indian Ocean world and the coastal regions of South Asia intensified gradually over the first half of the second millennium. During this period, the Song (960–1279) and Yuan (1271–1368) courts were in frequent contact with maritime polities in the South China Sea and across the Bay of Bengal. Seafaring merchants from China also successfully established commercial networks that, in the 12th and 13th centuries, extended to the Coromandel and Malabar coasts of South Asia. By the time Zheng He 鄭和 (1371–1433) sailed on his maiden voyage in 1405, Chinese traders and courts were no longer passive participants in Indian Ocean trade and diplomacy. Not only were Chinese seafaring merchants able to bypass intermediaries and procure goods directly from foreign markets, court officials from China also had the naval prowess to demand submission from polities located as far away as South Asia. Indeed, the maritime frontiers of Ming China during the reign of the Yongle 永樂 emperor (1403–24) extended to the coastal regions of South Asia, the main destination of the first three voyages of 'Admiral' Zheng He.

Zheng He's engagement with South Asia, a region he visited during each of his seven expeditions between 1405 and 1433, was multifaceted and included places (such as Bengal) that he did not travel to personally. It involved the use and demonstration of military power in order to construct a Chinese world order on behalf of the Yongle emperor, who desperately sought to legitimise his usurpation of the Ming throne. The solicitation and ferrying of tributary missions, court-sponsored commercial activities and the search for Buddhist relics were also part of these expeditions. The objectives of the Zheng He-led expeditions to South Asia fit with the arguments made by Geoffrey Wade in this volume (see Chapter 2) and in his earlier works about the Ming court's pursuit of domination in the maritime regions. Indeed, the activities of Zheng He and other Ming eunuchs in South Asia were also associated, as in the case of Southeast Asia, with seeking the submission of foreign rulers, procuring exotic treasures and artefacts and legitimising the reign of the Yongle emperor. Focusing on these objectives of the Zheng He expeditions, this chapter outlines the complex and multilayered relationships between the Ming court and South Asia during the reign of the Yongle emperor. These encounters differed significantly from those of previous periods and were never replicated again by any future court in China. In fact, the Zheng He expeditions marked the culmination of the maritime interactions between South Asia and China that grew rapidly after the 10th century. The main difference was the unprecedented role of the state in directing the interactions. While the abrupt end to the expeditions in 1433 led to the re-emergence of private merchant networks as key facilitators of these linkages, the arrival of European colonial polities in the 16th century yet again changed the dynamics of maritime contacts between South Asia and Ming China.

Engaging with the maritime world

Confucian officials at Chinese courts since the Han dynasty (206 BCE–220 CE) had tried unsuccessfully to curtail the commercial motives of foreign tribute carriers. While the court scribes portrayed the arrival of these missions as acceptance of vassal status by foreign polities, in reality most of the carriers were traders who sought to exploit the tribute system by selling their merchandise in local markets for considerable profit. During the Song dynasty, the court eventually recognised the commercial intention of the tribute carriers and tried to incorporate the practice into its fiscal system. It gave various incentives to foreign traders, including commercial privileges and tax breaks, and encouraged them to bring other merchants to Song China.[1] During the Song, because the overland routes to and beyond Central Asia were blocked by the semi-nomadic polities such as the Liao (907–1125) and Jin (1115–1234), the court paid greater attention to maritime commerce than during previous dynasties. As a result of these policies and encouragements, exchanges with the Indian Ocean region developed rapidly in the 11th and 12th centuries. The period also witnessed the development of shipbuilding technology and navigational skills in China and the emergence of Chinese communities abroad.[2]

Many of the policies with regard to promoting maritime commerce continued during the subsequent Yuan period. Unlike the Song, however, the Yuan court under Qubilai Khan (r. 1260–94) was actively involved in demanding submission from maritime polities through official missions and naval attacks. Between 1280 and 1296, for example, 13 missions were dispatched to strategic locations in the coastal regions of South Asia. Seven of these went to Kollam on the Malabar coast and six went to the Ma'bar polity on the Coromandel coast. These Yuan missions, which took place against the backdrop of punitive naval raids on Japan, Champa and Java, were intended to extract tributary missions.[3] Through these tributary missions Qubilai wanted to project himself as the legitimate 'Khan' in a politically fragmented Mongol world. It is likely that during Qubilai's reign a distinction was made between tributary missions with commercial motives and those that arrived to legitimise the Mongol ruler in China. This distinction may have been made and enforced by scrutinising the background of the tribute carriers and through verifications by court officials who personally travelled to foreign polities.

The Ming court, under the founding ruler the Hongwu 洪武 emperor (r. 1368–98) and subsequently the Yongle emperor, followed the Yuan court's policy in aggressively seeking tributary missions from maritime polities, including those in South Asia. The policies instituted by the Hongwu emperor, including his ban on private Chinese traders engaging in foreign trade, had a significant impact on maritime commerce, diplomatic interactions and the formation of Chinese diasporic networks. The Hongwu emperor also established a strict policy on tribute missions, restricting and punishing those who attempted to carry out commercial activities.[4] Aware of Qubilai's failed maritime strategy, the Hongwu emperor warned his heirs not to use Ming China's naval abilities to invade polities in the maritime realm. The threat to the Ming empire, according to the Hongwu emperor, lay in the northern borderlands and not in the coastal regions.[5]

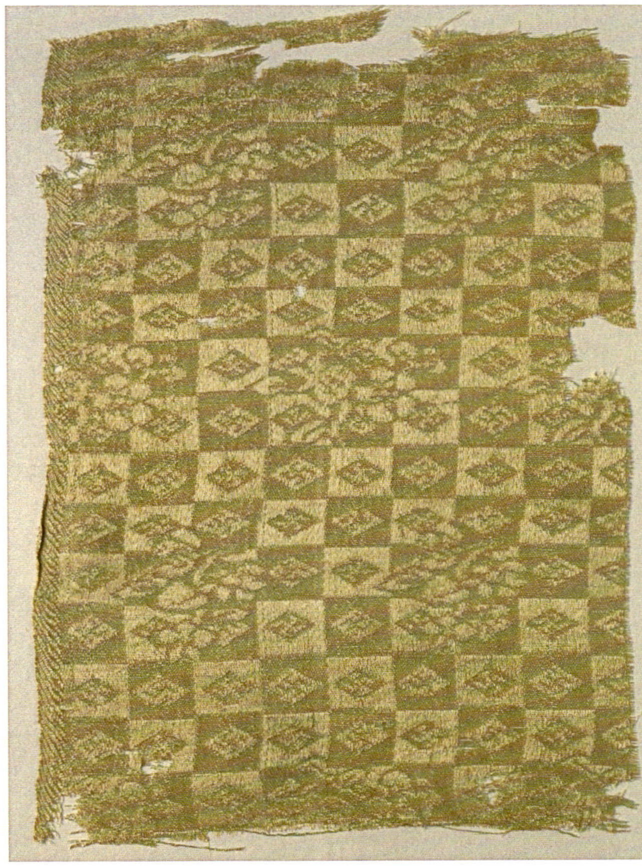

Plate 3.1 Patterned silk fragment, 1300–1600. Nanjing, Suzhou or Hangzhou. Silk damask, height 19cm, width 14cm. Victoria and Albert Museum, London, given by the Reverend Dr Franz Bock (1823–99), V&A 7052-1860

By the time the Yongle emperor usurped the Ming throne in 1402, private commercial networks of Chinese merchants based in Southeast Asia had become active in Indian Ocean trade. Using Southeast Asian ports as their bases, these private merchants conducted trade with Ming China as well as with the coastal regions of South Asia. One of the aims of the Zheng He expeditions may well have been to bring the commercial exchanges along the Ming coast, and the networks of private Chinese traders based abroad, under state control. The intention was also to install friendly regimes at key nodal points of the Indian Ocean world. All this was done through the demonstration of naval power, evident from the size and number of ships, the large contingent of soldiers and the advanced weaponry carried by Zheng He's armada.[6] Within this context, it is worth noting that the South Asian polities with which the Ming court pursued diplomatic relations were either located in strategic sectors of the Indian Ocean and/or had emerged as important trading destinations for Chinese merchants.

Maritime power and diplomacy

The terminus of Zheng He's first three expeditions was Calicut (*Guli* 古里, now Kozhikode), the leading centre for intra-Indian Ocean commerce and the main exporter of pepper from the Malabar coast. Prior to Zheng He's arrival

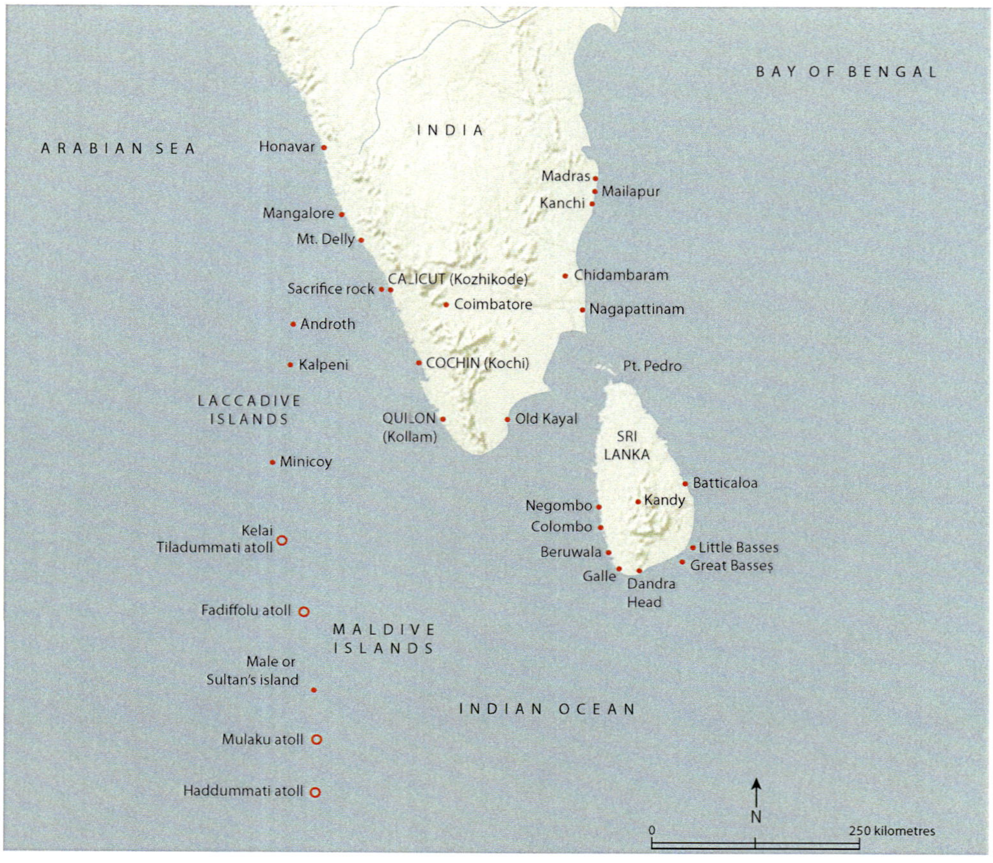

Plate 3.2 Map of southern India

on the Malabar coast, another eunuch emissary sent by the Yongle emperor, Yin Qing 尹慶 (active 1400–10), had visited the region. The *Ming Veritable Records* reports that in 1403 the Ming court sent Yin Qing to Melaka (*Manlajia* 滿剌加) and Cochin (*Kezhi* 柯枝, now Kochi) to 'confer upon the kings of these countries "spangled-gold" silk gauze drapes and parasols together with patterned fine silks and coloured silks as appropriate' (**Pl. 3.1**).[7] Yin Qing returned to China in 1405, with 'rulers' of Samudera (*Sumendala* 蘇門答剌), Melaka and Calicut.[8] While during the Zheng He expeditions, rulers of several maritime polities seem to have personally led tributary missions to the Ming court, it is more likely that the people Yin Qing brought with him were simply officials or traders from the three foreign polities. The aim may have been to legitimise Yongle emperor's accession through the display of foreign tributary missions at the court. This was, in fact, the first time after the Yongle emperor usurped the Ming throne that envoys had arrived in China from these three polities.

Yin Qing's destination in South Asia, as noted in the *Veritable Records*, was Cochin (**Pl. 3.2**), which was not yet a major port or commercial site on the Malabar coast. Neither was Melaka an important centre of trade or maritime communication when Yin Qing arrived. Rather, it was during the course of Zheng He's expeditions that both Cochin and Melaka developed into nodal points of Indian Ocean interactions. In fact, the Ming court played a critical role in transforming these two sites from obscurity to preeminence in their respective regions. This was perhaps done in order to access local resources and establish Ming bastions at key locations of the Indian Ocean world.[9] The Ming court's objectives entailed displacing existing powers at these sites. While the support for Melaka came at the expense of supplanting Samudera as the main chokepoint in the Straits of Melaka, Cochin may have been chosen over Calicut for its pepper supplies and as a base for westward exploration of the Indian Ocean.

When Yin Qing returned with the 'rulers' of Samudera, Melaka and Calicut, the Ming court 'commanded that these native leaders all be enfeoffed as kings of their countries, that they be provided with seals and patents and that variegated silks and clothing be conferred upon them'.[10] Ma Huan 馬歡 (d. *c.* 1460), who accompanied Zheng He in 1413, 1421 and 1431, seems to suggest that this enfeoffment of the ruler of Calicut was carried out by Zheng He in 1407, when he delivered a silver seal and gifts of 'hats and girdles of various grades' to the ministers of Calicut.[11] Ma Huan also describes how the Calicut king, planning to send tribute to the Ming court, ordered foreign craftsmen residing in his land to make a jewelled girdle for the Chinese emperor. This girdle, studded with precious stones and large pearls, was made with 50 *liang* of 'fine red gold' that had been processed into threads 'as fine as a hair'.[12]

The embassies sent by Calicut offered local products to the Ming court, which in return presented various gifts to the South Asian envoys and treated them to lavish banquets. Paper money, copper cash, silk gauzes and other silk fabrics, gilded brocades and porcelain were frequently presented to the envoys and the rulers of Calicut.[13] The list of return gifts, which were often more valuable and in greater quantities than the tribute offerings, clearly indicates the Ming court's attempt to induce foreign polities to send tributary missions on a regular basis. Embassies from Calicut continued to arrive at the Ming court until about 1435, but a decline in

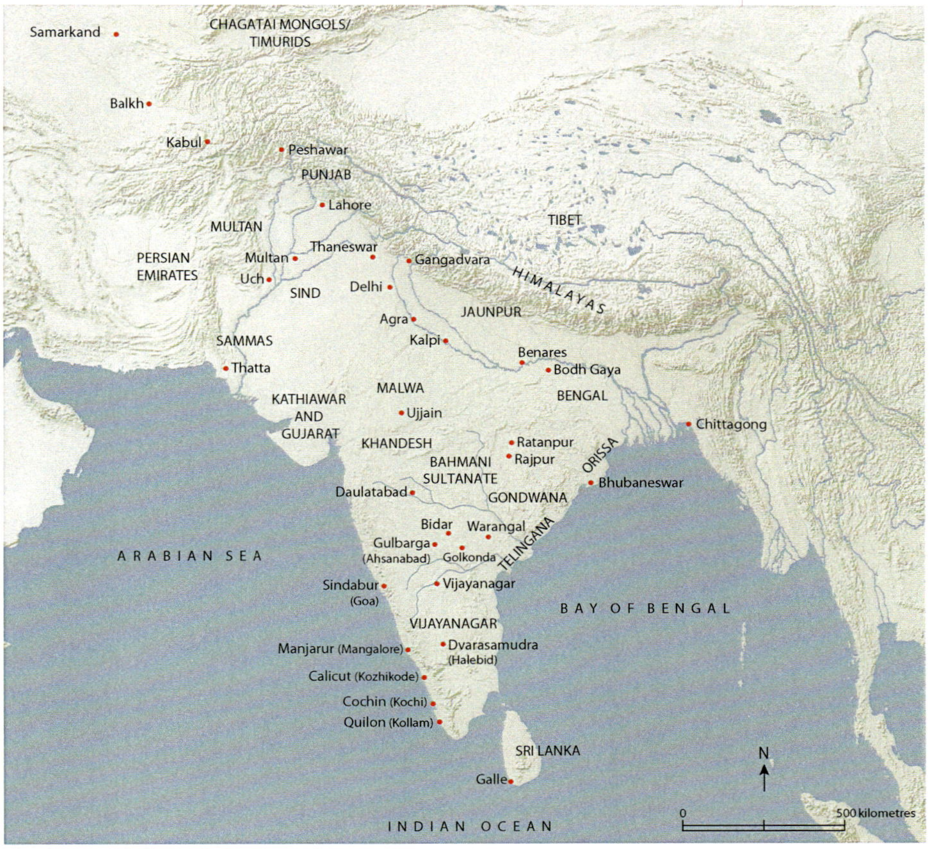

Plate 3.3 Map of Bengal-Jaunpur

intensity can be discerned after 1417, when the Yongle emperor granted special status to Cochin. Although the 18th-century *Ming shi* 明史 (*History of the Ming*) states that envoys from Calicut took precedence over those from other maritime polities, Cochin may have been the more important ally for the Ming court on the Malabar coast. In 1405, when Yin Qing returned to the Ming court, the Cochin representative was conspicuously missing and instead, as noted above, the 'ruler' of Calicut accompanied the Ming envoy. This seems to be an indication of the existing conflict between Calicut and Cochin in the early 15th century. Ming sources make it clear that Calicut was not only a leading trading hub in the Indian Ocean, but it was also a place where Muslim merchants (mostly of Arab origin) exerted significant political and economic power. Some of these merchants, especially those invested in foreign trade, funded the expansionist policies of the Zamorin, the ruler of Calicut. They may have been the ones who lobbied the Zamorin to invade Cochin, which was quickly emerging as the main rival port on the Malabar coast. Sometime in the late 15th century, the Zamorin did in fact occupy Cochin and install his representative as the king of the port-city.[14] Through the missions of Yin Qing and Zheng He the Ming court was probably aware of this rivalry between Calicut and Cochin and decided to intervene in 1416–17 by granting special status to Cochin and its ruler Keyili 可亦里.[15]

As part of his fifth expedition, which sailed from China in 1417, Zheng He was asked to confer a seal upon Keyili and enfeoff a mountain in his kingdom as the *zhenguo zhi shan* 鎮國之山 ('Mountain Which Protects the Country'). The Yongle emperor composed a proclamation that was inscribed on a stone tablet and carried to Cochin by Zheng He. Both of these were rare acts by the Ming court. Only three other polities, Melaka (in 1405), Japan (in 1406) and Brunei (in 1408), received a similar privilege. These stone tablets were significantly different from the trilingual inscription installed in Sri Lanka mentioned below. While the latter was inscribed to promote trading connections with foreign merchant communities, the proclamations sent to Melaka, Japan, Brunei and Cochin were intended to establish political relations with key polities, with perhaps the offer of military protection in times of need. 'All were intended', as Wang Gungwu has noted, by the Yongle emperor to seal 'closer relations between his empire and the four countries concerned'.[16] This exceptional relationship may have been established with Cochin because the Ming court decided to support an emerging port (i.e. Cochin) over the Muslim-dominated Calicut.[17]

After the cessation of the Zheng He expeditions, the Zamorin not only invaded Cochin, but also seems to have banned Chinese merchants from trading on the Malabar coast. The Christian traveller Joseph of Cranganore provides the following report about the absence of Chinese merchants in Calicut in the early 16th century:

> These people of Cathay are men of remarkable energy, and formerly drove a first-rate trade at the city of Calicut. But the King of Calicut having treated them badly, they quitted that city, and returning shortly after inflicted no small slaughter on the people of Calicut, and after that returned no more. After that they began to frequent Mailapetam, a city subject to the king of Narsingha; a region towards the East, ... and there they now drive their trade.[18]

The Ming court's attempt to intervene in local disputes was not limited to the Malabar coast. It also got involved in a

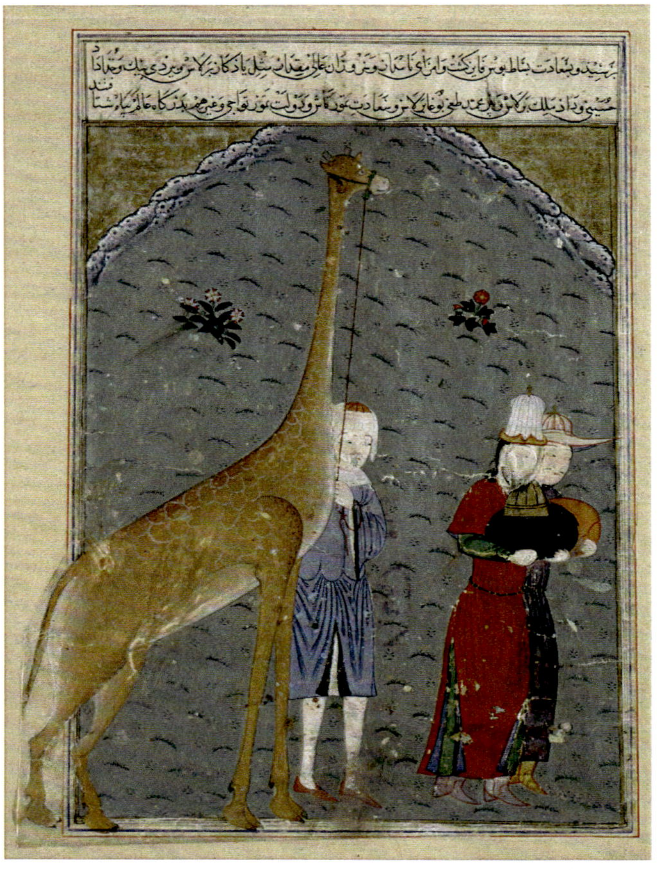

Plate 3.4 Timur receiving gifts from the Egyptian ambassadors, dated 16th July 1436 (Dhu'l-Hijja 839), Shiraz, Iran. Album leaf, ink, opaque watercolour and gold on paper, height 17.8cm, width 24cm. Worcester Art Museum, Jerome Wheelock Fund, 1935.26

conflict between Bengal and its neighbouring Jaunpur Sultanate (**Pl. 3.3**). In 1420, the king of Bengal complained to the Yongle emperor that Jaunpur forces had carried out several military raids on its territory. In response to the complaint, the Ming court dispatched the eunuch Hou Xian 侯顯 (active 1403–27) and others 'with Imperial orders of instruction for them [i.e. Bengal and Jaunpur], so that they would both cultivate good relations with their neighbours and would each protect their own territory'.[19] The entourage led by Hou Xian arrived in Bengal in August or September 1420 and was welcomed with a grand reception. It was Hou Xian's second visit to the region and this time he seems to have brought along Chinese soldiers, who were all presented with silver coins by the ruler of Bengal. The entourage then proceeded to Jaunpur to convey the Yongle emperor's message and try to resolve the territorial dispute peacefully.[20]

The rulers of Bengal evidently knew about Ming naval power and its interventions in other maritime regions prior to lodging the complaint. In fact, Bengal had sent at least eight embassies to the Ming court before 1420 and traders from the region were actively engaged in Indian Ocean commerce.[21] Hou Xian himself had visited the region in 1415. Thus, by 1420, the rulers, officials and traders in Bengal must have been very familiar with the Ming court's intentions to exert its power in the maritime world.

The list of products offered to the Ming court by the representatives of Bengal differed noticeably from those presented by other South Asian polities. The most remarkable of these gifts were the giraffes (**Pl. 3.4**) that arrived at the Ming court in 1414 and 1438.[22] Horses of different grades, parrots of various colour and pigeons were also presented by the representatives of Bengal. Like the giraffes, the horses presented to the Ming court were not of local origin. Rather, they were imported either from the Middle East or from Yunnan and then transshipped to China, a trading link that had existed prior to the Ming period.[23] Horses and exotic animals had also long been important components of foreign tributary offerings to the courts in China. The gifts offered by Bengal to the Ming court suggest an awareness of the tributary traditions of the Chinese court and the demands of the Chinese markets. Such knowledge may have come not only from the extensive networks of traders from Bengal, but also from the ethnic Chinese who seem to have been working in/for Bengal. The *Veritable Records* reports of two such Chinese representatives: Chen Deqing 陳得清, who is mentioned as the interpreter from the Bengal polity, and Song Yun 宋允, who is recorded as a person from Bengal and credited with bringing tribute missions to Ming China.[24] While Chen arrived in 1438, Song was at the Ming court in 1439.[25] After the cessation of the Zheng He expeditions, networks of private traders became the main maritime links between South Asia and Ming China. Within this context, ethnic Chinese traders, most likely those based in Southeast Asia, played an important role in initiating tributary missions from South Asia to the Ming court.

Sri Lanka (**Pl. 3.5**) was the fourth key polity in South Asia that frequently sent tribute missions to the Ming court. Unlike the other South Asian polities discussed above, however, the Ming court was involved in a major military conflict on the island. Prior to the conflict, the Ming court was aware of the importance of Sri Lanka in maritime commerce, the sacred Buddhist sites on the island and the main ethno-linguistic trading guilds in the region. This detailed knowledge about Sri Lanka is evident from the trilingual inscription composed in 1409 and subsequently taken to the island by Zheng He (see **Pl. 2.8**). Written in Chinese, Tamil and Persian, the languages of the three main trading groups on the island, the inscription evoked the virtues of the Buddha, a Tamil avatar of the Brahmanical deity Śiva and Allah separately in each of these languages.[26] The stone tablet, found in Galle on the southwest coast and now at the National Museum of Sri Lanka in Colombo, was set up, according to Fei Xin (*c.* 1385–*c.* 1436), who travelled with Zheng He on four occasions, to honour the 'peaceful government [of this country] through [our] imperial plan'.[27]

The military conflict in Sri Lanka took place when Zheng He arrived in the region to erect the trilingual tablet during his third expedition, which embarked from the Chinese coast in October–November 1409. Passing through Champa, Java, Melaka and Samudera, the ships led by Zheng He reached Galle in 1410. The 48 ships in Zheng He's armada carried 27,000 people, many of whom were soldiers. According to Ming sources, the 'king of Sri Lanka' had 'insulted' Zheng He when he reached the island during his first expedition in 1405–7. For his third voyage, Zheng He seems to have come prepared to battle the 'king', named Yaliekunaier 亞烈苦奈兒 or Aliekunaier 阿烈苦奈兒 ([Vira] Alakéswara or Alagakkonāra). Zheng He defeated

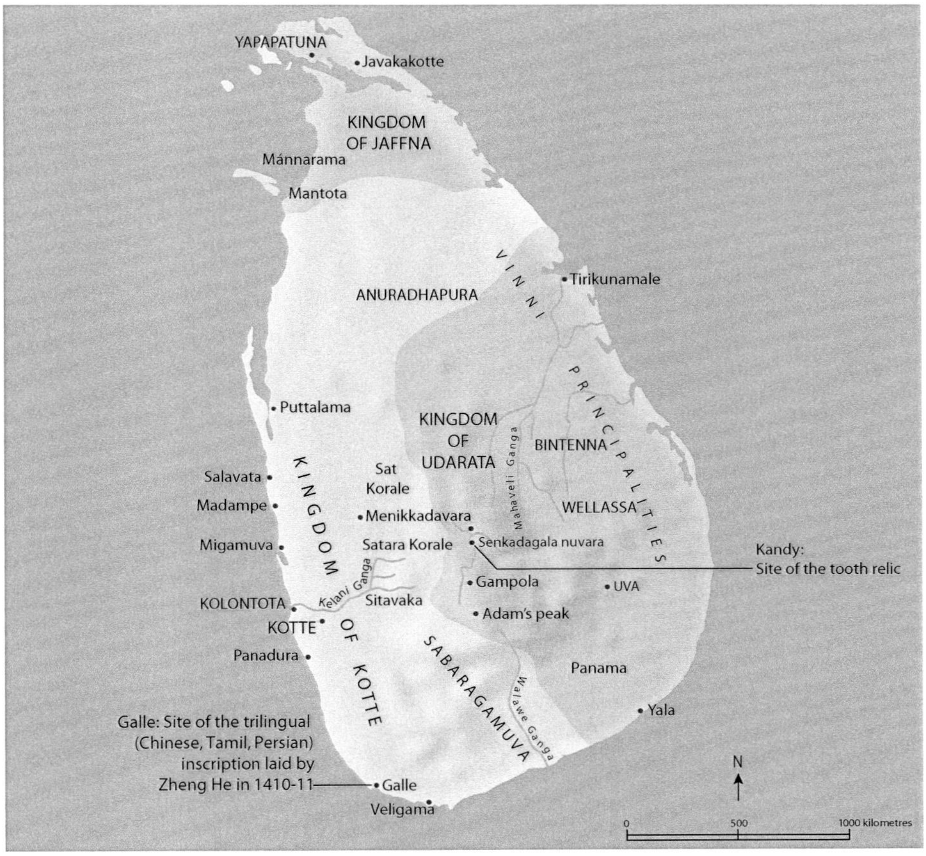

Plate 3.5 Map of Sri Lanka

and captured Yaliekunaier, and took him back to the Ming court. While Yaliekunaier was pardoned, the Ming court placed its own representative, a person whose name is recorded in Chinese as Yebanaina 耶巴乃那 ([Parākramābahu] Apana?), in charge of the region.[28] In addition to perhaps trying to exert control over the strategic location in the Indian Ocean through an appointed representative, the military conflict with Yaliekunaier, as noted below, may have been connected to the Yongle emperor's intention to also procure the famous Tooth Relic of the Buddha from Kandy.

The outcome of the Ming court's diplomatic interactions with South Asian polities, its interference in local disputes and even the military conflict in Sri Lanka is not clear. Tribute missions from South Asia were most frequent during the first six expeditions of Zheng He, which took place in tandem with missions led by several other eunuchs. The display of naval power, the use of military force and, as outlined in the next section, official trade may have triggered these tribute missions. Soon after the Zheng He expeditions ended, however, the tribute missions from South Asia to the Ming court also declined. The Ming rulers who succeeded the Yongle emperor did not need to legitimise their rule; there was also little support at the Ming court for the expensive maritime expeditions that augmented the power of the eunuchs. Without the presence of the Ming naval armada, South Asian polities, even those that benefited from the intervention of the Ming court, found it unnecessary to send tribute missions or engage in official trade. As a consequence, after the mid-15th century networks of private traders emerged as the only maritime links between South Asia and Ming China.

Trading for the court

The ban on maritime trade by the Hongwu emperor, as pointed out above, triggered an outflow of Chinese traders from the coastal regions of Ming China to locations in Southeast Asia, including places such as Sumatra and Java. In Palembang, for example, there seem to have been several such groups of Chinese settlers who traded with the Ming as representatives of foreign regions. These traders subsequently expanded their networks into the Bay of Bengal and the Arabian Sea regions. The Chinese settlements in Southeast Asia were places where traders from other regions of the Indian Ocean also congregated. By the time Zheng He embarked on his first expedition, merchants based in Southeast Asia, Chinese as well as non-Chinese, may have been controlling much of the maritime trade between South Asia and Ming China. The Zheng He expeditions resulted in the introduction of a new pattern of trading interaction that was conducted under the supervision of Ming officials. The commodities procured through these official transactions were not all meant for markets in Ming China. Rather, the selling of these goods at other foreign ports by the Ming representatives was also common. Thus Zheng He and the Ming court through its naval expeditions played a significant role in intra-Asian commerce between 1405 and 1433.

The Hongwu emperor's ban on maritime trade did not prevent foreign merchants from conducting business in Ming China. This can be discerned from an entry dated 1403 in the *Ming Veritable Records*. When a Muslim named Hazhi Mahamo Qilanni 哈只馬哈沒奇剌泥 and others came from the polity called Lani 剌泥 to offer tribute of local products, it was pointed out by the court official that

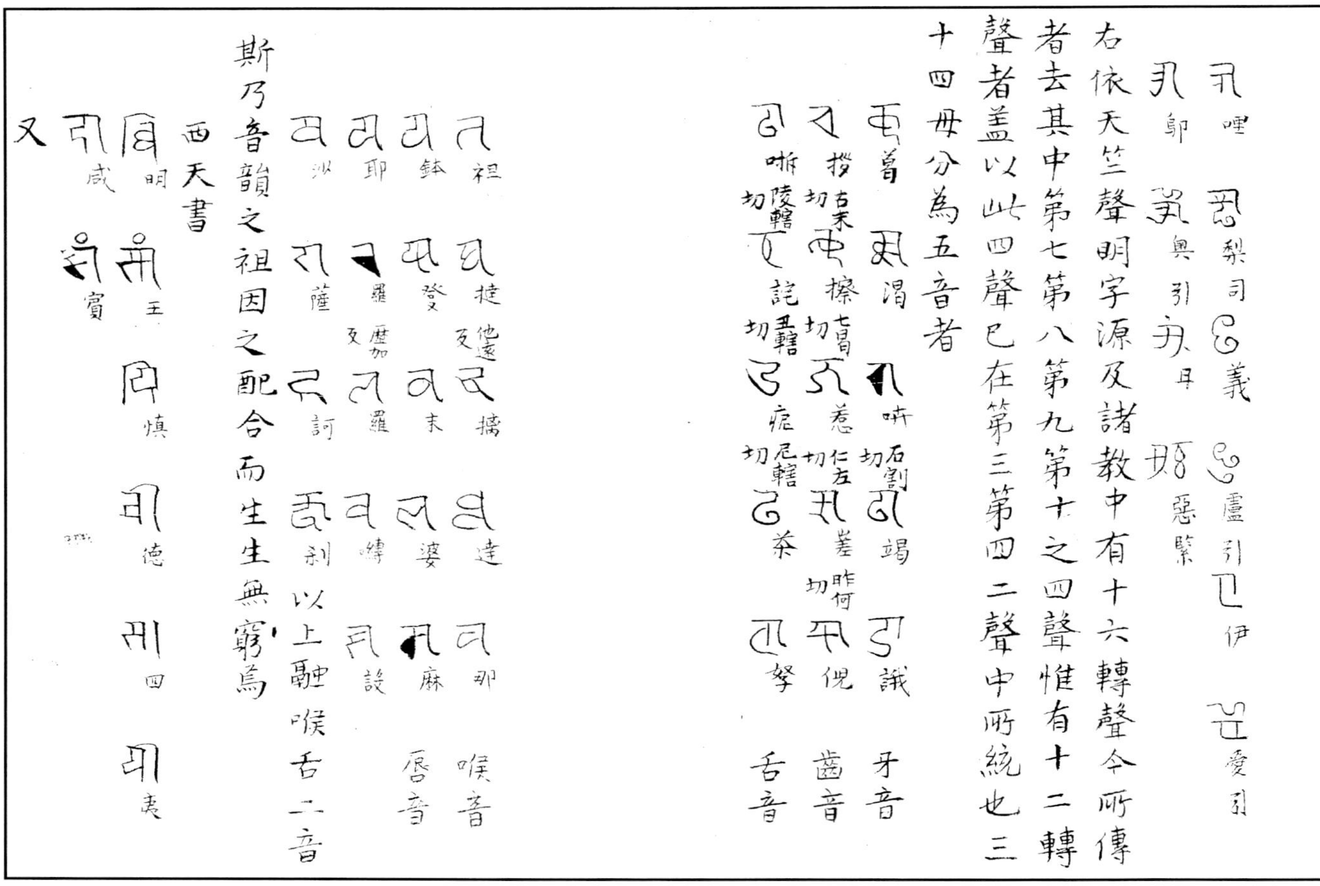
右依天竺聲明字源及諸教中有十六轉聲今所傳者去其中第七第八第九第十之四聲惟有十二轉聲者蓋以此四聲已在第三第四二聲中所統也三十四母分為五音者

斯乃音韻之祖因之配合而生生無窮焉

西天書

Plate 3.6 Bengali lexicon from the *Extensive Records of the Four Barbarian [Regions]* (*Siyi guangji* 四夷廣記) by Shen Maoshang 愼懋賞, 16th century. Ink on paper, height 27.8cm, width 16.7cm. The National Central Library, Taipei

the group had also brought pepper to trade in China. They requested that a tax be levied on the commodity. The Yongle emperor objected:

> Commercial taxes are levied by the state in order to restrain those engaging in the inferior occupation [commerce]. How can we use taxes for our benefit! The *yi* 夷 are now inclining towards virtue and coming from distant places, and you wish to appropriate their profits. The resulting loss and disgrace to the propriety of the country will outweigh by 10,000 times the amount received from them! This is not to be permitted![29]

T'ien Ju-Kang has argued that as a result of Zheng He's expeditions, the significance of pepper in Ming China changed 'from being a precious commodity to one in common use'.[30] The use of pepper as payment to court officials and military personnel during the later years of the Yongle emperor, T'ien contends, was the main reason for this change. The sale of pepper in China was monopolised and regulated by the state. It was also used by the state to address the issue of inflation caused by the drop in the value of paper money. Given the growing interest in acquiring pepper it is not surprising that Calicut was the main destination of Zheng He's first three voyages. The support for Cochin as an alternative source for procuring pepper, therefore, could also be related to this increasing domestic demand for the commodity.

The Ming court's interest in procuring pepper from South Asia is evident from the records of Ma Huan and Fei Xin, both of whom offer detailed descriptions of the availability of pepper, its cultivation and its price at various South Asian ports they visited. In Calicut, for example, Ma Huan notes that pepper was grown 'extensively' in the gardens established by people living in the mountainous region of the polity.[31] After it ripened, it was dried and sold to 'big pepper-collectors', who transported the commodity to an official storehouse. Both the local sale of pepper from this official storehouse and its supply to foreign traders were monitored and taxed by local authorities. In Cochin, on the other hand, there was no state monopoly on the production, transportation and sale of pepper, which was, according to Ma Huan, the only local product that the emerging port traded.[32] There were private warehouses in Cochin, owned by wealthy families, Fei Xin reports, where pepper was stored.[33] It was then sold directly to foreign merchants, without state supervision. Perhaps because of the lack of state monopoly, the price of pepper was about 34 per cent cheaper in Cochin than in Calicut. But it was still 25 per cent more expensive than the pepper available in Samudera.[34] Unlike Calicut and Samudera, however, in the early 15th century Cochin had limited presence of foreign traders and perhaps had more reserves of pepper for export than either of the others.

The Malabar coast was also a place where Zheng He and his entourage procured goods that arrived from elsewhere in the Indian Ocean. In Cochin, the Chetty merchants collected gemstones, pearls and aromatic goods for resale to the Ming representatives.[35] Similarly in Calicut, horses, coral, pearls, frankincense, putchuck (a medicinal root) and amber were brought from other regions for transit trade.

Horses were perhaps the most important of these transit goods destined for China. According to Fei Xin, horses were brought to the Malabar coast from West Asia, bred locally and 'transferred' for hundreds or thousands of coins for onward sale.[36] To purchase these transit goods and local products such as pepper, the Ming officials offered gold, silver, silk, blue-and-white porcelain, pearls, musk, quicksilver and camphor. While some of these objects came from China, others, such as camphor, originated in Southeast Asia.

Ma Huan describes the procedure through which trading activity took place between the representatives of the Ming court and local traders in Calicut.[37] While the two Muslim chiefs of Calicut oversaw the commercial transactions, a Chetty trader and a local broker participated in the purchase of goods from the Ming officials. One of the commanders from the Ming fleet was responsible for fixing the date for trade. On that designated date, commodities were displayed, prices agreed upon and a written agreement executed. After the sale of goods by the Chinese, the locals exhibited their merchandise. The prices were negotiated and paid with silk, the price of which was fixed in the written agreement.

For Fei Xin, Sri Lanka was inferior only to Java in terms of its importance in maritime trade.[38] The fact that the island produced several types of precious stones and gems, as well as pearls, is noted by both Fei Xin and Ma Huan (see discussion by Craig Clunas in Chapter 27 of this volume). Musk, hemp-silk, blue-and-white porcelain, copper coins, gold and silver objects and camphor were used by the Ming representatives to purchase goods from Sri Lanka. The trilingual inscription set up by Zheng He on the island suggests that the Ming representatives conducted trade with Tamil and Persian merchant guilds in addition to other local traders. From the nearby islands of the Maldives and Laccadives, the Chinese procured ambergris and perhaps also cowries.

Bengal seems to have been a leading trading partner of the Ming court and the Chinese traders who had settled in Southeast Asia. Cotton, textiles, precious stones and gems (mostly acquired from other regions of the Indian Ocean) and kingfisher feathers were some of the commodities sold to the Chinese. In return, the local merchants received gold and silver objects, silk fabrics, blue-and-white porcelain, copper coins, musk, vermilion, quicksilver and pepper. Ma Huan mentions that the ruler of Bengal owned ships that were sent to trade with foreign polities.[39] It was perhaps through such shipping networks that the giraffes presented to the Yongle emperor reached Bengal. In fact, the gifting of giraffes seems to have been a fairly common aspect of long-distance commercial interactions during the early 15th century.[40]

The extensive trading relations between Bengal and Ming China, official as well as the indirect private commerce through Southeast Asia, might explain how Bengali script (**Pl. 3.6**) and a list of more than 200 Bengali words transcribed in Chinese found their way into the 16th-century Ming work *Siyi guangji* 四夷廣記 (*Extensive Records of the Four Barbarian* [*Regions*]). The work, which includes words related to terrestrial objects, types of clothing, commodities, names for birds and animals, etc., indicates the continued importance of the South Asian coastal regions to Chinese merchants even after the state-sponsored commercial activity ceased. Much of this trade was conducted through Melaka and other ports in Southeast Asia where Chinese traders had established their diasporas.[41] These sites were also places where traders from Bengal and Gujarat had settled and engaged in commercial exchanges with their Chinese counterparts. While the fact that the Chinese continued to visit South Asia after the 1450s is suggested by the report by Joseph of Cranganore cited above, the extensive trading activity of Chinese and South Asian merchants is found in several Portuguese records, including one by Tomé Pires, the Portuguese envoy to Ming China in the early 16th century.[42]

The enduring interest in Buddhist South Asia

In 1403, soon after he ascended to the Ming throne, the Yongle emperor sent an invitation to the Fifth Karmapa (Deshin Shekpa, 1384–1415) of Tibet. Carried by Hou Xian, the same person who later visited Bengal in 1415 and 1420 by the maritime route, the invitation requested the Karmapa to visit the Ming capital and perform rituals for the deceased parents of the Yongle emperor. A little over three years later, in 1407, the Karmapa accompanied by Hou Xian arrived in Nanjing. After conducting several ceremonies at the capital, the Karmapa also visited Mount Wutai (**Pl. 3.7**), the perceived abode of the bodhisattva Mañjuśrī.[43] In 1408, the Yongle emperor invited to the Ming capital Tsongkhapa (1357–1419), the other important Tibetan leader, who, however, declined the invitation. In 1413, when Hou Xian

Plate 3.7 View of the Buddhist pilgrimage site Mount Wutai, located in Shanxi province southwest of Beijing

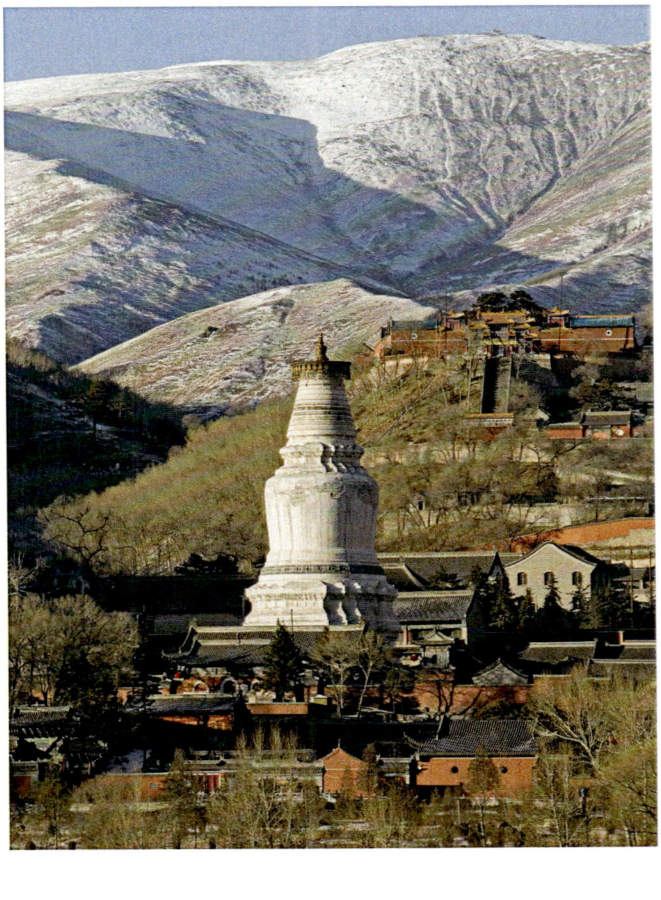

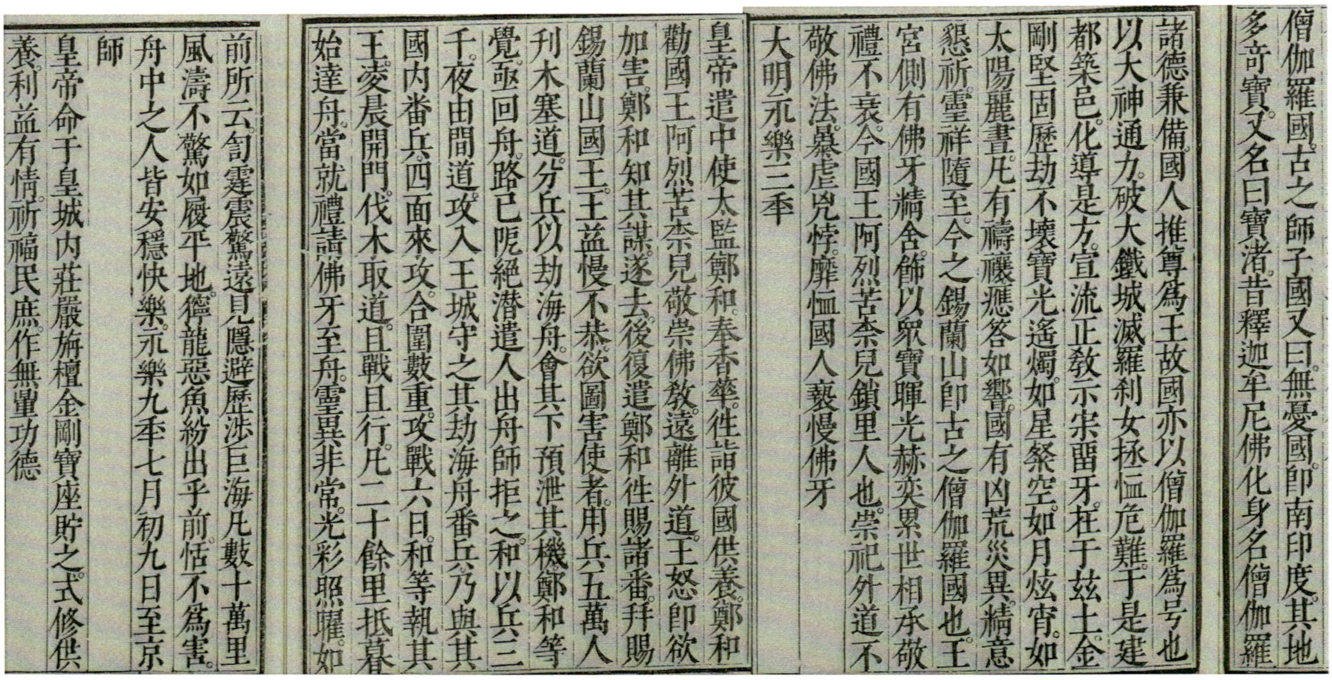
僧伽羅國古之師子國又曰無憂國即南印度其地
多奇寶又名曰寶渚昔釋迦牟尼佛化身名僧伽羅
諸德兼備國人推尊為王故國亦以僧伽羅為号也
以大神通力破大鐵城滅羅刹女拯恤危難于是建
都築邑化導是方宣流正教示寂留牙在于茲土金
剛堅固歷劫不壞寶光遥燭如星粲空如月炫宵如
太陽麗晝凡有禱禳應答如響國有凶荒災異精意
懇祈靈祥隨至今之錫蘭山即古之僧伽羅國也王
宮側有佛牙精舍飾以衆寶暉光赫奕累世相承敬
禮不衰今國王阿烈苦奈兒鎖里人也崇祀外道不
敬佛法暴虐兇悖靡恤國人褻慢佛牙
大明永樂三年
皇帝遣中使太監鄭和奉香華往詣彼國供養鄭和
勸國王阿烈苦奈兒敬崇佛教遠離外道王怒即欲
加害鄭和知其謀遂去後復遣鄭和往賜諸番并賜
錫蘭山國王王益慢不恭欲圖害使者用兵五萬人
刊木塞道分兵以劫海舟會其下預泄其機鄭和等
覺亟回舟路已阨絕潛遣人出舟師拒之和以兵三
千夜由間道攻入王城守之其劫海舟番兵乃與其
國内番兵四面來攻合圍數重攻戰六日和等執其
王凌晨開門伐木取道且戰且行凡二十餘里抵暮
始達舟當就禮請佛牙至舟靈異非常光彩照耀如
前所云訇霆震驚遠見隱避歷涉巨海凡數十萬里
風濤不驚如履平地獰龍惡魚紛出乎前恬不為害
舟中之人皆安穩快樂永樂九年七月初九日至京
師
皇帝命于皇城内莊嚴旃檀金剛寶座貯之式修供
養利益有情祈福民庶作無量功德

Plate 3.8 ***Records of the Western Regions [Visited During] the Great Tang Dynasty (Da Tang xiyu ji*** **大唐西域記) in the *Jiaxing Tripiṭaka* (*Jiaxing zang* 嘉興藏), *juan* 11, *c.* 1579–1707. Ink on paper. The Palace Museum, Beijing**

was sent to Nepal, perhaps to bring the South Asian monk Śāriputra 實哩沙哩卜得囉/室利沙 (also known as Paṇḍita 板的達, 1335–1426) to Ming China,[44] the eunuch passed through Tibet and met Tsongkhapa, presumably to again urge him to visit the Ming court.[45] Śāriputra had an audience with the Yongle emperor in 1414 and was tasked to build the replica of the Mahābodhi temple in Beijing, known today as the Wutasi 五塔寺. The temple in *vajrāsana* (金剛寶座) style was designed by Śāriputra but was completed only in 1473. McKeown correctly notes that the arrival of Śāriputra and the order to build the replica of the Indian temple in Beijing were part of the Yongle emperor's attempt to associate himself with not only his father's legacy as the founder of the dynasty, but also that of Qubilai as a *cakravartin* (universal) ruler.[46]

This interest in Buddhism expressed by the Yongle emperor, and in particular the episodes related to inviting Tsongkhapa to the Ming capital and the building of the replica of the Mahābodhi temple, is also linked to Zheng He and his maritime expeditions. A note added to the Ming-dynasty edition of Xuanzang's 玄奘 (602?–64) *Da Tang xiyu ji* 大唐西域記 (*Records of the Western Regions [Visited During] the Great Tang Dynasty*) suggests that the military actions undertaken by Zheng He in Sri Lanka in 1410–11 may have been related to obtaining the famous Tooth Relic of the Buddha housed in Kandy. Originally written in the middle of the 7th century, Xuanzang's record of his travels was included in the Chinese Buddhist Tripiṭaka. The first woodblock printed edition of the Chinese Tripiṭaka appeared in the 11th century and was reprinted several times, with various textual additions. During the Ming period there were six printed editions of the work. In the *Jiaxing zang* 嘉興藏 (*Jiaxing Tripiṭaka*) composed in 1676, a note is added to Xuanzang's chapter that deals with Sri Lanka (**Pl. 3.8**). This note most likely originated from *Ming beiben* 明北本 (*Ming Northern Edition*) or the *Yongle beizang* 永樂北藏 (*Yongle Northern Tripiṭaka*) edition, which was compiled between 1421 and 1440.[47] Translated into English by Li Rongxi, it reads:

> The country of Siṁhala, known as the 'Land of Lions' in olden times, and also called the 'Country of No Sorrow', is south of India. As it produces plenty of rare gems, it is also named the 'Precious Island'. Formerly, Śākyamuni Buddha transformed himself into a man named Siṁhala, and as he was a man possessing all virtues, he was made king by the people of the country. Therefore it was also called the country of Siṁhala. With his great supernatural powers, he destroyed the great iron city, annihilated the *rākṣasīs*, and rescued the victims who were in peril. Then he constructed a capital city and built towns to convert and guide the local people. After having propagated the right teachings, he passed away, leaving a tooth behind in this country. It is adamantine and will last for many *kalpas* without being damaged. It issues a precious light like a brilliant star, like the moon shining in the night, or the sun brightening the daytime. Whenever a prayer is said to it, it responds as swiftly as an echo. In times of natural disaster, an earnest prayer will bring instant divine auspiciousness. What is now called the Mountain of Ceylon was the country of Siṁhala in ancient times. Beside the royal palace is a temple for the Buddha's Tooth Relic, decorated with various gems and shining with great brilliance. It has been worshipped from generation to generation without negligence. The reigning king A-lie-ku-nai-er is a native of Soḷī. He worships heretics, does not venerate the Triple Gem, is a brutal and tyrannical ruler, has no feeling of pity for his people, and blasphemes the Buddha's Tooth Relic.
>
> In the third year of the Yongle period [1405] of the great Ming dynasty, the Emperor dispatched the eunuch Zheng He as an imperial envoy to send incense and flowers to that country and make offerings [to the Tooth Relic]. Zheng He exhorted King A-lie-ku-nai-er to respect Buddhism and keep away from heretics. The king was enraged and intended to kill the envoy. Having got wind of the intrigue, Zheng He went away. Afterward he was sent again to bestow gifts on various foreign

countries, and he visited the king of the mountain of Ceylon, who was all the more arrogant and disrespectful, and attempted to kill the envoy. The king mobilised fifty thousand troops to fell trees to obstruct the road and sent a contingent to ransack the seagoing vessels. At that juncture a subordinate official leaked the secret, and Zheng He and his men, having realised the situation, at once tried to return to their ships. As the road had been cut off, they could only secretly send some men out, but the captors of the ships would not allow them to go on board. Zheng He, commanding three thousand soldiers, made an assault by a shortcut at night and took possession of the royal city.

The native troops who had captured the ships joined forces with the native soldiers on land and launched a counterattack from all four sides. They besieged the royal city with a tight encirclement and fought for six days. Zheng He and his men captured the king and opened the city gate, and after cutting down trees to make a way, they moved away while fighting. Going for more than twenty *li*, they reached their ships in the evening. They brought the Buddha's Tooth Relic on board with due ceremony. It emitted a brilliant light in a most unusual manner as mentioned above, while a peal of thunder rumbled with such a loud crash so that people at a great distance saw the lightning and hid themselves. The ships sailed on the great sea without encountering a windstorm, [and they were as safe] as if they were walking on dry land. Ferocious dragons and mischievous fishes emerged before the ships but caused no harm. All the people on board the ships were safe and happy.

On the ninth day of the seventh month on the ninth year of Yongle [1411] they returned to the capital, and the Emperor ordered that a precious diamond seat [made of sandalwood] be prepared in the imperial city for the Tooth Relic, in order to make offerings to it for the benefit of living beings and the welfare of the people, so that they might perform countless meritorious deeds.[48]

Except for the concluding section describing the removal of the Tooth Relic from Sri Lanka, the episode described in this note is remarkably similar to the *Ming Veritable Records* account of the conflict between Zheng He and the Sri Lankan ruler Aliekunaier mentioned above. More importantly, this note also very closely resembles a letter from the Yongle emperor written to Tsongkhapa that bears the date 11 March 1413. Found in 1959 at the Potala Palace in Lhasa, the letter similarly highlights the fact that Zheng He took the Tooth Relic from Sri Lanka and that a 'precious diamond seat made of sandalwood' 莊嚴栴檀金剛寶座 (perhaps a sandalwood replica of the Mahābodhi temple) had been made to house it.[49] Both these sources, which are the earliest records on Zheng He's military action in Sri Lanka and one penned by the emperor himself, are confirmations of the relic's having been brought to Ming China. It would fit with the Yongle emperor's other Buddhist endeavours and aims mentioned above.[50]

In 1412, shortly after the Zheng He mission returned from Sri Lanka, the Yongle emperor initiated the building of the the Da Baoensi 大報恩寺 (Great Monastery of Filial Gratitude) and the so-called 'Porcelain Pagoda' (*Liuli ta* 琉璃塔) in Nanjing in memory of his parents (see discussion by Clarence Eng in Chapter 20 of this volume).[51] Zheng He was one of the persons put in charge of overseeing the Buddhist constructions and is later reported to have donated a large sum of money towards their completion.[52] Hou Xian's

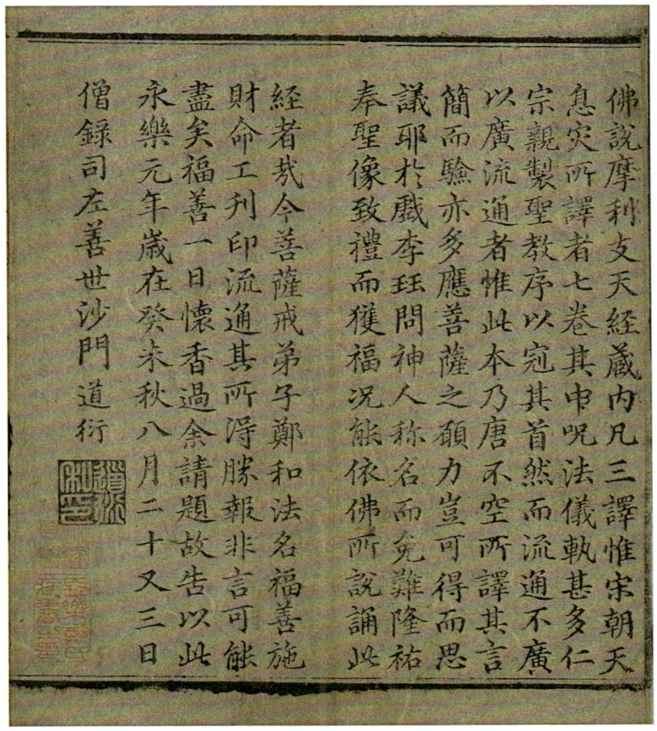
佛說摩利支天經藏内凡三譯惟宋朝天
息灾所譯者七卷其中呪法儀軌甚多仁
宗親製聖教序以冠其首然而流通不廣
以廣流通者惟此本乃唐不空所譯其言
簡而驗亦多應菩薩之願力豈可得而思
議耶於戲李玨問神人称名而免難隆祐
奉聖像致禮而獲福況能依佛所說誦此
經者哉今菩薩戒弟子鄭和法名福善施
財命工刊印流通其所得勝報非言可能
盡矣福善一日懷香過余請題故告以此
永樂元年歲在癸未秋八月二十又三日
僧録司左善世沙門道衍

Plate 3.9 Colophon of a sūtra dedicated to Mārīcī, dated 1403. Printing ink on paper. National Library of China

mission to Tibet and Nepal, carrying Yongle's letter to Tsongkhapa, took place soon after the construction of these monuments started. It is possible that the Tibetan lama was invited in connection with consecrating the temple and the pagoda. Although Tsongkhapa declined the invitation, his disciple Śākya Yeshé (1354–1439) is known to have reached the Ming court in 1415.[53]

From the above episodes it is clear that the Yongle emperor was involved in several Buddhist activities from the time he usurped the throne. They also indicate that he was familiar with Buddhist teachings and cognisant of their political use and implications. Much of this familiarity with Buddhism must have come from the Yongle emperor's association with the monk Daoyan 道衍 (Yao Guangxiao 姚廣孝, 1335–1418). Daoyan had been close to the Yongle emperor since before he usurped the throne. Later, he was involved in justifying the usurpation as the editor of various Ming records, including the *Veritable Records* of the Yongle reign.[54] Daoyan was also the person who bestowed the bodhisattva precepts upon Zheng He and wrote a colophon for a Buddhist text that the admiral offered to the Buddhist divinity Mārīcī (**Pl. 3.9**). These connections between the Yongle emperor, Daoyan and Zheng He might have resulted in the decision to procure the Tooth Relic from Sri Lanka, an important artefact used by Buddhist rulers to legitimise their political authority.[55] In a genealogy of Daoyan found in Changle city, Fujian province, the monk is reported to have accompanied Zheng He on his maritime expedition in 1411.[56] This was the same expedition that was responsible for bringing the Tooth Relic to Ming China. Although not an entirely convincing source of information, the genealogy, which was copied in 1940, seems to imply that Daoyan may have been in Sri Lanka when Zheng He procured the Tooth Relic for the Yongle emperor.

The early Ming attitude towards Buddhism has been characterised as 'pragmatic' or even as one of 'suppression', while at the same time 'acknowledging the utilitarian value of Buddhism for state ideology'.[57] Scholars have also noted the personal interest in Buddhism among some of the early Ming rulers and, at the same time, their restrictive policies, especially with regard to the wealthy Buddhist monastic institutions. The Yongle emperor's acquisition of the Tooth Relic and invitations to the Tibetan lamas, which took place during the first decade of his rule, clearly demonstrate this 'utilitarian value' of Buddhism in early 15th-century China.

Concluding remarks

Zheng He's expeditions ceased little over six decades before Vasco da Gama reached Calicut in 1498. Vasco da Gama's arrival at the Malabar coast inaugurated the period of European expansion in Asia, including the control of the commercial networks linking South Asia and China. In fact, the Portuguese quickly occupied Cochin and Melaka and were the first Europeans to assert their role in intra-Asian trade. For Robert Finlay and Geoff Wade, there are similarities between the methods used by Zheng He and the early Portuguese in exercising control over the key nodes of Indian Ocean commerce.[58] Parallels can also be found in their desire to procure pepper from the Malabar coast and the interest in the Tooth Relic from Sri Lanka, which seems to have miraculously reappeared during the time of Portuguese colonisation.[59] The European colonial powers, like the Chinese court, realised that a physical presence in South Asia was necessary to assert maritime superiority in the Indian Ocean.

At this very end of the pre-colonial phase of China's interactions with South Asia, several centuries of exchanges coalesced during the Zheng He expeditions. The Buddhist connections that defined the first millennium were again evident because of the Yongle emperor's interest in monks, relics and the need to legitimise his reign through the use of Buddhism. It also marked the culmination of a period of intense maritime commercial relations and diplomatic contacts between the two regions. The circulation of people, goods and knowledge were also vigorous and as multifaceted as in the past, which is revealed from the presents of giraffes and horses to the Ming court, the detailed records of Ma Huan and Fei Xin and the Bengali-Chinese lexicon. The first half of the 15th century was, therefore, on the one hand the climax of the past interactions between China and South Asia, and on the other hand a watershed, transiting within a century to a new phase that would be defined by European colonial domination.

Notes

1 Hartwell 1989; Sen 2003, 151–5.
2 Lo 2012.
3 Sen 2006a.
4 Li Kangying 2010.
5 Wang 1968.
6 Levathes 1994; Wade 2005a; Dreyer 2007.
7 *MSL Taizong shilu* 24.5b (1/10/壬申); Wade 2005b, http://epress.nus.edu.sg/msl/entry/7.
8 *MSL Taizong shilu*, 46.2a–b (3/9/癸卯); Wade 2005b, http://epress.nus.edu.sg/msl/entry/514.
9 On the establishment of a *guanchang* 官廠 ('government deport') at Melaka and its use in advancing Ming maritime domination in the South China Sea region, see Wade 2014. Similar attempt to transform a previously obscure location into a site of preeminence may have also taken place at the Swahili coast of Africa. For details, see Sen forthcoming.
10 *MSL Taizong shilu*, 46.2a–b (3/9/癸卯); Wade 2005b, http://epress.nus.edu.sg/msl/entry/514.
11 Mills 1970, 138.
12 Mills 1970, 146.
13 Ptak 1989.
14 Menon 1970; Malekandathil 2001, 35.
15 Sen 2011, 80, n. 96.
16 Wang 1968, 57.
17 Sen 2011.
18 Yule 1875, II, 391.
19 *MSL Taizong shilu* 229.1b (18/9/乙亥); Wade 2005b, http://epress.nus.edu.sg/msl/entry/2690.
20 Sen 2006b.
21 Bagchi 2012; Ray 1993.
22 Church 2004.
23 Chakravarti 1999.
24 *MSL Yingzong shilu*, 47.6b (3/10/丁卯); Wade 2005b, http://epress.nus.edu.sg/msl/entry/733 [Chen Deqing] and *MSL Yingzong shilu*, 54.7b (4/4/甲辰); Wade 2005b, http://epress.nus.edu.sg/msl/entry/949 [Song Yun].
25 Sen 2011, 65–6.
26 Bandaranayake *et al.* 1990, 217–19; Nagel 2001; Liu Yingsheng 2008.
27 Fei Hsin 1996, 64.
28 Sen 2014. On Yebanaina, see Karashima 1978.
29 *MSL Taizong shilu*, 24.9a-b (1/10/甲戌); Wade 2005b, http://epress.nus.edu.sg/msl/entry/13.
30 T'ien Ju-Kang 1981, 187.
31 Mills 1970, 143.
32 Mills 1970, 135.
33 Fei Hsin 1996, 67.
34 Mills 1970, 135, n. 3.
35 Mills 1970, 136.
36 Fei Hsin 1996, 69.
37 Mills 1970, 140–3.
38 Fei Hsin 1996, 63.
39 Mills 1970, 165.
40 Roşu 1982.
41 Sen 2005.
42 Cortesão 1944, vol. 2, 229 ff.
43 Berger 2001; Sperling 1983, 74–135.
44 McKeown 2010.
45 Sperling 1982; Sperling 1983, 146–7.
46 McKeown 2010, 137–54.
47 Ji *et al.* 1985, 880, n. 5. The passage, however, does not appear in the existing versions of the Ming Northern Edition.
48 Li Rongxi 1996, 353–5; original text in Xuanzang and Bianji, T. 2087: 938c–939a.
49 Su Bai 1996, 213–14.
50 Discussion of some of the Sri Lankan sources likely pertaining to the armed conflict between Zheng He and the local 'ruler' can be found in Hettiaratchi 2003 and Sen 2014.
51 He Xiaorong 2000, 104; Zhang Huiyi 2007.
52 He Xiaorong 2000, 104–5; He Yunao 2007; Gong and Pan 2008.
53 Sperling 1982.
54 Tsai Shih-shan 2001, 44.
55 Sen 2014.
56 Chi 2005, 769.
57 Brook 1994; Wu Jiang 2008, 23.
58 Finlay 1992; Wade 2005a.
59 Strong 2004, 193.

Chapter 4
Causes and Consequences of the Ming Intervention in Vietnam in the Early Fifteenth Century

Kenneth M. Swope

The august founder of the Ming dynasty, the Hongwu 洪武 emperor (r. 1368–98), while recognising the need for security, was also wary of the costs of warfare, noting:

> The ancients had a saying: 'Expanding territory is not the way to lasting peace. Troubling the people is the road to disorder.' … I feel that as the various small *man* 蠻 and *yi* 夷 countries [to the south] are obstructed by mountains, are across the seas or are secluded in some corner, they do not pose a danger to China. I will certainly not attack them.[1]

He later enjoined his successors from doing so as well, though in fact the founder himself was not immune to the lures of territorial expansion. Nevertheless, his own son, the Yongle 永樂 emperor (r. 1403–24), violated this injunction even more explicitly and embarked upon a costly two decade-long effort to formally annex the Kingdom of Annan (Annam or Đại Việt, modern-day northern Vietnam) to the Ming as the province of Jiaozhi 交趾.[2] While this action has traditionally been understood as a manifestation of Yongle's vainglory and desire to legitimise his reign after having usurped the throne from his nephew, the Jianwen 建文 emperor (r. 1399–1402), it can also be viewed within the broader context of Ming grand strategy, which was to 'manifest awe' (*wei* 威) both domestically and abroad so as to maintain hegemony and preserve regional security.[3] Ideally, as noted in the ancient Chinese military classics, awe could be maintained with a fairly circumscribed expenditure of resources, but there were also times when only blunt military force would suffice.[4] Indeed, as seen repeatedly in Ming military interventions in Southeast Asia during the 15th century, there were times when military force was the preferred method of establishing awe.[5] In this sense it served as an important adjunct to regular diplomatic relations as embodied in the so-called 'tributary system' and could even be seen as an object lesson for neighbouring powers.[6] The present chapter will consider the Ming intervention in Vietnam within this light and also discuss some of the broader unintended ramifications of the Ming decision to intervene in Vietnam.[7]

The term tributary (or tribute) system is a catch-all shorthand for the way Chinese empires generally conducted foreign relations and trade. On the one hand, it was designed to ensure some level of security and international primacy for the Chinese empire. But it was also an important component of domestic legitimation. As one scholar has remarked:

> No sharp line divided the conditions for maintaining international harmony from those for ensuring social and political order within the Middle Kingdom. The tribute system mediated between international and domestic harmony; hence, it was perceived as extending the emperor's power as well as Chinese civilisation to distant realms, while external threats to the empire, such as barbarian attack or mistreatment of an imperial embassy, were taken as evidence of domestic weakness.[8]

Thus it was imperative upon the Chinese monarch to restore order among the tributary states so as to reify his status as the rightful Son of Heaven. Of course the degree to which Chinese monarchs actually did this was predicated upon both the perceived strategic interests of the empire at any given time and the predilections of the reigning monarch and his advisers. Certain rulers tended to be much more interventionist, and domestic political conditions could influence such decisions as emperors sought to assert themselves at home by virtue of policy successes abroad. The two most prominent examples of this in the Ming period are the Wanli 萬曆 (r. 1573–1620) emperor's decision to intervene in Korea in 1592 (which also had serious security implications for the Ming) and the Yongle emperor's decision to intervene in Vietnam, discussed here.[9]

The Ming intervention in Vietnam was connected to a succession dispute.[10] A usurper named Hồ Quý Ly (*c.* 1335–*c.* 1407) had killed off most of the incumbent royal Trần family and placed himself, then his son on the throne.[11] Though dubious of his claims, after investigating the matter the Ming eventually accepted his explanation that the royal line had died out and that the new ruler was related to the old king, and they prepared to invest the Hồ as rulers of Annam. However, in preparation for this recognition the Yongle emperor firmly chastised the prospective Hồ ruler and reinforced his own status as the true Son of Heaven with the right to intervene and control the situation.[12] This was part of the general Ming strategy of 'manifesting awe' vis-à-vis tributaries so as to maintain a strategic balance of power in favour of the Ming. Of course it must also be kept in mind that the Ming sources, upon which the present study relies, tend to portray things from the perspective of the Ming court and its interests. They also tend to downplay the level of tributary agency and manipulation of the system for their own ends, though certainly one can see that at work in the present case.

But in the autumn of 1404 a Trần refugee reached Nanjing and recounted the story of the usurpation, requesting Ming aid in restoring the throne to the Trần family. Though as dubious of this man's claims as they had initially been of the Hồ, the Ming decided to investigate again.[13] Ming suspicions were confirmed when a group of Annamese envoys on a tribute mission reportedly saw the Trần claimant in the Ming capital and confirmed the man's tale, weeping and bowing before their 'rightful king'.[14] Yongle was enraged that he had been deceived and vowed to teach the usurpers a lesson:

> Who could have known he had killed the ruler and usurped the throne, changed the dynastic title and adopted a reign title, treated the people cruelly and attacked neighbouring states! The spirits of Heaven and Earth will not tolerate this. Even the ministers and people are deceitful. That is a country full of criminals. How can this be tolerated?[15]

The Ming then issued an edict demanding that the Hồ renounce their claims and accept the Trần claimant as the rightfully invested Ming tributary ruler. Perhaps sensitive to the fact that he himself was a usurper, the Yongle emperor again stressed his role as the Son of Heaven and denounced the duplicitous and regicidal activities of the Hồ .[16] Fearful of the possibility of a full-scale Ming invasion, Hồ Quý Ly claimed that he had no knowledge of the Trần heir's survival and acceded to the demand that his son give up the throne in order to buy time for his own military preparations.[17] Even at this stage the Ming emperor, occupied with military operations on multiple fronts including in southwest China (see discussion by Geoffrey Wade in Chapter 2 of this volume), seemed willing to compromise somewhat, even promising to enfeoff the Hồ pretender as a duke so long as the Trần were restored to the throne.[18] But because he did not trust the Hồ he sent the commanders Huang Zhong 黄中 (d. *c.* 1413) and Lü Yi 吕毅 (d. 1409) with some 5,000 troops as a royal escort.[19] However, Hồ did not meet the escort party at the border as promised. When the Ming commanders inquired as to the nature of his absence they were told that he was ill. Though suspicious, Huang Zhong proceeded through thick forests that caused his troops to break formation. As a driving rain poured down, his men were subsequently ambushed in a narrow defile and nearly annihilated just after they crossed the Vietnamese border.[20] The Ming forces tried to advance to engage the enemy but the Vietnamese cut a bridge so the Ming could not advance.

Interestingly enough, even after they had attacked the Ming escort force and killed the Trần claimant, the Vietnamese professed that they had no desire to oppose the Ming, and, at least according to Ming sources, their emissary bowed before Huang Zhong, stating:

> We distant *yi* dare not oppose the Great Nation, nor harm the Imperial army. It is just that Tianping is really but an unrelated commoner and not a relative of the Chens. He dared to engage in artful deceit, misleading the Emperor and giving trouble to the army. Death could not expiate all his crimes. Now, fortunately he has been killed. As an apology to the Son of Heaven, my king will send a memorial admitting guilt, noting that when the Imperial troops came from far off, our small country, being poor, did not have sufficient supplies to long support and maintain them.[21]

Huang Zhong pulled back because he was allegedly outnumbered twenty to one and returned to China to report to the Yongle emperor.[22] The emperor was predictably enraged and addressed the Duke of Chengguo 成國公, Zhu Neng 朱能 (1370–1406), saying, 'How dare this petty rascal ruler insult me! This cannot go unpunished, how can I not use the army?'[23] Zhu Neng nodded and replied, 'The traitorous bandit's crimes are indeed great and cannot be countenanced in Heaven or Earth. Your ministers request that we bring your Heavenly Awesomeness to bear upon him and exterminate him in one stroke.'[24] The Ming ruler then charged the usurper with 20 great crimes and assembled a punitive expedition. These crimes included hindering an official Ming emissary, resisting Ming troops, occupying officials' homes and hurting the people, and deliberately deceiving the Ming so as to obtain tributary investiture.[25]

Though Yongle couched the war as a righteous effort to restore the legitimate ruling line, its framing and prosecution also speak to larger concerns of grand strategy. Among the crimes the Vietnamese were accused of were attacking their southern neighbour, the kingdom of Champa, as well as incursions into Laos and, perhaps most significantly, into southwest China.[26] All of these areas were under the purview of the Son of Heaven and his claims to universal rule would be seriously undermined if he proved unable to defend them and come to the aid of loyal tributaries.[27] His father had repeatedly asserted Ming suzerainty over these lands, even incorporating some of their mountains and rivers in official Ming imperial sacrifices.[28] So although he was violating his father's injunction against invading a neighbour, the Ming ruler was performing his function as the legitimate ruler of the world in punishing the wicked. Yongle was careful to note that the Ming regarded all who violated the rules of investiture as criminals. As the emperor proclaimed:

> The bandit minister Li Jili 黎季犛 (Hồ Quý Ly) and his son Cang 蒼 of Annan 安南 [Annam] repeatedly killed rulers of the country and slaughtered their families. They grabbed power in the country and duplicitously usurped the throne, levied harsh and extortionate taxes and legally raped the people. There was much complaint in the region but no one to seek recourse from. Moreover, they have let their soldiers loot and plunder and invade neighbours' fiefs [i.e. lands of other tributary states]. Despite repeated imperial instructions they have deceitfully disobeyed orders and wallowed in their evil. Now I have ordered generals to lead the army to save the people and punish [the Hồ] for their crimes. The army will be mobilised on the 16th day of this month. I have specially proclaimed this so the spirits will assist them.[29]

Three days later Yongle appointed Zhu Neng the Generalissimo in Charge of Pacifying the Yi, with Mu Sheng 沐晟 (1368–1439) as Vice Commander of the Left and Zhang Fu 張輔 (1375–1449) Vice Commander of the Right.[30] Though contemporary sources claim the Ming force included as many as 800,000 troops, most modern estimates place the figure at slightly more than a quarter of that.[31] In any case, it was a huge force designed to overawe the Vietnamese with both numbers and firepower, as the Ming troops were equipped with the latest in military technology. Indeed, the reliance upon superior technological prowess was a hallmark of the Ming military throughout the dynasty and a key component of Ming grand strategy. It was particularly noteworthy in conflicts where the Ming could smash less well-equipped foes in stationary positions such as the ones they encountered in the wars of colonial expansion in China's southwest lands of Yunnan and Guangxi, which were only under nominal control at this early stage in the dynasty. In fact, just prior to the punitive campaign in Vietnam, the Ming had been aggressively establishing pacification commissions in the southwest as footholds for Chinese settlement and as a means for control and influence in more far-flung Tai and Burmese polities (see discussion by Geoffrey Wade in Chapter 2 of this volume).[32]

In their announced role as liberators of the people Yongle enjoined the troops to refrain from despoiling tombs, seizing goods, raping women or engaging in other evil acts.[33] He also said they should not violate local laws and should not 'recklessly advance in greedy pursuit of profit', a command which seems to have been directed at military commanders seeking glory and reward for their achievements. In particular he noted that the military expeditions of the Song and Yuan dynasties into Yunnan had failed because the commanders were greedy and had contended with one another.[34] Therefore the emperor explicitly instructed his commanders to cooperate and not become jealous of one another's achievements. Moreover, at least according to the Chinese sources, the initial goals seem to have been modest. Once the criminals were brought to justice, the Trần were to be restored to their throne. Publicly at least Yongle evinced no desire for the annexation of Annam.

A deeper examination of the build-up for war, however, suggests that it might not have been as impromptu as the emperor suggested. First of all, as noted above, the Ming had been engaging in a policy of southward expansion and territorial consolidation since the foundation of the dynasty. They were actively involved in relations with the polities of mainland Southeast Asia and were just embarking upon the famed naval expeditions to the so-called Western Oceans (*Xiyang* 西洋). Extensive preparations for war were made, including accumulating lots of clothing and special medicine for the rough Vietnamese climate. In addition to the huge land forces assembled in Yunnan and Guangxi, some units were sent ahead by sea to occupy towns and prepare for advancing Ming armies.[35] Moreover, there were hawkish elements within the court who advocated the annexation of Annam, and at least one geographic work published in 1394 had described Annam as part of the empire.[36] All of these suggest that the Ming were anticipating a long stay and had possibly been planning for the annexation of Vietnam for some time, with the Yongle emperor perhaps seeing it as just another step in his consolidation of power and establishment of legitimacy.[37] In any case such a move, coupled with his unprecedented use of naval power, accords well with the emperor's persistent desire to manifest awe at his rule.[38]

It was a gorgeous day when the Yongle emperor personally oversaw the troops departing the capital, and he confidently predicted victory. But the large army did not proceed particularly fast, and its commander Zhu Neng died in the tenth month of 1406 before even reaching the border. He was replaced by Zhang Fu, who would prove to be by far the most adept Ming commander in the ensuing decade until his final recall to China in 1416, well before the ultimate Ming defeat. The larger Ming invasion force was alert for ambushes and much better prepared, with extensive supplies and stores of medicine, in addition to large numbers of firearms.[39] It is noted that among the Ming commanders initially sent to chastise the Vietnamese in 1406 were the *Shenji jiangjun* 神機將軍 ('heavenly firearms commanders') Cheng Kuan 程寬 (active *c.* 1400) and Zhu Gui 朱貴 (*c.* 1370–1420).[40] This force consisted of some 75,000 troops, under 20 commanders mustered from all over the Ming empire.[41] Sun Laichen suggests that in this era about 10 per cent of Ming troops were equipped with firearms (**Pls 4.1–4.5**), though my research indicates that they strove to reach higher ratios when possible.[42] Clearly this was designed to overawe their presumably numerically and technologically inferior enemy.

The use of firearms is noteworthy in that it appears to have been standard operating procedure for the Ming to use guns as force multipliers and against technologically inferior foes in particular, where it was believed they could be overawed into ready submission. Hence we see their use in the initial conquest of Yunnan in the 1380s and throughout the Ming period in campaigns of expansion in the southwest.[43] Zhang Wen has recently argued that firearms were integral in the incorporation of formerly aboriginal lands into the regular administrative structure of the Chinese empire in the late imperial era, suggesting that the relationship between superior military technologies and bureaucratic administrative advances in China was in fact

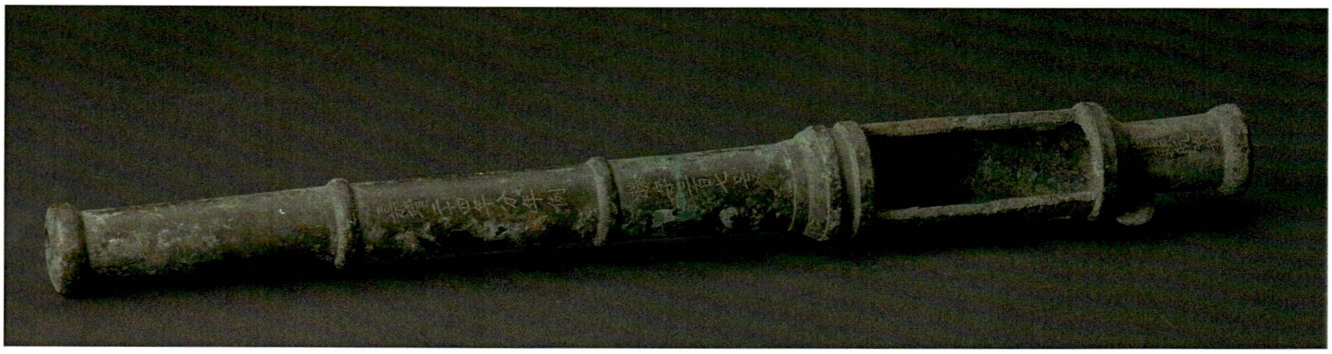

Plate 4.1 Chinese bronze cannon, Ming dynasty, dated 1545 (Jiajing reign). Length 64.5cm. The Capital Museum, Beijing

similar to the processes taking place in Southeast Asia, a topic which will be touched upon below.[44]

Aided by their superior firepower and logistics, in early 1407 the Ming advanced in multiple wings and smashed through formidable Vietnamese defences rather easily.[45] They forced Hồ Quý Ly to torch and abandon his Western Capital while using firearms and new tactics to frustrate the war elephants sent against them, for example concentrating fire at the handlers and the trunks of the animals.[46] Notably, the Ming supposedly deployed firearms to great effect against Vietnamese elephants in the bloody street fights for control of the Eastern Capital.[47] But the Ming were still apparently impressed enough with the war elephants that they took some back as war booty to China, including them among the 235,000 livestock they claimed to have captured.[48]

According to Chinese accounts, after the Ming captured the capital, a large number of Vietnamese officials begged to be formally incorporated into the empire on account of the total extermination of the Trần royal line by the Hồ.[49] The Ming acceded to this 'request', citing earlier Chinese control of the region as a precedent, and administrative offices were established in accordance with the manner in which the Ming governed other frontier regions.[50] Vietnam was formally annexed as the province of Jiaozhi on the first day of the sixth month of 1407 [5 July 1407].[51] This would prove to be significant in the long-term development of Vietnam, for it ultimately facilitated the greater centralisation of the state and aided in its wars: first of liberation against the Ming and subsequently in campaigns of expansion to the south and the west. Though many Vietnamese were enlisted into the Ming governmental structure within Vietnam itself, the Ming also forcibly deported thousands of tradesmen and artisans to Nanjing, including gunsmiths.[52] Additionally, some were assigned to the School for the Sons of State (*guo zi xue* 國子學) and trained as students, perhaps to serve as envoys later.[53]

Finally, again exercising the rights of the Yongle emperor as the Son of Heaven, Zhang Fu selected handsome young boys to be sent to the Ming capital for castration and palace service.[54] This is significant for a number of reasons. First of all, distributing eunuchs was the right of the emperor, and tributary states often presented the Ming emperor with gifts of eunuchs.[55] By forcibly taking these young boys Zhang Fu was asserting the right of his monarch to tribute, though that distinction would soon be erased with the formal annexation of Vietnam. Next, in part because of his status as usurper and again in contravention of his father's express wishes, the Yongle emperor had grown particularly dependent upon the eunuch establishment in his government. Producing more eunuchs with at least some knowledge of his newest province and its language could prove useful to the emperor in the long term.

The gunsmiths, however, have hitherto drawn the most attention from scholars, in part because several Ming

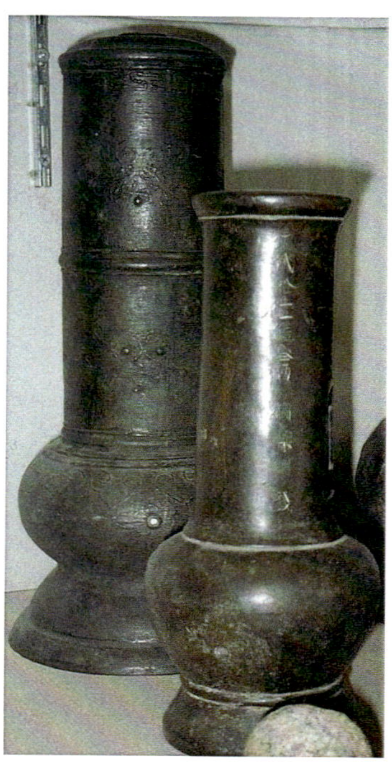

Plate 4.2 Two Chinese-style bombards (left: LSb 19241; right: LSb 19233). The one on the right contains an inscription in Chinese, although some of the characters are indistinct. History Museum of Vietnam, Hanoi

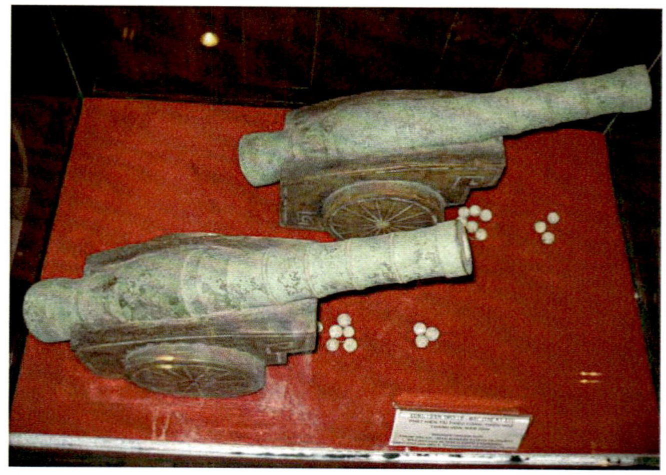

Plate 4.3 Two small bronze cannons, late 16th century. Military Museum, Hanoi

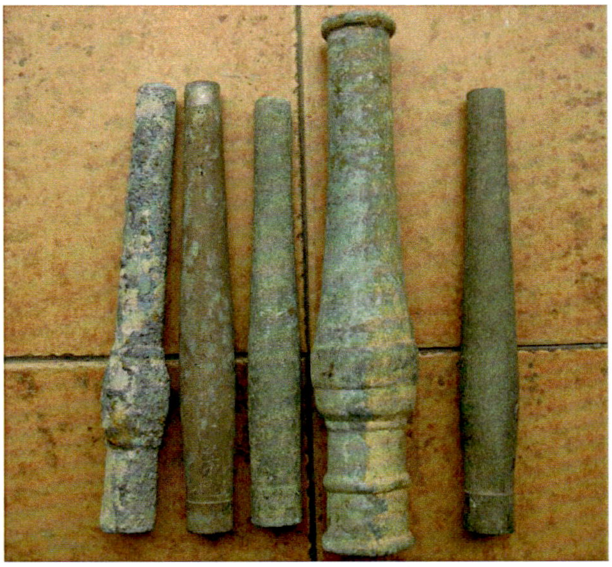

Plate 4.4 Vietnamese handguns in Mr Guo's shop at the antique market in Nanning, Guangxi

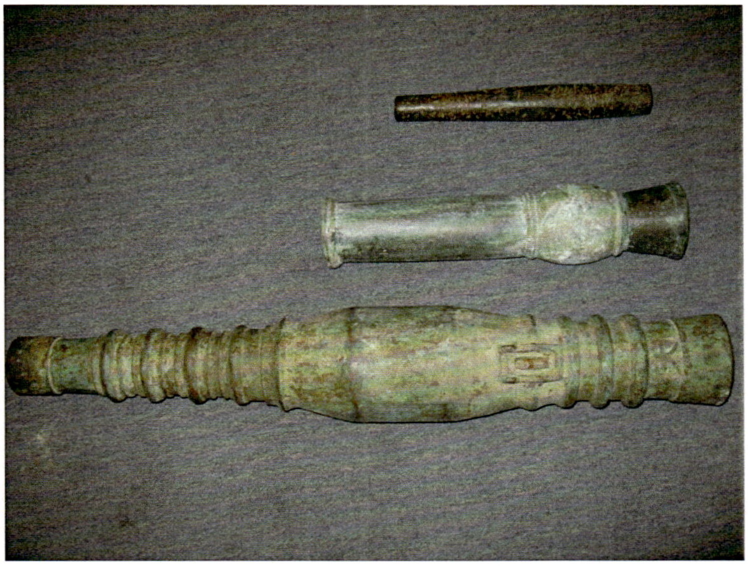

Plate 4.5 The three firearms in Mark Rapoport's possession at the 54 Traditions

sources highlight their importance. In fact, according to the 18th-century *Ming shi*, the Yongle emperor decided to establish the Firearms Division (*shenji ying* 神機營) in the capital in the early 15th century after the Ming captured new firearms and firearms experts during their invasion and occupation of Vietnam.[56] As we have seen, such later claims are false, since the Ming already had a very advanced armaments industry prior to the invasion. Nonetheless this claim (and the fact that Vietnamese artisans were deported) reveals that there was in fact a good deal of technological exchange taking place in Asia in the wake of the collapse of the Mongol Yuan dynasty (1271–1368) in China. It also attests to the Ming desire to assert themselves firmly at the apex of the reconstituted tributary system. As tributary overlords and colonial masters it was their prerogative to extract resources, human and otherwise, from their subject states. In bringing these artisans to China, the Yongle emperor was forcibly underscoring this fact and exercising his rights as the Son of Heaven. In fact, in addition to working in the Firearms Division, there is evidence that Vietnamese artisans assisted in the construction of the Yongle emperor's new capital in Beijing.[57]

Furthermore, as will be demonstrated below, such exchanges were not that unusual, as the Ming were always looking to gain a military edge over their rivals as part of their grand strategy. Though the Ming generally led the way in technological innovation and dissemination of new technologies, Ming emperors and military commanders were astute enough to recognise and adopt superior technologies and tactics, no matter what their origins. This can be seen in the Ming request for war elephants from Vietnam to aid in its pacification of recalcitrant tribal groups in the southwest.[58] It is also evidenced by the Ming adoption of so-called 'wooden wad' technology from Vietnam to increase the range of their 'fire lances' (*shen qiang* 神槍), upon encountering this technology during their occupation of Vietnam in the early 15th century.[59] (The term *shen qiang* is ambiguous. In pre-Ming times it could denote a primitive flamethrower of sorts, but in the Ming it just generically means 'gun' and appears to be used in that sense here, most likely to refer to forerunners of the arquebus.) Thus, when the Ming eagerly adopted superior Western military technologies such as the 'red barbarian cannon' and the arquebus from the Portuguese at the beginning of the 16th century, they were in fact operating within a well-established framework consistent with their grand strategic goals.[60]

Additionally, while the Mongols have long been recognised as major transmitters of military technology throughout the globe, until recently scholars have paid far less attention to the important role played by the succeeding Ming dynasty in continuing these efforts, albeit not always intentionally. Indeed, some scholars have identified the Ming as the world's first 'gunpowder empire' and have suggested that the dissemination of Ming firearms technology to Southeast Asia was critical in regional power struggles and state formation.[61] Moreover, even as they sought to protect their gunpowder technology from falling into the hands of potential foes, the Ming recognised how this technology could contribute to regional stability and hence shared it with their allies, most notably Joseon Korea. Likewise, they sought to keep it secret from their enemies, including the Vietnamese. As will be seen below, the Ming inability to maintain this key technological edge would be an important, but not the only, factor in their eventual defeat in Vietnam.

But initially Ming technological prowess carried the day and it seemed that Vietnam would be pacified even more easily than Yunnan. When Zhang Fu returned to the capital a year later in 1408, the Yongle emperor personally hosted a banquet in his honour. In particular the emperor praised him for overawing the enemy but Zhang deflected the compliment, crediting the emperor's sage planning and the backing of the state for his success.[62] In the assessment of Lo Jung-pang the Ming victory achieved the Yongle emperor's two grand strategic aims of frontier security and the restoration of China's ascendant position on the international scene, though it could also be argued that it merely reinforced these aims while actually extending Ming influence considerably, at least in the short term.[63] A song was composed in commemoration of the pacification of Annam, Zhang was promoted to a dukedom and his stipend was raised considerably.[64] The other states around Vietnam were also suitably impressed and were loath to challenge the military might of the Ming.[65] So in this sense the Yongle emperor achieved additional strategic aims without having to resort to military action in these other places. But rebellion soon broke out in Vietnam due to taxation woes, administrative difficulties and agitation by Trần claimants. There is also considerable evidence suggesting that Ming eunuch pacification commissioners were exorbitant in their demands for luxury items, particularly gemstones.[66]

Mu Sheng was initially dispatched from Yunnan to handle matters but he was unsuccessful, and Zhang Fu was again dispatched to Vietnam in 1409. He enjoyed quick success, defeating the Trần rebels, rejecting their claims to legitimacy and refusing their request to seek investiture from the Ming. Zhang executed the last Trần claimant and Vietnam again seemed to be under control, prompting his recall to China. This was a pattern that would be repeated over the next several years. Even the Yongle's emperor's promise to remit taxes for three years if the people returned to their old occupations and abandoned their resistance was unsuccessful in quelling dissent. In a situation eerily reminiscent of the American experience centuries later, the Ming in Vietnam would consistently win major battles with their superior firepower only to see rebel groups spring up as soon as Ming troops left an area.[67] The rebel leader Lê Lợi (1385–1433) would eventually emerge as the most intractable of these freedom fighters and it was he who would eventually drive the Ming out of Vietnam.[68] Over time the Vietnamese captured and started manufacturing their own firearms, evening the technological balance.

This process in turn had serious implications for the Vietnamese state later and should be seen as perhaps the most significant of the unintended consequences of the Ming invasion. In light of the mounting evidence to the contrary, it is surprising that many military historians continue to ignore the fact that Asians not only invented gunpowder technologies, but improved upon them and used them to great effect long before the coming of Western gun traders.[69] Moreover, innovations in the manufacture and deployment of gunpowder weapons often proved critical in state-building efforts and in the maintenance of regional stability, a process historians have often confined to the Western experience.[70] Yet, as Peter Lorge has recently provocatively argued, Europeans only began to exploit profitably gunpowder technologies when their states became more like the imperial bureaucratic Chinese state.[71] By extension, the same argument can be made for Southeast Asian states, most notably Vietnam. While much has been made of Vietnamese cultural and institutional borrowing from Ming China and its importance in the maturation of the Vietnamese state, until recently far less attention has been paid to military borrowings.[72] Just as they did with the tributary system itself, the Vietnamese adopted and adapted military technologies to suit their own ends and advance their position vis-à-vis their neighbours.

As the Ming occupation wore on, firearms proved useful time and again in aiding the Ming to quickly quell Vietnamese uprisings.[73] Particularly striking from a military perspective on the Ming invasion of Vietnam is the variety of weapons they used and the variety of settings in which they were utilised, attesting to their adaptability and readiness to employ firearms, in contradistinction to Western characterisations of the Ming as pacifistic and uninterested in military technologies. The Ming deployed firearms in breaking elephant charges, attacking heavy fortifications, and on ships. In at least one case they used their firepower to overwhelm defenders using heavy crossbows against them.[74] All told, the Ming left an occupation force of some 87,000 scattered in 39 citadels around the country, though most were concentrated in the Red River delta area.[75] These would be bolstered by frequent infusions of new troops as circumstances dictated, the Ming quickly coming to the realisation that their forces were insufficient and that military force alone could not suffice to bring the Vietnamese to heel.[76]

Over time, however, the Ming would also lose their technological advantage. The Vietnamese were already aware of the benefits of firearms in warfare and had used them effectively against the Chams (in what is now southern Vietnam) in the 1390s. So when the resistance began in earnest, one of the first things the rebels did was establish arsenals to manufacture weapons. In fact, this was most likely an extension of preparations begun by Hồ Quý Ly in anticipation of a Ming invasion.[77] And as the rebels acquired more and more Ming firearms, the tide of the occupation started to turn. As one Vietnamese source noted, 'their firearms piled up and their gunpowder stores were filled'.[78] This was nowhere more evident than in the successful Vietnamese siege of Xương Giang that signalled the end of Ming power in Vietnam.[79] Vietnamese sources confirm that despite their own establishment of arsenals, most of their weapons were captured from the Chinese or brought to them by defectors. Since many Vietnamese served as assistant commanders and vice commanders and as officers in guards and companies (the colonial administration mirroring that of the Ming), it can be reasonably presumed that these men gained training in the use of firearms and passed this on to the rebels when they joined the resistance movement.

This would not be the only case of unintentional technology transfer on the part of the Ming. Deserters apparently transmitted Ming firearms technology to Burma in the early 1500s after a Ming rout of the Maw Shans (as the Burmese called the Shan polities) in a border clash, and Ming guns most likely entered the rest of Burma and northeast India around the same time via traders.[80] The Vietnamese refused Ming demands to return captured weapons after peace was restored between the states in the 15th century.[81] This Ming request in itself is ironic given that they claimed to have acquired 135,900 horses, cows and elephants and over 2,000,000 weapons in their initial 1407 conquest of Vietnam as part of their tributary exactions.[82] Significantly, the Ming used the elephants not only for parades and in the imperial menagerie (see discussion by Jonathan Hay in Chapter 5 of this volume), but also for military operations, a practice that continued right up until the end of the Ming dynasty.[83]

More significant perhaps than the sheer numbers of weapons (inflated or not) are the kinds of technologies the Chinese acquired, or more accurately, the refinements to existing technologies. First of all, as noted above, the Vietnamese seem to have refined the design of the fire lance by placing a wooden wad behind the arrow made of ironwood, which was native to the region. This greatly extended the effective range of the weapon out to some 300 paces.[84] The technique is not found in older Chinese guns, but has been found in specimens dating from 1415. The Vietnamese also appear to have devised a priming pan lid to prevent fuses on matchlocks from getting wet in the steamy tropical climate. Surviving Chinese guns from as early as 1415 possess this innovation, which has not been reliably confirmed in Ming weapons prior to 1410.[85] Moreover, this innovation was also apparently incorporated into European-style cannon manufactured in China over the next 150 years, though the technique was abandoned in the late 16th century as more modern European firearms made their appearance in East Asia.[86]

These improvements were most likely introduced by the aforementioned Vietnamese craftsmen sent to Nanjing in the wake of the initial Ming invasion. Altogether some 17,000 captives were taken back to China and at least some were renowned as firearms experts. Their lives were spared in exchange for their service in the Ming Ministry of Works.[87] Their descendants served the Ming until 1489, and the official Hồ Nguyên Trừng (胡元澄, ?1374–?1446) was later honoured in China as a god of firearms.[88] Later Ming records indicate that certain firearms had been transmitted from Vietnam and adopted to great effect against the Mongols, but Li Bin and Sun Laichen have persuasively argued that it was these improvements, rather than the weapons themselves, that were transmitted from Vietnam. And a Qing era source specifically states that what the Ming acquired in the invasion of Vietnam were 'firearms techniques', after which they established the firearms training division so as to drill the men in the use of firearms.[89] Nonetheless, this testifies to the importance of technological diffusion and exchanges between the states of Asia prior to the Western engagement in the region and highlights regional dynamism in the early modern era.

In the other direction, after the withdrawal of the Ming in 1427, the Lê dynasty (1428–1527) in Vietnam added specialised firearms units to its military and created many warships equipped with heavy cannon for its navy. Firearms arsenals were also added to pre-existing arsenals.[90] To facilitate greater weapons production, much copper and other materials were imported into Vietnam from Yunnan and other provinces of southern China, and illegal trade in weapon-making materials flourished. The Vietnamese in turn transmitted this technology as they fought their neighbours to the south and west, most notably in the decisive defeat of Champa in 1471.[91]

Furthermore, in addition to manufacturing and deploying Chinese-derived weapons against their Cham foes, the Vietnamese reorganised their military organisation along Chinese lines and encouraged their military officers to study the Chinese military classics (*Wujing qishu* 五經七書), by instituting military examinations modelled after those of the Ming.[92] Thus, while scholars such as John Whitmore have long contended that bureaucratic and administrative centralisation spurred by the Ming occupation was crucial to the Vietnamese defeat of Champa,[93] only recently have scholars recognised the fact that improved Chinese-derived military technology was a vital component of this process. It also aided additional Vietnamese expansion to the west. In fact, archaeological and textual information suggests that so many firearms were being manufactured in Vietnam in the late 15th century that the government had to establish additional weapons depots specifically for the storage of firearms.[94]

In any event, it seems reasonable to assume that firearms played a critical role in state formation and consolidation in Asia in the 15th and 16th centuries and that the majority of the firearms in question – almost all of them prior to 1511 – were Chinese in origin or derived from Chinese rather than European models. Likewise it is striking how many features of the Chinese bureaucratic state, whether consciously adopted and copied as in the case of the Vietnamese, or coincidentally mimicked as in other cases, are present in these emerging polities. In this sense Peter Lorge's assertion that European states became more 'modern' militarily and organisationally by becoming more like the Chinese state seems perfectly tenable.[95] It also reveals an unintended consequence of the Ming practice of overawing neighbours.

In addition to its obvious significance for the histories of China and Vietnam respectively, the Ming decision to invade its southern neighbour needs to be considered within the broader context of Ming grand strategy and the desire of the Ming to assert and maintain its hegemony in Asia. As Geoffrey Wade has noted in Chapter 2 of this volume, Ming efforts in Vietnam were certainly colonial in nature but also carried out in conjunction with the great naval expeditions, which were a form of maritime proto-colonialism whereby the Ming sought to extend their own commercial and political interests by means of both diplomacy and force.[96] In this light the Ming needs to be viewed more dynamically as an expansionist early modern gunpowder empire that presaged the later activities of the Spanish and Portuguese in certain key respects. And while some have interpreted the Ming defeat in Vietnam as the 'beginning of China's fall from her position of preeminence',[97] the fact that the Ming successfully repulsed Japan's invasion of Korea more than 150 years later as well as the reconstruction of the tributary system by the Qing attests to the viability of both the Chinese empire and the system itself.

Ming actions were also, as demonstrated herein, very important for subsequent political and administrative developments in Southeast Asia and for commercial and technological dissemination. Though not as well known as ceramics, Ming firearms also made their way around Asia and became an important commodity, despite the efforts of the Ming state to restrict their movement in hopes of maintaining their military superiority. Indeed, the consequences of the Ming occupation of Vietnam would resonate for centuries and lead to just the kind of 'domino effect' feared by 20th-century Cold Warriors, with states falling prey to Vietnamese imperialism based in part on the Chinese model. Additionally, the Ming were not above importing superior military technologies from their neighbours, tributaries and even outsiders in the interest of retaining their position at the apex of the tributary hierarchy. Thus, far from being a passive, non-competitive imperial power as some have suggested, the Ming empire was in fact a dynamic, realistic hegemonic power much in line with its early modern contemporaries and even ahead of them in certain respects.

Notes

1 Wade 2005b, http://epress.nus.edu.sg/msl/entry/840, original text in *MSL Taizu shilu* 68.4a–b (4/9/辛未).
2 Tsai, Shih-shan Henry 2001; *DMB*, 355–65; Chao Zhongchen 1995.
3 Ming grand strategy has been the subject of much recent research that attempts to put it within the broader context of Chinese history and strategic culture, e.g. Johnston 1995; Wang Yuan-kang 2011, 101–80. I examine these and other works and take up the subject of Ming grand strategy in much greater detail in Swope forthcoming.
4 Some scholars suggest that the Ming deliberately refrained from using force most of the time, but still maintained a military presence by more subtle means such as stationing Ming officials in far-flung ports; Ptak 1998, 24–6.
5 On Ming military interventions in Southeast Asia in general in this era, including during the expeditions led by the eunuch Zheng He, see Wade 2008, and also Chapter 2 by the same author in this volume.
6 The classic English language overview of the tributary system remains Fairbank 1968. For relations with Southeast Asia in particular see Wang Gungwu 1968 and 1998. For a recent examination of the significance of the tributary system in maintaining Ming hegemony in Asia see Kang 2010.
7 I generally refer to the polity known as Đại Việt, which more properly refers to the more northern part of today's nation of Vietnam, as Vietnam throughout the present piece. For a recent overview of Ming–Vietnamese relations, see Zheng Yongchang 1997.
8 Finlay 1991, 6.
9 For a detailed analysis of the background context and the reasons Wanli decided to intervene in Korea, see Swope 2013 (also Swope 2009, which discusses that war in its entirety). On Yongle's grand strategic concerns see Ptak 1998, 28.
10 For a detailed discussion of the Ming dispute with the Hồ see Zheng Yongchang 1997, 26–36.
11 Hồ Quý Ly was able to take advantage of unrest in Annam caused by repeated invasions from Champa, the kingdom based in what is now southern Vietnam. *DMB*, 797; Tsai, Shih-shan Henry 2001, 178–9, and Whitmore 1985, 73–4.
12 Chao Zhongchen 1995, 340. For the original references see *MSL Taizong shilu* 19.3a–b (1/4/辛酉) and *Taizong shilu* 25.11b (1/11/丁卯), translated in Wade 2005b, http://epress.nus.edu.sg/msl/entry/24 and http://epress.nus.edu.sg/msl/entry/34.
13 *GQ*: Tan Qian 1978, 968. For details on the process of usurpation, see Whitmore 1985, 53–63, and *MSJSBM* 1997, 343–6. Also see *MS*, 8324.
14 Chao Zhongchen 1995, 341.
15 *MSL Taizong shilu* 37.3a–b (2/12/壬辰); Wade 2005b, http://epress.nus.edu.sg/msl/entry/346.
16 *MSL Taizong shilu* 38.3b–4a (3/1/甲寅); Wade 2005b, http://epress.nus.edu.sg/msl/entry/527.
17 Chao Zhongchen 1995, 341, and *DMB*, 799.
18 Chao Zhongchen 1995, 341.
19 *MSJSBM* 1997, 345.
20 *MSJSBM* 1997, 345–6. Also see *HMTJ*, 423.
21 *MSL Taizong shilu* 52.6a–7a (4/3/丙午); Wade 2005b, http://epress.nus.edu.sg/msl/entry/875. The Chens are the Trần and Tianping 天平 is the Chinese rendering of the claimant's name, Thiên Bình.
22 Chao Zhongchen 1995, 342.
23 *MSJSBM* 1997, 346.
24 *MSJSBM* 1997, 346. For a slightly different version of the exchange between Yongle and Zhu Neng, see *MSL Taizong shilu* 53.4b–5a (4/4/癸未) as cited in Wade 2005b, http://epress.nus.edu.sg/msl/entry/876. Also Chao Zhongchen 1995, 343–4.
25 The crimes as listed in the *Ming shilu* are enumerated and discussed in Zheng Yongchang 1997, 50–2. Also see Zhang Xiumin 1992, 193–5.
26 See Chao Zhongchen 1995, 343–4.
27 Concerning the emperor's right to exercise 'divine chastisement', see Lo Jung-pang 1970, 161–2.
28 Wang Gungwu 1998, 305.
29 Chao Zhongchen 1995, 344. The original in *MSL Taizong shilu* 56.1a (4/7/戊子). For a slightly variant translation, see Wade 2005b, http://epress.nus.edu.sg/msl/entry/901.
30 All these commanders had served Yongle loyally in his war of usurpation and in campaigns in the southwest. Zhang Fu's daughter was one of the emperor's concubines. See *DMB*, 64–6, Zhang Xiumin 1992, 191–210, and *MS*, 4219–24 for biographies of Zhang Fu.
31 *MS*, 4220, and *MSJSBM* 1997, 346. For the modern estimates see Wade 2005a, 43, and Whitmore 1985, 89.
32 Wade 2008, 584–7.
33 Chao Zhongchen 1995, 345.
34 See Zhang Xiumin 1992, 192, and Chao Zhongchen 1995, 345.
35 Chao Zhongchen 1995, 346.
36 Lo Jung-pang 1970, 164.
37 The emperor had previously claimed that 'since ancient times Annam had comprised administrative divisions of China'. See Wade 2008, 588, n. 43.
38 A number of scholars have recently drawn attention to the military and grand strategic implications of the naval expeditions, but it should be noted that Lo Jung-pang pointed this out nearly 50 years ago. See Lo Jung-pang 1970, 174–5.
39 On Ming strategy and planning, see Chao Zhongchen 1995, 345–6. For a list of major command assignments, see *HMTJ*, 426.
40 *MSJSBM* 1997, 346–7.
41 For a detailed discussion of Ming troop dispatches and a table with specific dates, see Zheng Yongchang 1997, 36–50.
42 Sun Laichen 2003, 498. Some sources give the outrageously high figure of 800,000 Ming troops being mobilised for the campaign in Annam, e.g. Chao Zhongchen 1995, 339. This biography offers an overview of the Ming occupation of Vietnam on 339–51. Also see Zheng Yongchang 1997, 46 concerning the figure of 800,000. On firearms ratios among Ming troops, see Swope 2009, especially ch. 2.
43 Li Bin 1995, 149. On their use in the late Ming during the suppression of the rebellion of the Miao chieftain, Yang Yinglong 楊應龍 (d. 1600), see Swope 2011.
44 Zhang Wen 2008.
45 *MS*, 4220, and Zhang Xiumin 1992, 196.
46 *HMTJ*, 429–30, and *MSJSBM* 1997, 348.
47 *MS*, 4220.
48 Zhang Xiumin 1992, 199.
49 *MSJSBM* 1997, 349.
50 *MS*, 4221.
51 See Zhang Xiumin 1992, 199.
52 All told the Ming claimed to have captured over 2.8 million Vietnamese (*man ren* 蠻人) but this figure must be inflated. See Zhang Xiumin 1992, 198.
53 Zhang Xiumin 1992, 46.
54 Zhang Xiumin 1992, 198–201.
55 See Tsai, Shih-shan Henry 1996, 14–17.
56 *MS*, 2264.
57 Zhang Xiumin 1992, 119–23; Clunas and Harrison-Hall 2014, 50.
58 Whitmore 1985, 41.
59 On this technology, see Li Bin 1995, 150–2; and Sun Laichen 2006, 89–93.
60 On the adoption of foreign technologies, see *MS*, 2264–5.
61 Sun Laichen 2000.
62 Zhang Xiumin 1992, 199.
63 Lo Jung-pang 1970, 174.
64 Chao Zhongchen 1995, 347.

65 Wang Gungwu 1998, 318–19.
66 Chao Zhongchen 1995, 348–51.
67 Chao Zhongchen 1995, 349–51.
68 For a biography of Lê Lợi, see *DMB*, 793–7.
69 See the discussion in Lorge 2008, 7–10. Also see Sun Laichen 2003, 495–7.
70 For the classic formulation of the Military Revolution thesis in relation to the West, see Parker 1996. On the relationship of military efficacy to state formation see Tilly 1990.
71 Lorge 2008, 9.
72 On the institutional and cultural fronts see Whitmore 1985 and Woodside 1988. On Chinese military influence on Vietnam and vice versa see Sun Laichen 2006.
73 Sun Laichen 2006, 79–80.
74 *GQ*: Tan Qian 1978, 979.
75 Whitmore 1985, 112.
76 Chao Zhongchen 1995, 351. On continued Ming dispatches of troops and the debates surrounding the efficacy of such policies, see Zheng Yongchang 1997, 71–82.
77 Whitmore 1985, 84, and Lo Jung-pang 1970, 171.
78 Quoted in Sun Laichen 2006, 77. Translation slightly modified.
79 Sun Laichen 2006, 88.
80 Sun Laichen 2003, 501–6.
81 *MS*, 8325.
82 *MSJSBM* 1997, 349. The figure given in this source for the weapons is over twenty million, but that must be due to a copyist's error. See Wang Yuan-kang 2011, 153.
83 On the acquisition of exotic animals as manifestations of imperial power, see Robinson 2013b, 288–303.
84 Li Bin 1995, 151–2; Sun Laichen 2006, 89–91.
85 Sun Laichen 2006, 91–5.
86 Sun Laichen 2008, 86–7.
87 Sun Laichen 2006, 91–2.
88 Li Bin 1995, 156.
89 Long Wenbin 1998, 1183.
90 Sun Laichen 2006, 95.
91 Sun Laichen 2006, 98–105.
92 Sun Laichen 2008, 76–7.
93 Whitmore 1985, 129–30.
94 Sun Laichen 2008, 79.
95 Lorge 2008, 21.
96 Wade 2005a, 51–5.
97 On the defeat as a blow to Ming prestige, see Lo Jung-pang 1970, 154.

Chapter 5
Green Beijing: Ecologies of Movement in the New Capital *c.* 1450

Jonathan Hay

Cities may be the largest premodern structures in China that art historians take as an object of study. The Chinese city takes on various guises in art-historical writing. We encounter it at times as a configuration of architectural forms and spaces, and at other times as a frame for diverse practices of art-making. More selectively, it sometimes takes form as a network of urban and extra-urban sites that were especially important for the production and reception of art. Illuminating as such characterisations of the city are, they tend to underplay a dimension of urban experience – movement – that the modern city-dweller is liable to see as fundamental. Some might argue that our contemporary awareness of the city as a constellation of movement is irrelevant to a 15th-century Chinese city, especially one like Beijing that had major symbolic functions. However, I raise the question of movement not in order to collapse differences between past and present, but on the contrary to suggest that movement provides an analytic lens through which we can gain a sharper sense of those very differences.

To craft movement as an analytic lens, one approach might start from 21st-century thinking on the city. This approach would posit that it is illusory to attribute to any city an essential, stable form; instead, urban form crystallises in perception and use, which happen in real time and are socially and culturally mediated. But since the study of Chinese art in English is by definition an intercultural affair, this first approach can never be enough in itself. When one works on another culture or another time period, it is also necessary for both scholarly and ethical reasons to try to reconstruct that culture's self-understanding, as far as one can. We would also need to adopt a second, more archival approach, therefore, in order to ask how 15th-century Beijingers themselves thought about urban movement. Ultimately, though, it is at the intersection between these two very different approaches, the theoretical and the philological, that movement could become the analytic lens needed.

In this short chapter, I cannot craft the lens itself but I may be able to locate the intersection where it could usefully operate. My starting point is a linguistic observation. Whereas the English language does not have a word in common usage to denote either form-in-movement or place-in-movement, the Chinese language does. The relevant term is *shi* 勢. *Shi* equally describes material forms such as mountains or garden rocks, and ephemeral configurations such as the balance of forces at a particular moment in a battle or a chess game. For the former, we might use a translation like 'stance' or 'structural propensity' or 'lines of force', and for the latter 'state of play' or 'current configuration'.[1] *Shi* is equally applicable to form, space and place, and I shall try to show that it can be usefully applied to the city of Beijing *c.* 1450 (**Pl. 5.1**). What kinds of movement would a mid-15th-century inhabitant of the city have thought of as structuring the *shi* of Beijing at any given moment? Three in particular would have come to mind, I think. The first is energy flow, which in Chinese cosmological thought up to and beyond this period was the very condition of existence. Beijing was configured from many different kinds of energy flow, but I only have space to discuss two: one that is tangible, water, and another that is

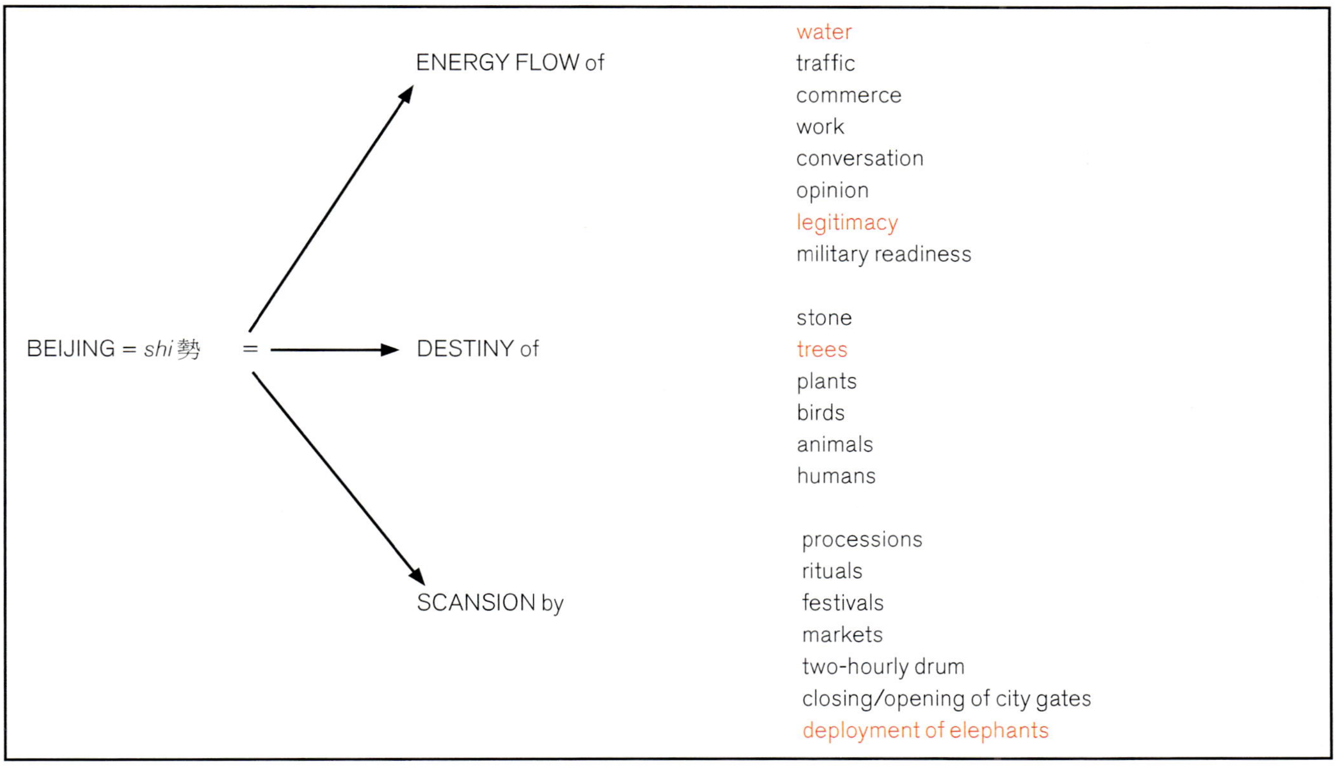

Plate 5.1

intangible, legitimacy. The second kind of movement has a partly arbitrary character: destiny. Like ourselves, 15th-century Chinese often associated destiny with human beings, and one could certainly explore human destinies in the Beijing context. My interest, however, is in non-human destinies, specifically the destinies of trees. Finally, balancing these first two unpredictable forms of movement was the controlled regularity that I will call scansion. From an art-historical point of view, scansion is particularly associated with monuments.[2] I will focus here on one type of living monument, the elephant, in its relation to architectural monuments.

The 1450 moment

Before entering this strange world in which water, legitimacy, trees and elephants share something in common, let me first introduce the city in question. In 1450, Beijing had no paved roads. It was dusty when the weather was dry and muddy when it rained. Since there was no sewer system, it stank. If one could afford it, one avoided walking as much as possible and either rode a horse or took a palanquin. Because the privileged classes rarely walked along the main streets, there were no trees there to provide shade from the summer heat. The person who went out for the day, no matter how he or she travelled, was liable to come home dirty.[3]

Before the Ming capital of Beijing was ever imagined, there was the Mongol Yuan dynasty (1271–1368) capital of Dadu 大都. Dadu (on whose site Beijing was later built) was located at the northwestern edge of a vast flood basin extending all the way to the sea. To the west and north it was ringed by protective mountains (**Pl. 5.2**). The Mongols built their city around a large lake. They constructed their palaces either side of this lake, with the Forbidden City on the east side, and annexed the lake's southern part for the walled imperial city within which the palaces were situated. The lake-centred site on which Dadu was built had a long history of prior imperial associations under the Liao (907–1125) and Jin (1115–1234) dynasties, but Dadu was the first city to enclose the lake within its walls. When the Ming dynasty was founded in 1368, it inherited this great city, which the Mongols had simply abandoned when they retreated north. However, because the Ming dynasty established its own principal capital in south China, in Nanjing, it downgraded the former Dadu and renamed it Beiping 北平. Beiping was far too big for its new function. The new Ming administration redrew the city's perimeter, therefore, so that the new northern wall excluded the northern third of Dadu, and it also moved the southern wall slightly to the south. The result was a smaller, squarer walled city that enclosed most but not all of the city's population (**Pl. 5.3**).[4] The area just outside the new southern wall was somewhat populated, but was not walled in.

Just after 1368 the Ming administration also refurbished one section of the Yuan imperial palace for use as the palace of the Prince of Yan. The prince, Zhu Di 朱棣 (1360–1424), was at that point just a boy who was growing up near his father, the Hongwu 洪武 emperor (r. 1368–98), in Nanjing. But in 1380, when he reached the age of 20, Zhu Di took possession of his Beiping palace, which became his base for the next 20 years, until 1399. Not long after, in 1402, Zhu Di seized the throne and became the Yongle emperor. Within a year he decided that the imperial capital should no longer be Nanjing but instead Beiping, now renamed Beijing, meaning the Northern Capital. In 1406 the order went out to start gathering the necessary construction materials. That process, together with overcoming the opposition of southern officials, took 11 years. The serious work of

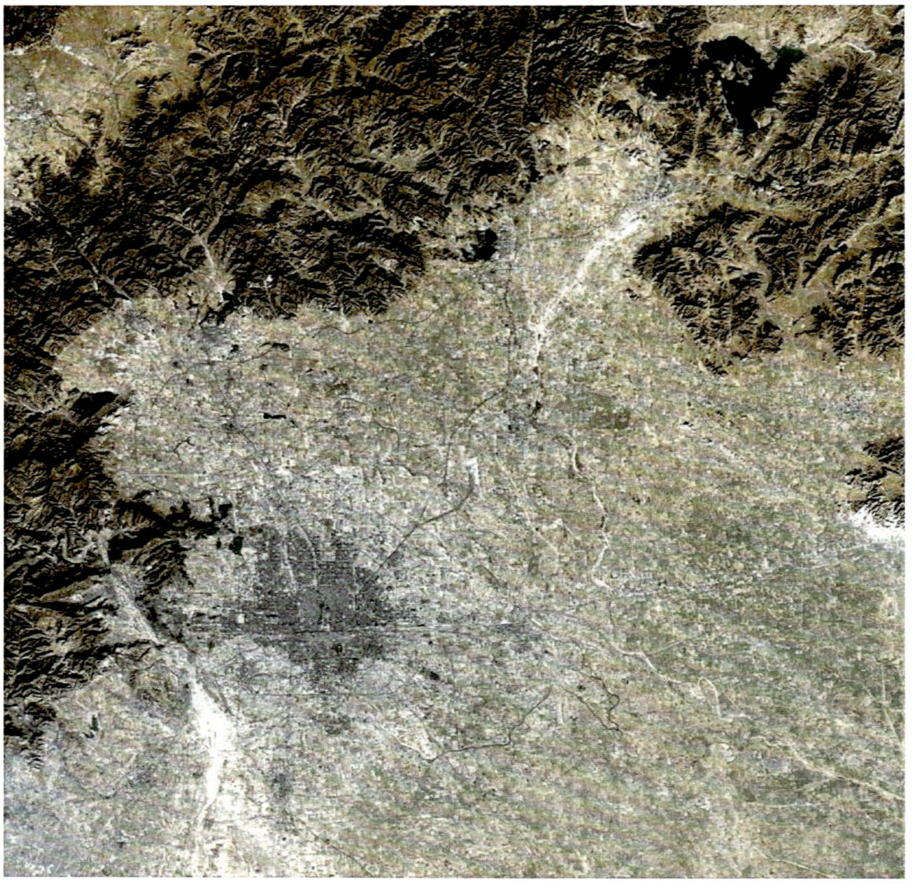

Plate 5.2 Satellite image of Beijing municipality

construction started only in 1417, therefore, when Zhu Di moved to Beijing to supervise the work. After four years enough had been done for the court to move entirely to Beijing. At the beginning of 1421 the city was duly designated the principal capital of the empire.[5]

Thirty years later, in 1450, the city had settled into its new role. During the intervening three decades construction had not stopped, as the city's architects and builders gradually worked their way through the important building projects that had been omitted from the initial five-year push. The following is a summary of the Beijing construction timeline:

- 1403: Beiping is renamed Beijing.
- 1406–17: accumulation of materials necessary to transform Beijing into the new capital.
- 1409–16: construction of Changling mausoleum.
- 1417–20: construction of the Forbidden City, major ritual sites and major government buildings.
- 1421: Beijing is designated the new capital.
- 1421: destruction by fire of three major palace halls.
- 1424–7: expansion of Changling mausoleum.
- 1437–9: construction of city gates and associated structures.
- 1440–1: reconstruction of the three major palace halls burned down in 1421, and strengthening of the walls of the Forbidden City.
- 1442: construction of the remaining major government offices.
- 1445: strengthening of the city wall, and replacement of wooden bridges at the city gates by stone bridges.[6]

In addition, trees had grown, residential neighbourhoods had crystallised and commerce had established itself.[7] In retrospect, 1450 can be seen as a special moment, because the city was fully in place, so to speak, but the population had not yet started to explode. But 1450 was also a special moment in a bad sense, both for China and for Beijing. Two years earlier, in 1448, the Mongols had invaded north China, and in 1449 they had captured in battle the emperor of the day, the Zhengtong 正統 emperor (r. 1436–49, later Tianshun 天順 1457–64). In 1450, Zhengtong's younger brother ruled China as the Jingtai 景泰 emperor (r. 1450–6), but with the threat of illegitimacy hanging over him. Moreover, the country had entered the same economic depression that afflicted most of Eurasia during the mid-15th century.[8] Furthermore – and this partly explains the economic problems – the 1440s and 1450s were marked by repeated climatic anomalies and natural disasters, including flooding within the city of Beijing.[9] This was Beijing's temporal situation in 1450. Now I want to consider the city's configuration as a place-in-movement.

Flows: water

Without water and the hydraulics that kept water flowing, Beijing could not have operated as a city at all. It was the availability of water in the Beijing area that had made it a preferred site for an urban centre for hundreds of years. As we have seen, there had long been a large lake there, which by the 15th century had been broken up into a series of smaller lakes.[10] The water for these lakes, and for Beijing more generally, came from two sources. First, Beijing was located within the watershed of the Yongding 永定 River, which runs southeast from northern Shanxi province and at one point comes close to Beijing. The city was located in the

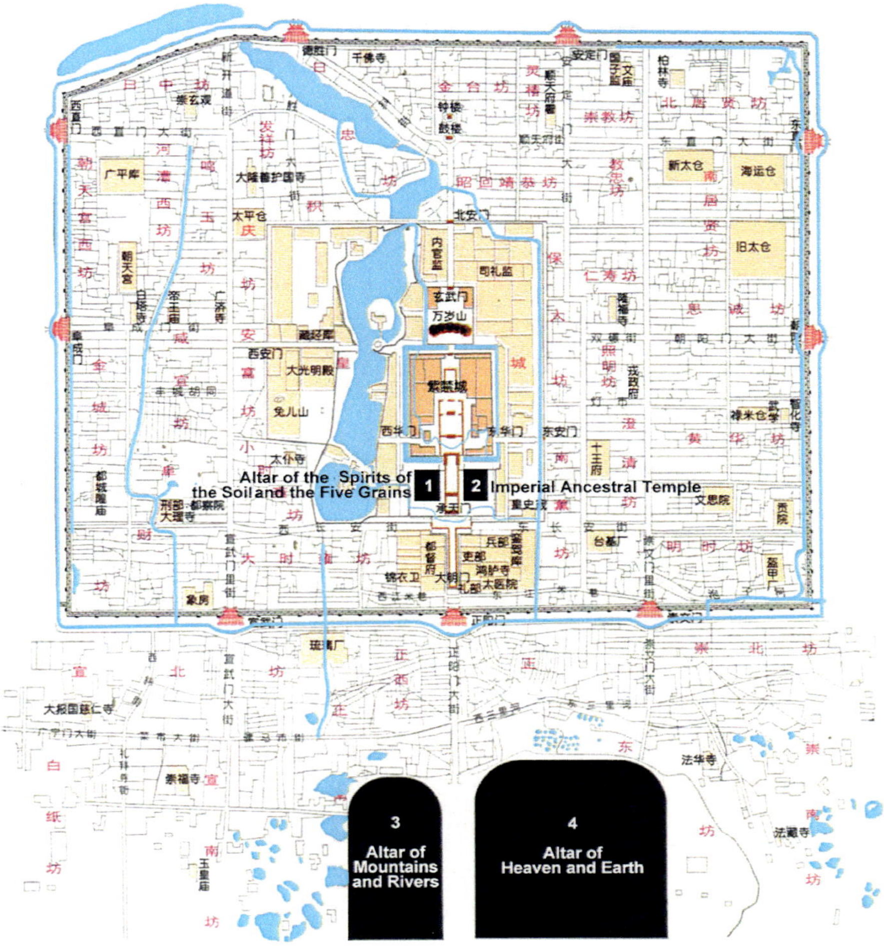

Plate 5.3 Map of Beijing, *c.* 1450, with the major ritual sites marked

higher-altitude northwestern part of the Yongding River flood zone, which provided the city with underground rivers and springs that contributed to the lakes. But the lakes also had the benefit of the runoff from the mountains to the north and northwest through the Gaoliang 高粱 River; the runoff also separately reached the moat of the city through the Qingshui 清水 River. When the new city walls were created at the very beginning of the Ming dynasty, the northern wall was constructed on the south bank of an east–west canal that had run through the city. That canal then became the northern moat. At its western end, the wall cut through the northernmost section of the lake. Once Beijing was established, the water from the Gaoliang River was diverted to the part of the lake within the city, which further shrunk the part outside the city wall. Further shrinkage was caused by rice cultivation in that area, which the Yongle emperor encouraged in order to keep his southern officials happy.[11]

The city's drinking water came partly from the lakes and partly from wells that tapped into underground springs of the Yongding River flood zone. In order to guarantee that drinking water remained a public good, the wells were almost all located in temples. In the 14th century the Mongols had built a canal, partly using aqueducts, all the way from Jade Spring Mountain in the mountains to the north in order to ensure a private supply of drinking water for the palace (**Pl. 5.4**).[12] Under the Ming, however, the palace came to depend instead on water from the lakes. The lake water reached the Forbidden City through two dedicated canals. But the old Jade Spring (Yuquan 玉泉) canal still ran north–south through the west of the city.[13]

The area's natural water resources were not enough in themselves to allow Beijing to function as the capital of the empire. The city could not have been constructed in the first place without man-made waterways to bring to Beijing the wood, stone and bricks necessary to construct the city. To the west, the early 15th-century Ming emperors followed the example of the Mongols and the Jurchen before them by maintaining dykes in order to fix the Yongding River in its course where it came closest to Beijing; the Yongding River was a major transportation route for the building materials and fuel that the city needed. Equally important, the dykes protected Beijing from flooding – flooding that was the result of soil erosion caused by progressive deforestation of the areas around the river over centuries.[14]

To the east of the city, Yongle inherited from the Yuan dynasty a canal system that linked Beijing to Zhigu 直沽 (renamed by him Tianjin), which was both the terminus of the Grand Canal and a maritime port. Because Beijing's altitude was so much higher than Tianjin's, the canal was constructed like a stairway, with dozens of locks. The link to Tianjin was crucial because Beijing depended on tax grain from north-central China and south China, and on all sorts of other products that came from the south. A century earlier, in the early 14th century, tax grain had largely been transported by sea, and the system had been so successful that the northern section of the lake functioned as a port

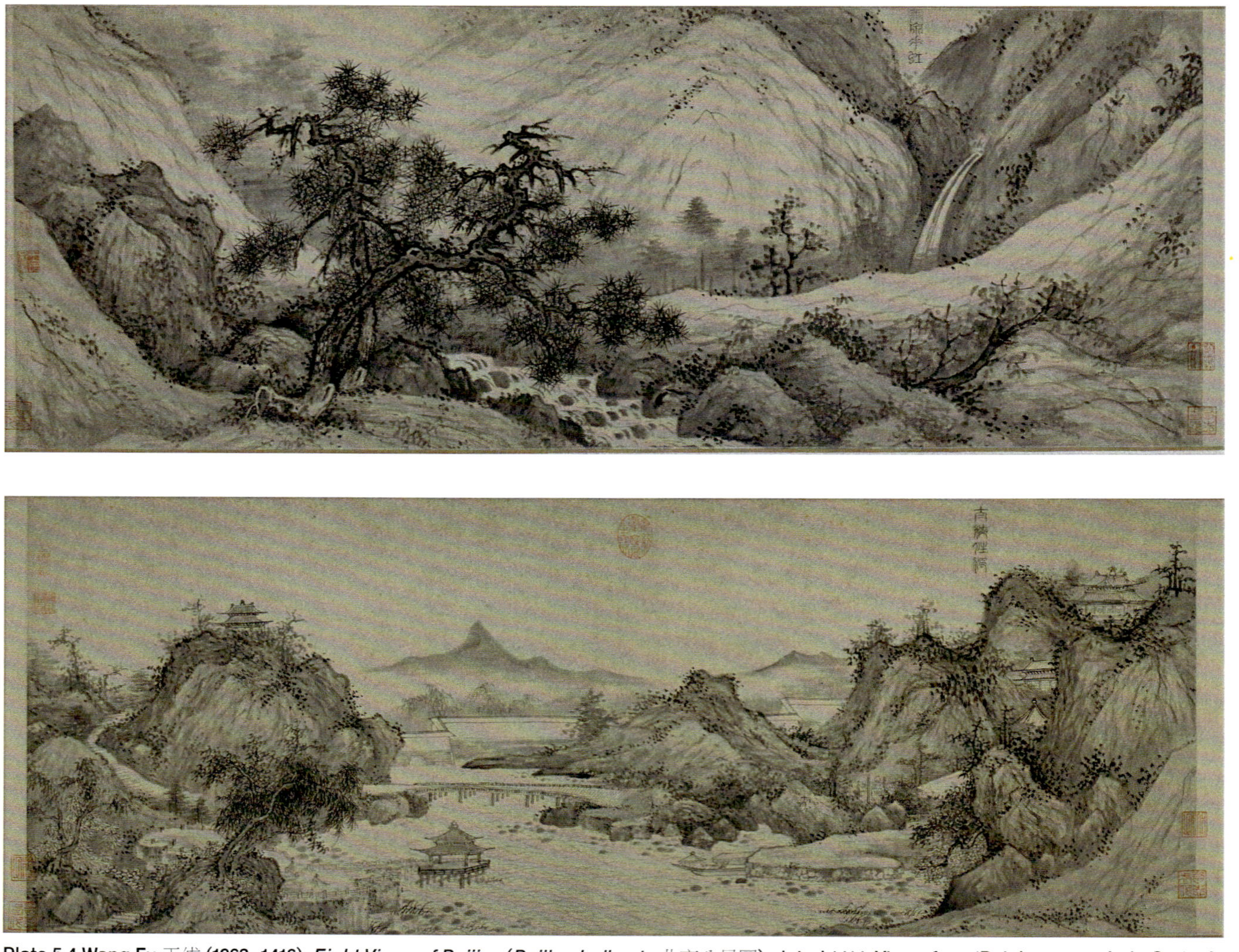

Plate 5.4 Wang Fu 王绂 (1362–1416), *Eight Views of Beijing* (*Beijing bajing tu* 北京八景圖), dated 1414. Views four, 'Rainbow over Jade Spring' and two, 'Clear Ripples at Taiye Lake'. Handscroll, ink on paper, height 42.1cm, length 2006.5cm. National Museum of China

inside the city of Dadu.[15] But by the beginning of the 15th century, the lake was no longer available as a port and the canals from Beijing to Tianjin were silted up and in disrepair. Between 1409 and 1413, one of those canals, starting from the southeast corner of Beijing, was opened up again by dint of a massive campaign of hydraulic intervention, and a gateway port was created at Zhangjiawan 張家灣. This project was part of a larger Ming policy of shifting the transportation of tax grain away from the ocean, where it was vulnerable to pirates, to the Grand Canal. The policy worked increasingly well up through the early 1430s. Subsequently, however, between the drying up of water sources and the breaching of dykes after heavy rains, canal access to Beijing became undependable and had to be combined with overland transportation.[16]

Plate 5.5 Makara water spout, Temple of Heaven, Beijing

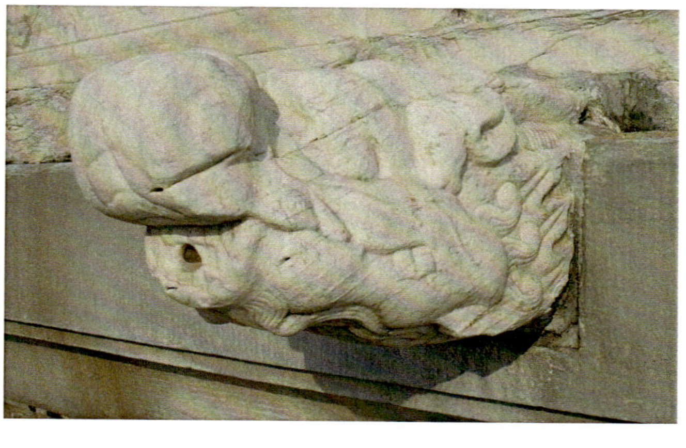

The architectural symbol of the importance of water in Beijing *c.* 1450 was the makara waterspout, which animated the marble platforms of palace halls, ritual altars, temples and bridges (**Pl. 5.5**). The makara (*jing* 鯨 or *yu long* 魚龍) is a sea monster, so it makes sense that it was already omnipresent in Yuan-dynasty Dadu, when there was a particularly active connection to the sea. Under the Yongle emperor the Ming court was also very involved with maritime trade (see Chapters 3, 12, 22 and 27 by Tansen Sen, Zhao Zhongnan, Sally Church and Craig Clunas in this volume), so it is no surprise that the makara remained omnipresent in the new capital of Beijing. But by 1450 the Ming court had turned away from the ocean, and the makara began its gradual transformation in popular consciousness into a type of dragon.

Flows: legitimacy

The flow of water ensured the city's demographic and economic health. But the political health of the new capital depended on the flow of something much more intangible, a

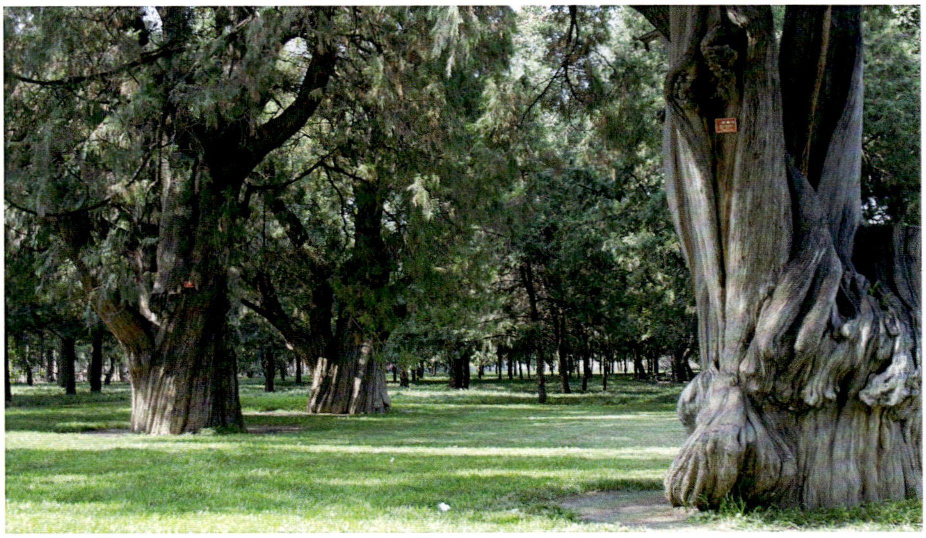

Plate 5.6 Twelfth-century cypresses at the former Altar of Heaven and Earth (today the Temple of Heaven)

legitimacy that was at once spiritual and political. The emperor, as the Son of Heaven and the possessor of Heaven's Mandate, exercised authority through the sword, the eunuch-led security services and the courts, but he derived his authority from a realm beyond the human. He had to be very careful not to allow his reserve of legitimacy to be depleted. It had to be regularly topped up, a little bit like modern electric batteries. The battery chargers for political legitimacy were the ritual sites at which the emperor on a regular schedule solemnly plugged himself in to the forces of the beyond. Because they were so important, the Yongle emperor made sure that these sites were all in place at the end of his initial four-year building campaign (see **Pl. 5.3**). The Altar of Heaven and Earth (*Tianditan* 天地壇) was the most important: the circular stone altar itself was located within a building at the centre of a site that covered some 500 acres in the southern outskirts of the city, just east of the central axis (on the other side of the axis was the Altar of Mountains and Rivers, *Shanchuantan* 山川壇).[17] It had inner and outer precincts; the outer precinct was used to raise the animals used in the sacrifices. Much closer to the palace were two other ritual sites that were almost as important. The first was the Altar of the Spirits of the Soil and the Five Grains (*Shejitan* 社稷壇), which had a small precinct of some 60 acres located just south of the Forbidden City, to the west of the central axis (see **Pl. 5.3**). The second was the Imperial Ancestral Temple (*Taimiao* 太廟), which stood across from it on the other side of the axis (see **Pl. 5.3**). The Ming conducted these various sacrifices annually and, as in earlier times, the processions were huge, choreographed affairs.[18]

The locations of the major ritual sites were carefully chosen to take advantage of existing resources. Long before the Mongols built a city around the lakes, the entire area had been a magnet for Buddhist temples. Some temples were decommissioned so that their trees could be integrated into ritual complexes. The Altar of the Spirits of the Soil and the Five Grains occupied the former location of a Buddhist temple, Xingguosi 興國寺 (Temple Revitalising the State), that dated to the Liao dynasty, and inherited trees that had been planted there more than three centuries before. A few of those trees – all junipers –are still growing there today. The Altar of Heaven and Earth was on the site of an Altar of Heaven dating from the Jurchen Jin dynasty, and took advantage of the cypresses that had been planted in the 12th century, some of which also survive (**Pl. 5.6**). The trees are at some distance from one another, forming a natural hall, with a tree canopy forming the roof.[19] To keep the battery charger metaphor, ancient trees functioned as attractors of spiritual energy. At all the major ritual sites, the ritual specialists planted many more trees. There were veritable forests at the sites of the Altars, and the Imperial Ancestral Temple was surrounded by junipers on all four sides: one surviving example is said to have been planted by the Yongle emperor himself.[20]

The fact that some temples were decommissioned does not mean that temples in general were seen as unimportant. Within Dadu's city walls in the 14th century, and subsequently within Beijing's city walls in the 15th, many of these temples survived along with their ancient trees. In the case of decommissioned temples, their trees sometimes became part of the gardens of residential mansions, such as the mansion of the chief architect of Yongle's Beijing, the Vietnamese eunuch, Ruan An 阮安 (d. 1453).[21] However, the 1420s, 1430s and 1440s also saw the repair and refurbishment of the majority of the 193 pre-Ming-dynasty temples, monasteries and shrines that stood within the Beijing city walls, and the construction of many new ones at imperial and private initiative.[22] Much the same thing happened outside the city walls, in the near outskirts and more distant suburbs, on all four sides: to the northwest, for example, there were 97 temples by 1470.[23] Here we have to view Beijing in its role as capital of the empire. In early Ming political thought, the equilibrium of the empire depended in part on the harmony of the centre. The sponsorship of religious establishments by eunuchs, imperial bodyguards and the court itself had many purposes, but one was to promote this harmony – not just by creating a peaceful ambience, or symbolising civic values, but magically as it were, by concentrating spiritual energy in the place where it mattered most. As the centre of the empire, therefore, Beijing was expected to have the densest concentration of religious establishments of any city. Equally, it was expected that the most important of these religious establishments, both inside and outside the city walls, would be imperially sponsored.

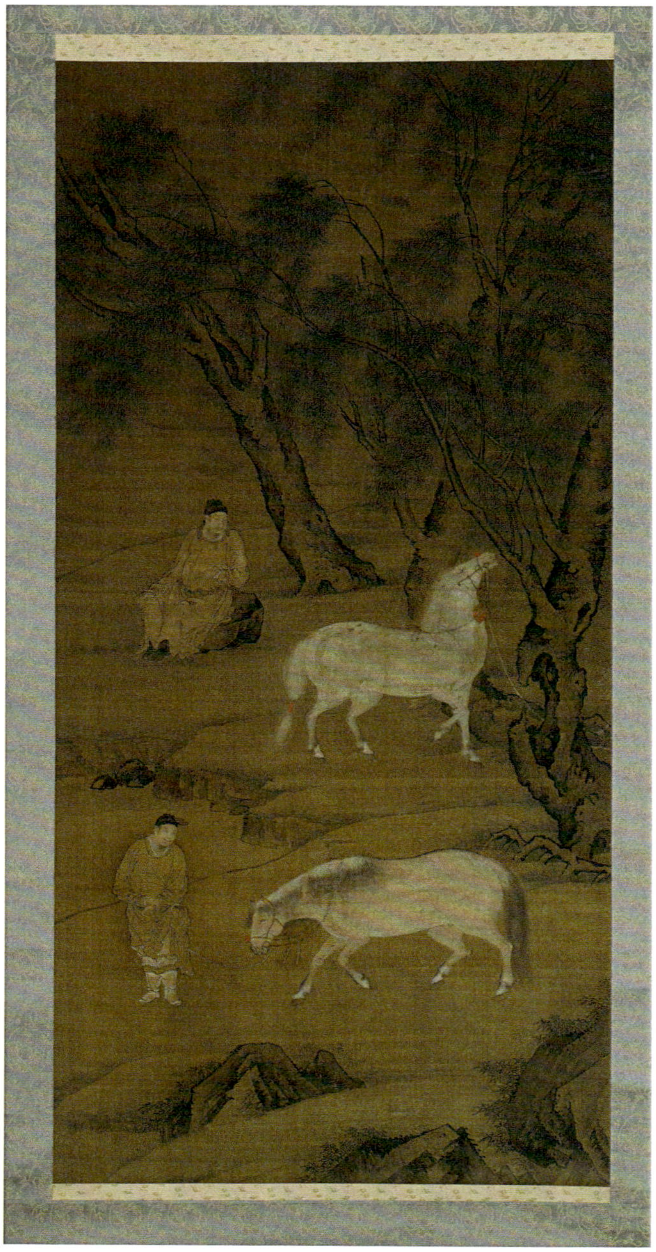

Plate 5.7 Anonymous, *Horses and Grooms under Willow Trees*, dated 1450. Hanging scroll, ink and colour on silk, height 170.6cm, width 81.5cm. Museum of Fine Arts, Boston, Special Chinese and Japanese Fund, 17.1

And this imperial sponsorship, backed up by visits and gifts, provided the emperor with another way of topping up his reserve of spiritual and political legitimacy.

Destiny: trees

We have just seen that the planting of evergreens at ritual sites and in temples led to happy destinies for a great many trees as living monuments. Other kinds of tree were also fortunate. Along the sides of the lakes there were old willows, which we often see in Ming court paintings depicting horses, because the horses of the imperial stables were taken to the lakes to bathe (**Pl. 5.7**). In grand residential gardens there were not only landmark trees but also a deliberate variety of tree types. We can clearly see this variety in 15th-century garden portraits such as *Elegant Gathering in the Apricot Garden* (*c.* 1437, see **Pl. 11.1**). The great palace gardens, of course, had the most varied range of trees. The southernmost lake just west of the Forbidden City was full of diverse trees that had been planted or transplanted by the Mongols. The transplanted trees were chosen for their rarity and beauty, and some were already huge at the time of transplanting.[24] The Yongle emperor also established an orchard garden immediately north of the Forbidden City with an artificially created hill as its dominant feature.[25] He further created a small but important temple garden in the north of the Forbidden City. The linked cypresses that still stand inside the gate of the temple (Qin'an dian 欽安殿) date from the 15th century.[26]

But these trees were but a fraction of the number of those that were less lucky in their destinies. If you were a tree living in any of the mountainous areas near Beijing – the hills to the west of the city, Mount Yan 燕山 to the north, the northern part of the Taihang 太行 Mountains or Mount Wutai 五臺山 to the southwest, or in fact anywhere within striking distance of the capital – your chances in the early 15th century of dying a natural death in the forest were not good. Beijing was a big city that was rapidly filling up with all sorts of buildings that needed wood for construction. Moreover, the city was located in a region that got very cold in the winter, and the principal fuel in the 15th century was not coal but firewood and charcoal. Not only were the lumber and charcoal industries rapaciously commercial, but the government ensured its own charcoal supply in Beijing by imposing annual quotas of supply that military garrisons all over north China had to meet. The result, as one might imagine, was the acceleration of a deforestation process that had begun centuries earlier. At the beginning of the 15th century there were still parts of the northern Taihang Mountains that were dense ancient forest; by 1475 the same areas were bare as a bone.[27]

The new capital's effects on the destinies of trees were also felt much further afield. The construction entailed the building and refurbishment of countless formal buildings – in the Forbidden City, in temples and monasteries across the city, at the ritual altars and other state ritual sites, at the Ming imperial tombs, and in the splendid mansions of high officials, generals, eunuchs and merchants. Nanmu, cypress and fir logs in particular were needed for pillars to hold up the immensely heavy roofs of temple and palace halls (**Pl. 5.8**). So, in the early 15th century, the destiny of a nanmu, cypress or fir tree that had grown to a great size in the distant provinces of Sichuan, Guizhou or Hunan was very likely to be cut down and turned into a pillar or beam in a Beijing building. The logs were floated down the Yangtze River, past Nanjing to Yangzhou, where they were then transported via the Grand Canal to Tianjin, then Tongzhou, and finally Beijing.[28]

Scansion: elephants

Many other rare and special nonhumans – animal, vegetable and mineral – were integrated into the Beijing environment. Among these were elephants, many looked after by Vietnamese mahouts who had accompanied them as war booty or tribute from Champa.[29] The elephant stable (*xunxiangsuo* 馴象所) was located in the southwest of the city. There was one training ground a little to the north, and

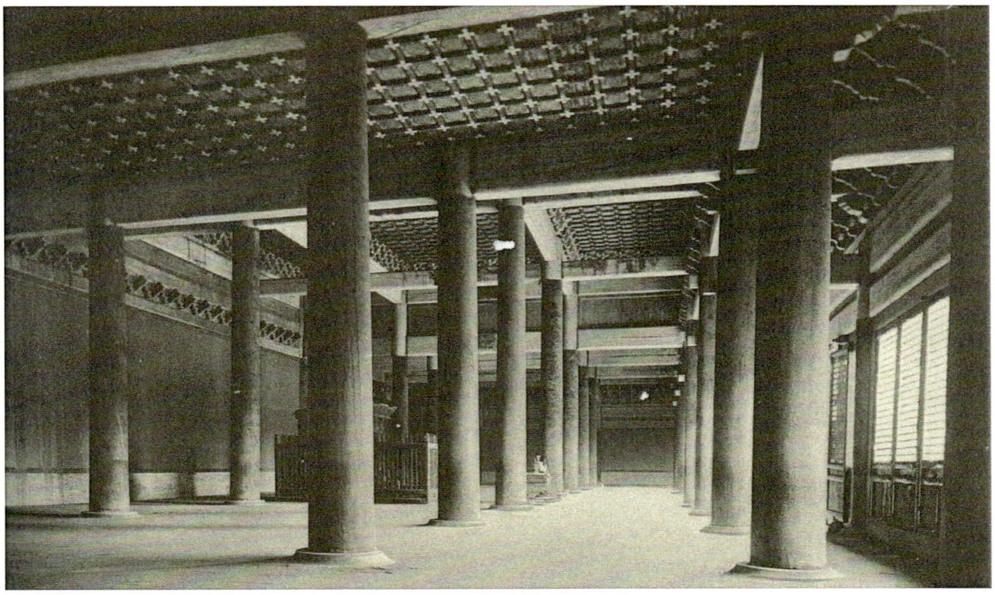

Plate 5.8 Interior of the Sacrificial Hall at Changling mausoleum of the Yongle emperor, *c.* 1424 (Boerschmann 1925, pl. 86)

another in the grounds of the imperial stables. Like the bathing of horses in the lake, the bathing of the elephants in the city moat was a public spectacle.

Under the Mongols, elephants had been working animals; it was elephants that moved huge transplanted trees into the Yuan palace gardens.[30] Under the Ming, however, elephants were ceremonial animals, whose main role was to modify both court space and urban space on a temporary basis.[31] Like old trees, they were living monuments, but unlike trees they could easily be moved about. At court, on any day when the emperor was holding an audience, three pairs of elephants were stationed in front of the Meridian Gate, standing facing each other on either side of the main axis (**Pl. 5.9**). Elephants took on a more public visibility on ritual occasions. The Beijing population got to see elephants on the emperor's birthday, on New Year's Day and on the winter solstice, all of which were marked by the stationing of elephants at the gates of the Forbidden City. And then, once a year, when the emperor made offerings at the Imperial Ancestral Temple, ten pairs of elephants flanked the road from Fengtian Gate to the temple itself. Finally, for the imperial sacrifices at the Altar of Heaven and Earth, 26 caparisoned elephants were led out of the elephant stables in pairs to stand either side of the major gateways and crossroads that the imperial procession passed through, and at a bridge the procession passed over,

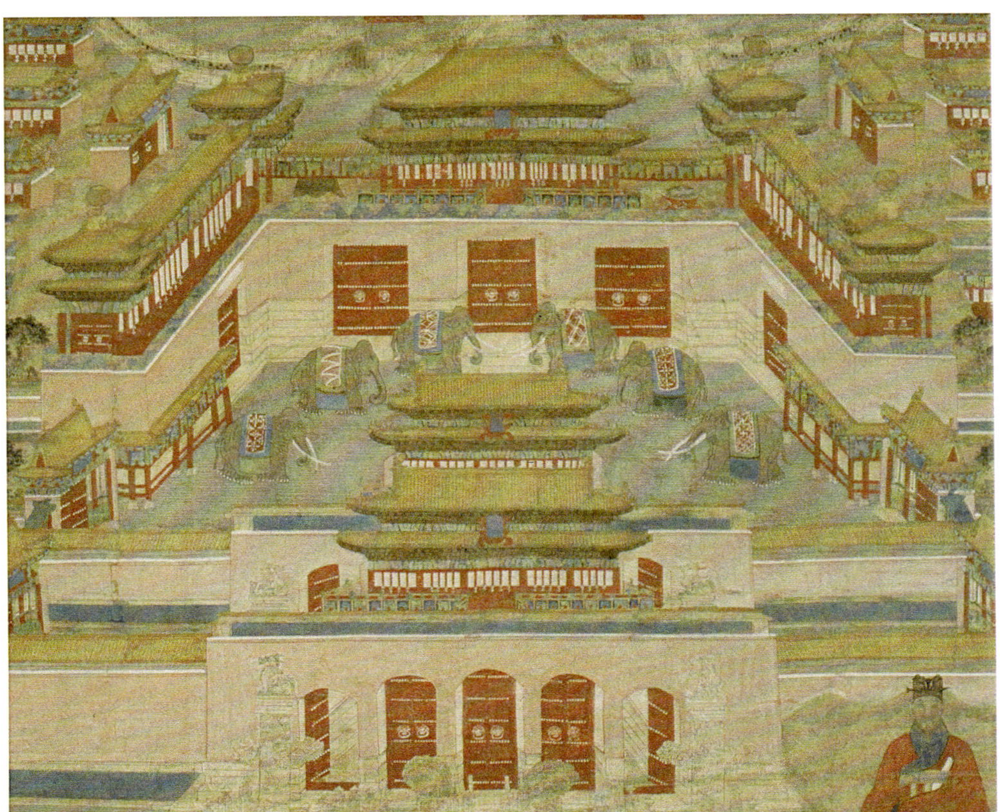

Plate 5.9 Anonymous, *Palace and Gardens of the Ming Dynasty* (detail of Pl. 6.13), Ming dynasty. Hanging scroll, ink and colours on silk, image: height 183.8cm, width 156cm; with mount: height 317cm, width 163cm. Nanjing Museum

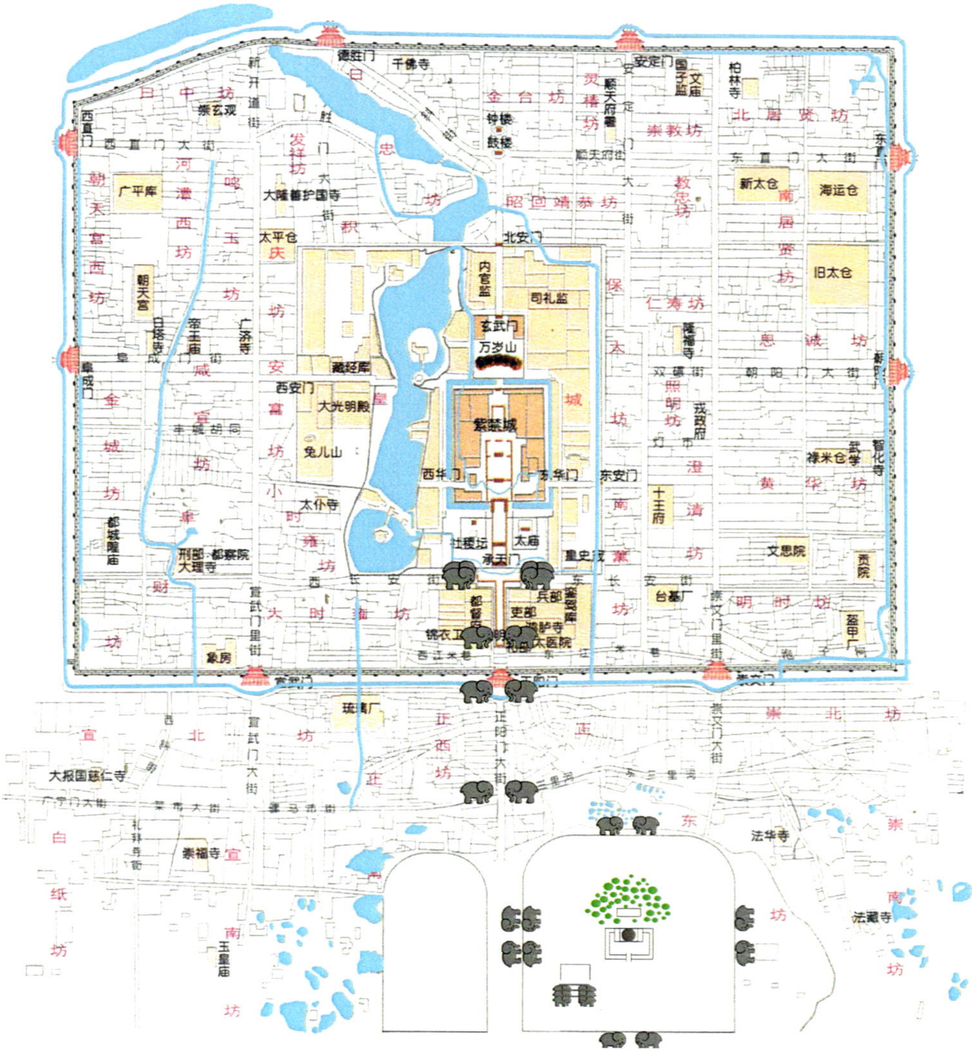

Plate 5.10 Map of Beijing, *c.* 1450, with the deployment of elephants for the emperor's visit to the Altar of Heaven and Earth to conduct sacrifices

as well as at the three successive gates of the Sacrificial Hall at the altar in question (**Pl. 5.10**). Some of the elephants must have knelt rather than stood, since the Yongle-period sculpted stone elephants on either side of the spirit road leading to the Ming imperial tombs include both kneeling and standing animals (**Pl. 5.11**). Elephants also had a second role within the procession: one pair of elephants pulled each of the two main chariots of the imperial procession to the sacrificial altar in question.[32] Elephants were thus as much part of the scansion of Beijing life as the two-hourly beating of the drum at the Drum Tower.

Plate 5.11 Stone elephant from the Spirit Road leading to the Ming imperial tombs, dated to the Yongle period, 1403–24

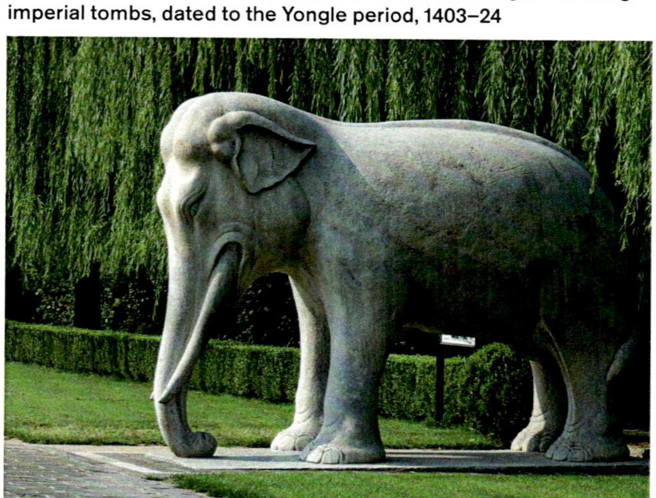

Thinking of Beijing as being at each moment a place in movement and a structure of movement helps us to get away from seeing the city simply as a frame for human activity. It allows us to see Beijing as a place where human beings understood themselves to be in constant interaction with non-human activity and movement. As a form of ecological awareness, this is very different from our own, and not necessarily any better or worse: it possessed its own sharpness of vision – perhaps a stronger sense of connectedness, for example – but one only has to think of the deforestation of the Taihang Mountains and the flooding that it caused to see that Ming ecological thinking had its own blind spots. Putting movement back into our picture of Beijing also allows us to see that the Ming state treated the urban space of the capital as plastic. This plasticity operated on different time-scales, from the one-day scale of a procession to the multi-generational and often multi-century scale of a tree's lifetime.

Plasticity is one important corollary of a conception of the city as *shi*. At the outset of this chapter I mentioned that there is no obvious English translation of *shi*. Place-in-movement and form-in-movement are among the awkward translations that result. There do, however, exist specialist art-historical terms of recent coinage that do the same kind of conceptual work. One is 'situation'. I used this term above in a temporal sense to describe Beijing's historical conjuncture around 1450. But one can also characterise the city itself in all its plasticity as a situation, in which case one comes close to the place-in-movement dimension of the Chinese concept of *shi*.[33] For the form-in-movement dimension, though, a more useful concept may be 'scape', one which I have been developing in an ongoing series of publications.[34] 'Scape', as I use the term, denotes the perceptual emergence of provisionally stable form in an artwork. These two terms, situation and scape, belong to a contemporary art-historical frame of reference that can accommodate non-Western analytic concepts like *shi* as well. This is the intersection at which movement can be developed as one useful analytic lens through which to explore the specificity of the Chinese past.

Notes

1 Owen 1992, 590–1.
2 On scansion, see Hay forthcoming.
3 On these unpleasant conditions, see Gao Shouxian 2004.
4 I gratefully acknowledge the help of Sylvia Wu and Jiaqi Liu in preparing the maps in **Pls 5.3** and **5.10**.
5 See Hou Renzhi 1979; Wan Yi 1990; Jiang Shunyuan 1991.
6 See Hou Renzhi 1979; Jiang Shunyuan 1991; Xu Weidong 2002; Chen Xibo and Han Guanghui 2010. See also Wang Jidong 2011.
7 Han Dacheng 1991.
8 Atwell 2002.
9 Yin Junke 2003.
10 Zhang Bizhong 1999.
11 The preceding account is based on the following studies: Yin Junke 2003; Li Xiaocong 2002.
12 Wang Fu's two paintings in **Pl. 5.4** show water springing from the mountains at Jade Spring and the destination of the water: the lake around which the Yuan Forbidden City was built; note the waterspout through which the water arrives. Although Wang Fu's authorship has been contested by Kathlyn Liscomb (1988–9), I do not find her arguments convincing.
13 Hou Renzhi 1979.
14 Yin Junke 2003.
15 Shi Cunlong 2008a.
16 On the canal system connecting Beijing to the Grand Canal, see Hou Renzhi 2001; Shi Cunlong 2008b.
17 The Altar of Mountains and Rivers would later become the Altar of Agriculture (*Xiannongtan* 先農壇), and the Altar of Heaven and Earth would become the Altar of Heaven (*Tiantan* 天壇).
18 On Beijing ritual sites in this period, see Deng Wenlin 2002.
19 This formalised forest literalises the Song-dynasty architectural metaphor that treats wood pillars as tree trunks and the bracketing system holding up the roof as brackets and leaves. See Feng Jiren 2012.
20 On trees at Beijing ritual sites, see note 19. See also Anami 2004.
21 At the end of his life, Ruan An had his residence turned back into a temple. On Ruan, see Wang Jidong 2011; Yang Chunyu 2011.
22 The figure of 193 used here comes from Naquin 2000, 114.
23 Naquin 2000, 259.
24 The modern Zhongnanhai, currently inhabited by Chinese Communist Party leaders. See Jiang Shunyuan 1992, especially 83–4; Yan Chongnian 1991.
25 The modern Jingshan Park. See Zheng Lianzhang 1990; Wang Hong 2002.
26 The modern Imperial Garden. On its earlier existence as the Qin'an Dian garden, see Wang Zilin 2007; Huang Ximing 1990.
27 On the supply of wood to Beijing, see Gao Shouxian 2006; Liu Xu and Chen Xibo 2010; Feng Zuxiang, Zhang Caite and Jiang Yuanzhen 2008; Tian Peidong 2012; Wen Zhenjun 2007. Unfortunately, it was not until the late 15th century that the Ming emperors got involved in reforestation, and even then they paid attention only to frontier places where the absence of forest made China vulnerable to invasion.
28 Wen Zhenjun 2007.
29 For reasons of national security, in 1453 the elephant handlers were not allowed to return to their own country, despite their pleas to be released from service. See MSL *Yingzong shilu*, 225 (Jingtai 4/first month/ninth day [17 February 1453]). I would like to thank Bruce Rusk for his generous help with research on elephants in 15th-century Beijing.
30 Yan Chongnian 1991, 232.
31 For the regulations governing the deployment of elephants, see *DMHD*, *juan* 228, 1121 'Xunxiangsuo' 馴象所.
32 A 16th-century handscroll in the National Palace Museum entitled *Heralding Departure* (*Chujing tu* 出警圖) depicts an imperial procession to the imperial tombs in which one elephant draws a chariot, preceded by a row of three elephants with ornaments on their backs; Na Chih-liang 1970, figs 13 and 14.
33 For a discussion of paintings as situations, see Hay 2007, especially 453–5.
34 Hay 2007; Hay 2010, 448–52.

Chapter 6
Painting of the Imperial Palace and Zhu Bang

Yu Hui

Translated by Luk Yu-ping

This chapter will focus on a Ming-dynasty hanging scroll entitled *Portrait of an Official in Front of the Beijing Imperial Palace* in the British Museum collection (**Pl. 6.1**). The discussion is divided into three sections. Firstly, it will analyse the painting itself and the main figure depicted in it, identified as Kuai Xiang 蒯祥 (1398–1481). Secondly, it will discuss the painter Zhu Bang 朱邦 (active mid to late Ming) to whom the painting is attributed, his life and his surviving works. Thirdly, it will compare and discuss several works that are similar to the painting in the British Museum, in order to understand who might have painted these works, their characteristics and function, as well as to explore the pattern of development and change in this type of imagery.

Kuai Xiang and the *Portrait of an Official in Front of the Beijing Imperial Palace*

Portrait of an Official in Front of the Beijing Imperial Palace measures 170cm in height and 110.8cm in width. A signature that reads Fengxi 豐溪 is visible on the right side of the painting, which is the shortened form of Fengxi daoren 豐溪道人 (Master of Fengxi) – one of the sobriquets of the painter Zhu Bang.[1] Below it is a seal mark in relief that reads *Zhu Bang zhi yin* 朱邦之印 (seal of Zhu Bang) (**Pl. 6.2**). In his article from 1972, Roderick Whitfield noted that this seal mark is identical to one found on another painting in the British Museum entitled *Fishermen in a River Gorge*, which he also considers to be an authentic work by Zhu Bang (**Pl. 6.3**).[2] His view can be accepted without doubt. There are some fine landscape paintings of the Zhe school (*Zhepai* 浙派) and Jiangxia 江夏 school in the British Museum. This is very much related to the importance that Professor Whitfield placed upon them while he was working at the then Department of Oriental Antiquities in the 1970s and 1980s. The main figure dressed in red in the *Portrait of an Official in Front of the Beijing Imperial Palace* should be Kuai Xiang, who was alive during the early part of Zhu Bang's life. This will be discussed further later in this chapter.

In the painting, Kuai Xiang is shown holding a tablet, standing to the left of Jinshuiqiao 金水橋 (Bridge of Golden Water) of Chengtianmen 承天門 (Gate of Heavenly Succession; renamed Tiananmen 天安門 or Gate of Heavenly Peace during the Qing dynasty). Behind him are Wumen 午門 (Meridian Gate), Fengtianmen 奉天門 (Gate for Worshipping Heaven) and Fengtiandian 奉天殿 (Hall for Worshipping Heaven). Fengtianmen and Fengtiandian were renamed Taihemen 太和門 (Gate of Supreme Harmony) and Taihedian 太和殿 (Hall of Supreme Harmony) in the Qing dynasty. In front of Kuai Xiang are Da Ming men 大明門 (Gate of the Great Ming) and Zhengyangmen 正陽門 (Gate of the True Yang). The Chinese characters for Wumen are now clearly visible in gold following conservation work on the painting for the exhibition *Ming: 50 years that changed China* at the British Museum in 2014.[3]

Kuai Xiang was born in Xiangshan village 香山村 next to Tai Lake 太湖 in Wu 吳 county in modern Jiangsu province.[4] He was revered as the leader of the Xiangshan group of artisans (*Xiangshan bang* 香山幫, literally Fragrant Mountain Gang), also known as the Wushan school 吳山派. Xiangshan village is renowned for its carpentry tradition.

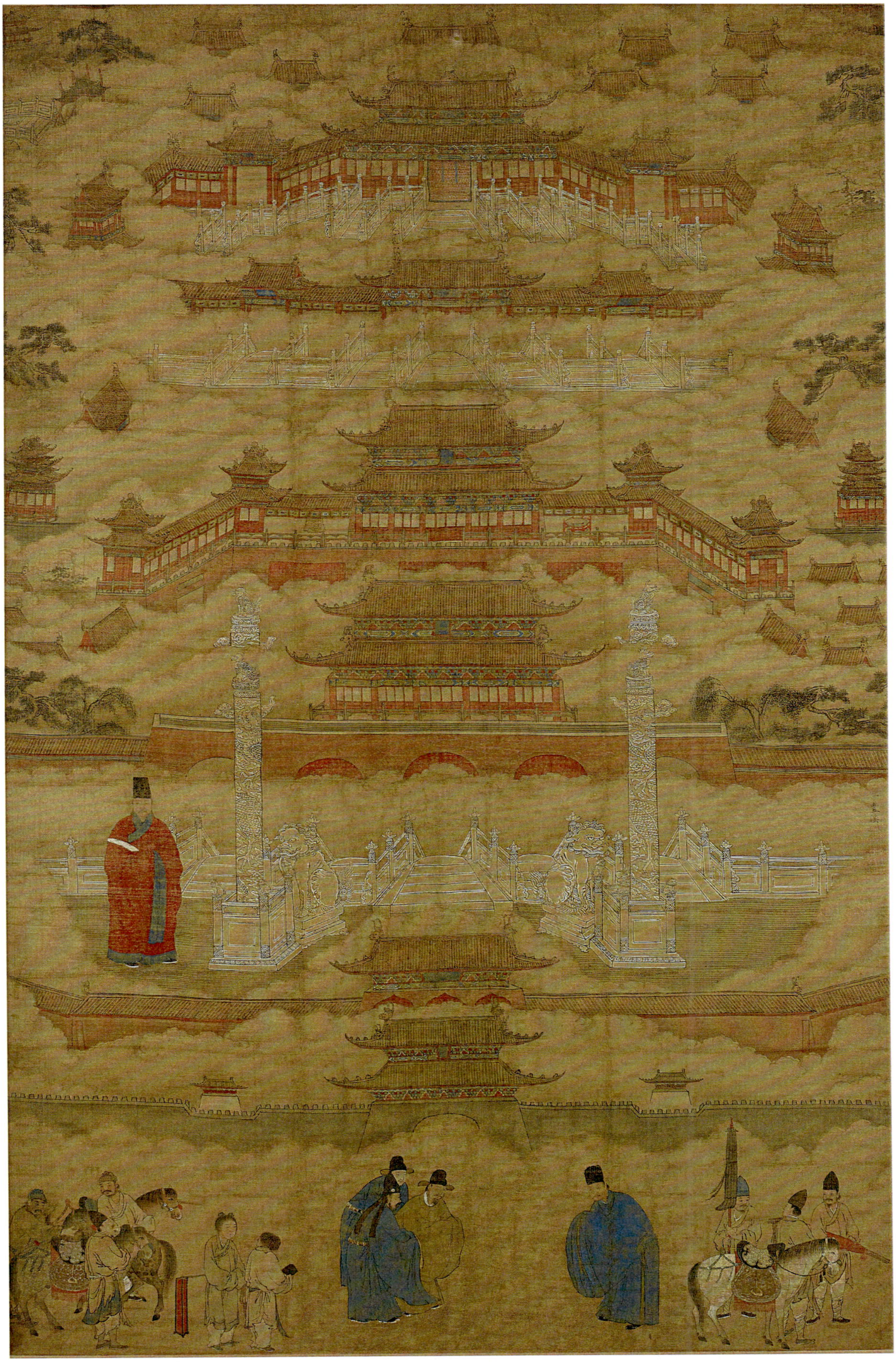

Plate 6.1 Anonymous, *Portrait of an Official in Front of the Beijing Imperial Palace* (*Beijing gongcheng tu* 北京宮城圖), *c.* 1480–1580. Hanging scroll, ink and colours on silk, image height 170cm, width 110.8cm; with mount height 204cm, width 114cm. British Museum, London, 1881,1210,0.87.CH

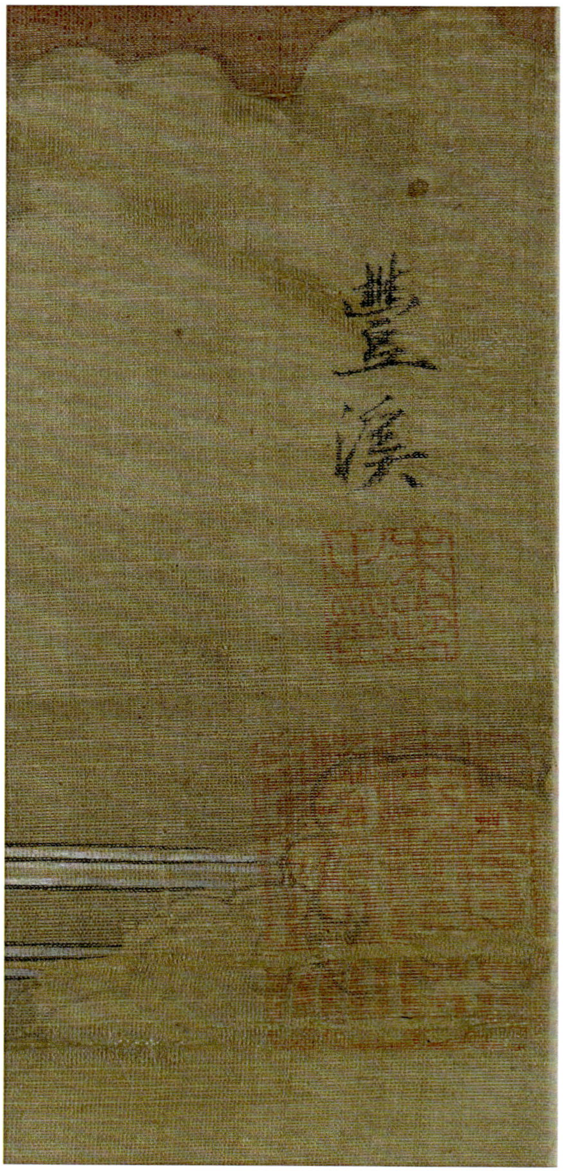

Plate 6.2 Seals and signature on *Portrait of an Official in Front of the Beijing Imperial Palace*. Signed Fengxi 豐溪; seal in relief 'Seal of Zhu Bang' (*Zhu Bang zhi yin* 朱邦之印); seal in intaglio 'Sleeping soundly without dreams leisure seal' (*Hanhou wumeng xian zhang* 酣齁無夢閒章)

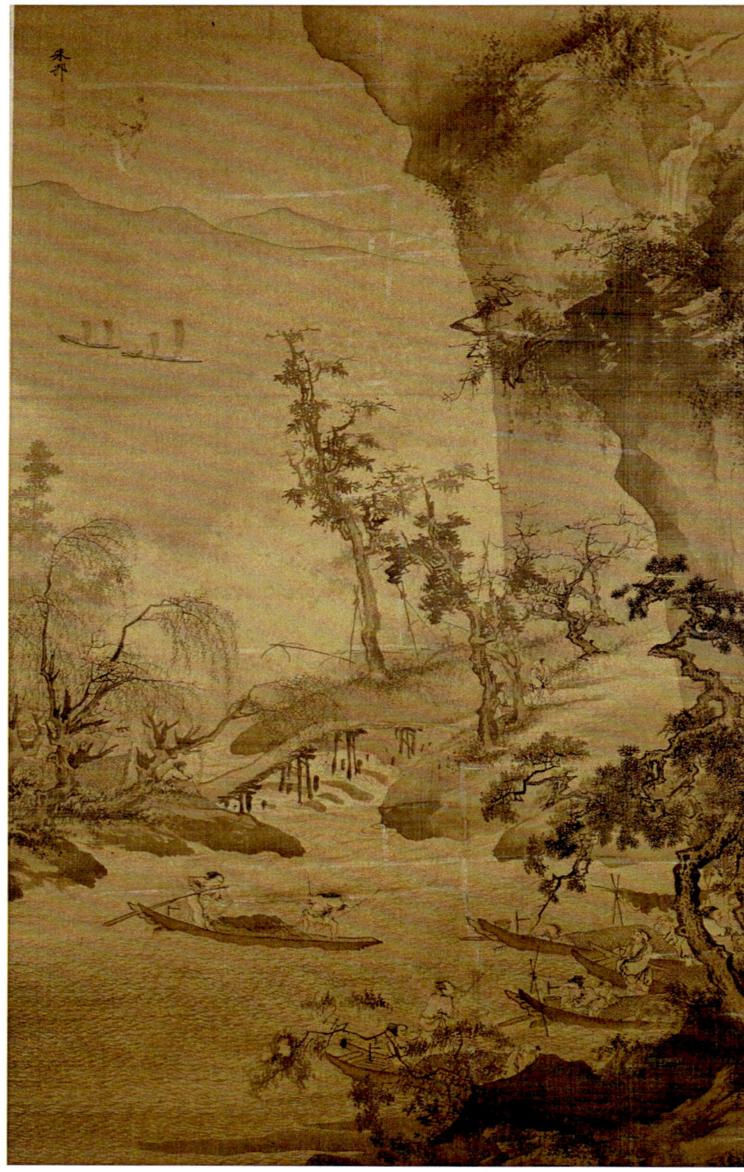

Plate 6.3 Anonymous, *Fishermen in a River Gorge* (*Xigu yufu* 溪谷漁父), Ming dynasty, 1522–66. Signed Zhu Bang 朱邦; seal in relief 'Seal of Zhu Bang' (*Zhu Bang zhi yin* 朱邦之印); Seal in intaglio 'Old Woodcutter of Mount Jiulong' (*Jiulong shanqiao laosou* 九龍山樵老叟). Hanging scroll, ink and colours on silk, image height 159.5cm, width 100.5cm; with mount height 290cm, width 130.5cm. British Museum, London, 1912,0529,0.3

As early as the Spring and Autumn period (771–476 BCE), artisans from the area participated in building the palace of the King of Wu 吳王 (528–473 BCE). Kuai Xiang's father Kuai Fu 蒯福 is said to have managed major official building projects.[5] At the beginning of his reign, the Hongwu 洪武 emperor (r. 1368–98) relocated artisans from around the empire to Nanjing in order to construct a new imperial palace at the capital. One of the most important groups was from Xiangshan. The Wu region was the base from which the Ming conquered China, so most of the artisans working for the Ming imperial court came from there. Because of this, the imperial palaces in both Nanjing and Beijing came to be constructed under the supervision of the Xiangshan group. The young Kuai Xiang followed his father into the carpentry trade, very quickly mastering the necessary skills, including the mortise and tenon technique, and how to calculate the amount of materials needed for construction. *Huang Ming ji lüe* 皇明紀略 (*Brief Records of the August Ming*) records that:

> In the capital there is a Vice-Minister Kuai's Alley. Kuai was a native of Xiangshan of the Wu region and a carpenter. During the Yongle reign, he was summoned to build the Great Inner (imperial palace). Every hall and elevated building, as well as winding corridors and bent eaves, he could draw by free-hand, all of which matched the emperor's intentions. He reached the position of the Vice Minister of Works, and his descendants continued his work.
>
> 京師有蒯侍郎衚衕，蒯為吳香山人，斲工也，永樂間召建大內，凡殿閣樓榭，以致回廊曲宇，隨手圖之，無不稱上意者，位至工部侍郎。子孫猶世其業。[6]

Legends about Kuai Xiang say that he could simultaneously draw a pair of dragons facing each other using both hands and they would match perfectly when folded. The Ming palace in Beijing was modelled on the imperial palace in Nanjing. Kuai Xiang was involved in the construction of both palaces, as well as temples, and civil and military bureaus.[7] In particular, he led the rebuilding of the three main halls, Fengtian 奉天, Huagai 華蓋 and Jinshen 謹身, at the imperial palace in Beijing in 1441, after they were destroyed by fire caused by lightning during the fourth month of 1420. At the end of the Tianshun 天順 reign (1457–64), he oversaw the construction of the emperor's mausoleum known as the Yu 裕 Mausoleum of the Thirteen Ming Tombs (*Ming shisan ling* 明十三陵).

Among the many professions involved in building construction work in ancient China, carpenters are known as the 'Head of the Hundred Works' (*baigong zhi shou* 百工之首) and usually control the most important parts of a project. The team led by the head carpenter has a decisive role to play in procedures ranging from determining the basic and overall design, to the arrangement and setting of the frames of the buildings. Other processes such as masonry, roof tiling, lacquering and papering are largely dependent on the work of the carpenters. Kuai Xiang was promoted from the Head of Artisans to Aide at the Work Project Office (*Yingshansuo cheng* 營繕所丞), finally becoming Left Vice-Minister (*Zuo shilang* 左侍郎) of the Ministry of Works in 1456. The Chenghua 成化 emperor (r. 1465–87) purportedly referred to Kuai Xiang as 'Kuai Lu Ban' 蒯魯班, comparing him to the legendary artisan Lu Ban 魯班 (507–444 BCE) of the Spring and Autumn period.[8]

According to the *Veritable Records*, Kuai Xiang reached the official rank of second grade and was given a grade one salary, but he continued to live a humble life and maintained his down-to-earth artisanal character.[9] In 1481 he passed away at the age of 84 while still serving as the Left Vice-Minister of the Ministry of Works.[10] *Ming shi* 明史 (*History of the Ming*) of the 18th century makes no mention of Kuai Xiang; instead, information about him has to be found in other writings and local legends. The limited attention that scholars paid to him may be due to his profession as an artisan. As noted above, the place where Kuai Xiang lived was known by locals as 'Vice-Minister Kuai's Alley'. Although this place no longer exists, the author believes that Suzhou Alley (Suzhou hutong 蘇州胡同), which is located around 2km southeast of the Forbidden City, was where artisans and merchants from Suzhou gathered during the Ming and Qing (1644–1911) dynasties. Kuai Xiang's former residence should have been near this place.

Kuai Xiang was buried south of his native place of Xiangshan village. His high official status at the imperial court became a source of motivation for other Xiangshan artisans and led to the emergence of more carpentry groups from the area. Although other carpentry leaders appeared after Kuai Xiang, such as Xu Gao 徐杲 (16th century) and Yao Canting 姚灿庭 of the Qing dynasty, they did not reach the achievements of Kuai Xiang. Today we can still see the skilfully made carpentry tools once used by the Xiangshan group in the museum commemorating Kuai Xiang located next to his tomb.

One scholar has questioned whether Kuai Xiang was buried at Xiangshan village, suggesting that the tomb now identified as Kuai Xiang's actually belonged to his grandparents, while the man himself may have been buried in the surroundings areas of Beijing.[11] The *Veritable Records* only states that Kuai Xiang was 'granted a burial according to regulations' (*ci jizang ru li* 賜祭葬如例) without specifying that he was buried near the capital.[12] This decree should mainly refer to the bestowal of funds by the imperial court to pay for Kuai Xiang's burial. According to Ming court customs, only officials and eunuchs who were from Beijing would be buried around the capital, while officials who were not from Beijing would normally be buried back at their native place. The 23rd generation descendant of Kuai Xiang is still alive today and has not expressed any doubt as to the burial site of his ancestor. The identity of the occupant of Kuai Xiang's tomb should not be in question.

The painter Zhu Bang

There is very little information about the painter Zhu Bang. According to *Huashi hui yao* 畫史會要 (*Outline of the History of Painting*) and *Ming hua lu* 明畫錄 (*Records of Ming Painting*), Zhu Bang, *zi* Zhengzhi 正之 (or Jinzhi 近之), is also known by the sobriquets Jiulongshan qiao 九龍山樵 (Woodcutter of Mount Jiulong), Fengxi yusou 豐溪漁叟 (Old Fisherman of Fengxi), Hanhou daoren 酣齁道人 (Master of Drinking and Snoring), Yinsou 隱叟 (Reclusive Old Man), and others.[13] He was a native of Anhui province, either from Xin'an 新安 (present-day She 歙 county) or Xiuning 休寧, and was skilled in painting landscape and figures in a style comparable to his Zhe school contemporaries Zheng Wenlin 鄭文林 (fl. 1522–66) and Zhang Lu 張路 (1464–1538). Based on his sobriquets, the author believes that Zhu Bang was an uninhibited painter with scholarly characteristics, who enjoyed drinking and excess. He was active in the middle and later parts of the Ming dynasty, and painted in an untrammelled style in the same vein as the works of Wu Wei 吳偉 (1459–1508), who was the leader of the Jiangxia school 江夏派, which was a branch of the Zhe school. The life of Zhu Bang is shrouded in mystery. There are no records of his activities, nor are there any records of him working in the Ming imperial court. *Portrait of an Official in Front of the Beijing Imperial Palace* can provide additional information about Zhu Bang's life. It is highly probable that at the end of the Chenghua reign, especially in 1481 when Kuai Xiang passed away, Zhu Bang was in Beijing looking for work opportunities. The Zhu clan was a distinguished clan in Anhui, and Anhui artisans also participated in the building of the imperial palaces in Nanjing and Beijing. It is possible that Zhu Bang was hired by members of the Xiangshan group from Suzhou to produce the painting. However, Zhu Bang's depiction of the Forbidden City and the surroundings of the Chengtian Gate in the painting are not very detailed or accurate (see below). This suggests that he had never stepped foot inside the Forbidden City and had never worked as a painter at the imperial court; instead he was a painter who worked among common people. Wu Wei served at the imperial court during the Chenghua reign. Around the age of 20 he was summoned by the emperor, and given the title of Embroidered-uniform Military Guard serving at Renzhidian 仁智殿 (Hall of Benevolent Wisdom).[14] If Zhu Bang was in Beijing during this time, he would have had the opportunity to meet Wu Wei. The two men had many reasons to socialise, given their shared love

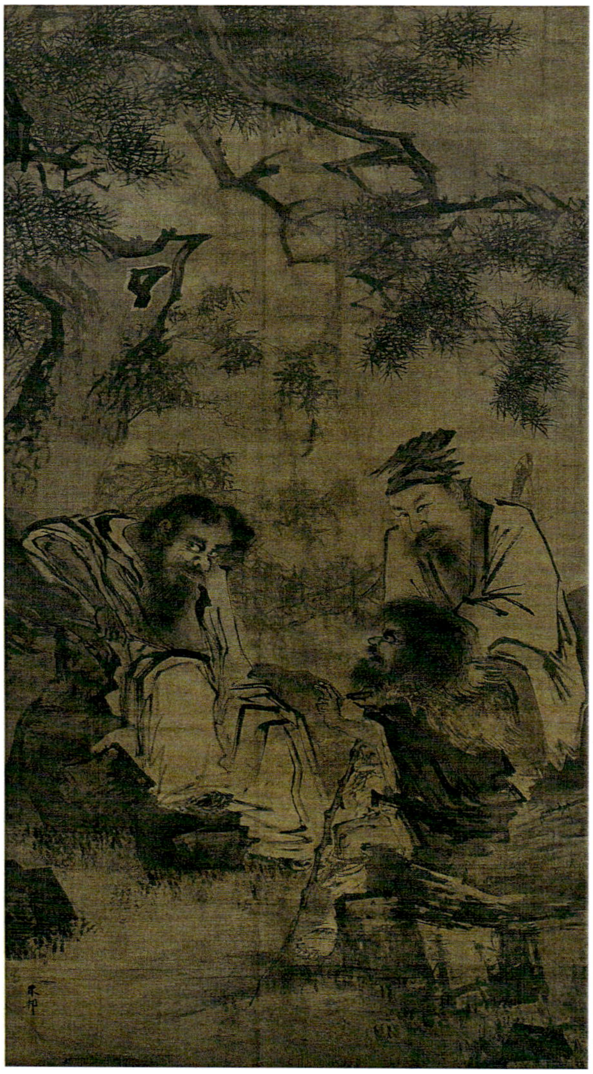

Plate 6.4 Attributed to Zhu Bang 朱邦, *Figures* (*Renwu tu* 人物圖), Ming dynasty, 16th century. Ink on silk, height 193cm, width 102cm. The Palace Museum, Beijing

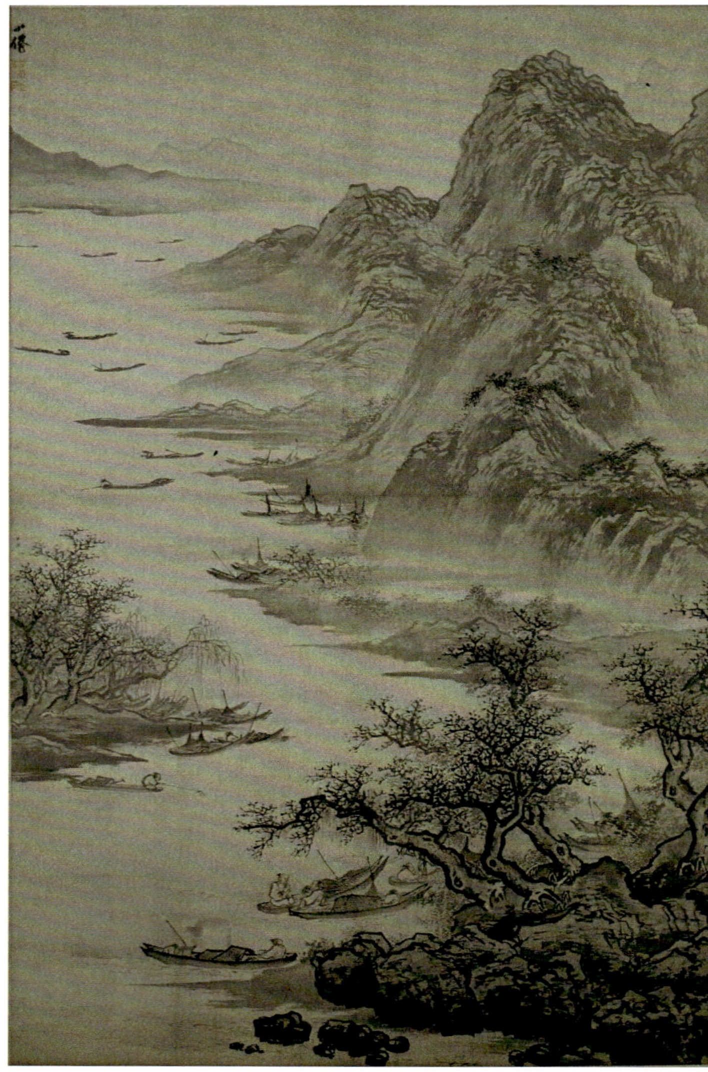

Plate 6.5 Wu Wei 吳偉 (1459–1508), *Amusement of Fishermen in a River Landscape* (*Jiangshan yule tu* 江山漁樂圖). Hanging scroll, ink and colour on paper, height 270cm, width 174.4cm. The Palace Museum, Beijing

of drinking, as well as their similar personalities and painting styles.

Eight paintings by Zhu Bang are currently known to have survived. The Palace Museum in Beijing has a work entitled *Figures* (*Renwu tu* 人物圖) with Zhu Bang's signature visible on the bottom left (**Pl. 6.4**). This painting depicts three of the Eight Daoist Immortals (Tieguai Li 鐵拐李, Zhongli Quan 鐘離權 and Lü Dongbin 呂洞賓) conversing under pine trees. The brushwork is broad, powerful and carefree, and the use of ink is impassioned. In addition to the *Portrait of an Official in Front of the Beijing Imperial Palace*, the British Museum has another painting by Zhu Bang entitled *Fishermen in a River Gorge*, noted earlier (see **Pl. 6.3**). It also carries Zhu Bang's signature, below which are two seals that read '*Zhu Bang zhi yin* 朱邦之印' (seal of Zhu Bang) in relief and '*Jiulong shanqiao…sou* 九龍山樵□叟' (Old Woodcutter of Mount Jiulong) in intaglio.[15] The painting depicts a river beneath a cliff face, where fishermen can be seen cooking and returning home in the evening. This type of subject matter belongs to the genre of the 'amusement of fishermen' (*yule* 漁樂), which was favoured by painters of the Zhe and Jiangxia schools, especially Wu Wei, evident in his monumental scroll *Amusement of Fishermen in a River Landscape* (*Jiangshan yule tu* 江山漁樂圖) (**Pl. 6.5**). Using broad and fluent brushstrokes, Zhu Bang captures a clear sense of depth in the misty scene. He uses his brush to lighten the outlines of the rocks on the mountains, and freely applies light ink with a large brush. Compared to the rough and energetic landscape paintings of Wu Wei and others of the Jiangxia school, Zhu Bang's use of brush and ink is even more untrammelled, and he pays greater attention to the sense of depth with rich variations in ink tones that generate a sense of the mist and moisture in a watery landscape.

The Anhui Museum has two works by Zhu Bang that are similar in style to the paintings discussed above. One is *Selling Fish in the Snowy River* (*Xuejiang maiyu tu* 雪江賣魚圖) (**Pl. 6.6**), which is comparable to *Fishermen in a River Gorge* in the British Museum; the other is *Immortal Lü* (*Lü xian tu* 呂仙圖) (**Pl. 6.7**), similar to *Figures* in the Palace Museum, Beijing. Also of the latter type is *Walking Alone in Empty Mountains* (*Kongshan duxi[illegible] tu* 空山獨行圖) (**Pl. 6.8**) in the Princeton University Art Museum, and *Traces of a Beast in a Pine Forest* (*Songlin shouji tu* 松林獸迹圖) (**Pl. 6.9**) in the Guangdong Museum. On the whole, Zhu Bang's *xieyi* 寫意

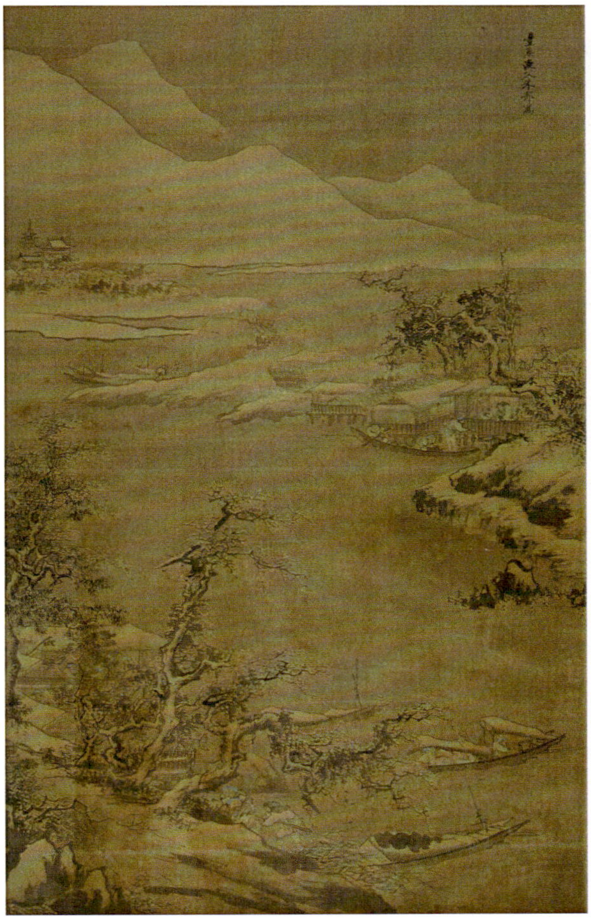

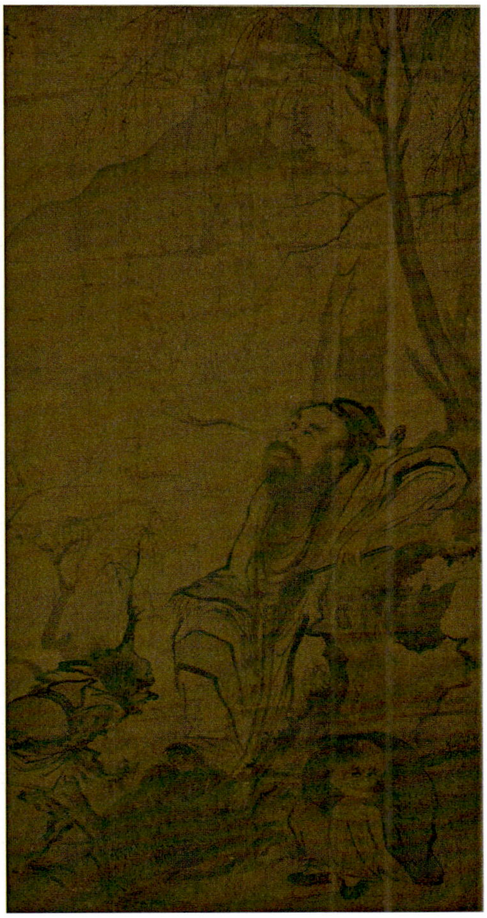

Plate 6.6 (left) Attributed to Zhu Bang 朱邦, *Selling Fish in the Snowy River* (*Xuejiang maiyu tu* 雪江賣魚圖), Ming dynasty, 16th century. Hanging scroll, ink and colours on silk, height 163.3cm, width 101.5cm. Anhui Museum

Plate 6.7 (right) Attributed to Zhu Bang 朱邦, *Immortal Lü* (*Lü xian tu* 呂仙圖), Ming dynasty, 16th century. Hanging scroll, ink and colour on silk, height 184cm, width 96.1cm. Anhui Museum

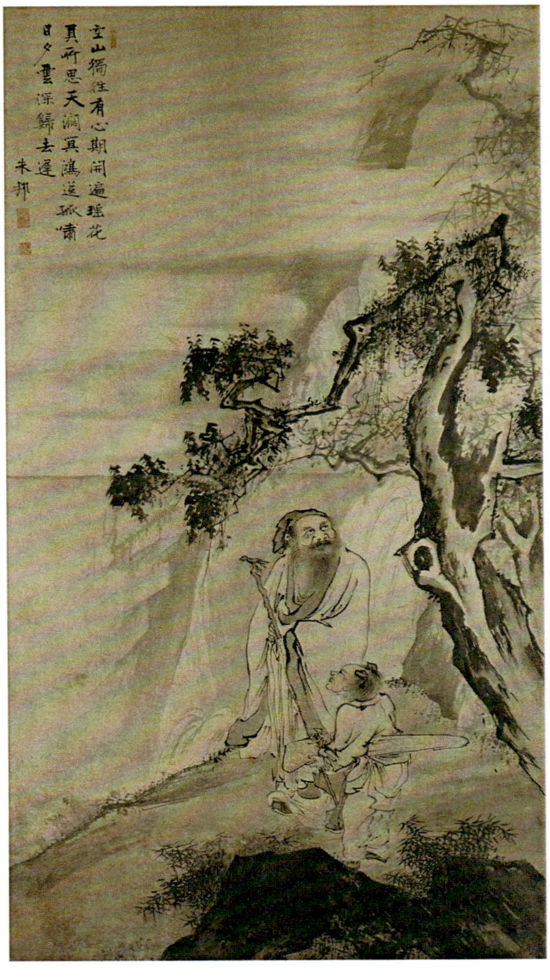

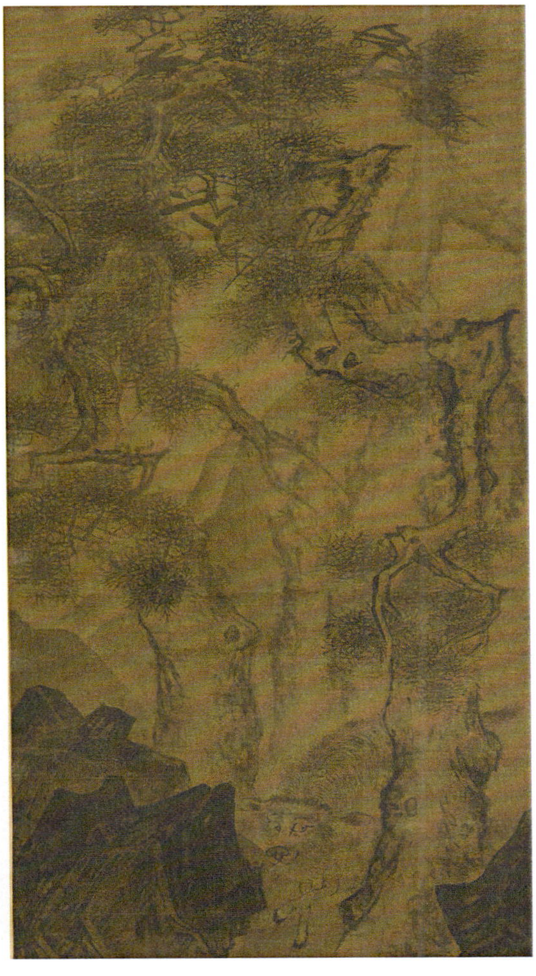

Plate 6.8 (left) Attributed to Zhu Bang 朱邦, *Walking Alone in Empty Mountains* (*Kongshan duxing tu* 空山獨行圖), Ming dynasty, 16th century. Hanging scroll; ink and light colour on paper, image height 161cm, width 91.5cm; with mount height 249cm, width 102.1cm. Princeton University Art Museum, Gift of DuBois Schanck Morris, Class of 1893 y1947-135

Plate 6.9 (right) Attributed to Zhu Bang 朱邦, *Traces of a Beast in a Pine Forest* (*Songlin shouji tu* 松林獸跡圖), Ming dynasty, 16th century. Hanging scroll, ink on silk, height 121.5cm, width 65.5cm. Guangdong Museum

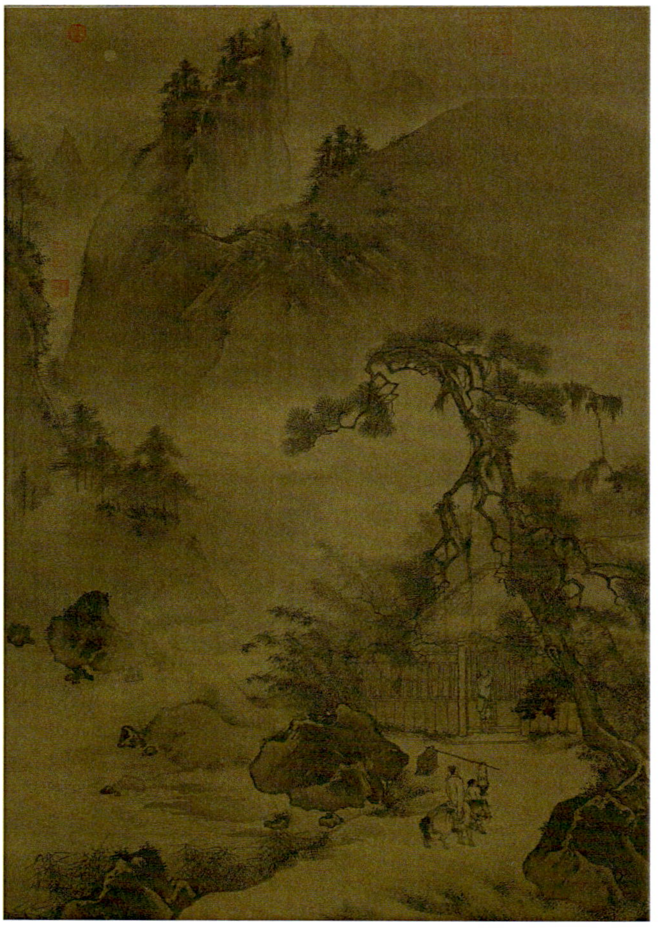

Plate 6.10 Anonymous, *Returning Home on a Moonlit Night* (*Xiye guizhuang tu* 夕夜歸莊圖), Ming dynasty, early to mid-16th century. Hanging scroll (mounted on panel), image height 155.1cm, width 107.1cm. Freer Gallery of Art, Smithsonian Institution, Washington, D.C., Gift of Charles Lang Freer F1916.401

(sketching the idea) paintings usually have several areas of broad brushstrokes and heavy ink that are used to invigorate the composition.

The Freer Gallery of Art in Washington, D.C. has an anonymous painting entitled *Returning Home on a Moonlit Night* (**Pl. 6.10**) that has been linked to Zhu Bang. In the past this painting was attributed to a Tang-dynasty painter, Lu Hong 盧鴻, but this has been refuted by James Cahill, who suggested that it is a work by Zhu Bang, based on comparisons to an anonymous painting in the Osaka City Museum of Fine Arts.[16] Using an anonymous painting to verify the painter of another anonymous painting seems insufficiently convincing. Although *Returning Home on a Moonlit Night* contains texture strokes (*cunfa* 皴法) that are similar to Zhu Bang's 'large axe cut' texture strokes (*da fu pi cun* 大斧劈皴), Zhu Bang tends to pay closer attention to the use of ink, especially the rhythm and nuances of light ink. *Returning Home on a Moonlit Night* can only be considered a late work of the Zhe school, and does not fit easily into Zhu Bang's stylistic oeuvre. The identity of the painter of this work awaits further research.

The existence of *Portrait of an Official in Front of the Beijing Imperial Palace* contradicts the record that Zhu Bang only had a broad and free painting style, noted above. Instead, he also painted in a more elegant style. *Picking Lotuses* (*Cailian tu* 采蓮圖) (**Pl. 6.11**) in the National Art Museum of China is another example that has a poetic atmosphere, and is similar to the more refined style of the painting in the British Museum. Based on his surviving works, it seems that Zhu Bang's painting style falls into two main categories: one is *gongbi* 工筆 (skillful brush) in colour and the other is *xieyi* (sketching the idea) using monochrome ink. Zhu Bang's early career would have been dominated by the former style, while his subsequent career was dominated by the latter.

Versions similar to *Portrait of an Official in Front of the Beijing Imperial Palace*

There are four known hanging scroll paintings that depict the same subject matter as *Portrait of an Official in Front of the Beijing Imperial Palace* (hereafter the Zhu Bang version). They are *Imperial Palace in Beijing* (*Beijing gongcheng tu* 北京宮城圖) in the National Museum of China, hereafter the National Museum version (**Pl. 6.12**); *Palace and Gardens of the Ming Dynasty* (*Mingdai gongyuan tu* 明代宮苑圖) in the Nanjing Museum, hereafter the Nanjing Museum version (**Pl. 6.13**); *Painting of Xu Gao* (*Xu Gao xiang* 徐杲像) and *Imperial Palace of the Ming Dynasty* (*Mingdai gongdian tu* 明代宮殿圖), both in the National Palace Museum, Taipei (**Pls 6.14–15**). All of these works are by anonymous Ming painters. Their composition and style are largely similar, except that in the case of the Zhu Bang version, the figure of Kuai Xiang is depicted on the left of the painting instead of the right.

It is possible to determine which of these five versions were painted by court painters and which were not, based on the accuracy of the palace architecture they depict. One point that is very easily overlooked is the direction of the pointed cloud-heads extending from the four *huabiao* 華表, ceremonial columns that are located inside and outside of the Chengtian Gate – they should all be positioned so that the cloud-tail points outwards (**Pl. 6.16**). The design of this type of structure had reached maturity by the Ming dynasty, and could not be freely changed. Another example of a Ming-dynasty ceremonial column can be found at Lingxingmen 欞星門 (Elite Star Gate; restored in 1754) at the Temple of Confucius in Qufu, Shandong province. The cloud-tails on

Plate 6.11 Attributed to Zhu Bang 朱邦, *Picking Lotuses* (*Cailian tu* 采蓮圖), Ming dynasty, 16th century. Handscroll, ink on paper, height 22.8cm, width 110cm. National Art Museum of China

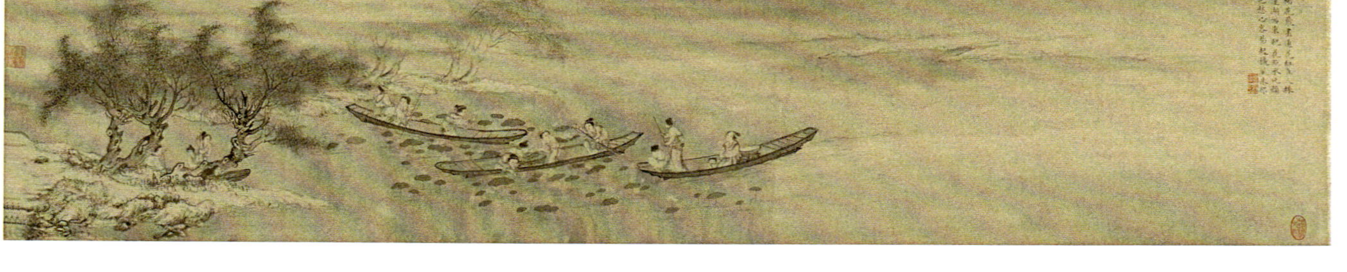

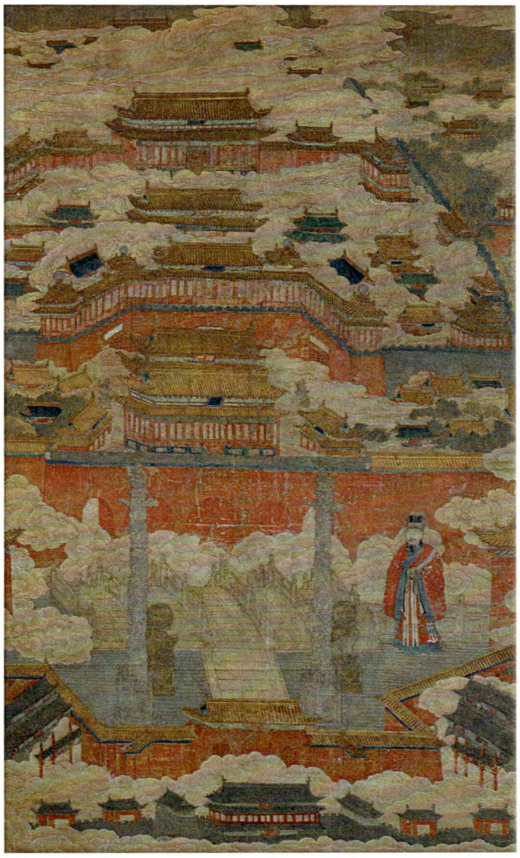

Plate 6.12 Anonymous, *Imperial Palace in Beijing* (*Beijing gongcheng tu* 北京宮城圖), early Ming period. Hanging scroll, ink on silk, height 169.5cm, width 100cm. National Museum of China

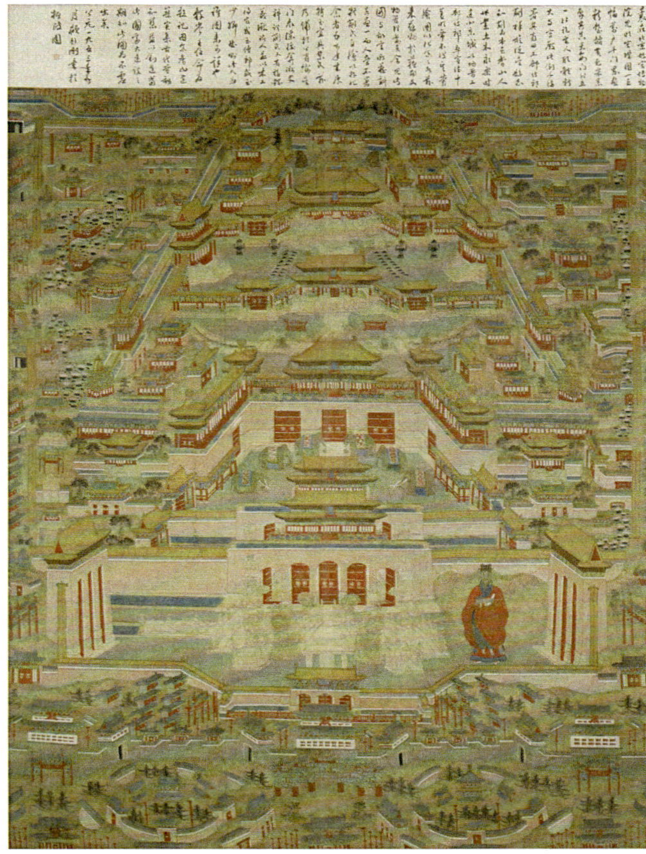

Plate 6.13 Anonymous, *Palace and Gardens of the Ming Dynasty* (*Mingdai gongyuan tu* 明代宮苑圖), Ming dynasty. Hanging scroll, ink and colour on silk, image height 183.8cm, width 156cm; with mount height 317cm, width 163cm. Nanjing Museum

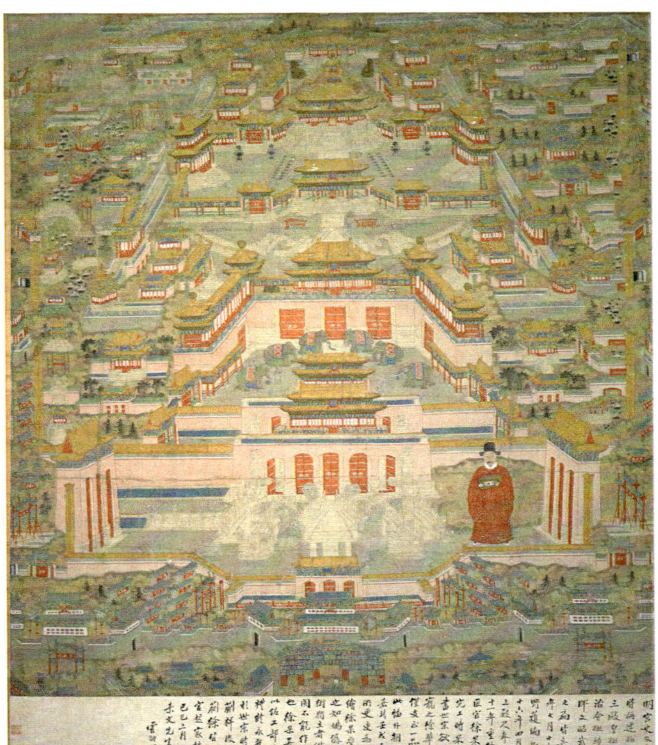

Plate 6.14 Anonymous, *Painting of Xu Gao* (*Xu Gao xiang* 徐杲像), 1522–72, with the inscription by Kan Duo 闞鐸 (1875–1934). Hanging scroll, ink and colour on silk, height 169cm, width 156cm. National Palace Museum, Taipei

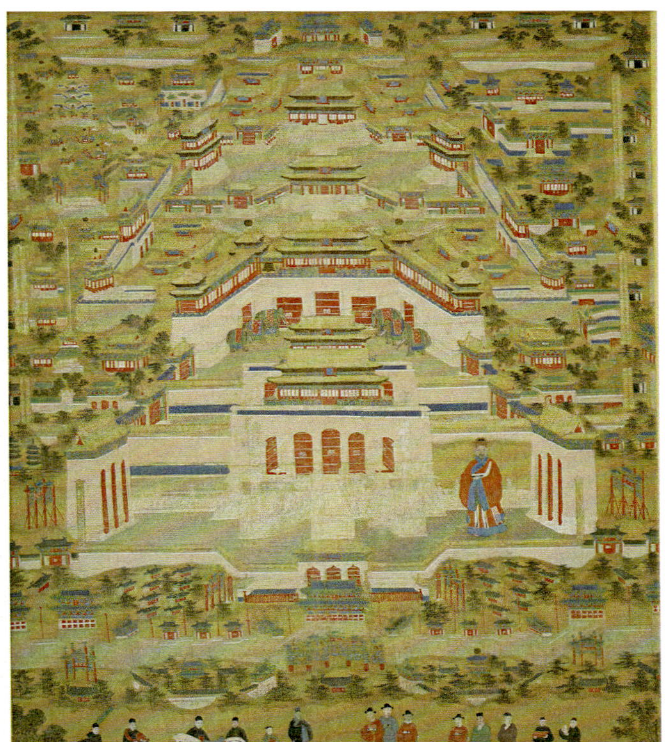

Plate 6.15 Anonymous, *Imperial Palace of the Ming Dynasty* (*Mingdai gongdian tu* 明代宮殿圖), Ming dynasty. Hanging scroll, ink and colour on silk, height 209cm, width 173cm. National Palace Museum, Taipei

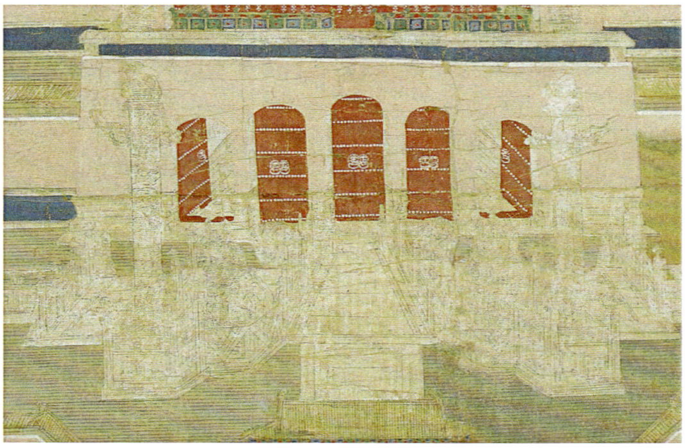

Plate 6.16 Detail of the cloud-heads of the ceremonial columns in Pl. 6.15. National Palace Museum, Taipei

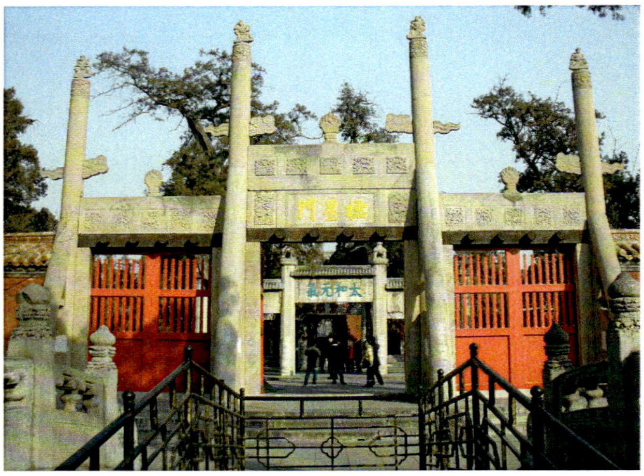

Plate 6.17 Lingxing Gate of the Temple of Confucius, Qufu

this column are also pointing outwards and cloud inwards (**Pl. 6.17**). A painter who has never set foot inside the Forbidden City is unlikely to paint them accurately. Instead, he would simply follow other people's renderings and imagine the design, which could easily lead to mistakes.

The paintings that correctly depict the cloud-heads of the four ceremonial columns inside and outside Chengtian Gate also tend to portray the architectural components of the buildings in a structured way, while those that have mistaken the direction of the cloud-heads are less orderly in their representation of the buildings, and less successful in conveying a sense of being present at the scene. This difference suggests that a painter's accuracy in his depiction of the Forbidden City was derived from observation of the actual place. Based on this analysis, *Painting of Xu Gao*, *Imperial Palace of the Ming Dynasty* and the National Museum version can be categorised as works by court painters who had been to Jinshui Bridge as well as the area around Chengtian Gate of the Forbidden City, which were inaccessible to ordinary people.

It should be noted that both the Zhu Bang version and the National Museum version were not produced by court painters. In the Zhu Bang version, the location of Kuai Xiang is incorrect. Since he was the Left Vice-Minister of the Ministry of Works, which was a part of the civil official hierarchy, he should be standing on the right side of the composition next to the Chengtian Gate. Duan Gate 端門, which should be located behind the Gate, is missing from the painting. Moreover, the cloud-heads of the ceremonial columns in both the Zhu Bang and National Museum versions are pointing in the wrong direction. The architectural elements in the two paintings are also not very clearly rendered. For these reasons, it can be inferred that the painters of these two works had not been to the Forbidden City before and hence could not have been employed by the imperial court. Instead, they would have had to base their works on other people's compositions, so it is not surprising that their treatment of details such as the direction of the cloud-heads on the ceremonial columns is incorrect.

Based on the discussion above, we can conclude that there are two basic models for paintings of this type in circulation during the Ming dynasty. One is a version created by a painter working outside of the court milieu who was unfamiliar with palace architecture, represented by the Zhu Bang version; the other is by a court painter, exemplified by *Imperial Palace of the Ming Dynasty*. The Zhu Bang version was probably the earlier of the two, painted not long after Kuai Xiang's death in 1481. This is suggested by the scene depicted in the bottom part of the painting, which shows Ming officials and members of the gentry standing and bowing to each other outside the Zhengyang Gate. This is the path that one must take to travel to Suzhou, located

Plate 6.18 Detail of Pl. 6.1 showing soul-guiding banner and soul-guiding lantern

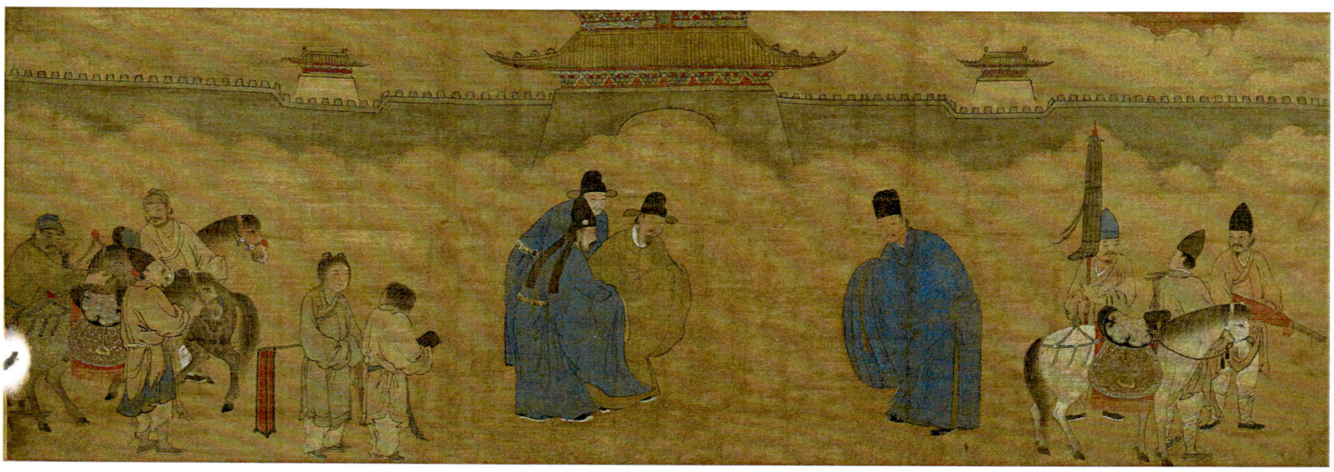

south of Beijing. Attendants are shown carrying items related to funeral customs used to welcome the soul of the deceased (**Pl. 6.18**): soul-guiding banners (*yinhun fan* 引魂幡) and a soul-guiding lantern (*yinhun deng* 引魂燈), also known as 'following-the-body lantern' (*suishen deng* 隨身燈) during the Ming dynasty. Their inclusion in the painting suggests the returning of Kuai Xiang's body and soul to his native place. According to ancient customs, it was necessary to summon and guide the soul of the deceased before and during the journey when bringing the deceased back to his native place for burial. This provides reassurance to family members that both the body and soul of the deceased have been properly interred. Some farming villages in Jiangnan still practice this custom today, while tools of the ritual can be found in folk museum collections. They are quite similar to those depicted in the Zhu Bang version. The painting captures an important moment in the funeral arrangements for Kuai Xiang. It is unlikely to have been painted for the imperial court, since the silk surface of the painting is not sufficiently fine. Instead, it was most likely painted for the builders and carpenters of the Xiangshan group according to their wishes. Normally a painting depicting the ritual of summoning the soul can only be painted shortly before the funeral. In 1481 when Kuai Xiang died, Zhu Bang was probably still in Beijing, and maybe even in the area of the Suzhou Alley. It is possible that he accepted a commission from the Xiangshan group to paint this work, which commemorates Kuai Xiang and expresses the group's concern for his afterlife.

Depictions of the ritual to summon the soul can be found in other Ming dynasty images. For example, a woodblock-printed illustration of chapter 65, 'Funeral of Li Pinger' (*Li Pinger chubin tu* 李瓶兒出殯圖) in the novel *Jin ping mei* 金瓶梅 (*Plum in the Golden Vase*), shows a procession carrying ceremonial banners that follows a winding path towards the burial grounds (**Pl. 6.19**). This image and the objects the figures carry are similar to the scene depicted in the lower part of the Zhu Bang version.

Likewise, *Imperial Palace of the Ming Dynasty* portrays the summoning of the soul of the deceased in its lower section (**Pl. 6.20**). The main figure in this painting could be Kuai Xiang as well. The work must have been painted by a court painter, perhaps from the Work Project Office of the Ministry of Works, probably for artisans working at the imperial court. The spread of this composition beyond the court provided other painters with an initial model that they could follow. Over time, portrayals of the summoning and guiding of the soul disappeared from the lower part of the composition. Instead, subsequent paintings were used in the same manner as images of deities by providing a focal point for court and Xiangshan group artisans to conduct commemorations and make offerings.

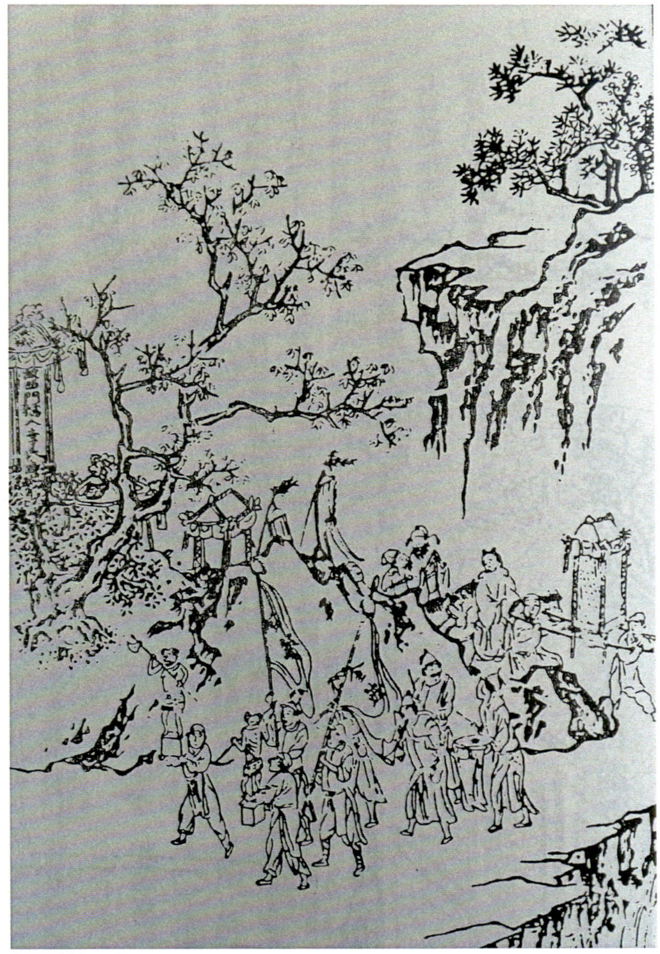

Plate 6.19 'Funeral of Li Pinger' from *Plum in the Golden Vase* (*Jin ping mei* 金瓶梅), reprint of the Chongzhen edition (Jinan, 1989)

After Kuai Xiang another talented artisan, Xu Gao, emerged at the Ming imperial court. *Painting of Xu Gao* (see **Pl. 6.14**), also known as *Imperial Palace of Beijing* (*Beijing gongdian tu* 北京宮殿圖), is based almost entirely on the Zhu Bang version. In an inscription below the painting, Kan Duo 闞鐸 (1875–1934) identifies the main figure depicted in the painting as Xu Gao, which he probably learned from the painting's title label. He writes that:

> Initially [Xu Gao] assisted Vice Minister of Works Lei Li in the renovations of Yongshougong (Palace of Eternal Longevity), and was recognised by Shizong (Jiajing emperor). At the time people said that he was the one succeeding Kuai Xiang.
>
> 初以佐工部侍郎雷禮修永壽宮，受知於世宗，時人謂為蒯祥後一人而已。

Plate 6.20 Detail of Pl. 6.15, showing the scene of the summoning of the soul of the deceased

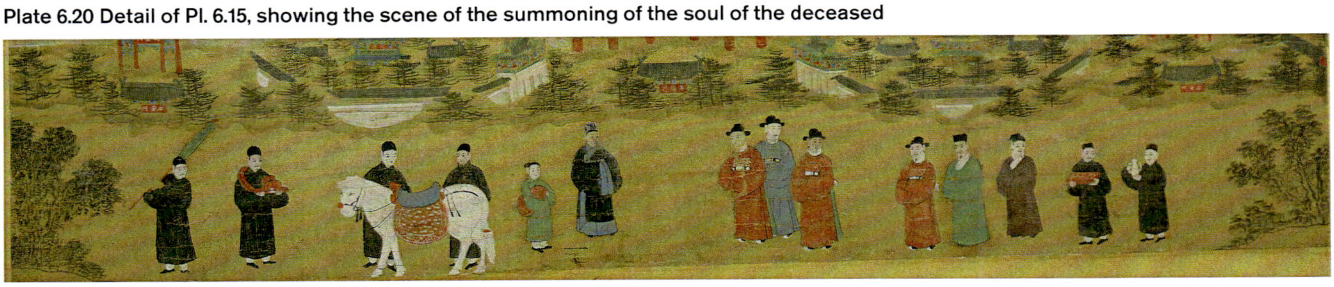

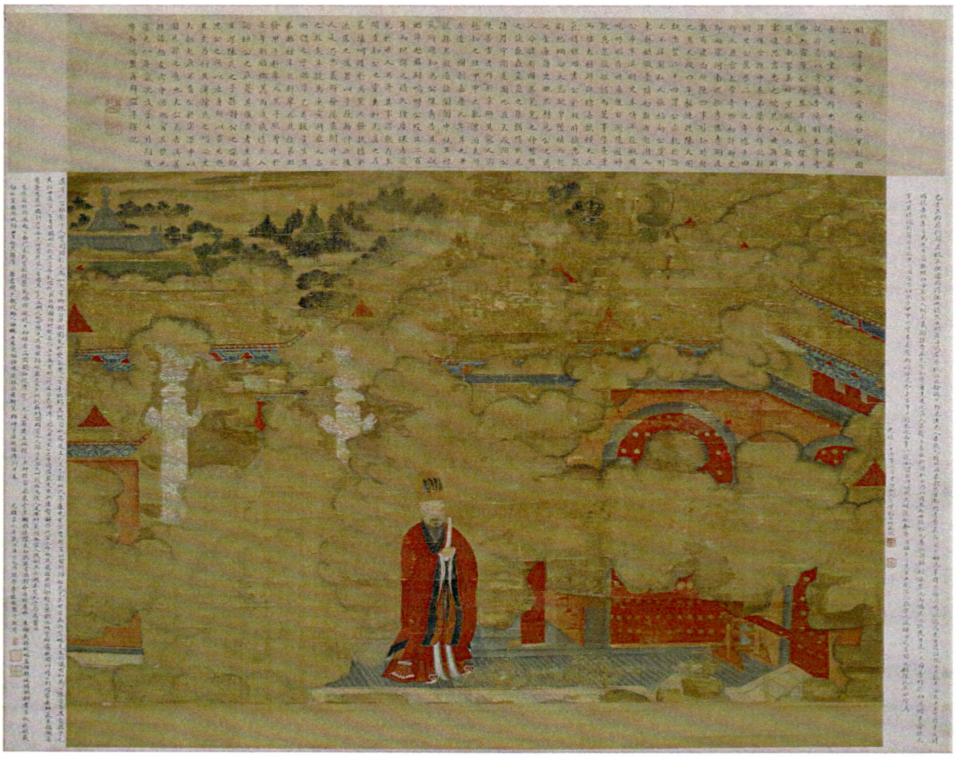

Plate 6.21 Anonymous, *Early Court Audience* (*Zaochao tu* 早朝圖), Ming dynasty, 17th century. Hanging scroll, ink and colours on silk, height 102.4cm, width 140cm. The Palace Museum, Beijing

During the Jiajing 嘉靖 reign (1522–66), Xu Gao participated in the rebuilding of the three main halls and the Yongshou Palace of the Forbidden City, reaching the position of Minster of Works with a rank of grade two. The depiction of the architecture in *Painting of Xu Gao*, as well as the ceremonial columns, basically matches Ming standards, so that it must be a court painter who created this work, an honour that is commensurable with Xu Gao's elevated position. There is no scene depicting the summoning and guiding of the soul in the painting, and it should have been painted after the burial of Xu Gao. It is likely that official artisans hired court painters to create this work based on the Zhu Bang version depicting Kuai Xiang as a way to commemorate Xu Gao.

The composition of the Zhu Bang version also became a model for the portrayal of officials attending court during the Ming dynasty. For example, the Nanjing Museum version has an inscription above the painting by Gu Jiegang 顧頡剛 written in 1953 in Zhuozhengyuan 拙政園 (Humble Administrator's Garden) in Suzhou, in which he identifies the main figure in the painting as Kuai Xiang on the basis of the National Museum version that he once saw at the Palace Museum, Beijing. However, the identity of this figure still needs to be verified. In the bottom section of the painting is Yongdingmen 永定門 (Externally Pacified Gate), which was completed in the tenth month of 1553 during the Jiajing reign, 82 years after the death of Kuai Xiang. Thus, this painting was probably meant to commemorate a Ming official who had passed away after 1553. The depiction of the ceremonial column and architecture basically accords with the design and regulations of that time, so a court painter who was familiar with the Forbidden City must have produced this work.

Another example of this subject matter is *Early Court Audience* (*Zaochao tu* 早朝圖) in the Palace Museum, Beijing (**Pl. 6.21**). An inscription above the painting written by Xu Hongqing 許鴻磬 during the Daoguang 道光 reign (1821–50) identifies the subject matter as the early court audience of Chen Boyou 陳伯友 (1601 *jinshi*) who was the Minister of the Court of Imperial Sacrifices. Chen Boyou is shown holding his tablet and standing next to the ceremonial column to the left of Chengtian Gate, while waiting to attend an early court audience at the imperial palace. After the Zhengde reign (1506–21), emperors became less diligent with court audiences – the Wanli 萬曆 emperor (r. 1573–1620) did not attend court audiences for several decades – so fewer paintings were produced of this subject matter. *Early Court Audience* was made after the death of Chen Boyou, and should have been used to commemorate him. The way that the painter has depicted the surroundings of the palace shrouded in morning mist is rather confusing. In particular, the details and arrangement of the buildings do not correspond with reality; for instance, the roof tops of the main halls of the imperial palace are painted in black rather than yellow. The gate of the building to the left of Chen Boyou also lacks specificity. This suggests that the painter of this work did not come from the imperial court.

The Royal Ontario Museum, Toronto, also has a painting similar to the Zhu Bang version, entitled *Portrait of a Civil Official Awaiting Audience* (**Pls 6.22–3**).[17] The painting depicts an official standing to the right of Jinshui Bridge. The cloud-heads of the ceremonial column are pointing in the wrong direction, so this work could not have been produced by a court painter; instead, he must have been a highly skilled painter working outside of the imperial court who based the painting on the Zhu Bang version. These examples show that the composition and mode of representation in the Zhu Bang version were recognised by officials and also served as a model for painters outside of the court environment.

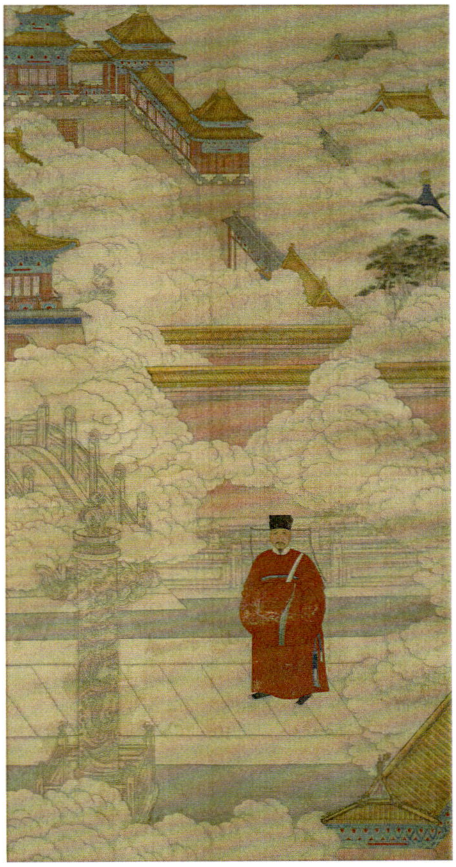

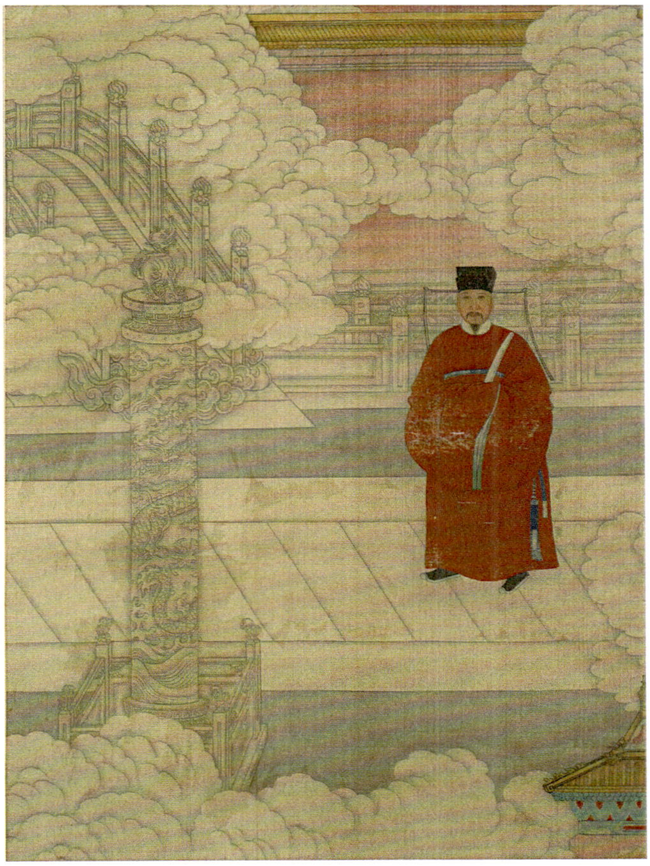

Plates 6.22–6.23 (left) Anonymous, *Portrait of a Civil Official Awaiting Audience* (*Shangchao wenguan xiang* 上朝文官像), 18th century; (right) detail of official. Hanging scroll, ink and colours on silk, height 161.5cm, width 82cm. Royal Ontario Museum, The George Crofts Collection, Gift of Mrs H. D. Warren, 921.32.102

Conclusion

The five related paintings, including the Zhu Bang version, and the two examples based on it, show the spread and recognition of this distinct composition by painters working inside and outside of the imperial court. They also reveal the respect that painters working in different environments felt towards a master artisan like Kuai Xiang. Conversely, this master artisan, who was an official of the second grade with a grade-one salary, was not mentioned by Confucian scholars of the late Ming and Qing dynasties who wrote the *Ming History*. This suggests their condescension towards leading artisans. Zhu Bang and other painters depicted Kuai Xiang as a towering figure in front of Chengtian Gate of the Forbidden City. Such a composition is unprecedented in the history of China. In the authoritarian system of the Ming dynasty, not only was this composition allowed but it was emulated by other painters. It is likely that it had the approval of the ruling Chenghua emperor, which suggests the extraordinary status that Kuai Xiang achieved. Furthermore, the Zhu Bang version, or *Portrait of an Official in Front of the Beijing Imperial Palace*, provides valuable information about the painter's possible activities in Beijing. This type of commemorative painting probably once existed in greater numbers, used by various branches of the Xiangshan group to commemorate their leader Kuai Xiang, but this has been forgotten by posterity.

Based on sources relevant to *Portrait of an Official in Front of the Beijing Imperial Palace*, we can find a series of images that appear to look roughly the same, connected by stylistic and representational elements. Due to differences in each painter's role and experiences and variations in the architecture depicted, the function of paintings like Zhu Bang's version changed, and their composition was also modified over time. This provides additional visual material for the study of painting history and the history of social customs in the Ming dynasty.

Notes

1 Mu Yiqin 1985, 79.
2 Whitfield 1972, 293, fig. 14.
3 For a summary of the conservation work done on this painting, see Qiu Jin Xian and Luk Yu-ping 2014.
4 For summaries of Kuai Xiang's biography see Cao Xun 1996; Meng Fanren 2011, 62–3.
5 Huang Yu 1999, *juan* 8, 155–6.
6 Huang Fulu 1985, 34.
7 Meng Fanren 2011, 62–3.
8 Meng Fanren 2011, 62.
9 *MSL, Xianzong shilu, juan* 213.7b–8a (17/3/辛丑).
10 The date of his death is recorded in *MSL, Xianzong shilu, juan* 213.7b–8a (17/3/辛丑).
11 Cao Xun 1996, 87–8.
12 *MSL, Xianzong shilu, juan* 213.8a (17/3/辛丑).
13 Zhu Mouyin 1631, *juan* 4; Xu Qin 1986, *juan* 1, 8. Also recorded in Mu Yiqin 1985, 79.
14 This is from an inscription by Song Lian 宋濂 on Wu Wei's *Figures in Four Sections* (*Renwu si duan* 人物四段) in the Shanghai Museum.
15 Whitfield 1972, 293, fig. 11.
16 Cahill 1985, 133–4.
17 I would like to thank Klaas Ruitenbeek, Director of the Museum für Asiatische Kunst (Asian Art Museum) in Berlin, for this information.

Chapter 7

The Empress' Dragon Crown: Establishing Symbols of Imperial Authority in the Early Ming

Luk Yu-ping

The crown is one of the most spectacular parts of a Ming empress' costume.[1] Surviving portraits of empresses in the National Palace Museum, Taipei, portray the splendour of these headdresses (**Pl. 7.1**). Dome-shaped and with curved panels extending from the back, they are decorated with precious stones, pearls and gold. Not only are they items of opulence, they are also rich in symbolism, and are impressive ways of communicating imperial authority and status. This chapter focuses on the crowns of empresses, and to a lesser extent on their ceremonial robes, as a way to explore how 'empress-ship' was conceptualised in Ming China in the period 1400 to 1450 – a topic that so far has not been explored in scholarship. It begins by identifying the features of crowns worn by early Ming empresses in comparison with those of previous dynasties. It will then consider how elements of the empress' crown defined her position within the imperial family through the organisation of sumptuary laws. It will argue that the common appellation of empress' crowns as *fengguan* 鳳冠 (phoenix crown) and the assumption that phoenixes alone represented empresses in the Ming dynasty need to be reconsidered.

Ming-dynasty emperors were polygamous, continuing a well-established institution in China's history.[2] Emperors were expected to bear children with multiple women in order to safeguard the imperial line. The 18th-century official *Ming shi* 明史 (*History of the Ming*) records that the founder of the dynasty, the Hongwu 洪武 emperor (r. 1368–98), had 15 named consorts who bore him many sons and daughters.[3] Based on a Song-dynasty system, Ming consorts were graded according to ten ranks and divided

Plate 7.1 Anonymous, ***Official Portrait of Empress Xu, Wife of the Yongle Emperor***, **Ming dynasty, Beijing. Album leaf, ink and colours on silk, height 65.7cm, width 52.1cm. National Palace Museum, Taipei**

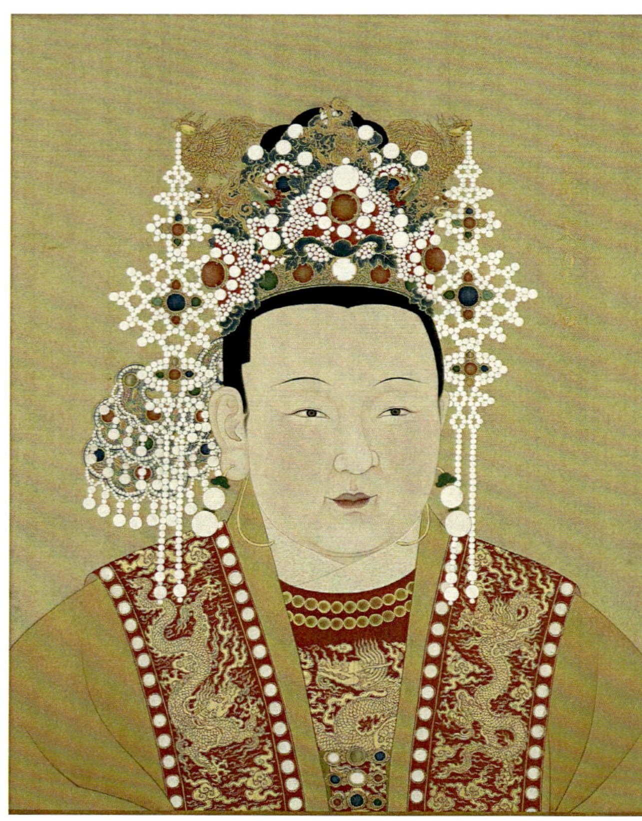

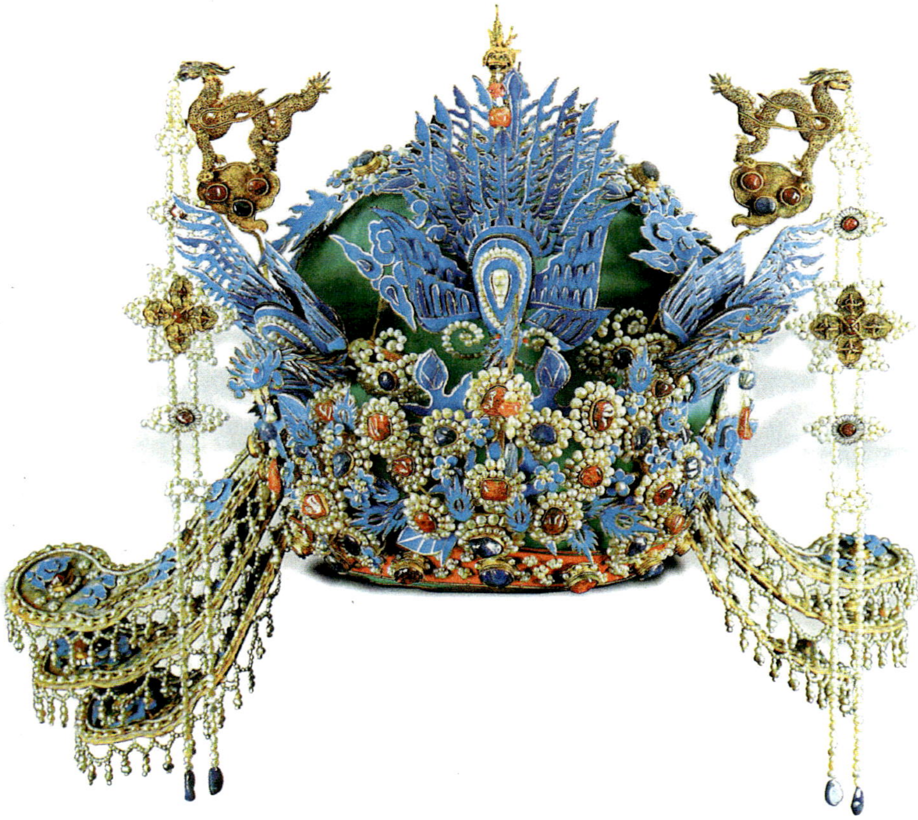

Plate 7.2 The crown of Empress Wang (1564–1620), wife of the Wanli emperor. Gold, pearls, kingfisher feathers and coral, height 35.5cm, width 20cm. Dingling Museum, Beijing

into four categories.[4] These were empress (*huanghou* 皇后), secondary consorts (*huangguifei* 皇貴妃; *guifei* 貴妃; *fei* 妃), third-class consorts (*pin* 嬪) and minor consorts. Although emperors could have multiple consorts, there could only be one principal wife who held the status of empress. The hierarchy for consorts was expressed in many ways, such as in the material goods and ritual deference to which these women were entitled. In turn, these distinctions further separated them from princesses, wives of officials, women who served at the imperial courts and ordinary women outside of the court milieu. Sumptuary laws made clear the intended exclusiveness of certain insignia and precious materials according to rank. Crowns are a good example of this.

So far, four crowns belonging to Ming empresses have been discovered by archaeologists (**Pl. 7.2**).[5] They were all found in the Dingling 定陵 (Ding Mausoleum), the only excavated Ming imperial tomb, and the burial site of the Wanli 萬曆 emperor (r. 1573–1620) and two of his consorts.[6] The excavation report was not specific regarding the condition of the crowns, except that some of the pieces were scattered.[7] Images of the crowns in their reconstructed state were published.[8] These can give a general impression of empress' crowns, but they cannot serve as substitutes for early Ming examples, since not only were they reconstructed, but the design of crowns most likely changed over time. Instead, we have to rely on textual and pictorial sources for more specific information. The *Da Ming huidian* 大明會典 (*Collected Statutes of the Great Ming*), first compiled in the Hongwu reign and published in 1503 and 1587, records in detail the ceremonial dress code for empresses and other members of the imperial household.[9] It includes the codes initially established by the Ming founder, which were then elaborated upon by the Yongle 永樂 emperor (r. 1403–24) and modified in the 16th century under the Jiajing 嘉靖 emperor (r. 1522–66).[10] Sections of this book are illustrated; for example, the chapter relating to the costumes of imperial women contains woodblock-printed images of an empress' crown (**Pl. 7.3**), ceremonial robe (**Pl. 7.4**), belt and possibly a tablet.[11] Another important source of information is the portraits of empresses in the National Palace Museum collection, Taipei, noted earlier. These survive as a set of half-length portraits in album form, mounted together with the portraits of Ming emperors, forming an official imperial genealogy.[12] Judging from descriptions in the *Statutes*, these portraits depict the imperial couple in *changfu* 常服 (routine court dress) rather than the most formal first-grade ceremonial attire, *lifu* 禮服. While we cannot confirm whether these sources are indicative of actual practice, they can be interpreted as models of how emperors and empresses were expected to look and dress. In some instances, image and text correspond closely to each other. In her portrait, Empress Xu 徐 (1362–1407), principal consort of the Yongle emperor, is shown wearing a high crown made with a black fabric base, decorated with a gold frontal dragon and flanked by a pair of gold phoenixes facing away from each other (see **Pl. 7.1**). These are surrounded by floral and foliage ornaments made of precious materials. Long strings of pearls with flower-shaped ornaments known as *zhujie* 珠結 (pearl knot) hang from the mouths of the phoenixes.[13] There are two additional phoenixes facing each other near the front of the crown and the curved panels at the rear are also ornately decorated with the divine bird. The sections of the empress' robe and shawl that are visible in the portrait are

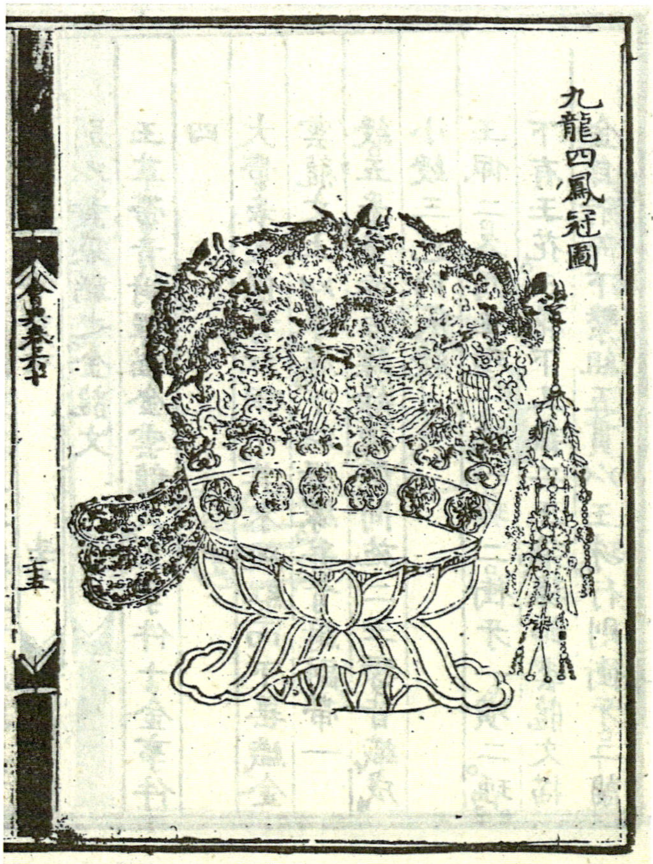

Plate 7.3 Empress's crown in *Collected Statutes of the Great Ming* (*Da Ming huidian*大明會典), reprint of the 1587 edition (Taipei 1963), *juan* 60.35, p. 1084

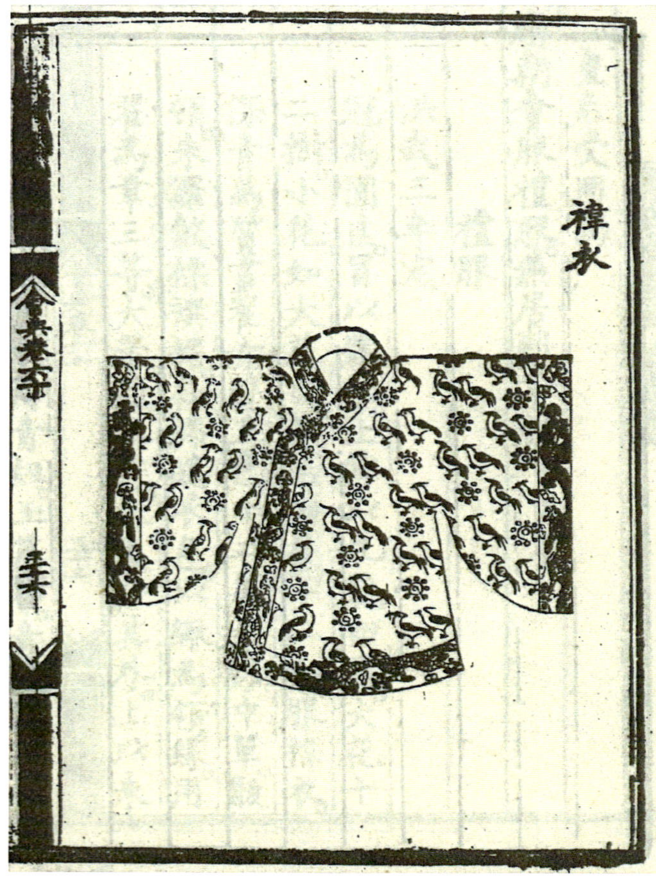

Plate 7.4 Empress' robe in *Collected Statutes of the Great Ming* (*Da Ming huidian*大明會典), reprint of the 1587 edition (Taipei 1963), *juan* 60.36, p. 1084

embroidered with dragon motifs. Empress Xu's appearance in her portrait matches the Yongle-period description of an empress' routine court dress in the *Statutes*, including specific details such as the red coral that highlights the mouth and crown of the phoenixes near the front of the headdress.[14]

Empresses in China's history did not always wear crowns as part of their ceremonial outfit. The *Zhouli* 周禮 (*Rites of Zhou*), dating from the 3rd century BCE, names the ceremonial costumes worn by emperors and empresses, which formed the basis for imperial dress codes of subsequent dynasties.[15] According to the *Zhouli*, empresses wore robes that were decorated with colourful pheasant motifs, known by various names such as *zhi* 雉, *hui* 翬 and *di* 翟. This design continued in the Ming dynasty on the first-grade ceremonial costumes of empresses. However, the same text makes no mention of matching headdresses for empresses, even though those worn by emperors are listed. It was only centuries later during the Song dynasty (960–1279) that crowns officially became a part of the written dress code for empresses.[16] Prior to this, elite women wore a variety of headdresses, wigs as well as elaborate hair ornaments that appeared to be dictated more by fashion than by official regulation.[17] According to the *Song shi* 宋史 (*History of the Song*), consorts could wear crowns decorated with nine pheasants and four phoenixes.[18] In 1139, after the capital moved to the south, the dress code was amended to stipulate specifically that only empresses wore a 'dragon phoenix flower hairpin crown' (*long feng hua chai guan* 龍鳳花釵冠).[19] Portraits of Song empresses in the National Palace Museum, Taipei, confirm that elaborate crowns had indeed become a part of the standard accoutrement of empresses. It is beyond the scope of this chapter to trace the development of empress' crowns in China, but interactions with steppe cultures in the north where elite women customarily wore tall gilded crowns, as well as links with ornate decoration on religious icons, are potentially worthwhile avenues for further research.[20]

In the portraits of Song empresses, also in the National Palace Museum, Taipei, we find crowns that are similar in design to those from the Ming dynasty.[21] The crown depicted in the portrait of Empress Yang 楊 (1162–1232) of the Southern Song dynasty (1127–1279), for instance, contains many of the elements inherited by the Ming. It is dome-shaped, with a principal dragon motif surrounded by smaller dragons, phoenixes and flowers, as well as curved panels extending from the back (**Pl. 7.5**). Perhaps this is the 'dragon phoenix flower hairpin crown' mentioned in the *History of the Song*. While there are clear similarities between the crowns depicted in Song and Ming portraits, there are also a number of significant differences. One distinctive feature of Song crowns that does not appear on the Ming versions is the small figures located among the dragons and phoenixes. In Empress Yang's portrait, some of these figures are riding the mythical creatures; others are positioned as a procession along the rim. This feature can also be found in the portraits of other Song empresses, none as spectacularly rendered as in the portrait of Empress Liu 劉 (969–1033), consort of Zhenzong 真宗 (r. 997–1022). In this portrait, the empress is shown with a crown decorated with a large group

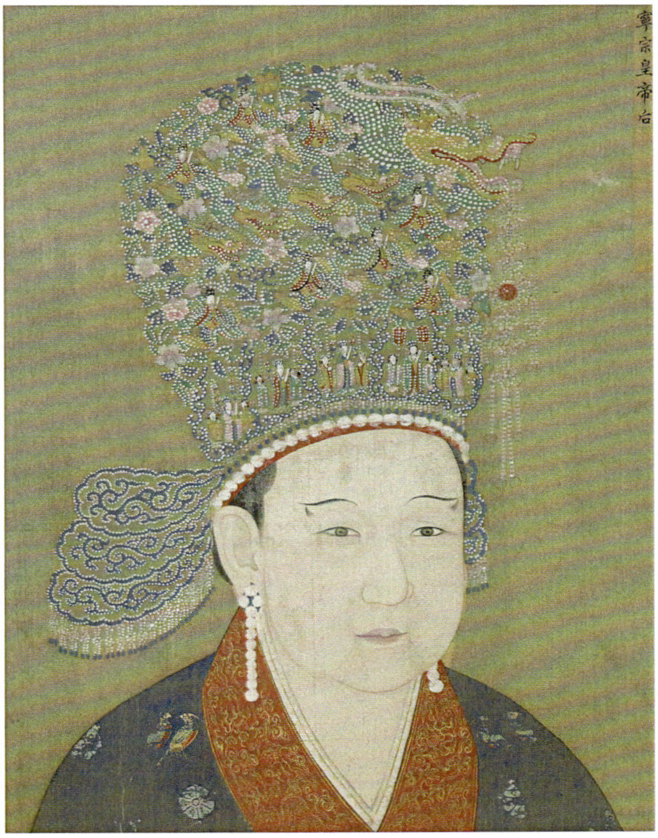

Plate 7.5 Anonymous, *Official Portrait of Song Empress Yang, Wife of Emperor Ningzong*, Southern Song dynasty. Album leaf, ink and colour on silk, height 56.2cm, width 45.7cm. National Palace Museum, Taipei

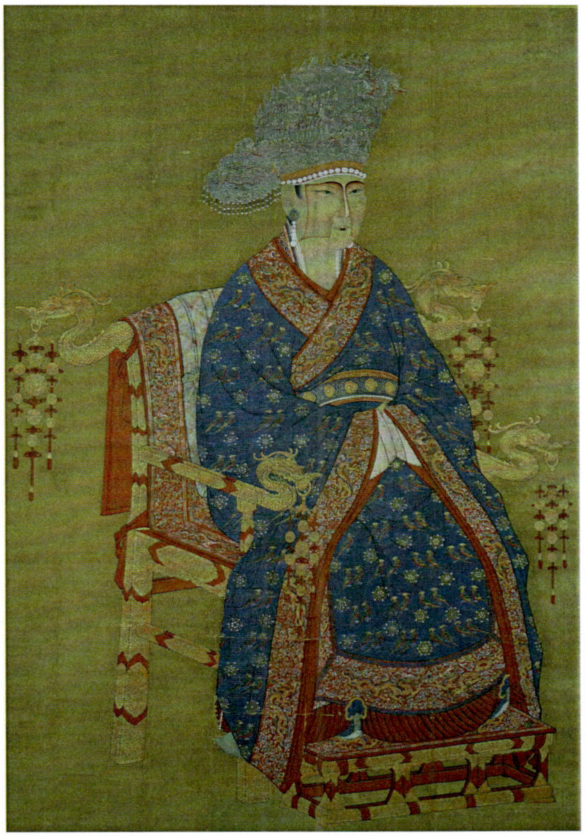

Plate 7.6 Anonymous, *Official Portrait of Song Empress Liu, Wife of Emperor Zhenzong*, Northern Song dynasty. Hanging scroll, ink and colour on silk, height 177cm, width 120.8cm. National Palace Museum, Taipei

of female figures appearing as though they are rising upwards, at the apex of which is a single, clearly larger, female figure riding a dragon (**Pl. 7.6**).[22] Her unusual facial make-up may be a revival of an earlier fashion that gives the impression of a purple veil.[23] Hui-shu Lee has identified the figures as representations of the Queen Mother of the West (Xiwangmu 西王母) and her entourage.[24] The Queen Mother of the West is a goddess with ancient origins who was widely venerated from the Han dynasty (206 BCE–220 CE).[25] Interestingly, although Song records do not mention this feature on empress' crowns, it is referred to in the sumptuary laws of the Jurchen Jin dynasty (1115–1234) that ruled the north of China around the time of the Southern Song dynasty.[26] In the Ming period, this feature no longer appeared on the decorations of empresses' crowns.

Another notable difference between crowns depicted in Song and Ming portraits is the greater emphasis in the latter on precious materials. The viewer's eyes are drawn to the different types and sizes of stones and pearls in the Ming portraits. Their clear outlines and shading highlight the lustre and three-dimensionality of the enormous gems inset into gold. By comparison, the visual impact of the crowns in Song portraits lies in the plethora of smaller elements that cover them. Pearls also feature prominently there, including apparently as facial decoration, but they tend to be smaller and are usually of uniform size. The significance of gemstones in early Ming culture is discussed by Craig Clunas in Chapter 27 of this volume. Since China did not possess a rich source of gemstones, historically they had to be imported. Zheng He's 鄭和 (1371–1433) maritime voyages and tribute from neighbouring lands provided a supply of these precious materials, which were most likely the source of the large stones decorating early Ming empresses' crowns as well as other imperial jewellery during the period 1400 to 1450. According to Clunas, the preference for gold and gems in the Ming can be viewed as part of 'pan-Eurasian high elite material culture', and may be related to the continuation of Mongolian elite taste in the Ming, or at least a consequence of the increased trade that was made possible by the earlier Mongol empire.[27]

In recent years, scholars have shed light on the importance of the Mongolian legacy in Ming culture, including in dress.[28] So far, empresses' crowns have not been considered as an example of this. At first glance, the distinctive headdress known as *gugu* 罟罟 worn by Mongolian elite married women bears little resemblance to Ming crowns. It is cylindrical and widens towards the top; its exterior is decorated with precious materials and bird feathers attached at the top.[29] However, Ming empress' crowns are related to Mongolian examples in the prominent 'pearl knots', hangings with bejewelled flower designs that fall on both sides of the wearer's face, reaching below the shoulders.[30] Examples of Yuan empresses' portraits, such as that of Empress Chabi (1227–81), wife of Qubilai Khan (1215–94), show comparable double pearl hangings (**Pl. 7.7**). These are attached to a teardrop-shaped jewelled pendant known as *yaner* 掩耳 (ear cover).[31] This feature is not found at all in Song portraits. Instead, they show a single hanging

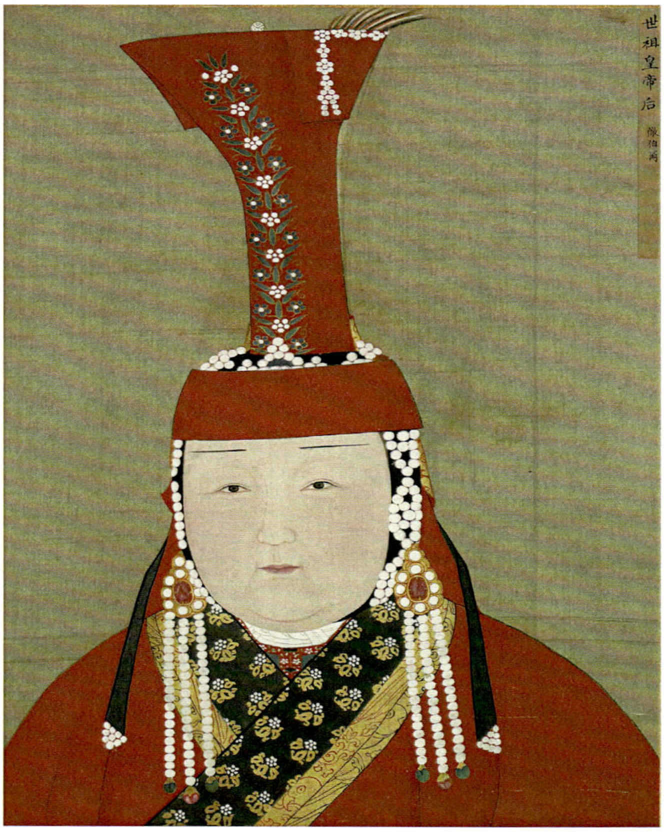

Plate 7.7 Anonymous, *Official Portrait of Yuan Empress Chabi, Wife of Qubilai Khan*. Album leaf, ink, colour and gold on silk, height 61.2cm, width 47.6cm. National Palace Museum, Taipei

with flower design attached to the mouth of a central dragon motif on the crowns.[32] How this double hanging pearl feature on Ming crowns is related to steppe customs will require further research. But it is interesting to note that long pendants attached to crowns were a feature of gold crowns from the Silla kingdom (57 BCE–935 CE) in the Korean peninsula, which in turn may be connected to crowns found in the Afghanistan region.[33]

Plate 7.8 Gold phoenix pendant, dated 1432, *Yinzuoju* 銀作局 (Jewellery Service). Height 14.2cm, width 7.8cm; weight 72.4g. Hubei Provincial Museum, excavated from the tomb of the Prince Zhuang of Liang and Lady Wei at Zhongxiang, Hubei province

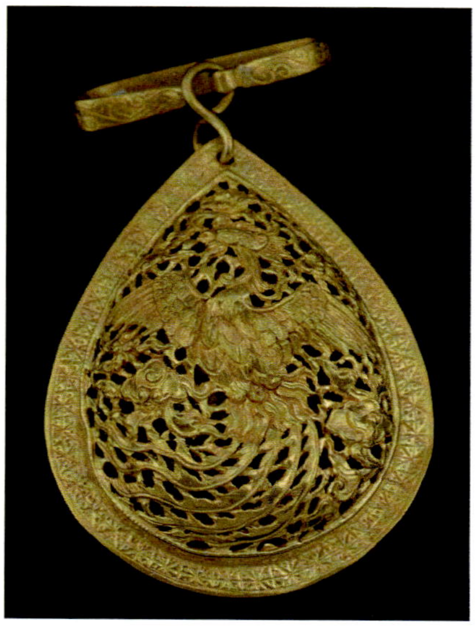

Judging from the above discussion, it is clear that the design of Ming empresses' crowns did not simply revive earlier customs, but rather elements of the past were selectively appropriated and modified. The Ming dynasty also continued a regulation that began in the Southern Song dynasty, whereby only the empress among imperial women was allowed to reproduce the dragon motif on her costume. Surviving Ming dynasty records provide detailed dress codes that elucidate this distinction. As noted earlier, the routine crown of Empress Xu depicted both dragons and phoenixes. The significance of this is clear when it is compared to the dress code of lower-ranked consorts. According to the *Statutes*, the routine court dress of secondary consorts (*huangfei* 皇妃) includes a crown of *luan* 鸞 and *feng* 鳳, and a robe embroidered with images of these two mythical birds with similar appearances.[34] *Feng* is usually translated as 'phoenix', whereas there is no consensus on the English equivalent of *luan*.[35] Both appear on the routine court costume of the heir's consort, while only *feng* appears on the costume of the wives of princes.[36] The same observation can be made of first-grade ceremonial costumes: the empress wore a crown with nine dragons and four phoenixes, with a large dragon at the centre.[37] This crown is paired with a dark blue robe decorated with pheasant (*di* 翟) motifs. Secondary consorts wore a crown of nine pheasants and four phoenixes and a robe decorated with further phoenixes, as did the heir's consort.[38] The burial objects of Lady Wei 魏 (d. 1451), wife of Prince Zhuang of Liang 梁莊王 (1411–41), excavated from their shared tomb in Zhongxiang 鍾祥, Hubei 湖北 province, include finely crafted examples of jewellery depicting phoenixes with elaborate tail feathers, which would have been appropriate for her rank (**Pl. 7.8**).[39] Ming sumptuary laws contradict a common assumption that the phoenix represented the empress. In fact, according to the *Statutes*, the emblem that distinguished an empress from other imperial and royal women during the early Ming dynasty was not the phoenix but the dragon, or the dragon in combination with other divine birds. Indeed, in the context of ceremonial costumes, the textual records indicate that the phoenix might even be lower in prestige than the pheasant in the hierarchy of motifs, since the ordinary costume of a prince's consort could only be decorated with phoenixes.

The importance of the dragon as an emblem of the empress becomes more pronounced in the portraits of empresses that succeed Empress Xu in the period 1400 to 1450. The portrait of Empress Zhang 張 (d. 1442), consort of the Hongxi 洪熙 emperor (r. 1425), appears very similar to that of her predecessor (**Pl. 7.9**). They both wear the same costumes and the overall design of their crowns appears the same. However, when considered closely, the crown depicted in Empress Zhang's portrait clearly differs from the earlier example and descriptions in the *Statutes*. The phoenixes that adorned Empress Xu's crown have all been replaced by dragons, including the decoration on the curved extensions at the back of the crown. The dragons on Empress Zhang's crown are also larger in size and fiercer, with powerful bodies and flame-like forms emanating from them. Rather than a 'phoenix crown', her crown can be more aptly

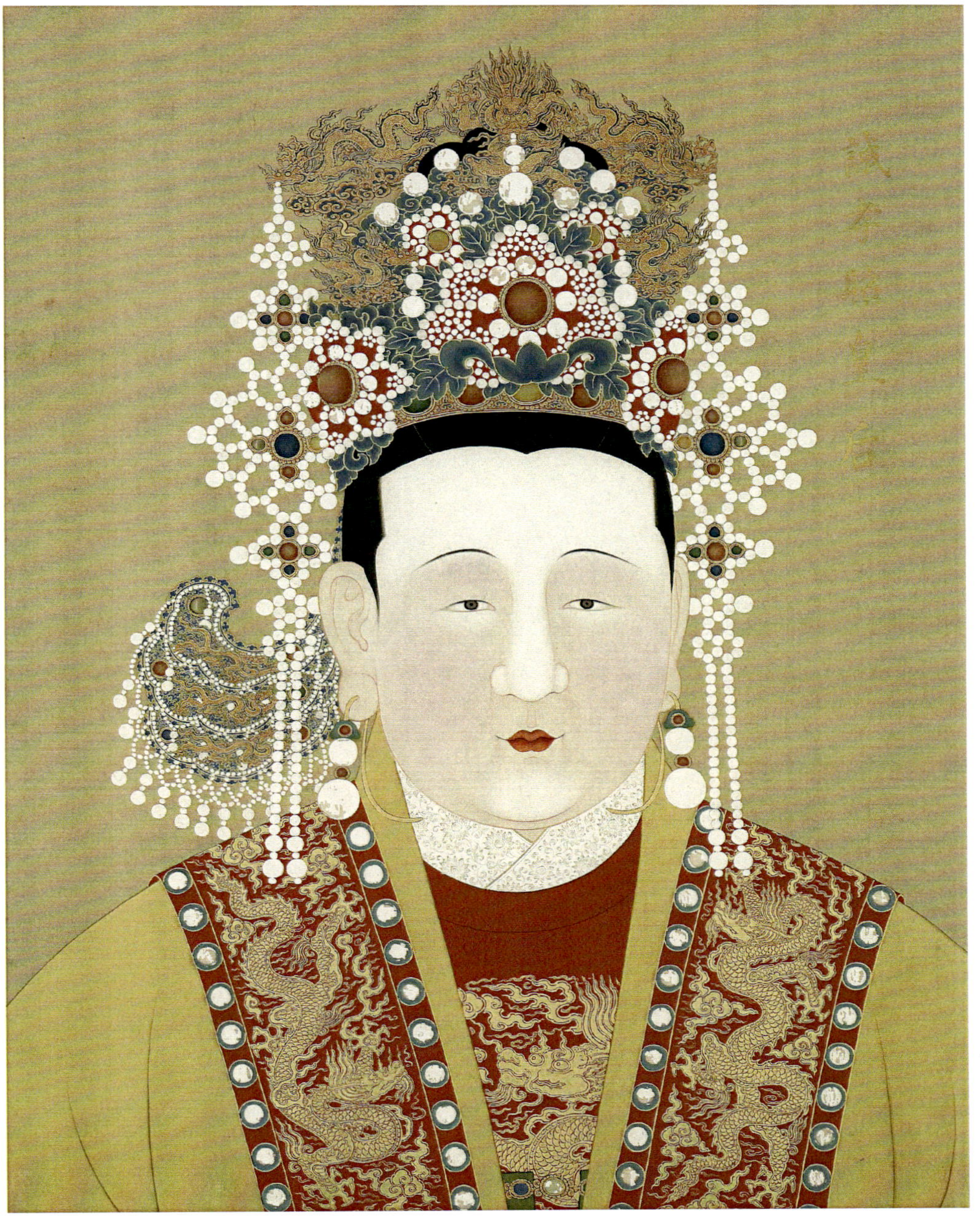

Plate 7.9 Anonymous, *Official Portrait of Empress Zhang, Wife of the Hongxi Emperor*, Ming dynasty, Beijing. Album leaf, ink and colours on silk, height 65.5cm, width 51.5cm. National Palace Museum, Taipei

described as a 'dragon crown'. This 'dragon crown' is repeated in the subsequent portrait of Empress Sun 孫 (d. 1462) (**Pl. 7.10**), the wife of the Xuande 宣德 emperor (r. 1426–35), and to a lesser extent in the portrait of Empress Qian 錢 (d. 1468) (**Pl. 7.11**), wife of the Zhengtong 正統 emperor (r. 1436–49), the last emperor of the period in question. There is indication that this design was not purely pictorial, but may be based on actual practice. The *Statutes* record that a woman chosen to be empress first received her set of routine ceremonial costume together with her conferring document and other gifts while she was at her natal home in a process known as *naji* 納吉 (presenting the auspicious).[40] Notably, the crown she receives is named in the text as *Jinlong zhucui yanju guan* 金龍珠翠燕居冠 ('Swallow residence' crown with gold dragon, pearls and kingfisher feathers; 'swallow residence' refers here to a more informal crown).[41] This suggests that it was the dragon which was recognised as the identifying motif of the crown for an empress' routine court dress.

The observation that the dragon was a principal emblem of the early Ming empress has broader implications that are worth considering. In the *Statutes*, sumptuary laws that dictate imperial and royal dress refer to ceremonial objects made of different materials, not only textiles and jewellery. Empresses' objects that were made of other materials and also decorated with dragon motifs include a jade belt, a jade hanging pendant, a wooden stand for her seal and a wooden container for her gilded conferring document.[42] Given its wider application, perhaps the empress' association with the dragon or dragon-and-phoenix motifs could be extended beyond costume to imperial furnishing more broadly, such as lacquer wares, porcelain and other items that decorated the spaces inhabited by imperial women. For example, consider the impressive carved red lacquer table in the Victoria and Albert Museum collection dated to the Xuande period that was most likely produced in the imperial lacquer workshop known as the 'Orchard Factory' (*Guoyuanchang* 果園廠) (**Pl. 7.12**). The drawer fronts and top of the table

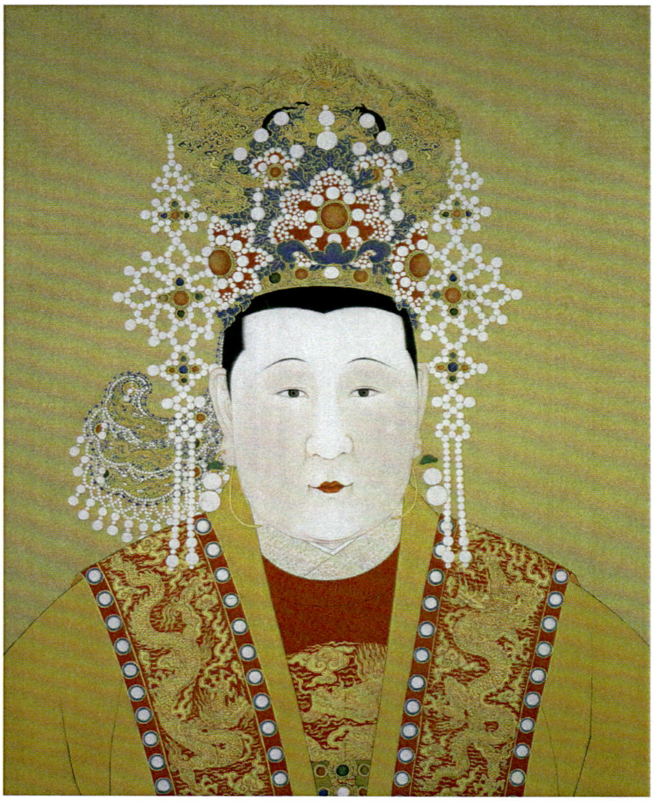

Plate 7.10 Anonymous, *Official Portrait of Empress Sun, Wife of the Xuande Emperor*, Ming dynasty, Beijing. Album leaf, ink and colours on silk, height 65.7cm, width 51.8cm. National Palace Museum, Taipei

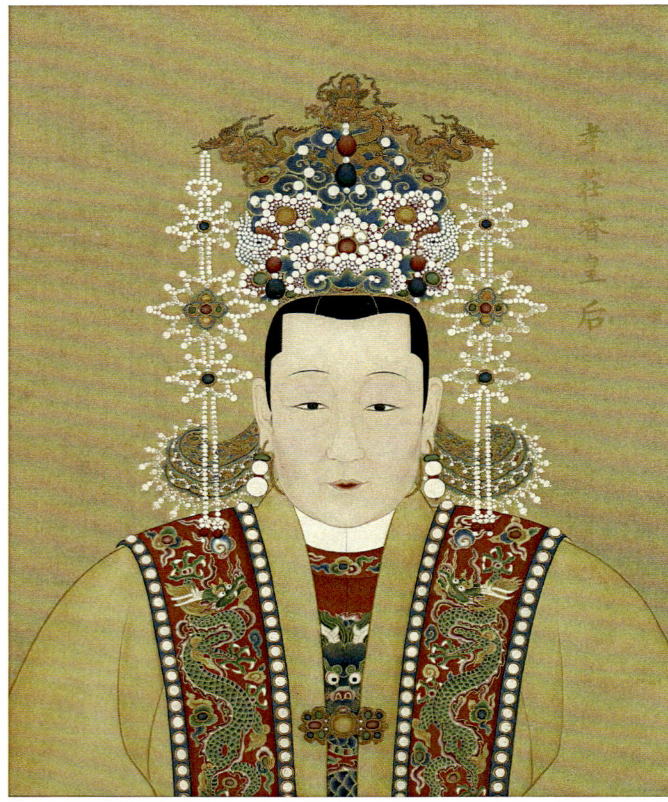

Plate 7.11 Anonymous, *Official Portrait of Empress Qian, Wife of the Zhengtong Emperor*, Ming dynasty, Beijing. Album leaf, ink and colours on silk, height 63.5cm, width 52.3cm. National Palace Museum, Taipei

are carved with rising dragons and descending phoenixes against a ground of blossoms and foliage. A conventional interpretation would be that the dragon represented the emperor while the phoenix represented the empress.[43] However, based on sumptuary laws, perhaps this piece of elaborately decorated furniture was produced specifically for the residence of the empress in the Forbidden City in Beijing during the Xuande reign. Similarly, early Ming imperial wares that depict only phoenixes or a combination of divine birds, such as a blue-and-white porcelain dish in the British Museum also dated to the Xuande period, might be more suitable for a lower-ranked consort rather than the empress herself (**Pl. 7.13**). As a result of considering sumptuary laws, it may be possible to review the function and intended audience of particular kinds of objects produced for the imperial and royal courts in the early Ming dynasty.

Scholars have observed that dragons became widespread as an imperial emblem on costume and decorations during the Ming and into the Qing dynasty (1644–1911), culminating in the iconic imperial 'dragon robe'.[44] This is another example of the Ming appropriating past traditions. Dragons have ancient significance in China and associations with rulership. For example, in order to legitimise his rule, the founder of the Han dynasty encouraged the myth that his mother conceived him after dreaming of a dragon.[45] Earlier it has been noted that the exclusive use of the dragon motif was part of the sumptuary laws of the Song dynasty. At the same time, the dragon motif was also 'established on the accoutrements of the steppe culture' from at least the Western Jin period (265–316). It was a 'unifying heraldic symbol', reserved for the ruler and his elite guards under the Mongols.[46] It was probably for this reason that the two-antlered, five-clawed dragon was banned from general use during the Yuan dynasty (1271–1368). Thus, the greater importance of the dragon as an emblem for both emperors and empresses during the Ming dynasty may have drawn upon a wider pan-Asian recognition of the dragon as a symbol of elite power and authority, in addition to its rich meanings within China's history.

For empresses specifically, changes to the model design of their crowns raise interesting questions concerning the ways that female authority was conceptualised and visualised. The depiction of 'dragon crowns' in portraiture aligns the empress more closely with the emperor in the visual language of imperial authority. The format of the album portraits accentuates this visual connection, as the portraits of emperors dressed in their routine court robes embroidered with dragon roundels are mounted opposite the portraits of empresses. In practice, this connection would have been visible to officials and palace staff during ceremonial occasions, beginning with the imperial wedding ceremony. The invention of a 'dragon crown' suggests the possibility for a powerful imperial woman to appropriate symbols of masculine imperial authority and be represented in closer displays of union with the emperor as his partner. It does not seem coincidental that the first Ming empress to be portrayed with a crown completely decorated with dragons was Empress Zhang, the closest that the Ming dynasty had to a female regent.[47] Female regency was prohibited under the Hongwu emperor for fear of their threat to the throne.[48] Empress Zhang came to power due to her long life as well as her acumen. She outlived both her husband, the Hongxi

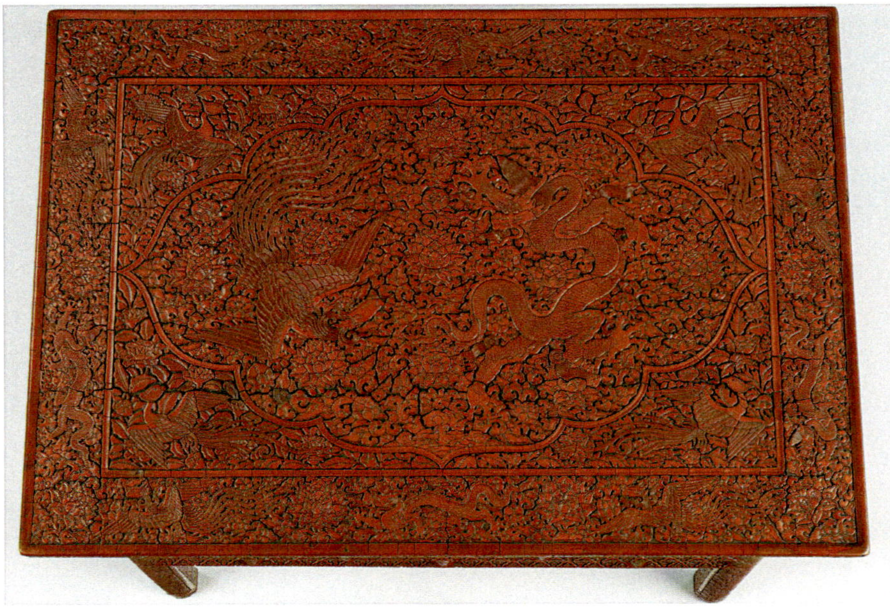

Plate 7.12 Carved red lacquer table. Lacquer on a wooden core, gilded metal fittings, Xuande mark and period, 1426–35, Beijing. Height 79.2cm, width 119.5cm, depth 84.5cm. Victoria and Albert Museum, London, FE.6:1 to 4-1973

emperor who ruled for only one year, and her son, the Xuande emperor. The *History of the Ming* records that she had 'thorough knowledge of the government affairs of China and abroad' (*Zhongwai zhengshi mo bu zhouzhi* 中外政事莫不周知), and made most of the major military and state decisions during the early part of the Xuande reign.[49] Moreover, she enjoyed extraordinary visibility in the wider realm. In 1429, the Xuande emperor accompanied her on a visit to the newly built imperial tombs where they were greeted by crowds of people who had gathered at the site.[50] On this journey, the empress summoned a peasant woman to enquire about her livelihood, and with the emperor tasted the foods that were offered. The importance of her role as mentor to the emperor and as a model empress is expressed in the historical records. Judging from the portraits, her successor Empress Sun appeared to model herself completely on the then dowager empress, including in terms of the portrayal of her facial features.

On the other hand, the adoption of an imperial symbol that is conventionally associated with the emperor on the costumes of empresses suggests a reduction in the scope for a distinct visual language of female authority, such as the representation of the Queen Mother of the West and her entourage that were a feature on the crowns of Song empresses. Instead, the emblem of dragons that Ming empresses share with emperors and princes stresses their place as wife and mother in the imperial bloodline, so that empress-ship was conceptualised and integrated even more firmly within the patriarchal system than before. The greater emphasis on the patriline suggested by the empress' dragon emblem is consistent with broader changes in society from the Yuan dynasty onwards. As Bettine Birge observes, there was a shift towards 'Confucian patrilineal ideals' in China as a result of the 'confrontation between Chinese and Mongol culture in the thirteenth and fourteenth centuries'.[51] New marriage and inheritance laws were established that favoured men over women, essentially stripping women of their property rights and their freedom to remarry.[52] These laws were adopted and promoted under the Ming dynasty.[53] This is not to suggest that there was a direct causal link between the design of empress' crowns and marriage and property laws. However, given their symbolic significance, changes to the design of crowns and other aspects of regalia could be symptomatic of broader trends in normative gender relations, which the emperor and empress personally embodied.

Within the 50 years in question, we can observe a range of experiences in empresses' lives. This was a period that saw the contributions of Empress Zhang and Empress Xu to court culture. Empress Xu's strong character is suggested by the account that when she was still a princess she mobilised army wives to defend Beijing while her husband was away on a military campaign.[54] As an empress, she is known for the publication of religious and didactic texts that were presented as diplomatic gifts and distributed to members of the court and beyond.[55] Yet it was also within this period that

Plate 7.13 Blue-and-white porcelain dish, Xuande mark and period, 1426–35, Jingdezhen. Height 4.5cm, diameter 20cm. British Museum, London, 1973,0726.361

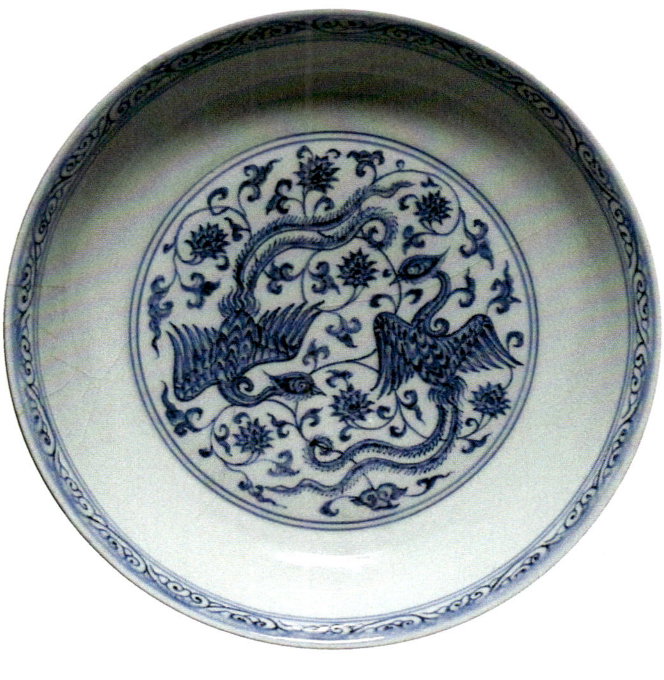

Empress Hu 胡 (d. 1443), first empress of the Xuande emperor, was deposed on the grounds that she did not bear any sons, only one daughter.[56] Although not directly related to empresses, it is important to remember that the sacrifice of childless consorts at the death of the emperor was practised during this period. This cruel custom of immolation was not abolished until the Tianshun 天順 (r. 1457–64) reign in 1464.[57] Patrilineality was an embedded part of Chinese history and Ming empresses were not unique in facing the challenges it presented. Further research is needed to understand the specific ways that Ming empresses and other imperial women of the period negotiated their position, how they engaged in the shaping of empress-ship, identity and imperial authority, and how this developed over time, so that we can begin to fill a significant gap in our understanding of this important group of makers and performers of Ming court culture.[58]

Lastly, if the crowns of Ming empresses can be more aptly described as 'dragon crowns', then where did the notion of the 'phoenix crown' to denote an empress' headdress come from? Preliminary evidence suggests that this term was in fact a later, Qing dynasty, development. *Qinding Da Qing huidian* 欽定大清會典 (*Imperially Sponsored Collected Statutes of the Great Qing*) states that Qing empresses' first-rank ceremonial costume included a robe embroidered with five-clawed dragons and a headdress embellished with gold filigree phoenixes.[59] Lower-ranked consorts were entitled to a headdress with fewer phoenixes, and princesses to one with pheasants.[60] They wore robes embroidered with dragons, but these were called *mang* 蟒 rather than *long* 龍 to distinguish their wearer's rank.[61] Surviving portraits of Qing empresses, where their crowns are decorated with phoenixes but without any dragons, are consistent with these codes.[62] The design of headdresses decorated with phoenixes spread beyond the court to become the customary headdress of a bride at her wedding.[63] It is most likely through its wider distribution that 'phoenix crown' became embedded in the popular lexicon.

Notes

1 I am using the translation 'crown' for *guan* 冠 to highlight its importance as a symbol of the empress' rank. It functions differently from European royal crowns that are tied to the state and inherited. In China, the crown together with other aspects of imperial costume was part of the wearer's property and was buried with them upon their death. There is no crowning ceremony as such in the coronation (or marriage) of an empress. On the Ming imperial marriage ceremony, see Hsieh Bao Hua 2003.
2 On the polygamy of Chinese emperors, see McMahon 2013.
3 *DMB*, 389–90.
4 Hsieh Bao Hua 2003, 101. See also Soullière 1987.
5 Zhongguo shehui kexue yuan *et al.* 1990, vol. 1, 205–6.
6 The Wanli emperor had two consorts buried with him, Xiaojing (d. 1611) and Xiaoduan (1564–1620), both née Wang. Xiaoduan was his empress, while Xiaojing was the mother of the future Guangzong and was posthumously interred with him.
7 Zhongguo shehui kexue yuan *et al.* 1990, vol. 1, 205.
8 Images of two of the crowns are in Zhongguo shehui kexue yuan *et al.* 1990, vol. 2, nos 114–16.
9 *DMHD*, *juan* 60.
10 Franke 1968, 178.
11 *DMHD*, *juan* 60.32a–39b, images on 60.35a–36b.
12 A full set of the portraits is reproduced in black and white in *DMB*. According to textual sources, full-length hanging scroll portraits of Ming empresses also once existed. There is one hanging scroll portrait of Empress Ma (d. 1382), wife of Hongwu, in the same collection, but it was added to the collection between 1744 and 1815. See Zhang Naiwei 1990, 395–400. Portraits of Empresses Ma and Xu that matched the hanging scroll portraits of their husbands, the Hongwu and Yongle emperors, are mentioned in Tan Qian 2006, 103.
13 *DMHD*, *juan* 60.37a–b.
14 *DMHD*, *juan* 60.37b.
15 Emperors' costumes are recorded in Lin Yin 1987, *juan* 5 under *sifu* 司服, 221–4; empresses' costume is in *juan* 2 under *nei sifu* 內司服, 81–2. Also discussed in Chen Gaohua and Xu Jijun 2002, 89–90.
16 Zhou Xun and Gao Chunming 1988, 93.
17 Zhou Xun and Gao Chunming 1988, 92–9.
18 Tuotuo *c.* 1345, *juan* 151.
19 Tuotuo *c.* 1345, *juan* 151.
20 For an example of a Liao dynasty crown worn by a princess, see Shen Hsueh-man 2006, 102–3.
21 Xu Wenyao 2013, 80.
22 Lee Hui-shu 2010, 59.
23 Liu Heping 2003, 135–6.
24 Lee Hui-shu 2010, 59.
25 Little 2000, 276–7.
26 Tuotuo 1975, *juan* 43, 978.
27 See Chapter 27 by Craig Clunas in this volume.
28 For instance Robinson 2008.
29 Watt 2010, 80–1; Jia 2005.
30 I am grateful to Professor Jessica Rawson for pointing this out to me.
31 Jia Xizeng 2005, 221–2.
32 This is consistent with the description of an empress' crown in *Jin shi*. See Tuotuo 1975, 978.
33 For examples of Silla crowns, see Lee Soyoung and Leidy 2014, 50–3.
34 Wang Qi 1988, under *niaoshou* 鳥獸, nos 2 and 3.
35 Hargett 1989, 238.
36 *DMHD*, *juan* 60.47a–50b, 59b–62a.
37 *DMHD*, *juan* 60.32a–34a.
38 *DMHD*, *juan* 60.39b–41b, 47a–48b.
39 On this tomb, see Hubei sheng wenwu kaogu yanjiusuo and Zhongxiang shi bowuguan 2007. The excavated objects are discussed in Clunas 2013, 139–64, especially Lady Wei 151–64; Clunas and Harrison-Hall 2014, figs 57, 58.
40 Hsieh Bao Hua 2003, 114.
41 *DMHD*, *juan* 67.8a.
42 *DMHD*, *juan* 60.33b, 38b–39b.
43 Clunas and Harrison-Hall 2014, 107. This interpretation of the phoenix and dragon combination is frequently repeated. For example, Bartholomew 2006, 55.
44 Cammann 1952; Lin Yeqiang 2009, 32.
45 Sung 2009, 122.
46 Kuehn 2011, 210–11.
47 On Empress Zhang, see Soullière 1987, 350–5.
48 *MS* 1984, 113, 3503.
49 *MS* 113, 3512.
50 *MS* 113, 3512.
51 Birge 2002, 290.
52 Birge 2002, 280; Bernhardt 1999.
53 Birge 2002, 277–9.
54 *MS* 113, 3510. For Empress Xu's biography, see *DMB*, 566–9.
55 Clunas and Harrison-Hall 2014, 60–1; Soullière 1987.
56 *MS* 113, 3513.
57 The end of the practice is recorded in *MS* 113, 3515–16.
58 For the author's attempts to explore this area, see Luk 2016a and 2016b. Keith McMahon has recently published a book about imperial women from the Song to Qing dynasties.
59 Kun 1963, *juan* 58.
60 Kun 1963, *juan* 58, 1876–85.
61 [illegible] Yeqiang 2009, 33–4. Lin explains that *mang* and *long* are not [illegible]ply differentiated by the number of claws.
62 Many of the portraits of Qing emperors and empresses have been published, such as in Beiping gugong bowuyuan 1931.
63 Xu Wenyao 2013, 80.

Chapter 8
Early Ming Ceramics: Rethinking the Status of Blue-and-White

Jessica Harrison-Hall

All over the world, 'Ming' has become shorthand not only for valuable porcelain of all periods but for preciousness more broadly.[1] This is despite the fact that many Ming ceramics were mass produced and much was globally exported. For example, 57,000 pieces of porcelain were sent through the reciprocal trade in return for 'tribute' in the single year of 1383 to Thailand, Java and other Southeast Asian states.[2] Today other Ming ceramics have become rare multi-million pound treasures, possessed by a few. Liu Yiqian 劉益謙, a Shanghai billionaire, bought the Meiyintang collection's Chenghua 成化 period *doucai* 斗彩 'chicken cup', made between 1464 and 1487, from Sotheby's Hong Kong sale on 8 April 2014 for the world record price of HK$281.24 million (nearly £24 million). He caused a social media storm by paying for it on his American Express card and drinking tea from it just as the Qianlong emperor did.[3] With this paradox in mind, this chapter explores the status of blue-and-white in the early 1400s in a variety of contexts, with perhaps surprising results.

In the 1400s, Ming Chinese porcelain was still so rare in Italy that it was considered a material suitable for presentation to God, representing perhaps a zenith of material wealth.[4] There was no direct trade between China and Europe at this time and so luxury goods came to Italy indirectly, via the Middle East or Africa. One of the earliest representations of Ming blue-and-white porcelain from Jingdezhen is seen in a *Madonna and Child* (**Pl. 8.1**) by

Plate 8.1 Francesco Benaglio (*c.* 1432–92), *Madonna and Child*, late 1460s. Tempera on panel transferred to canvas, height 80.7cm, width 56.2cm. National Gallery of Art, Washington, D.C. Widener Collection, 1942.9.44

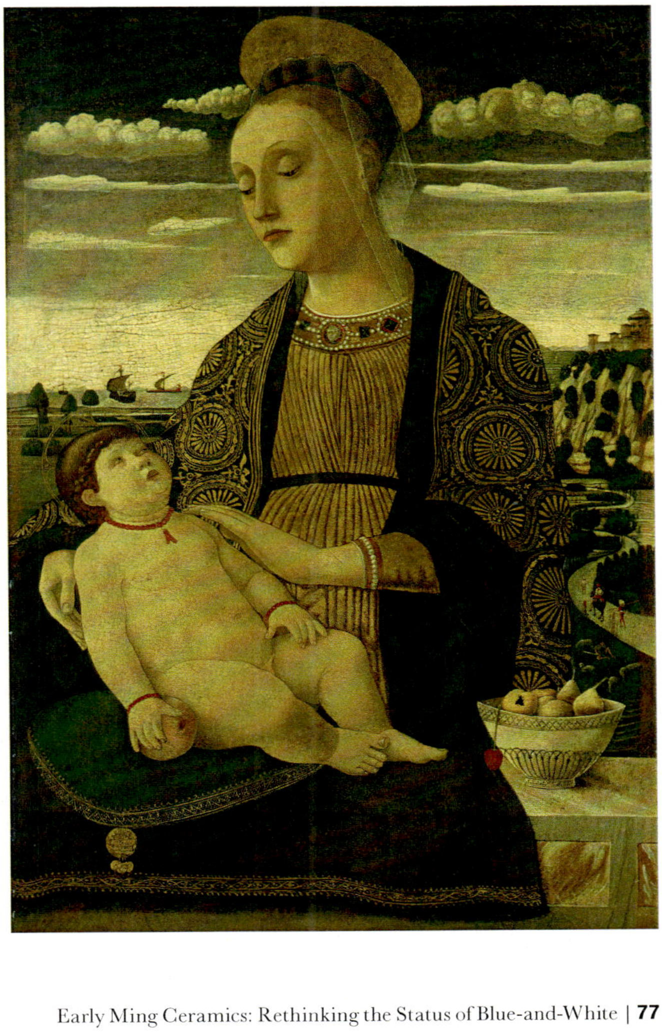

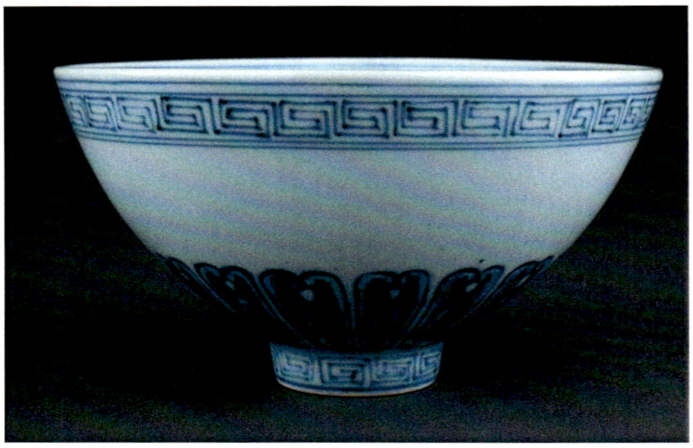

Plate 8.2 Blue-and-white porcelain bowl, Xuande mark and period, 1426–35, Jingdezhen. Height 9cm, diameter 15.9cm. Sir Percival David Collection, PDF 681

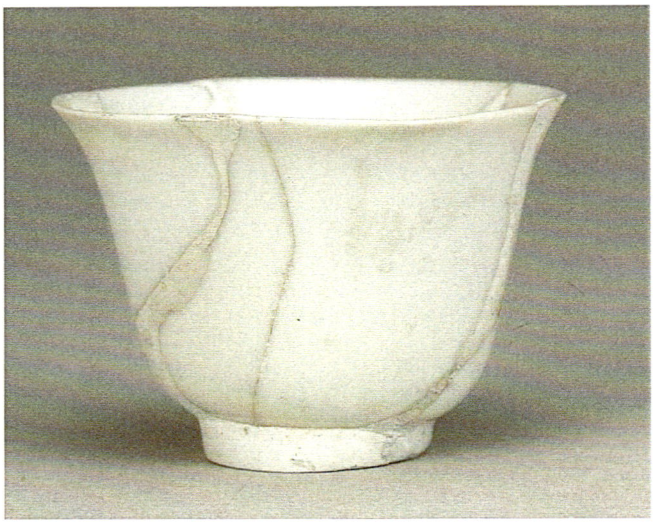

Plate 8.4 Small white glazed cup, excavated at Zhushan, Xuande mark and period, 1426–35. Height 4.6cm, diameter 6.2cm. Jingdezhen Institute of Ceramic Archaeology, Jingdezhen, Jiangxi province

Francesco Benaglio (*c.* 1432–92), an Italian Renaissance artist who painted this work in the late 1460s. Benaglio was also responsible for painting, in the late 15th century, with Michele da Verona (1470–1536/1544), frescoes in the Lavagnoli Chapel of the Church of S. Anastasia, Verona. These show Christ preaching on the seashore with a backdrop of trading vessels of the types which would have transported the porcelain.[5]

The type of bowl shown here (**Pl. 8.2**) was first made in the Yongle era 永樂 (1403–24) and then copied in the Xuande 宣德 period (1426–35), but the design was not subsequently used again until the style was revived in the Qing dynasty (1644–1911).[6] Yongle period wares tend to have darker, more intense blue designs and so the paler blue of this bowl suggests that the artist was representing a piece of porcelain of the Xuande era. Its accurate depiction here suggests he saw rather than imagined the bowl.

Nearly 50 years later, at the beginning of the 1500s, Chinese porcelain was still so rare in Italy that antique Ming blue-and-white was represented in the *Adoration of the Magi* by Andrea Mantegna (1431–1506) (**Pl. 8.3**).[7] Scholars have suggested that Mantegna contracted the sides of the Yongle period bowl slightly so that, filled with gold coins, it could fit in the hands of the wise man in this scene, which was painted between 1495 and 1505.[8] However, excavations at Jingdezhen have revealed white vessels of exactly this form and proportions from the Yongle and Xuande strata (**Pl. 8.4**).[9] As almost every shape was made in the full range of colours and designs, it is likely that a blue-and-white version existed of exactly these same proportions. Hongzhi 弘治 period blue-and-white bowls dating between 1488 and 1505 bear no resemblance to the bowl in the painting,[10] demonstrating that the blue-and-white bowl depicted by Mantegna was certainly a Yongle era piece and therefore an antique rather than an object that was created at the same time as the picture. During the course of the British Museum exhibition the possibility of this being Vietnamese was discussed. However,

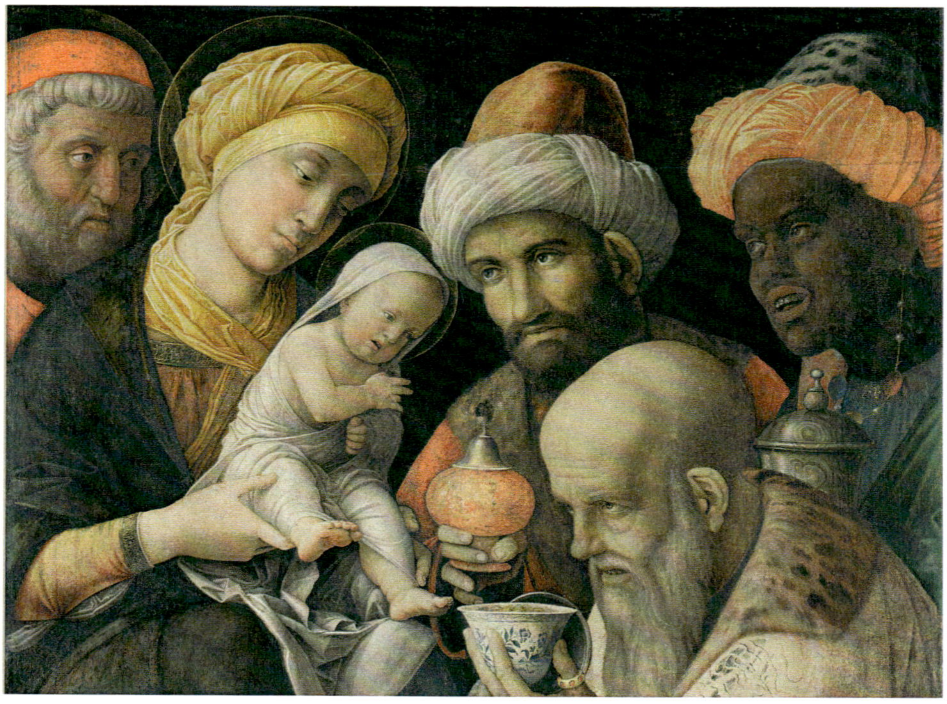

Plate 8.3 Andrea Mantegna (1431–1506), *Adoration of the Magi*, 1495–1505, Italy. Distemper on linen, height 48.6cm, width 65.6cm. The J. Paul Getty Museum, 85.PA.417

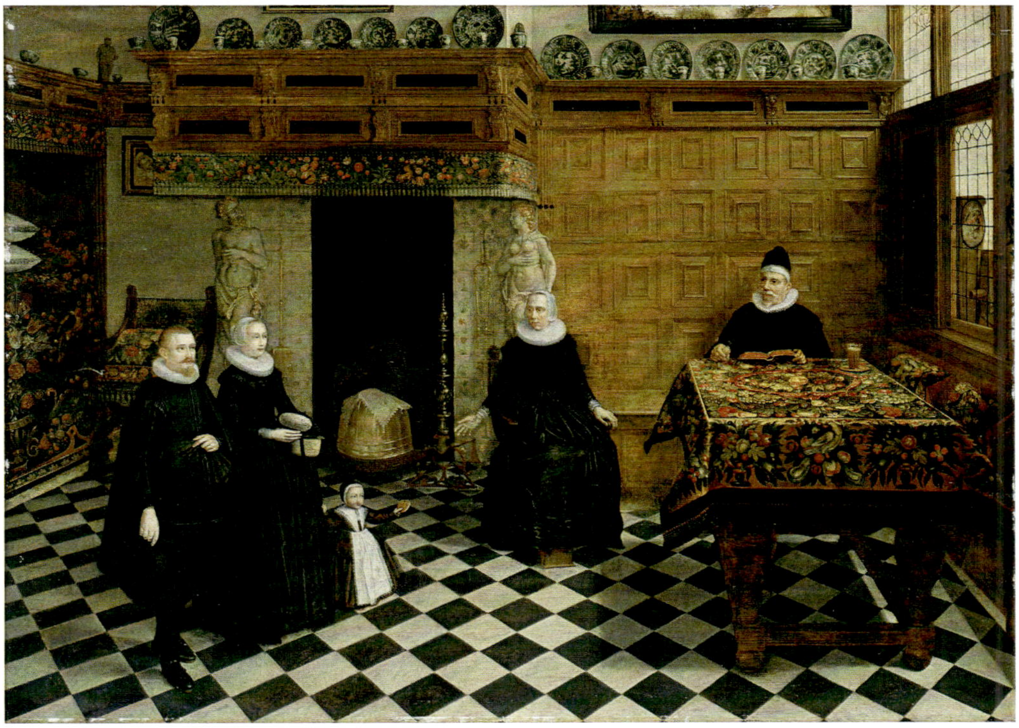

Plate 8.5 Anonymous, *The Visit*, *c.* 1630–5, Dutch school, Enkhuizen. Oil on wood, height 85.7cm, width 117.6cm. Museum of Art and History, Geneva, Dépôt de la Fondation Lucien Baszanger, Genève, 1967 (inv. no. BASZ 0005)

Vietnamese ceramics are putty coloured and no example of this form has been excavated to date.[11]

By the end of the Ming, Chinese porcelain was flooding into Europe, first Portugal and Spain, and later into Holland and England. It became commonplace in middle-class homes, as we see in this anonymous Dutch School oil painting, *The Visit*, of 1630–5 (**Pl. 8.5**). Here a family is depicted in an interior with black and white chequered tiles, wood panelling, tapestries and a frieze of blue-and-white *kraak* porcelain[12] on a shelf at the top of the wall. The enormous amount of porcelain vessels recovered from the Dutch East India Company testifies to the scale of the later Ming trade.[13] Chinese porcelain is never portrayed as a present for Christ in European paintings of the later Ming period, from the 1550s to 1640s. By this time it was not a magical treasure but a high-quality luxury good. It was no longer exclusively owned by aristocrats who received gifts from African and Middle Eastern courts, but was also in the possession of members of the middle classes who acquired it at auction from sales of vast cargoes shipped directly from China.[14] Some porcelains of the late Ming that were made exclusively for European customers with coats of arms or in European shapes appear in lavish still-life oil paintings (**Pl. 8.6**), such as a famous *Pronkstilleven* ('ornate still life') of 1638 by Willem Claesz Heda (1594–1680).[15] Here, Chinese porcelain is simply a luxury vessel in which to serve small fish alongside other Ming porcelain vessels used to serve wine. Its status has dramatically declined.

Beyond Europe, in the Middle East the status of Chinese porcelain was similarly high in the early Ming. It was considered to be a suitable gift for kings, as we can see in this courtly scene in a garden, made in about 1444 (**Pl. 8.7**). This album painting shows three kneeling Ming courtiers at the Timurid court and four Persian men carrying tables laden with early Ming porcelains, which perhaps had been presented as courtly gifts. The scene is from the *Shahnama* (*Book of Kings*), the Iranian national epic poem that combines legend and historical fact to tell the stories of Persian history from the earliest times to the Arab invasions of 651.[16] The *Shahnama* is not only great literature, but demonstrates the importance of political legitimacy and correct political behaviour. Illustrated manuscripts of the *Shahnama* exist in every style of Persian painting from 1330 onwards.[17]

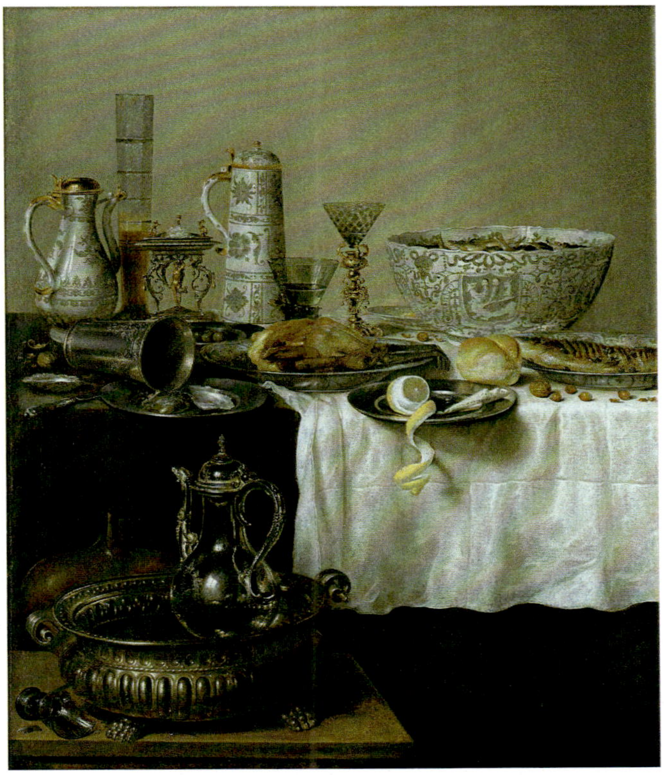

Plate 8.6 Willem Claesz Heda (1594–1680), *Breakfast Still Life*, dated 1638. Oil on canvas, height 118.4cm, width 97.5cm. Hamburger Kunsthalle, Hamburg, Inv.: 5504

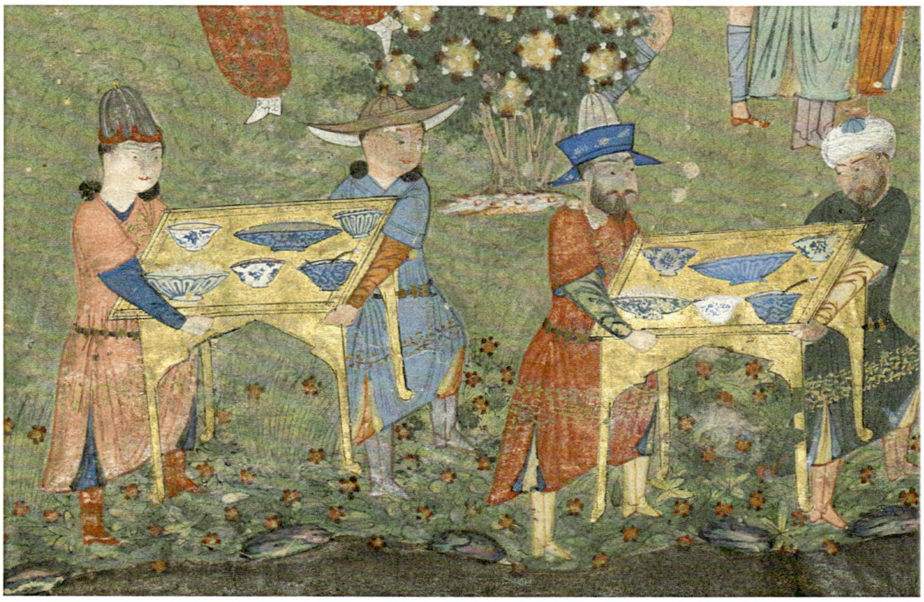

Plate 8.7 A courtly scene in a garden (detail), left folio of a double-page frontispiece (recto) illustration from the *Shahnama* (*Book of Kings*) of Abu'l-Qasim Manur Firdawsi (*c.* 934–*c.* 1020), *c.* 1444. Shiraz, Iran. Opaque watercolour, gold and silver on paper, height 32.7cm, width 22cm. Cleveland Museum of Art, 1956.10

From Samarqand to Vietnam, imitations in local materials are indications of the status of these blue-and-white materials in non-Chinese court contexts. A Timurid example in the Ulugh Beg Observatory Museum in Samarqand precisely copies Yongle era designs derived from small-format fan or album leaf paintings of a bird on a flowering branch.[18] Copies made in Vietnam between 1430 and 1480 can be even closer to the Ming originals, as demonstrated by the close comparison between a Vietnamese bowl decorated with a blue-and-white dragon and made in the Red River delta kilns, now in the Metropolitan Museum of Art, and the Chinese Xuande original on which it is based, an example of which is in the British Museum.[19]

Given the high status of early Ming blue-and-white porcelain in 15th-century Europe, the Middle East and Southeast Asia, what was the situation in China itself? In popular discourse blue-and-white has been associated directly with the personal use of the early Ming emperors.[20] However, the reality may be very different, and perhaps blue-and-white, while ordered for court use, was not actually used by the emperor personally at all, and was instead used for palace decoration and distribution to princes, high-ranking palace eunuchs and loyal ministers. To support this idea, I offer three observations: the first on reign marks; the second on the absence of blue-and-white in direct association with the emperor; and the third, visual evidence of the actual use of blue-and-white in the early Ming.

The first observation is about marks. A legible clerical script was used in the Yongle and Xuande eras between 1403 and 1435 to mark textiles, bronzes, cloisonné and lacquer wares. An impressive embroidered tangka, measuring over three metres in height and more than two metres in width, with a Yongle presentation mark, depicting Rakta Yamari and his consort trampling on the Lord of Death, was kept in the Jokhang (ཇོ་ཁང) Monastery, Lhasa.[21] Bronze ritual objects

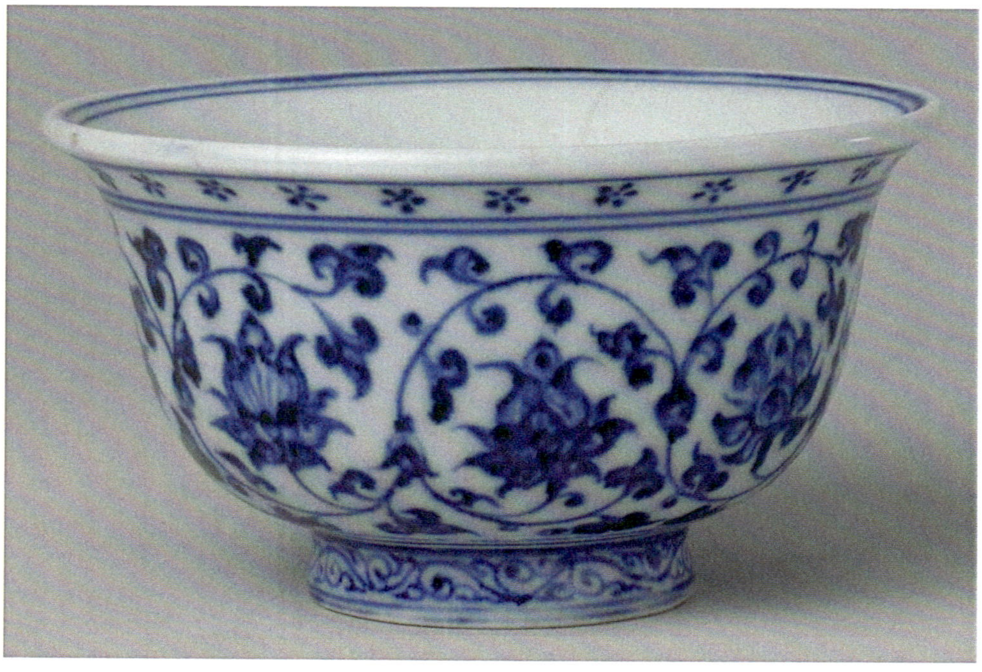

Plate 8.8 Blue-and-white porcelain cup, *yashou bei* 壓手杯. Yongle mark and period, 1403–24, Jingdezhen. Height 4.9cm, diameter 9.2cm. The Palace Museum, Beijing

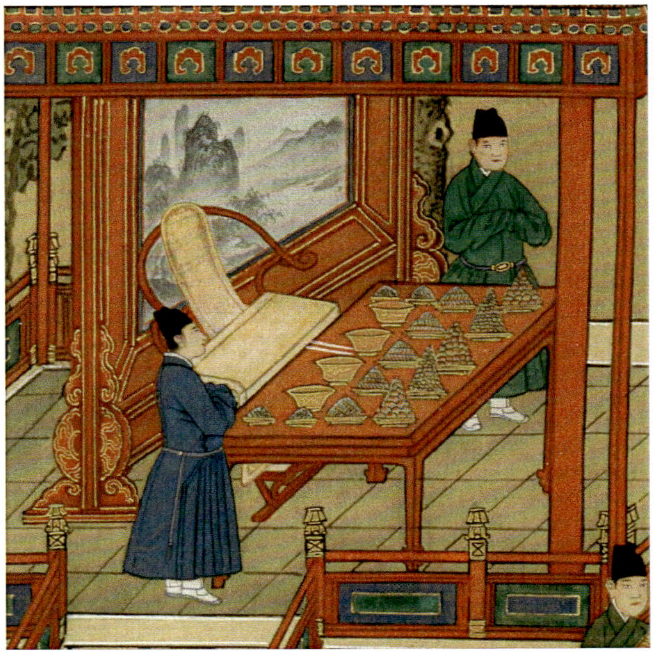

Plate 8.9 Anonymous, *Amusements in the Xuande Emperor's Palace* (*Zhu Zhanji xingle tu* 朱瞻基行樂圖), detail showing food table. Xuande period, 1426–35, or Chenghua period, 1465–87. Handscroll, ink and colours on silk, image height 36.6cm, length 687cm, with mount, height 38.5cm, length 1044cm. The Palace Museum, Beijing

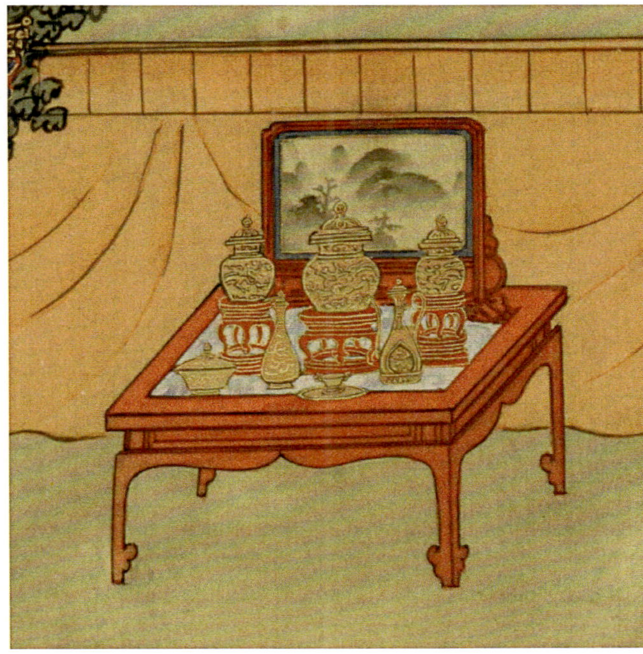

Plate 8.10 Anonymous, *Amusements in the Xuande Emperor's Palace* (*Zhu Zhanji xingle tu* 朱瞻基行樂圖), detail showing drink table. Xuande period, 1426–35, or Chenghua period, 1465–87. Handscroll, ink and colours on silk, image height 36.6cm, length 687cm; with mount, height 38.5cm, length 1044cm. The Palace Museum, Beijing

such as demon-quelling staffs (*khaṭvāṅga*) were sometimes marked in a four-character Yongle seal script.[22] Bronze sculptures were marked either with the character 'to present' (*shi* 施) or the character meaning 'made' (*zhi* 製).[23] These marks were frequently copied.[24] No Yongle marked cloisonné pieces survive but there are several examples with Xuande marks.[25] Lacquer pieces marked with both types of inscription were presented by the imperial court to other courts both within China and abroad. For example, a gift from the Ming court to the Ashikaga shoguns of Japan is recorded in the well-known inventory of 1403, which lists 58 items that were diplomatic gifts, including carved red lacquer.[26]

Very few genuine examples of underglaze blue Yongle marks survive. There are three blue-and-white cups in the Palace Museum, Beijing, known as *yashou bei* 壓手杯 (**Pl. 8.8**).[27] There are a few others of this type worldwide, but they are very rare. What is surprising is that their four-character Yongle marks are written in a clerical script. All other marked porcelains of this period are marked with an archaic seal script mark, the form of which connects the Yongle emperor with China's ancient past, perhaps helping to legitimise his position as ruler. This disparity probably means that blue-and-white porcelain was considered less important than the copper-reds and 'sweet white' wares, which use an archaic seal script for their date mark.[28] Marks on porcelain are, of course, introduced in the Yongle reign.[29] There are no genuine reign marks of the Ming founder, the Hongwu emperor. It is typical of the Yongle emperor's desire to legitimise his position and proclaim his authority that he should have begun a tradition that would last until the end of the imperial era.

A second observation relates to the emperors' personal use of blue-and-white in the early 1400s.We know the copper-red and pure white vessels were used for rituals,[30] but what about the vessels used in the emperor's own dining practices? Here it will be suggested that blue-and-white was used for palace ornament, palace entertainment and palace gifts, but that the emperor himself did not use it at all. Although the material evidence is slim, it does tend to support this argument.

One Ming court painting shows a wonderful banquet for one (**Pl. 8.9**), prepared for the emperor, who is depicted pitching arrows into a golden pot while he is watched by his personal palace attendants. They hold red lacquer trays filled with snacks, and gold decanters to pour wine into a gold cup. This scene appears towards the end of a scroll that has already depicted the emperor playing and watching archery, polo and a form of mini-golf. After these exertions he needed a hearty meal. The table is set with 14 golden food dishes piled high, and in front of these dishes are four gold bowls, perhaps containing other delicacies or soups. There is just one pair of gold chopsticks, of the kind excavated from the tomb of Prince Zhuang of Liang 梁莊王 (1411–41) and his wife Lady Wei 魏 (d. 1451), but there is no blue-and-white porcelain visible.[31]

The nearby drinks table (**Pl. 8.10**) has three jars for wine on red lacquer stands, a covered mixing bowl, a wine bottle, cup and decanter. These are decorated with designs of dragons among clouds, but they are all made of gold. The detailing is very specific. The lacquer table is inlaid with a multi-colour stone top in the same style as the four tables buried in Prince Huang of Lu's 魯荒王 (1370–89) tomb in Shandong.[32] The texture of the curtains, the leaves of the trees and the ground are all carefully depicted, and the very blue pigment needed to represent blue-and-white is used as a border in the stone screen behind the vessels. Yet there are no blue-and-white porcelains here. The gold vessel forms that are shown on the lacquer table are all familiar to us

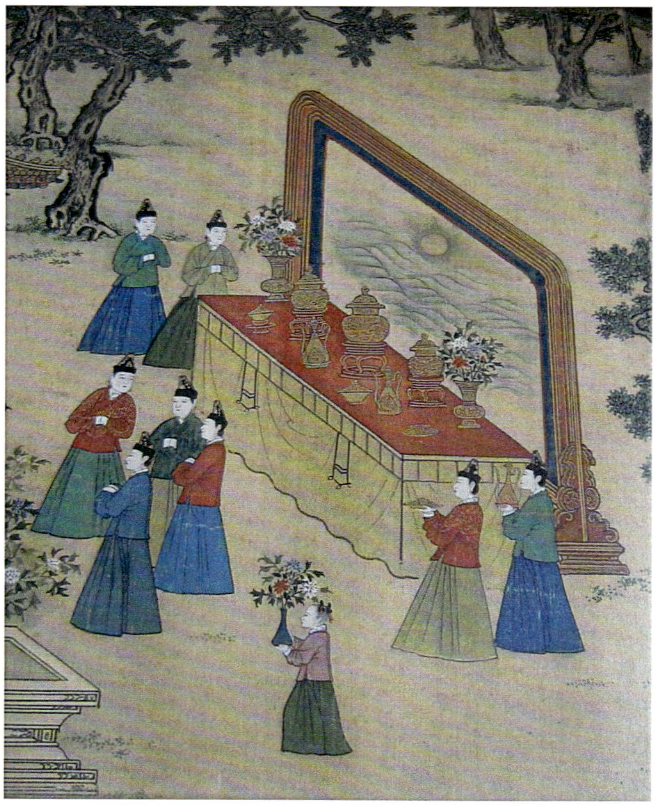

Plate 8.11 Detail of palace women serving drinks in gold vessels from *Amusements in the Four Seasons* (*Siji shangwan tu* 四季賞玩圖), c. 1426–84, Beijing. Handscroll, ink and colours on silk, height 35cm, width 780cm. Private collection

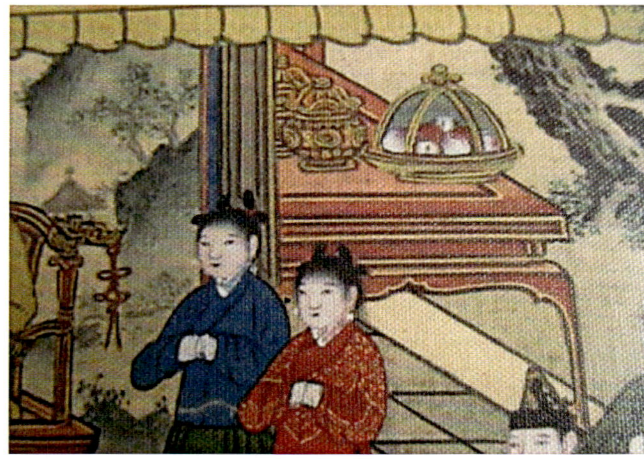

Plate 8.12 Detail of vessels on the table with cover from *Amusements in the Four Seasons* (*Siji shangwan tu* 四季賞玩圖), c. 1426–84, Beijing. Handscroll, ink and colours on silk, height 35cm, width 780cm. Private collection

from blue-and-white wine vessels. In other words, the court artist had the skill to represent blue-and-white, and the vessels existed at the time. They are absent from this picture because they were not for the emperor's own use and therefore not required on his personal drinks table.

This painting is not unique, and if we look at another three handscrolls depicting palace amusements we see the same situation. Drinking and eating vessels for the emperor's own use are depicted in a detail showing palace women serving drinks (**Pl. 8.11**), but again the vessels shown are gold and not blue-and-white. The stem cup with cover and stand could have been painted in blue-and-white. Plenty of blue-and-white examples of this form survive. Two blue-and-white stem cups were excavated at the tomb of Prince Zhuang of Liang, one with a dragon and one with a scene of court ladies.[33] So we can see that blue-and-white porcelain is suitable for a princely court, but not for the emperor himself. In place of blue-and-white the emperor is served either with gold or perhaps even with a 'sweet white' glazed stem cup.

Other blue-and-white vessels in the tomb of Prince Zhuang of Liang are not for the personal use of the prince but for storage, as is evidenced by four large blue-and-white jars.[34] The other stem cups in the tomb were white wares with dragons, originally gilded, whose designs were free from glaze and so fired orangey-red.[35] The *jue* 爵 cups on the silver tray from the same tomb could well have been made in porcelain. Both white and blue-and-white versions exist in heirloom collections and have been excavated,[36] but here higher status materials – silver and gold – are used instead.[37] Clearly, ritual vessels were governed by sumptuary laws.

If we go back to the imperial court, a detail from the scroll painting of *Amusements in the Four Seasons* shows the emperor watching a group of eunuchs gathering lotus flowers from a boat in a palace lake, with refreshments of wine and food kept ready behind a screen (**Pl. 8.12**). Again, all of the vessels used to hold the wine and food are gold; there is no blue-and-white. Gold wine jars are shown and a large serving dish filled with peaches is either white ware or more probably gold, but it is certainly not blue-and-white porcelain, even though these shapes existed in that material. The dish covers shown in this detail are a reminder of the imperfect impression that we have from the materials that have been handed down to us. Although the early Ming gives us more information than earlier eras, we are still without so much of the organic and fragile material which would provide a more complete picture.

The third observation offered here relates to how blue-and-white porcelain was used. It is not the case that the emperors did not have blue-and-white in the palace – quite the reverse. However, it is here proposed that they neither drank nor ate from blue-and-white, but instead ordered it for their vast households and for enormous banquets they held. Reading descriptions of the tribute missions or the orchestrated rituals,[38] one is overwhelmed by a sense of the sheer number of people who would have needed official hospitality. This then makes sense when we read about the vast orders completed by the kilns in Jingdezhen.

From details in these imperial amusement paintings, we can see blue-and-white porcelain being used for garden furnishings such as barrel seats and flower pots (**Pl. 8.13**). Blue-and-white flower pots of the early Ming have been excavated (**Pl. 8.14**); they must have been used to decorate the palace in the same way as Jun ware flower pots.[39] Blue-and-white porcelain overall played an important role in decorating the new palace in Beijing, both in its interiors and its gardens. Dozens of large tanks for rearing fish and water plants would have been positioned inside and outside in the Forbidden City, although few survive today.[40] Even the smallest palace environment had blue-and-white, including tiny bird feeders for water and hemp seeds or cricket cages.[41]

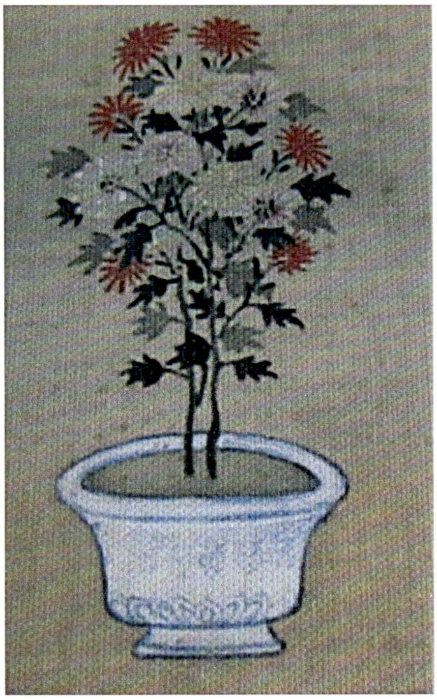

Plate 8.13 Detail of blue-and-white flower pot from *Amusements in the Four Seasons* (*Siji shangwan tu* 四季賞玩圖), *c.* 1426–84, Beijing. Handscroll, ink and colours on silk, height 35cm, width 780cm. Private collection

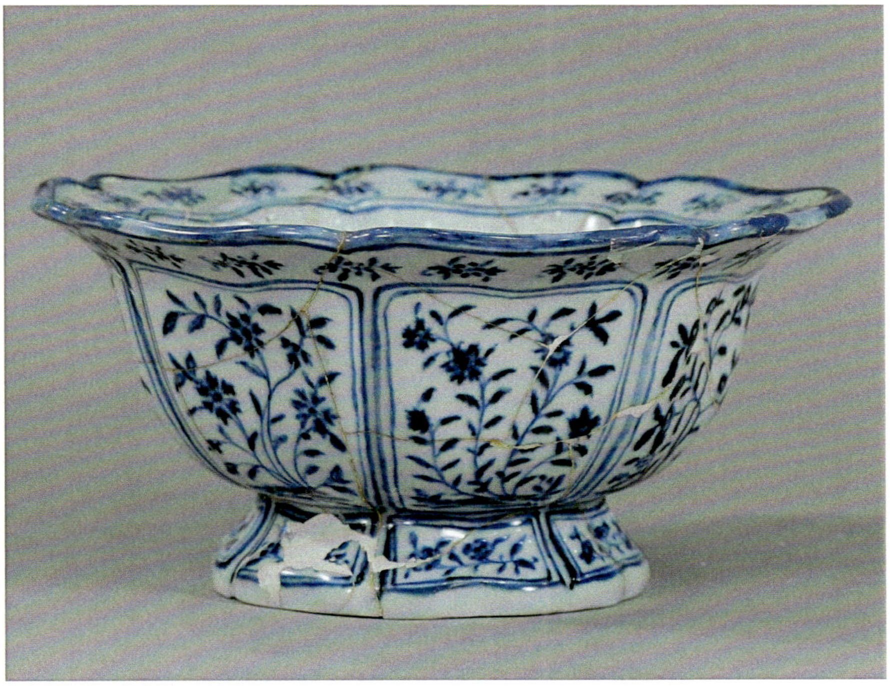

Plate 8.14 Blue-and-white porcelain flower pot excavated from Jingdezhen, Xuande period, 1426–35. Height 12.4cm, diameter 24.4cm. Jingdezhen Institute of Ceramic Archaeology, Jingdezhen, Jiangxi province

Of course, all this blue-and-white porcelain was produced under court orders. The designs on beautiful Yongle period vessels are entirely derived from small-format court paintings, perhaps for album leaves or fans. They are, it must be stressed, a new invention of the Yongle era. The clay body is made in a new way, as is the glaze, and the vessels are fired to new, higher temperatures, creating glossier glazes. The range of novel shapes in the early 1400s is extraordinary, many of them derived from the forms of Central Asian or Middle Eastern metalwork, glass and jade. Whether this new cosmopolitan style was a result of the international sea voyages or land tribute missions, or whether it was a response to objects left behind by the Mongol court which were then copied, is still uncertain. Many of these forms must have been purely decorative, even if the original on which they were based was not.

Plate 8.15 Detail of the brazier and monochromes from *Lantern Festival Celebrated in Emperor Xianzong (Chenghua)'s Palace* (*Xianzong yuanxiao xingle tu* 憲宗元宵行樂圖), dated 1485, Beijing. Handscroll, ink and colours on silk, height 37cm, length 624cm. National Museum of China

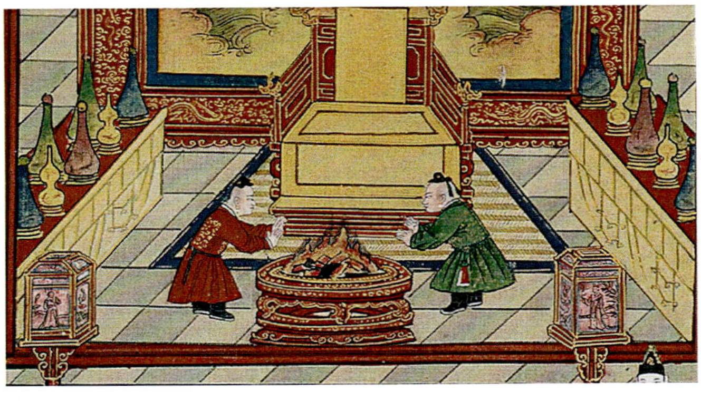

Palace ceramics were colourful in the 1400s and many of the types represented in the paintings do not survive at all, although we know that the glazes could be achieved. A detail of the National Museum of China's painting of the palace enjoying the lantern festival (**Pl. 8.15**) has a vivid scene of two boy eunuchs warming their hands over a coal-burning brazier. On either side of them are long tables with symmetrical arrangements of porcelain vases glazed in single colours – red, yellow, blue and green. They are catching the reflection of the flames in their glazes. Coloured vases are known from later periods but have not survived

Plate 8.16 Detail of pedlars from *Lantern Festival Celebrated in Emperor Xianzong (Chenghua)'s Palace* (*Xianzong yuanxiao xingle tu* 憲宗元宵行樂圖), dated 1485, Beijing. Handscroll, ink and colours on silk, height 37cm, length 624cm. National Museum of China

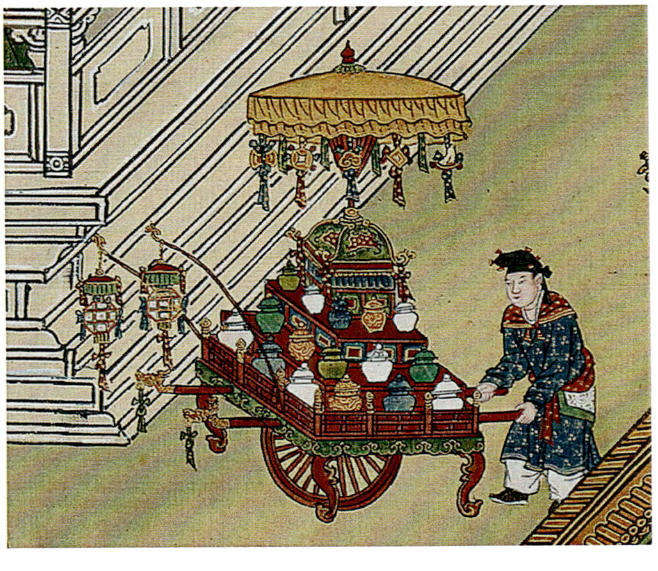

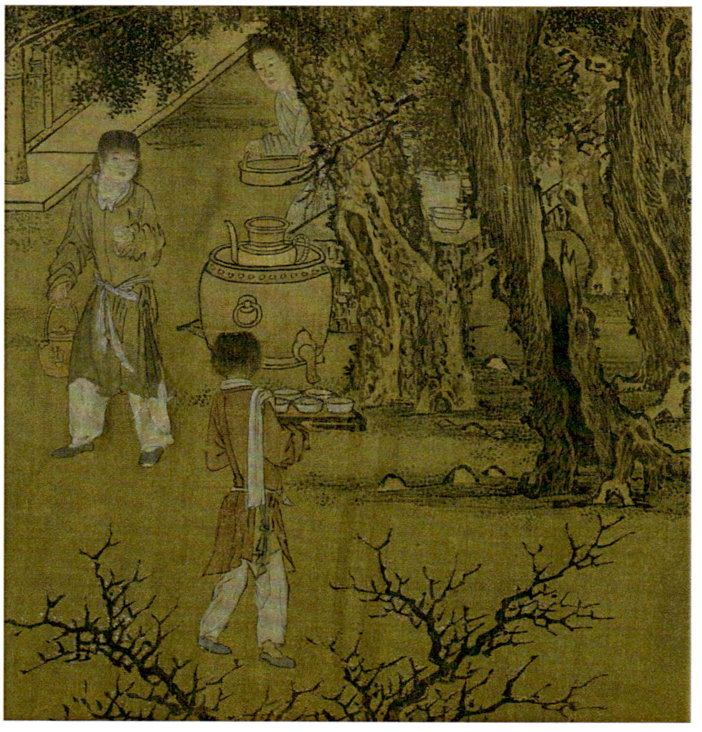

Plate 8.17 Detail of wine vessels in *Elegant Gathering in the Apricot Garden* (*Xingyuan yaji tu* 杏園雅集圖), dated 1437, Beijing. Handscroll, ink and colours on silk, height 37.5cm, width 240.7cm. Metropolitan Museum of Art, New York, Purchase, the Dillon Fund Gift 1989 (1989.141.3)

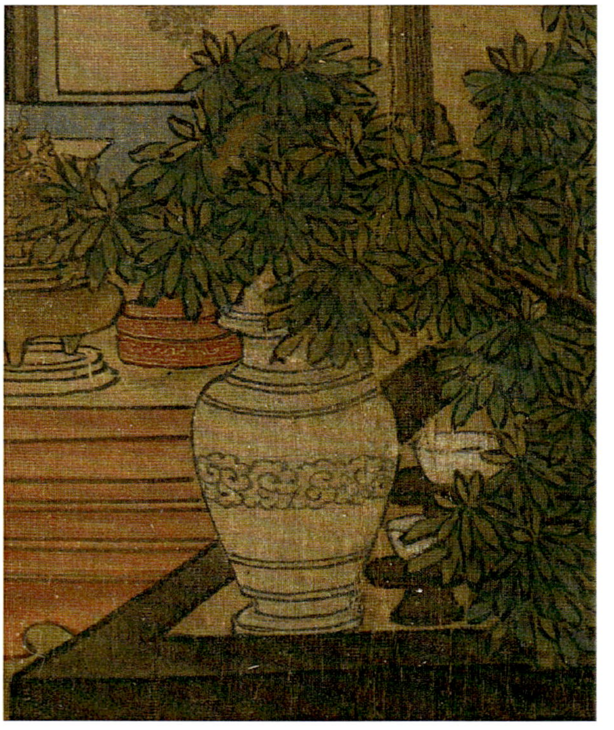

Plate 8.18 Detail of blue-and-white jar in *Elegant Gathering in the Apricot Garden* (*Xingyuan yaji tu* 杏園雅集圖), dated 1437, Beijing. Handscroll, ink and colours on silk, height 37.5cm, width 240.7cm. Metropolitan Museum of Art, New York, Purchase, the Dillon Fund Gift 1989 (1989.141.3)

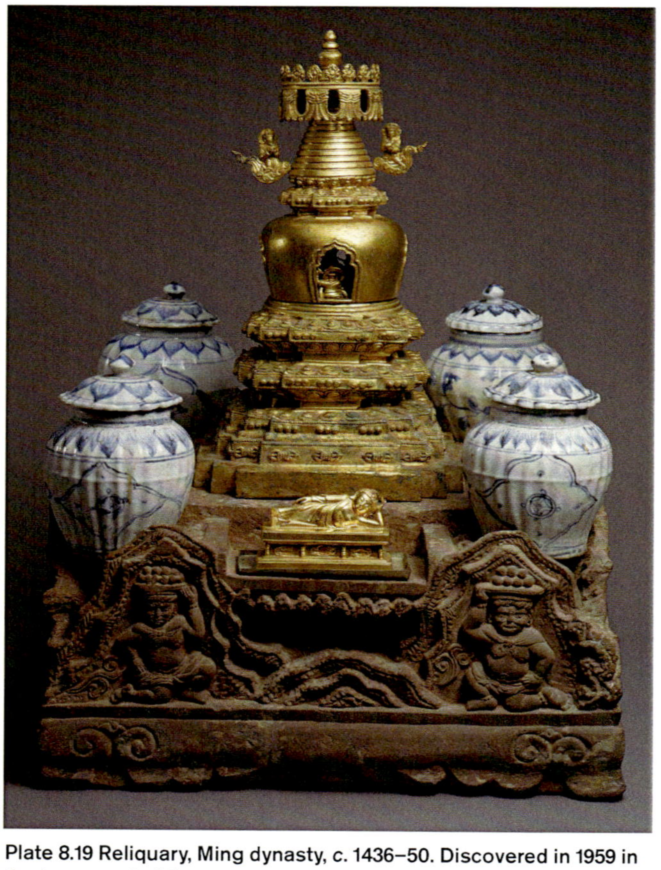

Plate 8.19 Reliquary, Ming dynasty, *c.* 1436–50. Discovered in 1959 in the basement of the stupa at Hongjue Temple, Niushoushan, Nanjing, Jiangsu province. Gilt bronze, height 32.7cm. Nanjing Museum

from this era in these shapes, although vessels with these glazes in other shapes are known.

The court aesthetic of Ming China in the early 15th century favoured overall patterns, exuberance and bright colours. We see this in the furnishings and fabrics for daily court use, not to mention the scarlet pillars and buttercup-yellow roof tiles of the Forbidden City. Broken pots, excavated at Jingdezhen, all date to the Yongle era and demonstrate the range of colour combinations experimented with at that time.[42] Many of the colour combinations that we associate with the 16th century were in fact already in use in the early 15th century. We also know from surviving pieces that these new colours – emerald green, coffee brown, sky blue – were made in the early Ming. Purple and sky-blue vessels in a range of table wares were made at Juntai in early Ming shapes, as well as flower pots of the same colours. It is the full range of shapes which has not survived, skewing our understanding of the material culture of the period.

For the festivals, eunuchs dressed up as itinerant salesmen (**Pl. 8.16**) so that the imperial household could play at shopping. Ceramics and other collectables were brought in to the palace. These would have included items from other kilns, such as Longquan, which produced goods both for the court and for the local market in the 1400s,[43] and their Jingdezhen copies.[44] Very little that was new in the way of ceramic technology was invented after the Yongle era until we reach the 18th century.

Finally, it is worth noting that we do see blue-and-white ceramics depicted in non-imperial contexts of the early Ming. In a scene of the scroll, *Elegant Gathering in the Apricot Garden*, of 1437 (see **Pl. 11.1**), male and female servants prepare wine and snacks for the three Yangs, who represent

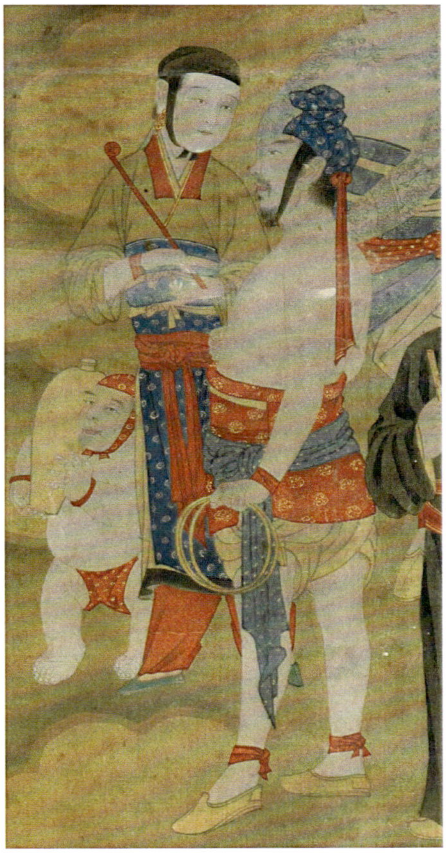

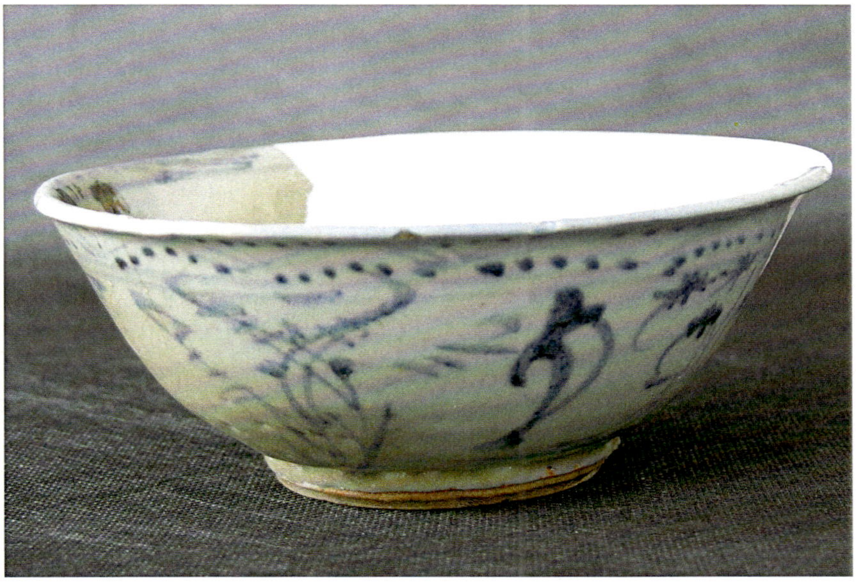

Plate 8.20 (left) Detail from *Assembly of Artists and Scholars of Various Talents and Schools of Former Times* (*Wanggu jiuliu baijia zhu shi yishu zhong* 往古九流百家諸士藝術眾), *c.* 1459, Shanxi or Beijing. Hanging scroll, ink, colours and gold on silk, Image: height 118cm, width 61.5cm; with mount: height 190cm, width 89cm. Shanxi Museum, from Baoningsi, Youyu county

Plate 8.21 (above) Blue-and-white porcelain bowl, early 15th century. Height 5.8cm, diameter 14.4cm. Nanjing Shipyard Museum

the power behind the child Zhengtong emperor. They are served wine in white porcelain bowls, but use blue-and-white storage jars from which the wine is decanted (**Pl. 8.17**). On another table in the painting is a blue-and-white jar next to two cups on lacquer stands (**Pl. 8.18**). So this material does appear on the drinks tables of powerful bureaucrats.

In addition to pictorial evidence, at least one actual surviving example shows the relationship between blue-and-white ceramics and a powerful (but non-imperial) individual close to the court. This gilt-bronze miniature *dagoba*, the Himalayan form of an Indian stupa, contains the reliquary in the centre (**Pl. 8.19**). The four blue-and-white porcelain jars around it are for storing fragrant herbs. Li Tong 李童 (d. 1453), a court eunuch who served as Director of Imperial Accoutrements under the Xuande emperor, donated this reliquary, under his Buddhist name Li Fushan 李福善, to the Hongjuesi 宏覺寺 (Monastery of Vast Awakening) at Mount Niushou 牛首山 near Nanjing, as an act of perpetual offering.[45] Li Tong was also the principal patron of the Fahaisi 法海寺 (Monastery of the Sea of the Law) in the western suburbs of Beijing.[46] As head of the Department of Imperial Accoutrements, he was able to bring together the work of the finest imperial craftsmen working in clay, stone and metal.

Very few representations of ordinary people in the early 15th century exist from China, and even fewer of the objects they owned. Ceramics do however appear in the *Shuilu* set of ritual paintings from Shanxi. An amusing example of this is an acrobatic act showing a strong man, a woman and a dwarf holding a porcelain vase (**Pl. 8.20**), part of an act (still being performed in 2011 in Shanghai) in which the small man tosses the vase into the air from the top of a human pyramid and catches it without breaking it. Another man in this group, who is tattooed all over with blue dragons, prompts further thoughts about the exclusivity of that imperial emblem. At the Nanjing shipyards, some poor-quality blue-and-white porcelain has been excavated (**Pl. 8.21**) dating to the early 1400s,[47] suggesting that low-quality blue-and-white wares fired at non-imperial kilns were available on the open market. High-quality products were tightly controlled by the court.

To conclude, in the 15th century outside China – in Europe, the Middle East and Southeast Asia – Ming blue-and-white porcelain was regarded as an extremely high-status commodity. In the 16th and 17th centuries it was still a luxury, if one of widespread reach. In China, the picture may well be very different, and perhaps blue-and-white, while ordered for court use, was not actually used by the emperor personally and was instead utilised as a palace ornament or for items for broader court use. This attitude to ceramics once again connects the early Ming to the Yuan period.[48] It may be that while in Europe blue-and-white porcelain was initially regarded literally as a gift fit for God, in China itself it was not regarded as being fit for use by the Son of Heaven.

Notes

1 Pierson 2013, 57–80 explores the idea of 'Ming vases' and their pricelessness.
2 Brook 2010, 219.
3 http://news.nationalpost.com/2014/07/24/chinese-billionaire-liu-yiqian-sparks-outrage-by-drinking-out-of-500-year-old-chicken-cup-worth-38m/.
4 Spriggs 1965.
5 Martin 2001.

6 For an overview of Yongle and Xuande porcelain see Harrison-Hall 2001, 93–142. For an almost identical Xuande period blue-and-white pot see Pierson 2004, 46, no. 681, and for a Yongzheng Qing copy see Pierson 2004, 111, no. C.649.
7 Carr 1997.
8 Carr 1997, 82.
9 Chang Foundation 1998, cat. 53, 59 and 230, which illustrates a Xuande mark and period one and discusses Yongle versions.
10 An example in the British Museum donated by Dale and Patricia Keller is Asia 2010,3007.31; see also Goddio, Pierson and Crick 2000.
11 Guy and Stevenson 1997; for excavations of 15th-century Vietnamese blue-and-white bowls see Bui Minh Tri and Nguyen-Long 2001, 218–20.
12 Canepa 2008; Rinaldi 1989; Canepa 2015.
13 van der Pijl-Ketel 2008, 65–76.
14 Ströber 2013. Thijs Weststeijn has a different argument about this in Weststeijn 2014.
15 Spriggs 1965; Corrigan, van Campen and Dierks 2015, 264–7.
16 Roxburgh 2005; Hillenbrand 2004.
17 Titley 1977.
18 Carswell 2000, 100, fig. 108.
19 Harrison-Hall 2014, 60, figs 6–7.
20 Ming wares commissioned by the courts are often associated with the emperors' personal use or taste perhaps to lend them greater public appeal. See Krahl 1995.
21 Hong Kong Urban Council *et al.* 1995, cat. 25; Henss 1997.
22 For examples in the Metropolitan Museum of Art see no. 2015.500.6.28; Watt and Leidy 2005, 74; and in the British Museum see Clunas and Harrison-Hall 2014, 231, fig. 202.
23 von Schroeder 2001.
24 For Xuande bronzes with later marks see Lu Pengliang 2014.
25 On cloisonné see Quette 2011, and Brinker and Lutz 1989.
26 Figgess 1962–3.
27 For an example in the Palace Museum see Geng Baochang 2002, 128–9; see also Geng Baochang 1993, 29 for an original Yongle example and two copies.
28 For excavated examples of Yongle marked white wares see Chang Foundation 1996, cat. 110; and for Yongle marked copper-reds see Beijing daxue kaogu wenbo xueyuan 2007, 20, fig. 50.
29 Bruce Rusk, 'Reignmakers: Ming Imperial Production and Its Imitators', China Project Workshop, Institute of Fine Arts, New York University, November 2011.
30 On the use of ceramics for new ritual use in the early Ming, see discussion by Shih Ching-fei in Chapter 13 of this book.
31 Hubei sheng wenwu kaogu yanjiusuo and Zhongxiang shi bowuguan 2007, 35–6.
32 Shandong bowuguan and Shandong sheng kaogu yanjiusuo 2014, col. pls 92–5.
33 Hubei sheng wenwu kaogu yanjiusuo and Zhongxiang shi bowuguan 2007, 75–80.
34 Hubei sheng wenwu kaogu yanjiusuo and Zhongxiang shi bowuguan 2007, 72–3.
35 Hubei sheng wenwu kaogu yanjiusuo and Zhongxiang shi bowuguan 2007, 85.
36 White *jue* excavated in 1982: see Shoudu bowuguan 2007, cat. 18. Blue-and-white *jue* and mountain stand made in the Yongle period are in the National Palace Museum; another was excavated in 1999 and is now in the Jingdezhen Institute of Ceramic Archaeology: see Liang Sui 1999, 132.
37 Clunas 1987, 83–7.
38 Roxburgh 2010; Thackston 2001.
39 Gugong bowuyuan 2013; Eskenazi Ltd 2013.
40 Pierson 2004, 34.
41 Liu Xinyuan 1995; for bird feeders see Chang Foundation 1998, 230–9.
42 Chang Foundation 1996.
43 Ye Yingting and Hua Yunong 2005; Zhejiang sheng wenwu kaogu yanjiusuo *et al.* 2009.
44 For Xuande period Jingdezhen-made copies of Longquan celadons see Liang Sui 1999, 249–55.
45 McLoughlin 2014, 44.
46 Toyka 2014, 73–150.
47 Nanjing shi bowuguan 2006, col. pl. 29, nos 4, 5.
48 Shi Jingfei 2003; Gerritsen 2012.

Chapter 9
Zhu Quan, A Prince who Changed Ming Musical History

Joseph S.C. Lam

Zhu Quan 朱權 (1378–1448) may have been a loser in early Ming politics but arguably won lasting renown through the role he played in musical transformations in the empire's second century.[1] Manipulated to support his elder brother Zhu Di's 朱棣 (1360–1424) capture of the Ming throne, and dispatched in 1403 to live as a prince (*wang* 王) under court surveillance in peripheral Nanchang 南昌 in Jiangxi province, Zhu Quan could not act on centre stage in Ming culture and politics during the critical years of 1400–50. However, he exercised his princely power and resources to continue and change the performing arts of the period, shaping their subsequent developments and interpretations. He changed Ming musical history.

Zhu Quan is now a seminal figure in Chinese cultural and musical history. Many scholars have examined his biography and legacy, and in particular, his treatises on early Ming drama and music.[2] Few, however, have discussed how he actually received, developed and transmitted the performing arts of his time.[3] Many questions remain to be answered. For example, what and how do his palace poetry (*gongci* 宮詞), dramatic scripts, theoretical treatises and *qin* 琴 (seven-string zither) tablatures tell us about his artistic career and its historical significance?

Recently Yao Pinwen 姚品文, a leading Chinese scholar of Zhu Quan studies, has suggested that the prince engaged consciously in cultural construction and bequeathed a princely, if not imperial, legacy for posterity, transcending the political one that he was not destined to build.[4] Yao's suggestion is insightful and instructive, because it opens new possibilities for interpreting Zhu Quan's creativity and significance in Ming cultural and musical history. Elaborating on Yao's suggestion, this chapter argues that Zhu Quan strategically consumed and produced drama and music, not only as a creative and talented artist but also as an authoritarian and benevolent patron and disciplinarian. He effectively disciplined the performing arts of his time and shaped their subsequent developments.

To develop this interpretation of Zhu Quan's role in Chinese cultural and musical history, this chapter will examine his preserved works in the media of drama and music, identifying data on his consumption and production of early Ming performing arts, and demonstrating how he authentically continued with what his predecessors and contemporaries had established, and creatively transformed what he had appropriated into his personal statements. This is why and how he managed to bequeath to posterity a legacy that is artistically, biographically, culturally and historically representative and significant.

A precocious and productive prince

Born in 1378 as the 17th son of the Ming founder Zhu Yuanzhang 朱元璋 (1328–98), and dying in 1448, Zhu Quan lived a long and productive life.[5] Allegedly, he wrote, compiled or published more than a hundred works addressing a variety of topics in astronomy, Confucianism, Daoist liturgy, medicine, military crafts and the performing arts of literature, music and theatre. The majority of the prince's writings are now lost; much was allegedly destroyed during the imperial court's suppression of the 1519 rebellion that Zhu Chenhao 朱宸濠 (1479–1521),

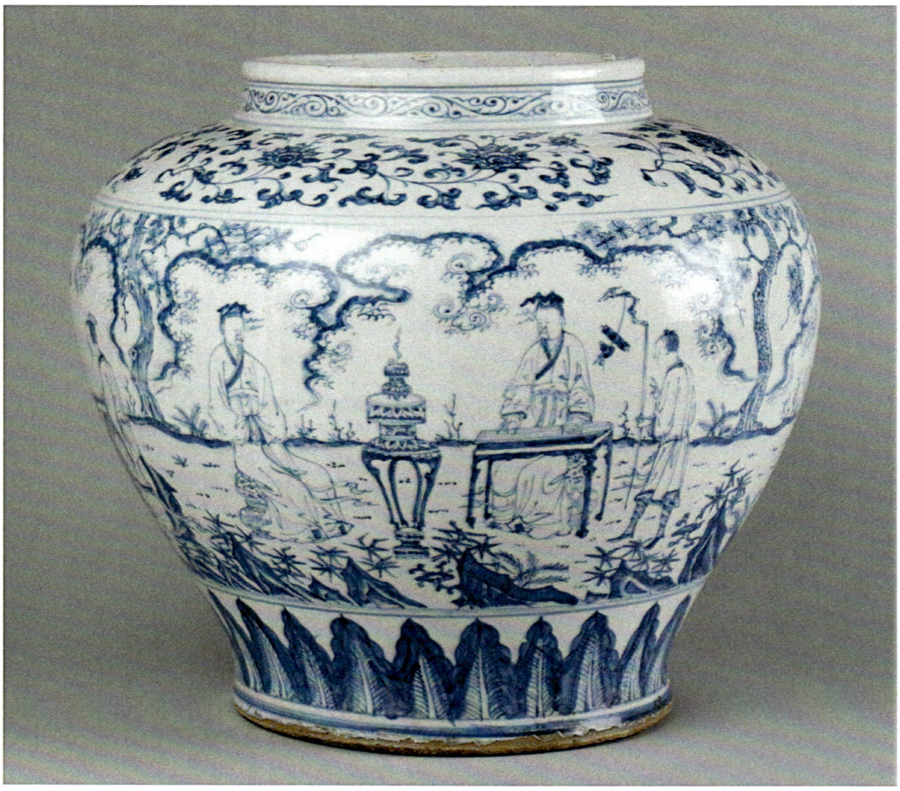

Plate 9.1 Wine jar showing a man playing a *qin*, Ming dynasty, 1436–49 (Zhengtong reign), Jingdezhen, Jiangxi province. Porcelain with underglaze cobalt-blue decoration, height 35.6cm, diameter 39.4cm. Victoria and Albert Museum, London, 6840-1860

Prince of Ning 寧王 and Zhu Quan's great-grandson, launched from Nanchang.[6] Judging from surviving works and the known titles of destroyed treatises, however, Zhu Quan wrote or finalised most of his writings after arriving at Nanchang in 1403 at the age of 26. Living an artistic and princely life there for 45 years, he produced a great deal; he obviously had all kinds of help from his artistic-cultural partners and servants.

As precocious as Zhu Quan was, he would hardly have figured as a mature producer and consumer of drama and music before his arrival in Nanchang. As a young and ambitious prince actively involved in military and political affairs around the struggles for the Ming throne, he would not have had the erudition and time required to comprehensively and effectively develop his artistic and scholarly enterprise. As described by Yao Pinwen, Zhu Quan's *Tongjian bolun* 通鑒博論 (*A General Discussion of Dynastic Histories*) and *Han Tang mishi* 漢唐秘史 (*A Secret History of the Han and Tang Dynasties*) are more educational and historical exercises than original and substantive treatises.[7] And as his reconstructed bibliography shows, more than half of his writings address Daoist topics. Only after 1403 did he become an active Daoist.

Among Zhu Quan's preserved works, three are now studied as historically significant works of Chinese drama, literature and music; these are the *Taihe zhengyinpu* 太和正音譜 (*A Formulary of Correct Tones for a Period of Great Harmony*, 1407),[8] the *Shenqi mipu* 神奇秘譜 (*A Treasured Score of Celestial and Distinctive Qin Compositions*, 1425)[9] and a series of over 70 palace poems (*c.* 1408).[10] Comprehensive and sophisticated in content and scope, these writings illustrate early Ming performing arts and artistic living with a degree of detail that few other contemporary documents provide, rendering it clear that Zhu Quan produced and consumed drama and music expressively and strategically.

Artistic and imperial upbringing

This strategic consumption was possible because he grew up as an artistic and scholarly man. Nurtured by an imperial father and educated by erudite teachers, he diligently and practically learned the craft of rulership. Having regularly participated in court, military and ritual exercises, the prince insightfully grasped artistic, intellectual and practical facets of civil and military arts. By the time he was dispatched, in 1393 at the age of 16, to preside at his assigned princedom in Daning 大寧, in present-day Inner Mongolia, Zhu Quan operated as a young, versatile and well-informed prince-general-artist-scholar. Supporting his overseeing of the princedom and furthering his artistic and intellectual education and pursuits was a critical group of scholar-officials, palace entertainers, servants and maids, in addition to recruited commoner artists and craftsmen.

That Zhu Quan grew up amid music is attested by his palace poems, or *gongci*. Around the year 1408, Zhu wrote a series of palace poems reflecting his experiences with music performed inside the palace. Poem 2 reports that orchestral music floated over palace halls and pavilions, and Poem 67 notes how processional music accompanied movements of imperial dignitaries.[11] Poem 4 notices how *qin* performers (**Pl. 9.1**) practised elegant music inside moonlit palace venues, while Poem 10 chronicles young palace maids learning to sing 'Picking Lotus' and other womanly songs. In a number of palace poems, Zhu Quan alludes to individual palace women playing the flute or *pipa* to enhance musically their feminine charm or lament their loneliness.

The genre of *gongci* is distinctive within Chinese poetry for highlighting imperial men's impressions of palace women's lives and sentiments. As a result, *gongci* ignores many other types of palace musical performances. For example, Zhu Quan's palace poems do not allude to musical performances of state sacrifices and state banquets held inside court and ritual sites, nor to the theatrical shows presented inside private mansions or wine parlors (*jiulou* 酒樓) and other public entertainment institutions of the capital.

As reported by official Ming documents such as the *Ming shi* 明史 (*History of the Ming*) and the *Da Ming huidian* 大明會典 (*Collected Statutes of the Great Ming*), the imperial Ming court enjoyed many musical performances by trained court musicians.[12] Zhu Yuanzhang promoted drama and music as a tool of governance and self-cultivation.[13] He instituted three court offices to handle ritual and entertainment music:[14] the Shenyueguan 神樂觀 (Imperial Music Office), the *Jiaofangsi* 教坊司 (Office of Entertainment Music) and the *Zhonggusi* 鐘鼓司 (Music Office of the Inner Court). Zhu Yuanzhang promoted not only Confucian *yayue* 雅樂 ('civilised music') but also current and vernacular operas, the exhortative functions of which he fully grasped and actively manipulated. Thus he had the *Pipaji* 琵琶記 (*The Lute*) regularly performed, promoting this drama about filial piety and other social virtues as a luxury necessary for elite and moral living.[15] To ensure his princes enjoyed and learned from performances of moral theatre, he dispatched them to their princedoms with copies of some 1,700 dramatic scripts.[16] To provide for official music performances within princedoms, he had them institute music offices with fixed numbers of performers: 36 musicians would perform at sacrificial rituals and 27 at formal banquets and other secular functions. In addition, each princedom would have two eunuch music officers whose job was to oversee musical entertainments inside princely palaces.[17] Early Ming regulations on music at the princedoms were official but idealistic. Entertainment and the musical needs of a princely household obviously demanded much more activity than that which two eunuch music officers could provide or oversee. Throughout the Ming dynasty, princely palaces self-indulgently, and even forcefully, recruited more local musicians than were officially allowed.[18] In other words, the dramatic-musical world of Ming China that Zhu Quan or any other Ming prince experienced was much more complex and expansive than the selective picture painted by his palace poetry.[19]

Moral plays and accurate lyrics

This princely musical experience nurtured Zhu Quan's personal creativity and strategic use of musical theatre to assert his artistic, Daoist and moralist self. He is known to have produced at least 14 dramas; two have been preserved, demonstrating how he continued the creative practices of Chinese theatre and implemented his father's teaching on using the medium as an artistic and didactic tool of governance. Like other traditional Chinese dramatists, Zhu Quan scripted new dramas based on culturally familiar stories and popular characters. He wrote new aria lyrics according to pre-existing tunes (*qupai* 曲牌), aligning musical and textual structures such as melodic and linguistic tones, number of phrases, phrase lengths, and rhyme and cadence schemes. His new lyrics were sung with known, if not old, melodies.

Zhu Quan was a conservative and didactic dramatist. He employed standard theatrical vocabulary, stage and performance practices, and dramatic forms and styles to produce credible and meaningful shows that are, by 21st-century criteria, more ideological than entertaining.[20] Zhu Quan is not a celebrated popular dramatist in the history of Chinese drama and theatre. As the script of *Zhuo Wenjun siben Xiangru* 卓文君私奔相如 (*Zhuo Wenjun Elopes with Sima Xiangru*) shows, Zhu creatively twisted a popular and subversive story about romantic elopement into a morality play on gendered ideals and virtues.[21] It lectures on masculine ambition and feminine submission at the expense of the dramatic and romantic excitement that eloping characters might be expected to evoke.

Zhu Quan portrayed Sima Xiangru (*c.* 179–117 BCE), the male protagonist in the play, as an ambitious and proud young man travelling with books and a sword to pursue riches and fame. Aside from his erudition and ambition, he has little that would physically or socially attract women. He pales against handsome, smart and passionate characters, such as Scholar Zhang Junrui 張君瑞 in the drama *Xixiangji* 西廂記 (*Romance of the Western Chamber*). Similarly, Zhu Quan's characterisation of Zhuo Wenjun, the female protagonist of his play, shows her as more wifely than charming. As scripted, she is desirable and virtuous principally because she will not forget her duty to serve her man – like a dutiful wife, she drives the carriage in which she and Sima Xiangru elope. This dutiful Zhuo Wenjun hardly flirts like Chen Miaochang 陳妙常, the accidental nun in *Yuzanji* 玉簪記 (*Jade Hairpin*) who seduces her man by playing *qin* music with him. The contrast between Zhu Quan's play and other earlier or later Ming dramas attests to the prince's prioritising of moralistic concerns over dramatic entertainment. For Zhu Quan, theatre was less an entertainment than a means of personal and communal cultivation and expression, an ideal and function that orthodox Ming China appeared to have some success in implementing throughout the second century of the empire.[22]

Systematising theatre and arias

To make theatre an expressive and social tool, Zhu Quan gave it discipline by regulating the composition and performance of its dramatic arias. Around 1407, Zhu Quan compiled his *Taihe zhengyinpu* as an ideological account of contemporary theatre and as a pioneering and practical formulary on linguistic and structural attributes of 353 fixed tunes for northern arias (*beiqu qupai* 北曲曲牌). With a mixture of materials taken from earlier writers and insights derived from his own experiences and theories, the document shows how the prince continued and developed early Ming theatre and aria composition.

As it is now preserved and known, *Taihe zhengyinpu* includes a preface and a miscellany of seven lists or reports. The preface is a concise exposition of the prince's didactic promotion of drama as a means of governance and cultural cultivation, an aesthetic learned from his father. The remaining texts present a mixture of pre-existing materials and original arguments. They include a list of 15 styles of dramas and arias (*yuefuti* 樂府體); a list of nine literary structures (*duishi* 對式); a list of names for 187 Yuan and 17 Ming dramatists and criticisms on their works; a classification of drama into 12 types; a register of 535 titles of northern drama (*zaju* 雜劇), 471 of which were authored by

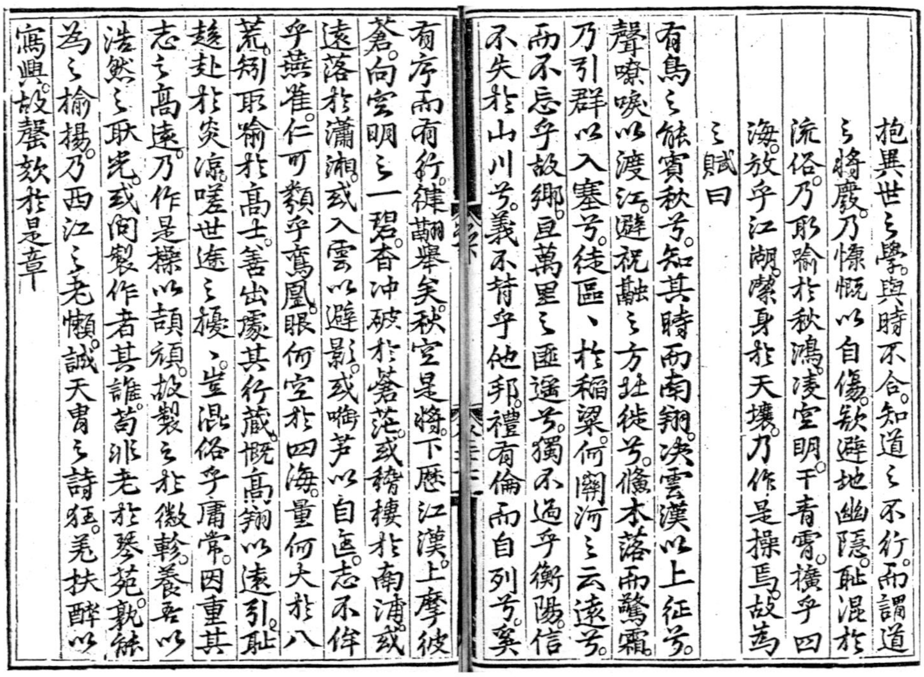

抱異世之學與時不合知道之不行而謂道之將廢乃慷慨以自傷欲避地幽隱恥混於流俗乃取喻於秋鴻凌空明干青霄橫乎四海放乎江湖潔身於天壤乃作是操焉故為之賦曰

有鳥之翩賓秋兮知其時而南翔浚雲漢以上征兮聲嘹唳以渡江避祝融之方壯徙兮儵木落而驚霜乃引群以入塞兮徒區區於稻粱何渺河之云遠兮而不忘乎故鄉豈萬里之匪遥兮獨不過乎衡陽信不失於山川兮義不背乎他邦禮有倫而自列兮奚有序而有行健翮舉矣秋空是翔下歷江漢上摩彼蒼向空明之一碧杳沖破於蒼茫或稽棲於南浦或遠落於瀟湘或入雲以避影或啣芦以自匿志不作乎燕雀仁可類乎鸞鳳眼何空於四海量何大於八荒翔取喻於高士善出處其行藏慨高翔以遠引恥趍赴於炎涼嗟世途之榛榛豈混俗乎庸常因重其志之高遠乃作是操以頡頏披製之於徽軫養吾以浩然之耿光或閱製作者其誰茍非老於琴苑孰能為之揄揚乃西江之老懶誠天胄之詩狂羌扶醉以寓興故鼇欵於是章

Plate 9.2 Zhu Quan 朱權 (c. 1378–1448), *Wondrous and Secret Notation* (*Shenqi mipu* 神奇秘譜), reprint of the 1425 Hongxi edition (Beijing, 1956). Pages showing the preface for *Qiuhong*

known Yuan dramatists; a listing of 110 works by nameless librettists, and 41 by male and professional entertainers (*changfu* 娼夫); biographical notes on 36 master singers who performed as elite artists and not as commercial entertainers, and whose performance Zhu had witnessed; a musical-theoretical discussion of the five classes of relative pitches, the twelve standard pitches and eleven musical mode-scales; and a series of prescriptions on singing practices.

Much of the information discussed in the seven texts or reports is taken from pre-existing sources, which scholars have now identified as Zhong Sicheng's 鍾嗣成 (fl. 1320s) *Luguipu* 錄鬼譜 (*A Registry of Deceased Masters*) and Zhi An's 芝庵 *Changlun* 唱論 (*A Discussion on Singing Practices*; prior to 1341). Some traditional arguments preserved in *Taihe zhengyinpu* are idiosyncratically adjusted by Zhu Quan to underscore the use of drama and theatrical performance as a means of governance and self-cultivation. For example, arguments that valorise honourable commoner performers (*liangjia* 良家), at the expense of Buddhists and professional and commoner entertainers, expose the prince's authoritative and opinionated personality.

Zhu Quan compiled *Taihe zhengyinpu* to transform ideologically dramatic theories and practices of his time; as such, it attests to the prince's historical agency and creative context. Born and raised in Nanjing in the south, the prince had spent his late boyhood and early manhood travelling and fighting many battles in northern China. He thus had the opportunities to become knowledgeable about the language of both northern and southern dialects. Being a sensitive dramatist and musical performer, he realised how effective composition and performance of dramatic lyrics depended on the correct matching of tune and melodic structures with the linguistic tones of spoken or sung words in the lyrics. Exercising his creative and systematising urges, he developed categories and rules to help composers, performers and audience to engage expressively with theatrical singing of arias.[23]

Early Ming China needed such categories and rules because it experienced drastic and rapid changes in language, drama and other expressive and regional practices. Since Jin and Yuan times, many northern Chinese had migrated to the south, singing northern arias (*beiqu* 北曲) in their newly adopted homes. Socially and politically valorised as a genre of sophisticated and superior performing arts, northern arias flourished in the south and were sung by both northerners and southerners. Those who were neither native nor experienced speakers of northern Chinese dialects needed help to compose and perform northern arias. It is this need that prompted the writing and publication of tutorials and theoretical guides on composing and performing theatrical arias, such as Zhou Deqing's 周德清 *Zhongyuan yinyun* 中原音韵 (*Phonology of the Central Plains*), compiled around 1324.[24] A dictionary of 5,866 words divided into 19 groups of rhymes, Zhou's reference work prescribes how the words can be used in *beiqu* compositions and performances. However, it presents few concrete examples of how the words can be composed and performed to fit *qupai* structures.

The task of producing a comprehensive and practical formulary on the fixed northern aria tunes fell to Zhu Quan – or rather he was the first to grasp the need for such a reference work. The task and the materials needed to complete the task, however, were beyond the scope of any one person to manage single-handedly. Linguistic words and tones are communal properties and codes that no individual could create by themselves. Being a politically marginalised, ideologically driven, scholarly and artistically gifted prince, Zhu Quan became the historical player who had the ability and resources to tackle the task. As a princely and musical scholar, he was able to collect and organise the linguistic-oral-aural data needed to produce an instructive and meaningful formulary.

His collection, selection and classification of northern aria fixed tunes according to scale-modes, and his annotation of the linguistic attributes of words in the lyrics of

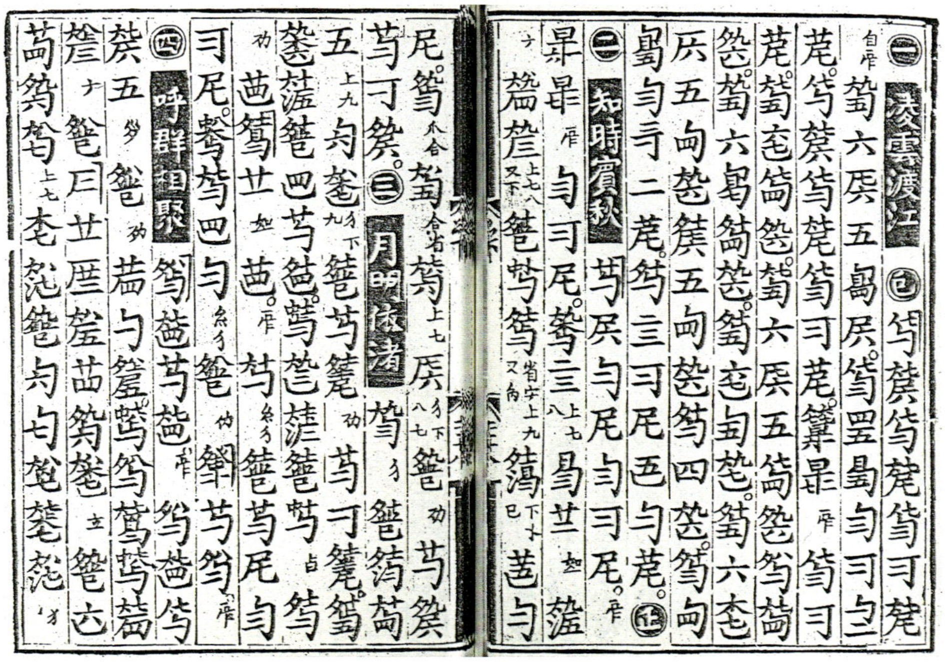

Plate 9.3 Zhu Quan 朱權, (*c.* 1378–1448), *Wondrous and Secret Notation* (*Shenqi mipu* 神奇秘譜), reprint of the 1425 Hongxi edition (Beijing, 1956). Pages showing notation for *Qiuhong*

353 arias, were Herculean tasks, particularly for the first time. If Zhu Quan finalised *Taihe zhengyinpu* around 1407, when he was barely 30 years old and had been settled in Nanchang for only four short years, then this shows the diligence of his application to the task at this time. It is most likely that he had or summoned substantive help from compilation partners in his princedom.

Such help neither diminishes Zhu Quan's achievement and contribution to Chinese drama nor negates his seminal role as an artist and theorist-teacher in the history of northern aria composition and performance. As a matter of fact, acceptance of the existence of this help promotes a more realistic understanding of how the prince achieved his legacy in Chinese drama and performance. Historically speaking, *Taihe zhengyinpu* has been most influential; it was and still is consulted by all concerned with northern drama composition and performance.

Continuing and developing *qin* music

Like *Taihe zhengyinpu*, Zhu Quan's *Shenqi mipu* of 1425 also attests to his role as a legacy-building and rule-formulating consumer and producer of performing arts. At present, this work remains the earliest extant, comprehensive and decipherable notated source of Chinese *qin* music.[25] As such, it establishes the prince's unique contribution to the genre's historical continuity and change since early Ming China. By the Southern Song and Yuan period (1127–1368) in China, *qin* music had become an elite and male performing art, and contemporaneous practitioners had developed their own aesthetics and composition-performance styles, producing exclusive compilations of their notated music. Unfortunately, no such notated sources from the Southern Song or earlier times have been preserved today. Only the titles of prominent works, such as *Zixia dongpu* 紫霞洞譜 (*Qin Music Anthology of the Purple Cloud Cave*), have been referenced in many historical documents.[26]

As an informative and unique document, *Shenqi mipu* occupies a seminal place in Chinese musical history. As such, it raises many questions as to how and why Zhu Quan notated and explained *qin* music, and how he compiled a verifiable record of the creation and transmission of the *qin* music repertory, theory and performance practices from Tang and Song times, which has remained historically influential through the Ming and down to the present. As it is now known, *Shenqi mipu* is a mature document, with practically all the standard features displayed by *qin* anthologies subsequently published in Ming and Qing China. These include, for example, comprehensive tablature signs, declarative and explanatory prefaces, modally classified repertories, critical annotations and programmatically suggestive titles and subtitles for individual works. It is unlikely that Zhu Quan created this comprehensive system of notational and explanatory features by himself. In fact, he clearly acknowledged the source of his system, and the tablature scores of his anthology affirm his statement. In his preface to the anthology, the prince revealed that he had collected Song and earlier *qin* scores, practised and edited them, a fact demonstrated by notational inconsistencies found in the anthology.[27]

As it is now preserved, the *Shenqi mipu* divides into three fascicles of 61 compositions. The first fascicle preserves 15 compositions in six distinctive scale-modes from Tang, Song or earlier times; the second fascicle includes 26 contemporary or recent works in five distinctive scale-modes; and the third fascicle holds 20 works in five modes. One composition in the last group, namely *Qiuhong* 秋鴻 (*Autumn Geese*), is often discussed as an original composition by the prince (**Pls 9.2–9.3**).[28] Many of the *qin* compositions preserved in *Shenqi mipu* were and still are traditional favourites. Their names include, for example, *Meihua sannong* 梅花三弄 (*Three Variations of Plum Blossom*), *Liushui* 流水 (*Flowing Water*) and *Xiaoxiang shuiyun* 瀟湘水雲 (*Water and Mist of the Rivers Xiao and Xiang*).

Zhu Quan prepared his anthology to preserve a tradition that he deemed authentic and representative of civilisation in

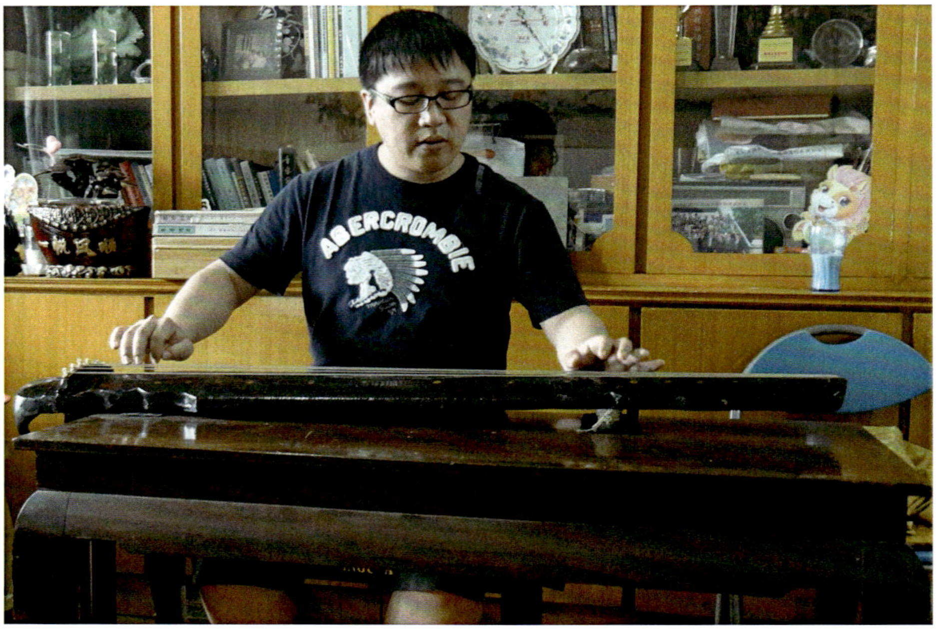

Plate 9.4 Gu Yongxiang playing *Feibao lianzhu* 飛瀑連珠 (*Drops of Water Flying Down from the Fall like Linked Pearls*)

China. In his preface for the document, he provided a brief history of the genre and explained his motives for producing the anthology, which can be briefly summarised here.[29] He argues that ancient sages had instituted music by fixing the five tones and performing them on seven-stringed *qin* zithers, musical instruments that embodied heavenly and earthly forces, producing music that helped gentlemen cultivate their benevolent hearts. In the centuries immediately preceding the Ming, Buddhists and other undesirable people had abused the music, and thus only a limited number of compositions were authentically practised in early Ming. To remedy the situation, Zhu Quan chose to preserve authentic compositions, namely either those he had personally learned, practised and edited or those his five assistants had learned and collected from different *qin* masters. The notated music in the *Shenqi mipu* was distinctive because it not only expressed the prince's heart and mind but also demonstrated how individual master musicians performed their own melodies and rhythms. In order to anthologise accurately *qin* music for posterity, the prince spent 12 years performing and correcting every detail of the collected works. The anthology, he claims, should be treasured by all who aspire to revive ancient and authentic music.

Zhu Quan's *qin* manifesto is historically representative of those artistic, elitist, idealist, moralist and scholarly *qin* connoisseurs of Ming and Qing China. What the prince declared is musically substantiated by his notated music: when deciphered and performed, they make celestially intriguing melodies and rhythms. Since the 1950s, when 20th-century *qin* masters realised the historical importance of *Shenqi mipu* and began to transcribe and then perform its notated music, the subtly contrasting styles and individualistic features in the historically different repertories preserved in the anthology have become more and more obvious. Zhu Quan's claim to historical authenticity and musical sophistication is winning more and more admirers.

Zhu Quan won and is still winning because his *qin* aesthetics and practices are organic and coherent. He is known to have made *qin* instruments himself. Practical and meticulous knowledge about *qin* instruments is what anchors and authenticates both his theories and his notated music. Currently two historical and extant Ming *qin* are considered as authentic instruments made by the prince. One is the renowned *Feibao lianzhu* 飛瀑連珠 ('Drops of Water Flying Down from the Fall like Linked Pearls') (**Pl. 9.4**); it is now owned by Gu Zechang 顧澤長 (b. 1941), a retired *qin* master and professor of Shenyang Conservatory of Music.[30] He inherited the instrument from his great-grandfather, Gu Xiaogeng 顧少庚, who acquired it in the late 1880s from a Mr Lu Changsen 陸長森 of Changsha.

Lu purchased the *qin*, which was previously owned by a Li Zhuo 李拙 of Xiangping 襄平 in present-day Liaoning province, in 1864. As Li reported, he discovered the instrument among a pile of dusty old things. Knocking on the wood of the instrument, he heard its resonant sounds, and then identified a text inscribed inside its body. This declares the instrument to be a '*qin* of central harmony, personally crafted by the Yun'an Daoist, of the Ming imperial clan (*Huang Ming zongshi yun'an daoren qinzuo zhongheqin* 皇明宗室雲庵道人亲造中和琴). Superbly built, the instrument measures 118cm long and features a shoulder width of 19.9cm. It still sounds resonant and sweet, a sonic confirmation of Zhu Quan's ideological and sophisticated production and consumption of *qin* music and musical instruments.[31]

Concluding remarks

Reviewing Zhu Quan's ideology for and systematisation of Chinese drama and music, one might ask how personal biography, official institutions and the forces of Ming culture and history interactively or singularly defined his distinctive and influential legacy. There is no doubt that a critical force came from those early Ming social-political struggles which robbed him of opportunities to implement his political ambitions, generating his tragic life, and transforming him into an impressive cultural-musical consumer and producer. Another critical force is the fortuitous convergence of his princely power and command of available resources with his artistic talents and personal ambitions to make a difference for the Ming empire and its people.

Many Ming princes stamped their personal marks on Ming history. Besides Zhu Quan, however, only two other princes achieved comparable historical status and bequeathed to posterity towering legacies in drama and music. The first is Zhu Youdun 朱有燉 (1379–1439), who authored a critically acclaimed and preserved repertory of northern dramas.[32] The second is Zhu Zaiyu 朱載堉 (1536–1611), who authored a collection of books on musical history and theories, collectively known as the *Yuelü quanshu* 樂律全書 (*Complete Collection of Zhu Zaiyu's Musical Treatises*); it includes what is arguably the earliest thesis on equal tuning and temperament in world music.[33]

All three Ming princes benefited from their privileged positions, which provided them with the training, resources and human assistance that allowed them to produce and consume Ming performing arts the way they did. Only Zhu Quan, however, had the ambition to discipline composition and performance of dramatic arias and *qin* music, and produced effective prescriptions and notations for their practices that are still consulted by 21st-century composers and performers. By comparison with the other two, Zhu Quan's legacy is the most systematising, and its influence on Ming, Qing and contemporary Chinese music is most clear and verifiable. Even if Zhu Quan's disciplining of Ming drama and *qin* music was more theoretical and princely than practical and nationwide, he posthumously shapes their historical interpretations and narratives. Ming musical history cannot be told without reference to Zhu Quan and his legacy.

Notes

1 For a concise description of Zhu Quan's biography and extant writings, see *DMB*, 305–7.
2 CNKI China National Knowledge Infrastructure (www.cnki.net), a website of Chinese academic research and current publications, for example, lists 350 items comprising journal articles, MA and Ph.D theses under the heading of 'Zhu Quan'.
3 Most available Chinese studies gloss over the issues; see for example Zhong Le 2013 and Zhang Zehong 2014.
4 Yao Pinwen 2013, 193, 204–10, 294.
5 Unless specified, biographical and bibliographical data about Zhu Quan's biography and writings follow those presented in Yao Pinwen 2013.
6 For two studies on the rebellion, see Chan 1976 and Jiang Fenglan 1997.
7 Yao Pinwen 2013, 42–8.
8 Yao Pinwen (annotated) 2010.
9 Zhu Quan 1981.
10 Zhu Quan 1987.
11 The poems have no titles; for convenience of identification, I have sequentially numbered them as they are presented in Zhu Quan 1987.
12 Zhang Tingyu 1984 and Shen Shixing 2007.
13 Lam 1998, 37–54.
14 Shen Shixing 2007, 104: 569–71; 183: 931–2; 226: 1110–12.
15 Li Zhenyu 2010, 54–64.
16 Li Zhenyu 2010, 58.
17 Liu Ruoyu 1980, 39–41.
18 Shen Shixing 2007, 56: 354.
19 For a survey of theatrical performances at the Ming court, see Li Zhenyu 2010.
20 Xu Zifang 2003.
21 Zhu Quan 1979, *juan* 7.
22 Li Kehe 2010.
23 This interpretation is stimulated by Luo Di's arguments on the historical rise and musical features of *beiqu*; Luo Di 2013.
24 Zhou Deqing 1978.
25 There are many general descriptions of Zhu Quan's *Shenqi mipu* and a number of musicological studies on technical and historical aspects of the anthology; see, for example, Xu Guanhua 2005; Xu Jian 2012, 235–43.
26 See Zhang Huaying 2013, 1–15, 52–7, 339.
27 See Wu Wenguang 2008 and Zhang Huaying 2005, 132–3.
28 Xu Jian 2012, 224–7; Yan Xiaoxing 2013.
29 Goormaghtigh and Yung 1997.
30 Liu Yi 1988.
31 View Gu Yongxiang 2014 [www.youtube.com/watch?v=ooXQiSFc8y4&feature=em-upload_owner#action=share] for an audio-visual clip of his playing of *Yiguren* 憶故人 (*Remembering People of the Past*) on the *qin*; Gu Yongxiang is the son of Gu Zechang. View also Song Ming 2013 for clear pictures of the instrument.
32 Idema 1985.
33 Zhu Zaiyu 1996.

Chapter 10
Fashioning the Imperial Legacy: Yang Shiqi and the *Record of Imperial Pronouncements*

Peter Ditmanson

On 29 January 1443, one year before his death, Yang Shiqi 楊士奇 (1365–1444), the leading grand secretary at the Ming imperial court, wrote a preface for his completed *Record of Imperial Pronouncements of Three Reigns* (*Sanchao shengyu lu* 三朝聖諭錄).[1] He cited his old age – he was 78 *sui* (77 years of age) – and he referred to his decades of service to the throne. He was, he explained, one of the first to answer the call in 1402 to serve the Yongle 永樂 emperor (r. 1403–24) upon his accession, 'correcting the great succession' (*zheng datong* 正大統) after usurping the throne from his nephew, the Jianwen 建文 emperor (r. 1399–1402). In his preface, Yang posed a rhetorical questioning of his own compilation: should the secrets of the court be preserved in a private work?

The question indicates Yang's recognition that this kind of record, an account of things that emperors had said to him, was not the norm, and that he had done something new in his day. 'In reply', he explained, 'I say that my fear is that the bountiful splendour of my sovereigns might vanish. Why should I have other concerns?' And he argued that there were precedents for this kind of work, harking back to the 11th-century Song dynasty statesmen Ouyang Xiu 歐陽修 (1007–72) and Sima Guang 司馬光 (1019–86), who had produced similar works: Ouyang's *Record of Memorials on Affairs* (*Zoushi lu* 奏事錄), and the *Debates on [the Prince of] Pu* (*Pu yi* 濮議) and *Sima Guang*'s *Records by Hand* (*Shoulu* 手錄). These accounts, claimed Yang, had 'recorded the interactions between ruler and ministers at that time, comprehensively and in detail, such that they reflect an era of a brilliant and capable match between them'. Such compilations, then, created a moral mirror for reflection on the personal dynamics that make effective governance possible and explain the virtue of his own compilation. 'And so in what I have recorded, there is sagely virtue, there is sagely admonition, and there is special favour. I only fear that I have not recorded the details. Why should I have other concerns?'

Official records of the pronouncements of these emperors had already been compiled. The *Ming Veritable Records* (*Ming shilu* 明實錄), a large bureaucratic aggregate account of edicts, memorials and events, had been compiled for the Yongle and Hongxi emperors in February of 1430, under the supervision of Yang Shiqi and others. The *Veritable Record* of the Xuande emperor was compiled in May of 1438, also under Yang. These records were for consultation only by the emperor and the top officials of the bureaucracy, the grand secretaries and Hanlin officials, and these materials did not circulate further. One set were stored in a special stone chamber built for this purpose, while another was kept in the library of the Grand Secretariat (*Neige* 內閣).[2]

Along with the *Veritable Records*, for each emperor the court produced a collection of *Precious Admonitions* (*baoxun* 寶訓), composed of pronouncements of the ruler on important subjects of significant political or philosophical import. The term *Precious Admonitions* can be traced back to ancient times, but in the early Ming, the inspiration to compile this record was the iconic *Governing Essentials of the Zhenguan Reign* (*Zhenguan zhengyao*, 貞觀政要) of Tang Taizong 唐太宗 (r. 627–49).[3] From the Yongle reign onwards, the *Precious Admonitions* were produced and presented at court in tandem with the *Veritable Records*. And like the *Veritable Records*, the

Precious Admonitions were not intended to circulate widely, but were chiefly intended to be 'revered by the sons and grandsons' of the imperial line, as the Xuande emperor put it.[4]

Now, in 1443, as one of the leading architects of these official accounts of the Ming emperors and their courts, Yang was asserting his right – and his responsibility – to record and transmit his own private collection of imperial pronouncements. He did not indicate the audience for which he was writing, but his invocation of the writings of Ouyang Xiu and Sima Guang suggest that he intended the work to contribute to the broader 'literati' discourse on the political order of the realm. Writing a preface to the work introduced it to a readership and signalled that it was intended for circulation. The *Record of Imperial Pronouncements* was part of a large body of material that Yang published at this time. He also published his *Record of Memorials and Responses* (*Zoudui lu* 奏對錄), a collection of his presentations at court, and his *Record of Compositions on Behalf* (*Daiyan lu* 代言錄), a collection of edicts and pronouncements that he had drafted for the emperors over the years.[5] His collection of his own writings, including poetry, biographies, eulogies, epitaphs and inscriptions, had been published a little over two years earlier, in 1440, a vast compilation that confirmed his role as one of the most prolific writers of the era.[6] In a preface to Yang's collected works, Yang's close colleague Huang Huai 黃淮 (1367–1449) waxed in superlatives on Yang's literary achievements and linked them with the glories of the dynasty itself:

> In our dynasty, since the Great Ancestor, the August Emperor initiated his cultured enterprise, generations of the learned have emerged in splendour! And the writings of Master [Yang] testify to the brilliance of our predecessors, soaring aloft. How many could do that! And during that era, he has matched their pace, how many could do that![7]

This chapter examines the *Record of Imperial Pronouncements* as a new source of information on the imperium that began to circulate to the world beyond the Ming court in the 1440s. On the one hand, as one of the few documents on this period in circulation, Yang's 'private' record was highly influential in shaping the image of the Yongle emperor and his son and grandson for the larger reading public. On the other hand, Yang's work set an important precedent of personal narratives by retiring high-level officials in the Ming court.

Yang completed his *Record of Imperial Pronouncements* at a crucial time. The emperor's grandmother, Empress Dowager Zhang 張 (1379–1442), the stabilising force in the regency, had died two months earlier, an event that Yang noted in his preface. The Zhengtong 正統 emperor (r. 1436–49), who had come to the throne at age eight, had recently turned sixteen, and was beginning to take over the affairs of the court for himself. Yang's generation of court statesmen were dying off. Yang Rong 楊榮 (1371–1440) had died two years earlier. Yang Pu 楊溥 (1372–1446) was nearly 70. Other powerful figures had come to play a more dominant role at court. The Director of Ceremonial, one of the most influential positions in the court, was the eunuch Wang Zhen 王振 (d. 1449), a power rival, cultivating an array of important relationships with prominent civil and military officials, and with the emperor himself.[8] With the waning power of the regency and the attentions of the wilful young emperor divided, it is not surprising that Yang Shiqi now sought to assert a long-standing personal bond between grand secretaries and successive emperors, and to affirm his own vision of the court.

There were, in Yang's day, few sources of information for people across the realm about the events and personalities at the Ming court. There is no evidence that the *Dibao* (邸報) or *Capital Gazette* circulated in the early Ming, although it did exist in earlier times. Little is known about the *Capital Gazette* in Ming times, except for anecdotal evidence, none of which appears before the late 15th century.[9]

The *Court Diary* (*Qijuzhu* 起居注) was established by the founding Hongwu 洪武 emperor (r. 1368–98), who appointed prominent officials to serve as the court diarist. In his own way, he was following previous dynastic precedents. He was eager to restore the rites of an idealised antiquity, in which history was recorded in real time – his actions and deeds passed down for posterity. He seems to have lost interest in this practice in his later paranoid years. And there is no mention of the court diary in the *Veritable Records* after 1382. Although some sources have suggested otherwise, there is reason to be sceptical that the post of court diarist existed until it was formally restored in the late 16th century, under the Wanli 萬曆 emperor (r. 1573–1620).[10] Court records, including the *Court Diary*, when one existed, were indeed used to compile the *Veritable Record*, but this, as noted above, did not circulate.

In 1402, when the Yongle emperor usurped the throne from his nephew, he sought to rewrite history so that the years of the Hongwu reign went down to 1402.[11] But there is little to indicate that this history was available to anyone beyond the immediate confines of the court. The *Record of Responding to Heaven and Pacifying the Troubles* (*Fengtian jingnan ji* 奉天靖難記) recounted the events leading up to the usurpation, and overlaps with the *Veritable Records* of the Yongle reign.[12] This text is often widely believed to have been composed and published in the early years of the Yongle reign, as a justification of the usurpation. But there is surprisingly little evidence that the text was actually composed at that time, and there in fact seems to be no written references to the text before the late 16th century. It appears in a few private library catalogues in the 17th century.

For the broader 'literati' public in the early 15th century, information on the usurpation of 1402, and indeed, the early history of the dynasty, would not have been readily available in any form. Of course, for public consumption, the Yongle emperor did produce vast public monuments to attest to the validity of his succession. The remarkable Da Baoensi 大報恩寺 (Great Monastery of Filial Gratitude), with its spectacular pagoda, was erected on the edge of Nanjing (see discussions by Marsha Haufler and Clarence Eng in Chapters 16 and 20 of this volume). And he ordered the construction of a vast stone stele to attest to his filial piety.[13] The project had to be redesigned when it became clear that the Yongle emperor's ambitions far exceeded the possible, and a smaller (but still immense) version of the stele was erected not far from the tomb site of his father on Mount Zhong. Yongle's own *Veritable Records* were delayed by the early death of his son, the Hongxi emperor. The records were eventually completed in 1430, and it seems that a more relaxed political environment prevailed from about this time, after the historical narrative of the Yongle usurpation and reign was resolved.

As David Robinson has shown us (see Chapter 1 in this volume), Ming emperors actively cultivated their image, following the grammar and imagery of power that predominated across much of Asia. Yang Shiqi and his peers played a role in this development of the martial imperial image. They were frequently commanded by their ruler to compose commemorative poems on the various hunts and military manoeuvres, to celebrate the martial vigour of the sovereign.

In the *Record of Imperial Pronouncements*, however, Yang sought to cast the court in a different light, with an emphasis on the sovereigns' civil virtues, moral composure and personal relationships with the members of the court. Yang wrote in the staid formal language of the 'Chancellor Style' (*Taigeti* 台閣體), one that he and his peers had cultivated over the first decades of the 15th century. In poetry and in prose, this style was clear and bland, a register of language with a confident vision of order, putting the world to right through an idealised narrative where, as Yang says in his preface, the Ming throne is passed down from one sage to the next – the world as it should be.

As one might expect, Yang himself plays a prominent role in these accounts and many of them are solitary exchanges between him and the emperor. As the sole witness to these interactions and with so many of his colleagues from that era dead, Yang had the liberty to reconstruct the character of the emperors and the court as he saw them. The short anecdotes found in the *Record of Imperial Pronouncements* thus offered his idealised and highly personal image of the ruler. In Yang's telling, the three emperors he served were sagacious and moral, but also intimate and highly deferential towards the civil officials at court.

In several of the anecdotes, Yang portrays the Yongle emperor and his son and grandson as deeply engaged in various aspects of 'literati' culture. In several entries, the emperor exchanges comments on the classical heritage with Yang and others. These discussions are not particularly deep or profound: in one, Yongle insists that these scholars verify their claims on the *dao* 道 with passages from the classics.[14] The point is not to show the emperor's scholarly prowess, but simply his familiarity with and deference to the Neo-Confucian corpus and the literary traditions of his courtiers. Elsewhere, Yang recorded another exchange with Yongle's son, Hongxi, focused on the literature of Ouyang Xiu, the prominent Song *litterateur* who came from Luling 盧陵, in Jiangxi province, also Yang Shiqi's home. Ouyang was widely considered to be the paragon of fine literary writing and Yang was one of his chief proponents. Here, he records the Hongxi emperor praising both his literary style and his moral rectitude: 'Writing that is not based on the correct way, this is useless writing. An official who is unable to speak directly is a disloyal official. Ouyang is truly a credit to Luling as a gentleman. Shiqi, you should so strive!'[15] Taught by Yang Shiqi in his minority, the Hongxi emperor here perfectly recites his teacher's point of view, a clear articulation of the principles behind the 'Chancellery literary style'.

In another entry, Yang offers one rare example of the Yongle emperor defending Neo-Confucian teachings against critics. Aside from the formal compilations of the '*Great Compendia*' of the Four Books, Five Classics and the Neo-Confucian writings on human nature and moral principle, the *Wujing daquan* 五經大全, *Sishu daquan* 四書大全 and *Xingli daquan* 性理大全, the Yongle emperor and his courtiers personally expressed few opinions on the Neo-Confucian tradition.[16] But in this story, the emperor is presented as its staunch defender. In the second year of his reign, 1404, an elderly minor scholar from Raozhou in Jiangxi, Zhu Jiyou 朱季友 (n.d.) presented books to the throne that criticised the major Song Neo-Confucian masters, Zhou Dunyi 周敦頤 (1017–73), Zhang Zai 張載 (1020–77), the Cheng brothers, Cheng Hao 程顥 (1032–85) and Cheng Yi 程頤 (1033–1107), and Zhu Xi 朱熹 (1130–1200). According to Yang, 'His Highness read it and reacted in severe anger, saying "He is a scholar-thief (*ruzhizei* 儒之賊)!"' The emperor then showed the writings to the others in attendance. The officials condemned the work and recommended that the author be punished and his works destroyed. Hu Guang noted that since the author was in his 70s, burning his writings might be sufficient. The emperor then declared: 'Slandering the former worthies and destroying the correct way is uncommonly criminal. By controlling him We can set an enduring example'. Then he ordered that Zhu be returned to Raozhou and that local officials there give him a beating and investigate his house to ensure that all his writings were destroyed. He then said to the courtiers, 'Eliminating evil must be done thoroughly. Destroying his writings is truly appropriate!'[17]

This account had already appeared in much briefer form in the *Veritable Records* of the Yongle reign.[18] Here Yang added greater emphasis to the emperor's indignation, indicating a more personal investment in the teachings of Neo-Confucianism. And further, Yang emphasised the emperor's deference to the advice of his officials. As this story was buried in the non-circulating *Veritable Records*, Yang here retold it to promulgate the image of an emperor fully committed to the teachings and counsel of his civil official. Throughout Yang's collected records, the emperors are depicted as showing careful deference and solicitude towards their officials. The relationships are shown to be personal and intimate. This is particularly clear in one entry in which a member of court died suddenly:

> In June of the sixth year of Yongle [1408], the Minister of Rites, Zheng Ci 鄭賜, died. Before this, his duties in the Rites Ministry had been many. Ci confided to his vice minister, Zhao Gong 趙玑, that he was anxious and ill. Frequently while memorialising at court, he would lose track and the emperor disliked it.
>
> That morning, the death was urgently announced. The Hanlin officials were summoned and [His Highness] asked, 'We had not heard that Ci was ill, how could he have lost his life?' Before any of them answered, I approached and said, 'I observed that Ci had been ill for several days. But he was afraid and did not dare to retire, which would have been better so that he could seek medical care. Yesterday evening, I was standing with Ci outside the Youshun Gate, and his physical strength was so impaired that he fell to the ground. Those around were startled that from his mouth and nose, the air was exhaled, but not

inhaled. I urgently ordered his aides to take him outside the Meridian Gate.'

His Highness did not wait for me to finish speaking and said to all the Hanlin officials, 'Ci was a gentleman and the care for him was insufficient. Have the eulogists send an official to eulogise him.' And he ordered the Works Ministry to send a coffin.

That evening, when Huang Huai and I finished memorialising on matters and withdrew, His Highness called me back. And he said, 'You should have come earlier and hinted something to me. We had misjudged Ci. From now on, when something is going on, just speak directly about it, without hiding it.'

This account is a telling one. The death of Zheng Ci is mentioned in the *Veritable Records*, along with a brief biography and a description of the emperor's fondness for him, but not the circumstances of his sudden collapse. Here, Yang portrays the Yongle emperor as caring and concerned, regretful for his impatience, and worried that the weighty matters of his office have led him to overlook the welfare of one of his ministers. The ruler gives his attention to the details of propriety and thoughtfulness in dealing with the dead official. And significantly, he calls for further direct and honest communication, greater intimacy, between himself and grand secretaries like Yang.

In another entry, this same intimacy is portrayed as the Yongle emperor is engaged in the personality dynamics of his grand secretaries:

In the winter of the fifth year of Yongle [1407], one day Hu Guang was alone at the Wuying Gate submitting a petition. His Highness read it and praised it repeatedly. Then he casually said, 'Yang Shiqi's literary talent is unmatched nowadays, but Huang Huai often can't stand this. Why is it?' [Guang] replied, 'Huai has governing talents, but Shiqi's literary talent is superior in simplicity and clarity, harmonising the mind without forcing it. It seems that Xie Jin valued Shiqi and myself and took Huai lightly, and so Huai is disgruntled.' His Highness said, 'I know that you also can't stand Huai. I am not fooled by all of this.'

Guang bowed his head and withdrew. He said to me, 'May my children and grandchildren, generation after generation, never dare to forget this!' After this, we two were more attentive to Huai.

The emperor is, as always, the ultimate authority and arbiter at the court, but here, that authority is drawn down to a personal level. Deeply knowledgeable in the literary enterprise of his secretaries (again, Yang Shiqi is shown in an impressive light), the emperor closely follows the competitive relationships between them.

In anecdotes concerning the Yongle emperor's son, the Hongxi emperor, Yang appears somewhat more assertive, though carefully remaining within the bounds of propriety. In one anecdote in the first month of the Hongxi emperor's ascent to the throne, Yang vehemently argues against the extra titles and salaries granted to him. Even as the emperor grows impatient, Yang insists that the added portion of his salary could support 60 soldiers instead. Finally Hongxi relents, declaring, 'We will carry out your wish'.[19] In the anecdotes on the Hongxi and Xuande emperors, Yang was more vocal in commenting directly on political and economic issues faced by the court and on conditions within the empire. While these two reigns marked a significant departure from the policies of the Yongle reign, however, Yang emphasised a seamless continuity from one ruler to the next.

With the latter two reigns, Yang further emphasised the closeness and intimacy that he enjoyed with the rulers. This is most readily apparent in one of his last meetings with the Hongxi emperor, who died of a heart condition less than a year after ascending the throne. After the ruler observed a baleful astronomical sign, he took it as an indication that his life was coming to an end. Yang recorded a last exchange with the emperor and another leading official, Jian Yi 蹇義 (1364–1435). The emperor reminisced about his years as the heir apparent, governing from the capital when his father was on campaigns. These had been difficult times, as his more martial younger brother, Zhu Gaoxu 朱高煦, the Prince of Han 漢王 (1380–1426), had persistently insinuated himself with the Yongle emperor by ridiculing and insulting him, in hopes of replacing him as heir apparent. Yang had been sent to prison for a short time for defending the heir against his brother's charges.[20]

'When I was regent (*jianguo* 監國) for those twenty years, with the slander that was raised, and Our heart was troubled, we three held together. Relying on the brilliance and benevolence of my imperial father, we were able to bring things to completion.' His words trailed off. Yi and I were both in tears. I said in response, 'Now we are safe from danger and at peace, thanks to the kindness of the former emperor, and the sincerity of Your Highness. There is no more need for your Eminence to worry.' His Highness said, 'After I depart from this world, who will know of the unity of mind and singular sincerity between the three of us?' And he thereupon issued two edicts and two seals to the two of us. I received a seal that said, 'Yang the Pure' (*Yang zhen* 楊貞), and the edict said such-and-such. We received these and withdrew. In a little over a month, the funeral took place. Alas! How painful![21]

Yang's personal account of these private moments with the dying emperor present a jarring level of disclosure. In this moment, Hongxi casts off the hierarchy of ruler and subject, 'the three of us' (*wusan* 吾三) here delineating a unified intimacy. Yang takes this as an apology for the times that he and Jian Yi suffered on behalf of the heir apparent.

Throughout these stories, Yang's portrayal of the ruler is far removed from the official imperial image. As David Robinson has shown, that public image was carefully cultivated with a broader pan-Asian audience in mind, an image of martial vitality and awe. Military campaigns and hunting expeditions presented grand visual spectacles, celebrated in paintings and in poetry. The rulers in Yang's accounts, however, offer a striking contrast. As we have seen, they are intimately engaged with their civil staff and sharing in the values and culture of the 'literati'.

One can well imagine that Yang Shiqi, at the end of his long distinguished career, compiled the *Record of Imperial Pronouncements* to burnish his own credentials and to ensure that history saw his service to these emperors in a good light. But it is also clear that Yang produced his own private record as a foil against the other powerful forces emerging at the court of the impressionable Zhengtong emperor. The imperial image in the early Ming was always malleable, continually reshaped by the contending factions at court and by the whims of the ruler himself. Yang clearly sought to push back against these other forces, drawing on the personal authority of his four decades at court, to present a narrative asserting that the imperial legacy was a largely civil one.

To this end, Yang produced an unofficial 'private' record aimed at an audience beyond the court, presenting a ruler sensitive to 'literati' concerns and values. In the recounting of intimate exchanges between the ruler and his secretaries, Yang seems to have redefined the protocol for disclosure of imperial affairs. Thus he found the need to defend himself in his preface. The *Record of Imperial Pronouncements* was the first record of the Ming court compiled for circulation to a readership beyond it.

The *Record of Imperial Pronouncements* was republished frequently over the course of the dynasty. By the early 16th century, it appeared in anthologies like the *Collection of Illuminations of the Good* (*Mingliangji* 明良集) by Huo Tao 霍韜 (1487–1540).[22] In the tumultuous years of the Zhengde (1506–21) and Jiajing (1522–66) reigns, scholars like Yang Yiqing 楊一清 (1454–1530) cited Yang Shiqi's work as one of the important sources to learn about the interactions between ruler and minister, as the *Veritable Records* were unavailable.[23] In his compilation on the Hanlin Academy, the Cantonese scholar Huang Zuo 黃佐 (1490–1566) cited Yang's *Record of Sagely Proclamations* as representing an ideal age. On the etiquette for submitting memorials, he cited examples from Yang's work, indicating that things were done properly in those days. 'One can see', he exclaimed, 'how ruler and minister worked together.'[24]

Yang Shiqi's work established a significant precedent. By the end of the 1440s, the court was plunged into chaos with the capture of the Zhengtong emperor at Tumu, the ascent of his half-brother as the Jingtai emperor and the abrupt restoration of Zhu Qizhen as the Tianshun emperor in 1457. In the wake of this tumult, the grand secretaries and other high court officials in succeeding generations began to publish their own private memoirs, airing their views and opinions and versions of events at court to an interested reading public.[25] Through works such as Li Xian's 李賢 (1408–67) *Daily Record of the Tianshun Reign* (*Tianshun rilu* 天順日錄), people learned about the court in narratives that were more boldly divergent from the official narrative of the *Veritable Records*.

Over the course of the dynasty, it was Yang Shiqi's portrait of Yongle, along with his son and grandson, that circulated through the realm. Yang's vision of these rulers became the dominant and the most cited one for the rest of the dynasty. In these accounts the rulers are portrayed in a flattering light, but they are also cut down to size. They are concerned and worried rulers who confide in their trusted advisors. Yang's image of the Yongle emperor is particularly striking, for here we are drawn far away from the imagery of the warrior king who contends on the northern steppe, and are closer to a sagely and very human Yongle, widely celebrated as an ideal over the course of the dynasty.

Notes

1 Yang Shiqi 1998, 387–415. The preface is on 387–8.
2 For an account of the Ming *Veritable Records*, see Xie Guian 1995 and Franke 1961.
3 On the compilation of the first Ming *Precious Admonitions*, see Niu Jianqiang 2000.
4 See the imperial preface to the *Taizong baoxun* in Lü Ben *et al.* 1996, 53.784.
5 For an account of Yang Shiqi's works and their publication, see Yang Shiqi 1998, 1–3.
6 For an inventory of Yang's writings, see Li Jinggeng and Huang Peijun 2008.
7 Yang Shiqi 1998, 1.
8 On the career of Wang Zhen, see Hammond 2002. On the politics of the early Zhengtong reign, see Twitchett and Grimm 1988, 306–9.
9 For a study of the *Capital Gazette* in Ming times, see Yin Yungong 1990.
10 See, for example, Huang Zuo 1560–6, 1.13a–14a.
11 For a summary of the historical revisions under the Yongle emperor, see Chan 2005.
12 For a comprehensive study of this text, see Wang Chongwu 1948.
13 Yang Xinhua and Lu Haiming 2001, 616–17.
14 Yang Shiqi 1998, 387.
15 Yang Shiqi 1998, 394.
16 See Ditmanson 1999, ch. 7.
17 Yang Shiqi 1998, 387.
18 *MSL Taizong shilu* 33.581 (2/7/壬戌) [28 August 1404].
19 Yang Shiqi 1998, 400.
20 On the machinations of Zhu Gaoxu against his brother, see Chan 1988, 210 and 278.
21 Yang Shiqi 1998, 403–4.
22 For a description, see the prefatory comments by the editors of the *Sikuquanshu*, e-SKQS 53.18a–b.
23 Yang Yiqing n.d., 18.44a.
24 Huang Zuo 1560–6, 6.7b.
25 For an overview of several of these private narratives that emerged in the 1460s and beyond, see the extensive notes in the 'Selected Bibliography' of De Heer 1986.

Chapter 11

Politics or Entertainment? Examining Jiangxi Scholar Officials and Zhejiang Painters through the Lens of the *Elegant Gathering in the Apricot Garden*

Yin Ji'nan

Translated by Luk Yu-ping

This chapter reflects a portion of ongoing research on the early Ming dynasty painter Xie Huan 謝環 (1377–1452) and his series of works on the theme of the *Elegant Gathering in the Apricot Garden* (*Xingyuan yaji tu* 杏園雅集圖).[1] These survive today in two versions, one in the Metropolitan Museum of Art, New York (**Pl. 11.1**), and the other in the Zhenjiang Museum (**Pl. 11.2**).[2] The initial plan was to elaborate on a history of the formation and transformation of the *Elegant Gathering in the Apricot Garden* as a concept and as literary and visual documents, and to expand the geographic field of enquiry to include all of East Asia. It was a complicated task. In 1437 nine scholar officials led by Yang Shiqi 楊士奇 (1365–1444) first created the concept of the *Elegant Gathering in the Apricot Garden*; Xie Huan in turn produced an image to match this. The notion of an *Elegant Gathering in the Apricot Garden* could be perpetuated through literary channels, while paintings of the theme were disseminated within connoisseurial channels, and the subsequent woodblock-printed version circulated even more widely through the publishing world.[3] One example of this broader circulation is Xu Lun's 許論 (1487–1559) *Two Garden Gatherings* (*Eryuan ji* 二園集) (**Pl. 11.3**), produced around 1560, containing text and images of the works *Elegant Gathering in the Apricot Garden* and *Birthday Gathering in the Bamboo Garden* (*Zhuyuan shouji tu* 竹園壽集圖).[4]

This chapter deals with the history of the construction of a literary and visual trope, one which involves nine Ming-dynasty scholar officials and one painter (who was a military attaché or *wuguan* 武官 at the time). These are tropes which have been replicated and transformed through time and through various readings of both text and image. In 1477 Ni Yue 倪岳 (1444–1501) and Li Dongyang 李東陽 (1447–1516) viewed a version of the *Elegant Gathering in the Apricot Garden* together at a gathering hosted by Ni Yue of Hanlin officials who had passed the metropolitan examination in the same year (*Hanlin tongnian hui* 翰林同年會). He invited the painter Gao Sixun 高司訓 to paint the event, and he himself penned a record accompanying the painting.[5] Ni Yue's father, Ni Qian 倪謙 (1415–79), was sent as ambassador to Korea's Joseon court in 1449, where he participated in poetic exchanges and other literary activities with Korean scholar officials (see discussion by Lee Soomi in Chapter 24 of this volume). Later in 1459, Zhang Ning 張寧 (1426–96) was also sent as envoy to Korea, and had similar poetic exchanges and gatherings with court members there.[6] Both Ni Qian and Zhang Ning were scholar officials who had some degree of interaction with Xie Huan's work.[7] Might they have shared their knowledge of the *Elegant Gathering in the Apricot Garden* concept and scroll in this foreign court? That is a different field of enquiry.

In 1503 Li Dongyang hosted a gathering of ten men who had passed the metropolitan examination in the same year (*Shi tongnian hui* 十同年會) and invited an anonymous painter to compose a similarly titled scroll (*Shi tongnian hui tu* 十同年會圖), now in the Palace Museum, Beijing.[8] In 1499, the Minister of Revenue Zhou Jing 周經 (1440–1510) held a 'Birthday Gathering in the Bamboo Garden' (*Zhuyuan shouji* 竹園壽集圖) attended by 14 scholar officials including Wu Kuan 吳寬 (1435–1504) and Xu Jin 許進 (1437–1510). He invited a court painter to record the event in a scroll

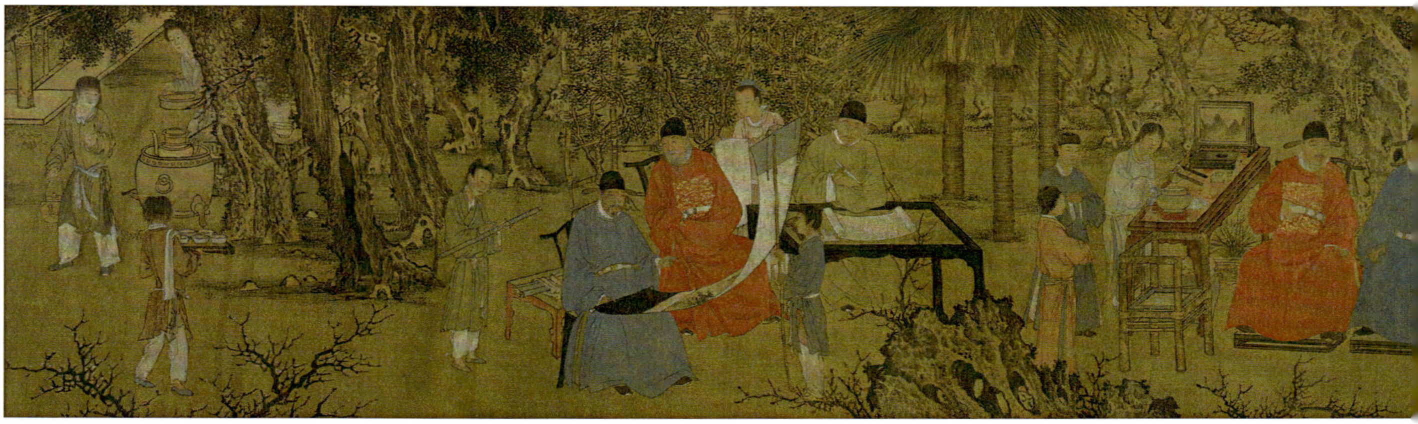

Plate 11.1 Anonymous, after Xie Huan 謝環 (1377–1452), *Elegant Gathering in the Apricot Garden* (*Xingyuan yaji tu* 杏園雅集圖), dated 1437, Beijing. Handscroll, ink and colours on silk, height 37.5cm, width 240.7cm. Metropolitan Museum of Art, New York, Purchase, the Dillon Fund Gift 1989 (1989.141.3)

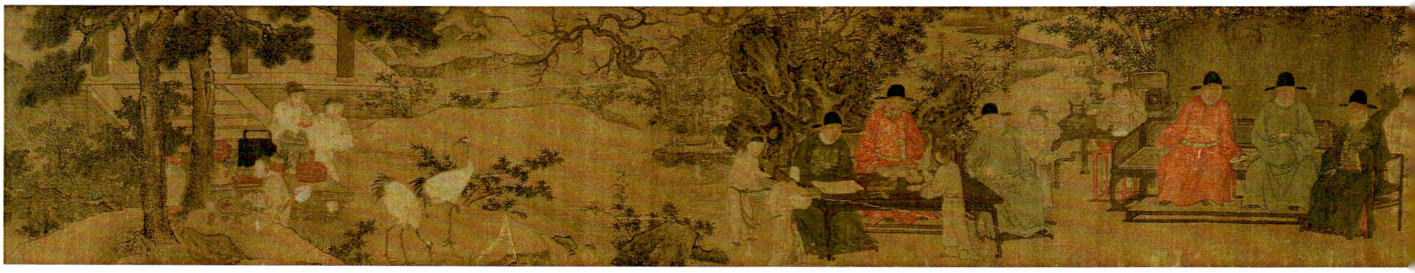

Plate 11.2 Anonymous, after Xie Huan 謝環 (1377–1452), *Elegant Gathering in the Apricot Garden* (*Xingyuan yaji tu* 杏園雅集圖), dated 1437. Handscroll, ink and colours on silk, height 37cm, width 401cm. Zhenjiang Museum, Jiangsu province

painting.[9] Wu Kuan had previously viewed the *Elegant Gathering in the Apricot Garden* scroll, and in 1503 participated in a gathering of 'five who are alike' (*Wu tong hui* 五同會), in this case referring to five officials who had much in common, and penned a preface to the event.[10] Fifty years later, Xu Lun, son of Xu Jin who participated in the *Birthday Gathering in the Bamboo Garden*, saw a version of the *Elegant Gathering in the Apricot Garden* in Taiyuan 太原, Shanxi 山西 province, in 1550.[11] In 1560, as noted above, he published woodblock-printed versions of the *Elegant Gathering in the Apricot Garden* and the *Birthday Gathering in the Bamboo Garden* scrolls, which were by then in his own collection. The trope retained its vitality into the Qing dynasty (1644–1911). As late as 1791 Weng Fanggang 翁方綱 (1733–1818) viewed the Zhenjiang version of the *Elegant Gathering in the Apricot Garden* in the collection of Chu Pengling 初彭齡 (d. 1825); this event is memorialised in his lengthy colophon.[12]

This discussion will be limited to the Zhenjiang version of the *Elegant Gathering in the Apricot Garden* and to Xu Lun's woodblock print of the same work. These two share a similar pictorial model that has been influential over the course of history. I agree with the view of the Taiwanese scholar Wu Sung-feng 吳誦芬 that this was Xie Huan's pictorial model.[13] The basic literary and visual evidence of this model provides sufficient material to engage in art-historical enquiry, as opposed to dwelling on questions of authenticity, which become of lesser importance.

The four-character title inscription (*Xingyuan yaji* 杏園雅集) on the Zhenjiang version of the *Elegant Gathering in the Apricot Garden* is absent from Xu Lun's woodcut version. The inscription serves to emphasise the location and the nature of the event: the location was the home of Grand Secretary Yang Rong 楊榮 (1371–1440) in eastern Beijing, and the event was a gathering of scholars. From Yang Shiqi's preface we can ascertain that he is more interested in the erudite nature of the gathering, and not in its pictorial substantiation. By contrast, the postscript (*houxu* 后序) authored by Yang Rong emphasises the image and the visual evidence provided within.

The date of the gathering is the first day of the third month in 1437. It would indeed have been the season when apricot blossoms were in flower, and a day that ministers and scholar officials would have been off duty or at rest. With the exception of Xie Huan, there were nine scholar officials present. The colophons connect this group of nine men to the subject matter *Nine Elders of the Mountain of Fragrance* (*Xiangshan jiulao* 香山九老) (**Pl. 11.4**) of the Tang dynasty (618–907), made famous by the poet Bai Juyi 白居易 (772–846).[14] There is only one apricot tree visible in the composition, an ancient tree whose flowers are in bloom. Based on the description written by the garden's host Yang Rong, there ought to be a proliferation of trees in the garden, but instead we see more evidence of evergreens and bamboo. The guests at the gathering confront the viewer directly, almost to hint that we as viewers are standing among the apricot forest, which lies off the bottom edge of the picture surface. The garden guests are appreciating the proliferation of apricot blossoms, but we are unable to share in the object of their appreciation. The apricot flowers they behold are mere imagined objects for us, which is quite poetic.

What is the nature, and indeed the purpose, of this image? Is it primarily intended for entertainment, or does it have a political meaning? What kind of impression is it

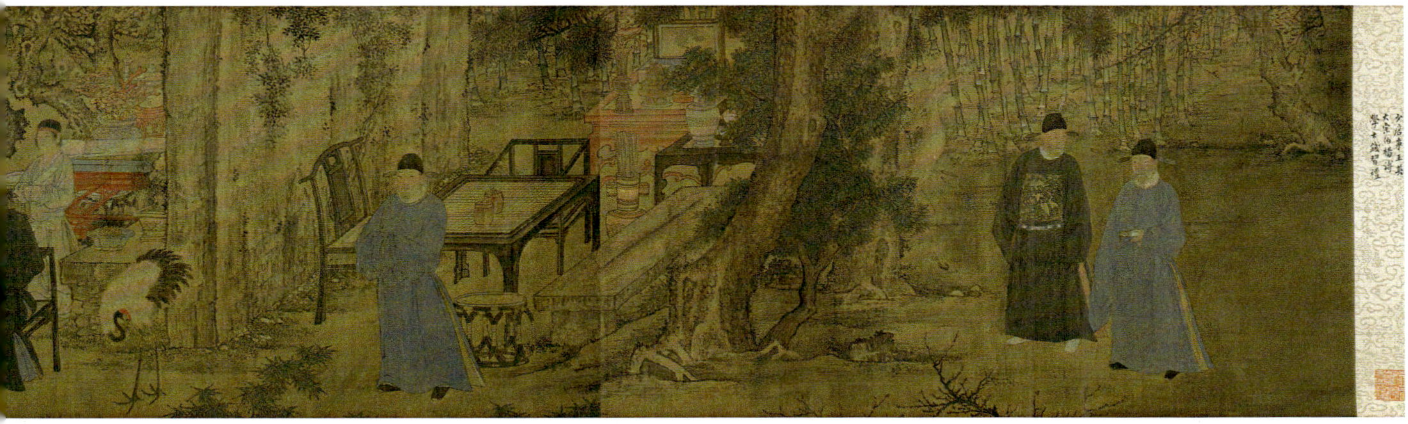

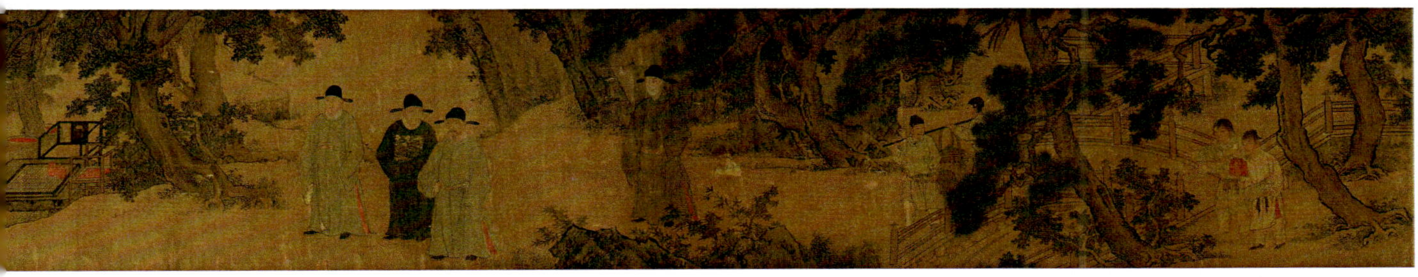

meant to leave on the viewer? The prefaces to the painting left by Yang Shiqi and Yang Rong certainly emphasise its political flavour. Yang Shiqi begins with this statement:

> Gentlemen of ancient times when at leisure would not pass a day when they forget all under the heaven and the state.
>
> 古之君子，其閒居未嘗一日而忘天下國家也。

Yang Rong concludes with a similar sentiment:

> Although in receiving the emperor's grace one must know recompense, even in enjoyment one must beware of idleness and excess. Even though I am old, I still wish to follow behind various gentlemen and be encouraged.
>
> 雖然感上恩而圖報，稱因宴樂而戒怠荒，予雖老，尚願從諸公之後而加勉焉。

From one opening to one conclusion, the colophons express political sentiments. Similar sentiments are evidenced in every poem recorded in the scroll.

Judging from the images, it seems that the dress of the people in the woodblock version of the *Elegant Gathering in the Apricot Garden* is more closely related to Yang Rong's description, as with the proverbial 'clothes and hat are smart and imposing, their grey hairs are shining' (*Yiguan weiran, huafa jiaoying* 衣冠偉然，華髮交映). On this point, I agree with Wu Sung-feng's view. Attire is often linked to bureaucratic systems and represents the social relationships and status of the wearer. The painting is separated into three sections, the middle section being the central part of the image and the left section acting as a secondary focus. Yang Shiqi, Yang Rong and Wang Zhi 王直 (1379–1462) appear in the first central section; Yang Shiqi is in the very central position, the host of the gathering Yang Rong is in attendance to his left, and Wang Zhi is at his right. This arrangement of figures asserts Yang Shiqi's prominence. At the time, Yang Shiqi was an official of rank 1b (*cong yipin* 從一品), Yang Rong was the same, while Wang Zhi was ranked 4a (*zheng sipin* 正四品). In the painting's 'sub-focus' to the left, Yang Pu 楊溥 (1372–1446) is located at the centre; he was ranked 2a (*zheng erpin* 正二品), and to his right is Wang Ying 王英 (1376–1449), also ranked 2a; to the left is Qian Xili 錢習禮 (1373–1461), an official ranked 5b (*cong wupin* 從五品). The third section of the scroll depicts three scholar officials walking. They are respectively Zhou Shu 周述 (d. 1439), Li Shimian 李時勉 (1374–1450) and Chen Xun 陳循 (1385–1462), all ranked 5b. The very central figure among the three sections is Yang Shiqi.

At this point in their careers Yang Shiqi shared the same official rank and title as Yang Rong. Because Yang Shiqi was tutor for both the Hongxi 洪熙 emperor (r. 1425) and the Xuande 宣德 emperor (r. 1426–35), and for many years accompanied these two rulers while they were on duty in Nanjing, he was in extremely close proximity to the ruler. From 1424 to 1444 Yang Shiqi was in effect the chief ministerial figure within the Grand Secretariat, so that his political life would have been at its apex in 1437, the date of the gathering where he was the pre-eminent figure. At this time the Zhengtong 正統 emperor (r. 1436–49) was only 11 years old; the entire realm was under the control of Empress Dowager Zhang 張 (d. 1442), widow of the Xuande emperor, working with a cohort of senior officials led by Yang Shiqi.

Was this an impromptu gathering, or a pre-planned party? Yang Rong's description seems to reflect spontaneity. 'Various gentlemen of the official council' (*guange zhugong* 館閣諸公) arranged to meet at his home, whereupon he then

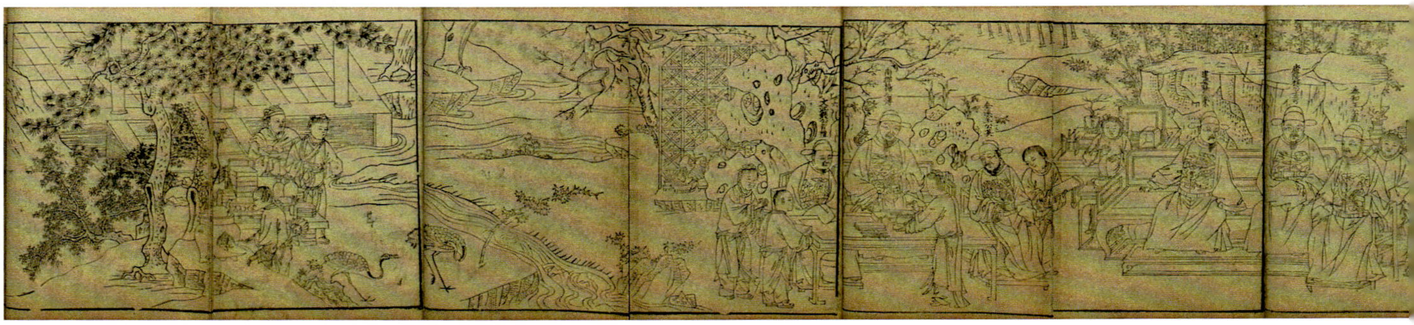

Plate 11.3 *Two Garden Gatherings* (*Eryuan ji* 二園集), c. 1560. Each page: height 21cm, width 14.7cm. Woodblock print, ink on paper. Chinese Rare Book Collection, Library of Congress, Washington, D.C.

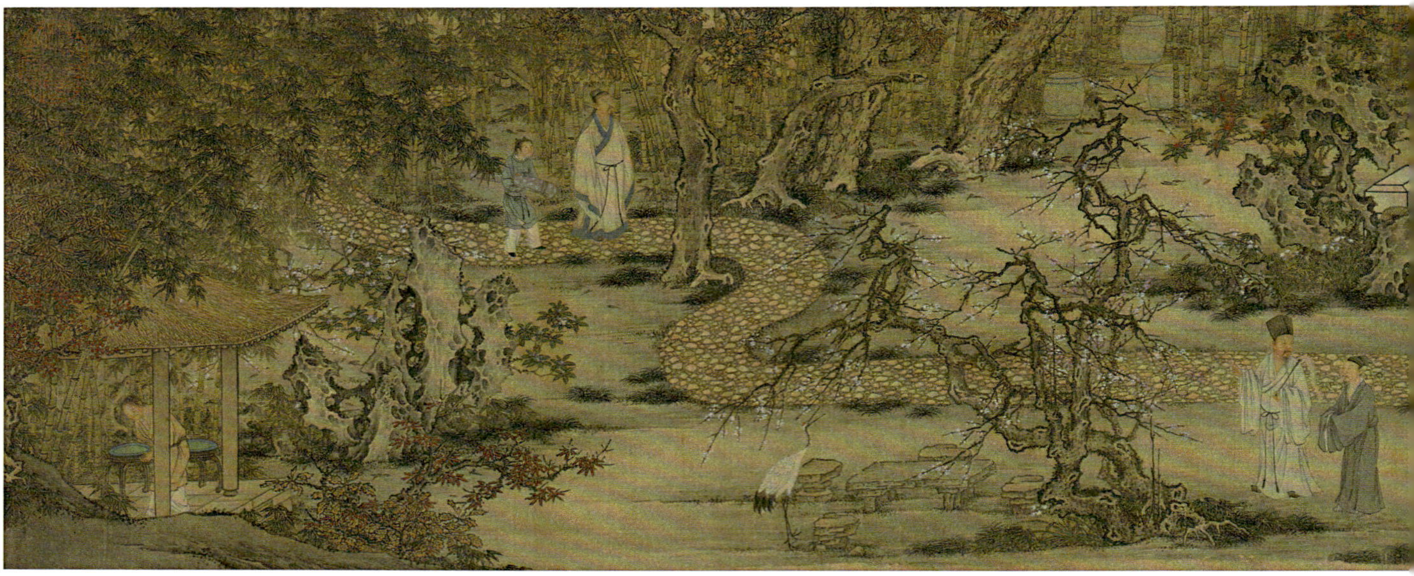

Plate 11.4 Attributed to Xie Huan 謝環 (1377–1452), *Nine Elders of the Mountain of Fragrance* (*Xiangshan jiulao tu* 香山九老圖), 1426–52. Handscroll, ink and colour on silk, height 30.6cm. The Cleveland Museum of Art, Bequest of Mrs A. Dean Perry 1997.99

invited everyone to Yang Rong's Apricot Garden. The painter Xie Huan's arrival seems unexpected, as if he had no foreknowledge of the gathering. From beginning to end, Yang Rong, as host and owner of the garden, does not give any suggestion that he was responsible for inviting everyone to the gathering. Thus the organiser of this gathering could very well have been Yang Shiqi, the central figure in the scroll, as well as the oldest member (at 73 years old) with the highest official status. It was a known habit of Yang Shiqi to hold gatherings in the private residences of others. For example, on the 26th day of the 12th month of 1422 Yang Shiqi held a 'Western City Feast' (*Xicheng yanji* 西城宴集) in the home of Chen Jingzong 陳敬宗 (1377–1459) in western Beijing.[15] The public reasons given for the gathering at Yang Rong's home were that it was the official season for the blossoming of apricot trees, just then in full flower, and that Yang Rong's Apricot Garden was just east of Chang'anmen 長安門 (Gate of Eternal Peace) and near Taijichang 台基廠, thus providing a central location convenient for scholar officials arriving from different directions.

From the pictorial representation we learn the important fact that not a single official from the northern part of the empire came to the Apricot Garden gathering. Despite the fact that the Yongle 永樂 emperor (r. 1403–24) had been combating the powerful cliques of southern landlords since his accession in 1403, this gathering is attended exclusively by officials from the southern region of the Ming realm. Moreover, of the southerners, there were no officials present from the provinces of Zhejiang or Jiangsu (*Nan zhili* 南直隸); of the other eight participants – with the exception of Yang Pu from Shishou 石首 in Huguang 湖廣 province – everyone at the gathering hailed from the single province of Jiangxi.[16] Their precise places of origin are as follows:

Yang Shiqi: Taihe 泰和 county, Jiangxi

Wang Zhi: Taihe 泰和 county, Jiangxi

Chen Xun: Taihe 泰和 county, Jiangxi

Wang Ying: Jinxi 金溪 county, Jiangxi

Qian Xili: Jishui 吉水 county, Jiangxi

Li Shimian: Anfu 安福 county, Jiangxi

Zhou Shu: Jishui 吉水 county, Jiangxi

This cannot be a coincidence, and in fact on the contrary seems to have happened by design. In a certain sense, this gathering can be understood as having the subversive flavour of a 'gathering of clansmen'. The same had been true of the 'Western City Feast' which Yang Shiqi had convened in the home of Chen Jingzong in 1422; of the 17 guests present there, 14 were from Jiangxi, and only three were

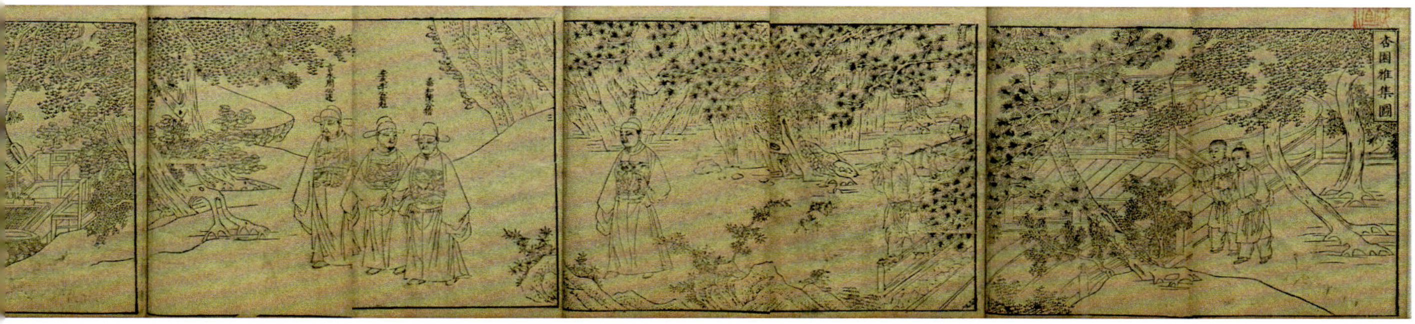

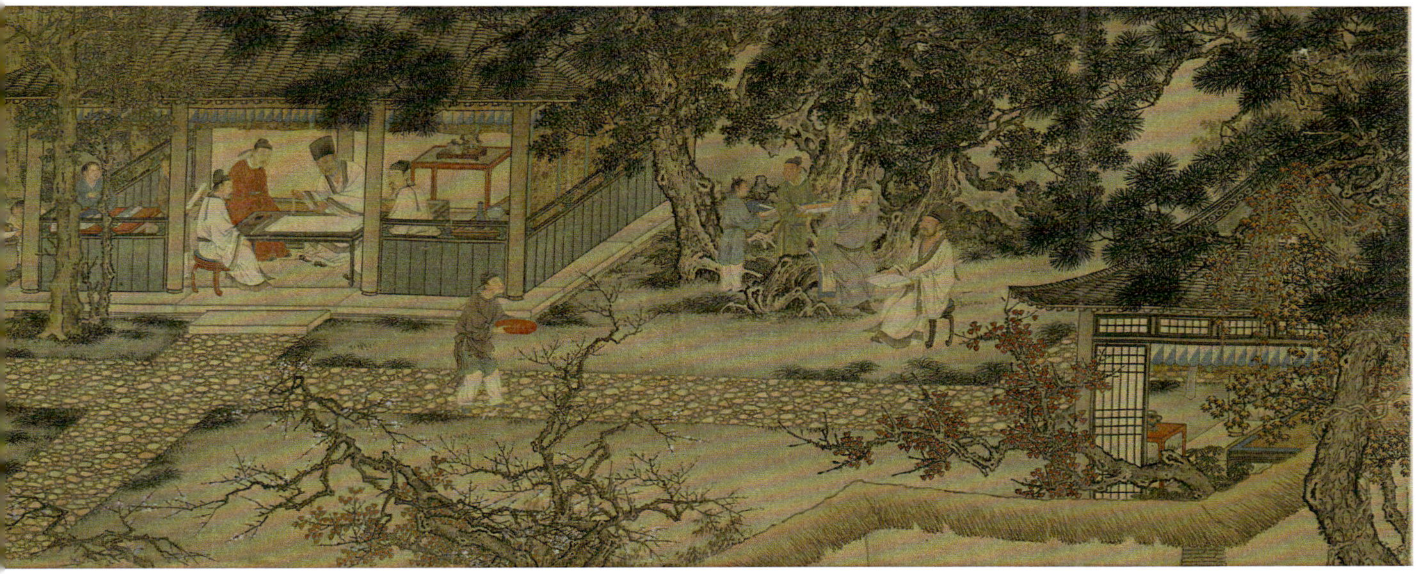

from Zhejiang. The location on that occasion was not the home of a Jiangxi native – and again nor was it Yang's own home – but rather was that of a Zhejiang native. Chen Jingzong had passed his metropolitan examinations and was awarded his *jinshi* degree in 1404, a year in which Yang Shiqi served as the official presiding over the examination system, thus putting him in the position of the younger man's mentor. At least one other guest at the 'Western City Feast' was a *jinshi* who had passed the exams in the same year of 1404, thus making him a classmate of Chen Jingzong, and equally beholden to Yang Shiqi.

It is thus relatively easy to grasp that this gathering, held in the private garden of Yang Rong (hailing from Fujian) and to which Yang Pu (from Huguang) was invited, was not a simple sabbatical celebration among senior court officials. Instead, it had the subtle flavour of a semi-private meeting of native Jiangxi officials. Only two of the nine officials at the Apricot Garden did not hail from Jiangxi (Yang Rong and Yang Pu); moreover, the undisputed leader of the Jiangxi connection within officialdom was none other than Yang Shiqi himself. This painting therefore can be seen as highlighting a crucial geographical characteristic of early Ming-dynasty politics.

From among the guests at the Apricot Garden gathering, Wang Ying, Wang Zhi, Li Shimian and Zhou Shu shared not only their Jiangxi roots, they had also passed their *jinshi* examinations in the same year of 1404 (when Yang Shiqi was an examiner). They shared a very close relationship. Wang Zhi and Chen Xun both shared the same origins as Yang Shiqi, in that all three were from Taihe county in Jiangxi. The *Elegant Gathering in the Apricot Garden* is thus also a reflection of the powerful status of Jiangxi officials at court. In earlier works on similar subject matter, such as *Nine Elders of the Mountain of Fragrance* (*Xiangshan jiulao tu* 香山九老圖) and *Elegant Gathering in the Western Garden* (*Xiyuan yaji tu* 西園雅集圖), the locality of the officials is diverse.[17] This differs from the clear prominence given to Jiangxi officials in the *Elegant Gathering in the Apricot Garden*. In addition to Yang Shiqi, 17 officials participated in the earlier 'Western City Feast', and essentially all of them had passed their metropolitan examinations in 1404. But geographical factors were important on this occasion too. Participants in this 'Western City Feast' included Zeng Qi 曾棨 (1372–1432), Wang Ying, Yu Xuekui 余學夔 (1372–1444), Qian Xili, Zhang Zonglian 張宗璉 (1374–1427), Chen Xun, Zhou Chen 周忱 (1381–1453), Peng Xianren 彭顯仁, Zhou Xu 周敘, Hu Tong 胡穜, Liu Chaozong 劉朝宗, Yu Zhengan 余正安 and Xiao Xingshen 蕭省身 (all 14 of these men were from Jiangxi), as well as Chen Jingzong, Gui Zongru 桂宗儒 and Zhang Chang 章敞 (all three of these men were from Zhejiang). Hu Tong, the son of Hu Guang 胡廣 (1369–1418), had entered the Hanlin Academy in 1418. Yang Shiqi wrote a preface expressly for the 'Western City Feast' which appears in his collected works *Dongli wenji* 東里文集 (Collected Works of Yang Shiqi).[18] But because no painter was in attendance on this occasion, we have no pictorial documentation of the event. We can see, however, that the foundation for Yang Shiqi's official power, based on a network of Jiangxi natives, had been established as early as 1404 among officials who passed the *jinshi* examination in that year. Not only did this grouping participate in the 'Western City Feast', but a portion of them were also in attendance at the Apricot Garden gathering over three decades later. These two gatherings both included a prominent number of Jiangxi 1404 *jinshi* officials.

In 1402, after the Yongle emperor defeated the Jianwen 建文 emperor (r. 1399–1402) and captured Nanjing, the structure and composition of the bureaucracy saw great changes. A Jiangxi network gradually came to replace the Zhejiang grouping of officials. During Zhu Yuanzhang's 朱元璋 (1328–98) time, military officials were drawn mostly from Anhui province, while civil officials came mostly from Zhejiang. Initially the cultured landlords of Jiangsu were excluded from power because of their relationship to Zhang Shicheng 張士誠 (1321–67), a rival of the Ming founder, but this began to change in the mid to late Ming dynasty. The Zhejiang connection had Song Lian 宋濂 (1310–81) and Liu Ji 劉基 (1311–75) as its chief representatives, so that officials from this province were heavily affected by their fall from power. During the Jianwen reign, Song Lian's student (and also a Zhejiang native) Fang Xiaoru 方孝孺 (1357–1402) was employed by the emperor himself, and became a symbol of the spirit of civil officialdom. After 1402, with the exception of Huang Huai 黃淮 (1367–1449, from Zhejiang) and Yang Rong (from Fujian), the remaining five Grand Secretariat officials were all from Jiangxi: Xie Jin 謝縉 (1369–1415), Yang Shiqi, Jin Youzi 金幼孜 (1367–1431), Hu Yan 胡儼 (1360–1443) and Hu Guang. In the 42 years between 1402 and 1444, the year that Yang Shiqi passed away, with the exception of Yang Rong's six years as Senior Grand Secretary (*Shou fu* 首輔), the three Jiangxi natives Xie Jin, Hu Guang and Yang Shiqi successively served as Senior Grand Secretary. We could therefore say that the configuration of official power during the Yongle reign was dominated by the Jiangxi lineage but with weaker Fujian and Zhejiang elements.

Beginning in the Yongle reign, the Jiangxi official network started to achieve political dominance, and at the same time its members also asserted influence on the literary arts with the so-called 'cabinet style' (*taige ti* 臺閣體) of poetic verse, which originated in the Jiangxi literary circles with Yang Shiqi as its archetypal practitioner (see discussions by David Robinson and Peter Ditmanson in Chapters 1 and 10 of this volume). But Jiangxi officials never took the lead in calligraphic or painting styles.[19] Conversely, although scholar officials in the Northern Song dynasty (960–1127), such as Su Shi 蘇軾 (1037–1101), never attained political dominance in their day, their place at the forefront of literature, calligraphy and painting is recognised by posterity. A later scroll, the *Gathering of Five who are Alike* (*Wu tong hui tu*) dated 1503 in the Palace Museum, Beijing, reflects the partial dominance of officials from the Jiangsu region during the mid-Ming dynasty, but it is not on par with the degree of political advantage that Jiangxi officials enjoyed as expressed in the *Elegant Gathering in the Apricot Garden* of 1437.

If we understand the *Elegant Gathering in the Apricot Garden* as an image of political power in 1437, how do we then understand the presence of the painter Xie Huan? Xie Huan hailed from Zhejiang, not Jiangxi. His appearance at the scene is intriguing. The two painters who worked on the 1499 scroll *Birthday Gathering in the Bamboo Garden*, Lü Wenying 呂文英 (1421–1505) and Lü Ji 呂紀 (b. 1477), were likewise from Zhejiang. It is known that Xie Huan and Yang Shiqi shared an amicable relationship; the bridge between them was the Zhejiang official Huang Huai. During the years 1403 to 1414, Huang Huai occupied a similar post to Yang Shiqi and other Jiangxi officials as mentor to the imperial princes, Zhu Gaochi 朱高熾 (1378–1425) (later the Hongxi emperor) and the imperial grandson Zhu Zhanji 朱瞻基 (1398–1435) (the Xuande emperor).[20] Huang Huai was also from Yongjia 永嘉 county, the same home locality as Xie Huan. According to research by the Wenzhou-based scholar Zhang Ruyuan 張如元, it was Huang Huai who recommended Xie Huan to the court, where he achieved fame as a professional painter.[21] Yang Shiqi was himself not a *jinshi* holder, but rather he came to court via introductions and recommendations (as was still possible in the very early Ming), in the same manner as Xie Huan. The man who first recommended Yang Shiqi was not, in fact, from Jiangxi. His recommender Wang Shuqying 王叔英 (d. 1402) hailed from Zhejiang and was a close friend of the distinguished Zhejiang scholar and official (and martyr in the cause of the Jianwen emperor) Fang Xiaoru. Importantly, this proves that Yang Shiqi had a close relationship to the Zhejiang cohort of officials from the very beginning of his career.

Huang Huai was thus an important link between the Jiangxi officials and the Zhejiang painter. He maintained a close relationship with the cohort of Jiangxi officials until 1427, when he retired to the Zhejiang countryside in his native Yongjia. On the eve of his departure from Beijing, the Jiangxi officials Yang Shiqi, Zeng Qi and Wang Ying sent poems commemorating his departure,[23] and in honour of the blossoming lotus flowers in front of his home, another of the Jiangxi officials, Wang Zhi, composed the *Preface to Poem of Auspicious Lotuses* (*Ruilian shi xu* 瑞蓮詩序).[24] As further testimony to the closeness of their relationship, in 1440 Huang Huai also composed a preface for Yang Shiqi's collected writings,[25] and when Yang Shiqi passed away in 1444, it was Huang Huai who wrote his funerary inscription.[26] Not only did Huang Huai endorse Xie Huan at court, he recommended other Zhejiang painters, Guo Chun 郭純 (1370–1444)[27] and Hu Zongyun 胡宗蘊,[28] to court as painters and calligraphers; he also recommended the painter Chen Zongyuan 陳宗淵 (b. 1370),[29] from Tiantai 天台 county in Zhejiang, for an official post in the Hanlin Academy. Guo Chun and Yang Shiqi are known to have had interactions, a fact that is testified to by Yang Shiqi's record of his visit to Guo Chun's studio, the 'humble hut' (*Pu zhai* 樸齋).[30]

There is one more Zhejiang scholar official who must be mentioned in this context, as previous art historians have yet to discuss him – this is Jiang Ji 蔣驥 (1378–1430), a consistent contact of Huang Huai who hailed from Qiantang 錢塘 city (modern Hangzhou 杭州) in Zhejiang. After his retirement in 1427, Huang Huai passed through Hangzhou on his way home, where the painter Dai Jin 戴進 (1388–1462) paid him a visit.[31] Shortly after, in 1428, Jiang Ji sent a letter from Beijing that discussed Dai Jin's entry to the court and talked of Dai's Beijing studio, called 'Snowy Bamboo Studio' (*Zhuxue shufang* 竹雪書房).[32] For this studio Dai asked Huang Huai to write an inscription, known as the *Record of the Snowy Bamboo Studio* (*Zhuxue shufang ji* 竹雪書房記). Whether Dai Jin worked at the imperial court is the subject of debate, but if he did, we can surmise that it was connected to Huang Huai. In addition, Yang Shiqi and Yang Rong both wrote poems for Dai Jin's studio.[33] Xie Huan inscribed a poem on Dai Jin's painting *Pine and Rock Pavilion* (*Songshi xuan tu* 松石軒圖). And on the occasion of Dai Jin's departure from Beijing, the Jiangxi official Wang Zhi also wrote him a departing poem.[34] When in 1428 Jiang Ji wrote to the retired Huang Huai about Dai Jin, he was by that time a lecturer at the Hanlin Academy. Jiang, together with Hu Guang, Yang Rong, Jin Youzi and Yang Pu, had all passed their *jinshi* exams in the same year of 1400. In 1430, after only 26 days of acting as Vice Minister of the Board of Rites, Jiang Ji suddenly passed away. It is possible that he was the direct advocate for Dai Jin's entry to the court, relying at this point on Huang Huai's powerful backing. Or perhaps it was Huang Huai who first introduced Dai Jin to Jiang Ji, who in his turn introduced Dai to his 'classmates' and contemporaries Yang Rong, Yang Pu and Jin Youzi. Whatever the possible scenarios, it appears that Huang Huai played a role in Dai Jin's meeting with Xie Huan, bringing these two important early Ming painters together.

Although Huang Huai was not himself present at the 1437 gathering at the Apricot Garden in Beijing, his presence and influence resonated throughout that event. Despite being a Zhejiang official, his relationship with the Jiangxi official cohort was always close, and it is this fact which helped ensure a special position for his protégé, the painter Xie Huan, at the Apricot Garden gathering. As for the other attendees – Wang Ying, Wang Zhi, Li Shimian and Zhou Shu – they shared a common background as officials and 1404 *jinshi* graduates. Despite the fact that Yang Shiqi had served as Minister Examiner during the *jinshi* exams of that year, the Chief Examiners in 1404 were the Jiangxi official Xie Jin and the Zhejiang official Huang Huai. Although Xie Jin had already passed away in 1415, Huang Huai was still alive during the time of the Apricot Garden gathering in 1437. He was a living 'mentor' to those who took the *jinshi* exams in 1404, and all of those officials who passed in that year were considered his 'students'. Huang Huai not only shared a native place of origin with Xie Huan, the two were by this point good friends of many years' standing.

It still remains slightly unclear as to why history has diluted the localist and political nature of the Jiangxi scholar officials' association that is so manifestly present in the *Elegant Gathering in the Apricot Garden*. This remains a question for future research.

Notes

1 The dates for Xie Huan are discussed in Yin Jinan 2007.
2 On the multiple versions of the painting, see Hearn 1999.
3 Clunas 1996, 64–6.
4 Clunas 1996, 64–6. A copy of *Eryuan ji*, *c.* 1560, is in the Chinese Rare Book Collection of the Library of Congress, Washington, D.C., accessible online at World Digital Library (https://www.wdl.org/en/item/296/).
5 See Li Ruoqing 2010, n. 31, citing Ni Yue 倪岳, *Qingxi mangao* 清溪漫稿 (*Writings from the Clear River*), *juan* 16.
6 Zhang Ning's journey to Joseon Korea is recorded in *Fengshi lu* 奉使錄 (*Record of Serving as an Envoy*).
7 On Ni Qian and Zhang Ning's relationship with Xie Huan, see Yin Jinan 2007.
8 On this event and scroll, see Yang Lili 2004a.
9 On this event and scroll, see Pan Shenliang 1988.
10 On this event and scroll, see Yang Lili 2004b. On Wu Kuan previously viewing the *Elegant Gathering in the Apricot Garden*, see Li Ruoqing 2010, n. 31.
11 This is recorded by Xu Lun in *Eryuan ji*.
12 See Lu Jiugao 1963.
13 Wu Sung-feng 2008.
14 Li Ruoqing 2010, 64–5.
15 Wu Sung-feng 2009.
16 Yang Shiqi *c.* 1445, 5.21b–23b.
17 Also discussed in Clunas 2014, 183–9, citing Dardess 1986.
18 Examples of these paintings can be found in the National Palace Museum, Taipei.
19 Yang Shiqi *c.* 1445, 5.21b–23b.
20 *Taige ti* as a style of calligraphy was associated with calligraphers like Shen Du 沈度 (1357–1434), who was not from Jiangxi.
21 For the biography of Huang Huai, see *DMB*, 665–6.
22 See Zhang Ruyuan 2007; also referred to by Yin Jinan 2007.
23 Yang Shiqi *c.* 1445, 7.12b–14a. 'Song shaobao Huanggong gui Yongjia shixu' 送少保黃公歸永嘉詩序 (*Preface to the Poem on Sending Off Master Huang to Yongjia*).
24 Wang Zhi *c.* 1465, 10.33a–34b.
25 See Yang Shiqi *c.* 1445, 1a–2b.
26 Huang Yongling 2006, *juan* 7.
27 Huang Yongling 2006, *juan* 10.
28 Huang Yongling 2006, *juan* 8.
29 Zhu Mouyin 1631, 4.15a.
30 Yang Shiqi *c.* 1445, 1.14a–15b.
31 On the life of Dai Jin, see Rogers 1993. This meeting is mentioned on 137–8.
32 Rogers 1993, 139.
33 Yang Weihua 2004, notes 19, 21.
34 Yang Weihua 2004, 82.

Chapter 12
The Gradual Termination of the Early Ming Voyages to the 'Western Ocean' and its Causes

Zhao Zhongnan

Translated by Luk Yu-ping

The voyages led by Zheng He 鄭和 (1371–1433) to the 'Western Ocean' (*Xiyang* 西洋, the area of maritime Southeast Asia west of Borneo extending into the Indian Ocean) were a major achievement in the history of Ming international relations, as well as a monumental feat in the maritime history of humankind. Six of Zheng He's seven voyages took place during the Yongle 永樂 reign (1403–24), while the seventh and final voyage occurred during the latter part of the Xuande 宣德 period (1426–35). Studies examining the achievements of these voyages by scholars in China and abroad have yielded fruitful results. There have been, however, relatively few systematic and in-depth investigations into the process and reasons behind the termination of Ming state-sponsored maritime voyages.

Suspension of the voyages in 1421

The beginning of the end of state-sponsored maritime voyages can be traced back to 1421, shortly after the completion of the transfer of the capital from Nanjing 南京 to Beijing 北京, and the destruction by fire of the three main halls of the newly built Forbidden City. On the 13th day of the fourth month of that year, the Yongle emperor issued an *Edict in Response to the Fengtian Hall Disaster* (*Fengtian dian zai kuan xu zhao* 奉天殿災寛恤詔), which clearly ordered the suspension of maritime activities, including shipbuilding and overseas trade.[1] The fire that destroyed the three main palace halls was interpreted as a divine warning to the Ming imperial court. Out of fear and respect for Heaven, the emperor called upon officials to reflect upon any errors that the imperial court had committed. In response, officials criticised the transfer of the capital to Beijing.[2] The decision to suspend maritime voyages also came about as officials reacted to the disastrous fire at the imperial palace. At the time, Zheng He's fleets were still at sea on their sixth maritime voyage. Given this and the character of the emperor, it is unlikely that he would have suspended maritime activities had it not been for broader problems within Ming society that made

Plate 12.1 Inside the Hall of Supreme Harmony (Taihedian 太和殿) of the Forbidden City, photo taken by Kazuma Ogawa in 1901. Tokyo National Museum

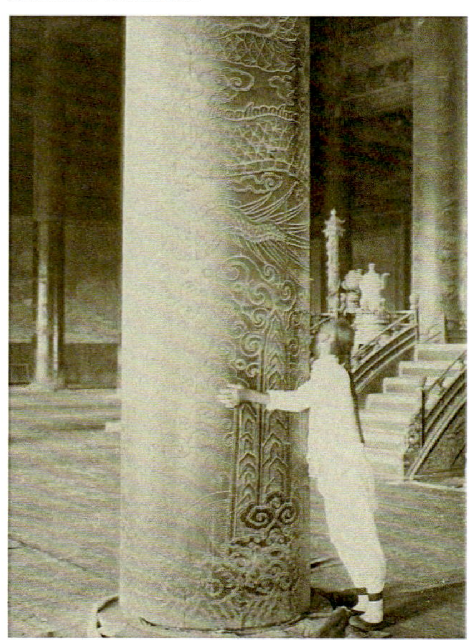

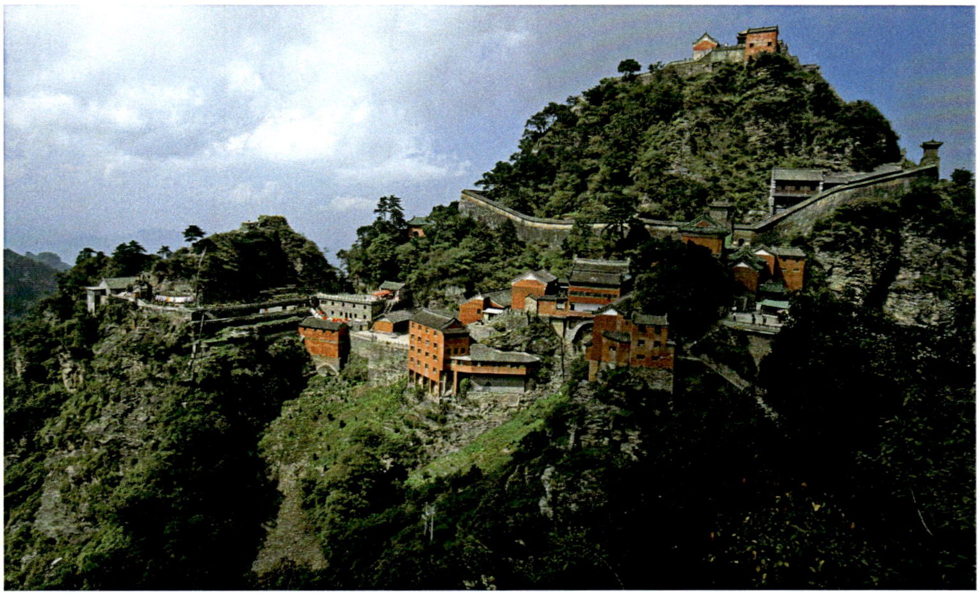

Plate 12.2 View of the Daoist temple complex at Mount Wudang, Hubei province

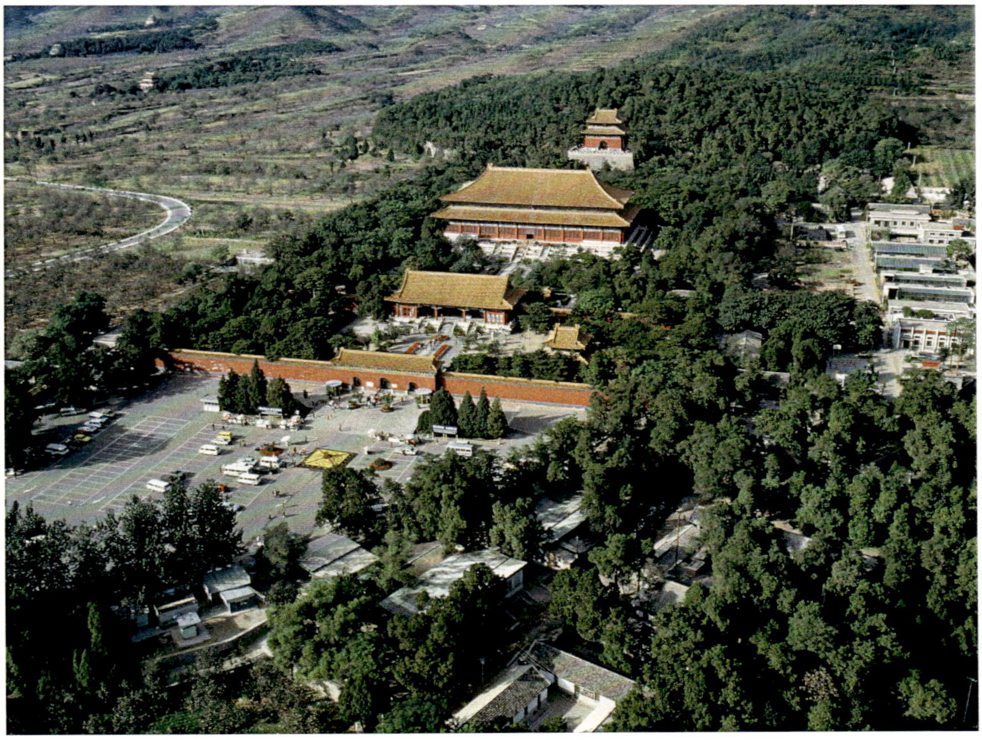

Plate 12.3 View of Changling 長陵, the Mausoleum of the Yongle emperor and Empress Xu. Part of the Ming imperial tombs on the outskirts of Beijing

it difficult for the voyages to continue. Specifically, there were three main reasons for the suspension of the voyages in 1421, which will be discussed below.

Firstly, the Ming dynasty under the Yongle emperor faced an over-depletion of its 'comprehensive state power' (*zonghe guoli* 綜合國力). Projects of unprecedented scale involving millions of people took place during the Yongle reign, including military campaigns to the north and south of the empire, the building of a new capital (**Pl. 12.1**) and imperial mausoleum, construction of a large temple complex at Mount Wudang 武當山 (**Pl. 12.2**), and the restoration of the Grand Canal. These projects took place almost concurrently, all requiring enormous investment of labour, material resources and finances, which significantly depleted the strength of the Ming state. It has been estimated that the cost of all of these projects combined would have been two or three times the revenue of the state, which the Ming government tried to manage through the conscription of free labour and resources.[3] Although this analysis is not entirely precise, the point it makes is convincing.

Under these circumstances, some major activities during the Yongle reign had to be suspended or stopped entirely since they were too costly and the resources that they consumed could not be replenished in time. For example, the construction of the Yongle emperor's mausoleum, Changling 長陵 (**Pl. 12.3**), was intermittent because of the demands of building the new capital in Beijing. As a result of the frequent campaigns in the north of China, the large-scale military operations against Annam could not be sustained, and only a small number of soldiers were left to defend a portion of the fortresses.[4] Similarly, it was difficult

A second reason for the suspension of state-sponsored maritime activities during the Yongle reign was the high cost of maintaining the fleets. The voyages led by Zheng He involved many ships of different sizes, populated by a crew of 20,000 to 30,000 people (see discussion by Sally Church in Chapter 22 of this volume).[7] In order to replenish supplies and maintain the condition of the ships, a large number of craftsmen were needed to conduct repairs at the ports and shipyards along the coast. A variety of timbers and materials, such as raw lacquer and *tung* oil for waterproofing surfaces, had to be prepared in advance or transported to the repair stations from across the country. Special timber was sourced from forests in Yunnan 雲南, Guizhou 貴州 and Huguang 湖廣 provinces, which was difficult to fell and transport. Moreover, Zheng He's fleets were manned with troops that were capable of intervening in local disputes by force, which required military expenditure. Thus, the fleets not only incurred expenses while they were at sea, but also after they had returned to China. One Ming source estimates that as a result of Zheng He's voyages, as much as six million *liang* of silver had been wiped off from the state treasury.[8] Archaeological excavations have also revealed the large scale of the Longjiang Shipyard (*Longjiang chuanchang* 龍江船廠) in Nanjing. As a principally agrarian society, the Ming dynasty could not cope with the financial burden of maintaining fleets of this size with only short gaps between voyages, while at the same time shouldering the costs of military campaigns and major building projects.

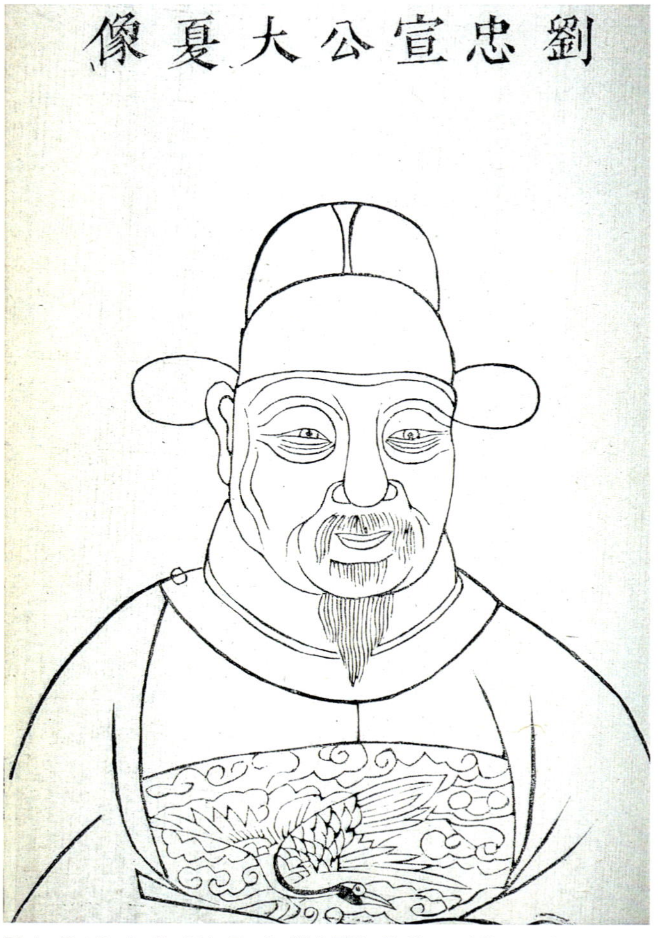

Plate 12.4 Portrait of Liu Daxia 劉大夏 in *Collected Illustrations of the Three Realms* (*Sancai tuhui* 三才圖會), published in 1609. SOAS Library, RM c.80.s.1, Portraits, *juan* 8, p. 31

to sustain the northern military campaigns because of insufficient provisions and funds for the troops. The Yongle emperor's final three military expeditions to the north were almost entirely instigated by the ruler himself through the force of his imperial authority. Other construction projects were not all completed during the Yongle reign, and instead had to be finished in stages later on. As such, the state-sponsored maritime voyages were only one of several large-scale projects that were stopped or put on hold during the latter part of the Yongle period.

While the Ming state during the early Yongle reign may have had the means to cope with a series of large-scale projects, this was not the case in the middle and later parts of the period. Zheng He's repeated voyages incurred large expenditures, as substantial rewards were given to foreign rulers and treasures were purchased at inflated prices. In addition, activities such as military campaigns, the transfer of the capital and construction of the imperial mausoleum resulted in the consumption of resources at an unprecedented rate that could not be replenished in time. This put the Ming population and society on the whole under financial strain.[5] Although the Yongle emperor still harboured thoughts of sending fleets on further maritime voyages in early 1424, and Zheng He and others were already making the necessary preparations, the plan did not materialise following the death of the emperor and the cost of other ongoing state projects.[6]

A third reason was that any material gains from the maritime voyages could not compensate for the vast quantities of resources consumed by projects undertaken during the Yongle reign. In preparation for each voyage, large amounts of silver, luxury goods and special local products, such as silk and porcelain produced at Jingdezhen, were collected to serve as capital for trade.[9] These items might be levied or purchased, which placed additional burdens on local populations and governments. It is impossible now to calculate accurately the profitability of trade conducted on Zheng He's voyages. Regardless of this, the goods that the fleets brought back to China would have been kept by the imperial court and not used to offset the depletion of material resources and corvée labour that formed the basis of military campaigns and building projects. In an economy that still relied heavily on physical assets, the treasures and special goods brought back from foreign lands could not be easily converted into official currency to purchase construction materials and provisions for the troops, or to provide an adequate salary for soldiers and labourers. Instead, these goods could only be enjoyed by the courts, without any benefit to ordinary people and society at large.[10] This was the view of the official Liu Daxia 劉大夏 (1436–1516) (**Pl. 12.4**) during the Chenghua 成化 reign (1465–87) on the possibility of resuming the voyages:

> Several hundred thousand units of money and food would be spent; soldiers and ordinary people would die in their tens of thousands. Even if the fleets returned with extraordinary treasures, how would that be of benefit to the state?
>
> 費錢糧數十萬，軍民死且萬計，縱得奇寶而回，於國家何益！[11]

As noted earlier, it has been claimed that Zheng He's voyages spent around six million *liang* of silver. This was out of seven million that they took with them.[12] The same source further records that the Yongle emperor gave the remaining funds to the Ministry of Works to pay for the construction of Da Baoensi 大報恩寺 (Great Monastery of Filial Gratitude) in Nanjing.[13] This claim is hard to verify.[14] The financial activities of the imperial court were often left unrecorded. However, money issued by the Ming government was known to be ineffective as a market currency at the time, while the building and decoration of the Da Baoen Monastery needed special materials that were not easily acquired through simple corvée labour or purchases from the market. It is thus feasible that unused silver from Zheng He's voyages, accepted by the market and not officially issued, was used to fund the building of the Monastery. This would have hastened the process of the monetisation of silver in Ming society. There is no record that other construction projects and military campaigns received the same exceptional financial support as the Da Baoen Monastery, even if they were more costly. Any silver remaining from the voyages would have supported very limited projects, while treasures brought back from the voyages could not be turned into currency to replenish the resources depleted by wars and construction. This resulted in a vicious cycle of spending that could not continue.

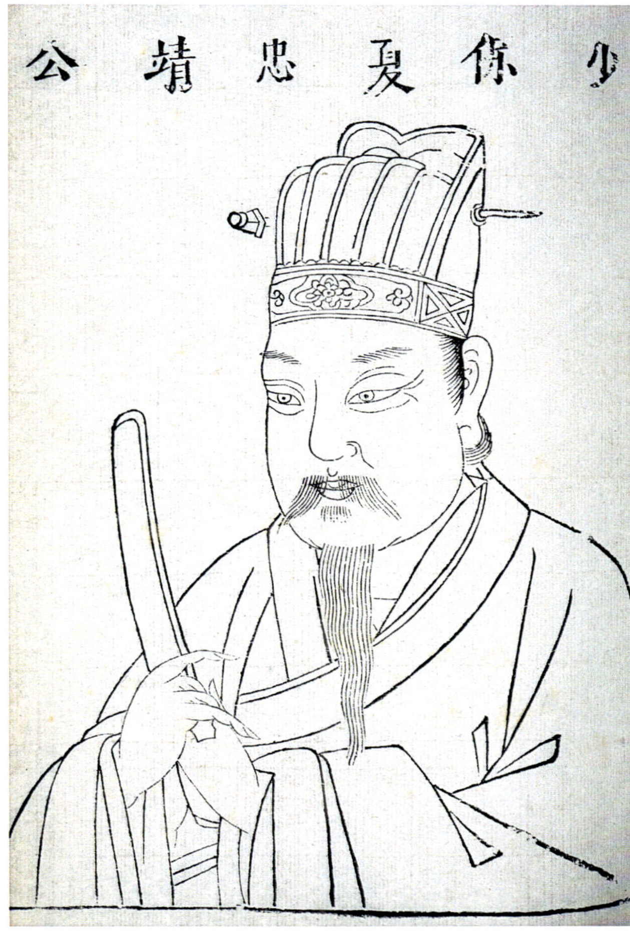

Plate 12.5 Portrait of Xia Yuanji 夏元吉 in *Collected Illustrations of the Three Realms* (*Sancai tuhui* 三才圖會), published in 1609. SOAS Library, RM c.80.s.1. Portraits, *juan* 8- additional, p. 10

Termination of the voyages during the Hongxi reign (1425)

After the enthronement of the Hongxi 洪熙 emperor (r. 1425), his officials drafted an edict on his behalf that ordered the suspension of treasure ship building activities. Ships that were docked at the ports in Fujian 福建 and Taichang 太倉 were recalled to Nanjing, and goods intended for overseas trade were returned to the inner palace for storage.[15] As noted above, several major projects from the Yongle reign were already unsustainable during the emperor's lifetime. Some of the projects even competed with each other over resources, while ministers increasingly voiced objections towards them. Tensions also existed between the Hongxi emperor when he was a prince and his father over his right to govern and inherit the throne. Thus, when he became ruler, the Hongxi emperor agreed with the views of his officials and terminated state-sponsored maritime voyages, in addition to other costly large-scale projects that had begun during his father's reign.[16]

Although the Hongxi emperor's enthronement edict was issued under his name, it was in fact drafted by the Grand Secretary Yang Shiqi 楊士奇 (1365–1444) based upon proposals from officials including Xia Yuanji 夏元吉 (1366–1430) (**Pl. 12.5**) and Yang Rong 楊榮 (1371–1440).[17] Thus, the content of the edict, including the declaration to terminate maritime voyages, expressed the shared attitude of officialdom. It shows the concern of Confucian scholar officials for the well-being of the state and the livelihood of ordinary people. More importantly, Zheng He's voyages were not simply commercial in nature; they were primarily political and diplomatic missions aimed at showcasing the might of the Ming state and its dominant status in the region. This included intervening in and pacifying local conflicts through military force along the way, and attempting to establish an ideal international order shaped by the Ming empire.[18] While the voyages did establish the Ming empire's central place in the tribute-trade system, and impressed upon kingdoms in Southeast Asia and the Indian Ocean the existence of a great power to their east, the cost of this enterprise was substantial. Zheng He's voyages, together with the Yongle emperor's other large-scale activities, had overstretched the limited capacity of the Ming state. Consequently, once the Hongxi emperor ascended the throne, he took a different path, and implemented tightening and stabilising policies, such as suspending state-sponsored maritime voyages and military campaigns, and even considered moving the capital back to Nanjing, in order to ease the burden on the Ming state.[19]

Furthermore, the Yongle emperor was a ruler who came to power through usurping the throne. One of the driving forces behind his large-scale activities, including cultural projects such as the compilation of the *Yongle dadian* 永樂大典 (*Great Canon of the Yongle Reign*), was the need to establish himself as an extraordinary emperor and to change the perception that he became emperor through questionable means, in order to enhance the legitimacy and rightfulness of his rulership.[20] The Hongxi emperor did not share this experience and attitude. To the contrary, the officials he relied upon used the suspension of large-scale, exorbitant projects to establish and enhance the standing of the new emperor and his senior government. There were clearly both proactive and reactive elements in the Hongxi emperor's decision to suspend state-sponsored maritime voyages.

The Hongxi emperor and his circle of advisors turned away from the Yongle emperor's taxing and outward-looking policies, and to an extent returned to the policies of the late Hongwu and Jianwen reigns, in order to enable society to return to a path of peace and stability. This marked the beginning of a period known as 'the rule of Ren and Xuan' (*Ren Xuan zhi zhi* 仁宣之治), referring to the Hongxi (Renzong 仁宗) and Xuande 宣德 (宣宗, r. 1426–35) reigns, which saw a more practical and stable kind of governance. This change was not only a turn to stability from one emperor to the next, but also an example of a wider process in which imperial rulership moved from the founding of a dynasty, towards pioneering activities, then stable development.[21] Moreover, compared to his father who possessed an extroverted martial character, the Hongxi emperor was more inward-looking and focused on preserving the achievements of the past. This difference in temperament is demonstrated in the divergent directions that the two men took in their policies. Even if the Ming state had remained strong, and tensions did not exist between him and his father, the Hongxi emperor still would not have actively advocated for the continuation of state-sponsored maritime voyages.

Suspension and resumption of the voyages during the Xuande reign (1426–35)

In the first five years of his reign, the Xuande emperor did not dispatch fleets on state-sponsored maritime voyages. Then in the sixth year of his reign (1431), Zheng He and his fleet was sent to the 'Western Ocean' once again. There are three main reasons for this change. Firstly, before 1431, Ming society and economy had not fully recovered to the level of the early Yongle reign. Secondly, since the Hongxi emperor had declared the suspension of the voyages in his enthronement edict, the Xuande emperor could not overturn this decision in the short term. In his own initial edict, the Xuande emperor had explicitly stated that he would abide by the orders given by his father when he ascended the throne.[22] Resuming state-sponsored voyages in the first few years of his reign would have given the impression that he had betrayed ancestral instructions and broken his own promises.

Thirdly, the presence of the senior official Xia Yuanji was an important factor in preventing the Xuande emperor from quickly resuming maritime voyages. Xia served as the Minister of Finance in the latter part of the Yongle reign, and resolutely opposed costly expansionist projects. His views were crucial in shaping the content of the Hongxi emperor's enthronement edict, which the Xuande emperor followed. The Xuande emperor was also personally close to Xia, since the official had guided and advised him when he was still the imperial 'grandson-heir' during the Yongle reign. After he became ruler, the Xuande emperor continued to ask for Xia's advice on many aspects of government, so that Xia occupied a pre-eminent position within officialdom.[23] The emperor would not have easily resumed state-sponsored voyages as long as Xia continued to oppose them.

The situation, however, changed from 1431 onwards. The strength of the Ming state had largely recovered, the effect of the Hongxi emperor's initial edict had faded, and Xia Yuanji had by then passed away. The three main obstacles to resuming maritime voyages were thus largely neutralised. Under these circumstances, the Xuande emperor could venture to resume sending fleets overseas. Moreover, unlike his father, he had enjoyed a very good relationship with the Yongle emperor, so he did not completely renounce the policies of the earlier ruler, but instead tried to reach a compromise between the positions of his two predecessors. This was his approach on the matter of state-sponsored maritime voyages: after an initial suspension, he resumed them once conditions allowed, making possible Zheng He's seventh and final voyage that took place from 1430 to 1433.

In his later years, the Xuande emperor had to issue multiple edicts aimed at lightening the burden on ordinary people of his own excessive spending on courtly pleasures and entertainment. Despite this, he had no intention of suspending state-sponsored maritime voyages. Ming imperial porcelain decorated with sea creatures and waves, which appeared during the Yongle reign and were related to maritime activities, became more widespread under the Xuande emperor. The motif can be found on a variety of surviving vessels in the same way as auspicious flora and fauna patterns.[24] These porcelain pieces were daily wares that accompanied the emperor in the imperial court. To an extent, the motif of sea creatures and waves, painted in different colours in a lively and refined manner, must have expressed the emperor's interest and attitude towards maritime voyages. On the 21st day of the ninth month of 1434, the Xuande emperor issued an *Edict to Suspend Collecting Materials in Response to Disaster* (*Xuzai tingzhi wuliao chi* 恤災停止物料敕) that ordered the Ministry of Works to stop collecting raw materials from Southern Zhili 南直隸 region (present-day Jiangsu, Anhui and Shanghai), which was suffering from natural disasters.[25] The edict did not, however, suspend preparations of materials for use on ships intended for maritime voyages; instead they would continue as planned.

Yet, three months later, on the first day of the first month of 1435, an *Edict to Hasten Labour* (*Chiyi chi* 馳役敕) was issued, addressed to the Ministry of Works and Li Long 李隆, a military official guarding Nanjing, which for the first time ordered the termination of all purchasing and manufacturing activities related to ships intended for maritime voyages.[26] It is likely that this edict was issued by senior officials under the emperor's name, since by this time the Xuande emperor was gravely ill and unable to attend court audiences. He would pass away two days later. On the day of his death, another *Edict to Stop Collecting and Capturing* (*Tingzhi caibu chi* 停止採捕敕) reaffirmed the ban on activities related to maritime voyages, in addition to the cancellation of the gathering of rare flora and fauna.[27]

Curiously, the *Edict to Stop Collecting and Capturing* was issued on the same day as the Xuande emperor's posthumous edict. Normally an emperor's posthumous edict would be drafted by an official appointed to the task, and issued under the deceased emperor's name. The timing of the *Edict to Stop Collecting and Capturing*, and the fact that it deals with matters that the Xuande emperor was fond of while he was alive, suggest the likelihood that it was originally drafted by senior officials intending to further curtail spending at the imperial court. But since the emperor had passed away, the document could only be distributed together with his posthumous edict.[28] The *Edict to Stop Collecting and Capturing* would appear in its entirety in the initial decree of the Zhengtong 正統 emperor (r. 1436–49), which was also drafted by Yang Shiqi.[29] In addition, shortly after the Xuande emperor's death, his mother Empress Dowager Zhang 張 (1379–1442) ordered the removal of all of his former playthings, such as cricket jars, from the palace.[30] This suggests that the edict to suspend state-sponsored maritime voyages was actually issued by senior officials with the support of the empress dowager at the time of the emperor's illness and death.

On a broader level, the pursuit of economic benefit had become an unavoidable social trend in China starting from the early Ming, and especially during the Xuande reign, given the rise of private maritime trade and local handicraft industries, the monetarisation of silver and the development of domestic and international commodity markets. The Ming empire also faced numerous problems at the end of the Xuande reign, which included excessive spending by the imperial court that affected state finances,[31] depreciation of the official currency,[32] and economic instability. Under these circumstances, the Ming government could not ignore economic considerations and other pressing social concerns, and risk investing vast resources into state-sponsored maritime voyages. Senior officials, together with the empress dowager and the eunuch Wang Zhen 王振 (d. 1449), took advantage of the circumstances and the opportunity to issue edicts to urgently correct the problems in rulership under the Xuande emperor during his later years. The fact that the Zhengtong emperor's enthronement edict makes no mention of state-sponsored maritime voyages can be considered the official end point of this enterprise. The death of Zheng He during his seventh voyage, in the Xuande reign, is another reason for its termination.

Attempt to resume the voyages and its abandonment during the Chenghua reign (1465–87)

Following the death of the Xuande emperor, the Zhengtong emperor ascended the throne at a very young age. He was guided by a group of senior officials who had long opposed maritime voyages, so resuming them was not possible at the time. The Jingtai 景泰 emperor (r. 1450–56), who became ruler after the Tumu 土木 debacle in 1449, concentrated his attention on internal affairs. He also did not consider sending fleets overseas. When the Zhengtong emperor retook the throne with the new reign title Tianshun 天順 (r. 1457–64), there were suggestions to resume state-sponsored voyages, but these were strongly and immediately opposed by officials who reasoned that the state had more pressing concerns, namely the threat spreading across the country of farmers leaving their farms to evade taxes.[33] The issue was dropped. The emperor largely continued policies from the early Zhengtong reign that was relatively stable, and maritime voyages were no longer considered.

The subsequent Chenghua emperor, however, with the support of eunuchs, did entertain thoughts of resuming state-sponsored voyages. This was, however, strongly opposed by officials such as Liu Daxia, quoted earlier, whose view was supported by the high-ranking Minister of War Xiang Zhong 項忠 (1421–1502).[34] But the enormous cost of the voyages and their perceived lack of benefit were not the only reason why officials opposed them. Another reason had to do with the fact that pepper (*hujiao* 胡椒) and sappanwood (*sumu* 蘇木), brought back by Zheng He's fleets from Southeast Asia, had been distributed to officials as wages over an extended period of time. During Zheng He's first voyage, they were brought back to China as rare goods. It is said that the spices commanded an official price that was 20 times higher than their value overseas.[35] Since pepper and sappanwood were considered rare and expensive, they were bestowed upon high-ranking officials and members of the aristocracy as a special reward.

Over time, however, the quantity of pepper and sappanwood brought back to China increased. Apart from Zheng He's voyages, foreign envoys also presented the spices as tribute. This led to the amassing of an enormous stockpile of spices. Oversupply caused the prices of pepper and sappanwood to depreciate rapidly in the market. Faced with spices laying to waste in storage, the Ming government decided to use pepper and sappanwood as a form of currency to give to labourers and soldiers, and as a part of the salary given to civil and military officials in Nanjing and Beijing. The earliest record of the distribution of pepper and sappanwood to officials as remuneration dates to 1422.[36] Later on, the proportion of spices fluctuated, but eventually the Ming government established a standard practice of allotting money as salary in the first half of the year and spices in the second half.[37]

Around 50 years later in 1471, perhaps due to the diminishing stock of spices and dissatisfaction among officials, pepper and sappanwood were at one point replaced by cloth from the imperial treasury as part of official salary.[38] However, the arrangement of distributing money in the first half of the year and spices in the second half to officials still continued.[39] This practice only stopped in 1481, when there was less than a year's salary worth of spices in storage and the emperor agreed to replace spices with other currency in the official salary.[40] Thus, from 1422 to 1481, that is for around 60 years in the early part of the Ming dynasty, part of the remuneration of officials in the two capitals was paid in the form of pepper and sappanwood. If one includes the years when these spices were distributed to labourers and soldiers during the Yongle reign, then the history of the Ming government imposing pepper and sappanwood as currency lasted for more than 70 years.[41]

The Ming government had in effect partially shifted its own financial crisis on to civil and military officials. Pepper and sappanwood were nearly worthless to officials at the time as there was no market for them, and no household needed the amount distributed. Officials who had devoted many years of their lives to serving the state struggled to eke out a living and support their families on their income. Not surprisingly, this led to deep dissatisfaction among officials. In fact, not only were the spices given as part of their salary worthless, the paper money and copper coins issued by the government were also not entirely accepted by the market as forms of currency.[42] Instead the monetisation of silver, which was not officially issued and had been used by the government to purchase spices and other foreign goods, grew in importance. Consequently, officials during the mid-Ming dynasty desired silver rather than spices in their salary. Although it was the government that forced spices on to officials, the original source of the spices was Zheng He's voyages, when they were purchased at inflated prices. The strong opposition voiced by officials in the two capitals towards resuming state-sponsored voyages was thus based on their personal interests as well as the interest of the state.

Zheng He's final voyage was completed in 1433 during the Xuande reign. Maritime voyages were not discussed again at the imperial court until 1471 during the Chenghua reign. This meant that there was a period of nearly 40 years when the ships built for long-distance journeys had been left idle, without adequate repair and maintenance. If the voyages resumed, the cost of preparing the ships would have been considerable and beyond what the Ming government could afford in the short term. Although the strength of the Ming state under the Chenghua reign exceeded that of the early Ming, various reasons such as the weakened authority of the emperor and government, and the lesser capability of the state to control local society, meant that the Ming empire could no longer concentrate resources on large-scale projects. The Chenghua emperor did not have the power and authority of the Yongle emperor, who could act wilfully to persist with military campaigns, transfer of the capital and maritime voyages with no regard for official opposition and the cost to the state. Moreover, the Ming economy had changed from a system based on physical assets towards one based on currency. The Ming imperial court was no longer able to levy forcibly all the material and resources needed for the fleets in the same manner as in the early Ming.[43] This change is another reason why the Ming dynasty could no longer continue state-sponsored maritime voyages.

The Yongle and Xuande emperors had additional incentive to continue the maritime voyages despite opposition, since they relied on 'treasure ships' (*baochuan* 寶船) to bring back precious goods from foreign lands to the imperial court. Decades later during the Chenghua reign, the imperial court had access to one million *liang* of silver annually in the treasury for expenses.[44] It could also depend on avenues such as the Bureau for Foreign Shipping (*Shibo si* 市舶司) situated along the southeastern coast to purchase high-grade imported foreign goods at far lower cost than dispatching fleets overseas.[45] In addition, during the Chenghua reign, only individual eunuchs supervising the Palace Treasury supported resuming the voyages. None of the most powerful members of the imperial court at the time, such as the eunuchs Huai En 懷恩 (d. 1488) and Liang Fang 梁芳 (fl. 1470), and the emperor's favourite consort Lady Wan 萬 (1428–87), expressed clear support for the idea. The Chenghua emperor himself did not share the ambition of the Yongle and Xuande emperors for long-distance maritime voyages. Thus, the termination of the voyages to the 'Western Ocean' was inevitable.

Notes

1 *HMZL* 6, 124.
2 *MS* 149, 4152.
3 Mote and Twitchett 1988, 276.
4 *MSJSBM* 1977, 22, 351.
5 *MSJSBM* 1977, 21, 337.
6 Xie Xie 1959, *juan* 18, 761, 766.
7 For instance, one estimation is given in *MS* 204, 7767.
8 Wang Shixing 1981, *juan* 1, 5.
9 Wan Ming 2014, 158.
10 This follows the view of Zhao Tiefeng 趙鐵峰 of Northeast Normal University in China.
11 Jiao Hong 1981, 150.
12 Wang Shixing 1981, *juan* 1, 5.
13 Wang Shixing 1981, *juan* 2, 23.
14 This follows the view of Professor Xia Weizhong 夏維中 of the Department of History at Nanjing University.
15 *HMZL* 9, 131.
16 Zhao Zhongnan 2005.
17 The edict is recorded in Yang Shiqi's literary compilation. See Yang Shiqi 1986, 582–6.
18 Ueda 2014, ch. 4.
19 Zhao Zhongnan 1997, 10.
20 Zhao Zhongnan 2015, 66.
21 Zhao Zhongnan 2008, 243.
22 *HMZL* 9, 146.
23 *MS* 149, 4152.
24 Liao Baoxiu 1998, 137.
25 *HMZL* 9, 174–5.
26 *HMZL* 9, 176.
27 *HMZL* 9, 176.
28 This follows the view of Zhang Jiaoyu 張兆裕 of the Chinese Academy of Social Sciences.
29 *HMZL* 9, 178.
30 Xie Xie 1959, *juan* 21, 883.
31 Zhao Zhongnan 2015, 551.
32 *MS* 81, 1964.
33 *MS* 164, 4458.
34 Jiao Hong 1981, *juan* 5, 150.
35 Wan Ming 2014, 146.
36 *MSL Xuanzong shilu* 9.8a, Hongxi 1/9/癸丑.
37 *MS* 82, 2003.
38 *MSL Xianzong shilu* 97.5b, 7/10/丁丑.
39 *MSL Xianzong shilu* 191.1b–2a, 15/6/辛卯.
40 *MSL Xianzong shilu* 214.7a, 17/4/甲子.
41 Wan Ming 2014, 148–51.
42 *MS* 81, 1964.
43 This follows the view of Professor Gao Shouxian 高壽仙 of the Chinese Academy of Governance.
44 *MS* 79, 1927.
45 Fang Zhiyuan 1996, 189, 193.

Chapter 13
The New Idea of Ritual Vessels in the Early Ming Dynasty: A Third System?

Shih Ching-fei

The new ritual vessels system established in the early Ming lies in two parts. Firstly, the long-standing tradition of making ritual vessels in ancient bronze shapes was almost abandoned. Secondly, porcelain was elevated as the primary material for important ritual vessels employed in worshipping ceremonies for both the state and local courts. The ritual vessels referred to in this chapter are those used for the state's most important ritual category of *jili* 吉禮 (auspicious or festivity rituals), including the worship of Heaven, Earth, the Sun and Moon, and the worship of ancestors in the *Taimiao* 太廟 (Imperial Ancestral Temple) and Confucius temples. In Chinese history, *li* 禮 (ritual propriety) was regarded as one of the important foundations for state rulership. It is thus crucial for a state to issue proper ritual regulations, and the substantial content of the ritual regulations relates to the Five Rites (*wuli* 五禮).

The Five Rites were festivity rituals (*jili* 吉禮), guest rituals (*binli* 賓禮), military rituals (*junli* 軍禮), congratulational rituals (*jiali* 嘉禮) and 'inauspicious rituals' (*xiongli* 兇禮, i.e. funeral rites). The system of the Five Rites reaches a mature stage in the Tang dynasty, and the changes between Tang and Song in the way of editing ritual books were regarded by scholars as a profound influence on the subsequent dynasties.[1] The Hongwu 洪武 emperor (r. 1368–98), founder of a newly established dynasty after a long period of Mongol rule, claimed to reinstate the ritual regulations of the Tang and Song dynasties and was keen to establish a proper ritual system from the very beginning of the Ming dynasty. Under his urging, *Da Ming jili* 大明集禮 (*Collected Rites of the Ming Dynasty*), also known as the 'early regulations of the Hongwu reign' (*Hongwu chuzhi* 洪武初制) was completed in 1370, but was not issued nor printed. It was supplemented and published in 1529, the ninth year of the Jiajing 嘉靖 reign (1522–66). However, at the same time, other edited ritual books including *Hongwu lizhi* 洪武禮制 (*Ritual Code of the Hongwu Reign*), collectively named the 'finalised codes of the Hongwu reign' (*Hongwu dingzhi* 洪武定制), were later issued during the Hongwu reign and were put into practice from the early to mid-Ming periods.[2] Due to space limitations I will focus here on ritual vessels employed during the early to mid-Ming periods. The picture becomes more complicated from the Jiajing reign onwards, due to the ritual changes of the so-called 'Great Ritual Controversy' (*Daliyi* 大禮議).[3]

According to the 18th-century *Ming Shi* 明史 (*History of the Ming*), in 1368 the Hongwu emperor quoted Confucius, saying:

> They served the dead as they would have served the living; they served the departed as they would have served those still present.
>
> 事死如事生，事亡如事存。[4]

Hongwu decreed that all the ritual vessels for ancestor worship in the Imperial Ancestral Temple should be made after the likeness of the services they used when living. No ancient ritual vessel shapes such as *bian* 籩 or *dou* 豆 should be used.[5] In the following year (1369), the Hongwu emperor issued another order, that all ritual vessels should be made of ceramic, which supposedly replaced all other materials which were employed at this time for ritual use.[6]

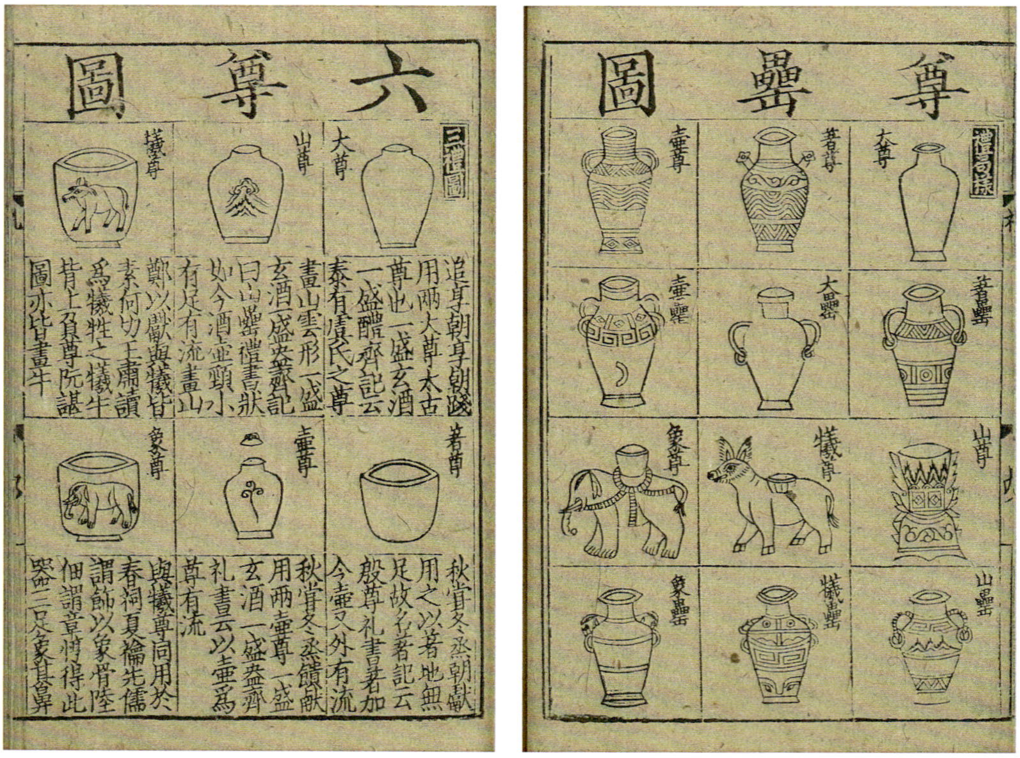

Plate 13.1 Two pages from the *Zuantu huzhu Zhouli* 纂圖互註周禮 (*The Rites of Zhou, Illustrated and Cross-Referenced*), Southern Song edition, National Library of China, pp. 17–18. a) *Liuzun tu* 六尊圖 (*Images of Six Vessels*) (left) after *Sanli tu* and b) *Zunlei tu* 尊罍圖 (*Images of Wine Vessels*) (right), after *Liju yang* 禮局樣 (*Ritual Service models*). *Liju yang* was the official ritual vessel models issued by the Southern Song government, based on the Xuanhe *bogu tu* system

This revolutionary change in ritual vessels, in tandem with the ritual reform of the early Ming dynasty,[7] was not limited to the ceremonies of the Imperial Ancestral Temple, but was also seen in the regulation for *jiaoshi* 郊祀 (suburban sacrifices) such as the sacrifices to Heaven, Earth and other gods, and later extended to the ceremonies of royal courts, local government and Confucian temples within the state.[8]

Although it is not certain to what extent this early Ming ritual policy was followed, we know that it was long lived. For almost 400 years this ceramic-oriented ritual practice lasted, at least up to the reign of the Yongzheng 雍正 emperor (1723–35) in the Qing dynasty. We learn this fact from the comments made by the Qianlong 乾隆 emperor (r. 1736–95), when he conducted systematic ritual reform in the 13th year of his reign (1748),[9] followed by the publication of a ritual book with illustrations, *Huangchao liqi tushi* 皇朝禮器圖式 (*Illustrated Regulations for Ceremonial Paraphernalia of the Imperial Court*) in the 24th year (1759).[10]

Almost every recent publication on early Ming ceramics mentions this unprecedented change by the Hongwu emperor in the 14th century. No one, however, has paid enough attention to this issue, leaving a number of further issues to be explored in the course of this chapter.

A third system: What was the main content of this change of ritual vessels?

Previous studies have shown that there were two distinguished systems of ritual vessels employed from at least the Song to the Yuan dynasty: the ritual vessel shapes for worshipping illustrated in the *Sanli tu* 三禮圖 (*The Illustrated Catalogue of Three Ritual Classics*) and those that followed the ancient bronze shapes illustrated in the *Xuanhe bogu tu* 宣和博古圖 (*The Xuanhe Illustrated Catalogue of Antiquities*) (**Pl. 13.1a–b**).[11] By the early Ming, with the introduction of the new idea of ritual vessels issued by the Hongwu emperor, these earlier systems were almost abandoned. We might view the new ideas of the early Ming dynasty as 'a third system' (or 'ceramic-oriented ritual vessel system' or 'Hongwu ritual vessel system'), in addition to the *Sanli tu* and *Xuanhe bogu tu* systems.

According to the illustration in *Da Ming huidian* 大明會典 (*Collected Statutes of the Great Ming*),[12] vessels for worshipping Heaven at the Circular Mound Altar (*Huangqiu* 圜丘), apart from *jue* 爵, *deng* 登, *xing* 鉶, *fu* 簠, *gui* 簋, *bian* 籩 and *dou* 豆, were all replaced by dishes or bowls made of ceramic (**Pl. 13.2**).[13] Interestingly, another order by the emperor came right after, which changed all the ritual vessels into porcelain. This change is not only limited to the state level but was also enforced in other princely courts, local government and Confucius temples as shown in documents.[14]

Recent studies on rituals and ritual vessels of the Song, Yuan, Ming and Joseon dynasties provide us with a better basis for further study. Hsieh Ming-liang's 謝明良 studies on the above-mentioned two systems of *Sanli tu* and *Xuanhe bogu tu* ritual vessels, which were employed after the 8th century in East Asian regions as shown in the cases of excavated burials of the Tang dynasty Empress Ai 哀 and the Yuan dynasty Wang 汪 family, help us identify the choices being made in different periods.[15] Chen Fang-mei 陳芳妹 and Hsu Ya-hwei 許雅惠 take a broader view of East Asian Confucian ritual practice. Hsu Ya-hwei studies the set of black pottery ritual vessels from the Yuan dynasty unearthed from Saiyinchidahu's 賽因赤答忽 tomb at Luoyang 洛陽, Henan, and argues that the ritual vessel shapes based on contemporary illustrated ritual books for county level, *Shaoxi zhouxian shidianyi tu* 紹熙州縣釋奠儀圖 (*Illustrated Shaoxi Confucius Worshipping Ceremony of Counties*), was possibly edited by Zhu Xi 朱熹 (1130–1200) during the Southern Song period (only the Qing edition survives today)

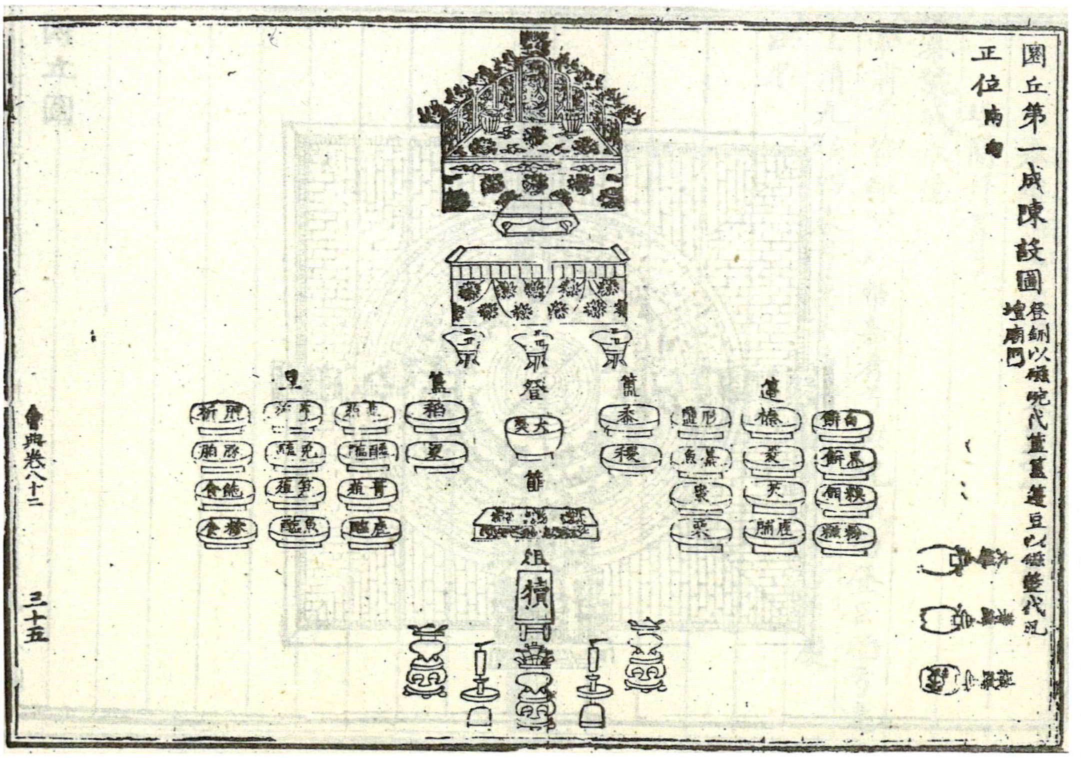

Plate 13.2 Illustration for display on the first level of the Circular Mound Altar (*Huanqiu diyicheng chenshe tu* 圜丘第一成陳設圖), *Da Ming huidian* 大明會典 (*Collected Statutes of the Great Ming*), reprint of the 1587 edition (Taipei, 1963), *juan* 82, p. 1298-1

on the basis of the *Xuanhe bogu tu* bronze vessel types.[16] Chen Fang-mei has surveyed Zhu Xi's ideas on the set of ritual vessels for the Sacrifice to Sages (*shidian* 釋奠) and discovered that Zhu Xi's ideal, as shown in the above-mentioned *Shaoxi zhouxian shidianyi tu* and other relevant visual materials on ritual vessels and actual objects, was not only practised widely in the East Asian region but also lasted for a long time after the 12th century.[17] Lee Dingeun 李定恩 looked into Joseon's fusion of the two systems, a decision made during Sejong's 世宗 reign (1397–1450) when it was not possible to obtain definitive information on the official ritual practice system from the Ming court.[18] However, in their studies, the Ming dynasty ritual system was relatively absent, as there was less evidence available for reference.

No pictorial evidence of early Ming ritual vessels survives today. The images included in *Da Ming jili* were printed in the ninth year of the Jiajing reign (1530) and claimed to follow the Hongwu emperor's initial edition of ritual practice.[19] This 16th-century edition of *Da Ming jili* is itself problematic, because its publication was a byproduct of the controversial ritual reconstruction known as the Great Ritual Controversy in the Jiajing period. Apart from the *jue* 爵 vessel (which remains a bronze-specific shape), it is difficult for scholars to differentiate ritual vessels from the other vessels and thereby establish a clear picture of early Ming ritual vessels, due to the use of porcelain in utilitarian forms.

However, there are some hints from objects with outstanding features or shapes identical to those pictured in ritual books, which might help us to explore this question a little further. It is helpful to compare the Ming dynasty ceramic-oriented system with the Joseon dynasty's *Jegidoseol* 祭器圖說 (*Illustrated Catalogue of Ritual Vessels*), compiled during the reign of King Sejong.[20] After being rejected by the Ming emperors in its request for ritual books, King Sejong's court decided to study the ritual practice on their own. The Joseon system is mainly based on Zhu Xi's ideal Sacrifice to Sages, which belongs to the *Xuanhe bogu tu* system (**Pl. 13.3a–b**; see also **Pl. 13.1** right). When they were uncertain about which form to use, they chose to keep both systems and thus fused them in some parts.[21]

Since there appears to be no early Ming illustration showing sets of ritual vessels, we will examine the objects themselves to explore this issue. Firstly, porcelain was the primary material chosen for important ritual vessels employed in worship ceremonies. Even the *bian* 籩 vessel, which is supposed to be made of woven bamboo, was replaced with porcelain in this system. Secondly, common porcelain shapes were given particular 'decoration' (symbols) to show ritual features. Thirdly, synthesised forms and decorations from the two previous systems were used.

We may find some ritual vessel examples closer to the *Sanli tu* or *Xuanhe bogu tu* system. However, more often we find a 'blended' or synthesised format that came from nowhere. A porcelain jar with seven bands of relief on the body and two rope-shaped handles, currently housed in the National Palace Museum, is a fitting example (**Pl. 13.4**). This creative form could be regarded as a *bian* or other ritual vessel among the set of early Ming ritual vessels. Other likely candidates appear hybrids of the two previous systems.

It is particularly interesting if we compare the situation with Joseon examples of *buncheon* 粉青 wares, in which there is a merging of the two systems of *Sanli tu* and *Xuanhe bogu tu*, as mentioned above. The Baur Foundation has a Ming ceramic jar incised with a cow-like animal on the belly (**Pl. 13.5**). This jar might have been made with reference to the *xizun* 犧尊 of the *Xuanhe bogu tu* system in *Da Ming jili* (**Pl. 13.6**). According to the *Da Ming jili* (usually), the animal was supposed to be made into a 3D vessel; in this case, the illustration of the animal was squarely transplanted on to the jar as a 2D motif. On the other hand, the depiction of an

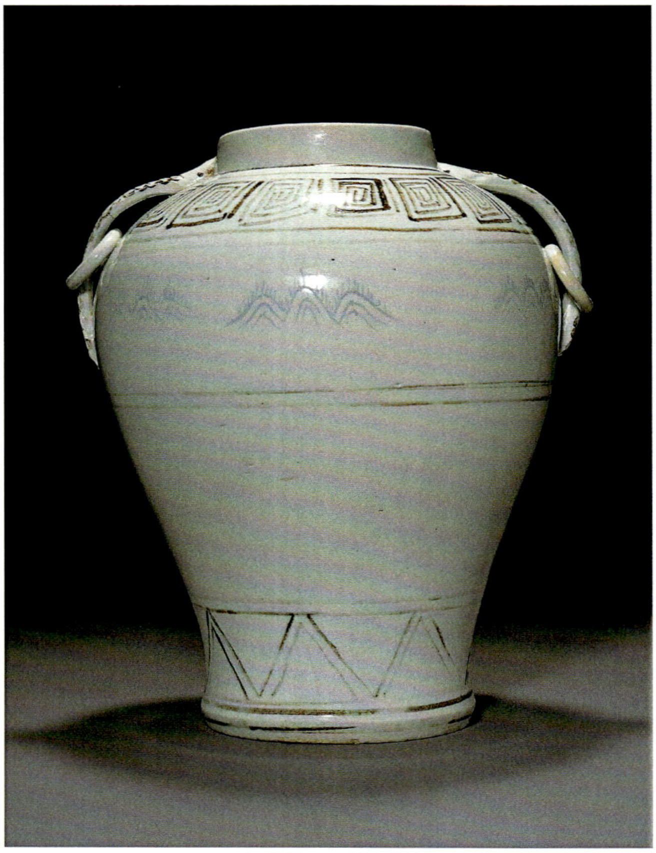

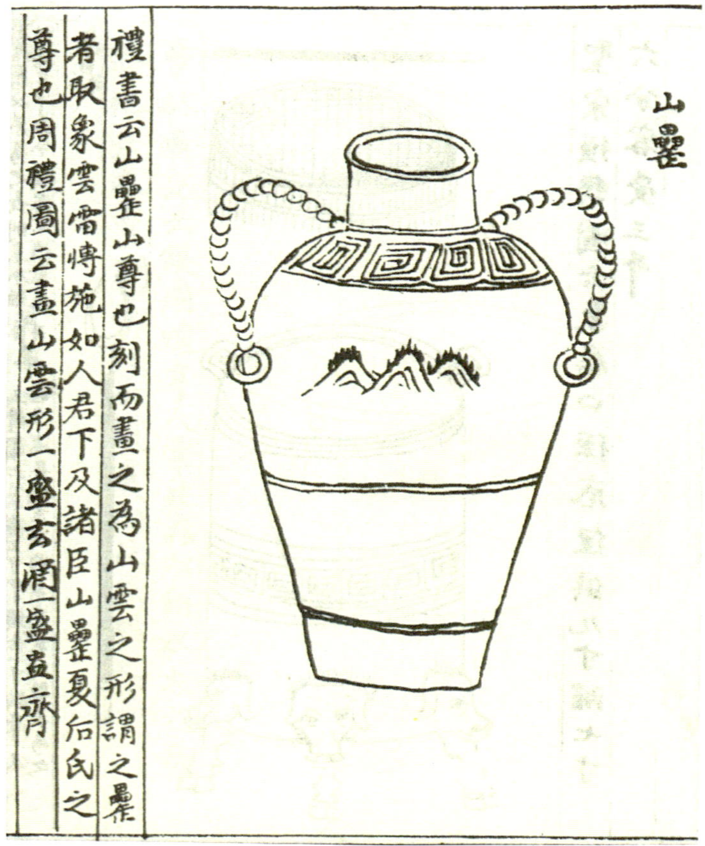

Plate 13.3a–b: a (left) Underglazed cobalt-blue and iron-brown *shanlei* 山罍, Joseon dynasty, 15th century. Height 27.8cm, diameter mouth 9.5cm, foot 11.8cm. Leeum, Samsung Museum of Art; b) (right) *Five Rites* (*Olyeui* 五禮儀) in *Annals of the King Sejong* (*Sejong Sillok* 世宗實錄), dated 1451, reprint of T'aebaeksanbon edition (Seoul, 1955)

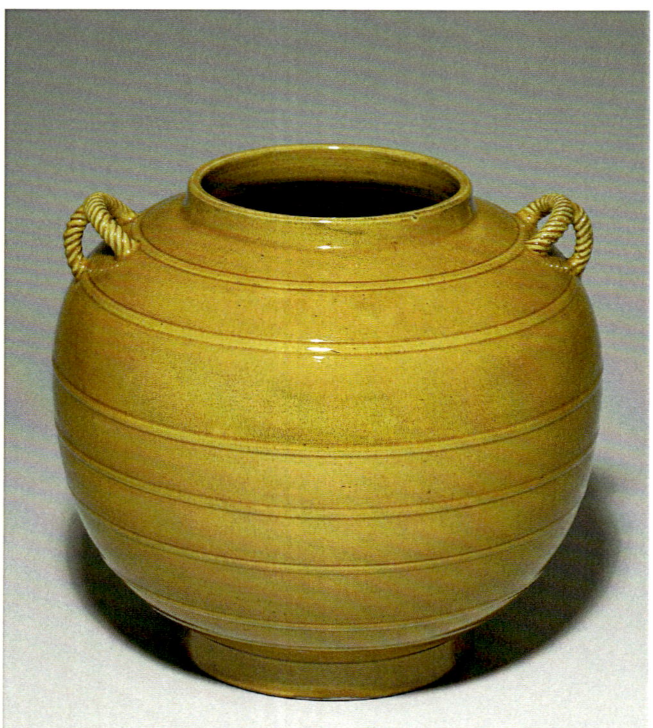

Plate 13.4 Yellow-glazed jar with two rope-shaped handles, 15th century. Height 23.2cm, diameter mouth 10cm, foot 11cm. National Palace Museum, Taipei

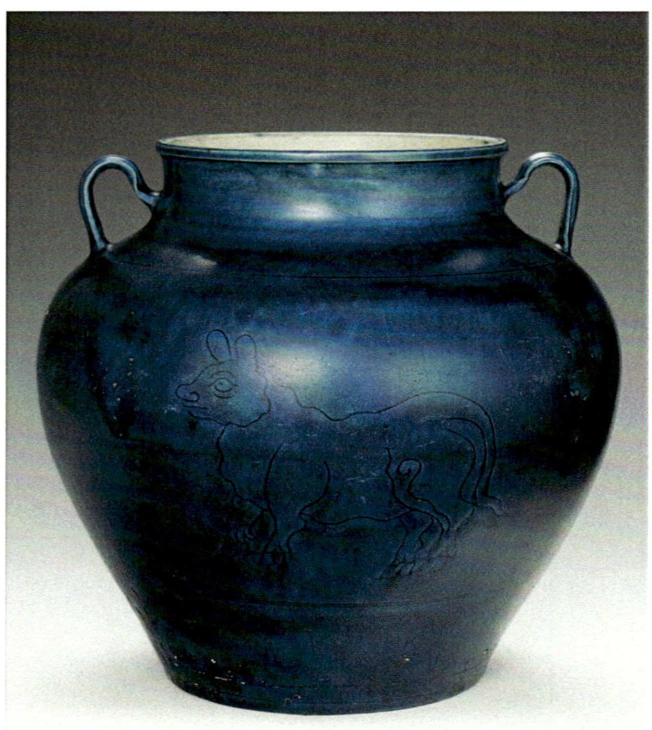

Plate 13.5 Blue-glazed porcelain jar (*xizun* 犧尊), Jiajing mark and period, 1522–66. Height 25.8cm. Baur Foundation, Museum of Far Eastern Art, Geneva

image (for example, an animal, mountain etc.) on a jar refers to the *Sanli tu* system (see **Pl. 13.1** left). We might also ask, why did this jar, made in the Jiajing period, not follow the conventions of the *Da Ming jili*?

Why was ceramic chosen as the primary material for ritual vessels?

The use of porcelain ritual vessels for ritual practice was a state order by the emperor, a forceful decree that must be followed by his court and people, especially at a time when ritual construction was of utmost importance to a new ruler trying to establish his legitimacy. Where did the Hongwu emperor get this new idea from?

It is understood that the frugality advocated by Hongwu in the early Ming period might explain the use of porcelain instead of bronze, when there was a shortage of coinage or copper. In addition, the making of vessel shapes in the likeness of the services that the ancestors used while living can also be explained by the Hongwu emperor's citation of Confucius, as previously mentioned. Why was ceramic chosen as the primary material for ritual vessels? According to earlier studies, we know that ritual vessels made of ceramic appeared from time to time in history: for example, some Song dynasty *guan* wares, Yuan dynasty black pottery or even Joseon *buncheon* wares. However, they were often meant as supplements or substitutes for bronze ritual vessels, when there were shortages of bronze models. These copied archaistic bronze styles. Scholars such as Qin Dashu 秦大樹 have suggested that some Yaozhou and Ding ware were produced in the shapes of ritual vessels in the Song dynasty.[22] These were likely to be sent to the court to supplement bronze ritual vessels. We learn from documents that the Southern Song government asked for the substitution of bronze vessels in ritual practices with ceramic ritual vessels produced in the Zhejiang area.[23]

The black pottery from the Yuan dynasty copied archaic bronze shapes based on the Xuanhe *bogu tu* system. More intriguing and oft-cited pieces are the 15th-century Joseon buncheon wares. These above-mentioned examples, however, show that ceramics were mainly chosen as substitutes or supplements when bronze or metal vessels were in short supply or lacking. In a few cases, ceramic wares were chosen because they adhered to ancient doctrines, such as *heguyi* 合古意 ('matching ancient doctrines') and *qi yong tao pao* 器用陶匏 ('employing vessels made of pottery and gourd'). The Ming dynasty is the first instance when ceramic itself was regarded primarily to serve as the material for ritual vessels in such a wide range of contexts, in their usual ceramic shapes, from the imperial to regional courts and local governments.

The last point, not to be overlooked, is the role of the lead official for early Ming ritual reform, Tao An 陶安 (1312?–68). According to the investigation by Hsieh Yu-chen 謝玉珍, Tao An was once appointed as the local prefect of Raozhou 饒州, where he might have learned about ceramic making in Jingdezhen; this might have inspired the proposal to employ ceramic as the primary material for ritual vessels.[24] This information is crucial to our discussion of the possible origins of this unprecedented change in ritual vessels. More supporting evidence for this speculation will be explored further in the future.

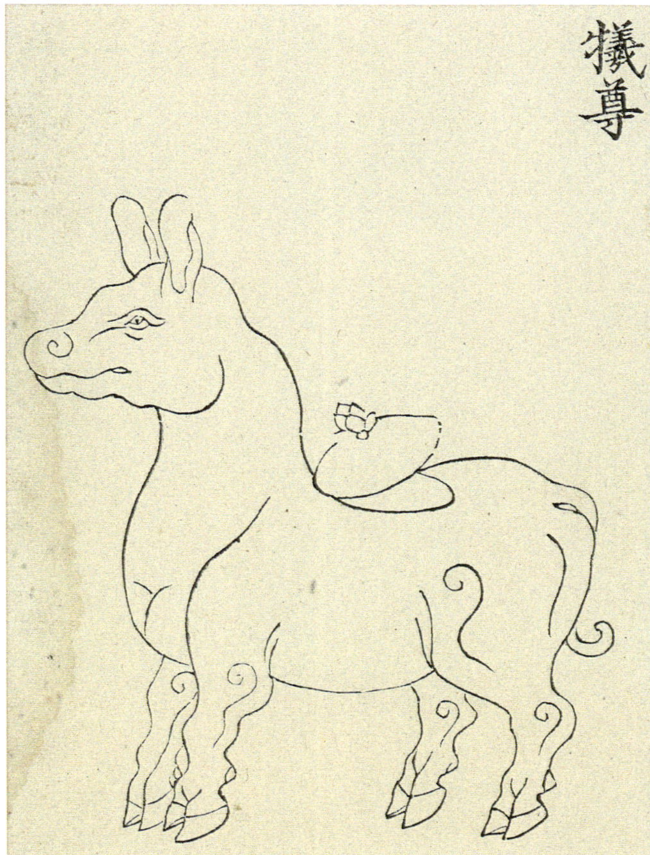

Plate 13.6 ***Xizun*** **犧尊 of** ***Xuanhe bogu tu*** **system in** ***Da Ming jili*** **大明集禮 (*****Collected Ceremonial of the Ming Dynasty*****), dated 1530. National Library of China**

What were the consequences of this new idea?

What interests us more is the question of the consequences of this unprecedented and revolutionary decision. What was its impact in the early Ming? One would immediately think of it as an important impetus leading to the establishment of the imperial kiln at Jingdezhen in the early Ming period. In addition, the features of ritual vessels also lead to the creation of particular forms of decoration and visual effects in imperial wares.

An obvious impact is the urgent and great demand for ceremonial vessels for ritual practices in the state and kingdoms, local governments and Confucius temples.[25] Liu Xinyuan noticed that porcelain had been employed for ceremonial use as early as the first year of the Hongwu reign for worshipping the emperor's ancestors at the Nanjing Taimiao.[26] Christine Lau tried to link extant Ming imperial wares to corresponding documents, especially the ritual vessels used in suburban sacrifices, including monochrome porcelain *jue* copying bronze-shaped bowls and dishes.[27] Hsieh Yu-chen explored many more relevant documents related to this issue and suggested that this decision by the Hongwu emperor might have led to the establishment of the imperial kiln during the early Ming dynasty.[28]

What signifiers for ritual vessels express their distinctiveness from other common utensils? It is difficult to differentiate ritual vessels from daily utensils made of ceramics. Almost no trace of archaic ritual shapes can be found apart from *jue* 爵 and *zhou* 舟 (or *he* 盉).[29] This is the main reason why scholars of ceramic studies do not pay too

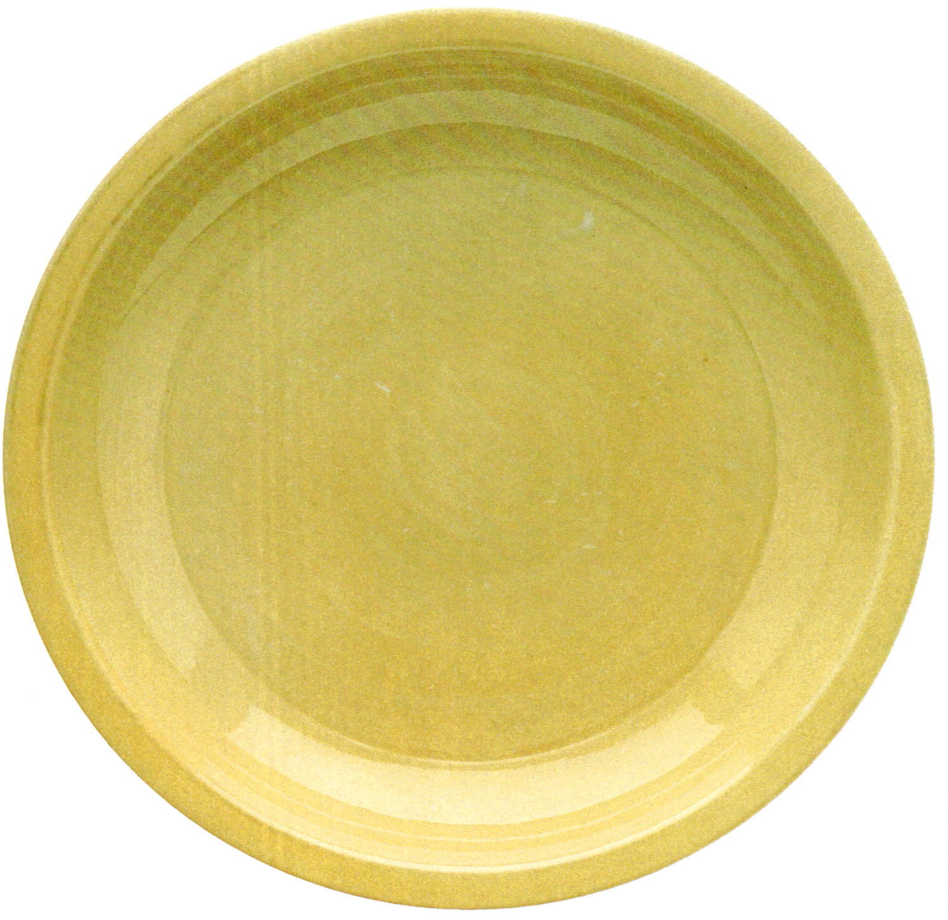

Plate 13.7 Yellow-glazed porcelain dish, Yongle period, 1403–24, Jingdezhen, Jiangxi province. Height 5.7cm, diameter 31.7cm. Sir Percival David Collection, PDF 582

much attention to this unprecedented decision. It is also the reason why scholars who work on the development of ritual vessels from the Tang dynasty onwards regard the Ming to early Qing as a cul-de-sac. Yet there are some traces of distinction that we can find on Ming ceramics. Previous scholars have also provided us with some hints.[30]

Does size of the vessels matter? Wang Guangyao 王光堯 from the Palace Museum suggested that the decision which he called 'the ceramification of ritual vessels' (*lijiqi ciqihua* 禮祭器瓷器化) and the 'daily-utensilification of ritual vessels' (*lijiqi riyongqihua* 禮祭器日用器化), decreed by the court to the princely courts, local provincial governments and Confucius temples, reminds us to pay attention to large-sized porcelains of the early Ming period for possible examples of ritual vessels, as no apparent bronze ritual vessels can be identified.[31] We also realise that the large-sized dishes of the early Ming period were not only seen in Jingdezhen wares but also in Longquan celadon, with similar designs.

In addition, colour is undoubtedly a good angle for investigation as we have both documents and objects to support it. Monochrome glazes were introduced to mark the ritual vessels for the worship of different gods. The regulations of the *Da Ming huidian* state that monochrome wares of blue, yellow, red and white glazes are to be used for the worship of Heaven, Earth, the Sun and the Moon. One would also agree that the urgent demand for monochrome glazes must have contributed to the technological advancement at the Jingdezhen imperial kiln in order to meet the regulations and demand.[32] The emergence of yellow glazes in the Hongwu and Yongle period can be regarded as important.[33] A Yongle-period yellow glazed dish in the Percival David Collection has gold painted lines on the rim (**Pl. 13.7**), showing its connection with metalware and so it is likely to have served as a ritual vessel.

Decoration is a key reference point in differentiating ritual vessels from common wares, and may also be an aspect that engages with the viewer more directly. Interestingly, if we look closer, we discover an animal image on the so-called *xizun* 犧尊 (animal-shaped wine vessel) in the illustration of ritual at the Circular Mound Altar (**Pl. 13.2**, below right); Hsieh Ming-liang has referred this to those with similar decorations.[34] An example is the blue-glazed jar of the Jiajing period from the Baur Foundation with an incised cow-like animal on the belly mentioned earlier (see **Pl. 13.5**). We find more examples of slightly different versions from the Hongzhi 弘治 period (1488–1505), with gold painting (**Pl. 13.8**). And we might also cite an example of a yellow-glazed *zhuzun* 著尊, a jar with animal heads on two sides near the neck, the gold-painted lines referring to metal (**Pl. 13.9**).[35] A blue-glazed jar of the Jiajing period with a mountain design on the belly should be regarded as a relevant ritual vessel. It stands for the *shanzun* 山尊 ('mountain' wine vessel), a type of vase with an 'mountain' image and part of a set of six vases, *liuzun* 六尊, used for offering wine (**Pl. 13.10**).

From the above discussion, we have learned that the unprecedented decision on ritual vessels was launched during the early Ming (late 14th century) ritual reform and its influence lasted for almost 400 years, until the early

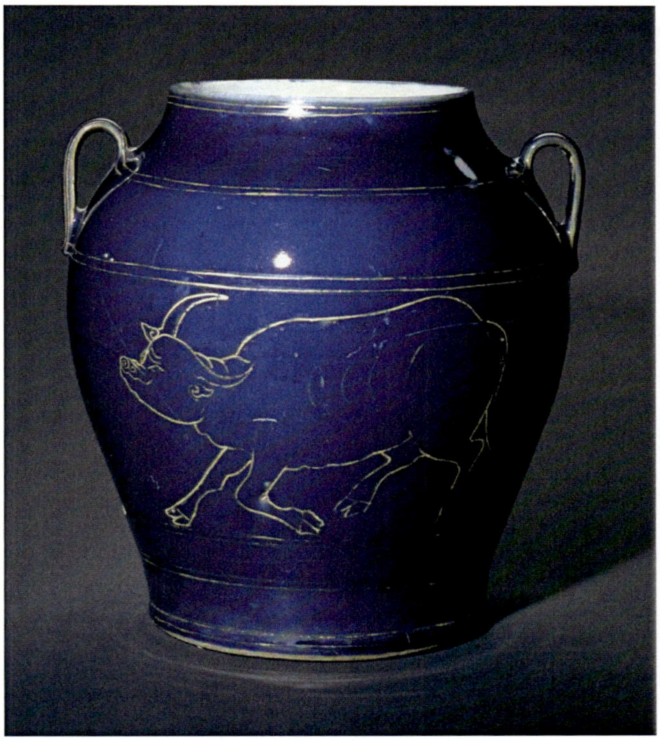

Plate 13.8 Blue-glazed porcelain jar, gold painted, Hongzhi period, 1488–1505, Jingdezhen, Jiangxi province. Height 32.2cm, diameter mouth 16.5cm, foot 18.5cm. The Palace Museum, Beijing

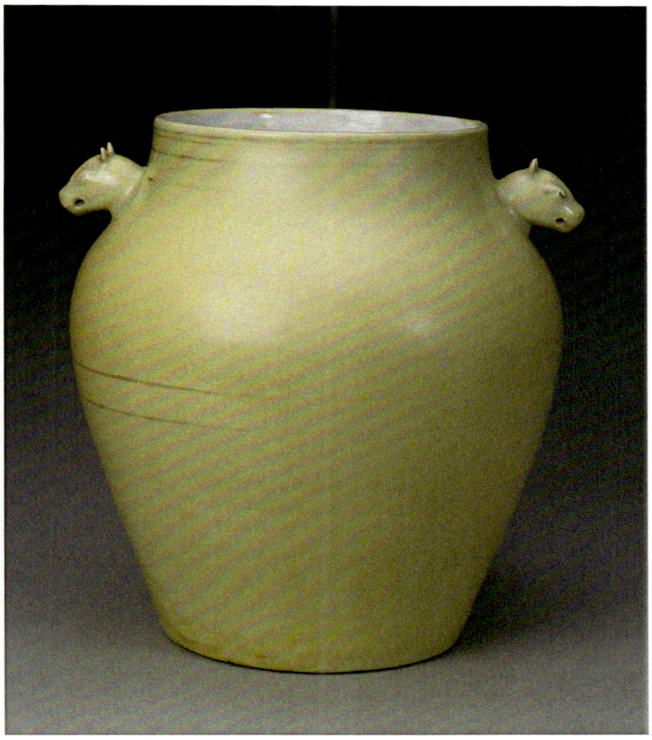

Plate 13.9 Yellow-glazed porcelain jar, *zhuzun* 著尊, Hongzhi period, 1488–1505, Jingdezhen, Jiangxi province. Height 32cm, diameter mouth 19cm, foot 17.5cm. The Palace Museum, Beijing

Qianlong period in the mid-18th century. In this reform, the long-standing tradition of making ritual vessels in ancient bronze shapes was almost abandoned, and porcelain was elevated as the primary material for important ritual vessels employed in ceremonies of worship from the state to the local governments. However, little attention has been paid to this issue.

Although we do not yet know the full picture of this third system, this chapter has sought to show that there are some traces of distinctiveness that enable us to explore the significance of this change in ritual vessels. We may well regard this ceramic-oriented system as a third system of ritual vessels in addition to the *Sanli tu* or *Xuanhe bogu tu* systems, as it is both different and distinct from these previous systems. The early Ming decision led to the establishment of a long-lived imperial kiln system and a ceramic-oriented system of ritual vessels in later Chinese material culture history.

But the frugality advocated by Hongwu in the early Ming period might explain why ceramic substitutes enjoyed an economic advantage. In addition, ceramic wares were chosen because they adhered to the ancient doctrines. We also saw why the vessel shapes should be made in the likeness of the services that the ancestors used while living, in the Hongwu emperor's citation of Confucius and Song Taizu. Lastly, a scholar's proposal that the early Ming ritual reformist Tao An might have played a crucial role in making such a decision, as he had previously served as the local prefect of Raozhou, deserves further exploration in the future.

Lastly, what are the consequences of this unprecedented decision, made during the early Ming, dictating that all ritual vessels should be made of ceramics? Firstly, it is likely

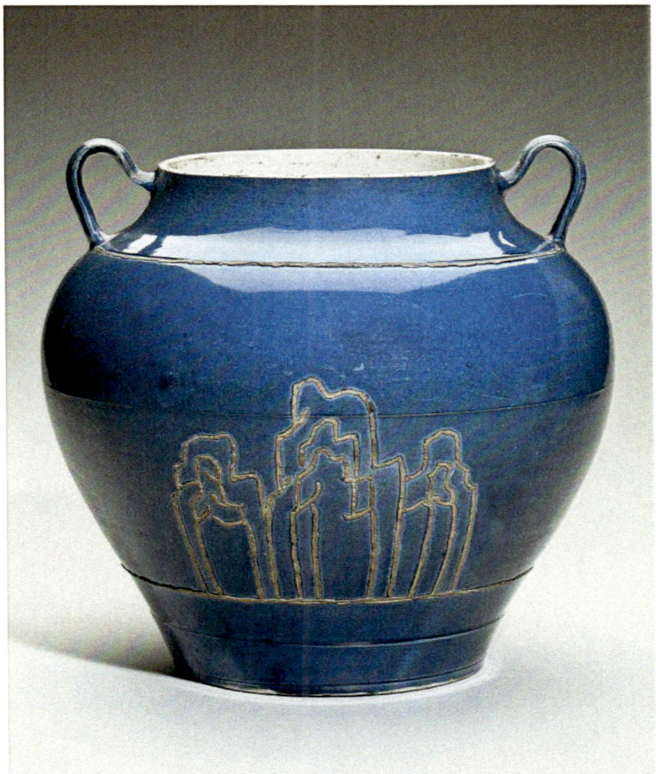

Plate 13.10 Blue-glazed jar with unglazed 'mountain' image, Jiajing mark and period, 1521–67. Height 25.2cm, width 25.5cm widest point. Private collection

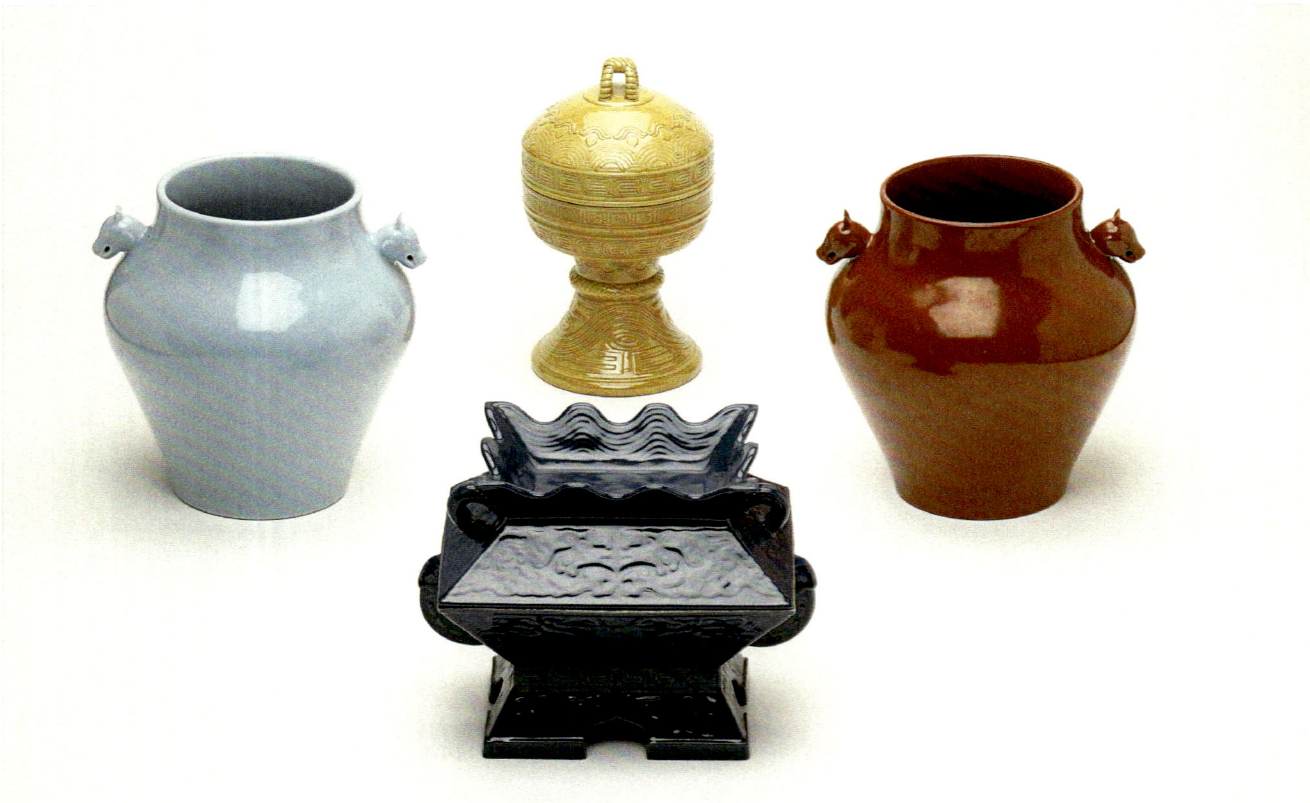

Plate 13.11 Porcelain ritual vessels, 18th–19th century. Height 14cm–27cm. Victoria and Albert Museum, London, C.526-1910, C.17&A-1968, FE.99-1970, C.483-1910

that the urgent demand for ceramic ritual vessels from the court to local levels led to the establishment of imperial ceramic production in the early Ming dynasty. It also prompted technological improvements, as shown in the case of the development of monochrome glazes in the early Ming period.

Without this ceramic-oriented system we would not see the lovely outcome, which were Qianlong's porcelain ritual vessels; although there was also a big change again in Qianlong's ritual vessel reform as presented in *Huangchao liqi tushi* (**Pl. 13.11**). In addition, useful references from Joseon-dynasty Korea would undoubtedly help us explore the situation of early Ming ritual practice in the future.[36]

Notes

1 Cheng Shuguo 1998, ch. 2. Chang Wen-chang provides a detailed review of previous studies on rituals in the Tang and Song dynasties. Chang Wen-chang 2012, 1–44.

2 Zhao Kesheng 2004–5, 54–7.

3 Fisher 1977; Huang Chin-hsin 1994; Zhao Kesheng 2008–12, 26–9.

4 *MS* 51, 1315.

5 *MS* 51, 1315. See also a similar record in *MSL Taizong shilu* 43.4a (2/6/丁亥).

6 *DMHD*, 2715.

7 According to Zhao Kesheng, the ritual reform of the Hongwu emperor was eventually settled in around the tenth year of the Hongwu reign. On early Ming ritual reform see Zhao Kesheng 2004–5, 54–7.

8 Hsieh Yu-chen 1995, 14–18; Wang Guangyao 2010, 75–9.

9 Kun Gang 1991, 645.

10 *Huangchao liqi tushi* was compiled during the Qianlong reign (1736–96). The 18-*juan* text was completed in 1759 and revised and printed in 1766. It is divided into six parts, describing sacrificial objects (*Jiqi* 祭器, *juan* 1–2), ceremonial objects (*Yiqi* 儀器, *juan* 3), caps and robes (*Guanfu* 冠服, *juan* 4–7), musical instruments (*Yueqi* 樂器, *juan* 8–9), insignia (*Lubu* 鹵簿, *juan* 10–12) and military objects (*Wubei* 武備, *juan* 17–18). Each object is illustrated and described as to its appearance, dimensions, the materials it is made of, which decoration it bears, the numbers of the particular object to be used during a certain ceremony and its actual use. For relevant studies on the arrangements and content of the book, see Medley 1957–9.

11 Chen Fang-mei 2005, 300–2. Hsieh Ming-liang 2006, 81–2. *Sanli tu* 三禮圖 (20 *juan*) collection on illustrated ritual vessels was compiled by Nie Chongyi 聶從義 (10th century). The present edition of *Sanli tu* is *Chongjiao Sanli tu* 重校三禮圖. See Nie Chongyi 1966. *Xuanhe bogu tu* 宣和博古圖 was compiled through 1111 to 1125 under the commission of Emperor Huizong of Song (r. 1100–25), and featured illustrations of some 840 vessels and rubbings from the imperial collection. Although it is not a ritual book, it contains the study of ancient bronze ritual vessels that Zhu Xi later adopted for the ritual vessel examples in his ideal Sacrifice to Sages and thus broadly influenced the ritual vessel system in the East Asian region. The present edition is edited by Wang Fu 王黻, *Chong xiu Xuanhe bogu tu* 重修宣和博古圖 (*Revised Xuanhe Illustrated Catalogue of Antiquities*). See Wang Fu 1983. Tsai Meifen reminds us that the debate on the choices of *Sanli tu* and *Xuanhe bogu tu* systems during the early Yuan period. Tsai Meifen 2001, 230–3. Craig Clunas has noticed that printed copies of the *Chong xiu Xuanhe bogu tu* were widely circulated in the 16th century during the Ming dynasty; see Clunas 2004, 97.

12 *Da Ming huidian* was submitted to the throne in 1497 and, after revision, officially issued and printed in 1509 in the Zhengde reign (1506–21). It is thus also called *Zhengde huidian* 正德會典 (*Collected Statutes of the Zhengde Reign*). The first version contained 180 *juan*, and after two supplements were added during the Jiajing 嘉靖 (1522–66) and Wanli 萬曆 (1573–1619) reigns, it reached its final size of 228 *juan* in the edition of 1597.

13 *DMHD*, 1298.

14 *DMHD*, 1446 and 2773.

15 Hsieh Ming-liang 2006, 81–2.

16 Hsu Ya-huei 2003. There are two editions of *Shaoxi zhouxian*

shidianyi tu that survive today. The one used in this chapter is the one in the *Shiku quanshu* 1986, vol. 648.

17 Chen Fang-mei 2011.

18 Lee 2013.

19 *Da Ming jili* is a collection of court rituals of the Ming dynasty. It was compiled under the supervision of Xu Yikui 徐一夔 and with a staff that included eminent Confucian experts including Liang Yin 梁寅, Liu Yu 劉于, Zhou Yuliang 周於諒, Hu Xingjian 胡行簡, Liu Zongbi 劉宗弼, Dong Yi 董彝, Cai Chen 蔡琛, Teng Gongying 滕公瑛 and Zeng Hu 曾魯. The compilation began in 1369 and was finished at the end of the following year. Xu Yikui 1963. However, it was not supplemented and published until the ninth year of the Jiajing reign (1530). For studies on *Da Ming jili*, see Zhao Kesheng 2004–5.

20 *JWS Sejong Sillok* 128.

21 Lee 2013.

22 For example Qin Dashu 2005, 64–73.

23 Tsai 2000, 327–8 Hsu Ya-hwei 2011, 13–17.

24 Hsieh Yu-chen 1995, 34.

25 Lu Minghua 1990, 146–7.

26 Liu Xinyuan 1985.

27 Lau 1993.

28 Hsieh Yu-chen 1995, 13–44.

29 Tsai 1996, 126.

30 Hsu Ya-hwei 2011; Chen Fang-mei 2011.

31 Wang Guangyao 2010, 75–9.

32 We also learn from documents that colour scheme was regarded as important in differentiating status. Tsai 1996, 129–30.

33 Cao Jianwen 2003–5.

34 Hsieh Ming-liang 2006, 73–6.

35 Wang Chong-ci 2008.

36 Pang Pyong-son 2001; Kim Yun-jeong 2007.

Chapter 14
Gifts of Good Fortune and Praise-Songs for Peace: Images of Auspicious Portents and Panegyrics from the Yongle Period

Lina Lin

Translated by Silin Chen

Early in his reign, the Yongle 永樂 emperor (r. 1403–24) asked officials to identify auspicious omens across the empire in order to support the legitimacy of his rule. Not only did officials search the provinces for accounts of propitious occurrences, they also recorded them in their writings and paintings. Many extant works from the period, produced by officials, are on the subject of auspicious signs. This chapter argues that such texts and images were intended to offset doubts about the legitimacy of the Yongle emperor's ascension to the throne, and to symbolically affirm Heaven's approval of his reign.[1]

According to the *Ming shi* 明史 *(History of the Ming)*, the physiognomist Yuan Gong 袁珙 (1335–1410) described the appearance of Prince Zhu Di 朱棣 (1360–1424), the future Yongle emperor, in regal terms, and identified him as the rightful Son of Heaven.[2] He purportedly told the prince:

> [You have] a dragon's walk and a tiger's step, a protruding forehead that reaches towards the Heaven, [these are signs of] the Son of Heaven of Great Peace. When you turn forty, and your whiskers reach below your navel, you will ascend the throne.
>
> 龍行虎步，日角插天，太平天子也。年四十鬚過臍，即登大寶矣。

Indeed, two years after his fortieth birthday, Zhu Di would become emperor. In his seated portrait in the National Palace Museum, Taipei, he is depicted with a long, wavy beard and a dark reddish complexion (see **Pl. 16.6**). Compared to earlier portraits of rulers from the Song dynasty (960–1279), this image is painted with more defined brushstrokes in the area of the face and costume. The Yongle emperor sits on a spacious, gem-encrusted throne, the back of which is in the shape of the character *shan* 山 (mountain). The arms of the throne are adorned with six dragon heads with tassels made of precious stones hanging from their mouths. Thrones of such extravagance do not appear in earlier imperial portraits. The use of lavish furnishings, like the references to imperial physiognomy, seems intended to bolster the legitimacy of a man who rose to power under violent circumstances.

The Yongle emperor usurped the throne from his nephew the Jianwen 建文 emperor (r. 1399–1402) following a bloody civil war. Auspicious omens were identified during his reign to support the rationale and legitimacy of his actions. It was believed that Heaven would generate propitious events to signal its approval of an emperor who possessed the mandate to rule, and who governed effectively and diligently. Many officials wrote poems to celebrate these omens, and paintings were produced to commemorate them.

The mystical beast *zouyu*

Auspicious omens included sightings of rare creatures and extraordinary occurrences in nature. In the fourth month of 1404, the Yongle emperor appointed his eldest son, Zhu Gaochi 朱高熾 (1378–1425), as his successor. In the ninth month of that year, the Prince of Zhou 周王, Zhu Shu 朱橚 (1361–1425), travelled to the capital to pay his respects, and presented the emperor with a mystical creature known as a *zouyu* 騶虞.[3] The *zouyu* is said to have the appearance of a white tiger, a nature that is humane and righteous, and the

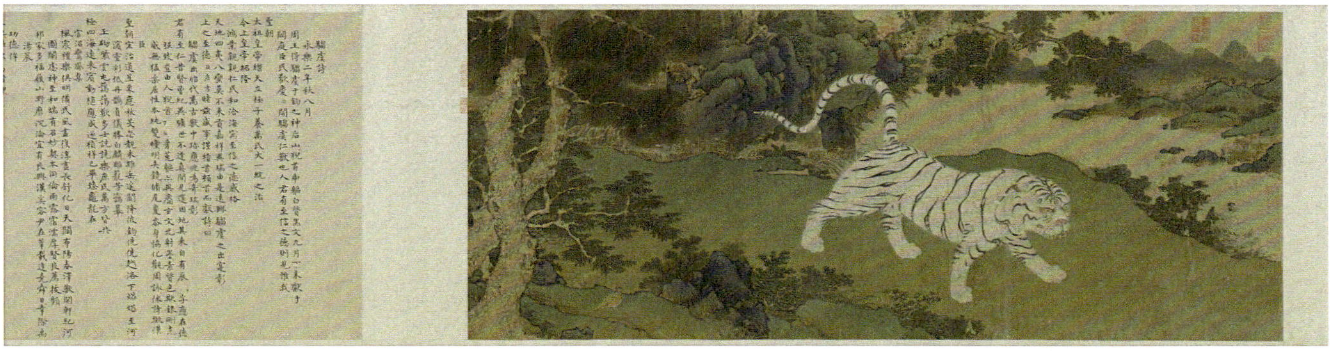

Plate 14.1 Anonymous, *Painting of Zouyu from the Inner Palace* (*Mingren neifu zouyu tu* 明人內府騶虞圖), Ming dynasty, *c.* 1404–5, Nanjing. Handscroll, ink and colours on silk, height 51.9cm, width 125cm. National Palace Museum, Taipei

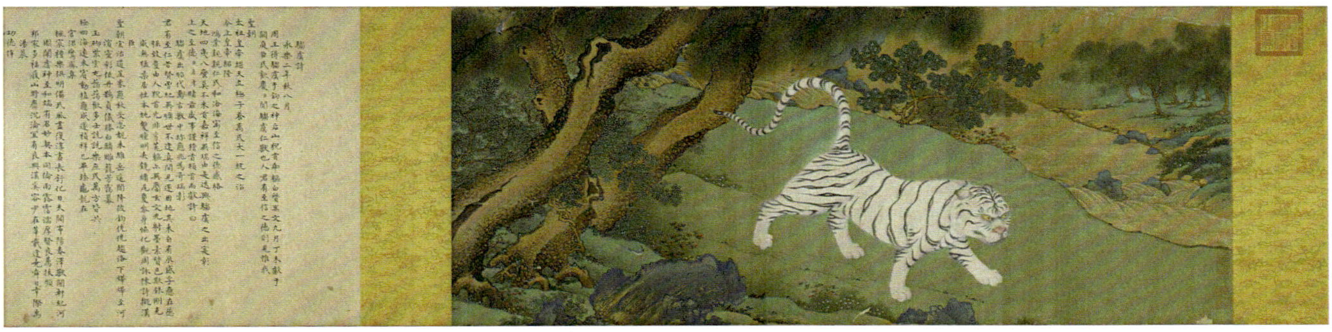

Plate 14.2 Anonymous, *Painting of Zouyu* (*Mingren hua zouyu tu* 明人畫騶虞圖), Ming dynasty, *c.* 1404–5. Handscroll, ink and colours on silk, height 54cm, width 129cm. National Palace Museum, Taipei

ability to foretell good and evil. According to Huang Zuo's 黃佐 (1490–1566) *Hanlin ji* 翰林記 (*Records of Hanlin Scholars*), the Prince of Zhou captured the *zouyu* while hunting in Junzhou 鈞州, his fiefdom in Henan 河南 province.[4] The record further states that officials wrote and presented odes on *zouyu* to the emperor. As confirmation of Heaven's approval, one month later the muddy Yellow River reportedly turned clear in Pucheng 蒲城 and Hejin 河津 counties.[5]

The National Palace Museum, Taipei, has two early Ming paintings depicting *zouyu* in its collection. One is known as *Ming Painting of Zouyu from the Inner Palace* (*Mingren neifu zouyu tu* 明人內府騶虞圖) (**Pl. 14.1**). The other is *Ming Painting of Zouyu* (*Mingren hua zouyu tu* 明人畫騶虞圖) (**Pl. 14.2**). Similar in size, composition and style, the two paintings would have been produced around the same time, based on the same sketch (*gaoben* 稿本).[6] They both depict a single *zouyu* prowling in a landscape painted with vibrant colours and outlines partially rendered in gold. The creature is shown with a swirling pattern on its forehead to indicate its curly fur. The dense canopy of pine needles and birds interspersed among flowers demonstrate fine brushwork, which suggests that the paintings were most likely produced by court painters. The same 27 colophons are inscribed after the painting in both scrolls. *Ming Painting of Zouyu* contains one additional colophon written by the official Yin Xiangbao 尹向寶 (fl. early 15th century), dated the eighth month of 1404. This difference between the two scrolls may have been the result of later remounting. The colophons are ordered according to the official rank of their writers, beginning with the monk-official and Junior Preceptor Yao Guangxiao 姚廣孝 (1335–1418), also known as Daoyan 道衍, who was the Yongle emperor's main strategist (see Chapter 16 by Marsha Haufler in this volume). Others include Jian Yi 蹇義 (1364–1435), Lü Zhen 呂震 (1365–1426), Hu Yan 胡儼 (1360–1443), Xie Jin 解縉 (1369–1415), Huang Huai 黃淮 (1367–1449) and Hu Guang 胡廣 (1370–1418) – all important officials of the Ming court. The poems praise the Yongle emperor and present *zouyu* as an auspicious sign of his rule. These paintings and colophons would have been produced after the Prince of Zhou's gift, made on the eighth day of the ninth month in 1404. The dating of the painting can be further narrowed down based on the title of one of the officials: Lü Zhen identifies himself as the Chief Minister of the Court of Judicial Review (*Dalisi qing* 大理寺卿) in his colophon. This is a title that he used until the ninth month of 1405, when he changed positions.[7] Hence the paintings would have been made before this date.

Miraculous manifestations of Zhenwu

Imperial religious activities, both Daoist and Buddhist, were frequent during the Yongle reign, and were intended to demonstrate that the emperor was a virtuous ruler who had the protection and support of divine powers. For instance, *Preface to Saintly Filial Poem on Auspicious Responses* (*Shengxiao ruiying shi you xu* 聖孝瑞應詩有序) records that the Yongle emperor held an audience with Daoist masters who came from across the empire at the temple Chaotiangong 朝天宮 (Palace in Homage to Heaven) in Nanjing during the eleventh month of 1406.[8] Leading up to and on the day of the emperor's visit to the temple, a series of auspicious signs were recorded:

> On the day of *guihai*, spiritual beings appeared at *Shenyueguan* (Imperial Music Office); on *jiazi* auspicious clouds appeared at Chaotian Palace; and on *yichou*, sweet dew fell on trees in the palace. On *bingyin*, when his Majesty's carriage visited

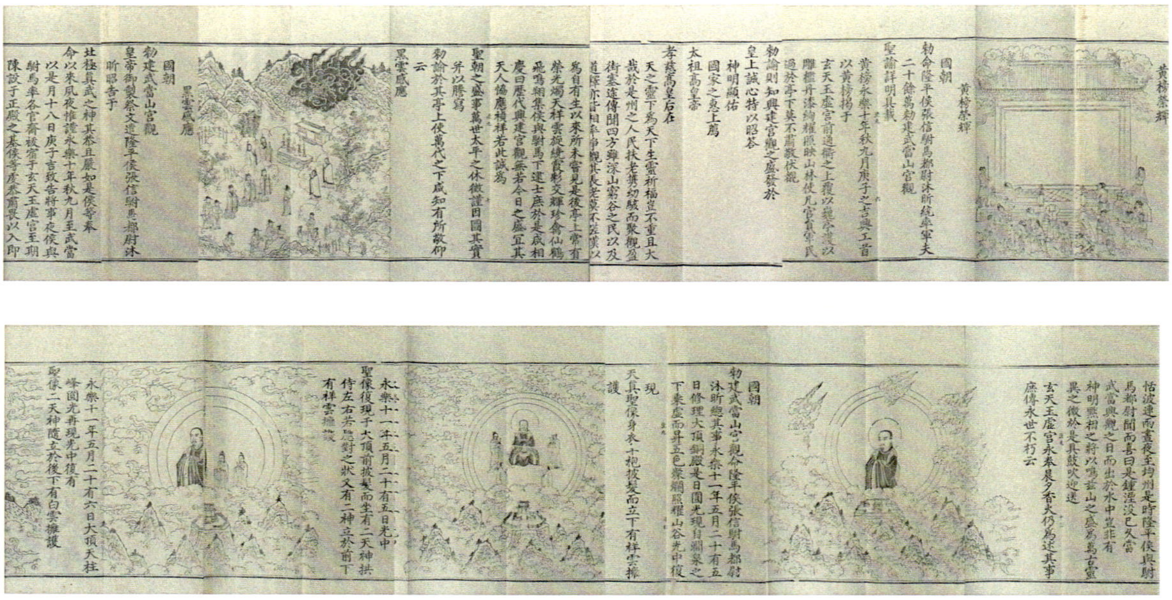

Plate 14.3 ***Catalogue of Auspicious Responses of the Supreme Emperor of the Dark Heaven of the Great Ming*** **(*Da Ming xuantian shangdi ruiying tulu* 大明玄天上帝瑞應圖錄), dated 1444–5. Printed ink on paper, each page: height 35cm, width 11.3cm. Bibliothèque National de France, Paris, Chinois 9546**

> Chaotian Palace again, auspicious clouds covered the altar, while hundreds of *luan*-phoenixes and cranes circled the air.
>
> 癸亥有神人見神樂觀，甲子卿雲見朝天宮，乙丑甘露降於宮樹。丙寅車駕復幸朝天宮，卿雲覆映壇上，鸞鶴數百翔舞旋繞。[9]

Of particular importance during the Yongle reign was the worship of the Daoist deity Zhenwu 真武, the Supreme Emperor of the Dark Heaven (*Xuantian shangdi* 玄天上帝) (see discussion by Maggie Chui Ki Wan in Chapter 15 of this volume). During the civil war, Zhu Di and his military counsellor, Daoyan, propagated the story of the manifestation of Zhenwu in order to motivate troops and win the obedience of the people. When the revolt started, a deity in armour with untied hair is said to have appeared in the sky, which Daoyan identified as Zhenwu and his teacher.[10] Zhu Di then 'dishevelled his hair and unsheathed his sword in response' (*Pifa bajian xiangying* 披髮拔劍相應).[11] The Yongle emperor credited the deity for his victory, which he expressed in an imperial edict dated to the third month of 1412:

> By the time of my reign, Zhenwu had spread numinous transformations, assisted the state, protected the people, and greatly manifested responses. From the beginning of my campaign 'to clear away disasters, in accordance with Heaven's will', [Zhenwu's] power and efficacy have been so notable, the resonance so numerous, that it is impossible to fully speak of them.
>
> 至我朝，真武闡揚靈化，陰佑國家，福庇生民，十分顯應。我自奉天靖難之初，顯著威靈，感應至多，言說不盡。[12]

After he ascended the throne, the Yongle emperor continued to venerate Daoism, especially Zhenwu. He commissioned the *Musical Stanzas on Mysterious Teachings Composed under the Imperial Aegis of the Great Ming* (*Da Ming yuzhi xuanjiao yuezhang* 大明御製玄教樂章), containing ritual music composed in tribute to the Dark Emperor Zhenwu. He ordered the construction and expansion of a major temple complex at Mount Wudang 武當山 in Hubei 湖北 province that venerated Zhenwu. After construction was largely completed in 1416, the emperor bestowed an elevated title on the mountain, naming it the 'Great Marchmount, Supreme Harmony Mountain' (Dayue Taiheshan 大嶽太和山), and personally composed an inscription for it that was carved on to a commemorative stele.[13]

According to the *Ming Veritable Records*, miraculous signs began to appear at Mount Wudang during 1413, the second year after construction of the temple complex began.[14] Auspicious five-coloured clouds gathered, and Zhenwu reportedly revealed himself many times at the mountain peak, at Zixiaogong 紫霄宮 (Palace of Purple Cloud) and Yuxugong 玉虛宮 (Palace of Jade Void).[15] Imperial edicts and Zhenwu's divine manifestations were recorded with detailed explanatory texts and illustrations in the *Catalogue of Auspicious Responses of the Supreme Emperor of the Dark Heaven of the Great Ming* (*Da Ming xuantian shangdi ruiying tulu* 大明玄天上帝瑞應圖錄), a version of which is compiled in the Daoist Canon (**Pl. 14.3a–b**).[16] A handscroll painting of this subject matter is in the Baiyun guan 白雲觀 (White Cloud Monastery), Beijing.[17] In total, 17 scenes are depicted in the version in the Daoist Canon. Six of these have specific titles summarising supernatural phenomena: 'Imperial Edict Illuminates' (*Huangbang ronghui* 黃榜榮輝), 'Dark Cloud Responds' (*Heiyun ganying* 黑雲感應), 'Jianlin (trees) Responds to Auspiciousness' (*Qianlin yingxiang* 騫林應祥), 'Betal-plum Tree Manifests Auspiciousness' (*Langmei chengrui* 榔梅呈瑞), 'Deity Leaves Behind Giant Tree Trunk' (*Shenliu jumu* 神留巨木) and 'Giant Bell Appears from the Water' (*Shuiyong hongzhong* 水湧洪鐘). The remaining 11 untitled scenes portray Zhenwu appearing at the mountain. Such representations of the deity helped to establish and spread an official image of Zhenwu during the Ming dynasty. Subsequently, after the capital was transferred to Beijing in 1421, Zhenwu, who was also the deity of the north, would become recognised as the divine protector of the emperor and the Ming empire.

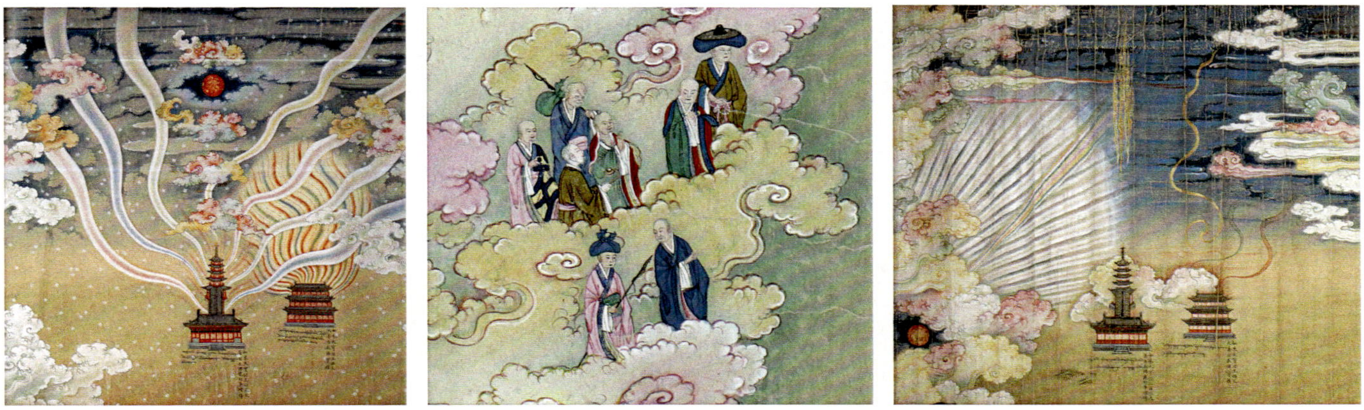

Plate 14.4a–c Details from *Miracles of the Mass of Universal Salvation Conducted by the Fifth Karmapa for the Yongle Emperor*, artist unknown, dated 1407. Handscroll, ink and colours on silk, height 66cm, width 4,968cm. The Tibet Museum, Lhasa

Miracles of the Fifth Karmapa

In addition to his patronage of Daoism, the Yongle emperor also showed a strong affinity for Tibetan Buddhism, starting from when he was still a prince. Lu Rong's 陸容 (1436–94) *Shuyuan zaji* 菽園雜記 (*Random Jottings from the Bean Garden*) records Zhu Di's belief in Tibetan Buddhism as demonstrated after one particularly bloody battle during the civil war:

> After the Great Battle of Baigou River, the battlefield was littered with the corpses of dead soldiers. Taizong (the Yongle emperor) remembered them and ordered their skulls to be collected and made into rosary beads. These were distributed to eunuchs to pray for the reincarnation of the dead. Some skulls that were deep and big were used to hold pure water on the Buddhist altar. These were called Heavenly Numinous Cups. All these were the teachings of *hu* monks.
>
> 太宗皇帝白溝河大戰，陣亡軍士積骸遍野。上念之，命收其頭骨，規成數珠，分賜內官念佛，冀其輪迴。又有頭骨深大者，則以盛淨水供佛，名天靈盌，皆胡僧之教也。[18]

In the second month of 1403, the Yongle emperor sent the eunuch Hou Xian 侯顯 (1365–1438) with a delegation to Tibet to meet with the Fifth Karmapa, Deshin Shekpa (1384–1415; also called Halima 哈立麻 in Chinese sources).[19] They convinced Deshin Shekpa to travel to Nanjing where he would perform a Mass of Universal Salvation (*Pudu da zhai* 普渡大齋) at Linggusi 靈谷寺 (Numinous Valley Monastery) for the emperor's deceased parents, the Hongwu 洪武 emperor (r. 1368–98) and Empress Ma馬 (1332–82), during the fifth month of 1407.[20] When the Yongle emperor's wife, Empress Xu 徐 (1362–1407), passed away in the seventh month, he asked Deshin Shekpa to perform a seven-day mass at Mount Wutai 五臺山.[21] The emperor treated Deshin Shekpa with the formality accorded to a prince and granted him the title of the 'Great Treasure Dharma King' (*Da bao fawang* 大寶法王).[22]

A long handscroll entitled *Miracles of the Mass of Universal Salvation Conducted by the Fifth Karmapa for the Yongle Emperor*, now in the Tibet Museum, depicts miracles that took place around the Lingu Monastery as a result of Deshin Shekpa's visit and the rituals he performed (**Pl. 14.4a–c**).[23] The scenes depicted follow a chronological order spanning 19 days in the second and third months of 1407. Many different miraculous phenomena are depicted in the scroll, including five-coloured clouds, multi-coloured radiance, a rain of heavenly flowers, sweet dew, arhats manifesting in the sky, clouds in auspicious shapes and circling cranes. The final scene records light emanating from the southwest and from the Karmapa's residence.[24] Each scene is inscribed with writings in five languages: Chinese, Persian, Tày, Tibetan and Mongolian.[25]

The Yongle emperor sought to build ties with Tibetan Buddhist leaders, using religion to placate Mongolian and Tibetan tribes, and to establish the prestige of the Ming government. In 1414, the emperor once again dispatched Hou Xian to Lhasa to invite Tsongkhapa (1357–1419) to visit China. Tsongkhapa sent in his place his student Śākya Yeshé (1354–1439), who arrived in Nanjing in the 12th month of that year.[26] During his stay, Śākya Yeshé performed religious rituals for the Yongle emperor; in return the emperor lavished treasures upon him, and bestowed on him the title 'Great Preceptor of State' (*Da guoshi* 大國師) during the fifth month of 1415. In 1416, Śākya Yeshé returned to Tibet, bringing with him the Yongle emperor's Tibetan edition of the Buddhist canon, *Kangyur*, now housed in the Sera Monastery in Tibet.[27] The Yongle emperor successfully used Buddhism to strengthen and unify the Ming state, while maintaining Confucianism as the basis of his ruling philosophy.

Auspicious beasts from abroad

During the Yongle reign, many foreign envoys travelled to the Ming imperial court to pay their respects, bringing with them valuable goods and rare animals as tribute. The arrival of foreign tribute could also be interpreted as an auspicious omen, which was recorded in paintings and poems. For instance, Xia Yuanji's 夏原吉 (1366–1430) *Poem to Saintly Virtue and Auspicious Responses* (*Shengde ruiying shi* 聖德瑞應詩), written in 1419, records that:

> Hormuz and other foreign states sent envoys with offerings of *qilin*, lions, heavenly horses, leopards, elephants, ostriches, zebras, antelopes, oryxes and parrots with five-coloured feathers. Also, Jiaozhi offered white crows, 'mountain phoenixes', a three-tailed turtle and other creatures.
>
> 海外忽魯謨斯等國，遣使來進麒麟、獅子、天馬、文豹、紫象、駝雞、福祿、靈羊、長角馬哈獸、五色鸚鵡等，又交趾進白烏、山鳳、三尾龜等物。[28]

With the support of the Yongle emperor, Zheng He 鄭和 (1371–1433) led six maritime voyages to territories along the

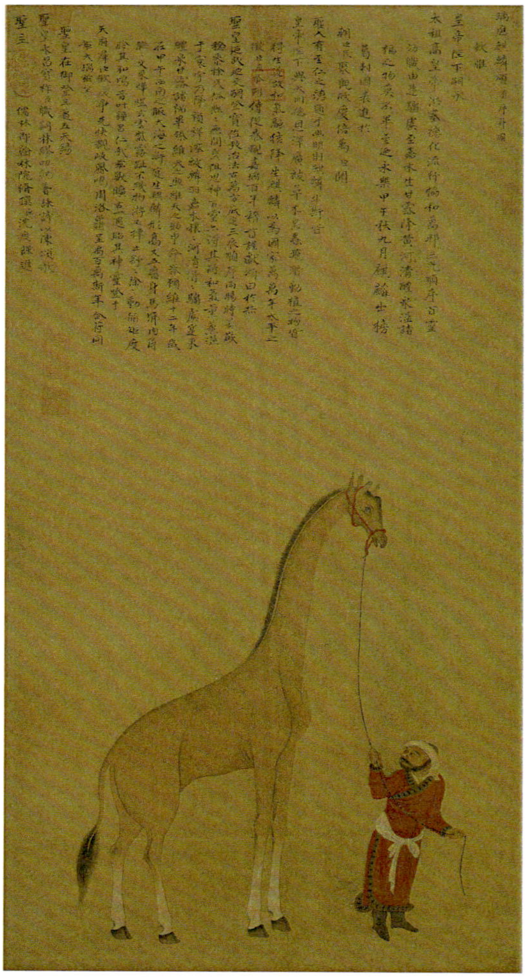

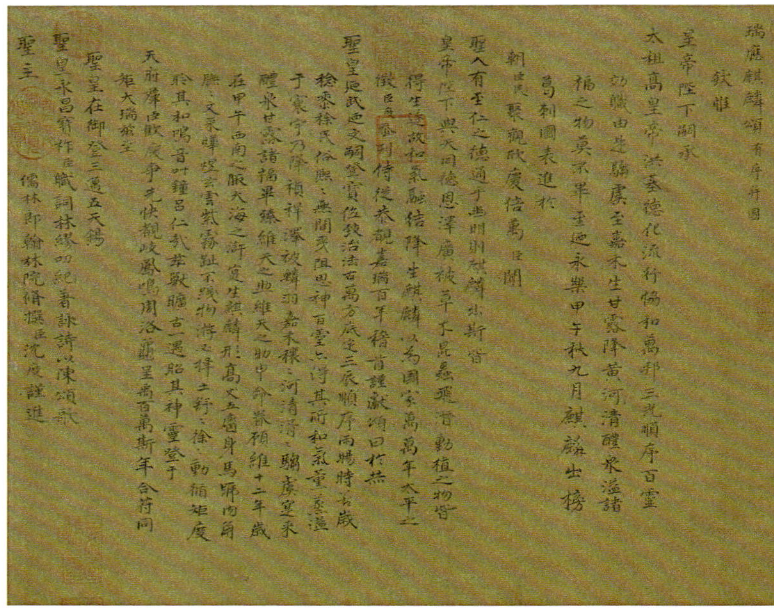

Plate 14.5a–b: a) (left) Anonymous, *Tribute Giraffe from Bengal* (*Mingren hua qilin Shen Du song* 明人畫麒麟沈度頌), calligraphy by Shen Du 沈度 (1357–1434), Ming dynasty, dated *c.* 1414. Hanging scroll, ink and colours on silk, image height 90.4cm, width 45cm. National Palace Museum, Taipei; b) (above) Calligraphy by Shen Du 沈度 on *Tribute Giraffe from Bengal* (*Mingren hua qilin Shen Du song* 明人畫麒麟沈度頌)

South China Sea and the Indian Ocean. In return, these regions sent envoys to the Ming court to offer tribute. In the summer of 1404, an envoy from Annam presented a white elephant to the emperor.[29] Zeng Qi 曾棨 (1372–1432) composed an *Ode to the White Elephant* (*Baixiang fu* 白象賦) to commemorate this gift. In the third month of 1409, an envoy from Jiaozhi 交趾 (in present-day northern Vietnam) offered another white elephant. Chen Gui 陳珪 (d. 1415) wrote to congratulate the emperor, but the emperor replied that white elephants are common and that congratulations were not necessary.[30]

In the ninth month of 1414, the ruler of Bengal (roughly Bangladesh today) sent the Yongle emperor a giraffe, which the Chinese thought was a *qilin* 麒麟.[31] According to the 2nd-century dictionary *Shuowen jiezi* 說文解字 (*Explaining and Analysing Characters*), a *qilin* is a benevolent beast that has the body of a deer, the tail of an ox and a single horn.[32] The *qilin* is believed to be the most auspicious of beasts, appearing only when the emperor is both rightful and benevolent. One theory suggests that it became equated with the giraffe because *qilin* sounded similar to *giri*, the Somali word for giraffe.[33] In 1414, Hanlin officials such as Shen Du 沈度 (1357–1434), Xia Yuanji, Jin Youzi 金幼孜 (1367–1431) and Li Shimian 李時勉 (1374–1450) all composed *Odes to Qilin* (*Qilin fu* 麒麟賦).[34] In 1415, Malin 麻林, today's Malindi of Kenya, sent an envoy bearing tributes of '*qilin*, heavenly horse and spiritual deer' (*qilin, tianma, shenlu* 麒麟、天馬、神鹿) to China.[35] The arrival of giraffes as tribute in China caused such a sensation that the envoy from Joseon Korea sent representatives to congratulate the emperor in Beijing.[36] It is also recorded in the official *Annals of the Joseon Dynasty* (*Joseon wangjo sillok* 朝鮮王朝實錄).[37] Both Bengal and Malindi are far from China. The arrival of two *qilin* in the Ming capital within a short span of time was understood as the direct result of the charismatic power of the Yongle emperor's virtue reverberating across vast distances.

A painting depicting the tribute giraffe from Bengal is in the National Palace Museum, Taipei (**Pl. 14.5a**).[38] It includes a transcription of Shen Du's ode to *qilin* (**Pl. 14.5b**), signed with the following:

> In autumn, the 9th month of the *jiawu* year of the Yongle reign [1414] … a sign of eternal peace in the state ... The real *qilin* is five *zhang* in height [approximately 16.6m]. It has the body of a river deer and the hooves of a horse … [it] walks slowly and steadily … Gentleman-Confucian and Senior Compiler in the Hanlin Academy, your servitor, Shen Du, respectfully presents.
>
> 永樂甲午（1414）秋九月，…以為國家萬萬年太平之徵。…實生麒麟，形高丈五。麕身馬蹄…舒舒徐徐…儒林郎翰林院脩撰臣沈度謹進。

Although Shen Du is named as the writer, the handwriting of the inscription does not resemble that of the Hanlin scholar. The written characters are not sufficiently regular in form. Extant calligraphy by Shen Du, such as *Album of Admonitions by Jingzhai* (*Jingzhai zhen* 敬齋箴) in the Palace Museum, Beijing, shows the grace and elegance of his

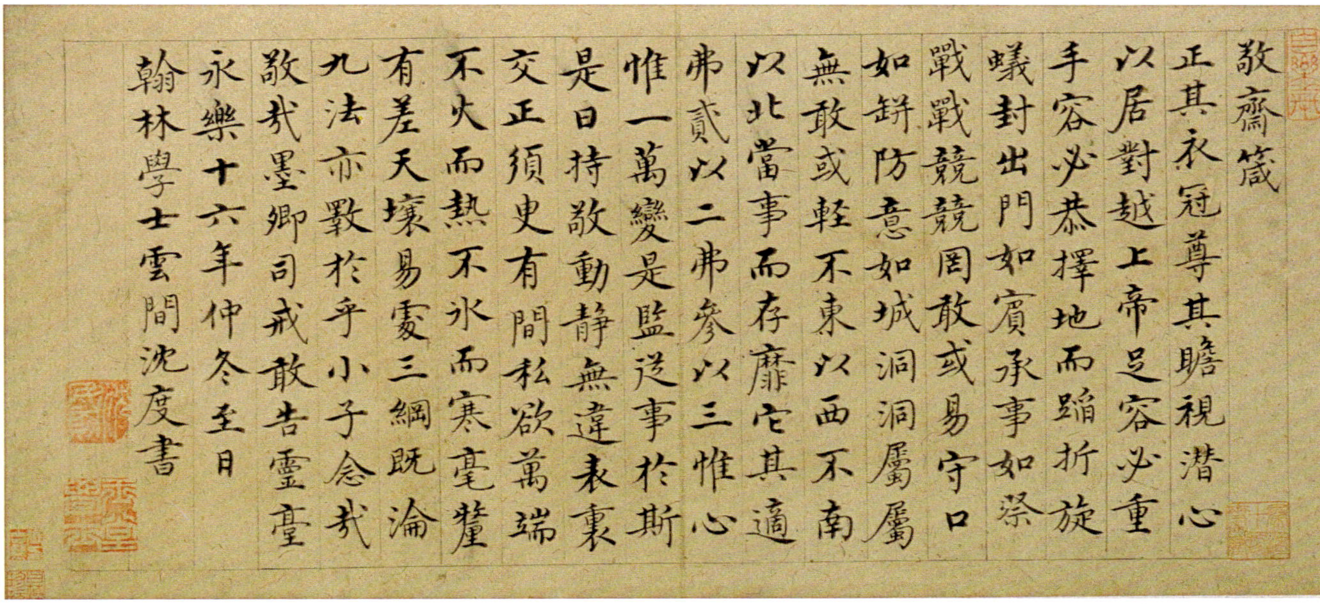

Plate 14.6 Shen Du 沈度 (1357–1434), *Album of Admonitions by Jingzhai* (*Jingzhai zhen* 敬齋箴), dated 1418. Album, ink on paper, height 23.8cm, width 49.4cm. The Palace Museum, Beijing

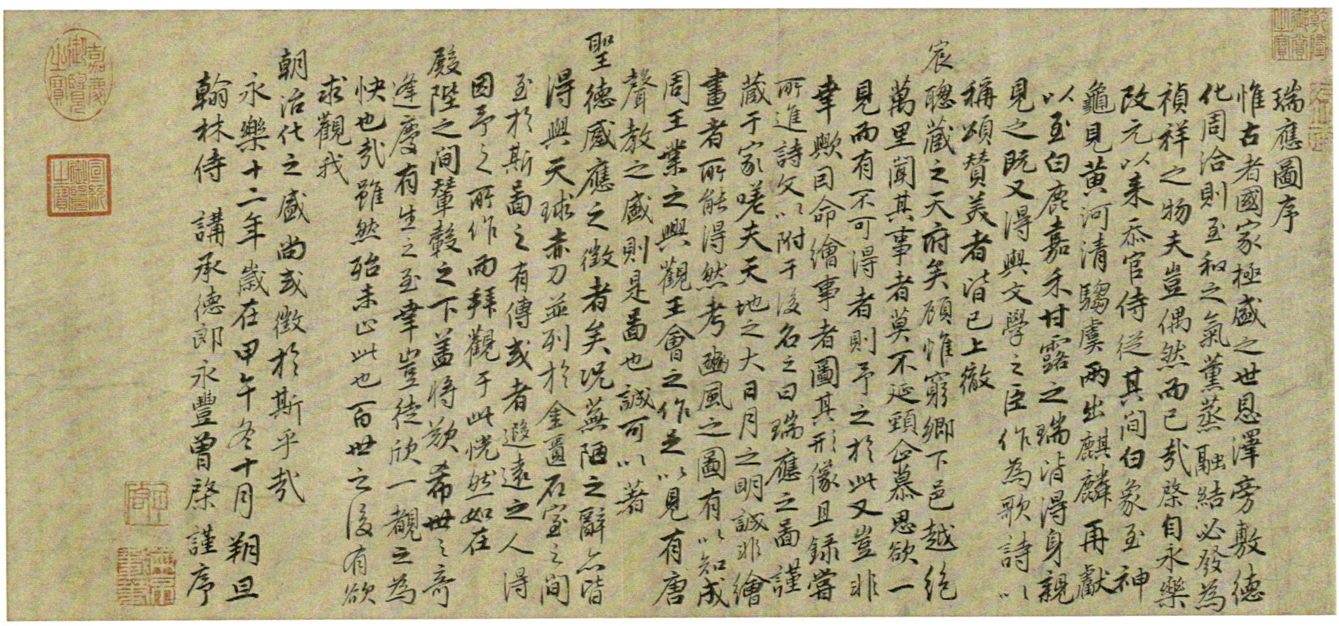

Plate 14.7 Zeng Qi 曾棨, Preface to *Pictures of Auspicious Responses* (*Mingren ruiying tu* 明人瑞應圖), dated 1414. Handscroll, ink and colours on paper, height 30cm, width 686.3cm. National Palace Museum, Taipei

calligraphy (**Pl. 14.6**). By comparison, the writing on the painting of the giraffe is slender and meticulous, and less rounded and regular. More conspicuously, the term *shenghuang* 聖皇 (saintly emperor) at the start of the third line from the left is indented rather than positioned above other lines in the inscription as a sign of respect to the ruler. A Hanlin scholar would never have broken a taboo like this. It is probable that the painting in the National Palace Museum, Taipei, was not intended for the emperor's own collection; instead, it may well have been painted by court painters as a reward to a minister. Paintings of this subject matter were in circulation during the Ming dynasty. For instance, Xie Zhaozhe 謝肇淛 (1567–1624) records in *Five Assorted Offerings* (*Wuzaju* 五雜俎) that:

> In the middle of the Yongle reign, [the emperor] received a *qilin*. He ordered paintings to be made of it, which were awarded to his ministers. I had the chance to see one of these at a friend's home.
>
> 永樂中曾獲麟，命工圖畫，傳賜大臣，余嘗於一故家得見之。[39]

Because the Yongle emperor had usurped the throne, he needed to use visual and literary means to support his legitimacy as emperor. Paintings and poems were created to record the arrival of numerous foreign envoys bearing symbolically significant gifts, such as the giraffe, interpreted as a *qilin*, to support the emperor's claim to the Mandate of Heaven. These are incorporated into a wider world of auspicious signs, as seen in the handscroll *Painting of Auspicious Responses* (*Mingren ruiying tu* 明人瑞應圖) by an anonymous Ming court painter in the National Palace Museum, Taipei (**Pl. 14.7**).[40] In his preface to the painting, Zeng Qi writes that:

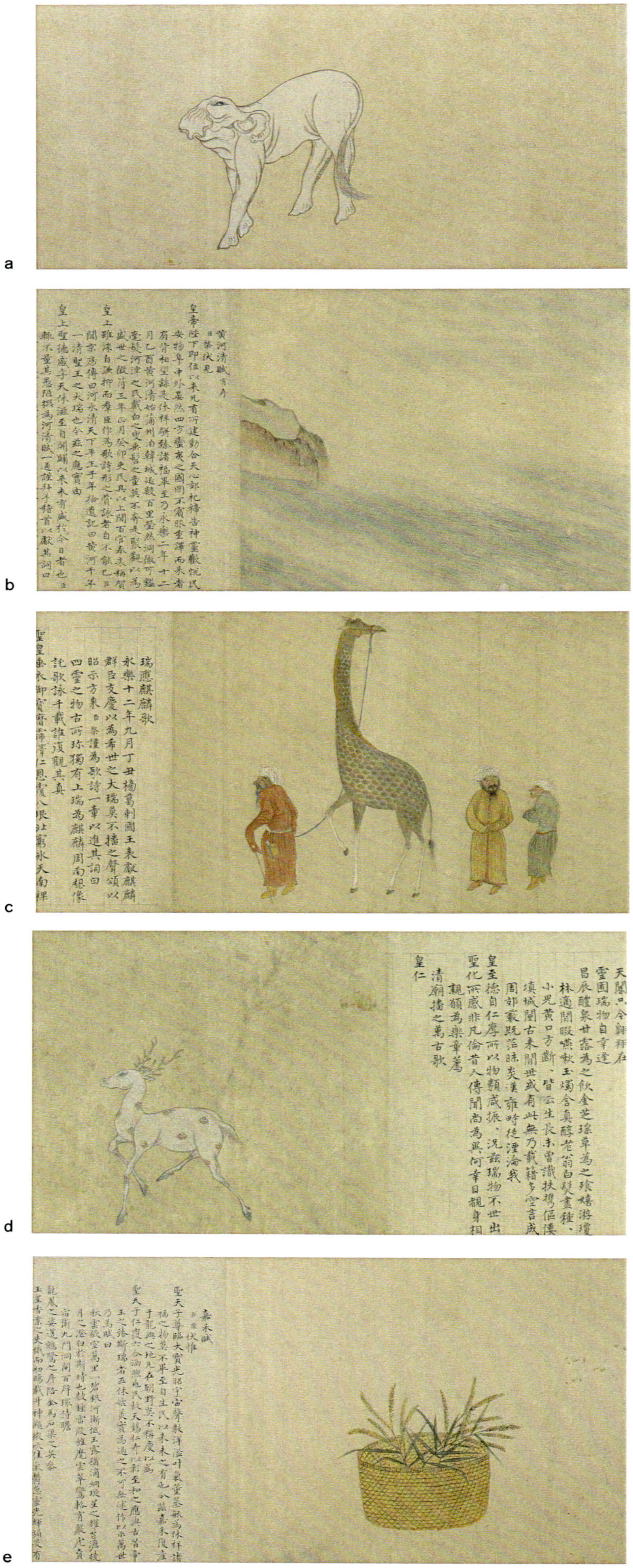

Plate 14.8a–e Anonymous, *Pictures of Auspicious Responses* (*Mingren ruiying tu* 明人瑞應圖), dated 1414. Handscroll, ink and colours on paper, height 30cm, width 686.3cm. National Palace Museum, Taipei; a) detail of a white elephant; b) detail of the clear Yellow River; c) detail of a *qilin*; d) detail of a white deer; e) detail of auspicious grains

> Since the beginning of the Yongle reign, my humble self has served as an official during this time. The white elephant came; the mystical tortoise appeared; the Yellow River turned clear; *zouyu* appeared twice, and *qilin* was offered twice, as well as other auspicious signs, such as the appearance of white deer, auspicious grain and sweet dew. All this I could personally witness, because painters were ordered to paint their image.
>
> 自永樂改元以來，忝官侍從其間。白象至，神龜見，黃河清，騶虞兩出，麒麟再獻。以至白鹿、嘉禾、甘露之瑞，皆得身親見之，因命繪事者圖其形象。

According to Zeng's preface, the painting was produced in the tenth month of 1414. There are five sections in the painting (**Pl. 14.8a–e**). From right to left they depict a white elephant, the Yellow River with its muddy water turning clear, a *qilin*, a white deer and auspicious grains with more than one ear of grain on each stem. An ode is inscribed after each image. Zeng, a native of Jiangxi, was the top metropolitan graduate of 1404, and the Deputy Chief Editor of the *Yongle da dian* 永樂大典 (*Great Canon of the Yongle Reign*). As Zeng's preface suggests, there should be eight rather than five scenes depicted in the scroll: divine tortoise, *zouyu* and sweet dew are mentioned but not shown. These sections may have been lost over time and the scroll subsequently remounted. The white elephant depicted commemorates the tribute from Annam in 1404; the river scene records the Yellow River turning clear in the winter of 1404; the *qilin* documents the giraffe arriving from Bengal in 1414; the white deer relates to a command from the Yongle emperor in 1406 ordering officials to compose odes about the topic. According to the *Veritable Records*, the people of Miyun county 密雲縣, Shuntian prefecture 順天府 (today's Beijing municipality) presented auspicious grain as tribute in 1409.[44] As a means of communication, painting could express a consistent theme through the repetition of an established formula. This painting, like others discussed above, is a symbolic celebration of a prosperous society and a just ruler, which held significance in reality. From a Ming perspective, such paintings and odes represented the voice of an era.

Celebrating the new capital

After assuming the throne, the Yongle emperor promoted officials and scholars from the previous reign, appointing them to positions in the imperial library. Seven men made up the Grand Secretariat, five of whom were from Jiangxi, including Xie Jin, Hu Guang, Yang Shiqi, Jin Youzi and Hu Yan. Only Yang Rong 楊榮 (1371–1440) and Huang Huai were not from Jiangxi. Instead they were from Jian'an 建安 in Fujian 福建 province, and Yongjia 永嘉 in Zhejiang 浙江 province, respectively. These officials played a particularly important role in recommending and promoting painters from their native towns. Hanlin officials were closely connected with court painters. Court painters served the imperial household, while Hanlin officials were attendants of the emperor, so their positions paralleled each other's. On occasion, a Hanlin official could be asked to paint for the emperor. An example of this is Wang Fu 王紱 (1362–1416) who worked at the imperial library during the early Yongle reign, later reaching the position of Secretariat Drafter because of his talent as a calligrapher. In 1409, Wang accompanied the Yongle emperor on his inspection trip to the north, and to Beijing in 1413. To record the two journeys, the emperor commissioned Wang to paint the *Eight Views of Beijing* (*Beijing bajing tu* 北京八景圖), now in the National Museum of China (**Pl. 14.9a–h**).[45]

The frontispiece to the painting is inscribed by Hu Guang in 1414. At the end of the scroll, there are odes written in the Eminent Court Official Style (*Taige ti* 台閣體) – a graceful writing style developed by scholars in the Yongle and Xuande reigns used to describe an age of peace and prosperity. The odes were written by 13 officials during a literary gathering. They include Hu Guang, Hu Yan, Yang Rong, Jin Youzi, Zeng Qi, Lin Huan, Liang Qian, Wang Hong, Wang Ying and Wang Fu. One of the inscriptions reads:

> The Saintly Son of Heaven arrived here like a soaring dragon. He commanded the construction of Beijing as the capital where people from myriad directions convened. Carriages patrolled and hunted in the surrounding areas; scholarly officials lined in procession … The roads in all four directions were even and straight, enabling the control of all regions. This is a firm foundation for imperial descendants to reign for ten thousand generations.
>
> 聖天子龍飛於兹，肇建北京為萬方會同之都，車駕幾載巡狩，而文學之臣多列扈從。…東南西北道里適均直，足以控制萬方，而為聖子神孫萬世磐石之基也。[46]

The eight views of Beijing that are depicted are: 'Sunset at Jintai' (*Jintai xizhao* 金台夕照), 'Clear Waves at Taiye Pond' (*Taiye qingbo* 太液晴波), 'Spring Clouds at Qionghua Island' (*Qiongdao chunyun* 瓊島春雲), 'Cascading Rainbow at Mount Yuquan' (*Yuquan chuihong* 玉泉垂虹), 'Layered Shades of Green at Juyong Pass' (*Juyong diecui* 居庸疊翠), 'Misty Trees at Jimen' (*Jimen yanshu* 薊門煙樹), 'Dawn Moonlight at Lugou Bridge' (*Lugou xiaoyue* 盧溝曉月) and 'Clearing Snow on West Mountain' (*Xishan jixue* 西山霽雪).[47] Each scene is followed by an inscription celebrating the grand achievements of the Yongle emperor. The scroll with its combination of paintings and poems may be interpreted as an attempt to generate interest for Beijing among officials in the south. It expresses the attitude of officials in support of the Yongle emperor's decision to move the capital from Nanjing to Beijing.

Officials celebrated the construction of the new imperial palace in Beijing by writing odes with reference to auspicious signs. For instance, *Ode to Imperial Virtues and Auspicious Responses* (*Shengde ruiying song* 聖德瑞應頌) mentions unusual radiance, grains with multiple ears, *lingzhi* 靈芝 fungus, sweet springs and dew, rabbits, *qilin*, *zouyu* and phoenixes. This work is part of *Odes Presented by Scholarly Officials of the Yongle Reign* (*Ming Yongle chao cichen xiansong* 明永樂朝詞臣獻頌), dated 1417, written by Hu Guang, Yang Rong and Jin Youzi, and now in the First Historical Archives of China.[48] As the title of the ode suggests, these signs were evidence that the Yongle emperor was a wise and capable ruler, whose actions, including the transfer of the capital, accorded with the will of Heaven.

Auspicious symbols in flower-and-bird paintings

Bian Wenjin 邊文進 (*c.* 1356–*c.* 1428) was an important court painter of flower-and-bird paintings (**Pl. 14.10**) who was active during the Yongle to Xuande reigns, and was

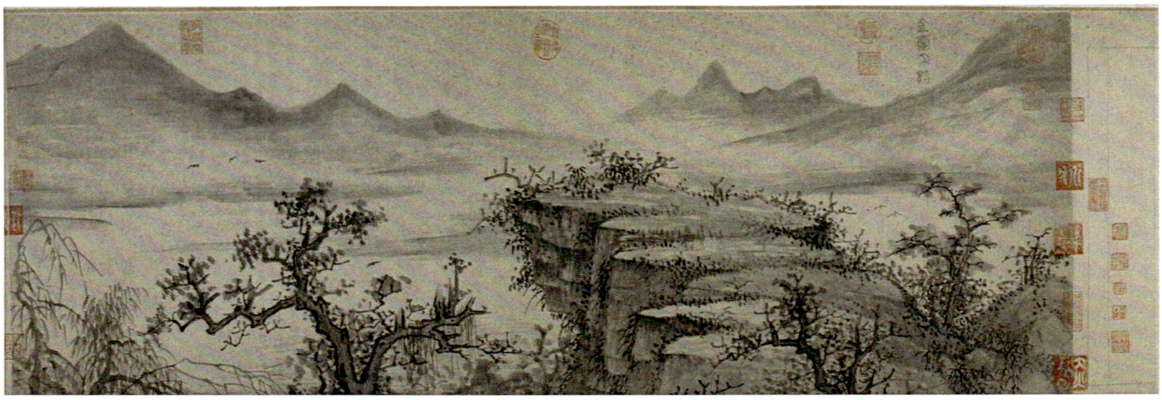

a) Sunset at Jintai (*Jintai xizhao* 金台夕照)

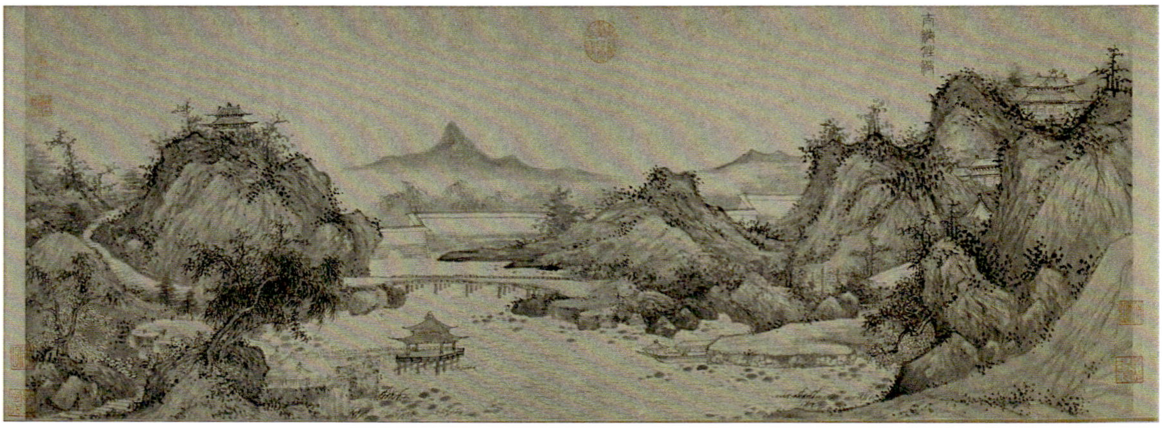

b) Clear Waves at Taiye Pond (*Taiye qingbo* 太液晴波)

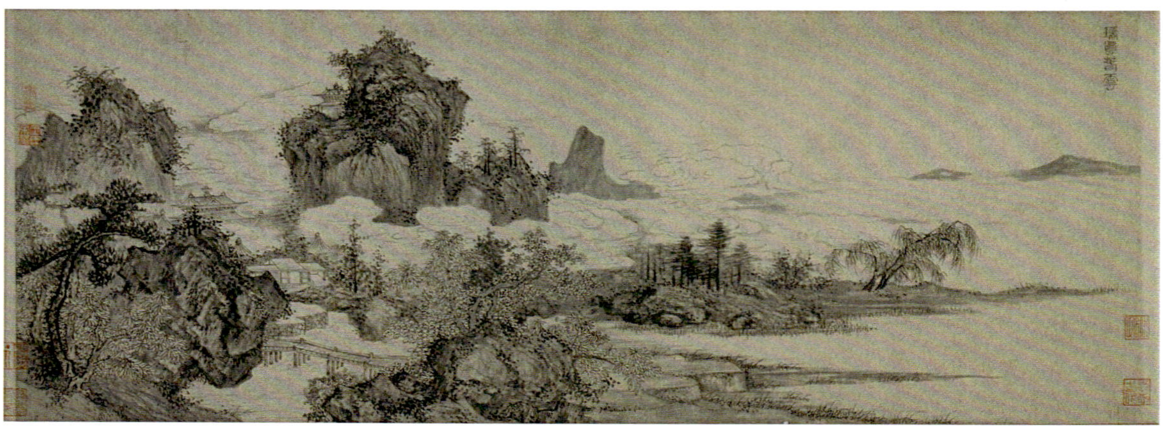

c) *Spring Clouds at Qionghua Island* (*Qiongdao chunyun* 瓊島春雲)

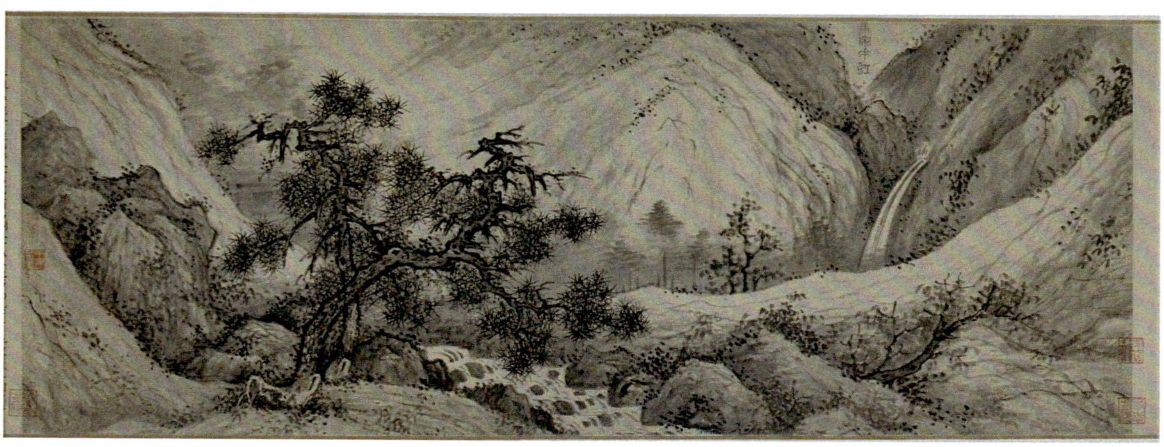

d) Cascading Rainbow at Mount Yuquan (*Yuquan chuihong* 玉泉垂虹)

Plate 14.9a–h Wang Fu 王紱, *Eight Views of Beijing* (*Beijing bajing tu* 北京八景圖), dated *c.* 1414. Handscroll, ink on paper, height 42.1cm, length 2006.5cm. National Museum of China

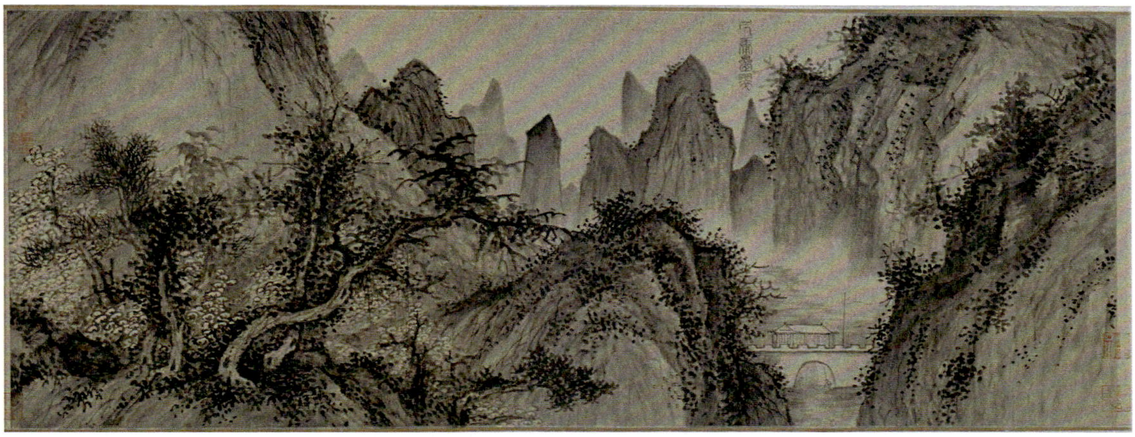

e) *Layered Shades of Green at Juyong Pass* (*Juyong diecui* 居庸疊翠)

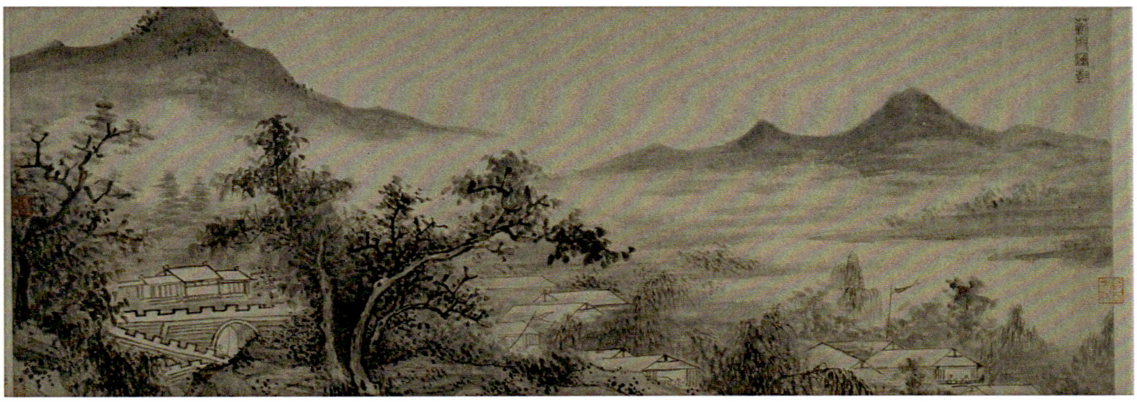

f) Misty Trees at Jimen (*Jimen yanshu* 薊門煙樹)

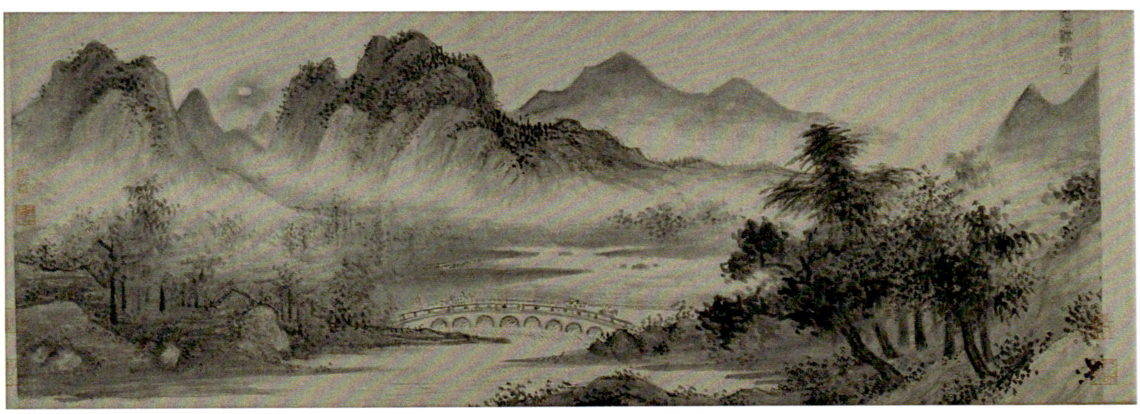

g) Dawn Moonlight at Lugou Bridge (*Lugou xiaoyue* 盧溝曉月)

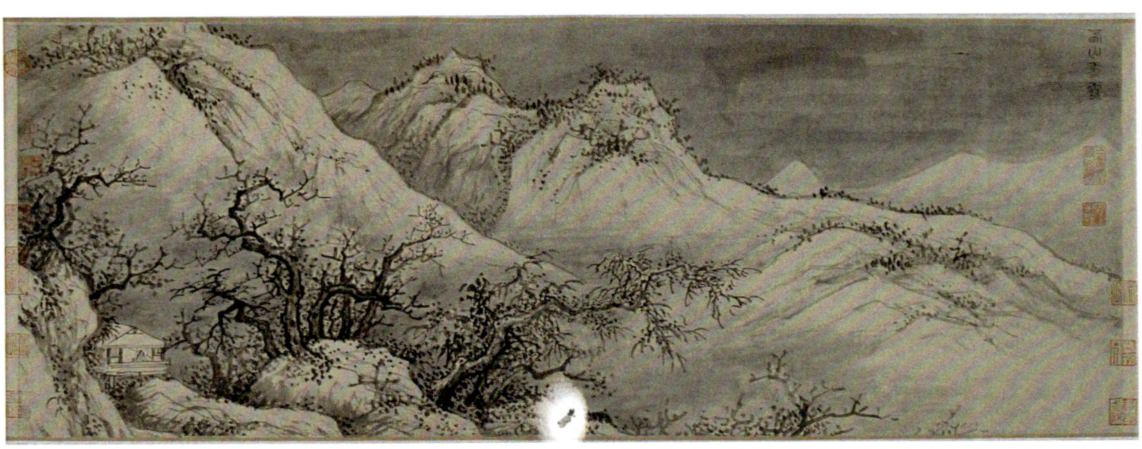

h) Clearing Snow on West Mountain (*Xishan jixue* 西山霽雪)

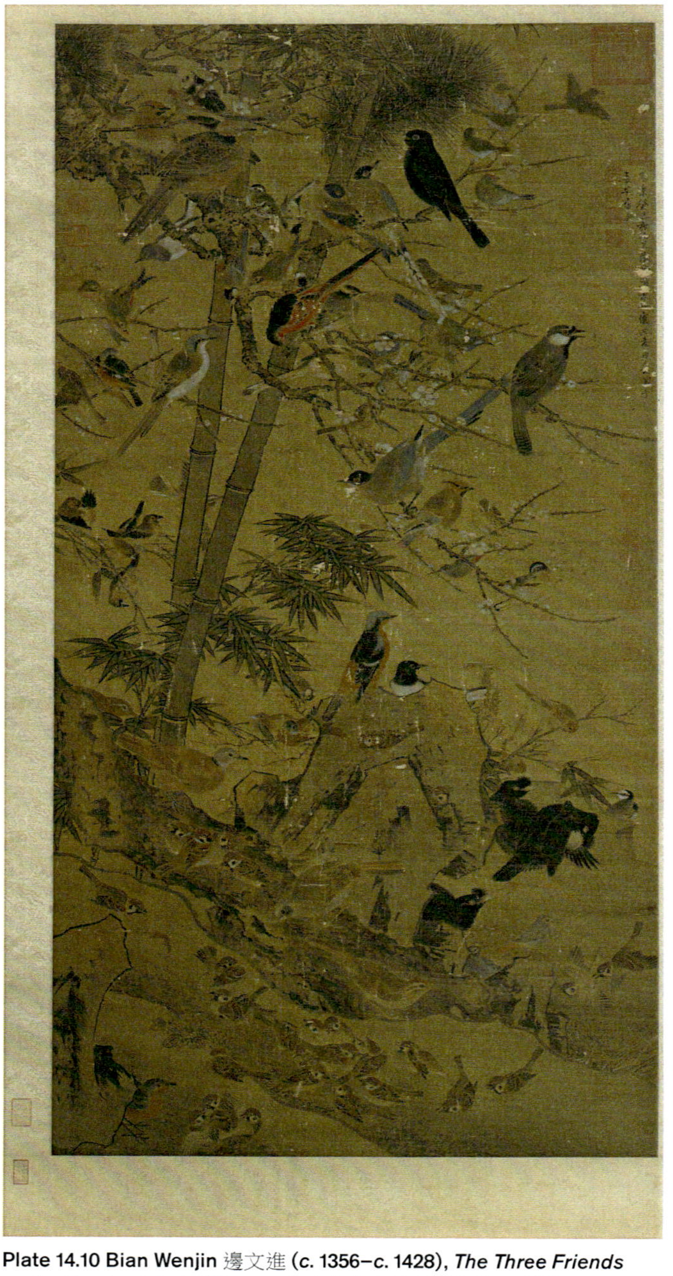

Plate 14.10 Bian Wenjin 邊文進 (*c.* 1356–*c.* 1428), *The Three Friends and a Hundred Birds* (*Sanyou baiqin tu* 三友百禽圖), *c.* 1413. Hanging scroll, ink and colours on silk, height 151.3cm, width 78.1cm. National Palace Museum, Taipei

Plate 14.11 Colophon of *The Three Friends and a Hundred Birds*

appointed official-in-attendance at the imperial court. According to He Liangjun's 何良俊 *Siyouzhai hualun* 四友齋畫論 (*Theory of Painting from the Studio of the Four Friends*), completed in 1573:

> The court designated Renzhi Hall to place painters. At one time the painters at the academy included specialists in figures, Jiang Zicheng; birds, Bian Jingzhao [Wenjin] from Longxi; landscapes, Shang Xi, Shi Rui, Ma Shi from Lianchuan, Li Zai, Ni Duan, and Chen Xian.
>
> 我朝特設仁智殿以處畫士，一時在院中者，人物則蔣子成，翎毛則隴西之邊景昭，山水則商喜、石銳、練川馬軾、李在、倪端、陳暹。[49]

Bian inherited the use of fine brushwork and vivid colours from the Northern Song painting tradition in the manner of Huang Quan 黃筌 (*c.* 903–65), while combining it with the style of Southern Song academic painters. In *Three Friends and a Hundred Birds* (*Sanyou baiqin tu* 三友百禽圖), in the National Palace Museum, Taipei (**Pl. 14.11**), he writes that:

> In the seventh month of the *guisi* year of the Yongle reign [1413], Bian Jingzhao [Wenjin] of Longxi painted *Three Friends and a Hundred Birds* at his official residence in Chang'an.
>
> 永樂癸巳秋七月，隴西邊景昭寫三友百禽圖於長安官舍。

In this inscription, Chang'an refers to Nanjing, the capital at the time. It is probable that the work was commissioned by the Yongle emperor before the capital was moved to Beijing. Pine, bamboo, plum blossom and rock motifs constitute the main structure of the painting. They are interspersed with nearly a hundred birds, creating a highly decorative quality. The brushwork outlining and texturing the rocks and plum branches is relatively loose, while the painting as a whole is painted using a refined and meticulous technique of outlines filled in with colours. Pine, bamboo and plum blossom, appearing as background in this painting, are known as the *Three Friends of Winter* (*Suihan san you* 歲寒三友), which has symbolised the moral virtue of a Confucian gentleman since Song-Yuan times. Many of the birds depicted in the painting, such as cranes, magpies, quails and sparrows, are often associated with auspicious meanings of happiness, majesty and status, in addition to representing virtue. The painting depicts nearly a hundred birds; these are analogous to many officials paying reverence to the emperor, and symbolise accordance with the will of Heaven. Many court paintings of the Ming dynasty have auspicious meaning. The title of the painting, *Three Friends and a Hundred Birds*, has a distinctly celebratory feeling which coincides with Ming imperial taste.

Conclusion

In China's history, auspicious omens were interpreted as signs of the peace and prosperity of the state. Propitious occurrences, such as grains with multiple ears on a stem, a muddy river turning clear, the appearance of phoenixes and *qilin*, were understood as Heaven's response to virtuous rulership and a flourishing society. In order to prove the legitimacy of rulership, Hanlin academicians composed celebratory odes under imperial order, to which paintings were added as records. These works documented auspicious signs, highlighted the peace and prosperity of the age and served as a form of political propaganda. Praising imperial grace and virtue became part of the literary activities of eminent officials as they attended to the wishes of the emperor. Producing these poems and paintings provided officials with a pathway to advancement. This was a distinctive phenomenon in Chinese politics.

Notes

1 For other discussions of this topic, see for instance Liscomb 2002 and Haufler 2014.
2 *MS* 299, 7643.
3 *MS* 299, 7643.
4 *MSL Taizong shilu* 34.2a–b (2/9/丙午).
5 Huang Zuo 1560–6, 11.15b.
6 *MSL Taizong shilu* 35.4b (2/10/乙酉).
7 On these two paintings, see Li Ruoqing 2012b; Liscomb 2002.
8 *MS* 151, 4179–80.
9 Yang Shiqi *c.* 1445, 54.4a.
10 Yang Shiqi *c.* 1445, 54.4a.
11 Chao Shin-yi 2011, 97, citing Fu Weilin 傅維鱗, *Mingshu* 明書 (*Book of Ming*), *c.* 1647, *juan* 160.
12 Fu Weilin 傅維鱗, *Mingshu* 明書 (*Book of Ming*), *c.* 1647, *juan* 160.
13 Yang Lizhi 1999, 20.
14 *DZ* 981.
15 *DZ* 981.
16 *MSL Taizong shilu* 140.4b–5a (11/6/戊申) and 262.2b (21/8/甲子).
17 Zhongguo daojiao xiehui and Suzhou daojiao xiehui 1994, 617–18.
18 *DZ* 959. On representations of this subject matter, see Little 2000, 302–5; Lin Sheng-chih 1999; Giuffrida 2008.
19 Little 2000, no. 111, 304–5.
20 Lu Rong 1494, 1.4a.
21 *MSL Taizong shilu* 17.5b (1/2/乙丑).
22 On this event, see Berger 2001; Haufler 2014, 237–8.
23 *MSL Taizong shilu* 69.7a (5/7/癸酉).
24 *MSL Taizong shilu* 65.1a–b (5/3/丁巳).
25 For discussions of this scroll, see Luo Wenhua 1995; Berger 2001; Jiang Cheng'an and Zheng Wenlei 2000; Whitfield 2014.
26 Whitfield 2014, 80.
27 Luo Wenhua 1995, 90; Haufler 2014, 238; Whitfield 2014, 72.
28 *MSL Taizong shilu* 159.3a (12/12/癸巳).
29 *MSL Taizong shilu* 101.176.1b (14/5/辛丑).
30 Xia Yuanji 2012, 17.
31 Zeng Qi's 曾棨 'Preface to Ode to the White Elephant' (*Baixiang fu youxu* 白象賦有序), in *GJTSJC*, *juan* 171, 782–3.
32 *GJTSJC*, *juan* 171, 782–3.
33 Yu Jideng 1981, *juan* 6, 111, 115.
34 *MSL Taizong shilu*, *juan* 155.1a–b (12/9/丁丑 and 戊寅).
35 Duan Yucai 2005, 475.
36 Feng Chengjun 1962, 55.
37 *JWS*, *juan* 171, 781–3.
38 *MSL Taizong shilu* 170.2b–3a, 13/11/壬子.
39 *MS* 7, 95.
40 Wu Han 1980, 262.
41 Church 2004.
42 Xie Zhaozhe 2001, *juan* 9, 3839.
43 On this painting, see Li Ruoqing 2012a; Liscomb 2002.
44 Yu Ruji *et al.* 1620, 2.28a–b.
45 For more on this work, see Liscomb 1988–9; Li Ruoqing 2009.
46 Transcribed in Sun Chengze 1761, 65.1b, 65.4a–b.
47 Translation of the eight views follows Liscomb 1988–9.
48 Zhongguo diyi lishi dang'an guan *et al.* 2001, 13–35.
49 He Liangjun 1984, 112.

Chapter 15
Enshrining the Dark Troops: The Printing of Daoist Books in the Early Ming Dynasty

Maggie Chui Ki Wan

Zhenwu 真武, or the Perfected Warrior, was the single most important Daoist deity in the Great Ming Empire. From the reign of the Yongle 永樂 emperor (r. 1403–24), who claimed to have received help from Zhenwu in the civil war that brought him to the throne, the deity was regarded as the protector of the Ming empire and the divine source of military power for Ming rulers.[1] Honoured with the exalted title 'Supreme Emperor of the Dark Heaven' (*Xuantian shangdi* 玄天上帝) or the Dark Emperor, Zhenwu was the only deity enshrined in one of the main halls situated along the central axis of the Forbidden City when Beijing was inaugurated as the capital in 1421.[2] Known as Qin'an dian 欽安殿 (Hall of Imperial Peace), this building was solely dedicated to Zhenwu when it was first established and has remained so down to the present day. The extant architecture of the Hall of Imperial Peace preserves many imperial religious artefacts, and its furnishings have been the subject of research.[3] What remains little known are five large paintings on paper adhering to the northern interior wall of the building.[4] Dated to the Ming dynasty, the central painting depicts the image of 'Five Dragons holding the Saintly (Zhenwu)' (*Wulong peng sheng* 五龍捧聖).[5] The remaining four panels, probably of a later date, portray a total of 12 martial figures, each holding weapons (**Pl. 15.1a–b**; **Table 1**). These figures are thunder marshals – active ritual agents responsible for subjugating demonic entities in a type of Daoist ritual called thunder rites (*leifa* 雷法). At either end of the eastern and western walls are images of the Inspectors of Years (*Zhinian* 值年), Months (*Zhiyue* 值月), Days (*Zhiri* 值日) and Hours (*Zhishi* 值時). The *Furnishing Archives of the Qing Palace* (*Qinggong chenshe dang'an* 清宮陳設檔案), compiled in 1756, 1840 and 1910, leaves no record of these painted figures except those in the central panel.[6] This chapter does not intend to investigate this particular set of paintings, but takes it as a point of departure for understanding the relationship between Zhenwu and thunder marshals in the Ming court during the first half of the 15th century. In particular, it considers the process whereby thunder marshals were accepted by the imperial court as the troops of Zhenwu, and the role of Daoist books in contributing to this process of religious change.

Compared with Zhenwu, thunder marshals have received far less scholarly attention and were seldom recognised as protectors of the Ming dynasty. Daoist studies in recent decades, however, have revealed the significant development of thunder traditions and liturgies in Chinese society from the Song dynasty (960–1279) onwards.[7] Mark Meulenbeld has shown that thunder rituals began as a kind of martial ritual developed by Daoists in the 12th century to establish judicial control over threats posed by illicit spirits that inhabited the local soil.[8] Drawing on the deified power of thunder, thunder rituals aim to search, interrogate and punish noxious spirits that cause unrest and calamities. Since at least the early 13th century, the major celestial organ responsible for disciplining deviant spirits within the Daoist jurisdiction has been the Thunder Inspectorate (*Leiting dusi* 雷霆都司), which reports directly to Zhenwu as the Dark Emperor.[9] The Inspectorate has the power to annihilate unruly spirits, or compel them to submit to the celestial jurisdiction headed by the Jade Emperor and

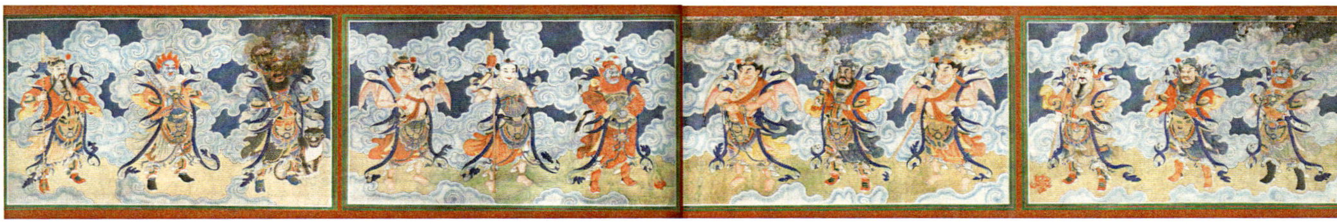

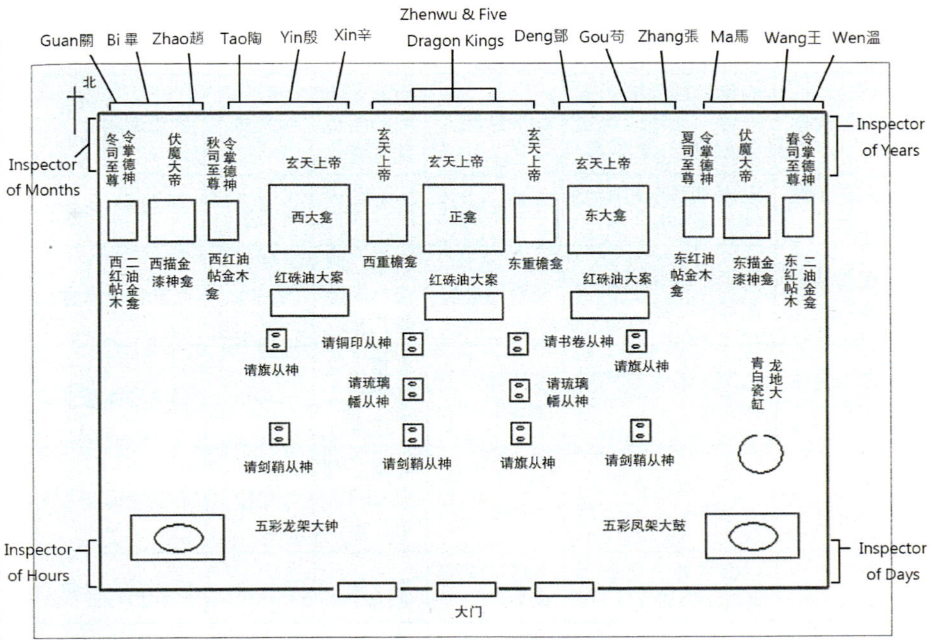

[图33] 钦安殿平面图

Plate 15.1a–b a) (above) Twelve Thunder Marshals. Painting on paper adhering to the northern interior wall of the Hall of Imperial Peace, Forbidden City, Beijing; b) (left) Floor plan of the Qin'an dian (Hall of Imperial Peace) with author's own addition of Marshals' names based on a plain floor plan found in Wang Zilin 2007, fig. 33

subsequently absorb them into the armies of the Thunder Division (*Leibu* 雷部). The thunder marshals discussed here were unruly spirits that had been incorporated into the divine troops of the Thunder Division after undergoing a Daoist process of transformation. Their connections with Zhenwu within the liturgical structure of Daoism were firmly established no later than the 13th century. While the thunder marshals constitute the lowest group of the liturgical structure, the Dark Emperor occupies a pivotal position, often regarded as second only to the Jade Emperor (Yuhuang 玉皇). Despite their inferior position, thunder marshals were reverenced and thunder rituals widely popular from the Southern Song, through the Yuan, to the Ming period.

Although both the Yuan and the early Ming courts patronised Zhenwu, they adopted very different strategies for dealing with the widespread cults of thunder marshals. As Meulenbeld incisively notes, the Yuan government

Table 1 Table showing the combination of Celestial Lords and Marshals as visually represented on different occasions in the 15th century

Celestial Lords & Marshals (year)	Deng 鄧	Xin 辛	Zhang 張	Tao 陶	Gou 苟	Bi 畢	Pang 龐	Liu 劉	Ma 馬	Zhao 趙	Wen 溫	Guan 關	Yin 殷	Wang 王
a. Hall of Imperial Peace (unknown)	✓	✓	✓	✓	✓	✓			✓	✓	✓	✓	✓	✓
b. *Scripture of the Jade Emperor* (1424)	✓	✓	✓	✓	✓	✓	✓	✓	✓	✓	✓	✓	✓	✓
c. *Golden Writings (Xuantian jiao dushu)* (1433)	✓	✓	✓	✓	✓	✓	✓	✓						
d. Ming Daoist Canon (*Zhengtong Daozang*) (1445)	✓	✓	✓	✓	✓	✓			✓	✓	✓	✓	✓	✓
e. Golden Hall at Mount Wudang (1473)	✓	✓	✓	✓	✓	✓			✓	✓	✓	✓		
f. Palace of Five Dragons at Mount Wudang (1483)									✓	✓	✓	✓		
g. Palace of the Southern Rock (Nanyangong) (1494)	✓	✓	✓	✓	✓	✓	✓	✓	✓	✓	✓	✓		

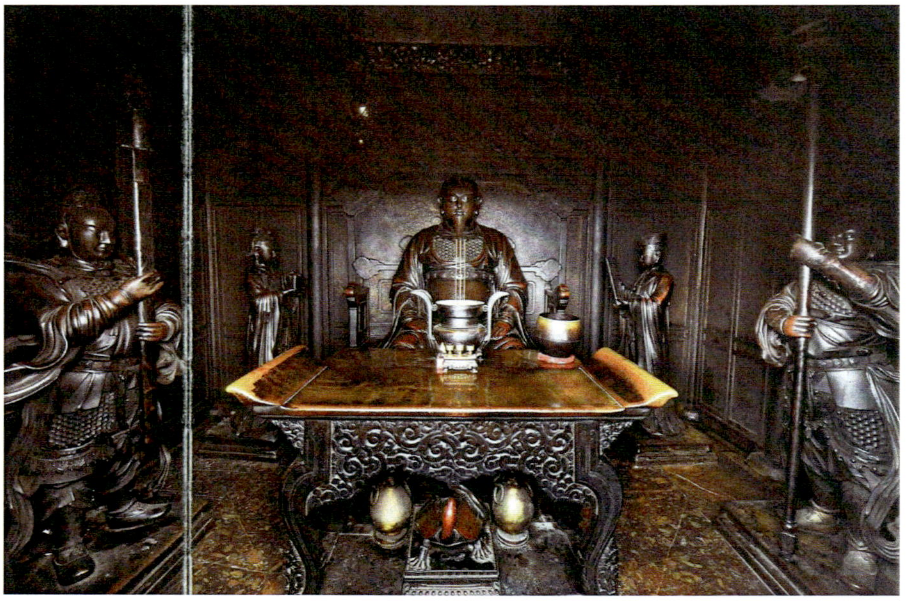

Plate 15.2 Statues of Zhenwu and four attendants in the Golden Hall, Palace of Supreme Harmony, Mount Wudang, Hubei, Ming dynasty, Yongle period (r. 1403–24)

strongly prohibited religious festivals and performances for territorial cults, including those involving thunder marshals, and imposed severe punishment on their organisers and soldiers of the imperial army who participated in them.[10] The Yuan government showed intense fear of local religious theatre because of its subversive potential for instigating mass rebellion. Moreover, such theatre performances often conveyed 'the notion of supernatural powers that may assist the living at times they are threatened by alien invasions', which undermined the rulership of the Mongol Yuan court.[11] After the fall of the Yuan, the subsequent emperors of the Ming dynasty adopted a radically different policy and endeavoured to harness the spirits of the local soil by employing masters of thunder ritual at court, asking them to transform unruly spirits into defenders of the empire. Meulenbeld even argues that the imperial patronage of Zhenwu who has command over demonic forces is one major aspect of the Ming project aimed at incorporating unruly spirits for the purpose of territorial protection.[12] True as that may be, thunder marshals did not receive imperial acknowledgement as protectors of the empire as Zhenwu did in the early Ming period. Indeed, thunder marshals were not recognised by the Ming court as the troops of Zhenwu until the second half of the 15th century.

Plate 15.3 Statue of Zhenwu in the Hall of Imperial Peace, Forbidden City, Beijing, Ming dynasty, Yongle period (r. 1403–24)

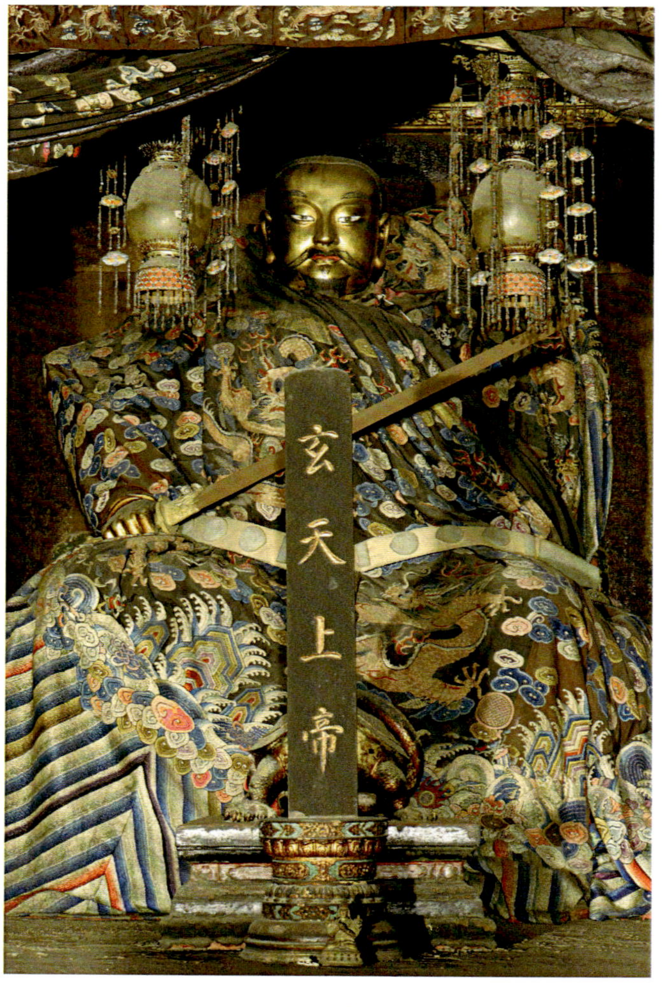

We can observe the change in the Ming court's attitude towards thunder marshals by studying imperial donations to temples at Mount Wudang 武當山, the sacred mountain of Zhenwu, in present-day Hubei province. Based on two gazetteers, both with the title *Gazetteer of the Great Mountain of Supreme Harmony* (*Dayue Taiheshan zhi* 大嶽太和山志), Noelle Giuffrida has compiled a summary showing imperial donations of statues of Zhenwu and his retinue to Mount Wudang throughout the Ming dynasty.[13] The Yongle emperor, who supported the reconstruction and renovation of Daoist temples on the mountain, is recorded to have donated one set of five statues to the Golden Hall (Jinding 金頂) at Taihegong 太和宮 (Palace of Supreme Harmony), situated at the peak of the mountain. This set, which remains installed in the Golden Hall, consists of statues of Zhenwu and four attendants, namely Numinous Official (*lingguan* 靈官), Jade Maiden (*yunü* 玉女), Flag Holder (*zhiqi* 持旗) and Sword Holder (*pengjian* 捧劍) (**Pl. 15.2**).[14] It closely resembles another set of five gilt bronze statues now preserved in the Hall of Imperial Peace in the Forbidden City, noted earlier, which is also said to have been produced under the auspices of the Yongle emperor (**Pl. 15.3**).[15] No

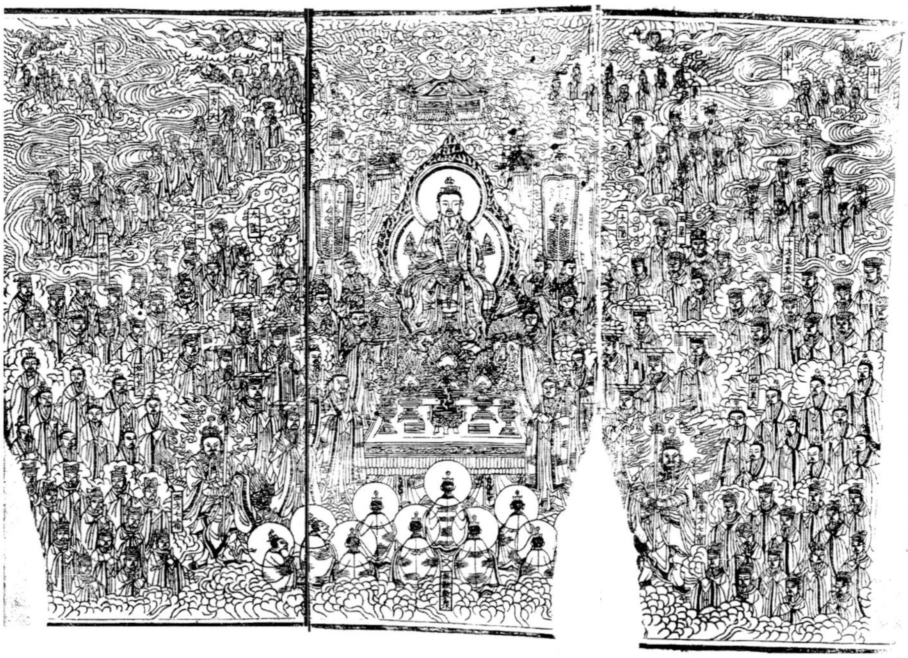

Plate 15.4 Frontispiece to the *Scripture on Salvation*, dated 1406. Accordion-bound woodblock printed book. National Central Library, Taipei, 312.2 09161

emperor is recorded to have donated statues to Mount Wudang subsequently until 1458, when the Tianshun 天順 emperor (r. 1457–64) sent statues of Zhenwu and his attendants to Yuzhengong 遇真宮 (Palace of Encountering the Perfected).[16] It was in 1473, over 50 years after the first donation made by the Yongle emperor, that the Chenghua 成化 emperor (r. 1465–87) commissioned a new set of statues for the Golden Hall. Most notably, this set not only included extremely high-quality statues of Zhenwu, his four attendants and a tortoise with a snake (a manifestation of Zhenwu), made from silver with gold decoration, but also ten gilt bronze statues of thunder marshals (see **Table 1e**).[17] On the same occasion, the Chenghua emperor also sent gilt bronze statues to Yuxugong 玉虛宮 (Palace of Jade Void), but they were only of Zhenwu, his four attendants and a tortoise with a snake.[18] The absence of thunder marshals in the imperial donations of the Yongle and Tianshun emperors points to the fact that the Ming court only began to acknowledge officially and worship thunder marshals as the dark troops of Zhenwu in the second half of the 15th century. Once the thunder marshals were accepted by the imperial court, however, their position in the state cult of Zhenwu became very prestigious indeed, with their statues being installed at the pinnacle of Mount Wudang.

The shift in the imperial court's attitude towards thunder marshals was marked and, in part, fostered by the printing of Daoist scriptures, compendiums and collections compiled by Daoist masters favoured by the emperor, princes and ordinary people. These Daoist publications suggest the rise of thunder marshals and their acceptance by the imperial family through writings and images. In particular, they demonstrate how thunder marshals were raised to the status of territorial protectors through fortifying and emphasising their ties with Zhenwu.

The earliest extant illustrated Ming Daoist scripture, the *Scripture on Salvation* (*Duren jing* 度人經), dated 1406, now in the National Central Library, Taipei, shows no trace of thunder marshals in the Daoist pantheon it records (**Pl. 15.4**).[19] Instead, the earliest datable printed scripture that portrays thunder marshals as part of the Daoist pantheon is an edition of the *Combined Scriptures of the Founding Acts by the Jade Emperor on High* (*Gaoshang yuhuang benxing jijing* 高上玉皇本行集經, hereafter *Scripture of the Jade Emperor*), dated 1424, in a private collection.[20] This work was originally produced through spirit-writing in the late Southern Song (1127–1279). Although it makes no mention of thunder marshals, it was nevertheless the fundamental scripture of the Qingwei 清微 (Pure Tenuity) school, a thunder ritual tradition that became prominent in the 13th century.[21] Exceptionally long with nine folded leaves, the first frontispiece in the 1424 edition depicts two supreme Daoist gods, the Celestial Worthy of the Primordial Beginning (Yuanshi tianzun 元始天尊) and the Jade Emperor, flanked by their retinue. The Four Saints (*Sisheng* 四聖), composed of Zhenwu in combination with Tianpeng 天蓬, Tianyou 天猷 and Leizu 雷祖, head the military bureaucracy of the pantheon.[22] They are followed by ten thunder marshals, namely Celestial Lords Xin 辛, Tao 陶, Pang 龐, Liu 劉 and Marshal Yin 殷 on the left, and Celestial Lords Deng 鄧, Zhang 張, Gou 苟, Bi 畢 and Marshal Wang 王 on the right (**Pl. 15.5a–b**; **Table 1b**).[23] Another four marshals with the surnames Ma 馬, Zhao 趙, Wen 溫 and Guan 關 are depicted together with Zhenwu as guardians on the last page of the scripture (**Pl. 15.6**). Although 14 thunder marshals are depicted with Zhenwu in the scripture, only four are presented as his subordinates, while the remainder attend to the Celestial Worthy of the Primordial Beginning and the Jade Emperor. This shows a sharp contrast with the imperial donation of statues to Mount Wudang in 1473, wherein ten thunder marshals were included as the retinue of Zhenwu (**Table 1e**).

Produced roughly around the same period as the 1424 edition of the *Scripture of the Jade Emperor* is a fully illustrated edition of the *Collected Glosses on the Precious Book of the Jade Pivot, Spoken by the Heavenly Worthy of Universal Transformation of the Sound of the Thunder of Responding Origin in the Nine Heavens* (*Jiutian yingyuan leisheng puhua tianzun yushu baojing jizhu*

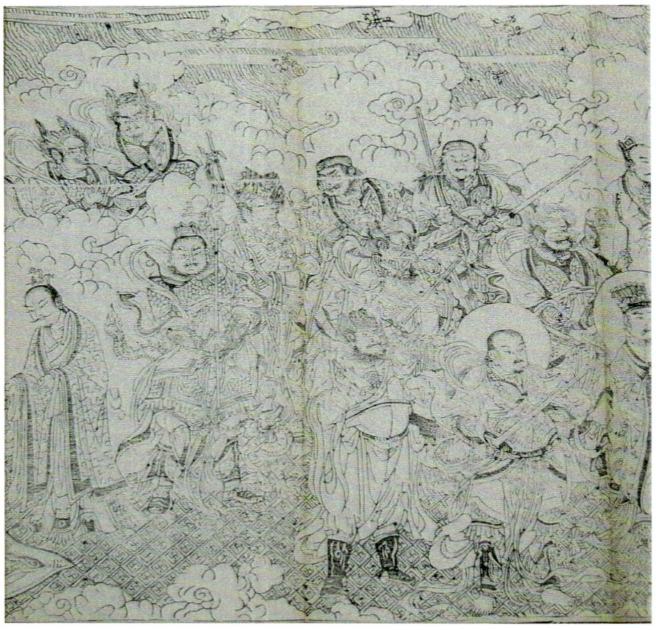
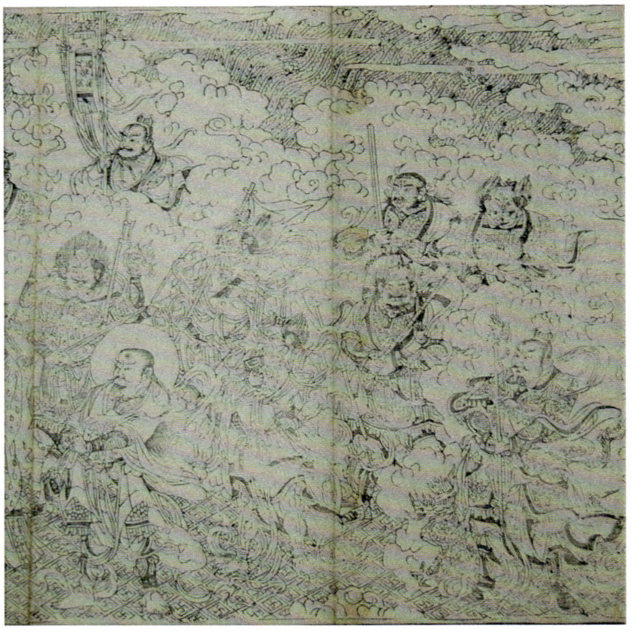

Plate 15.5a–b Frontispiece to the *Scripture of the Jade Emperor* (left and right), dated 1424. Accordion-bound woodblock printed book. Collection of Lee Hsien-kuang

九天應元雷聲普化天尊玉樞寶經集註; hereafter *Collected Glosses*) in the British Library. The *Collected Glosses* was compiled in 1333 as an annotated edition of the *Precious Book of the Jade Pivot* (*Yushu baojing* 玉樞寶經), the core scripture of the supreme Daoist god of thunder completed around the 12th century.[24] The British Library edition was printed from woodblocks made in the 15th century.[25] This edition was widely circulated and reproduced in prints and manuscripts, in both China and Korea.[26] It contains the images of 45 Daoist deities that are not found in the edition collected in the *Daoist Canon of the Zhengtong Reign* (*Zhengtong Daozang* 正統道藏, hereafter Ming Daoist Canon), and demonstrates how Zhenwu was related to the thunder marshals. This series of portraits was a Daoist ritual document called *lu* 籙 (register).[27] *Lu* is a list of spirits given to Daoists for them to summon and deploy during rituals. Poul Andersen has convincingly shown that the *lu* in the *Collected Glosses* is composed of two large categories of gods, namely masters and guardians (**Pls 15.7–8**), where the latter are subordinate to the former.[28] Designated as the Patriarch of Myriad Methods (*Wanfa jiaozhu* 萬法教主), Zhenwu heads the procession (see **Pl. 15.7**). He is identified here as the chief of all masters and guardians from different thunder-ritual traditions. His superior position is crucial for giving him the authority to subdue and mobilise thunder marshals if they became unruly during the ritual process. According to the *Secret Methods of Divine Fire of Pure Tenuity* (*Qingwei shenlie bifa* 清微神烈祕法), composed in the late 13th century, a Daoist

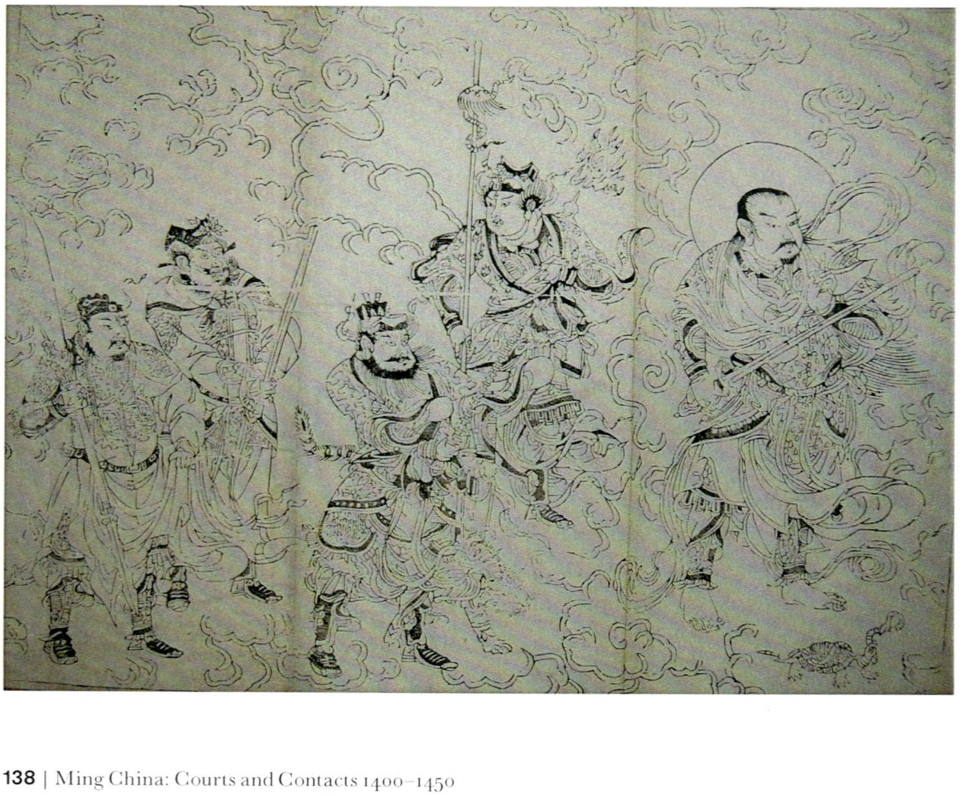

Plate 15.6 Guardian figures on the last page of the *Scripture of the Jade Emperor*, dated 1424. Accordion-bound woodblock printed book. Collection of Lee Hsien-kuang

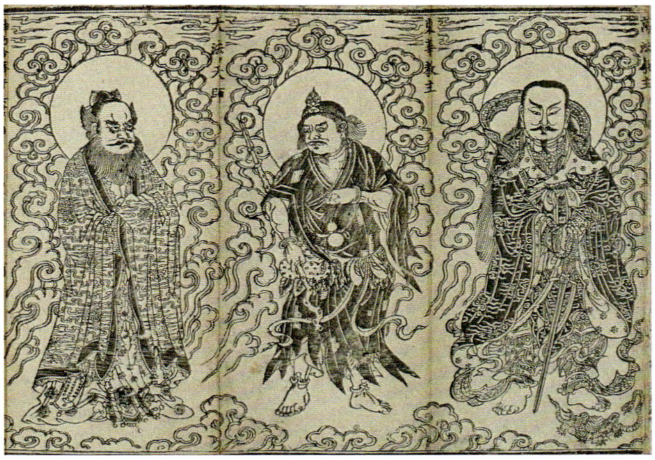

Plate 15.7 The first three deities shown in the British Library edition of the *Collected Glosses*, 15th or 16th century. Patriarch of Myriad Methods (Zhenwu) on the far right. Accordion-bound woodblock printed book. British Library, London, ORB.99/161

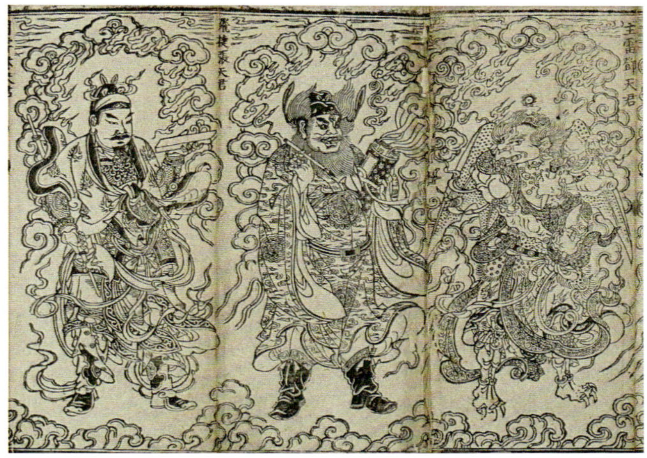

Plate 15.8 The seventh to ninth deities shown in the British Library edition of the *Collected Glosses*, 15th or 16th century. From right to left: Celestial Lords Deng, Xin and Zhang. Accordion-bound woodblock printed book. British Library, London, ORB.99/161

master can request Zhenwu to exercise his power as the Ancestral Master (*Zushi* 祖師) to force unruly thunder marshals to obey and undertake the tasks of generating thunderbolts and bequeathing rain.[29] As mentioned earlier, thunder marshals were all originally derived from demonic gods and described in Daoist ritual manuals as violent and savage beings demanding bloody sacrifices (see **Pl. 15.8**). They only transformed into gods through the Daoist ritual of sublimation.[30] Their demonic origins and immense martial power are explicitly visible when they are represented in colour, with red hair and blue bodies, wielding ritual weapons.[31] In liturgical manuals codified in the 13th and 14th centuries, Zhenwu was one of the supreme authorities who could command violent thunder deities.

The demonic nature of thunder marshals may well have accounted for their low profile in the imperial accounts of the Yongle period. Although the worship of thunder marshals as the dark troops of Zhenwu might have begun to flourish in the early 15th century, the Yongle emperor never explicitly associated himself with the military power of thunder marshals. His trusted Daoist master Zhou Side 周思得 (1359–1451), however, was a master of thunder rites and famous for his command over one particular thunder marshal called Numinous Official Wang (Wang *lingguan* 王靈官) or Marshal Wang. Zhou is said to have accompanied the Yongle emperor on his northern expeditions to Mongolia between 1410 and 1424, contributing to their success.[32] In 1420, Zhou built a Temple of Heavenly General (Tianjiang miao 天將廟) with a Hall of the Ancestral Master (Zushi dian 祖師殿) at the emperor's request, to venerate Marshal Wang and his master Sa Shoujian 薩守堅 (fl. 1141–78?), respectively. This temple formed the basis of the later expanded Dade guan 大德觀 (Temple of Great Virtue), one of the most important Daoist compounds in Beijing. Zhou continued to receive the imperial support of the Xuande 宣德 emperor (r. 1426–35), who appointed him as head of Dade Temple in 1426.[33]

In 1433, Zhou funded the printing of a 40-volume ritual compendium entitled *Golden Writings on the Great Achievement of Deliverance of the Numinous Treasure of Highest Clarity* (*Shangqing lingbao jidu dachengjinshu* 上清靈寶濟度大成金書, hereafter *Golden Writings*). Scholars have noted that Zhou inserted the gods of thunder into the most exalted liturgies in the *Golden Writings*.[34] On most occasions, however, Zhou invokes thunder marshals collectively as 'Officials and Generals of All Departments of the Thunderbolt' (*Leibu zhusi guanjiang* 雷部諸司官將). He only mentions the names of individual thunder marshals in a few cases, such as in the *jiao* 醮 (offering) ritual dedicated to the Dark Emperor Zhenwu.[35] Documents used in the ritual invoke thunder marshals, namely Deng, Xin, Zhang and Tao, referred to as the Four Great Celestial Lords of Thunderclap (*Leiting sida tianjun* 雷霆四大天君), and Gou, Bi, Pang and Liu, the Four Great Celestial Lords of the Thunder Gate (*Leimen sida tianjun* 雷門四大天君) (see **Table 1c**).[36] This is the same group of eight thunder marshals that can be found attending to the Jade Emperor in the frontispiece of the 1424 edition of the *Scripture of the Jade Emperor*, discussed earlier. Unlike the frontispiece, however, the offering document subsumes all eight marshals under the authority of Zhenwu. It also combines the eight marshals with Marshals Ma, Zhao, Wen and Guan, who were the only four subordinates of Zhenwu in the earlier scripture. This group of 12 thunder marshals would soon become the standard composition of the dark troops of Zhenwu, as evident when wooden statues of them were sent by the Hongzhi 弘治 emperor (r. 1488–1505) to Mount Wudang in 1494 (see **Table 1g**).[37] A painting dated to the early 15th century, now in the Herbert F. Johnson Museum of Art, Cornell University, portrays Zhenwu accompanied by eight of the 12 standard thunder marshals, including Celestial Lords Deng, Xin, Zhang and Tao and Marshals Ma, Zhao, Wen and Guan (**Pl. 15.9**). It seems that the incorporation of thunder marshals into the dark troops of Zhenwu had almost reached its final stage when Zhou Side completed the *Golden Writings* in 1433, with variations only in one or two of the marshals on different occasions.

The 45th Heavenly Master Zhang Maocheng 張懋丞 (1388–1447) wrote in his preface to the *Golden Writings* that Zhou Side had repeatedly performed the Ritual Offering of the Golden Register (*Jinlu jiao* 金籙醮), the most prestigious Daoist offering ritual, for the imperial court in accordance with the liturgical manuals laid down in the *Golden Writings*.[38]

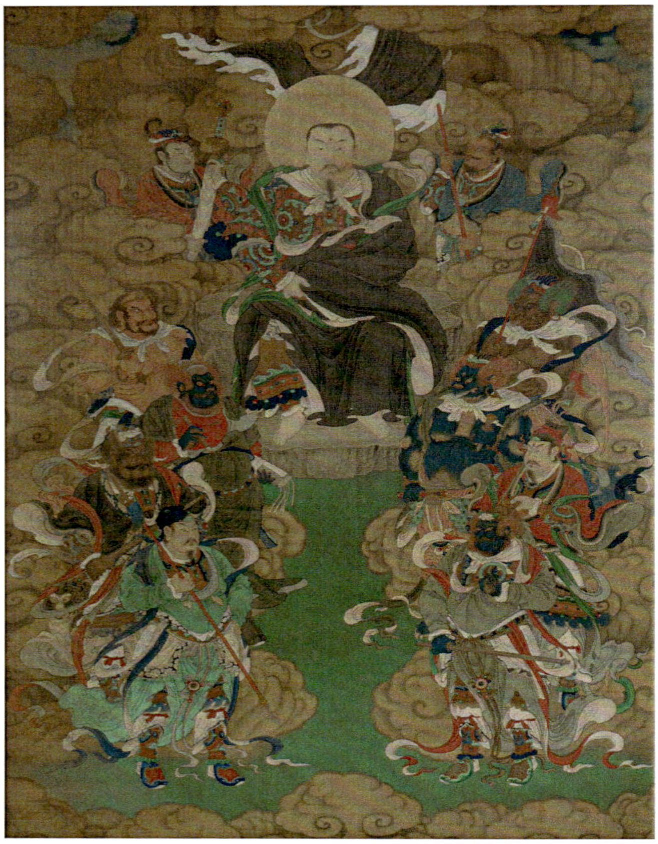

Plate 15.9 Zhenwu (Perfected Warrior) as Supreme Emperor of the Dark Heaven (*Xuantian Shangdi* 玄天上帝), early 15th century. Hanging scroll, ink and colour on silk, height 132cm, width 98cm. Herbert F. Johnson Museum of Art, Cornell University, George and Mary Rockwell Fund 2000.003

The printing of the *Golden Writings* can be considered as Zhou's attempt to legitimise the pivotal role of the thunder marshals in the imperial cult of Zhenwu. It also brought about the consolidation of the hierarchical relationship between Zhenwu and the individualised thunder marshals at the national level.

Zhou Side's effort was seconded by Zhu Quan 朱權 (1378–1448), Prince Xian of Ning 寧獻王, ten years later. Zhu was the younger brother of the Yongle emperor and one of the most renowned Daoists from the first generation of Ming princes. In 1444, Zhu Quan completed the *Jade Fascicles of Great Clarity on the Ultimate Way of the Heavenly Sovereign* (*Tianhuang zhidao taiqing yuce* 天皇至道太清玉冊, hereafter *Jade Fascicles*) in two volumes, and had it printed in his principality in Nanchang 南昌 in present-day Jiangxi 江西 province.[39] In the preface, Zhu claims that Daoism is the true faith of China and he, as a transcendent being, has composed the book to reveal the essence of the Dao and facilitate its dissemination in this world.[40] This encyclopaedic work presents Daoist teaching in all its aspects, including codes and regulations of major areas of Daoist liturgies. What demands particular attention is the chapter on rituals for making offerings to the divine. It stipulates the proper temple setting dedicated to the Dark Emperor, which should include the following:

> The Hall of the Dark Emperor should have the gods of the Thunder Division sculpted on either side; it should have the narrative of the Dark Emperor perfecting himself painted on the interior walls.
>
> 玄帝殿兩旁當塑雷部諸神，殿內壁上當畫玄帝修真事跡。[41]

Zhu Quan's instruction no longer mentions the presence of the four attendants (Numinous Official, Jade Maiden, Flag Holder and Sword Holder), but explicitly specifies thunder marshals as the retinue of Zhenwu in a temple setting. As Lucille Chia and Richard Wang have aptly noted, Ming princes produced books primarily aimed at the emperor, their imperial relatives and literati acquaintances, rather than a general audience.[42] Thus the target audience of the *Jade Fascicles* was likely to be the Ming emperor and the imperial family. His specification can be considered as his appeal for imperial recognition of thunder marshals as the dark troops of Zhenwu. His appeal was echoed favourably by the printing of the Ming Daoist Canon by the imperial court one year later.

In 1445, the Ming Daoist Canon, first compiled under the prescript of the Yongle emperor in 1406, was finally completed after 40 years of editorial work. It consists of 5,305 volumes in 480 boxes.[43] The first volume of scriptures in each box opens with a frontispiece, a rectangular pictorial composition covering seven leaves. An example taken from a fragmentary Ming-dynasty set of the Daoist Canon collected in Baiyun guan 白雲觀 (White Cloud Monastery), Beijing (**Pl. 15.10**), shares close similarities with the Wanli period reprint of the Daoist Canon dated 1598, now preserved in the Bibliothèque nationale de France, Paris.[44] The frontispiece shows a perfected being kneeling before the Three Pure Ones, the highest gods of the Daoist religion.

Plate 15.10 Frontispiece for a fragmented set of the Ming Daoist Canon, Ming dynasty, probably 16th century. Accordion-bound woodblock printed book. White Cloud Monastery, Beijing

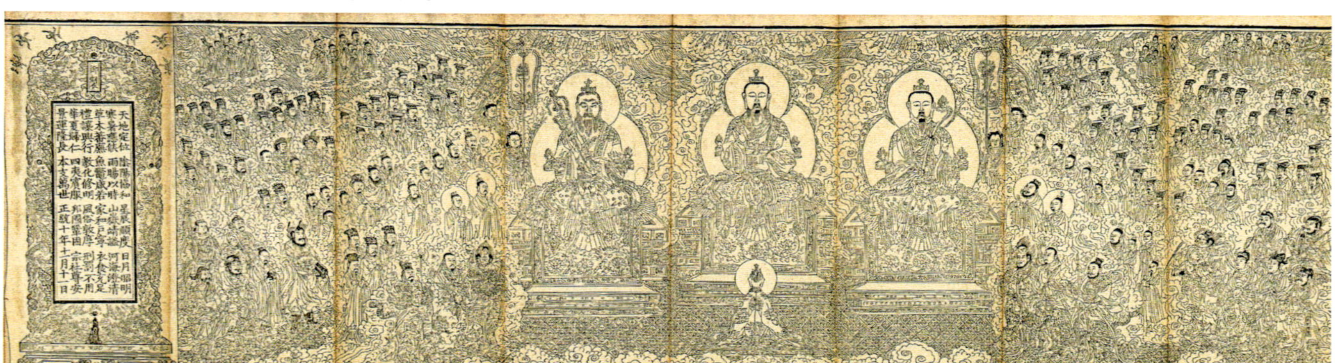

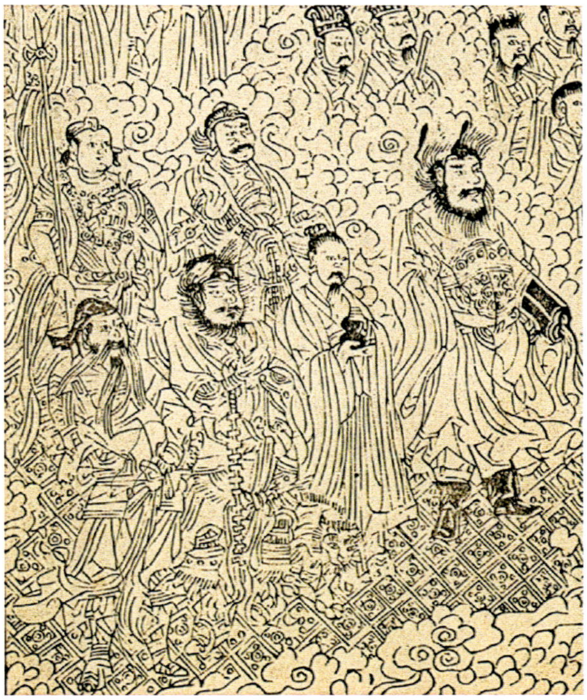

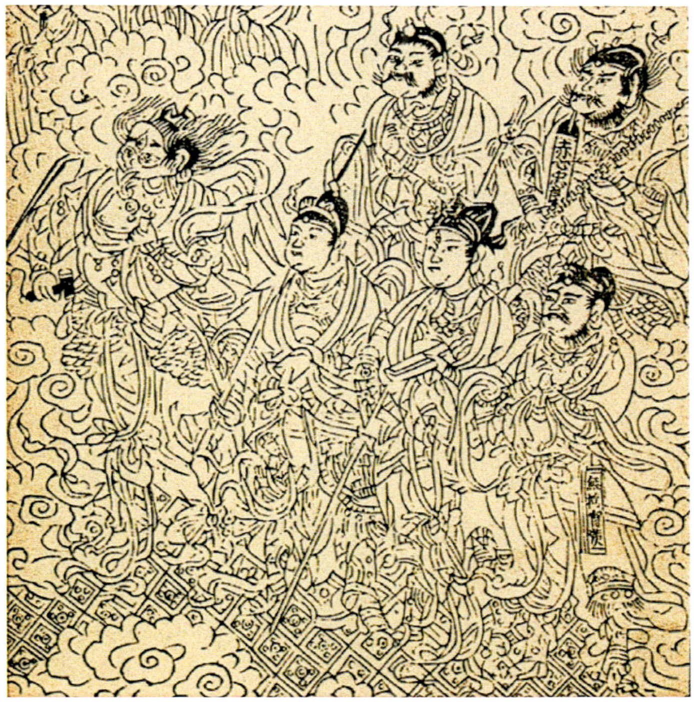

Plate 15.11a–b Details of Fig. 15.10. From front to back, right to left: (a) Celestial Lords and Marshals Xin, Tao, Zhao, Guan, Bi and Yin; (b) Celestial Lords and Marshals Wen, Ma, Zhang, Deng, Wang and Gou

Flanking the Three Pure Ones in the front row are the Four Saints, with Zhenwu on the left. Towards the two ends of the same row are twelve thunder marshals. They include Celestial Lords and Marshals Xin, Tao, Bi, Yin, Zhao and Guan on the left, and Deng, Zhang, Gou, Ma, Wen and Wang on the right (**Pl. 15.11a–b**, **Table 1d**). With the exception of Marshals Yin and Wang, these individualised thunder marshals in the frontispiece were the same ones that were made into statues and donated by the Chenghua emperor to Mount Wudang in 1473 (**Table 1e**). Although Ming emperors never sent statues of Marshals Yin and Wang to Mount Wudang, the two thunder marshals were depicted with the other ten thunder marshals in the paintings of Qin'an Hall in the Forbidden City, discussed earlier (**Table 1a**). In other words, the frontispiece for the Ming Daoist Canon and the paintings of Qin'an Hall share the same set of dark troops. It is likely that the latter were painted after the platoon of thunder marshals were standardised through the printing of the former. The depiction of thunder marshals in the frontispiece of the Ming Daoist Canon confirms that the imperial court had fully accepted the demonic thunder deities as territorial protectors by the middle of the 15th century.

The visual materials examined above show the collaborative efforts of Daoist masters favoured by the emperor, princes and ordinary people to position thunder marshals in the imperially endorsed Daoist pantheon, and to pave the way for the imperial recognition of thunder marshals as the troops of the Dark Emperor and the protectors of the Ming empire. Underlying their efforts are strong beliefs in the immense martial power of thunder marshals and an urge to raise the status of these gods in both the liturgical structure of Daoism and the Ming court rituals. The efforts matched well with the desire of the early Ming emperors to harness martial spirits through thunder rituals to protect the empire. The compilation and printing of Daoist scriptures and books in the early 15th century contributed to the consolidation of the pivotal position of thunder marshals in major Daoist rituals and the legitimisation of their ties with Zhenwu. The final recognition of the thunder marshals as part of the imperially endorsed Daoist pantheon was also authoritatively announced through the printing of the frontispiece for the Daoist Canon. As succeeding Ming emperors continued to reprint the Daoist Canon and grant copies to major Daoist temples all over the empire, the prestigious status of thunder marshals as the leading spiritual military force of the Great Ming became firmly established.[45]

If the first half of the 15th century was a formative period when individualised thunder marshals were in the course of becoming the core of Zhenwu's troops and attaining imperial recognition, the late Ming saw the full bloom of these processes. The Wanli 萬曆 emperor (1573–1620), for example, was personally involved in worshipping thunder marshals and commissioning the production of paintings and scriptures of thunder ritual traditions, in the hope of deploying thunder gods to pacify the court in times of trouble.[46] The close tie between Zhenwu and the thunder marshals also became the main storyline of the 17th-century vernacular novel *Journey to the North* (*Beiyou ji* 北遊記).[47] The novel describes how Zhenwu retrieved the 'Thirty-six Heavenly Generals' (*Sanshiliu tianjiang* 三十六天將) who escaped to earth. The 'Thirty-six Heavenly Generals' include the majority of thunder marshals described as the dark troops in this chapter. Their inclusion as main characters of a vernacular novel about Zhenwu marks the final stage of establishing their tie with Zhenwu – a tie that was no longer only implanted in the Daoist community but also infiltrated into the secular life of ordinary people in late Ming times.

Notes

The work described in this chapter was substantially supported by a grant from the Research Grants Council of the Hong Kong Special Administrative Region, China (Project no. CUHK 451513).

1 Chan 1997, 94–106; Chao Shin-yi 2011, 97, 108.
2 Naquin 2000, 120; Mote and Twitchett 1988, 209, 237.
3 Wang Zilin 2007, 144–75. The journal *Forbidden City* recently published a special issue (vol. 244) on the Hall of Imperial Peace, which includes some of the latest studies on its artefacts; Wang Zilin 2015.
4 I am deeply indebted to Wang Zilin and Luo Wenhua, researchers at the Palace Museum, Beijing, and Xu Xiaodong, Associate Director of the Art Museum, The Chinese University of Hong Kong, for their help in arranging my visit to the Hall of Imperial Peace in the summer of 2014.
5 Tao Jin 2015, 70.
6 Zhu Saihong 2013, 736, 770, 802, 826, 852, 874, 912.
7 Andersen 1996; Hymes 2002; Davis 2001; Li Zhihong 2011; Meulenbeld 2007; 2015.
8 Meulenbeld 2015, 101.
9 Meulenbeld 2015, 102.
10 Meulenbeld 2015, 121.
11 Meulenbeld 2015, 124–5.
12 Meulenbeld 2015, 132–4.
13 Giuffrida 2008, 123–32. One of the two Gazetteers was compiled by Ren Ziyuan 任自垣 (1350?–1431) in 1431 and updated by others in 1491 and 1494 to include material down to the Hongzhi reign. See Yang Lizhi 1999, 5–236. The other was a 17-*juan* work compiled by Wang Zuo王佐 in 1556 and updated by others in 1562 and 1583. As Giuffrida has noted, the list she compiled excludes the Yongle emperor's initial 'investment' to build and refurbish temples on Mount Wudang.
14 Hubei sheng bowuguan 2012, 145.
15 Wang Zilin 2007, 146.
16 Giuffrida 2008, 129.
17 Yang Lizhi 1999, 45–6, 286.
18 Yang Lizhi 1999, 45–6, 286.
19 For a study of this edition, see Wan forthcoming. Although Chao Shin-yi has shown that 'by the end of the twelfth century, the Thunder Rites had become a generic practice that was accepted by every major school, new or old, of Daoism' (Chao Shin-yi 2011, 52), there is little trace of thunder marshals in extant pictorial representations of the Daoist pantheon, such as temple murals and scripture frontispieces, from the Song and Yuan period. *Album of Daoist and Buddhist Themes* (*Daozi mopu* 道子墨寶) in the collection of the Cleveland Museum of Art is a rare example with the depiction of 30-odd thunder marshals. However, although the album was traditionally said to be painted in the Song dynasty, its dating remains debatable, with a scholar dating it to the early Ming period. See Gyss-Vermande 1991, 101. For the appearance of thunder marshals in Song and Yuan literary works, see Nikaidō Yoshihiro 2007.
20 For details of this edition, see Hsieh Tsung-hui 2013, 22–5. I am indebted to Hsieh Tsung-hui for providing me with the images.
21 Schipper and Verellen 2004, 1096–7.
22 The Four Saints are a group of Daoist spiritual guardians that appeared in the Northern Song period. Davis 2001, 74–9; Chao Shin-yi 2011, 25–7. However Yisheng 翊聖, originally one of the four guardians, was often replaced by 'Leizu' in the Ming period.
23 Within the limits of this chapter it is impossible to detail the iconographic features of each thunder marshal. For their iconography, see the Daoist Iconography Project: http://manoa.hawaii.edu/daoist–iconography/identify.html.
24 Schipper and Verellen 2004, 1092–3.
25 Wan Chui-ki 2010, 155, 168.
26 Miura 2005.
27 Andersen 2011.
28 Andersen 2012.
29 *DZ* 222, *juan* 1, 140–2. Chao Shin-yi 2011, 67–9, 76–7. All works from the Ming *Daozang* (Daoist Canon) are indicated by the abbreviation *DZ* with pagination cited according to the 1988 edition.
30 Meulenbeld 2007, 2–43.
31 The colourfully painted edition of the *Collected Glosses*, dated 1527, now in the Tenri Central Library (call no: 126–*i3*), is one of the best examples that show the powerful images of the thunder marshals.
32 Tian Rucheng 1958, *juan* 4, 44.
33 Zhou's biography is summarised in Ding Huang 1989; Meulenbeld 2007, 221–2.
34 Meudenbeld 2007, 223.
35 *Xuantian jiao dushu* 玄天醮都疏 (*Documents for the Dark Heaven Offering*) in Zhou Side 1992, *juan* 35, 463–4.
36 Zhou Side 1992, *juan* 35, 464.
37 Yang Lizhi 1999, 74, 287.
38 Zhou Side 1992, 1.
39 See Wang 2012, 68. For an introduction to the Daoist life of Zhu Quan, see xi–xix.
40 DZ 1483, *juan* 1, 357. For an introduction to this work, see Schipper and Verellen 2004, 947–8.
41 DZ 1483, *juan* 5, 404.
42 Chia 2006, 30; Wang 2012, 81.
43 Chen Guofu 1975, 179.
44 Delacour 2010, 167.
45 Chen Guofu 1975, 178.
46 Wan 2015.
47 Seaman 1987.

Chapter 16
Faces of Transnational Buddhism at the Early Ming Court

Marsha Haufler

In an essay published some years ago, I identified a portrait of the Chinese monk Daoyan 道衍 (1335–1418) in the Palace Museum, Beijing, as 'part of a network of images that linked the monasteries, the court and official culture' in the Ming dynasty (1368–1644) and later (**Pl. 16.1**).[1] Due to the transnational character of East Asian monastic Buddhism, this portrait can also be recognised as belonging to an international network of images. Its pictorial formula and aspects of the biography of its subject connect it with Sino-Japanese circuits of cultural exchange. Two almost contemporary textile portraits of the Tibetan cleric Śākya Yeshé (1354–1439?) were also part of an international web, but it was one that extended westwards from the Ming court to Tibet, where these works have been preserved (**Pls 16.2–3**).[2] Made in Ming imperial workshops for Tibetan viewers, these images combine visual elements drawn from Chinese imperial and Tibetan Buddhist sources. When viewed together, the portrayals of Daoyan and Śākya Yeshé evoke the complexity of the religious landscape of the early 15th-century Chinese court and its capital cities, Nanjing and Beijing, and show how the Ming-dynasty ruling house used different visual languages, much as it used multiple written languages, to address people of different cultures.

Daoyan was born in Suzhou 蘇州 prefecture in the lower Yangtze River region, the heartland of Han Chinese

Plate 16.1 Anonymous, *Portrait of Daoyan* (also known as Yao Guangxiao), c. 1403–18. Hanging scroll, ink and colours on silk, image: height 184.5cm, width 120.2cm; with mount: height 357cm, width 166cm. The Palace Museum, Beijing

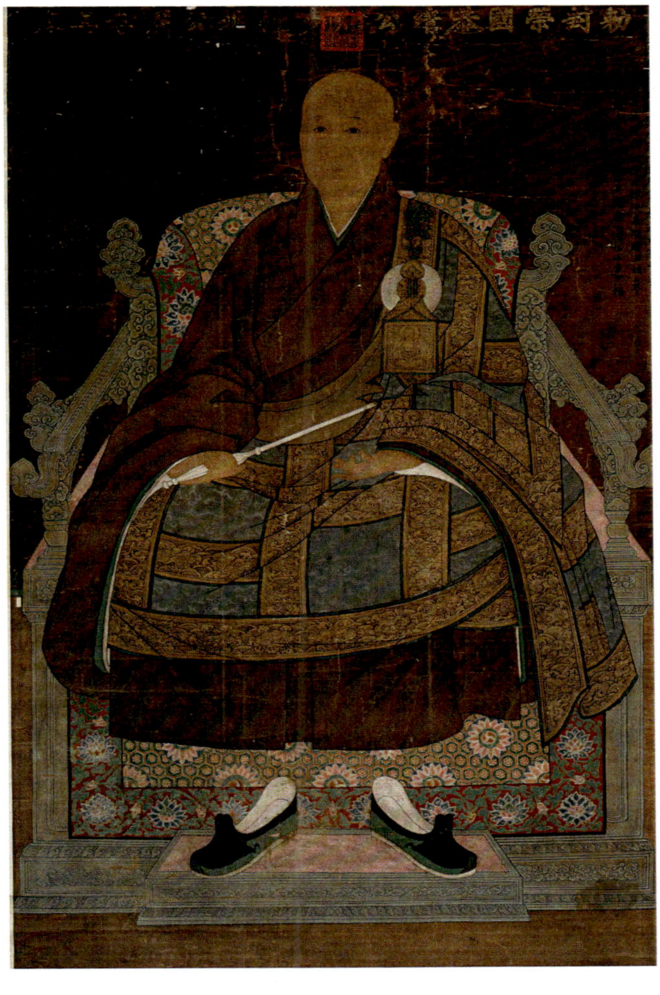

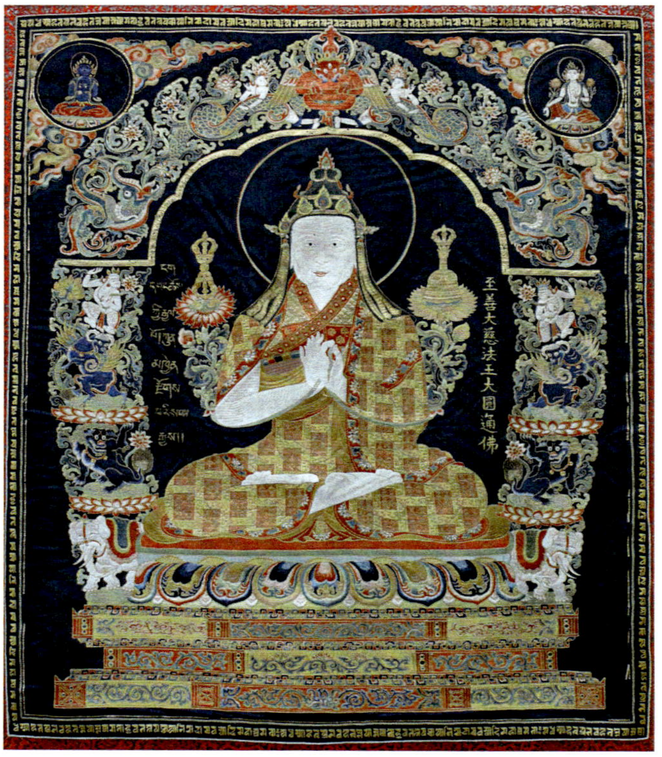

Plate 16.2 (above) Anonymous, *Portrait of Śākya Yeshé*, Ming dynasty. Silk embroidery, image height 76cm, width 65cm. Tibet Museum

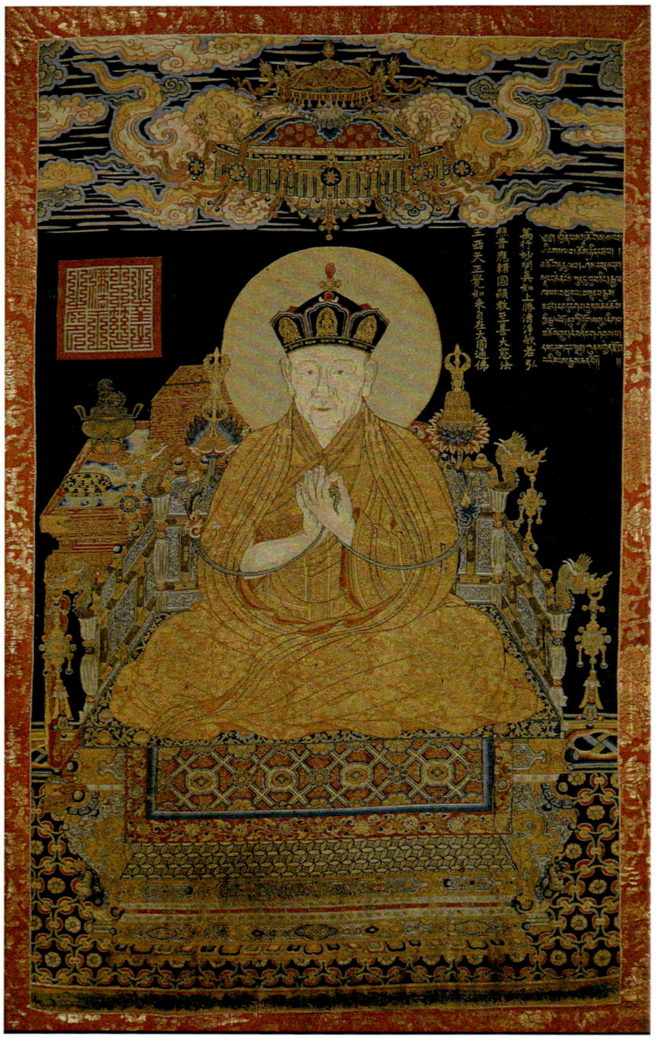

Plate 16.3 (right) Anonymous, *Portrait of Śākya Yeshé*, Ming dynasty. Silk tapestry, image height 108.5cm, width 63cm. Norbulingka Collection

scholarly culture in his time. He entered Miaozhian 妙智庵 (Marvellous Wisdom Hermitage) not far from his home at the age of 14, became a monk at 18, resided in various monasteries over the course of his life, and became an eminent master of the Linji 臨濟 school of Chan 禪 Buddhism.[3] Like other learned Buddhist monks, he was well versed in Chinese classical texts, wrote poetry and prose, and associated with leading scholars and artists in monastic and secular circles. Laymen and clerics, including visiting Japanese monks, prevailed upon his erudition and literary ability, soliciting encomia, prefaces, colophons and other occasional writings from him.[4] His early attainments were such that the eminent monk Zongle 宗泐 (1318–91) recommended him to the first Ming emperor in 1382. The emperor subsequently appointed him to accompany Prince Zhu Di 朱棣 (1360–1424) to his fief in Beiping 北平 (later Beijing), where Daoyan became abbot of Qingshousi 慶壽寺 (Celebrating Longevity Monastery). Also skilled in military strategy and divination, Daoyan became infamous for helping Zhu Di usurp the throne in 1402. The monk went on to have a distinguished career during the Yongle 永樂 reign period (1403–24). Within months of ascending the throne Zhu Di appointed him Left Buddhist Patriarch (*Zuo shanshi* 左善世) in the Central Buddhist Registry (*Senglu si* 僧錄司), which was given oversight of all the Buddhist monks and nuns in the country, and soon thereafter promoted him to Junior Preceptor of the Heir Apparent (*Taizi shaoshi* 太子少師). In an effort to convince the monk to return to secular life, the Yongle emperor restored his family name, Yao 姚, which Daoyan had given up when he left his family to enter a monastery, granted him a new personal name with a Confucian flavour – Guangxiao 廣孝, meaning 'to broaden filial piety' – and offered him various worldly enticements.

However, Daoyan declined to give up his religious calling, continued to dress as a monk when not at court and lived out his life in monasteries. When Daoyan died, the grieving emperor gave him a monk's funeral and a tomb pagoda in Fangshan 房山 county southwest of Beijing, personally composed the inscription for the memorial stele at the tomb and granted him a posthumous name and noble titles. In 1425, not long after the death of the Yongle emperor, his son and successor further bestowed upon Daoyan the title of Junior Preceptor (*Shaoshi* 少師, a very prestigious designation distinct from the lower-ranked Junior Preceptor of the Heir Apparent) and recognised him as a meritorious official of the Yongle reign deserving annual state offerings in the Imperial Ancestral Temple (*Taimiao* 太廟).[5] These secular honours are encapsulated by the inscription written in gold across the top of the Palace Museum portrait: 'The true countenance of Lord Yao Guangxiao, imperially ennobled Duke Gongjing of the State of Rong bestowed [with the title] Junior Preceptor'

(*Chifeng Rongguo Gongjing gong zeng shaoshi Yao gong Guangxiao zhenrong* 敕封榮國恭靖公贈少師姚公廣孝真容).

Once there were many portraits of Daoyan, including several connected with temples in Beijing.[6] Most portrayed him with a shaven head and dressed as a monk, as we see him in the Palace Museum scroll, but one lost painting reportedly depicted him in Ming court dress with a red robe, jade belt and 'Tang' court hat. Qingshousi, Daoyan's primary residence in Beijing, had one of the former type and perhaps the picture of him dressed for court as well.[7] In 1530 this monastery, by that time renamed Da Xinglongsi 大興隆寺 (Great Prosperity Monastery), received Daoyan's spirit tablet and state-sponsored offering rites when they were expelled from the Imperial Ancestral Temple after a zealous Confucian official complained about memorialising a monk in the imperial shrine.[8] Fire destroyed the monastery five years later and the fate of its portrait or portraits is uncertain.[9] Daoyan's tablet and official rites were then moved again, this time to the venerable Da Longshan huguosi 大隆善護國寺 (Great Flourishing Goodness Protecting the State Monastery) in the western part of the city.[10] This monastery also had a portrait of Daoyan as a monk, perhaps the one formerly at Da Xinglongsi, and it became one of the famous sights of the capital.[11] In an account of his visit to the monastery in 1599, the poet Yuan Hongdao 袁宏道 (1568–1610) testified to the portrait's power. He described Daoyan's appearance as natural and unrestrained and his eyes brilliant like a flash of lightning, and characterised the inscription written on the painting by the master himself as that of a true Chan monk.[12] This painting was lost by the mid-18th century,[13] but the apparent lifelikeness of the figure and Daoyan's self-inscription are enough to connect it with the Sino-Japanese tradition of monk portraiture wherein image and autograph combine to evoke a master's presence for his disciples and Dharma heirs.[14] A representative earlier example is the famous portrait of the Southern Song (1127–1279) Linji school master Wuzhun Shifan 無準師範 (1177–1249) given to his Japanese disciple Enni Ben'en 圓爾辯圓 (1202–80) in 1238 (**Pl. 16.4**).[15]

A poetic inscription written by the late Ming celebrity monk Zibo Zhenke 紫柏真可 (1543–1603) on the Palace Museum portrait of Daoyan associates it with another Beijing monastery and the Ming Sino-Japanese clerical network.[16] Zhenke's inscription refers to Daoyan's close relationship with the Japanese Linji school master Musho Tokushi 無初德始 (Ch. Wuchu Deshi, d. 1429). Musho accompanied a Japanese embassy to the Ming court in Nanjing early in the Hongwu period (1368–98) and remained in China to study, becoming the Dharma heir of Zongle, the cleric who recommended Daoyan to the Hongwu emperor. Musho met Daoyan at Qingshousi in Beiping; Daoyan found him congenial and took him as a 'Dharma nephew'. Musho continued his travels in China, but in 1402 Daoyan summoned him back to the capital, then Nanjing, where they picked up their friendship and deep conversations about Chan. In 1412, when Daoyan was planning to retire to a hermitage at Tanzhesi 潭柘寺 (Deep Pond and Wild Mulberry Monastery) in the Western Hills of Beijing, he petitioned the emperor to appoint Musho abbot of the monastery. The appointment was made, and Musho lived out his life there.[17] Daoyan was fond of Tanzhesi from his early days in Beiping and chose it for his old-age retreat, making it second in importance only to Qingshousi in his biography.[18] Tanzhesi established a memorial portrait hall for him with a painted image, presumably the Palace Museum scroll.[19] The large size (184.5 x 120.2cm), apparent realism and fine execution of this painting, along with the gold inscription including the posthumous title given to the master in 1425, suggest that it was done in that year or

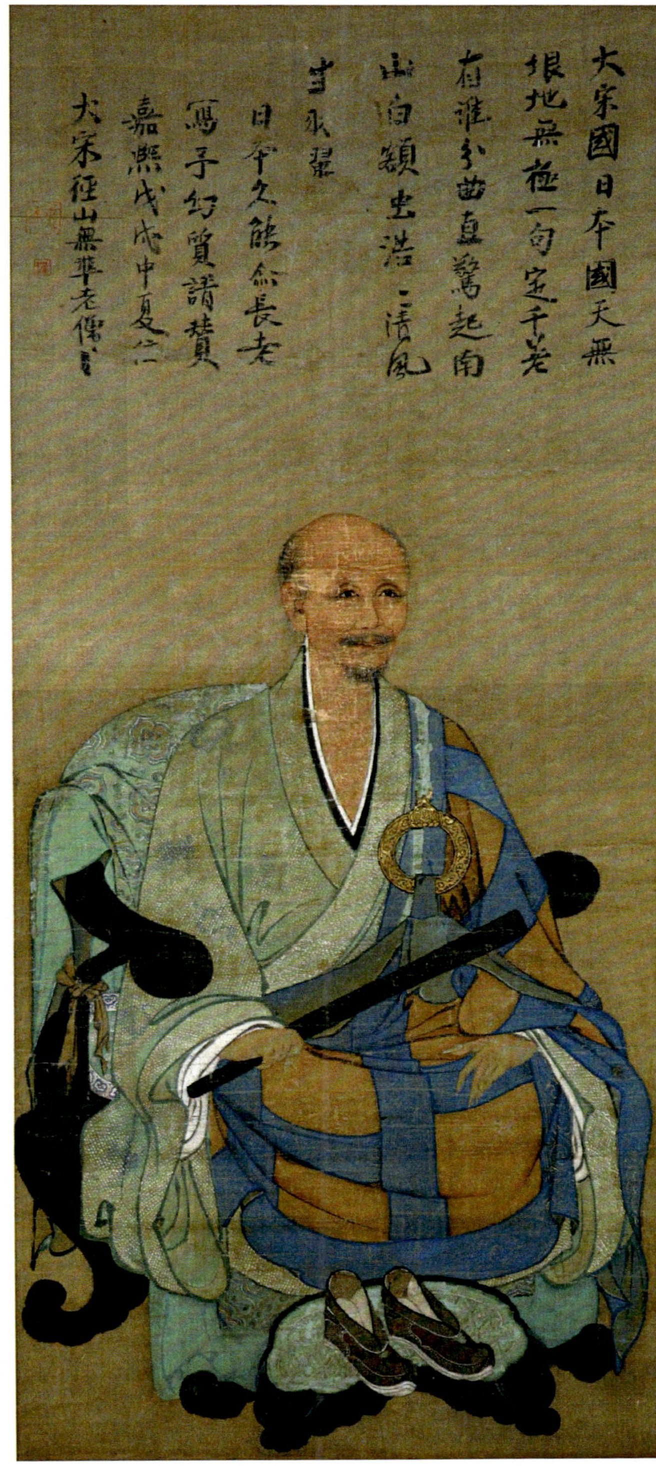

Plate 16.4 Anonymous, *Portrait of Master Wuzhun Shifan* (1177–1249), Southern Song, with an inscription dated 1238. Hanging scroll, ink and colours on silk, height 124.8cm, width 55.2cm. Tōfuku-ji, Kyoto, Japan

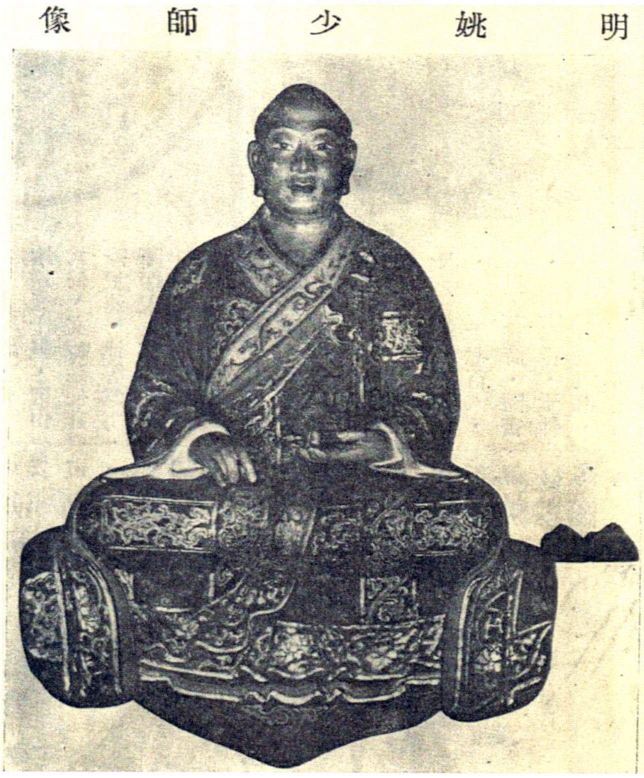

Plate 16.5 Portrait sculpture of Daoyan in Tanzhesi 潭柘寺 (Deep Pond and Wild Mulberry Monastery) (current whereabouts unknown), published in *Yilin yuekan* 藝林月刊 (*Art World Monthly*), no. 56 (1934), p. 7

shortly after by a court artist who had known Daoyan in life. Wang Zheng suggests that the court presented it to Tanzhesi before Abbot Musho died in 1429.[20] As the inscription by Zhenke and a second one dated to 1601 show, the portrait remained at Tanzhesi through the late Ming. It did not become famous like the portrait at Da Longshan huguosi, however. By the middle of the Qianlong period (1735–96) it had been removed from the monastery and acquired by the Qing court.[21] Daoyan's hermitage at Tanzhesi had a portrait sculpture of the master that survived into the 20th century (**Pl. 16.5**).[22]

Although the Palace Museum portrait is a posthumous image inscribed with court-bestowed titles rather than a work done in the master's lifetime and inscribed by the man himself, it still draws on the tradition of Chan portraiture represented by the 1238 portrayal of Song master Wuzhun in style and iconography. As in the Song portrait, Daoyan's face is rendered with soft washes of colour and highly individualised, his boldly outlined robes have weight and depth, and the designs on his garments and furnishings are finely detailed. Like Wuzhun, he sits cross-legged on a fabric-draped chair, having left his shoes on a low step below, and holds an abbot's ritual implement.[23] Specifically, he holds the fly-whisk traditionally used in Dharma exposition to punctuate remarks visually.[24] Both masters wear a gorgeous silk vestment, or *kāṣāya* (Ch. *jiasha* 袈裟), a highly symbolic garment, over a Chinese-style long-sleeved robe that wraps in front. The luxuriousness of these examples notwithstanding, the *kāṣāya* is basically a simple rectangular garment composed of strips and patches meant to recall the patchwork clothing made of discarded rags worn by the Buddha and his followers, representing their renunciation of worldly things. In Chan tradition, when passed from master to pupil, this garment came to signify the transmission of the Dharma.[25] Draped over the left shoulder and anchored by a ring over the heart, the *kāṣāya* is worn for formal occasions, notably when an abbot takes the high seat in a Dharma Hall to preach, thus playing the role of Buddha and becoming, in Robert Sharf's words, 'a living Buddha icon'.[26] The portrait of Wuzhun Shifan invokes the master in this iconic role, and the meanings implicit in the iconographic programme of this and many similar pictures must inform our understanding of the portrait of Daoyan.

Politics, however, are not far from the surface in either the portrait of Daoyan or that of Wuzhun. The beautiful silk robes worn by both masters reflect the longstanding court tradition of conferring fine monastic robes on favoured clerics.[27] Like Daoyan, Wuzhun enjoyed imperial favour, albeit of a more conventional sort based on his religious credentials. In 1232 the Song emperor Lizong 理宗 (r. 1224–64) summoned Wuzhun to court, where the master answered questions about Chan and expounded the Buddhist doctrine, and the emperor rewarded him with a golden *kāṣāya* (Ch. *Jinlanjia* 金襴袈), a vestment woven with patterns in gold thread and the name Buddha Mirror Chan Master (*Fojian chanshi* 佛鑒禪師).[28] It has been suggested that the portrait documents this occasion and shows the master wearing the imperially presented *kāṣāya*.[29] The imperial practice of bestowing golden *kāṣāya* continued in the Yongle period, and the opulent outer robe Daoyan wears in the Palace Museum portrait surely came from his sovereign.[30] His robes also accord with Ming court regulations for monastic dress that were established in 1382 and remained in effect through the 15th century. These regulations assigned robes of different colours to different categories of monks. As a Chan monk, Daoyan wears a brown common robe under his jade-green coloured *kāṣāya*. The *kāṣāya* borders with gold patterns were a luxury only permitted to monk officials of the Central Buddhist Registry.[31] The fabrics of Daoyan's *kāṣāya* are further distinguished by their patterns of propitious *ruyi* 如意 (as-you-wish) clouds that resemble the head of the *ruyi* sceptre and the *lingzhi* 靈芝 fungus of immortality.[32] This ceremonial garment is fastened with a knotted turquoise cord and a jade ring from which hangs a golden image of a seated Buddha, presumably another badge of rank.

While relying on a common pictorial tradition, the portraits of Wuzhun and Daoyan differ in significant ways, beginning with scale. The Song-dynasty scroll is smaller (124.8 x 55.2cm), making its subject less physically imposing than Daoyan.[33] Moreover, whereas Song and Yuan master portraits typically employ three-quarter views, Daoyan turns only slightly to his right and gazes almost directly at the viewer. His imposing chair is seen straight on, like those in later monk portraits and in imperial portraits such as that of the Hongzhi 弘治 emperor (r. 1488–1505).[34] In fact, the seat itself – broad, square, jade-coloured and ornate – invites comparison with the dragon thrones occupied by the Yongle and Xuande 宣德 (r. 1426–35) emperors in their portraits in the National Palace Museum, Taipei (**Pls 16.6–7**). The arms and the backrest of Daoyan's seat, however, are more

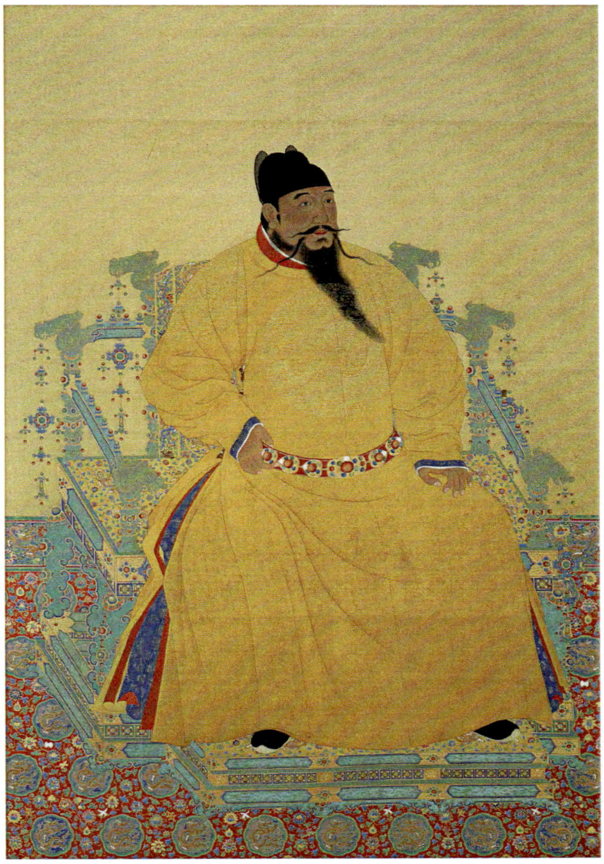

Plate 16.6 Anonymous, *Portrait of the Yongle Emperor*, Ming, 15th century. Hanging scroll, ink and colours on silk, height 220cm, width 150cm. National Palace Museum, Taipei

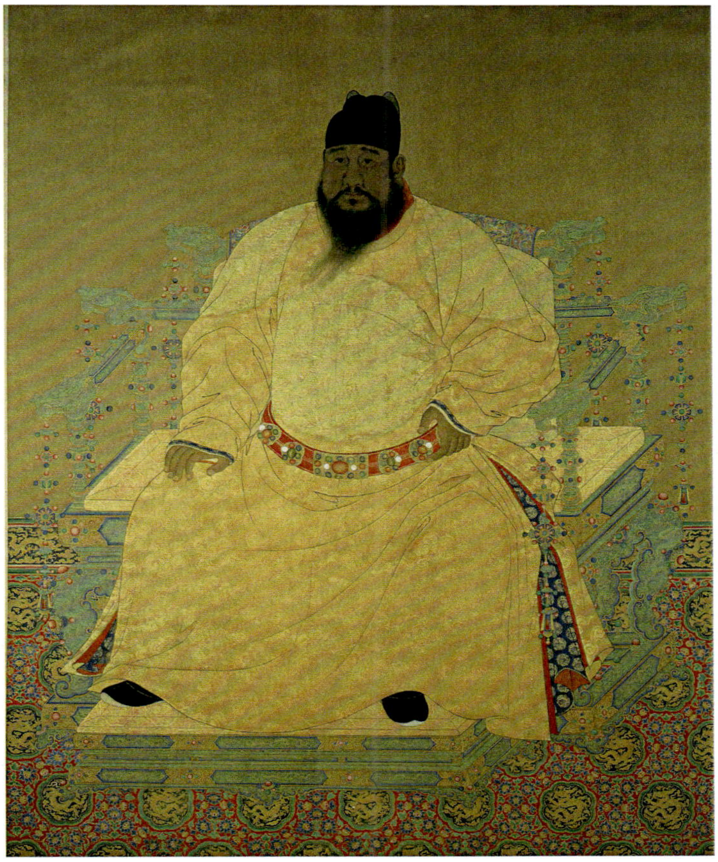

Plate 16.7 Anonymous, *Portrait of the Xuande Emperor*, Ming, 15th century. Hanging scroll, ink and colours on silk, height 215.8cm, width 171cm. National Palace Museum, Taipei

modestly adorned with *ruyi* cloud designs rather than with jewels and imperial dragons. The cloud patterns on his chair and *kāṣāya* immerse the master in allusions to Heaven and immortality. In sum, this grand imperial reworking of an old Buddhist portrait formula is a remarkably synthetic tribute, in text and image, to a man who in life moved between the great monasteries of the Ming capitals and the imperial palace, and in death received offerings in the Imperial Ancestral Shrine and Buddhist memorial halls.

The two early Ming textile portraits of the Tibetan hierarch Śākya Yeshé mounted as *thangkas*, one embroidered and the other produced in *kesi* (silk tapestry), likewise mix religious and political messages in communicating court favour (see **Pls 16.2–3**). They are recognised as products of Ming imperial ateliers that document the emperor's respect for Śākya Yeshé and the high position he enjoyed at court. Both portraits have received a great deal of attention since the *kesi* was introduced to modern readers in 1960 by an article on Tibetan cultural relics published in the Chinese journal *Wenwu* 文物 (*Cultural Relics*).[35] In a recent essay Xiong Wenbin 熊文彬 builds on the findings of Chinese and Tibetan scholars who have studied the *kesi* to shed new light on its production.[36] In the English-language literature, Dora Ching has examined the two portraits with great care in her analysis of developments in Ming imperial portraiture.[37] Observations by Xiong, Ching and others are echoed here, but the following discussion is concerned with other matters, especially with the portraits as vehicles of intercultural communication and as visual records of the diverse and often politicised Buddhist culture of the Ming courts and capitals where Chan and Tibetan Buddhism flourished side by side.

Śākya Yeshé, a younger contemporary of Daoyan, first arrived in China in 1415, during the Yongle period, as an emissary of his master Tsongkhapa (1357–1419), founder of the Gelug school of Tibetan Buddhism, and on imperial request, he performed esoteric rituals that brought forth miraculous celestial responses.[38] The Yongle emperor gave him an impressive honorific title and sent him off on his journey home in 1416 with lavish gifts of Buddhist images, scriptures and implements, clothing, silks, and gold and silver utensils, and dispatched more such gifts to him the following year.[39] Śākya Yeshé was invited back to the Ming court during the Xuande period and was received with even greater honour than before. In 1434 the emperor granted him an elevated title consisting of a long string of superlatives modifying the dual designation Dharma King of Great Compassion (*Daci fawang* 大慈法王) and Universally Penetrating Buddha (*Dayuan tongfo* 大圓通佛).[40] Both portraits are marked with versions of this title and are thus contemporary with or postdate this event. It is generally thought that the embroidered portrait, now in the Tibet Museum, was made on imperial order and bestowed upon Śākya Yeshé by the Xuande emperor. The same assumption was made about the *kesi* until recently, when the importance of the Tibetan inscription on the border below the portrait was recognised. As read by Xiong Wenbin, this inscription identifies two of Śākya Yeshé's disciples who bore lofty titles

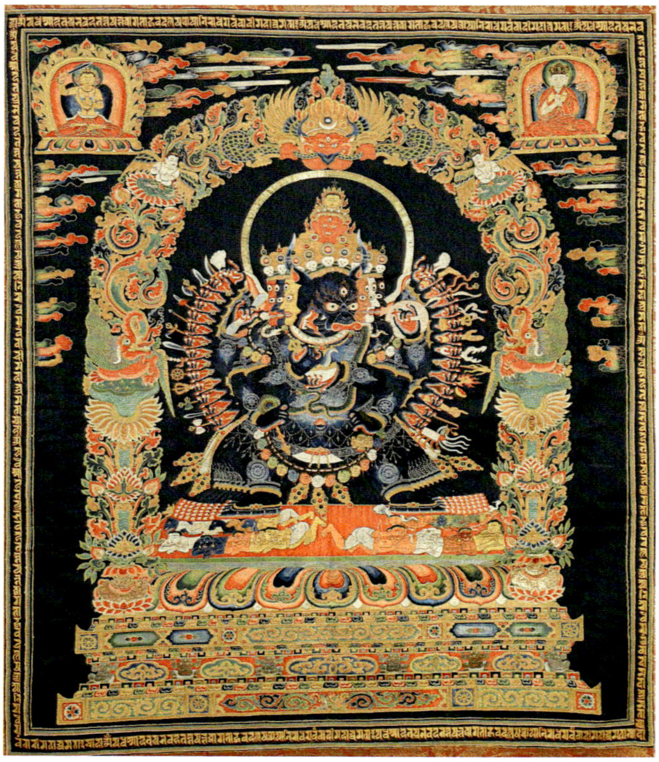

Plate 16.8 Vajrabhairava, Ming dynasty, *c.* 1434 (Xuande reign). *Thangka*, silk embroidery, image height 79cm, width 62cm. Potala Palace, Lhasa

awarded by the Ming court, Consecration Preceptor of State Amogha (Ch. Guanding Guoshi Amuge 灌頂國師阿木葛) and Preceptor of State Sonam Sherab (Ch. Guoshi Suonan Xirao 國師索南喜饒), as responsible for the *thangka*'s manufacture. Xiong proposes that this took place between 1434 and 1443 in an imperial weaving workshop in Jiangnan, the region south of the lower Yangtze River.[41] Until the late 20th century, it was kept at Sera Monastery in Lhasa, which was founded by Śākya Yeshé in 1418 and is recognised as one of the three great Gelug monasteries.[42]

Both portraits of Śākya Yeshé mix Chinese and Tibetan elements, but the latter dominate the embroidered image, the smaller of the two works (76 x 65cm) (see **Pl. 16.2**). From the Chinese tradition come the auspiciously coloured *ruyi* clouds and the degree of individualisation in the master's face. He is portrayed as a jowly, ageing man with puffy eyes and furrowed brow. He wears Tibetan garments, a sleeveless upper garment and a lower robe, under an opulent red-and-gold *kāṣāya* with floral borders. Like a Buddha, he sits in *vajra* (cross-legged) posture, facing forward, and makes the *dharmachakra mudra* (Dharma wheel or teaching hand gesture). An ornate Vajrasattva headdress signifies his perfection of yogic meditation and complete enlightenment.[43] His corporeality notwithstanding, the master inhabits an otherworldly realm of brilliant colours and strong colour contrasts, geometric order and fantastic creatures on a flat black ground. He is visually integrated into this divine world by the whiteness of his flesh, the triangular form of his posture, the flat geometric patterns of his *kāṣāya* uninterrupted by folds, and the fabulous red and golden lotus flowers he holds by their stems. The flowers magically support a golden *vajra* sceptre and *vajra* bell (*ghanta*) essential ritual implements of Vajrayana and attributes of a number of Tantric deities.[44] Śākya Yeshé's halo is rendered with a single fine gold line like the haloes of the deities in the upper corners of the composition, the blue figure of the primordial Buddha Vajradhāra on the left and White Tārā, the female Buddha of longevity, on the right. His lotus seat with inverted petals rests on a Mount Sumeru pedestal decorated with jewels, scrolling designs and upturned corners. Most spectacularly, he occupies a fantastic decorative niche, or 'arch of glory', composed of the 'six ornaments', white elephants, blue lions, winged rams, lotus-bearing *devas*, crocodilian *Makaras*, *Nāgas* or serpent deities and a crowning winged Garuda. The scrolling designs and arch of glory were Nepalese-inspired elements of Tibetan art echoed in temples of the Ming capitals and other parts of China where Tibetan Buddhism was practised.[45] The interplay between Chinese and Tibetan elements in the embroidered portrait continues in the bilingual inscriptions that proclaim Śākya Yeshé's temporal and eternal identities by giving the key parts of his imperially bestowed title: Supremely Good (*Zhishan* 至善) Dharma King of Great Compassion and Universally Penetrating Buddha. Thus enshrined, accompanied, haloed, liturgically equipped and labelled, Śākya Yeshé is presented as a Buddha and implicitly the emperor's guru, in accordance with the Tibetan practice of worshiping one's guru as a fully enlightened Buddha.[46] Finally, the icon is bordered by mantras written in gold *Läntsa* script, a decorative form of Sanskrit used in Tibet for such sacred texts.

Śākya Yeshé appears as a small secondary figure in a number of textile *thangkas* of meditational deities. One of these, an embroidered Vajrabhairava *thangka* (**Pl. 16.8**) in the Potala Palace, is comparable to the embroidered portrait in size (79 x 62cm) and composition, and it shares motifs such as the red-topped lotus seat with a single layer of inverted petals, Mount Sumeru pedestal with upturned corners, decorative niche topped by *Makaras* and a Garuda, and auspicious coloured clouds. Also like the portrait, this Vajrabhairava *thangka* is framed by a *Läntsa*-script border.[47] There are, of course, significant iconographic variations, from the shapes of the clouds to the use of lotus columns to support the *Makaras* of the ornate niche. Nevertheless, the visual formula suggests that both works came from a series or set of images, albeit not from the same one.

The larger (109 x 64cm), more impressive *kesi* portrait of Śākya Yeshé (see **Pl. 16.3**) shares a number of features with the embroidered image, including attention to the individuality of the master's face. He appears thinner and older in the *kesi* but again has a deeply lined face, sagging jaws and accentuated eye sockets. Presumably the artists worked from a painting that provided a fairly detailed report on his physiognomy in the manner of the portrait of Daoyan. Śākya Yeshé's Buddhahood is also signified in many of the same ways in the *kesi* as in the embroidery: he again has a halo, sits in a fully frontal *vajra* posture, makes the teaching *mudra*, and holds the stems of lotus flowers, one supporting a *vajra* sceptre and the other a *vajra* bell. His lotus-flower seat, however, is very discreetly placed under the step below his throne, perhaps due to its visual incongruity with the rest of the physical environment, and rather than being enshrined in a Tibetan-style arch of glory, he is protected and glorified by a cloud-borne, jewelled canopy typical of Ming Buddhist paintings.

While expressing Śākya Yeshé's divinity in visual terms intelligible to virtually any Buddhist of the time, the *kesi* portrayal is temporally localised like a Chinese ancestor or an imperial portrait by the depiction of material goods signifying the subject's worldly status. The palatial furnishings – the carpet, the marble-topped red lacquer table with gold-filled incised designs and the magnificent throne – are meticulously detailed. The throne is similar in general form and scale to the one occupied by Daoyan, but it is far more lavish. Inset with jewels and fitted with carved dragon heads holding jewelled lotus pendants, it resembles the dragon thrones depicted in the portraits of the Yongle and Xuande emperors.[48] Śākya Yeshé's chair is, of course, less luxurious than the imperial seats, with four rather than six dragons, and the carpet beneath it is less exquisitely patterned than those under the emperors' thrones, as was appropriate to his lower but still exalted status as a Dharma King.

In the tapestry as in the embroidered portrait, Śākya Yeshé wears Tibetan-style upper and lower garments and a patchwork-patterned *kāṣāya*. Here, however, the ensemble is topped by a heavy meditation cloak with gold-on-gold patterns of imperial dragons, *ruyi*-shaped clouds and other auspicious motifs, recalling references in the *Ming Veritable Records* (*Ming shilu* 明實錄) to gold damask cloaks given to an emissary sent by Śākya Yeshé and others in 1423.[49] The master's ornate black hat features a red jewel set on top of a gold *vajra*, a red sun and white crescent moon on the crown, and five plaques bearing golden Buddha images to resemble the five-Buddha initiation crown used in Vajrayana rituals. This hat, which has been identified as an imperial gift, became a standard part of Śākya Yeshé's iconography.[50]

Overall, the words and material goods in the picture match Ming court records of what was bestowed upon eminent Tibetan clerics, including monks' clothing, fine silk fabrics, gold and silver vessels, ritual objects, Buddhist images, scriptures, official titles and seals of office. In the *kesi* portrait Śākya Yeshé is awash in such imperial gifts. On his left, rendered in gold in Chinese and Tibetan, is the full title granted him by the Xuande emperor in 1434. To his right is a copy of the red impression of his imperially bestowed seal, with the legend reading 'Seal of the Supremely Good Dharma King of Great Compassion' written in the nine-fold seal script (*jiudie zhuan* 九疊篆) style preferred for official seals. Although the *vajra* and *vajra* bell are the master's standard attributes, they also correspond to the emperor's gifts of ritual implements, as do the bronze (or copper) incense burner with a cover in the shape of a lion and the tortoise shell incense box on the table. The red *sūtra* case decorated with gold dragon designs, also on the table, recalls gifts of Buddhist scriptures. This remarkable collection was certainly intended to convey the exquisitely deferential treatment accorded Śākya Yeshé at the Ming court, but it also evokes, perhaps more importantly, the reciprocal nature of his relationship with the emperor: he gave the emperor enlightening teachings, efficacious rites and religious status, and received in return court rituals, royal status and a grand array of prestige objects.

All this visual information is luxuriously packaged in fine *kesi*, a medium that imparts value through its demanding technique, capacity for delicate design and subtle coloration, and durability. As the old saying goes, 'an inch of *kesi* is worth an ounce of gold'. From the Song dynasty onwards, *kesi* was used to emulate and copy fine paintings. In the Yuan dynasty, imperial workshops led by the Nepalese master Anige (1245–1306) and his followers translated Buddhist subjects and imperial portraits into woven images.[51] In light of this tradition, making a portrait of Śākya Yeshé in *kesi* was an inspired diplomatic stroke that honoured its Tibetan subject with a dazzling display of Chinese artistry and craftsmanship.[52]

As noted above, Śākya Yeshé appears as a small secondary figure in a number of textile *thangkas* of meditational deities.[53] Placed in the upper right corner in these works, he is shown seated cross-legged on an inverted lotus pedestal within an elaborate arch, much as he appears in the embroidered portrait, but he wears a black hat designed like a five-Buddha crown and an enveloping cape like those pictured in the *kesi* portrait.[54] In other words, these small images combine features seen in both the embroidered and *kesi* portraits of the master. The primary subjects of these *thangkas* match those listed in the Tibetan inscription under the *kesi* portrait. According to this inscription, along with the portrait, Śākya Yeshé's followers Amogha and Sonam Sherab sponsored images of Kālacakra Chakrasaṃvara, Hevajra, Vajrabhairava and Mahachakra. Xiong Wenbin's Chinese rendering of this inscription does not specify the medium of the images, but he identifies them as *kesi thangkas*.[55] We do not know if they contained small images of Śākya Yeshé. Nevertheless, it is not much of a stretch to imagine that his disciples would have honoured their guru's relationship to the great meditational deities by commissioning images like the *kesi* Chakrasaṃvara *thangka* (68 x 56cm), formerly in the Carolyn and Wesley Halpert collection, where Śākya Yeshé occupies the upper right corner and is paired with Vajradhāra on the left.[56] A *kesi* Hevajra *thangka* with the same composition and border belongs to the Potala Palace, and a very similar *kesi* of Vajrabhairava reportedly remains in the Yumbu Lakhar temple in the Yarlung valley in central Tibet.[57]

In sum, the *kesi* portrait of Śākya Yeshé is special by virtue of its documentation and reasonably rare medium, and is distinguished from the embroidered portrait by its mixture of mundane and extramundane references, with the visual weight tipped to the former. However, both portraits were simultaneously icons, visual counterparts to written accounts of Śākya Yeshé's lavish reception by the Yongle and Xuande emperors, and vehicles for communicating the court's esteem for the master and the new but already powerful Gelug order that he represented.

Stepping back to look at the portraits of Śākya Yeshé and Daoyan in the same frame, it is easy to find general connections between them. They belong to the same era, possibly even the same decade, and share basic concerns with their subjects' physiognomy, discipline-specific ritual regalia, and material indicators of status. All three bear the highest titles bestowed on their subjects by the Ming court, in each case rendered in gold. The differences between the

Chapter 17
The Early Ming Imperial Atelier on the Tibetan Frontier

Karl Debreczeny

A great deal of Tibetan Buddhist art was created in the early Ming imperial workshops, both for use at court and as part of complex diplomatic exchanges with Tibetan hierarchs. This has not been the traditional understanding of the Ming, which is typically described as expending a great deal of energy to reassert an ethnic Chinese identity in the wake of Mongol rule. Indeed the early Ming court followed Mongol precedents in drawing on a Tibetan model for creating an imperial Buddhist vocabulary symbolic of divine rule, and Tibetan Buddhism continued as a faith of the powerful within the inner court. First this chapter will introduce early Ming interest in Tibetan Buddhism and its artistic production and use at court. Then it will focus on an example of the political use of such objects: a site on the Sino-Tibetan frontier, Qutansi 瞿曇寺 (Gautama Monastery), the Ming court's close involvement being (in part) one element of a larger strategy to secure its borders.[1]

Ming imperial interests in Tibetan Buddhism

With the decline of Buddhism in India in the 13th century, Tibet became the new holy land to the west and source of Buddhist learning. Tibetan Buddhism became particularly important in Inner Asian models of kingship and found support in the courts of the Tanguts and the Mongols. In a Ming painting (**Pl. 17.1**), for instance, from a set related to the 'Water-Land' (*shuilu* 水陸) rite from Baoningsi 寶寧寺 (Precious Peace Monastery), an arhat is depicted writing in Tibetan, which had become by this time the medium of the faith.

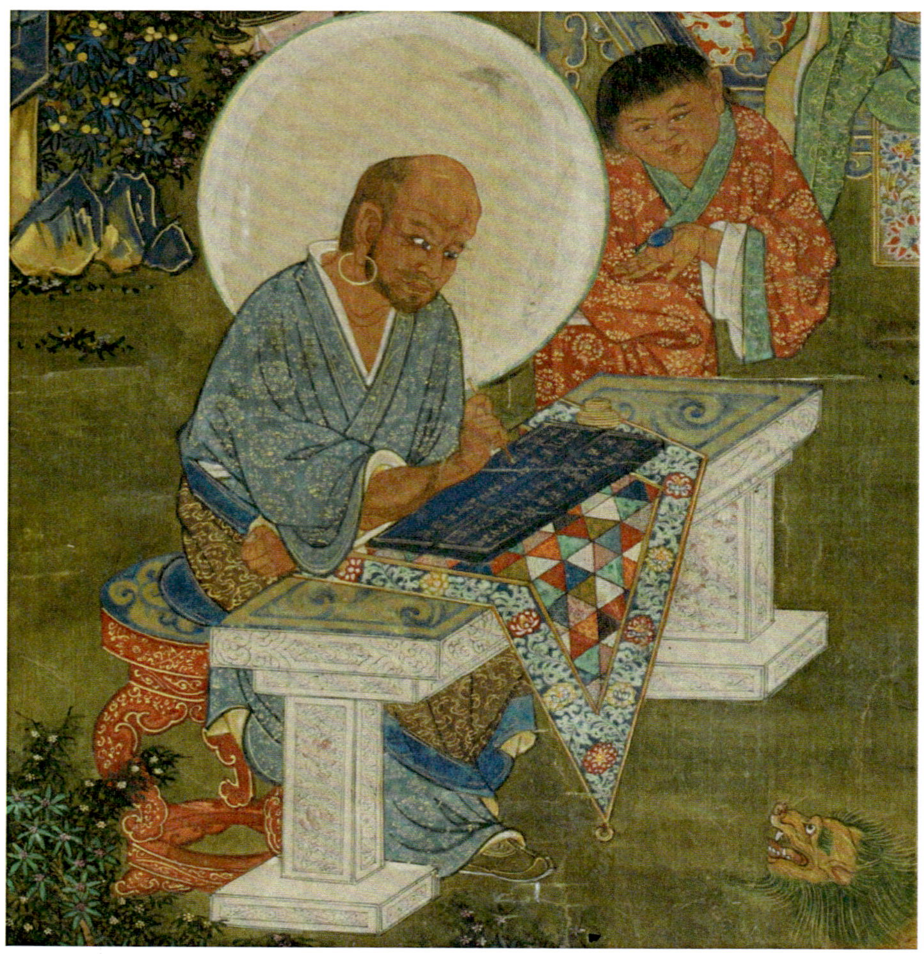

Plate 17.1 Arhat depicted writing Tibetan, detail from a set of 'Water-Land' (*shuilu* 水陸) ritual paintings from Baoningsi 寶寧寺, Shanxi province, Ming dynasty, c. 1449. Ink, colours and gold on silk, height 120cm, width 61cm. Shanxi Museum

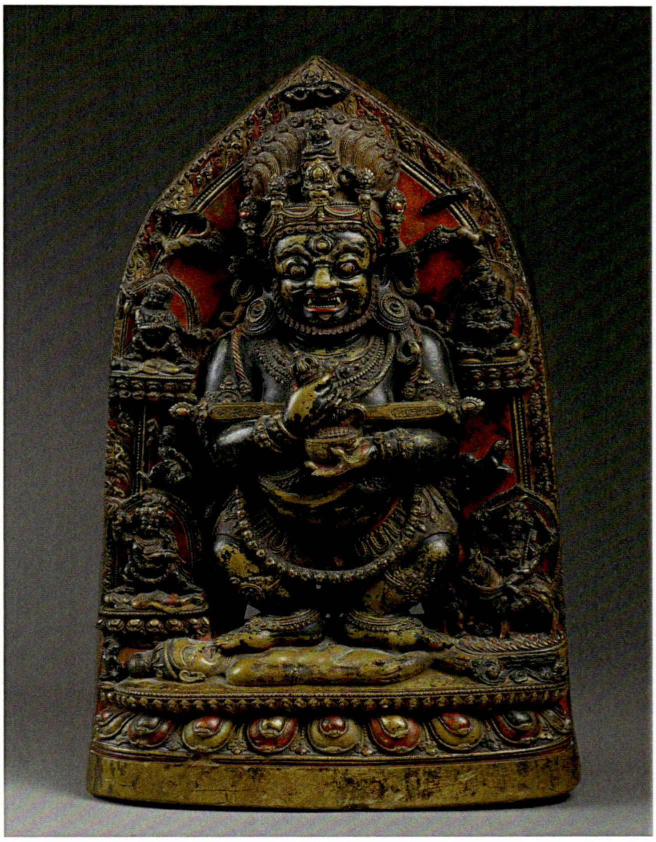

Plate 17.2 Panjaranātha Mahākāla (Tib. Gur gyi mgon po); inscription names Qubilai Khan and Imperial Preceptor Phakpa, dated 1292. Lithographic limestone partially gilded and polychromed, 47 x 285cm. Musée Guimet, Gift of L. Fournier (MA 5181)

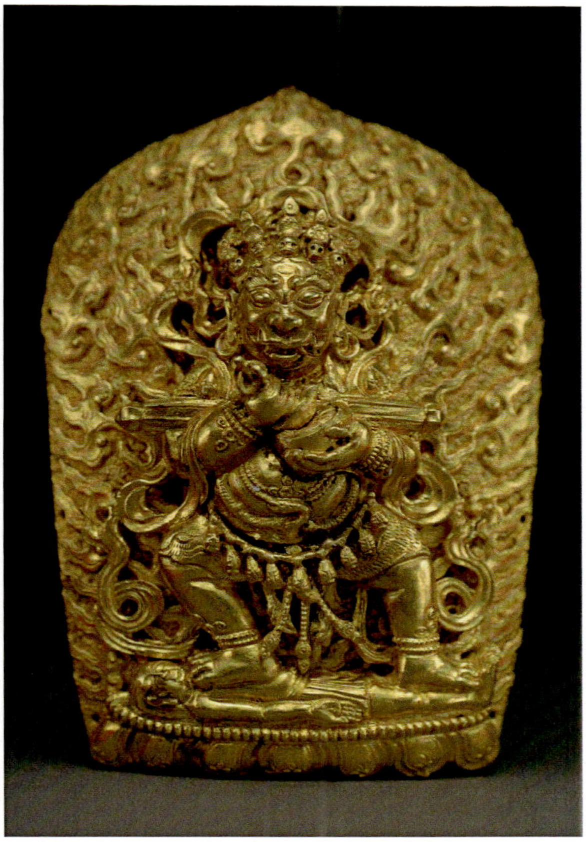

Plate 17.3 Statue of Mahākāla, excavated from the tomb of Prince Zhuang of Liang (1411–41) and Lady Wei at Zhongxiang, Hubei province, *c.* 1411–41. Nanjing or Beijing imperial workshops. Gold, height 9.4cm, width 5.4cm, depth 1cm, weight 114g. Hubei Provincial Museum

The first official expression of Ming interest in Tibetan Buddhism came only a few years after the Ming dynasty was founded, when in 1375 the first Ming emperor Hongwu 洪武 (r. 1368–98) sent a letter of praise to the Fourth Karmapa Rolpai Dorjé (Rol pa'i rdo rje; 1340–83), who had held one of the highest positions at the former Yuan court. Tibetans provided a model of sacrosanct rulership and esoteric means to power for the Mongol empire. The Yuan Imperial Preceptor (*dishi* 帝師), the highest religious authority in the land, was always Tibetan. The Hongwu emperor, formerly a monk under the previous Yuan system, would have been familiar with their role.[2] Indeed continuity can be traced in the Tibetan patriarchs who served both the late Yuan and early Ming courts.[3]

The form of Mahākāla as Pañjaranātha (Tib: Gur gyi mgon po) (**Pl. 17.2**) was a centrepiece of Mongol imperial Buddhism, and the most potent symbol of Tibetan esoteric power in the Yuan pantheon. A sculpture of this emanation of Mahākāla made by the Nepalese head of the Yuan imperial atelier Anige 阿尼哥 (1244–78/1306) for Qubilai Khan's final conquest of the Song dynasty (960–1279) became emblematic of both Qubilai's rule and the Yuan imperial lineage.[4] While that sculpture was lost with the fall of the Qing, this sculpture dated 1292 bears an inscription naming Qubilai Khan (1215–94) and his Tibetan Imperial Preceptor Phakpa ('Phags pa).[5] A striking continuation of this Tibetanised visual language of sacral rule in the Ming can be found in an object (**Pl. 17.3**) among the goldwork excavated from the tomb of Prince Zhuang of Liang 梁莊王 (1411–41), a large (9.4cm) gold hat ornament in this form of Mahākāla.[6] While the goldsmith did not understand the form perfectly, Pañjaranātha can be recognised by the stick (*gaṇḍi*) balanced across his arms. It seems a powerful political statement that Yongle's grandson would prominently display an image of the most potent symbol of Yuan power and sacral authority upon his head.

The Yongle emperor

It was Hongwu's son Ming Chengzu (1360–1424), commonly known by his reign title Yongle 成祖 (r. 1403–24), who was the first Ming emperor to establish significant ties with Tibetan patriarchs, and recently there has been some acceptance that he was probably a believer in Tibetan Buddhism. One thing that emerged very clearly from various angles in the Ming conference held at the British Museum in 2014 is that the Yongle emperor consciously modelled a number of his policies closely on those of Qubilai Khan, and this extends to his engagement with Tibetans as well.[7] As an imperial prince he was granted the former Mongol capital in Beijing. He took up residence in the former Mongol palace, opening the former imperial libraries and treasures which had been preserved and sealed, and retained some of the Yuan palace eunuchs who were left there.[8] This was likely one of the direct conduits of Mongol imperial culture, which would have included Tibetan Buddhist practices, into the future Yongle court. Moreover the Yongle emperor is known in Tibetan sources, such as *The Blue Annals*, as Ye Wang (Ye dbang), 'The Prince of Yan 燕', his previous title as the prince of the Beijing area, suggesting that the Yongle emperor, who was not the crown prince, was well acquainted with Tibetans, and they with him, during his early career in Beijing during the Hongwu era.[9]

The visit of the Fifth Karmapa

The most significant event in Sino-Tibetan relations during the early Ming was the visit of the Fifth Karmapa, Deshin Shekpa (De bzhin gshegs pa; 1384–1415) (**Pl. 17.4**), to the early Ming capital of Nanjing in 1407. The Karmapa taught Yongle's courtiers and several members of his family while he stayed in Nanjing for almost a year, and among those who received instruction was Empress Xu 徐 (1362–1407).[10] In dealing with the Karmapa, Yongle consciously drew parallels in his own actions to Qubilai Khan's relationship with his Tibetan Imperial Preceptor Phakpa during the founding of the previous Yuan dynasty. Yongle also bestowed on the Karmapa the title *Dabao fawang* 大寶法王, or 'Great Precious King of the Dharma' – the same title Qubilai had bestowed on Phakpa when the former declared himself Great Khan. According to Tibetan sources, Yongle expressed an interest in recreating their priest-patron relationship, and made a similar offer to send troops into Tibet in order to install the Karmapa as the temporal ruler and forcibly convert all monasteries to his order, an offer similarly declined. Yongle's offer parallels Qubilai's offer to Phakpa, as does the response, which was to decline in favour of religious plurality.[11]

Plate 17.4 Fifth Karmapa (1384–1415) and the Yongle emperor (r. 1403–24), *c.* 18th century. Pigments on cotton, height 100cm, width 60cm. Current location unknown

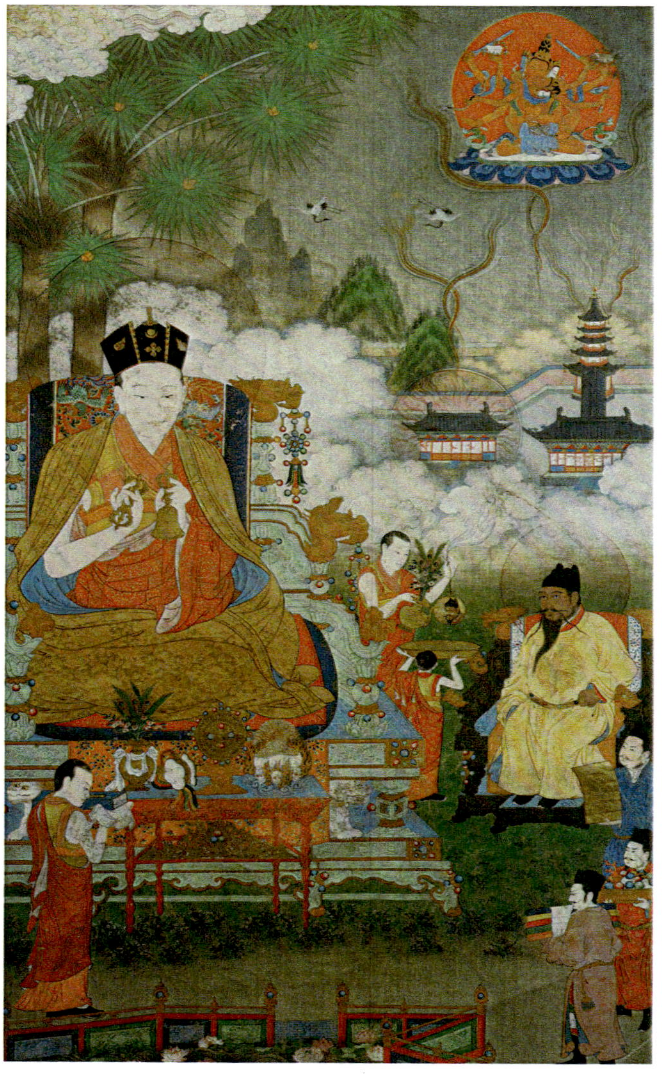

The Karmapas were of particular interest to Yongle as there exists a Buddhist path to legitimisation through empowerment, namely the path of the *cakravartin* ruler which the Mongols had employed, and the Karmapas, who were either the final imperial preceptors of the Yuan empire or held a comparable position in the waning years of the Mongol court, were by this time the primary transmitters of this esoteric power.[12] Yongle thus invited the Fifth Karmapa to court in 1403, barely a year after coming to power, and received various initiations. After the Karmapa's visit Yongle indeed styled himself a *cakravartin* ruler, and some Tibetan sources obligingly describe Yongle as a *cakravartin* king after these events, specifically an iron-wheel *bālacakravartin*: 'one who turns the wheel of the doctrine by force'.[13] In the portrait of the Karmapa (see **Pl. 17.4**) we see this relationship codified: Yongle is receiving consecration as a sacral ruler, with a mirror reflecting Yongle's visage while water is poured on it from a ritual vessel. One can see that this painting both reproduces the official Yongle portrait exactly, at lower right, and, above him, directly quotes from the 1407 miracle handscroll produced by Yongle court painters.[14]

Visual evidence for continuity from the Mongol Yuan in the artistic production of the Ming imperial atelier is the presence of an already fully mature Sino-Tibetan artistic synthesis in the early years of the 15th century, the most famous examples being the bronzes of the Yongle period.[15] Yuan court prototypes for these Yongle Buddhist images can be found in Yuan woodblock printings and locally in the surviving stone carved images on the Juyong Pass 居庸關 (1345) which date to the final years of the Mongol empire in China.

Images made in the Ming workshops and sent to Tibet were copied and had a profound effect on Tibetan art, from entire genres such as arhat painting to particular images, such as the famous 'Udayana Buddha', represented by the impressive gilt bronze with a Xuande 宣德 reign mark (1426–35) in the Musée Cernuschi, known to Tibetans as 'the Sandalwood Lord of China' (*rgya nag gi tsandan jo bo*) which was both reproduced and venerated.[16] For example, a large painting of this Buddha with a Yongle reign mark (1412) can still be found on display at Nénying (gNas rnying) Monastery, in Tsang province, Tibet.[17] A copy of a handscroll recording miracles the Karmapa performed while in the capital Nanjing (1407), sent to the Karmapa's seat Tsurphu (mTshur phu) Monastery, became one of the primary models for an entire Tibetan style, the painting tradition of the Karmapa Encampment (Karma sGar bris).[18]

One of the most famous visual manifestations of Yongle's engagement with Tibetan Buddhism is this same monumental 50-metre long handscroll known as the *Miracles of the Mass of Universal Salvation Conducted by the Fifth Karmapa for the Yongle Emperor* (in Chinese known as *Pudu Ming Taizu changjuan tu* 普渡明太祖長卷圖) in the Tibet Museum. It recordsthe miraculous occurrences during memorial services performed by the Fifth Karmapa in 1407 at Nanjing's largest imperially sponsored temple, Linggusi 靈谷寺 (Numinous Valley Monastery), for the Hongwu emperor and Empress Ma, along with Hongwu's parents, in a series of 49 narrative scenes (see **Pl. 14.4a–c**).[19] On one level this painting can be viewed as containing an ulterior motive, as rumours circulated of Yongle's possible Mongol or Korean ancestry after he seized the throne from his nephew with assistance from Mongol cavalry in 1402. Questioning Yongle's ethnicity – denying his very Chinese identity – has also been a typical means by which to isolate and marginalise his interests in Tibetan Buddhism.[20] The manner in which Yongle came to power naturally put a cloud over his reign and made him concerned about the image of his own legitimacy. The handscroll had a clear political agenda in confirming the legitimacy of Yongle's reign, and made use of similar strategies that the Mongol court employed to project power across Asia, such as the multilingual inscriptions found on this handscroll, as also seen on Yuan public works such as the aforementioned Juyong Pass.

Beyond such well-publicised projects is the 1413 missive scroll which the Yongle emperor sent to the Fifth Karmapa describing the famous eunuch admiral Zheng He's 鄭和 (1371–1433) voyage to Sri Lanka and capture of the Buddha's tooth relic.[21] The scroll mentions the participation of the eunuch Hou Xian 侯顯 (active 1403–27), Yongle's main envoy to the Tibetans and bearer of the 1413 letter, who had already been in Tibet for four years before the voyage. In it the emperor also describes his own visionary experiences, which clearly went beyond the bounds of what would be required in diplomacy.[22] Therefore to limit Ming motivations in the patronage of Tibetan art to politics alone is to limit our own view, for religious faith and political acumen are not mutually exclusive, and it would be a mistake to project 21st-century cynicism on to the 15th century.

The Zhengde emperor

While discussions of Ming court interest in Tibetan Buddhism tends to be limited to the Yongle emperor, he was by no means the most extreme among Ming rulers in his adoration of Tibetan Buddhism. Tibetan art continued to receive significant court patronage, especially under emperors Xuande and Chenghua 成化 (r. 1465–87), but the Zhengde 正德 emperor (r. 1506–21) was an enthusiastic patron of Tibetan Buddhism who took his zeal to a level few had dared. According to the Qing dynasty *Wuzong waiji* 武宗外紀 (*Unofficial History of the Emperor Wuzong*): 'At that time the emperor studied Tibetan scripture, and converted to that religion. He dressed as a Tibetan monk, and practised Dharma at court.'[23] He was also proficient in the Tibetan language, kept many Tibetan monks around him, and built a Tibetan Buddhist temple within the Forbidden City.[24]

According to Tibetan sources Zhengde adopted the Tibetan name Rinchen Palden (Rin chen dpal ldan) and, incredibly, even went so far as to style himself an emanation

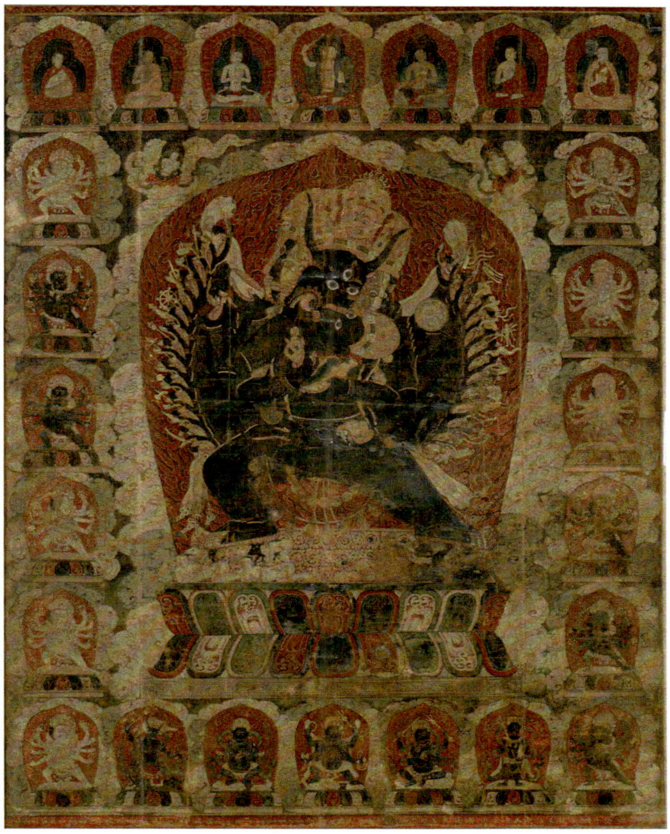

Plate 17.5 Vajrabhairava, dated 1512. Ink and colour on silk, height 129.5cm, width 99cm. University of California, Berkeley Art Museum and Pacific Film Archive, Gift of James and Dorothy Cahill (1982.13)

of the Seventh Karmapa (1454–1506). Far from wishful thinking on the part of Tibetans, this assertion, and the mission of the eunuch envoy who carried these tidings, was received rather coldly by the Karmapa's court.[25] Testament to some of Zhengde's religious interests are found in the form of an invitation sent with the eunuch Liu Yun 劉允 in 1515 to the Eighth Karmapa (1507–54) with many gifts. The letter of invitation in Chinese and Tibetan was preserved at Tsurphu Monastery.[26] A detailed Tibetan account of this ill-fated mission is also recorded in *A Scholars' Feast* (*mKhas pa'i dga' ston*, 1545), which further relates that the Chinese were insulted by the cold reception they received and took back all the gifts, only to be robbed on their return trip.[27] This is one of the few Chinese missions for which there is a detailed record in Tibetan sources, and it is especially valuable as it was recorded by a firsthand witness; the author Pawo Tsuklak Trengwa (dPa' bo gTsug lag phreng ba; 1504–66) was one of the Eighth Karmapa's own disciples. The account even includes an incredulous Tibetan explanation of what a eunuch is. The very concept must have been alien to a culture where a sizeable percentage of the male population was celibate without resorting to mutilation.[28]

Richardson thus identified the Tibetan name Rinchen Palden 領占班丹 on *thangkas* such as the one illustrated here (**Pl. 17.5**) as none other than the emperor himself.[29] Marsha Weidner (Haufler) has further contextualised this painting by identifying the occasion of its commission as the emperor's birthday.[30] As we can see, demand for Tibetan objects within the Ming court was strong, and the impetus for their creation multivariate.

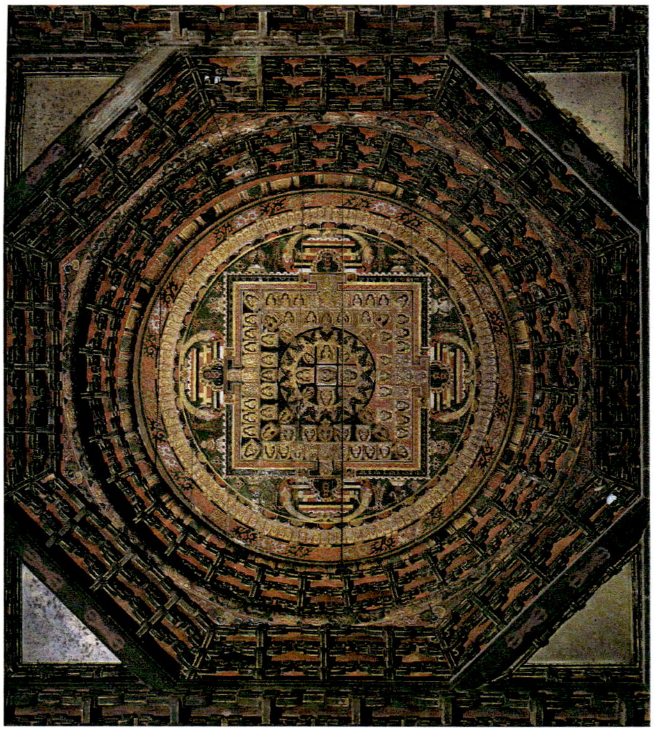

Plate 17.6 Vairocana *Maṇḍala*, central bay, Fahai Monastery, Beijing. Built between 1439–41 by the Ming court eunuch Li Tong (d. 1453)

Broader court engagement: Fahaisi

Moving beyond the emperor's personal engagement with Tibetan Buddhism, Fahaisi 法海寺 (Sea of the Law Monastery), completed in 1443, is a small private temple on the outskirts of Beijing.[31] While the basic architectural and painting programmes of Fahai Monastery are clearly Chinese, a subtle Tibetan presence is observable in various Tibetan forms that appear throughout the temple. For example, on the ceilings in the three coffered bays over the central altar are three large *maṇḍala* (**Pl. 17.6**), which are linked to Tibetan mortuary liturgy, such as the central Vairocana, which is specifically related to the *Purification of All Bad Rebirths Tantra* (*Sarva-durgati-pariśodhana Tantra*).[32] In this way the Tibetan *maṇḍalas* on the ceiling are linked functionally to the Chinese 'Water-Land' ritual paintings on the walls (**Pl. 17.7**), in their role of salvation for the dead. Within Fahai Monastery's wall paintings subtle Tibetan elements can also be found; for instance, among the Chinese courtly attire in Indra and Brahmā's royal procession on the north wall of Fahai Monastery, only Mārīcī (see **Pl. 17.7**, centre right) is given the distinctive five-leaf crown and *vajra* chignon finial, similar to contemporaneous painted images in Tibet and Sino-Tibetan bronzes produced at the Ming court.

Eunuchs at the Ming court

Fahai Monastery's principal patron was a eunuch of the inner court who served as director of all imperial artists, the Directorate of Imperial Accoutrements (*Yuyongjian* 御用監). The fact that Tibetan borrowings appear specifically at this small private temple seems to be a result of the intersecting layers of the eunuch bureaucracy at the Ming court, both in their roles as the controllers of the imperial construction apparatus, the Ministry of Works and as the official imperial envoys to Tibetan patriarchs. Thus the eunuchs were in close contact with the Tibetan clerics at court, often becoming their personal patrons, and directly oversaw the artists who made these images.

Evidence of a significant Tibetan presence at Fahai Monastery is found in ten Tibetan names on the back of the

Plate 17.7 'Water-Land' ritual paintings (note Mārīcī wearing Tibetan-inspired 5-leaf crown). North wall, Fahai Monastery, Beijing

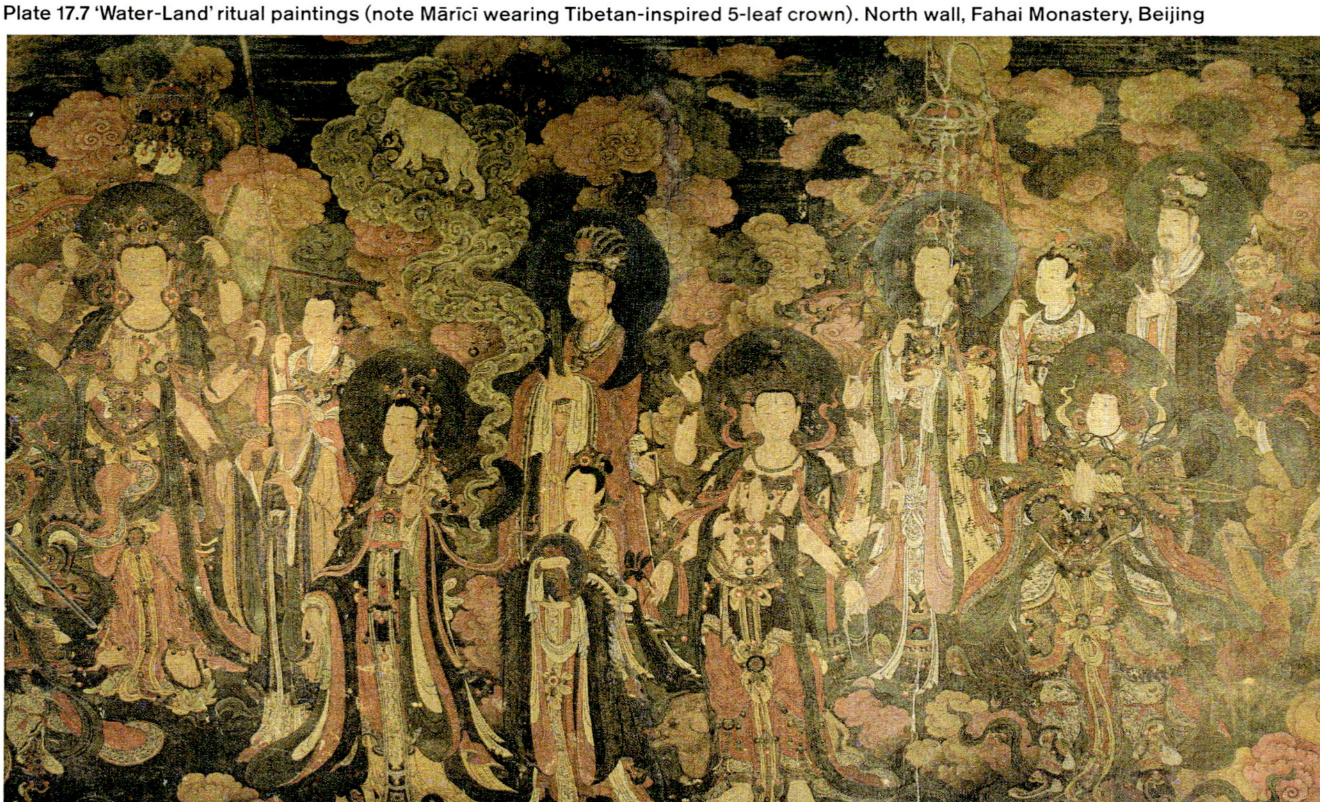

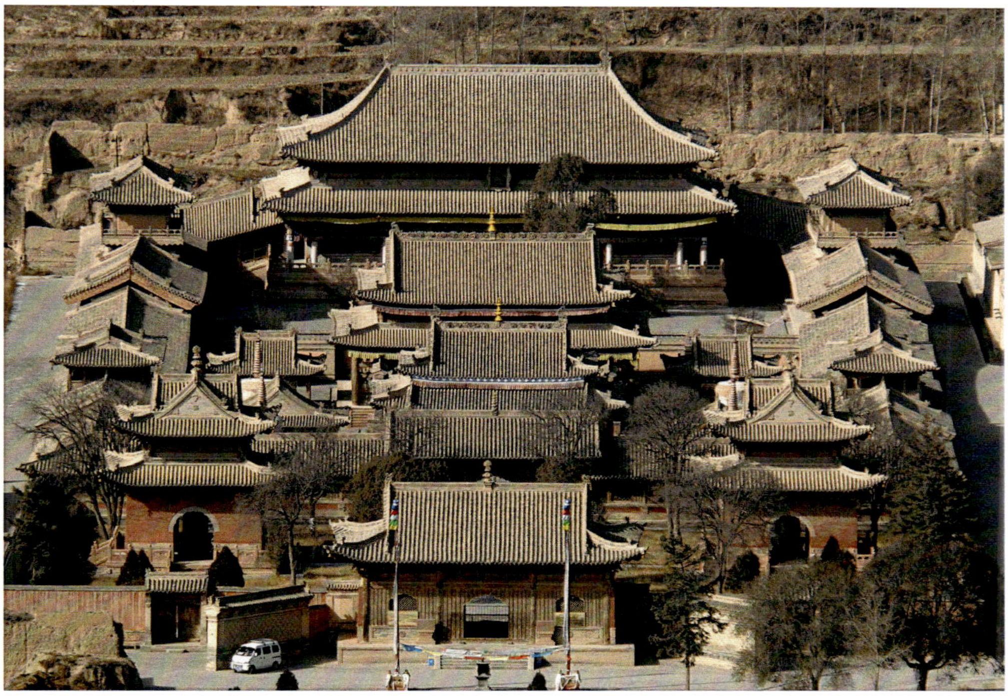

Plate 17.8 Qutan Monastery 瞿曇寺 (Tib: Gro tshang rdo rje 'chang), Qinghai

'Record of Fahai Monastery' stele. The first name, Śākya Yeshé (Śākya ye shes 釋迦也失; d. 1435), is that of the founder of Sera Monastery, who was sent in Tsongkhapa's (Tsong kha pa; 1375–1419) stead to the Yongle court.[33] The third name, Palden Tashi (dPal ldan bkra shis 班丹紮釋), is the most interesting in the context of this discussion, for he not only appears to have played a role in the founding of Fahai Monastery, but also was abbot of Qutan Monastery, in Qinghai, far away on the Sino-Tibetan boarder, a provincially located temple built with imperial sponsorship.[34] Palden Tashi was directly involved with Buddhist practice in Beijing and wielded significant influence within the National Buddhist Registry, the *Senglusi* 僧錄司. He served as the Fifth Karmapa's translator at court in Nanjing in 1406, translated numerous Tibetan texts into Chinese (presumably for Chinese court practitioners of Tibetan Buddhism) and ordained several Ming officials – including some of those sent to expand Qutan Monastery.[35] The eunuchs Hou Xian (who had served with the famous eunuch admiral Zheng He) and Yang Sanbao 楊三寶 are recorded as having travelled in the company of Palden Tashi.

Qutan Monastery (Tib. Gro tshang rdo rje 'chang)

Qutan Monastery (Tib. Gro tshang rdo rje 'chang) (**Pl. 17.8**) was founded in 1392 in present-day Ledu 樂都 county, 43km east of Xining in modern-day Qinghai province. Its location is described on one of its own early Ming dedicatory stele (1425) as being on the border connecting with the western kingdoms (Tibet), and thus at the meeting of the northwest Ming frontier and the eastern border of the Tibetan province of Amdo. Qutan Monastery is one of the earliest expressions of Ming court interest in Tibetan Buddhism, and an examination of local Tibetan chronicles and Chinese imperial records reveals that Qutan Monastery was dependent on the Ming court's support and protection. In turn, its patronage was part of a larger Ming Sino-Tibetan border strategy to establish an alliance between the local authorities and the imperial court.[36] If one maps where Ming garrisons end, one finds that a network of such court-supported temples takes over.[37]

The early Ming court repeatedly sent eunuchs to inspect and participate in the construction of Qutan Monastery, marking it as an important court construction project on the Chinese empire's periphery, at least until it was eclipsed by the founding of the major Geluk (dGe lugs) monastery of Kumbum Jampa Ling (sKu 'bum byams pa gling) outside of Xining in 1506. This quick fall into relative obscurity prevented later large-scale renovations and expansions at Qutan Monastery, preserving the early 15th-century structure and painting relatively intact.

Qutan Monastery, like Fahai Monastery, is Chinese in architecture, with a mixed Chinese and Tibetan painting and statuary programme. The outer painted gallery depicts the life of the Buddha in blue-green Chinese landscape painting, while inside the halls the paintings appear Tibetan in both style and iconography, and it is on these halls that I will focus.[38]

Although Qutan Monastery was initially founded by Sangyé Tashi (Sangs rgyas bkra shis; d. 1414) in 1392, the bulk of its construction took place under imperial patronage in the early 15th century, during the tenure of his nephew, the aforementioned Palden Tashi. Palden Tashi is recorded as being appointed abbot of Qutan Monastery by the Yongle emperor in 1408.[39] He was a monk of the Karma Kagyü (bKa' brgyud) order, but also maintained close ties to Sakya (Sa skya), an orientation reflected in the wall paintings of the monastery – which is important for their dating.

First stage of construction (1392)

Tibetan and Chinese sources include five bilingual stele *in situ* dated to roughly the first quarter of the 15th century. Comparing them to extant visual material at Qutan Monastery, we can sketch a three-stage chronology for the

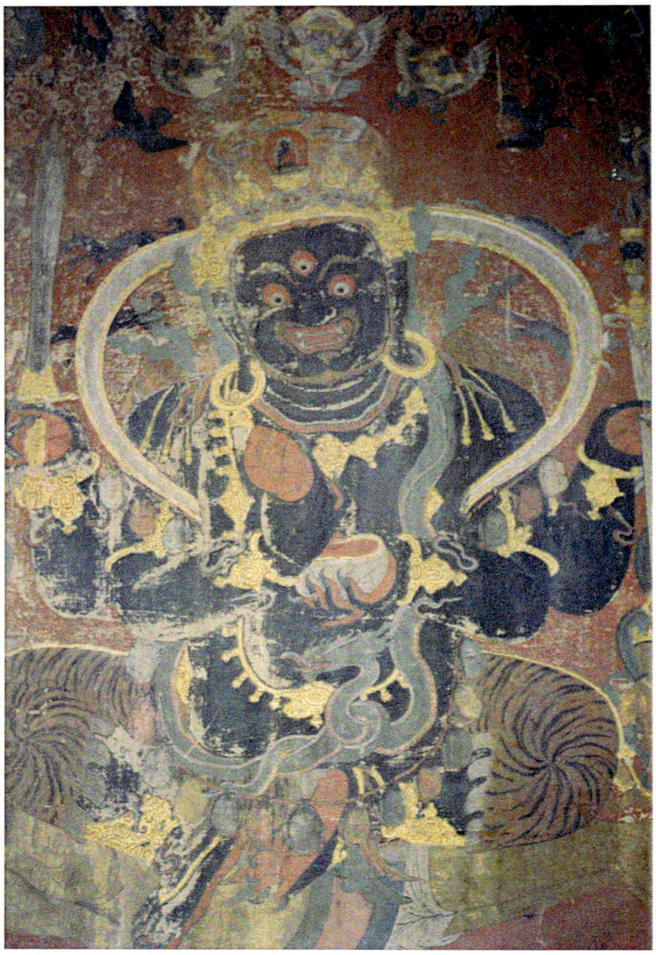

Plate 17.9 Four-Armed Mahākāla (primary protector of Kagyü order). South wall, east door wall, Qutan Hall, Qutan Monastery

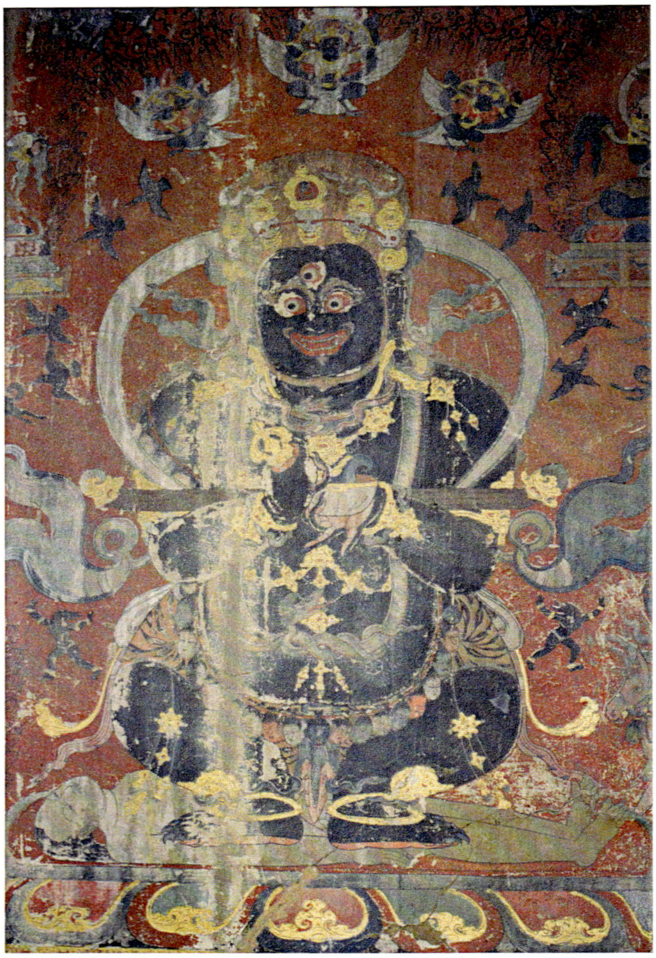

Plate 17.10 Pañjaranātha Mahākāla (primary protector of the Sakya Order). South wall, west door wall, Qutan Hall, Qutan Monastery

temple. A local Tibetan history, the *History of the Dharma in Amdo* (*mDo smad chos 'byung*; 1865), gives an account of the founding and initial painting and sculpture programme of Qutan Monastery, which is recorded as being largely Tibetan:

> In the four directions were erected earth-subduing stūpas, and the principal images of the central chapel (Qutandian 瞿曇殿) were the Buddhas of the Three Times and their close disciples (the Eight Great Bodhisattvas). In the left flanking Hall of the Protectors were statues of Four-Armed Mahākāla and Pañjaranātha Mahākāla together with attendants. In the wall paintings were Six-Armed Mahākāla with his retinue of seventy-five forms of Mahākāla, and Four-Armed Mahākāla with attendants residing here together with the blessed [image of] Dharmarāja ... Because it had an [image of] Achima (A phyi ma), it is known as the 'Achi Protector Chapel'.
>
> In the right-flanking chapel was the Great Sakya Stūpa. In the paintings on its sides were Vajradhara inside each of four gates which themselves resembled *dānyukaṭaka* stūpas. And in sequence were countless assemblies of deities of the Anuttara Tantra class and the three other tantra classes (Kriyā, Caryā and Yoga), such as Kālacakra, Saṃvara, Hevajra and a form of Bhairava according to the Ko (sKo) tradition; many tutelary deities (*yi dam*) of the Nyingma class such as Vajrakīla, the Four Guardian Kings, various *Dharma*-protectors, Guardians of the Ten Directions, together with G[illegible] Nāga on the tips of light rays; and the pillars on the [differ[illegible]] levels which appeared to be supported by the many hands of offering deities, etc. These things are renowned as apparitions of miraculous form. Qutan Monastery's abbot Kal Zangpa (sKal bzang pa) said that these were intended as auspices for the construction of the Vajradhara Chapel (Longguodian 隆國殿).[40]

Qutan Hall (Tib. dBus su lha khang)

Murals inside Qutandian 瞿曇殿 (Gautama Hall) (1392) seem to be Ming works, and iconographic evidence within wall paintings themselves supports this assessment: those inside the hall contain Kagyü and Sakya imagery, such as the Four-Armed Mahākāla (**Pl. 17.9**) – primary protector of the Kagyü order – and Pañjaranātha Mahākāla (**Pl. 17.10**) – primary protector of the Sakya order. One also finds paintings of hierarchs of Kagyü and Sakya orders, such as Sakya Paṇḍita. This Kagyü/Sakya presence is significant for dating the Qutan Hall's wall paintings, as Qutan Monastery was originally a Kagyü temple, but with close ties to the Sakya, until it changed sectarian affiliation and came under the Geluk order's control in the mid-15th century. If Qutan Hall had been repainted later under Geluk stewardship one would expect Geluk content. However, none is present inside the hall; Geluk imagery is only evident outside in the later 18th-century vestibule (repaired in 1782), such as the founder of that monastic order, Tsongkhapa.

However Tibetan in style and iconography the wall paintings may appear at first glance, Chinese painters' hands are revealed in numerous small details, such as the skull crown of Pañjaranātha (**Pl. 17.10**) – which is painted in the same manner as a Mingwang 明王 (**Pl. 17.11**) found in

Chinese temples such as Pilusi 毗盧寺 (Vairocana Monastery) – strung together through the eye sockets. In the depiction of Four-Armed Mahākāla (see **Pl. 17.9**) one also finds a dragon-like garland depicted with horns, curling snout and spiny ridge, and shorts are placed modestly on figures – otherwise depicted nude, which is characteristic of Chinese production of Tibetan Buddhist imagery.

The only wall paintings within Qutan Hall executed in an outwardly Chinese manner are the small scenes of the *Fifty-three Visits of Sudhana* which run in two registers along the lower section of the east and west walls, where the figures are clearly dressed as Chinese courtiers. Cleverly hidden within the 14th visit, in an architectural panel used as a horizontal cartouche, is a badly abraded Tibetan inscription which appears to contain a Yongle reign date: 'Ta'i Yung lo bsten' (Da Yongle 大永樂) 'closely arranged [in the] Great Yongle [reign]'. This would confirm an early Ming date for the painting of the murals (that is, during the period of imperial involvement), though slightly later than the hall's founding.

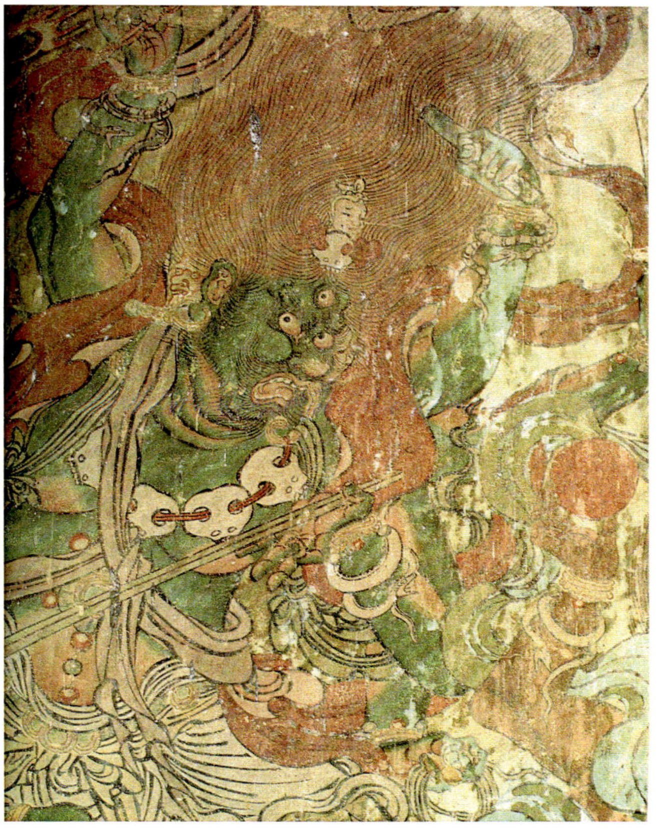

Plate 17.11 Detail of Kṣitigarbha, mid-16th century. Pilu Monastery, Hebei province

Second stage of construction (1418)

The *History of the Dharma in Amdo* goes on to describe the second stage of construction and ornamentation of Qutan Monastery during the early 15th century:

> In the lifetime of the Yongle and Xuande emperors, the official Samten Zangpo (bSam gtan bzang po) erected images of Śākyamuni and Vajradhara. Thirteen temples and the monastic servants of monastic estates of seven valleys were bestowed. Golden seals were given to the brothers Palden Zangpo (Palden Tashi)[41] and Sonam Gyaltsen (bSod nams rgyal mtshan), his (Sangye Tashi's) own nephews. In particular patents which were clear expressions of praise over a period of time and a self-arisen image of the Buddha were given [by the Yongle Emperor] to Palden Zangpo, and a chapel a day's distance from the palace was built with state funds to house it. The statue resided in the Jo khang of Blazing Jewel Light (Baoguang Hall) as the chief image.[42]

Baoguang Hall (Tib. Jo khang rin chen 'od 'bar)

Baoguangdian 寶光殿 (Hall of Blazing Jewel Light) was built in 1418. The iconographic programme of Baoguang Hall is identical to Qutan Hall, just built on a grander scale. Elaborate knots (**Pl. 17.12**) in the sashes of the deities on the side walls of Baoguang Hall are clearly derived from a Chinese repertoire – again confirming the presence of Chinese painters' hands in the Tibetan imagery. A similar

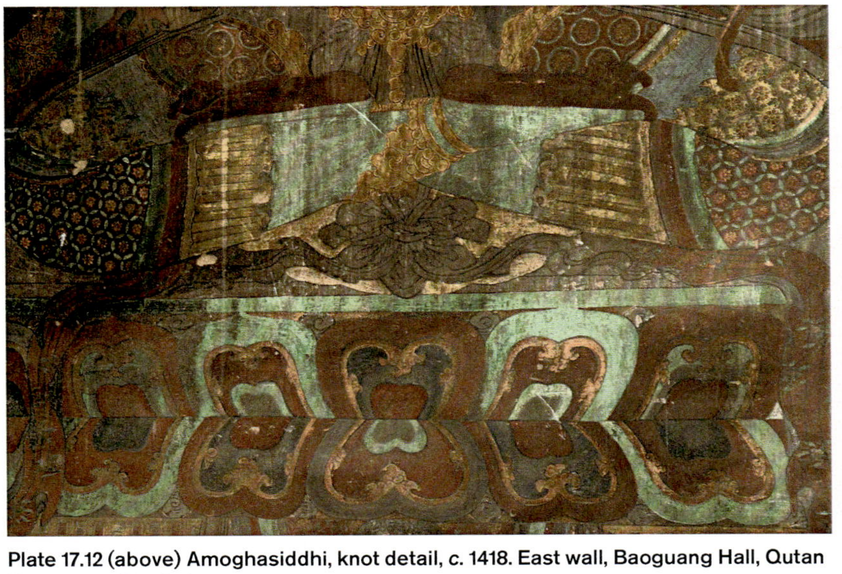

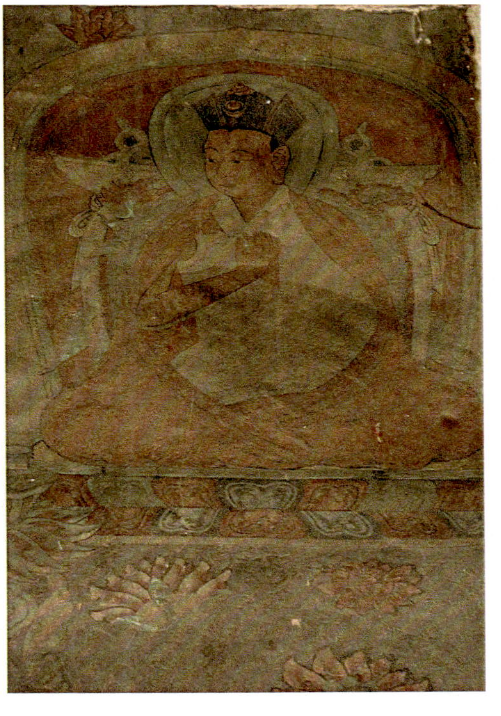

Plate 17.12 (above) Amoghasiddhi, knot detail, *c.* 1418. East wall, Baoguang Hall, Qutan Monastery, Qinghai

Plate 17.13 (right) Detail of a Karmapa (Fifth Karmapa, Deshin Shekpa (1384–1415)?), *c.* 1418. North wall, Baoguang Hall, Qutan Monastery, Qinghai

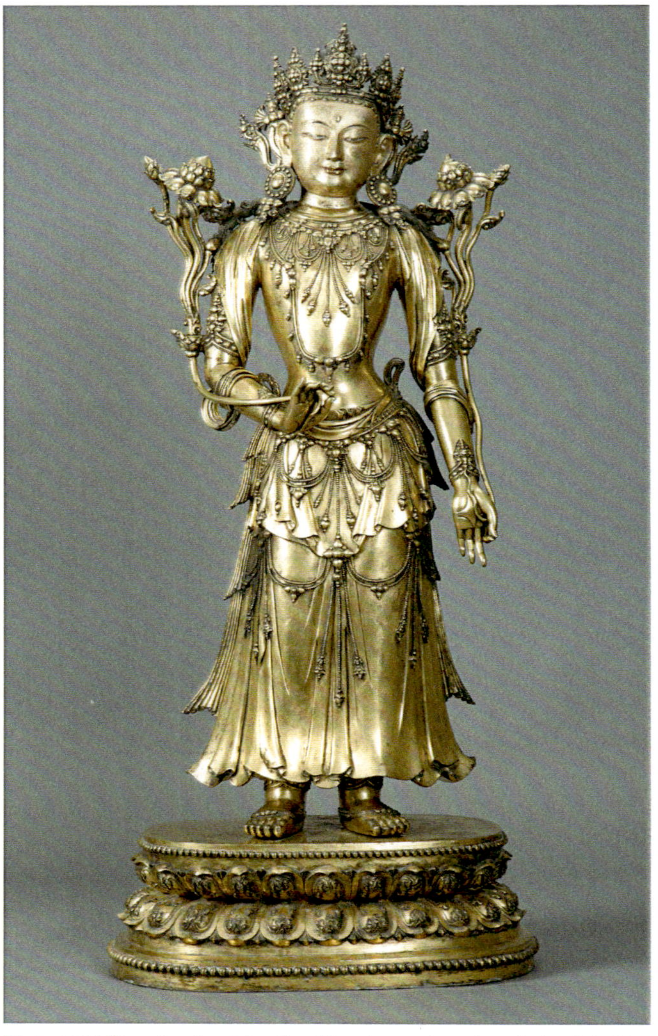

Plate 17.14 Standing bodhisattva, Yongle mark and period, 1403–24. Gilded bronze, height 145cm. Qinghai Provincial Museum

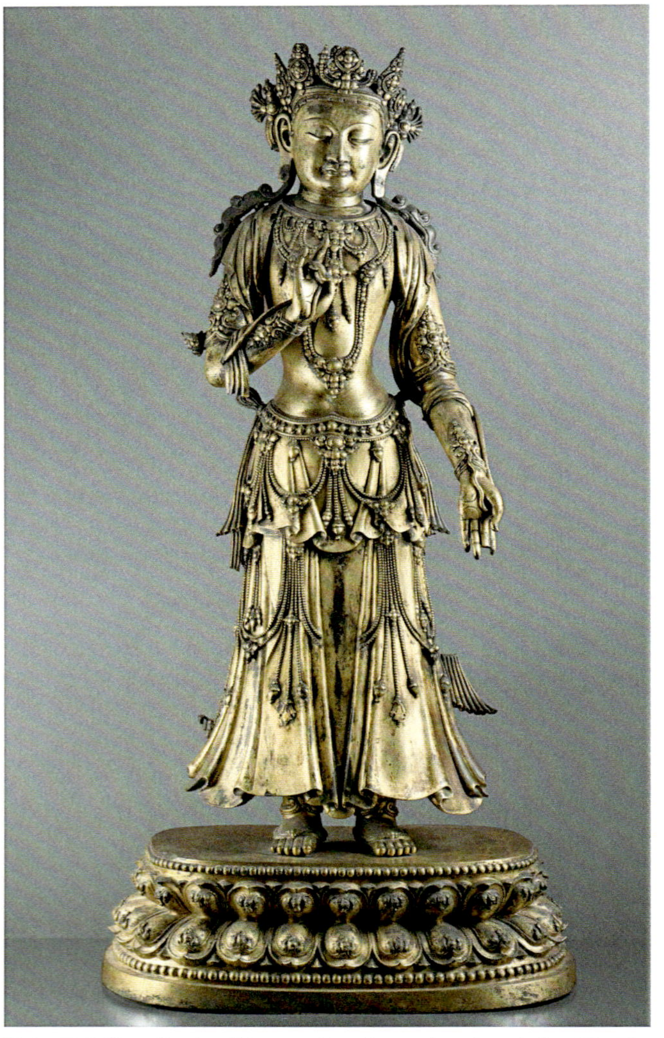

Plate 17.15 Standing bodhisattva, Yongle mark and period, 1403–24. Gilded bronze, height 136cm, width 45cm, length 66cm. Musée Cernuschi, Paris, bequeathed by Pauline Tarn/Renée Vivien, 1909, M. C. 5173

mixture of Kagyü and Sakya imagery is found in this hall, indicating these are also original early 15th-century paintings, most dramatically represented by a Karmapa (**Pl. 17.13**). This is most likely the Fifth Karmapa previously discussed. At the time of the hall's construction, the abbot of Qutan Monastery is recorded as having been the Fifth Karmapa's personal disciple and translator at the Ming court.

A brief account of the casting of Baoguang Hall's central image, a gilt-bronze Buddha, is given in the *Imperial Bestowal of Qutan Monastery's Golden Buddha Image Stele* (*Yuzhi Qutansi jinfoxiang bei* 御制瞿曇寺金佛像碑), dated 1418. In this inscription Yongle evokes the image of King Indrabhūti of Oḍḍiyāna – the Indian historical model of devout rule. Enhancing the aura of piety in the emperor's act is a story familiar to the making of sacral images across traditions, designed to increase the efficacy of the image:

> Though the artisans worked for a long time they could not complete it, until one day when they went out for food, leaving the workshop deserted, the divine body manifested itself. This frightened and amazed everyone and was seen as a magical manifestation of the powers by the buddhas and bodhisattvas, thus completing the work in a single casting.[43]

Thus this image was known as a miraculously self-arisen image (*rang 'byung*), a special class of sacred image within Tibetan tradition, sent west by the court as an offering to Qutan Monastery's abbot.

Qutan Monastery was once well appointed with such gilt bronzes (**Pl. 17.14**) produced at the Ming court, as evidenced by a near life-sized bodhisattva with a Yongle reign mark (1403–24), most likely one of the Eight Great Bodhisattvas which once flanked a central triad. These are recorded as created in imperial workshops and sent west, suggesting a pattern of other statuary, and gives some potential context to the nearly identical sculpture (**Pl. 17.15**) in the Musée Cernuschi as well. The trilingual Yongle reign date inscriptions on both sculptures in Chinese, Sanskrit and Tibetan are unusual and reinforce their close connection.

Third stage of construction (1427)

The *History of the Dharma in Amdo* goes on to describe the third stage of construction and ornamentation of Qutan Monastery nine years later in 1427:

> After that, on the walls are pictures of the rainbows that variously appeared like globes, pillars and wheel spokes when

> the temple praised as the 'Hall of Enriching the State' was founded by the Xuande emperor in fulfillment of his father's wishes. By the power of the king's faith an image of Vajradhara descended from the sky. The statue [which was installed there] is renowned among the Chinese as a relic of the Yongle emperor. It is recorded in a stele that to fulfill the wishes of the Emperor's heart, [the image] came from the land of the gods for the benefit of sentient beings of the human realm.[44]

Longguo Hall (Tib. Srid skyong gling)

The halls of Qutan Monastery become increasingly splendorous in their imperial architecture as one moves toward the rear of the complex; Longguodian 隆國殿 (Hall of Enriching the State) (see **Pl. 21.3** in this volume) is said to be based on the blueprint of Fengtiandian 奉天殿 (Hall of Service to Heaven) in Beijing's Forbidden City. The description in the *History of the Dharma in Amdo* implies that Longguo Hall was built as the Yongle emperor's memorial hall, a statement reiterated in the bilingual dedicatory *Imperial Bestowal of Qutan Monastery's Rear Hall Stele* (*Yuzhi Qutansi houdian bei* 御制瞿曇寺後殿碑) dated the second year of Xuande (1427).[45] It is also implied that this memorial hall was built by Xuande in conjunction with the Yongle emperor's funerary rites.

Eunuchs on the periphery

Longguo Hall contains a 'Long Life to the Emperor' (*huangdi wansui* 皇帝萬歲) inscription on a wooden placard which records that it was: 'built in … the second year of Xuande [1427] by Meng Ji 孟繼, Shang Yi 尚義, Chen Xiang 陳享 and Yuan Qi 袁琦, eunuchs of the Directorate of Imperial Accoutrements'. This Director of Imperial Accoutrements, Meng Ji, was sent by the Ming court to personally supervise the construction of Longguo Hall. Such a high-ranking officer of the imperial construction apparatus was almost certainly accompanied by numerous high-ranking master craftsmen from the imperial atelier, and Longguo Hall's architectural workmanship has been favourably compared to other inner court productions by eunuchs, such as Fahai Monastery and Zhihuasi 智化寺 (Transformation of Wisdom Monastery) in Beijing. It seems likely that this Yuan Qi on the Qutan Monastery tablet is the same Chinese official to whom Palden Tashi gave full ordination vows in 1434, seven years after the completion of Longguo Hall.[46]

Supporting evidence which further expands our understanding of the eunuch Meng Ji's role in the construction of Qutan Monastery is found in a set of Chinese archival records of successive generations of imperial edicts for donations to the temple (1651): 'During the Yongle period imperial envoys such as the eunuch Meng 孟 and commander Tian Xuan 田選, respecting the imperial edict(s), built the two halls, Baoguang and Longguo, and erected a stele record'.[47] It would seem from various textual evidence that both Baoguang and Longguo halls, as well as the covered gallery and eight of the subsidiary halls, were conceived of as part of the same construction project by the Yongle emperor, and it is stated directly that Xuande was 'fulfilling the wishes of his father', and thus completing his vision.

Conclusion

This short chapter has only scratched the surface of Tibetan art vis-a-vis the Ming court, both for use in the centres of power and its application on the periphery. Textual evidence suggests that Qutan Monastery was only one example of a larger pattern of imperial patronage along the Ming-Tibetan frontier. However Tibetan in iconography the imagery within Qutan Monastery's halls may appear at first glance, Chinese painters' hands are revealed in various subtle formal elements. This suggests that the Chinese painters of the early Ming imperial atelier were able to adjust the style and iconography of their paintings between Tibetan (within the halls) and Chinese (in the outer gallery). While one might be tempted to dismiss the Tibetan elements that appear in otherwise Chinese architectural contexts found at temples such as Qutan Monastery as simply resulting from their close proximity to the Sino-Tibetan border – in other words, as a marker of their 'regionalism' or 'provincialism' – evidence presented here suggests that a more complex and imperially sponsored formation of Sino-Tibetan art was operative in the Ming court, both in the centre of power, Beijing, and in the outer reaches of the empire.

To put it another way, as Shane McCausland observed in his remarks after the presentation of this paper at the British Museum conference, this evidence suggests a Ming royal awareness and participation in regional and blended modes of artistic practice, their awareness of the agency of such patronage, and that all of this was indeed part of Ming policy. I would add that, rather than a Ming innovation, this was built on a firm foundation of Mongolian precedence in order to project themselves as rulers on the Inner Asian model, moulded in the image of Qubilai Khan.

Notes

1 This chapter is an abbreviated discussion based on chapters 2 and 3 of my dissertation, 'Ethnicity and Esoteric Power: Negotiating Sino-Tibetan Synthesis in Ming Buddhist Painting' (Debreczeny 2007), some of the findings of which were previously published in Debreczeny 2003. Thanks to Elliot Sperling, Shane McCausland, Yu-Ping Luk, Craig Clunas and Jessica Harrison-Hall.

2 Hongwu patronised several Tibetan lamas and their monastic projects, including Qutan Monastery's founder Sangyé Tashi (Sangs rgyas bkra shis; Ch. Lama Sanluo 剌麻三囉; d. 1414) in Qinghai province. See Sperling 2001.

3 For instance, the head of the Sakya order Kunga Tashi Gyaltsen (Kun dga' bkra shis rgyal mtshan; 1349–1424) played an important political role in both Yuan and Ming court connections with Gyantse (rGyal rtse).

4 This sculpture of Mahākāla was counted among the objects of inheritance symbolic of Mongol rule alongside Chinggis Khan's spirit banner and the imperial seal. For more on the political role of Mahākāla (and Pañjaranātha in particular) within the Mongol empire see Grupper 1979 and Debreczeny 2014.

5 Stoddard 1985.

6 Prince Zhuang of Liang (1411–41), was a grandson of Yongle and brother of Xuande. At least one other golden image of Pañjaranātha Mahākāla was also found in the same tomb, along with other Tibetan Buddhist imagery. See Hubei sheng wenwu kaogu yanjiusuo and Zhongxiang shi bowuguan 2007; and Hubei sheng bowuguan 2007.

7 Also explored in Robinson 2008.

8 Tsai 2001, 29–33.

9 Sperling 1983, 74–6.

10 Tsai 2001, 84.

11 Sperling 1983.
12 Sperling 2004.
13 Sperling 1983, 140.
14 See Clunas and Harrison-Hall 2014, 54, fig. 29 and 239, fig. 208.
15 For example Clunas and Harrison-Hall 2014, 227, fig. 195, and 229, fig. 199.
16 'Standing Buddha', Xuande reign mark (1426–35), gilt bronze. Height 64cm, Musée Cernuschi, M.C.686. See Clunas and Harrison-Hall 2014, 207, fig. 175. The statue was believed to have been commissioned by the Indian king Udayana of Kosambi/Kausambi. The sandalwood statue was believed to have been brought to China in the 4th century by way of Khotan and inspired many copies. See Tanaka 1999, 52; Jackson 1996, fig. 42; Jackson 2012, 175, fig. 8.19.
17 See Jackson 2012, 173–6.
18 See Debreczeny 2007, 104–7; and Jackson 2009, 96–7.
19 See Patricia Berger 2001; and Clunas and Harrison-Hall 2014, 239, fig. 208.
20 For example, Fong Wen and Watt 1996, 329.
21 The scroll is now among the holdings of the Board of Management for Cultural Relics of the Autonomous Region of Tibet, described in Xizang zizhiqu wenwu guanli weiyuan hui 1981, which reproduces the Chinese text. The Tibetan text is not published. Sperling 2011.
22 Sperling 2011.
23 Mao Qiling 1982.
24 The *Wuzong wai ji* confuses *fan* 番 (Tibetan) with the homophone *fan* 梵 (Sanskrit), a common mistake in Chinese sources.
25 See Richardson 1959, 6–8, and Appendix B, 16–17; and Sperling 1980a.
26 Translated by Richardson 1959, 6–8, and transliterated in Appendix B, 16–17.
27 dPa' bo gTsug lag phreng ba 1986, *mKhas pa'i dga ston*, 1241; Richardson 1958, 151–3.
28 Sperling 1980a.
29 Richardson 1975.
30 Weidner 2009a.
31 See Debreczeny 1997, 2003, and 2007. For an image of the exterior see Clunas and Harrison-Hall 2014, 36, fig. 14.
32 Debreczeny 2003, 51; and Debreczeny 2007, 97–148 (especially 134–6). These *maṇḍala* are also described in detail in Toyka-Fuong 2010, though their function and how they fit into the overall programme of the temple are not discussed.
33 For a translation of Śākya Yeshé's biography see Debreczeny 1997, 50–58. On Śākya Yeshé at the Ming court and his possible involvement with the founding of Fahai Monastery see Debreczeny 2007, 138–42. For an image see Clunas and Harrison-Hall 2014, 242, fig. 209.
34 For a translation of Palden Tashi's biography see Debreczeny 2007, Appendix II, 399–414. For an image see Clunas and Harrison-Hall 2014, 245, fig. 211.
35 It seems likely that the eunuch Yuan Qi on Qutan Monastery's 1427 Wansui Tablet is the same Chinese official to whom Palden Tashi gave full ordination vows (see p. 161 and Debreczeny 2007, 151 and 181).
36 Qutan Monastery's abbots also played an important role in the formulation of early Ming policies towards Tibet. See Sperling 2001.
37 Tuttle 2011.
38 Sadly space constraints here prevent me from delving into the beautiful wall paintings in the surrounding covered gallery which depict the life of the Buddha. Suffice it to say, there are only a few subtle hints of a Tibetan context in the surviving 11 panels of Ming paintings, but more overt Tibetan elements do appear in the later Qing restorations (*c.* 1837–8). On the covered gallery see Xie Jisheng and Liao Yang 2006b.
39 However, his 'appointment' may be nothing more than nominal recognition of Palden Tashi's abbotship at Qutan Monastery, as this was true for many of the largely ceremonial appointments and titles bestowed on Tibetan patriarchs and local rulers by the Ming court, following the traditional uncle-nephew system of succession.
40 dKon mchog bstan pa rab rgyas 1987, 171–2.
41 Palden Zangpo (dPal ldan bzang po) is another name for Palden Tashi. See Debreczeny 2007, 150, 218.
42 dKon mchog bstan pa rab rgyas 1987, 172. This would correspond to the construction of Baoguang Hall and the bestowal of its main image, a golden Buddha, as recorded in a pair of bilingual stele: the 'Yongle Imperial Decree Stele of 1418' (永樂十六年瞿曇寺皇帝敕諭碑; Tib: rGyal po'i lung gis) dated to the twenty-second day of the first month of the sixteenth year of the Yongle period (1418), and the 'Imperial Bestowal of Qutan Monastery's Golden Buddha Image Stele' (御制瞿曇寺金佛像碑; Tib: *rGyal pos gser sku la bstod pa'i rdo ring*) dated to the first day of the third month of the sixteenth year of Yongle (1418) located in front of the temple (see Xie Zuo 1982, 83–9). The stele gives the name of the hall in Chinese as Baoguang Hall (Tib: B'u gwong sde), while the *mDo smad chos 'byung* gives the Tibetan name Jo khang Rin chen 'od 'bar, both meaning 'Blazing Jewel Light', and clearly describing the same hall.
43 'Imperial Bestowal of Qutan Monastery's Golden Buddha Image Stele' reproduced in Xie Zuo 1998, 86–9.
44 dKon mchog bstan pa rab rgyas 1987, 172.
45 Both Tibetan and Chinese texts are reproduced in Xie Zuo 1998, 96–100.
46 dKon mchog bstan pa rab rgyas 1987, 681. See also Debreczeny 2007, 151 and 181.
47 Xie Zuo 1998, 61.

Chapter 18

Religious Consciousness and Beliefs in the Ming Tombs of Princes and Royal Family Members in Hubei Province

Yuan Wenqing

Translated by Luk Yu-ping

The founder of the Ming dynasty, Zhu Yuanzhang 朱元璋 (1328–98), established a system of princely enfeoffment that aimed to use blood relations to maintain control of the empire. Royal princes were sent to live away from the capital, usually in major cities and economically prosperous areas around China. The Hubei 湖北 region possessed favourable environmental conditions, a flourishing economy and rich cultural heritage. Located in the central plains, it was also an area of political and military importance. Consequently, it became one of the regions where the largest number of Ming princes was enfeoffed, and where the most Ming royal tombs have been discovered and excavated to date. One of the interesting features of Ming royal tombs found in Hubei is the diverse religious elements they reveal. This chapter examines the archaeological finds from several major Ming royal tombs in the region, focusing on material that expresses the beliefs and religious inclinations of the tomb occupants.

Hubei province during the Ming dynasty

Hubei province is located in central China along the middle section of the Yangtze River. It has long enjoyed fame as a fertile 'land of fish and rice' (*Yumi zhi xiang* 魚米之鄉) with developed agricultural and fishing economies. The saying 'Huguang's harvest meets the needs of all under Heaven' (*Huguang shou, tianxia zhu* 湖廣熟, 天下足) suggests the richness of this region.

In 1364, Zhu Yuanzhang conquered the Jingxiang 荊湘 region and established the Huguang Branch Secretariat (*Huguang xing zhongshusheng* 湖廣行中書省). In 1376, after the founding of the Ming dynasty, this became the Huguang Provincial Administrative Commission (*Huguang buzheng shisi* 湖廣布政使司), which oversaw an area that included present-day Hubei and Hunan 湖南 provinces. The territory that remains part of present-day Hubei includes six prefectures (*fu* 府) – Wuchang 武昌, Hanyang 漢陽, Huangzhou 黃州, De'an 德安 (now Anlu 安陸), Jingzhou 荊州 and Xiangyang 襄陽; two departments (*zhou* 州) – Anlu 安陸 (now Zhongxiang 鐘祥) and Mianyang 沔陽; as well as E'xi 鄂西, where a Military Command of Soldiers and Civilians of the Shizhou Guard (*Shizhou wei junmin zhihui shisi* 施州衛軍民指揮使司) was established. In 1531, Anlu department became Chengtian 承天 prefecture. The basic administrative and organisational structure of modern Hubei was thus formed.

With its prosperous economy and rich culture, Hubei nurtured many accomplished individuals during the Ming dynasty. Renowned officials include Yang Pu 楊溥 (1372–1446), a member of the early Ming Grand Secretariat, and Zhang Juzheng 張居正 (1525–82), Grand Secretary of the Wanli 萬曆 reign (1573–1620). The brothers Yuan Zongdao 袁宗道 (1560–1600), Yuan Hongdao 袁宏道 (1568–1610) and Yuan Zhongdao 袁中道 (1570–1623), as well as Zhong Xing 鐘惺 (1574–1624) and Tan Yuanchun 譚元春 (1586–1637), were writers who left important marks in the history of Chinese literature. The 'sage of medicine' Li Shizhen 李時珍 (1518–93) was also a native of the province.

In addition, the religious culture of Hubei was well developed and influential during the Ming dynasty. Mount Wudang 武當山 at Shiyan 十堰 is a renowned Daoist centre that flourished under the patronage of the Yongle 永樂 emperor (r. 1403–24) in the early Ming. Huangmei 黄梅 is a sacred Chan Buddhist site that has been the focus of pilgrimage since the Tang dynasty (618–907). Yuquansi 玉泉寺 (Monastery of Jade Spring) at Dangyang 當陽, the Duobao fota 多寶佛塔 (Buddhist Pagoda of Many Treasures) of Guangdesi 廣德寺 (Monastery of Spreading Virtue) at Xiangyang 襄陽 and the Daoist temple complex at Mount Wudang are all classified as major historical and cultural sites protected at national level.

The spread of Ming royal family members in Hubei province

Thirteen princely lineages were established in Hubei during the Ming dynasty. Among the royal descendants who were enfeoffed there, 45 were princes of the first rank (*qinwang* 親王) and 50 were commandery princes (*junwang* 郡王). Together with princesses and lower-ranked princes with titles such as Defender-General of the State (*Zhenguo jiangjun* 鎮國將軍), Bulwark-General of the State (*Fuguo jiangjun* 輔國將軍) and Supporter-General of the State (*Fengguo jiangjun* 奉國將軍), an extensive royal clan was established.

Four of the Ming founder's sons were given titles and subsequently enfeoffed in Hubei. Three of them established royal courts in the region during their father's reign (1368–98). They were Zhu Zhen 朱楨 (1364–1424), Prince Zhao of Chu 楚昭王, in Wuchang; Zhu Bo 朱柏 (1371–99), Prince Xian of Xiang 湘獻王, in Jingzhou; and Zhu Dong 朱楝 (1388–1414), Prince Jing of Ying 郢靖王, in Zhongxiang. A fourth prince, Zhu Zhi 朱植 (1378–1424), Prince Jian of Liao 遼簡王, was relocated to Jingzhou during the Yongle period.

The Hongxi 洪熙 emperor (r. 1425), the fourth emperor of the Ming dynasty, had three sons who were enfeoffed in Hubei: Zhu Zhanshan 朱瞻墡 (1406–78), Prince Xian of Xiang 襄憲王, in Xiangyang; Zhu Zhan'gang 朱瞻堈 (1406–53), Prince Xian of Jing 荊憲王, in Qichun 蘄春; and Zhu Zhanji 朱瞻垍 (1411–41), Prince Zhuang of Liang 梁莊王, in Zhongxiang.

The Chenghua 成化 emperor (r. 1465–87), the eighth emperor of the Ming dynasty, also had three sons who were enfeoffed in Hubei: Zhu Youyuan 朱祐杬 (1476–1519), Prince Xian of Xing 興獻王, in Zhongxiang; Zhu Youlun 朱祐棆 (1478–1501), Prince Hui of Qi 岐惠王, in Anlu; and Zhu Youzhi 朱祐榰 (1481–1545), Prince Ding of Shou 壽定王, in Anlu.

The Jiajing 嘉靖 emperor (r. 1522–66), the 11th emperor of the Ming dynasty, had one son enfeoffed in Hubei: Zhu Zaizhen 朱載圳 (1537–65), Prince Gong of Jing 景恭王, in Anlu. The emperor also posthumously enfeoffed his elder brother Zhu Houxi 朱厚熙 (1500) as Prince Huai of Yue 岳懷王 in Zhongxiang. Likewise, the Wanli emperor (r. 1573–1620), the 13th emperor of the Ming dynasty, had one son enfeoffed in Hubei: Zhu Changrun 朱常潤 (1594–1647), Prince of Hui 惠王, in Jingzhou.

A significant number of tombs belonging to individual princes, consorts and royal couples have been excavated in Hubei province. They include those of Prince Jian of Liao (Jingzhou), Prince Zhao of Chu (Wuchang), Prince Xian of Xiang (Jingzhou), Prince Zhuang of Liang (Zhongxiang) and Prince Jing of Ying (Zhongxiang). Important archaeological discoveries of tombs belonging to other Ming royal family members have also been made in Wuchang, Jingzhou, Xiangyang and Qichun.

Religious elements in the Ming royal tombs in Hubei province

The excavated Ming royal tombs in Hubei show distinct religious elements. Analysis of tomb settings and burial objects can reveal the different beliefs of Ming princes and their family members. This chapter will consider archaeological finds from the tombs of Prince Zhao of Chu, Prince Xian of Xiang, Prince Jing of Ying and Lady Guo 郭 (d. 1414), Prince Zhuang of Liang and Lady Wei 魏 (d. 1451), Lady Liu 劉氏 (d. 1560), the secondary consort of one of the princes of Jing, and other family members of the Prince of Jing lineage at Qichun, in order to discuss their religious characteristics and influences.

Daoist features in the tomb of Prince Zhao of Chu

Prince Zhao of Chu, Zhu Zhen, was the sixth son of Zhu Yuanzhang. He became the Prince of Chu in 1370, and was enfeoffed in Wuchang in 1381. In 1424, he died of illness and was buried at Mount Lingquan 靈泉山 with the posthumous title *zhao* 昭.[1] The Hubei Provincial Institute of Cultural Relics and Archaeology led the excavation of the tomb in 1991.[2] The form of the tomb, its burial objects and the burial practice it reveals are unique among Ming royal tombs excavated to date.

The tomb complex of Prince Zhao of Chu is monumental in scale, with majestic above-ground architecture, which corresponds to Ming regulations. However, the underground site itself is very small and consists of a single chamber. It is the only example of its kind among the excavated tombs of contemporary first-rank princes, which are normally arranged in the shape of the Chinese character *ya* 亞.

Moreover, the tomb of Prince Zhao of Chu contains the smallest number of burial objects so far found in tombs of first-rank princes from that time. The only objects indicating his rank are a conferring tablet and a royal seal. He was not buried with any ceremonial headdresses; his belt is made of gold mounts with wooden plaques (instead of plaques made of precious stones), and there is no evidence of human sacrifices or wooden figurines in the tomb. On the whole, this can be considered a 'simple burial' (*bozang* 薄葬).

In addition to being modest in terms of size and burial objects, the interior setting of Prince Zhao of Chu's tomb is notable as five talismans or 'numinous tablets' (*lingpai* 靈牌) have been placed at the east, south, west, north and central parts of the burial chamber. Furthermore, in front of the coffin platform is a stone altar table (**Pl. 18.1**), on top of which are five bronze ceremonial offering objects (*wugong* 五供), consisting of an incense burner, two candlesticks and two vases. The form of the stone altar table bears a close resemblance to a bronze altar table found in the Golden Hall (*Jindian* 金殿) at the peak of Mount Wudang (**Pl. 18.2**). This suggests that the setting inside the tomb of Prince Zhao of Chu may have been emulating the Daoist features of the Golden Hall.

There are clearly distinct Daoist elements in the tomb of Prince Zhao of Chu, which may help to explain the simple burial that was afforded the prince. Instead of emphasising lavish burials, Daoists believe in seeking to attain

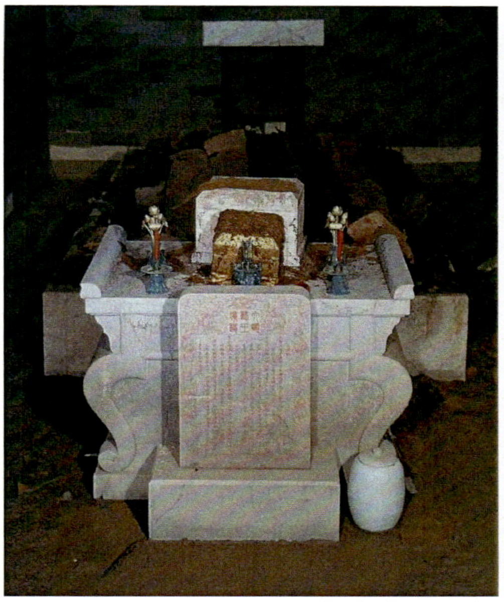

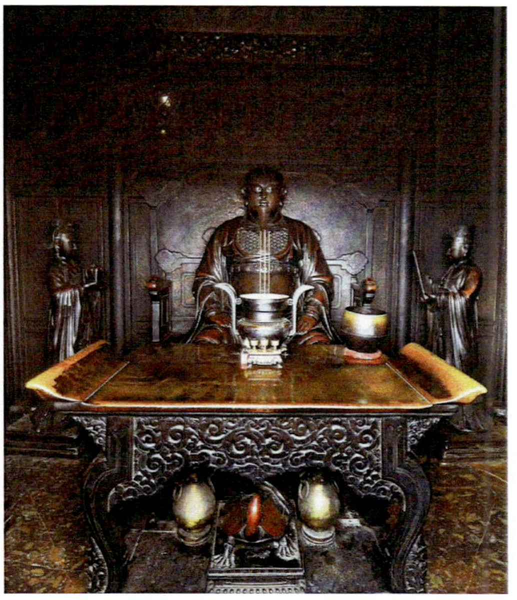

Plate 18.1 (left) Stone altar table in the tomb of Prince Zhao of Chu (1364–1424)

Plate 18.2 (right) Bronze altar table in the Golden Hall, Mount Wudang

transcendence to the divine (*yuhua shengtian* 羽化升天). It is possible that Prince Zhao of Chu was a lay Daoist follower (*xinshi* 信士 or *jushi* 居士) during his lifetime.

The absence of distinct Daoist elements in the tomb of Prince Xian of Xiang

Prince Xian of Xiang, Zhu Bo, was the 12th son of Zhu Yuanzhang.[3] In 1378, he became the Prince of Xiang, and in 1385 he was enfeoffed in Jiangling 江陵, present-day Jingzhou. In 1399, the Jianwen 建文 emperor (r. 1399–1402) denounced the prince, causing him to commit suicide with his consort Lady Wu 吳 in a fire. The emperor imposed upon him the posthumous title *li* 戾 (criminal). Under the Yongle emperor, his posthumous title was changed to *xian* 獻 (contributor) and he was granted a burial without his corpse (*yiguanzhong* 衣冠塚; literally, tomb with garment and hat), next to the Daoist Taihuiguan 太暉觀 (Abbey of Great Radiance) in Jiangling 江陵, where it was guarded by official clerics.

Among the four first-generation Ming princes enfeoffed in Hubei, only the personal beliefs of Prince Xian of Xiang have been clearly recorded. He was known to have venerated Daoism while he was alive. He was well versed in Daoist teachings and used the Daoist-style sobriquet 'Follower of the Purple Void' (Zixuzi 紫虛子).[4] During the first month of 1399, the prince participated in a Daoist offering ritual at Mount Wudang, at the conclusion of which he tossed a gold figure of a dragon, a jade disk and a jade tablet on to the mountain, which were buried.[5] In 1982, these items were discovered underneath Cijian Platform 賜劍台 in front of Zixiaodian 紫霄殿 (Hall of Purple Cloud). The carved inscription on the jade tablet provides evidence of the prince's profound belief in Daoism:

> Now Prince of Xiang, disciple of the Three Effulgences, from the Great Cavern of the Mysterious Capital of Highest Clarity, at the present Upper-prime Festival, establishes the Numinous Altar of the Three Effulgences of Great Radiance at the Abbey of Great Radiance (Taihuiguan), to perform the Great Universal Heavenly Offering of the Numinous Treasure of the Supreme Cavern of Mystery that Venerates the Perfected, Performs Teachings, Benefits the State and Its People, and Delivers the Living and the Dead, with 1200 parts in total, over 5 days and nights. Now that the performance of the Way has been complete, the tablet is tossed into the numinous mountains. Praying to deities and transcendents for longevity across generations and ascension towards Highest Clarity. Perfected Being of the Five Marchmounts, the most sagely and most numinous, one begs for the deletion of the record of sins, and for one's name to be raised to the Nine Heavens. Calling upon the numinous mountains, this message is relayed by the golden dragon. In the first year of the Jianwen reign [1399], in the *yimao* year, the first month *shenshuo* of the fifteenth day *bingwu*. The Ritual Master of the Scripture and Register of the Great Cavern of Highest Clarity, subject Zhou Sili, announces this at the auspicious lands of Mount Wudang.
>
> 今謹有上清大洞玄都三景弟子湘王，以今上元令節，開建太暉觀太暉三景靈壇，啟修無上洞玄靈寶崇真演教福國裕民濟生度死普天大齋，計一千二伯（百）分，通五晝宵。今則行道事竟，投簡靈山。願神願仙，長生度世，飛行上清。五嶽真人，至聖至靈，乞削罪錄，上名九天，請詣靈山，金龍驛傳。建文元年歲次已卯正月申朔十五丙戌。上清大洞經籙法師臣周思禮于武當山福地告聞。[6]

In December 1997, the Jingzhou Museum undertook a rescue excavation of the tomb of Prince Xian of Xiang.[7] Among the burial objects found in the tomb are a royal seal made of wood covered in gold leaf, and a relatively large quantity of wooden figurines. The only burial object that has some connection to religion is a string of 12 bronze coins, inscribed with auspicious sayings such as 'Peace under Heaven' (*tianxia taiping* 天下太平) and 'Winds are regular and rain fall in season' (*fengtiao yushun* 風調雨順). The setting of the tomb and other burial objects do not show clear Daoist or other religious elements. It seems that since the tomb was a burial without the prince's corpse, all the arrangements were made according to Ming court regulations, and the prince's religious beliefs when he was alive were not featured.

The equal representation of Confucianism, Buddhism and Daoism in the tomb of Prince Jing of Ying and Lady Guo

Born in 1388, Prince Jing of Ying, Zhu Dong, was Zhu Yuanzhang's 24th son. In 1391 he was made the Prince of

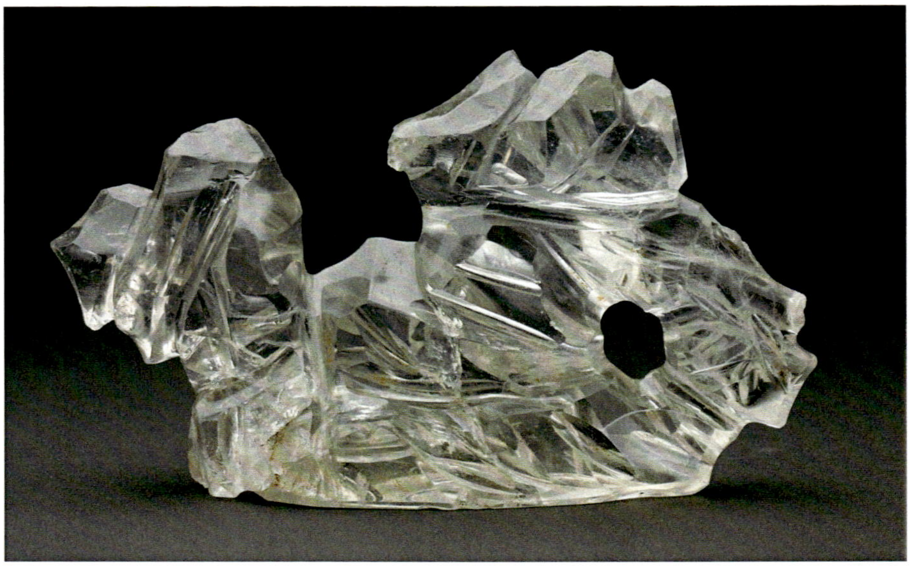

Plate 18.3 Crystal brush rest, excavated from the tomb of Prince Jing of Ying (1388–1414). Hubei Provincial Museum

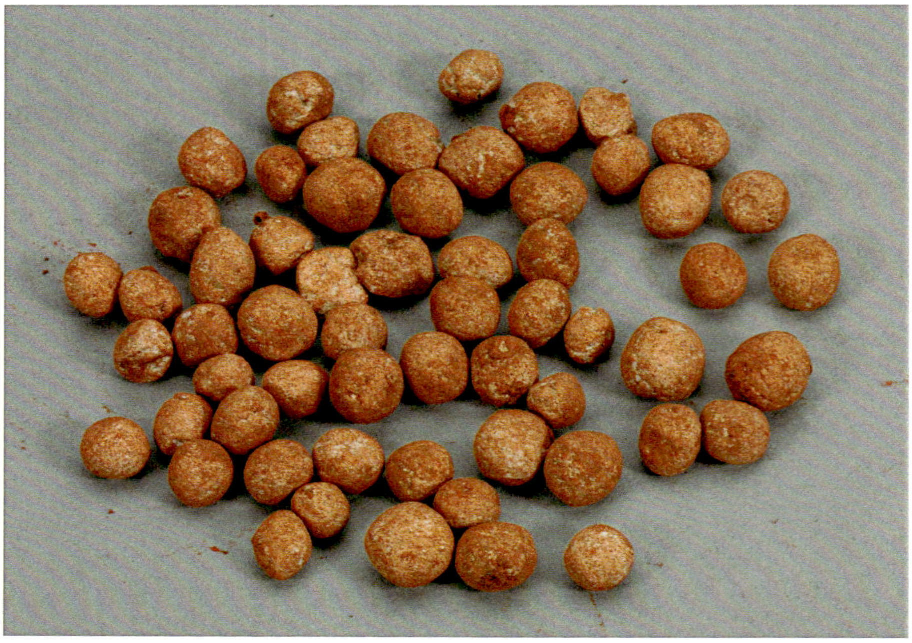

Plate 18.4 Elixirs used in Daoist practice, excavated from the tomb of Prince Jing of Ying (1388–1414). Hubei Provincial Museum

Ying, and was enfeoffed in Anlu (present-day Zhongxiang City) in 1408.[8] He passed away at the age of 27 in 1414 and was granted the posthumous title *jing* 靖. His consort Lady Guo 郭 (d. 1414) died shortly after him. The tomb that the couple share has been excavated by the Hubei Provincial Institute of Cultural Relics and Archaeology.[9]

The underground tomb consists of five chambers arranged in the shape of the Chinese character *ya* 亞, which conforms to burial practices at the time. The coffins of the couple are placed side by side on top of a platform. Six further bodies have been discovered in the tomb; they are believed to have been sacrificed. The east and west chambers of the tomb each contain three red-lacquered wooden coffins that have decomposed, but traces of them can still be observed. There are also signs that porcelain vases were once placed in front of the heads of the coffins. These correspond with actual vases that have been discovered in the tomb. Judging from dental remains, the six people who were sacrificed in the burial had not yet reached adulthood. The phenomenon of human sacrifice is relatively rare in the Ming royal tombs of Hubei, although according to textual sources it was customary for the burials of early Ming emperors. The tomb of Prince Jing of Ying and Lady Guo provides archaeological evidence of this cruel practice in the early Ming period.

Religious features in the tomb of Prince Jing of Ying and Lady Guo can be observed mainly in its burial objects, which highlight an equal representation of Confucian, Buddhist and Daoist elements.

Prince Jing of Ying is buried with items that he favoured in life, mostly functional scholarly objects, including *duan* 端 and *she* 歙 inkstones, a mountain-shaped crystal brush stand (**Pl. 18.3**), a bronze water-dropper in the shape of a three-legged toad and an agate paperweight in the shape of a dragon-beast. The back of the *she* inkstone is inscribed 'Studio of the Book Hermit' (*Shuyin zhai* 書隱齋), which denotes the name of the prince's study. This suggests the prince was a 'Confucian scholar' who was well versed in the classics.

Elixirs (*xiandan* 仙丹) used in Daoist practices have also been discovered in the tomb (**Pl. 18.4**). This is a very important

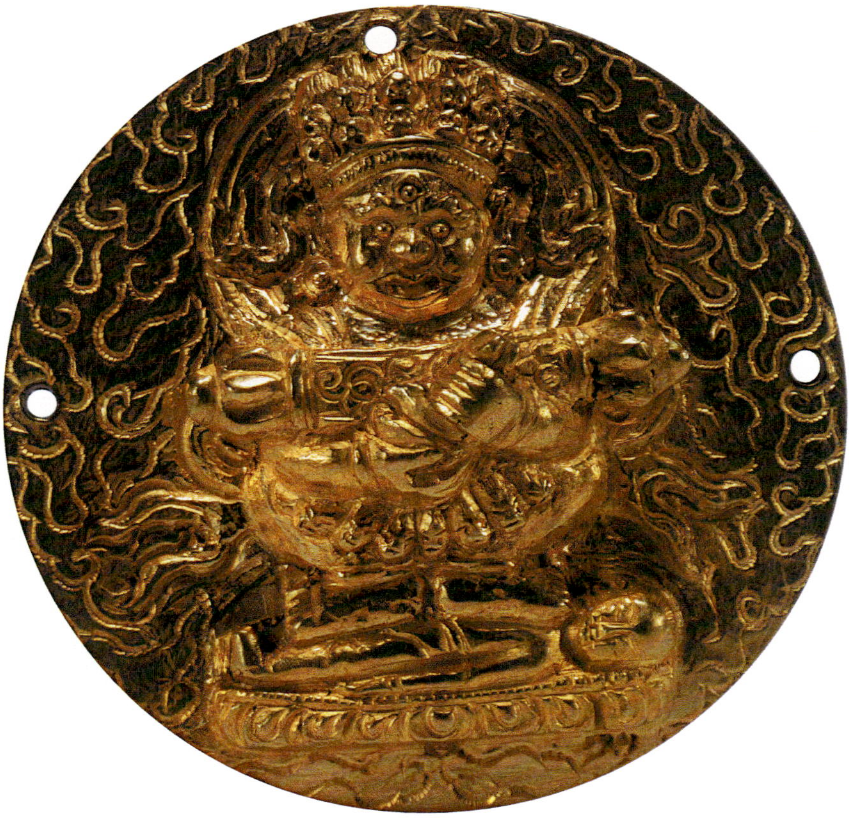

Plate 18.5 Plaque of Mahākāla, excavated from the tomb of Prince Zhuang of Liang (1411–41) and Lady Wei (d. 1451) at Zhongxiang, Hubei province. Gold, height 3.1cm, weight 27.4g. Hubei Provincial Museum

discovery. The consumption of elixirs is related to Daoism, and it provides evidence of the prince's belief in the religion. It may also offer a reason for the prince's premature death.

Lady Guo's burial objects contain relatively more Buddhist items, such as *vájra* (stylised thunderbolt) and Buddhist prayer beads. These show that Lady Guo, and probably Prince Jing of Ying, venerated Buddhism as well.

Buddhist elements in the tomb of Prince Zhuang of Liang

Prince Zhuang of Liang, Zhu Zhanji , was the ninth son of the Hongxi emperor. Born in 1411, he was made the Prince of Liang in 1424, and was enfeoffed in Anlu (present-day Zhongxiang) in 1429. In 1441, he passed away due to illness. Ten years after his death, his consort Lady Wei 魏氏 (d. 1451) passed away and was interred in the same tomb. From April to May 2001, a rescue excavation was conducted on the tomb under the supervision of the Hubei Provincial Institute of Cultural Relics and Archaeology.[10]

Prince Zhuang of Liang lived during the Yongle to the Zhengtong periods, while Lady Guo lived into the Jingtai reign – a time when the Ming economy was at its peak. A large number and variety of high-quality gold, silver and jade vessels, as well as jewellery and precious stones, have been found in the tomb. These have survived in good condition.

Among the many gold objects buried in the tomb, some of the most striking are Tibetan Buddhist objects: images of the deities Mahākāla (**Pl. 18.5**; see also **Pl. 17.3**) and Garuda, Sanskrit *bījas* (seed syllables) (**Pl. 18.6**), a mantra tablet (**Pl. 18.7**) and *vájra* thunderbolts (**Pl. 18.8**). There are

Plate 18.6 Seed syllables, excavated from the tomb of Prince Zhuang of Liang (1411–41) and Lady Wei (d. 1451) at Zhongxiang, Hubei province. Gold, left: height 2.8cm, width 2cm; right: height 2.9cm, width 2.1cm. Hubei Provincial Museum

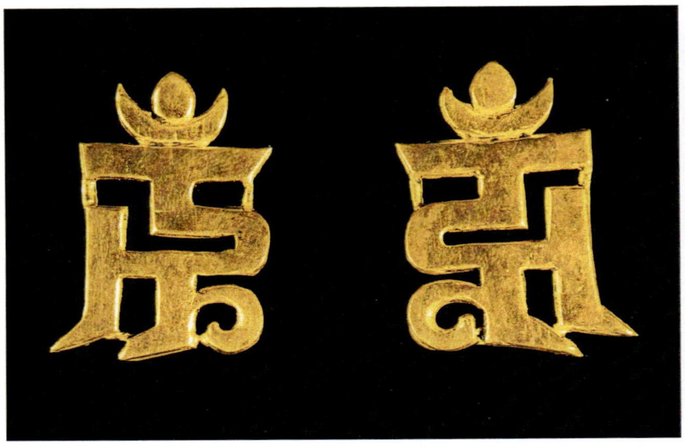

Plate 18.7 Mantra tablet, excavated from the tomb of Prince Zhuang of Liang (1411–41) and Lady Wei (d. 1451) at Zhongxiang, Hubei province. Gold, weight 9.4g, diameter 5.3cm. Hubei Provincial Museum

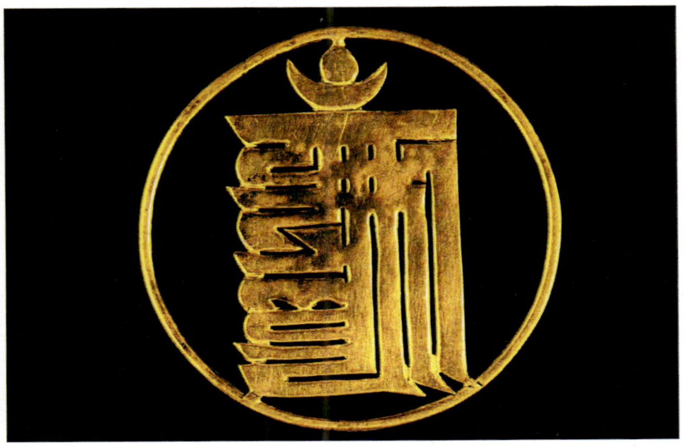

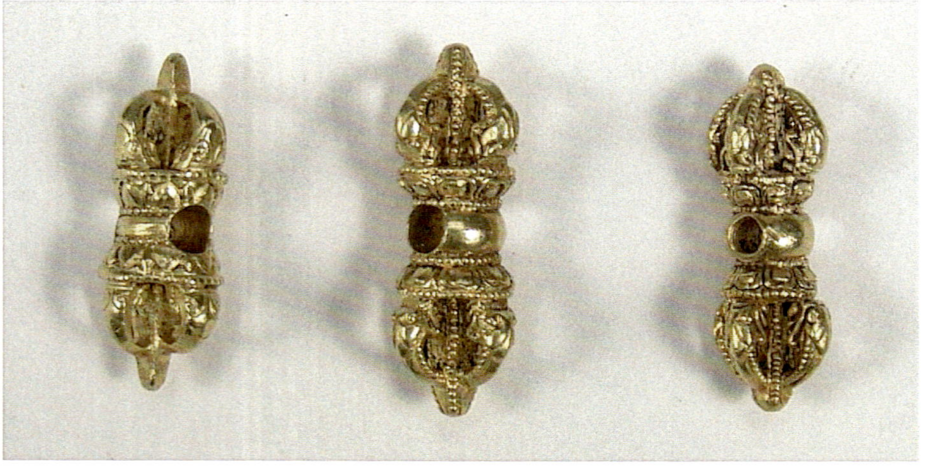

Plate 18.8 *Vájra* thunderbolts, excavated from the tomb of Prince Zhuang of Liang (1411–41) and Lady Wei (d. 1451) at Zhongxiang, Hubei province. Gold, length 2.4cm–2.6cm. Hubei Provincial Museum

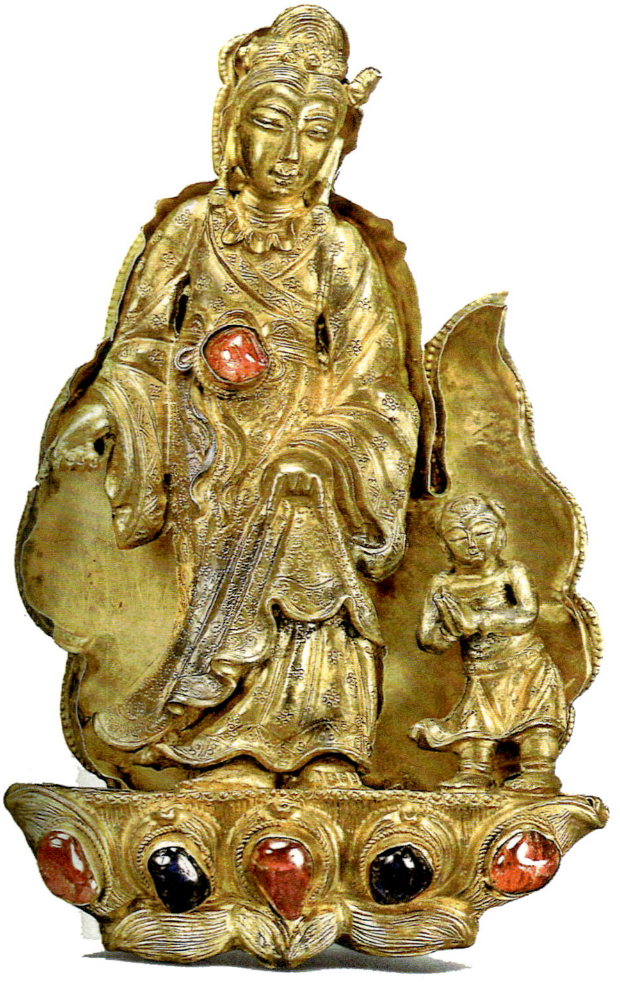

Plate 18.9 Figure of the Bodhisattva Guanyin, excavated from the tombs of Ming royal family members located in Qichun. Gold with semi-precious stones, height 8.6cm, width 5.4cm, weight 39g. Hubei Provincial Museum

also gold-covered wooden prayer beads, prayer beads made of crystal and bone, jade and bone head beads, as well as jade in the shape of an endless knot and turquoise in the shape of a double-fish, both Buddhist symbols.

These burial objects indicate that the tomb occupants were followers of Tibetan Buddhism, which flourished during the Yuan dynasty (1271–1368). The various sects of the religion were still venerated by the Ming courts during the Hongwu and Yongle periods. The large number of Tibetan Buddhist objects in the tomb of Prince Zhuang of Liang and Lady Guo reflects the popularity of Tibetan Buddhism in the upper echelons of society at the time. The discovery of these precious objects is significant for the understanding of social attitudes, Sino-Tibetan relations and the spread of Tibetan Buddhism to the interior of China during the early Ming dynasty.

Buddhist and Daoist elements in the tombs of the Prince of Jing lineage

The Prince of Jing of the first generation, Zhu Zhan'gang, was the sixth son of the Hongxi emperor. He was made Prince of Jing in 1424 and enfeoffed in Jianchang 建昌 (present-day Nancheng 南城 county) in Jiangxi province in 1429. In 1445, he was re-enfeoffed in Qizhou (present-day Qichun). The title of the Prince of Jing was subsequently passed down to eleven princes over ten generations.

While a considerable number of artefacts have been found in the tombs of royal family members of the Prince of Jing lineage, there is a paucity of information based on scientific excavations. The only archaeological findings that have been published are on the tomb of Lady Liu 劉 (d. 1560), who was the second consort of Prince Duan of Jing 荊端王, Zhu Houquan 朱厚烇 (d. 1553).[11] The burial goods excavated from her tomb mainly consist of gold, silver and bronze items. Among the many gold and silver objects, there are gold hairpins in the shape of phoenixes and flowers, gold pendants, gold phoenix crowns, gold rings inlaid with gems, and a silver cup and box, all of which are of high quality. Objects with religious significance include gold and silver coins for the deceased inscribed '*a mi tuo fo*' 阿彌陀佛 (Amitābha) and '*zao sheng tian jie*' 早生天界 (quick rebirth in heaven), which are clearly related to Buddhism. *Tianjie* 天界 (heaven) in this context refers to one of the ten dharma realms of Buddhism that pertains to the condition of rapture.

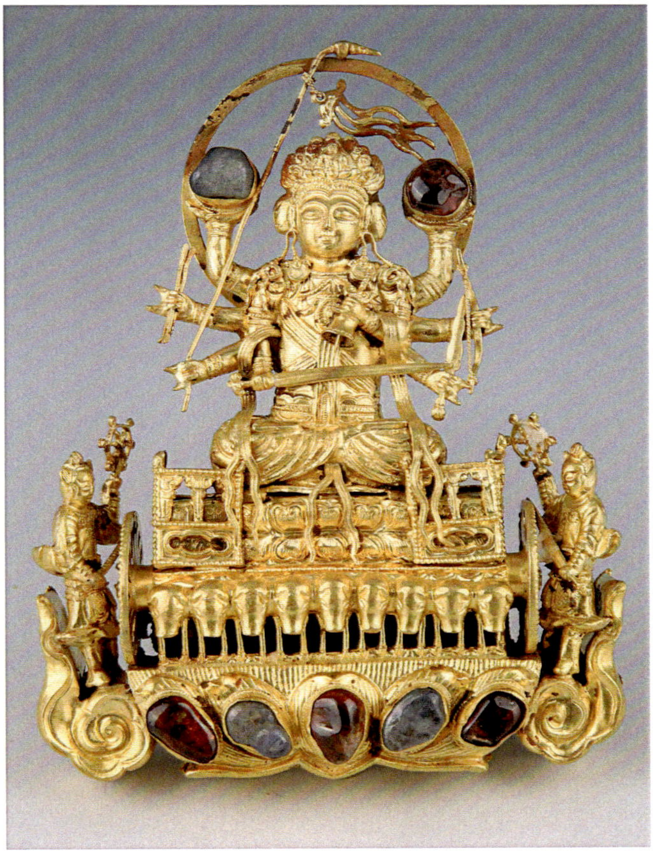

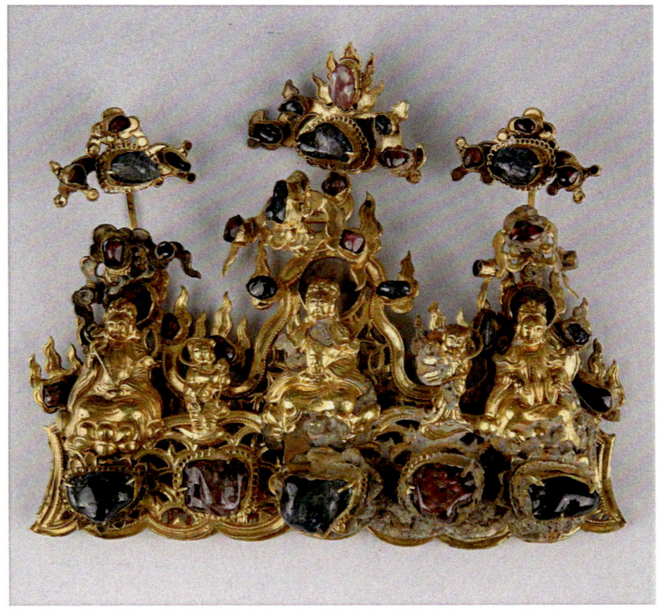

Plate 18.10 (left) Figure of Mārīcī, excavated from the tombs of Ming royal family members located in Qichun. Gold with semi-precious stones, height 11.7cm; width 8.8cm, depth 2cm, weight 129.9g. Qichun Museum, Qichun, Hubei province

Plate 18.11 (above) Figure of the Three Pure Ones, excavated from the tombs of Ming royal family members located in Qichun. Gold with semi-precious stones, height 12cm, width 14cm, weight 136.6g. Qichun Museum, Qichun, Hubei province

A larger number of religious objects made of gold and silver have been found in the tombs of Ming royal family members located in Qichun. Among the discoveries are Han Chinese Buddhist images, such as of the Bodhisattva Guanyin 觀音 (**Pl. 18.9**), as well as Tibetan Buddhist subject matter, such as the deity Mārīcī (**Pl. 18.10**). A representation of the Three Pure Ones (*Sanqing* 三清), the supreme deities of Daoism (**Pl. 18.11**), is particularly notable, as it is rare among gold and silver images from the period. While these objects are undoubtedly luxury items owned by royal family members of the Prince of Jing lineage, they are also objects that provide their owners with spiritual solace and support.

Conclusion

Analysis of the royal tombs in Hubei reveals many burial customs and objects that are closely related to religious beliefs. Princes and royal family members, from different areas and time periods, held diverse religious attitudes.

Historically, Confucianism, Buddhism and Daoism intermingled, influenced and propelled one another. In their engagement with different religions, members of the Ming royal family selected aspects that suited their needs. On the whole, the strategy of the Ming government towards religions involved accommodation, utilisation and control. Confucianism remained the basis for governing the state, as expressed in the Ming founder's instruction to his sons:

> To explain the classics and histories, cultivate one's moral character, connect the ancient and the present, so that one can carry the weight of the state of all under Heaven.
>
> 講說經史，蓄養德性，博通古今，庶可以存籍天下國家之重[12]

Diversity in religious attitudes led to diversity in religious life. This is evident in the tombs and burial objects of Ming princes and their relatives. Religious accommodation and appropriation had become the mainstream. This shows that Ming royal family members still had considerable freedom to make their own choices with regards to religious beliefs.

Notes

1 Zhu Zhen's biography is recorded in his tomb epitaph. See Hubei sheng wenwu kaogu yanjiusuo *et al.* 2003, 17.
2 Hubei sheng wenwu kaogu yanjiusuo *et al.* 2003. For discussions in English about this tomb, see Clunas 2005–6, 3–7; Yang Xiaoneng 2006, 43–4.
3 For the biography of Prince Xian of Xiang, see *MS* 117, 3581. For discussions in English about this prince, see Clunas 2013, 54–5.
4 For a discussion of Ming princes and Daoism, including Prince Xian of Xiang, see Wang 2012.
5 Wang Yucheng 1994, 148–9.
6 Transcribed from tablet. See also Wang Yucheng 1994, 148.
7 Jingzhou bowuguan 2009.
8 Prince Jing of Ying's biography is recorded in his tomb epitaph. See Yuan Wenqing, Long Yongfang and Zhou Daiwei 2007, 50.
9 Yuan Wenqing, Long Yongfang and Zhou Daiwei 2007; Yuan Wenqing and Zhou Daiwei 2007.
10 Hubei sheng wenwu kaogu yanjiusuo and Zhongxiang shi bowuguan 2007. For discussions of this tomb in English, see Clunas 2013, ch. 5; Clunas 2005–6, 7–11; Yang Xiaoneng 2006, 44–5.
11 Xiaotun 1958.
12 *MSL Taizu shilu* 63.1a, 4/閏3/己未.

Chapter 19
Paper Money of the Ming Dynasty: Examining the Material Evidence

Caroline R. Cartwright,
Christina M. Duffy and Helen Wang

In recent years there has been unprecedented interest in the Ming paper money in the British Museum and British Library collections. Much of this interest was prompted by the inclusion of a Ming note in the British Museum/BBC project 'A History of the World in 100 Objects'. People involved in the production of the radio series, the website, the book and the CD longed to describe the note in a superlative way.[1] But, the Ming notes are not the world's earliest paper money, the earliest surviving or the most enduring notes in history.[2] They are not even particularly beautiful examples of Ming dynasty printing. It is well known that the notes were made of mulberry paper, but the sources give different botanical terms: some say *Morus alba* and others *Broussonetia papyrifera*. In order to address this question of which type of mulberry was used, the Ming Dynasty Paper Money Project was initiated. Fourteen Ming dynasty notes in the collections at the British Museum and British Library were analysed in the first combined microscopic examination of Ming paper money. This is a pioneering study, providing unprecedented data for Ming dynasty papermaking and is likely to be of interest to historians of Ming painting, book production and printmaking. Preliminary findings were first presented at an international and interdisciplinary workshop on Ming paper money at the British Museum in May 2013; then at the *Ming: 50 years that changed China* exhibition and 'Ming China: Courts and Contacts' conference on 9 October 2014, and at the 'Chinese Paper Money AD 1000–1450' workshop at the British Museum on 11 October 2014. A full report of the microscopical analysis was published in the *British Museum Technical Research Bulletin* in autumn 2014.[3] The present chapter starts with a short section on provenance, and then follows with a summary view of what the curator sees when looking at Ming notes and how much more can be ascertained through the expertise of both the plant scientist and the imaging scientist.

Outline history of the collections

The Ming Dynasty Paper Money Project looked at 14 Ming notes: nine in the British Museum and five in the British Library. Although the Museum and Library are today separate institutions, they were previously one single institution. In the early 1970s there was a small collection of world paper money in the Museum's Department of Coins and Medals, and there was also a collection of world paper money in the Department of Printed Books, in the Museum's library. The former remained in the British Museum while the latter was moved to the newly formed British Library, explaining why there are Ming notes in both institutions.[4]

In 1977, David Wilson, Director of the British Museum, initiated a planning committee to discuss the development of the Museum. One of the outcomes of those discussions was that the Department of Coins and Medals should collect paper money, and in 1979 Virginia Hewitt was appointed as the Museum's first Curator of Paper Money. At that time the Museum's paper money collection was housed in two filing cabinets, with each note mounted in a card frame. Gradually, these were transferred to a new housing, with each note placed inside a Melinex envelope and housed within acid-free card casing. The nine Ming notes currently

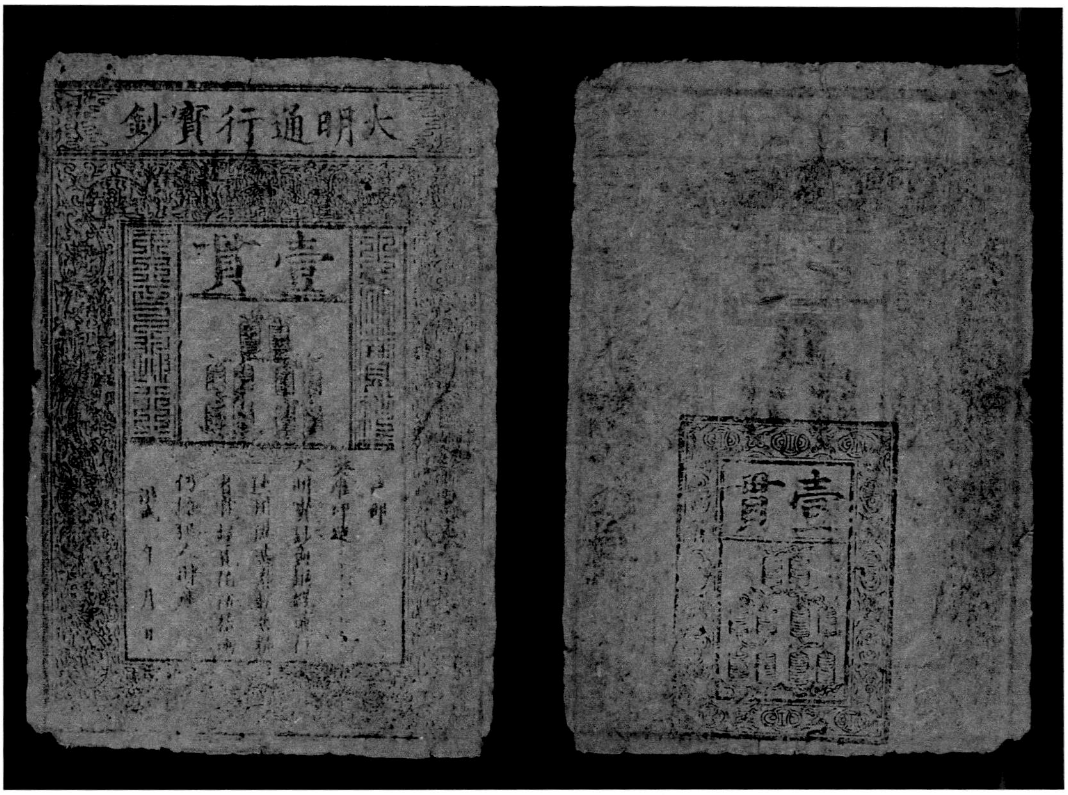

Plate 19.1 Ming dynasty paper money *Da Ming tongxing baochao* 大明通行寶鈔 for one string, front and back, issued in 1375. Ink on paper, height 34.1cm, width 22.2cm. British Museum, London, donated by Miss E.G. Hingley, 1942,0805.1

in the Museum collection were acquired in 1913 (from H.A. Ramsden), in 1942 (donated by E.G. Hingley) and in 2009 six notes were donated by the ifs School of Finance (previously known as the Chartered Institute of Bankers, whose paper money collection had been on loan to the Museum since 1987). Another note was transferred from the Museum's handling collection in the 21st century.

Henry Alexander Ramsden (1872–1915) was a well-known collector of East Asian money. Based for some time in Japan, he was the President of the Yokohama Numismatic Society and General and Foreign Manager of Jun Kobayagawa Co. (Jun Kobayagawa being his brother-in-law). Much of his collection was purchased by John Reilly Jr (1883–1935), whose papers, including details of Ramsden's collection, are in the archives of the American Numismatic Society in New York. A handwritten note records that this Ming note was 'found inside a Buddha of the Ming period'. Almost nothing is known about Emily Georgina Hingley. The British Museum database records that she donated Chinese antiquities to the Museum in 1942 and died in 1948.[5]

The notes from the ifs School of Finance were once part of the Avonmore collection, belonging to Frederick Ernest Catling (d. 1947), of Avonmore Road, West Kensington, London. Catling was an engraver and collector of paper money, and his collection, known as the Avonmore collection, was assembled over 50 years (then stolen in the 1930s and recovered following an advertisement in a newspaper). He sold his collection to the Institute of Bankers in 1946. The Institute of Bankers became the Chartered Institute of Bankers in 1987 and the ifs School of Finance in 2006. The collection of paper money was given to the British Museum in 2009.

The Ming notes in the Museum's library were housed within the Department of Printed Books, under the charge of a certain Mr Grimley, who was also responsible for the philatelic collection. Each Ming note was placed between two sheets of glass, with the edges sealed. Of the five notes, three are still housed in this way and two were removed from the glass so that they could be examined as part of this project. The provenance of these notes has yet to be determined.

At the moment, it is not known how Ramsden, Hingley and Catling acquired their Ming notes. However, there is some anecdotal evidence suggesting that Ming notes were found inside Buddhist statues in Beijing during the Boxer Rebellion of 1900–1; inside a Buddha statue in the collection of Sophus Black (1882–1960), a Dane who was working and living in China from 1902–31; and buried inside the Beijing city wall in the 1930s. All of these claims need to be researched and validated. There are Ming notes in other collections around the world, and it is possible that they came from the same or similar sources. It would also be useful to know more about Ming notes in Chinese collections. However, for the time being, this data is not readily available, and it is impossible to estimate the total number of Ming notes that have survived.

Ming notes as part of China's monetary history and Ming dynasty material culture

Helen Wang

To the curator's naked eye, the Ming notes in the British Museum and British Library collections all look fairly similar (**Pl. 19.1**). They are large, grey notes, printed in black on both sides, and with three red seal impressions stamped on the notes. They are all of the same denomination for one string (*guan*貫) of coins, and are all dated to the Hongwu reign (1368–1398). Ming notes were

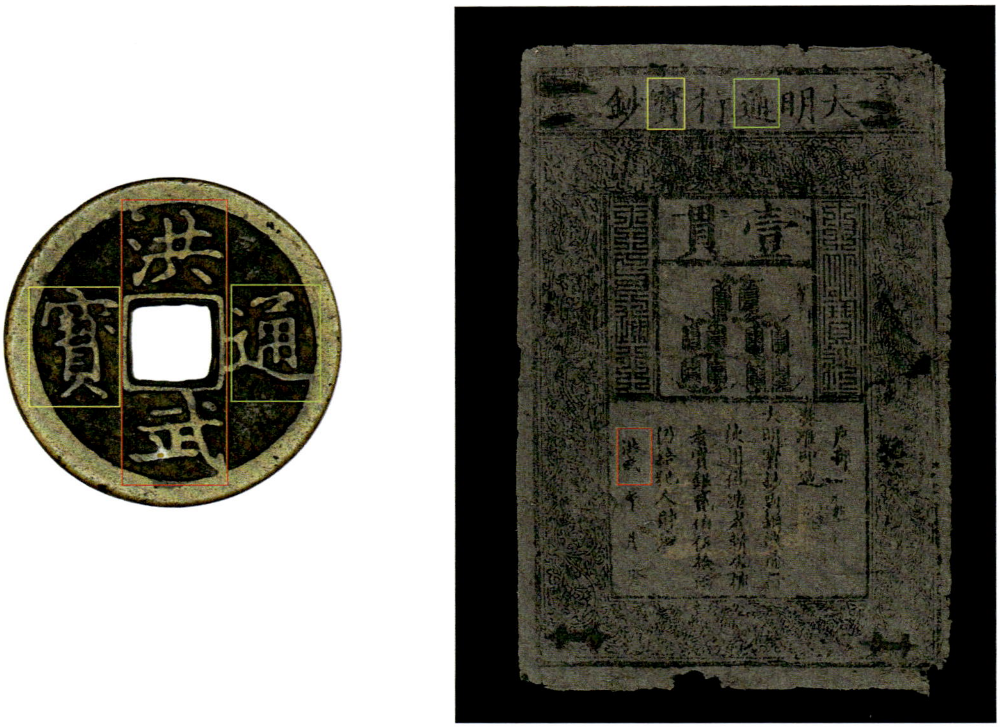

Plate 19.2 The same concepts of money seen on Ming coins and paper money: *Hongwu tongbao* 洪武通寶 coin and *Da Ming tongxing baochao* 大明通行寶鈔. British Museum, London, 1870,0507.14712.154; and CIB,EA.263

first issued in 1375 and were more or less abandoned by the 1430s owing to the discrepancy between their transactional value and their face value. However, all surviving notes have inscriptions giving the Hongwu reign period, including posthumous issues; and the year, month and day are never filled in.

The notes have the name printed in large characters across the top: *Da Ming tongxing baochao* 大明通行寶鈔 ('Great Ming Circulating Treasure Certificate'). The notes are often referred to simply as *baochao* 寶鈔 ('treasure certificate'), where *bao* 寶 conveys the notion of 'treasure' and *chao* 鈔 is the physical paper note. The term *tongxing baochao* 通行寶鈔 on the notes corresponds with the *tongbao* 通寶 found on the *Hongwu tongbao* 洪武通寶 coins (**Pl. 19.2**), and Da Ming 大明 was widely used as the dynasty's name, for example in inscriptions on ceramics.

Many of the features of Ming notes clearly derive from the paper money of earlier dynasties.[6] They have a similar height to width ratio, and the essential elements (e.g. name, denomination, seal-script panels, information and date) are all present, though occasionally arranged in different positions. Even the string of coins presented as an image (of 1,000 coins arranged in ten groups of 100) at the centre of the Ming notes has its origins in the design of Jin dynasty (1115–1234) paper money. In the *Zhenyou baoquan* 貞祐寶券 note for 50 strings in the Shanxi Museum collection, the denomination is given as 50 strings, and five bundles of ten strings are depicted at the very top of the note (**Pl. 19.3**).

The name of the Ming notes follows that of the *Zhiyuan tongxing baochao* 至元通行寶鈔 notes issued by the Yuan emperor Qubilai (r. 1260–94) in 1287 (**Pl. 19.4**), but replaces the reign period with the name of the Ming dynasty. The *Zhiyuan tongxing baochao* was Qubilai's second note, its name being a development of his first – the *Zhongtong yuanbao jiaochao* issued in 1260. *Zhiyuan* refers to the reign period (1264–94); *yuanbao* ('primordial treasure') refers to silver ingots; *jiao* ('exchange') to the function; and *chao*, again, to the paper note. These names developed out of earlier terms for paper money: for example, *baoquan* ('treasure voucher') printed on Jin dynasty (1115–1234) notes, and *jiao* and *chao*, both associated with paper money since the Song dynasty (960–1279).

Although Ming notes were issued in several denominations (100-, 200-, 300-, 400-, 500-*wen* and 1-*guan* notes were issued from 1375 onwards; and 10-, 20-, 30-, 40-, 50-*wen* notes from 1389), almost all of the surviving notes are for 1-*guan* and depict a string of 1,000 coins, in ten groups of 100 coins. This image is misleading, however, as the notes were not convertible, and when it came to exchanging different forms of money (for instance, for paying taxes in the form specified by the state), the value of the *guan* was determined by the current rate of exchange.[7]

The vertical panels on either side of the denomination on Ming notes each present four characters written in a stylised nine-fold seal script (*jiudiezhuan* 九疊篆 / *jiudiewen* 九疊文). The panel on the right reads *Da Ming baochao* 大明寶鈔 ('Great Ming treasure certificate'); and the one on the left reads *Tianxia tongxing* 天下通行 ('to circulate under heaven'). While we can think of the ninefold seal script in the context of official seals of the Ming dynasty, its use on paper money clearly derives from the seal script panels on earlier Jin notes and the 'Phags-pa script panels on the Yuan notes.

On the Ming notes, the instructions for use, in the large box in the lower half of the note, read in columns from right to left. On the far right is the name of the issuing office. This is important as it provides one of the few ways of dating Ming notes. Between 1375 and 1380, Ming notes were issued by the Secretariat (*Zhongshusheng* 中書省), and thereafter by the Ministry of Revenue (*Hubu* 戶部). Almost all of the notes surviving today were issued by the latter. A few notes issued by the Secretariat have been excavated from tombs near Jiangyin, in Jiangsu province: two from a tomb in Luqiao,

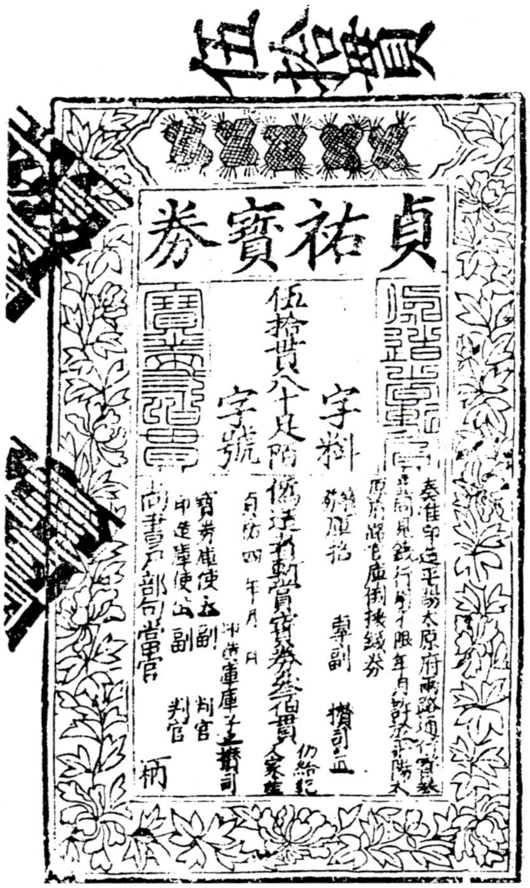

Plate 19.3 *Zhenyou baoquan* 貞祐寶券 for 50 strings, Jin dynasty, 1213–16 (Zhenyou reign). Height 33.7cm, width 17.9cm. Shanxi Museum

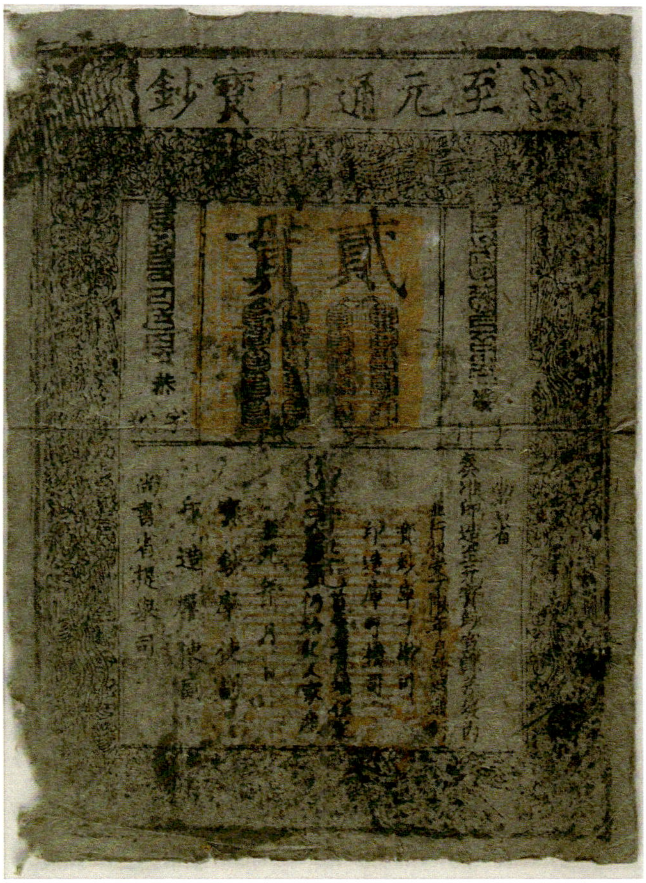

Plate 19.4 *Zhiyuan tongxing baochao* 至元通行寶鈔 for two strings, Yuan dynasty, 1264–94 (Zhiyuan reign). Height 29.8cm, width 21.4cm. Shanghai Museum

about 26km north of Jiangyin, found in 1988 (for 1 string and 200 cash), and five from a tomb in Changjing, about 40km southeast of Jiangyin, found in 2004 (three for 300 cash and two for 200 cash).[8] The rest of the inscription is the same on all notes: '[The Ministry of Revenue/Secretariat], with Imperial sanction, has manufactured and printed Great Ming treasure certificates for circulation alongside bronze coins. Those using counterfeit notes will be executed. Informants will receive 250 *liang* of silver and the entire property of the criminal.' The final column gives the date of issue as 'the … day of the … month of the … year of the Hongwu reign period', though the three blanks were never filled in, and the reign name was never changed.

All three red seal impressions stamped on Ming notes (two on the front and one on the back) are six-character inscriptions in nine-fold script. Those on the front read *Da Ming baochao zhi yin* 大明寶鈔之印 ('Seal of the Great Ming treasure certificate'), *Baochao tijusi yin* 寶鈔提舉司印 ('Seal of the supervisorate of treasure certificates') and the one on the back *Yinzao baochao ju yin* 印造寶鈔局印('Seal of the office of treasure-certificate-printing'). The latter two name the two main government organisations involved in the production and issue of paper money.

These are the basic design features found on Ming dynasty paper money, and although they are usually considered in the context of numismatics and the history of Chinese money, they should also be reviewed as part of the much larger world of Ming material culture.

Scanning electron microscopic identification of fibres in Ming dynasty paper money

Caroline R. Cartwright

Traditionally Ming dynasty paper money was thought to be made from mulberry bark fibres, although it was not known (or stated) which of the Moraceae family was involved, e.g. *Morus alba* (white mulberry), *Morus australis* (formerly *M. bombycis*) (Chinese mulberry), *Broussonetia papyrifera* (paper mulberry) or *Broussonetia kazinoki* (Japanese paper mulberry/chu). Recent interest in Ming dynasty paper money prompted scientific examination of the Ming notes in the British Museum (nine originals, one reproduction and four later forgeries) and the British Library collections (two out of five analysed). For this study, reference material associated with papermaking during the Ming dynasty was sourced from China and Japan and included: paper mulberry (*Broussonetia papyrifera*), Japanese paper mulberry (*Broussonetia kazinoki*), white mulberry (*Morus alba*), Chinese mulberry (*Morus australis*), snailseed vine (*Cocculus trilobus*), hibiscus/cotton rosemallow (*Hibiscus mutabilis*), different types of bamboo (Bambuseae tribe), sandalwood (*Dalbergia* sp.), rice straw (*Oryza sativa*), wheat straw (*Triticum* sp.), cotton (*Gossypium* sp.), hemp (*Cannabis sativa*), ramie (*Boehmeria nivea*), jute (*Corchorus* sp.), rattan (*Calamus* sp.), flax (*Linum* sp.), gampi (*Wikstroemia canescens*) mitsumata (*Edgeworthia* sp.), abaca (*Musa textilis*) and silk (from mulberry silkworm, *Bombyx mori*, larvae cocoons).

Collection	Registration number	*Broussonetia papyrifera* paper mulberry	*Morus alba* white mulberry	*Morus australis* Chinese mulberry	*Bambuseae tribe* bamboos	*Hibiscus mutabilis* hibiscus	*Oryza sativa* rice	*Triticum* sp. wheat	*Cannabis sativa* hemp
British Museum	1913,1011.30	■	■	■	■	■			■
British Museum	1942,0805.1	■	■						
British Museum	OR.9730	■	■	■	■				■
British Museum	CIB.EA.260	■	■	■	■				■
British Museum	CIB,EA.261	■	■			■			
British Museum	CIB,EA.262	■	■			■			
British Museum	CIB,EA.263	■	■					■	
British Museum	CIB,EA.264	■	■	■	■	■	■	■	■
British Museum	CIB,EA.265	■	■	■	■				■
British Library	ORB 40/862	■	■	■	■				
British Library	ORB 40/863	■	■						■

Table 1 Identifications of selected sampled Ming dynasty notes in the British Museum and British Library collections. Key: filled cell = fibres and other plant cells present from this taxon

Examination of tiny samples (that were so minute that their source was undetectable) taken from the Ming notes and the comparative reference specimens was undertaken in the Hitachi S-3700N variable pressure scanning electron microscope (VP SEM) using the backscatter electron detector.[9] From the outset of the VP SEM examination, it was clear that many different types of fibres and other plant cells were present in the samples taken from the original British Museum Ming notes and from two of the British Library examples (**Table 1**). As these tiny samples were removed from a single specific location on each note, the identifications presented in **Table 1** cannot be interpreted as being representative of all fibre types used for the manufacture of Ming paper money. There may be other plant fibres in unsampled areas of the notes already studied as well as in notes not yet available for study. Single location sampling also means that the identified taxa in **Table 1** cannot be presented quantitatively or even semi-quantitatively, so a simple present/absent notation has been used.

Plate 19.5 VP SEM image of *Broussonetia papyrifera* (paper mulberry) fibres from Ming dynasty paper money. British Museum, London, 1913,1011.30

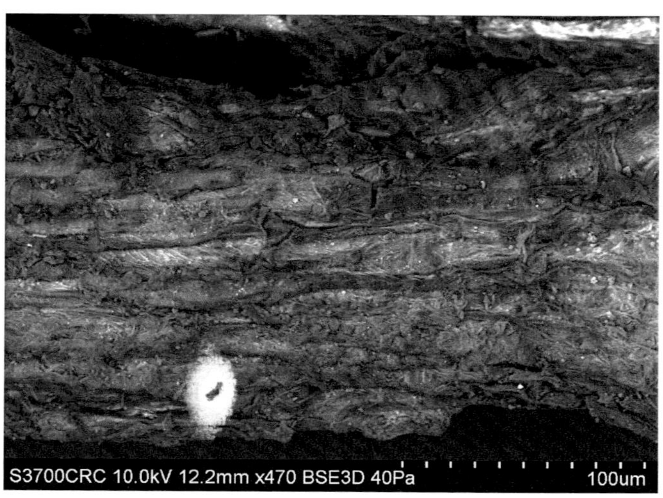

Identification of genus or species was possible through the VP SEM examination of Ming note samples at appropriate magnifications. A single SEM view was not sufficient to characterise each sample or fibre type, so many SEM images were captured for each of the Ming notes and reference specimens. Specialist botanical expertise was crucial for the identification of the fibres and other plant cells present in Ming dynasty paper money, not least because the morphological features of these cells had been greatly altered during the paper-making processes. Identification was only possible where sufficient diagnostic features were present in association with one another, and where these features were not compromised by fungal hyphae, ink, pigments, dirt, encrustation or deterioration. It is self-evident that fibre atlases and online fibre databases were not useful for comparative purposes in this particular study; such resources invariably illustrate modern textbook examples of fibres in pristine condition.

The VP SEM analyses revealed surprising results; although fibres from white mulberry and paper mulberry (**Pl. 19.5**) had been used, all of the notes contained several different types of fibres and other plant cells, including bamboo (**Pl. 19.6**), rice straw, wheat straw, hibiscus and hemp, as well as other types of mulberry, such as Chinese

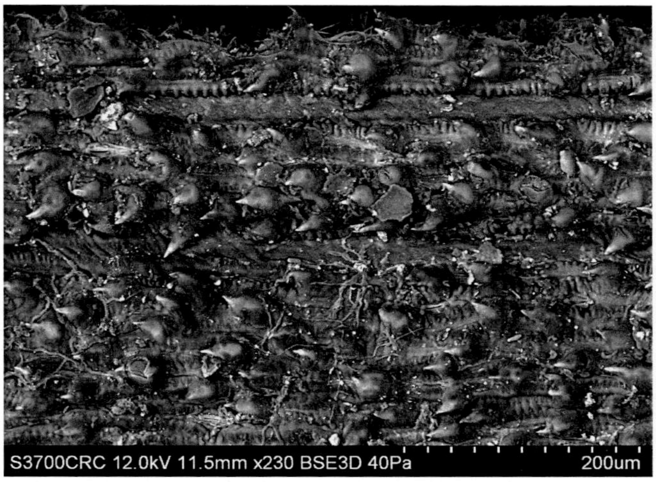

Plate 19.6 VP SEM image of bamboo leaf cells from Ming dynasty paper money. British Museum, London, CIB,EA 264

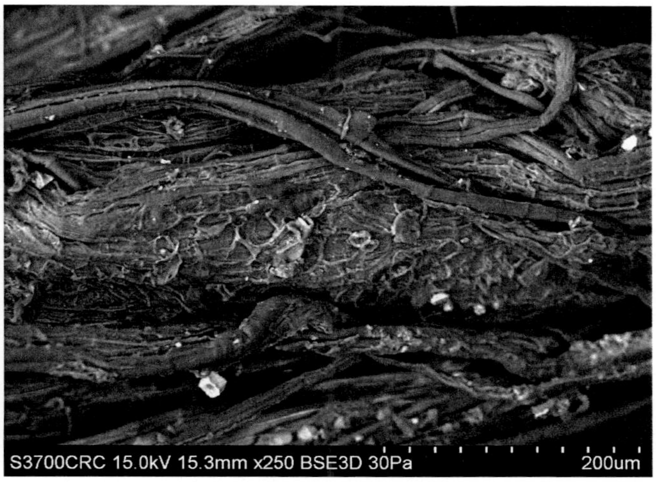

Plate 19.7 VP SEM image of *Morus australis* (Chinese mulberry) fibres from Ming dynasty paper money. British Museum, London CIB.EA.260

mulberry (**Pl. 19.7**).[10] This appears to make the Ming paper money comparable in composition to other types of early Chinese paper.[11]

Further research is needed to establish whether Ming paper money was made of recycled materials, which might explain why there is a range of plant types in apparently different condition, possibly reflecting different production intensity. Although tiny samples were taken from the Ming notes studied recently,[12] given that the Hitachi S-3700N VP SEM has a large chamber that can accommodate a specimen size up to 300mm in diameter (and 110mm in height at an analytical working distance of 10mm), in the future it is possible that fragments of Ming paper money from other collections that do not exceed these dimensions could be put directly into the VP SEM chamber for very carefully monitored scientific examination without the need for sampling.

Visualising separate components of digital images using colour space analysis

Christina M. Duffy

The recent increase in the digitisation of cultural heritage material has created vast amounts of digital assets. These assets undoubtedly enable greater public access and reduce the handling of valuable materials, but have only more recently become recognised as datasets worthy of research in their own right.

Digital images are captured in what is known as a colour space, most typically in the RGB colour space, representing the percentage of the red, green and blue components combined. This colour space is called trichromatic which assumes that it is possible to generate any colour using a combination of the three primary colours R, G and B. As such, any RGB colour space image can be separated into three individual monochrome images, which differ in pixel values, providing new ways of visualising an image. This separation of an image into its constituent components can reveal hidden information by highlighting nuances which are difficult to distinguish in the combined RGB image.

A colour space is not a physical property, but rather an attribute of visual perception that allows reproducible representations of colour in analog and digital applications. It is typically specified by three parameters (but can be more), and it is the relationships between these parameters which characterises a particular colour space. While separating an RGB image down into its individual components can be useful, more information can be retrieved from digital images by converting into other colour spaces and examining those components. Mathematical algorithms enable the parameters of one colour space to be transformed into another. These transformations are helpful for making colour descriptions more intuitive such as by describing colours in terms of their hue, saturation and luminance.

Cultural heritage material is often composed of several different types of inks and pigments overlying a substrate such as paper, papyrus or parchment. In an attempt to separate these constituents visually, the Luv colour space was identified as having great potential.[13] The Luv colour space was developed by researchers to overcome problems found in other colour spaces where the differences between two colours were sometimes not perceivable by the human eye. By describing the colour in terms of one component of lightness (L), and two components of chromacity (u and v), those differences were noticeable.

Microscopical examination of fibres in Ming dynasty paper money[14] highlighted the visual difference between the black pigment used to state the terms of the money's use, and the red pigment used for impressing seals indicating the note's authenticity. Black pigment was found to be well absorbed and attached to pulped fibres resulting in good overall legibility (**Pl. 19.8**). However, red pigment (**Pl. 19.9**) was identified as being particulate in nature and not coating the fibres as readily as black pigment. This poor distribution of red pigment resulted in an overall loss in clarity of the seal lineation, rendering any study of these demarcations very difficult. This was especially the case in areas where the seal is obscured by overwritten black pigment.

To overcome this illegibility and to generate images where the seal and ink could be studied separately, digital images of the British Library and British Museum Ming dynasty paper money notes were transformed from their RGB colour spaces into the LCHLuv colour space. LCHLuv

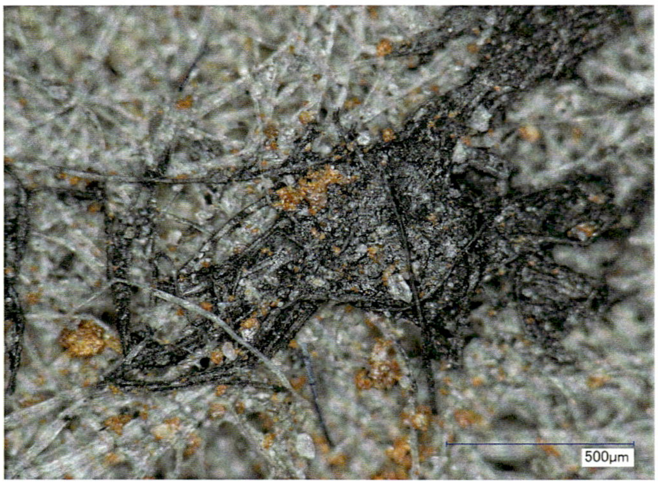

Plate 19.8 Microscopy image of black pigment in BM 1942,0805.1 at x200 magnification captured using a Keyence VHX 2000 E series digital microscope

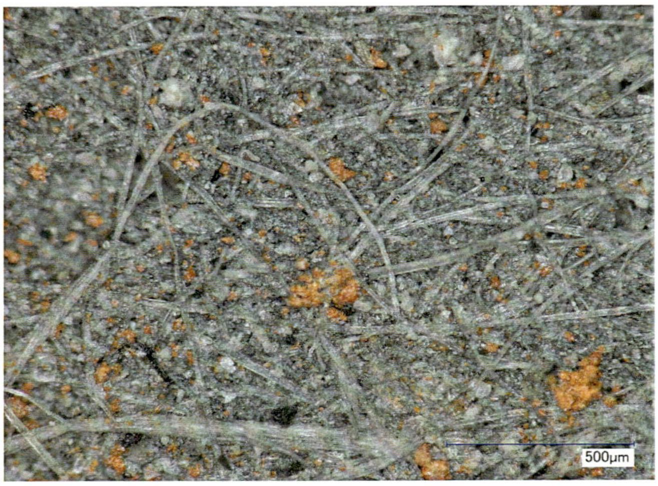

Plate 19.9 Microscopy image of red pigment in BL ORB 40/863 at 200x magnification captured using a Keyence VHX 2000 E series digital microscope

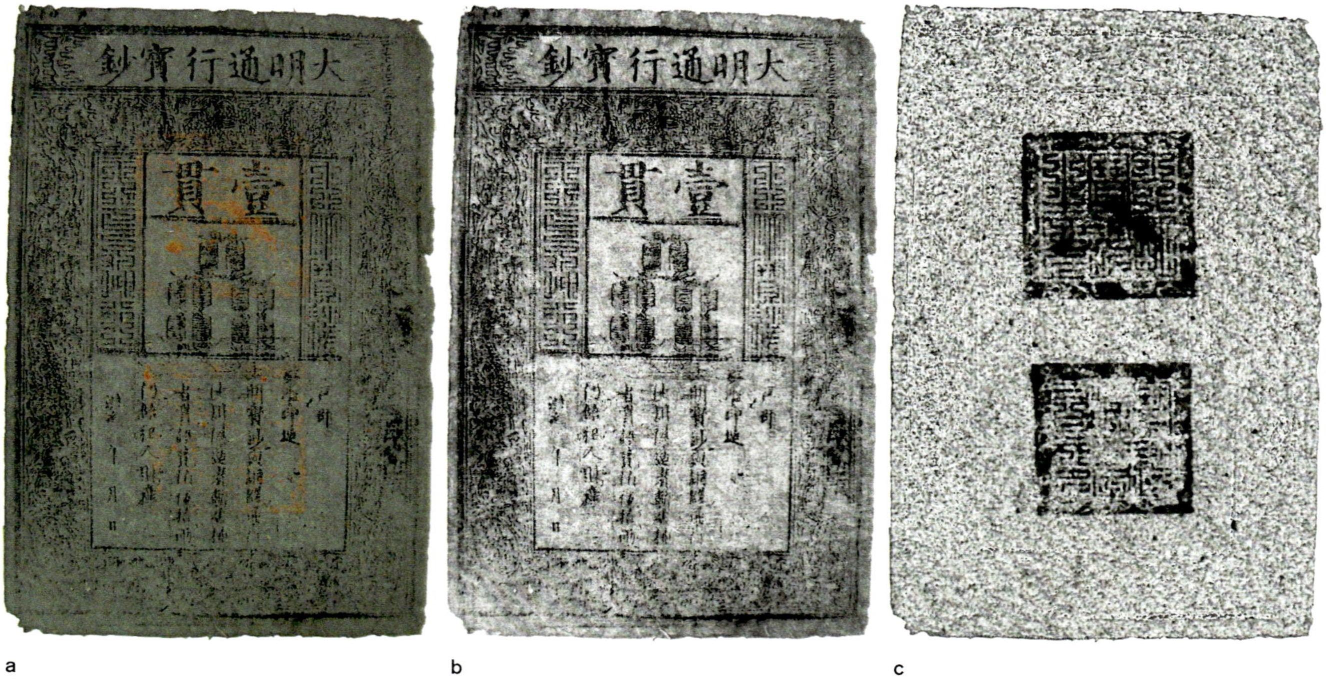

Plate 19.10a–c a) Original RGB image of BL ORB 40/863; b) Black pigment only in LCHLuv L colour space; c) red seal pigment in LCHLuv C colour space

is a luminance-chrominance colour space which is described by one component representing luminance or 'lightness' (L), and two components representing 'colour intensity' (C and H). It is a direct derivative of the Luv colour space as described earlier.

Pl. 19.10a shows a digital image of British Library note ORB 40/863 captured using a Nikon D40 camera. The image was saved in JPG format in standard RGB colour space and imported into ImageJ, an open source image processing and analysis software package, for colour space conversion. ImageJ has a plugin architecture which allows for extensible programming. Two plugins, Colour Transformer, and Colour Space Converter, were used in ImageJ to convert the RGB image of ORB 40/863 (**Pl. 19.10a**) into the LCHLuv colour space. The L and C components of this colour space are shown in **Pl. 19.10b–c**. The two monochrome images show the black pigment has been completely separated from the red pigment allowing ease of study of the separate constituents.

The results are impressive. Other imaging techniques such as multispectral and hyperspectral imaging will certainly provide a more in-depth analysis of the constituent materials, but these techniques can be expensive to install and require some technical expertise to manage. Colour space analysis is a powerful and affordable method requiring only a digital image and freely available software.

Concluding remarks

The aim of our presentation at the conference was to share the results of our pioneering research into Ming paper money. Although the sample of 14 notes was small, the analysis and imaging were done to the highest specifications and the results provide unprecedented data. This data is relevant not only for Ming paper money, but also for Ming dynasty papermaking, and is important for historians of Ming painting, book production and printmaking. The design of Ming paper money places it clearly in the context of the development of paper money in Chinese history, but key features and expressions are also found in other media such as seals and ceramics, thereby placing Ming paper money in a much broader cultural context.

Notes

1 MacGregor 2010, 465–9; http://www.bbc.co.uk/ahistoryoftheworld/.
2 The earliest paper money was the 'flying cash' *feiqian* of the Tang dynasty (618–907). The earliest surviving paper money is from the Jin dynasty (1115–1234). While the paper money issued by Qubilai Khan during the Yuan dynasty (1271–1368) was very successful, the demise of Ming paper money served as a 400-year deterrent to government-issued paper money. See von Glahn 2005 and H. Wang 2014.
3 Cartwright, Duffy and Wang 2014.
4 The following information in this section is from personal communication with Joe Cribb, former Keeper of the Department of Coins and Medals, British Museum, and from the Museum's database (http://www.britishmuseum.org/research/collection_online/collection_object_details.aspx).
5 Hingley donated the Ming note (1942,0805.1 in the Department of Coins and Medals) and a book made of ten leaves of engraved jade (1942,1012.1 in the Department of Asia).
6 von Glahn 2005. See also Zhou Xiang 2004; and Nei Menggu qianbi yanjiu hui and Zhongguo Qianbi bianjibu 1987.
7 Peng 1993, 537–635. See also von Glahn 1996.
8 Wu and Diao 2005.
9 For full details see Cartwright, Duffy and Wang 2014.
10 Cartwright, Duffy and Wang 2014.
11 See Hunter 1978; Tsien 1985.
12 Cartwright, Duffy and Wang 2014.
13 Duffy 2014 (http://www.bl.uk/eblj/2014articles/pdf/ebljarticle22014.pdf).
14 Cartwright, Duffy and Wang 2014.

Chapter 20
The Porcelain Pagoda: A Persisting Enigma

Clarence Eng

This chapter concerns a structure that was arguably the biggest art object constructed during the Ming period. Imposing and magnificent, the Da Baoensi ta 大報恩寺塔 (Great Monastery of Filial Gratitude Pagoda) in Nanjing was a spectacle for miles around, gleaming by daylight and lantern-lit at night. It was public art on a massive scale, designed to be seen, to command admiration and to convey a powerful statement, though what that statement *was* precisely is open to interpretation. However, though famous in its time, it is now an enigma, having been painstakingly dismantled during the Taiping uprising in 1856. It is known today largely from contemporary sketches and descriptions, and from architectural fragments scattered in collections worldwide.

The early history of this pagoda is obscured by the subsequent reworking of official records precisely for the period in question, and our transmitted knowledge appears to date largely from the late Ming or early Qing dynasty. However, there is consensus on events and on many of its features, though rather less agreement on why or even how it was built. The initial parts of this chapter will concentrate on the harder evidence, examining first those surviving fragments that can confidently be attributed to this structure before considering some remains that are less clearly ascribable. It will then address the possible inspiration for this pagoda with its unusual detailing, and finally it will discuss outstanding questions for which there are presently no good answers.

The firm evidence

This narrative commences with the Tianxisi 天禧寺 (Monastery of Heavenly Blessings), which stood across the city moat from the Jubaomen 聚寶門 (Gate of Collected Treasures) (today's Zhonghuamen 中華門) on the southern side of Nanjing's city wall. This temple had origins before the Tang dynasty, but by the early Ming it was in a sorry state. Urgent renovation was undertaken by the Hongwu 洪武 emperor (r. 1368–98) who memorialised its completion in 1388. Subsequently it fell again into disrepair and also suffered fire damage early in the reign of the Yongle 永樂 emperor (r. 1403–24), who commissioned its rebuilding. Some work may have begun as early as 1407, but major reconstruction began in 1412, specifically on the 15th day of the 6th month of the 10th year of Yongle.[1] The temple was renamed the Da Baoen Monastery and the project included a new pagoda, to be called the Da Baoen Monastery Pagoda. Contemporary sketches show this structure located behind the main Buddha Hall on a centralised site, probably in the same place as at least one precursor structure.[2] Researchers note that although work began in 1412 the new pagoda may first have been proposed under Hongwu (**Pl. 20.1**).[3]

The pagoda took 19 years to build, being dedicated in 1428 and finally completed in 1431.[4] Sadly, architecture was never until recent times considered a subject worthy of serious attention by Chinese scholars, nor were descriptions written in the expectation that a structure might itself cease one day to exist. In consequence, no contemporary accounts or drawings indicating architectural detailing appear to have survived. Much of our descriptive information dates

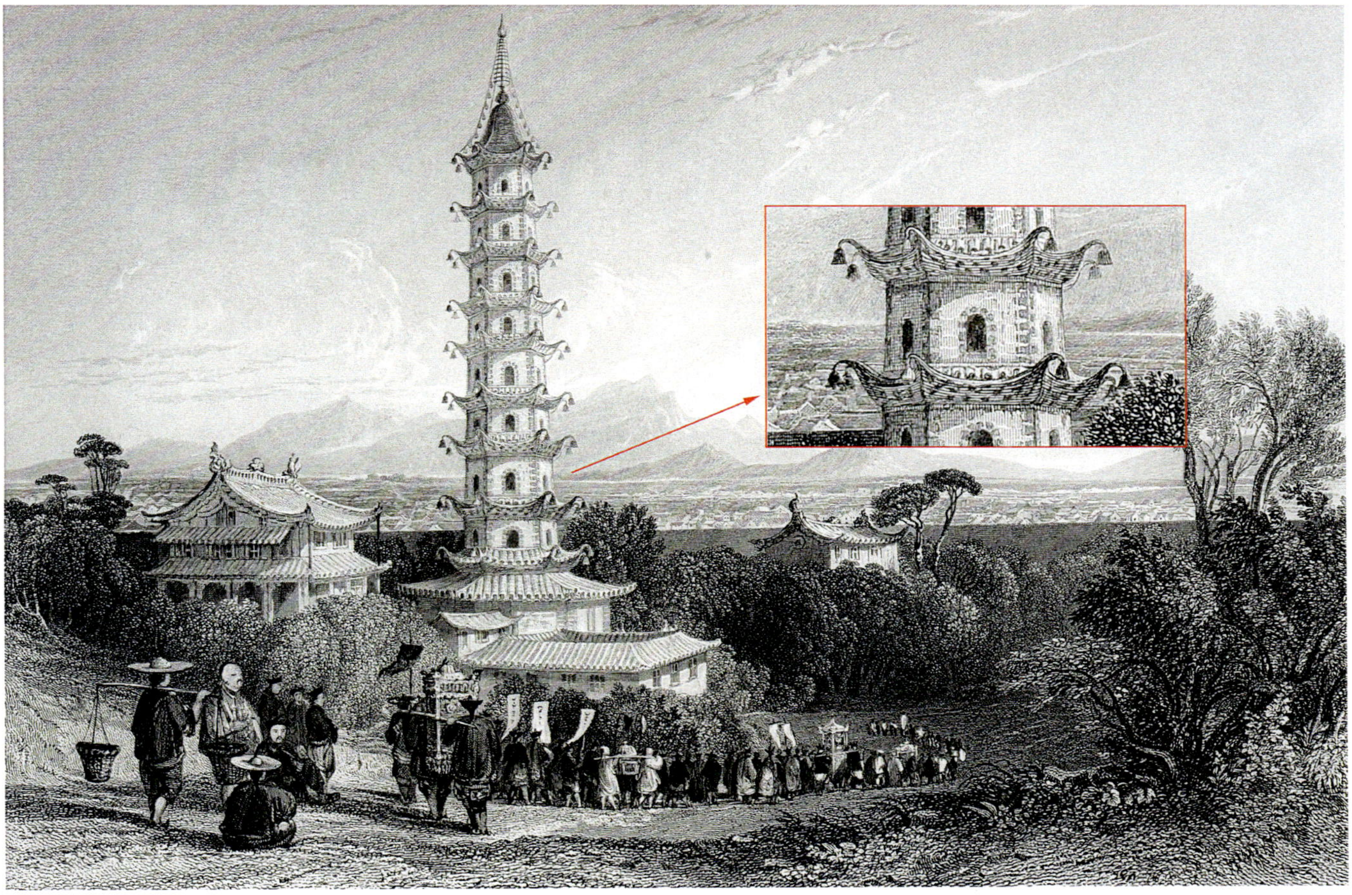

Plate 20.1 A print of the Porcelain Pagoda (and detail), one of a series made in Nanjing by Thomas Allom in the late 1830s or early 1840s (after Allom 1858–9, facing p. 162, first published 1843)

from the 17th century and later, in short narratives by European visitors, particularly in the 1840s after the Treaty of Nanjing, and in sketches by both Chinese and European travellers.[5] The pagoda was finally reduced to rubble in 1856, having been laboriously dismantled over two years by the Taiping rebels to deny its use as a vantage point for besieging government troops.

Though descriptions differ in matters of detail (especially concerning colours and ornament) they and surviving sketches agree on the main features. The pagoda was octagonal with a recorded height equivalent to 102m including its *cha*-post (steeple), and a brickwork height of between 80 and 90m. It was one of the tallest buildings in the nation at the time, having nine storeys with that at ground level sheltered by an encircling ambulatory.[6] Sketches suggest that the structure had only a modest architectural batter (taper), with the illusion of height given mainly by progressive diminution of detailing on successive higher storeys. Each storey was defined by a shallow tiled roof, supported by either *faux* timber brackets or corbelling (sketches differ) and hung (we are told) with bells at the eaves corners and lit after dark by oil lamps in niches. At each level, four decorated arched openings led onto a balustrade. The structure was surmounted by a finial bearing a precious vessel and nine discs, this assembly stabilised (in conventional fashion) by chains anchored to the eaves corners of the main roof.

Fragments of the pagoda have entered collections outside China since the 1870s, and new material stored in Nanjing has emerged from excavations since the 1950s. The challenge is to identify pieces which can be ascribed to the pagoda itself, rather than to the temple site generally, or to other contemporary sites in imperial Nanjing. Not unique to the Da Baoen Monastery Pagoda, but frequently occurring in early Ming imperial sites in Nanjing are glazed ceramic materials of exceptional quality and finish.

The pagoda earned its unique fame, and indeed its colloquial name, *Liuli ta* 琉璃塔 (the 'Glazed Pagoda' or the 'Porcelain Pagoda' to European travellers) from its white glazework cladding. It was a continuous light show, glistening in sunlight and brilliantly lit by capiz-shell lanterns at night. Accounts also mention other colours; green, red and yellow on the roofs defining each storey and green balustrades. Thomas Allom's account mentions on each storey 'open doorways…..their arches elegantly turned with glazed tiles …… in all variation of colour, representing deities, demons and monsters…'[7].

Supporting these descriptions were significant finds made in excavations during 1958–9 at the village of Yunhuatai 藝花臺 at Mount Jubao 聚寶山, about 1.5km southwest from the pagoda site. Some 73 official kilns are recorded to have been set up in the early Ming to assist the construction of the new imperial capital, and Mount Jubao was evidently an important part of this system, having several cross-draft kilns.[8] Prominent amongst the finds were large architectural components in polychrome stoneware. These parts were unused and unblemished and many were components of arched openings shaped as lobed and cusped ogees of

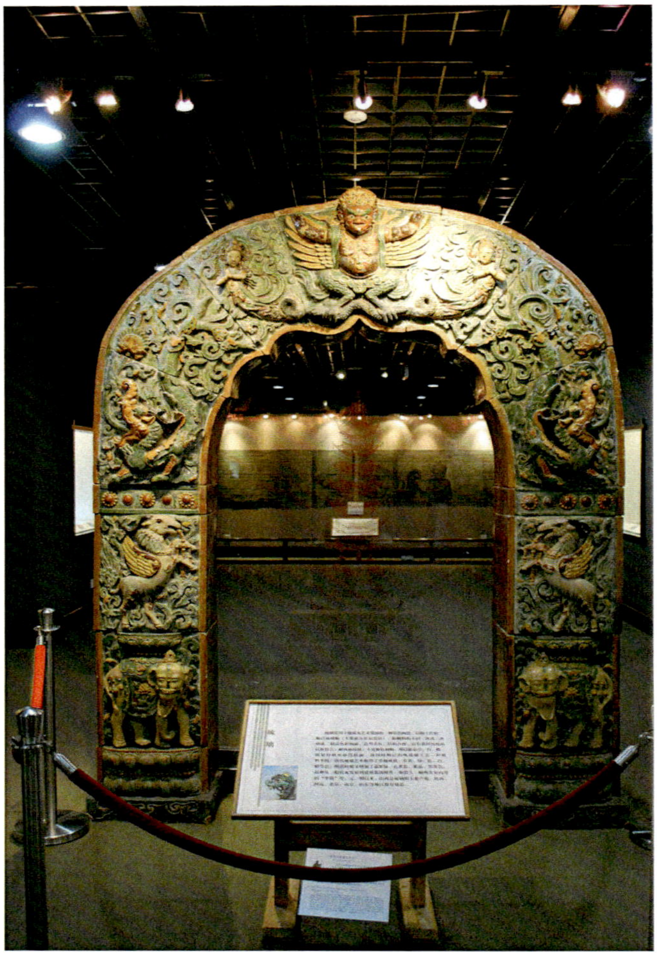

Plate 20.2a Reconstruction of arch-surround of the Da Baoen Monastery Pagoda in the Nanjing Museum

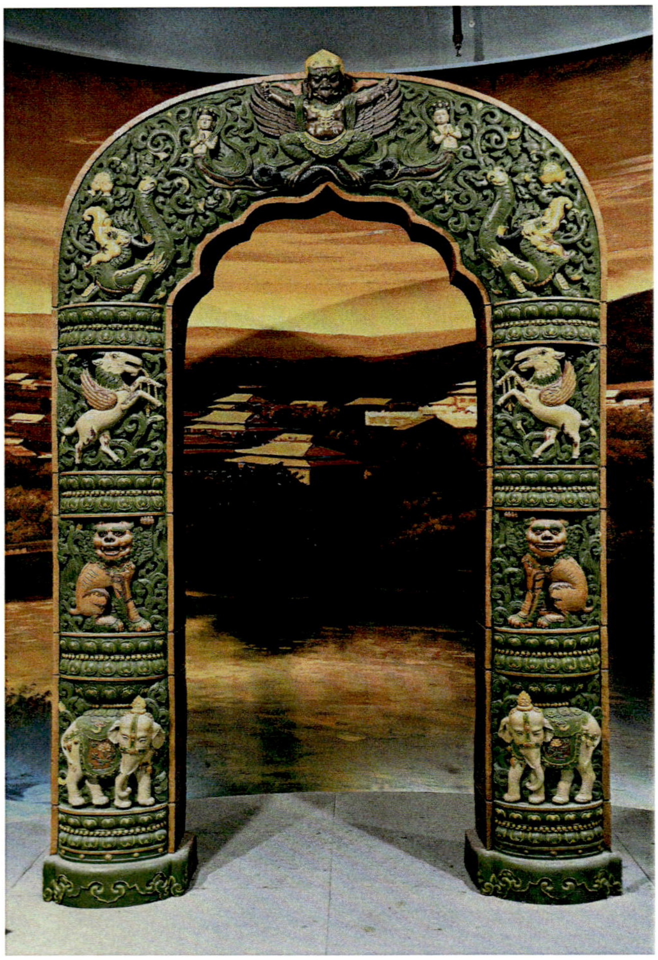

Plate 20.2b Reconstruction of arch-surround of the Da Baoen Monastery Pagoda in the Nanjing Municipal Museum

different sizes. They are glazed primarily in four colours; brown, green, yellow and black. By their similarity, these finds confirm the provenance of collection specimens which have long been thought to be from the pagoda, and their unused condition supports reports of parts being made in triplicate to provide replacement spares.[9] Some of the original spares may indeed have been used for repairs to the upper three storeys when in 1801 the pagoda was struck by lightning.

The greater part of these finds are stored at the Nanjing Municipal Museum from which four pieces were displayed in the *Ming: 50 years that changed China* exhibition at the British Museum.[10] Three of these exhibits are components of arch surrounds. From the parts found at Mount Jubao, the two leading Nanjing museums (the Nanjing Municipal Museum and the Nanjing Museum) have assembled tentative reconstructions of these arch surrounds (**Pl. 20.2a–b**).

The arch components depict Buddhist motifs from a *torana*, a composition that frames depictions of enlightened beings and portrays the 'six perfections' of the enlightened mind. At the top is a *garuda*, 'the devourer' and 'lord of birds' in both Hindu and Buddhist traditions, flanked by *nagas*, serpent spirits from the underworld. A similar composition, employing differently modelled representations, appears on the arch from 1345 in the Yuan dynasty Cloud Terrace at Juyong Pass 居庸關, north of Beijing.

Below this are outward-facing *makaras*, water demons with trunks and upwardly extended tails, and next are inwardly facing winged goats on their hind legs. At the base are inward-facing caparisoned elephants bearing flat-topped lotus pedestals which seemingly support the weight of the creatures above. The reconstructions by the two museums differ. That at the Nanjing Municipal Museum is 'taller' and, above the elephants, additionally incorporates inward-facing lions with raised paw, a combination that is said to symbolise the combined strength of the two animals.[11] This reconstruction also incorporates more floral 'spacers' which appear to be designed specially to fit these side-jambs. Missing from both reconstructions are *devas*, young gods representing the sixth 'perfection', who in a full *torana* would come between the winged goats and the *makaras*. These may yet remain to be discovered.

The reconstructions in Nanjing resemble some features of high-relief figures carved in wood which embellish the top and side of each drawer panel of a hexagonal sutra cabinet at Zhihuasi 智化寺 (Transformation of Wisdom Monastery) in Beijing. This cabinet is believed to have survived from the foundation of the temple in 1440.[12]

The objects in the *Ming: 50 years that changed China* exhibition have other significant features seen most clearly in the piece depicting a winged goat. First, it bears on one side a location code of four Chinese characters reading *jizi yiyou* 已字一右. Researchers at the Nanjing Museum believe these are from a fail-safe numbering sequence based on the *Qianzi wen* 千字文 (*Thousand Character Classic*), by which *ji* 已 would

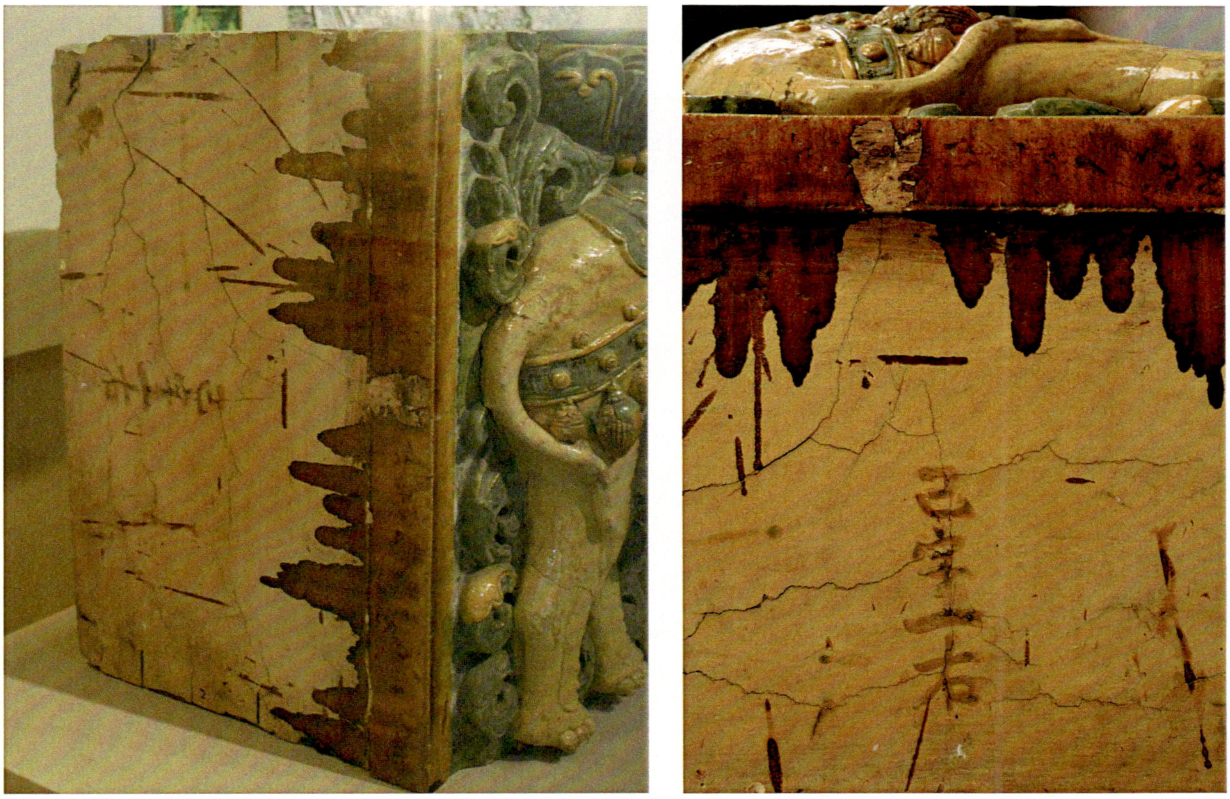

Plate 20.3 A location code, thought to be based on the *Qianzi wen* 千字文 (*Thousand Character Classic*) and reading '173 - 2', first on right'. Nanjing Municipal Museum

translate as '173' and *zi* 字 as the number '2'. The remaining two characters might then follow a similar convention, or simply indicate '1' ('first') on the 'right' **Pl. 20.3**).

Second, this and other pieces from side-jambs are penetrated vertically by a moulded cavity more typical of stonemasonry techniques but here pre-formed to receive a tenon to brace the jamb against lateral forces. The cavity functions also (perhaps fortuitously) to reduce the fired mass, in places reducing the clay thickness to 20cm and assisting the safe escape of water vapour in the kiln (**Pl. 20.4**).

The larger components, such as those in the exhibition, are roughly cube shaped, measuring approximately 50cm across each face, and each weighing over half a ton; all qualities that challenge the frequent practice outside China to label them as 'tiles'. They are better understood as 'architectural components'. Other similarly designed pieces from Mount Jubao differ in size, as do examples in museum collections. This supports depictions of the pagoda which show its height being visually emphasised not by architectural batter, but by progressive diminution of applied features on higher storeys. Variations in finish and colour palette suggest also that different craft workshops may have been involved in the glazework (**Pl. 20.5a–b**).

These components are moulded in ceramic, but their complex integral cavities come from the design repertoire of stonemasons. This unusual combination of skills suggests cooperation for a clearly exceptional project between traditionally distinct craft groups. To date the identity of these craftsmen is not known. However, though lobed ogee arches are exotic to China, they are ubiquitous in Middle Eastern and European architecture of the same period, which suggests a likely direction of influence.

The body material for these parts is dense, fine grained and impermeable with many of the physical qualities of stoneware. There are contemporary accounts of special white clays being brought to Mount Jubao from Dangtu county in Taiping prefecture, some 90km upstream in Anhui province.[13] Taiping is renowned for its porcelain stone kaolin clays and also for its white-wares production. Samples

Plate 20.4 The blocks supporting the side-jambs of the arches are penetrated vertically by a stepped cavity shaped to accept a brace, strengthening the arch as a load-bearer. Nanjing Municipal Museum

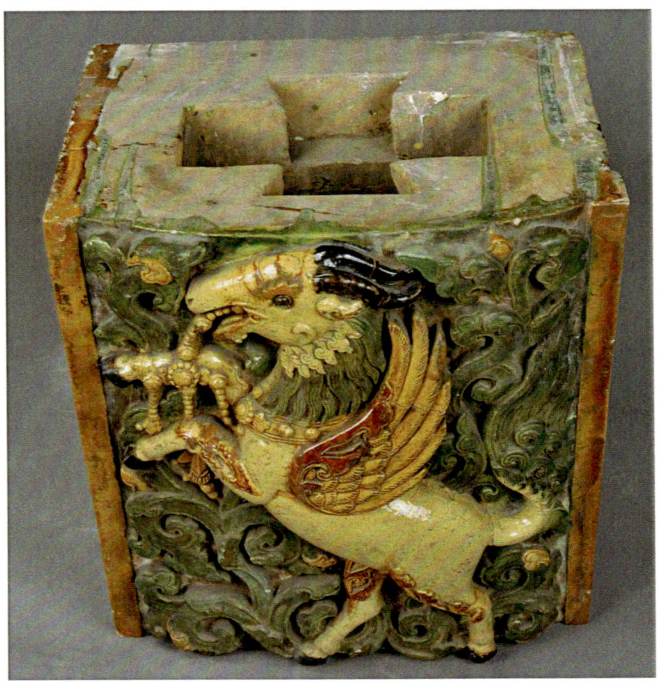

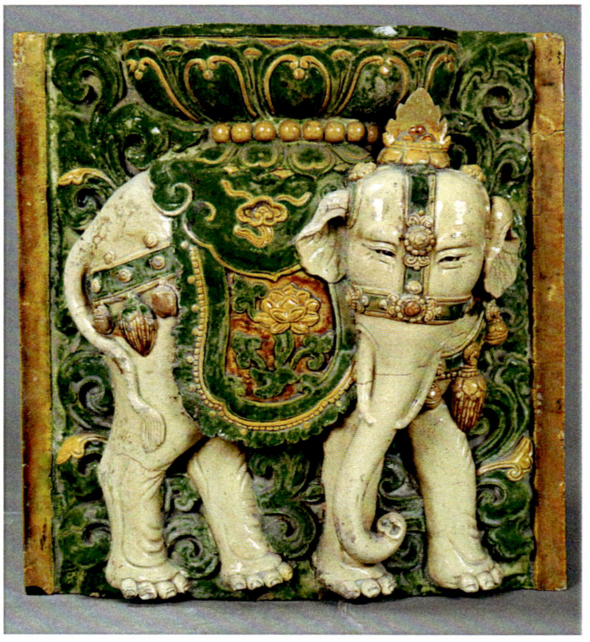

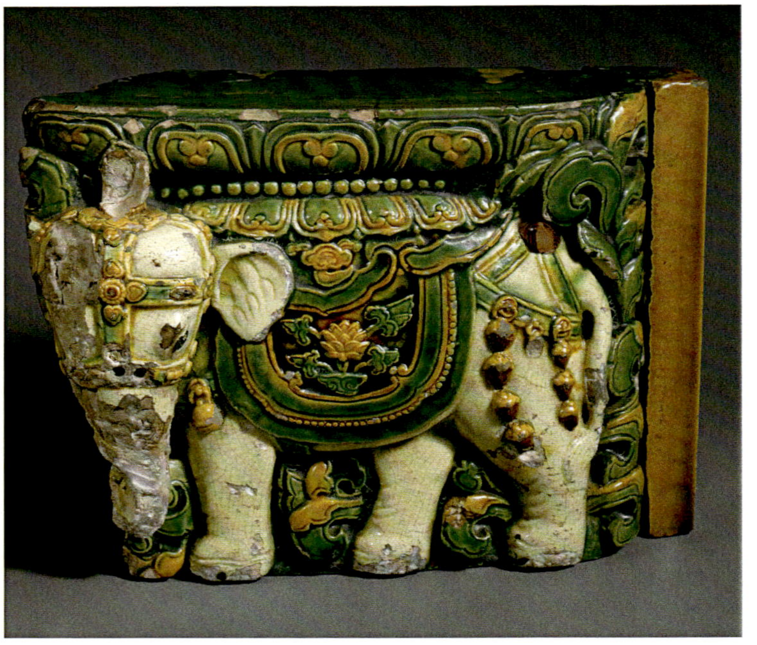

Plate 20.5a–b Components for arch surrounds differ in size, showing that the apparent height of the pagoda was emphasised by diminution in size of ornament on higher storeys: a) *c.* 1412–31. Height: 51cm, width: 47.6cm, depth: 39.5cm. Nanjing Municipal Museum; b) *c.* 1412–31, Height 23.5cm, width 33cm, depth 15.2cm. The Metropolitan Museum of Art, New York, purchase by subscription, 1879 (79.2.789)

of body material from the pagoda have been compared with material from Dangtu by researchers at the Palace Museum in Beijing. Detected silica and alumina levels of 70% and 20% are typical for Yongle-period porcelains from Jingdezhen and this, together with a sintering temperature for the Da Baoen Monastery Pagoda samples of 960–980° +/- 20° centigrade, is consistent with the possibility that these are porcelain clays fired to near-stoneware temperatures.[14]

The other uniquely prominent quality of the pagoda is the white cladding which earned it the sobriquet 'Porcelain Pagoda'. Many collections possess porcelain bricks formed with an 'L'-shaped profile and bearing a white *tianbai* 甜白 ('sweet white') glaze carefully applied to just one external face at the base of the 'L'.[15] They are found in sizes ranging from 17 to 37cm along the long edge, and a cache of some 2,200 pieces was discovered at Dongmentou 東門頭 at the imperial kilns in Jingdezhen, confirming their production source (**Pl. 20.6a–b**).[16]

Accounts refer to the pagoda being clad in white 'tiles', but for some time it was not clear whether these bricks indeed were those 'tiles' and, if so, how they were installed. Clearly, a flat, rectangular or square facing-tile would have been an easier shape to produce. However, a flat tile may have been difficult to fix given the unreliable adhesive quality of mortars in the early Ming, which were best used only under compression as a levelling medium. Researchers have debated whether these 'L' profile bricks might have been for corbelling, but this would have required that at least *two* external faces be glazed. However, Allom's account offers a cogent answer. He noted that 'porcelain slabs' lined both the interior and exterior faces, and they were 'fixed in the masonry by means of deep keys, cut like a half T in the brick'.[17] This suggests that the cladding was achieved by mounting these bricks back-to-back in mirror-pairs that were held in position by the brickwork in which they were embedded, with their single glazed faces presenting an uninterrupted external finish (**Pl. 20.7**).

There is one last category of components which can be attributed to the pagoda, by association with finds from Mount Jubao, from contemporary descriptions and by

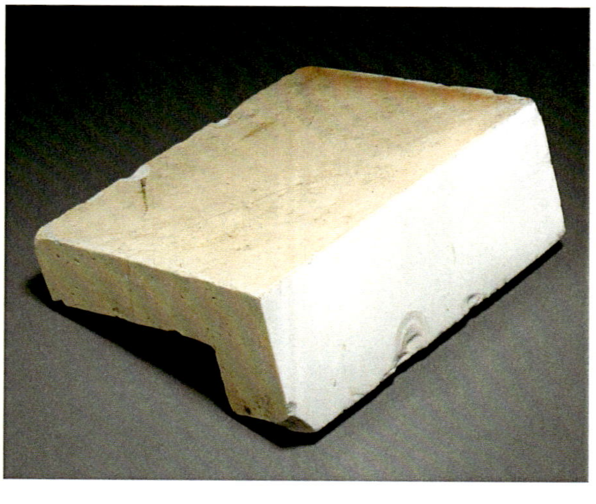

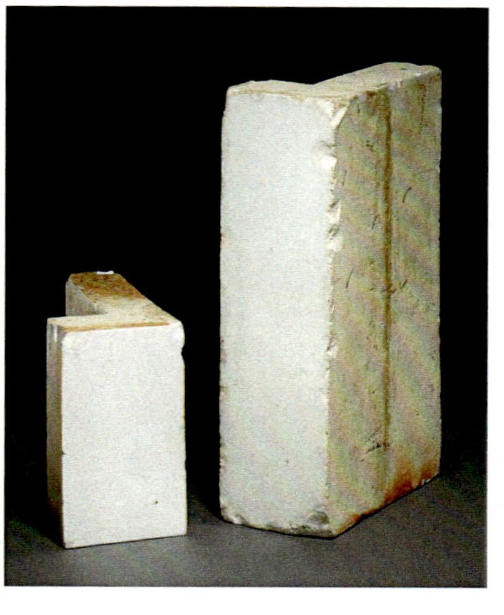

Plate 20.6a–b Porcelain cladding pieces from the Da Baoen Monastery Pagoda: a) Yongle period, 1412–19, Jingdezhen. Height 3.7cm, width 18.8cm, depth 14.9cm. Sir Percival David Collection, PDF. A. 458; b) Yongle period, *c.* 1412–19. Length 13cm and 37cm. British Museum, London, Franks.32

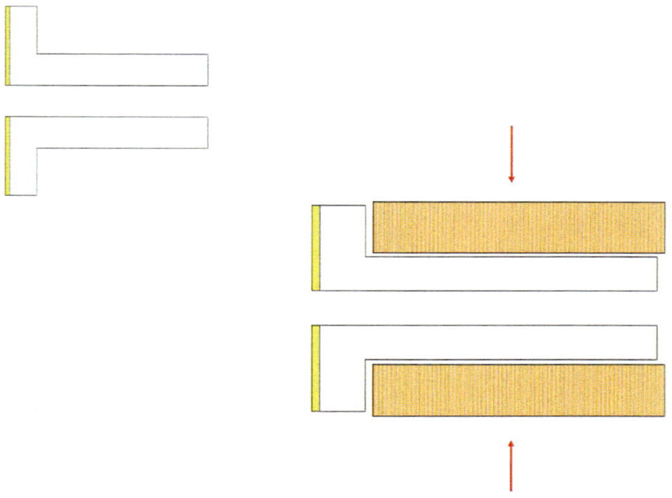

Plate 20.7 Probable fixing method for facing-bricks

recent archaeological finds at the pagoda site. These are stoneware wall-tiles with integrally moulded notches and tongues at the back which engage with corresponding fixings set into the wall.

There are two designs. One bears in *bas relief* a crossed *vajra* (thunderbolt) motif in yellow with a red ceramic 'jewel' at its centre on a green ground banded by yellow. This design matches descriptions (by Loch) of 'walls all lined with square porcelain tiles, each separate one embossed with a small device in the centre...' Fragments matching unused examples from Mount Jubao were found on the pagoda site in 2008.[18] The other design has polychrome green and yellow floral scrolls decorated in perfect register to provide a continuous 'textile brocade' pattern. Again, examples have been found at both Mount Jubao and on the pagoda site which match examples in private and museum collections.[19]

Parts attributable to the temple site but not necessarily to the pagoda

Some ceramic parts in collections match finds excavated from Mount Jubao and the Da Baoen Monastery, but are not noted in contemporary descriptions of the pagoda, and therefore cannot yet be confidently associated with the pagoda (and not another building nearby).

Among these are what *may* be floor tiles, because they are flat surfaced, thin and have no integral fixings at the back to suggest they are for walls. They are decoratively glazed and meticulously finished, but specimens are few. Two types are described below; one is in blue and white and the other in polychrome. However, no such floor tile has yet been found *in situ*, and there is no evidence in China of floors being laid with decorative glazework until very modern times. Even the most prestigious palace halls in the Ming and Qing dynasties were floored with specially commissioned and laboriously made dense grey unglazed flooring bricks (*jinzhuan* 金磚), a speciality of Suzhou, from where with difficulty they were transported for the major imperial halls in Beijing. Given that plain unglazed flooring was reserved for the most exalted halls, it would be surprising (if these finely colourful tiles were indeed also for floors) that rules of *lèse-majesté* or sumptuary apparently failed to discourage the use by lesser individuals of a decoratively superior product.[20]

The first example is a porcelain tile decorated in underglaze blue. Two complete pieces in the British Museum are 23cm² in size.[21] Similar tiles excavated in Nanjing and at Jingdezhen were found not to be decorated in the traditional 'blue-and-white' of porcelain tablewares. Instead they were produced painstakingly by covering the entire surface with cobalt underglaze colouring and then scraping into this the design whose revealed white body-colour was then highlighted with trailed white slip. They are referred to as *landi baihua zhuan* 藍地白花磚 ('blue-ground white decorated bricks', or more simply 'white on blue'). Five different patterns have been identified, and sherds found at the Da Baoen Monastery in Nanjing are matched by samples excavated in the Xuande stratum at the imperial kilns at Zhushan 珠山 in Jingdezhen where they were produced.[22] As mentioned, it is not certain that they were floor tiles, or even ever used in Nanjing, but might perhaps have been in transit via the capital for another destination (**Pl. 20.8a–d**).

The other example is represented by two almost complete pieces: one in the Sir Percival David Collection on display at the British Museum and the other at the Victoria and Albert Museum in London. They are moulded and incised polychrome stoneware pieces bearing a (repeating) design of confronted dragons and cloudlets in green on a yellow ground. Their pattern matches sherds excavated at the Da Baoen Monastery. Significantly, the pieces in London are trapezoidal, 28cm long, 2cm thick and tapering very slightly from a curved edge measuring approximately 19cm. Their shape suggests that they were made for a circular laying pattern and they have undercut edges, which suggests they could be floor tiles.[23] The taper angle of the specimen in the Sir Percival David Collection is 2.64° which, given the other dimensions, suggests a circular pattern with a diameter of 8.55m. A laying pattern of such a size could have been accommodated at many levels within the pagoda. However, none of the contemporary accounts mentions such a distinctive circular feature, and Loch's account describes a principal chamber that is *square*.

Other pieces in collections which claim provenance from the pagoda though not yet attributable are parts of wall decorations and roof finials, many of which match complete pieces found at Mount Jubao and fragments excavated at various sites in Nanjing. Prominent among these are

a) Private collection in Nanjing

b) Excavated from Jingdezhen 1993. Jingdezhen Institute of Ceramic Archaeology

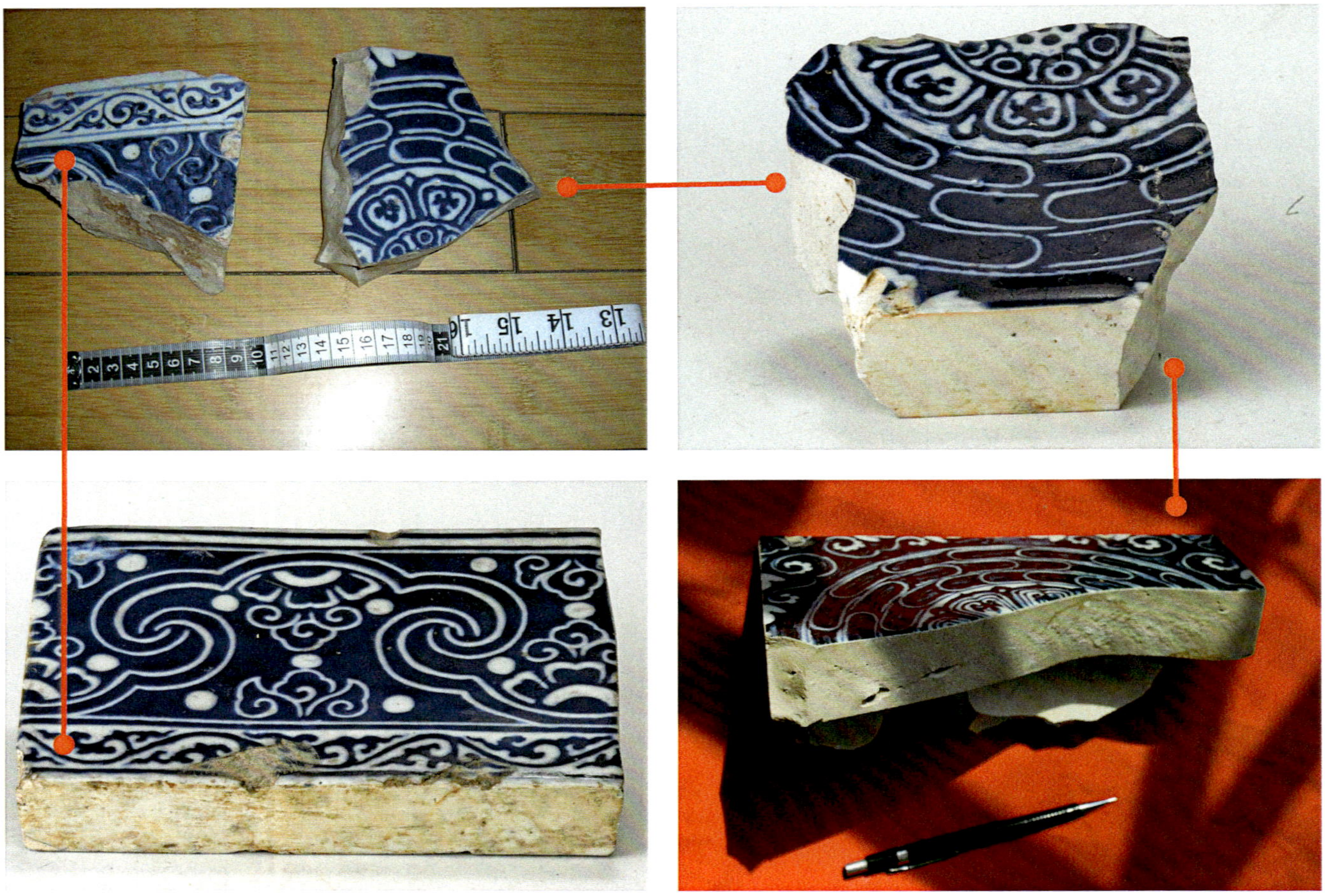

c) Excavated from Jingdezhen 1993. Jingdezhen Institute of Ceramic Archaeology

d) Excavated from the Da Baoen Monastery Pagoda site 2009. The Museum of Ceramic Specimens, Humanity College, Nanjing Art University

Plate 20.8a–d Unusual 'white on blue' underglaze decorated porcelain tiles which may be floor tiles. Fragments excavated in Nanjing match specimens found at Jingdezhen. They are similar to two complete specimens in the British Museum (registration numbers 1993,1027.1-2)

distinctive polychrome components in yellow and green. Remarkably, it seems that polychrome glazework appeared on imperial roofs and architectural detailing in early Ming Nanjing, but subsequently only on walls and never on roofs in imperial projects in Beijing.[24]

Partially addressed questions about the Da Baoen Monastery pagoda

The jury is still out on *why* the Da Baoen Monastery project was begun, or to *whom* its pagoda was dedicated. The dedicatory stele erected by Yongle in February 1424, early in the same year that he perished on his fifth campaign against the Mongols, dedicates the project with emphatic filial piety to his august deceased father and his august deceased mother, clearly meaning the Hongwu emperor and the Empress Ma 馬 (1332–82). It describes the renaming of the temple and prays that the project will bring good fortune to the spirits of 'my deceased father and mother above [i.e. in heaven]' and it records that the project is 'near completion'.[25] A later dedicatory stele, erected by Yongle's grandson Xuande in 1428, records the ancestral names associated with the project and, understandably, reaffirms Yongle's filial dedication from four years previously.[26]

Yongle may have been haunted by the suggestion that Empress Ma might not be his biological mother, and the stele inscription clearly aims to refute this and emphasise his legitimacy. It also complements the assertion being made by Yongle's administration that his nephew the Jianwen 建文 emperor (r. 1399–1402) was an illegitimate and rightfully deposed usurper.[27] However, interpretations differ, and some researchers have suggested that the project may have been dedicated at one time to Yongle's Empress Xu 徐 (1362–1407), and also that there may be complex political sub-texts in the renaming of the temple.[28]

Clues to this may be implied by homophones of its new name. Its renaming from Tianxi Monastery to the Da Baoen Monastery Pagoda is described in some detail in the 1424 stele. Homophones and associated meanings for the important character *bao* 報 include familiar and frequently used forms such as:

褒 as in *bao*$_1$ *yi* 褒義 (praise or commend)

寶 as in *bao*$_3$ *ta* 寶塔 (a treasure pagoda)

保 as in *bao*$_3$ *cun* 保存 *bao shou* 保守 (preserve or maintain and keep watch over)

報 as in *bao*$_4$ *en* 報恩 (pay a debt of gratitude) or *bao fu mu en* 報父母恩 (filial gratitude)

抱 as in *bao*$_4$ *qian* 抱歉 (to be sorry, to regret)

There are also more subtle homophones that might have appealed to concerns amongst the educated elite regarding the parentage and accession of the incumbent emperor:

> 報 as in *bao*$_4$ *xiao* 報曉 (herald the dawn), with *xiao*$_3$ 曉 (dawn) itself a homophone of *xiao*$_4$ 孝 (filial piety),

and finally (and perhaps also subtly suggestive):

> 胞 as in *bao*$_1$ *xiong*, *bao di* 胞兄,胞弟 (twin brothers, literally 'born from the same womb').

Various texts including the stele inscriptions record that repairs to the *temple* were largely complete by 1424 and it was dedicated in 1428, though its pagoda was not completed until 1431, after 19 years.

Why the project took so long is unclear. It seems that '100,000 soldiers, skilled craftsmen and miscellaneous labourers' were allocated to the task, under the supervision of the Directorate of Palace Servants and a Vice Minister of Works, an administrative structure which was then typical for military organisation in Nanjing.[29] Whether this manpower number is accurate, or simply a figurative indication for 'many', or indeed whether this effort was even maintained is unclear, and it is difficult to relate it to the reported cost of the project. There are references by the late Ming or early Qing to a project cost of 2.5 million taels (ounces) of silver, and by the 1840s both Allom and Loch refer to a surprisingly accurate figure of 2,485,484 ounces, but there seems to be no earlier recorded figure, nor is it clear whether this sum was for the whole temple or only for the pagoda.[30]

If '100,000 men' can be taken to approximate a real figure, labour costs might be guessed from early- to mid-Ming pay rates for agricultural labour of about 5–6 taels per man-year.[31] On this basis, wages would have cost 500,000–600,000 taels per year, at which rate 2.5 million taels would not have lasted more than five of the 13 years of the project. It is possible of course that the labour force fluctuated, or that some (the soldiers?) were paid from other funds or were even corvée labour, or a combination of all these factors. It has been suggested that some 1,700 specialist artisans who were assigned to the dedicated kilns at Mount Jubao may have been reassigned to Beijing for the palace building projects there.[32]

Whatever happened, work on the pagoda was well behind plan by March 1428 when the Xuande emperor ordered Zheng He to take command of the project. The Yongle emperor had meanwhile died in 1424 on campaign in Mongolia, to be followed in rapid succession by his son the Hongxi 洪熙 (r. 1425) emperor, who expired suddenly and was in turn succeeded in 1425 by *his* son the Xuande emperor.

Zheng He 鄭和 (1371–1433) in his role as commander of the imperial maritime expeditions is discussed elsewhere in this volume but there are elements from his background which are pertinent to his role in this project. First, he had previously served with distinction under Yongle as Director of the Palace Household in which position he was responsible for all palace construction. This was before his appointment in 1404 as Commander of the Imperial Fleet. After the fleet was eventually laid up in 1424, Zheng He retained his command but in 1425 was also appointed Defender of Nanjing with responsibilities for domestic order and civil administration, and it was in this rôle that in 1428 he took over the Da Baoen Monastery project, presumably rekindling his former skills as superintendant of palace construction.[33]

Second, Zheng He was a Muslim descendant of a former Yuan dynasty Governor of Yunnan (an expatriate appointed by Qubilai Khan from a distinguished family in Bukhara) and very possibly retained contacts with the Muslim community in Nanjing and other nearby cities. However, it is most unlikely that in these final three years of construction he could have influenced the design of the pagoda and its exotic Central Asian or Middle Eastern features. The detailed design, including these features, would have been agreed between architects and patrons at the very start of such a monumental project.[34]

There are a number of possible reasons for the delay in completing the pagoda. The structure was new and unique in design, and it was located beside the city moat on a site with high ground water. Similar waterlogged sites in Nanjing had already necessitated special foundations under parts of the city wall, and the pagoda's monolithic design made it a heavy structure. For these wet soil conditions, the choice of impervious stoneware for important supports such as arch surrounds was sensible, and designing them as structurally strong ogees with lateral bracing gave the building great strength. The penalty was that the design necessitated innovative kiln techniques and also long-distance transport of special clays, rather than the use of locally sourced clays as would have been customary for ordinary glazework.[35] The height of the pagoda was not itself a new challenge, but a major complication was the design requirement for its apparent height to be accentuated by adjusting the dimensions of ornament and applied decoration on successively higher storeys. This meant that *each* of the nine storeys required parts (such as arch surrounds) that were specially designed to scale, then fired at high temperature and then glazed. Each of these components would have been a craft masterpiece in its own right, with little opportunity for division of labour.

This organisational complication was exacerbated by the white porcelain bricks with which much of the structure was clad (internally also, we are told by Allom). Each storey would have required cladding parts with tailored dimensions and, with no means in those times for post-forming, each piece needed to be delivered ready for use. Numerous different parts were required, including spacers, half-bricks, corbels, squinches and external corners (with re-entrant angles for internal corners), all made to close tolerances in different component sizes for each of the nine storeys. Furthermore, with these parts coming by a tortuous route overland and by water from Jingdezhen, the delivery to Nanjing of damaged or ill-fitting parts would have been unwelcome. Even with mass production and division of labour, logistics and production control must have been daunting.

Behind the difficulties of construction, there were almost certainly serious additional 'centrally inspired' interruptions of resources. Da Baoen Monastery was a state project and

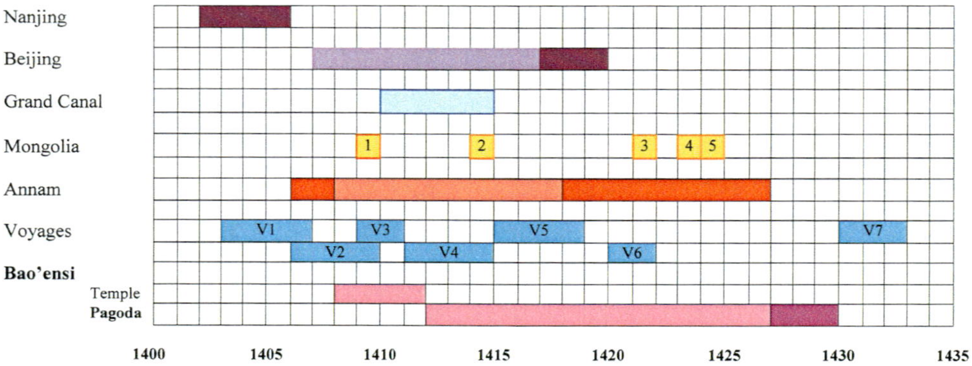

Plate 20.9 Competition for state resources in China 1400–33

undoubtedly merited 'fast-track' priority on resources, not least because its progress would have been conspicuously visible on the city roofline from the imperial palace. However, there were distractions, many of which certainly commanded higher priority, and this is best seen as a timeline (**Pl. 20.9**), which indicates how various projects of national importance were simultaneously inter-linked financially and hence capable of creating immovable blockages for important but lesser local projects such as this pagoda. The 'northern' projects around Beijing, the Grand Canal and the repeated Mongolian campaigns would ultimately continue until Yongle's death, and were matched in the south by equally costly 'foreign policy' targets such as the Annam campaign and Zheng He's expeditionary voyages.

Some important but still outstanding questions

I would like finally to list various questions for which there are presently no ready answers, some of which link with ongoing studies on cultural transmission.

We do not know who designed the pagoda.[36] Whilst in many respects its conceptual design follows conventional preceding forms, there are elements of its detailing which are remarkable, in particular the use of lobed ogee arches. These are not unique in China. There are other examples including another site in Nanjing, the Linggusi temple, where a fireproof sutra repository of revolutionary design had already been completed in 1381 (**Pl. 20.10a–b**). However, these arch forms are not Chinese. They are seen in various locations stretching across Central Asia to the Near East and into Western Europe. Many of these date from the late Yuan or early Ming (contemporaneous with the Late Gothic in Europe).

The porcelain cladding is an obviously unique quality, and the Da Baoen Monastery Pagoda has an ingenious solution for a challenging design requirement, but the broader question concerns the use of keys and tenons for fixing such parts. Curiously, the cladding solution adopted for the Da Baoen Monastery Pagoda was very different from the applied brickwork used by the builders of the 'Iron Pagoda' (Tieta 鐵塔) at Youguosi 佑國寺 (Protecting the State Monastery), Kaifeng 開封, nearly 400 years earlier. Keys and tenons that would normally be cut in stone are foreign to Chinese building traditions of timber-frame structures, movable partitions and brickwork in-fill. The use of ceramic masonry keys in China is rare but not unique, but none matches in boldness and quality the

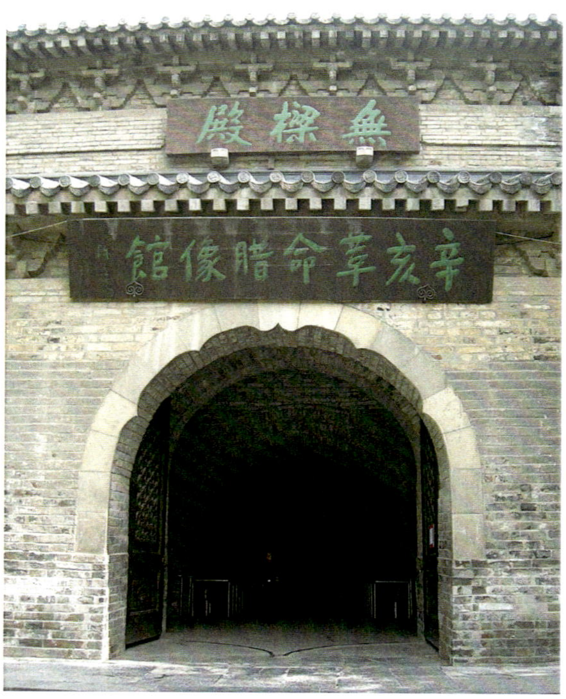

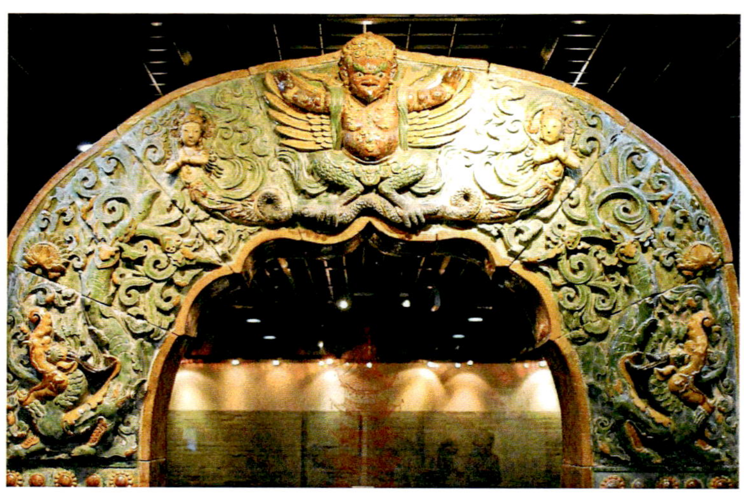

Plate 20.10a–b: a) (above) Detail of reconstruction of lobed ogee arch surround from Da Baoen Monastery Pagoda in the Nanjing Museum; b) (left) Lobed ogee arch of Wuliangdian 無梁殿 (Beamless Hall) at Linggusi 靈谷寺 (Numinous Valley Monaste , Nanjing

massive load-bearers seen in the arch surrounds at the Da Baoen Monastery.[37] These are more typical of solutions found in the Near East, or in the vaulted arches of European churches.

As mentioned, rare technical skills were needed to fire the larger pieces of monolithic stoneware. These are uniquely large, certainly for China and possibly anywhere. There is no record of who the kiln masters were or where they came from. The polychrome glaze of the more ornate parts (applied in a separate, second firing) was unusually fine but probably well within the technical capability of Ming craft workshops in and around Shanxi province, the northern centre for glazework expertise. We know that Shanxi craft workshops managed and led the glazework kilns for the Yuan palaces of Dadu, and later for the Ming and Qing palaces of Beijing.[38] However, there is no record that connects Shanxi craftsmen with work on the imperial projects in Nanjing, and there were differences in the finish of Ming palace halls in Nanjing and Beijing. For instance, polychrome glazes ornamented prestigious buildings (including this pagoda) in Nanjing but subsequently in imperial Beijing, even with Shanxi glazework craftsmen clearly on hand, multi-coloured finishes for roofs were entirely assembled from *monochrome*-glazed components. The polychrome glazework seen in Nanjing could have been the work of Shanxi craftsmen, but the source of expertise for designing and first-firing at high-temperature the monumental stoneware components is presently unclear.

Finally, it is not even certain how this pagoda was constructed. No descriptions of pagoda building have survived generally. Marks on walls of brick-built pagodas suggest that bamboo scaffolding was sometimes used, but for a structure of this height there would have been concerns for stability, even before the addition of heavy static loads of arch components or the dynamic stress of hoists and pulleys. Particularly difficult to explain with no contemporary record of construction techniques is how the builders would have installed the heavy timber *cha*-post or steeple. This was a heavy post cut from a single massive tree which stood suspended on cantilevers within the upper third of the pagoda. It was customarily installed from above in the final stages of construction.[39] At least one group of researchers suggests the use of a continuous ramp on which earth was mounded around each successive storey, providing a progressively elevated temporary working platform which was subsequently removed on project completion.[40]

In conclusion, we now know much of how the Da Baoen Monastery Pagoda looked but we do not know who built it or indeed how it was built. This has not diminished local ambitions, and there is a project under way in Nanjing, on the original site, to construct a concrete, glass and steel structure of similar height which will serve as a visitor education centre. A Chinese conglomerate is believed to have contributed RMB 1 billion towards the project, and this in purchasing power parity is broadly equivalent to the 2.5 million taels which the original pagoda is said to have cost.

Notes

1 The earlier 1407 date is suggested by Carrington Goodrich and Fang in *DMB*, 363. They associate the rebuilding with the death of Yongle's Empress Xu in 1407 and the subsequent project in her honour. Wang Cheng-Hua 1998, 19, notes the commencement year. Thomas Allom quotes the specific day from records kept by monks at the monastery. He also notes the project cost (discussed later) and records the architect as 'Shelang-Hwang' (possibly transliteration for Huang Shilang (?), but no similar name appears in sources examined). Allom 1858–9, 164–5.

2 In addition to **Pl. 20.1**, see also Eng 2014, 247, figs 8.13 and 8.15 for reproductions of sketches by John Nieuhoff (after Nieuhoff 1669, 84) and by Xu Hu (active early 19th century).

3 Thorp 1988, 115.

4 Transcriptions of a 1424 stele erected by Yongle and of Xuande's 1428 dedicatory stele are recorded in Zhang Huiyi 1938 *juan* 5, 22–5.

5 Nieuhoff 1669, 79–85. A longer account was published in 1843 by Captain Granville G. Loch in Loch 1843, 180–1. See also Allom 1858–9, 162. These accounts date from times when the purpose and function of pagodas were still not fully understood in the West. Salient extracts appear in Eng 2014, 246–8.

6 *HDACA* 1986, 196. See also Kerr and Wood 2004, 516.

7 Allom 1858–9, 164–5.

8 Nanjing bowuyuan 1960.

9 Thorp 1988, 115.

10 Clunas and Harrison-Hall 2014, figs 190–1.

11 Beer 1999, 88–90.

12 Whilst the figures which appear in the Cloud Terrace *torana* are similar in form and sequence to those in the reconstruction at the Nanjing Municipal Museum (the fuller of the two reconstructions in Nanjing), additional guardian figures appear in the sequence at the Zhihua Monastery, which also uses its *makaras* as decorative column-heads away from the *torana* sequence in the panel frames. The Zhihua Monastery sutra cabinet is surprisingly fortunate to have survived the turbulent history of the temple. The *garuda* at the head of each of its panels is a motif rarely seen in China (especially in the North) and reflects Hindu iconography more commonly observed (outside India) in Southeast Asia and the Indonesian archipelago. Kenneth Hammond notes that its presence in this temple, supposedly since its 1440 dedication, might be a legacy of the Mongol acceptance of Tibetan Lamaist Buddhism during the Yuan dynasty, a patronage which continued under the Yongle emperor. See Hammond 2001, 194. Beijing wenbo jiaoliuguan 2005, 132–9.

13 *DMHD*, *juan* 190. See also Lu Maocun 1996; Wang Guangyao 2004.

14 Ding, Kang and Miao 2011. See also Wood 1999, 67.

15 The *tianbai* glaze, a brilliant white, sometimes with a hint of green, was one of the glazes developed in Jingdezhen in the early 15th century during the quest for ever whiter glazes. See Wood 1999, 66–7.

16 Harrison-Hall 2001, 523.

17 Allom 1858–9, 164–5, cited by Krahl 1991, 55, with acknowledgement to J. and H. Espir.

18 See Eng 2014, 248.

19 See Eng 2014, 185 and also Eng 2008, 277.

20 Though no glazed floor tiles of any kind have yet to be found *in situ*, depictions exist of what may be monochrome tiles. For example in an Early Tang Dynasty mural painting of a dance in a palace setting at the Dunhuang grottoes in Cave 220 (south wall), monochrome tiles in four shades appear to be laid as floor tiles in diaper pattern. However, this mural may depict an imaginary setting and its detail not necessarily inspired by real life. For image, see Fan 2004, 73, fig. 62. From the Ming dynasty, a two-tone composition appears on the flagstone floor of a pavilion in a handscroll from 1484, in Clunas and Harrison-Hall 2014, 62, fig. 38. In the same catalogue (p. 102, fig. 91) and in another medium, a carved lacquer dish depicts what appears to be patterned tiles on a pavilion terrace. However, these are almost certainly depictions of unglazed flooring bricks with a patterned moulded surface intended to afford better grip outdoors in inclement weather. Such tiles were already well developed by the Tang dynasty and can be

seen, for instance, on the pavilion terraces, though not inside the main halls, in the remains of the *Da Ming gong* 大明宮, the former Tang imperial palace in today's Xian.

21 Clunas and Harrison-Hall 2014, 111. See also Eng 2014, 200.

22 Chang Foundation 1998, 122, 294–5, pls F18–21. See also Eng 2014, 201 regarding specimens excavated recently in Nanjing.

23 Floor tiles, with undercut edges to leave a triangular void for mortar to assist levelling, were well developed in China before the Tang dynasty. See *HDACA* 1986, 187.

24 For relevant illustrations, please refer to Eng 2014, 71, 185–6. See also Eng 2008, 278, 344.

25 I am most grateful to Dr Eileen Hsu Hsiang-Ling for her valuable advice on the epigraphy of the stele inscriptions.

26 The inscriptions are transcribed in Zhang Huiyi 1938, *juan* 5, 24–6. In addition, a recent commentary by Chen Pingping 2011, indicates additional material from a history of the temple compiled by its monks in 1807 and entitled *Zhe yi fancha zhi* 折疑梵刹志 (*Records Clarifying Questions of a Buddhist Monastery*) (primary source not yet sighted).

27 Tsai, Shih-shan Henry 2001, 22, 89, 141.

28 Wang Cheng-Hua 1998, 19–21 suggests that the filial assertions of the 1424 stele may have been inspired by Yongle's decision to move the capital to Beijing, leaving behind in Nanjing the tombs of his parents. Watt and Leidy (2005, 18) suggests that it honours 'his parents' but commemorated his supposed real mother (the Imperial concubine). Allom (1859, 163) quotes local histories (preserved by the monks at the temple) which record that the pagoda was dedicated to 'the Empress' which, from Allom's context, suggests that this was Yongle's consort, the Empress Xu. This interpretation is supported independently in *DMB*, 363 which suggests that in 1413, as an act of filial piety, Yongle's three sons, Gaochi 高熾 (the future Hongxi emperor), Gaoxu 高煦 and Gaosui 高燧 jointly commemorated the pagoda in honour of their mother, who died in 1407.

29 Dreyer 2007, 142. The employment of soldiers and artisanal workers together on such a project is mentioned in announcements and imperial orders from 1413 included in an appendix to Zhang Huiyi 1938, 125.

30 Thorp 1988, 115. See also Allom 1859, 163; Loch 1843, 205 (Appendix).

31 Huang 1974, 280–5.

32 Thorp 1988, 115. See also Watt and Leidy 2005, 20.

33 Tsai, Shih-shan Henry 2001, 203. See also Dreyer 2007, 137, 140; *DMB*, 197.

34 For Zheng He's role as 'defender' of Nanjing and Xuande's detailed instructions up to and including project completion, see Dreyer 2007, 140–2.

35 Eng 2014, 239–51.

36 Names of 'builder-administrators' for palace projects in Nanjing and Beijing are sometimes recorded but not it seems those active during this period. These officials were in any case unlikely to have made the detailed designs for the projects.

37 The Xiudingsi 修定寺 at Anyang in Henan province is a fine (and also unique in China) example of ceramic architectural construction using tenons and keys, in this case to fasten the elaborate external earthenware brick ornamentation to an inner wall. It originated in the 6th century, was destroyed and rebuilt in the late 7th century. It was extensively restored in the Ming Jiajing period (1522–66) but was pillaged for its fine ornamental brickwork in the 1920–30s, and most recently restored (with replacement ornamental bricks) in the 1970s. Samples of its decorative bricks have been dated through thermoluminescence to the Tang dynasty. The British Museum (amongst others) displays one of these bricks. See Portal 1990; Swart and Till 1990, 64–76; Cao 2005; Steinhardt 2014, 211–13.

38 Hsu, Eileen Hsiang-ling (forthcoming). See also Hsu 2012.

39 In Buddhist teaching the *cha* post is said to symbolise the rotational axis of the universe and is a vestigial component of early Indian stupas which were precursors of Chinese and East Asian pagodas. Some researchers now believe it may have served a practical purpose also in acting as a counter-pendulum in earthquakes. See Eng 2014, 97–8, 229–30; Ueda 1995; *HDACA* 1986, 211; Hu Shiping 1991.

40 See Thorp 1988, 115 and also *HDACA* 1986, 194–213.

Chapter 21
Architecture of the Early Ming Court: A Preliminary Look

Aurelia Campbell

On the architecture of the early Ming dynasty (1368–1644), the eminent 20th-century Chinese architectural historian Liang Sicheng (1901–72) wrote:

> With the founding of the capital at Beijing at the beginning of the fifteenth century, there appeared, principally in the official architecture of the court, a style of marked departure from the tradition of the Song [(960–1279)] and Yuan [(1271–1368)] dynasties. The change is very abrupt, as if some overwhelming force had turned the minds of the builders toward an entirely new sense of proportion.[1]

Liang's observations indicate that a new architectural style had been worked out sometime during the construction of the two Ming capitals at Nanjing and Beijing.[2] What did this architectural style look like? In what ways did it differ from the architecture that preceded it and came after it? What was the reason for the sudden change? This chapter offers some preliminary answers to these questions.

Because so few buildings from the first Ming capital at Nanjing survive, it is almost impossible to study court architecture during the reign of the Hongwu emperor (1368–98). But from the reign of his son, the Yongle emperor (1403–24), enough buildings exist to flesh out significantly our understanding of what is called the 'official Ming architectural style' (*Mingdai guanshi jianzhu* 明代官式建築). This term refers to buildings constructed under imperial edict and managed by the government's Ministry of Works (*Gongbu* 工部), which follow distinct layouts, structures and patterns of ornamentation.[3]

Yongle was a prolific builder, arguably more so than almost any other Chinese emperor until that point. In addition to constructing the palaces at Beijing, he was involved in several architectural projects outside of the capital. Three of the best-preserved buildings commissioned by Yongle are Ling'endian 祾恩殿 (Hall of Eminent Favour) (1416) (**Pl. 21.1**), the sacrificial hall at Yongle's tomb, Changling 長陵, located in the Changping 昌平 district north of Beijing[4]; Zixiaodian 紫霄殿 (Hall of Purple Cloud) (**Pl. 21.2**), the main hall of

Plate 21.1 Ling'endian 祾恩殿 (1416), the sacrificial hall at Yongle's tomb, Changling 長陵, Changping 昌平, north of Beijing

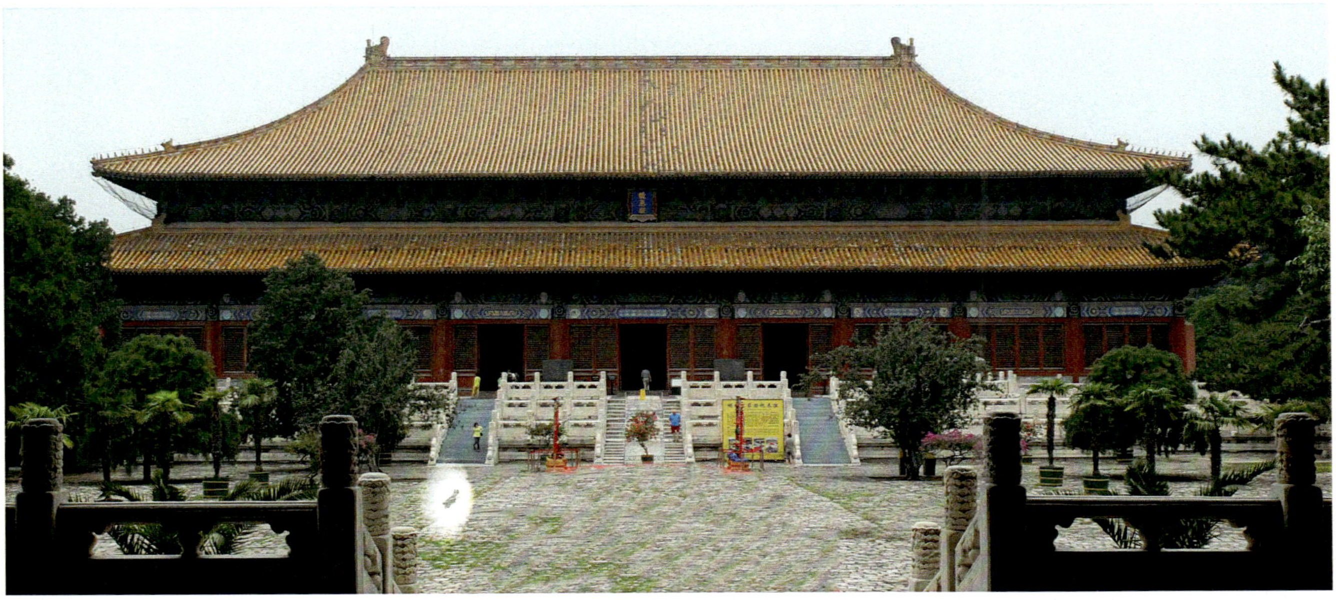

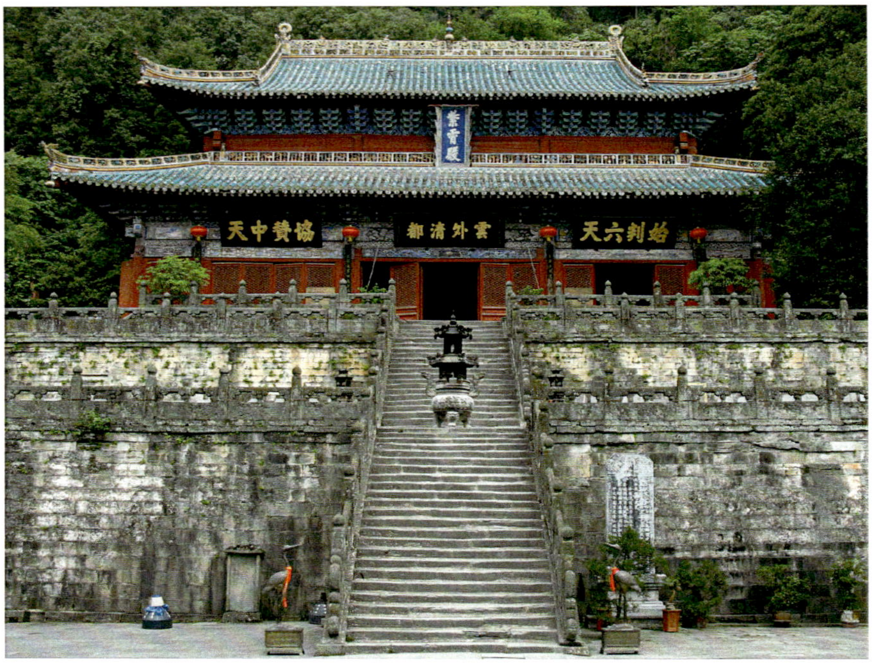

Plate 21.2 Zixiaodian 紫霄殿 (1412), the main hall of Zixiaogong 紫霄宮, Mount Wudang 武當山, Hubei province

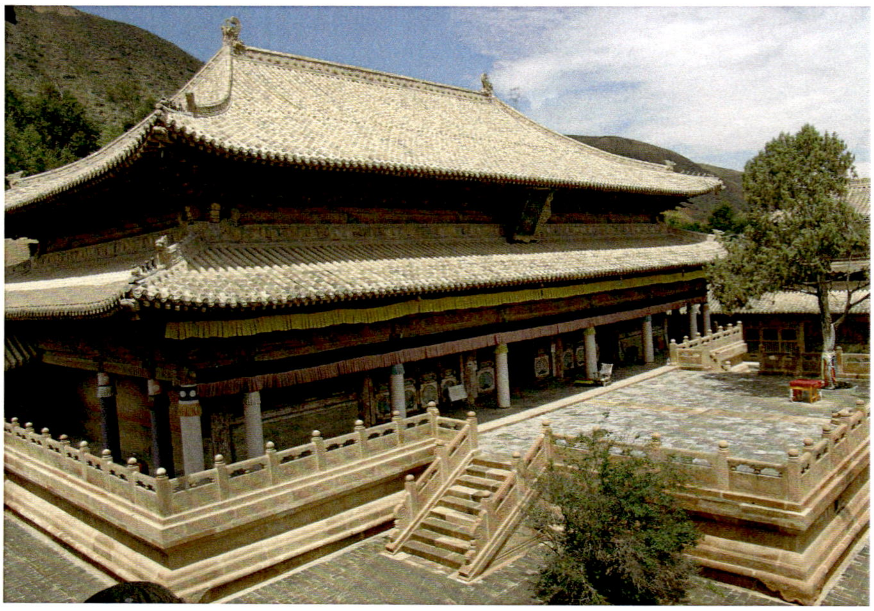

Plate 21.3 Longguodian 隆國殿 (1427), the main hall of Qutansi 瞿曇寺, a Tibetan Buddhist monastery in Ledu 樂都, Qinghai province

Zixiaogong 紫霄宮 (1412), one of the largest Daoist temples on Mount Wudang 武當山 in Hubei province (see also Chapters 14 and 21)[5]; and Longguodian 隆國殿 (Hall of Enriching the State) (1427) (**Pl. 21.3**) the main hall of Qutansi 瞿曇寺 (Gautama Monastery), a Tibetan Buddhist monastery in Ledu 樂都, Qinghai province (see also discussion by Karl Debreczeny in Chapter 17 of this volume).[6]

Ling'endian, Zixiaodian and Longguodian were all constructed within 15 years of each other under the direction of officials dispatched from the imperial capital. Typologically, they are analogous in that they are all the main halls of their respective architectural complexes. Considering these similarities, one might expect the halls to look more alike than they actually do. Indeed, the initial visual impacts of these buildings differ quite significantly. Yet a close examination of these buildings' structures reveals that they actually share an underlying logic because the same basic principles governed their construction. These principles reflect a shift away from the ones outlined in the Song dynasty government construction manual *Yingzao fashi* 營造法式 (*Treatise on Architectural Methods*) of 1103[7] and towards the widely different set of rules put forth in the Qing (1644–1911) court's building manual, *Gongcheng zuofa* 工程做法 (*Imperial Specifications for State Buildings*) (*c.* 1734).[8] Nonetheless, the official Ming architectural style should not be understood merely as a passive transitional style between the Song and the Qing. Rather, the many early Ming architectural developments reveal a deliberate attempt to simplify and standardise the construction process, a possible outcome of the extraordinary task of building two Ming capitals within just a few decades of each other. To demonstrate this point, this chapter focuses on three specific elements: the module system, the bracket-set types and the relationship between the bracket-sets and the bays in these three halls.

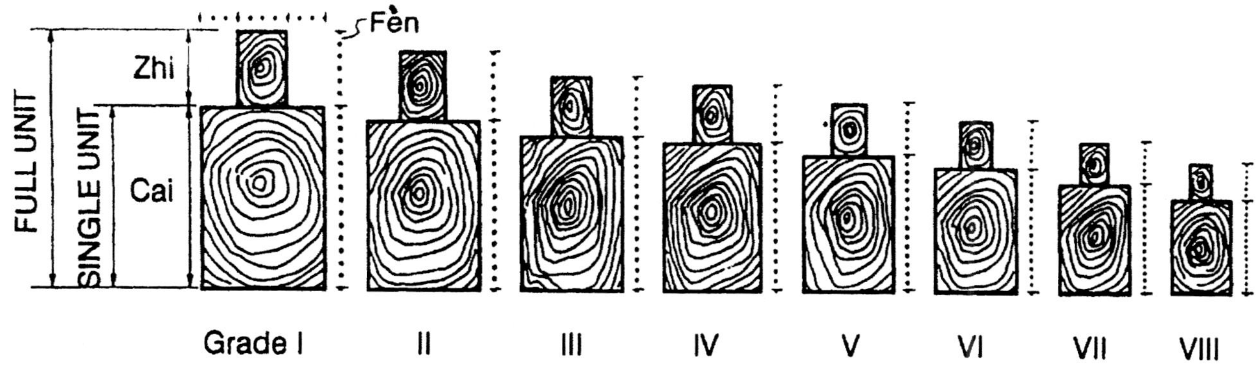

Plate 21.4 Eight grades of modules outlined in the *Yingzao fashi* 營造法式 (after Guo Qinghua 1998, p. 7)

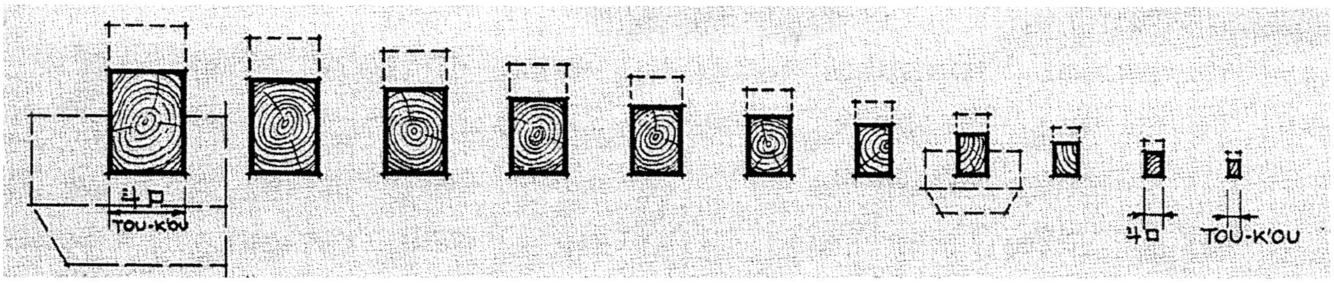

Plate 21.5 Eleven grades of modules outlined in the *Gongcheng zuofa* 工程做法 (after Liang Sicheng 2005, p. 18)

Modules

Traditional Chinese timber-frame architecture is based on a modular system, meaning that a standard module is used to calculate the dimensions of the rest of the structural members. In the Song dynasty *Yingzao fashi* the module was known as *cai* 材. The dimensions of the *cai* were equal to the cross-section of the bracket-set arm (*gong* 栱), which was both the smallest and the most frequently used structural member.[9] In the Song, the size of the module and the overall scale of the building were in direct proportion. Therefore, a small module yielded a small building and a large module yielded a large building.[10] The *Yingzao fashi* outlines eight grades (*deng* 等) of *cai* (**Pl. 21.4**). The largest and highest rank *cai* (Grade One) measures nine *cun* 寸 in height and six *cun* in width (approximately 28 x 19cm), while the smallest and lowest rank *cai* (Grade Eight) measures 4.5 *cun* in height and three *cun* in width (approximately 14 x 9cm).[11]

It is important to keep in mind that no actual building from the Tang or Song periods actually conforms completely to the rules outlined in the *Yingzao fashi* because the purpose of the manual was not to guide the construction of buildings, but rather to 'summarise the [architectural] knowledge from previous dynasties'.[12] For example, even though Dongdadian 東大殿 (East Main Hall) at Foguangsi 佛光寺 (Monastery of Buddha Light) (857) employs a Grade One module (approximately 9.4 x 6.4 *cun*, or 30 x 20.5cm) on the *Yingzao fashi* scale, it only has seven bays across the front, not the nine or eleven required for a true Grade One building as outlined in the *Yingzao fashi*.[13]

In the Qing dynasty *Gongcheng zuofa* the module is called *doukou* 斗口. *Doukou* (literally 'block mouth') refers to the opening in the capital block into which the arm of an inter-columnar bracket-set (*pingshenke* 平身科) – or a set between, as opposed to on top of, the columns – was inserted. Like the *cai*, the dimensions of the *doukou* are equal to the cross-section of the bracket-arm.[14] The *Gongcheng zuofa* outlines eleven grades of *doukou* (**Pl. 21.5**) in contrast to the *Yingzao fashi*'s eight grades of *cai*.

In theory, the largest and highest rank *doukou* (Grade One) was 8.4 *cun* in height x 6 *cun* in width (approximately 27 by 19.5cm) while the smallest (Grade Eleven) was 1.4 in height x 1 *cun* in width (approximately 4.5 by 3.2cm).[15] However, in practice, the first through third grades were almost never used; most high-rank buildings used only the seventh, eighth or ninth grades. For instance, Taihedian 太和殿 (Hall of Supreme Harmony) (1695), the largest hall in the Forbidden City, eleven bays across the façade, only employs a Grade Seven *doukou*, which was 4.2 *cun* in height and 3 *cun* in width (approximately 13.3 x 9.5cm).[16] That such an eminent building as Taihedian uses such a relatively low-grade module means that by the 18th century the module's size was significantly less important in determining the overall rank of a building than it was in the Song.

How large were the modules used in the Yongle buildings discussed here? Was the size of the module closely linked to the rank of the architecture, as it was in the Song? Or had it already declined in importance, as was the case in architecture of the Qing?

The width of the modules used at Zixiao Hall, Ling'en Hall and Longguo Hall range from 3 to 3.5 *cun* in width (**Table 1**). This is consistent with the module sizes of other imperial buildings from around the same time, which range from about 3.15 to 4.1 *cun* in width (**Table 2**). These modules correspond to the eighth, or lowest, grade in the *Yingzao fashi* scale and are roughly the same size as the module used at Taihedian. Because the transition to a smaller module was already well underway by the Yuan period, it would be incorrect to assume that smaller modules suddenly appeared in the early Ming.[17] However, based on the three halls examined here, it is clear that in the early 15th century a major shift had occurred whereby even the highest rank imperial Ming halls employed relatively small modules –

Table 1 Module sizes in the three halls

Hall name	Date	Number of façade bays	Module (*doukou*) width in cm/*cun*
Zixiaodian[20]	1412	5	10.5cm/3.3 *cun*
Ling'engdian[21]	1416	9	9.5–10cm/3–3.15 *cun*
Longguodian[22]	1427	7	11cm/3.5 *cun*

Table 2 Module sizes in other Ming buildings

Hall name	Date	Number of façade bays	Module (*doukou*) width in cm/*cun*
Yuzhengong main hall 遇真宮大殿[23]	1417	3	10cm/3.15 *cun*
Shenwumen chenglou 神武門城樓[24]	1420	7	12.5–13cm/3.9–4.1 *cun*
Shejitan front hall 社稷壇前殿[25]	1425	5	12.5cm/3.9 *cun*
Fahaisi main hall 法海寺大殿[26]	1439	5	9cm/2.83 *cun*
Zhihuasi Wanfoge 智化寺萬佛閣[27]	1444	5	8cm/2.5 *cun*
Taimiao front hall 太廟前殿[28]	1545	11	12.5cm/3.9 *cun*
Taimiao middle hall 太廟中殿[29]	1545	9	12.5cm/3.9 *cun*
Taimiao rear hall 太廟後殿[30]	1545	9	12.5cm/3.9 *cun*

smaller, even, than those used in the non-imperial Buddhist and Daoist temples that survive from the Yuan period.[18] Therefore, we can conclude that beginning in early Ming there was indeed a significant weakening of the link between the size of the module and the overall rank of a building, a trend that persisted in the Qing.[19]

What significance lies in the shrinking of the module? As I have explained above the size of the module corresponded to the cross-section of the bracket-set arm. Therefore, much smaller modules meant much smaller bracket-sets. By the early Ming dynasty carpenters had figured out ways to support the roof eaves more efficiently by using beams that projected past the façade of the building.[31] This meant that the large and complex bracket-set types that we see in the Tang and Song dynasties had become unnecessary structurally.[32] By creating smaller and less complicated bracket-sets, carpenters could save considerable amounts of time in the construction process. Furthermore, timber materials could be better economised and costs reduced.

The issue of saving wood during the Yongle reign is somewhat tricky. On one hand, for the construction of his capital, the Yongle emperor seemed to gather old-growth *nan* 楠 timbers from the southwest of his empire without any reservations whatsoever regarding cost or environmental waste.[33] At the same time, textual records document the immense difficulties involved in obtaining these woods, which took four or five years to reach the capital and

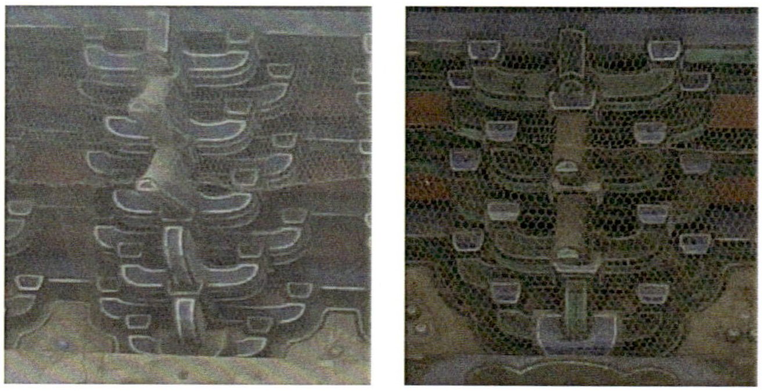

a)

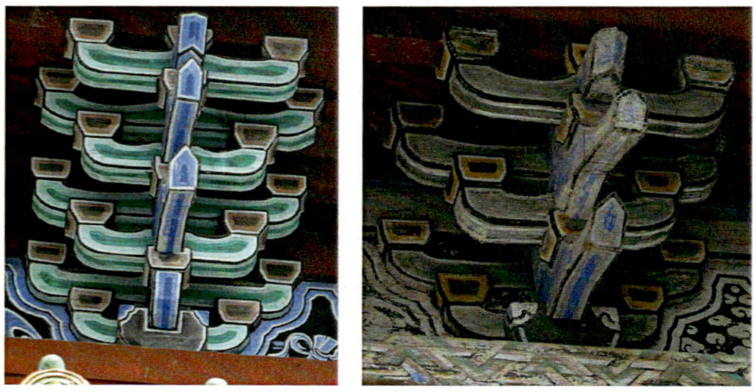

b)

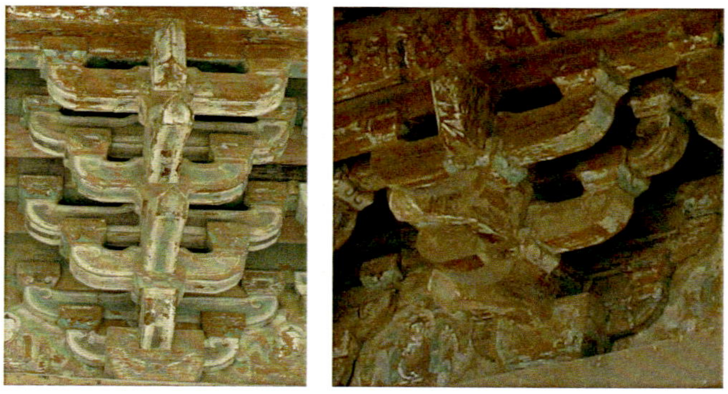

c)

Plate 21.6a–c: a) Ling'endian top (left) and bottom (right) bracket-sets; b) Zixiaodian top (left) and bottom (right) bracket-sets; c) Longguodian top (left) and bottom (right) bracket-sets

Table 3 General characteristics of bracket-sets[34]

	Ling'endian	**Zixiaodian**	**Longguodian**
Bracket-set types (upper eaves)	9-*cai*, double-*qiao*, double-*ang*, rear tail supporting an inclined member 九踩重翹重昂後尾起斜杆	7-*cai*, single-*qiao* double-*ang*, rear tail supporting an inclined member 七踩單翹重昂後尾起斜杆	7-*cai*, single-*qiao*, double-*ang*, level rear tail七踩單翹重昂斗拱後尾平置
Bracket-set types (lower eaves)	7-*cai*, single-*qiao*, double-*ang liujin* rear tail七踩单翘重昂後尾溜金	5-*cai*, double-*ang*, *liujin* rear tail 五踩重昂後尾溜金	5-*cai*, double-*ang*, level rear tail 五踩重昂斗拱後尾平置

exhausted an extraordinary amount of manpower.[35] Furthermore, immediately following the Yongle reign, the need to conserve *nan*-wood construction materials had evidently already been recognised at the imperial level.[36] Therefore, although it may not have been the highest priority of Yongle himself, it seems logical to conclude that builders had been devising techniques to make the best possible use of materials since at least the Song dynasty and that these methods were finally carried out on a large scale in the early Ming. The reduction of the module size was no doubt at least in part a result of this concern.

Bracket-set types

Ling'endian, Zixiaodian and Longguodian are all double-eave structures, which means they have two layers of bracket-sets. At all the halls, the bracket-sets supporting the top eave employ two more tiers (*cai* 踩) – or projections perpendicular to the building's façade – than those that support the bottom eave.[37] Qi Yingtao has observed that the most eminent Ming dynasty buildings, such as halls that directly served the emperor, employ nine-tier brackets on the top and seven-tier sets on the bottom, whereas less illustrious buildings, such as Buddhist temples, use seven-tier bracket sets on the top and five-tier sets on the bottom.[38] This is consistent with the evidence preserved in the three halls examined here, where Ling'endian (**Pl. 21.6a**), one of the most important Ming halls for making state sacrifices, employs nine- and seven-tier sets and both Zixiaodian and Longguodian, the main halls in a Daoist and a Buddhist temple, respectively, use seven- and five-tier bracket sets (**Pl. 21.6b–c**).

At Zixiaodian and Longguodian, the bracket types are identical to each other: seven-tier, single projection (*qiao* 翹),[39] double false cantilever (*chongjia'ang* 重假昂) on the top and five-tier double false cantilever sets on the bottom (**Table 3**).[40] The fact that the same bracketing appears both in the five-bay Zixiaodian and the seven-bay Longguodian suggests that in early Ming official architecture the number of tiers in a bracket-set was not dictated by the size or number of bays in a building, but rather by the importance of the architecture to the state. This point is also supported through the example of the three main halls aligned along the central axis of the *Taimiao* 太廟 (Imperial Ancestral Temple) (1545) (**Pl. 21.7**), which all employ seven-tier sets even though the buildings are five, nine and eleven bays across the façade.[41]

The bracket-sets of Ling'endian, Zixiaodian and Longguodian, and in fact all brackets in official Ming architecture, employ the 'filled-heart' technique (*jixinzao* 計心造) outlined in the *Yingzao fashi*, in which bracket arms perpendicular to the building façade support a 'crisscross'[42] of both parallel and perpendicular bracket arms (**Pl. 21.8a**). Bracket-set techniques that were once popular in the Song and the Yuan, such as the 'stolen heart' (*touxinzao* 偷心造) (consisting mostly of perpendicular rather than parallel projecting bracket arms) (**Pl. 21.8b**) and 'single-arm' (*dangongzao* 單栱造) (a single-tier bracket parallel to the wall plane) (**Pl. 21.8c**), disappeared in the early Ming. This indicates a newfound level of simplification in bracket-set types.[43]

The parts of the bracket-set invisible from the outside reveal additional likenesses among the three halls. Ling'endian and Zixiaodian, and in fact all the high rank Yongle period buildings at Mount Wudang, employ a special kind of bracket known as *liujin* 溜金.[44] *Liujin* is a vestige of the more structurally complicated true cantilever (*ang* 昂) used in the pre-Ming periods.[45] In the *liujin* bracket, the rear tail of the false cantilever of the inter-columnar sets extends well

Plate 21.7 ***Taimiao*** **太廟 (Imperial Ancestral Temple) (1545), Beijing**

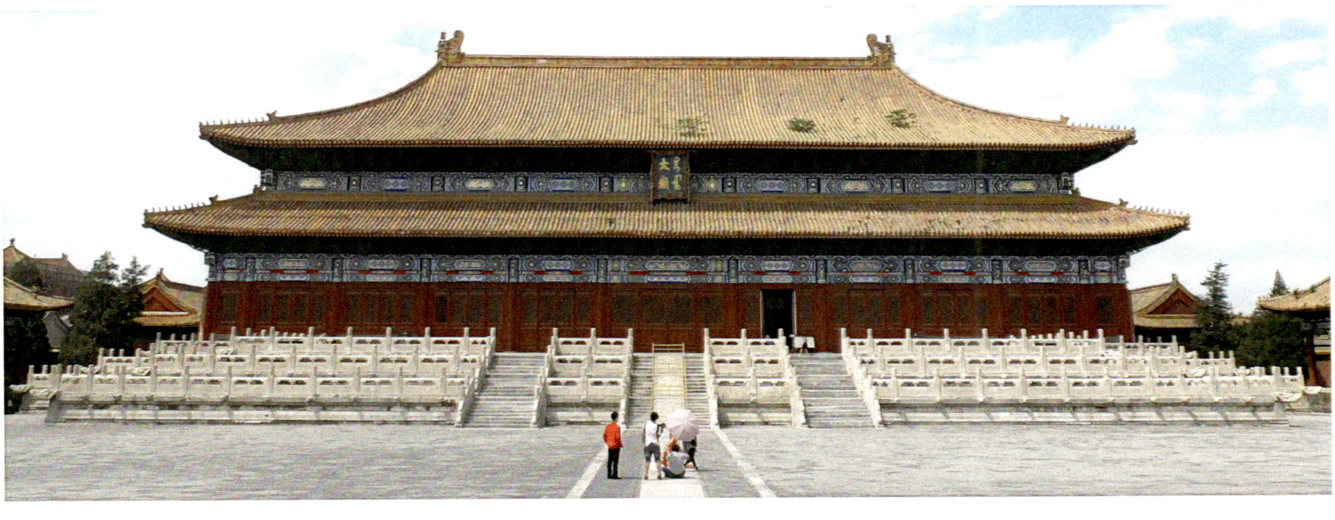

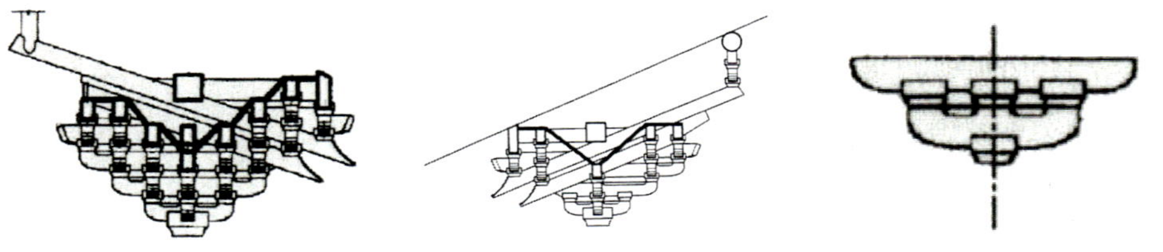

a) b) c)

Plate 21.8a–c: a) 'Filled-heart construction' (*jixinzao* 計心造) bracket-set; b) 'Stolen heart construction' (*touxinzao* 偷心造) bracket-set; c) 'Single-arm construction' (*dangongzao* 單栱造) bracket-set (after Guo Daiheng 2009, p. 664)

inside the building to support the lowest eave purlin (*jinheng* 金桁) and is often elaborately carved underneath (**Pl. 21.9a–b**).[46] These early Ming buildings reveal that the *liujin* brackets, which are typically associated with official-style Qing architecture, were already in use by the early 15th century.[47]

In sum, in the early Ming dynasty bracket-set construction was simplified and standardized in the following ways: (1) In buildings with double-roof eaves, the brackets that supported the top eaves consistently employed two more tiers than those that supported the bottom eaves. (2) The distribution of the number of tiers used in a bracket corresponded to the function of a building: state buildings possessed larger sets than those serving as Buddhist or Daoist temples. (3) The number of bracket-set tiers was not related to the number of bays across a building's façade, but rather to the importance of the building. (4) There was a noticeable simplification in the variety of bracket-set types beginning in the early Ming. Finally, (5) *liujin* brackets, traditionally associated with Qing architecture, were widely used, even in imperial buildings lying far outside the capital, such as the Daoist temples on Mount Wudang.

Spacing of inter-columnar sets

As mentioned above, by the early Ming period, the size of the module and resulting bracket-set was no longer as important in determining the rank of a building as it was in the Song. Instead, the number of inter-columnar bracket-sets became the new indicator of rank and status. The *Yingzao fashi* stipulates that, regardless of the width of the bay, there were to be two inter-columnar bracket-sets in the central bay and one each in the corner and flanking bays.[48] This was the number of inter-columnar sets most frequently used in the Yuan dynasty. By the early Ming, however, it seems that the more brackets that were used, the better. Ling'endian, for instance, uses eight sets in its central bay, while Zixiaodian and Longguodian each use six and four sets, respectively. Perhaps unsurprisingly, at 10.30m, Ling'endian also has the widest central bay; Zixiaodian's central bay is the second widest, measuring 8.37m, and Longuodian's is the narrowest, measuring 6.60m (**Table 4**). Thus the more inter-columnar brackets a building employed, the wider its bays were, and the higher its overall architectural rank was.[49] We can therefore conclude that from the early Ming onwards a close relationship had developed between the width of the bays and the number of inter-columnar bracket-sets used.[50]

By the Qing dynasty this relationship became more fully codified. The Qing *Gongcheng zuofa* required each inter-columnar bracket-set cluster to be spaced at a distance of eleven *doukou* modules and the width of a bay to be determined by multiplies of eleven *doukou*.[51] For example, in the Qing dynasty a bay containing six inter-columnar bracket-sets possessed a total width of 77 *doukou*, and a bay with four sets measured 55 *doukou* in width.[52] In fact, in the *Gongcheng zuofa*, the module was not only used to calculate the distance between the bracket-sets and the bay width, but almost every other aspect of the building as well, including the cross-sections of the beams, pillars and purlins.[53] This was not the case in the *Yingzao fashi*. In the Song, bracket-sets were unevenly spaced. Moreover, although the module was

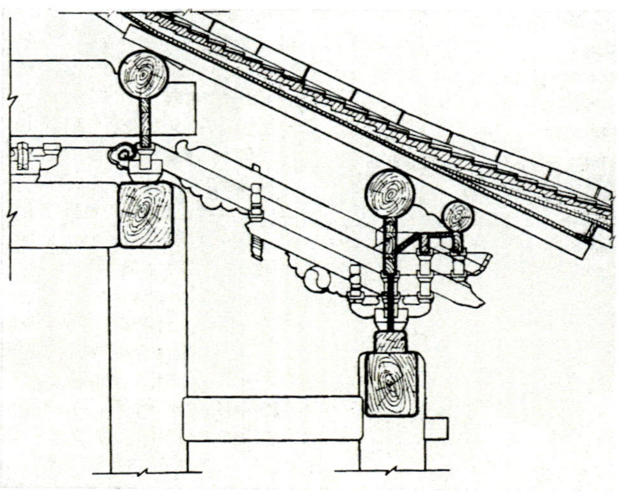

a)

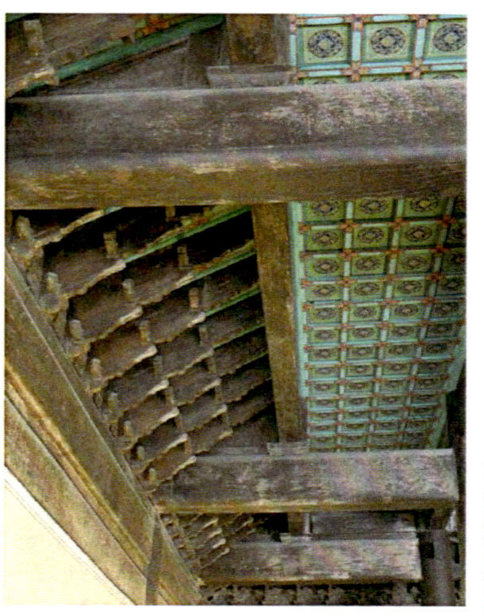

b)

Plate 21.9a–b: a) Line drawing of *liujin dougong* 溜金斗栱 (after Wang Xiaoqing 2006, p. 449); b) *liujin dougong* tails inside Ling'endian

Table 4 Width of bay (in metres)[54], number of intercolumnar bracket-set clusters and distance between the bracket-set clusters (in *doukou*)[55]

	Ling'endian	Zixiaodian	Longguodian
Façade:			
Central bay (*mingjian* 明間)	10.30m,[56] 8 sets, 11.5 *doukou*	8.37m, 6 sets, 11.4 *doukou*	6.60m, 4 sets, 12 *doukou*
First flanking bays (*cijian* 次間 1)	7.20m, 6 sets, 10.4 *doukou*	6.39m, 4 sets, 12.1 *doukou*	5.70m, 4 sets, 10.4 *doukou*
Second flanking bays (*cijian* 2)	7.20m, 6, sets, 10.4 *doukou*	N/A	5.70m, 4 sets, 10.4 *doukou*
Third flanking bays (*cijian* 3)	7.20m, 6 sets, 10.4 *doukou*	N/A	N/A
Side bays (*shaojian* 梢間)	6.70m, 6 sets, 10.4 *doukou*	2.56m, 1 set, 12.1 *doukou*	2.12m, none, 19.3 *doukou* (?)
Side:			
Central bay	10.30m, 9 sets, 9.6 *doukou*	5.94m, 4 sets, 10.8 *doukou*	7.74m, 4 sets, 14.1 *doukou*
First flanking bays	6.70m, 6 sets, x[57]	3.66m, 2 sets, 11.1 *doukou*	3.82m, 2 sets, 11.6 *doukou*
Side bays	2.80m, 2 sets, x[58]	2.56m, 1 set, 10.1 *doukou*	1.92m, none, 17.4 *doukou* (?)

used to calculate the cross-sections of the other structural members, it was not yet used to determine the widths of the bays.[59] Similarly, in the three Ming halls examined here, the spacing between the bracket-sets in the central bay is not set at eleven, but fluctuates between 10.3 to 12.1 *doukou* modules. The width of the central bay at Longguodian, for instance, is 60 *doukou* and there are four bracket-set clusters, meaning that they are spaced at 12 *doukou* intervals. The spacing of the bracket-sets also differs depending on whether they are located in the central bay (*mingjian* 明間), the flanking bays (*cijian* 次間) or the corner bays (*shaojian* 梢間). For instance, whereas the bracket-sets in the central bay at Ling'endian are spaced at 11.5 *doukou*, those in the flanking and corner bays are spaced at 10.4 *doukou* (**Table 4**).

These buildings reveal that in the early Ming the number of inter-columnar bracket sets became a primary expression of a building's rank. Moreover, although we do see some evidence of a close relationship between the number of bracket sets and the width of the bays, it is also clear that these early Ming buildings did not yet determine the width of the bays based on the 11-*doukou* rule later outlined in the *Gongcheng zuofa*.[60] Even though the system of bracket-set spacing was not set precisely at 11 *doukou* in the early Ming period, the more or less stable 10 to 12 *doukou* distances in the three Yongle halls examined here undoubtedly set the stage for the standardisation that was finally achieved in the Qing.

Conclusions

Upon first glance Ling'endian, Zixiaodian and Longguodian look quite different from each other. However, a closer investigation of their structures reveals that they were built according to the same basic architectural principles as each other. The style they embody, now known as the official Ming architectural style, was novel at the time, having been worked out in the first 60 or so years of the Ming dynasty. In comparison with pre-Ming buildings, those built in the early 15th century are highly simplified and standardised. The new Ming architectural style can be understood as the product of efforts to facilitate carpenters' workloads and also to save wood during the intense period of construction of the two Ming capitals. Indeed, as we can tell from the halls examined here, the official Ming architectural style was a one-size-fits-all model that was designed to move across wide geographical territories. Once the structures were built, it was likely up to the local craftsmen to apply superficial decoration according to regional customs, based on the functional demands of the halls or in response to site-specific geographic constraints. It is no doubt these superficial decorations that account for the halls' immediately recognisable differences and obscure their many underlying consistencies.

Notes

I would like to thank Rui Zhu and Alexandra Harrer for their helpful comments on a draft of this chapter.

1 Liang and Fairbank 2005, 103.
2 The palaces in Nanjing were constructed in three phases: between 1366 and 1367 the basic scale and layout of the buildings was arranged; from 1375 to 1377 most of the palace buildings were constructed; and in 1392 they were expanded. The palaces in Beijing were constructed between 1416 and 1420, but were rebuilt and expanded several times throughout the Ming and Qing dynasties. See Pan 2009, 112–18 for an introduction to the palace architecture in Nanjing under Hongwu and in Beijing under Yongle. For a study on the construction dates of Yongle's capital at Beijing see Li Xieping 1995, 34–64.
3 Guo 2005, 1–2. It is important to mention that each new dynasty developed its own official architectural style. According to Fu Xinian, official architecture can be understood in contrast to vernacular architecture. Fu argues that whereas vernacular architecture evolves organically at a consistent rate, depending on such factors as geography, climate and culture, because it is controlled and standardised by the government, official architecture instead develops in stages, with significant changes being made under each new dynasty. Fu 1999, 91.
4 Little has been published on the architecture of Ling'endian. See Liu Dunzhen 1933 and Li Qianlang 2009 for an introduction.
5 Between 1413 and 1424 Emperor Yongle constructed dozens of Daoist temples over a 60km-wide area of Mount Wudang. On this architectural complex, see Wudangshan zhi bianzuan weiyuanhui 1994, 123–69; Hubei sheng jianshe ting 2005; and de Bruyn 2010, especially ch. 12.
6 Qutansi was consecutively supported by the Hongwu, Yongle, Hongxi and Xuande emperors. Although the construction of Longguodian was finished in the second year of the Xuande (1427) reign, the project was initiated during the reign of Yongle. On the architecture of Qutansi see Wu Cong 1994; Debreczeny 2007, 158–90; and Campbell 2011, 127–45.
7 For an overview and history of the *Yingzao fashi* see Glahn 1981, Glahn 1975 and Glahn 1984; and Guo Qinghua 1988. For annotated and punctuated versions of the *Yingzao fashi* see Liang Sicheng 1983 and (Song) Li Jie 2006.
8 On the *Gongcheng zuofa* see Liang Sicheng 2006 and Wang Puzi 1995.
9 Harrer 2010, 44.

10 Or, in the words of Qinghua Guo, 'the module controls the scale'. Guo 1988, 6.

11 These calculations are based on Song dynasty measurements in which one *cun* is roughly equal to 3.12cm. The modules also correspond to the number of bays across the façade and to different building types. See Li Jie 2006, 24–5 for the original text outlining the module ranking system. For this information organised into a clear table see Guo Daiheng 2009, 642.

12 Chen Mingda 1998.

13 Fu Xinian 2001, 647. It may well be that because in the Tang dynasty builders did not yet have the technical means to fabricate delicate timber-frame constructions they 'over-dimensioned' everything in order to ensure structural stability. Nonetheless, the *Yingzao fashi* clearly testifies to the perceived importance of the module size in determining the overall rank of a building. I would like to thank Alexandra Harrer for bringing this point to my attention. 'Over-dimensioned' is Harrer's terminology.

14 Liang Sicheng 2005, 19–20.

15 Sun Dazhang 2009, 399. These calculations are based on Ming dynasty measurements in which one *cun* is roughly equal to 3.175cm. See Guo Huayu 2005, 127.

16 Sun Dazhang 2009, 399.

17 See Pan Guxi 2009, 450–4 for an explanation of the major structural changes that occurred during the Yuan dynasty.

18 Examples include Yonglegong Sanqingdian 永樂宮三清殿, five bays, 6.6 x 4.4 *cun* (20.7 x 13.5cm); Yonglegong Chunyangdian 永樂宮純陽殿, five bays, 6 x 4 *cun* (18.0 x 12.5cm); Guangsheng Shang si Mituodian 廣勝上寺彌陀殿, five bays, 5.25 x 3.5 *cun* (16.5 x 11cm); Zhenrusi Dadian 真如寺大殿, three bays, 4.4 x 3 *cun* (13.5 x 9cm). Pan Guxi 2009, 452.

19 This point can be illustrated by comparing the three-bay wide Main Hall of Zhenrusi (1320) to the nine-bay wide Ling'endian. Despite their obvious differences in size and rank, both halls employ modules of 3 *cun*.

20 Bai, He and Wang 2009, 91.

21 Bai, He and Wang 2009, 91.

22 Bai, He and Wang 2009, 91; Wu Cong 1994, 39; and Qi Yingtao 1992, 326. Guo Huayu provides different figures for the module widths of the three halls: Zixiaogong, 7.6–8cm/2.4–2.5 *cun*; Ling'endian, 9.5cm/3.0 *cun*; Longguodian, 7.6–8.0cm/2.4–2.5 *cun*. Guo Huayu 2005, 128. I am following Bai and Wu's figures because they are consistent with each other.

23 The module size is an approximate figure based on the remains of this building. Bai, He and Wang 2009, 91.

24 Bai, He and Wang 2009, 91.

25 Bai, He and Wang 2009, 91. Guo gives 11.5–12cm/3.62–3.78 *cun* for the module width. Guo Huayu 2005, 128.

26 Guo Huayu 2005, 128.

27 Bai, He and Wang 2009, 91.

28 Qi Yingtao 1992, 326.

29 Qi Yingtao 1992, 326.

30 Qi Yingtao 1992, 326.

31 See Pan Guxi 2009, 451 for a technical description of the ways in which beams were used to support brackets.

32 This does not mean, however, that bracket-sets became purely ornamental. Recent scholarship has demonstrated that Ming and Qing brackets still served a structural function even though they had shrunken in size. Guo Huayu 2005, 142.

33 Yu Zhuoyun thus concluded that '...because [the forests in Sichuan] were so vast and the supply of wood plentiful, there was an endless stream of timber travelling between the province and the timber yards in Beijing'. Yu Zhuoyun and Hutt 1987, 20. The 60 massive *nan* wood pillars used at Ling'endian, which soar 13m in height and measure 1.17m in diameter, offer a glimpse of just how large the timbers used for imperial construction during the Yongle reign could be. Nonetheless, the column dimensions at Ling'endian should not be considered typical of all Ming buildings, but only the very highest-ranking ones.

34 Bai, He and Wang 2009, 93.

35 For example, a Ming dynasty text records: '照得楠杉大木，產在川貴湖廣等處，差官採辦，非四五年不得北京' ('The great *nan* and *shan* timbers are produced in Gui[zhou], Hu[nan], and Guang[zhou]. An official dispatched to collect the timbers would not return to Beijing for four or five years'). For more on this subject see Zhou Qiwen 2012, 139. Ming records also reveal that it was difficult for even 1,000 men to move a single felled timber: '一木初臥，千夫難移'. Another text mentions that 700 or 800 men were required: '拽運輒至七八百人'. Lan Yong 1994, 94. Eventually Ming regulations specified the number of individuals required to move trunks of certain sizes. A trunk of *nan* wood seven *zhang* 丈 tall, and one *zhang*, two-to-three *chi* 尺 in circumference, for example, required 500 men: '崇楠木一株，長七丈，圍圓一丈二三尺者，用拽運夫五百名。' Gao Shouxian 2006, 28.

36 For example, a text dating to 1431 mentions that Xuande issued an order to stop the waste of *nan* timber materials stored in the Beijing timber yards: '有不當用，切勿妄廢。若本大材而工匠斲小用之，罪亦不貸. When there are [timber materials] not being used, do not rashly waste them. If carpenters chop these large timbers for trivial purposes, they will be punished without pardon.' See Jiang Shunyuan 2002, 244.

37 The formula used to calculate the number of tiers in a bracket set is the following: twice the number of projecting steps (2x *chucaishu* 出踩數) +1 = a bracket set of y-*cai* 踩. Harrer 2010, 580.

38 Qi Yingtao 1992, 336.

39 *Qiao* 翹 are *gong*-shaped (*gongxing* 弓形) wooden members that project outwards from the central line of the block atop which they sit. It is the same thing as the Song dynasty *huagong* 華栱 (see footnote below). Wang 2006, 418.

40 A so-called 'false cantilever' (*jia'ang* 假昂) refers to the result of the end of a projecting bracket-arm (*huagong*) has been carved to look like a true cantilever (*ang* 昂), but which, instead of serving a structural function is merely decorative. In the early Ming it was common for buildings to have two false cantilevers.

41 Qi 1992, 335.

42 Guo Qinghua 2002, 50.

43 Qi 1992, 336.

44 Bai, He and Wang 2009, 92.

45 The cantilever is a diagonal member resting on a fulcrum that capitalises on the upward thrust created by the massive load on one end to support the weight of the roof eave on the other end. Lothar Ledderose gives a very clear explanation in English of the cantilever's function in timber-frame architecture. See Ledderose 2000, 122–3.

46 For more on *liujin* brackets see Guo Huayu 2002, 281–9.

47 Pan Guxi 2009, 458–9.

48 '凡于闌額上坐櫨科安鋪作者，謂之 '補間鋪坐。' 當心間需用補間鋪坐兩科朵，次間及梢間各用一朵' ('The bracket sets atop the cap blocks atop the architrave are called 'intercolumnar bracket-sets. The central bay needs two sets of inter-columnar bracket sets while the flanking and corner bays each need one'). Li Jie 2006, 34.

49 It is important to mention that the link between the bay width and the number of brackets may actually have been dictated by a structural problem. On account of the decreasing size of the module and the smaller bracket-arms that came along with it, the number of bracket-sets may have been increased in order to provide enough support for the heavy load of the roof: the larger the building, the wider the bay spans, and the more bracket-sets required. Guo Huayu 2005, 142.

50 For more on this phenomenon see Zhang Shiqing 1999, 92.

51 Zang Shiqing 1999, 92.

52 Guo Huayu 2005, 49.

53 Sun Dazhang 2009, 398–9.

54 Bai, He and Wang 2009, 88–9.

55 Guo Huayu 2005, 147.

56 Guo Huayu (2005, 140) gives 9.83m for the width of the Ling'endian *mingjian*.

57 No measurements provided.

58 No measurements provided.

59 See Zhang Shiqing 1999 for a detailed explanation of this development.

60 Guo Huayu 2005, 49.

Chapter 22
Investigating Zheng He's Ships: What is Known and Knowable?

Sally K. Church

By far the most controversial but most essential issue regarding the ships that were used on Zheng He's 鄭和 15th-century maritime expeditions is their size. According to the biography of Zheng He in the 'Official Ming History' (*Ming shi* 明史), compiled in 1739, these 'Treasure Ships' (*baochuan* 寶船) were 44 *zhang* 丈 long and 18 *zhang* wide.[1] If we take the standard equivalent of the *zhang* in the Ming period, which is 3.11m,[2] the dimensions work out to approximately 137m by 56m, or 449ft by 184ft. Most maritime historians and shipbuilding engineers, both Western and Chinese, say that a wooden ship of this period could not possibly have been this big. To help visualise this size, an American football field is 110m long and 49m wide; one of Zheng He's ships would have been both longer and wider than this. The *USS Minnesota*, a steel battleship built in 1905 and decommissioned in 1924 after fighting in the First World War, was only slightly longer (139m) than the length that the *Ming shi* gives for Zheng He's ships, but considerably narrower (24m), obeying the principle espoused by some naval architects that a longer ship should be proportionally narrower.[3] Thus another problem with the dimensions given in the *Ming shi* is that such a ship is proportionally wide in the beam, with a length to width ratio of 2.45, as opposed to the *Minnesota*'s 5.79. Because it was made of steel, the *Minnesota* would have been much stronger on the high seas than a wooden sailing ship of that size, particularly before diagonal braces were invented by Robert Seppings in the early 19th century.[4] However, the *Ming shi* is a highly respected work of Chinese history, and it is difficult to ignore the dimensions recorded in it entirely. Consequently, there is a great deal of controversy over the entire matter among historians. In my view, Zheng He's ships could not have been 450ft long; their length was more likely to have been about 250ft. This chapter provides the essence of my argument, which I have set out at greater length in another paper,[5] and ties it into the Ming context set out so exquisitely by the British Museum exhibition *Ming: 50 years that changed China*.[6]

Louise Levathes' book *When China Ruled the Seas* includes an illustration by Jan Atkins of a colossal Zheng He ship dwarfing Christopher Columbus's *Santa Maria* by comparison (**Pl. 22.1**).[7] Although Zheng He's ship seems incredulously large in this illustration compared to the *Santa*

Plate 22.1 Christopher Columbus's *Santa Maria* compared to Zheng He's ship (after Levathes 1994)

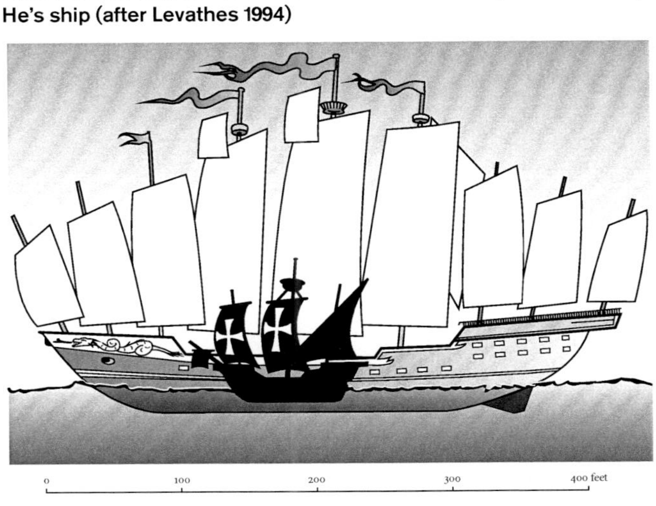

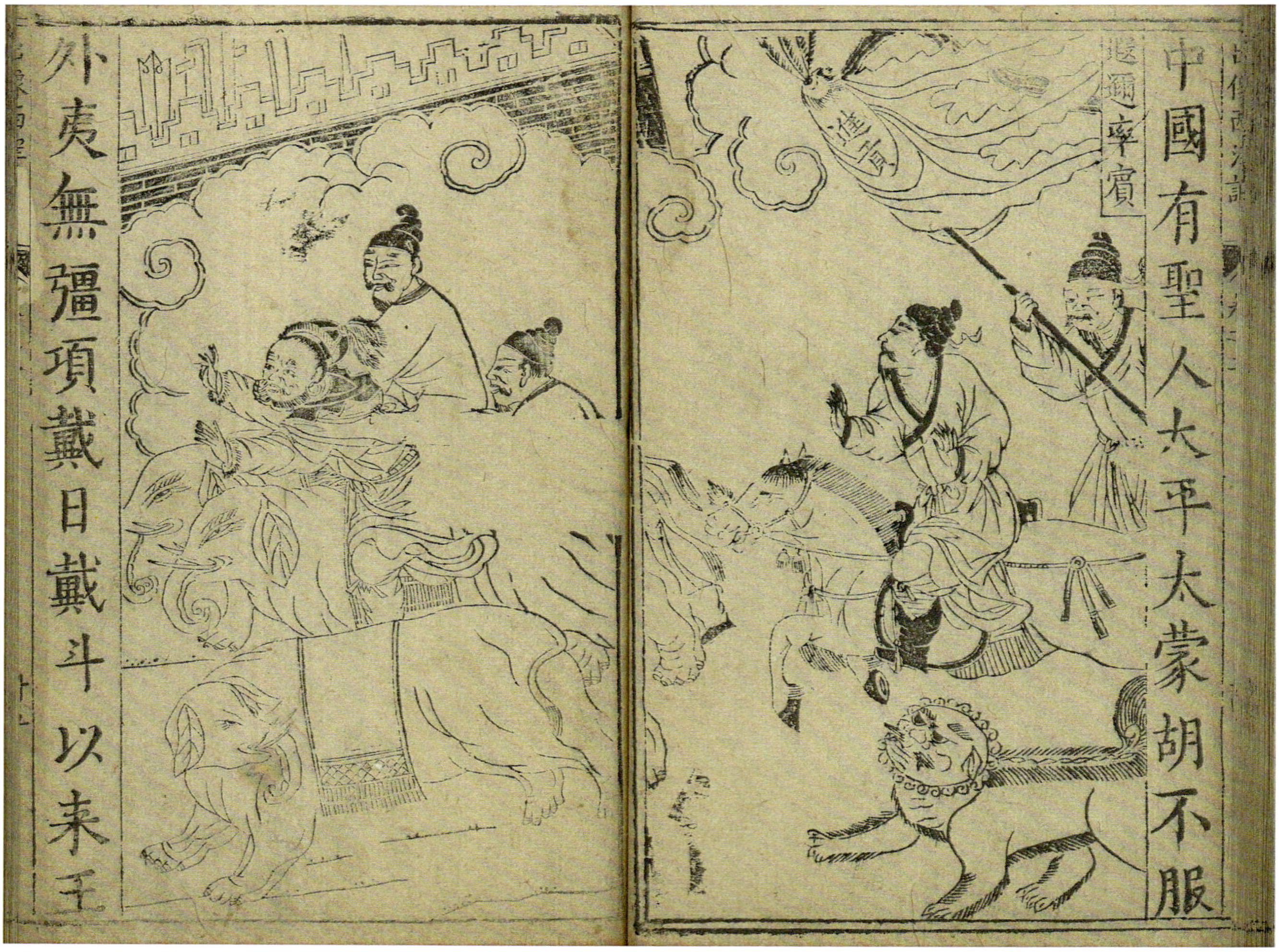

Plate 22.2 *The Adventures of the Eunuch of the Three Treasures in the Western Oceans* (*Sanbao taijian xiyangji* 三寶太監西洋記) by Luo Maodeng 羅懋登, written in 1597. This page shows foreigners bringing tribute of elephants. Woodblock-printed, ink on paper. National Library of China

Maria, the drawing is in fact an accurate representation of both the dimensions as given in the *Ming shi* and those of Columbus's ship. The illustration also depicts the ship as having nine main masts, a detail that betrays the source on which it is based. The idea that Zheng He's largest ships had nine masts seems to derive from the novel about Zheng He's exploits entitled *The Adventures of the Eunuch of the Three Treasures in the Western Oceans* (*Sanbao taijian xiyangji* 三寶太監西洋記), written in 1597 by the otherwise unknown writer Luo Maodeng 羅懋登 (**Pl. 22.2**). The novel lists five classes of ship in the fleet, giving the number of ships for each type, the number of masts, the dimensions in *zhang* and the length-to-beam ratio. These details are presented in **Table 1**.

The similarity of the length to beam (width) ratios of these five hypothetical ships seems to suggest scientific accuracy. However, the ratio should in fact not be the same for all sizes of ship – this would not accord with the principle mentioned above that longer ships should be proportionally narrower.[8] Moreover, the total number of ships given in the first column of the table (1,384) is also astronomical by comparison with any of the estimates given in the historical sources, which range from 48 to 250.[9]

Table 1 Five types of ship as presented in *The Adventures of the Eunuch of the Three Treasures in the Western Oceans*

No. of ships	No. of masts	Type of ship	Dimensions (*zhang*)	L/W ratio
36	9	treasure ships	44.4 x 18	2.46
700	8	horse transport ships	37 x 15	2.47
240	7	grain supply ships	28 x 12	2.33
300	6	personnel ships	24 x 9.4	2.55
108	5	warships	18 x 6.8	2.64

The question of the size of Zheng He's ships became particularly important around the turn of the 21st century when it was suggested that a replica ship should be built and sailed on the high seas for the 600th anniversary of the first voyage that was coming up in 2005. The pressing question, then hotly debated, was how large this replica should be. In the end, no replica was built in time for the anniversary, largely because it could not be agreed what size to make it. Leading up to the anniversary, there was a lively debate on whether the replica should be constructed according to the dimensions in the *Ming shi*, or whether something smaller and more reasonable in terms of time, manpower, materials and expense should be designed. With regard to materials, primarily meaning wood, it is possible to use the figures that are available for British 'ships of the line' to calculate roughly that a 44-*zhang* ship would have required approximately 24,600 trees.[10] The environmental impact of a replica project of such a scale is staggering to contemplate

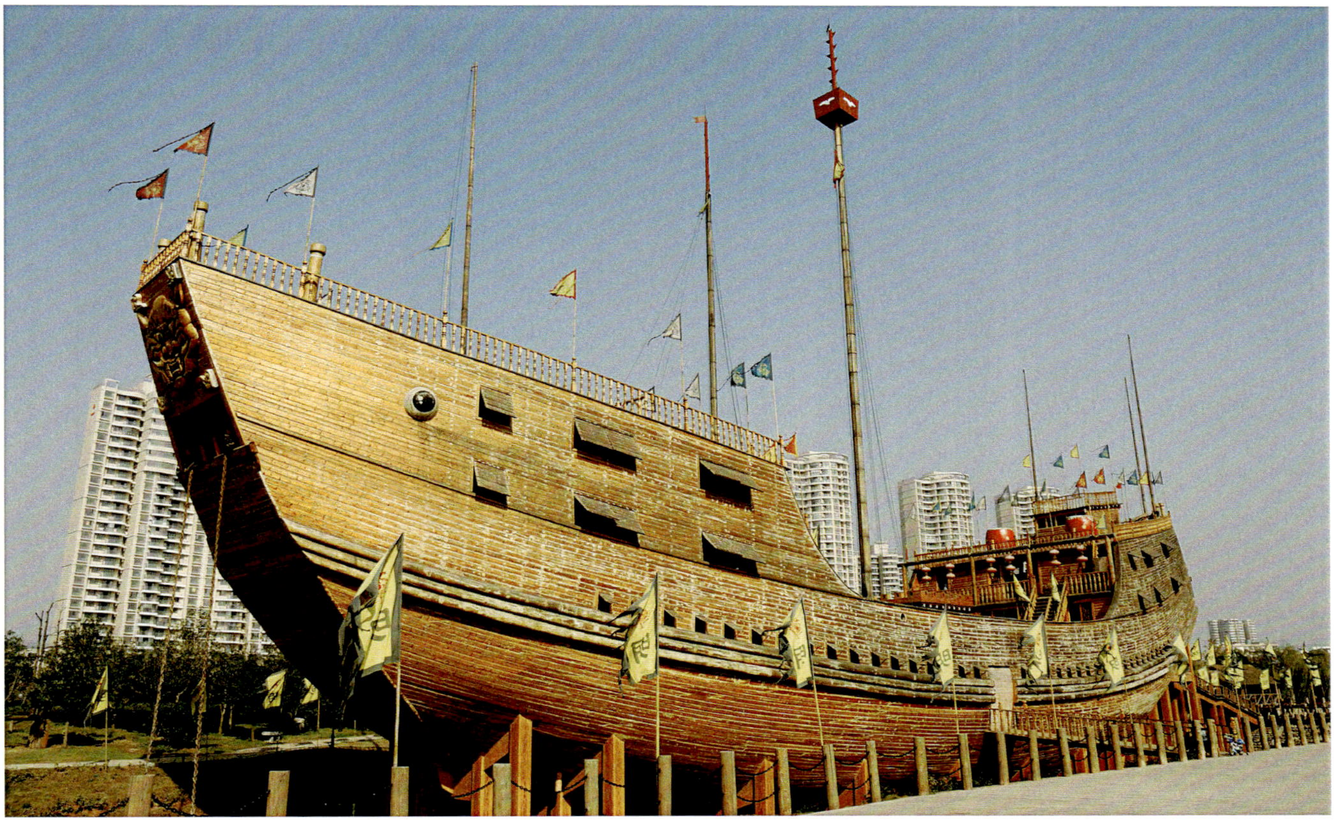

Plate 22.3 A full-size replica of Zheng He's treasure ship in Nanjing Treasure Shipyard Relic Site Park

and this was a consideration for the planners of the 600th anniversary. A fleet of 62 ships of this size (the number of ships given in the *Ming shi* for the first voyage) would have required about 1,525,200 trees. Moreover, the ships would have lasted only about ten years before they had to be completely rebuilt. Therefore, over the 28 years of the voyages, they would have needed to be reconstructed three or four times, bringing the total up to 4,575,600 or even six million trees.[11] This would have included not only fir, but also more expensive and exotic woods of teak and cedar for parts of the ships requiring extra strength, such as rudders and tillers.[12] Shipbuilding was not the only demand on China's forests at the time; the new capital was being built in Beijing from approximately 1407 onwards, which also required huge amounts of high-quality wood. Thus the effect of just these two of Emperor Yongle's ambitious projects on the environment and the economy, even if the ships were half the dimensions given in the *Ming shi*, was enormous, not to mention the pressure on the infrastructure which would have been required to transport the trees from their points of origin.

Another issue is time: there does not seem to have been enough time for ships of such a large size to be built. Emperor Yongle came to the throne in the second half of 1402. In 1403 he announced the plan to launch these expeditions, and the first voyage set sail in July 1405. This means that all 62 ships had to have been built in less than two years, which is remarkable given that a single replica half the size, which is now being built with modern technology in Nanjing, has been under construction for almost six years (**Pl. 22.3**). More will be said about this replica later.

Between the 580th anniversary in 1985 and the 600th anniversary in 2005, the possibility of building a replica for the big celebration stimulated a substantial amount of research into the size of these ships. Scholars made all sorts of speculations and calculations, attempting to make sense of the dimensions given in the *Ming shi*. One scholar suggested that the length and beam of the ships may have been reversed, and a decimal point introduced, yielding dimensions of 18 *zhang* long by 4.4 *zhang* wide.[13] Another argued that the measurement given as length was actually the product of the length multiplied by the beam.[14] Still others dispensed with the *Ming shi* entirely and looked back to the dimensions of earlier ships in China's long maritime tradition. The trouble with comparing ships from other periods and contexts is that in the end it is difficult to draw precise conclusions about Zheng He's ships from these earlier ships. The essential difficulty with the issues surrounding Zheng He's ships is that not enough information about them survives.

Despite the reverence in which the *Ming shi* is held by some scholars, it should be remembered that in general the official histories of China are secondary, not primary, sources. Although they were compiled from primary sources, this did not occur until the subsequent dynasty. Thus while Zheng He's expeditions took place between 1405 and 1433, the *Ming shi* was not completed until 300 years later, almost 100 years into the Qing dynasty. By that time, not only those involved in the voyages, but even those who could remember the voyages were gone. The history was also compiled, not by shipbuilders or scientists of any kind, but by literati, educated in the Confucian classics. The most likely explanation for the unrealistically large dimensions in

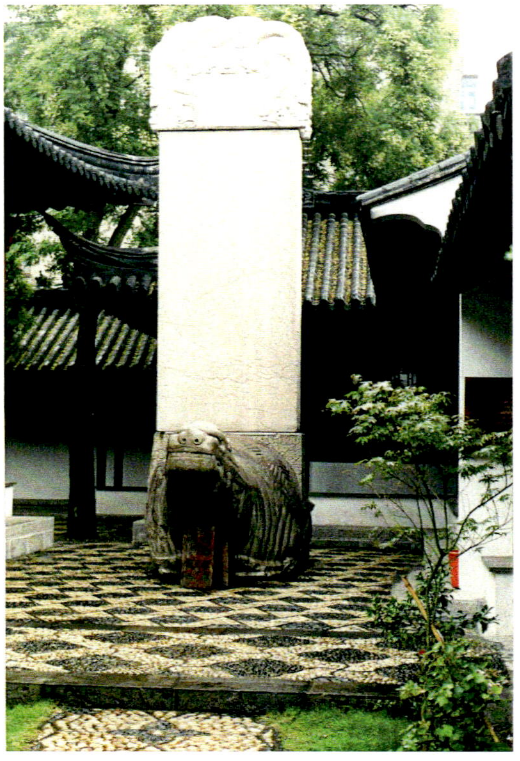

Plate 22.4 (left) Stele in Jinghai Temple, reconstructed in 1980s

Plate 22.5 (right) Rubbing of the Jinghai Temple stele

the Ming history is that the compilers found these figures in the sources and copied them without thinking carefully about whether they made sense.[15]

Moreover, all the documents that had been in the official government archives concerning the voyages had disappeared. According to one source, the documents were destroyed in the Chenghua reign period (1465–87), due to a power struggle between Confucian scholars and eunuchs. From Zheng He's time onwards, eunuchs had become associated with ambitious maritime ventures, and they became more powerful as the years went on. It seems that in order to thwart the plans of the eunuch Wang Zhi 汪直 to launch military expeditions, the Confucian scholar Liu Daxia 劉大夏, Vice President of the Ministry of War, destroyed all the documents in the archives relating to Zheng He's voyages.[16]

Despite this unfortunate obliteration of the official written record, references to the voyages have surfaced in a number of sources. The trouble is that the surviving sources are still scanty, and information about the ships in them is quite rare. It is scattered among different sources, and does not fit together as a neat whole. We might have the length and beam of one ship, the complement of another, the mast height of a third, and the rudderpost length of a fourth, but no record of the dimensions of a single ship from the fleet in its entirety.

One point that seems fairly certain is that there were many different sizes of ship on these voyages. In addition to the 62 enormous ships mentioned by the *Ming shi*, other sources refer to 100–250 ships in the fleet. There were probably ships of many different sizes and purposes. Gong Zhen 鞏珍, a staff member on the final voyage in 1431–3, refers to specially designated water ships,[17] and there may have been other specialised types. Although the novel cannot entirely be trusted, it does suggest that there were specific types of ships for different purposes (see **Table 1**). It is well documented that there were 27,000 to 28,000 people (including crew and passengers) on most of the voyages. In order to transport so many, the fleet would have needed quite a number of ships. Various calculations of the number of ships based on these personnel figures have been made, which will be examined more closely later in the chapter.

Another difficulty is the lack of images. There are certainly no drawings of the ships that we could in any way term 'scientific'. The few images we have do not provide accurate details, but just give a general impression. There are three main sets of illustrations that shed some light on the size of the ships and these will be discussed below.

We also do not completely understand the measurement units used to build these ships. While we know how long the Ministry of Works *chi* 尺 (foot) was, there were other types of *chi* in use as well. We have references to a shipbuilding *chi*, a Huai *chi* 淮尺, a tailor's *chi*, a construction *chi* and others, specialised according to profession, reminiscent of the English baker's dozen. The length of a *chi* also changes over time from one dynasty to another, and differs from place to place. Whether the Ministry of Works *chi* was the standard used in shipbuilding we do not know. Two wooden foot-rulers have been found in the Treasure Shipyard, both about 31cm long.[18] They provide enticing evidence, but there is no way to tell when they were dropped into the basins.

As for the sources and what they say, there are three types of source now extant: written works, illustrations and archaeological evidence. For the written works, in addition to the *Ming shi*, we have the *Ming Veritable Records* (*Ming shilu* 明實錄), three first-hand accounts, one anonymous itinerary, some stone inscriptions and some unofficial histories. As we have seen, the *History of the Ming* mentions only the length and beam measurements. There are no figures for depth or any other details. The *Veritable Records* contains some information, but not about the size of the ships. It gives details about the numbers of ships that were built, and where and when they were constructed, repaired or modified.[19] It also mentions that some ships were built from scratch, while others were converted (*gaizao* 改造) from grain transport ships. Under Yongle's reign the overseas grain transport ships that the preceding Yuan dynasty had relied upon for south-to-north grain transport were largely phased out; the construction of the new capital in Beijing had necessitated refurbishment of the canal system to allow grain to be transported on inland waterways instead of by sea. Interestingly this meant that some of the existing grain transport ships no longer used for that purpose were converted into treasure ships for Zheng He's voyages. Instances of these conversions are recorded in the *Shilu*.

The three first-hand travel accounts, those of Ma Huan 馬歡, Fei Xin 費信 and Gong Zhen, unfortunately say very little about the ships.[20] They comment that the vessels were enormous, but do not specify the size. There are hints about the size, however, such as when it is mentioned that in some ports the large ships of the fleet had to moor offshore while people and goods were transported into port on smaller ships. Again, all we can tell from these accounts is that the ships were very large.

One piece of rather more meaty information is provided by Gong Zhen, who says that 200–300 men were required to operate the sails, anchors and rudders of the ships.[21] From these figures we can perhaps obtain a rough idea of their size. With such a small complement, however, these would not be 44-*zhang* ships. According to one expert, a 44-*zhang* ship would have needed 8,000 men to man it.[22] The *USS Minnesota* was manned by 838 men and 42 officers, but as a steel ship it would have needed far fewer men than a wooden ship. In an anonymous itinerary for the seventh expedition, found in Zhu Yunming's 祝允明 (1461–1527) miscellany *Qianwen ji* 前聞記 (*Record of Things Heard*) (*c.* 1500), the number of people sailing on the voyage is given as 27,550, broken down into the following categories of passengers and crew on board:

> Officers; troops serving under the banners; group-leaders (*huozhang*, literally 'fire-leaders'); helmsmen; anchormen; interpreters; business-factors; accountants; doctors; iron-anchor mechanics; caulkers; scaffold-builders; other craftsmen; sailors; and boatmen.[23]

Another source of information about the size occurs on one of the stone stelae that were set up in China and in other places that Zheng He visited. Words inscribed on stone are often thought to be more trustworthy than written records. One of them was at the Jinghaisi 靜海寺 (Calm Sea Monastery)in Nanjing, where Zheng He went to pray for smooth sailing before he set out on his voyages (**Pl. 22.4**). It mentions the size of the ships (**Pl. 22.5**). The inscription says: 'in the third year of Yongle (1405), the ships were 2,000 *liao* 料 . . . and in the seventh year (1409) they were 1,500 *liao*'. The appearance of yet another unit for the size of the ships, the *liao*, creates new problems. It seems to have been a unit of capacity, used for calculating the amount of grain and other goods to be transported. The scholar Lo Jung-pang reckons that it was 500 pounds, in which case the 2,000-*liao* ships would have been 500 tons and the 1500-*liao* ships 375 tons.[24] However, this is just an estimate and should not be taken as the final word.

As noted above, scholars have made various calculations in attempts to figure out the size of the ships from the scanty and scattered information that is available. Professor Xin Yuan'ou, a shipbuilding engineer at Shanghai Jiaotong University, whose paper 'A Technical Analysis of the Size of Zheng He's Ships' (*Guanyu Zheng He baochuan chidu de jishu fenxi* 關於鄭和寶船尺度的技術分析) first excited my interest in this topic, was the one who estimated that each of the 20,000 ton ships (his estimate for the 450ft size) would have required 8,000 men to man it. If the figure of 27,000 people in each fleet is correct, and if 8,000 men were required for each ship, there would have been fewer than four ships in the entire fleet, not the 62, 100 or 250 that have been mentioned in the sources. For this reason, the figure of 8,000 men as a complement must be incorrect. This is one argument for saying that the ships cannot have been the 20,000 ton size.

Starting out from the smallest possible complement, the estimate by Gong Zhen of 200–300 people per ship would work out to 112 ships (27,000 people divided by 250, the average of his 200–300 figure). This figure for the number of ships is at least within the range mentioned in the sources. The number of vessels given in two almost identical inscriptions contemporary with the voyages is 100 – these are the Liujiagang and Changle inscriptions, both dated 1431, discovered in Taicang (near present-day Shanghai) and Fujian (near Fuzhou), respectively. This number sounds suspiciously like an estimate that has been rounded off. It works out to 270 men per ship, which falls within the range estimated by Gong Zhen. Professor Xin also tries dividing 27,000 by 62 to determine the average number of men per ship on the first voyage, obtaining 436 men per ship. However, this calculation does not take into account the existence of smaller ships as well. A similar operation carried out for the 48 ships mentioned by Fei Xin for the third voyage yields 563 men per ship. From these efforts, Xin concludes that Lo Jung-pang was correct and the ships were probably about 500 tons in capacity and 800 tons in displacement. He estimates that they were about 250ft in length, and this is the size I have settled on as most likely to be correct.

In China today there is sometimes fierce disagreement among scholars on this subject. Those who argue that the Ming history must be right and believe that Zheng He's ships were 44 *zhang* long form one camp, and those who say they were 2,000 *liao* in size form another. These two groups take their positions very seriously and have sometimes almost come to blows. I witnessed a heated debate at the 600th anniversary conference in July 2005, in which an elderly scholar with strong views nearly fainted. Since then, Chinese maritime historians have become less strident on the matter and have agreed to disagree, but there are still strong feelings on the issue.

In recent years, some members of the small ship camp have formed a group called the Beijing Association for the Study of Zheng He and Maritime Culture (*Beijing Zheng He yu Haiyang wenhua yanjiu hui* 北京鄭和與海洋文化研究會), which is currently building a replica of a 2000-*liao* treasure ship at the Treasure Shipyard in Nanjing. The overall specifications of this ship are as follows:

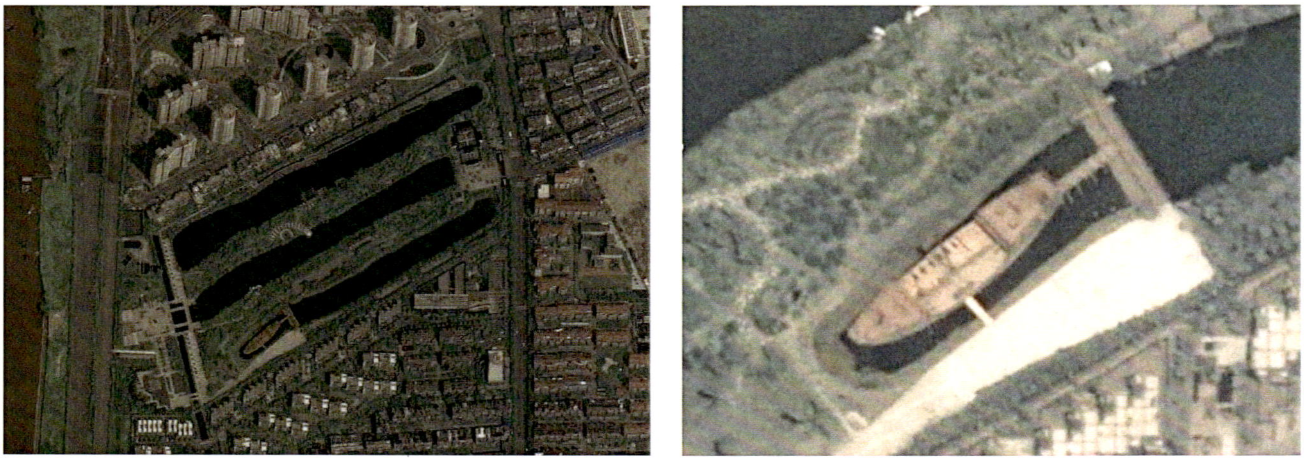

Plate 22.6a–b Google map images, showing the actual ship under the construction

Total length: 71.1m	Draught: 4.6m
Length at waterline: 63.05m	Loaded displacement: 1,810 tons
Beam 14.05m	Height of main mast: 38m[25]
Depth: 6.1m	

This replica is thus just under the 250ft size which in my view is most realistic. One of the wonders of modern technology is that one can zoom in on Google Earth and see the replica under construction at the Treasure Shipyard in Nanjing, occupying one end of basin 6 (**Pl. 22.6a–b**).

There are three main sets of illustrations relevant to the size of the ships. The first is the Mao Kun 茅坤 map, which dates from the 1620s. In Chinese it is called *Zheng He hanghai tu* 鄭和航海圖 (*Zheng He's Navigation Chart*),[26] while in English it has been called 'the Mao Kun map' because it was preserved in a collection of military texts called *Wubei zhi* 武備志 (Treatise on Military Preparedness) held in the library of Mao Kun 茅坤 (1512–1601), which was printed in 1621 (**Pl. 22.7**) by his grandson Mao Yuanyi 茅元儀 (1594–1641) and presented to the throne in 1628. This is probably not the actual sailing chart used on Zheng He's voyages – it is perhaps a copy, or a copy of a copy – but it includes compass directions and the lengths of time (in watches, *geng* 更) that it takes to sail between certain destinations, as well as drawings of the shorelines as seen from the sea. It is therefore a valuable source of information. While there are no images of ships in the map itself, the 40 folios of the map are followed by four

Plate 22.7 *Treatise on Military Preparedness* or *Records of Armaments and Military Provisions* (*Wubei zhi* 武備志). Tianqi period edition, 1621–7. Woodblock-printed, ink on paper, National Library of China

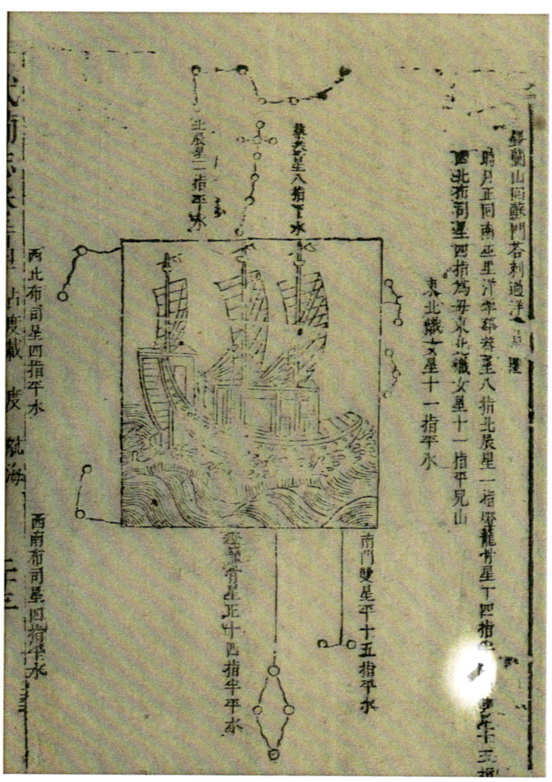

Plate 22.8 (left) Drawing of 11.07m long rudderpost comparison with a man; (right) Wood rudderpost. Length 10.06m. Nanjing Treasure Shipyard Relic Site Park

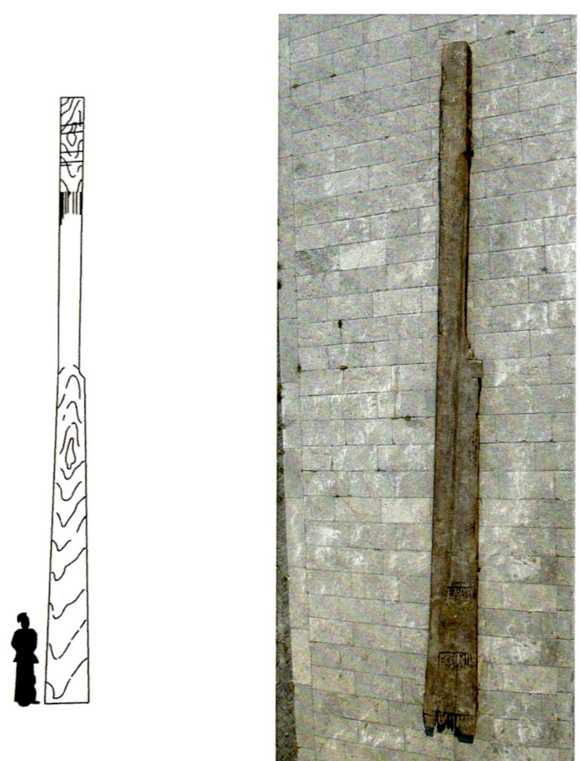

so-called 'stellar diagrams',[27] which indicate how to position a ship in line with the constellations in order to sail across the two long expanses of open water along Zheng He's route where coastal sailing is impossible. These expanses are firstly across the Bay of Bengal from Southeast Asia to India and back, and secondly from Calicut to Hormuz and back. The ships depicted in these stellar diagrams are sketchy, but they present an image of small ships with only three masts rather than gigantic ships. They even show a particular type of rudder that is consistent with the 11.07m long rudderpost found at the shipyard in 1957 (**Pl. 22.8**).[28]

The second source of images is the illustration included in a religious text telling how the goddess Tianfei 天妃 (Celestial Spouse) protects sailors.[29] The important thing about this text is its date – 1420 – exactly contemporaneous with the voyages, compared to the illustrations in the Mao Kun map, which cannot be pinpointed before the 1620s. In this picture Zheng He's ships are of a modest size with three main masts and two subsidiary ones (**Pl. 22.9**).

The third source of illustrations is the *Longjiang Shipyard Treatise* (*Longjiang chuanchang zhi* 龍江船廠志) of 1553 by Li Zhaoxiang 李昭祥 (fl. 1537–53).[30] The Longjiang Shipyard was located in Nanjing near the Treasure Shipyard where the ocean-going ships were built. It produced much smaller ships than the Treasure Shipyard, mostly military ships for policing the inland waterways, but there was some overlap between the two shipyards in construction and supplies.[31] The *Treatise* provides illustrations of the 24 models of ship built at the shipyard, and these are accompanied in most cases by their dimensions. They are all of different sizes, and some are fortunately named according to their size, expressed in *liao*. There are 400-, 300-, 200-*liao* ships and smaller ones as well. Some scholars have tried to extrapolate the information given for the 400-*liao* ship to determine the dimensions of the 2,000-*liao* type. André Wegener Sleeswyk devised a formula for calculating the *liao* of a ship by multiplying its length, beam and depth (measured in *chi*) together, and raising it to the power of two-thirds.[32]

One of the illustrations of the 24 ships in the *Treatise* is of the 'ocean-going ship' (*haichuan* 海船). Enticing though it is to see this illustration, and to think it might represent Zheng He's ships, a disappointing inscription appears in the space where the dimensions are usually given saying: 'There is no information about the dimensions of this ship' (*chidu wukao* 尺度無考). Thus by 1553, only 120 years after the end of the voyages when the *Treatise* was written, the specifications for the long-distance sailing ships had already been forgotten, even in the precise place where they had been constructed. Despite this lack of information, the illustration itself at least provides a vague image that someone at the shipyard had of the ship at the time. Although it looks large, it has only four main masts, not nine (**Pl. 22.10**). While not scientific, the illustrations described above give the general impression that Zheng He's ships were not the gargantuan constructions depicted in the Atkins illustration (see **Pl. 22.1**).

There have been several archaeological discoveries of note. In addition to the rudderpost discovered in the Treasure Shipyard in 1957,[33] two others of similar sizes were

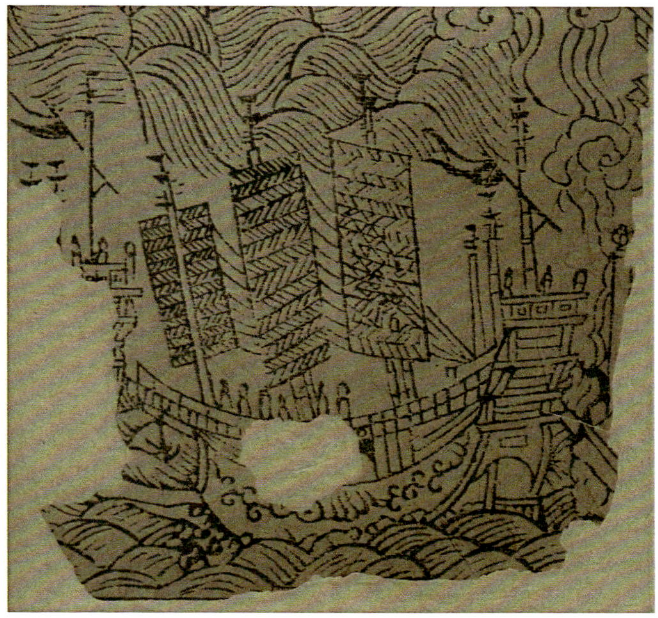

Plate 22.9 Ship from 'Sutra spoken from on high of the miraculous efficacy of Tianfei in salvation from distress' (*Taishang shuo Tianfei jiuku lingying jing* 太上說天妃救苦靈應經), dated 1420. Woodblock printed, ink on paper. National Library of China

found in approximately the same location during the excavation of the shipyard in 2003–4. While the 1962 study of the first find claims to prove that Zheng He's ships could have been the size stated in the *Ming shi*, it considers these ships to be *shachuan* 沙船, or 'sand-ships', shallow ships used primarily for inland transport, which I believe to be a

Plate 22.10 *Longjiang Shipyard Treatise* (*Longjiang chuanchang zhi* 龍江船廠志) by Li Zhaoxiang 李昭祥 (fl. 1537–53), 1553. Page showing ocean-going ship (*haichuan* 海船). The Bodleian Libraries, The University of Oxford, Chin.e.455/117-119

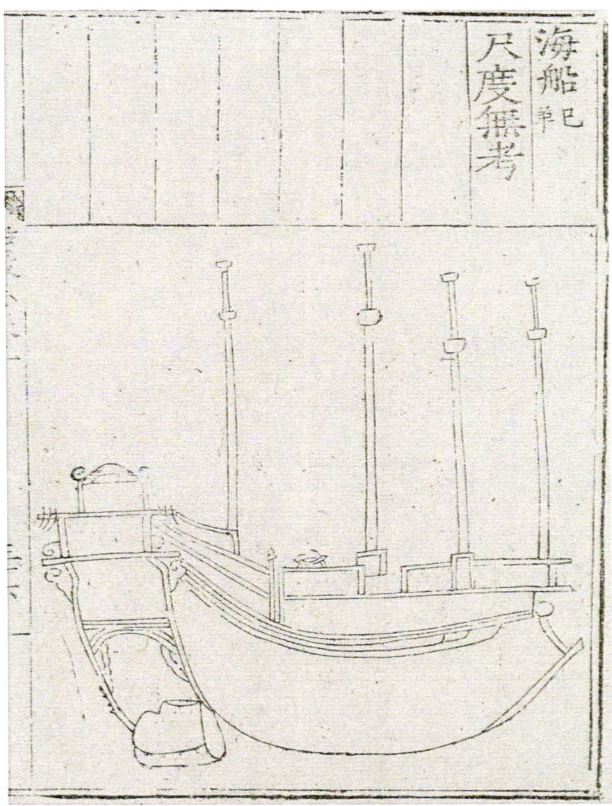

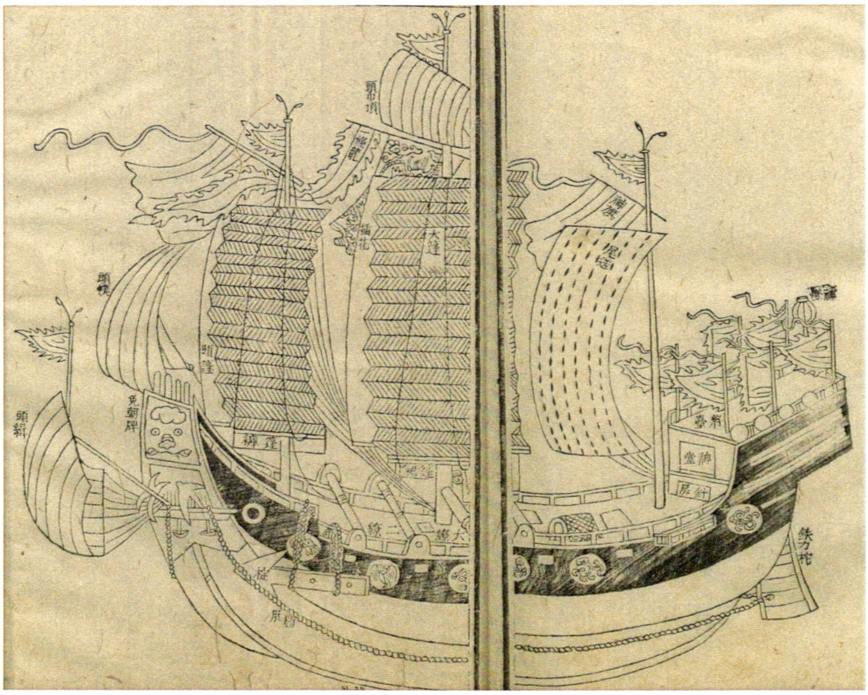

Plate 22.11 ***The Annals of Ryukyu*** **(*Liuqiu guo zhi lüe* 琉球國志略) by Zhou Huang 周煌, published in 1759. Shurun tang edition, National Library of China**

mistake. It also proposes a formula for determining ship size from rudderpost size that is based on a modern propeller-driven steel ship, and a rudder of a completely different shape – made for shallow-water rather than deep-water sailing. More recently, scholars have been saying that Zheng He's ships must have been deep-bottomed *fuchuan* 福船 style ships (like the Ryukyu ship, **Pl. 22.11**) in order to survive on the high seas.[34] In the illustrations in **Plate 22.12**, showing the various sizes of treasure ship compared to the size of the rudderpost, an 11.07m long rudderpost appears like a toothpick compared to a ship that is 137m long or even half that size. The archaeological report of the Nanjing Treasure Shipyard itemises thousands of objects that were excavated there (including nails and pieces of wood), but nothing conclusive was found to indicate that the ships were of the order of 450ft long.

It was mentioned above that two foot-rulers were found in the Treasure Shipyard, both about 31cm long, thus conforming to the size of the Ministry of Works foot. Another clue to the length of the foot is provided in a completely unexpected source. The Ming paper money note

Plate 22.12 Three sizes of ship compared to the size of the rudderpost

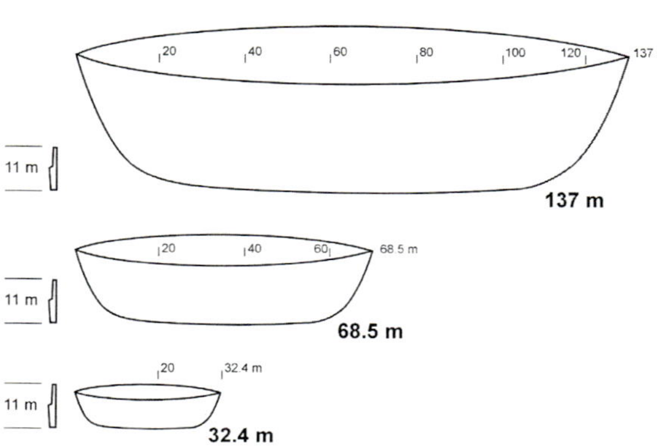

(see **Pl. 19.1**) is exactly one Chinese foot long, and was designed this way to standardise the size of a foot. The samples that survive can therefore be used to confirm the size of a Ministry of Works foot in the Ming period.[35] Although, as mentioned above, it is not absolutely certain that this is the length of the foot used as a standard for shipbuilding, it is not likely to be far off. It should be noted that the prominent scholar and shipbuilding engineer Xi Longfei 席龍飛 uses 28.3cm as the standard shipbuilding foot measure, based on a ruler discovered in Fujian.[36]

One important piece of archaeological evidence is the shipyard itself. Many of the original 13 basins, shown on a map of Nanjing from the Second World War (**Pl. 22.13**) have now been filled in and transformed into sites for apartment buildings. Only three of the original basins now survive, basins 4, 5 and 6 (**Pl. 22.14**). Basin 6 is the only one to have been excavated. Its 400m length leaves plenty of room for three 137m long treasure ships lengthwise, but it is only 40m wide. Therefore, 56m wide treasure ships would not fit in the basin. This seems to be conclusive evidence that the ships built in this shipyard were not 44 by 18 *zhang*.

In 2010, a further archaeological exploration turned up an inscription in what is thought to be the tomb of Hong Bao 洪保, another eunuch, saying that he sailed on a ship that was 5,000 *liao* in size.[37]

Studies by Chinese scholars are becoming more and more sophisticated and rigorous, as historians increasingly collaborate with engineers and scientists. Of course there is always hope that future archaeological finds will uncover more ships and discoveries related to Zheng He's voyages and will answer the questions posed above. However, only the discovery of a 44-*zhang* ship will settle the matter of whether they were ever this big. Until further evidence is found, it appears that the best we can say is that the ships were probably about 250ft long, which is still a substantially large ship.

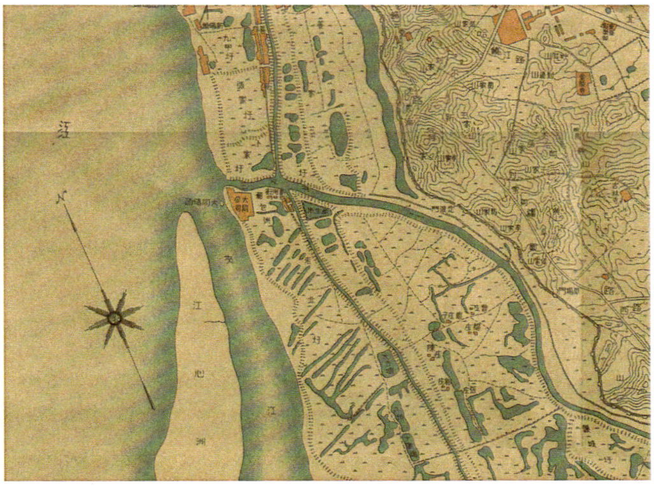

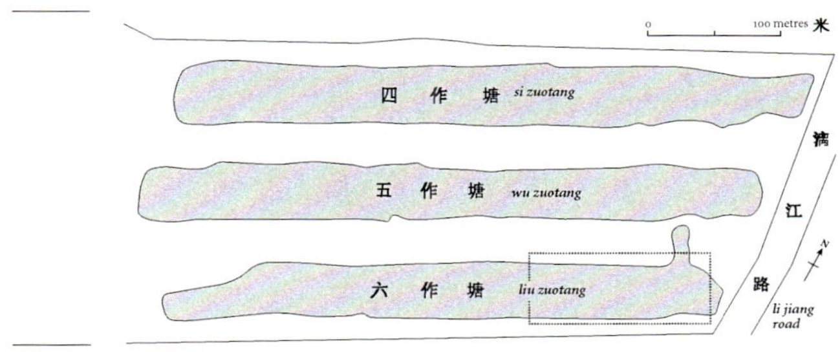

Plate 22.13 (left) Map of Nanjing in 1944, showing the 13 basins on the eastern shore of the Yangtze River. Nanjing Municipal Museum

Plate 22.14 (above) Illustration from Nanjing Archaeological Report of shipyard excavation; the rectangle at the bottom right represents the length and width of a hypothetical 137m x 56m treasure ship

Notes

1 *MS*: *j*. 304, 7766–8.
2 According to the work that has been done on Ming weights and measures, the standard Ministry of Works foot (*chi* 尺) is 31.1cm long. There are ten *chi* in one *zhang*, hence one *zhang* is 3.11m. Qiu Guangming 1992.
3 The *Minnesota* had a draft of 7.5m and a displacement of 16,000 tons. It was one of six ships that belonged to the 'Connecticut-class' of steel battleships built for the US Navy between 1903 and 1908. See https://en.wikipedia.org/wiki/Connecticut-class_battleship (accessed 15 April 2016), and US Department of the Navy, Office of the Chief of Naval Operations 1969, 374–5. Charles E. Gibson tells of the way in which ships in the West became proportionally longer and narrower as they advanced from the Elizabethan era to the 17th century. See Gibson 1958, 127.
4 See Seppings 1818, 1–8. The article is available online at http://www.bruzelius.info/Nautica/Shipbuilding/Seppings%281818%29.html (accessed 16 April 2015).
5 Church 2005.
6 Clunas and Harrison-Hall 2014.
7 Levathes 1994, 21.
8 Xin Yuanou 2002, 1–20.
9 Pao Tsun-p'eng adds up various figures for ship numbers in the sources and comes up with a total of 317 ships in the fleet. See Pao Tsun-p'eng 1961, 24–5.
10 The ships of the line were a 'type of sailing warship that formed the backbone of the Western world's great navies from the mid-17th century through the mid-19th century' (http://www.britannica.com/technology/ship-of-the-line) (Accessed 15 April 2016); Edye 1832; Albion 1926, 9.
11 Church 2005, 32.
12 In the excavation of the Treasure Shipyard, most of the wood was found to be *Cunninghamia lancelota* (sometimes called 'China-fir' (though it is not a fir)). See Nanjing shi bowuguan 2006, 112–14.
13 Xi Longfei and He Guowei 1985, 95, referring to Yang You, Yang Zongying and Huang Genyu 1981, esp. 20.
14 Han Zhenhua 1988.
15 Some editions of Ma Huan's travel account, *Yingya shenglan* 瀛崖勝覽, contain the dimensions as given in the *Ming shi*, and one or more of these may have been the source that the editors used to compile this official history. However, the earliest and most authentic edition does not have them. This is the *Jilu huibian* 紀錄匯編 edition published by Shen Jiefu 沈節甫 (*jinshi* 1559) in approximately 1617. It is thought to be the closest to the first edition produced in 1451. The three later editions that do contain the dimensions are: the *Chaoshuo ji* 鈔說集 edition (dated after 1617), the *Sanbao zhengyi ji* 三寶征彝集 manuscript (also dated after 1617) and the *Qi shi Dansheng tang* 祁氏淡生堂 manuscript of 1620. In these works, the dimensions are not integrated into the text but written on the blank pages before the book begins as if added later as an afterthought.
16 Yan Congjian's 嚴從簡 *Shuyu zhouzi lu* 殊域周咨錄 of 1574, *Zhongwai jiaotong shiji congkan* 中外交通史籍叢刊 series, vol. 13 (Beijing 1993), *j*. 8, p. 306. J.J.L. Duyvendak translates the story of the documents' destruction see Duyvendak 1938, 341–412, esp. 395–6.
17 Gong Zhen 1961, 12.
18 Nanjing shi bowuguan 2006, 66–7, col. pl. 13.
19 A table of the information about the construction of ships provided in the *Shilu* can be found in Church 2005, 18–19.
20 These accounts are *Yingya shenglan* (1451, first preface 1416), *Xingcha shenglan* 星槎勝覽 (1436) and *Xiyang fanguo zhi* (1434), respectively.
21 Gong Zhen 1961, 12.
22 Xin Yuanou 2002.
23 Zhu Yunming, 'Down to the Western Oceans' (*Xia Xiyang* 下西洋), quoted in Mills 1970, 15.
24 Lo Jung-pang 1955, esp. 493, n. 18.
25 These dimensions were first given in the association's promotional literature in 2009, and published in the journal produced by the association. See Zhao Zhigang 2008–9, esp. 103.
26 Xiang Da 1961b.
27 This is Mills' designation, see Mills 1970, 29, 253, 335–46.
28 As noted below, two additional rudderposts of similar size have been found there. See Nanjing shi bowu guan 2006, 112–14.
29 The full title of this text is: *Taishang shuo Tianfei jiu kuling yingjing* 太上說天妃救苦靈應經. It is discussed by Jin Qiupeng 金秋鵬 2000. The illustration is reproduced in Wang Bomin 1988, ill. no. 30, 32–3.
30 I have used the edition in *Xuanlantang congshu xuji* 玄覽堂叢書續集; and also the modern edition edited by Wang Lianggong 王亮功 (1999).
31 The interrelationships between the two shipyards are discussed in Church 2011; Church 2010.
32 Sleeswyk 1996.
33 Zhou Shide 1962.
34 The Ryukyu ship illustration is found in Zhou Huang, original date 1759 (Daoguang edition, *c*. 1830), 33b–34a.
35 Zhu Zaiyu 1998. On Zhu Zaiyu 朱載堉 (1536–1611) as the inventor of as the inventor of equal temperament in music, see Robinson 1980.
36 Xi Longfei 1999, 272–3.
37 Anon. 2014.

Chapter 23
'Trees and Stones Are Only What They Are': Translating Ming Empire in the Fifteenth Century

Carla Nappi

> You walk for days among trees and among stones. Rarely does the eye light on a thing, and then only when it has recognised that thing as the sign of another thing: a print in the sand indicates the tiger's passage; a marsh announces a vein of water; the hibiscus flower, the end of winter. All the rest is silent and interchangeable; trees and stones are only what they are.[1]

As we sit and read, Marco Polo (1254–1324) (as stylised by Italian writer Italo Calvino) recounts the feeling of a journey that leads to a city called Tamara. Tamara is a city of signs. The traveller along her streets is surrounded by images that point, warn, encourage or describe. Even her buildings are themselves signs: their form and placement signify the roles they play within Tamara's broader urban ecology. The goods on display along her streets accrue value only insofar as they signify other things. In wandering among the signs of Tamara with Marco Polo, our knowledge of the city (like his) never quite moves beyond the surface. We leave Tamara, according to him, without actually having discovered it. What the city might be beneath this thick coat of signs remains a mystery after we leave her streets.

In Calvino's book, Tamara is just one of many cities that Marco Polo describes to Yuan ruler Qubilai Khan (1260–94) in the course of a conversation about the spaces of the ruler's empire that the Venetian explorer has visited in his travels: a city that exists as a mirror-image, a city of dead things and a city that cannot be expunged from the mind once it has been experienced. But Tamara takes on special meaning as a city that becomes a text, and a text made up only of signs and names:

> Your gaze scans the streets as if they were written pages: the city says everything you must think, makes you repeat her discourse, and while you believe you are visiting Tamara you are only recording the names with which she defines herself and all her parts.[2]

This chapter takes Tamara and her signs as inspiration to look anew at the ways Ming translators also related cities and text. Ming students and instructors of translation mapped distant spaces and languages on gridded glossary pages, naming the categories and signs of foreign experience and finding equivalences in documentary Chinese. To understand these translators' practices – especially their creation and use of bilingual glossaries – is to comprehend how they used signs on a page to create new kinds of equivalence. The translators' signs weren't quite tiger paw prints or hibiscus flowers: instead, these men read lines, sounds and images. But in doing so, they similarly encountered and created foreign peoples as constellations and combinations of symbols. By understanding them in this way, and by exploring the consequences of reading their practices as such, we can bring Ming history into dialogue with a larger set of questions about identity, ontology and empire in the early modern world. These texts can help us think anew about Ming objects by inviting us to consider not just what kinds of objects circulated in the early Ming, but also how we can use the early Ming to rethink objects themselves, from what and where they emerge and how they are constituted through literary technologies. This chapter will ultimately suggest that knowing a world and its objects is knowing what it looks like to be the same. The material world – as we encounter and know it – is a world of sameness.

In order to get there, let us first visit the Yongle 永樂 court (r. 1403–24).

'A print in the sand ... a tiger's passage'

Tigers stalked the capital of the Yongle emperor. They did not walk along its streets, but instead across the pages of its foreign language glossaries. And so *ba-er-si* 巴兒思 or 把兒思 prowled the Mongolian and Gaochang 高昌 glossaries. *Po-lang-ke* 迫郎克 populated the pages of Persian glossaries. *Gong* 供 roamed through Tibetan glossaries, and *si* 思 padded through Thai glossaries.

The Yongle emperor had prompted the creation of this multilingual paper bestiary in the fifth year of his reign (1407) after winning the throne in a bitter battle against his nephew, the erstwhile Jianwen 建文 emperor (r. 1399–1402). He was in the midst of a campaign to subjugate Annam (Northern Vietnam), and the eunuch Zheng He 鄭和 (1371–1433) had just returned from the first voyage of his treasure fleet.[3] Zheng He arrived at court laden with gifts, envoys and stories from the many foreign states his troops had visited. Yongle rewarded him and his men before immediately hatching plans for their next assignment to the south, which the emperor planned at the same time as an extended campaign against Mongolia in the north.

As the membranes of this Ming world became increasingly porous, the empire was increasingly incapable of sustaining communications using written Chinese alone. Therefore, in order to protect and expand it, in 1407 the Yongle emperor created a Translators' College (*Siyi guan* 四夷館).[4] Initially part of the Hanlin Academy, the College included eight bureaus devoted to a range of languages that were crucial for diplomatic communication between the Ming empire and states that did not use the Chinese script. The Mongolian (*Dada* 韃靼) Bureau handled diplomatic exchange between the Ming court and any state officials or others who preferred to use the Mongolian language in written communication. The Jurchen (*Nüzhen* 女真) Bureau was established to translate between Chinese and an Altaic language that had become politically crucial in the Jin dynasty (1115–1234) when North China was under Jurchen rule.[5] The Huihui 回回 Bureau handled texts from areas that were known to practise Islam and that submitted documents in Persian, although the term *huihui* could also be used to describe texts in Arabic script. A wide territory fell under its jurisdiction: Samarqand, Arabia, Turfan, Champa, Java, Cambodia, Melaka and, remarkably, Japan.[6] There was a Tibetan (*Xifan* 西番) Bureau responsible for Tibetan literary and diplomatic texts; a Gaochang 高昌 Bureau responsible for documents in Uighur script; a Baiyi 百夷 Bureau that covered many polities and subprefectures around what is now Yunnan; and a Myanmar (*Miandan* 緬甸) Bureau. The Sanskrit (*Xitian* 西天) Bureau produced and translated sutras and other classic literature – its extant 'glossaries' (*yiyu* 譯語) are in fact Sanskrit texts copied out with Chinese glosses on pronunciation – and its officials were also responsible for written communication with India.[7] In addition to the eight original bureaus founded by the Yongle emperor in 1407, a ninth bureau devoted to Babai 八百, a script used in Yunnan, was added in 1511.[8] A tenth bureau for an early version of the Thai language (*Xianluo* 暹羅) was added in 1578.[9] Each of these bureaus was charged with translating a particular foreign script to and from Chinese, training students and officials in the relevant language and creating written materials as study aids, and to facilitate translation between the script and Chinese.[10]

Students came to the College through various routes and performed many different sorts of functions once established there. The earliest students at the College were culled from the Imperial Academy and the instructors were recruited from a pool of local interpreters who were native or fluent speakers of the relevant languages. Later students were allowed to enter the College by examination, and many managed to buy or bribe their way in. By the late 16th century, positions at the College had largely become hereditary: when an instructor died, his son often took over his job.[11] Students were typically examined every three years, at which point they either failed (and could retake the test twice more during the regular three-year cycle before being ejected from the College), or were rewarded with a promotion. After three of these tests – or nine years of training – a student was qualified as an instructor. Once establishing himself as a capable translator, in addition to teaching and studying foreign scripts, a student or instructor could also be called upon as a calligrapher. He might alternatively be sent to a border station, where he would translate and produce documents for the court and occasionally teach Chinese classical literature and culture to foreign envoys.

The students and faculty at the College left a dispersed documentary archive of traces of a variety of materials meant to aid in the study and practice of translation. Students were responsible for learning, and in principle were periodically examined on, the most commonly used terms in the language they worked with. These included manuals for recognising and producing the alphabets of foreign scripts like Persian, Mongolian and 'Phags-pa. They also included bilingual compilations of *laiwen* 來文, which were paired memorials in Chinese and a range of languages that were of diplomatic importance to the state. In addition, translators produced bilingual sets of poems that were ostensibly intended to aid in their practice, which was based in part on the memorisation of vocabulary. Aside from Sanskrit verses that were (like the other extant materials from that bureau) actual Buddhist texts, most of the bilingual poems composed by the bureaus were likely created by teachers and students as learning exercises.[12] Each bureau composed two examples of verse in five- or seven-character units: each word was rendered both in Chinese and in foreign script with a Chinese gloss, with a complete Chinese-only version of the poem also provided as a reference. The poems are laid out on each page in the direction of the original non-Chinese script. The Persian poems, for example, are read from right-to-left, with one line of verse continuing across all the pages of the document before the reader would have had to flip back to the first page to read the next line, and do the same for that line. In contrast, the Thai poems are read top-down and right-left on each page. For the most part, these were not particularly attractive literary works, but they served the purpose of helping students become capped and salaried translators. Some students and instructors at the Thai Bureau, for example, wrote a ditty that helped them remember basic terms like moon and mountain, person and plant, and hot and cold.[13]

The language bureaus were also charged with creating bilingual glossaries full of words and phrases that were arranged in topical categories: Heavenly Bodies and Phenomena; Precious Objects; Human Affairs; Geography and the Land; Writing and Records; Types of People; Buildings; The Human Body; Directions; Numbers and Counting; Birds and Beasts; Flowers and Trees; Tools and Implements; Cloth and Clothing; Colours; Food and Drink; and Time and Calendrics. A section for Commonly Used Terms functioned as a miscellany of words that did not fit elsewhere. Some glossaries included other categories that included important vocabulary not subsumed in the typical glossary topics: the Tibetan instructors added a section for Aromatic Drugs, for example, and one for Classical or Religious Terminology. Each glossary page had columns of paired terms that were sometimes related to each other, with the entries in each topical category often beginning with the most simple and familiar, and ending with specialised terminology that was specific to the documents in a particular script. Readers would begin at the top right of each page and read down each column until arriving at the left edge and turning to the next set of words. For each entry, the translators provided three components: a word in foreign script, a translation into Chinese and a Chinese transliteration of the way the foreign term sounded. Some glossaries were clearly the work of several people, with at least one responsible for each script: the scripts on some extant glossaries seem to have been written at different times, and likely by different hands.

Like prints in the sand marking the passage of a tiger, the terms on these glossary pages marked the passage of objects across and through Ming imperial languages of translation: suns and moons, rivers and roads, vegetables and trees. Ming translators' glossaries were full of the traces of these objects and more. Reading these glossaries not just as translators' tools but also as collections of objects allows us to understand Ming history as it might inform a broader history of objects and traces thereof.

'A marsh … a vein of water'

In the early 15th century, the Yongle emperor had founded not just a Translators' College, but also a machine for generating and then codifying possible ways of being the same for things in the Ming world. Those included ways of being a human body, ways of being a colour and even possible ways of being a mother or a son. This sameness was systematised though the education and practices of Ming translators.

Understood in this way, Ming translators' glossaries were not just inscriptions produced by imperially sanctioned translators of diplomatic documents, but were also paper technologies for generating new likenesses and new ways of being the same. At one level, this was happening when translators decided to classify a particular term in a specific glossary category: when a Mongolian translator included terminology for 'pearls' within Precious Objects instead of Birds and Beasts, for example, he mapped the physical universe of the Mongolian and Chinese languages in a particular way. At another level, when translators equated a Persian term with a particular Chinese term, the juxtaposition of those two terms subtly expanded the meaning of each and created a new way of being the same for each of them. We cannot attribute these juxtapositions to the intentions of particular translators who might have decided to equate particular terms – the glossaries may well have been products of multiple hands writing multiple scripts and working collaboratively, and the extant glossaries are often devoid of the kinds of paratexts that might be used to ascribe authorship to them. Still, the texts themselves performed equivalence and accomplished the work of generating and inscribing likenesses.

In creating these texts, Ming translators were actually changing the material landscape of the dynasty insofar as they were changing the way it was defined and understood. That landscape was in part created through Ming practices of synonymy, and translators' glossaries both recorded traces of these practices and helped enact them. This phenomenon was not local to the particular context of Ming translation. One of the most important ways that we come to know the world of objects in general is through synonymy: deciding what things are the same as other things and in what ways. A definition is just a statement of a series of ways of being the same as other things. The way a marsh, for Calvino, announces the presence of a vein of water, so a term like *he* 河 in a glossary announces the fact that this is a river. And as the marsh is part of what it is to be that vein of water, so *he* makes up part of what it is to be a river. The names we have for things become part of how we understand those things, by becoming part of the constellation of traces from which they emerge and become present to us. Names thus become an integral part of the things themselves. At the same time, the way that synonymy was enacted by Ming translators generated a very specific set of relations. The terms included in translators' glossaries were ostensibly culled from, and intended to aid in translating, documents of diplomatic importance to the Ming state. The particular kinds of equivalence were therefore shaped by the nature of Ming diplomatic relations with other states and the documentary traces that those relations produced. Diplomatic (or in some cases, religious or literary) documents were anatomised into individual units of vocabulary and then fitted onto a grid of glossary categories. What it was to be the same, for these translators, was thus the result of a disciplining process that transformed foreign documents into a shape that could be used and consumed by Ming readers and writers.

That disciplining proceeded according to the practical needs of translators and interpreters. Translators' College glossaries were meant to aid script-based translation of written documents, and thus foreign terminology was included, translated and integrated into the Chinese glossary system to the extent that it was useful to writers and readers. In contrast, consider the terms included in the glossaries of another Ming organ of translation, the Interpreters' Station (*Huitong guan* 會同館). These texts were geared toward assisting oral interpreters in learning and using the vocabulary that was vital to carrying out their duties at the station. Intended for spoken conversation, they only included Chinese transliterations of foreign terms and did not include foreign scripts.[14] They were typically organised according to the same categories as the Translators' College texts, though some editions contained additional rubrics. One Korean glossary, for example, contained separate sections for the names of the heavenly stems and earthly branches, and for the names of the trigrams from the *Yijing* 易經 (*Classic of Changes*).[15] Judging from the terms and phrases included in the Station glossaries, interpreters had many kinds of interactions with visiting merchants and envoys. They commented on travel conditions and the state of the roads and buildings of the capital and its environs, and were well armed with phrases that described the conditions of rivers and directions for fording them, crossing bridges, travelling along roads, using wells and negotiating city walls. They spoke of the various stages of the night watch, the times of the day and the year and they commented on changes in the seasons. They learned the names for flowers, plants, trees, animals and foodstuffs that would typically come up in conversation with foreign envoys – not just lice and butterflies, but also glow-worms and mad dogs and silver-haired horses. (In the glossaries for Mongol and Jurchen languages, this could include many names for different varieties of horses, signalling the importance of the animals for trade with those groups.) They learned how to instruct envoys on the proper etiquette for inhabiting households in the capital: no running around, for example, and no burning the doors and windows down (*guanfang buxu zuojian* 官房不許作踐; *men chuang buxu shaohui* 門窓不許燒毀).[16] They learned the terms for instruments used for cooking, playing music and maintaining horses and livestock; words for madmen, scarred men, belt makers, hat makers and idiots, hunchbacks, tanners and people with harelips. They learned how to talk about actions, from meditating to agreeing to sitting, and included special terms for 'not becoming a useful person', for asking in detail, for requesting wine and for bringing in horses. They learned how to talk about body parts and things that one could do with and to them, emotions, illnesses and qualities of character. The nature of some of the phrases in these glossaries gives us a sense that interpreters were not solely called upon to perform duties within the walls of the Station or even the capital: they were also sent to accompany envoys on their travels. Thus, some interpreters' glossaries included multi-word phrases on Human Affairs that would ostensibly have been of use to foreign envoys staying at the hostel: 'That's ugly', or 'I'm drunk!'[17] Interpreters at the Station could consult the handbook for instructions on how to direct foreign envoys in practical matters for navigating the roads, how to chat about the weather, how to direct envoys in matters of court etiquette and what to say to envoys who were on their way back home after visiting the Ming.

The kinds of relations that the Interpreters' Station glossaries generated were based on an assumption of embodied performance: they were equivalences of gesture or oral utterance, to be invoked in a context where the primary goal was face-to-face communication, discipline, entertainment and/or stewardship. We can compare this to the kinds of equivalence generated by the Translators' College glossaries and other textual materials, which assumed a context of archivable ink on a page, where the equivalences would be experienced as written text rather than spoken physical action. This contrast is interesting insofar as it draws our attention to the situatedness and locality of a quality we may otherwise take for granted: the state of being the same.

So, how does this help us understand *these* objects in *these* glossaries at this point in the Ming? And why does that matter?

'A hibiscus flower ... the end of winter'

The objects inscribed into Ming translators' texts collectively made up a traveller's landscape, whether that traveller was ultimately at home in the Chinese language and exploring non-Chinese documents, or vice versa. In Calvino's city of Tamara, the objects experienced by the traveller were not in themselves meaningful: instead, they stood only as signs for other, absent things. A hibiscus flower was not meaningfully experienced as itself, but instead only as an indication that spring was near. We might consider translators' glossaries in a similar sense. As much as they performed equivalence in the ways explained above, they also inscribed difference: each term in Persian, Tibetan, Mongolian or another script immediately called attention to itself as distant from the object it named even as it was part, on some level, of it. If it was included in a College glossary, it signalled its own morphological difference from Chinese terms (through the body of its script, through the transliteration of its sound into Chinese characters) and thus from the scriptural body of the Ming, even as it became part of it by becoming partnered with Ming Chinese terms on the page. Therefore, in a way the vocabulary collected in Ming College glossaries can be read as signs of difference, of absence from the legible heart of the Ming empire and of illegibility that needed translating. Vocabulary in the Interpreters' Station glossaries signalled a different kind of distance: there, each of the terms was offered in a transliterated Chinese script and the presence of a glossary signalled some kind of a distinction in oral cultures and a resulting potential problem through in-person communication. In both cases, translators' vocabulary was a sign of a distance that needed to be overcome.

Even if it could not entirely be overcome, however, that distance could potentially be controlled. And that control was enacted by translators' practices of synonymy, of making foreign terms – and thus objects, and actions and ways of speaking – functionally equivalent to Ming Chinese ones. The Translators' College and the bureaus subsumed within it systematised these ways of being the same, and did so using fairly consistent rubrics. Each of the bureau glossaries that were used for practical and pedagogical purposes by students and instructors included virtually the same categories. Many of the glossary categories began with the most commonly used terms and proceeded to more specialised terms that were specific to the documentary contexts of particular languages. Because of that, there was significant overlap in the vocabulary included in the early pages of most of the bureau glossaries at the College and Station. As a result, the different language glossaries are also related to each other: looking at *tian* 天 (Heaven) across the bureau glossaries (and the translation and language-learning practices that these glossaries form traces of) gives us a way of expanding our notion of *tian* and relating the terms that translators equated with it not only to *tian* but also to one another: thus *abka*, *tngri*, and the heavens in other scripts and languages become the same. And this was the case not just for heaven, or for things like tigers and stones, but also for actions and modes of being, like 'walking', saying 'yes' or 'sitting'. As we explore connections and contacts in the Ming world, it is useful to keep in mind that those linkages could take many different forms, and the production of sameness by Ming translators was one important way that the early Ming formed new relationships and brought a new landscape of (language, translated) objects into being. And just as Tamara's hibiscus flower signalled a transformation as well as an ending in pointing travellers ahead to a new season, a foreign term in a foreign script in a Translators' College glossary signalled both a limit to communication and a transformation that transgressed that limit.

'Trees and stones … only what they are'

As the traveller makes her way to Calvino's city of Tamara, there are objects she does not see. If a thing does not signal another thing, it escapes her notice. She walks for days among trees and stones without seeing them: trees and stones, after all, are only what they are. Beyond Tamara, Calvino's book is peppered with other cities distinguished by their relationships to signs. Zirma, a city of memories and redundancies populated by blind men, madmen and girls raising pumas. Zoe, a city whose buildings and spaces and objects are indistinguishable from one another. Hypatia, a city that embodies a fantastically unconventional relationship between objects, images, language and signs, where the musicians hide in tombs and beautiful women wait in the stables. Olivia, a city of peacocks and sarcasm that challenges the traveller's relationship between words and things. In each case, as we read, a page becomes a world full of things that are always pointing to other things. The documentary traces of Ming translators – especially the bilingual glossaries they made and used – can be read in a similar light. The things strewn across its pages are meaningful, are included and are significant only insofar as they point the reader to other things: to a foreign script, to another state, to a particular way of gridding material reality and ultimately to distance itself.

Notes

1 Calvino 1972, 13.

2 Calvino 1972, 14.

3 Zheng He returned with his fleet in October 1407. On the seven voyages of his fleet, see Dreyer 2007. Dreyer interprets the voyages of Zheng He as a display of Ming power, in contrast to the popular account of Zheng He as a benign explorer.

4 On the dating of the founding of the *Siyi guan* to 1407, and on scholarly disagreement over which month it was founded in (November/December or April), see Pelliot 1947, 207–90, 227–8.

5 By the late 16th century, this bureau seems to have been an extinct or at least defunct part of the College: throughout the 15th and 16th centuries the Jurchen people preferred to write and read Mongolian even while they spoke Jurchen.

6 Wang Zongzai 1924, 10b–22b. In the 1695 Qing ver[illegible] of the *Siyi guan kao* by Jiang Fan, *Huihui* was added as an additional region administered by the *Huihui* Bureau. See Jiang Fan 1997. Classification under the *Huihui* bureau would have meant that Japan was sending Persian documents to China for official communication.

7 The Sanskrit Bureau seemed to be a problem for the College. According to a popular story, in the early days of the College one Qin Junchu 秦君初 (1385–1441) faked his way through the imperial exams and into a position as Sanskrit Bureau translator by memorising or sneaking a copy of a sutra into the exam, copying it out in Sanskrit and attaching it to the end of his exam paper. His deceit was not discovered until a century after his death, when instructors at the Bureau wanted to compile a glossary like that of their peers and had no model. They consulted the *Huayi yiyu* compiled by Qin during his days teaching at the Bureau, expecting it to contain translations of pertinent terms and ideas like the other glossaries, and found only a recopying of a Buddhist sutra, the *Manjusri-Nama-Samgiti* (Chanting of the Names of Manjusri).

8 Pelliot 1947, 229.

9 Pelliot 1947, 229.

10 A number of articles and essays have studied the *Siyi guan* and *Huitong guan*. The interested reader should consult Hirth 1888; Wild 1945; Pelliot 1947; Kane 1989, esp. 90–9; Crossley 1991, 38–70; and Nappi 2015. Many of the early works rely on the foundational work by French Sinologist (educated in medicine as well) Jean-Pierre Abel-Rémusat. See Abel-Rémusat 1826. Several short articles through the early 20th century reported discovering new manuscripts of the text in European collections in London, Paris, Berlin and St Petersburg. See, for example, Ross 1908, 689–795, which discusses a manuscript that likely originated in the *Huitong guan*.

11 This option was implemented after several directors of the College complained about the quality of the students who were securing places through examination or bribery. According to these complaints, the classrooms were full of rich boys who had neither the aptitude for learning nor an interest in studying the languages to which they were assigned. The entrance examinations, he protested, were irrelevant to the work the men actually did upon enrolling in the College, and the privileged sons of wealthy officials threatened to undermine the work of the entire institution. After one particularly strident complaint from a College Director in the 16th century, the court implemented his suggestion that a new set of students should be chosen from among the blood relations of the current College translators. For the full text of the 1566 memorial sent by Director Xu Jie 徐階 (1494–1574) to the Jiajing 嘉靖emperor (r. 1522–66), along with a commentary by Gao Gong 高拱, see Lü Weiqi 1928, 193–7.

12 The 1695 *Siyi guan kao* by Jiang Fan includes examples of poems used to aid in the memorisation of vocabulary from the eight bureaus extant in 1695: Persian, Uighur, Tibetan, Thai, Burmese, Sanskrit, Baiyi and Babai. Some of the poems are titled, and most include the names of the authors, all of whom were translators of the College. These were most likely student assignments, as each bureau set includes the names of one or two officials who composed the poems (it is unclear whether they did so in foreign or Chinese script), and the names of student translator-officials who translated them.

13 Jiang Fan 1997, 719–20.

14 See the *Chaoxian* 朝鮮 glossary from the Awa no Kuni collection at Cornell University for prefatory remarks on the whole series of 13 glossaries, based on an edition compiled by Mao Ruizheng茅瑞徵 (*jinshi* 1601; fl. 1597–1636, *zi* Bofu伯符), who had written the *Huang Ming xiangxu lu*皇明象胥錄 (*Record of the Interpreters of the August Ming*) (1629), a treatise on tribute states of the Ming, and other texts on military and foreign relations. The edition also included a preface by Zhu Zhifan朱之蕃 (1564–?, *jinshi* 1595 [optimus]), a senior official in the Hanlin Academy who was famed for his calligraphy. Zhu had been sent as an envoy to Korea in 1605, perhaps explaining why his preface to the work appeared at the beginning of the Korean glossary. The glossaries included in the Awa no Kuni collection are Ming products, but more precise dating is unknown. See Davidson 1975. Because some of these countries communicated in writing with the Ming using Chinese, they didn't need script glossaries.

15 Huo Yuanjie 1979, with Zhu Zhifan preface.

16 Kane 1989, 244.

17 These examples can be found in the Human Affairs (*renshi*) section of the Ryukyu glossary from Huo Yuanjie 1979, 94. Numerous other cases are included in the many Interpreters' glossaries. There are several examples from the Awa no Kuni Bunko glossaries.

Chapter 24
Building Cultural Authority in Early Joseon Korea (1400–1450)

Lee Soomi

Translated by Oh Seung Hee and Jeong-Spencer Eunjin

The period from 1400 to 1450 was a time of major cultural and political change in Korea. Following the founding of the Joseon dynasty in 1392, this era saw the state ideology shift from Buddhism to Neo-Confucianism. Taejong (r. 1400–18), the third king of the dynasty, eliminated senior officials and their relatives in order to clear the way for his son Sejong (r. 1418–50) to seize power.[1] He established policies aimed at reducing the estates owned by Buddhist temples across the country that were enforced by Sejong after he became king. By 1424, only 18 Buddhist temples of the Contemplative (*Seon* 禪) school and 18 of the Textual (*Gyo* 教) school would remain out of the tens of thousands of temples that had previously existed. Slaves and land owned by temples also became the possession of the government.[2] Consequently, the position of Buddhism, a central power in the previous Goryeo dynasty (918–1392), was severely damaged.[3]

This chapter explores how Sejong eradicated the cultural legitimacy of the past dynasty and propagated the new cultural authority of the Joseon dynasty (1392–1897) following this turbulent period. Over the three decades of his reign, Sejong established an institutional foundation for the arts and accomplished many cultural achievements.[4] Examining this aspect of his reign reveals that events such as the demolition of cultural symbols of the Goryeo dynasty and nationwide enshrinement of portraits of the founder of the Joseon dynasty, hitherto thought to be unrelated, were actually closely intertwined and aimed at creating a centralised state that was governed by literature and the arts. This chapter also studies how poetry, calligraphy and painting were used for the purpose of forging an emotional bond between the king and scholar officials, and as a means to manage symbols of kingship during the Joseon period.

After the political situation stabilised and the authority of the Goryeo dynasty was subdued, Sejong successfully established his new cultural policy to enhance the dignity of the Joseon dynasty. Although Neo-Confucianism was established as the state ideology, belief in Buddhism lingered among the populace and, to an extent, respect for the perceived role of Buddhism in maintaining a stable society. In order to inculcate fully Neo-Confucianism into Joseon society, Sejong employed symbols and the arts in sophisticated ways to communicate his ideas to his subjects.

Sejong's treatment of royal portraits

Royal portraits were among the most significant symbols of rulership in dynastic Korea. It is, therefore, important to examine how Sejong managed the portraits of the Joseon founder Taejo (1335–1408; r. 1392–98), born Yi Seonggye 李成桂, and the royal portraits of the Goryeo dynasty that he inherited. By doing so, we will be able to understand the process whereby the authority of the Goryeo dynasty was overthrown and the cultural authority of the Joseon dynasty was established.

Prior to Sejong's rule, a series of royal portrait halls (*jinjeon*) were established to house the portraits of Taejo.[5] The first of these halls, named Junweonjeon, was built during the second month of 1398 at the king's birthplace of Yeongheung, Hamgyeong province (**Pl. 24.1**). In the following month of the same year, another portrait hall, Jipgyeongjeon, was established in Gyeongju, the capital of the ancient Silla

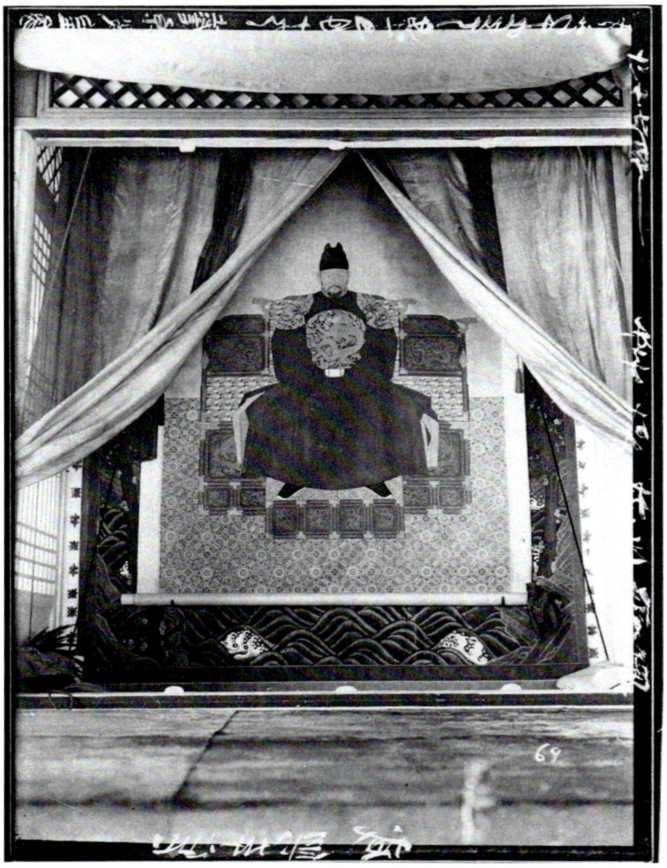

Plate 24.1 *Portrait of Taejo* 太祖御眞 in Yeongheung Junweonjeon 永興 濬源殿, photograph taken in 1913. National Museum of Korea

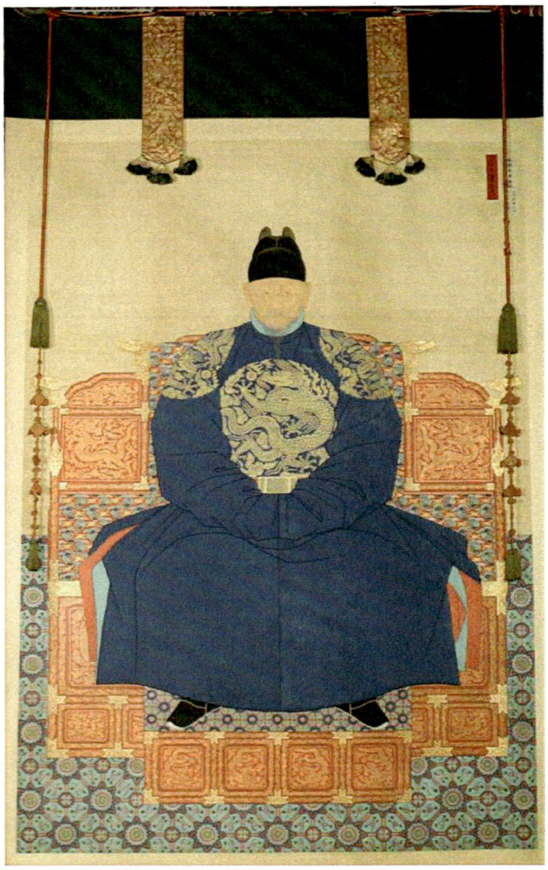

Plate 24.2 *Portrait of Taejo* 太祖御眞, dated 1872, Jeonju Gyeonggijeon 全州 慶基殿. Hanging scroll, colour on silk, height 218cm, width 150cm. Royal Portrait Museum, Jeonju City

Kingdom (57 BCE–935 CE). By 1405, a portrait of Taejo had also been enshrined in Pyeongyang, the capital of the Goguryeo kingdom (37 BCE–668 CE). After Taejo passed away in 1408, portraits of him were enshrined in Hanyang, the capital of the Joseon dynasty, and Jeonju, his ancestral seat. The only extant portrait of Taejo is in Jeonju. It is a copy dated 1872, produced by court painters based on the original image that no longer survives (**Pl. 24.2**).[6]

At the beginning of his reign, Sejong considered the use of portraiture in ancestral rituals to be misguided.[7] Sejong's policies, however, shows that his attitude towards royal portraits and their halls gradually changed. In particular, he began to consider the importance of the Portrait Halls of King Taejo, and ordered the production of new portraits of the former king, as well as copies of existing ones.[8] During the first year of his reign in 1419, Sejong oversaw the completion of the final Portrait Hall of King Taejo, which his father Taejong had begun in the previous year. Significantly, this hall was located in Gaeseong, which was the capital city of the vanquished Goryeo dynasty. Thus, the portraits of Taejo were distributed and enshrined in locations of particular political significance to the king and the history of Korea. Moreover, the enshrinement ceremony of Taejo's portrait in Gaeseong was recorded in detail, setting it apart from previous enshrinements that were not well documented, which suggests the likelihood that the event was politically motivated.[9]

Once Sejong completed the project of enshrining Taejo's portraits, he turned his attention to the royal portrait paintings and statues of the Goryeo dynasty. When Taejo became the first Joseon king in 1392, he ordered the statues of the kings of the Goryeo dynasty to be moved from Gaeseong to Majeon in Gyeonggi province.[10] The number of ceremonial enshrinements of Goryeo royal portraits was then gradually reduced. In 1426, Sejong ordered the incineration of all the preparatory drawings of the portraits of kings and queens of the Goryeo dynasty that were stored in the Bureau of Painting (Dohwawon), and the half-length royal portraits kept in Jeongneung.[11] Although burning can be interpreted as a conventional way of disposing sacred objects,[12] Sejong's act was more of a symbolic severance of the legitimacy of the Goryeo dynasty. According to the *Veritable Records of the Joseon Dynasty*, in 1427 and 1428, Sejong further ordered the burial of the portraits and the statues of King Taejo Wang Geon 王建 (877–943; r. 918–43), founder of the Goryeo dynasty, and King Hyejong (912–45; r. 943–5), as well as portraits of those who contributed to the former dynasty in proximity to the king's royal tomb in Gaeseong.[13] Finally, Sejong finished this task with the burial of 18 portraits of Goryeo kings in 'enclosed and pristine lands (屛處潔地)' in 1430.[14]

One of the royal images buried near the tomb of the founder of the Goryeo dynasty in Gaeseong has been excavated.[15] It is a bronze statue that is believed to be a representation of Wang Geon that was buried near his tomb (**Pl. 24.3**). Remnants of a silk belt were found together with the bronze statue, suggesting that the statue may have originally been dressed in a silk garment.[16] According to Ro

Myoung-ho, this statue of Wang Geon was the most sacred object in the ancestral rituals of the Goryeo dynasty, even more so than the royal portrait paintings.[17] Burial of this statue by Sejong during the Joseon dynasty must have been an act of considerable political significance.

By burning and burying the portraits and statues of Goryeo kings, part of the most significant symbols of the Goryeo dynasty were eliminated. They were replaced by portraits of the rulers of the new Joseon dynasty in 1430, just 11 years after Sejong established the final Royal Portrait Hall of King Taejo in 1419.

Sejong's promotion of literary activities

Sejong was able to accomplish the delicate task of removing the inheritance of the former dynasty because he had the support of scholar officials whom he had nurtured at the Hall of Worthies (Jiphyeonjeon 集賢殿), the Royal Academic Institute, since 1420.[18] These scholar officials advised Sejong on state projects and provided him with concrete justifications for undertaking them based on historical sources. Jiphyeonjeon scholars also played an important role in carrying out major cultural enterprises during this period, such as the invention of the Korean alphabet Hangeul in 1443, the publication of the poetry collection *Songs of Flying Dragons* (*Yongbi'eocheonga* 龍飛御天歌), the first work published in Hangeul, between 1442 and 1447, and the production of a revised version of the *Illustrated Guide to the Three Bonds* (*Samgang haengsildo* 三綱行實圖) in 1434 with Korean material (see discussion by Sarah Schneewind in Chapter 25 of this volume).[19]

By encouraging opportunities for interaction with his subjects, Sejong achieved political consensus and mitigated antipathy surrounding the controversy over the way in which he had became king in place of his older brothers. He attended daily royal lectures, where he read Confucian classics and discussed state affairs with Jiphyeonjeon scholars. After ascending to the throne, Sejong frequently held banquets for officials and royal family members. According to the *Veritable Records of the Joseon Dynasty*, on the eighth day of his enthronement Sejong held a banquet in honour of his father during which he wrote poems with one of his elder brothers, Prince Hyoryeong (1369–1486), and danced with scholar officials 'amid great pleasure'.[20] Sejong continued to hold banquets for royal family members and toasted them until Taejong passed away.[21]

Sejong also participated in poetry gatherings with royal princes and scholar officials. Poetry exchange, calligraphy and painting were important means for fostering an intimate bond between Sejong, royal princes and officials. For instance, Sejong attended a poetry gathering held at his uncle Prince Hyoryeong's new pavilion Huiwujeong 喜雨亭 in 1447. There, the king commanded the crown prince, his third son Prince Anpyeong (1418–53), as well as officials Seong Sammun 成三問 (1418–56) and Yim Wonjun 任元濬 (1423–1500), to compose poems.[22] It is believed that two paintings were produced at the gathering: *Night Banquet at Huiwujeong* (*Huiwujeong yayeondo* 喜雨亭夜宴圖) and *Pleasure of the Moon along the Riverbank* (*Imgang-wanwoldo* 臨江玩月圖).[23]

Royal princes, in particular Prince Anpyeong, often played a key role as a mediator when the king sought poetry

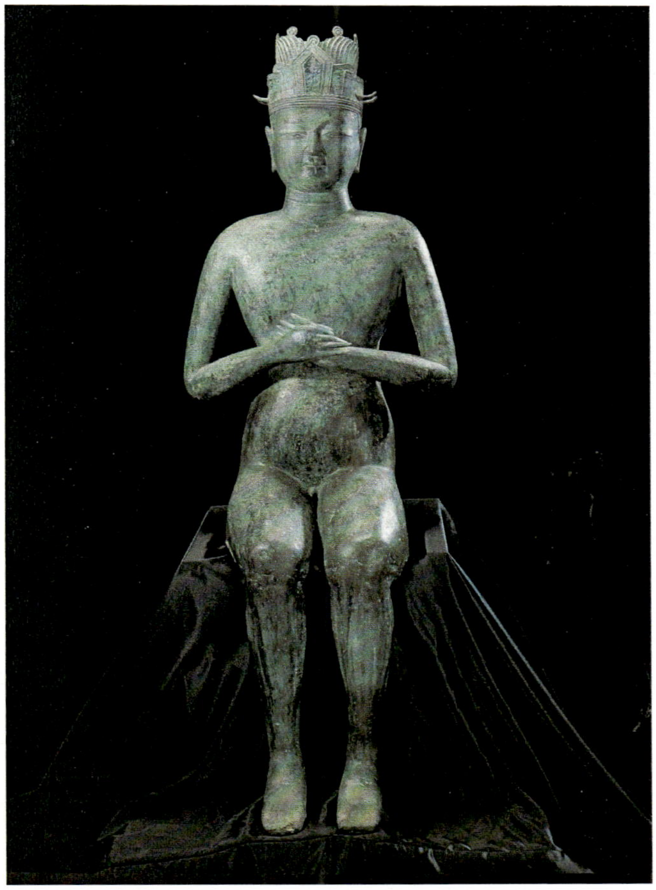

Plate 24.3 Statue of King Taejo Wang Geon, founder of the Goryeo dynasty, excavated at Hyeonneung in Gaeseong. Bronze, height 138.3cm. The Korean Central History Museum, Pyeongyang

from officials. For instance, in 1442, at the recommendation of Prince Anpyeong, Sejong travelled to Icheon to visit a thermal spring in the company of the prince and many officials. After returning to the palace, Prince Anpyeong commissioned a painting and poems from 17 scholars to commemorate the visit. Munjong (r. 1450–2), who was the crown prince at that time, also composed an archaistic phrase, mounted it with a painting, and commanded Sin Sukju 申叔舟 (1417–75) to write a preface. In 1444 when Sejong visited a thermal spring in Cheongju, Prince Anpyeong and nine attending officials replied to the *Poem on Sweet Spring Water* (*Yecheon si* 醴泉詩) with 30 poems of their own. It is assumed that these poems were made into a scroll by the prince, most eulogising the king's virtue.[24] Princes were also patrons in their own right. A particularly impressive example is the painting *Dream Journey to the Peach Blossom Land* (*Mong-yudowondo* 夢遊桃源圖) (**Pl. 24.4**). Commissioned by Prince Anpyeong, it is a visualisation of his dream, painted by An Gyeon 安堅 (active *c.* 1440–70) with colophons and poems written by 21 scholars.[25]

A precedent for the exchange of poetry between ruler and officials can also be found in the Goryeo dynasty. It was, however, practised more collectively and on a larger scale in the Joseon dynasty. Sejong's poetry exchange with Jiphyeonjeon scholars further aimed to enhance the quality of poetry and calligraphy.[26] The *Veritable Records of the Joseon Dynasty* records that Sejong openly expressed dissatisfaction over standards in the literary arts during a large banquet

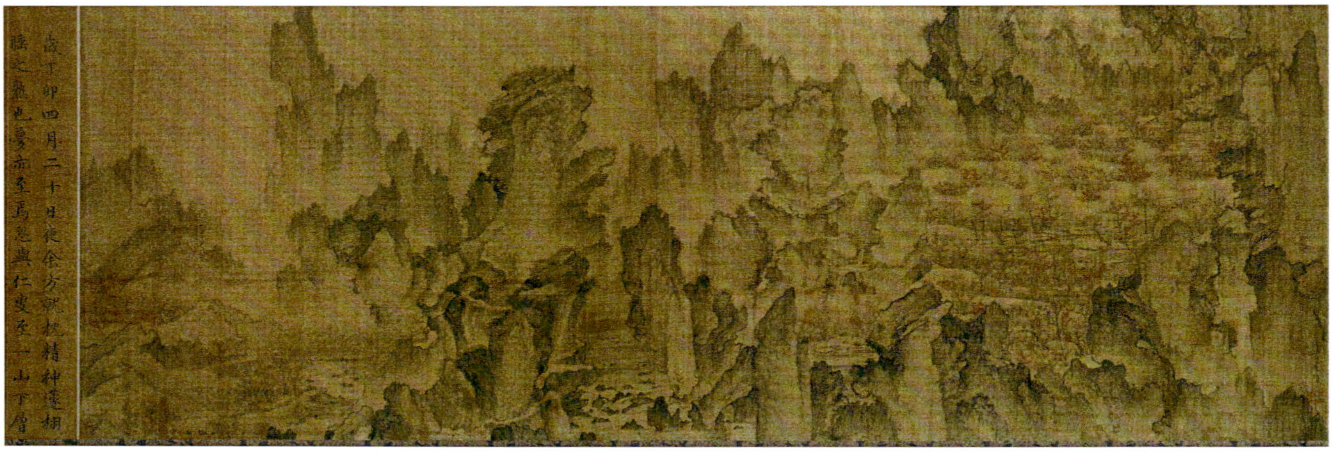

Plate 24.4 An Gyeon 安堅 (active c. 1440–70), *Dream Journey to the Peach Blossom Land* (*Mong-yudowondo* 夢遊桃源圖), dated 1447. Handscroll, ink and colours on silk, height 38.7cm, width 106.1cm. Tenri Central Library

held at the royal palace of Gyeonghoeru on the eighth day of the sixth month of 1435. Addressing princes, the grand secretary and 53 scholars, he said:

> Why is there now a lack of those who correctly abide by instructions and announcements (*xungao*)? Confucian scholars are not fond of the study of poetry because I have not admired the study of poetry. 'Writing poetry and prose is a skill of little consequence,' so even though later generations say that a certain era is not fond of the study of poetry, surely it is harmless. Yet, among sages of ancient times, there were none who were not adept at writing poetry and prose. I am also inclined to the study of poetry. If there are those on high who are fond of it, then who would not be fond of it?
>
> 何今時尚乏訓誥(詁)之正者耶。儒生不好詩學，專由予不尚詩學之故也。詞章末藝，後世雖云某代不尚詩學，固無害也。然前古聖賢，未有不兼能詩賦者。予亦有意於詩學，上有好者，孰不好焉。[27]

Sejong then assembled scholar officials to compose poetry. In response to this, 47 officials dedicated poems with alternating lines of 5 words and 7 words to the king, which were made into a scroll. In his speech, Sejong expressed wariness towards literary activities, while promoting their importance. Under Neo-Confucianism, the king was expected to avoid becoming too immersed and distracted by literary interests. In order to justify his support of literary cultivation, Sejong asserted that writing and exchange of poetry with officials were a part of internal and external administration. Sejong's own view of culture spread among scholar officials and through to the wider society. In addition, Sejong emphasised the quality of calligraphy. For example, in the fifth month of 1442, the king commissioned an album of rubbings from stone inscriptions and distributed it to officials as models for practising calligraphy.[28]

Plate 24.5 Anonymous, *Eight Steeds of Taejo* (*Taejo Paljundo* 太祖八駿圖), dated 1705. National Museum of Korea

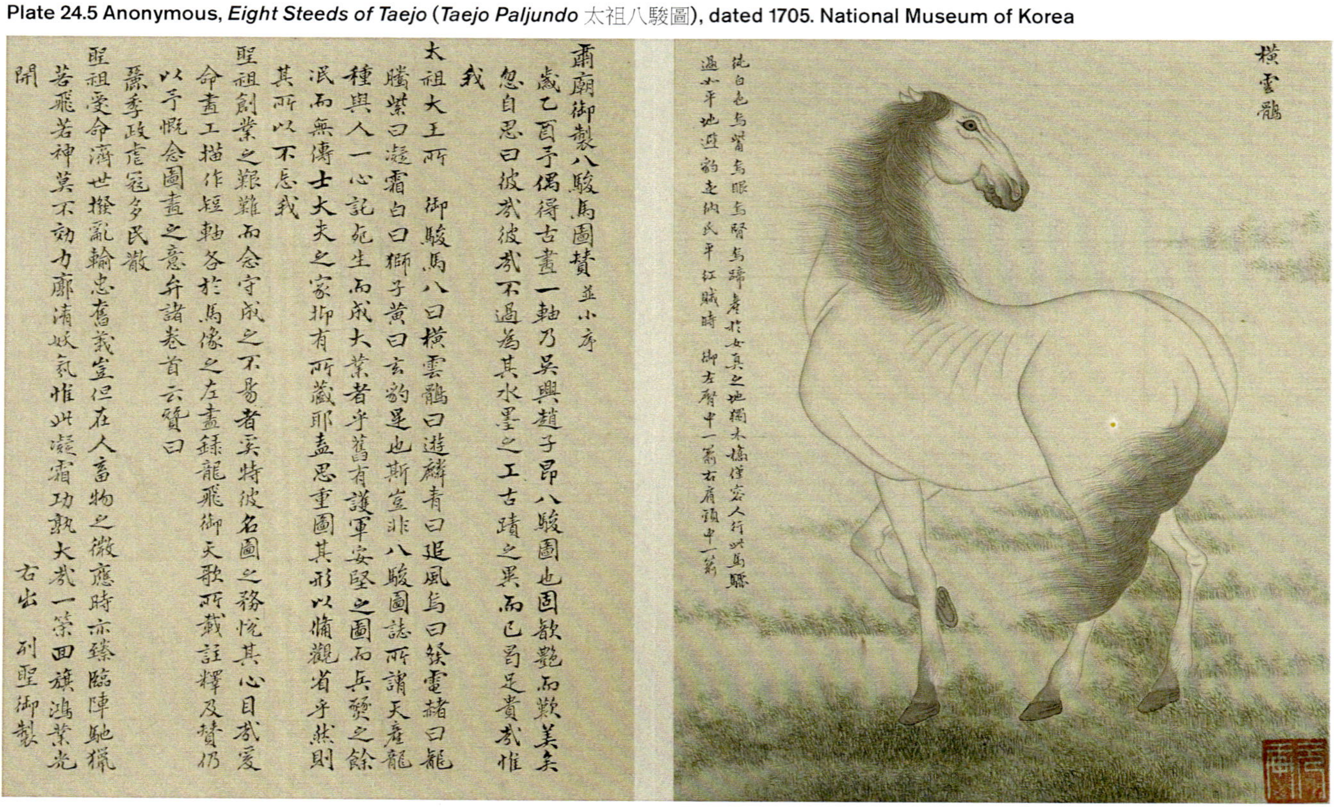

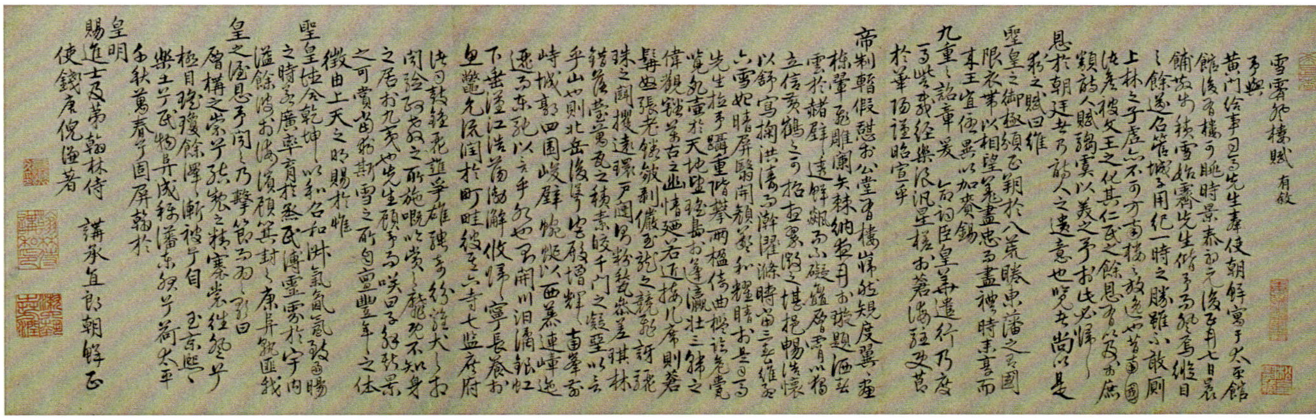

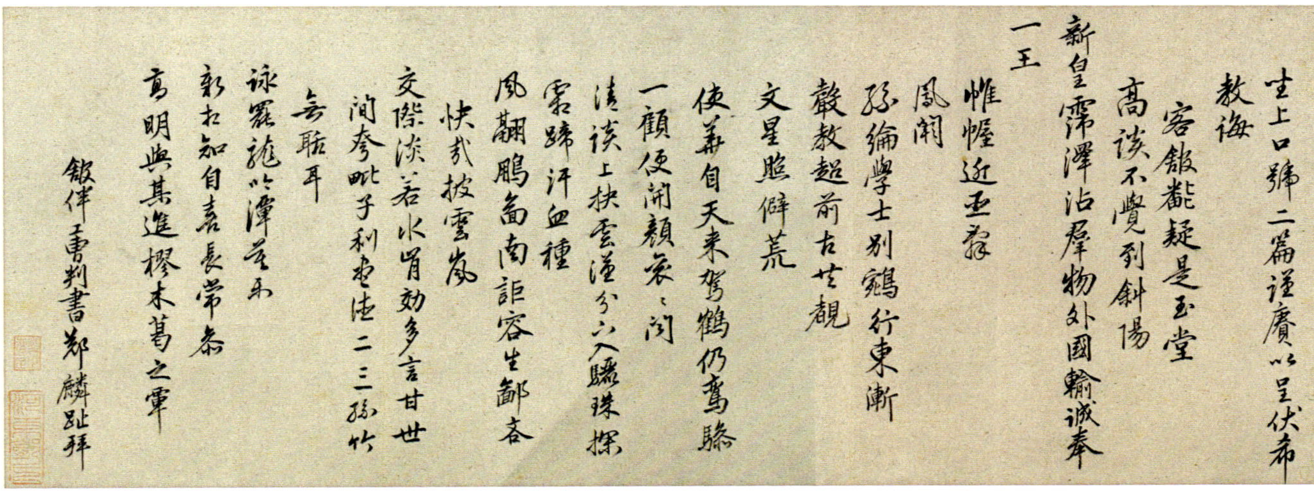

Plates 24.6–24.7 Poems written by Chinese and Korean scholars (*Bong sa Joseon changhwa sigwon* 奉使朝鮮倡和詩卷), dated 1450, remounted in 1905, Hanseong (modern-day Seoul), Korea. Ink on paper, height 33cm, length 160cm. National Museum of Korea, Seoul, Sin 14149

In 1446, Sejong commanded An Gyeon, the most distinguished court painter at the time, to paint the *Eight Steeds of Taejo* (*Taejo Paljundo* 太祖八駿圖) – a depiction of the eight horses that the founder of the Joseon dynasty once rode.[29] This painting is no longer extant, but there is a later version of it dated to 1705 in the National Museum of Korea (**Pl. 24.5**). The 'eight steeds' of Taejo is referred to in Canto 70 of the epic poetry anthology *Songs of the Flying Dragons Flying to Heaven*, noted earlier, which consists of poems glorifying the heroic achievements of the ancestors of the Joseon dynasty. In the following year, Sejong commissioned a smaller version of the painting and ordered officials to compose poems on the topic as a test of their literary abilities. Seong Sammun won first place out of eight leading officials, including Yi Gyejeon 李季甸 (1404–59), Yi Seokhyeong 李石亨 (1415–77), Sin Sukju and Seo Geojeong 徐居正 (1420–88). The poems written by these officials were then mounted together with the small painting as a scroll and stored at Jiphyeonjeon.[30] Furthermore, *After Records on the Eight Steeds by Jiphyeonjeon* was set as an examination topic in the metropolitan civil service examination that was held once every ten years.

Sejong's commission of paintings and writings on the *Eight Steeds of Taejo* was highly strategic. It promoted the achievements of historical figures of significance to Joseon and elicited declarations of loyalty from officials, thereby reinforcing the legitimacy of the dynasty and his rule. At the same time, the dissemination of these works meant that the writings of leading scholar officials of the period would be shown, compared and discussed by a wider audience. This in turn encouraged scholar officials to become more competent intellectual leaders, with finely honed abilities in poetry writing, in addition to possessing a profound knowledge of Neo-Confucian classics. Throughout the process, Sejong was able to exhibit his cultural leadership by commanding officials to compose poems, thereby communicating his ideals of Neo-Confucian governance and cultural sentiments.

Poems shared by envoys in Joseon

The result of Sejong's promotion of literary cultivation among scholar officials can be found in the handscroll of *Poems Shared by Envoys in Joseon* (*Bongsa Joseon changhwa sigwon* 奉使朝鮮倡和詩卷) in the National Museum of Korea. Around 1,600cm in length, it consists of a frontispiece with the title of the scroll, followed by prose and poems, and colophons written by Tang Hanti 唐翰題 (1816–75) and Luo Zhenyu 羅振玉 (1866–1940) of the Qing dynasty (1644–1911). The scroll was mounted in its present condition in 1905.[31] This scroll records the literary exchanges between Ni Qian 倪謙 (1415–79) (**Pl. 24.6**), an envoy from Ming China, and Jiphyeonjeon scholars, including Jeong Yinji 鄭麟趾 (1396–1478) (**Pl. 24.7**), Seong Sammun (**Pl. 24.8**) and Sin Sukju (**Pl. 24.9**). The writings were composed during Ni Qian's one-month stay in Joseon when he, together with his deputy Sima Xun 司馬恂 (?–1466), delivered the imperial

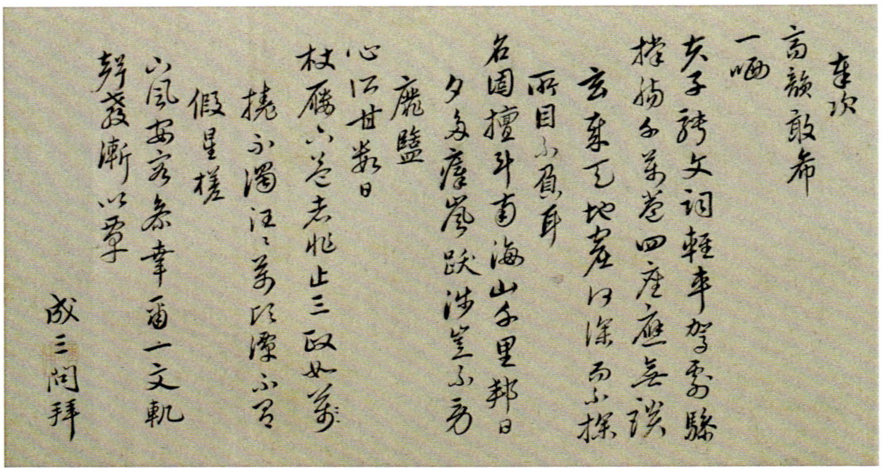

Plates 24.8–24.9 Poems written by Chinese and Korean scholars (*Bong sa Joseon changhwa sigwon* 奉使朝鮮倡和詩卷), dated 1450, remounted in 1905, Hanseong (modern-day Seoul), Korea. Ink on paper, height 33cm, length 160cm. National Museum of Korea, Seoul, Sin 14149

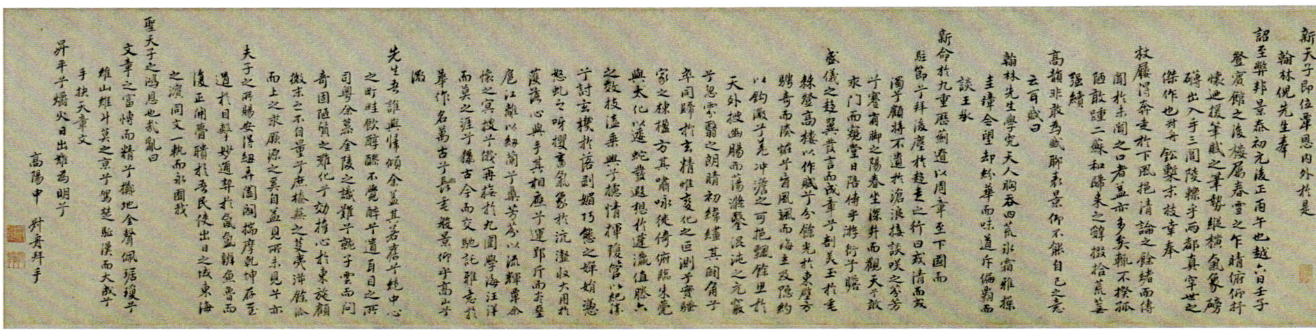

message to Sejong proclaiming Jingtai 景泰 (r. 1450–56) as the newly enthroned emperor of China. They left Beijing on the 13th day of the 12th month of 1449, and the imperial messenger in Gyeongbok Palace, Seoul, was informed of their arrival on the first day of the first leap month of 1450.[32]

Ni Qian and Sima Xun's visit to Joseon Korea was one of 36 envoys that the Ming sent to Joseon during the Sejong period – the highest number dispatched to any single king during the Ming dynasty. Prior to this visit, the early Ming court usually sent eunuchs as its main representative to Joseon. In 1450, following the turmoil of the battle at Tumu Fort when the Zhengtong 正統 emperor (r. 1436–49) was captured by Oirat Mongols, the Ming court chose instead to send Ni Qian who was then Expositor-in-waiting of the Hanlin Academy, and Sima Xun who was the Supervising Secretary of the Office of Scrutiny for Justice, suggesting the importance placed upon the visit. The arrival of two well-educated officials from China was anticipated by Joseon scholars who saw this as an opportunity to display their literary talents through poetry exchanges. The resulting poems held national and diplomatic significance, and were subsequently compiled and published by the Joseon court in the *Anthology of Brilliant Flowers* (*Hwanghwa jip* 皇華集).[33] Ni Qian also recorded the poems that he wrote and exchanged with Joseon scholars, which were published in *Chapters from the Liao Sea* (*Liaohai pian* 遼海篇). The scroll *Poems Shared by Envoys in Joseon* consists of poems most likely selected by Ni Qian who mounted them as a scroll after his return to Beijing.[34]

Thirty-five pieces of writing from Ni Qian's envoy in 1450 were recorded in the scroll. All of them are poems, except for *Ode to Ascending a Pavilion after Snow* (*Xueji denglou fu* 雪霽登樓賦) by Ni Qian and the reply to it by Sin Sukju, both written in a prose form. When Ni Qian composed a poem, Joseon officials Jeong Yinji, Sin Sukju and Seong Sammun replied with poems in the same rhythm. In total, Ni Qian wrote 15 poems; Sin Sukju, Jeong Yinji and Seong Sammun each wrote six poems. The poetry and prose in the scroll were written in the composer's own hand.

Ni Qian was impressed by what he witnessed when he arrived in Joseon. In a poem recorded in *Anthology of Brilliant Flowers*, Ni Qian describes his visit to the temple at the Royal Confucian Academy (Seonggyun'gwan 成均館) on the third day of the first month in 1450:

> In the early morning I visited the temple at the Royal Academy… Well-dressed literati are happily seated; youthful students joyfully stand in rows. How could the winds of culture especially reach the Eastern Seas [Joseon]? Saintly transformation now spreads to the remotest corners of the world.
>
> 曉向成均謁廟堂… 濟濟衣冠忻在坐，青青衿佩喜成行。文風豈特覃東海，聖化于今遍八荒。[35]

Seeing through the lens of the Ming empire, Ni Qian interpreted the cultivation of Joseon scholars as the consequence of the virtue of Chinese civilisation and its replication. It is not surprising that there were those in Joseon Korea who felt antipathy towards the envoy and considered him arrogant. The *Veritable Records of the Joseon Dynasty*, for instance, describes Ni Qian in unflattering terms while acknowledging his literary talents:

> Ni Qian was talented and untrammelled. During his journey [in Joseon] he composed several tens of poems; he combined them into one copy and posted it on the walls of the Taepyeong'gwan [guesthouse for Ming envoys]. He also wrote an ode *Ascending a Pavilion* for it to be hung at the pavilion. People may mock him for being arrogant with his talent… Ni Qian and others at first did not accept gifts, but later they accepted them, and even demanded them.

倪謙多才放曠，途中題詠累數十篇，聯爲稿，榜于太平館壁。又書所作登樓賦，以掛于樓，或者譏其逞才驕矜… 謙等初不受贈遺，後乃受之，至有求索如此。[36]

This sense of competitiveness extended both ways. On one occasion, Ni Qian sensed the desire of the Minister of Works, Jeong Yinji 鄭麟趾, to challenge him in poetry. This took place after he composed the poem describing the scene at the temple of the Royal Confucian Academy. When Ni read Jeong's poem, he was stunned and said:

> Early on when I composed the poem on visiting the temple, I had intended to praise [Joseon] for being non-Chinese (*yi*) yet still valued culture. Unexpectedly Jeong Yinji (Minister of Works) responded to my poem at the banquet, seemingly with condescension. I followed and replied to his work. From then onwards, whenever I had to reply to his poems, I would reply immediately after reading them, finishing in a moment's time. Then all were shocked and impressed.
>
> 初作謁廟詩，本以嘉其夷而右文也，不意工曹席間吟和，似有陵騁意，隨和還之。自此凡和其詩，俱觀罷卽答，頃刻而就，始皆驚服。[37]

The above quote, recorded in Ni Qian's own poetry anthology, shows his self-flattering reminiscence of his experience in Joseon Korea. On the other hand, some Joseon scholars thought Ni Qian's literary talent was overrated. For example, Seong Hyeon 成俔 (1439–1504) mentions in *Yongjae chonghwa* 慵齋叢話 (*Sayings from the Yong Studio*) that,

> At the time the Jiphyeonjeon scholar Jeon Seong saw his [Ni Qian's] poem, laughed at it and said: 'This poem is written by a pedantic and outmoded instructor-official. I can beat him with only one of my sleeves rolled up.'
>
> 是時集賢儒士全盛 見詩哂之曰：眞迂腐教官所作，可袒一肩而制之。[38]

The *Veritable Records of the Joseon Dynasty* further stress that Ni Qian and Jeong Yinji grew close and exchanged poems every day after the incident at the banquet.[39] It records that Ni Qian finally praised Jeong Yinji after they wrote poems and drank together, saying that 'one night's conversation with you is more valuable than ten years of reading books (*Yu jun yiye hua, sheng du shinian shu* 與君一夜話, 勝讀十年書)'.[40]

Joseon scholars thought that their exchange of poetry was not simply a means of communication but also a way of manifesting their cultural pride.[41] They believed that literary ability would be one way to change the Ming envoy's attitude of superiority towards them and to overcome the hierarchy between the two states.[42] Writing poetry was, therefore, not a personal matter, but had broader implications for the government. Sejong created an institutional system that encouraged officials to become highly cultivated scholars adept in the literary arts who could act as competent representatives of Joseon Korea in its key diplomatic relationship with Ming China.

After laying the foundation for his political power by discarding the Goryeo dynasty's royal portraits and statues while enshrining the portraits of the Joseon founder Yi Seonggye across the country, Sejong proceeded to establish Joseon's cultural authority in earnest. Sejong encouraged opportunities for literary activities in order to communicate with scholar officials and royal family members, and to consolidate his relationship with them. The king shared his Neo-Confucian cultural vision through poetry and painting, and elicited responses from scholar officials. Poems and paintings produced under these circumstances had political implications, functioning as an expression of unity between the king and scholar officials. Through his policies, Sejong successfully established the new cultural authority of the Joseon dynasty within 50 years of its foundation.

Notes

1. On culture during the Sejong period in general, see Sejongdaewang ginyeom saeophoe 1984–6; Hanguk jeongsin munhwa yeonguwon 2001.
2. *JWS Sejong sillok* 24 (6/4/庚戌) and (6/4/丁巳); Yi Seong-mu 2001, 20–1.
3. The fall in the status of Buddhism during the early Joseon period is also well reflected in the change of clerical system. Ryu 2002.
4. Studies on the art of the Sejong period include Ahn 1982, 61–71; Choi 2001; Hong and Chang 2009.
5. See detailed studies on this by Cho Insoo. Cho 2004; Cho 2006.
6. On the portrait of Taejo at Gyeonggi Royal Portrait Hall, see Lee 2005; Lee 2010. For a catalogue of Gyeonggi Royal Portrait Hall, see Jeonju National Museum 2005.
7. Ro 2004, 169–71; *JWS Sejong sillok* 55 (14/1/丙子).
8. Cho 2006, 178–9.
9. *JWS Sejong sillok* 5 (1/8/庚辰).
10. *JWS Taejo sillok* 1 (1/7/丁未 and 8/壬戌).
11. *JWS Sejong sillok* 8 (8/5/壬子).
12. Cho 2006, 168.
13. *JWS Sejong sillok* 37 (9/8/乙丑), *Sejong sillok* 41 (10/8/庚辰).
14. *JWS Sejong sillok* 60 (15/6/丙申).
15. Ro 2006, 226–36.
16. There is a record indicating that a garment was offered after an ancestral ceremony at Goryeo Taejo Jinjeon. See *Goryeosa* 21, Sinjong (6/9/甲午).
17. Ro 2004, 195.
18. Kang 1998.
19. Kim 1982.
20. *JWS Sejong sillok* 1(1/8/乙未).
21. Song 2008.
22. Yi Jong-mook 2001, 249–53.
23. On the *Night Banquet at Huiwujeong*, see Seo Geojeong, 'Huiwujeong yayeondo si' 喜雨亭夜宴圖詩 (The Poem for the Painting of Night Banquet at Huiwujeong Pavillion), in Seo 2004, vol. 2, 110–12. On the *Pleasure of the Moon along the Riverbank*, see Seong Sammun, 'Seongsuchan yimgang wanwoldo si seo' 成修撰臨江翫月圖詩序 (Seong's Preface for the Painting and Poem of the Pleasure of the Moon along the Riverbank, in Sin Sukju 1988, vol. 15, 117–18. The text is accessible in Hanguk gojeon jonghap DB, http://db.itkc.or.kr/itkcdb/mainIndexIframe.jsp.
24. Yi Jong-mook 2001, 247–9; *JWS Sejong sillok* 104, (26/4/辛丑).
25. On *Dream Journey to the Peach Blossom Land*, see Ahn 1991, 107–19.
26. Yi Jong-mook 2008, 171–4. For the exchange of poetry between Prince Anpyeong and contemporary literati, see Yi Jong-mook 2001.
27. *JWS Sejong sillok* 68 (17/6/戊申).
28. *JWS Sejong sillok* 69 (24/5/丁亥).
29. On the *Eight Steeds of Taejo*, see Cheong 1991.
30. Cheong 1991, 12; JWS *Sejong sillok* 117 (29/8/丁丑).
31. On this scroll, see Sin 2004.
32. *JWS Sejong sillok* 127, (32/1st leap month/丙午).
33. The first version of *Hwanghwa jip*, called *Gyeong'o bon* 庚午本, is a collection of poems which Ni Qian and Sima Xun exchanged with Joseon officials in 1450. However, *Gyeong'o bon* does not appear to be compiled in Korea. It is assumed that *Gyeong'o bon* was included when Hwanghwa jip was published as a series in the reign of King Seonjo referring to *Liaohai pian* of China. Kim 1999.
34. Sin 2004, 300–9.
35. *Hwanghwa jip*, 'Al munmyo' 謁文廟 (Visiting the Confucian Temple printed in 1773. The text is accessible in National Library of Korea DB (http://viewer.nl.go.kr:8080/viewer/viewer.jsp).

36 *JWS Sejong sillok* 127 (32/1st leap month/甲子).

37 Ni Qian, 'Zheng gongcao jianhe jixi yongyun yi da zhu' 鄭工曹見和即席用韻以答注 (Minister of Works Jeong's Impromptu Reply in Rhyme), in *Liaohai pian* 遼海編 (*Chapters from the Liao Sea*). See Yin Mengxia and Yu Hao 2003, vol. 1, 523.

38 Seonghyeon 成俔 (1439–1504), *Yongjae chonghwa* 慵齋叢話 (*Assorted Writings of Yongjae*), vol. 1. The text is accessible in Hanguk gojeon jonghap DB, http://db.itkc.or.kr/itkcdb/mainIndexIframe.jsp.

39 *JWS Sejong sillok* 127 (32/1st leap month/戊申).

40 *JWS Sejong sillok* 127 (32/1st leap month/癸丑).

41 On the role of poetry in diplomacy between the Joseon and Ming, see Kim 1999, 322–34.

42 Kim 1999, 324–6.

Chapter 25
The *Book of the Five Relationships*: Thoughts on Mid-Fifteenth-Century Court Confucianism

Sarah Schneewind

Did a Joseon book inspire a Ming court compilation?
In the first half of the 15th century, Great Ming adopted luxuries and signs of power from across Eurasia, and from Africa and the Middle East. Joseon Korea sent, not always willingly, brushes and paper, gold and pickles, concubines and eunuchs, chefs and animals.[1] But neither books nor written moral instruction seem likely imports from what the Ming saw as a lowly tributary. Rather striking, therefore, is a suggestion made in the *Dictionary of Ming Biography* (hereafter, *DMB*), published in 1976, that the *Wulun shu* 五倫書 (*Book of the Five Relationships*), was 'an imperial undertaking… initiated in the Xuande period, possibly as a result of the Korean publication in 1434 of the elegantly illustrated book of exempla, *Samgang haengsil* 三綱行實 [*-do* 圖, or *The Illustrated Guide to the Three Bonds*]'.[2] This chapter will assess the likelihood of Joseon influence and how to think of the book as an 'imperial undertaking', and use the two books to complicate the common view of Confucianism as a strict, oppressive and hierarchical system.

One can imagine the Xuande 宣德 emperor (r. 1426–35) receiving a Korean book from a consort or a mission, admiring it in the same way as he did so many Korean products, and perhaps deciding that a complimentary imitation would be timely in around 1434 when Ming was losing, and Joseon gaining, ground against the Jurchens in the north.[3] None of the references given in the *DMB* entry, however, justifies the hypothesis. With respect to timing, King Sejong (r. 1418–50) started the discussion of what became the *Samgang haengsil-do* (hereafter, *Samgang*) in 1428; was given a draft in 1432; ordered printing on 4 June 1434; and ordered distribution on 24 December 1434. The fastest travel time from Seoul, capital of Joseon, to Beijing was 34 days, and the Xuande emperor died on 31 January 1435. His last six days of life could not have sufficed for him to select and rework items from various histories and classics for the *Wulun shu* as the preface added in the Zhengtong 正統 period (r. 1436–49) says he did.[4] Nevertheless, it is possible that Sejong sent a proof to the Ming court earlier in 1434, or a partial mock-up even earlier, given that another book had been sent for approval in 1422.[5] In short, timing alone cannot tell us whether or not Xuanzong admired *Samgang* and began *Wulun shu* in imitation.

Another factor undermines the imitation hypothesis more definitively. The two collections share many stories, but no organisational features.[6] *Samgang* has three fascicles devoted to the Three Bonds: the bond of child to parent, minister to ruler and wife to husband. *Samgang* includes 111 stories of filial children (*xiaozi* 孝子), 110 of loyal officials or loyal subjects (*zhongchen* 忠臣) and 110 of fiercely devoted women (*lienü* 烈女). *Wulun shu*, by contrast, contains 62 chapters that are unevenly divided among categories (see below). *Samgang* grants each exemplar his or her prose story and a poem, both in Chinese, and an illustration. (Hangul prompts were added to later editions.) *Wulun shu* includes only prose accounts. *Samgang* rigidly confines each exemplar to one woodblock, while *Wulun shu* runs text from page to page in the usual way. What this means is that the reader of *Samgang* first encounters a pictorial narration of the story, then turns the page to read about him or her.[7] On the face of it, the two books share little in terms of appearance.

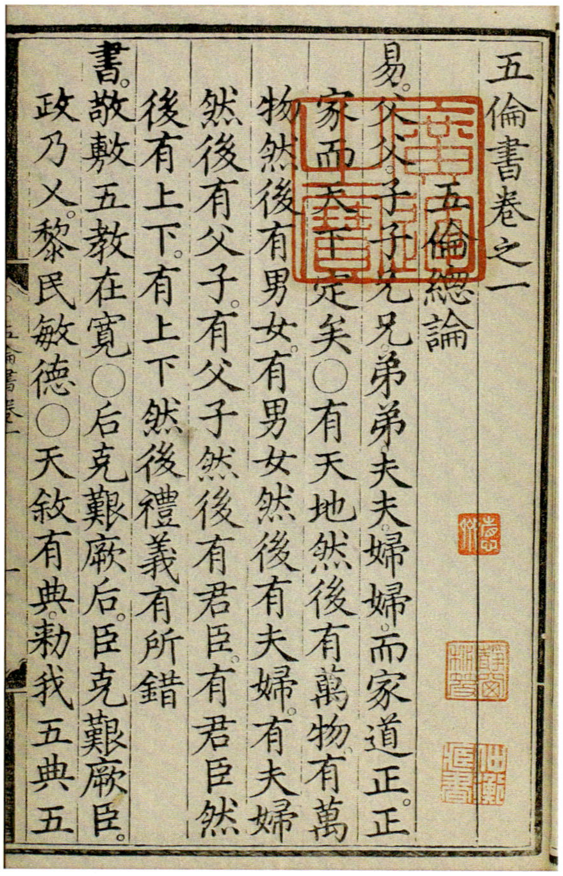

Plate 25.1 First page of *Book of the Five Relationships* (*Wulun shu* 五倫書), dated 1447. Woodblock printed, ink on paper, height 37cm. Princeton University Library, East Asian Library, TC328/1212

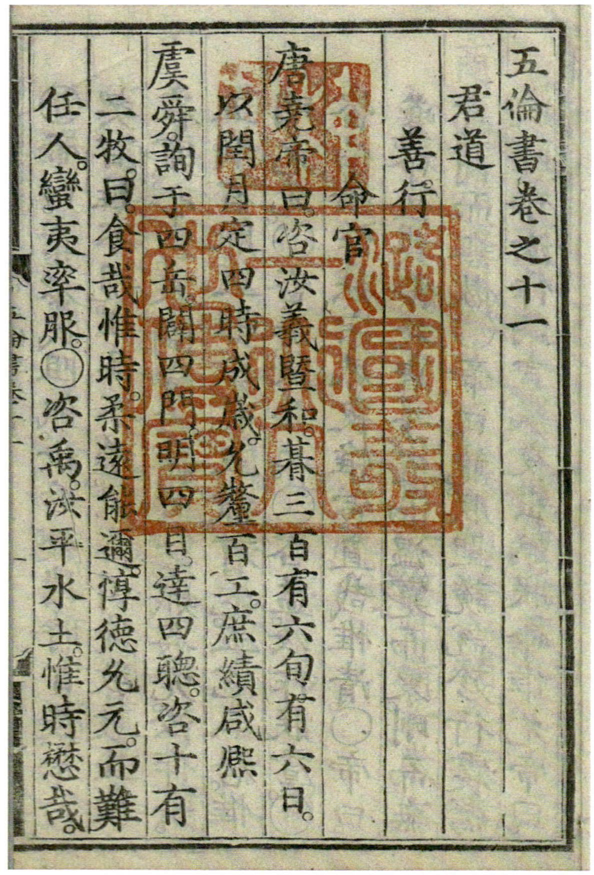

Plate 25.2 *Book of the Five Relationships* (*Wulun shu* 五倫書), imperial edition with seal of the Kings of Lu, dated 1447. Woodblock printed, ink on paper, height 35cm. The Bodleian Libraries, The University of Oxford, Backhouse 421

Yet we may still ask whether *Samgang* had the kind of flawless beauty the Xuande emperor appreciated. An extant example of *Wulun shu* from the Xuande court is in the Princeton University Library and the Bodleian Library, University of Oxford (**Pls 25.1–2**). There is debate as to whether the 1434 edition of *Samgang* is extant, but the 1982 reprint is believed to be the closest to the original (**Pls 25.3–4**), so I rely on that here. The two books share the formal features of the finest palace productions: double borders, on the centre fold thick black mouths inside elephant trunks, blackened fishtails with scalloped white strips and decorative circles above the central title lines. Both books were punctuated on the blocks. *Wulun shu* was larger: the court edition is about 40 x 23cm by my measurement, compared to *Samgang*'s reported not quite 27 x 17cm. *Wulun shu* was carved in large, elegant standard script (*kaishu* 楷書), and printed on high-quality tree-bark paper.[8] The imperial Qing catalogue notes its great purity.[9] *Samgang* is, if anything, less elegant, although the pictures make it more appealing. More to the point, since many beautiful Ming palace printed books had reached Joseon by 1428, it is more likely, as Young Kyun Oh concludes, that they influenced the look of *Samgang* and not the other way around.

The purpose of the *Samgang haengsil-do*

Yet books from the Ming court shaped *Samgang* only so far. More significant were debates that were taking place at the Joseon court. King Sejong and his team of officials were shaping a Neo-Confucian realm centred on filiality and ritual for all, and governed by a powerful king wielding the *Great Ming Code* (*Da Ming lü* 大明律). Other aristocrats or *yangban*, however, understood Neo-Confucianism as supporting hereditary status and upper-class privilege.[10] In 1428, the court learned that a commoner had killed his father. A high minister deplored the patricide as a case of 'a person of lower status killing one of higher status', but for Sejong patricide was in a class of its own.[11] Wives will go around killing their husbands, he says, and servants their masters; a patricide, by contrast, strikes at the very heart of a kingly order built on filial piety.[12] To transform all his subjects, down to 'ordinary people living in the alleys and lanes', Sejong initially ordered the ethnically Uighur Joseon scholar Seol Sun 偰循 (?–1435) to revise an earlier work on filial children.[13] Ministers insisted on the addition of wifely exemplars to strengthen new patrilineal ideals in order to curb the property rights and independence that Goryeo elite women had formerly enjoyed. When Sejong countered with a proposal to include officials who had remained true to their lords in adversity, Seol Sun in turn insisted on giving dignity to scholar-officials by adding exemplars who had loyally remonstrated with rulers about their behaviour.[14]

Samgang focuses on ascriptive hierarchy and the duty of subordinates. Within each category, the Chinese exemplars come in chronological order, followed by the Korean exemplar in chronological order, but royalty are moved to

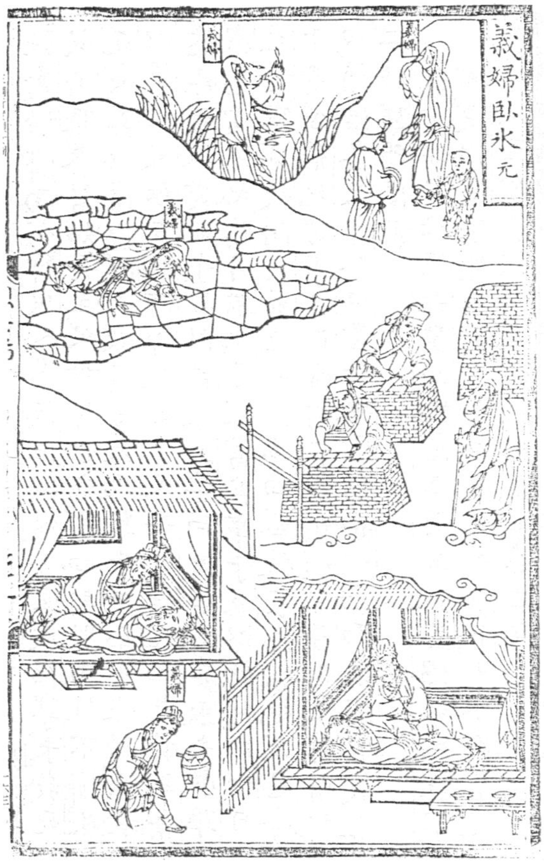

Plate 25.3 *The Illustrated Guide to the Three Bonds* (*Samgang haengsil-do* 三綱行實圖), reprint of the 1432 edition (Seoul, 1982). Page showing the illustration of righteous wife Zhang

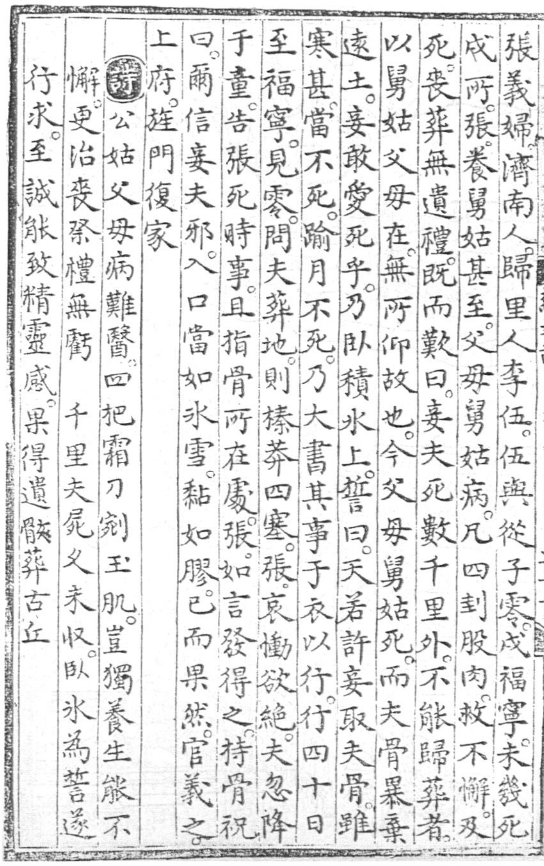
三綱行實烈女圖
張義婦濟南人歸里人李伍伍與從子零戍福寧未發死
戍所張養舅姑甚至父母舅姑病凡四刲股肉救不懈及
死喪葬無遺禮既而歎曰妾夫死數千里外不能歸葬者
以舅姑父母在無所仰故也今父母舅姑死而夫骨暴棄
遠土妾敢愛死乎乃臥積氷上誓曰天若許妾取夫骨雖
寒甚當不死踰月不死乃大書其事于衣以行行四十日
至福寧見零問夫葬地則榛莽四塞張哀慟欲絕夫忽降
于童告張死時事且指骨所在處張如言發得之持骨祝
曰爾信妾夫邪入口當如氷雪黏如膠已而果然官義之
上府旌門復家
詩 公姑父母病難醫四把霜刀剜玉肌豈獨養生能不
懈更治喪祭禮無虧 千里夫屍久未收臥氷為誓遂
行求至誠能致精靈感果得遺骸葬古丘
一六四

Plate 25.4 *The Illustrated Guide to the Three Bonds* (*Samgang haengsil-do* 三綱行實圖), reprint of the 1432 edition (Seoul, 1982). Page showing the text of righteous wife Zhang

the beginning regardless of timing.[15] The chronologically nonsensical arrangement of illustrations puts emperors and officials higher on the page than commoners; and kings, official buildings, fathers, husbands, graves and funerals above subjects, houses, sons, wives and living quarters.[16]

Most fundamentally, the Three Bonds formulation valorises fixed hierarchy over other Confucian values. It demands absolute filiality of the child (and daughter-in-law), loyalty-to-the-death of the minister (and subject) and fierce devotion of the wife (or widow), without reciprocal obligations on the part of parents, rulers or husbands. Invented by the Han toady and patrilinealist Ban Gu 班固 (32–92), the formula also served Zhang Zhidong 張之洞 (1837–1909) at the other end of imperial history as a bastion against egalitarian challenges.[17] The Three Bonds was not the only option Confucianism offered: Joseon later made other choices, and *Wulun shu* refers to the Three Bonds but relies on another formulation.[18]

The dating of *Wulun shu*

Korean influence on *Wulun shu* seems unlikely. Was it an 'imperial undertaking'? The attribution to the Xuande emperor in the preface may have been fiction given that he died a decade before its publication. The preface itself, putatively by his son, may have been ghost-written, perhaps by Grand Secretary Yang Shiqi 楊士奇 (1365–1444), as a way to camouflage teachings meant for the teenage Zhengtong emperor as teachings from him to others, in the name of his father.[19]

If the Xuande emperor did work on the project, it clearly fell into abeyance until some eight years after his death. Two kinds of confusion surround the dating of *Wulun shu*. First, the *DMB* gives conflicting information. One entry records that the book was 'finished and printed in 1443', leading to speculations about an imaginary delay in one county's acquisition of the book.[20] But another entry correctly gives 1443 as the year Liu Yan 劉儼 (1394–1457), a new metropolitan graduate (*jinshi* 進士), was assigned to work on the compilation.[21] Further sources show that the team included other men from the Hanlin Academy (*Hanlin yuan* 翰林院), such as Lü Yuan 呂原 (1418–62), Yang Ding 楊鼎 (1410–85) and Qian Xili 錢習禮 (1373–1461), all metropolitan graduates who later lectured the emperor on the classics.[22]

Second, the *DMB* entry on Liu Yan dates the printing of *Wulun shu* to Zhengtong 13 (1448), but accounts in the *Veritable Records* for the year 1447 clearly state that the Zhengtong emperor ordered the printing of the book on 27 April and the building of 40 storerooms for its woodblocks and copies on 25 September.[23] On 27 October 1448, copies of the book were sent to Confucian schools across the empire.[24] The source for the incorrect dating in *DMB* may be *Hanlin ji* 翰林記 (*Records of the Hanlin Academy*), which mistakes the year of the book's dissemination for the year of its completion. This error is compounded by a later comprehensive catalogue, which adds the correct month of the preface of the book, but in the wrong year.[25] The *Hanlin ji* author Huang Zuo was perhaps misled by a rather funny memorial of 1448:

The teachers and students of the Confucian schools of the empire, having received from above the gift of the *Wulun shu*, are constantly coming to the capital to express their thanks for this grace, neglecting and abandoning their task of study. We request that from now on, upon their receiving it, it be considered sufficient that they face the court to express thanks for this grace. The emperor agreed.

禮部奏：天下儒學師生蒙賜五倫書籍，往往赴京謝恩，荒廢學業，乞令就彼望闕謝恩為便。從之。[26]

The *Veritable Records* dates the *Wulun shu* quite clearly: its compilation started or re-started in 1443; the completed book was printed in 1447; and it was promulgated in 1448.

Comparing the contents of *Wulun shu* and *Samgang*

Although each had been discussed before, Mencius was the first to list five 'cardinal human relations' (*renlun* 人倫), without calling them 'the Five Relationships':

> Between parent and child (literally, father and son) there is affection; between ruler and minister righteous propriety; between husband and wife distinction; elder and younger [brother] follow precedence; friends share good faith.
>
> 父子有親，君臣有義，夫婦有別，長幼有序，朋友有信。[27]

The Neo-Confucians built on this formulation, making explicit that the fourth relation refers to brothers. *Wulun shu* builds on that tradition, as **Table 1** shows, following the 'Doctrine of the Mean' in putting ruler-minister ahead of parent-child.[28]

Accordingly, *Wulun shu* differs from *Samgang* in a number of ways. First, the opening chapter of *Wulun shu* surveys the set of five relationships through brief quotations, and the other chapters cover each side of each dyadic relationship with both 'fine words' (*jiayan* 嘉言, a phrase from the *Book of Documents*) and 'good deeds' (*shanxing* 善行, a phrase from the *Record of Rites*).[29] Second, the 'fine words' sections provide a theoretical component, with quotations from all of the Confucian Five Classics and Four Books, and a dozen later works by writers including the Song Neo-Confucians. Third, the Five Relationships formula includes the relatively equal relations of 'brothers' and 'friends'. Fourth, *Wulun shu* goes further to include sections on daughters, mothers, uncles, aunts, lineage relatives and 'teacher-student.'

A fifth and important difference is that *Wulun shu* makes demands of both parties. *Samgang* contains not one single 'devoted husband'.[30] *Wulun shu* includes 11 devoted husbands or fiancés. Most are men who refuse to desert the partners of their early obscurity for new, high-ranking wives, but there is also one husband who refuses to add concubines. The newly successful men of Song times in this category refuse to abandon wives or fiancées who are not only lowly, but also disabled (since birth status as such had diminished in importance since Tang times). For instance, one new examination graduate whose betrothed had gone dumb stands up to the demands of his elder brother that he choose someone able to advance the family interests:

> If I do not marry this girl, for her whole life she will never have a married home… To cast someone off because of illness, how could that accord with human feeling?
>
> 此女某若不娶，平生遂無所歸。…因即疾而遂棄，豈人情哉。[31]

Emotional sincerity is central in *Wulun shu*. An entry on Liu Tingshi 劉庭式 (fl. *c.* 1078–85) tells how he had contracted early to marry the daughter of a local neighbour. He earned his metropolitan degree, and could have made a better match since the betrothal silk had not yet been sent over to formalise the agreement. Moreover, the girl had gone blind. But, when someone urged a different match, Liu laughed and said:

> My heart is already promised to her! How could I turn my back on my earlier intentions? 吾心已許之矣。豈可負吾初心哉。

Table 1 Table of contents from *Wulun shu*

Category	Subcategory	Subtopics	Appended relationships	# of chapters (*juan*)	Which *juan*?
The Five Relations				1	1
Way of the Ruler	Fine words			2	2–3
	Good deeds	49	(The final 5 subsections are on royal women.)	19	4–23
Way of the Minister	Fine words			1	24
	Good deeds	42		28	25–53
Way of the Parent	Fine words			½	54
	Good deeds		Mothers, uncles, aunts	1 ½	54–5
Way of the Child	Fine words			½	56
	Good deeds		Daughters, wives	1 ½	56–8
Way of the Husband and Wife	Fine words			½	59
	Good deeds		(Separate subsections on husbands and wives.)	½	59
Way of Elder and Younger Brothers	Fine words			½	60
	Good deeds		Lineage	½	60
Way of Friends	Fine words			½	61
	Good deeds		Teacher-student	1 ½	61–2

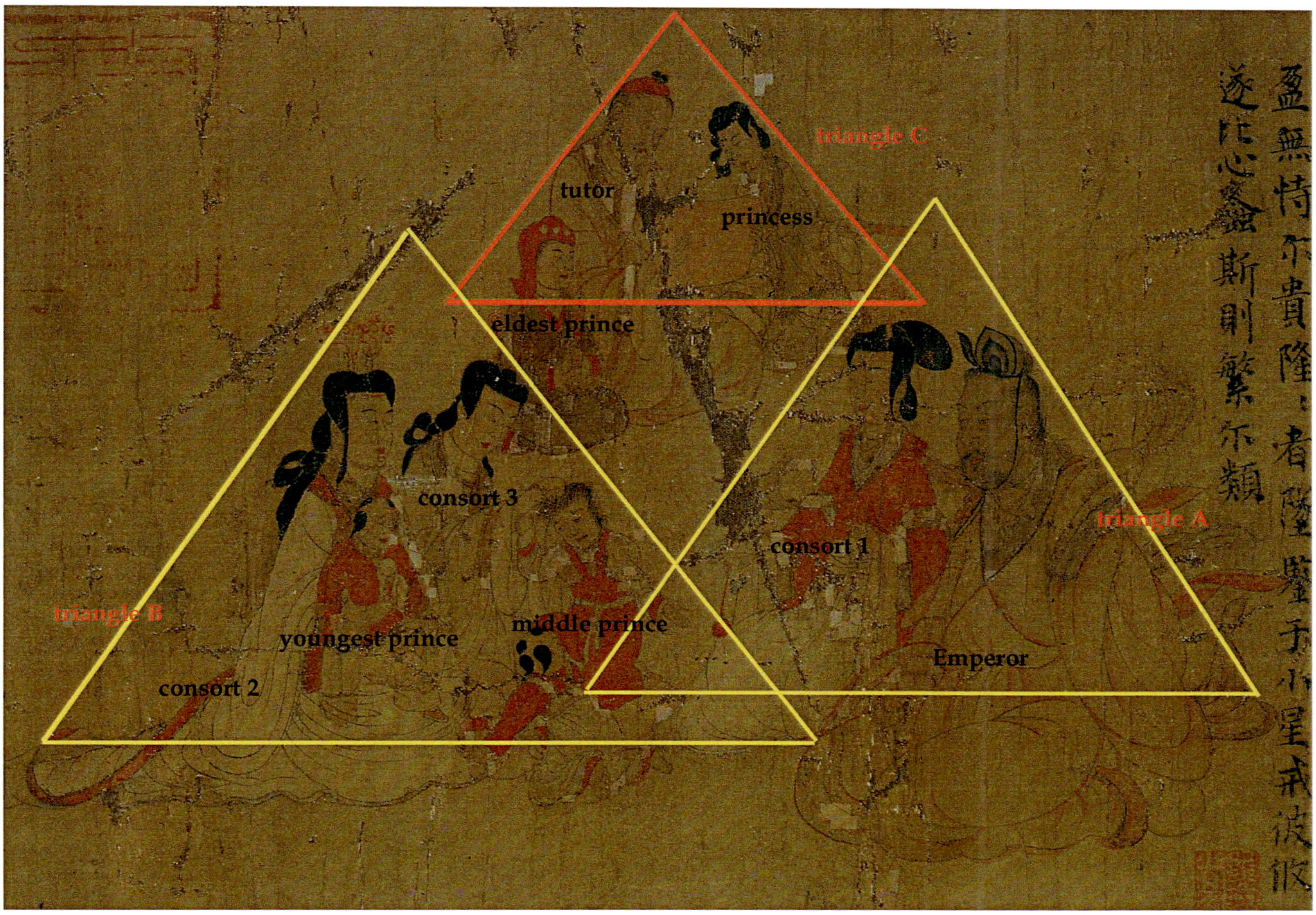

Plate 25.5 After Gu Kaizhi (顧愷之) (344–405), *Admonitions of the Instructress to the Court Ladies* (*Nüshi zhen tu* 女史箴图), detail of family scene, *c.* 400–500s. Handscroll, ink and colours on silk, height 24.37cm, length 343.75cm. British Museum, London, 1903,0408,0.1

They married, and she bore several children before dying. After several years, when Liu still had not remarried, a colleague said to him: 'Grief is born of love; love is born of sexual desire. In this case, where does your love come from? What does your grief come from?' Liu replied:

> I only know that I have lost my wife, and that's all. If I trace it back in reasoning that sex produces love and love produces grief, then the sexual desire will weaken, the love will fall into abeyance, and my grief will also be forgotten. Then, indeed, any rippling sleeve in the marketplace, with dallying eyes that beckon to the heart, could be made a wife!
>
> 吾知喪吾妻而已。吾如緑色而生愛緑愛而生哀。色衰愛弛。吾哀亦忘。則凡楊袂倚市。目挑而心招者。皆可以為妻也。[32]

The point is the humanity and moral value of all parties, and the individual's development of his natural conscience – not obedience to hierarchy or family interest.

In *Wulun shu*, superiors hold as much responsibility as privilege. One account tells of the exemplary brother Minister Niu Hong 牛弘, whose younger brother liked to drink. Minister Niu arrived home one evening to find his wife furious because the bibulous brother had shot their cart ox; he did not even reprimand his brother, but simply bore it, like his namesake the ox.[33] Similarly, a family head recorded in the 'lineage' section, when asked how the family had managed to stay together for nine generations, took a brush and he wrote 'Forbearance' (*ren* 忍) 100 times on a piece of paper.[34] He did not speak of forcing or even educating inferiors into obedience. Such is Confucian harmony in *Wulun shu*. Compared with the punishing one-sided obligations of the 'Three Bonds', or with the contemporary European 'Great Chain of Being', the Five Relationships offers a capacious and humanist utopianism.

Further, the 'Five Relationships' formulation chosen by the Ming court for this book undermines any equation of 'Confucianism' with 'family values'. The model instead is a set of dyadic relationships, of which two are not family relations. Exemplars are fiercely conscientious individuals who sometimes speak and act against both the wider family interest and the orders of seniors, precisely in order to carry out the mutual, if unequal, obligations of a particular dyad. Dora Ching, pointing out the paucity of visual representations of the family in imperial China, discusses the *Admonitions of the Instructress to the Court Ladies* (*Nüshi zhen tu* 女史箴圖) in the British Museum, traditionally attributed to Gu Kaizhi 顧愷之 (344–405) but dated to *c.* 400–500, as a rare portrayal of an ideal complete family.[35] To my eye, however, the painting shows a 'family' broken into dyads, whose overlapping relations of superiority are very difficult to represent properly all together. Ching's analysis highlights the way in which the bodies of the adults set boundaries that protect and confine the children, but actually the eldest prince and the princess royal form part of the lines of the overall pyramid, leaving their backs unprotected (**Pl. 25.5**). We can see the pyramid as comprised three smaller triangles: at the lower right sit husband (ruler) and wife; on the left mothers and children, with the older son more central than but no taller than his brother, and the secondary consorts bent in less dignity and with the tops of their heads slightly below that of the empress; and at the top, teacher-student, so that the eldest son (and heir) is above both his brothers – but his sister is distressingly above him, or possibly just further back. With overlapping age, generation, gender and status hierarchies, as well as the mutual responsibilities of each dyad to represent, it is small wonder that few painters attempted whole family portraits.[36]

The ruler-minister relationship in *Wulun shu*

A sixth difference between *Wulun shu* and *Samgang* is that the former focuses on governance rather than social hierarchy. Governance dominates even some stories of family exemplars: the first 'devoted husband' listed, for instance, wins office because the respect he and his wife show one another demonstrates that he has sufficient virtue to govern commoners.[37] A man of early Ming times listed under 'Way of the Father' wrote to his son with advice about incorruptibility in office; when bureaucratic backbiting sent the son to jail, the father's letter surfaced, and so impressed the emperor that he released the son and rewarded the father.[38] Nominally a compendium of all relationships, this book focuses on the responsibilities of the ruling class.

The ruler-minister relation dominates the compilation: it receives 50 chapters, about 80 percent of the book, analysed according to 91 topics.[39] The categories of rulers' 'good deeds', which were often just utterances, are: sagely virtue, sagely study, respecting Heaven, following ancestral laws, sagely filiality, the virtue of humility, warnings about the need for caution, warnings about desires, frugality, esteeming good faith, constant discernment (of others' minds and qualities), rites and music, taking sacrifice seriously, establishing the heir apparent, harmony among relatives, fiefs, virtuous transformation, diligence in governing, systems of rule, commanding officials, seeking advice, listening to and accepting advice, nourishing the aged, revering Confucian scholars, promoting study, nourishing talent, recognising others, seeking out the wise, employing the wise, benevolence to commoners, emphasising agriculture, rectifying names, rewarding those who contribute, praising and commending, rewards and punishments, eliminating heterodoxy, mercy in punishment, forgiving trespasses, managing troops, managing horses, commanding generals and controlling barbarians.[40]

Each category spans history, sometimes from the very beginning through early Ming. Frugal behaviour, for instance, is demonstrated by 28 rulers from the sage-king Yao 堯 to Yongle 永樂 (r. 1403–24).[41] There is some intertextuality: after a Han emperor appears, for instance, three articles refer to him directly. Over time change appears: the first 12 articles involve frugality on the part of the ruler himself, sometimes explicitly to benefit the people; in medieval times, frugality encompasses ministers and palace women; in the Song (960–1279) frugality is demanded even of commoners. While *Wulun shu* was being compiled, unrest caused by imperial demands made the examples condemning requisitions from the people highly topical.

The categories of good deeds for ministers illustrate the many tasks and challenges facing officials at all levels: assisting (the ruler's) virtue, making basic plans for the dynasty, regulating ritual, regulating appointments, regular assessments of officials, selection of officials, preserving the law, insisting on doing right, constancy in doing right (in both often despite pressure from rulers), reproving and warning (the ruler), impeachments, loyal righteousness, knowing the main principles, administration, transforming people through teaching, correcting popular customs, having mercy on commoners, soothing words, the encouragement of agriculture, equalising tax burdens, emptying jails, preparing against drought, rescuing people from natural disasters, water management, the soldier-cultivation system, serving as an ambassador, military tactics (this has the most sections), border defence, eliminating bandits, suppressing and pacifying, relating to the people with kindness and good faith, orthodox study, diligence and determination, tireless labour, perspicacity, knowledge, loyal reverence, virtuous self-control and tolerance (with respect to those who wrong you), incorruptibility, modest yielding, not taking advantage and quiet retirement.[42] 'Loyalty' (*zhong* 忠) appears twice: as 'loyal righteousness' (*zhong yi* 忠義), which in the examples given in the book usually means dying for one's country at the hands of invaders and rebels; and as 'loyal reverence' (*zhong jin* 忠謹), meaning expressions of ritual reverence for the ruler that exceed common practice. One exemplar's story in this category concludes: 'Because of his loyalty, the emperor often followed his advice'.[43]

Although Confucian relationships were dyadic, this list shows that within the ruler-minister relation there lurked a third term: *min* 民, meaning subjects or commoners. In fact, the dyad *junchen* 君臣 is ambiguous, sometimes meaning ruler-minister, sometimes ruler-subject. Throughout the Ming, emperors and officials often praised or blamed one another in terms of whether they helped or harmed the populace. The triad ruler-minister-subject appears from the earliest proclamations right through the last emperor's suicide note at the end of the dynasty: he criticised himself, but also blamed his officials for the disaster and asked the rebels not to harm a single one of the common people.[44] We could say that in Ming this third term – the people – actually mediated the relationship between ruler and minister in their ideological and political pronouncements.[45]

The uses and legacy of *Wulun shu*

We could see *Wulun shu* as imperial propaganda. The Hongwu and Yongle emperors and their empresses star in most of the chapters on rulers; in the frugality section, for instance, the average number of lines of text per ruler is five, but the Hongwu emperor gets 14. Ming emperors are also recorded as recognised exemplars from the period, thus partaking of their glory. The preface to *Wulun shu* boasts about how the dynasty has nourished, in people's daily lives, the closeness of parent and child, the righteousness between ruler and minister, the differentiation of husband and wife, the orderly precedence of brothers and the good faith between friends, bringing decades of peace.

After the initial wide promulgation of *Wulun shu*, rulers especially bestowed the book upon princes who requested it;

the Zhengtong emperor himself was the first to do this, in 1449.[46] His successor also honoured officials with this gift, giving it to the top metropolitan graduate in 1451 and Hanlin chancellor Ke Qian 柯潜 (1423–73); in 1448 to the most long-lived Ming official, Wei Ji 魏驥 (1374–1471); and in about 1451 to Li Kui 李奎 (1389–1457), who like some others constructed a special building to house it.[47] *Wulun shu* was among the many rewards (alternating with punishments) granted to the Mongolian Ming general Mao Qara 毛哈喇 (1394–1468); he told his son and grandson, who later died alongside him battling Mongol forces:

> Loyalty and righteousness are all in here. You should respectfully learn it thoroughly. Do not neglect this!
>
> 忠義盡在是矣汝等奉誦之毋忽。[48]

As a gift, *Wulun shu* was part of a larger set of imperial publications and writers also drew on it in this capacity. It provided the epigraph for the treatise on music by Prince Zhu Zaiyu 朱載堉 (1536–1611).[49] Li Dongyang 李東陽 (1447–1516) lists it with other imperial books in an examination essay, noting that the books were widely read, even by commoners.[50] A commentary by Xia Liangsheng 夏良勝 (1480–1538) on the fundamental text 'Doctrine of the Mean' includes a Yongle edict he had read about in the *Wulun shu*.[51] A Mongolian scholar in Henan annotated it for students.[52]

The collection served as a source for early Ming history.[53] Many notable scholar-officials, such as Wei Jiao 魏校 (1483–1543) and Yang Yiqing 楊一清 (1454–1530), mention reading it.[54] Officials drew on it right away for precedents: a memorial of 9 June 1450 references a saying of the Yongle emperor on wide consultation with officials, and another of 15 June 1450 cites it on taking personal responsibility for sacrifice.[55] Wang Shu 王恕 (1416–1508) used a Yongle utterance from *Wulun shu* to discuss rites to Confucius.[56] Another memorial urged the ruler to attend to heavenly portents as *Wulun shu* shows the Hongwu emperor doing.[57] A 16th-century official used it as 'reliable evidence' of early Ming processes of advice and consent.[58] Urging active daily teaching by the throne to guide officials and commoners, Qiu Jun 邱濬 (1418–95) quoted from *Wulun shu* the Yongle emperor's description of beginning his mornings with quiet-sitting.[59] The compilation promoted imperial centrality, and it may have been key in preserving specific sayings and actions of the early Ming rulers. But it recorded officials too: Ye Sheng 葉盛 (1420–74) wrote that in his time, only *Wulun shu* recorded the important contributions of early Ming general Liu Jiang 劉江 (fl. *c.* 1370).[60]

Government offices reprinted *Wulun shu* whole, but like other palace works, its wide audience meant that it also stimulated commercial editions and imitations, some illustrated.[61] It also justified other collections. In 1457–8, Han Yong (1422–78) collected Ming poems in Jiangxi 江西 province, where he had served for about eight years before being sidelined.[62] His preface refers to the classical role of poetry in reflecting popular opinion and thus the quality of rule. He celebrates the successive Ming 'sages' for nourishing human talent and virtue, so that talent is rising, music is stirring and everyone from the nobility down to the cotton-wearers of the hills and forests is recreating antiquity – especially in Jiangxi. But not *only* there, of course: just as the Sagely Son of Heaven has promulgated *Wulun shu*, Han writes, we scholar-officials will be able to collect recent poems more broadly, once the completion of the national gazetteer has ushered in a true period of 'instituting rites and making music'.[63] Han, as both beneficiary and partner of the glorious throne, claims the right to compile poetry/public opinion himself.

Given the long history of remonstrance, this partnership did not preclude sharp criticism. During a severe drought in 1493, the Hongzhi emperor called for frugality and for straight talk. Li Dongyang responded in May with a characteristic Mencian critique, referencing comments on the timely use of natural resources.[64] Resources are limited, he writes, as the current impoverishment of both subjects and state coffers shows. They can only be 'inexhaustible' if the ruler sets an example by respecting frugality; and to encourage that, Li condenses a story from *Wulun shu* in which the Yongle emperor meditates on how his frequent ceremonial changes of clothing remind him of Empress Ma, his putative mother, personally mending for the royal family, and of the joy such thrift brought his father, the Hongwu emperor. Li reminds his own ruler that the founder of the Ming, and his attending ministers, had set the Empress Ma's thrift as a 'law for ten thousand generations' (*wei wanshi fa* 為萬世法), a judgement reinforced by it being recorded by the Xuande emperor in *Wulun shu*.[65] If the emperor sets the example, the whole bureaucracy will follow suit, 'managing finances with all their might' (*jingying jili* 經營極力).[66] But the book enables Li to go beyond encouragement. Before telling the story of Empress Ma mending, Li borrows a saying originally from the *Tang tongdian*, then quoted by Taizu 太祖 of the Song dynasty (r. 960–76), and included just above, in the section on rulers' frugality in *Wulun shu*:

> Just because there is one man ruling the whole empire, it does not mean that the whole empire is an offering to that one man. Well, if the empire is not an offering to one man, to whom is it an offering? The point is that it is not a private possession!
>
> 以一人治天下不以天下奉一人。夫天下不以一人將誰奉乎。不私其有之謂也。[67]

Song Taizu directed this saying at his womenfolk as they draped their palace in expensive fabrics. The contrast with Empress Ma's mending relates it directly to Li's memorial, enabling him to anticipate the attack by Huang Zongxi 黃宗羲 (1610–95) in 1663 on rulers who take the realm as their own family estate and squeeze every penny from the people to enrich themselves and their heirs, rather than working hard to benefit all.[68]

Conclusion

The *Wulun shu* made an impact; among other things, the label '*wulun*' (Five Relations) became common only after its publication. To assess the *DMB*'s summary statement about it, quoted at the start of this chapter: the Korean *Samgang* probably did not inspire the compilation. The Xuande emperor may have started the project, but even if he did, most of the work was probably done under his eldest son. Moreover, *Wulun shu* was an 'imperial undertaking' only in a loose sense. It was compiled by at least four of the sharpest minds in the country during the mid-Ming shift of initiative away from the throne and into the hands of ministers. Scholar-official Ni Qian 倪謙 (1415–79) wrote that *Wulun shu*, Taizu's *Great Warning* (*Yuzhi da gao* 御制大誥) and two collections compiled under the Yongle emperor urging secret good deeds and filiality all showed how the Ming emperors, like the sage-kings, led through rites and education.[69] But in fact *Wulun shu* is not like the others. Aside from the preface, *Wulun shu* is not written in the emperor's voice, and it targets not ordinary people, but the powerful, as did Liu Yan's next project, the *Mirror for Rulers* (*Lidai junjian* 歷代君鑑). My brief introduction has overlooked the contemporary relevance of the work as well as the Hanlin Academy authors, who may have discussed their work on *Wulun shu* somewhere at more length than I have found.[70] But I propose that this fascinating, beautiful, mid-15th century court production may be best understood as a Hanlin work of history offering practical moral guidance to both rulers and ministers in their joint responsibility to the country and the people.

Notes

I am grateful to Young Kyun Oh, Sixiang Wang, David Robinson, Julia Murray, Bruce Tindall and the conference organisers.

1 Clark 1988, 290–1; Ye Quanhong 1991, 134; *MSL Xuanzong shilu* 96.9b (7/10/辛未) and for tribute missions in the Xuande period pp. 108.3a, 108.4a, 108.10a, 108.13b, 108.14a, 110.1b, 110.3b, 110.4b, 113.13a, 115.4a–b.
2 *DMB*, 970.
3 Clark 1988, 288.
4 Huang Yuji *c.* 1690, 11.41.
5 Oh 2013, 96 and personal communication 3 June 2014. For the journey, see Wang Sixiang 2013.
6 For example, *Samgang* has 26 stories of Yuan-era wives, *Wulun shu* has 11. Six are the same; but the wording varies, and all of the overlapping stories come from the official history of the Yuan (*Yuanshi* 元史).
7 See Oh 2013, 105 for a brilliant interpretation of this arrangement.
8 For discussion of these features, see Jang 2008, 125–8 and Oh 2013, 94 ff. My measurement is of the Harvard rare book copy; Jang reports on a smaller one that may be the Harvard microfilmed edition.
9 Yu Minzhong 1775, 9/11–12.
10 Deuchler 1992, 26–7, 115–17.
11 Oh 2013, 53.
12 Oh 2013, 61.
13 Oh 2013, 62.
14 Deuchler 1992, ch. 1. Oh 2013, 75. This combines Oh's explanation and my speculation.
15 Oh 2013, 100.
16 Oh 2013, 117.
17 Rather ungrateful, considering that Ban's own younger brother rescued him from prison. See Zhu Zhanji 1443, 60/9. Ban Gu writes: 'What is it I call the Three Bonds? Ruler–minister, father–son, husband–wife.' See Ban Gu *c.* 80, 7/1.
18 King Sejo (r. 1455–68) ordered his ministers to compile a *Record of the Five Relationships*. See *Sejo sillok* 36.23b (1465/7/25#2). In 1518, a group of scholars supplemented *Samgang* with an *Illustrated Guide to Two Relationships*. See Oh 2013, 227; Zhu Zhanji 1443, preface and 62/14.
19 Y[illegible]g Shiqi wrote a poem about *Wulun shu*; see Yang Shiqi *c.* 1445, 58/[illegible]6.
20 *DMB*, 293; Brook 1996, 106; Brook 1998, 652, 654.
21 *DMB*, 970. Liu Yan eventually got in trouble for among other things failing his own son in an examination. See his epitaph in Xu Hong 1505, 8/19.
22 On Lü Yuan, see his epitaph in Li Xian *c.* 1470, 20/23, and in Xu Hong 1505, 8/12; his 1462 death notice in *MSL Yingzong shilu* 346.5a (6/11/庚申); and his biography in Liao Daonan 1545, 3/32. On Yang Ding, see his death notice in *MSL Xianzong shilu* 267/3a–b (21/6/甲午). On Qian Xili, see Wang Zhi *c.* 1465, 24/59. Peng Shi 彭時 (1416–75) may also have worked on the collection, while at the National University; see Li Xian *c.* 1470, 15/16.
23 *DMB*, 970. *MSL Yingzong shilu* 151.8b (12/3/己丑) (printing), 157.5a (12/8/乙亥) (storage). *MS* 8/98/2425-6 reports that the Xuande emperor made the book and the Zhengtong emperor prefaced and printed it. See also Jang 2008, 122 n. 22, but the citation to the *Huidian* should be to the *Yingzong shilu*.
24 *MSL Yingzong shilu* 170.7b (13/9/癸丑).
25 Huang Zuo 1560–6, 13.10b; the catalogue is *Qianqingtang shumu*, Huang Yuji *c.* 1690, 11/41.
26 Memorial from the Ministry of Rites (*Libu* 禮部). Yu Ruji *et al.* 1620, 94/26, and *MSL Yingzong shilu* 172.6a (13/11/庚子).
27 *Mengzi* 34A.
28 Xia Liangsheng *c.* 1530, ch. 20.
29 They were bound variously: the Qing catalogue lists five versions in 32, 60 or 62 fascicles, in four or six cases. Yu Minzhong 1775, 9/11–12.
30 Oh 2013, 173.
31 Zhu Zhanji 1443, 59/7, story of Zheng Shutong 鄭叔通.
32 Zhu Zhanji 1443, 59/6–7, from *Songshi* 宋史, 459/1. Husbandly fidelity may have political overtones like wifely fidelity.
33 Zhu Zhanji 1443, 60/17.
34 Zhu Zhanji 1443, 60/26.
35 Ching 2013, 277.
36 That it is a royal family, exceptionally, which was portrayed as a group may underline problems with the view that the imperial family was 'the pattern and model of all families within the empire'. See Clunas 2013, 94. Ordinary wives could not be demoted to concubine, nor vice versa; imperial consorts could be shifted around. Ordinary sons inherited equally; there was only one throne.
37 Zhu Zhanji 1443, 59/4.
38 Zhu Zhanji 1443, 54/4. Ye Chunji 1570–4, 14/12–13 cites this case from *Wulun shu*.
39 Ni Qian 1493, 25/16–17 notes this unevenness of categories.
40 Zhu Zhanji 1443, Table of Contents 1–7.
41 Zhu Zhanji 1443, 7/1–8.
42 Zhu Zhanji 1443, Table of Contents 7–15.
43 Zhu Zhanji 1443, 51/7.
44 *MS* 2/24/335.
45 A mid-19th century primer includes the three terms together: ruler (*jun* 君), shown as originally having handlike elements on both sides of a box (*kou* 口), is explained as facing forwards, while both minister (*chen* 臣) and people (*min* 民) face right towards the sovereign. 'To recline' (*wo* 臥) is explained as depicting both ministers and ordinary folk kowtowing to the sovereign. Bai 2005, 131.
46 See *MSL Yingzong shilu* 179.13b (14/6/丙子), 206.7b (2/7/ 戊午), 209.3a (2/10/庚午); *MSL Xiaozong shilu* 132.7a (10/12/壬辰); *MSL Shizong shilu* 205.3a (16/10/乙卯), 205.2a (16/10/癸丑). Other bestowals: *MSL Yingzong shilu* 212.8a (3/1丙辰) (an official's wife); *MSL Yingzong shilu* 216/11a (3/5/戊辰) (a new county school); *MSL Wuzong shilu* 171/11a–b (14/2/辛卯) (replacement copy in Confucius's hometown); and *MSL Shizong shilu* 174/5b (14/4/ 己巳) and 180/6b (14/10/甲寅).
47 On Ke Qian, see epitaph by Wang Yu王 (1422–95, js. 1451), in Xu Hong 1505, 13/11, who like Huang Zuo 1560–6 (16/16) adduces the gift to prove how good ruler–minister relations were then. On Wei Qi, see Mao Qiling *c.* 1690, 73/4. On Li Kui, see Xie Min and Tao Cheng 1731, 40/32.
48 Xu Hong 1505, 17/8. *DMB*, 1039–40.
49 Zhu Zaiyu *c.* 1600, 1/1.
50 Li Dongyang 1516, 38/21. See He 2013, 113–14.
51 Xia Liangsheng *c.* 1530, 12/77.
52 Kuang Yuche and Ren Chongyue 1984, 51.
53 Jang 2008, 169. Historian Chen Jian noted this use of *Wulun shu*

and other court compilations. See Xiang Yannan 1993, 55. A 1467 memorial cites both *Wulun shu* and the *Veritable Records*. See *MSL Xianzong shilu* 46.7b–8a (3/9/己卯).

54 Wei Jiao *c.* 1545, 16/25; Yang Yiqing *c.* 1526, 18/44. A government student and scholar mention the utility of the compilation. See Ke Shangqian 1545 14/8.

55 *MSL Yingzong shilu* 191.23b (1/4/癸卯), 192.4b–5b (1/5/己酉).

56 Wang Shu *c.* 1510, 8/15a. See also Yu Ruji *et al.* 1620, 68/4; and *MSL Xiaozong shilu* 12/1a (1/3/戊辰).

57 Memorial by Zhang Mou 章懋 (1437–1522), in Huang Xun 1551, 9/8.

58 Lu Can *c.* 1552, 5/7.

59 Qiu Jun 1620s, 7/50.

60 Ye Sheng 1465–72, 37/4, 7.

61 Jang 2008, 161, citing Sakai, *Zōho Chūgoku zensho no kenkyū* 增補中國善書の研究, 81. Rather than prohibiting commercial reprints, the court occasionally tried to assure accuracy by fining sloppy printers, as in an order of 1523. See Jang 2008, 177–8. Thirteen years later, William Tyndale was hanged for printing a Bible in English.

62 *DMB*, 498–9.

63 Han Yong *c.* 1480, 11/1–2. *DMB*, 498ff.

64 *MS* 2/15/187; *DMB*, 877; Li Dongyang 1516, 39/12.

65 Zhu Zhanji 1443, 7/8; Li Dongyang 1516, 39/12.

66 Li Dongyang 1516, 39/12.

67 Li Dongyang 1516, 39/10–11

68 de Bary and Huang 1993, 91–2.

69 Ni Qian 1493, 25/16–17.

70 See a brief mention in Lü Yuan 1480–1520, 10/6a.

Chapter 26
Looking East, Looking West: The Artistic Connections of Ming China and Timurid Iran

Priscilla Soucek

The many ways in which Iran was connected to China over the centuries, both by land and by sea, complicates the isolation of any particular period of that relationship. This ambiguity is especially pronounced for the period 1400–50 due to the lingering presence of East Asian visual symbols that had been popularised in Iran during the time of Mongol domination from the middle of the 13th century to the middle of the 14th century. When we see a 15th-century painting from Iran or Central Asia that includes Chinese elements, it is often difficult to know whether these should be viewed as a lingering reflection of the Mongol era, or newly acquired features deriving from more recent contact with Ming China.

Although Mongol governmental control over Iran had collapsed by the 1350s, the cultural and artistic legacy of the Ilkhans, the branch of the Mongol dynasty who had ruled Iran, survived to varying degrees in the regional successor states that were created within its former boundaries. In some cases the consistent use of a similar design or motif in both the Mongol and Ming periods, such as the association of dragons with governmental authority, underscores the cultural continuity in significant aspects of the visual vocabulary of the region. For example, dragons and long-tailed birds appear prominently in the decoration of a Mongol palace erected in north-west Iran in the 1250s and are also featured in court paintings of the post-Mongol period.[1] These same creatures appear repeatedly in the court arts of 15th-century Iran. For example, golden dragons embellish the white umbrella carried over the head of a prince in an early 15th-century painting from Tabriz that is thought to depict a local ruler of the Jalayirid dynasty that ruled the region between the collapse of the Ilkhanid Mongol state and the rise of the Timurids (**Pl. 26.1**).[2] As will be demonstrated below, dragons are also associated with royal power in paintings made for various members of the Timurid dynasty.

The period of 1400–50 under discussion coincides with Timurid domination over Iran and Central Asia. It opens with the final years of Timur's life (who died in 1405) and encompasses the entirety of the reign of his son and eventual successor, Shah Rukh (r. 1407–47). Timur's empire had been created by reconnecting the fragmented polities that arose as successors to the Mongol Empire in Iran and Central Asia. Unfortunately, he devoted more energy to these conquests than to converting his extensive holdings into a stable and integrated state. As a result, shortly after his death the various regions of his empire began to pursue more or less independent paths. Consequently, regional variations in artistic production began to appear as different local rulers gave varying degrees of importance to patronage of the arts; local artistic connections with China also differed in form and content.

Timur's life extended only to the first five years covered by the exhibition at the British Museum, but the impact of his conquests and of his attitude towards artistic production can serve as a point of departure. In important respects the fundamental objective of Timur's conquests was to reconstruct the Mongol empire with the presumed goal of making his own family its legitimate rulers in perpetuity. This objective is evident not only from the focus of his military campaigns, but also from more personal aspects of his life. He sought to bolster his political legitimacy by attaching himself to the family of Chinggis Khan in any possible way. He ruled in the name of a titular Mongol descendant whose importance was symbolic rather than practical. He sought out and married female members of the Chinggisid family, which permitted him to use the coveted title of *Güregen* or 'son-in-law'.[3]

Timur also appears to have viewed the Ming rulers as obstacles to his eventual goal of reconstructing the broad expanse of the Mongol state. A Spanish envoy to Timur's court, Ruy González de Clavijo, who witnessed several royal audiences during his visit to Samarqand in the autumn of 1404, describes the ways in which Timur showed his contempt for Chinese officials sent from the Ming court to collect tribute from him. He not only sought to humiliate them by relegating them to an inferior position among his guests, but also addressed them in insulting language. In addition, they were detained for some time before being allowed to return to China, and without the payment from him that they had been sent to collect.[4]

Although none of the other Timurids attempted to assert control over the territory of the Ming state, other facets of Timur's legacy continued to shape their artistic patronage. Following a policy previously used by the Mongols, whenever he conquered an area, Timur treated skilled craftsmen as booty to be used as he saw fit. If their skills were deemed useful, those individuals could be forced to leave their homes and move to his capital, Samarqand, in order to execute projects under his command.[5]

The artistic consequences of these forced relocations instigated by Timur are most easily documented in architecture. For example, in the cemetery zone of Samarqand known as the Shah-i Zindeh, tombs belonging to female members of Timur's immediate family can be divided between those that are decorated with the techniques and designs already established in Samarqand by the last quarter of the 14th century, prior to Timur's seizure of the city, and those which display decorative systems introduced to the region in the early 15th century by builders and tile-makers who had been transferred to Samarqand from the Iranian cities of Shiraz, Yazd and Isfahan.

A mausoleum in the Shah-i Zindeh, known as the tomb of Shad-i Mulk Agha and erected through the patronage of Timur's elder sister, Turkan Agha (d. 1386), to serve both as her own tomb and that of her daughter who had died in 1371, continues the architectural and decorative traditions that had been established in Samarqand by the 1360s and which are evident in some of that complex's earliest documented structures such as the tombs from the 1340s and 1350s.[6] In addition to an elaborate programme of geometric ornament, the tiles of Shad-i Mulk Agha employ stylised lotus blossoms shown in profile. These floral designs indicate that at least one East Asian decorative feature had already been integrated into the artistic repertoire of Samarqand tile makers by the last quarter of the 14th century.

This local Samarqand approach to architectural decoration contrasted with the new techniques and designs that were introduced by craftsmen forcibly transferred to

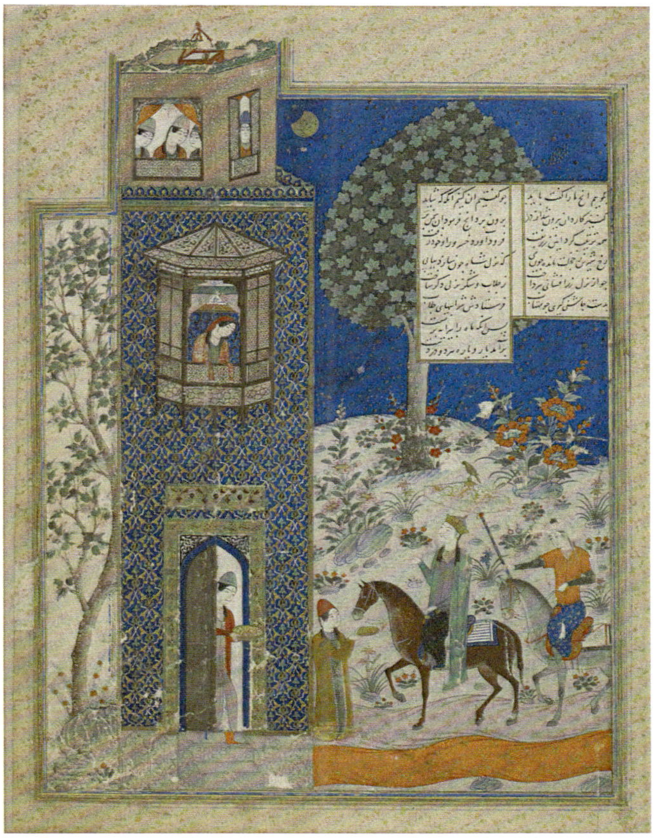

Plate 26.1 Page showing Khusraw at Shirin's castle in Nizami, *Khusraw wa Shirin*, dated 1406–10, Tabriz. Ink, opaque watercolour and gold on paper, height 25.7cm, width 18.4cm. Freer Gallery of Art, Smithsonian Institution, Washington, D.C., Purchase F1931.36

Samarqand after Timur's campaigns in western Iran in the 1380s and 1390s. These new trends are represented by a tomb erected by another of Timur's sisters, Shirin Bika Aqa, for either her own use or that of her family.[7] The tomb's portal is surmounted by a vertically ribbed vault, while its exterior surfaces are covered with tiles executed in the laborious technique of cut-tile mosaic that had been developed in western Iran. Comparable vaults and ornamentation are still preserved in late 14th or early 15th-century structures erected in Tabriz, Isfahan and Shiraz.[8] The consequences of Timur's policy of moving craftsmen from one region to another is more easily documented in architecture than in the production of portable works of art, but some objects may reflect the application of a similar practice of transferring skilled craftsmen from one region to another in order to execute a royal commission. The fact that Timur's grandson Ulugh Beg (1394–1449) also inherited at least some of his grandfather's transplanted craftsmen is indicated by the fact that after his accession to the throne in 1411, he issued a decree permitting transplanted Syrian ceramic specialists to return to their homes.[9] Ulugh Beg's decision to release Timur's conscripted workers, however, does not exclude the possibility that he acquired other specialised artisans.

Although Ulugh Beg did not emulate his grandfather's passion for territorial expansion, the fact that his dominion included Timur's capital, Samarqand, may well have provided him with the opportunity to embrace other aspects of the latter's policies. It is known, for example that he too

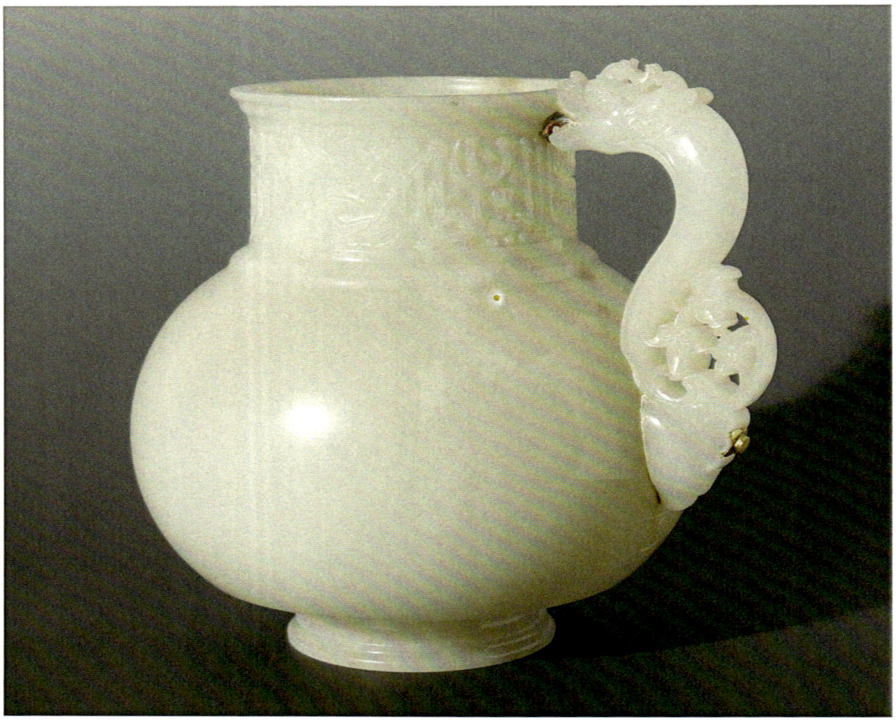

Plate 26.2 Pale green jade jug, inscribed with the titles of Ulugh Beg b. Shah Rukh, *c.* 1425–38, Samarqand. Height 14.5cm, diameter 16cm. Calouste Gulbenkian Foundation, Lisbon, Inv. 328

married female descendants of Chinggis Khan, which permitted him to use the same honorific title of *Güregen,* or 'son-in-law' used by his grandfather. The coins struck by Ulugh Beg made reference to his grandfather by employing a symbolic device associated with him as well as his name.[10] Ulugh Beg's special connection with his grandfather is also suggested by the fact that in 1425 he arranged for the transportation of a large slab of black jade from the region of Qarshi in Transoxiana to Samarqand where he had it carved and placed over Timur's grave. The texts inscribed on it include a description of the circumstances under which he had acquired this stone.[11] The particulars about who had shaped this slab of black jade and inscribed it with a text are not known, but Ulugh Beg's appreciation of this material is evident in the three jade drinking vessels which were inscribed with his name. Two of them, one in the British Museum (see **Pl. 1.5**), the other at the Bharat Kala Bhavan in Banaras, are made of green jade and have dragon handles.[12] The third example, now in the Calouste Gulbenkian Foundation Lisbon, was fashioned from a pale green stone and was clearly modelled after a metalwork object of a type known to have been produced in Herat; its principal ornament consists of Ulugh Beg's name and titles (**Pl. 26.2**).[13] The far-flung territories inhabited by Timur's descendants led to a proliferation of princely courts including those in the city of Herat, the residence of his son, Shah Rukh, as well as one at Shiraz in south-west Iran, which was the successive residence of two of Timur's grandsons, Iskandar Sultan b. Umar Shaikh (r. 1404–14) and Ibrahim Sultan b. Shah Rukh (r. 1414–35). Shiraz, renowned as the birthplace and residence of several important Persian authors including Sa'di (d. 1292) and Hafiz (d. 1389), had by the later 14th century become a major centre for the production of literary manuscripts.[14]

Manuscripts made for both Iskandar Sultan and Ibrahim Sultan contain images revealing the two prince's respective possession of objects of Chinese manufacture. The texts of their books contain the classics of Persian literature, but the ways in which those books were decorated provides insight into the new artistic currents reaching the Timurid dominions from Ming China. These examples will be taken in chronological order, beginning with a consideration of Iskandar Sultan's manuscripts and then turning to one associated with Ibrahim Sultan.

Iskandar Sultan's short but tumultuous life highlights the competing quests for political power and military superiority among Timur's descendants in the years following the latter's death in 1405. Iskandar Sultan's court historian, Mu'in al-din Natanzi, claims that Iskandar received an official envoy sent to him by the Yongle emperor. This envoy, whose journey from China is said to have taken two years, reached Shiraz in 1412–13 with an official letter and various Chinese objects, and was sent back to China with a letter in Iskandar's name as well as 'Iranian rarities'.[15] Iskandar, whose excessive ambition brought him into conflict with his Timurid relations and ultimately led to his execution in 1415 on the orders of his uncle Shah Rukh (r. 1409–47) whose position as Timur's successor had been accepted by the other members of the dynasty, appears to have viewed his relations with the Chinese emperor as a confirmation of his own exalted status.

The most clear-cut link between Iskandar's association of East Asian visual symbols with his own political ambitions comes in an illustration in a manuscript anthology made for him which is now in the collection of the British Library (**Pl. 26.3**) a book that is sometimes called 'Iskandar's Miscellany'. The picture in question illustrates a story in the *Iskandar-name* of Nizami describing how that prince sought the advice of a reclusive sage who lived in a mountain retreat. This painting's starry sky, and the fact that the young prince is led by a servant carrying a candle, indicate that this visit is nocturnal.

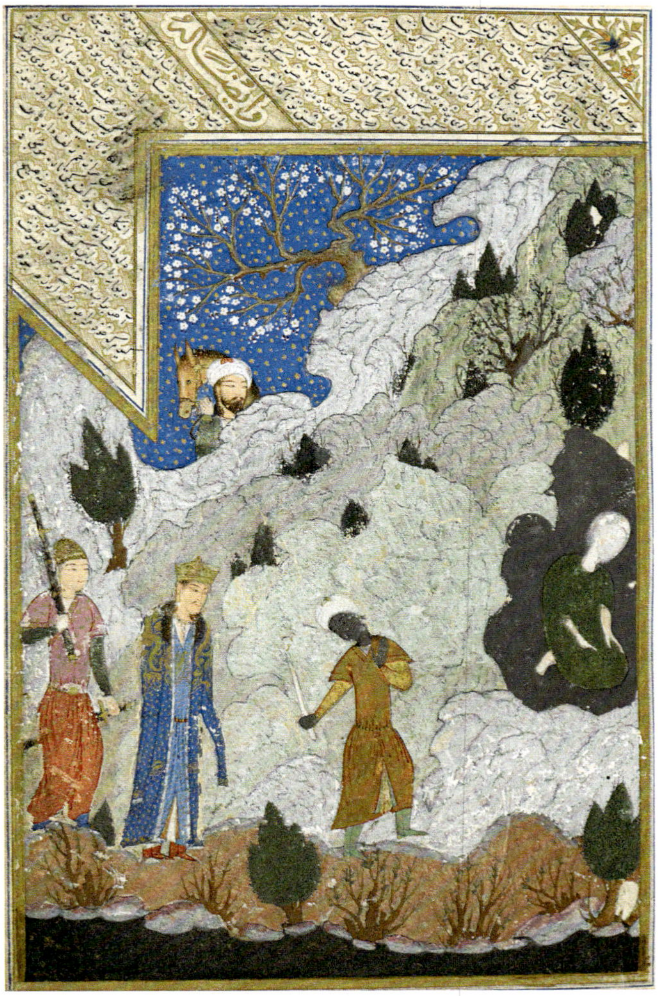

Plate 26.3 'Iskandar visiting a sage in his cave at night', from *Anthology* made for Iskandar Sultan b. Umar Shaikh at Shiraz, *c.* 1412. Height 18.4cm, width 12.7cm. British Library, London, Add. 27261, fol. 230r

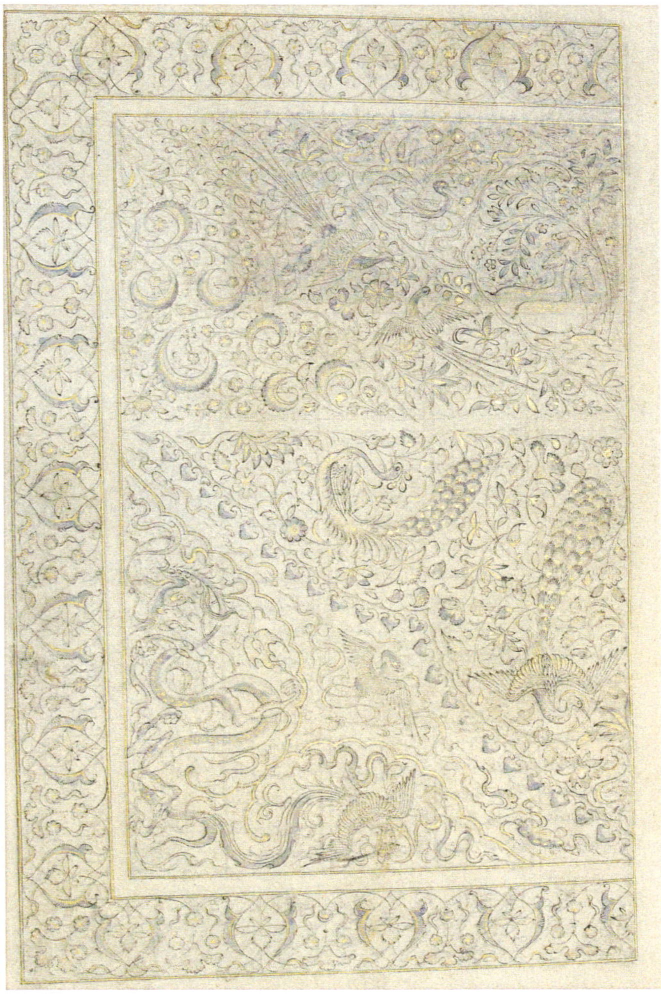

Plate 26.4 Illuminated page showing designs for cloud-collar embroideries, *Anthology* of Iskandar Sultan, dated 1410–11. Tempera and gold dust on paper, height 27.4cm, width 17.2cm. Calouste Gulbenkian Foundation, Lisbon, L.A. 161, fol. 130a

The princely message of this image is enhanced by the fact that Iskandar wears both a crown and a gold-embroidered fur-trimmed robe. Although the design of his garment's gold-embroidered decoration can be seen only in part, its main feature appears to be a pair of sinuous dragons whose tails are visible on his shoulders and sleeves. A similar dragon appears as a marginal decoration on another page of this manuscript on fol. 542r. Although this dragon lacks the exact configuration of the dragons used to embellish robes worn by members of the Ming imperial family, the connection between this creature and Iskandar's princely status would have been clear to a viewer in Iskandar's day.

The inclusion of designs which appear to replicate Chinese embroidery patterns on other pages of Iskandar's manuscripts suggest that such patterns held a special interest for this Timurid prince. One of these drawings executed in ink with touches of colour appears to be a kind of sampler with several patterns on the same page (**Pl. 26.4**). The most prominent of them show one quarter of the design for a kind of cusped medallion known as a 'cloud collar' that was traditionally placed on the shoulders of Chinese robes such as one embellished with dragons made for a Ming prince that was excavated in Shandong province.[16] A manuscript made for Iskandar Sultan in the Gulbenkian Foundation in Lisbon contains designs that show a variety of exotic bird with an exceptionally long tail, often described as a 'simurgh'. Depictions of this exotic type of bird were produced in Iran during the period of Mongol domination during late 13th and early 14th centuries when it was often combined with dragons.[17] Iskandar's page shows a pair of long-tailed birds framed in a lobed border which resembles the ornaments that decorate the shoulders of Ming dragon robes.[18] The presence of textile decorations of Chinese origin in paintings made for Iskandar Sultan is not surprising for silk textiles were a standard component in the gifts sent to foreign dignitaries by Chinese rulers.

The location of Shiraz in proximity to the Persian Gulf port of Hormuz gave it particular importance during the period of voyages to the Near East carried out by the Ming fleets led by the Muslim admiral, Zheng He, between 1414 and 1433.[19] Both Shah Rukh in Herat and his son Ibrahim Sultan in Shiraz are known to have participated in an exchange of envoys with the Ming rulers, and traces of those exchanges are reflected in books made for these Timurids at their respective courts.

The removal of Iskandar from control over the key city of Shiraz provided an opportunity for Shah Rukh to install his own son, Ibrahim Sultan, as the ruler of that important

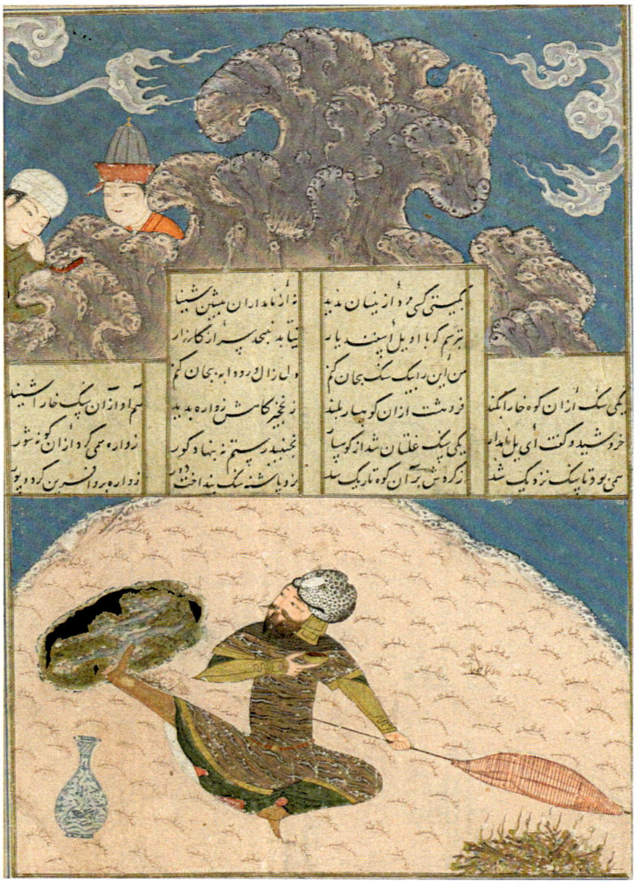

Plate 26.5 'Rustam deflects a rock', in Firdawsi, *Shahnama*, 1430s. Opaque watercolours, ink and gold on paper. The Bodleian Libraries, The University of Oxford, MS Ouseley Add. 176, fol. 272b

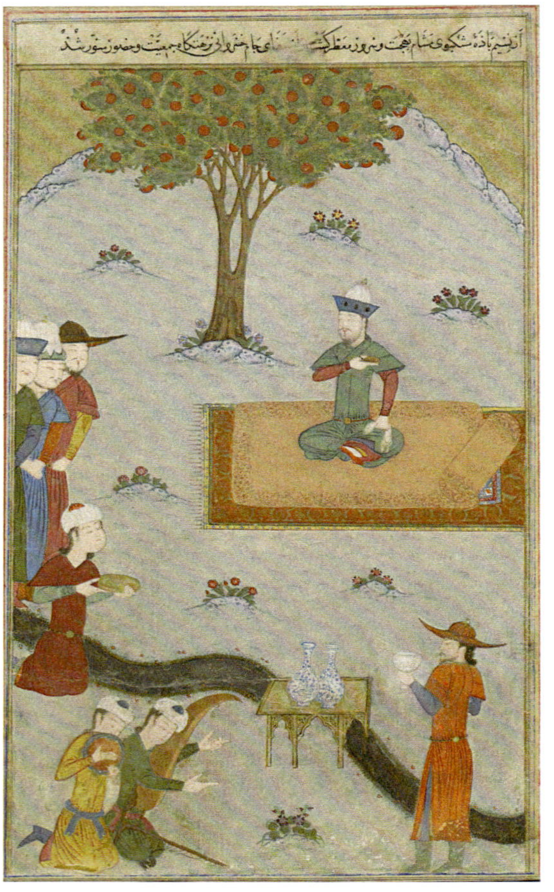

Plate 26.6 'Timur celebrates his conquest of Delhi in December 1398', page from a dispersed copy of *The Zafarnama* (*Book of Victories*) by Sharaf al-din Ali Yazdi, copied by Ya'qub ibn Hasan known as Siraj al-Husayni al-Sultani at Shiraz for Ibrahim Sultan b. Shah Rukh, 1436. Harvard Art Museums/Arthur M. Sackler Museum, Bequest of Abby Aldrich Rockefeller, 1960.198

Plate 26.7 A page from a *Shahnama* manuscript depicting Faridun enthroned in the palace of Zahhak, dated 1444. Height 24.2cm, width 23.2cm. Bibliothèque nationale de France, Suppl. Persan 494

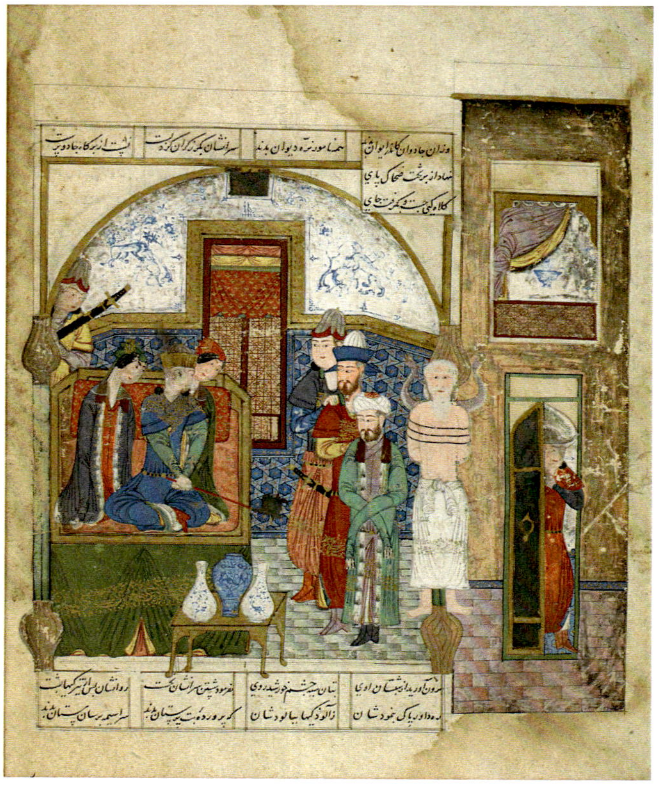

centre. Pictorial evidence linked to the reign of Ibrahim Sultan provides the clearest indication of the way in which the Zheng He voyages contributed to the distribution of Chinese ceramics in the Near East. In addition to these well-known voyages, Chinese ceramics also appear to have been distributed by land-based convoys.[20]

As was the case with the luxurious Chinese textiles that appear to have reached Shiraz during the reign of Iskandar Sultan, most of the information about the appearance of Ming ceramics in Timurid Iran comes from vessels depicted in manuscripts made at Timurid courts in Shiraz and Herat. Three paintings from Shiraz ranging in date from *c.* 1430 to 1444 suggest that the volume and variety of Chinese ceramics in use at the court in Shiraz grew with time.

The first example comes from a copy of the *Shahnama* of Firdawsi made for Ibrahim Sultan and believed to date from the 1430s.[21] One of this manuscript's spare compositions focuses on the hero Rustam who deflects a rock with his right foot while seated on the ground drinking from a golden cup and roasting meat on a spit over a fire (**Pl. 26.5**). The solitary Chinese blue-and-white bottle on the ground beside him is decorated with a landscape that includes a bird swimming on a small pond. This same object is depicted on another folio of this *Shahnama* manuscript depicting Firdawsi's conversation with the court poets of Ghazni. In

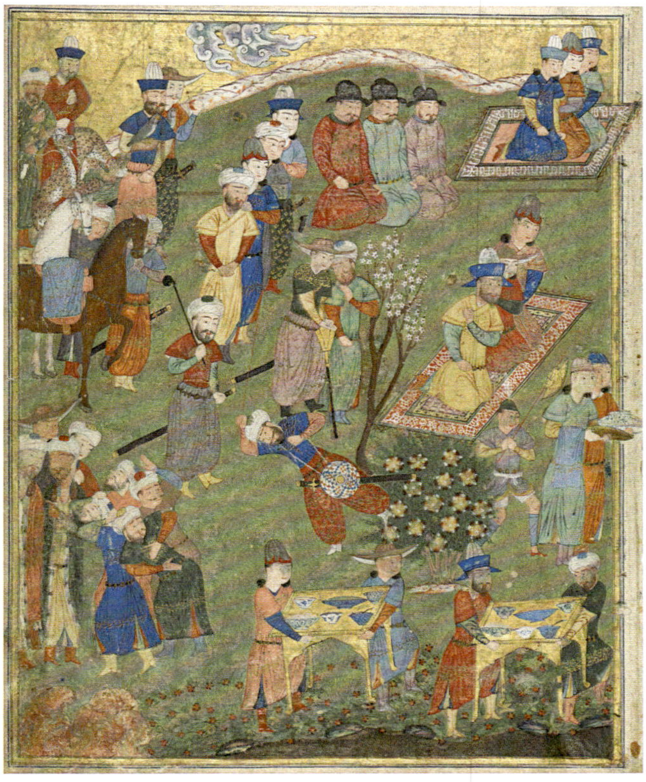

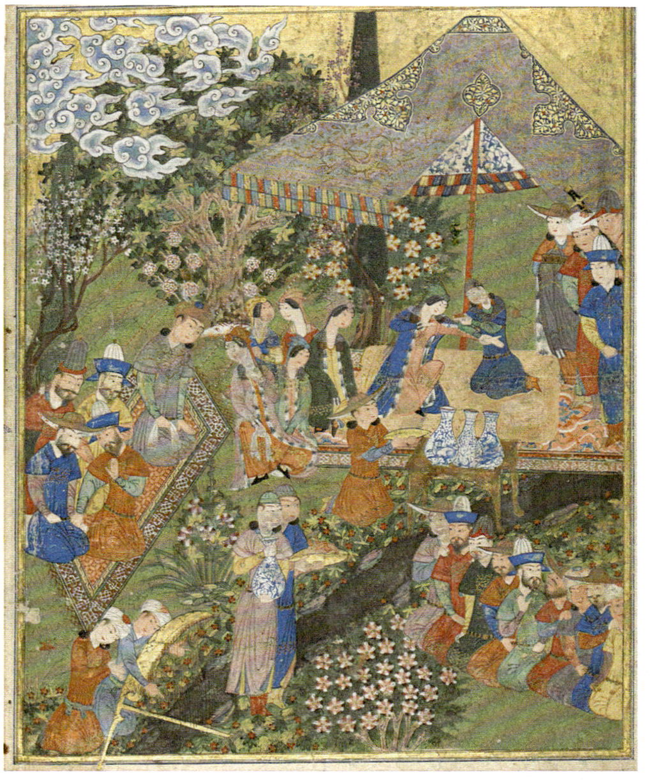

Plate 26.8a–b: a) (left) 'A princely banquet in a garden', left folio of double page frontispiece (recto) illustration from the *Shahnama* (*Book of Kings*) of Abu'l-Qasim Manur Firdawsi, 1444, Shiraz, Iran. Opaque watercolour, gold and silver on paper, height 32.7cm, width 22cm. The Cleveland Museum of Art, John L. Severance Fund 1956.10; b) (right) Manuscript of the *Shahnama* of Firdawsi, 1444. Opaque watercolour, gold and silver on paper. The Cleveland Museum of Art, J. H. Wade Collection, 1945.169

this case, the ceramic bottle sits in solitary splendour on a golden dish.[22]

A very similar blue-and-white bottle appears in the next example, a page from a dispersed manuscript of a history of Timur's life, known as the *Zafarnama,* which was written for Ibrahim Sultan by his court historian Sharaf al-din Ali Yazdi (**Pl. 26.6**). Timur once again drinks from a shallow golden bowl while courtiers stand beside him or entertain him. This painting contains the depiction of three different Chinese ceramic objects. An attendant grasps the lower portion of a stem-cup and a pair of blue-and-white bottles sit on a small golden table; one of these is decorated with a swimming bird and the other has a landscape scene.

The final example is a double-page painting now detached from its parent manuscript dated to 1444 that can be found in the Bibliothèque nationale de France (**Pl. 26.7**).[23] This painting now in the Cleveland Museum of Art (**Pls 26.8a–b**) suggests that the ceramic collection at Shiraz had been augmented since it depicts 18 separate objects. Two are sets of six bowls of varying sizes and shades of blue. Each group of objects rests on a golden table that is carried by two men. Another attendant carries a pair of larger blue-and-white dishes one of which serves to cover the other. The number of blue-and-white bottles has also grown, the pair seen in the *Zafarnama* illustration has now become four. Three bottles sit side-by-side on a small brownish red table and a fourth is carried by one of the prince's attendants.

The most surprising feature of this double-paged frontispiece, however, is the fact that it also depicts three Chinese men who kneel on the ground behind two groups of local courtiers who kneel on small carpets. Although it is tempting to connect the presence of these Chinese visitors with the great variety of Chinese ceramic vessels depicted in this painting, its connection with a manuscript of 1444 means that this image post-dates the culmination of the Zheng He voyages by more than a decade. Although historical evidence confirms that the cessation of his travels did not signal the end of all contacts between the Timurids and the Ming court, the identity of these particular visitors has yet to be established.

The *Shahnama* manuscript in Paris, to which this page belongs, appears to have been produced at the Timurid court of Shiraz because its scribe, who signs as Muhammad al-Sultani, was the court calligrapher for Ibrahim Sultan. As the latter had died in 1434, a decade before this manuscript was produced, the youthful prince depicted in the painting would appear to be his son and heir, Abdallah b. Ibrahim (r. 1434–46). This Paris *Shahnama* and its frontispiece now in Cleveland argue for the stability of the Timurid court in Shiraz in the years following Ibrahim Sultan's death, both with respect to the production of illustrated manuscripts and in maintaining relations with Ming China. The most tangible consequences of that relationship is the continued collecting and use of Ming blue-and-white ceramics at court functions.

Embroidered textiles and blue-and-white ceramics were not the only kinds of Chinese materials known to the Timurids. Another medium is a kind of heavy coloured and decorated paper that differs in several ways from the traditional kinds of paper used in Iran and Central Asia for the transcription of various kinds of texts. The composition of the ink used by Near Eastern scribes required that they

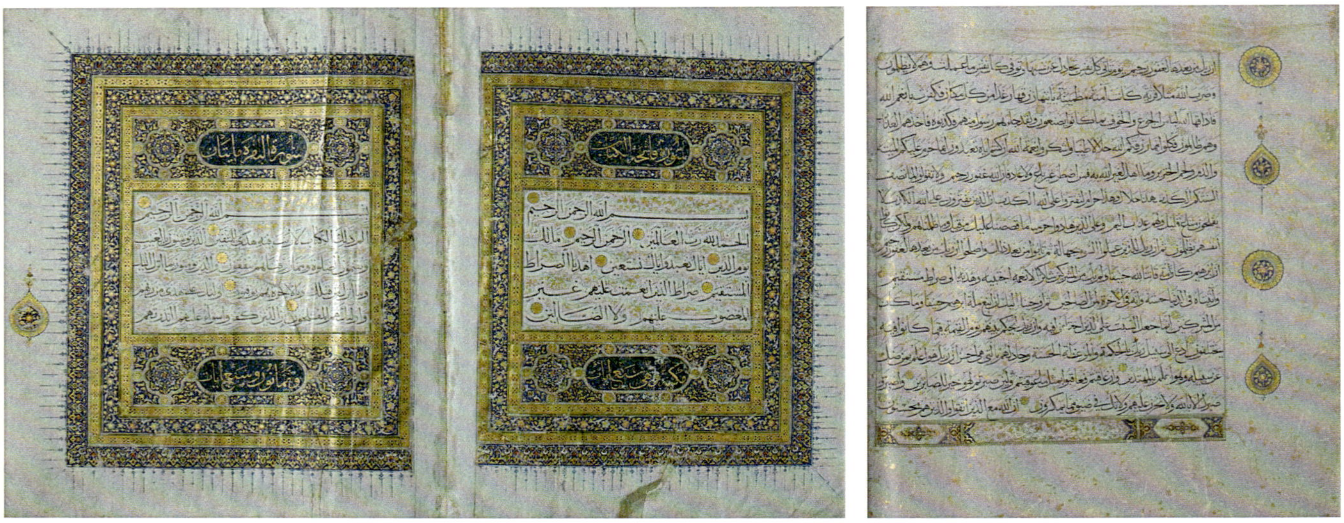

Plates 26.9–10 Sections of a Qur'an written on Chinese gold-sprinkled paper, attributed to the Timurid court at Herat. Illumination attributed to the Muhammad Juki illuminator, *c.* 1440. Leather, paper, ink, colours and gold, book: 44.5 x 38.1cm, manuscript: 30.5 x 26.7cm. Detroit Insitute of Arts, City of Detroit Purchase, 30.323

write on paper which had been smoothed and covered with a coating of starch. The paper made and used in Iran and Central Asia is well suited to this technique of writing. During the reign of Shah Rukh, however, a very different type of paper was used to copy a few manuscripts. It was much heavier than ordinary paper, was dyed in various colours, decorated with gold and had a smooth and waxy surface. Some volumes contain the classics of Persian literature and some carry the text of the Qur'an. Dated examples suggest that most of these manuscripts were produced in the 1430s or 1440s.[24]

A Qur'an now in Detroit is a good example of this group. The two opening pages of its text are its most lavishly ornamented pages and have been published in a number of

Plate 26.11 Preface to the *Shahnama* of Firdawsi, text composed by Baysunghur b. Shah Rukh, Herat, *c.* 1444. Gouache on paper, height 24.7cm, width 13.5cm. Royal Asiatic Society, Persian 239 fol.3b

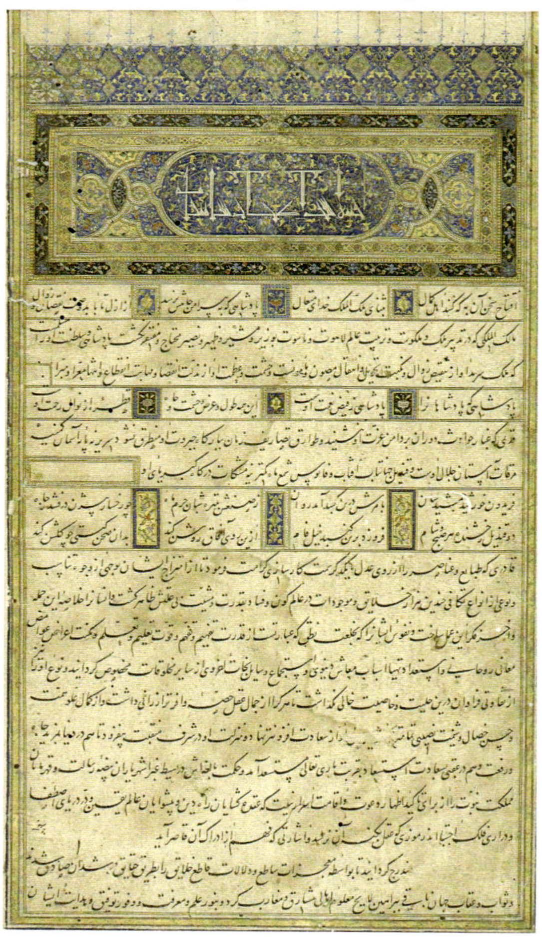

Plate 26.12 'Gushtasp plays polo before the Qaysar', illustration from the *Shahnama* of Firdawsi, *c.* 1444. Gouache on paper, height 22cm, width 15cm. Royal Asiatic Society, Persian 239 fol.252a

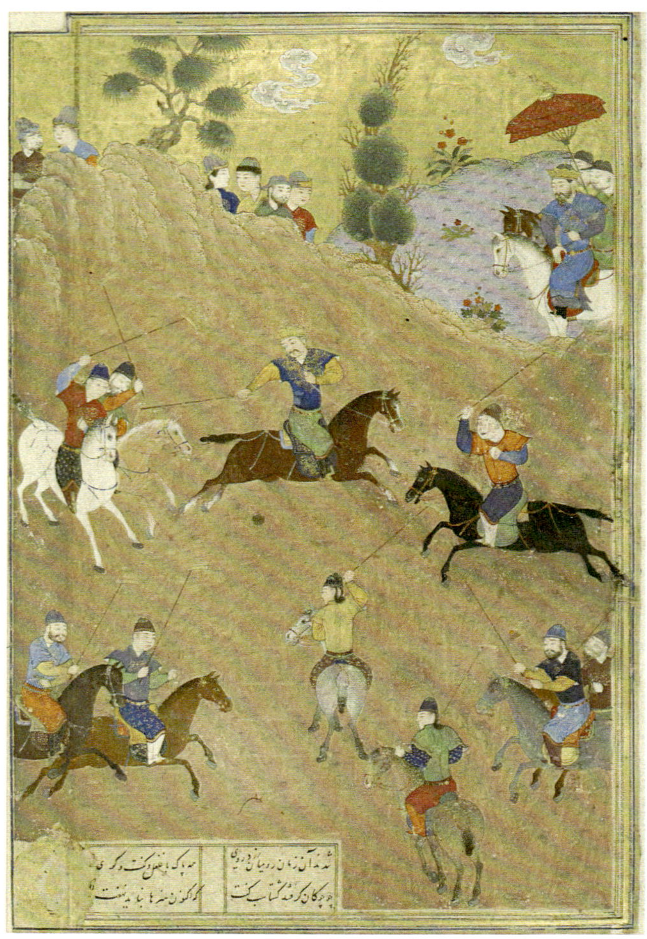

exhibition catalogues.[25] Although various aspects of this manuscript deserve a more detailed study, the remarks here will focus on its unusual paper and the striking parallels between the decorative repertoire of this Qur'an's opening illumination and that in a copy of Firdawsi's *Shahnama*, now at the Royal Asiatic Society in London where it is known as Ms 239. Internal documentation in this book Ms. 239 demonstrates that it was produced for a Timurid Prince, Muhammad Juki b. Shah Rukh. His name and titles are included in dragon-embellished banners depicted in some of the paintings.[26] Although manuscript illumination in 15th-century Timurid manuscripts is highly conventional, the Detroit Qur'an and the *Shahnama* in the Royal Asiatic Society share idiosyncratic features in the design of their golden borders, the tonality of their colours and the execution of their intricate frames which divide the surface of the page into discrete compartments (**Pls 26.9–10**). These similarities suggest that both manuscripts were produced in close proximity to each other in both time and space. The *Shahnama* copy is thought to date to the 1440s and to have been made in Herat so the same provenance can thus be suggested for the Detroit Qur'an. Another distinctive feature of Muhammad Juki's *Shahnama* is that it depicts one of its heroes, Gushtasp, in a fashion analogous to the painting of Iskandar Sultan discussed earlier in this chapter. He wears a golden crown and the shoulders of his garment are embroidered with golden dragons (**Pls 26.11–12**). The question of whether this princely figure should be interpreted as a depiction of Shah Rukh's son Muhammad Juki has been raised, but so far no conclusive answer had been provided.[27]

Aside from its highly decorated opening pages, the visual drama of the Detroit Qur'an is created by the unusual paper on which it is copied. Ten different colours of heavy paper decorated on one side with gold are used for the volume's individual gatherings. In one case, the Qur'an's text has been written over an upside-down landscape vignette that shows a grape vine rooted in a golden hillside. The plant's branches, leaves, tendrils and grape clusters are visible between the words of Quran 16: 119–28.

This brief survey of Ming-Timurid artistic relations between 1400 and 1450 demonstrates that Timur's descendants included Chinese textiles, ceramics and paper in their courtly life and ceremonies. Both the quality of these objects or materials and their distant origin must have enhanced their value to the rulers in the various centres of Timurid power. This general conclusion does not exclude the possibility, however, that individual Timurid rulers placed more particular and personal interpretations on their ownership of such precious goods.

Notes

1 Masuya 2002.
2 Brend 2010, 18–19, pl. 11.
3 Manz 1989, 14, 17, 57.
4 Bailey 1992, 12.
5 Watt 2002, 63–73; Golombek and Wilber 1988, vol. 1, 34–43.
6 Golombek and Wilber 1988, cat. nos 12–14, pls 20–6.
7 Golombek and Wilber 1988, cat. no. 17, pls 30–4.
8 Golombek and Wilber 1988, cat nos 214, 220–1, pls 415–26, 434–45.
9 Golombek 1996, 124, 129.
10 Barthold 1963, 178.
11 Barthold 1963, 100–5; Blair 2006, Grabar 1957, 347, 553–5.
12 Clunas and Harrison-Hall 2014, 263, fig. 222.
13 Blair 2000, 29–31; Lentz and Lowry 1989, 144, 161, figs 46, 57; Komaroff 1992.
14 See Wright 2013.
15 Soucek 1996, 84–5.
16 Clunas and Harrison-Hall 2014, 72, fig. 54.
17 Masuya 2002.
18 Clunas and Harrison-Hall 2014, fig. 54, 72.
19 Bailey 1996, 10.
20 Bailey 1996.
21 Now in the Bodleian Library where it has the shelfmark of Ouseley Add. 176. See Brend and Melville 2010, 118–20.
22 Brend 2010, 28, pl. 20.
23 Stchoukine 1954, no. 27, p. 46; Robinson 1954, 105.
24 Blair 2000.
25 Lentz and Lowry 1989, 78–9, 332.
26 Brend 2010, 116–17.
27 Brend 2010, 106–7.

Chapter 27

Precious Stones and Ming Culture, 1400–1450

Craig Clunas

The poem with which the interpreter Ma Huan 馬歡 (b. *c.* 1380) prefaces his account of the early Ming imperially ordered oceanic voyages, commanded by the eunuch admiral Zheng He 鄭和 (1371–1433), opens stirringly:

> The emperor's glorious envoy received the divine commands,
>
> 'proclaim aloud the silken sounds, and go to the barbarous lands' …

And it continues, in describing the armada's reception in foreign parts:

> Here when the heavenly writing came, a happy clamour meeting,
>
> Chieftains and heads of the barbarous tribes all vied to give it greeting.
>
> Tribute of southern gold, rare gems, from distant parts appear;
>
> Grateful, admiring our virtue, they show themselves loyal, sincere …
>
> Mountains high and mighty waves I ere then saw but few;
>
> Unwonted gems and jewels rare I now begin to view.[1]

Even by the standards of early 15th-century court panegyric, hardly famed as one of the high points of Chinese verse, this is not great poetry. But, as this chapter will argue, it is not by accident that 'southern gold' (*nan jin* 南) and 'rare gems' (*yi bao* 異寶), or 'unwonted gems and jewels' (*yi bao qi zhen* 異寶奇珍) glitter in this poem with which Ma Huan opened his *Overall Survey of the Ocean Shores* (*Ying ya shenglan* 瀛涯勝覽), a text which was probably written after the first voyage in 1416. In fact, they are the only specific objects of foreign 'tribute' he mentions in this prefatory verse. Gemstones, and objects inlaid with gemstones, have lain outside the mainstream of research into Chinese art and material culture, largely because until recently scholars have had so few examples to examine. Although the literary evidence for the use of table vessels in precious metals is ample, the number of surviving artefacts in museums, prior to recent archaeological discoveries, has been small.[2] The same is true *a fortiori* with regard to precious metal vessels and objects enhanced with gemstones. The few surviving

Plate 27.1 Toothpick box with chain, Ming dynasty, 15th century. Gold and gems, length 9.1cm, with chain 25.2cm, weight 83g. Rietberg Museum, Zurich, Collection Alice and Pierre Uldry. Inv. No. U 301 GS

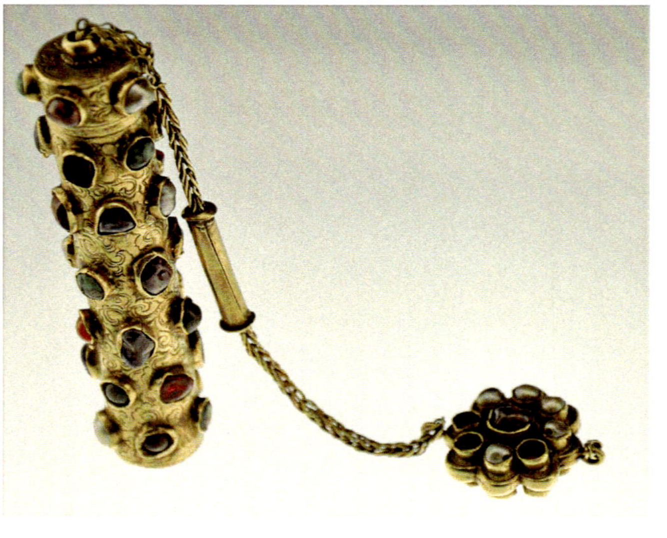

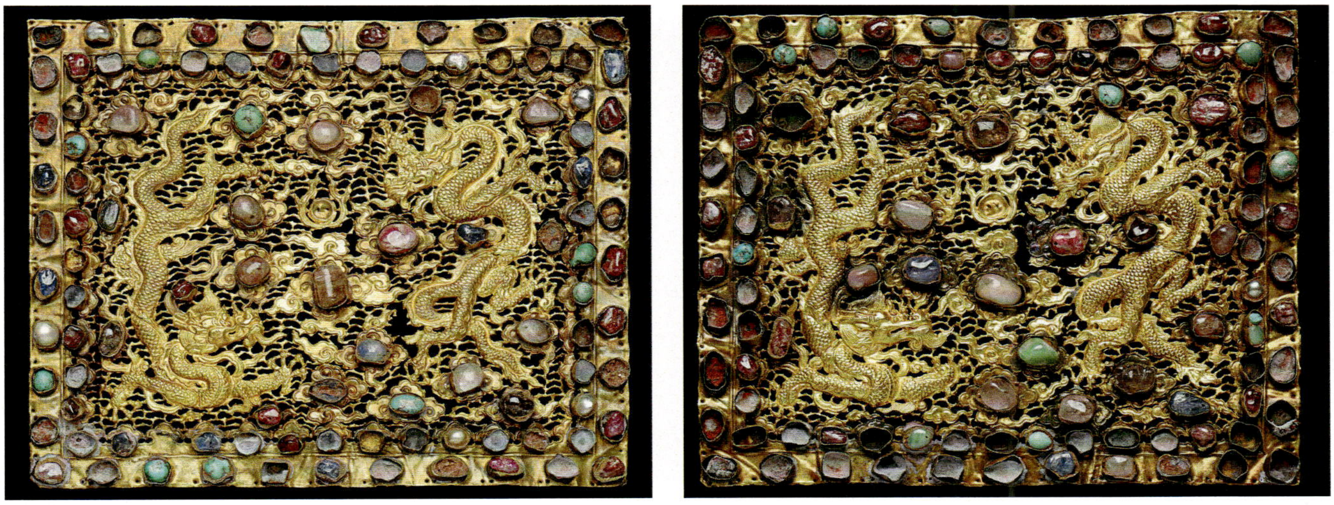

Plate 27.2 Pair of gold pillow ends inlaid with semi-precious stones, Xuande period, 1426–35, Beijing or Nanjing. Gold, rubies, turquoise and other precious and semi-precious stones, height 14.47cm, width 18cm each. British Museum, London, 1949,1213.1-2

examples outside China, such as a gem-encrusted gold toothpick case in the Rietberg Museum, Zurich (**Pl. 27.1**) or a pair of pillow ends in the British Museum (**Pl. 27.2**), have lacked a context in which to understand them, excavated as they were in the early 20th century in uncontrolled conditions. Indeed, the latter objects were for many years catalogued and displayed as ornamental plaques for sewing on clothing, a sort of luxury rank badge, and their true function as ornamental pillow ends has only recently been recognised. But in more recent years significant excavations in China have greatly enhanced our understanding of the types, functions and range of precious metal objects in the early Ming, and many aristocratic tombs have yielded up material of this type.[3] Now, through a closer examination of the significant quantity of such material excavated from the tomb of Prince Zhuang of Liang 梁莊王 (1411–41) at Zhongxiang in Hubei province, and by reading that material in the light of a survey (necessarily sketchy) of its historical and cultural context, it is possible to make the preliminary claim, which it is hoped will be tested through further research, for the importance of such objects in Ming courtly life. This was an importance out of all proportion to their quantity, indeed one which conversely is derived from their very rarity.

It was not just rhetorically, or in verse, that gems were sought out by the maritime voyages of the Yongle (1403–24) and Xuande (1426–35) reigns. A eunuch memorial of 1458 claims that 'the stock [of gems brought back by Zheng He] is close to exhaustion', suggesting that it was sufficient for courtly needs through the first half of the 15th century, which encompassed the short lifetime of Prince Zhuang of Liang.[4] It is worth therefore taking a closer look at exactly what stones of which types are found in this extraordinary complex of objects (**Pl. 27.3**). The tomb of Zhu Zhanji 朱瞻垍, ninth son of the Hongxi emperor (r. 1425), first and last Prince of Liang, contains 111 items inlaid with some 18 different types of precious stones, numbering 772 stones in all; it is slightly unclear from the excavation report whether this figure also includes the 21 loose gems (**Pl. 27.4**) which may have come adrift from their settings (the tomb itself was flooded centuries ago), or which may simply have been included as loose stones. It is a reasonable presumption that most if not all of these items were gifts to the prince from the central imperial courts, and manufactured in imperial workshops in Nanjing or Beijing. None of the stones has been cut, rather they are polished only, but they include some

Plate 27.3 Group of gold and gem-encrusted hairpins, excavated from the tomb of Zhu Zhanji, Prince Zhuang of Liang (1411–41), and of Lady Wei (d. 1451) at Zhongxiang, Hubei province, *c.* 1403–51, Nanjing or Beijing. Gold, jade, precious and semi-precious stones, maximum length 20.5cm. Hubei Provincial Museum

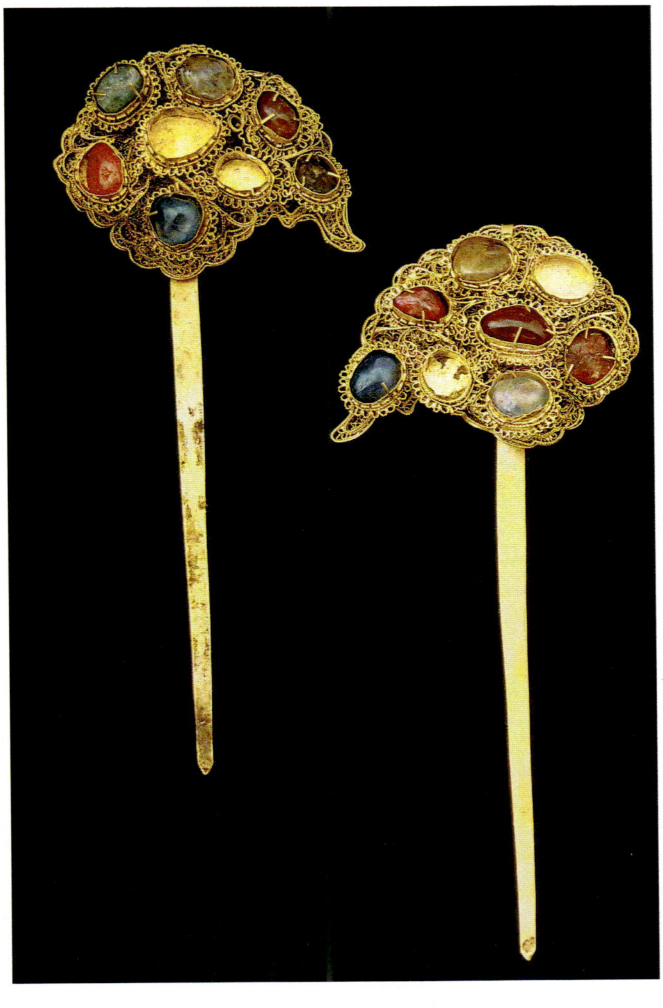

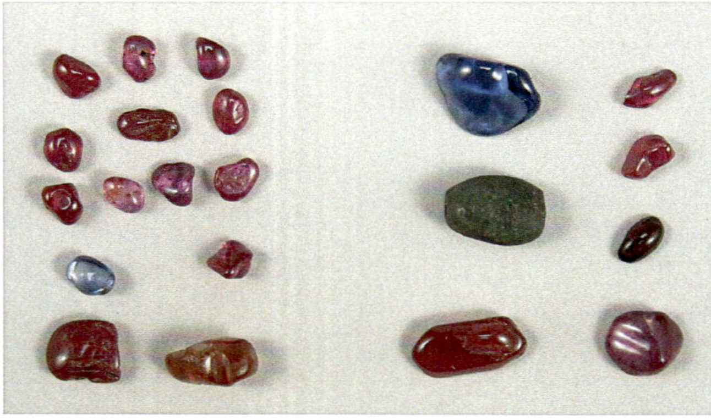

Plate 27.4 Loose gems excavated from the tomb of Zhu Zhanji, Prince Zhuang of Liang, and of Lady Wei at Zhongxiang, Hubei province. Hubei Provincial Museum

gems of particularly large size and high quality. The largest single group of stones is the rubies, of which there are 175, as opposed to 147 sapphires and 52 turquoise (there are no diamonds); rubies also predominate among the loose stones, 17 of which display the seductive red gleam of this rarest of the four major gemstone types (diamond, emerald, sapphire and ruby). One of the loose stones has been scientifically tested, proving it to be a true ruby, or corundum (aluminium oxide Al_2O_3 coloured with chromium), as opposed to a balas ruby or spinel which despite visual similarities is mineralogically quite different (aluminium magnesium oxide $MgAl_2O_4$).[5] Jewellery and items of personal adornment form the great majority of the objects inlaid with gems, although it is clear that in this period it was also the practice on occasion to inlay vessels and objects, not just jewellery, of various kinds. Although the gold vessels from the Prince Zhuang of Liang tomb are all plain, a ewer and a basin of unknown provenance now in the Philadelphia Museum of Art, and included in the British Museum exhibition *Ming: 50 years that changed China*, are decorated not only with an incised pattern of dragons and clouds similar in execution to those on the Rietberg Museum toothpick case, but also with a quantity of gems and semi-precious stones, and the now-empty settings for many more.[6] Stones are also inset into the hilt of an elaborate 'jewel sword' with courtly connections, the gems forming the eyes of the lion-like beast which grips the blade in its mouth.[7] And jewels of all sorts decorate both the thrones of Ming emperors and the headdresses of their consorts as they are portrayed in formal court portraiture.[8] However, in the case of Prince Zhuang and his consort Lady Wei 魏 (d. 1451), the great majority of the jewels they possessed seem to have been worn on the body, on hat buttons in his case, and on hairpins, earrings, finger rings and bracelets in hers.

Given their numerical and visual predominance in the Prince Zhuang of Liang tomb (note for example their centrality in each plaque of the great gold filigree belt (**Pl. 27.5**), which will be further discussed below), and also for reasons of space, this chapter will concentrate on the rubies, noting only in passing that, despite their visual dissimilarity, red rubies and blue sapphires are, in terms of their basic chemistry, the 'same thing' (with different trace impurities accounting for the hue), and they tend to be found in close proximity to each other in nature.[9] But where did they come from? As Lin Meicun has pointed out in an important recent essay, China is generally poorly supplied with the major types of gemstone, which historically have been sought outside its borders. Lin identifies three major phases in the East–West cultural exchange of gems. One is to be situated in the late Eastern Han period (25–220), when the influx of Buddhism also brought with it the important symbolic role which gems have played in that religion, as for instance in the concept of 'seven jewels', Chinese *qi bao* 七寶, after the Sanskrit *sapta-ratnāni*, a term of wide usage though of fluctuating content. It has even been argued by some scholars that there is in fact a 'theological-economic link' between this idea and an upsurge in Sino-Indian trade in the first centuries AD.[10] A second phase identified by Lin Meicun as being crucial to the influx of gems to China is to be found in the Yuan period, with its opening of both trans-Eurasian and oceanic trade routes, when the classic Arabic lapidary texts such as that of Ahmad al-Tīfāshi (1184–1253) may have become known in China. The third phase is situated in the early Ming, associated in particular with the Zheng He voyages, a phase for which the tomb of Prince Zhuang of Liang offers our best material evidence.[11]

Rubies are mined today, and indeed have been mined for centuries, in a relatively limited number of places. Closest geographically to the Ming borders are the particularly prolific ruby mines of Mogok, now in northern Myanmar, but in the early 15th century controlled by the Shan state of Mong Mit, itself part of a larger Shan polity of Hsenwi.[12] The scholarship of Sun Laichen has provided us with an account of the key part that an overland trade in gems played in state formation among the Shan. The trade was partially controlled from the Chinese side by 'supervising eunuchs' (*zhen shou tai jian* 鎮守太監) based at the provincial capital of Yunnanfu (modern Kunming) from 1425, who acquired material directly on behalf of the imperial court, but it was also partly in the hands of Chinese private traders who ventured to the Shan regions. The trade seems to have flourished particularly after 1450.[13] Geoff Wade's exhaustive coverage of references to Southeast Asia in the *Ming Veritable Records* (*Ming shi lu* 明實錄) shows almost nothing in the way of gems arriving as 'tribute' at court from the Shan states before that date; in fact, there is only one such reference, relating to the presentation in 1396 by Si Lunfa 思倫發 (father of the more famous Shan chieftain Si Renfa 思任發/ Thonganbwa, fl. 1400–45) of 'elephants, horses, gold, precious stones'.[14] Apart from this reference, we do hear of envoys from Sulu, Melaka and Xianluo (modern Thailand) presenting 'precious stones' in 1417, 1419 and 1438 respectively, while in 1436 a righteous envoy to the former colony of Jiaozhi (northern Vietnam) is recorded refusing a bribe of 'gold and precious stones'.[15] The mere absence of a record in the *Veritable Records* cannot be taken as convincing evidence that an event did not take place, but it may well be that 'tribute' was not the principal route by which rubies got into China. Of course, the rubies in the Prince Zhuang of Liang gold belt may indeed have come from the Mogok mines, but if they did so they are much more likely to have come via intermediaries elsewhere; gems are, after all, supremely portable items. The chronicler of the Zheng He

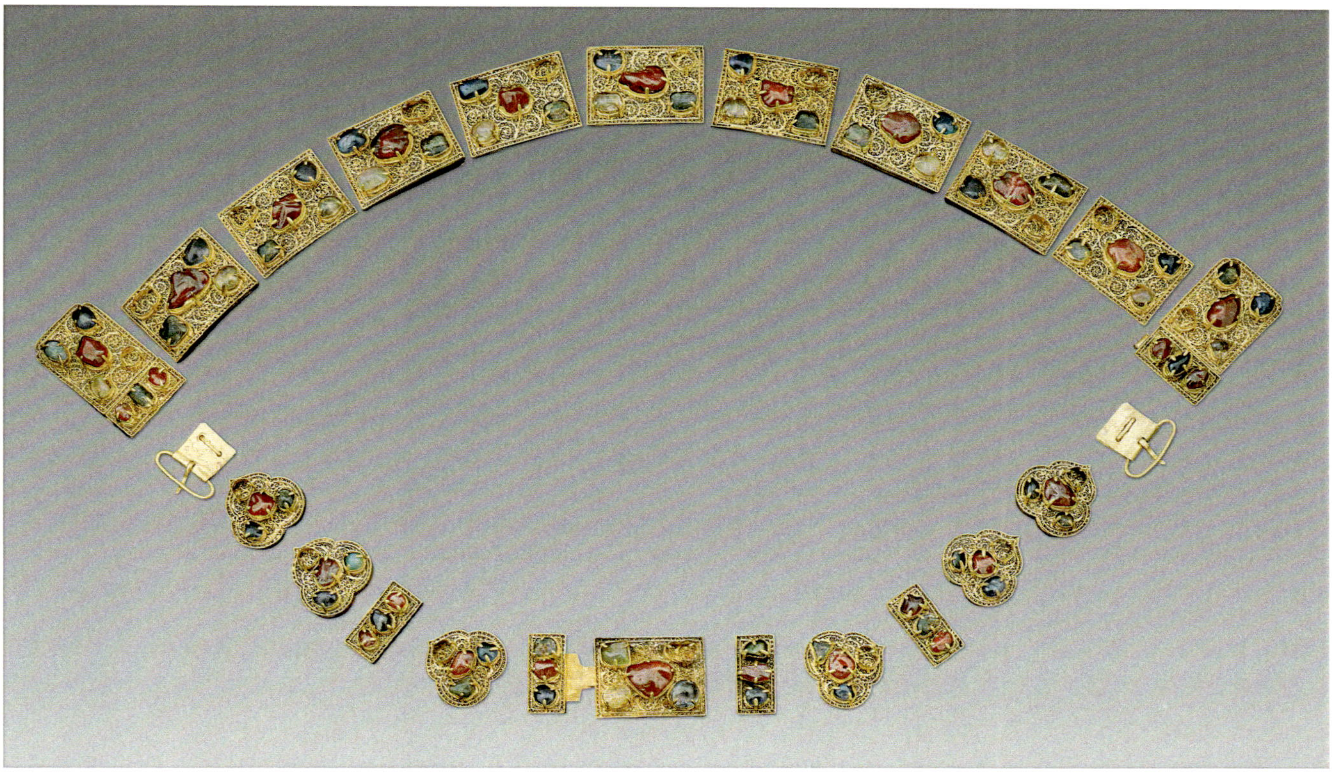

Plate 27.5 Gold belt set with gems excavated from the tomb of Zhu Zhanji, Prince Zhuang of Liang, and of Lady Wei at Zhongxiang, Hubei province. Yongle or Hongxi period, c. 1403–25, Nanjing or Beijing. Gold, precious and semi-precious gems, total length 65cm, overall weight 641.9g; largest piece: height 6cm, width 3.5cm. Hubei Provincial Museum

voyages, Ma Huan, tells us that, in Java, 'Gold, all kinds of precious stones (*bao shi* 寶石), and all varieties of foreign goods are sold in great profusion';[16] Java was a port of trade, not a point of gem production, and his note demonstrates merely that Chinese private or court-sponsored agents did not have to go directly to the mines to get the stones. He remarks too on the ready availability of gemstones in Xianluo (which played the same port-of-trade role), and on the gem-trading activities (still pursued today) of the Chettiar merchants of Cochin (now Kochi) and Calicut (now Kozhikode) in modern Kerala, on the southwest coast of India; however, these were again principally middlemen, rather than mining entrepreneurs.[17] An equally or even more likely source of rubies for the early Ming court was the island of Sri Lanka, the crucial point of intersection between the trade routes of the eastern and western parts of the Indian Ocean, and a land of semi-mythical riches, identified for example by Arab writers as the original site of Eden, and by the Venetian traveller Niccolò de' Conti (1395–1469), who was in Asia at the very time of the Zheng He voyages, as a particularly rich source of gems.[18] In 1283, one of Sri Lanka's rulers had written to a Mamluk sultan of Egypt with the proud boast: 'I have a prodigious quantity of pearls and precious stones of every kind', while at least five diplomatic missions to the Ming from King Parakramabahu VI (r. 1412–68) took place between 1416 and 1459, and the island was the site of one of Zheng He's most forceful interventions, testified to on the trilingual Galle stele inscription, with its implicit claim that Chinese (not Sinhala) is the successor to Sanskrit as the central Buddhist language.[19] Sri Lanka is the subject of the longest single gem-related passage in Ma Huan's *Overall Survey of the Ocean Shores*, where he writes, a propos of the mountain 'at the side of the king's residence':

> The interior of the mountain produces red *yagu* 雅姑, blue *yagu*, yellow *yagu*, blue *milan* 米藍 stones, *xilani* 昔剌泥, *kumolan* 窟沒藍, and other such [stones]; they have each and every precious stone. Whenever heavy rain occurs, the water rushes out of the earth and flows down amidst the sand; they search for and collect [the stones], and that is how they get them. There is a common saying that the precious stones are in truth the crystallised tears of Buddha the patriarch.[20]

J.V.G. Mills, Ma Huan's translator and editor, has done his best to make sense of the terminology here, as heir to a long tradition of learned wrangling going back at least to the great French sinologist, and notably combative controversialist, Paul Pelliot (1878–1945). However, there is very little point in trying to work out what such terms 'really' mean in contemporary parlance, or to tie 15th-century usage to modern definitions on a one-to-one basis. The naming of gemstones has always been (and remains) unstable and fluctuating, touching as it does on essentially unresolvable issues of the intersection between cultural value, commercial worth and the chemistry of rocks. But what is important to note in the early Ming context is that the terminology is not in origin Chinese, but is borrowed from neighbouring languages, as part of the interaction of Arab, Persian and Mongol vocabularies with Chinese, attendant on the Chinggisid hegemony in Eurasia. *Yagu* is from the Arabic *yāqūt* and first appears in the late Yuan text *Nan cun chuo geng lu* 南村輟耕錄 of 1366 by Tao Zongyi 陶宗儀 (*c.* 1316–*c.* 1402), in his discussion of various kinds of 'Muslim stones' (*huihui shitou* 回回石頭), although he uses the much more complicated graphic forms 鴉鶻 to render the word *yagu*.[21]

Despite the fact that Tao does discuss other types of 'red stones', it still seems likely that a 'red *yagu*' is what today we are calling a ruby or a spinel. They were, on Ma Huan's testimony, available at many points on the Indian Ocean littoral, at Aden for instance, in addition to those places already mentioned.[22] At Hormuz on the Persian Gulf there were red *yagu* but also red *la* 剌, which Mills identifies as the Persian word *lal*, meaning the balas ruby or spinel. It might be speculated that these are in fact the same stones as the *lazi* 蠟子 which are mentioned in the antiquarian text *Ge gu yao lun* 格古要論 of 1388 as coming from 'the Southern and Western Barbarian regions' and as being 'often [found] embossed on bracelets, bowls, cups and rings'.[23] Spinels were mined at Badakhshan, which straddles the modern Afghanistan/Tajikistan border and was then within the Timurid empire, to which the coastal city-state of Hormuz was then theoretically a vassal. The fact that Ma Huan's only specific mention of *la* comes in relation to the closest point he got to the Timurid empire is not without interest. Hormuz was also, Ma tells us, the source of 'fine vessels of jade' (*mei yu qi min* 美玉器皿), attesting to its connections with the sources of that stone deep in Central Asia, in an area also not at that point under Ming control.[24] Badakhshan is almost certainly the source of the magnificent 170-carat spinel stone in the British crown jewels known romantically since the early 19th century as the 'Black Prince's Ruby', first recorded in 1685 but quite possibly in circulation well before that.[25] There is no direct evidence for gems as part of the 'tribute' brought by any of the 78 official Timurid missions to the Ming court between 1387 and 1504 (unless they are concealed under the generic label of *fang wu* 方物, 'local products').[26] However, as in the case of the rubies of Mogok, this does not mean that the spinels of Badakhshan did not make their way by other means into the Ming empire, and the Timurid connection, which will be discussed below, is certainly an important one.

If we turn from issues of supply to those of consumption, we might ask what gems mean in the Ming context. In her magisterial cultural history of gemstones and jewellery in the early modern West, the art historian Marcia Pointon has written, 'Jewellery exists both as a unique material manifestation that blends the natural world with the skill and ingenuity of human endeavour and as ideas circulated and debated'. It acts as 'a means of conveying what is most precious in a non-material as well as a material sense'.[27] For China, we have barely begun to think about these issues, and the literature on gems is very meagre in comparison to that on the cultural value of, for example, jade. So what follows has to be speculative, an agenda for further work rather than settled conclusions, and is meant as a suggestion of several possible lines of enquiry.

One of these might be to think more intensively about the religious symbolism of jewels, in its relationship to actual material culture. A modern listing of Chinese Buddhist terminology makes the point about *bao* 寶 – 'jewel' or 'gem' – that 'this term often qualifies that which touches on the Buddha or Buddhism'.[28] This is certainly borne out by the standard English dictionary of Chinese Buddhist terms, which has no fewer than 44 entries where *bao* is the headword; these include *bao dian* 寶典 ('the scriptures'), *bao guo* 寶國 ('the Pure Land'), *bao shu* 寶樹 ('the jewel-trees of the Pure Land'), *bao zang* 寶藏, for Buddhism itself, and *bao che* 寶車 ('the precious cart'), i.e. the one vehicle, the Mahāyāna.[29] If a 'jewel cart', *bao che* 寶車, had such a meaning, it is hard to imagine that a *baochuan* 寶船, ('jewel ship', as the mightiest of Zheng He's ships were called), lacked such resonances altogether. We might also recall the concept of the Buddhist 'three jewels' (*San bao* 三寶), referenced in Zheng He's inscription of Xuande 11 [1431], recounting the miracles of the goddess Tianfei at Changle, and which later became attached to the man himself in literature and folklore.[30] Ma Huan, we might remember, reports the Sri Lankan belief that gems are the tears of the Buddha, a rare case in which not just actual gems but the lore about gems is being translated into the imaginary of the Ming empire. The term *bao* is also equally often seen as an attribute of sovereignty, as in terms such as *bao zuo* 寶座 ('throne'), or the *bao xun* 寶訓 ('Precious Instructions'), a set of texts 'containing the most important imperial edicts and orders … officially ordered for publication',[31] or even the *tong bao* 通寶 ('circulating treasure'), coins which bore the imperial reign mark and were issued only by the Ming state.

We might also ask to what extent gems were important simply because they came from outside the Ming. Like the appearance of a tribute *qilin* from Bengal, they partake of the concept of *rui* 瑞, the numinous or auspicious aspect of unusual phenomena. This is perhaps particularly so in the case of rubies, in that they seem to have a rather limited history in China prior to the Yuan period, when they appear bearing a foreign name and trailing all the allure of the exotic. Two balas rubies, or spinels, were indeed found, along with a cache of other gemstones (sapphires, topaz, chalcedony), inside a magnificent Tang dynasty (618–906) gilded silver pot excavated as part of the Hejiacun hoard in the outskirts of Xi'an in 1970. But it remains the case that for this early period 'rubies are not easily identifiable in literary and historical sources', and even the exhaustive erudition of the great scholar of exotic imports to early China, Edward Schafer, cannot cite a Tang Chinese word which refers specifically to a ruby or spinel; they were little known (and certainly not written about) then.[32] However, they predominate visually in the Ming material from the half century 1400–50, and, as we have seen, are numerically the largest single group of stones in the Prince Zhuang of Liang tomb. Does this prominence relate simply to more copious sources of supply at this period, following on from the exploitation of both land and sea routes of engagement with the rest of Eurasia? Or does it relate to changed tastes on the part of the Chinese elite, tastes which they might perhaps have shared with contemporaries elsewhere? It certainly seems to be the case that there was something of a craze for rubies, for gems of a predominantly red hue (as indeed there was for red ceramics), in many of the courts of Eurasia in the 14th and early 15th centuries. Rashid al-Din describes the garden laid out by the Ilkhanid Ghazan Khan near Tabriz in 1302, with its 'golden throne inlaid with rubies and other gems'.[33] In the same part of the world a century later, rubies and spinels were to be the Timurid gem par excellence, as when the gardens of the emir Timur himself were described in Persian poetry in these terms:

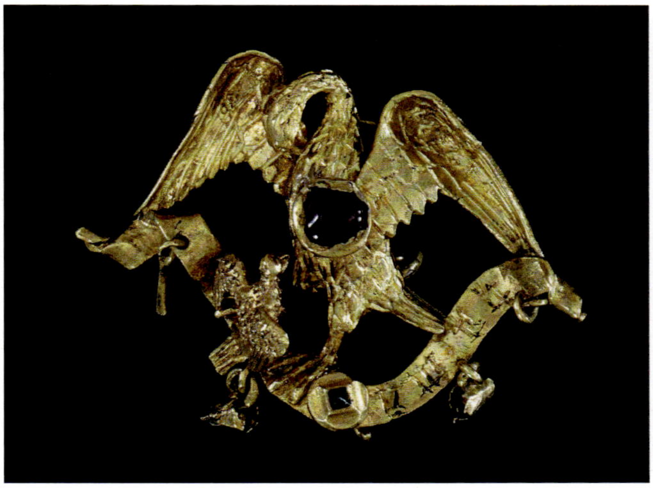

Plate 27.6 Pendant in the form of a pelican, *c*. 1440–60, Franco-Burgundian. Gold set with ruby, height 2.95cm, width 3.58cm. British Museum, London, Franks Bequest AF 2767

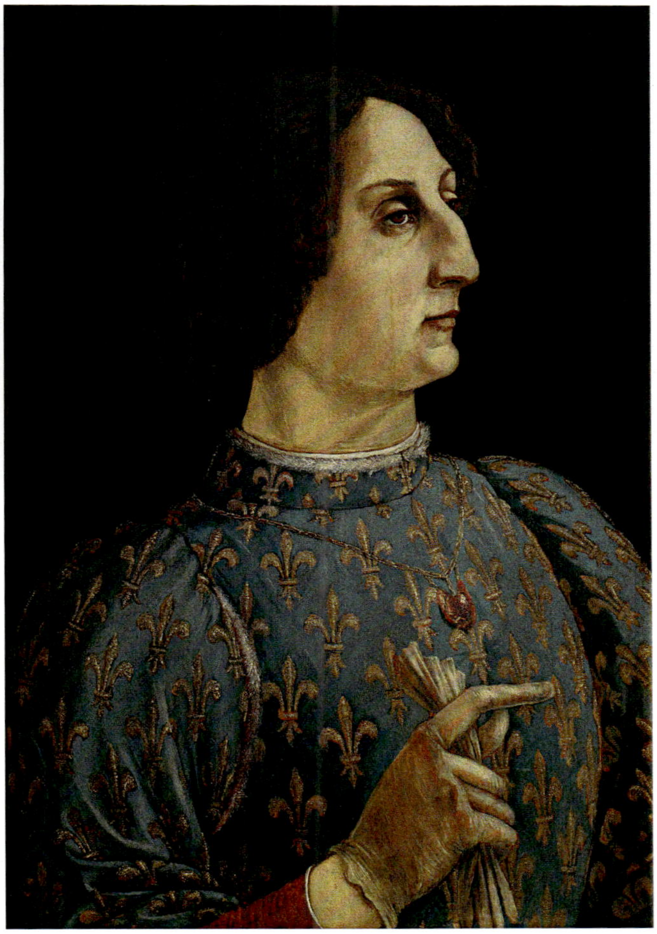

Plate 27.7 Antonio Pollaiuolo (1433–98) and Piero Pollaiuolo (1443–96), *Portrait of Galeazzo Maria Sforza*, *c*. 1471. Tempera and oil on cypress panel, height 65cm, width 42cm. Galleria degli Uffizi, Florence

> Highland and lowland, steppe and plain, were turned into pleasure parks like the gardens of paradise,
>
> Forage herbs became tulips, stones became rubies and pearls, grass became elixir, and the ground became gold.[34]

The Castilian ambassador Ruy González de Clavijo (d. 1412), in Samarqand in 1403, is our source for the observation that Timur 'wore on his head a tall white hat on the crown of which was displayed a balas ruby'.[35] For the Mughal rulers of India in later centuries, rubies were a key sign of their Timurid ancestry, and they explicitly sought out inscribed gems, several of which survive today, in Iran.[36] The flash of red attracted the eye in other parts of the world too at just this time. In South India the Tamil text *Līlātilakam*, written at Travancore between 1375 and 1400, innovatively uses the simile of rubies and coral in place of the more usual 'pearls and coral' (*maṇi-pravāḷam*) to describe the interlacing of Sanskrit and vernacular vocabularies in elegant prose.[37]

In Europe during the same era, as well as the possible case of the 'Black Prince's Ruby' (if not definitively medieval), noted above, rubies (which may also in fact be spinels) glitter prominently in the earliest surviving crown of an English queen, the so-called 'Bohemian' or 'Palatine' crown, attested as part of the English crown jewels in 1399.[38] They appear in a gold-and-ruby Burgundian badge showing the pelican in her piety (**Pl. 27.6**), as well as on the breast of the Duke of Milan, Galeazzo Maria Sforza (1444–76), whose favourite red gems all had their own nicknames (**Pl. 27.7**).[39]

It is perhaps not leaning too heavily on the evidence to postulate the sense of a gold-and-gems aesthetic combination (with rubies, the rarest of the four major gem types, particularly prominent) to set beside golden textiles as one element of a pan-Eurasian high elite material culture (to set alongside, for example, the taste for fine horses, hunting hounds and trained raptors). Is such a gold-and-rubies aesthetic in the Chinese context (and this must of necessity be highly speculative) an inheritance of a specifically Mongol glamour or, to put it more conservatively, one which at least owes its dissemination to the Mongol hegemony, and then to the 'last gasp of the *pax Mongolica*'[40] in an early 15th-century era of peace in Central Asia? Gold was certainly a colour sacred to the Mongols, with a cosmological as well as a material significance;[41] to what extent did its use in combination with red stones become a broadly understood visual language of grandeur and status in a range of post-Mongol polities? And do red gems perhaps have a specifically Ming cosmological significance, in terms of the 'five phases' cosmology of which colour symbolism was just one aspect? At first sight, this is perhaps an attractive line of argument. It is still quite common in the literature to see a claim to the effect that red was 'the symbolic colour of the Ming dynasty' and hence red gems 'a metaphor of royalty'.[42] But the contemporary evidence for this is in fact sparse. The idea that dynastic succession, the overthrow of one house by another, was governed by the order of the 'Five Phases' (or 'Five Virtues', *wu xing* 五行), such as water, fire, etc., and hence that each dynasty had 'its' colour, certainly carried considerable credence in early Chinese political thought. But by the Northern Song period (960–1127) this had been comprehensively dismissed by intellectuals such as Ouyang Xiu 歐陽脩 (1007–72), and the theory's role in explicit dynastic legitimation seems to have rapidly diminished; it does not appear as an argument in any of the official Ming sources authored by the Confucian elite.[43] There is however some evidence that fire (and hence

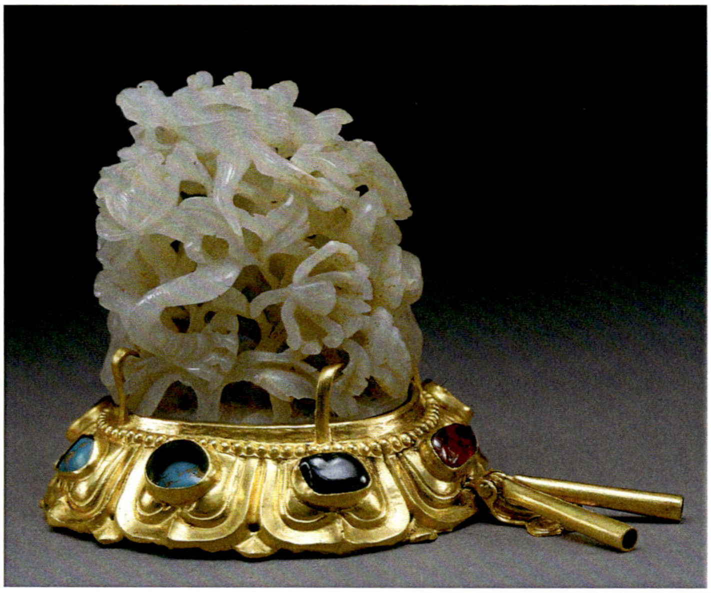

Plate 27.8 Hat-top ornament, excavated from the tomb of Zhu Zhanji, Prince Zhuang of Liang, and of Lady Wei at Zhongxiang, Hubei province, *c.* 1424–41, Nanjing or Beijing. Jade, gold, semi-precioius and precious gems, height 6.3cm, diameter 6.6cm. Hubei Provincial Museum

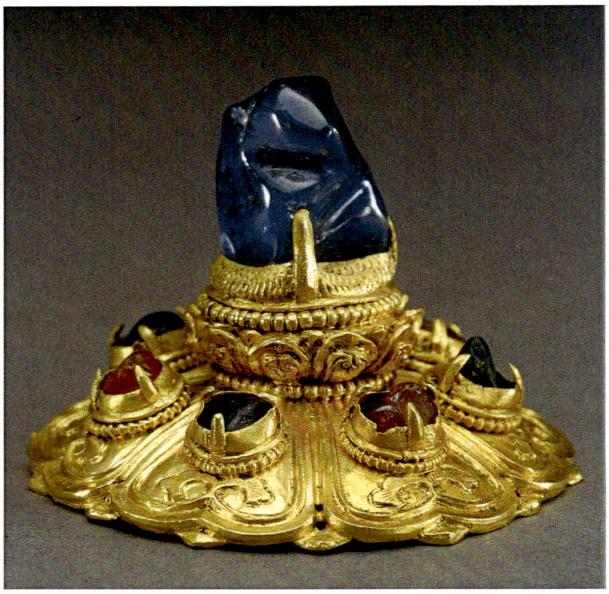

Plate 27.9 Gold hat-top ornament, excavated from the tomb of Zhu Zhanji, Prince Zhuang of Liang, and of Lady Wei at Zhongxiang, Hubei province, *c.* 1420–41, Nanjing or Beijing. Gold with seven gem stones, height 3.9cm, width 5.2cm. Hubei Provincial Museum

the colour red) was promulgated as the supporting virtue of the peasant armies who fought against the Mongols at the end of the Yuan dynasty. These armies included (but were not restricted to) those led by the Ming founder Zhu Yuanzhang, fire having been sometimes seen as the phase indicative of the Song dynasty, which they ostensibly (at least initially) fought to restore.[44] It is very tempting therefore to posit the material evidence as telling us something about beliefs which might have been held within the imperial clan about the protective force of the colour red, even if these beliefs go unrecorded in sources written by those subscribing to the now-orthodox position that it was the ruler's virtue, and not the preordained succession of Five Phases, which governed the rise and fall of dynasties. Certainly the red rubies are by far the most prominent of the five differently coloured gemstones in the filigree gold plaques that make up the magnificent princely belt excavated from the tomb of Prince Zhuang of Liang (see **Pl. 27.5**). The use of 'red, white, blue, yellow, black' (in that order, and here the term used for 'red' is *chi* 赤) is ordained

Plate 27.10 Gold hat-top ornament, excavated from the tomb of Zhu Zhanji, Prince Zhuang of Liang, and of Lady Wei at Zhongxiang, Hubei province, *c.* 1424–41, Nanjing or Beijing. Gold with ten gem stones, height 7.5cm. Hubei Provincial Museum

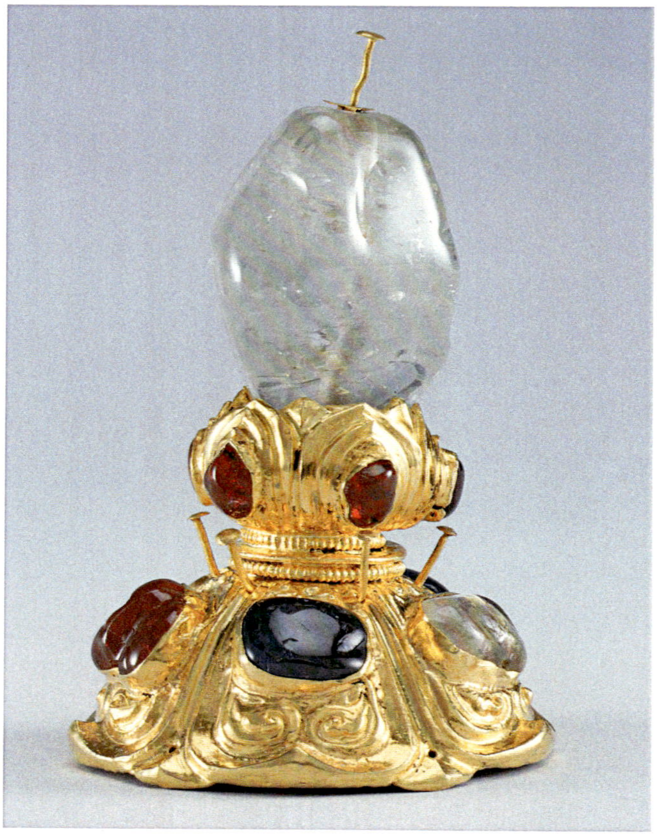

Plate 27.11 Gold hat-top ornament, excavated from the tomb of Zhu Zhanji, Prince Zhuang of Liang, and of Lady Wei at Zhongxiang, Hubei province, *c.* 1424–41, Nanjing or Beijing. Gold with 18 gem stones, height 3.4cm. Hubei Provincial Museum

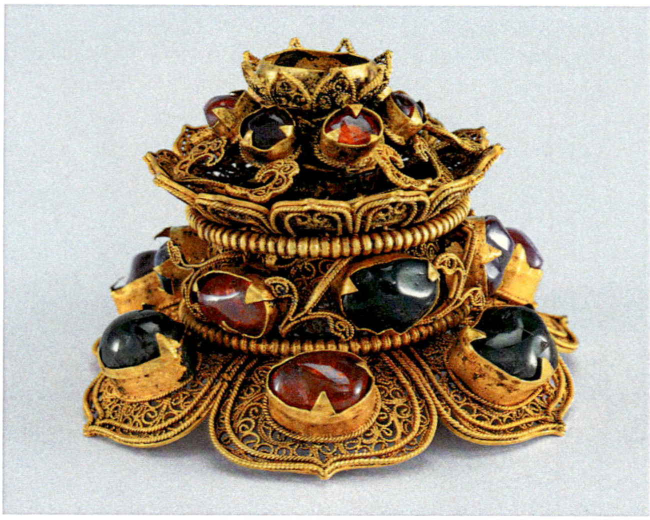

in the context of belt ornaments in the relevant section of dress regulations for imperial princes found in the *Da Ming huidian* 大明會典 (*Collected Statutes of the Great Ming*).[45] The Prince Zhuang belt conforms to this prescription to a degree, except that blue gems are substituted for white, and the black ornaments provided by organic materials such as wood or rhinoceros horn have all perished due to immersion in water, leaving one empty collet on each plaque.[46] Does the prominence of rubies then have a cosmological significance? While not ruling this out, it seems wiser to consider that such prominence may owe as much to the rarity, and hence value, of rubies in a pan-Eurasian context of multiple successor states to Mongol hegemony, all equally aware of what constituted glamorous and splendid princely accoutrements.

In the Chinese case, the early Ming inheritance from the Yuan in the realm of elite material culture is certainly becoming ever more evident. Although the excavators of the Prince Zhuang of Liang tomb initially assigned all the gem-encrusted hat buttons (**Pls 27.8–11**) to the Yuan period, on the grounds presumably of their similarity to hat ornaments seen in Yuan imperial portraiture, it seems more prudent to share the scepticism of Lu Xixing and David Robinson, preferring to see these rather as a Ming continuation of a Yuan format, one of many.[47] Even so, there is a degree of divergence within this (admittedly small) body of objects, with the example shown in **Plate 27.11** displaying a completely different aesthetic to those shown in **Plates 27.8–10**, where the solid settings contrast with the elaborate filigree of the former piece. And the variety does not stop there: **Plate 27.8** is dominated by an elaborate openwork jade carving of a dragon, while **Plates 27.9–10** culminate in a single large vertical gem. A hat button of this latter type, topped by a red gem, is visible atop the central figure in the anonymous but certainly early Ming-period scroll, *Hunting by a Lake*, now in the Palace Museum, Beijing (**Pl. 27.12**), and they appear in several 15th-century imperial portraits as well. As we have seen, such hat buttons were also very much a Timurid fashion; indeed the Ming envoy Chen Cheng 陳誠 (d. after 1457), who was in the Timurid capital of Herat in 1414–15, observed how the dandies of the city 'have gems and jewels on their heads to manifest their extravagance'.[48] One other object type with a similarly wide range might be the kind of jewel-encrusted belt now under discussion, which along with jewelled robes played a prominent part in diplomatic exchange across Eurasia.[49] A Yuan ambassador gave the Delhi sultan Muhammad b. Tughluq an example of the latter (along with slave girls, textiles, aromatics and weapons) in 1340.[50] In Ma Huan we read how the King of Calicut, in South India:

> wished to send tribute; [so] he took fifty *liang* of fine red gold and ordered the foreign craftsmen to draw it out into gold threads as fine as a hair; these were strung together to form a ribbon, which was made into a jewelled girdle with incrustations of all kinds of precious stones and large pearls ...[51]

At this high end of precious metal working, shared technical traditions could cover large areas of the premodern world. There are for example very close similarities of technique and decoration between Indian and Chinese silver filigree work of the 18th century, such

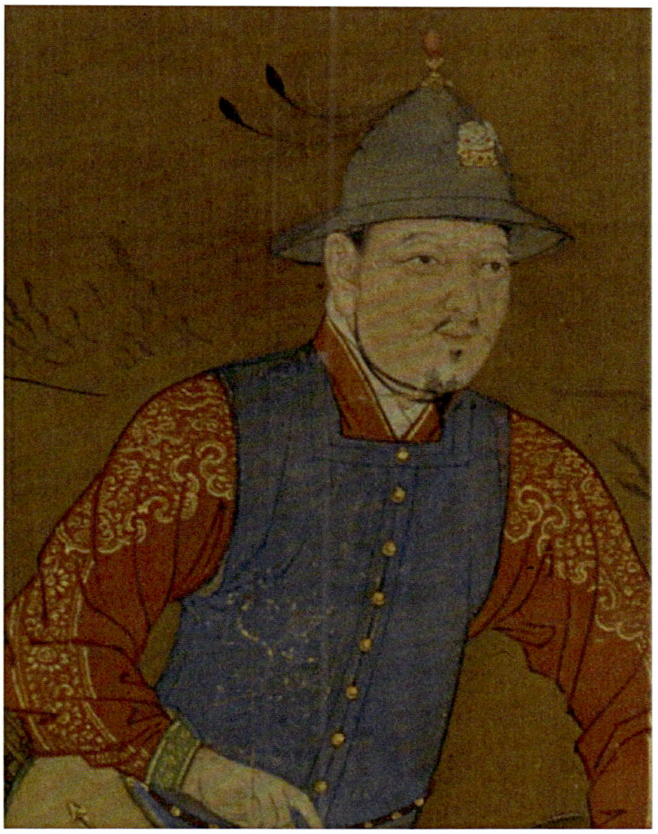

Plate 27.12 Detail from ***Hunting by a Lake*** (***Hupan shelie tu*** 湖畔射獵圖), ***c.*** **1426–35, Beijing. Ink and colour on silk, image height 107cm, width 123.5cm, with mount height 208cm, width 142cm. The Palace Museum, Beijing**

that individual objects have been variously identified as both Indian and Chinese in manufacture.[52] While there can be no suggestion that the Prince Zhuang of Liang belt is actually of Indian manufacture, it is reasonable to posit that it partakes of an internationally understood language of esteem and kingly exchange. At the very least, it recalls the 'golden waist belts' which the ruler of Bengal gave to the Chinese ambassador Hou Xian 侯顯 (like Zheng He, a eunuch) in 1415, or the 'two gold belts inlaid with jewels' which the ruler of the Arab state of Aden presented to the Ming envoy who turned up on his shores.[53] Thus from Hubei to Bengal to Aden, and arguably further to the west as well, a gold belt studded with gems (and perhaps particularly with red gems) was a meaningful shared symbol of sovereign esteem, along with the fierce and exotic animals and fine horses and weapons which similarly had passed as gifts between princes throughout the 14th and into the 15th century.[54] These astonishing objects help us to think outside the framework of nationally bounded cultures and artistic traditions and to see the ways in which courts of many kinds mediated contact and exchange in a world where the cosmopolitan allure of the Great Khans continued to gleam and glitter.

Notes

Particular thanks go to Peter Ditmanson, Jérôme Kerlouegan and David Robinson for readings of this chapter, which helped to sharpen the argument and provided several key references.

1 Mills 1970, 73–5; the Chinese text consulted is that also used by Mills: Ma Huan 1955, 1–2. See also Wan Ming 2005.
2 Clunas 1987.
3 For convenient surveys see Nanjing shi bowuguan 2004, also Yang Zhishui 2011.
4 Sun Laichen 2010, 172.
5 Hubei sheng wenwu kaogu yanjiusuo and Zhongxiang shi bowuguan 2007, I, 206, 317–21, 322–7.
6 Clunas and Harrison-Hall 2014, 85.
7 Clunas and Harrison-Hall 2014, 152–3.
8 E.g. Clunas and Harrison-Hall 2014, 54, 58.
9 Morgan 2008, 1.
10 Elverskog 2010, 35, citing Liu Xinru 1994, 177.
11 Lin Meicun 2014, 76, 83.
12 Fernquist 2005, 297–8.
13 Sun Laichen 2010, 172, 175.
14 *MSL Taizu shilu* 244.2b–4a (29/2/庚寅), Wade 2005b, http://epress.nus.edu.sg/msl/entry/3081.
15 *MSL Taizong shilu* 192.1a (15/8/甲申), Wade 2005b, http://epress.nus.edu.sg/msl/entry/2440; *MSL Taizong shilu* 216.1a (17/9/丙午), Wade 2005b, http://epress.nus.edu.sg/msl/entry/2637; *MSL Yingzong shilu* 38.5b–6a (3/1/癸卯), Wade 2005b, http://epress.nus.edu.sg/msl/entry/701; *MSL Yingzong shilu* 20.3a–b (1/7/戊申), Wade 2005b, http://epress.nus.edu.sg/msl/entry/218.
16 Mills 1970, 90; Ma Huan 1955, 9.
17 Mills 1970, 105–6, 141, 143; Ma Huan 1955, 21, 45, 47.
18 Elverskog 2010, 83; Mills 1970, 64.
19 Hall 2010, 112, 116–17.
20 Mills 1970, 127–8 (romanisation converted to pinyin); Ma Huan 1955, 37.
21 Tao Zongyi 1980, *juan* 7, 84–5.
22 Mills 1970, 155; Ma Huan 1955, 58.
23 David 1971, 126 identifies *lazi* as 'wax opals', but the description seems to fit rubies or spinels at least as well (not least because of the reference to their great value), and it is noteworthy that there is no alternative term for these stones in this text.
24 Mills 1970, 170; Ma Huan 1955, 67.
25 Keay 2012, 92–3.
26 Zhang Wende 2006, 266–74.
27 Pointon 2009, 3.
28 Raguin 1985, 278.
29 Soothill and Hodous 1937, 476–8.
30 Full text in Vermeer 1991, 113.
31 Franke 1968, 199.
32 Michaelson 1999, 120–1 (thanks to Carol Michaelson for this reference); Schafer 1963, 334.
33 O'Kane 1993, 250.
34 Balabanlilar 2007, 28–9.
35 Alexander 2004, 142 (thanks to David Robinson for this reference).
36 Dale 1998, 46; for an example of a necklace containing such engraved spinels, see Watson 2008, 124.
37 Freeman 1998, 38–65 (58).
38 Keay 2012, 19.
39 McCall 2013, 459.
40 Elverskog 2010, 197.
41 Gerritsen 2012, 249–50.
42 Li He and Knight 2008, 52.
43 Liu Pujiang 2007 (thanks to Peter Ditmanson for this reference).
44 Liu Pujiang 2007, 536–7; Chen Gaohua 1979 (thanks to David Robinson for this reference).
45 Shen Shixing 2007, *juan* 60, 377.
46 Hubei sheng wenwu kaogu yanjiusuo and Zhongxiang shi bowuguan 2007, I, 169–70.
47 Lu Xixing 2012; Robinson forthcoming.
48 Rossabi 1983, 53.
49 For a Timurid example in the Metropolitan Museum of Art see http://www.metmuseum.org/toah/works-of-art/1989.87a-l [accessed 10 September 2015].
50 Sen 2006b, 432.
51 Mills 1970, 146; Ma Huan 1955, 49.
52 E.g. a silver box, Victoria and Albert Museum 1982, no. 337, and Archer, Rowell and Skelton 1987, no. 188.
53 Sen 2005, 508; Mills 1970, 159; Ma Huan 1955, 58.
54 Robinson 2013b, 285–7.

Chapter 28
Ming Ceramics Discovered in Kenya and Some Related Issues

Qin Dashu

From 2010–13, Peking University and the National Museum of Kenya undertook a project entitled 'Sino–Kenyan Cooperative Archaeological Project in Lamu Archipelago Areas',[1] sponsored by the Ministry of Commerce of the People's Republic of China. As part of this project, the School of Archaeology and Museology of Peking University carried out excavations and also conducted a thorough study of Chinese ceramics unearthed in Kenyan coastal areas from previous archaeological excavations and surveys.

Research on Chinese ceramics in Kenya's coastal areas

The joint archaeological team from Peking University and the National Museum of Kenya conducted three studies of Chinese ceramics unearthed in Kenya. The examined objects were from 37 sites or shipwrecks located through formal excavation and investigations at locations along the Kenyan coast from 2010 to 2013. These included Fort Jesus in Mombasa,[2] the Gedi Ruins of Malindi,[3] the site of Shanga on Pate Island[4] and the Manda town ruins on Manda Island.[5] Chinese ceramics of unknown provenance held at the Fort Jesus Museum, the Gedi Ruins Museum and the Lamu Museum were also examined. A total of 9,552 Chinese ceramic sherds were collected and studied from these varied sources. An additional 1,060 Chinese ceramic sherds uncovered during the excavation projects and a small number of Japanese and Southeast Asian ceramics were analysed and sorted. In terms of scale, this Kenyan coastal project is the second biggest of all the sites around the Indian Ocean rim to have yielded finds of Chinese ceramics. The largest project is the work on Chinese ceramics from the site of Fustat, the old town of Cairo.[6]

The project proceeded as follows: 1) selecting and piecing together ceramic sherds excavated from Kenyan coastal sites; 2) conducting a typological study identifiying the place of manufacture, the classification of types and dating the finds; 3) compiling statistics according to their types; 4) measuring, cataloguing and illustrating the samples (**Pl. 28.1**), and photographing all the ceramics with a colour chart in raw format; 5) creating a database of Chinese ceramics from the coastal areas of Kenya and publishing the final report. The research methodologies were as follows:

Plate 28.1 The China-Kenya joint archaeology team illustrating Chinese ceramics unearthed in Kenya

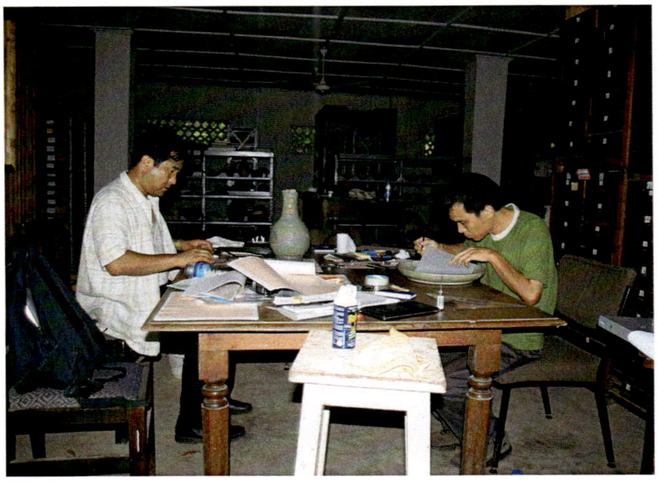

1. The identification of production areas or kiln origins and the dating of objects were mainly done by visual observation. To ensure the reliability of the results, experts of each type of ware were invited to review these findings. For example, researchers familiar with Yue, Longquan, Jingdezhen and Fujian kiln sites from Zhejiang and Fujian Provincial Archaeological Institutes as well as the Palace Museum in Beijing were invited to Kenya to participate in the evaluation of these ceramics. Archaeometric analysis of unearthed ceramics was performed by Associate Professor Cui Jianfeng of Peking University who visited Kenya twice to conduct the on-site elemental analysis of the Chinese ceramics. The Thermo-Fisher Scientific's Niton XL3t 900 handheld x-ray fluorescence (XRF) analyser was used to analyse the glazed surface of the samples. The data of ten elements, Zirconium (Zr), Strontium (Sr), Rubidium (Rb), Thorium (Th), Iron (Fe), Manganese (Mn), Titanium (Ti), Scandium (Sc), Calcium (Ca) and Potassium (K), was collected for statistical analytical purposes. The underglaze colour elements of some of the Yuan dynasty blue-and-white wares, underglaze copper red wares and the blue-and-white wares in Fort Jesus Museum were analysed to identify the sources of the pigment materials and their dating. More than 1,000 records were made. The handheld analyser has proven effective in the identification of kiln origins. Therefore, the results are reliable and have served as the foundation for further research.
2. Each of the 37 sites of the Kenyan coastal area where Chinese ceramics were found have been investigated and five sites were excavated by our team. All 9,552 Chinese shards were treated as one unit. After dating and identifying their production kiln, shards were analysed in detail. Since the 1960s, research on Chinese ceramics from the sites located along the Indian Ocean rim has focused on identifying the types of wares at each individual site at a particular time. With a detailed statistical study, a better understanding of the export of Chinese ceramics can be achieved.
3. Archaeological information was extracted from each sample. Some types of Chinese porcelain shards were unearthed in large numbers and were sorted using archaeological typological methods. As a result, they can be studied from different perspectives in the future.

As the preliminary study is now complete, the researchers involved in the project, including the author, are engaged in analysing the materials obtained in Kenya, comparing and contrasting them with Chinese ceramics found around the Indian Ocean rim at other sites as well as in China itself, in addition to the eventual writing of the final report. The reports of some of these areas are, however, complete and have yielded some significant preliminary results.[7] This chapter will discuss some of these findings, focusing specifically on Ming ceramics found at Kenyan coastal sites as well as some important related issues of the Ming dynasty's ceramics trade and its history in general.

General overview of the Chinese ceramics excavated from Kenyan coastal areas

East Africa, or more precisely the terminal of the South China Sea and Indian Ocean rim, was an important node in trading networks. Starting from the 9th century, cities in modern-day Kenya and Tanzania were important locations in the trading circle of the Indian Ocean rim. Unearthed ceramic wares found in East Africa show that there was a long history of the exportation of Chinese ceramics to this region. A number of Changsha (**Pl. 28.2**) and Ding wares of the 9th century, Yue wares of the 10th century (**Pl. 28.3**) as well as 10th-century Fanchang white wares of Anhui province have been unearthed in Kenyan coastal areas. Research has shown that the large scale export of Chinese ceramics by sea began in the mid-8th century and rapidly reached a peak in the late Tang to early Northern Song dynasty in the 9th–10th centuries.[8] During this period a range of ceramic exports reached East African coastal areas, which were the terminals of Chinese ceramic exportation. At this time, however, the ceramics were imported through entrepôts.

Chinese ceramics discovered in East Africa show that a second peak was reached during the late Southern Song to early Ming dynasty in the 13th to early 15th centuries when Chinese merchants travelled to the East Africa regions.[9]

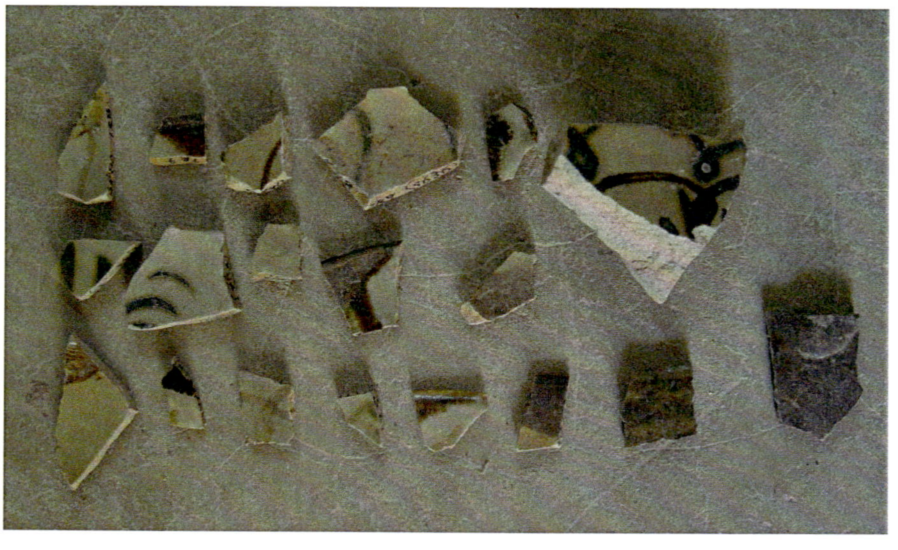

Plate 28.2 Changsha ware shards of the 9th century unearthed from Shanga site, Pate Island

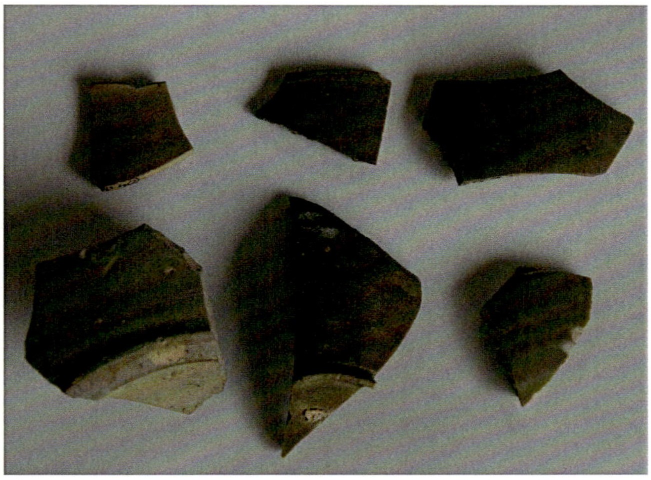

Plate 28.3 Yue ware shards from the 10th century unearthed from the site at Shanga, Pate Island

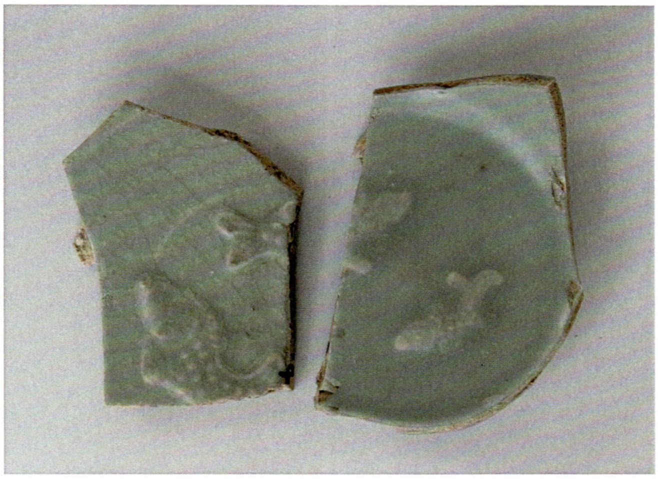

Plate 28.4 Longquan wares from the 13th century excavated from the site at Mambrui, Kenya

During this second phase, the quantity of Chinese ceramics discovered in East Africa increased tremendously and Longquan wares formed the majority of exported goods (**Pl. 28.4**). This was the most prosperous era in the trading of Chinese ceramics in the region before the later colonial period. The most important episode during the early Ming dynasty was Zheng He's navigations. Zheng He visited Africa at least twice and according to researchers, landed at a few sites along the Kenyan coast. The Chinese ceramics discovered in the coastal areas of Kenya provide key material evidence of Zheng He's presence in Africa as this chapter will discuss.

In the 15th and 16th centuries, East Africa was the first stop for Westerners when they entered the Indian Ocean. In 1498, Vasco da Gama landed in Malindi after rounding the Cape of Good Hope. The Portuguese controlled East Africa during the 16th century, and used it as a springboard to establish colonies east of Africa. The trade route of Lisbon–Malindi–Goa–Melaka was created and eventually extended to the southeast region of China. During this period, the volume of ceramic trade expanded rapidly and even surpassed that of previous eras.

The coastal areas of Kenya that represent the Swahili region of East Africa played a strategic role in the ancient trade circle of the South China Sea to the Indian Ocean, and in the global trade system that gradually evolved in the 15th and 16th centuries. The Chinese ceramics that have been unearthed in these areas were important trade wares and through tracing their export from China to regions along the Indian Ocean rim, it is possible to obtain a better understanding of the wider changes that occurred over time in the history of Chinese maritime trade.

The Ming dynasty represents a crucial period in the history and development of Chinese maritime trade and the Chinese ceramics discovered in Kenya demonstrate the state of ceramic exports at this time, especially to the Indian Ocean rim regions. Among the 9,552 pieces of Chinese ceramics unearthed from the 37 sites or museum collections studied, 2,523 items (26.41%) are Ming ceramics. Among the Ming ceramics, 753 objects (29.85%) are from the early Ming, 171 (6.78%) are mid-Ming (Chenghua to Zhengde reigns) and 1,599 (63.38%) are from the late Ming to colonial period. Chinese ceramics unearthed from two key sites in Kenyan coastal regions and the accompanying data will be used as evidence to discuss two important issues surrounding the export of Ming ceramics.

The 'Ming Gap' in Chinese ceramic exports during the early Ming

The term 'Ming Gap' was coined by Tom Harrisson in light of the fact that no sign of trading activity during the Ming dynasty had been found, not even in the form of broken pieces of ceramics, along 100 miles of the coast of southwest Borneo despite the discovery of millions of sherds from the pre-Ming period in the area.[10]

In 2004, Roxanna M. Brown, then Director of the Southeast Asian Ceramics Museum at Bangkok University, confirmed the existence of a 'Ming Gap'. She listed 15 shipwrecks containing Chinese and Southeast Asian ceramics discovered in the Southeast Asia region to show that Ming dynasty policies banning or curtailing private foreign trade caused the end of the ceramic trade that up until this point had been monopolised by China. Dr Brown identified two types of shortages: a general scarcity of Chinese ceramic during the years 1325–80 and a severe shortfall of specifically blue-and-white porcelain in 1352–1487. These two shortages were again referred to by Brown as the 'Ming Gap'.[11] Her views were well received by academics and the 'Ming Gap' became a common feature in discussions among experts in connection with the Ming dynasty's export of ceramics and believed by many to be a consequence of the Ming dynasty's ban on private overseas trade.

The phenomenon of the almost non-existence of blue-and-white Chinese ceramics during the late Yuan and early Ming has been partially proved in the East Africa coastal areas. Only a few Yuan dynasty blue-and-white shards were found in Kenya and almost no early Ming blue-and-white shards have been discovered. However, it is incorrect to say that no Chinese ceramics were exported during the early Ming period. Dr Brown's conclusions relied on ceramics recovered from shipwrecks discovered in Southeast Asia and it should be pointed out that these do not always provide a complete picture of the trading situation because materials

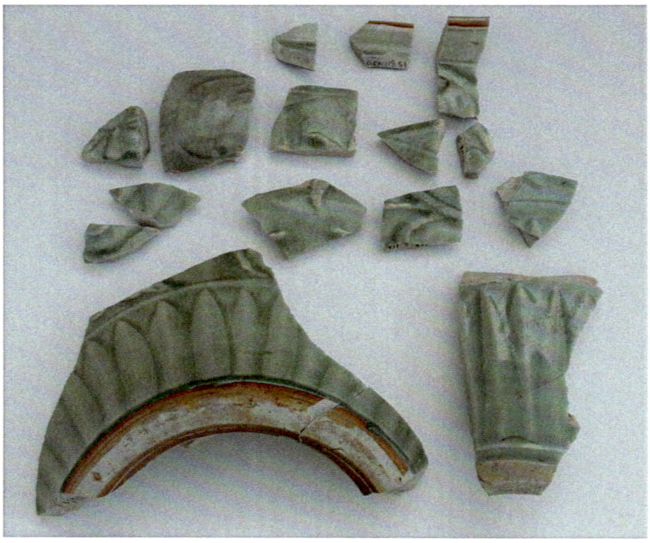

Plate 28.5 Longquan ware shards from the early Ming period (early 15th century) unearthed from Gedi Ruin

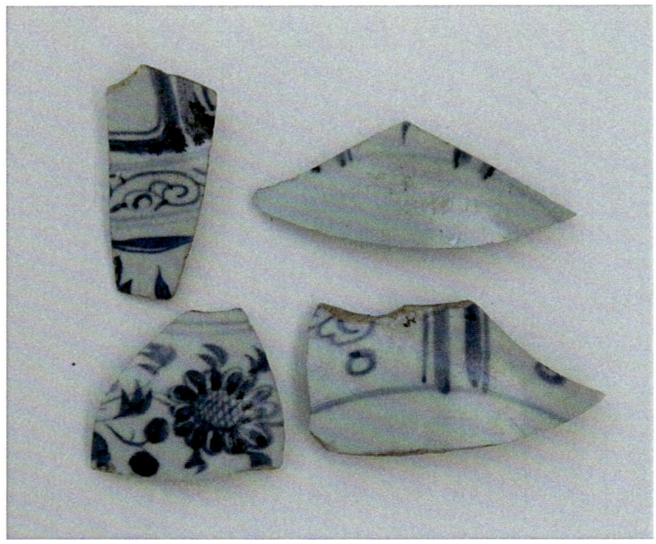

Plate 28.6 Blue-and-white shards from the Yuan dynasty unearthed from Gedi Ruin

recovered in underwater discoveries are unhelpful in terms of context. In order to examine the quantity of Chinese ceramic exports from a chronological perspective, studying a coherent context or stratum of an ancient trading site is a better way of understanding the issue of the evolution of the export of Chinese ceramics.

Research by our team as part of this project in the coastal areas of Kenya shows that the absence of export ware during

Plate 28.7 Underglazed copper-red Yuhuchun vase unearthed from Gedi Ruin (restored)

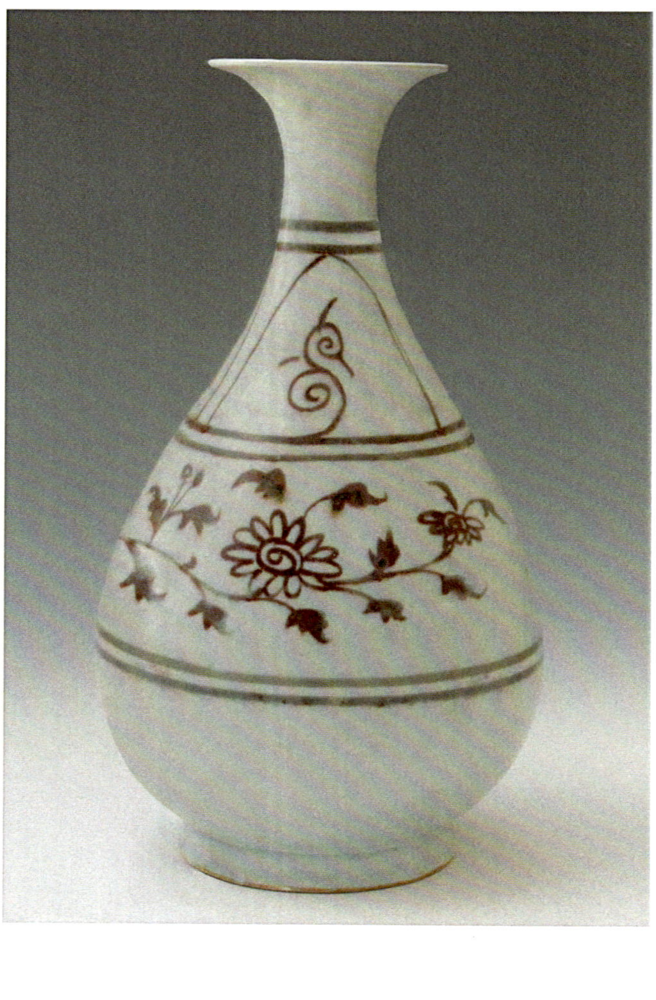

the late Yuan to the Hongwu reign (1325–98) in the early Ming period is due to the fact that there is not enough material from shipwrecks to cover this period in time. However, there are sufficient discoveries on land to show that the 'Ming Gap' did not exist at this time. The Longquan kilns have been extensively excavated in recent years and the dating of late 14th and 15th century wares is now more securely linked to archaeological evidence from the production sites in the Longquan area of Zhejiang province. A large quantity of Longquan ware dating to this period has been discovered along the coast of Kenya (**Pl. 28.5**), in addition to a few blue-and-white (**Pl. 28.6**) and underglaze copper-red wares from Jingdezhen (**Pl. 28.7**).

Following on from this, we can now use data derived from our investigation of Chinese ceramics unearthed from the Gedi Ruins on the outskirts of Malindi to examine thoroughly the state of Chinese ceramic exports during the late Yuan to early Ming periods. The Gedi site is located 15km southwest of Malindi in the central part of the Kenyan coastal region. It was the largest and most important ancient settlement in the region and judging by the size of the site, academics believe that it was a settlement of 3,000 people. On the basis of archaeological excavation and related research, scholars estimate that it was built in the 12th or 13th century. It slowly developed into a prosperous settlement and lasted until the 16th century when it was abruptly abandoned. James Kirkman was in charge of archaeological excavations at the site for a period of more than ten years from 1948[12] and it is the most extensively excavated site in the Kenyan coastal area. As part of our project, we conducted research on all the ceramic pieces (a total of 1,257) excavated from the site, identifying the areas of production and determining the dates of manufacture.[13]

In terms of the production areas, 732 pieces (58.23%) were Longquan wares (including Longquan type wares made in the broader area of Longquan in China), 469 (37.71%) were made in Jingdezhen, 30 (2.39%) were Fujian wares, 14 (1.11%) were from Guangdong, 1 (0.08%) was Cizhou ware and 6 pieces (0.48%) remain unidentified. An investigation into the Longquan wares revealed that almost none of them could be dated to the Southern Song and most of them were from the Yuan and early Ming dynasty. Only four pieces were dated to the mid-Ming.

In terms of production date, the findings were as follows:

- Apart from the six pieces of unidentified wares, only two (0.16%) of the 1,251 pieces of datable wares could be attributed to the Southern Song and they are both Qingbai wares of Jingdezhen.
- Of the total number of items, 289 pieces (23.1%) were dated to the early and middle period of the Yuan dynasty (1276–1332). Among these wares, 256 (88.58%) were Longquan wares, 30 (10.38%) were Fujian, 2 (0.69%) were from Guangdong and 1 piece (10.35%) was Cizhou ware.
- There were 217 pieces (17.35%) of the total items that could be dated from the late Yuan to early Ming period (1333–1403).[14] Among these objects, 182 pieces (83.87%) were Longquan wares (including Longquan Type) and 35 (16.13%) pieces were from Jingdezhen, including some blue-and-white shards.
- Early Ming pieces from the Yongle to Xuande reign (1403–35) totalled 292 (23.34%). During this period, 290 items (99.32%) were Longquan wares and 2 (0.68%) were Jingdezhen wares, mostly dating from the Yongle to Tianshun reign period (1403–64).
- One hundred (7.99%) of the total number of items were dated to the mid-Ming (Chenghua to Zhengde reign, 1465–1521). During this period, 4 pieces (4%) were Longquan wares, 90 (90%) were from Jingdezhen, of which most were blue-and-white, and 6 (6%) were Guangdong wares.
- There were 351 pieces (28.06%) of the total number of items that could be dated to the late Ming (Jiajing, Longqing, Wanli and Tianqi reigns, 1522–1627). During this period, 345 pieces (98.29%) were from Jingdezhen and 6 pieces (1.71%) were Guangdong wares (all shards of a storage jar).

The statistics surrounding the Chinese ceramics from the Gedi Ruins, especially the figures from the late Yuan and early Ming period, show that the quantity of exported Longquan wares was much larger than that of Jingdezhen wares at this time. The issue of resolving the problem of the 'Ming Gap' is related to an increase in knowledge concerning the dating of Longquan ware. The alleged lack of Chinese ceramic exports during the early Ming is due to the fact that the early Ming Longquan celadons have been incorrectly dated to the Yuan period.[15] As a result, it is now clear that the scale of ceramic export at this time was not small, but was in fact dominated by Longquan wares. In her study Roxanna Brown also mentioned that there was no export of blue-and-white ceramics from the late Yuan to the end of the Chenghua reign (1352–1487), but this has also been disproved as blue-and-white and underglaze red wares of the late Yuan and early Ming have been discovered in Kenya as shown in this chapter.

In examining the Chinese ceramics discovered at sites in the South China Sea and the Indian Ocean rim, it is possible to believe that the commonly held notion that the Zheng He navigations represented the peak of a new trading era is contradicted by the fact that there are seemingly only limited archaeological discoveries of materials from this period. Indeed this does seem to cast doubt on the nature of Zheng He's navigations and the true extent of trade during this period.[16] However, Longquan wares unearthed from many sites related to Zheng He and this period have previously been dated to the Yuan period or even earlier to the Southern Song. Therefore, after studying and comparing these wares with kiln site finds in China and other Longquan wares, these finds unearthed in Africa and even from other regions of the Indian Ocean rim can be re-dated as early Ming products. If we distinguish the Yuan and early Ming Longquan wares correctly, and apply statistical analysis to them, we come to the conclusion that the early Ming was in fact an extended part of the peak of Chinese ceramic exports that had developed since the Yuan dynasty.

The official export of Longquan ware during the early Ming

The excavation of the Fengdongyan kiln in 2006 confirmed that this was the production site of official Longquan wares from the early Ming period, as recorded in historical literature.[17] The excavation results improved our

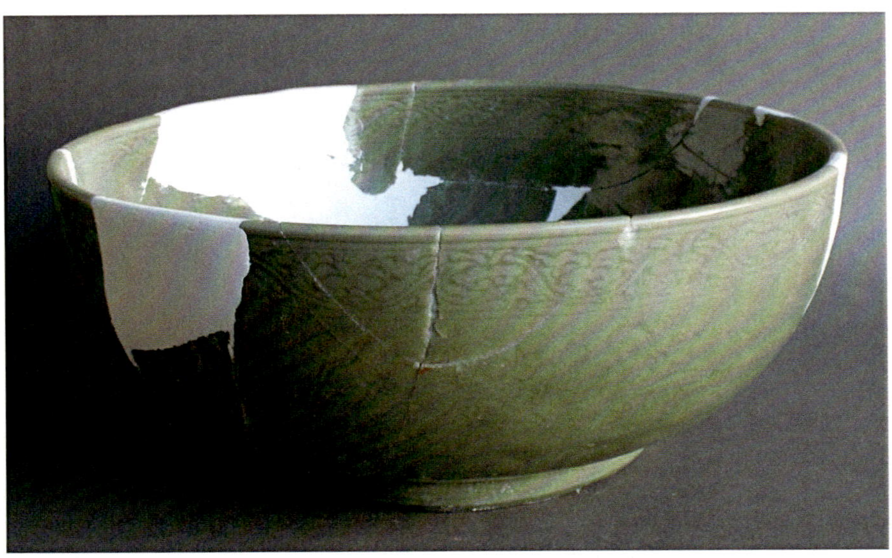

Plate 28.8 Large official Longquan ware bowl, Hongwu period, 1368–98, unearthed from Fengdongyan kiln site, Dayao, Longquan. Height 16.4cm; diameter 40cm

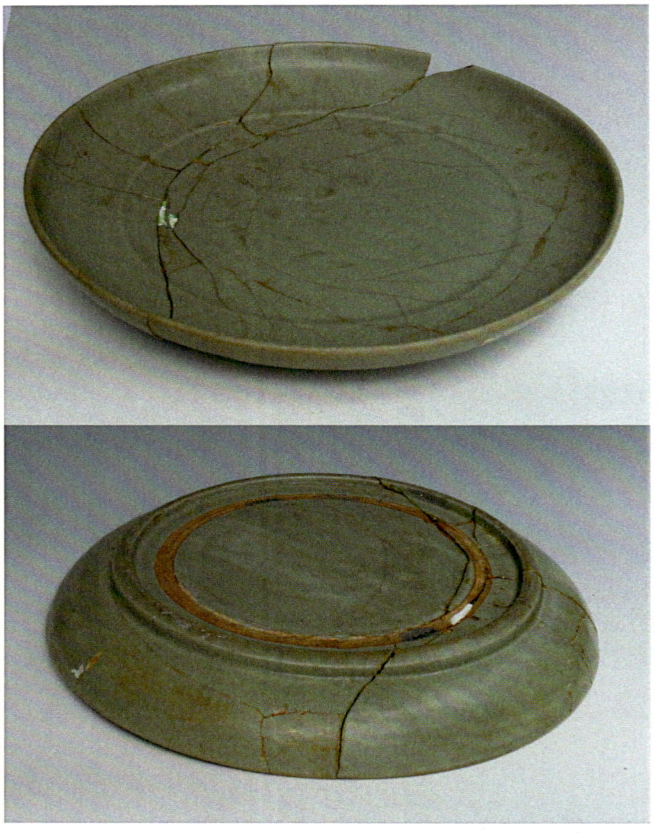

Plate 28.9 Official Longquan dish unearthed from Ungwana site, Kenya

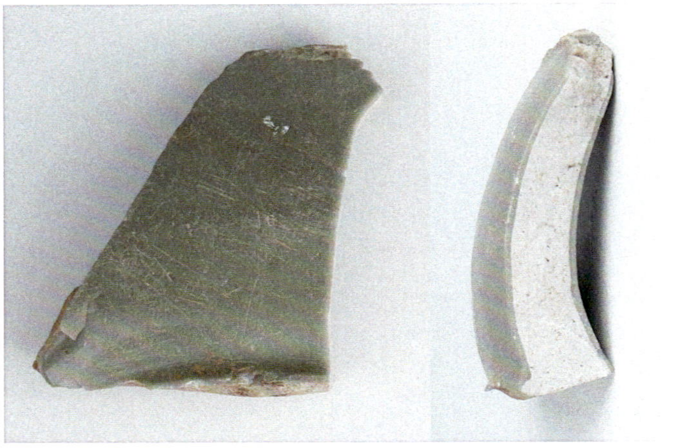

Plate 28.10 Official Longquan shard of a large bowl unearthed from the site at Mambrui

understanding of these official wares that acted as a form of tribute from Chinese kilns to the imperial court at this time. The objects were finely made, with regularly and neatly formed thick bodies. Thick green glaze had been applied evenly and the glaze has a notable gloss (**Pl. 28.8**). The unglazed ring on the base for supporting the object during firing was always very regular in shape, showing that great care had been taken when scraping away any unwanted glaze. The shape of the objects and the decorative designs were quite similar to the official blue-and-white wares of Jingdezhen. This is a distinctive feature and in this respect they were unlike the regular Longquan wares used by the ordinary people of the period.[18] Through use of this feature, our team identified some of the Longquan wares unearthed from the Kenyan coastal areas as early Ming official wares. These include the celadon dish with incised lotus from Ungwana (**Pl. 28.9**), the incised celadon bowl from Ishakani in Coast province, the celadon bowl with moulded medallion from the Gedi Ruins and the sherds of official Longquan wares found at the sites of Shanga, Pate Island and Mambrui (**Pl. 28.10**).

Plate 28.11 The large official Longquan dish collected in Topkapı Palace Museum, Istanbul, Turkey

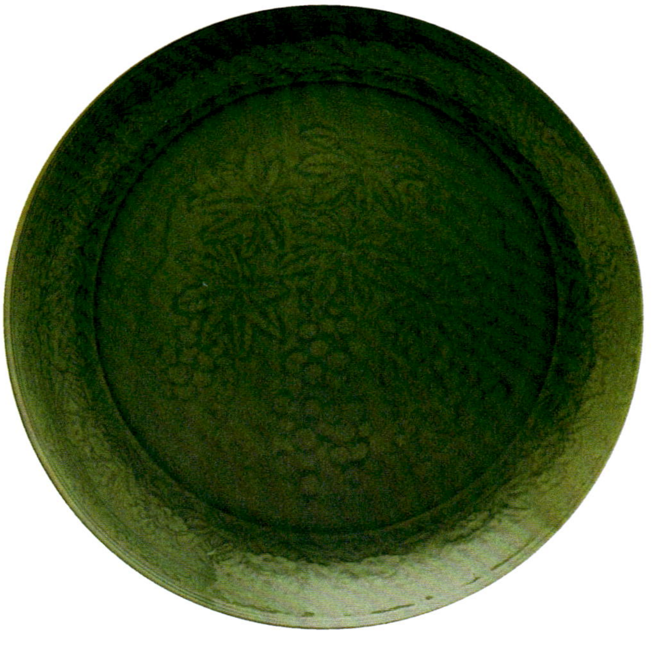

In order to have a better understanding of the early Ming Longquan wares found in East Africa, I have carefully studied the examples of celadon produced as tribute in Longquan. Family tombs of even the most important officials of the Ming court such as Xu Da 徐達 (1332–85), Mu Ying 沐英 (1345–92) as well as princes and marquises do not contain this type of tribute ware from Longquan. Of the hundreds of early Ming Longquan wares unearthed from tombs throughout the country, not one example of this type has been found. There are about 20 to 30 pieces of this type of Longquan official ware in the Beijing Palace Museum, most of them handed down from ancient times.[19] This confirms the exclusive nature of the tribute wares, which were made only for the imperial court. However, such wares have also been discovered at important places overseas. For example, the Topkapı Saray in Istanbul has a large collection of these types of Longquan wares (**Pl. 28.11**).[20] This means that early Ming Longquan wares might have been used for trading and that Longquan tribute wares designed by the imperial court were specially made as gifts for foreign countries. This is recorded in the *Collected Statutes of the Great Ming* under the entry of 'Ministry of Works'.[21] Therefore, Longquan official wares were ordered by the Ministry of Works, used on official occasions and presented as gifts to other countries. The popular large dishes and bowls of the Yongle reign might have been made in Longquan kilns specifically for the voyages of Zheng He so that they could be presented as gifts to the rulers of the countries he visited. In any case, these discoveries of imperial wares provide strong evidence that Zheng He visited the coastal areas of Kenya.

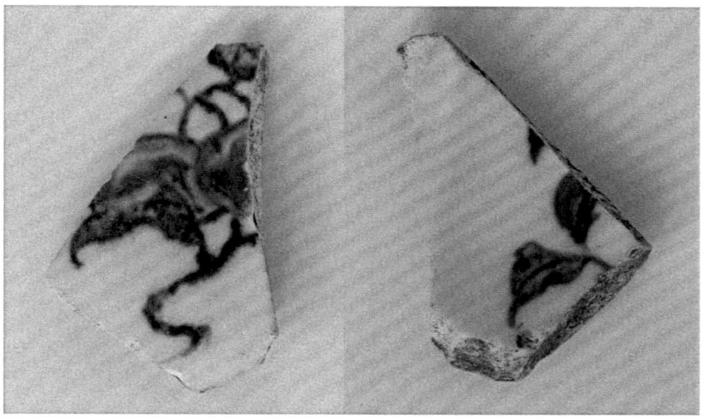

Plate 28.12 Jingdezhen official kiln blue-and-white shard excavated at the site of Mambrui

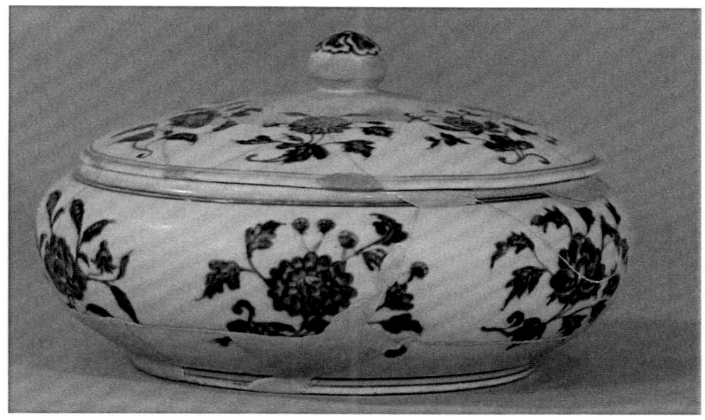

Plate 28.13 Jingdezhen official kiln blue-and-white jar with lid, excavated from Dongmentou, Zhushan, Jingdezhen in 1994. Height 14.8cm; diameter 25.8cm. Jingdezhen Institute of Ceramic Archaeology

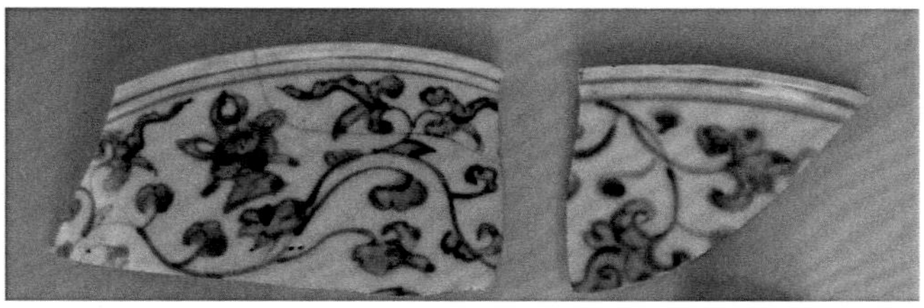

Plate 28.14 (above) Jingdezhen blue-and-white shards of Hongzhi to Zhengde period excavated from Mambrui site

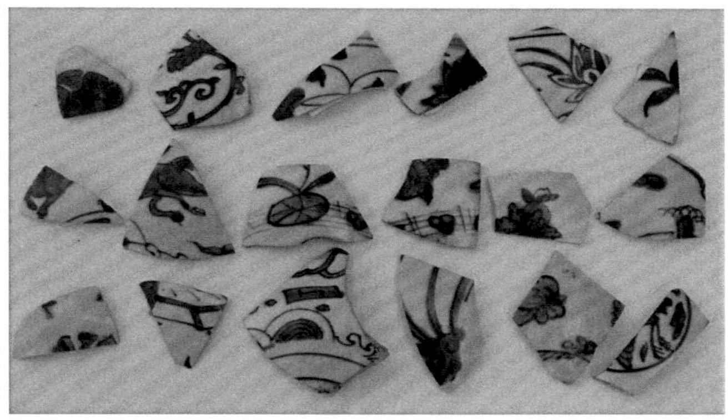

Plate 28.15 (right) Jingdezhen blue-and-white shards of Jiajing reign unearthed form Gedi Ruin

A Chinese researcher studying the 14 locations of East Africa on the 'Zheng He Navigation Chart' (*Zheng He hanghai tu* 鄭和航海圖) has identified seven locations where Zheng He probably landed. The name 'Man Ba Che' (慢八撤) marked on the chart has been identified as Mambrui.[22] Significantly, excavations at the site of Mambrui by our joint archaeological team have yielded a piece of blue-and-white imperial ware of the Yongle reign (**Pl. 28.12**) which may come from a blue-and-white jar with a lid from the official kiln of the Yongle reign (**Pl. 28.13**) and a *Yongle tongbao* 永樂通寶 (Circulating treasure of the Yongle era) coin.[23] An official Longquan ware shard was also found at the same site (see **Pl. 28.10**). These archaeological materials provide conclusive evidence that Zheng He visited Kenya in East Africa and that Mambrui was one of the possible places where he landed.

The increase of Chinese ceramics during the mid-Ming period

During the Chenghua, Hongzhi and Zhengde reigns (1465–1521), the quantity of Chinese ceramics at the Gedi Ruins and Mambrui increased tremendously, representing a brief upturn in Indian Ocean rim maritime trade controlled by the Arabs and Persians. For a long period of time, the coastal areas of East Africa maintained a close relationship with West Asia and the Middle East. The dominance of Arab and Persian trade ended when the Portuguese came to Africa. From the end of the Xuande reign to the early years of the Chenghua reign (1436–65), there was an extremely low level of Chinese ceramic production and trade and we found very few shards from this period in Kenya. However, starting from the Chenghua reign, Chinese ceramic production increased and the scale of ceramic export became relatively large during a short period of time (**Pls 28.14–15**). This was the result of internal changes within the Ming dynasty when the manufacture of various products that represented the development of market economy increased and had an impact on society. The silver standard of the monetary system was formed in this period which needed more silver in exchange for material goods. This caused a shortage of silver and consequently led to stronger reliance on imported silver.[24] The rapid commercialisation of goods resulted in the flourishing of illegal trade along the coastal regions of China and ceramics were one of the most important cargos in this illicit trade. Consequently, Chinese porcelain of this period is found in fairly large numbers along the Indian Ocean rim and Southeast Asia, thereby reflecting the whole trading system of the entire Ming dynasty and not just that of East Africa.

Notes

I hereby wish to acknowledge Jessica Harrison-Hall and Dr Virginia L. Bower who have helped proofread and improve this chapter. Their dedication is much appreciated. Gratitude also goes to Dr Li Baoping for his continuous work on improving the text.

本研究為“國家社會科學基金重大項目《非洲出土中國古代外銷瓷與海上絲綢之路研究》”（項目批准號：15ZDB057）的成果之一。本研究得到指南針計劃專項項目“東非地區出土中國古代外銷瓷的綜合研究”的資助。 This article is one of the outcomes of a major research project funded by the China National Social Science Fund: 'The Study on Chinese Export Ceramics Found in Africa and the Maritime Silk Road' (Project Number: 15ZDB057), with the support of China National Planning Office for Philosophy and Social Science. It is also supported by the 'Integrated Research on the Exported Ceramics of Ancient China Found along the Coast of East Africa', which was sponsored by the Compass Plan Project of State Administration of Cultural Heritage.

1 In 2011 the government dissuaded the team from undertaking excavation and research for security reasons.
2 Kirkman 1974.
3 Kirkman 1954.
4 Horton *et al.* 1996.
5 Chittick 1984.
6 Qin 1995.
7 Liu Yan *et al.* 2012; Qin *et al.* 2014.
8 Qin 2013.
9 The famous Yuan dynasty navigator Wang Dayuan (1311–?), author of *Daoyi Zhilüe* (*A Simplified Description of the Ocean's Shores*), made his two major trips from Quanzhou on merchant ships. His first trip was in the first year of Zhishun (1330) when he travelled to Somalia and Mozambique. The second trip was in the third year of Zhiyuan (1337) when he returned to Mozambique. Both of his trips were on merchant ships, indicating that Chinese merchants had already been to Africa by this time. Wang Dayuan recorded more than 220 places in Asia, Africa and Australia in *Daoyi Zhilüe*: 'What I recorded is what I visited, experienced and what I saw and heard. Legends and stories are not mentioned in this book' (Wang Shixing 1981). Ma Huan, the author of *Yingya Shenglan* (*The Overall Survey of the Ocean's Shores*), who participated in three of Admiral Zheng He's maritime expeditions, complimented Wang Dayuan's documentation: 'After visiting and seeing in person, I know what the author of *Daoyi Zhilüe* documented are real facts' (Ma Huan 1985).
10 Harrisson 1958; Tai 2011.
11 Brown 2005; Brown 2009.
12 Kirkman 1954.
13 A preliminary report was published about our study of Chinese ceramics unearthed from the Gedi Ruins in 2012. However, some more shards from the Gedi Ruins were found in storage during the course of our investigations in 2013. Because of this, the statistics used in this chapter are slightly different from those in the brief report. See Liu Yan *et al.* 2012.
14 Longquan ware from the late Yuan and early Ming dynasty are very similar which is why we have considered them as coming from one time period.
15 In 2006, the Zhejiang Provincial Institute of Cultural Relics and Archaeology and the School of Archaeology and Museology at Peking University formed a joint archaeological team to conduct an excavation on the Fengdongyan kiln site at Dayao, Longquan city (Zhejiang sheng wenwu kaogu yanjiusuo *et al.* 2009). During the excavation, the strata of the Hongwu and Yongle periods were discovered. Among the Yongle strata, three shards with the incised date of the Yongle reign were unearthed and thus confirmed the reliability of the date of the strata. Subsequently, some researchers have continued detailed comparative studies on the unearthed materials from the strata of the Yuan, early Ming and mid-Ming periods (Xu Jun 2009; Shen Jun 2014). These studies have significantly enhanced our knowledge about the early Ming Longquan ware, followed by the discovery that many formerly identified Longquan ware of the Yuan dynasty are actually products from the early Ming period.
16 Wang *et al.* 2014.
17 Zhejiang sheng wenwu kaogu yanjiusuo *et al.* 2009.
18 Xu 2009.
19 Qin *et al.* 2009.
20 Krahl 2001.
21 In *Da Ming huidian*, vol. 194, 'Ministry of Works no. 14', the entry of 'pottery wares' recorded: 'In the 26th year of Hongwu reign edict: Firing of imperial wares and others must have designs of the examples approved, the materials and labours calculated. If large quantity has been counted, the potters shall be sent to the capital for setting up the kilns and for the production of the porcelain. If less quantity has been counted, works are delegated to Raozhou state and Chuzhou state under the order of Ministry of Works.' (Shen Shixing 2007). We know from this record that Raozhou 饒州 State (present-day Jingdezhen 景德镇) and Chuzhou 處州 State (present-day Longquan 龍泉) both accepted official orders from the government to produce imperial objects. They made ordered objects from sample designs and requested the same standards of production. A further record consulted has shown that Longquan undertook the manufacture production of official wares from the 26th year of Hongwu reign (1393) to the first year of Chenghua (1465).
22 Shen Fuwei 2004.
23 China had long exported copper coins through smuggling since ancient times. The coins were mainly used as raw materials to recast as new objects. Despite numerous government edicts forbidding the exportation of copper coins since the Song dynasty, the smuggling of these coins continued. Therefore, a copper coin of *Yongle tongbao* found overseas does not necessarily mean that the findspot was one reached by Zheng He's voyage. But, if the coin is taken into consideration with the Longquan official ware sherds and the Jingdezhen Yongle official blue-and-white sherds discovered in Mambrui, they become relatively secure evidence for the argument that Zheng He's fleet had landed there.
24 Wan 2004.

Chapter 29
Traces of the Zheng He Voyages in Late Ming Navigational Materials

Timothy Brook

During the first half of the 15th century, the Ming imperial household famously dispatched seven expeditions under the command of the eunuch Zheng He 鄭和 (1371–1433), as well as many smaller maritime embassies under other command, to the rulers of what we now call South and Southeast Asia. The navigational knowledge and nautical lore these expeditions would have required to reach destinations around the Indian Ocean – and having reached them, could have enlarged in turn – must have been enormous. 'Must have been', because almost nothing of this knowledge survived in the public record in China in later times. Whatever charts, route guides (known to Elizabethan Englishmen as 'rutters') and voyage diaries were produced in the course of engaging in this vast diplomatic traffic were deposited with the imperial household. There they were embargoed as state intelligence to which only the court could be privy, and eventually destroyed. Not a shred of primary documentation survives from the Ming central administration, and yet traces are to be found in certain late Ming sources.

Three well-known documents of the late Ming reveal, however, that some of this knowledge escaped the centripetal vortex of the political centre.[1] One is the so-called 'Laud rutter', named in honour of Archbishop William Laud

Plate 29.1 Laud rutter or *Dispatched on Favourable Wind* (*Shunfeng xiangsong* 順風相送) in Chinese, 16th century. The Bodleian Libraries, The University of Oxford, MS.Laud Or.145

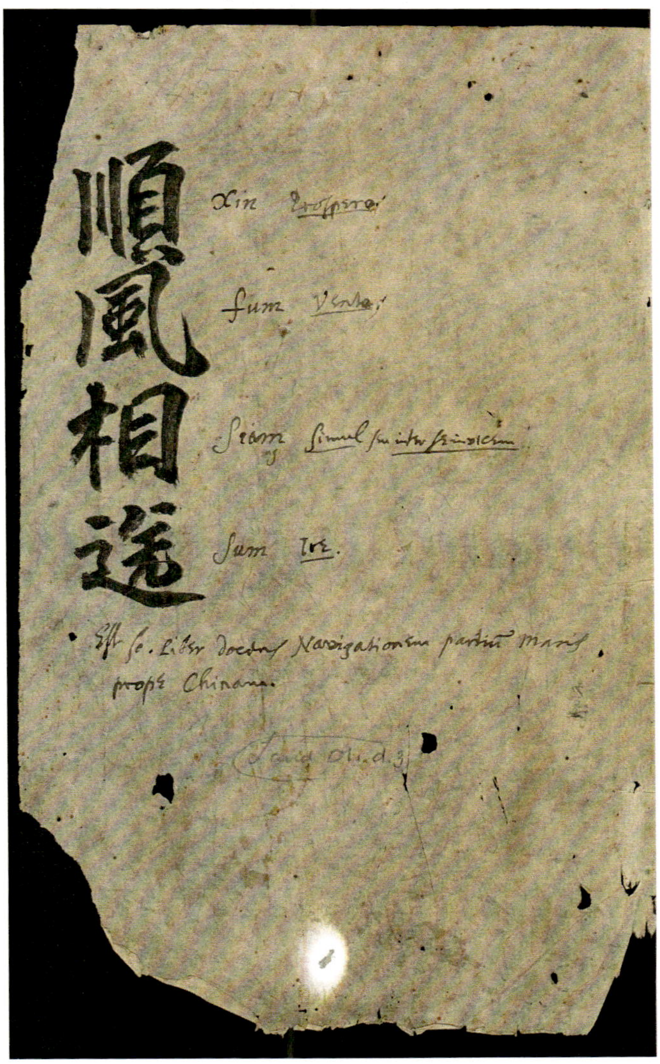

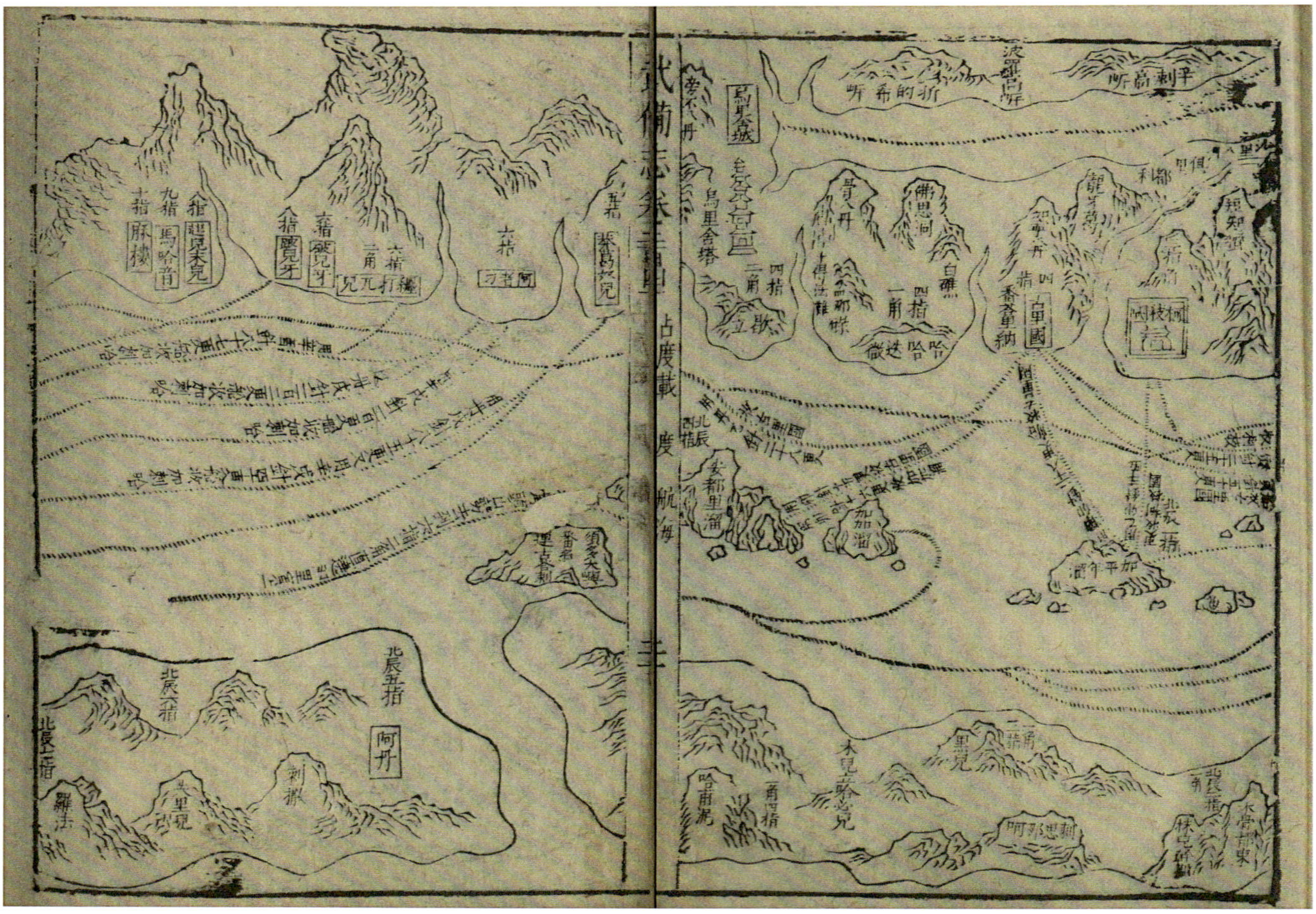

Plate 29.2 ***Treatise on Military Preparedness*** **(*Wubei zhi* 武備志), 240.20a–b. Tianqi period edition, 1621–7. National Library of China**

(1573–1645) who presented it to the Bodleian Library at Oxford in 1639, presumably after it had been in his possession for some years.[2] A rutter is a handbook listing the distances and directions that a mariner should take when following a maritime route. The Laud rutter is a compilation that presents all the routes from China to Southeast Asia and the Indian Ocean in a one-fascicle manuscript handwritten in Chinese (**Pl. 29.1**). As the anonymous but literate editor relates in his preface, his book is not an actual rutter but an edited compilation based on handwritten records that he was able to acquire. The correctness of the data presented in the text he attributes entirely to the Zheng He voyages, noting that 'in the first year of Yongle [1403] envoys were ordered to go to the countries of the Western Ocean to present edicts, and so had multiple opportunities to compile and correct [knowledge of] compass routes'.[3] Probably acquired by an agent of the East India Company in the first two decades of the 17th century, the Bodleian manuscript must originally have belonged to a Chinese merchant working outside China in the commercial networks around the South China Sea. Had this manuscript not been removed from circulation and deposited in a foreign library, it would never have survived to the 1930s, when the historian Xiang Da 向達 (1900–66) transcribed it during an academic sojourn in Oxford. State jealousy of frontier knowledge and private jealousy of craft knowledge, a deadly combination from the historian's point of view, would otherwise have conspired to guarantee its destruction.

The next exception to the disappearance of the knowledge that the Zheng He expeditions used and generated is the set of route charts (**Pl. 29.2**) which Mao Yuanyi 茅元儀 (1594–1640) compiled in the late 1610s and included as chapter 240 of his grand survey of military affairs, *Wubei zhi* 武備志 (*Treatise on Military Preparedness*). These charts, which vary in scale from page to page, show the principal routes along which the eunuch envoys and their military entourages passed. These routes are marked as dotted lines on the water without great precision, though many are annotated in great detail with the compass bearings marking the route. This is navigational information of a precise sort, indicating that Mao Yuanyi had access to a source preserving detailed first-hand knowledge of the Zheng He sailings. It has been suggested that Mao's source was a private record that his grandfather, Mao Kun 茅坤 (1512–1601), acquired in the mid-16th century while working on *Chouhai tubian* 籌海圖編 (*Illustrated Compendium on Maritime Defence*), a massive official compilation of data concerning coastal administration at the height of piracy in the Jiajing era (1522–66). If he ever had it, Mao Kun did not draw on it for his project, as far as we can detect. By the time of Mao Yuanyi, information concerning navigation routes to the Indian Ocean no longer excited state sensitivity. Even to members of the court in the Tianqi era (1621–7), it was obvious that Chinese ships, and indeed ships from all over the world, were plying these routes in numbers that defied the presumption that this knowledge should be construed as secret.

The final exception to the loss of navigational information from the 15th century differs in many ways from the previous two. This is Zhang Xie's 張燮 *Dongxi yang kao* 東西洋考 (*Study of the Eastern and Western Seas*) completed in 1617, the ninth chapter of which is devoted to navigational information. Zhang produced the book in response to a request for information on maritime matters from the magistrate of Haicheng 海澄 county, who had jurisdiction over Moon Harbour (Yuegang 月港), the port in Zhangzhou 漳州 prefecture from which merchants were setting forth in ever greater numbers through the Wanli era (1573–1620). That a local official in this period should want this information signals a significant reversal in the vector of maritime knowledge back from the private sector to the state sector, where it was no longer regarded as contraband. Zhang's book was not published at the time, but it was not embargoed and circulated well enough to have survived until it was published in a mid-19th-century collectanea.[4]

Dongxi yang kao postdates the Laud rutter. Like the Laud editor, Zhang has heavily edited and reorganised the information he had drawn from pilots' rutters rather than simply reproduce a primary document from the 15th century. In fact, Zhang is not much interested in what happened in the 15th century at all, but instead restricts the material he includes to that which is of relevance to the present. He divides his route data into the standard late Ming categories of 'water routes within the harbour' (meaning the coastal zone off Zhangzhou and Quanzhou 泉州), 'Western Ocean compass routes' (the network of routes running southwards down the coast of continental Southeast Asia) and 'Eastern Ocean compass routes' (the network of routes running eastwards out to the Pescadores and the Philippines and down to Borneo). Both the eastern and western route networks end at points beyond which Chinese junks did not sail. The Western Ocean routes stop at Aceh at the northern end of Sumatra, as that marked the westernmost port at which Chinese vessels called. That Zheng He and company went beyond Aceh is of no account to Zhang Xie. He is curious as to how contemporary information is overlaid on earlier knowledge, and in suitable scholarly fashion tracks some of that knowledge back to sources from the Song and before, but for him history is past. The traces of Zheng He's voyages in *Dongxi yang kao* are thus rather faint, nothing more than curious footnotes that help construct the story of the state of play of Ming maritime networks as of 1617.

Stepping back from Zhang Xie, we can observe that knowledge of the Zheng He voyages survived in private commercial circles not because late Ming captains were intent on pursuing the political or geostrategic purposes that struck fear into imperial hearts. (Bear in mind that the expeditions were initiated because the Yongle emperor, facing a severe legitimacy deficit as a usurper and for nepoticide, hoped that the presentation of tribute by foreign rulers would demonstrate to a domestic audience that he enjoyed the mandate of Heaven).[5] Ming merchants in fact had no interest in such matters. If information about the routes Zheng followed was important to them, it was because these were simply the routes that every navigator sailing out of Ming coastal waters took. Memories of Zheng

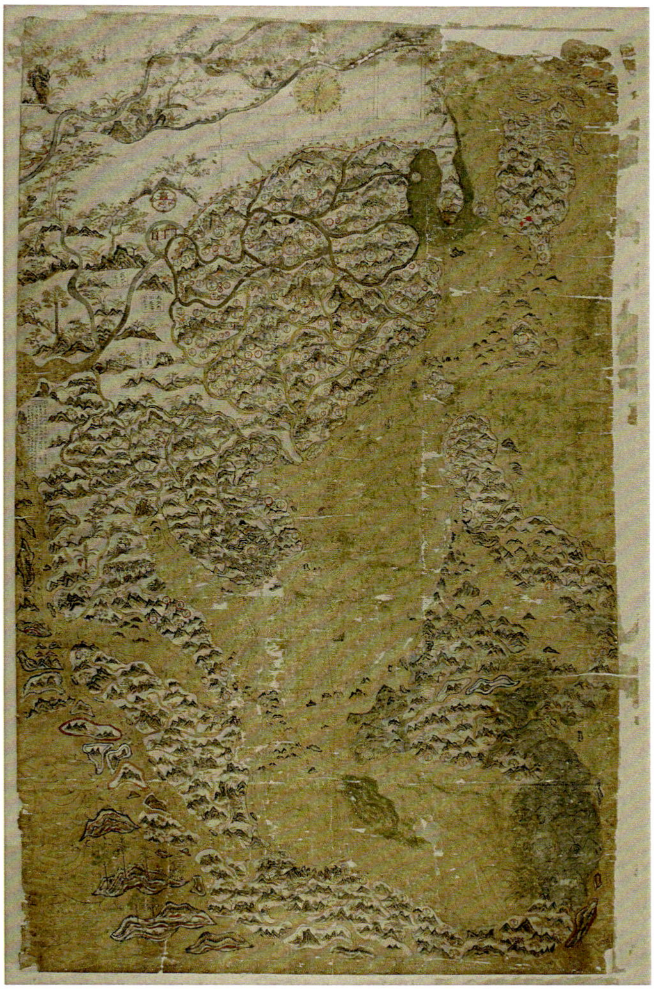

Plate 29.3 The Selden map of China, *c.* 1608. Watercolour and ink on paper, height 160cm, width 100cm. The Bodleian Libraries, The University of Oxford, MS. Selden supra 105

He had no monopoly on these routes; he simply travelled in the same sea lanes that everyone else used. What for the Ming court was diplomatic knowledge was for mariners practical knowledge. Still, that portion of navigational knowledge that by the late Ming had no practical application was preserved. Conspicuous in this regard are the instructions for sailing across the Indian Ocean. This was a traverse that Chinese ships made in the 15th century but not in the 16th, when the ingress of armed Portuguese vessels into the region discouraged the Chinese from sailing beyond the Straits of Melaka. The editors of the Laud rutter and *Wubei zhi* nonetheless both elected to include information about sailing routes across the Indian Ocean, even though no one was using this knowledge in the late Ming – which is why Zhang Xie left it out. The fact that these routes may have been moribund for a century did not dissuade the other two. Nor, as we are about to see, did it discourage the creator of a fourth late Ming document of Chinese maritime lore, the Selden map (**Pl. 29.3**).

The Selden map is the first Chinese map since the Yuan dynasty to situate China in relation to the world beyond its shores in a way that takes account of the actual distances separating any one place on the map from any other, particularly maritime sites outside the realm.[6] Probably drawn about 1608 by a Chinese cartographer working in the

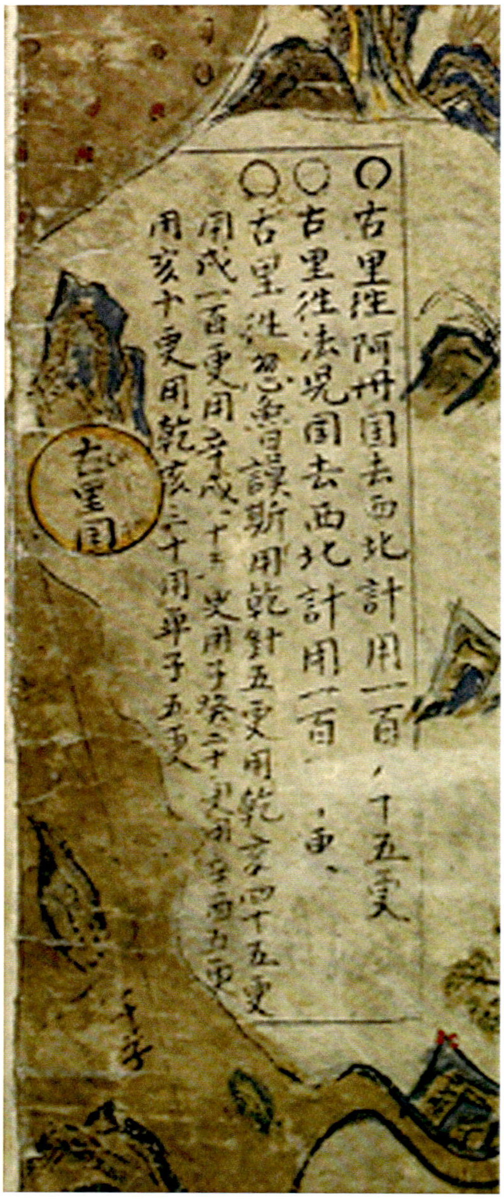

Plate 29.4 The Calicut colophon of the Selden map

western Javanese port of Bantam, it is also unique in depicting sailing routes, a feature not previously found on any other chart on this scale anywhere in the world. Radiating from a point in the Taiwan Strait off Moon Harbour into several networks extending north, east and south directions, these lines show the viewer where cargo vessels travelled, attesting the map as a whole to be a presentation of commercial rather than political knowledge. When examined alongside the routes recorded in the Laud rutter and *Dongxi yang kao*, the route networks on the Selden map roughly correspond to what is found in those books, though with minor variations – the existence of which is significant in indicating a degree of variability in knowledge, and in turn in the unknown sources of that knowledge.

The routes on the Selden map extend across and beyond the entirety of what are now known as the East and South China Seas, extending as far southeast as the Moluccas and as far west as the end of the Melaka Strait. Accordingly, the routes the eunuch armadas followed coincide with only about a third of the routes on the chart, a reminder that whatever the Selden map is, it is *not* a record of Zheng He's travels. On close inspection, however, the Zheng voyages have left a clear trace on the map in the form of a rectangular colophon at the left-hand edge of the map directly to the east of a city marked as Calicut (Chinese *Guli* 古里, modern Kozhikode, Kerala State, south India). In the 15th century, Calicut was the main trade entrepôt between West and East Asia; European travellers during the centuries before and after the 15th regularly referred to 'ships from Calicut' when describing maritime trade in the Indian Ocean.[7] But Calicut is on the southwest coast of India, not where the Selden cartographer has put it in roughly where we would locate Rangoon, thereby collapsing completely the Bay of Bengal. Mislocating Calicut so radically goes against the considerable topographical accuracy that the map otherwise displays, indicating that the cartographer had no knowledge of the Indian Ocean. Placing it where he has is surely of no help to sailors. Still, he felt compelled to include the port and the colophon for epistemological reasons that we will return to at the end of this chapter.

The colophon (**Pl. 29.4**) presents a series of three directions from Calicut to the south coast of Arabia, each marked by a circle, which in translation I transpose to consecutive numbering:

(1) from Calicut to the country of Aden, go northwest for 185 watches.

(2) from Calicut to the country of Dhofar, go northwest 150 watches.

(3) from Calicut to Hormuz, sail on a 315° bearing for 5 watches, on a 322½° bearing for 45 watches, on a 300° bearing for 100 watches, on a 292½° bearing for 15...watches, on a 7½° bearing for 20 watches, on a 277½° bearing for 5 watches, on a 330° bearing for 10 watches, on a 322½° bearing for 30 watches, and on a bearing of true north for 5 watches.

(1) 古里往阿丹國，去西北，計用一百八十五更。

(2) 古里往[佐]法兒國，去西北，計用一百五十更。

(3) 古里往忽魯謨斯，用乾針五更，用乾亥四十五更，用戌一百更，用辛戌一十五更，用子癸二十更，用辛酉五更，用亥十更，用乾亥三十，用單子五更。

The Calicut colophon consists of three types of data: destination, direction and distance. The destinations are three ports along the south coast of the Arabian peninsula, west to east: Aden at the mouth of the Red Sea; Dhofar in Oman, a port known today as Salalah; and Hormuz at the mouth of the Persian Gulf. Distance is measured in *geng* 更 or watches, the distance a boat travelling at normal speed can cover during a tenth of a 24-hour day. Depending on the estimated speed one chooses, this works out at between 10 to 15 nautical miles (16 to 24km) per watch.[8] Curiously, the data for the three directions are not reported equally. For Aden and Dhofar, the colophon provides each with only an approximate direction (northwest) and a cumulative distance. These distances are noteworthy. The colophon gives the distance from Calicut to Aden as 185 watches. At a speed of 4 knots, this figure converts to 1,850 nautical miles (nmi). Given that the distance by air is just over 1,800 nmi, this figure is strikingly accurate. The figure of 150 watches for Calicut to Dhofar is less so. The air distance is just over

1,300 nmi, which should entail a reduction of the Calicut–Aden distance by 55 watches, whereas the figure in the colophon of 150 watches is only 35 watches less than the Aden route. The distance given for the route to Hormuz is even less reliable. The actual air distance is 1,450 nmi (i.e. between the distances to Dhofar and Aden), yet the watches listed in the directions add up to 235, far longer than either of the other two. This discrepancy may reflect the difference between sailing on open water and following a coastal route: the one on a straight-line course, the other on a more zigzag route compounded by the slower speed needed to negotiate the south of the Persian Gulf. The air distance to Hormuz being about 1,450 nmi, however, the addition of 90 watches seems more than the irregularity of a coastal route can explain. More useful for analysis are the directional details the Calicut colophon provides for the route to Hormuz, which it reports as a sequence of nine segments, each with its compass bearing and distance. The density of data compared to that for the other two routes may be the effect of the source the Selden cartographer used; it may also indicate that Hormuz was, at least in Chinese memory, more important than the other two ports.[9]

For comparative purposes, consider how these three routes are described in the Laud rutter. The route to Aden is there broken into five segments, of which the longest by far is the fourth, which extends for 125 watches on a 277½° bearing.[10] In addition, the Laud rutter furnishes a total distance of 176 watches, 9 watches shorter than the 'Calicut' colophon to the Selden map – which at a slightly faster average speed of 4.2 knots is as approximately accurate as that map. The route from Calicut to Dhofar in the Laud rutter is dominated by two compass bearings, 292½° and 285°, again well to the south of a true northwest bearing.[11] What the Laud rutter and the Selden map do agree on is distance; both report that the journey from Calicut to Dhofar takes 150 watches. The data for comparing the distance to Hormuz in the two documents is poor, but the detail of compass bearings in the Calicut colophon makes for a good comparison. The description of this route in the Laud rutter reads as follows:

> Set out on a 322½° bearing. Once you have left the breakwater and draw 15 fathoms,[12] sight the North Star at a height of 4 fingers and the Southern Cross exactly at 11½ fingers, then take a 330° bearing for 5 watches until you reach the white shoals. Follow the coast of the island and take a 337½° bearing for 5 watches to reach Dingdebaxi 丁得把昔*. Sight the North Star at a height of 7½ fingers. If the winds are good, cross the sea between a 307½° bearing and a 300° bearing for 100 watches to Guma* 姑馬 Island. If the winds are contrary, follow a 300° bearing for 85 watches. . . . Sight as though from the back of the North Star at a height of 4½ fingers, then follow the coast of the island and set a course of 277½° for 5 watches to reach the head of Jialita* 伽里塔 Island. Sail between a 337½° and a 330° bearing for 3 watches to reach the ferry at Tiwi (Ch. *Diewei* 迭微), then 322½° for 5 watches to reach Malishiji* 麻里實吉, then 292½° to reach Turtle Island. . . . Sail between 330° and 322½° for 4 watches . . ., then 322½° for 25 watches to reach Shalacemo* 沙剌側抹 [Qalhat?] Hill. . . . Sail due north for 5 watches to reach Hormuz.
>
> 開船乾亥，離石欄，水十五托，看北辰星四指，燈籠星正十一指半，单亥五更取白礁，沿山使用壬亥四十五更，取丁得把昔，看北辰星七指半，好風過海，乾戌单戌一百更姑馬山（若戧風，单戌八十五更……見看被身形北辰星四指半，沿山使用辛酉五更取伽里塔山頭，壬亥，单亥三更取迭微討水，乾亥五更取麻里實吉，辛戌取龟山…单亥及乾亥四更…乾亥廿五更取沙剌側抹山，…用單子五更取忽鲁謨斯。[13]

Between the Laud rutter and the Selden map the sequences of bearings and watches are substantially comparable:

> Laud rutter: 322½° – 330° (5 watches) – 337½° (5) – 307½°/300° (100) – 277½° (5) – 337½°/330° (3) – 322½° (5) – 292½° – 330°/322½° (4) – 322½° (25) – 0° (5);
>
> Selden map: 315° (5) – 322½° (45) – 300° (100) – 292½° (15) – 7½° (20) – 277½° (5) – 330° (10) – 322½° (30) – 0° (5).

The two versions are notably close in their final legs. The Laud rutter advises the pilot to get on close to a 330° bearing for 42 watches from Hormuz, whereas the map colophon recommends taking the 330° bearing 3 watches earlier. The rutter plots the rest of the course in five segments, whereas the map reduces the changes of course to two. Both end on a bearing heading due north into Hormuz for the last 12 hours of the voyage. Their closeness is hardly surprising, for one would expect the navigational data for entering the narrower passages of coastal waters to tolerate less variation than courses plotted on the open sea. More strikingly, on the open sea both prescribe a course of 300° for 100 watches (though the Laud rutter advises shifting off that course after 85 watches if the winds are contrary). We need not assume that the coincidence of directions is merely a sign that the route was unitary or that both texts conform to some standard of accuracy we might want to idealise. More important for our purpose, which is to understand how knowledge of the Zheng He voyages percolated through time, is the stubborn fact that the two texts do not transcribe the route in exactly the same way, in terms either of how they segment it or of what bearings and distances they assign to each segment. Their directions overlap at many points without precisely reproducing each other. That they are not identical reinforces the point earlier made with regard to the first two routes on the Calicut colophon: sailing instructions from the 15th-century expeditions circulated in variants, and their variations were absorbed and repeated by those who were producing new documents about the turn of the 17th century, when the sea lanes in this part of the world were once again coming alive with traffic.

This conclusion is further reinforced when we turn to another of the four exceptions to lost knowledge listed at the beginning of this chapter, Mao Yuanyi's visual transcription of the Zheng He routes in *Wubei zhi*. The final panel in his album, which shows sea routes in the western half of the Indian Ocean, underscores the importance of Calicut as the chief entrepôt for trading networks in this region. From its prominent position in the upper right-hand corner of the panel radiate half a dozen routes, each annotated as going either to or from Calicut. Deciphering the opposite terminus of these routes is difficult, given the somewhat chaotic arrangement of bodies of land in and around the Indian Ocean. The routes that appear to be linked to Calicut are annotated as follows:

(1) for your ship to reach Calicut, [take] a bearing of 45° for 50 watches and of 60° for 25 watches and you reach your destination.

(2) follow a 97½° bearing for 25 watches and you reach your country of destination.

(3) follow a 82½° bearing for 28 watches and your ship reaches Calicut.

(4) follow a 90° bearing for 15 watches and you reach [indecipherable]; then follow a 90° bearing for 16 watches and you reach Jiamao* 加卯.

(5) follow a 105° bearing for 28 watches and you reach Calicut.

(6) follow a 300° bearing for 85 watches, then a 292½° bearing for 40 watches, and your ship reaches Qalhat.

(1) 船收古里國，艮针五十更，寅針二十五更，收相接。

(2) 用乙卯針二十五更，收相接國。

(3) 用甲卯針二十八更，船收古里國。

(4) 用卯針十五更，收□□□，用卯針十六更，收□□□。

(5) 用丹[单]乙針二十八更，收古里國。

(6) 用丹[单]戌針八十五更，又用辛戌針四十更，船收加刺哈。[14]

Only two of these routes actually name the port at the other end of the route, neither of which is Aden, Dhofar or Hormuz. Aden is clearly marked on the map, but without being explicitly connected by a route line to anywhere. Otherwise the Arabian peninsula fades off beyond the left-hand edge of the chart, giving no indication of where the Persian Gulf might lie. The navigational data in Mao Yuanyi's Zheng He atlas are accordingly not easy to correlate with either the Calicut colophon or the Laud rutter. The only readily useful comparator is the sixth route, from Calicut to Qalhat, which lies across the mouth of the Persian Gulf from Hormuz. Mao's version lacks precision, but it does repeat the main compass bearing given in both the Calicut colophon and the Laud rutter of 300°. Not only that, but it replicates the advice in the Laud rutter that the pilot should turn off that compass bearing after 85 watches if the winds are not favourable. It then follows this data with the instruction to sail on a 292½° bearing, which corresponds to the next bearing on the Selden map, though the latter directs the pilot off that bearing after 15 rather than 40 watches and breaks down the remainder of the route into a more detailed series of segments. The Mao version ends at Qalhat – which may be a variant rendition of what the Laud rutter calls Shalacemo and which it locates five watches due south of Hormuz. Finally, the Mao chart severely reduces the distance by about 100 watches – which is almost perfectly in line with what the actual distance is.

Without Mao Yuanyi's source, we cannot recreate his reconstruction of the Zheng He sailing routes. We can, however, appreciate from the number of routes running in and out of Calicut which he records that the variations found between the Selden map and the Laud rutter are outnumbered by yet further now unknown variants, suggesting that an even wider trove of route documents survived down to the late Ming. What this observation does, of course, is simply strengthen the conclusion we drew earlier regarding the relative unity of data recorded in earlier sources and at the same time their internal inconsistency. For there to be this many variations, mostly minor, in the information transcribed into late Ming sources, there had to be a large body of records available at least in private archives, and possibly in state archives as well. This at least is what these three versions of the sea route from Calicut to Hormuz tell us.

The question these traces of the Zheng He voyages then raise is why the Selden cartographer – or indeed, why Mao Yuanyi or the editor of the Laud rutter – chose to include sailing directions from India to Arabia in their texts at all. One reason could be a sense of fidelity to one's sources: the obligation to be as complete in reporting knowledge of the past as possible. This explanation applies best to Mao Yuanyi, whose explicit concern is to show the routes that Zheng He's ships sailed. Mao is intensely interested in history, but his greater purpose is to provide information that may be of use in the future: to indicate all sea lanes that might become potential avenues of military attack. His book is a *bei zhi* 備志, a 'record to prepare for the future'. The Laud editor similarly looks back to the Zheng He voyages as he compiles his rutter, and yet he too declares that his purpose is to provide knowledge that will be of use to 'shipboard' (*zai chuan* 在船) men.[15] The knowledge he provides may rely on sources from the 15th century, but his intention is to make it available for future use. Zhang Xie provides something of a negative confirmation by *not* including Indian Ocean routes in *Dongxi yang kao*. His mandate was to produce an overview of current maritime practices, not a history. Accordingly, he left out the routes to and from Calicut. The rutters he consulted must have included them, but they were not relevant to his purpose. The Selden cartographer is similarly presentist in his concerns but takes a middle position. He is concerned to represent maritime routes as they were at the time he drew the map, which is why the north end of Sumatra exhausts the geographical extent of the routes he depicts. From this perspective, the Calicut colophon is not so much a curious exception as a telling inclusion. Like the Laud rutter and Mao's Zheng He atlas, it provides information that might some day become relevant to Chinese mariners. The Chinese knew very well that this was the zone from and into which the European merchants with whom they had contact were now trading; they were also encountering South Asian traders in considerable numbers travelling the trade corridors around the South China Sea.[16] By including data about these routes on his map, the Selden cartographer was tucking into his panorama of the Chinese maritime trading world information that one or more of his sources happened to furnish, and that could have future use. That Zheng He sailed these Indian Ocean routes two centuries earlier was of no particular account. The Calicut colophon may have preserved traces of the past, but its stronger intention was to provide traces of the future.

Notes

1 Further comments on these three sources may be found in Mills 1979.

2 The cover of the book bears a later inscription, *Shunfeng xiangsong* 順風相送 (*Dispatched on Favourable Winds*), which is how Chinese

scholarship tends to refer to the Laud rutter. It was reprinted in 1961 as the first of two navigational manuals in Xiang Da 1961b.

3 Xiang Da 1961b, 22.

4 Zhang Xie 1981.

5 Brook 2010, 93–4.

6 For the dating and authorship of the Selden map, see Brook 2013, 169–73.

7 Manguin 2009.

8 The speed of 6¼ knots has been widely used by Ming historians. At that speed, a ship would cover 150 nautical miles in 24 hours. Xiang Da, however, considered 4 knots a more realistic estimate for Ming junks. Equivalent to a daily distance of 100 nautical miles, this is a rate I find more accurate for reading the Selden map; see the discussion in Brook 2013, 95, 162.

9 On the earlier export of Chinese porcelain to Hormuz, see Sjostrand and Barnes 2001.

10 Xiang Da 1961, 80: 開船乾亥，離石欄外，水十五托，看北斗星四指，看燈籠星十一指半，单亥五更取白礁外過，乾戌五更平希星峪，用乾亥二十更，看北斗辰五指三角，看燈籠星正十指三角，平莽角雙儿，過.礁開洋，用辛酉一百二十五更平蕉塔那山，看北辰五指，燈籠星十指，取塔巴里付山，沿山一更，取小赤塔密儿，取水，巡山使单坤二十更，取阿丹碼頭.

11 Xiang Da 1961b, 80–1: 開船乾戌，，離石欄外，水十五托，单亥五更，取白礁外過，乾亥五更平希星山，单乾二十更，看北辰五指一角，燈籠十指一角，平莽角雙儿，過.礁頭開洋，辛戌五十更，看北辰六指三角，燈籠八指三角，单辛七十更，看北斗七指三角，燈籠七指三角，取祖法儿碼頭，泊船是也.

12 Zhang Xie explains in the introduction to the ninth chapter of *Dongxi yang kao* that a *tuo* 托, here translated as 'fathom', was defined locally as the distance between your hands with your arms outstretched.

13 Xiang Da 1961b, 78–9. Asterisks indicate that a place name is romanised from Chinese characters. On the identification of Diewei as Tiwi, the region southeast of Muscat, see Mills 1970, 222.

14 Mao Yuanyi 1628, 240.20a–b. On the identification of Jialaha as Kalhat/Qalhat, see Mills 1970, 188.

15 Xiang Da 1961b, 22.

16 Brook 2008, 84–116.

Bibliography

Abel-Rémusat, Jean-Pierre, 'De l'étude des langues étrangères chez les Chinois', in *Mélanges Asiatiques, ou Choix de morceaux de critique, et de mémoires relatifs aux religions, aux. sciences, à l'histoire, et à la géographie des nations orientales*, vol. 2, Paris, 1826, pp. 242–65.

Abu-Lughod, Janet, *Before European Hegemony: The World System A.D. 1250–1350*, Oxford, 1991.

Adamek, Wendi, 'Imaging the Portrait of a Chan Master', in Bernard Faure (ed.), *Chan Buddhism in Ritual Context*, London and New York, 2003, pp. 36–73.

Ahn Hwi-joon 안휘준, 'Sejongjo ui misul' 세종조의 미술 (Art of the Sejong Period), *Sejongjo munhwa ui jaeinsik* 세종조 문화의 재인식 (*New Understanding of the Culture under the Reign of King Sejong*), Seongnam, 1982.

Ahn Hwi-joon 안휘준, *An Gyeon gwa Mong'yu dowondo* 안견과 몽유도원도 (*An Gyeon and A Dream Journey to the Peach Blossom Land*), Seoul, 1991.

Ahn Hwi-joon 안휘준, *Hanguk misul gwa munhwa* 한국미술과 문화 (*Korean Art and Culture*), Seoul, 2000, pp. 120–33.

Albion, Robert Greenhalgh, *Forests and Sea Power: The Timber Problem of the Royal Navy, 1652–1862*, Cambridge, MA, 1926.

Alexander, David, 'Pisanello's Hat. The Costume and Weapons Depicted in Pisanello's Medal for John VIII Palaeologus: A Discussion of the Saber and Related Weapons', *Gladius* 24, 2004, pp. 135–86.

Allom, Thomas with Rev. G.N. Wright and D.J.M. Tate, *The Chinese Empire Illustrated: Being a Series of Views from Original Sketches, Displaying the Scenery, Architecture, Social Habits etc., of that Ancient and Exclusive Nation*, London, 1858–9.

Amitai, Reuven, *Mongols and Mamluks: The Mamluk-Ilkhanid War, 1260–82*, Cambridge, 1995.

Amitai, Reuven, 'Mamluks of Mongol Origin and their Role in Early Mamluk Political Life', *Mamlūk Studies Review*, vol. 12, no. 1, 2008, pp. 119–37.

Anami, Virginia S., *Encounters with Ancient Beijing: Its Legacy in Trees, Stone and Water*, Beijing, 2004.

Andersen, Poul, 'Taoist Talismans and the History of the Tianxin Tradition', *Acta Orientalia* 57, 1996, pp. 141–52.

Andersen, Poul, 'The *Yushu jing* and the Qingwei Tradition', paper presented at the International Conference on Song Daoism organised by the Centre for Studies of Daoist Culture, The Chinese University of Hong Kong, 22–3 September 2011.

Andersen, Poul, 'The Register and Illustrations of the *Yushu jing* and the Uses of the Scripture in China and Korea', paper presented at the workshop 'Icons, Charts and Talismanic Scripts: Daoist Visual Culture' at Dartmouth College, Hanover, NH, 22–4 May 2012.

Anon., '*Nanjing Zutangshan shehui fuliyuan zai shigong guocheng zhong faxian Mingdai duzhijian taijian Hong Bao mu*' 南京祖堂山社會福利院在施工過程中發現明代都知監太監洪保墓 (The Discovery of the Grave of the Ming Eunuch Hong Bao, while Doing Work on the Social Welfare Institute of Zushantang, Nanjing), http://www.sssc.cn/a/20110427/130387330843676.shtml.

Anon., 'Xia Xiyang' 下西洋 (Down to the Western Oceans), in Zhu Yunming 祝允明 (ed.), *Qian wen ji* 前聞記 (Stories from the Past), in *Jilu huibian* 紀錄彙編 (Collection of Records), vol. 12, *juan* 202, pp. 36b–38a.

Archer, Mildred, Rowell, Christopher and Skelton, Robert, *Treasures from India: The Clive Collection at Powis Castle*, London, 1987.

Aris, Michael and Aung San Suu Kyi (eds), *Tibetan Studies in Honour of Hugh Richardson*, Warminster, 1980.

Atwell, William S., 'Time, Money, and the Weather: Ming China and the "Great Depression" of the Mid-Fifteenth Century', *Journal of Asian Studies*, vol. 61, no. 1, 2002, pp. 83–113.

Atwood, Christopher, 'Historiography and Transformation of Ethnic Identity in the Mongol Empire: The Öng'üt Case', *Asian Ethnicity*, vol. 15, no. 5, 2014, pp. 514–34.

Ayalon, David, 'The Wadifiya in the Mamluk Kingdom', *Islamic Culture*, vol. 25, 1951, pp. 89–104.

Ayalon, David, 'The Auxiliary Forces of the Mamluk Sultanate', *Der Islam*, vol. 65, 1988, pp. 13–37.

Bagchi, Prabodh Chandra, 'Political Relations between Bengal and China in the Pathan Period', in *India and China: Interactions through Buddhism and Diplomacy, A Collection of Essays by Professor Prabodh Chandra Bagchi*, comp. Bangwei Wang and Tansen Sen, London, 2012, pp. 109–35.

Bai, Limin, *Shaping the Ideal Child: Children and Their Primers in Late Imperial China*, Hong Kong, 2005.
Bai Ying 白穎, He Congrong 賀從容, and Wang Guixiang 王貴祥, 'Wudangshan Nanyangong Xuandidian fuyuan yanjiu' 武當山南巖宮玄帝殿復原研究 (Research into the Restoration of Dark Emperor Hall of Nanyan Palace in Mount Wudang), in Wang Guixiang 王貴祥 (ed.), *Zhongguo jianzhu shilun huikan, di er ji* 中國建築史論匯刊第2辑 (Collected Writings on History of Chinese Architecture, vol. 2), Beijing, 2009–10, pp. 81–106.
Bailey, Gauvin A., 'The Stimulus: Chinese Porcelain Production and Trade with Iran', in Lisa Golombek, Robert B. Mason and Gauvin A. Bailey (eds), *Tamerlane's Tableware: A New Approach to the Chinoiserie Ceramics of Fifteenth- and Sixteenth-Century Iran*, Costa Mesa, CA, 1996, pp. 7–15.
Balabanlilar, Lisa, 'The Lords of the Auspicious Conjunction: Turco-Mongol Imperial Identity on the Subcontinent', *Journal of World History* 18, no. 1, 2007, pp. 1–39.
Ban Gu 班固, *Baihu tongde lun* 白虎通德論 (Universal Discussions at the White Tiger Hall), *c.* 80, e-SKQS.
Bandaranayake, Senake, Dewaraja, Lora, Silva, Roland and Wimalaratne, K.D.G. (eds), *Sri Lanka and the Silk Road of the Sea*, Colombo, 1990.
Barnhart, Richard *et al.*, *Painters of the Great Ming: The Imperial Court and the Zhe School*, Dallas, 1993.
Barthold, Vasili Vladimirovich, *Four Studies on the History of Central Asia*, vol. II, *Ulugh-Beg*, trans. V. and T. Minorskhy, Leiden, 1963.
Bartholomew, Terese Tse, *Hidden Meanings in Chinese Art*, San Francisco, 2006.
Beer, Robert, *The Encyclopedia of Tibetan Symbols and Motifs*, London, 1999.
Beijing daxue kaogu wenbo xueyuan 北京大學考古文博學院, Jiangxi sheng wenwu kaogu yanjiusuo 江西省文物考古研究所 and Jingdezhen shi taoci kaogu yanjiusuo 景德鎮市陶瓷考古研究所, 'Jiangxi Jingdezhen Ming Qing yuyao yizhi fajue jianbao' 江西景德鎮明清御窯遺址發掘簡報 (Brief Excavation Report on Imperial Kiln of the Ming and Qing Dynasties Located in Jingdezhen City, Jiangxi Province), in *Wenwu* 文物 (*Cultural Relics*), no. 5, 2007, pp. 4–47.
Beijing wenbo jiaoliuguan 北京文博交流館, *Gucha zhihua si* 古剎智化寺 (*The Ancient Zhihua Temple*), Beijing, 2005.
Beiping gugong bowuyuan 北平故宮博物院 (ed.), *Qingdai dihou xiang* 清代帝后像 (*Portraits of Emperors and Empresses of the Qing Dynasty*), Beijing, 1931.
Ben Cheneb, M. and Suter, H., 'Ibn al-Bannā'', in M.Th. Houtsma, T.W. Arnold, R. Basset and R. Hartmann (eds), *Encyclopaedia of Islam, First Edition (1913–1936)*, Brill Online, 2015.
Berger, Patricia, 'Miracles in Nanjing: An Imperial Record of the Fifth Karmapa's Visit to the Chinese Capital', in Marsha Weidner (ed.), *Cultural Intersections in Later Chinese Buddhism*, Honolulu, 2001, pp. 145–69.
Bernhardt, Kathryn, *Women and Property in China, 960–1949*, Stanford, 1999.
Birge, Bettine, *Women, Property, and Confucian Reaction in Sung and Yüan China (960–1368)*, Cambridge, 2002.
Birge, Bettine, 'Women and Confucianism from Song to Ming: The Institutionalization of Patriarchy', in Paul Jakov Smith and Richard von Glahn (eds), *The Song–Yuan–Ming Transition in Chinese History*, Cambridge, MA and London, 2003, pp. 212–40.
Blair, Sheila S., 'The Decorated Papers used in Manuscripts in Later Islamic Times', *Muqarnas* 17, 2000, pp. 24–36.
Boerschmann, Ernst, *Chinesische Architektur*, vol. 1, Berlin, 1925.
Boxer, C.R., 'The Dutch East India Company and the China Trade', *History Today* 29, no. 11, 1979, pp. 741–50.
Brend, Barbara, *Muhammad Juki's Shahnama of Firdausi*, London, 2010.
Brend, Barbara and Melville, Charles, *Epic of the Persian Kings: The Art of Ferdowsi's Shahnameh*, Cambridge, 2010.
Brinker, Helmut and Kanazawa, Hiroshi, *Zen Masters of Meditation in Images and Writings*, Zurich, 1996.
Brinker, Helmut and Lutz, Albert, *Chinese Cloisonné: The Pierre Uldry Collection*, New York, 1989.
Broadbridge, Anne, *Kingship and Ideology in the Islamic and Mongol Worlds*, Cambridge, 2008.
Brook, Timothy, *Praying for Power: Buddhism and the Formation of Gentry Society in Late-Ming China*, Cambridge, MA, 1994.
Brook, Timothy, 'Edifying Knowledge: The Building of School Libraries in Ming China', *Late Imperial China*, vol. 17, no. 1, 1996, pp. 93–119.
Brook, Timothy, 'Communications and Commerce', in Denis C. Twitchett and Frederick W. Mote (eds), *The Cambridge History of China: Volume 8, The Ming Dynasty, 1368–1644, Part 2*, Cambridge, 1998, pp. 579–707.
Brook, Timothy, *Vermeer's Hat: The Seventeenth Century and the Dawn of the Global World*, London, 2008.
Brook, Timothy, *The Troubled Empire: China in the Yuan and Ming Dynasties*, Cambridge, MA, 2010.
Brook, Timothy, *Mr Selden's Map of China: The Spice Trade, a Lost Chart and the South China Sea*, London, 2013.
Brown, Roxanna M., 'Ming Ban-Ming Gap: Southeast Asian Shipwreck Evidence for Shortages of Chinese Trade Ceramics', in Pei-kai Cheng (ed.), *Proceedings of the International Conference: Chinese Export Ceramics and Maritime Trade, 12th–15th Centuries*, Hong Kong, 2005.
Brown, Roxanna M., *The Ming Gap and Shipwreck Ceramics in Southeast Asia: Towards a Chronology of Thai Trade Ware*, Bangkok, 2009.
Bu Liansheng 步連生, '*Ming Xuande shi nian diaozao de Bandan Zhashi xiang – fei chuanshuo zhi Yao Guangxiao xiang*' 明宣德十年雕造的班丹札釋像 – 非傳說之姚廣孝像 (The Image of Bandan Zhashi Carved in the Tenth Year of Xuande of the Ming Dynasty – Not the Alleged Image of Yao Guangxiao), *Wenwu* 文物 (*Cultural Relics*), no. 7, 1979, pp. 82–6.
Buddhist Studies Authority Database Project, http://authority.ddbc.edu.tw/person/.
Bui Minh Tri and Nguyen-Long, Kerry, *Vietnamese Blue and White Ceramics*, Hanoi, 2001.
Byrd, Vickie C., Hamilton, Kathy A. and Johnson, Nancy R. (eds), *Tibet: Treasures from the Roof of the World*, Bowers Museum of Cultural Art, Santa Ana, CA, 2003.
Cahill, James, *Parting at the Shore: Chinese Painting of the Early and Middle Ming Dynasty, 1368–1644*, New York and Tokyo, 1985.
Calvino, Italo, *Invisible Cities*, San Diego and New York, 1972.
Cammann, Schuyler, *China's Dragon Robes*, New York, 1952.
Campbell, Aurelia, 'The Impact of Imperial and Local Patronage on Early Ming Temples at the Sino-Tibetan Frontier', Ph.D diss., University of Pennsylvania, 2011.
Canepa, Teresa, 'Kraak Porcelain: The Rise of Global Trade in the Late 16th and Early 17th Centuries', in Luísa Vinhais and Jorge Welsh (eds), *Kraak Porcelain: The Rise of Global Trade in the Late 16th and Early 17th Centuries*, London, 2008, pp. 17–63.
Canepa, Teresa, 'Silk, Porcelain and Lacquer: China and Japan and their Trade with Western Europe and the New World, 1500–1644. A Survey of Documentary and Material Evidence', Ph.D diss., Leiden University, 2015.
Cao Jianwen 曹建文, 'Ming Hongwu guanyao diwen huangyouci de faxian ji qi shidai kaozheng' 明洪武官窑低温黄釉瓷的发现及其时代考证 (The Discovery of Low-fired Yellow-glazed Porcelains from the Official Kiln in the Hongwu Period of the Ming Dynasty and its Dating), *Dongnan wenhua* 東南文化 (*Southeast Culture*), 2003–5, pp. 73–5.
Cao Xun 曹汛, 'Kuai Xiang de shengping niandai he jianzu zuopin 蒯祥的生平年代和建築作品' (The Life of Kuai Xiang and His Building Works), *Beijing jianzhu gongcheng xueyuan xuebao* 北京建築工程學院學報 (*Journal of Beijing Institute of Civil Engineering and Architecture*), vol. 12, no. 1, March 1996, pp. 83–8.
Cao Xun 曹汛, 'Xiudingsi jianzhu kaogu you san ti' 修定寺建築考古又三題 (The Xiudingsi Temple, Architecture, Archaeology and Three Questions), *Jianzhushi* 建築師 (*The Architect*), no. 6, 2005, pp. 106–13.
Carr, Dawson W., *Andrea Mantegna: 'The Adoration of the Magi'*, Los Angeles, 1997.
Carswell, John, *Blue and White: Chinese Porcelain around the World*, London, 2000.
Cartwright, Caroline R., Duffy, Christina M. and Wang, Helen, 'Microscopical Examination of Fibres Used in Ming Dynasty Paper Money', *British Museum Technical Research Bulletin*, 8, 2014, pp. 105–16.
Chakravarti, Ranabir, 'Early Medieval Bengal and the Trade in Horses: A Note', *Journal of the Economic and Social History of the Orient*, vol. 42, no. 2, 1999, pp. 194–211.

Chan, Hok-lam, 'The Yung-lo, Chien-wen, Hung-Hsi, and Hsuan-te Reigns', in Frederick W. Mote and Denis C. Twitchett (eds), *The Cambridge History of China: Volume 7, The Ming Dynasty, 1368–1644, Part 1*, Cambridge, 1988, pp. 182–304.

Chan, Hok-lam, '"Zhenwu shen. Yongle xiang" chuanshuo suyuan' 「真武神・永樂像」傳說溯源 (Tracing the Sources of the Legend 'the God Zhenwu, the Image of Yongle'), in Hok-lam Chan, *Mingdai renwu yu chuanshuo* 明代人物與傳說 (*Essays on Ming Personages and Legends*), Hong Kong, 1997, pp. 87–127.

Chan, Hok-lam, 'Xie Jin (1369–1415) as Imperial Propagandist: His Role in the Revisions of the "Ming Taizu shilu"', *T'oung Pao*, second series, vol. 91, 2005, pp. 58–124.

Chang Foundation 鴻禧美術館, *Jingdezhen chutu Mingchu guanyao ciqi* 景德鎮出土明初官窯瓷器 (*Imperial Hongwu and Yongle Porcelain Excavated at Jingdezhen*), Taipei, 1996.

Chang Foundation 鴻禧美術館, *Jingdezhen chutu Ming Xuande guanyao ciqi* 景德鎮出土明宣德官窯瓷器 (*Xuande Imperial Porcelain Excavated at Jingdezhen*), Taipei, 1998.

Chang Wen-chang 張文昌, *Zhi li yi jiao tianxia: Tang Song lishu yu guojia shehui* 制禮以教天下--唐宋禮書與國家社會 (*Establishing 'li' to Civilize 'tien-hsia': Ritual Books and Historical Changes in Tang and Song China*), Taipei, 2012.

Chao Shin-yi, *Daoist Ritual, State Religion, and Popular Practices: Zhenwu Worship from Song to Ming (960–1644)*, London and New York, 2011.

Chao Zhongchen 晁中辰, *Ming Chengzu zhuan* 明成祖傳 (*Biography of Ming Chengzu*), Beijing, 1995.

Chen Fang-mei 陳芳妹, 'Zhui sandai yu dingyi zhijian: Songdai cong "kaogu" dao "wangu" de zhuanbian' 追三代於鼎彝之間 – 宋代從「考古」到「玩古」的轉變 (Seeking the Three Dynasties among the Ritual Vessels of Old: The Song Dynasty Move from 'Investigating Antiquity' to 'Appreciating Antiquity'), *Gugong xueshu jikan* 故宮學術季刊 (*The National Palace Museum Research Quarterly*), vol. 23, no. 1, 2005, pp. 267–332.

Chen Fang-mei 陳芳妹, '"Yu sandai tongfeng": Zhuxi dui dongya wenhua yixiang de xingsu chutan' 「與三代同風」: 朱熹對東亞文化意象的形塑初探 (Sharing the Moralizing Influence of the Three Dynasties: Zhu Xi's Shaping of East Asian Cultural Imagery), *Guoli Taiwandaxue meishushi yanjiou jikan* 國立臺灣大學美術史研究集刊 (*Taida Journal of Art History*), no. 31, 2011, pp. 61–150.

Chen Gaohua 陳高華, 'Yuandai nongmin qiyijun minghao xiaoding' 元代農民起義軍名號小訂 (Names of the Armies of the Peasant Rebellion in the Yuan Dynasty), *Nankai daxue xuebao* 南開大學學報 (*Nankai Journal*) 2, 1979, pp. 95–6.

Chen Gaohua 陳高華 and Xu Jijun 徐吉軍 (eds), *Zhongguo fushi tong shi* 中國服飾通史 (*The General History of Chinese Clothing*), Ningbo, 2002.

Chen Guofu 陳國符, *Daozang yuanliu kao* 道藏源流考 (*Studies on the Origins and Development of the Daoist Canon*), Taipei, 1975.

Chen Jian 陳建, *Huang Ming tong ji* 皇明通記 (*Comprehensive Accounts of the August Ming*), repr. Beijing, 2008.

Chen Mingda 陳明達, 'Zhongguo gudai mujiegou jianzhu jishu (Nan Song zhi Ming, Qing)' 中國古代木結構建築技術 (南宋至明清) (Technologies of Ancient Chinese Wooden Architecture: Southern Song to Ming and Qing), in Chen Mingda 陳明達 (ed.), *Gu Jianzhu yu diaosu shi lun* 古建築與雕塑史論 (Discussion on Ancient Chinese Architecture and Sculpture), Beijing, 1998, pp. 217–18.

Chen Nan 陳楠, *Mingdai Daci Fawang yanjiu* 明代大慈法王研究 (*Research on the Great Compassion Dharma King of the Ming Dynasty*), Beijing, 2005.

Chen Pingping 陳平平, 'Jianlun xian wei ren zhi de yi bu Jinling Dabao'en si zhuanzhi jiqi lishi he xianshi jiazhi' 簡論鮮爲人知的一部金陵大報恩寺專志及其歷史和現實價值 (Notes on A Little-known Special Record of Jinling Dabao'en si Temple), *Nanjing Xiaozhuang Xueyuan Xuebao* 南京曉莊學院學報 (*Journal of Nanjing Xiaozhuang University*), January 2011, pp. 38–44.

Chen Xibo 陳喜波 and Han Guanghui 韓光輝, 'Ming Beijing cheng yingjian shiliao caiban yanjiu' 明北京城營建石料採辦研究 (A Study of Stone Procurement for the Construction of Ming Beijing), *Beijing shehui kexue* 北京社會科學 (*Social Science of Beijing*), 2010, no. 2, pp. 98–103.

Cheng Shuguo 陳戍國, *Zhongguo lizhi shi: Sui Tang Wudai juan* 中國禮制史: 隋唐五代卷 (*History of the Rites System in China: Sui, Tang and Five Dynasties*), Changsha, 1998.

Cheong Beong-mo 정병모, 'Gungnip jung'ang bangmulgwan sojang *Paljun do*' 국립중앙박물관 팔준도 (*Painting of the Eight Steeds* in the National Museum of Korea), *Milsul sahak yeongu* 미술사학연구 (*Korean Journal of Art History*), vol. 189, March 1991, pp. 3–26.

Chi Jingjia 池敬嘉, 'Yao Guangxiao sui Zheng He xia Xiyang lice' 姚廣孝隨鄭和下西洋蠡測 (Analysis of Yao Guangxiao's Expedition to the Western Oceans with Zheng He), in *Chuancheng wenming, zouxiang shijie, heping fazhan: Jinian Zheng He xia Xiyang 600 zhounian guoji xueshu luntan wenji* 傳承文明 走向世界 和平發展：紀念鄭和下西洋600 週年國際學術論壇論文集 (*Carry on Civilization, Open to the World, For Peace and Development: Proceedings of International Academic Forum in Memorization of 600th Anniversary of Zheng He's Expedition*), Beijing, 2005, pp. 766–72.

Chia, Lucille, 'Publications of the Ming Principalities: A Distinct Example of Private Printing,' *Ming Studies* 54 (2006), pp. 24–70.

Ching, Dora C.Y., 'Tibetan Buddhism and the Creation of the Ming Imperial Image', in David M. Robinson (ed.), *Culture, Courtiers, and Competition: The Ming Court (1368–1644)*, Cambridge, MA, 2008, pp. 321–64.

Ching, Dora, 'Shadows in Life and Death: Family Portraiture', in Jerome Silbergled, Dora C.Y. Ching and P.Y. and Kinmay W. Tang Center for East Asian Art (eds), *The Family Model in Chinese Art and Culture*, Princeton, 2013, pp. 275–300.

Chittick, N., *Manda: Excavations at an Island Port on the Kenya Coast*, Nairobi, 1984.

Cho Insoo 조인수, 'Joseon chogi Taejo eojin ui jejak gwa Taejo jinjeon ui unyeong' 조선 초기 태조 어진의 제작과 태조 진전의 운영' (Political Significance of Royal Portraits in the Early Joseon Period), *Misulsa wa sigak munhwa* 미술사와 시각문화 (*Art History and Visual Culture*), vol. 3, Seoul, 2004, pp. 116–53.

Cho Insoo 조인수, 'Sejongdae ui eojin gwa jinjeon' 세종대의 어진과 진전 (Royal Portraits and Jinjeon in the Sejong Period), in hangsan Ahn Hwi-joon gyosu toeim ginyeom nonmunjip ganhaeng wiwonhoe 항산 안휘준 교수 퇴임 기념 논문집 간행위원회 (Publication Committee for Collection of Papers Commemorating the Occasion of Professor Ahn Hwi-joon's Retirement) (ed.), *Misulsa ui jeongnip gwa hwaksan* 미술사의 정립과 확산 (*The Establishment and Expansion of Art History*), Seoul, 2006, pp.160-179.

Choi Wansu 최완수, 'Sejong sidae ui geurim gwa geulssi' 세종시대의 그림과 글씨 (Painting and Calligraphy of the Sejong Period), *Sejong munhwasa daegye: eumak misul pyeon* 세종문화사대계: 음악, 미술편 (A Compendium of Cultural History under King Sejong: A volume of Music and Art), Seoul, 2001, pp. 373–469.

Church, Sally K., 'The Giraffe of Bengal: A Medieval Encounter in Ming China', *The Medieval History Journal*, vol. 7, no. 1, 2004, pp. 1–37.

Church, Sally K., 'Zheng He: An Investigation into the Plausibility of 450-ft Treasure Ships', *Monumenta Serica*, vol. 53, 2005, pp. 1–42.

Church, Sally K., 'Two Ming Dynasty Shipyards in Nanjing and their Infrastructure', in Jun Kumura (ed.), *Shipwreck ASIA: Thematic Studies in East Asian Maritime Archaeology*, Adelaide, 2010, pp. 32–49.

Church, Sally K., 'Traces of a Memory: References to Zheng He's Voyages in the Longjiang Shipyard Treatise', in Shanghai Chinese Maritime Museum (ed.), *Zhongguo hanghai wenhua zhi diwei yu shiming* 中國航海文化之地位與使命 (The Position and Mission of China's Maritime Culture), Shanghai, 2011, pp. 97–109.

Clark, Donald, 'Sino-Korean Tributary Relations under the Ming', in Denis C. Twitchett and Frederick W. Mote (eds), *The Cambridge History of China: Volume 8, The Ming Dynasty, 1368–1644, Part 2*, Cambridge, 1998, pp. 272–300.

Clunas, Craig, 'Some Literary Evidence for Gold and Silver Vessels in the Ming Dynasty (1368–1644)', in Michael Vickers and Julian Raby (eds), *Pots and Pans: A Colloquium on Precious Metals and Ceramics*, 1987, pp. 83–7.

Clunas, Craig, *Fruitful Sites: Garden Culture in Ming Dynasty China*, Durham, 1996.

Clunas, Craig, 'The Other Ming Tombs: Kings and Their Burials in Ming China', *Transactions of the Oriental Ceramics Society*, LXX (2005–6), pp. 1–16.

Clunas, Craig, *Empire of Great Brightness: Visual and Material Cultures of Ming China, 1368–1644*, London, 2008.

Clunas, Craig, *Screen of Kings: Royal Art and Power in Ming China*, London, 2013.

Clunas, Craig, '*Wen*: The Arts of Peace', in Craig Clunas and Jessica

Harrison-Hall (eds), *Ming: 50 Years that Changed China*, London, 2014, pp. 158–203.
Clunas, Craig and Harrison-Hall, Jessica (eds), *Ming: 50 Years that Changed China*, London, 2014.
Cohen, Paul, *History in Three Keys: The Boxers as Event, Experience, and Myth*, New York, 1997.
Corrigan, Katrina H., van Campen, Jan and Diercks, Femke with Janet C. Blyberg, *Asia in Amsterdam: The Culture of Luxury in the Golden Age*, New Haven and London, 2015.
Cortesão, Armando, *A Translation of the Suma Oriental of Tomé Pires, an Account of the East, from the Red Sea to Japan, Written in Malacca and India in 1512–1515*, 2 vols, London, 1944.
Crossley, Pamela K., 'Structure and Symbol in the Ming-Ch'ing Translator's Bureaus (ssu-i kuan)', *Central and Inner Asian Studies* 5, 1991, pp. 38–70.
Dale, Stephen Frederic, 'The Legacy of the Timurids', *Journal of the Royal Asiatic Society*, 3rd series, 8.1, 1998, pp. 43–58.
Daoist Iconography Project: http://manoa.hawaii.edu/daoist-iconography/identify.html
Dardess, John, *Confucianism and Autocracy: Professional Elites in the Founding of the Ming Dynasty*, Berkeley, 1983.
Dardess, John, *A Ming Society: T'ai-ho County, Kiangsi, in the Fourteenth to Seventeenth Centuries*, Berkeley, Los Angeles and London, 1986.
David, Sir Percival, *Chinese Connoisseurship: The Ko Ku Yao Lun, The Essential Criteria of Antiquities*, London, 1971.
Davidson, Jeremy H.C.S., 'A New Version of the Chinese-Vietnamese Vocabulary of the Ming Dynasty', *Bulletin of the School of Oriental and African Studies*, vol. 38, no. 2, 1975, pp. 296–315.
Davis, Edward, *Society and the Supernatural in Song China*, Honolulu, 2001.
de Bary, William Theodore and Huang Zhongxi, *Waiting for the Dawn: A Plan for the Prince: Huang Tsung-hsi's* Ming-i tai-fang lu, New York, 1993.
de Bruyn, Pierre-Henry, *Le Wudang Shan: Histoire des Récits Fondateurs*, Paris, 2010.
De Heer, Philip, *The Care-Taker Emperor: Aspects of the Imperial Institution in Fifteenth-Century China as Reflected in the Political History of the Reign of Chu Ch'i-yü*, Leiden, 1986.
Debreczeny, Karl, 'Fahai Temple and Tibetan Influence at the Early Ming Court', MA thesis, Indiana University, 1997.
Debreczeny, Karl, 'Sino-Tibetan Artistic Synthesis in Ming Dynasty Temples at the Core and Periphery', *The Tibet Journal*, vol. xxviii, nos 1–2, Spring–Summer 2003, pp. 49–108.
Debreczeny, Karl, 'Ethnicity and Esoteric Power: Negotiating Sino-Tibetan Synthesis in Ming Buddhist Painting', Ph.D diss., University of Chicago, 2007.
Debreczeny, Karl, *The Black Hat Eccentric: Artistic Visions of the Tenth Karmapa*, Rubin Museum of Art, New York, 2012.
Debreczeny, Karl, 'Imperial Interest Made Manifest: sGa A gnyan dam pa's Mahākāla Protector Chapel of the Tre shod Maṇḍala Plain', in Roberto Vitali, Gedun Rabsal and Nicole Willock (eds), *Trails of the Tibetan Tradition: Papers for Elliot Sperling*, Dharamshala, 2014, pp. 129–66.
Delacour, Catherine, *La voie du tao: un autre chemin de l'être*, Paris, 2010.
Deng Wenlin 鄧文林, 'Taimiao Shejitan Jingshan Dagaodian de bianqian' 太廟社稷壇景山大高殿的變遷 (Historical Changes of the Imperial Ancestral Temple, the Altar of the Spirits of the Soil and the Five Grains, Jingshan, and Dagao Palace), in *Zhongguo Zijincheng xuehui lunwen ji* 中國紫禁城學會論文集 (*Collected Essays from the Conference on China's Forbidden City*), vol. 2, Beijing, 2002, pp. 117–22.
Deuchler, Martina, *The Confucian Transformation of Korea: A Study of Society and Ideology*, Cambridge, MA, 1992.
Ding Huang 丁煌, 'Guoli zhongyang tushuguan cang Ming Xuande banian kanben *Shangqing lingbao jidu dacheng jinshu sijuan* chuyan – Daozang shisoushu xilie yanjiu zhi yi' 國立中央圖書館藏明宣德八年刊本「上清靈寶濟度大成金書四卷」初研——道藏失蒐書系列研究之一 (A Preliminary Research on the Four-volume *Golden Writings on the Great Achievement of Deliverance of the Numinous Treasure of Highest Clarity* of the Xuande Reign, Collected in National Central Library), *Guoli chenggong daxue lishi xuebao* 國立成功大學歷史學報 (*Cheng Kung Journal of Historical Studies*) 15, 1989, pp. 221–54.
Ding Yinzhong 丁銀忠, Kang Baoqiang 康葆強, Miao Jianmin 苗建民 *et al.*, 'Nanjing bao'ensita liuli goujian taiti yuanliao laiyuan de keji yanjiu' 南京報恩寺塔琉璃構件胎體原料來源的科技研究 (Scientific Investigation into the Provenance of Body Materials for Glazework at the Nanjing Da Baoen Monastery Pagoda), *Zhongguo Taoci* 中國陶瓷 (*Chinese Ceramics*), 2011, no. 1, pp. 70–5.
Ditmanson, Peter, 'Contesting Authority: Intellectual Lineages and the Chinese Imperial Court from the 12th to the 15th Centuries', Ph.D diss., Harvard University, 1999.
Ditmanson, Peter, 'Imperial History and Broadening Historical Consciousness in Late Ming China', *Ming Studies*, no. 71, May 2015, pp. 23–40.
dKon mchog bstan pa rab rgyas, *mDo smad chos 'byung* (History of the Dharma in Amdo, 1865, repr. Gansu, 1987.
dPa' bo gTsug lag phreng ba, *Dam pa'i chos kyi 'khor lo bsgyur ba rnams kyi byung pa gsar bar byed pa mKhas pa'i dga ston* (A Scholars' Feast), 1545, repr. Beijing, 1986.
DMB: Carrington Goodrich, L. and Fang Chaoying (eds), *Dictionary of Ming Biography: 1368–1644*, The Ming Biographical History Project of the Association for Asian Studies, 2 vols, New York and London, 1976.
DMHD: Li Dongyang 李東陽 and Shen Shixing 申時行 (eds), *Da Ming huidian* 大明會典 (*Collected Statutes of the Great Ming*), Dongnan shubaoshe facsimile of 1587 edn, Taipei, 1963.
Dreyer, Edward, *Early Ming China*, Stanford, 1982.
Dreyer, Edward L., *Zheng He: China and the Oceans in the Early Ming Dynasty 1405–1433*, New York, 2007.
Du Huiyue 杜慧月, *Mingdai wenchen chushi Chaoxian yu Huanghua ji* 明代文臣出使朝鮮與皇華集 (Ming-dynasty Scholar Official Envoys to Joseon and the Anthology of Brilliant Flowers), Beijing, 2010.
Duan Yucai 段玉裁, *Shuowen jiezi zhu* 說文解字注 (Descriptions of Text and Explanation of Characters Annotated), Taipei, 2005.
Duffy, Christina M., 'The Discovery of a Watermark on the St Cuthbert Gospel using Colour Space Analysis', *British Library Electronic Journal*, 2014, http://www.bl.uk/eblj/2014articles/pdf/ebljarticle22014.pdf
Duindam, Jeroen, *Dynasties: A Global History of Power, 1300–1800*, Cambridge, 2016.
Duyvendak, J.J.L., 'The True Dates of the Chinese Maritime Expeditions in the Early Fifteenth Century', *T'oung Pao*, vol. 34, 1938, pp. 341–412.
DZ: *Daozang* 道藏 (*Daoist Canon*), repr. Beijing, Shanghai and Tianjin, 1988.
DZ 222: *Qingwei shenlie bifa* 清微神烈祕法 (*Secret Methods of Divine Fire of Pure Tenuity*).
DZ 649: *Taishang laojun shuo Tianfei jiu kuling yingjing* 太上老君說天妃救苦靈應經 (*Sutra Spoken from on High of the Miraculous Efficacy of Tianfei in Salvation From Distress*).
DZ 959: *Da Ming Xuantian shangdi ruiying tulu* 大明玄天上帝瑞應圖錄 (*Catalogue of Auspicious Responses of the Supreme Emperor of the Dark Heaven of the Great Ming*).
DZ 981: *Da Ming yuzhi xuanjiao yuezhang* 大明御製玄教樂章 (*Musical Stanzas on Mysterious Teachings Composed under the Imperial Aegis of the Great Ming*).
DZ 1483: Zhu Quan 朱權, *Tianhuang zhidao taiqing yuce* 天皇至道太清玉冊 (*Jade Fascicles of Great Clarity on the Ultimate Way of the Heavenly Sovereign*).
Edye, John, *Calculations Relating to the Equipment, Displacement, etc. of Ships and Vessels of War*, London, 1832.
Elverskog, Johan, 'The Story of Zhu and the Mongols of the 17th Century', *Ming Studies*, vol. 50, 2004, pp. 39–76.
Elverskog, Johan, 'The Legend of Muna Mountain', *Inner Asia*, vol. 8, 2006, pp. 99–122.
Elverskog, Johan, *Buddhism and Islam on the Silk Road*, Philadelphia and Oxford, 2010.
Elvin, Mark, *The Retreat of the Elephants: An Environmental History of China*, New Haven and London, 2004.
Eng, Sunchuan Clarence, 'The Use of Ceramic in Chinese Late Imperial Architecture', Ph.D diss., London University, 2008.
Eng, Clarence, *Colours and Contrast: Ceramic Traditions in Chinese Architecture*, Leiden, 2014.
Eskenazi Ltd, *Junyao*, London, 2013.
Fairbank, John King (ed.), *The Chinese World Order: Traditional China's Foreign Relations*, Cambridge, MA, 1968.
Fairbank, John K., Reischauer, Edwin O. and Craig, Albert M., *East Asia: Tradition and Transformation*, Boston, 1973.

Fan Jinshi 樊錦詩, *Dunhuang shiku* 敦煌石窟 (*Dunhuang Grottoes*), Beijing, 2004.
Fan Yuming 范玉明, 'Kesi *Zhishan Daci Fawang xiang* de zhizuo' 緙絲《至善大慈法王像》的 製作 (Production of the *kesi* 'Portrait of Zhishan Daci Fawang'), 2009, http://www.szgmx.cn/lwxs1.asp?lwid=24650.
Fang Zhiyuan 方志遠, *Chenghua huangdi da zhuan* 成化皇帝大傳 (*Biography of the Chenghua Emperor*), Shenyang, 1996.
Farmer, Edward L., *Zhu Yuanzhang and Early Ming Legislation: the Reordering of Chinese Society Following the Era of Mongol Rule*, Leiden, 1995.
Faure, Bernard, '*Quand l'habit fait le moine:* The Symbolism of the Kāsāya in Sōtō zen', *Cahiers d'Extrême-Asie*, no. 8, 1995, pp. 335–69.
Faure, Bernard (ed.), *Chan Buddhism in Ritual Context*, New York, 2003.
Fei Hsin, *Hsing-ch'a sheng-lan: The Overall Survey of the Star Raft*, trans. J.V.G. Mills, rev., anno. and ed. Roderich Ptak, Wiesbaden, 1996.
Fei Xin 費信, *Xingcha shenglan* 星槎勝覽 (The Overall Survey of the Star Raft), ed. Feng Chengjun 馮承鈞, 1938, repr. Taipei, 1962.
Feng Chengjun 馮承鈞, *Yingya shenglan jiaozhu* 瀛涯勝覽校注 (*Annotated General Survey of the Ocean Shores*), repr. Taipei, 1962.
Feng Jiren, *Chinese Architecture and Metaphor: Song Culture in the* Yingzao Fashi *Building Manual*, Honolulu, 2012.
Feng Zuxiang 馮祖祥, Zhang Caite 張菜特 and Jiang Yuanzhen 姜元珍, 'Mingdai caimu zhi yi ji qi biduan' 明代採木之役及其弊端 (The Ming Dynasty Lumber Corvée and Its Abuses), *Beijing linye daxue xuebao: shehui kexue ban* 北京林業大學學報: 社會科學版 (*Journal of Beijing Forestry University: Social Sciences*), 2008, no. 2, pp. 48–51.
Fernquist, Jon, 'Min-gyi-nyo, the Shan Invasions of Ava (1524–27), and the Beginnings of Expansionary Warfare in Toungoo Burma: 1486–1539', *SOAS Bulletin of Burma Research*, vol. 3, no. 2, 2005, pp. 284–395.
Figgess, John, 'A Letter from the Court of Yung Lo', *Transactions of the Oriental Ceramic Society*, 1962–3, no. 34, pp. 97–100.
Finlay, Robert, 'The Treasure Ships of Zheng He; Chinese Maritime Imperialism in the Age of Discovery', *Terrae Incognita*, vol. 23, 1991, pp. 1–12.
Finlay, Robert, 'Portuguese and Chinese Maritime Imperialism: Camões's *Lusiads* and Luo Maodeng's *Voyage of the San Bao Eunuch*', *Comparative Studies in Society and History*, vol. 34, no. 2, 1992, pp. 225–41.
Fisher, Carney, 'The Great Ritual Controversy in Ming China', Ph.D diss., University of Michigan, 1977.
Fong Wen C., 'Imperial Portraiture in the Song, Yuan, and Ming Periods', *Ars Orientalis*, no. 25, 1995, pp. 47–59.
Fong Wen and Watt, James C.Y. *et al.*, *Possessing the Past: Treasures from the National Palace Museum, Taipei*, New York, 1996.
Foulk, T. Griffith and Sharf, Robert H., 'On the Ritual Use of Ch'an Portraiture in Medieval China', *Cahiers d'Extrême-Asie*, no. 7, 1993–4, pp. 149–219.
Franke, Wolfgang, 'The Veritable Records of the Ming Dynasty', in W.G. Beasely and E.G. Pulleyblank (eds), *Historians of China and Japan*, London, 1961, pp. 60–77.
Franke, Wolfgang, *An Introduction to the Sources of Ming History*, Kuala Lumpur, 1968.
Freeman, Rich, 'Rubies and Coral: The Lapidary Crafting of Language in Kerala', *Journal of Asian Studies*, vol. 57, no. 1, 1998, pp. 38–65.
Fu Xinian 傅熹年, *Shilun Tang zhi Mingdai guanshi jianzhu fazhan de mailuo jiqi yu defang chuantong de guanxi* 試論唐至明代官式建築發展的脈絡及其與地方傳統的關系 (Discussion of the Development of Tang to Ming Dynasty Official Architecture and its Relationship to Regional Traditions), *Wenwu* 文物 (*Cultural Relics*), 1999, no. 10, pp. 81–93.
Fu Xinian 傅熹年, *Zhongguo Gudai jianzhu shi, di er juan* 中國古代建築史 第二卷 (*History of Traditional Chinese Architecture*, vol. 2), Beijing, 2001.
Gao Deyang 高德暘, *Jie an ji* 節菴集 (*Collected Writings of Jie Abbey*), in *Siku quanshu cunmu congshu* 四庫全書存目叢書 (*Extant Compendia from the Complete Library of the Four Treasuries*), Jinan, 1995–7, *ji* 29.
Gao Shouxian 高壽仙, 'Mingdai Beijing jiedao gouqu de guanli' 明代北京街道溝渠的管理 (The Management of Streets and Drainage System in Ming Beijing), *Beijing shehui kexue* 北京社會科學 (*Social Science of Beijing*), 2004, no. 2, pp. 102–7.
Gao Shouxian 高壽仙, 'Mingdai Beijing yingjian shiyi shulüe' 明代北京營建事宜述略 (Records of Building Beijing in the Ming dynasty), *Lishi dang'an* 歷史檔案 (*Historical Archives*), no. 4, 2006, pp. 23–32.
Ge Sang Ben 格桑本 and Qinghai sheng wenhua ding 青海省文化廳 (eds), *Qutansi* 瞿曇寺 (*Qutan Monastery*), Chengdu, 2000.
Geng Baochang 耿寶昌, *Mingqing ciqi jianding* 明清瓷器鑑定 (*Ming and Qing Porcelain Identification*), Beijing, 1993.
Geng Baochang 耿寶昌 (ed.), *Mingchu qinghuaci* 明初青花瓷 (*Early Ming Blue-And-White Porcelain*), Beijing, 2002.
Gerritsen, Anne, 'Porcelain and the Material Culture of the Mongol-Yuan Court', *Journal of Early Modern History*, vol. 16, no. 3, 2012, pp. 241–73.
Gibson, Charles E., *The Story of the Ship from the Earliest Days to the Present*, London, 1958.
Giuffrida, Noelle, 'Representing the Daoist God Zhenwu, the Perfected Warrior, in Late Imperial China,' Ph.D thesis, University of Kansas, 2008.
GJTSJC: Jiang Tingxi 蔣廷錫 *et al.* (ed.), *Gujin tushu jicheng* 古今圖書集成 (*Synthesis of Books and Illustrations Past and Present*), Taipei, 1976.
Glahn, Else, 'On the Transmission of the Ying-tsao fa-shih', *T'oung Pao*, vol. 61, 1975, pp. 232–65.
Glahn, Else, 'Chinese Building Standards in the 12th Century', *Scientific American*, vol. 244, issue 5, 1981, pp. 162–73.
Glahn, Else, 'Unfolding the Chinese Building Standards: Research on the *Yingzao fashi*', in Nancy Steinhardt (ed.), *Chinese Traditional Architecture*, New York, 1984, pp. 47–57.
Goddio, Franck, Pierson, Stacey, and Crick, Monique, *Sunken Treasure: Fifteenth Century Chinese Ceramics from the Lena Cargo*, London, 2000.
Goldsmith, Oliver, *The Citizen of the World: Or Letters from a Chinese Philosopher, Residing in London, to his Friends in the East*, 2 vols, Dublin, 1769.
Golombek, Lisa, 'The Ceramic Industry in Fifteenth-Century Iran: An Interpretation', in Lisa Golombek, Robert B. Mason and Gauvin A. Bailey (eds), *Tamerlane's Tableware: A New Approach to the Chinoiserie Ceramics of Fifteenth- and Sixteenth-Century Iran*, Costa Mesa, CA, 1996, pp. 124–39.
Golombek, Lisa and Subtelny, Maria (eds), *Timurid Art and Culture: Iran and Central Asia in the Fifteenth Century*, Leiden, 1992, pp. 144–57.
Golombek, Lisa and Wilber, Donald, *The Timurid Architecture of Iran and Turan*, 2 vols, Princeton, 1988.
Gong Bai 龔拜 and Pan Qun 潘群, 'Zheng He chongxiu Da Bao'en si kaolüe' 鄭和重修大報恩寺考略 (Brief Examination of the Renovation of the Great Baoen Temple by Zheng He), *Zheng He yanjiu* 鄭和研究 (*Zheng He Research*), vol. 69, no. 1, 2008, pp. 10–19.
Gong Zhen 鞏珍, *Xiyang fanguo zhi* 西洋番國志 (Treatise on the Foreign Nations of the Western Ocean), Beijing, 1961.
Goody, Jack, *Renaissances: The One or the Many?*, Cambridge and New York, 2010.
Goormaghtigh, George and Bell Yung, 'Preface of *Shenqi Mipu*: Translation with Commentary', *ACMR Reports*, vol. 10, no. 1, 1997, pp. 1–7.
Goryeosa DB, http://www.krpia.co.kr.
GQ: Tan Qian 談遷, *Guoque* 國榷 (*Discussions About the [Ming] State*), 10 vols, Taipei, 1978.
Grabar, Oleg, 'Review of *Epigrafika Vostoka* (*Oriental Epigraphy*) by V.A. krachkovskaya', *Ars Orientalis* 2, 1957, pp. 547–56.
Gregory, Scott W., 'Daydreaming Dynasty: The Eunuch Sanbao's Journeys in the Western Seas and "Present-Day" Fiction of the Ming', *Ming Studies*, no. 70, November 2014, pp. 10–28.
Grupper, Samuel M., 'The Manchu Imperial Cult of the Early Ch'ing Dynasty: Texts and Studies on the Tantric Sanctuary of Mahakala at Mukden', Ph.D diss., Indiana University, 1979.
Gugong bowuyuan 故宮博物院, *Junci yaji: Gugong bowuyuan zhencang ji chutu junyao ciqi huicui* 鈞瓷雅集: 故宮博物院珍藏及出土鈞窯瓷器薈萃 (*Selection of Jun Ware: The Palace Museum's Collection and Archaeology Excavation*), Beijing, 2013.
Guo Daiheng 郭黛姮, *Zhongguo gudai jianzhu shi: Song, Liao, Jin Xixia jianzhu* 中國古代建築史: 宋、遼、金、西夏建築 (*History of Traditional Chinese Architecture: Architecture of the Song, Liao, Jin and Xixia*), Beijing, 2009.
Guo Huayu 郭華瑜, *Shilun Mingdai de liujin dougong* 試論明代的溜金斗栱 (A Preliminary Discussion on *Liujin* Brackets in the Ming dynasty), in Yu Zhuoyun 于倬雲 and Zhu Chengru 朱誠如 (eds),

Zhongguo Zijincheng xuehui lunwenji, di er ji 中國紫禁城學會論文集, 第二輯 (*Collected Writings from the Forbidden City Study Society*), Zijincheng chubanshe, Beijing, 2002.
Guo Huayu 郭華瑜, *Mingdai guanshi jianzhu damuzuo* 明代官式建築大木作 (*The System of Major Carpentry in Official Buildings of the Ming Dynasty*), Nanjing, 2005.
Guo Qinghua 郭清華, '*Yingzao Fashi*: Twelfth-Century Chinese Building Manual', *Architectural History*, vol. 41, 1988, pp. 1–13.
Guo Qinghua 郭清華, *A Visual Dictionary of Chinese Architecture*, Victoria, 2002.
Guy, John and Stevenson, John, *Vietnamese Ceramics: A Separate Tradition*, Chicago, 1997.
Gyss-Vermande, Caroline, 'Les Messagers divins et leur iconographie', *Arts Asiatiques* vol. 46, no. 1, 1991, pp. 96–110.
Hall, Kenneth R., 'Ports-of-trade, Maritime Diasporas, and Networks of Trade and Cultural Integration in the Bay of Bengal Region of the Indian Ocean: *c.* 1300–1500', *Journal of the Economic and Social History of the Orient* 53, 2010, pp. 109–45.
Hammond, Kenneth J., 'Beijing's Zhihua Monastery: History and Restoration in China's Capital', in Marsha Weidner (ed.), *Cultural Intersections in Later Chinese Buddhism*, Honolulu, 2001, pp. 189–208.
Hammond, Kenneth J., 'The Eunuch Wang Zhen and the Ming Dynasty', in Kenneth J. Hammond (ed.), *The Human Tradition in Premodern China*, Wilmington, 2002, pp. 143–56.
Han Dacheng 韓大成, 'Mingdai Beijing jingji shulüe' 明代北京經濟述略 (An Overview of the Beijing Economy under the Ming Dynasty), *Beijing shehui kexue* 北京社會科學 (*Beijing Social Sciences*), 1991, no. 4, pp. 93–105.
Han Yong 韓雍, *Xiangyi wenji* 襄毅文集 (Collected Works of Han Yong), *c.* 1480, e-SKQS.
Han Zhenhua 韓振華, 'Lun Zhongguo chuan de chuanliao ji qi jisuan faze' 論中國船的船料及其計算法則 (On the *liao* in Chinese Ships and Methods for Calculating It), *Haijiao shi yanjiu* 海交史研究, 1988, no. 1, pp. 197–205.
Hanguk gojeon jonghap 한국고전종합DB, http://db.itkc.or.kr/itkcdb/mainIndexIframe.jsp.
Hanguk jeongsin munhwa yeonguwon 한국정신문화연구원 (Academy of Korean Studies), *Sejong sidae ui munhwa* 세종시대의 문화 (*Culture under Sejong's Reign*), Seoul, 2001, pp. 20–1.
Hargett, James M., 'Playing Second Fiddle: The *Luan*-Bird in Early and Medieval Chinese Literature', *T'oung Pao*, second series, vol. 75, 1989, pp. 235–62.
Harrer, Alexandra, 'Fan-shaped Bracket-Sets and their Application in Religious Timber Architecture of Shanxi Province', Ph.D diss., University of Pennsylvania, 2010.
Harrison-Hall, Jessica, *Ming Ceramics in the British Museum*, London, 2001.
Harrison-Hall, Jessica, 'Creating Ripples on the Ming Pond', *Arts of Asia*, vol. 44, no. 6, November/December 2014, pp. 57–63.
Harrisson, T., 'The Ming Gap and Kota Batu, Brunei (With an appeal for help)', *The Sarawak Museum Journal*, vol. 8, June 1958, no. 11 (new series), no. 26 (old series), pp. 273–7.
Hartwell, Robert, 'Foreign Trade, Monetary Policy and Chinese "Mercantilism"', in Kinugawa Tsuyoshi (ed.), *Collected Studies on Sung History Dedicated to James T.C. Liu in Celebration of his Seventieth Birthday*, Kyoto, 1989, pp. 453–88.
Haufler, Marsha, 'Beliefs: Miracles and Salvation', in Craig Clunas and Jessica Harrison-Hall (eds), *Ming: 50 Years that Changed China*, London, 2014, pp. 206–53.
Hay, Jonathan, 'The Mediating Work of Art', *Art Bulletin* 89, no. 3, Fall 2007, pp. 435–59.
Hay, Jonathan, *Sensuous Surfaces: The Decorative Object in Early Modern China*, London, 2010.
Hay, Jonathan, 'Monument', *RES: Anthropology and Aesthetics*, vol. 67/68 (2016/17), forthcoming.
HDACA: Zhang Yuhuang (ed.), *The History and Development of Ancient Chinese Architecture*, Beijing, 1986.
He Liangjun 何良俊, *Siyouzhai hualun* 四友齋畫論 (*Theory of Painting from the Studio of the Four Friends*), in Yu Kun 俞崑 (ed.), *Zhongguo hualun leibian (shang)* 中國畫論類編（上） (*Categorized Compilation of Chinese Painting Theory, vol. 1*), Taipei, 1984.
He Xiaorong 何孝榮, *Mingdai Nanjing siyuan yanjiu* 明代南京寺院研究 (*Research on the Ming Dynasty Temples and Monasteries at Nanjing*), Beijing, 2000.
He Yuming, *Home and the World: Editing the 'Glorious Ming' in Woodblock-printed Books of the Sixteen and Seventeenth Centuries*, Cambridge, MA, 2013.
He Yunao 賀雲翱, 'Zheng He yu Jinling Da Bao'en si guanxi kao' 鄭和與金陵大報恩寺關係考 (Examination of the Connections between Zheng He and the Great Bao'en Temple in Nanjing), *Dongnan wenhua* 東南文化 (*Southeastern Culture*), vol. 198, no. 4, 2007, pp. 48–53.
Hearn, Maxwell, 'An Early Ming Example of Multiples: Two Versions of *Elegant Gathering in the Apricot Garden*', in Judith G. Smith and Wen Fong (eds), *Issues of Authenticity in Chinese Painting*, New York, 1999, pp. 221–58.
Henderson, Gregory and Hurvitz, Leon, 'The Buddha of Seiryōji: New Finds and New Theory', *Artibus Asiae*, vol. 19, no. 1, 1956, pp. 4–55.
Henss, Michael, 'The Woven Image: Tibeto-Chinese Textile Thangkas of the Yuan and Early Ming Dynasties', *Orientations*, vol. 28, no. 10, November 1997, pp. 26–39.
Henss, Michael, *Buddhist Art in Tibet: New Insights on Ancient Treasures: A Study of Paintings and Sculptures from 8th to 18th Century*, New Delhi, 2012.
Hettiaratchi, S.B., 'Studies in Cheng-Ho in Sri Lanka', in Chen Xinxiong 陳信雄 and Chen Yunu 陳玉女 (eds), *Zheng He xia Xiyang guoji xueshu yantaohui lunwen ji* 鄭和下西洋國際學術研討會論文集 (*Collection of Essays from the International Workshop on the Zheng He's Expeditions to the Western Oceans*), Taipei, 2003, pp. 91–109.
Hillenbrand, Robert (ed.), *Shahnama: The Visual Language of the Persian Book of Kings*, Aldershot, 2004.
Himalayan Art Resources, http://www.himalayanart.org/.
Hirth, F., 'The Chinese Oriental College', *Journal of the China Branch of the Royal Asiatic Society*, vol. 22, 1888, pp. 203–19.
HMTJ: Chen Jian 陳建, *Huang Ming tongji* 皇明通紀 (*Comprehensive Annals of the Imperial Ming*), 2 vols, Beijing, 2008.
HMZL: Fu Fengxiang 傅鳳翔 (ed.), *Huang Ming zhaoling* 皇明詔令 (*Imperial Edicts in the Ming Dynasty*), SKQS, Jinan, 1995.
Ho Peng Yoke, *Li, Qi and Shu: An Introduction to Science and Civilization in China*, Seattle and London, 1985.
Hong Kong Urban Council *et al.*, *Heaven's Embroidered Cloths: One Thousand Years of Chinese Textiles*, Hong Kong, 1995.
Hong Sunpyo and Chang Chin-sung, 'Peace under Heaven: Confucianism and Painting in Early Joseon Korea', in Lee Soyoung (ed.), *Art of the Korean Renaissance, 1400–1600*, New York, New Haven and London, 2009, pp. 65–90.
Horton, M.C., Brown, H.W. and Mudida, N., *Shanga: The Archaeology of a Muslim Trading Community on the Coast of East Africa* (vol. 14), London, 1996.
Hou Renzhi 侯仁之, 'Yuan Dadu cheng yu Ming Qing Beijing cheng' 元大都城與明清北京城 (Yuan Dadu and Ming-Qing Beijing City), *Gugong bowuyuan yuankan* 故宮博物院院刊 (*Palace Museum Journal*), 1979, no. 3, pp. 3–21.
Hou Renzhi 侯仁之, 'Gudai Beijing yunhe de kaizao he shuailuo' 古代北京運河的開鑿和衰落 (The Opening and Decline of the Grand Canal at Beijing in Ancient Times), *Beijing guihua jianshe* 北京規劃建設 (*Planned Development in Beijing*), 2001, no. 4, pp. 8–12.
Hsieh Bao Hua, 'Empress' Grove: Ritual and Life in the Ming Palace', *Research on Women in Modern Chinese History*, no. 11, December 2003, pp. 99–187.
Hsieh Ming-liang 謝明良, 'Ji Tang gongling aihuanghou mu chutu de taoqi' 記唐恭陵哀皇后墓出土的陶器 (The Ceramics Excavated from the Tomb of Empress Ai of Tang), *Gugong Wenwu Yuekan* 故宮文物月刊 (*The National Palace Museum Monthly of Chinese Art*), no. 296, 2006, pp. 68–83.
Hsieh Tsung-hui 謝聰輝, *Xin Tiandi zhi ming: Yuhuang, Zitong yu feiluan* 新天帝之命：玉皇、梓潼與飛鸞 (*Command of the New Heavenly Emperor: Jade Emperor, Zitong and Flying Phoenixes*), Taipei, 2013.
Hsieh Yu-chen 謝玉珍, 'Mingchu guanfang yongqi de renwuwen' 明初官方用器的人物紋 (The Early Ming Official Wares Decoration with Figure Image), MA diss., Soochou University, 1995.
Hsu, Eileen Hsiang-ling, 'Green, Amber, and Cream: The Forgotten Art of "Liuli" Glazed Ceramics in Ming China', *Record of the Princeton University Art Museum*, vol. 71/2, 2012–13, pp. 36–57.
Hsu, Eileen Hsiang-ling, *Monks in Glaze: the Yixian Luohan and Ceramic Workshops in Ming China*, forthcoming.

Hsu Ya-hwei 許雅惠, '*Xuanhe bogu tu* de jianjie liuchuan: yi Yuandai Saiyin Chidahu mu chutu de taoqi yu *Shaoxi zhouxian shidianyi tu* weili' 《宣和博古圖》的「間接」流傳–以元代賽因赤答忽墓出土的陶器與《紹熙州縣釋奠儀圖》為例 (The 'Indirect' Transmission of the Hsuan-ho po-ku-t'u Earthenware from the Tomb of Sai-yin Ch'ih-ta-hu and the Shao-hsi chou-hsien shih-tien i-t'u), *Guoli Taiwandaxue meishushi yanjiou jikan* 國立臺灣大學美術史研究集刊 (*Taida Journal of Art History*), no. 14, 2003, pp. 1–26.
Hsu Ya-hwei 許雅惠, 'Nansong jinshi shoucang yu zongxing qingjie' 南宋金石收藏與中興情結 (Antiquarian Trends in the Dynastic Revival of the Southern Song), *Guoli Taiwandaxue meishushi yanjiou jikan* 國立臺灣大學美術史研究集刊 (*Taida Journal of Art History*), no. 31, 2011, pp. 1–60.
Hsu Ya-hwei 許雅惠, 'Songdai fugu tongqifeng zhi yuwai chuanbo chutan: yi shier zhi shiwu shiji de Hanguo weili' 宋代復古銅器風之域外傳播初探—以十二至十五世紀的韓國為例 (Revival of Antiquity outside China? – A Preliminary Study of the 'Archaistic Style' in Sino-Korean Artifacts from the Twelfth to the Fifteenth Century), *Guoli Taiwandaxue meishushi yanjiou jikan* 國立臺灣大學美術史研究集刊 (*Taida Journal of Art History*), no. 32, 2012, pp. 103–70.
Hu Guang 胡廣, *Hu wen mu gong wen ji* 胡文穆公文集 (*Collected Writings of Hu Guang*), in *Siku quanshu cunmu congshu* 四庫全書存目叢書 (*Extant Compendia from the Complete Library of the Four Treasuries*), Jinan, 1995–7, *ji* 29.
Hu Shiping, 'The Earthquake-Resistant Properties of Chinese Traditional Architecture', *Earthquake Spectra*, vol. 7, no. 3, 1991, pp. 355–90.
Huang Fulu 皇甫錄, *Huang Ming ji lüe* 皇明紀略 (*Brief Records of the August Ming*), repr. Beijing, 1985.
Huang, Chin-hsin 黃進興, *Youru shengyu: quanli, xinyang yu zhengdangxing* 優入聖域–權力、信仰與正當性 (Entering the Master's Sanctuary: Power, Belief and Legitimacy in Traditional China), Taipei, 1994.
Huang, Ray, *Taxation and Government Finance in 16th century Ming China*, Cambridge, 1974.
Huang Wei 黃薇 and Huang Qinghua 黃清華, 'Guangdong Taishan Shangchuandao Huawanping yizhi chutu ciqi ji xiangguan wenti' 廣東臺山上川島花碗坪遺址出土瓷器及相關問題 (Ceramics Unearthed from the Shangchuan Island of Taishan, Guangdong, and its Related Issues), *Wenwu* 文物 (*Cultural Relics*), no. 5, 2007, pp. 78–88.
Huang Ximing 黃希明, 'Zijincheng gongting yuanlin de jianzhu tese' 紫禁城宮廷園林的建築特色 (Characteristics of Palace Garden Construction in the Forbidden City), *Gugong bowuyuan yuankan* 故宮博物院院刊 (*Palace Museum Journal*), no. 4, 1990, pp. 38–46.
Huang Xun 黃訓, *Ming chen jingji lu* 名臣經濟錄 (*Record of Writings on Statecraft by Famous Ming Officials*), 1551, e-SKQS.
Huang Yongling 黃永陵 (ed.), *Huang Huai wen ji* 黃淮文集 (*Collected Writings of Huang Huai*), Beijing, 2006.
Huang Yu 黃瑜, *Shuang huai sui chao* 雙槐歲鈔 (*Annual Notes of the Two Huai Trees*), Beijing, 1999, repr. 2012.
Huang Yuji 黃虞稷, *Qianqingtang shumu* 千頃堂書目 (*Book Catalogue of the Qianqing Hall*), *c.* 1690, e-SKQS.
Huang Zuo 黃佐, *Hanlin ji* 翰林記 (*Record of the Hanlin Academy*), 1560–6, e-SKQS.
Hubei sheng bowuguan 湖北省博物館 (ed.), *Liangzhuang wang mu: Zheng He shidai de guibao* 梁莊王墓——鄭和時代的瑰寶 (*The Tomb of Prince Liangzhuang: Treasure of the Era of Zheng He*), Beijing, 2007.
Hubei sheng bowuguan 湖北省博物馆 (ed.), *Dao sheng wanwu: Chu di daojiao wenwu* 道生萬物：楚地道教文物 (*The Tao Gives Rise to Ten Thousand Things: Taoist Relics from the Chu Region*), Beijing, 2012.
Hubei sheng jianshe ting 湖北省建設廳, *Wudangshan gujianzhu qun* 武當山古建築群 (*The Traditional Architectural Complex of Mount Wudang*), Beijing, 2005.
Hubei sheng wenwu kaogu yanjiusuo 湖北省文物考古研究所 *et al.*, 'Wuchang Longquanshan Ming Chuzhao wang mu fajue jianbao' 武昌龍泉山明代楚昭王墓發掘簡報 (Brief Report on the Excavation of the Ming-dynasty Tomb of Prince Zhao of Chu at Mount Longquan in Wuchang), *Wenwu* 文物 (*Cultural Relics*), no. 2, 2003, pp. 4–18.
Hubei sheng wenwu kaogu yanjiusuo 湖北省文物考古研究所 and Zhongxiang shi bowuguan 鐘祥市博物館 (eds), *Liangzhuang wang mu* 梁莊王墓 (*Mausoleum of Prince Liang Zhuangwang*), Beijing, 2007.
Hucker, Charles O., *A Dictionary of Official Titles in Imperial China*, Stanford, 1985.
Hunter, Dard, *Papermaking: The History and Technique of an Ancient Craft*, New York, 1978, pp. 201–23.
Huntington, John C., Bangdel, Dina and Thurman, Robert A.F., *The Circle of Bliss: Buddhist Meditational Art*, Columbus, OH, 2003.
Huo Yuanjie 火原潔, *Huayi yiyu* 華夷譯語 (*Sino-foreign Glossaries*), repr. Taipei, 1979.
Hwanghwa jip 황화집 皇華集 (*Anthology of Brilliant Flowers*), 1773, National Library of Korea's collection.
Hymes, Robert, *Way and Byway: Taoism, Local Religion, and Models of Divinity in Sung and Modern China*, Berkeley, Los Angeles and London, 2002.
Idema, Wilt, *The Dramatic Oeuvre of Chu Yu-tun*, Leiden, 1985.
Im Yonghan 임용한, 'Oirat ŭi wihyŏp kwa Chosŏn ŭi pang'ŏ chŏllyak' 오이라트의 위협과 조선의 방어전략 (The Oirat Threat and the Chosŏn Dynasty's Strategies of Defence), *Yŏksa kwa silhak* 역사과실 (*History and Practical Learning*), vol. 46, 2011, pp. 42–70.
Jackson, David P., *A History of Tibetan Painting: The Great Tibetan Painters and their Traditions*, Vienna, 1996.
Jackson, David P., *Patron and Painter: Situ Panchen and the Revival of the Encampment Style*, New York, 2009.
Jackson, David P., *The Nepalese Legacy in Tibetan Painting*, New York, 2010.
Jackson, David P. *et al.*, *Mirror of the Buddha: Early Portraits from Tibet*, New York, 2011.
Jackson, David P., *The Place of Provenance: Regional Styles in Tibetan Painting*, New York, 2012.
Jang, Scarlett, 'The Eunuch Agency Directorate and the Ming Imperial Publishing Enterprise', in David Robinson (ed.), *Culture, Courtiers and Competition: The Ming Court (1368–1644)*, Cambridge, MA, 2008, pp. 116–87.
Jeonju National Museum, *Wang ui chosang gyeonggi geon gwa taejo iseonggye* 왕의 초상, 경기전과 태조 이성계 (*Joseon Royal Portraiture: King Taejo's Image and the Gyeonggi Royal Portrait Hall*), Jeonju, 2005.
Ji Xianlin 季羨林 *et al.*, *Da Tang Xiyu ji jiaozhu* 大唐西域記校注 (*Annotation of the Records of the Western Regions [Visited During] the Great Tang [Dynasty]*), Beijing, 1985.
Jia Jun 賈珺, 'Mingdai *Eryuanji* yanjiu' 明代《二園集》研究 (Study on Two Garden Records of the Ming Dynasty), *Zhongguo jianzhu shilun huikan* 中國建築史論彙刊 (*Journal of Chinese Architectural History*), no. 2, 2013, pp. 334–76.
Jia Xizeng 賈璽增, 'Guguguan xingzhi tezheng ji yanbian kao' 罟罟冠形制特徵及演變考 (Features and Evolution of *gugu* Headdresses), in Zhao Feng 趙豐 and Shang Gang 尚剛 (eds), *Sichou zhi lu yu Yuandai yishu guoji xueshu taolunhui lunwenji* 絲綢之路與元代藝術國際學術討論會論文集 (*Proceedings of the International Conference on the Silk Road and Yuan Dynasty Art*), Hong Kong, 2005, pp. 210–25.
Jiang Cheng'an and Zheng Wenlei (eds), *Precious Deposits: Historical Relics of Tibet, China*, vol. 3, 2000, Beijing.
Jiang Fan 江繁, *Siyi guan kao* 四譯館考 (Study of the Translators' College), in *Siku quanshu zongmu* 四庫全書總目 (*Catalogue of the Complete Library of the Four Treasuries*), vol. 272, Jinan, 1997, pp. 671–728.
Jiang Fenglan 江鳳蘭, 'Qianxi Ningwang Chenhao panluan zhi yuanyin ji zhunbei' 淺析寧王宸濠叛亂之原因及準備 (A Preliminary Analysis of the Reasons and Preparations of Prince Ning Zhu Chenhao's Rebellion), *Jiangxi jiaoyu xueyuan xuebao* 江西教育學院學報 (*Journal of Jiangxi Education Academy*), April 1997, pp. 1–3.
Jiang Shunyuan 姜舜源, 'Yuan Ming zhi ji Beijing gongdian yange kao' 元明之際北京宮殿沿革考 (Change and Development in Beijing Palaces during the Yuan-Ming Transition), *Gugong bowuyuan yuankan* 故宮博物院院刊 (*Palace Museum Journal*), 1991, no. 4, pp. 88–94.
Jiang Shunyuan 姜舜源, 'Lun Beijing Yuan Ming Qing sanchao gongdian de jicheng yu fazhan 論北京元明清三朝宮殿的繼承與發展' (On Continuity and Development in the Palaces of the Yuan, Ming, and Qing Dynasties), *Gugong bowuyuan yuankan* 故宮博物院院刊 (*Palace Museum Journal*), 1992, no. 3, 77–87.
Jiang Shunyuan 姜舜源, 'Ming Qing chaoting Sichuan caimu yanjiu' 明清朝廷四川采木研究 (Research into Sourcing Wood from Sichuan for the Ming and Qing Palaces), in Yu Zhuoyun 于倬雲 and Zhu Chengru 朱誠如 (eds), *Zhongguo Zijincheng xuehui lunwenji, di er ji* 中國紫禁城學會論文集, 第二輯 (*Collected Writings from the Forbidden City Study Society*), Beijing, 2002.

Jiang Yikui 蔣一葵, *Chang'an kehua* 長安客話 (*A Visitor's Remarks on the Capital*), *c.* 1603, repr. Beijing, 1980.
Jiang Yonglin, *The Mandate of Heaven and the Great Ming Code*, Seattle and London, 2011.
Jiao Hong 焦竑, *Yu tang cong yu* 玉堂叢語 (*Comments from Jade Hall*), Beijing, 1981.
Jin Ao 金鰲, *Jinling dai zheng lu* 金陵待徵錄 (*Corrective Record of Jinling*), 1844, repr. Taipei, 1983.
Jin Qiupeng 金秋鵬, 'Qijin faxian zuizao de Zheng He xia xiyang chuandui tuxiang ziliao –*Tianfeijing* juanshou chatu' 迄今發現最早的鄭和下西洋船隊圖像資料 — 《天妃經》卷首插圖 (The Earliest Hitherto Discovered Illustration of Zheng He Going to the South Seas in the Sūtra on the Celestial Spouse (*Tianfeijing*)), *Zhongguo keji shiliao* 中國科技史料 (*Chinese Historical Materials of Science and Technology*) vol. 21, no. 1, 2000, pp. 61–4.
Jin Weinuo 金維諾, 'Fahaisi bihua 'Dishifantian tu' 法海寺壁畫 '帝師梵天圖' (The 'Indra Iconography' of the Wall Paintings of Fahai Temple), *Meishu yanjiu* 美术研究 (*Art Research*), no. 3,1959, pp. 24–7.
Jin Weinuo 金維諾, 'Fahaisi bihua "Dishifantian tu" de yuanyuan yi chengjiu' 法海寺壁畫 '帝師梵天圖' 的源源以成就 (The Origins and Achievements of the 'Indra Iconography' of the Wall Paintings of Fahai Temple), in Jin Weinuo 金維諾 (ed.), *Beijing Fahaisi bihua* 北京法海寺壁畫 (*The Fahai Temple Frescoes*), Shijiazhuang, 2001.
Jing Anning, 'The Portraits of Khubilai Khan and Chabi by Anige (1245–1306), a Nepali Artist at the Yuan Court', *Artibus Asiae*, vol. 54, no. 1/2, 1994, pp. 3–54.
Jingzhou bowuguan 荊州博物館, 'Hubei Jingzhou Ming Xiangxian wang mu fajue jiabao' 湖北荊州明湘獻王墓發掘簡報 (Brief Report on the Excavation of the Ming Tomb of Prince Xian of Xiang in Jingzhou, Hubei), *Wenwu* 文物 (*Cultural Relics*), no. 4, 2009, pp. 43–60.
Jixiang 際祥, *Jingcisi zhi* 淨慈寺志 (*Records of the Jingci Monastery*), Hangzhou, 1888; *Hanji dianzi wenxian ziliao ku* 漢籍全文資料庫 (*Scripta Sinica database*), Taipei, http://hanchi.ihp.sinica.edu.tw/ihp/hanji.htm.
Johnston, Alistair Ian, *Cultural Realism: Strategic Culture and Grand Strategy in Chinese History*, Princeton, 1995.
JWS: *Joseon wangjo sillok* 朝鮮王朝實錄 DB (*Veritable Records of the Joseon Dynasty*), National Institute of Korean History, http://sillok.history.go.kr/main/main.jsp.
Kane, Donald, *The Sino-Jurchen Vocabulary of the Bureau of Interpreters*, Bloomington, 1989.
Kang Mun-sik 강문식, 'Jiphyeonjeon chulsin gwan'in ui hakmungwan gwa jeongchigwan' 집현전 출신 관인의 학문관과 정치관 (Academic and Political Vision of Jiphyeonjeon Scholars), *Hanguksaron* 한국사론 (*The History of Korea*), vol. 39, June 1998, pp. 90–7.
Kang, David C., *East Asia Before the West: Five Centuries of Trade and Tribute*, New York, 2010.
Karashima, Noburu, 'The Yeh-pa-nai-na Problem in the History of Sri Lanka: A Review Based on New Chinese Sources', in Leelananda Premayilleke, Karthigesu Indrapala and J.E. van Lohuizen-de Leeuw (eds), *Senarat Paranavitana Commemoration Volume*, Leiden, 1978, pp. 98–106.
Kares, Jean, 'Translation of Medium: Kesi Meets Painting', *Textile Society of America Symposium Proceedings*, 2008, Paper 279, http://digitalcommons.unl.edu/tsaconf/279.
Karmay, Heather, *Early Sino-Tibetan Art*, Warminster, 1975.
Kawachi Yoshihiro 河内良弘, *Mindai Nyoshinshi no kenkyū* 明代女真史の研究 (*History of the Jurchen in the Ming Period*), Kyoto, 1992.
Ke Shangqian 柯尚遷, *Zhouli quan jing shi yuan* 周禮全經釋原 (*Source of Explanations on the Complete Classic of the Rites of Zhou*), 1545, e-SKQS.
Keay, Anna, *The Crown Jewels: The Official Illustrated History*, London, 2012.
Kerr, Rose and Wood, Nigel, *Joseph Needham, Science and Civilization in China*, vol. 5, part 12, *Ceramic Technology*, Cambridge, 2004.
Kieschnick, John, 'The Symbolism of the Monk's Robe in China', *Asia Major*, vol. 12, no. 1, 1999, pp. 9–32.
Kieschnick, John, *The Impact of Buddhism on Chinese Material Culture*, Princeton, 2003.
Kim Eun-jeong 김은정, 'Gyeong'o bon *Hwanghwa jip* pyeonchan gyeong'wi wa simun suchang ui uimi' 경오본 황화집 편찬경위와 시문수창의 의미 (Publication of gyeong'o version of *Hwanghwa jip* and the Meaning of Exchange Poems), *Hanguk hansi yeongu* 한국한시연구 (*Study of Korean Classical Poetry*), vol. 7, 1999, pp. 307–16, 333–4.
Kim Won-yong 김원용, '*Samgang haengsildo* e daehayeo' 삼강행실도에 대하여 (On the *Illustrated Guide to the Three Bonds*), *Samgang haengsildo* 삼강행실도 (*The Illustrated Guide to the Three Bonds*), Seoul, 1982, pp. 3–8.
Kim Yun-jeong 金允貞, '15세기明朝宮廷用磁器의제작체계와관리' 〈十五世紀明朝宮廷用瓷器之製作體制與管理〉 (The System and Management in Production of Ming Imperial Ware)', 미술을 통해 본 동아시아사中國史學會–第55回學術發表會論文集 (*The 55th Conference Proceeding of Institution of Chinese History*), Daegu, 2007, pp. 26–40.
Kirkman, James S., *The Arab City of Gedi*, Oxford, 1954.
Kirkman, James S., *Fort Jesus: A Portuguese Fortress on the East African Coast*, Oxford, 1974.
Kitajima Manji 北島万次, 'Eirakuteiki ni okeru Chōson ōkoku no sakuhō to kōeki' 永楽帝期における朝鮮王国の冊封と交易 (Investiture and Trade with the Kingdom of Chosŏn during the Yongle Period), in Tanaka Takeo (ed.), *Zenkindai no Nihon to Higashi Ajia* 前近代の日本と東アジア (*Early Modern Japan and East Asia*), Tokyo, 1995, pp. 197–215.
Kojima Tsuyoshi 小島毅, '嘉靖の礼制改革について' (The Reformation of Ritual in the Jiajing Era), *Toyo bunka kenkyushyo kiyo* 東洋文化研究所紀要 (*Memoirs of the Institute of Oriental Culture*) 117, 1992, pp. 117, 381–426.
Komaroff, Linda, 'Persian Verses of Gold and Silver: Inscriptions on Timurid Metalwork', in Lisa Golombek and Maria Subtelny (eds), *Timurid Art and Culture*, Leiden, 1992, pp. 144–57.
Komaroff, Linda and Carboni, Stefano (eds), *The Legacy of Genghis Khan: Courtly Art and Culture in Western Asia, 1256–1353*, New York, 2002.
Krahl, Regina, *Chinese Ceramics in the Topkapi Saray Museum, Istanbul*, 3 vols, London, 1986.
Krahl, Regina, 'Glazed Roofs and Other Tiles', *Orientations*, March 1991, pp. 47–61.
Krahl, Regina, *The Emperor's Broken China Reconstructing Chenghua Porcelain, An Exhibition of Chinese Porcelains of the Chenghua Period (1465–87) Recently Excavated from the Imperial Kiln Site at Jingdezhen in South China at Sotheby's*, London, 1995.
Krahl, Regina, 'Chinese Ceramics in the Topkapi Saray Museum, Istanbul', in Ayse Ucok (ed.), *Chinese Treasures in Istanbul*, Istanbul, 2001, pp. 40–101.
Kuang Yuche 匡裕徹 and Ren Chongyue 任崇岳, 'Pingdingshan menguzu Ma shi kaoshu' 平頂山蒙古族馬氏考述 (Research into the Mongolian Ma Clan of Mount Pingding), *Zhongnan minzu xueyuan xuebao (Zhexue shehui kexue ban)* 中南民族學院學報 (哲學社會科學版) (*Journal of South-central University for Nationalities (Philosophy and Social Science)*), no. 4, 1984, pp. 49–54.
Kuehn, Sara, *The Dragon in Medieval East Christian and Islamic Art*, Leiden and Boston, 2011.
Kun Gang 崑岡 (ed.), *Qinding Da Qing huidian* 欽定大清會典 (*Imperially Endorsed Collected Statutes of the Great Qing*), Taipei, 1963.
Kun Gang 崑岡 (ed.), *Da Qing huidian shili* 大清會典事例 (*Statutes of the Great Qing with Precedents and Examples*), Beijing, 1991.
Kyūshū Kokuritsu Hakubutsukan 九州国立博物館 (ed.), *Seichi Chibetto: Potara-kyū to tenkū no shihō* 聖地チベット: ポタラ宮と天空の至宝 (*Tibet: Treasures from the Roof of the World*), Tokyo, 2009.
Lam, Joseph Sui Ching, *State Sacrifices and Music in Ming China (A.D. 1368–1644): Creativity, Orthodoxy and Expressiveness*, Albany, 1998.
Lan Yong 藍勇, 'Ming Qing shiqi de huang mu cai ban' 明清時期的皇木採辦 (The Procurement of Wood for Imperial Use in the Ming and Qing Period), *Lishi yanjiu* 歷史研究 (*Historical Research*), no. 6, 1994, pp. 86–98.
Lau, Christine, 'Ceremonial Monochrome Wares of the Ming Dynasty', in Rosemary E. Scott (ed.), *The Porcelains of Jingdezhen*, PDF Colloquies on Chinese Art and Archaeology in Asia, no. 16, London, 1993, pp. 83–100.
Ledderose, Lothar, *Ten Thousand Things: Module and Mass Production in Chinese Art*, Princeton, 2000.
Lee, Jung Eun 李定恩, 'Joseonwangjo Sejong sillok Jegidoseol ui jejeongbaegyeong gwa Joseon chogi yejemisul ui hyeongseong' 『세종실록』 '祭器圖說'의 제정배경과 조선초기 예제 미술의 형성 (Background and meaning of 'Pictorial Illustrations of Ritual

Vessels' in Annals of the King Sejong and Creation of Ritual Art in the Early Joseon), in *Dongasia ui gungjungmisul: Kim Hongnam gyosu jeongnyeon toeim ginyeom nonmungip* 東亞細亞之宮廷藝術：金紅男教授退休紀念論文集 (*Court Art in East Asia : Collection of Essays Commemorating the Occasion of Professor Kim Hongnam's Retirement*), Seoul, 2013, pp. 256–79.

Lee Hui-shu, *Empresses, Art, and Agency in Song Dynasty China*, Seattle, 2010.

Lee Soomi 이수미, 'Taejo eojin ui 'jejak gwa bong an' 태조어진의 제작과 봉안 (Production and Installation of Portrait of King Taejo), *Wang ui chosang gyeonggi geon gwa taejo iseonggye* 왕의 초상, 경기전과 태조 이성계 (*Joseon Royal Portraiture: King Taejo's Image and the Gyeonggi Royal Portrait Hall*), Jeonju, 2005, pp. 228–41.

Lee Soomi 이수미, 'Gyeonggi geon ui weonbonjeok seongkeok jaekeomto' 경기전 태조어진의 원본적 성격 재검토 (Re-examining the Characteristics that Denote the Original Image of King Taejo at the Gyeonggi Royal Portrait Hall), *Joseon wangsil gwa jeonju* 조선왕실과 전주 (*Jeonju: The Origin of the Joseon Dynasty*), Jeonju, 2010, pp. 234–42.

Lee Soyoung and Leidy, Denise Patry, *Silla: Korea's Golden Kingdom*, New York, 2014.

Lentz, Thomas W. and Lowry, Glenn D., *Timur and the Princely Vision: Persian Art and Culture in the Fifteenth Century*, Los Angeles, 1989.

Levathes, Louise, *When China Ruled the Seas: The Treasure Fleet of the Dragon Throne, 1405–1433*, Oxford, 1994.

Li Bin 李斌, 'Yongle chao yu Annan de huoqi jishu jiaoliu', 永樂朝與安南的火器技術交流 (The Exchange of Firearms Technology with Annam in the Yongle Period), in Zhong Shaoyi 鐘少異 (ed.), *Zhongguo gudai huoyao huoqi shi yanjiu* 中國古代火藥火器史研究 (*Studies on Ancient Chinese Firearms*), Beijing, 1995, pp. 147–58.

Li Bozhong, 'Was There a "Fourteenth-Century Turning Point"? Population, Land, Technology and Farm Management', in Paul Jakov Smith and Richard von Glahn (eds), *The Song–Yuan–Ming Transition in Chinese History*, Cambridge, MA and London, 2003, pp. 135–75.

Li Dongyang 李東陽, *Huai lu tang ji* 懷麓堂集 (*Collected Works of Huailu Hall*), 1516, e-SKQS.

Li Dongyang 李東陽 and Shen Shixing 申時行 (eds), *Da Ming Hui Dian* 大明會典 (*Collected Statutes of the Great Ming*) (*DMHD*), Dongnan shubaoshe facsimile of 1587 edn, Taipei, 1963.

Li He and Knight, Michael, *Power and Glory: Court Arts of China's Ming Dynasty*, San Francisco, 2008.

Li Jie 李誡, *Yingzao fashi* 營造法式 (*Treatise on Architectural Methods*), *Wenyuange Qinding Siku quanshu* 文淵閣欽定四庫全書 (*Wenyuan Copy of the Complete Library in Four Sections*), Beijing, 2006.

Li Jinggeng 李精耕 and Huang Peijun 黄佩君, 'Mingdai "Taigeti" mengzhu Yang Shiqi shiwen quxiang chutan' 明代台閣體盟主楊士奇詩文取向初探 (On the Orientation of the Poetry and Prose of Yang Shiqi, Leading Figure of the 'Grand Secretariat Style'), *Jiangxi shehui kexue* 江西社會科學 (*Jiangxi Social Sciences*), no. 11, 2008, pp. 113–17.

Li Kangying, *The Ming Maritime Trade Policy in Transition, 1368 to 1567*, Wiesbaden, 2010.

Li Kehe 李克和, 'Zhu Quan quxue yanjiu' 朱權曲學研究 (A Study of Zhu Quan's Theories on *Qu* Arias), in *Ming Qing qulun ge'an yanjiu* 明清曲論個案研究 (*Case Studies on Ming and Qing Theories on Qu Arias*), Beijing, 2010, pp. 1–26.

Li Qianlang 李乾朗, 'Changling Ling'endian' 長陵祾恩殿 (The Hall of Eminent Favour of the Changling Tomb), *Zijincheng* 紫禁城 (*Forbidden City*), no. 5, 2009, pp. 18–25.

Li Rongxi (trans.), *The Great Tang Dynasty Record of the Western Regions*, Berkeley, 1996.

Li Ruoqing 李若晴, 'Yanyun ru hua – Beijing bajing tu kaoxi' 燕雲入畫 – 北京八景圖考析 (The Capital in Painting – A Study of the *Eight Views of Beijing*), *Xin meishu* 新美術 (*New Arts*), no. 6, 2009, pp. 27–35.

Li Ruoqing 李若晴, 'Yutang yiyin: *Xingyuan yaji tu* juan kaoxi' 玉堂遺音：《杏園雅集圖》卷考析 (Remaining Sounds from the Jade Hall: Analysis of the *Elegant Gathering in the Apricot Garden* Scroll), *Meishu xuebao* 美術學報 (*Art Journal*), no. 4, 2010, pp. 60–9.

Li Ruoqing 李若晴, 'Xia er xiang feng – "Mingren hua ruiying tujuan" kaoxi' 遐邇向風:《明人畫瑞應圖卷》考析 (Analysis of the *Ming Painting of Auspicious Responses*), *Meishu yanjiu* 美術研究 (*Art Research*), no. 1, 2012a, pp. 42–6.

Li Ruoqing 李若晴, 'Zouyu ru xian: Ming Yongle "Zouyu tu" juan kao xi' 騶虞入獻：明永樂《騶虞圖》卷考析 (*Zouyu* as Tribute: Analysis of *Painting of Zouyu* from the Ming Yongle period), *Nanjing yishu xueyuan xuebao* 南京藝術學院學報 (*Journal of Nanjing Arts Institute (Fine Arts & Design)*), no. 3, 2012b, pp. 18–21.

Li Song 李松, 'Beijing Fahaisi' 北京法海寺 (Fahai (Sea of the Law) Temple in Beijing), *Xiandai foxue* 現代佛學 (*Modern Buddhism*), no. 4, 1963, pp. 37–42.

Li Xian 李賢, *Gurang ji* 古穰集 (*Collected Works of Li Xian*), *c.* 1470, e-SKQS.

Li Xiaocong, *Réflexions sur l'occupation de l'espace dans le vieux Pékin*, trans. Victoire Suro, Beijing, 2002.

Li Xieping 李燮平, 'Yongle Yingjian Beijing gongdian tanshi' 永樂營建北京宮殿探實 (Research on the Construction of Beijing Imperial Palace under Yongle's Reign), in Yu Zhuoyun 于倬雲 (ed.), *Zijincheng jianzhu yanjiu yu baohu* 紫禁城建築研究與保護 (*Research and Conservation of the Forbidden City Buildings*), Beijing, 1995, pp. 34–64.

Li Zhaoxiang 李昭祥, *Longjiang chuanchang zhi* 龍江船廠志 (Longjiang Shipyard Treatise), *Xuanlantang congshu xuji* 玄覽堂叢書續集 (*Additional Collectanea from the Xuanlan Hall*), vol. 117, facsimile of Jiajing (1522–67) edn, comp. Zheng Zhenduo 鄭振鐸, Nanjing, 1947.

Li Zhaoxiang 李昭祥, *Longjiang chuanchang zhi* 龍江船廠志 (Longjiang Shipyard Treatise), original date 1553, ed. Wang Lianggong 王亮功, Nanjing, 1999.

Li Zhenyu 李真瑜, *Mingdai gongting xijushi* 明代宮廷戲劇史 (*History of Theatre in the Ming Court*), Beijing, 2010.

Li Zhihong 李志鴻, *Daojiao tianxin zhengfa yanjiu* 道教天心正法研究 (*History and Ritual: A Study of Tianxin Zhengfa*), Beijing, 2011.

Li Zongwan 勵宗萬, *Jingcheng guji kao* 京城古蹟考 (*Study of Ancient Traces of the Capital*), 1745, repr. Beijing, 1981.

Liang Sicheng 梁思成, *Yingzao fashi* 營造法式 (*State Building Standards*), Beijing, 1983.

Liang Sicheng and Fairbank, Wilma, *Chinese Architecture: A Pictorial History*, Mineola, NY, 2005.

Liang Sicheng 梁思成, *Qing Gongbu 'Gongcheng zuofa celi' tujie* 清工部《工程做法則例》圖解 (*Imperial Specifications for State Buildings in Qing Dynasty*), Beijing, 2006.

Liang Sui 梁穗 (ed.), *Jingdezhen chutu Yuan Ming guanyao ciqi* 景德鎮出土元明官窯瓷器 (*Yuan and Ming Imperial Porcelains Excavated at Jingdezhen*), Beijing, 1999.

Liao Baoxiu 廖寶秀, 'Xuande guanyao ciqi fengfuxing zhi yanjiu' 宣德官窯瓷器豐富性之研究 (Research into the Richness of Xuande Imperial Porcelain), *Gugong xueshu jikan* 故宮學術季刊 (*The National Palace Museum Research Quarterly*), no. 1, 1998, pp. 87–154.

Liao Daonan 廖道南, *Diange cilin ji* 殿閣詞林記 (*Notes on the Forest of Words [of the Hanlin Academy] and the Halls and Offices [of the Grand Secretaries]*), 1545, e-SKQS.

Liao Yang 廖暘, 'Qutansi Qutandian tuxiang chengxu suyuan' 瞿曇寺瞿曇殿圖像程序溯源 (The Origins of the Iconographical Program of the Wall-Paintings in Qutan Temple of Qutan Monastery), *Gugong bowuyuan yuankan* 故宮博物院院刊 (*Palace Museum Journal*), no. 6, 2012, pp. 96–121.

Liew Foon Ming, 'The Luchuan-Pingmian Campaigns (1436–1449) in the Light of Official Chinese Historiography', *Oriens Extremus*, vol. 39, no. 2, 1996, pp. 162–203.

Liew Foon Ming, *The Treatises on Military Affairs of the Ming Dynastic History, (1368–1644): an annotated translation of the treatises on military affairs, chapter 89 and chapter 90: supplemented by the treatises on military affairs of the draft of the Ming Dynastic History: a documentation of Ming-Qing historiography and the decline and fall of the Ming Empire*, Hamburg, 1998.

Lin Meicun 林梅村, 'Zhubao yishu yu Zhongwai wenhua jiaoliu' 珠寶藝術與中外文化交流 (The Art of Jewellery and Cultural Exchange), *Kaogu yu wenwu* 考古與文物 (*Archaeology and Cultural Relics*), no. 1, 2014, pp. 76–88.

Lin Sheng-chih 林聖智, 'Mingdai Daojiao tuxiangxue yanjiu: Yi *Xuantian ruiying tu* wei li 明代道教圖像學研究：以《玄帝瑞應圖》為例 (Daoist Iconology of the Ming Dynasty – With *Auspicious Responses of the Dark Emperor* as a Case Study), *Meishushi yanjiu jikan* 美術史研究集刊 (*Taida Journal of Art History*), no. 6, 1999, pp. 133–91.

Lin Yeqiang 林業強, 'Ming Qing paofu longwen zashuo' 明清袍服龍

紋雜說 (Notes on Dragon Motifs on Ming and Qing Robes), in Zong Fengying 宗鳳英, Ling Yeqian 林業強 and Peter Lam (eds), *Chaotian jinxiu: Shengwenge cang Ming Qing gongting fushi* 朝天錦繡: 昇雯閣藏明清宮廷服飾 (*Heavenly Splendour: The Edrina Collection of Ming and Qing Imperial Costumes*), Hong Kong, 2009, pp. 31–43.
Lin Yin 林尹, *Zhouli jin zhu jin yi* 周禮今注今訳 (*The Rites of Zhou, with Modern Commentary and Translation*), Taipei, 1987.
Linrothe, Robert, *Paradise and Plumage: Chinese Connections in Tibetan Arhat Painting*, New York, 2004.
Liscomb, Kathlyn, 'The "Eight Views of Beijing": Politics in Literati Art', *Artibus Asiae*, vol. 49, 1988–9, pp. 127–52.
Liscomb, Kathlyn, 'Foregrounding the Symbiosis of Power: A Rhetorical Strategy in Some Chinese Commemorative Art', *Art History*, vol. 25, no. 2, April 2002, pp. 135–61.
Little, Stephen with Eichman, Shawn, *Taoism and the Arts of China*, Chicago, 2000.
Liu Dunzhen 劉敦楨, 'Ming Changling' 明長陵 (The Changling Tomb of the Ming Dynasty), *Zhongguo yingzao xueshe huikan* 中國營造學社匯刊 (*Bulletin of the Society for Research in Chinese Architecture*), vol. 4, no. 2, 1933.
Liu Heping, 'Empress Liu's "Icon of Maitreya": Portraiture and Privacy at the Early Song Court', *Artibus Asiae*, vol. 63, no. 2, 2003, pp. 129–90.
Liu Pujiang, 'The End of the Five Virtues Theory: Changes of Traditional Political Culture in China since the Song Dynasty', *Frontiers of History in China*, vol. 2, no. 4, 2007, pp. 513–46.
Liu Ruoyu 劉若愚, *Ming gongshi Jin'ao tuishi biji* 明宮史金鰲退食筆記 (*History of Ming Palace, Collected Notes about the Imperial Palace*), Beijing, 1980.
Liu Tung 劉侗 and Yu Yizheng 于奕正, *Dijing jingwu lüe* 帝京景物略 (*Description of the Scenery of the Imperial Capital*), 1635, repr. Taipei, 1969.
Liu Xinru, *Ancient India and Ancient China: Trade and Religious Exchanges, AD 1–600*, Delhi, 1994.
Liu Xinru, *Silk and Religion: An Exploration of Material Life and the Thought of People AD 600–1200*, Oxford, 1996.
Liu Xinyuan 劉新園, 'Mindai Hongwu tyo ni okeru to ketokuchin gokisyo sesa nendai ni tsuite' 明代洪武朝における用瓷と景德鎮御器廠設置年代について (The Date of Setting the Official Kiln in Jingdezhen in Hongwu Reign Period), in *Mikami Tsugio hakase kinen runbun shyo, Tojihen* 三上次男博士喜壽紀念論文集一陶磁篇 (*A Festschrift in Honor of Dr. Mikami Tsugi*, edition of ceramics), Tokyo, 1985, pp. 129–37.
Liu Xinyuan 劉新園, *Ming Xuande guanyao xishuai guan* 明宣德官窯蟋蟀罐 (*Ming Xuande Official Kiln Cricket Cages*), Jingdezhen, 1995.
Liu Xinyuan *et al.*, *Xuande Imperial Porcelain Excavated at Jingdezhen*, Taipei, 1998.
Liu Xu 劉旭 and Chen Xibo 陳喜波, 'Wuliu shijiao xia de Ming Beijing yingjian mucai caiban yanjiu: yi chuanmu caiban weili' 物流視角下的明北京營建木材採辦研究 —— 以川木採辦為例 (The Procurement of Lumber for Construction in Ming Beijing from the Point of View of Transportation), *Dili yanjiu* 地理研究 (*Geographical Research*), 2010, no. 8, pp. 1407–15.
Liu Yan 劉巖, Qin Dashu 秦大樹 and Kiriama, Herman, 'Kenniya binhaisheng Gedi gucheng yizhi chutu Zhongguo ciqi' 肯尼亞濱海省格迪古城遺址出土中國瓷器 (Chinese ceramics unearthed from Gedi Ruin of Coastal Province, Kenya), *Wenwu* 文物 (*Cultural Relics*), no. 11, 2012, pp. 37–60.
Liu Yi 劉憶, 'Ming Ningwang Zhu Quan yu Zhonghe qin' 明寧王朱權與中和琴 (Prince of Ning Zhu Quan and the Harmonious Qin He Produced), *Nanjing yishu xueyuan xuebao* 南京藝術學院學報 (*Journal of Nanjing Academy of Arts*), no. 4, 1988, pp. 53–4.
Liu Yingsheng 劉迎勝, 'Xilanshan bei de shiyuan yanjiu' 錫蘭山碑的史源研究 (Research on the Historical Sources for the Sri Lankan Stele), *Zheng He yanjiu* 鄭和研究 (*Zheng He Research*), vol. 72, no. 4, 2008, pp. 45–52.
Lo Hui-Yang 羅輝映, 'Lun Mingda "Daliyi"' 論明代「大禮議」 (Discussion on the Great Ritual Controversy of the Ming Dynasty), *Mingshi yanjiu luncong* 明史研究論叢 (*Collected Articles on Ming History*), vol. 3, 1985, pp. 167–88.
Lo Jung-pang 羅榮邦, 'The Emergence of China as a Sea Power During the Late Song and Early Yuan Periods', *Far Eastern Quarterly* 14, 4, August 1955, pp. 489–503.
Lo Jung-pang 羅榮邦, 'Intervention in Vietnam: A Case Study of the Foreign Policy of the Early Ming Government', *Tsing hua Journal of Chinese Studies*, vol. 8, 1970, pp. 154–85.
Lo Jung-pang 羅榮邦, *China as a Sea Power 1127–1368: A Preliminary Survey of the Maritime Expansion and Naval Exploits of the Chinese People during the Southern Song and Yuan Periods*, Singapore and Hong Kong, 2012.
Loch, Captain Granville G., *The Closing Events of the Campaign in China: the Operations in the Yang-tze-kiang and Treaty of Nanjing*, London, 1843.
Long Wenbin 龍文彬, *Ming huiyao* 明會要 (*Institutions of the Ming Dynasty*), 2 vols, Beijing, 1998.
Lopez Jr, Donald S. (ed.), *Critical Terms for the Study of Buddhism*, Chicago, 2005.
Lorge, Peter A., *The Asian Military Revolution: From Gunpowder to the Bomb*, Cambridge, 2008.
Lu Ben 吕本, *et al.* (eds), Huang Ming baoxun 皇明寶訓 (Precious Instructions of the Imperial Ming), SKQS, Tainan, 1996.
Lu Can 陸粲, *Luzi yu ji* 陸子餘集 (*Collected Works of Lu Can*), *c.* 1552, e-SKQS.
Lu Jiugao 陸九皋, 'Xie Tingxun *Xingyuan yaji tu* juan' 謝廷循 '杏園雅集圖'卷 (Xie Huan's *Elegant Gathering in the Apricot Garden* Scroll), *Wenwu* 文物 (*Cultural Relics*), no. 4, 1963, pp. 24–6.
Lu Maocun 盧茂村, 'Dangtuxian Mingdai liuliyao kaochaji' 當塗縣明代琉璃窯考察記 (Survey Report on Ming Period Liuli Kilns in Dangtu County), *Dongnan Wenhua* 東南文化 (*Southeast Culture*), 1996, no. 1, pp. 113–14.
Lu Minghua 陸明華, 'Mingqing huangjia cizhi jiqi yanjiu' 明清皇家瓷質祭器研究 (Studies of Imperial Porcelain Ritual Vessels in the Ming and Qing Dynasties), *Shanghai bowuguan jikan* 上海博物館集刊 (*Journal of Shanghai Museum*), no. 5, 1990, pp. 139–49.
Lu Pengliang 陸鵬亮, 'Xuande Bronzes: A Legend Re-examined', *Arts of Asia*, vol. 44, no. 6, November/December 2014, pp. 90–100.
Lu Rong 陸容, *Shuyuan za ji* 菽園雜記 (*Miscellaneous Records of the Bean Garden*), 1494, e-SKQS.
Lü Weiqi 呂維祺, *Siyi guan ze* 四譯館則 (*Regulations of Bureau of Translators*), 1775, repr. Kyoto, 1928.
Lu Xixing 陸錫興, 'Ming Liangzhuang wang mu maoding zhi yanjiu: jian lun Yuan Ming shidai damao he maoding' 明梁莊王墓帽頂之研究: 兼論元明時代大帽和帽頂 (The Study of Hat Ornaments from the Tomb of Prince Zhuang of Liang and Hats and Hat Ornaments of the Yuan and Ming Dynasties), *Nanfang wenwu* 南方文物 (*Cultural Relics of Southern China*), no. 4, 2012, pp. 96–100.
Lü Yuan 呂原, *Lü Wenyi gong quan ji* 呂文懿公全集 (*Comprehensive Collected Works of Lü Yuan*), 1480–1520, microfilm.
Luk Yu-ping, *The Empress and the Heavenly Masters: A Study of the Ordination Scroll of Empress Zhang (1493)*, Hong Kong, 2016a.
Luk Yu-ping, 'Celestial Mistress and Bodhisattva: Visualizing the Divine Identities of Two Empresses in Ming China (1368–1644)', in Melia Belli Bose (ed.), *Women, Gender and Art in Asia, c. 1600–1900*, London, 2016b.
Luo Di 洛地, 'Xuyan' 序言 (Preface), in Yao Pinwen 姚品文, *Wangzhe yue xuezhe: Ningwang Zhu Quan di yisheng* 王者與學者-寧王朱權的一生 (*A Prince and A Scholar: The Life of Prince of Ning, Zhu Quan*), Beijing, 2013, pp. 1–20.
Luo Wenhua 羅文華, 'Ming Dabao fawang jian Pudu dazhai changjuan' 明大寶法王建普度大齋長卷 (Miracles of the Mass of Universal Salvation), *Zhongguo zangxue* 中國藏學 (*Chinese Tibetology*), vol. 1, 1995, pp. 89–97.
Ma Huan 馬歡, *Yingyai shenglan* 瀛涯勝覽 (*General Survey of the Ocean Shores*), Feng Chengjun 馮承鈞 (ed.), repr. Beijing, 1955.
Ma Huan 馬歡, *Yingyai shenglan* 瀛涯勝覽 (*General Survey of the Ocean Shores*), Shen Jiefu 沈節甫 (ed.), *c.* 1617.
Ma Lan 馬蘭 (ed.), *Qinghai wenwu jingpin tuji* 青海文物精品圖集 (*Catalogue of Highlights of Cultural Relics from Qinghai Province*), Beijing, 1999.
MacGregor, Neil, *A History of the World in 100 Objects*, London, 2010.
Malekandathil, Pius, *Portuguese Cochin and the Maritime Trade of India, 1500–1663*, New Delhi, 2001.
Manguin, Pierre-Yves, 'Asian Shipbuilding Traditions in the Indian Ocean at the Dawn of European Expansion', in A.K. Sinha (ed.), *Approaches to History, Culture, Art, and Archaeology: Essays in Honour of Professor Om Prakash*, New Delhi, 2009.
Manz, Beatrice F., *The Rise and Rule of Tamerlane*, Cambridge, 1989.

Mao Qiling 毛奇齡, *Xiheji* 西河集 (Collected Works of Mao Qiling), e-SKQS.
Mao Qiling 毛奇齡, *Ming Wuzong wai ji* 明武宗外紀 (*A Supplementary History of Emperor Wuzong*), Shanghai, 1982.
Mao Yuanyi 茅元儀, *Wubei zhi* 武備志 (*Treatise on Military Preparedness*), 1628.
Martin, Lillian Ray, *The Art and Archaeology of Venetian Ships and Boats*, College Station, TX, 2001.
Masuya, Tomoko, 'Ilkhanid Courtly Life', in Linda Komaroff and Stefano Carboni (eds), *The Legacy of Genghis Khan: Courtly Art and Culture in Western Asia, 1256–1353*, New York, 2002, pp. 74–103.
McCall, Timothy, 'Brilliant Bodies: Material Culture and the Adornment of Men in North Italy's Quattrocento Courts', *I Tatti Studies in the Italian Renaissance*, no. 16, 2013, pp. 445–90.
McKeown, Arthur Philip, 'From Bodhgayā to Lhasa to Beijing: The Life and Times of Śāriputra (*c.* 1335–1426), Last Abbot of Bodhgayā', Ph.D diss., Harvard University, 2010.
McLoughlin, Kevin, *Ming: The Golden Empire*, Edinburgh, 2014.
McMahon, Keith, *Women Shall Not Rule: Imperial Wives and Concubines in China from Han to Liao*, Lanham, 2013.
Medley, Margaret, 'The "Illustrated Regulations for Ceremonial Paraphernalia of the Ch'ing Dynasty" in the Victoria and Albert Museum: Paper read by Miss Margaret Medley on 18th March, 1959', *Transactions of the Oriental Ceramic Society*, vol. 31, 1957–9, pp. 95–104.
Meng Fanren 孟凡人, *Mingdai gongting jianzu shi* 明代宮廷建築史 (*A History of Ming Palace Architecture*), Beijing, 2011.
Mengzi 孟子 (Mencius), http://ctext.org.
Menon, Sreedhara A., *A Survey of Kerala History*, Kottayam, 1970.
Meulenbeld, Mark, 'Civilized Demons: Ming Thunder Gods from Ritual to Literature', Ph.D diss., Princeton University, 2007.
Meulenbeld, Mark, *Demonic Warfare: Daoism, Territorial Networks, and the History of a Ming Novel*, Honolulu, 2015.
Michaelson, Carol, *Gilded Dragons: Buried Treasure from China's Golden Ages*, London, 1999.
Mills, J.V.G. (trans. and ed.), *Ma Huan, Ying-yai sheng-lan. The Overall Survey of the Ocean's Shores [1433]*. Hakluyt Society Extra Series 42, Cambridge, 1970.
Mills, J.V., 'Chinese Navigators in Insulinde about A.D. 1500', *Archipel* 18, 1979, pp. 69–93.
Minghe 明河, *Buxu gaoseng zhuan* 補續高僧傳 (*Supplement to Extended Biographies of Eminent Monks*), in *Xu zang jing* 續藏經 (*Extended Canon*), vol. 77, no. 1524, http://www.cbeta.org/result/normal/X77/1524_015.htm.
Miura, Kunio 三浦國雄, '"Yushu jing" no keisei to dempa' 「玉枢経」の形成と伝播 (The Formation and Propagation 'Yushu jing'), *Tōhō shūkyō* 東方宗教 (*Journal of Eastern Religions*), vol. 105, 2005, pp. 1–19.
Momoki Shiro, 'Đại Việt and the South China Sea Trade: From the 10th to the 15th Century', *Crossroads*, vol. 12, no. 1, 1998, pp. 1–34.
Morgan, Diane, *Fire and Blood: Rubies in Myth, Magic and History*, Westport, CT, 2008.
Morihira Masahiko 森平雅彦, *Mongoru hakenka no Kōrai: teikoku chitsujo to ōkoku no taiō* モンゴル覇権下の高麗：帝国秩序と王国の対応 (*Koryŏ under Mongol Hegemony: An Empire's Order and A Kingdom's Response*), Nagoya, 2013.
Mote, Frederick, 'The T'u-mu Incident of 1449', in Frank Kierman and John Fairbank (eds), *Chinese Ways in Warfare*, Cambridge, MA, 1974, pp. 243–72.
Mote, Frederick W. and Twitchett, Denis C. (eds), *The Cambridge History of China, Volume 7: The Ming Dynasty, 1368–1644, Part 1*, Cambridge, 1988.
Mou Fuli 牟復禮 (Frederick Mote) and Cui Ruide 崔瑞德 (Denis Twitchett), trans. Zhang Shusheng 張書生, *Jianqiao Zhongguo Mingdaishi* 劍橋中國明代史 (*Cambridge History of Ming China*), Beijing, 1992.
MS: Zhang Tingyu 張廷玉 (ed.), *Ming shi* 明史 (*History of the Ming*), Beijing, 1984.
MSJSBM: Gu Yingtai 谷應泰, *Ming shi jishi benmo* 明史紀事本末 (*Narrative of Events in Ming History from Beginning to End*), Beijing, 1977.
MSJSBM: Gu Yingtai 谷應泰, *Mingshi jishi benmo* 明史紀事本末 (Narrative of Events in Ming History from Beginning to End), in *Lidai jishi benmo* 歷代紀事本末, 2 vols, Beijing, 1997.
MSL: Zhongyang yanjiuyuan lishi yuyan yanjiusuo 中央研究院歷史語言研究所 (ed.), *Ming shilu* 明實錄 (*Veritable Records of the Ming Dynasty*), Taipei, 1962–6.
Mu Yiqin 穆益勤 (ed.), *Mingdai yuanti zhepai shiliao* 明代院體浙派史料 (*Historical Materials Pertaining to Court-style and Zhe School Painting in the Ming Dynasty*), Shanghai, 1985.
Murai Shōsuke 村井章介, 'Mōko shūrai to ibunka sesshoku' 蒙古襲来と異文化接触 (The Mongol Invasions and Contact with Foreign Cultures), in Han-Ilbon munhwa kyoryu kigŭm and Tongbuk'a yŏksa chaedan (eds), *Monggol ŭi Koryŏ-Ilbon ch'imgong kwa Han-Il kwan'gye* 몽골의 고려일본 침공과 한일관계 (Mongolian Attacks on Korea and Japan and Korean-Japanese Relations), Seoul, 2009, pp. 31–55.
Na Chih-liang, *The Emperor's Procession: Two Scrolls of the Ming Dynasty*, Taipei, 1970.
Nagel, Eva, 'The Chinese Inscription on the Trilingual Slabstone from Galle Reconsidered. A Case Study in Early Ming-Chinese Diplomatics', in H.-J. Weisshaar, H. Roth and W. Wijeyapala (eds), *Ancient Ruhuna. Sri Lankan-German Archaeological Project in the Southern Province*, vol. 1, Darmstadt, 2001, pp. 385–468.
Nanjing bowuyuan 南京博物院, 'Mingdai Nanjing Jubaoshan Liuliyao' 明代南京聚寶山琉璃窯 (Ming Liuli kiln at Mount Jubao, Nanjing), *Wenwu* 文物 (*Cultural Relics*), no. 2, 1960, pp. 41–8.
Nanjing shi bowuguan 南京市博物館, *Jin yu yu: Gongyuan 14 zhi 17 shiji Zhongguo guizu shoushi* 金與玉: 公元 14–17 世紀中國貴族首飾 (*Gold and Jade: The Aristocratic Jewelry from the 14th to 17th Century*), Shanghai, 2004.
Nanjing shi bowuguan 南京市博物館, *Baochuan chang yizhi: Nanjing Ming Baochuan chang liu zuotang kaogu baogao* 寶船廠遺址: 南京明寶船廠六作塘考古報告 (*Archaeological Remains from the Treasure Shipyard: Archaeological Report of the Ming Dynasty Treasure Shipyard No. 6 in Nanjing*), Beijing, 2006.
Nappi, Carla, 'Full. Empty. Stop. Go.: Translating Miscellany in Early Modern China', in Karen Newman and Jane Tylus (eds), *Early Modern Cultures of Translation*, Philadelphia, 2015.
Naquin, Susan, *Peking Temples and City Life, 1400–1900*, Berkeley, Los Angeles and London, 2000.
Nei Menggu qianbi yanjiu hui 内蒙古錢幣研究會 and Zhongguo Qianbi bianjibu 中國錢幣編輯部 (eds), *Zhongguo gu chao tu ji* 中國古鈔圖集 (*A Compilation of Pictures of Chinese Ancient Paper Money*), Beijing, 1987.
Ngulphu, Sonam Tsering, 'Shākya Yeshe', *Treasury of Lives*, published 2 March 2015, accessed 31 May 2016 (http://treasuryoflives.org/biographies/view/Shakya-Yeshe/5795).
Ni Qian 倪謙, *Ni Wenxi ji* 倪文僖集 (*Collected Works of Ni Qian*), 1493, e-SKQS.
Ni Yue 倪岳, *Qingxi mangao* 清溪漫稿 (*Writings from the Clear River*), in *Jinyin Wenjinge Siku quanshu* 景印文津閣四庫全書 (*Photofacsimile of the Wenjin Copy of the Complete Library in Four Sections*), Beijing, 2004, vol. 418.
Nie Chongyi 聶從義 (ed.), *Chongjiao Sanli tu* 重校三禮 圖 (*Revised Illustrated Catalogue of Three Ritual Classics*), in *Sibu chongkan sanbian* 四部叢刊編 *(The Four Branches of Literature Collection)*, vol. 3, Taipei, 1966a.
Nieuhoff, John, *An Embassy from the East-India Company to the Emperor of China*, trans. J. Ogilby, London, 1669.
Nikaidō Yoshihiro, 'Tongshu xiaoshuo li yuanshuai shen de xingxiang' 通俗小說裡元帥神的形象 (Images of Marshal Gods in Vernacular Novels), in Li Fengmao 李豐楙 and Liao Zhaoheng 廖肇亨 (eds), *Shengchuan yu shichan–Zhongguo wenxue yu zongjiao lunji* 聖傳與詩禪–中國文學與宗教論集 (*Hagiography and Chan/Poetry: The Essays on Chinese Literature and Religion*), Taipei, 2007, pp. 513–47.
Niu Jianqiang 牛建強, 'Ming chu "Da Ming rili" yu "Huang Ming baoxun" de zuanxiu' 明初《大明日歷》與《皇明寶訓》的纂修 (The Compilation of the 'Great Ming Daily Calendar' and the 'Precious Admonitions of the Imperial Ming' in the Early Ming period), *Shixueshi yanjiu* 史學史研究 (*Historiographical Research*), no. 1, 2000, pp. 67–70.
O'Kane, Bernard, 'From Tents to Pavilions: Royal Mobility and Persian Palace Design', *Ars Orientalis* 23, 1993, pp. 249–68.
O'Rourke, Kevin H. and Williamson, Jeffrey G., 'Did Vasco da Gama Matter for European Markets?', *Economic History Review*, vol. 62, issue 3, 2009, pp. 655–84.
Oh Young Kyun, *Engraving Virtue: The Printing History of a Premodern Korean Moral Primer*, Leiden, 2013.

Okada, Hidehiro, 'China as a Successor State to the Mongol Empire', in Reuven Amitai-Preiss and David O. Morgan (eds), *The Mongol Empire and its Legacy*, Boston and Cologne, 1999, pp. 260–72.

Ong Eng Ann, Alexander, 'Contextualising the Book-burning Episode during the Ming Invasion and Occupation of Vietnam', in Geoff Wade and Sun Laichen (eds), *Southeast Asia in the Fifteenth Century: The China Factor*, Singapore, 2010, pp. 154–68.

Ou Chaogui 歐朝貴, 'Da Ci Fawang Shijia Yeshi kesi xiang' 大慈法王釋迦也失緙絲像 (The *Kesi* Thangka Portrait of Śākya Yeshé), *Xizang yanjiu* 西藏研究 (*Tibetan Studies*), no. 3, 1985, pp. 125–6.

Owen, Stephen, *Readings in Chinese Literary Thought*, Cambridge, MA and London, 1992.

Pak Wŏn-ho 朴元熇, '"Jingnnan zhi yi" yu Chaoxian' 靖難之役與朝鮮 (The Jingnan War and Joseon), *Mingshi yanjiu* 明史研究 (*Ming History Research*), vol. 1, 1991, pp. 227–47.

Pak Wŏn-ho 朴元熇, *Myŏng-ch'o Chosŏn kwan'gyesa yŏn'gu* 明初朝鮮關係史研究 (*Relations between the Early Ming Dynasty and Joseon*), Seoul, 2002.

Pal, Pratapaditya, *Tibetan Paintings: A Study of Tibetan Thankas Eleventh to Nineteenth Centuries*, New York, 1984.

Pan Guxi 潘谷西, *Zhongguo gudai jianzhu shi, di si juan: Yuan, Ming jianzhu* 中國古代建築史: 第四卷 元明建築 (*Chinese Traditional Architecture*, vol. 4: *Yuan and Ming Architecture*), Beijing, 2009.

Pan Shenliang 潘深亮, 'Lü Wenying, Lü Ji hezuo *Zhuyuan shouji tu* qianxi' 呂文英、呂紀合作《竹園壽集圖》淺析 (Analysis of the *Birthday Gathering in the Bamboo Garden* by Lü Wenying and Lü Ji), *Gugong bowuyuan yuankan* 故宮博物院院刊 (*Palace Museum Journal*), no. 4, 1988, pp. 61–3.

Pang Pyong-son 方炳善, '中國御器廠與朝鮮分院' (The Chinese Imperial Kiln and its Choson Branch)《廣州分院與朝鮮陶瓷》(*Guangzhou branch and Choson ceramics*), Seoul, 2001.

Pao Tsun-p'eng 包遵彭, 'Zheng He xia xiyang zhi baochuan kao' 鄭和下西洋之寶船考 (On the Ships of Zheng He), *Guoli lishi bowuguan lishi wenwu congkan., Di yi ji*, 國立歷史博物館歷史文物叢刊第一輯 (*National Historical Museum Collected Papers on the History and Art of China*, 1st series), no. 6, Taipei and Hong Kong, 1961.

Parker, Geoffrey, *The Military Revolution: Military Innovation and the Rise of the West, 1500–1800*, 2nd edn, Cambridge, 1996.

Parker, Geoffrey, *Global Crisis: War, Climate Change and Catastrophe in the Seventeenth Century*, New Haven and London, 2013.

Pelliot, Paul, 'Le Hoja et le Sayyid Rusain de l'Histoire des Ming', *T'oung Pao*, vol. 38, issue 1–2, 1947, pp. 81–292.

Peng Xinwei, *A Monetary History of China*, trans. E.H. Kaplan, Bellingham WA, 1993, vol. 2.

Pierson, Stacey, *Illustrated Catalogue of Underglaze Blue and Copper Red Decorated Porcelains in the Percival David Foundation of Chinese Art, London*, London, 2004.

Pierson, Stacey, *From Object to Concept: Global Consumption and the Transformation of Ming Porcelain*, Hong Kong, 2013.

Poceski, Mario, '"Chan Rituals of the Abbots" Ascending the Dharma Hall to Preach', in Steven Heine and Dale S. Wright (eds), *Zen Ritual: Studies of Zen Buddhist Theory in Practice*, Oxford, 2008, pp. 83–111.

Pointon, Marcia, *Brilliant Effects: A Cultural History of Gem Stones and Jewellery*, New Haven and London, 2009.

Pollock, Sheldon, *The Language of the Gods in the World of Men: Sanskrit, Culture and Power in Premodern India*, Berkeley, Los Angeles and London, 2006.

Portal, Jane, 'A Tang Dynasty Tile in the British Museum', *Orientations*, March 1990, pp. 67–71.

Ptak, Roderich, 'China and Calicut in the Early Ming Period: Envoys and Tribute Embassies', *Journal of the Royal Asiatic Society of Great Britain and Ireland*, vol. 1, 1989, pp. 81–111.

Ptak, Roderich, *China and the Asian Seas*, Aldershot, 1998.

Qi Hong 祁紅 (ed.), *Fahaisi bihua* 法海寺壁畫 (*The Fahai Temple Frescoes*), Beijing, 1993.

Qi Yingtao 祁英濤, 'Beijing Mingdai dianshi mu jiegou jianzhu goujia xinzhi chutan' 北京明代殿式木結構建築構架形制初探 (A Preliminary Investigation into Structural forms of Ming Beijing Palace Wooden Architecture), in Qi Yingtao 祁英濤, *Qi yingtao gu jianzhu lunwenji* 祁英濤古建築論文集 (*Collected Writings of Qi Yingtao on Traditional Architecture*), Beijing 1992, pp. 325–41.

Qian Zhengkun 錢正坤, 'Qinghai Ledu Qutansi bihua yanjiu' 青海樂都瞿曇寺壁畫研究 (A Study of the Wall Paintings of Qutan Monastery, Ledu, Qinghai), *Meishu Yanjiu* 美術研究 (*Art Research*), no. 4, 1995, pp. 57–63.

Qin Dashu 秦大樹, 'Aiji Fusitate yizhi zhong faxian de Zhongguo taoci' 埃及福斯塔特遺址中發現的中國陶瓷 (Chinese Ceramics Found in the Ruins of Fustat, Egypt), *Haijiaoshi yanjiu* 海交史研究 (*Research into China Overseas Communications History*), no. 1, 1995, pp. 79–92.

Qin Dashu 秦大樹, 'Songdai taoci liqi de shengchan he shengchan jigou' 宋代陶瓷禮器的生產和生產機構 (The Production of the Song Porcelain Ritual Vessels), *Wenwu* 文物 (*Cultural Relics*), no. 5, 2005, pp. 64–73, 95.

Qin Dashu 秦大樹, 'Zhongguo gudai taoci waixiao de diyige gaofeng–9 zhi 10 shiji taoci waixiao de guimo he tedian' 中國古代陶瓷外銷的第一個高峰–9~10世紀陶瓷外銷的規模和特點 (China's First Ceramic Export Trade Peak – Focus on the Volume and Characteristics of Ancient Chinese Ceramics Foreign Trade in the 9th and 10th Centuries), *Gugong bowuyuan yuankan* 故宮博物院院刊 (*Palace Museum Journal*), no. 5, 2013, pp. 32–49.

Qin Dashu 秦大樹and Shi Wenbo 施文博, 'Longquan yao jizai yu Mingchu shengchan zhuangkuang de ruogan wenti' 龍泉窯記載與明初生產狀況的若幹問題 (The Ancient Literature Records on Longquan Ware and the Issues Related on Manufacture Situation in Early Ming Dynasty), in Zhejiang sheng wenwu kaogu yanjiusuo 浙江省文物考古研究所 *et al.* (eds), *Longquan dayao fengdongyan yaozhi chutu ciqi* 龍泉大窯楓洞巖窯址出土瓷 (Unearthed Ceramics of the Fengdongyan kiln site at Dayao, Longquan), Beijing, 2009, pp. 28–35.

Qin Dashu 秦大樹, Xu Huafeng 徐華烽 and Muchulla, Mohammed, 'Kenniya mengbasatana hao chenchuan chushui de Zhongguo ciqi' 肯尼亞蒙巴薩塔納號沉船出水的中國瓷器 (The Chinese Porcelain Salvaged from Mombasa Wreck in Kenya), *Gugong bowuyuan yuankan* 故宮博物院院刊 (*Palace Museum Journal)*, no. 2, 2014, pp. 6–24.

Qinghai sheng wenwuchu 青海省文物處 and Qinghai sheng kaogu yanjiusuo 青海省考古研究所 (eds), *Qinghai wenwu* 青海文物 (*Qinghai Cultural Relics*), Beijing, 1994.

Qiu Guangming 丘光明, *Zhongguo lidai duliangheng kao* 中國歷代度量衡考 (*Study of Chinese Measurement Units Through History*), Beijing, 1992.

Qiu Jin Xian and Luk Yu-ping, 'Conserving Two Ming Paintings at the British Museum', *Arts of Asia*, vol. 44, no. 6, November/December 2014, pp. 64–70.

Qiu Jun 邱濬, *Chongbian Qiongtai huigao* 重編瓊臺會稿 (*Revised Jointly Written Drafts of the Jade Terrace*), 1620s, e-SKQS.

Quette, Beatrice, *Cloisonné Chinese Enamels from the Yuan, Ming and Qing Dynasties*, New Haven and London, 2011.

Raguin, S.J., Yves, *Terminologie raisonée du Bouddhisme chinois*, Taipei, 1985.

Ray, Haraprasad, *Trade and Diplomacy in India-China Relations: A Study of Bengal during the Fifteenth Century*, New Delhi, 1993.

Ricca, Franco and Lo Bue, Erberto F., *Gyantse Revisited*, Florence, 1990.

Ricca, Franco and Lo Bue, Erberto F., *The Great Stupa of Gyantse: A Complete Tibetan Pantheon of the Fifteenth Century*, London, 1993.

Richardson, Hugh E., 'The Karma-pa Sect. A Historical Note', *Journal of the Royal Asiatic Society of Great Britain & Ireland (New Series)*, vol. 90, no. 3–4, July 1958, pp. 139–64.

Richardson, Hugh E., 'The Karma-pa Sect. A Historical Note. Part II', *Journal of the Royal Asiatic Society of Great Britain & Ireland (New Series)*, vol. 91, no. 1–2, April 1959, pp. 1–18.

Richardson, Hugh E., 'Tibetan Painting in China, a Postscript', *Oriental Art*, vol. 21, no. 2, Summer 1975, pp. 161–2.

Rinaldi, Maura, *Kraak Porcelain: A Moment in the History of Trade*, London, 1989.

Ro Myoung-ho 노명호, 'Goryeo Taejo Wang Geon dongsang ui yujeon gwa munhwajeok baegyeong' 고려 태조 왕건 동상의 유전과 문화적 배경 (The Bronze Statue of King Taejo of Goryeo Dynasty and its Cultural Background), *Hanguk saron* 한국사론 (*The History of Korea*), vol. 50, June 2004, pp. 149–212.

Ro Myoung-ho 노명호, 'Goryeo Taejo Wang Geon dongsang ui hwangje gwanbok gwa johyeong sangjing' 고려 태조 왕건 동상의 황제관복과 조형성 (The Emperor's Attire of the Bronze Statue of Goryeo Taejo Wang Geon and its Formative Symbol), *Bungnyeok ui munhwa yusan* 북녁의 문화유산 (*Treasures from The Korean Central History Museum*), Seoul, 2006, pp. 226–36.

Robinson, B.W., 'Origin and Date of Three Famous *Shah-Nameh* Illustrations', *Ars Orientalis*, vol. 1, 1954, pp. 105–12.
Robinson, David, 'The Ming Court and the Legacy of the Yuan Mongols', in David M. Robinson (ed.), *Culture, Courtiers, and Competition: The Ming Court (1368–1644)*, Cambridge, MA, 2008, pp. 365–421.
Robinson, David, *Empire's Twilight: Northeast Asia under the Mongols*, Cambridge, MA, 2009.
Robinson, David, 'Mongolian Migration and the Ming's Place in Eurasia', *Journal of Central Eurasian Studies*, vol. 3, 2012, pp. 109–29.
Robinson, David, 'Difficult Decisions in A Changing Time: Koryŏ's Relations with the Yuan and Ming Dynasties', paper presented at 'Koryo: Inner and Outer', University of Hawaii, Manoa, February 2013a.
Robinson, David, *Martial Spectacles of the Ming Court*, Cambridge, MA and London, 2013b.
Robinson, David, 'Migration and Memory: Chinggisid Narratives of the Early Ming', paper presented at 'Mobility and Transformations: Economic and Cultural Exchange in Mongol Eurasia', The Hebrew University of Jerusalem, June 2014.
Robinson, David, *Seeking Order in a Tumultuous Age: The Writings of Chŏng Tojŏn (1342–1398), a Korean Neo-Confucian*, Honolulu, 2016.
Robinson, David, *Empire's Shadow: The Ming Court in Eurasia*, forthcoming.
Robinson, Kenneth, *A Critical Study of Chu Tsai-Yü's Contribution to the Theory of Equal Temperament in Chinese Music*, additional notes by Erich F.W. Altwein, preface by Joseph Needham, Wiesbaden, 1980.
Rogers, Mary Ann, 'Visions of Grandeur: The Life and Art of Dai Jin', in Richard Barnhart *et al.*, *Painters of the Great Ming: The Imperial Court and the Zhe School*, Dallas, 1993, pp. 127–94.
Ross, Sir E. Denison, 'New Light on the History of the Chinese Oriental College, and a 16th Century Vocabulary of the Luchuan Language', *T'oung Pao*, vol. 9, issue 1, 1898, pp. 689–95.
Ross, Sir E. Denison, *Catalogue of the Arabic and Persian Manuscripts in the Oriental Public Library at Bankipore*, Calcutta, 1908.
Rossabi, Morris, 'Notes on Esen's Pride and Ming China's Prejudice', *The Mongolia Society Bulletin*, vol. 9, no. 2, 1970, pp. 31–9.
Rossabi, Morris, 'A Translation of Ch'en Ch'eng's *Hsi-yü fan kuo chih*', *Ming Studies*, vol. 17, no. 1, 1983, pp. 49–59.
Roşu, Arion, 'La Girafe dans la faune de l'art Indien', *Bulletin de l'École Française d'Extrême-Orient*, vol. 71, 1982, pp. 47–61.
Roxburgh, David J., *The Persian Album 1400–1600*, New Haven and London, 2005.
Roxburgh, David J., 'The "Journal" of Ghiyath al-Din Naqqash, Timurid Envoy to Khan Baligh, and Chinese Art and Architecture', in Lieselotte E. Saurma-Jeltsch and Anja Eisenbeiss (eds), *The Power of Things and the Flow of Cultural Transformations*, Berlin, 2010, pp. 90–113.
Ryu Gi-jeong 류기정, 'Joseon jeongi seungjeong ui jeongbi wa unyeong' 조선전기 승정의 정비와 운영 (Modification and Management of Buddhist Policy in the Early Joseon), *Cheongnam sahak* 청람사학 (*Journal of the Chongnam Historical Society*), vol. 5, 2002, pp. 61–73.
Saeki Kōji 佐伯弘次, 'Nihon shinkō iko no Rai-Nichi kankei' 日本侵攻以後の麗日関係 (Korean-Japanese Relations after the Mongol Invasion of Japan), in Han-Ilbon munhwa kyoryu kigŭm and Tongbuk'a yŏksa chaedan (eds), *Monggol ŭi Koryŏ-Ilbon ch'imgong kwa Han-Il kwan'gye* 몽골의 고려일본 침공과 한일관계 (*Mongolian Attacks on Korea and Japan and Korean-Japanese Relations*), Seoul, 2009, pp. 260–74.
Schafer, Edward H., *The Golden Peaches of Samarkand: A Study of T'ang Exotics*, Berkeley, Los Angeles and London, 1963.
Schipper, Kristofer and Verellen, Franciscus (eds), *The Taoist Canon: A Historical Companion to the Daozang*, Chicago and London, 2004.
Seaman, Gary, *Journey to the North: An Ethnohistorical Analysis and Annotated Translation of the Chinese Folk Novel Pei-yu chi*, Berkeley, 1987.
Sejongdaewang ginyeom saeophoe 세종대왕기념사업회 (Committee of King Sejong the Great Project) (ed.), *Sejong munhwasa daegye* 세종문화사대계 (*A Compendium of Cultural History under King Sejong*), vols 1–5, Seoul, 1984–6, pp. 373–469.
Sen, Narayan Chandra, 'Accounts of Bengal in Extensive Records on Four Foreign Lands', in Victor H. Mair, Nancy S. Steinhardt and Paul R. Goldin (eds), *Hawai'i Reader in Traditional Chinese Culture*, Honolulu, 2005, pp. 505–13.
Sen, Tansen, *Buddhism, Diplomacy, and Trade: The Realignment of Sino-Indian Relations, 600–1400*, Honolulu, 2003.
Sen, Tansen, 'The Yuan Khanate and India: Cross-Cultural Diplomacy in the Thirteenth and Fourteenth Centuries', *Asia Major*, vol. 29, nos 1–2, 2006a, pp. 299–326.
Sen, Tansen, 'The Formation of Chinese Maritime Networks to Southern Asia, 1200–1450', *Journal of the Economic and Social History of the Orient*, vol. 49, no. 4, 2006b, pp. 421–53.
Sen, Tansen, 'Maritime Interactions between China and India: Coastal India and the Ascendance of Chinese Maritime Power in the Indian Ocean', *Journal of Central Eurasian Studies*, vol. 2, 2011, pp. 41–82.
Sen, Tansen, 'Changing Regimes: Two Episodes of Chinese Military Interventions in Medieval South Asia', in Upinder Singh and Parul P. Dhar (eds), *Asian Encounters: Networks of Cultural Interactions*, New Delhi, 2014, pp. 62–85.
Sen, Tansen, 'The Impact of Zheng He's Expeditions on Indian Ocean Interactions', *Bulletin of the School of Oriental and African Studies*, forthcoming.
Seo Geojeong 서거정 徐居正, *Saga jip* 사가집 四佳集 (Collected Works of Saga), vol. 2, Seoul, 2004.
Seol Sun 偰循, *Samgang haengsil-do: yeollyeopyeon* 三綱行實圖：열녀편 (*Illustrated Guide to the Three Bonds*), *c.* 1434, repr. Seoul, 1982.
Seonghyeon 성현 成俔, *Yongjae chonghwa* 용재총화 慵齋叢話 (*Assorted Writings of Yongjae*), http://db.itkc.or.kr/itkcdb/mainIndexIframe.jsp.
Seppings, Robert, 'On the Great Strength Given to Ships of War by the Application of Diagonal Braces', *Philosophical Transactions of the Royal Society of London*, 1818, pp. 1–8, http://www.bruzelius.info/Nautica/Shipbuilding/Seppings%281818%29.html.
Serruys, Henry, 'Mongols Ennobled during the Early Ming', *Harvard Journal of Asiatic Studies*, vol. 22, 1959a, pp. 209–60.
Serruys, Henry, 'The Mongols in China during the Hung-wu Period', *Mélanges chinois et bouddhiques*, vol. 11, 1959b, pp. 1–328.
Shan Guoqiang 單國強, *Dai Jin* 戴進, Changchun, 1996.
Shandong bowuguan 山東博物館 and Shandong sheng kaogu yanjiusuo 山東省文物考古研究所, *Luhuang wang mu* 魯荒王墓 (*The Tomb of Prince Huang of Lu*), 2 vols, Beijing, 2014.
Shang Chuan 商傳, '*Ming chu zhuming zhengzhijia Yao Guangxiao*' 明初著名政治家姚廣孝 (The Famous Early-Ming Statesman Yao Guangxiao), *Zhongguo shi yanjiu* 中國史研究 (*Journal of Chinese Historical Studies*), no. 3, 1984, pp. 119–29.
Sharf, Robert H., 'The Idolization of Enlightenment: On the Mummification of Ch'an Masters in Medieval China', *History of Religions*, vol. 32, no. 1, August 1992, pp. 1–31.
Sharpe, Kevin, *Selling the Tudor Monarchy: Authority and Image in Sixteenth Century England*, New Haven and London, 2009.
Shen Fuwei 沈福偉, 'Zheng He baochuan de Dongfei hangcheng' 鄭和寶船的東非航程 (The East Africa Voyages of Zhenghe Treasure Fleets), in Wang Tianyou 王天有 and Wan Ming 萬明 (eds), *Zheng He yanjiu bainian lunwenxuan* 鄭和研究百年論文選 *(100 Years of Zheng He Studies: Selected Writings)*, Beijing, 2004, pp. 96–110.
Shen Hsueh-man, *Gilded Splendor: Treasures of China's Liao Empire (907–1125)*, New York, 2006.
Shen Jun 申浚, 'Yuan Ming shiqi longquan yao yanjiu' 元明時期龍泉窯研究 (The Study of Longquan Kiln in the Yuan and Ming Dynasties), Ph.D diss., Peking University, 2014.
Shen Mude 神穆德, *Tanzhe shan Xiuyun si zhi* 潭柘山岫雲寺志 (*Gazetteer of Xiuyun Temple, Mt Tanzhe*), 18th century, repr. Taipei, 1994.
Shen Shixing 申時行 (ed.), *Ming hui dian* 明會典, Wanli chao chongxiuben, Zhonghua shuju edn, Beijing, 2007.
Shi Cunlong 施存龍, 'Beijing Mengyuan shidai Dadu gang' 北京蒙元時代大都港 (The Dadu Port in Beijing during the Mongol Yuan Period), *Shuiyun kexue yanjiu* 水運科學研究 (*Water Transport Research*), no. 1, 2008a, pp. 45–9.
Shi Cunlong 施存龍, 'Mingdai Beijing Tongzhou gang he yunhe' 明代北京通州港和運河 (Ming Beijing's Tongzhou Port and the Grand Canal), *Shuiyun kexue yanjiu* 水運科學研究 (*Water Transport Research*), no. 3, 2008b, pp. 42–8.
Shih, Ching-fei 施靜菲, 'Meng Yuan gongting zhong ciqi shiyong chutan', *Meishushi yanjiu jikan* 15, 2003, pp. 169–93.
Shoudu bowuguan 首都博物館, *Jingdezhen Zhushan chutu Yongle guanyao ciqi* 景德鎮珠山出土永樂官窯瓷器 (*Yongle Imperial Porcelain Excavated in Zhushan, Jingdezhen*), Beijing, 2007.

Siggstedt, Mette, 'Forms of Fate: An Investigation of the Relationship between Formal Portraiture, Especially Ancestral Portraits, and Physiognomy (*xiangshu*) in China', in *International Colloquium on Chinese Art History, 1991, Proceedings, Painting and Calligraphy*, part 2, Taipei, 1992, pp. 713–48.

Sin Seung-un 신승운, 'Ye Gyeom ui Bongsa *Joseon changhwasikweon* e daehan yeongu' 예겸의 봉사조선창화시권에 대한 연구 (A Study on *Envoy's Offering of Poems from Joseon* by Ni Qian), *Seojihak yeongu* 서지학연구 (*Journal of the Institute of Bibliography*), vol. 28, 2004, pp. 297–344.

Sin Sukju 신숙주 申叔舟, *Bohanjae jip* 보한재집 保閑齋集 (*Collected Works of Bohanjae*), Seoul, 1988.

Sjostrand, Sten and Barnes, Claire, 'The *Turiang*: A Fourteenth-Century Chinese Shipwreck Upsetting Southeast Asian Ceramic History', *Journal of the Malaysian Branch of the Royal Asiatic Society* 74, no. 1, 2001, pp. 71–109.

Skaff, Jonathan, *Sui-Tang China and its Turko-Mongol Neighbors*, Oxford and New York, 2012.

Sleeswyk, André Wegener, 'The Liao and the Displacement of Ships in the Ming Navy', *The Mariner's Mirror*, vol. 82, issue 1, 1996, pp. 3–13.

Smith, Paul Jakov, 'Problematizing the Song-Yuan-Ming Transition', in Paul Jakov Smith and Richard von Glahn (eds), *The Song–Yuan–Ming Transition in Chinese History*, Cambridge, MA and London, 2003a, pp. 1–34.

Smith, Paul Jakov, 'Impressions of the Song-Yuan-Ming Transition: The Evidence from *Biji* Memoirs', in Paul Jakov Smith and Richard von Glahn (eds), *The Song–Yuan–Ming Transition in Chinese History*, Cambridge, MA and London, 2003b, pp. 71–110.

Song Hye-jin 송혜진, 'Sejong ui munye gamseong gwa yeonhoe ui jeongchi' 세종의 문예 감성과 연회의 정치 (King Sejeong's Literary Emotional Leadership and the Ceremony of Banquets in his Reign), *Onuerui dong'yang sasang* 오늘의 동양사상 (*The Oriental Thought in Today*), vol. 19, October 2008, pp. 98–9.

Song Lian 宋濂 *et al.*, *Yuanshi* 元史 (*History of the Yuan*), 1368–70, e-SKQS.

Song Ming 宋明, Taikong guqin zhi qinfu Guan Pinghu 'Liushui' yong qin 'Feibao lianzhu' 太空古琴之親撫管平湖《流水》用琴 "飛瀑連珠 (A Guqin Music Recording Sent to Outerspace: Guan Pinghu Performs 'Flowing Water' on the Qin named 'Feibao lianzhu'), http://www.douban.com/note/319869953, uploaded by Song Ming 6 December 2013.

Soothill, William Edward and Hodous, Lewis, *A Dictionary of Chinese Buddhist Terms*, London, 1937.

Soucek, Priscilla P., 'The Manuscripts of Iskandar Sultan: Structure and Content', in Lisa Golombek and Maria Subtelny (eds), *Timurid Art and Culture*, Leiden, 1992, pp. 116–31.

Soucek, Priscilla P., 'Eskandar b. 'Omar Sayx b. Timiur: A Biography', *Oriente Moderno*, n.s. 15 (76), no. 2, 1996, pp. 73–87.

Soullière, Ellen, 'Palace Women in the Ming Dynasty: 1368–1644', Ph.D diss., Princeton University, 1987.

Sperling, Elliot, 'The 5th Karma-pa and Some Aspects of the Relationship Between Tibet and the Early Ming', in Michael Aris and Aung San Suu Kyi (eds), *Tibetan Studies in Honour of Hugh Richardson*, Warminster, 1980a, pp. 279–89.

Sperling, Elliot, 'Liu Yun's Mission to Tibet', unpublished paper, 1980b.

Sperling, Elliot, 'The 1413 Ming Embassy to Tsong-khapa and the Arrival of Byams-chen Chos-rje Shākya Ye-shes at the Ming Court', *The Journal of the Tibet Society* 2, 1982, pp. 105–8.

Sperling, Elliot, 'Early Ming Policy toward Tibet: An Examination of the Proposition that the Early Ming Emperors Adopted a "Divide and Rule" Policy toward Tibet', Ph.D diss., Indiana University, 1983.

Sperling, Elliot, 'Notes on the Early History of Gro-tshang Rdo-rje-'chang and its Relations with the Ming Court', *Lungta* 14 (Spring), 2001, pp. 77–87.

Sperling, Elliot, 'Karma Rol-pa'i rdo-rje and the Re-Establishment of Karma-pa Political Influence in the 14th Century', in 'The Relationship between Religion and State (chos srid zung 'brel)', in Christophe Cüppers (ed.), *Traditional Tibet. Proceedings of a Seminar Held in Lumbini, Nepal, March 2000*, Lumbini, 2004, pp. 229–44.

Sperling, Elliot, 'Tibetan Buddhism, Perceived and Imagined, along the Ming-Era Sino-Tibetan Frontier', in Matthew Kapstein (ed.), *Buddhism Between Tibet and China*, Boston, 2009, pp. 155–80.

Sperling, Elliot, 'Tibetan Buddhism at the Imperial Courts of China', unpublished paper presented at the Global Buddhist Congregation, 28 November 2011, New Delhi.

Sperling, Elliot, 'Two Early Ming Missives to Karma-pa Hierarchs', in Tashi Tseringet *et al.* (eds), *Tibetan Studies in Honour of Rai Bahadur Athing T.D. Densapa*, forthcoming.

Spriggs, A.I., 'Oriental Porcelain in Western Painting', *Transactions of the Oriental Ceramic Society*, vol. 36, 1964–6 (1965), pp. 73–87.

Stchoukine, Ivan, *Les peintures des manuscrits timurides*, Paris, 1954.

Steinhardt, Nancy Shatzman (ed.), *Chinese Traditional Architecture*, New York, 1984.

Steinhardt, Nancy Shatzman, *Chinese Architecture in an Age of Turmoil, 200–600*, Honolulu and Hong Kong, 2014.

Stoddard, Heather, 'A Stone Sculpture of mGur mGon-po, Mahakala of the Tent, Dated 1292', *Oriental Art*, vol. 31, no. 3, Autumn 1985, pp. 278–82.

Ströber, Eva, *Ming: Porcelain for a Globalised Trade*, Stuttgart, 2013.

Strong, John S., *Relics of the Buddha*, Princeton, 2004.

Stuart, Jan and Rawski, Evelyn, *Worshiping the Ancestors: Chinese Commemorative Portraits*, Washington, D.C., 2001.

Su Bai 宿白, *Zang chuan Fojiao siyuan kaogu* 藏傳佛教寺院考古 (*Archaeology of Buddhist Temples in the Tibetan Tradition*), Beijing, 1996.

Sun Chengze 孫承澤, *Chunming mengyu lu* 春明夢餘錄 (*Record of a Remembered Dream of the Capital*), 1761, e-SKQS.

Sun Dazhang 孫大章, *Zhongguo gudai jianzhu shi, di wu juan: Qingdai jianzhu* 中國古代建築史, 第五卷: 清代建築 (*History of Traditional Chinese Architecture*, vol. 5, *Qing Architecture*), 2nd edition, Beijing, 2009.

Sun Laichen, 'Ming-Southeast Asian Overland Interactions, *c.* 1368–1644', Ph.D diss., University of Michigan, 2000.

Sun Laichen, 'Military Technology Transfers from Ming China and the Emergence of Northern Mainland Southeast Asia (1390–1527)', *Journal of Southeast Asian Studies*, vol. 34, no. 3, 2003, pp. 495–517.

Sun Laichen, 'Chinese Gunpowder Technology and Dai Viet, ca. 1390–1497', in Nhung Tuyet Tran and Anthony J.S. Reid (eds), *Viet Nam: Borderless Histories*, Madison, 2006, pp. 72–120.

Sun Laichen, 'Chinese-Style Gunpowder Weapons in Dai-Viet (Vietnam): The Archaeological Evidence', *Revista de cultura*, vol. 27, 2008, pp. 42–59.

Sun Laichen, 'Shan Gems, Chinese Silver and the Rise of Shan Principalities in Northern Burma', in Geoff Wade and Sun Laichen (eds), *Southeast Asia in the Fifteenth Century: The China Factor*, Singapore, 2010, pp. 169–96.

Sung Hou-mei, *Decoded Messages: The Symbolic Language of Chinese Animal Painting*, New Haven and London, 2009.

Swart, Paula and Till, Barry, 'The Xiudingsi Pagoda; a Buddhist Masterpiece Unveiled', *Orientations*, May 1990, pp. 64–76.

Swope, Kenneth M., *A Dragon's Head and a Serpent's Tail: Ming China and the First Great East Asian War, 1592–1600*, Norman, 2009.

Swope, Kenneth M., 'To Catch a Tiger: The Ming Suppression of the Yang Yinglong Miao Uprising (1587–1600) as a Case Study in Ming Military and Borderlands History', in Kenneth R. Hall and Michael Aung-thwin (eds), *New Perspectives on the History and Historiography of Southeast Asia: Continuing Explorations*, London, 2011, pp. 112–40.

Swope, Kenneth M., 'As Close as Lips and Teeth: Debating the Ming Intervention in Korea', in Peter A. Lorge (ed.), *Debating War in Chinese History*, Leiden, 2013, pp. 163–90.

Swope, Kenneth M., 'Manifesting Awe: Imperial Leadership and Grand Strategy in the Ming Dynasty', forthcoming.

Tai, Yew Seng, 'Ming Gap and the Revival of Commercial Production of Blue and White Porcelain in China', *Bulletin of the Indo-Pacific Prehistory Association, Additional Papers from the Hanoi Conference and Others*, vol. 31, 2011, pp. 85–92.

Tan Qian 談遷, *Zaolin zazu* 棗林雜俎 (*Miscellaneous Delicacies from the Jujube Grove*), repr. Beijing, 2006.

Tan Yiling 譚怡令, 'Bai qin bai shengyin yi dong yi xingqing – Bian Wenjin's *Sanyou bai qin*' 百禽百聲音 一動一性情一邊文進三友百禽 (The Sound of Many Birds, the Moving Nature of Each: Bian Wenjin's *Three Friends and a Hundred Birds*), *Gugong wenwu yuekan* 故宮文物月刊 (*The National Palace Museum Monthly of Chinese Art*), vol. 329, 2010, pp. 66–75.

Tanaka, Kimiaki, *Art of Thangka from Hahn Kwangho Collection: Vol. 2*, Seoul: Hahn Foundation for Museum, 1999.
Tao Jin 陶金, 'Qian'an yizhen: Qian'an dian cang Song Huizong yujian yu shier leijiang shengxiang hua' 欽安遺珍：欽安殿藏宋徽宗玉簡與十二雷將神像畫 (Treasures from the Hall of Imperial Peace: The Inscribed Jade Slips of Song Dynasty and the Twelve Celestial Guardians Painting), *Zijincheng* 紫禁城 (*Forbidden City*), vol. 244, no. 5, 2015, pp. 66–81.
Tao Zongyi 陶宗儀, *Nancun chuogeng lu* 南村輟耕錄 (*Conversation while Resting from Plowing*), Beijing, 1980.
Thackston, Wheeler M., *Album Prefaces and Other Documents on the History of Calligraphers and Painters*, Leiden, 2001.
Thorp, Robert L., *Son of Heaven: Imperial Arts of China*, Seattle, 1988.
Tian Peidong 田培棟, 'Ming zhengfu dui Taihangshan yu Yanshan linmu de kanfa – Mingdai Beijing de ranliao gongying wenti' 明政府對太行山與燕山林木的砍伐 (Ming Government Felling of Trees in the Taihang Mountains and on Mt Yan – Ming Beijing's Fuel Supply Problem), *Beijing lianhe daxue xuebao: renwen shehui kexue ban* 北京聯合大學學報: 人文社會科學版 (*Journal of Beijing Union University: Humanities and Social Sciences*) 10, no. 3, July 2012, pp. 51–4.
Tian Rucheng 田汝成, *Xihu Youlanzhi* 西湖遊覽志 (*Travel Record of the West Lake*), 16th century, repr. Beijing, 1958.
T'ien Ju-kang, 'Cheng Ho's Voyages and the Distribution of Pepper in China', *Journal of the Royal Asiatic Society of Great Britain and Ireland*, vol. 2, 1981, pp. 186–97.
Tilly, Charles, *Coercion, Capital, and European States, 990–1990*, London, 1990.
Titley, Norah M., *Miniatures from Persian Manuscripts: A Catalogue and Subject Index of Paintings from Persia, India, and Turkey in the British Library and the British Museum*, London, 1977.
Toyka, Ursula, *The Splendours of Paradise: Murals and Epigraphic Documants at the Early Ming Buddhist Monastery Fahai Si*, Sankt Augustin, 2014.
Toyka-Fuong, Ursula, 'Three Tibeto-Chinese Mandala Paintings of Around 1442', in Christian Luczanits and Erberto Lo Bue (eds), *Tibetan Art and Architecture in Context. PIATS 2006: Tibetan Studies: Proceedings of the Eleventh Seminar of the International Association for Tibetan Studies, Königswinter 2006*, vol. 20, Andiast, 2010, pp. 311–34.
Ts'ai Ho-pi 蔡和璧, 'Youguan Hongwu, Yongle guanyao de beijing' 有關洪武、永樂官窯的背景, *Hongxi wenwu* 鴻禧文物 (*Journal of Chang Foundation*), no. 1, 1996, pp. 130–1.
Tsai, Mei-fen 蔡玫芬, 'Guanfu yu guanyang: qianlun yingxian Songdai ciqi fazhan de guanfang yinsu' 官府與官樣—淺論影響宋代瓷器發展的官方因素 (Official Institution and Official Models: About the Official Elements that Influenced the Development of Song Ceramics), *Qianxinian Songdai wenwu dazhang* 千禧年宋代文物大展 (China at the Inception of the Second Millennium: Art and Culture of the Sung Dynasty, 960–1279), Taipei, 2000, pp. 321–37.
Tsai, Mei-fen 蔡玫芬, 'Zhuanxing yu qifa: qianlun taoci suochengxian de mengyuan wenhu' 轉型與啟發—淺論陶瓷所呈現的蒙元文化 (Development and Inspiration: A Preliminary Discussion on the Mongol Culture represented on Porcelains), *Dahan de shiji* 大汗的世紀 (*Age of the Great Khan*), Taipei, 2001, pp. 230–3.
Tsai, Shih-shan Henry, *The Eunuchs in the Ming Dynasty*, Albany, 1996.
Tsai, Shih-shan Henry, *Perpetual Happiness: The Ming Emperor Yongle*, Seattle, 2001.
Tsien, T.H., *Science and Civilisation in China, Vol. 5: Chemistry and Chemical Technology. Part I: Paper and Printing*, Cambridge, 1985.
Tuotuo 脫脫, *Jin shi* 金史 (*History of the Jin*), repr. Beijing, Zhonghua shuju, 1975.
Tuotuo 脫脫, *Song shi* 宋史 (*History of the Song*), *c.* 1345, e-SKQS.
Tuttle, Gray, 'Imperial Strategies in Transition: The Qinghai/Amdo Frontier Between Empire and Nation', Honolulu, March 2011.
Twitchett, Denis and Grimm, Tilemann, 'The Cheng-t'ung, Ching-t'ai and T'ian-shun Reigns, 1436–64', in Frederick W. Mote and Denis C. Twitchett (eds), *The Cambridge History of China, Volume 7: The Ming Dynasty, 1368–1644, Part 1*, Cambridge, 1988, pp. 305–42.
Twitchett, Denis C. and Mote, Frederick W. (eds), *The Cambridge History of China, Volume 8: The Ming Dynasty, 1368–1644, Part 2*, Cambridge, 1998.
Ueda, Atsushi, 'The Riddle of Japan's Quakeproof Pagodas', *Japan Echo*, vol. 22, Spring 1995, pp. 71–7.
Ueda, Makoto 上田信, trans. Gao Yingying 高瑩瑩, *Hai yu diguo: Ming Qing shidai* 海與帝國: 明清時代 (*Ocean and Empire: Ming and Qing Periods*), Guilin shi, 2014.
US Department of the Navy, Office of the Chief of Naval Operations, Naval History Division, Washington, D.C., *Dictionary of American Naval Fighting Ships*, Washington, D.C., 1969, vol. 4.
van der Pijl-Ketel, Christine, 'Kraak Porcelain Salvaged from Shipwrecks of the Dutch East India Company (VOC)', in Luísa Vinhais and Jorge Welsh (eds), *Kraak Porcelain: The Rise of Global Trade in the Late 16th and Early 17th Centuries*, London, 2008, pp. 65–76.
Veit, Veronika, 'The Eastern Steppe: Mongol Regimes after the Yuan (1368–1636)', in Nicola di Cosmo, Allen Frank and Peter Golden (eds), *The Cambridge History of Inner Asia: The Chinggisid Age*, Cambridge, 2009, pp. 157–65.
Vermeer, Eduard B., *Chinese Local History: Stone Inscriptions from Fukien in the Sung to Ch'ing Periods*, Boulder CO, 1991.
Vinhais, Luísa and Welsh, Jorge (eds), *Kraak Porcelain: The Rise of Global Trade in the Late 16th and Early 17th Centuries*, London, 2008.
Vitali, Roberto with Rabsal, Gedun and Willock, Nicole (eds), *Trails of the Tibetan Tradition: Papers for Elliot Sperling*, Dharamshala, India, 2014.
von Glahn, Richard, *Fountain of Fortune: Money and Monetary Policy in China 1000–1700*, Berkeley, 1996.
von Glahn, Richard, 'Imagining Pre-modern China', in Paul Jakov Smith and Richard von Glahn (eds), *The Song–Yuan–Ming Transition in Chinese History*, Cambridge, MA and London, 2003a, pp. 35–70.
von Glahn, Richard, 'Towns and Temples: Urban Growth and Decline in the Yangtze Delta, 1100–1400', in Paul Jakov Smith and Richard von Glahn (eds), *The Song–Yuan–Ming Transition in Chinese History*, Cambridge, MA and London, 2003b, pp. 176–211.
von Glahn, Richard, 'The Origins of Paper Money in China', in W.N. Goetzman and K.G. Rouwenhorst (eds), *The Origins of Value: The Financial Innovations that Created Modern Capital Markets*, New York, 2005, pp. 65–90.
von Schroeder, Ulrich, 'XX. Chinese Metal Sculptures of the Ming dynasty (1368–1644 AD)', in *Buddhist Sculptures in Tibet, Volume II, Tibet and China*, Hong Kong, 2001, pp. 1237–91.
Wade, Geoff, 'The Zheng He Voyages: A Reassessment', *Journal of the Malaysia Branch of the Royal Asiatic Society*, vol. 78, no. 1, 2005a, pp. 37–58.
Wade, Geoff (trans.), *Southeast Asia in the Ming Shi-lu: An Open Access Resource*, Singapore, 2005b, http://epress.nus.edu.sg/msl/.
Wade, Geoff, 'Engaging the South: Ming China and Southeast Asia in the Fifteenth Century', *Journal of the Economic and Social History of the Orient*, vol. 51, no. 4, 2008, pp. 588–97.
Wan, C.K. Maggie, 'Image and Efficacy: The Frontispieces to the Wanli Emperor's *Yushu jing*', *Artibus Asiae*, vol. 75, no. 1, 2015, pp. 45–82.
Wan, C.K. Maggie, 'Interactions between Daoist Rituals and Scriptural Illustrations in the Ming Dynasty – A Case Study of the *Duren jing*', in Deng Fei (ed.), *Proceedings of the Conference of Ritual and Image: The Integration of Chinese Religion and Art*, Beijing, forthcoming.
Wan Chui-ki 尹翠琪, 'Daojiao banhua yanjiu: Da Ying tushuguan cang "Yushu baojing" si zhu ben zhi niandai ji chahua kao' 道教版畫研究：大英圖書館藏《玉樞寶經》四註本之年代及插畫考 (Daoist Woodblock Prints: A Study of the Illustrations and Dating of the Glossed *Yushu baojing* Collected in the British Library), *Daojiao yanjiu xuebao: Zongjiao, lishi yu shehui* 道教研究學報：宗教、歷史與社會 (*Daoism: Religion, History and Society*), no. 2, 2010, pp. 135–218.
Wan Ming 萬明, 'Mingdai baiyin huobihua: zhongguo yu shijie de xinshijiao' 明代白銀貨幣化: 中國與世界連接的新視角 (Silver as Currency in the Ming Dynasty: New Perspective of the Connection between China and the Rest of the World), *Hebei xuekan* 河北學刊 (*Hebei Academic Journal*), no. 3, 2004, pp. 145–54.
Wan Ming 萬明, *Ming chaoben 'Yingya shenglan' jiaozhu* 明抄本《瀛涯勝覽》校註 (*Annotated Ming Manuscript of 'Overall Survey of the Ocean Shores'*), Beijing, 2005.
Wan Ming 萬明, *Zhongguo rongru shijie de bulü* 中國融入世界的步履 (*China Assimilating into the Footsteps of the World*), Beijing, 2014.
Wan Yi 萬依, 'Lun Zhu Di yingjian Beijing gongdian, qiandu de zhuyao dongji ji houguo' 論朱棣營建北京宮殿，遷都的主要動機及

後果 (On the Principal Motivations and Consequences of Zhu Di's Beijing Palace Construction and Transfer of the Capital), *Gugong bowuyuan yuankan* 故宫博物院院刊 (*Palace Museum Journal*), 1990, no. 3, pp. 53–61.

Wang Ao 王鏊, *Zhenze jiwen* 震澤紀聞 (*Zhenze's Miscellaneous Records*), in Shen Yunlong (ed.), *Ming Qing shiliao huibian* 明清史料彙编 (*Collection of Ming and Qing Historical Materials*), section 1, no. 3, Taipei, 1967.

Wang Bomin 王伯敏 (ed.), *Zhongguo meishu quanji* Huihua bian Banhua juan 中國美術全集 繪畫编: 版畫卷 (*The Complete Collection of Chinese Art: Paintings: Woodblock Prints*), Shanghai, 1988.

Wang Cheng-Hua, Material Culture and Emperorship: The Shaping of Imperial Roles at the Court of Xuanzong (r. 1426–35), Ph.D diss., Yale University, 1998.

Wang Chongwu 王崇武, *Fengtian jingnan ji zhu* 奉天靖難記注 (*Record of Responding to Heaven and Pacifying the Troubles, Annotated*), Shanghai, 1948.

Wang Chong-ci 王崇齊, 'Qianlun yuancang huangyou shuangshouer guan' 淺論院藏黃釉雙獸耳罐, *Gugong wenwu yuekan* 故宮文物月刊 (*The National Palace Museum Monthly of Chinese Art*) no. 298, 2008, pp. 88–101.

Wang Dayuan 汪大淵, Daoyi Zhilüe Jiaoshi 島夷志略校釋 (Collated and Annotated of Daoyi Zhilüe), Beijing, 1981, p. 15.

Wang Fu 王黼,(ed.), *Chong xiu Xuanhe bogu tu* 重修宣和博古圖 (*Revised Xuanhe Illustrated Catalogue of Antiquities*), in *Jinyin Wenjinge Siku quanshu* 景印文津閣四庫全書 (Photofacsimile of the Wenjin Copy of the Complete Library in Four Sections), vol. 840, Taipei, 1983.

Wang Guangyao 王光堯, 'Yuan Ming Qing sandai de guan liuli yao zhidu yanjiu' 元明清三代的官琉璃窯制度研究 (Studies on the Official Liuli Kiln Systems of the Yuan, Ming and Qing Dynasties), in Wang Guangyao 王光堯 (ed.), *Zhongguo gudai guanyao zhidu* 中國古代官窯制度 (*The System of Ancient Official Chinese Kilns*), Beijing, 2004, pp. 102–15.

Wang Guangyao 王光堯, *Mingdai gongting taoci shi* 明代宮廷陶瓷史 (*History of Ming Imperial Ceramics*), Beijing, 2010.

Wang Guanyu 王冠宇 and Wu Zhenlin 吳震霖, 'Cong tongci kaogu kan Zheng He xia xiyang de xingzhi' 從陶瓷考古看鄭和下西洋的性質 (Looking at Zheng He's Voyages through Ceramic Archaeology), *Gugong bowuyuan yuankan* 故宮博物院院刊 (*Palace Museum Journal*), no. 1, 2014, pp. 51–62.

Wang Gungwu, 'Early Ming Relations with Southeast Asia: A Background Essay', in John K. Fairbank (ed.), *The Chinese World Order: Traditional China's Foreign Relations*, Cambridge, MA, 1968, pp. 34–62.

Wang Gungwu, 'Ming Foreign Relations: Southeast Asia', in Denis C. Twitchett and Frederick W. Mote (eds), *The Cambridge History of China, Volume 8: The Ming Dynasty, 1368–1644, Part 2*, Cambridge, 1998, pp. 301–32.

Wang, Helen, 'Currency of Empire: Money in the Ming Dynasty', *Orientations*, vol. 45, no. 6, September 2014, pp. 2–7.

Wang Hong 王紅, 'Jingshan shiji kao' 景山史跡考 (The History of Coal Hill), in Shan Shiyuan 單士元 and Yu Zhuoyun 于倬雲 (eds), *Zhongguo zijincheng xuehui lunwen ji* 中國紫禁城學會論文集 (*Collected Essays from the Conference on the Forbidden City Society*), vol. 2, Beijing, 2002, pp. 123–30.

Wang Jidong 王繼東, 'Zhongguo Mingchao Beijing cheng yu Yuenan Ruanchao Shunhua cheng neizai wenhua lianxi chutan' 中國明朝北京城與越南阮朝順化城內在文化聯繫初探 (A Preliminary Investigation of the Cultural Relations Inherent in the Relationship between Ming Dynasty Beijing and Nguyễn Dynasty Huế), *Dongnanya zhi chuang* 東南亞之窗 (*Window on the South-east*), 2011, no. 16, pp. 43–9.

Wang Mintong 王民同, 'Zheng He shi heping youhao shizhe' 鄭和是和平友好使者 (Zheng He: The Envoy of Peace and Friendship), *Huizu yanjiu* 回族研究 (*Journal of Hui Muslim Minority Studies*), no. 1, 2003, pp. 43–8.

Wang Puzi 王璞子, *Gongcheng zuofa zhushi* 工程做法註釋 (*Imperial Specifications for State Buildings*), Beijing, 1995.

Wang Qi 王圻, *San cai tu hui* 三才圖會 (*Illustrated Compendium of the Three Powers*), Shanghai, 1988.

Wang, Richard G., *The Ming Prince and Daoism: Institutional Patronage of an Elite*, Oxford and New York, 2012.

Wang Shixing 王士性, *Guangzhi yi* 廣志繹 (*Further Elucidations on My Extensive Record of Travels*), 1597, repr. Beijing, 1981.

Wang Shu 王恕, *Wang Duanyi zouyi* 王端毅奏議 (*Memorials of Wang Shu*), *c.* 1510, e-SKQS.

Wang Sixiang 王思翔, 'A Game of Thrones: Knowledge, Diplomacy, and Dynastic Crisis in Choson-Ming Relations', paper presented at the Association of Asian Studies Conference, San Diego, 2013.

Wang Xiaoqing 王效清, *Zhongguo gudai jianzhu shuyu cidian* 中國古代建築術語辭典 (*Dictionary of Chinese Traditional Architectural Terms*), Beijing, 2006.

Wang Yi 王毅, '*Xizang wenwu jianwen ji (yi)*' 西藏文物見聞記 (一) (Notes on Tibetan Cultural Relics Seen and Heard About, Part 1), *Wenwu* 文物 (*Cultural Relics*), no. 6, 1960, pp. 41–8, 51.

Wang Yuan-kang, *Harmony and War: Confucian Culture and Chinese Power Politics*, New York, 2011.

Wang Yucheng 王育成, 'Ming Wudang shan jinlong yujian yu daojiao toulong' 明武當山金龍玉簡與道教投龍 (Gold Dragon and Jade Tablet at Mount Wudang and the Daoist 'Tossing of the Dragon' Ritual of the Ming), *Shehui kexue zhanxian* 社會科學戰線 (*Social Science Front*), no. 3, 1994, pp. 148–54.

Wang Zheng 王征, '*Zhi gong zui gong xing you dingpan – Nanxundian "Yao Guangxiao xiang" zhou kaoshi*' 知公罪公星有定盤–南薰殿《姚廣孝像軸》考釋 (Textual Research into the Portrait Scroll of Yao Guangxiao in the Nanxun Hall), *Zhongguo dianji yu wenhua* 中國典籍與文化 (*Chinese Classics and Culture*), no. 1, 2011, pp. 118–33.

Wang Zhi 王直, *Yi'an wenji* 抑庵文集 (*Collected Writings of Wang Zhi*), *c.* 1465, e-SKQS.

Wang Zilin 王子林, *Zijincheng yuanzhuang yu yuanchuang* 紫禁城原狀與原創 (*The Original Condition and Originality of the Forbidden City*), 2 vols, Beijing, 2007.

Wang Zilin 王子林 *et al.*, 'Tianyi zhenyou Qian'an dian de Xuanwu shengjing' 天一鎮佑欽安殿的玄武聖境 (Protection and Blessing of Tianyi Xuanwu's Sacred Realm at the Hall of Imperial Peace), *Zijincheng* 紫禁城 (*Forbidden City*), vol. 244, no. 5, 2015, pp. 16–129.

Wang Zongzai 王宗載, *Siyi guan kao* 四夷館考 (*Study of the Bureau of Translators*), Beijing, 1924.

Watson, Oliver, *Museum of Islamic Art, Doha, Qatar*, Munich, London, Berlin and New York, 2008.

Watt, James C.Y., 'A Note on Artistic Exchanges in the Mongol Empire', in Linda Komaroff and Stefano Carboni (eds), *The Legacy of Genghis Khan: Courtly Art and Culture in Western Asia, 1256–1353*, New York, 2002, pp. 63–73.

Watt, James C.Y. (ed.), *The World of Khubilai Khan: Chinese Art in the Yuan Dynasty*, New York, 2010.

Watt, James C.Y. and Leidy, Denise, *Defining Yongle: Imperial Art in Early 15th Century China*, New York, 2005.

Watt, James C.Y. and Wardwell, Anne E., *When Silk was Gold: Central Asian and Chinese Textiles*, New York, 1997.

Wei Jiao 魏校, *Zhuangqu yishu* 莊渠遺書 (*Posthumous Collection of Wei Jiao*), *c.* 1545, e-SKQS.

Weidner, Marsha (ed.), *Cultural Intersections in Later Chinese Buddhism*, Honolulu, 2001.

Weidner, Marsha, 'Xifang shoucang Ming chao Chenghua yu Zhengde shiqi Han Wei fengge de shengka' 西方收藏明朝成化與正德時期漢魏風格的省卡 (Sino-Tibetan Thangkas of the Chenghua and Zhengde Periods in Western Collections), *Gugong bowuyuan yuankan* 故宮博物院院刊 (*Palace Museum Journal*), October 2007, pp. 78–97.

Weidner, Marsha, 'Portraits and Personalities in the Temples of Ming Beijing: Responses to Portraits of the Monk Daoyan', in Naomi Noble Richard and Donald E. Brix (eds), *The History of Painting in East Asia: Essays on Scholarly Method*, Taipei, 2008, pp. 224–42.

Weidner, Marsha, 'Beyond Yongle: Tibeto-Chinese Thangkas for the Mid-Ming Court', *Artibus Asiae*, vol. LXIL, no. 1, 2009a, pp. 7–37.

Weidner, Marsha, 'Fit for Monks' Quarters: Monasteries as Centers of Aesthetic Activity in the Late Fourteenth Century', *Ars Orientalis*, no. 37, 2009b, pp. 49–77.

Weidner, Marsha Smith (ed.), *Latter Days of the Law: Images of Chinese Buddhism, 850–1850*, Honolulu, 1994.

Wen Zhenjun 溫震軍, 'Mingdai Jinbei bianguan humu yanjiu' 明代晉北邊關護木研究 (A Study of Forestry Protection in Northern Shanxi Border Areas under the Ming Dynasty), *Xinzhou shifan xueyuan xuebao* 忻州師範學院學報 (*Journal of Xinzhou Normal University*), 2007, no. 2, pp. 108–10.

West, Stephen H., 'Text and Ideology: Ming Editors and Northern

Drama', in Paul Jakov Smith and Richard von Glahn (eds), *The Song–Yuan–Ming Transition in Chinese History*, Cambridge, MA and London, 2003, pp. 329–73.

Weststeijn, Thijs, 'Cultural Reflections on Porcelain in the Seventeenth-century Netherlands', in Jan van Campen and Titus M. Eliens (eds), *Chinese and Japanese Porcelain for the Dutch Golden Age*, Zwolle, 2014, pp. 213–29.

Whitfield, Roderick, 'Che School Paintings in the British Museum', *Burlington Magazine*, vol. 114, no. 830, May 1972, pp. 283–95.

Whitfield, Roderick, 'Ming Pyrotechnics: The Xiaoling and the Linggusi in the 1407 Scroll', *Arts of Asia*, vol. 44, no. 6, November/December 2014, pp. 71–81.

Whitmore, John K., *Vietnam, Hồ Quý Ly, and the Ming*, New Haven, 1985.

Wild, Norman, 'Materials for the Study of the Ssu I Kuan (Bureau of Translators)', *The Bulletin of the School of Oriental and African Studies*, vol. 11, no. 3, 1945, pp. 617–40.

Wood, Nigel, *Chinese Glazes*, London, 1999.

Woodside, Alexander, *Vietnam and the Chinese Model: A Comparative Study of Chinese and Vietnamese Government in the First Half of the Nineteenth Century*, Cambridge, 1988.

Wright, Elaine J., *The Look of the Book: Manuscript Production in Shiraz, 1303–1452*, Washington, D.C., 2013.

Wu Cong 吳葱, 'Qinghai Ledu Qutansi jianzhu yanjiu' 青海樂都瞿曇寺建築研究 (Study of the Architecture of Qutan Monastery in Ledu, Qinghai), MA thesis, Tianjin University, 1994.

Wu Han 吳晗 (ed.), *Chaoxian Lichao shilu zhong de Zhongguo shiliao* 朝鮮李朝實錄中的中國史料 (*Chinese Historical Material in the Joseon wangjo sillok*), vol. 1, Beijing, 1980.

Wu Hongmei 吳紅梅 and Diao Wenwei 刁文偉, 'Jiangsu Jiangyin chutu de Da Ming tongxing baochao' 江蘇江陰出土的大明通行寶鈔 (Ming Dynasty Banknote Unearthed in Jiangyin, Jiangsu Province), *Zhongguo qianbi* 中國錢幣 (*China Numismatics*), no. 4, 2005, pp. 51–2, 86–7.

Wu Jing, *Enlightenment in Dispute: The Reinvention of Chan Buddhism in Seventeenth-Century China*, New York, 2008.

Wu Sung-feng 吳誦芬, 'Zhenjiang ben *Xingyuan yaji tu* de yiwen' 鎮江本《杏園雅集圖》的疑問 (The Study of *Elegant Gathering in the Apricot Garden*), *Gugong xueshu jikan* 故宮學術季刊 (*The National Palace Museum Research Quarterly*), no. 1, 2009, pp. 73–137.

Wu Wenguang 吳文光, *Shenqi mipu yuequan* 神奇秘譜樂詮 (*Musical Interpretations of Shenqi mipu*), Shanghai, 2008.

Wudangshan zhi bianzuan weiyuanhui 武當山志編纂委員會, *Wudangshan zhi* 武當山志 (*Gazetteer of Mount Wudang*), Beijing, 1994.

Xi Longfei 席龍飛 and He Guowei 何國衛, 'Shilun Zheng He baochuan' 試論鄭和寶船 (A Preliminary Discussion on Zheng He's Treasure Ship), in Jinian weida hanghaijia Zheng He xia xiyang 580 zhounian choubei weiyuanhui 紀念偉大航海家鄭和下西洋五百八十周年籌備委員會, Zhongguo hanghai shi yanjiuhui 中國航海史研究會 (eds), *Zheng He xia Xiyang lunwen ji, di yi ji* 鄭和下西洋論文集, 第一輯 (*Collected Papers on Zheng He's Voyages to the Western Seas*), Beijing, 1985, pp. 93–107.

Xi Longfei 席龍飛, *Zhongguo zaochuan shi* 中國造船史 (*History of Shipbuilding in China*), Wuhan, 1999.

Xia Liangsheng 夏良勝, *Zhongyong yanyi* 中庸衍義 (*Derivations of the Doctrine of the Mean*), *c.* 1530, e-SKQS.

Xia Yuanji 夏原吉, *Xia Yuanji ji* 夏原吉集 (*Collected Works of Xia Yuanji*), repr. Changsha, 2012.

Xiang Da 向達, *Liangzhong haidao zhenjing* 兩種海道針經 (*Two Maritime Rutters*), Beijing, 1961a.

Xiang Da 向達, *Zheng He hanghai tu* 鄭和航海圖 (*Zheng He's Maritime Rutter*), Beijing, 1961b.

Xiang Yannan 向燕南, '*Chen Jian "Huangming zizhi tongji" de bianzuan tedian ji yingxiang*' 陳建《皇明資治通紀》的編纂特點及影响' (The Characteristics and Influence of the Compilation of Chen Jian's 'Comprehensive Record in Aid of Governance of the August Ming'), *Shixueshi yanjiu* 史學史研究 (*Journal of Historiography*), no. 1, 1993, pp. 48–56.

Xiaotun 小屯, 'Liu niang jing Ming mu de qingli' 劉娘井明墓的清理 (Clearing the Ming tomb of Liu niangjing), *Wenwu cankao ziliao* 文物參考資料 (*Materials for the Study of Cultural Relics*), no. 5, Beijing, 1958, pp. 55–6, and plate.

Xie Guian 謝貴安, *Ming shilu yanjiu* 明實錄研究 (*A Study of Ming Veritable Records*), Taipei, 1995.

Xie Jisheng 謝繼勝 and Liao Yang 廖旸, 'Qinghai sheng ledu qutan si qutan dian bihua neirong bianshi' 青海樂都瞿曇寺瞿曇殿壁畫內容辨識 (Identifying the Content of the Murals in the Qutan Hall, Qutan Monastery, Ledu, Qinghai), *Zhongguo zangxue* 中國藏學 (*China Tibetology*), no. 2, 2006a, pp. 191–202.

Xie Jisheng 謝繼勝 and Liao Yang 廖旸, 'Qutan si huilang fochuan bihua neirong bianshi yu fengge fenxi' 瞿曇寺回廊佛傳壁畫內容辨識與風格分析 (Identifying the Contents and Analysing the Style of the Jataka Murals in the Ambulatory of Qutan Monastery), *Gugong bowuyuan yuankan* 故宮博物院院刊 (*Palace Museum Journal*), no. 3, 2006b, pp. 16–43, 155–6.

Xie Min 謝旻 and Tao Cheng 陶成, *Jiangxi tongzhi* 江西通志 (*Provincial Gazetteer of Jiangxi*), 1731, e-SKQS.

Xie Xie 謝燮, *Ming tongjian* 明通鑒 (*Comprehensive Mirror of the Ming*), Beijing, 1959.

Xie Zhaozhe 謝肇淛, *Wuzaju* 五雜俎 (*Five Assorted Offerings*), Shenyang, 2001.

Xie Zuo 謝佐, *Qutansi* 瞿曇寺 (*Qutan Monastery*), Xining, 1982.

Xin Yuanou 辛元歐, 'Guanyu Zheng He baochuan chidu de jishu fenxi' 關於鄭和寶船尺度的技術分析 (A Technical Analysis of the Size of Zheng He's Ships), *Chuanshi yanjiu* 船史研究 (*Marine History Studies*) 17, 2002, pp. 1–20.

Xiong Wenbin 熊文彬, '*Xizang Luobulinka cang Mingdai Da Ci Fawang xiang kesi tangka zai tan* 西藏羅布林卡藏明代大慈法王像緙絲唐卡再探 (Revisiting the *Kesi* Thangka Portrait of Da Ci Fawang in the Collection of the Norbulingka Palace in Tibet), *Zhongguo zangxue* 中國藏學 (*China Tibetology*), no. 3, 2014, pp. 154–9.

Xizang zizhiqu wenwu guanli weiyuan hui 西藏自治區文物管理委員會, 'Mingchao huangdi ci gei xizang chubusi gama huofo de liangjian zhaoshu' 明朝皇帝賜給西藏楚布寺噶瑪活佛的兩件詔書 (Two Ming Missives to Karmapa Hierarchs in Tsurpu Monastery, Tibet), *Wenwu* 文物 (*Cultural Relics*), no. 11, 1981, pp. 42–4.

Xu Guanhua 徐冠華, '*Shenqi mipu* chutan' 神奇秘譜初探 (A Preliminary Study on *Shenqi mipu*), MA thesis, Dongnan University, 2005.

Xu Hong 徐紘, *Huang Ming ming chen wan yan lu* 皇明名臣琬琰錄 (*Stele Records of Famous Officials of the August Ming*), 1505, e-SKQS.

Xu Jian 許健, *Qinshi xinbian* 琴史新編 (*A New Narrative of Qin History*), Beijing, 2012.

Xu Jun 徐軍, 'Cong fengdongyan yaozhi de fajue shixi Yuan Ming longquan qingci fenqi he tezheng' 從楓洞巖窯址的發掘試析元明龍泉青瓷分期和特征 (Approach of Study on Dating and Characteristics of Longquan Celadon in Yuan and Ming Period From Excavation on Fengdongyan Kiln Site), in Zhejiang sheng kaogu yanjiusuo 浙江省文物考古研究所 *et al.* (eds), *Longquan dayao fengdongyan yaozhi chutu ciqi* 龍泉大窯楓洞巖窯址出土瓷器 (Unearthed Ceramics of the Fengdongyan kiln site at Dayao, Longquan), Beijing, 2009, pp. 11–18.

Xu Lun 許論, *Eryuan ji* 二園集 (*Two Garden Records*), *c.* 1560.

Xu Qin 徐沁, *Ming hua lu* 明畫錄 (*Records of Ming Painting*), repr. Shanghai, 1986.

Xu Weidong 徐衛東, 'Mingchu neige de weizhi bianqian' 明初內閣的位置變遷 (The Changing Location of the Grand Secretariat at the Beginning of the Ming Dynasty), in *Zhonghua tongren xueshu lunji* 中華同人學術論集 (*Collected Essays of Collegiality in China*), Beijing, 2002.

Xu Wenyao 徐文躍, 'Mingdai de fengguan daodi shenme yang?' 明代的鳳冠到底什麼樣? (What does the Ming Dynasty Phoenix Crown Look Like?), *Zijincheng* 紫禁城 (*Forbidden City*), no. 2, 2013, pp. 62–85.

Xu Yikui 徐一夔 (ed.), *Da Ming jili* 大明集禮 (Collected Rites of the Ming Dynasty), in *Siku quanshu zongmu* 四庫全書總目 (*Catalogue of the Complete Library of the Four Treasuries*), Taipei, 1963, *juan* 82.

Xu Zifang 許子方, 'Zhu Quan ji qi zaju chuangzuo' 朱權及其雜劇創作 (Zhuan Quan and His Creative Writing of Dramas), in *Ming zajushi* 明雜劇史 (*History of Ming Zaju Drama*), Beijing, 2003, pp. 99–104.

Xuanzang 玄奘 and Bianji 辯機, *Da Tang Xiyu ji* 大唐西域記 (*Records of the Western Regions Visited During the Great Tang Dynasty*), T. (51) 2087.

Yan Chongnian 閻崇年, 'Lun Beijing gongyuan de minzu tezheng' 論北京公園的民族特徵 (On the National Characteristics of Beijing Gardens), *Zhongwai chengshi yanjiu* 中外城市研究 (*Research on Chinese and Foreign Cities*), no. 1, 1991, pp. 227–39.

Yan Congjian 嚴從簡, *Shuyu zhouzi lu* 殊域周咨錄 (*A Comprehensive Record on Foreign Countries*), 1574, repr. *Zhongwai jiaotong shiji congkan* 中外交通史籍叢刊 (*Collection of Historical Material Regarding Chinese-Foreign Communication Series*), vol. 13, Beijing, 1993.

Yan Xiaoxing 嚴曉星, 'Qiuhong niandai xinzheng' "秋鴻"年代新證 (New Evidence on 'Autumn Geese'), in *Qixian guyi* 七弦古意 (*Historical Expressions of Qin*), Beijing, 2013, pp. 19–33.

Yang Chunyu 楊春雨, 'Cong Mingchao Beijing cheng he Ruanchao Shunhua cheng kan Zhong Yue jianzhu wenhua jiaoliu' 從明朝北京城和阮朝順化城看中越建築文化交流 (Exchanges of Architectural Culture between China and Vietnam as Seen from Ming Dynasty Beijing and Nguyen Dynasty Hue), *Dongnanya zongheng* 東南亞縱橫 (*Southeast Asia Overview*), 2011, no. 6, pp. 45–9.

Yang Honglin 楊洪林, 'Ming Chengzu yu Wudangshan Zhenwu dadi' 明成祖與武當山真武大帝 (Ming Chengzu and Zhenwu of Mount Wudang), *Wudang xuekan* 武當學刊 (*Wudang Journal*), vol. 17, no. 4, December 1997, pp. 6–9.

Yang Lili 楊麗麗, 'Mingren *Shi tong nian tu* juan chutan' 明人十同年圖卷初探 (Investigation into the Ming *Painting of Ten of the Same Year*), *Gugong bowuyuan yuankan* 故宮博物院院刊 (*Palace Museum Journal*), no. 2, 2004a, pp. 100–12.

Yang Lili 楊麗麗, 'Shixi Mingren *Wu tong hui tu* juan' 試析明人《五同會圖》卷 (Analysis of the Ming Painting of *Five Who are Alike*), *Gugong bowuyuan yuankan* 故宮博物院院刊 (*Palace Museum Journal*), no. 7, 2004b, pp. 89–96.

Yang Lizhi 楊立志 (ed.), *Mingdai Wudang shan zhi erzhong* 明代武當山志二種 (*Two Gazetteers of Mount Wudang of the Ming Dynasty*), Wuhan, 1999.

Yang Shiqi 楊士奇, *Dong li ji* 東里集 (*Collected Works of Yang Shiqi*), *c.* 1445, e-SKQS.

Yang Shiqi 楊士奇, *Dongli bie ji* 東里別集 (*Other Works of Yang Shiqi*), Taipei, 1986.

Yang Shiqi 楊士奇, *Dongli wenji* 東里文集 (*Collected Writings of Yang Shiqi*), Beijing, 1998.

Yang Shiyu 楊士鈺, *Hou Xian zhuan* 侯顯傳 (*Biography of Hou Xian*), Lanzhou, 2008.

Yang Weihua 楊衛華, 'Dai Jin zhongnian jujing shijian xinkao' 戴進中年居京時間新考 (New Study into When Dai Jin Resided in Beijing during His Middle Age), *Meishu yanjiu* 美術研究 (*Art Research*), no. 4, 2004, pp. 80–3.

Yang Xiaoneng, 'Ming Art and Culture from an Archaeological Perspective, Part 1: Royal and Elite Tombs', *Orientations*, June 2006, pp. 40–9.

Yang Xinhua 楊新華 and Lu Haiming 盧海鳴, *Nanjing Ming Qing jianzhu* 南京明清建筑 (*Ming and Qing Architecture of Nanjing*), Nanjing, 2001.

Yang Yiqing 楊一清, *Guanzhong zouyi* 關中奏議 (Memorials from Guanzhong), *c.* 1526, e-SKQS.

Yang You 楊槱, Yang Zongying 楊宗英 and Huang Genyu 黄根余, 'Lüe lun Zheng He xia Xiyang de baochuan chidu' 略論鄭和下西洋的寶船尺度 (A Preliminary Discussion on the Size of Zheng He's Treasure Ships), in *Haijiaoshi yanjiu* 海交史研究 (*Maritime History Studies*) 3, 1981, pp. 11–22.

Yang Zhishui 揚之水, *Shehua zhi se: Song Yuan Ming jinyinqi yanjiu* 奢華之色: 宋元明金銀器研究 (*The Color of Luxury: Research on Gold and Silver Ware of the Song, Yuan and Ming Dynasties*), Beijing, 2011.

Yao Pinwen 姚品文, *Taihe zhengyinpu jianping* 太和正音譜箋評 (*An Annotated Edition of Zhu Quan's Formulary of Correct Tones for a Period of Great Harmony*), Beijing, 2010.

Yao Pinwen 姚品文, *Wangzhe yu xuezhe: Ning wang Zhu Quan di yisheng* 王者與學者：寧王朱權的一生 (*A Prince and A Scholar: The Life of Prince of Ning, Zhu Quan*), Beijing, 2013.

Ye Chunji 葉春及, *Shidong ji* 石洞集 (*Collected Works of Ye Chunji*), 1570–4, e-SKQS.

Ye Quanhong 葉泉宏, *Mingdai qianqi Zhong-Han guojiao de yanjiu* 明代前期中韓國交之研究 (*Research into Sino-Korean Relations in the Early Ming Dynasty*), Taipei, 1991.

Ye Sheng 葉盛, *Shuidong riji* 水東日記 (*Diary from East of the River*), 1465–72, e-SKQS.

Ye Yingting 葉英挺 and Hua Yunong 華雨農 (eds), *Faxian: Da Ming Chuzhou Longquan guan yao* 發現:大明處州龍泉官窯 (*The Discovery of the Ming Imperial Kiln at Longquan, Chuzhou*), Hangzhou, 2005.

Yi Jong-mook 이종묵, 'Sejongdae Jiphyeonjeon mun'in ui munhakhwaldong' 세종대 집현전 문인의 문학활동 (Literary Activities of Jiphyeonjeon Scholars in the Sejong Period), *Sejong sidae ui munhwa* 세종시대의 문화 (*Culture under Sejong's Reign*), Seoul, 2001, pp. 219–307.

Yi Jong-mook 이종묵, 'Joseon sidae eojesi ui changjak yangsang gwa geu uimi' 조선시대 어제시의 창작 양상과 그 의미 (Aspect of King's Poems and Its Meaning), *Gyujanggak* 규장각 (*Royal Library*), vol. 19, June 2008, pp. 171–4.

Yi Seong-mu 이성무, 'Sejongdae ui yeoksa wa munhwa' 세종대의 역사와 문화 (History and Culture in the Sejong Period), *Sejong sidae ui munhwa* 세종시대의 문화 (*Culture under Sejong's Reign*), Seoul, 2001, pp. 20–1.

Yin Jinan 尹吉男, 'Mingdai gongting huajia Xie Huan de yeyu shenghuo yu fang Mishi yunshan huihua' 明代宮廷畫家謝環的業餘生活與仿米氏雲山繪畫 (The Ming Court Painter Xie Huan's Life Outside Work and Emulation of the Mi-style Cloud and Mountain Painting), *Yishushi yanjiu* 藝術史研究 (*The Study of Art History*) 9, 2007, pp. 101–27.

Yin Junke 尹鈞科, 'Lun Yongding he yu Beijing cheng de guanxi' 論永定河與北京城的關係 (On the Relationship between the Yongding River and the City of Beijing), *Beijing shehui kexue* 北京社會科學 (*Social Science of Beijing*), no. 4, 2003, pp. 12–18.

Yin Mengxia 殷夢霞 and Yu Hao 于浩 (eds), *Shi Chaoxian lu* 使朝鮮錄 (*Records of Visiting Joseon*), Beijing, 2003.

Yin Yungong 尹韵公, *Zhongguo Mingdai xinwen chuanbo shi* 中國明代新聞傳播史 (*A History of Chinese News Dissemination in the Ming Dynasty*), Chongqing, 1990.

Yu Jideng 余繼登, *Diangu jiwen* 典故紀聞 (*Hearsay Notes on Statuary Precedents*), repr. Beijing, 1981.

Yu Lu 雨露 (ed.), 'Gudai tangka, chuanyue erlai de yidong simiao' 古代唐卡, 穿越而來的移動寺廟 (Ancient *Thangkas*, Movable Temples from the Past), 11 December 2014, http://qinghai.kaiwind.com/top/201412/11/t20141211_2165144.shtml.

Yu Minzhong 于敏中, *Qinding tianlu linlang shumu* 欽定天祿琳琅書目 (*Imperially Commissioned Bibliography of the Tianlu linlang Library*), 1775, e-SKQS.

Yu Minzhong 于敏中 *et al.*, *Rixia jiuwen kao* 日下舊聞考 (*Study of Ancient Accounts Heard in the Precincts of the Throne*), 1774, repr. Beijing, 1983.

Yu Ruji 俞汝楫 *et al.*, *Libu zhi gao* 禮部志稿 (*Gazetteer of the Ministry of Rites*), 1620, e-SKQS.

Yu Zhuoyun and Hutt, Graham, *Palaces of the Forbidden City*, New York, 1987.

Yuan Hongdao 袁宏道, annotated by Qian Bocheng 錢伯城, *Yuan Hongdao ji jianjiao* 袁宏道集箋校 (*Annotated Collection of Works by Yuan Hongdao*), Shanghai, 1981.

Yuan Shusen 袁樹森, *Tanzhe si* 潭柘寺 (*Tanzhe Monastery*), Beijing, 2001.

Yuan Wenqing 院文清 and Zhou Daiwei 周代瑋, 'Dakai Yingjingwang mu' 打開郢靖王墓 (Opening the Tomb of Prince Jing of Ying), *Wenwu tiandi* 文物天地 (*Cultural Relics World*), no. 12, 2007, pp. 86–9.

Yuan Wenqing 院文清, Long Yongfang 龍永芳 and Zhou Daiwei 周代瑋, 'Hubei sheng Zhongxiang shi Mingdai Yingjingwang mu fajue shouhuo zhongda' 湖北省鐘祥市明代郢靖王墓發掘收穫重大 (Important Discoveries in the Excavation of the Ming Tomb of Prince Jing of Ying in Zhongxiang of Hubei Province), *Jiangnan wenwu* 江漢考古 (*Jiangnan Archaeology*), no. 3, 2007, pp. 49–51.

Yule, Henry, *The Book of Ser Marco Polo the Venetian Concerning the Kingdoms and Marvels of the East*, 2 vols, London, 1875.

Zeng Qi 曾棨, *Ke Zeng xi shu xian sheng ji* 刻曾西墅先生集 (*Record of Ke Zeng, Gentleman of the Western Villa*), in *Siku quanshu cunmu congshu* 四庫全書存目叢書 (*Extant Compendia from the Complete Library of the Four Treasuries*), Jinan, 1995–7, *ji* 30.

Zhang Bizhong 張必忠, 'Shishahai de lishi bianqian' 仕刹海的歷史變遷 (Historical Transformations of Shishahai), *Beijing shehui kexue* 北京社會科學 (*Social Science of Beijing*), 1999, pp. 97–104.

Zhang Chunyan 張春燕, 'Guancang jingpin zhi yi – "Daci Fawang xiang" tangka' 館藏精品之一 – '大慈法王像'唐卡 (A Fine Piece in the Museum Collection: Portrait Thangka of Śākya Yeshé), 2011, p://www.tibetology.ac.cn/index.php?option=com_content&vi=article&id=5365&Itemid=218.

Zhang Huaying 章華英, *Guqin* 古琴 (*Ancient Zither*), Hangzhou, 2005.

Zhang Huaying 章華英, *Songdai guqin yinyue yanjiu* 宋代古琴音樂研究 (*A Study of Song Dynasty Guqin Music*), Beijing, 2013.

Zhang Huiyi 張惠衣, *Jinling Da Bao'ensi ta zhi* 金陵大報恩寺塔志 (*Records of the Pagoda of the Great Baoen Temple of Jinling*), Beijing, 1938.
Zhang Huiyi 張惠衣, *Jinling da Bao'en si zhi* 金陵大報恩寺志 (*Records of the Great Bao'en Temple of Nanjing*), Nanjing, 2007.
Zhang Junqi 張君奇, 'Qutansi bihua ji Fojiao gushi' 瞿曇寺壁畫及佛教故事 (The mural paintings in Qutan Monastery and the Buddhist story), *Qinghai Wenwu* 青海文物 (*Qinghai Cultural Relics*), 1992, no. 7, pp. 144–8.
Zhang Junqi 張君奇, 'Qinghai Ledu Qutansi' 青海樂都瞿曇寺 (Qutan Monastery, Ledu, Qinghai), *Qinghai wenwu yaowen* 青海文物要聞 (*Important News of Qinghai Cultural Relics*), May 1998.
Zhang Naiwei 章乃煒, *Qing gong shuwen* 清宮述聞 (*Jottings on the Qing Palace*), repr. Beijing, 1990.
Zhang Ning 張寧, *Fengshi lu*奉使錄 (*Record of Serving as an Envoy*), repr. Shanghai, 1936.
Zhang Ruyuan 張如元, *Wenzhou Xie Lingyun houyi yanjiu: Yongjia Heyang Xieshi jia ji kaoshi* 溫州謝靈運後裔研究: 永嘉鶴陽謝氏家集考實 (*Research into the Descendants of Xie Lingyun of Wenzhou: Investigation into the Family Compilations of the Xie Clan in Heyang, Yongjia*), Hangzhou, 2007.
Zhang Shiqing 張十慶, 'Gudai jianzhu de sheji jishu ji qi bijiao: shilun cong 'Yingzaofashi' zhi 'Gongcheng zuofa' jianzhu sheji jishu de yanbian he fazhan' 古代建築的設計技術及其比較——試論從《營造法式》至《工程做法》建築設計技術的演變和發展 (Discussing the Development of Designs and Construction Methods in Ancient Architecture from the Song Dynasty *yingzao fashi* Manual to the Qing Dynasty *gongcheng zuofa* Manual), *Huazhong jianzhu* 華中建築 (*Huazhong Architecture*), vol. 17, no. 4, 1999, pp. 92–8.
Zhang Shuxia 張淑霞 (ed.), *Beijing Fahaisi*北京法海寺 (*Fahai Temple in Beijing*), Beijing, 2001.
Zhang Wen 張文, 'Huoqi yingyong yu Ming-Qing shiqi xinan diqu de gaitu guiliu' 火器應用與明清時期西南地區的改土歸流 (The Use of Firearms and the Bureaucratization of Native Offices in the Southwest Region during the Ming and Qing), *Minzu yanjiu* 民族研究 (*Nationalities Research*), no. 1, 2008, pp. 85–94.
Zhang Wende 張文德, *Ming yu Tiemu'er wangchao guanxi shi yanjiu* 明與帖木兒王朝關系史研究 (A History of Ming–Timurid Relations), Beijing, 2006.
Zhang Xie 張燮, *Dong Xi yang kao* 東西洋考 (*Study of the Eastern and Western Seas*), 1840, repr. Taipei, 1981.
Zhang Xiumin 張秀民, *Zhong-Yue guanxi shilun wenji* 中越關係史論文集 (*Essays on the History of Sino-Vietnamese Relations*), Taipei, 1992.
Zhang Yuhuan 張馭寰and Du Xianzhou 杜仙洲, 'Qinghai Ledu Qutansi diaocha baogao' 青海樂都瞿曇寺調查報告 (The Investigation Report on Qutan Monastery, Ledu, Qinghai), *Wenwu* 文物 (*Cultural Relics*), no. 5, 1964, pp. 46–53, 59–60.
Zhang Yuhuang (ed.), *The History and Development of Ancient Chinese Architecture*, Beijing, 1986.
Zhang Zehong 張澤洪, 'Mingdai huangjia daoshi Zhu Quan ji qi yinyue lilun yanjiu' 明代皇家道士朱權及其音樂理論研究 (A Study of Zhu Quan, a Ming Dynasty Imperial Daoist and His Music Theory), *Huangzhong: Wuhan yinyue xueyuan xuebao* 黃鐘：武漢音樂學院學報 (*Huangzhong: Journal of Wuhan Conservatory of Music*), no. 2, 2014, pp. 30–5.
Zhao Kesheng 趙克生, 'Hongwu shinian qianhou de jili gaizhi chutan: yi jiao,miao, shejili wei zhongxi' 洪武十年前后的祭禮改制初探—以郊、廟、社稷禮為中心 (The Change of the Sacrificial Rite before and after The Tenth Year of Hongwu), *Dongnan Wenhua* 東南文化 (*Southeast Culture*), 2004–5, pp. 54–7.
Zhao Kesheng 趙克生, 'Jiajing shidai de jili da biange' 嘉靖時代的祭禮大變革 (The Ritual Reform in the Jiajing Period), *Xibeishida xuebao (shehuikexue ban)* 西北師大學報(社會科學版) (*Journal of Northwest Normal University- Social Sciences*), 2008–12, pp. 26–9.
Zhao Kesheng 趙克生, *Mingdai Guojia lizhi yu shehui shenghuo* 明代國家禮制與社會生活 (*Goverment Rituals and Society Lives in the Ming Dynasty*), Beijing, 2012.
Zhao Zengfu 趙增福, 'Qutansi bilang hua zhong de Fojiao gushi' 瞿曇寺壁廊畫中的佛教故事 (The Jataka Murals in the Ambulatory of Qutan Monastery), *Qi[illegible] wenwu* 青海文物 (*Qinghai Cultural Relics*), no. 7, 1992, pp. 144–8.
Zhao Zhigang 趙志剛, 'Qianglie de Zhongguo qixi: Zheng He baochuan fujian jilüe' 强烈的中國氣息: 鄭和寶船復建記略 (Exciting News in China: A Brief Record of the Reconstruction of Zheng He's Treasure Ship), *Zheng He yu haiyang wenhua yanjiu* 鄭和與海洋文化研究 (*Research into Zheng He and Maritime Culture*), no. 5, 2008–9, pp. 100–9.
Zhao Zhongnan 趙中男, 'Lun Zhu Gaochi de lishi diwei' 論朱高熾的歷史地位 (Evaluation of Zhu Gaochi's Historical Role), *Liaoning daxue xuebao* 遼寧大學學報 (*Journal of Liaoning University*), no. 5, 1997, pp. 5–10.
Zhao Zhongnan 趙中男, 'Zhu Di yu Zhu Gaochi de guanxi ji qi shehui zhengzhi yingxiang' 朱棣與朱高熾的關係及其社會政治影響 (The Social and Political Effects Caused by the Relationship between Zhu Di and Zhu Gaochi), *Hunan keji xueyuan xuebao* 湖南科技學院學報 (*Journal of Hunan University of Science and Engineering*), no. 3, 2005, pp. 120–5.
Zhao Zhongnan 趙中男, *Xuande huangdi da zhuan* 宣德皇帝大傳 (*Biography of the Xuande Emperor*), Beijing, 2008.
Zhao Zhongnan 趙中男, *Mingchao de guaidian* 明朝的拐點 (*Turning Points in the Ming Dynasty*), Beijing, 2015.
Zhejiang sheng wenwu kaogu yanjiusuo 浙江省文物考古研究所, Beijing daxue kaogu wenbo xueyuan 北京大學考古文博學院 and Longquan qingci bowuguan 龍泉青瓷博物館 (eds), *Longquan dayao fengdongyan yaozhi chutu ciqi* 龍泉大窯楓洞巖窯址出土瓷器 (*Unearthed Ceramics of the Fengdongyan kiln site at Dayao, Longquan*), Beijing, 2009.
Zheng Lianzhang 鄭連章, 'Wansui shan de shezhi yu Zijincheng weizhi kao' 萬歲山的設置與紫禁城位置考 (Investigation into the Establishment of Longevity Hill and Its Relationship to the Siting of the Forbidden City), *Gugong bowuyuan yuankan* 故宮博物院院刊 (*Palace Museum Journal*), no. 3, 1990, pp. 37–43.
Zheng Yongchang 鄭永常, *Zhengzhan yu qishou: Mingdai Zhong-Yue guanxi yanjiu* 征戰與棄守: 明代中越關係研究 (*Conquest and Surrender: Sino-Vietnamese Relations in the Ming Period*), Tainan, 1997.
Zheng Yonghua 鄭永華, 'Yao Guangxiao shiliao yi ze ji xiangguan zhu wenti – jian ji "Mingchu zhuming zhengzhi jia Yao Guangxiao" yiwen de xiuzheng yu buchong' 姚廣孝史料一則及相關諸問題 – 兼及《明初著名政治家姚廣孝》一文的修正與補充 (Historical Materials on Yao Guangxiao and Some Related Issues – With Amendments and Supplements for the Article 'The Famous Early-Ming Statesman Yao Guangxiao'), *Zhongguo shi yanjiu* 中國史研究 (*Journal of Chinese Historical Studies*), 2007, vol. 2, pp. 149–54.
Zheng Zihai 鄭自海, 'Ming chu wushi jueyu de waijiao jia, hanghai jia Hou Xian shilüe kao', 明初五使絕域的外交家、航海家侯顯事略考 (An Examination Into the Activities of the Early Ming Diplomat and Navigator Hou Xian, and his Five Missions to Remote Border Regions), *Zheng He yanjiu* 鄭和研究 (*Zheng He Research*), vol. 81, no. 1, 2011, pp. 44–50.
Zhong Le 鐘樂, 'Cong yinyue de jiaodu lijie Zhu Quan de gongci' 從音樂的角度理解朱權的宮詞 (Research on Zhu Quan's Palace Poems from A Musical Angle), MA thesis, Jiangxi Normal University, 2013.
Zhongguo daojiao xiehui 中國道教協會 and Suzhou daojiao xiehui 蘇州道教協會, *Daojiao da cidian* 道教大辭典 (*Great Dictionary of Daoism*), Beijing, 1994.
Zhongguo diyi lishi dang'an guan 中國第一歷史檔案館 *et al.*, *Zhongguo Mingdai dang'an zonghui* 中國明代檔案總匯 (*Collection of Archives of the Ming Dynasty*), Guilin, 2001.
Zhongguo huaxue yanjiu hui 中國畫學研究會, *Yilin yuekan* 藝林月刊 (*Art World Monthly*), no. 56, 1934, p. 7.
Zhongguo shehui kexue yuan 中國社會科學院 *et al.* (eds), *Dingling* 定陵 (*Dingling Mausoleum*), Beijing, 1990, vols 1 and 2.
Zhou Deqing 周德清, *Zhongyuan yinyun* 中原音韻 (*Phonology of the Central Plains*), Beijing, 1978.
Zhou Huang 周煌, *Liuqiu guozhi lüe* 琉球國志略 (*A Brief History of Ryukyu Kingdom*), 1759, repr. 1830.
Zhou Qi 周齊, *Mingdai fojiao yu zhengzhi wenhua* 明代佛教與政治文化 (*Buddhism and Political Culture during the Ming Period*), Beijing, 2005.
Zhou Qiwen 周崎文, 'Ming Qing nanmu caiban shi qiantan' 明清楠木採辦史淺探 (A Preliminary Investigation into the Procurement of Nanmu in the Ming and Qing dynasties), in Wang Ping 王萍 (ed.), *Mei cheng zai jiu: Jinsi nan zhi mei* 美成在久-金絲楠之美 (*Time-vested Beauty: The Elegance of Gold-shimmering Nanmu*), Beijing 2012.
Zhou Shide 周世德, 'Cong Baochuanchang duogan de jianding tuilun Zheng He baochuan' 從寶船廠舵杆的鑑定推論鄭和寶船

(Confirming the Hypotheses Regarding Zheng He's Treasure Ships in Light of the Rudderpost Discovered at the Treasure Shipyard), *Wenwu* 文物 (*Cultural Relics*), no. 3, 1962, pp. 35–40.
Zhou Side 周思得, *Shangqing lingbao jidu dacheng jinshu* 上清靈寶濟度大成金書 (*Golden Writings on the Great Achievement of Deliverance of the Numinous Treasure of Highest Clarity*), in *Zangwai Daoshu* 藏外道書 (*Daoist Texts Outside the Canon*), vols 16 and 17, repr. Chengdu, 1992.
Zhou Xiang 周祥, *Shanghai bowuguan cangpin yanjiu daxi:Zhongguo gudai zhichao* 上海博物館藏品研究大係:中國古代紙鈔 (*Studies of the Shanghai Museum Collections: Ancient Chinese Paper Money*), Shanghai, 2004.
Zhou Xun 周汛 and Gao Chunming 高春明, *Zhongguo lidai funü zhuangshi* 中國歷代婦女妝飾 (*Women's Adornment in China's Successive Dynasties*), Hong Kong, 1988.
Zhu fo pusa miaoxian minghao jingzhou 諸佛菩薩妙相名號經 (*Xylographs in Marvelous Images, Names, Sutras, and Dharanis of the Buddhas and Bodhisattvas*), 1431, repr. Beijing, 2011.
Zhu Mouyin 朱謀垔, *Huashi hui yao* 畫史會要 (*Outline History of Painting*), 1631, e-SKQS.
Zhu Quan 朱權, 'Zhuo Wenjun siben Xiangru' 卓文君私奔相如 (Zhuo Wenjun Elopes with Xima Xiangru), in Chen Wannai 陳萬鼐 (ed.), *Quanming zaju* 全明雜劇 (*Complete Ming Zaju Dramas*), repr. Taipei, 1979, *juan* 7.
Zhu Quan 朱權, 'Shenqi mipu' 神奇秘譜 (A Treasured Score of Celestial and Distinctive Qin Compositions), in *Qinqu jicheng* 琴曲集成 (*A Compendium of Qin Compositions*), repr. Beijing, 1981, vol. 1, pp. 94–169.
Zhu Quan 朱權, 'Gongci qishi shou' 宮詞七十首 (Seventy Palace Poems), in *Ming gongci* 明宮詞 (*Ming Palace Poems*), Beijing, 1987, pp. 1–5.
Zhu Saihong 朱賽虹 (ed.), *Gugong bowuyuan cang Qinggong chenshe dang'an* 故宮博物院藏清宮陳設檔案 (*Furnishing Archives of Qing Palace in the Collection of the Palace Museum*), Beijing, 2013, vol. 6.
Zhu Zaiyu 朱載堉, *Yuelü quanshu* 樂律全書 (*Complete Collection of Zhu Zaiyu's Musical Treatises*), Beijing, 1996.
Zhu Zaiyu 朱載堉, annotated by Feng Wenci 馮文慈, *Lü lü jing yi* 律呂精義 (*Essentials of Musical Harmonics*), repr. Beijing, 1998.
Zhu Zaiyu 朱載堉, *Yuelü quanshu* 樂律全書 (*Complete Compendium of Music and Pitch*), *c.* 1600, e-SKQS.
Zhu Zhanji 朱瞻基, *Wulun shu* 五倫書 (*Book of the Five Relationships*), 1443, repr. Shanghai, 2002

Contributors

Aurelia Campbell is Assistant Professor of East Asian art history at Boston College. She is currently completing a book entitled *Architecture and Empire in the Reign of Yongle, 1402–1424*, which investigates a far-flung network of buildings patronised by the Yongle emperor, including the Forbidden City in Beijing, a Daoist temple complex on Mount Wudang in Hubei province and a Buddhist monastery at the Sino-Tibetan frontier. Other current research interests include architectural ornamentation, Buddhist material culture and Tibetan architecture in China.

Carla Nappi is the Canada Research Chair of Early Modern Studies and Associate Professor of History at the University of British Columbia, Vancouver. She specialises in the history of China, science and translation.

Caroline R. Cartwright is the Senior Scientist and Wood Anatomist in the Department of Scientific Research at the British Museum. Her scientific expertise includes the identification and interpretation of organics such as fibres, wood, charcoal, macro plant remains, shell, ivory and bone from around the world in all time periods. She specialises in scanning electron microscopy and optical microscopy. Amongst her recent publications is the Invited Review 'The principles, procedures and pitfalls in identifying archaeological and historical wood samples' published in *Annals of Botany*.

Christina M. Duffy is the British Library's Imaging Scientist on the Conservation Science and Research team. She graduated with a degree in Physics with Astronomy from Dublin City University in 2007 before achieving a PhD from Imperial College London on Meteoritics and Planetary Science in 2011. She specialises in digital microscopy, multispectral imaging and image processing techniques. Recent major projects have included recovery of faded text from Magna Carta and a CT analysis of the St Cuthbert Gospel binding.

Clarence Eng 翁纯全 is a Research Associate in the Department of Art and Archaeology at the School of Oriental and African Studies (SOAS), University of London. His former career with Royal Dutch Shell included senior positions in Europe, South Asia and China. More recently, he has pursued academic interests in architectural history alongside broader enquiries into cultural and technological transmission across Central and East Asia. His recent book *Colours and Contrast: Ceramic Traditions in Chinese Architecture* extends earlier PhD research and he is a contributing author to *The Phoenix Mosque and the Persians of Medieval Hangzhou*, due for publication in 2016.

Craig Clunas is Professor in the History of Art Department at the University of Oxford. He has published extensively on the art history and culture of China, especially the Ming period (1368–1644). His books include *Art in China* (1997, second edition 2009), *Superfluous Things: Material Culture and Social Status in Early Modern China* (1991), *Fruitful Sites: Garden Culture in Ming Dynasty China* (1996),

Pictures and Visuality in Early Modern China (1997), *Elegant Debts: The Social Art of Wen Zhengming, 1470–1559* (2004), *Empire of Great Brightness: Visual and Material Cultures of Ming China, 1368–1644* (2007) and *Screen of Kings: Art and Royal Power in Ming China* (2013).

David M. Robinson is Robert H. N. Ho Professor in Asian Studies and Professor of History at Colgate University. His publications include the edited volume *Culture, Courtiers, and Competition: The Ming Court (1368–1644)* (2008) and the authored books *Bandits, Eunuchs, and the Son of Heaven* (2001), *Empire's Twilight: Northeast Asia under the Mongols* (2009), *Martial Spectacles of the Ming Court* (2013), and *Seeking Order in A Tumultuous Age: The Writings of Chŏng Tojŏn* (2016). His current book project, entitled *Empire's Shadow: The Ming Court in Eurasia*, examines the Ming court's engagement with the legacy of the Mongol empire.

Geoffrey Wade researches China–Southeast Asia interactions and comparative historiography. He received his PhD in History at the University of Hong Kong with a thesis entitled 'The *Ming Shi-lu* (Veritable Records of the Ming Dynasty) as a Source for Southeast Asian History, 14th to 17th Centuries'. His translations from the Ming shi-lu are online at: http://epress.nus.edu.sg/msl/. An edited volume *Asian Expansions: The Historical Experiences of Polity Expansion in Asia* was published in 2015.

Helen Wang is Curator of East Asian Money in the Department of Coins and Medals at the British Museum. Her recent publications include *Textiles as Money on the Silk Road* (co-edited with Valerie Hansen, 2013). She has been working closely with scientists Caroline Cartwright (British Museum) and Christina Duffy (British Library) looking down the microscope at Ming paper money in the British Museum and British Library collections.

Jessica Harrison-Hall is Head of the China Section at the British Museum and Curator of Chinese Ceramics and the Sir Percival David Collection. She has curated the permanent gallery for Chinese Ceramics and many exhibitions including *Ming: 50 years that changed China*. Other publications include *Ming Ceramics* (2001 translated into Chinese 2014), *Chinese Ceramics* (with Regina Krahl, 2009 translated into Chinese 2013), *Passion for Porcelain* (with L. Mengoni, H. Young and A. Dawson, 2012) and *Ming: Art, People and Places* (2014).

Jonathan Hay is Ailsa Mellon Bruce Professor at the Institute of Fine Arts, New York University. He has written widely on the visual and material culture of pre-modern China, and on the theory and method of art history. His major publications include *Shitao: Painting and Modernity in Early Qing China* (2001) and *Sensuous Surfaces: The Decorative Object in Early Modern China* (2010).

Joseph S.C. Lam 林萃青is Director of the Confucius Institute at the University of Michigan and Professor of Musicology, the School of Music, Theatre and Dance, the University of Michigan. A musicologist and sinologist, Lam specialises in the musics and cultures of Southern Song (1127–1275), Ming (1368–1644) and modern China (1900 to present). His most recent publications include: 'Music and Masculinities in Ming China' (*Asian Music*, 2011) and *Songdai yinyueshi lunwenji: lilun yu miaoshu/Historical Studies on Song Dynasty Music: Theories and Narratives* (Shanghai: Shanghai Conservatory of Music Press, 2012). Currently, he is working on a monograph entitled: *Kunqu, the Classical Opera of Globalized China*.

Karl Debreczeny is Senior Curator at the Rubin Museum of Art, New York. He completed his PhD in Art History at the University of Chicago. His research interests focus on exchanges between Tibetan and Chinese painting traditions, and has conducted field research in various locations along the Sino-Tibetan border. His publications include *The Black Hat Eccentric: Artistic Visions of the Tenth Karmapa* (2012); and 'Imperial Interest Made Manifest: sGa A gnyan dam pa's Mahākāla Protector Chapel of the Tre shod Maṇḍala Plain' (2014). His current project explores the intersection of religion, politics and art focusing on Tibetan Buddhism's role in the courts of North Asia from the 7th to 19th centuries.

Kenneth M. Swope is Professor in the Department of History at the University of Southern Mississippi. He completed his PhD from the University of Michigan. His research interests encompass the military, social, political and diplomatic history of early modern East Asia. He is the author of *Warfare in China since 1600* (2005), *A Dragon's Head and a Serpent's Tail: Ming China and the First Great East Asian War, 1592–1598* (2009) and *The Military Collapse of China's Ming Dynasty, 1618–1644* (2013). He is currently completing research for his new book on the Ming-Qing transition in Southwest China.

Lee Soomi 이수미 李秀美 is head of Fine Arts Department at the National Museum of Korea. She completed her PhD in Art History at Seoul National University, focusing on 'A Study on The City of Supreme Peace Screen Painting'. In 2002, she was awarded the Harvard-Yenching Institute Visiting Fellowship and was Visiting Curator in the Department of Asia at the British Museum during 2012. Her publications include the catalogues *The Return of the Oegujanggak Uigwe from France: Records of the State Rites of the Joseon Dynasty* (co-authored, 2011) and *Joseon Painters as Envoys to China* (co-authored, 2011).

Lina Lin (林莉娜) is Associate Researcher in the Department of Painting and Calligraphy at the National Palace Museum, Taipei, where she has been working since 1987. She completed her MA in Art History at the University of Kansas. She has published widely on Chinese painting, particularly from the imperial courts of the Ming and Qing dynasties, curated a special display on the Xuande Emperor of the Ming and participated in major exhibitions on the Qing courts of the Kangxi, Yongzheng and Qianlong emperors.

Luk Yu-ping 陸於平 is Curator (Chinese Collections) at the Asia Department of the Victoria and Albert Museum,

London. Previously, she was Project Curator of the exhibition *Ming: 50 years that changed China* at the British Museum, and Assistant Professor in the Department of Visual Studies at Lingnan University in Hong Kong. She completed her DPhil in the History of Art at the University of Oxford. Her first book *The Empress and the Heavenly Masters: A Study of the* Ordination Scroll of Empress Zhang *(1493)* was published by the Chinese University of Hong Kong Press in 2015.

Maggie Chui Ki Wan 尹翠琪 is Associate Professor in the Department of Fine Arts at The Chinese University of Hong Kong. She completed her DPhil at the University of Oxford. Her research focuses on the history of Chinese ceramics, Daoist art as well as art and religion in late imperial China. Her publications include *Jiajing Emperor and His Auspicious Words* (2008), *Image and Efficacy: The Frontispieces to the Wanli Emperor's Yushu jing* (2015) and *Daoist Scripture Frontispieces and their Archetypes* (2016). She is currently working on a book on Daoist prints of the Ming dynasty.

Marsha Haufler is Professor of Art History in the Kress Foundation Department of Art History at the University of Kansas. She completed her PhD in art history at the University of California, Berkeley. Her research has focused on Mongol patronage in Yuan China, Chinese women artists, Buddhism in the aesthetic life of later imperial China and Tibeto-Chinese art. Her publications include the edited volumes *Flowering in the Shadows: Women in the History of Chinese and Japanese Painting* (1990) and *Cultural Intersections in Later Chinese Buddhism* (2001), and the exhibition catalogues *Views from Jade Terrace: Chinese Women Artists 1300–1912* (1988) and *Latter Days of the Law: Images of Chinese Buddhism 850–1850* (1994) and a range of articles on later Buddhist art in China.

Peter Ditmanson is a Senior Research Fellow at Pembroke College, University of Oxford. He specialises in Chinese cultural intellectual history and Chinese traditional historiography. He has written articles on Ming political culture and the historiography of the Yongle emperor's usurpation of the throne in 1402.

Priscilla Soucek is John L. Loeb Professor in the History of Art in the Institute of Fine Arts at New York University. She completed her PhD at New York University. Her research interests focus on Persian and Arabic manuscripts, portraiture and the history of collecting. Her publications include *Content and Context of Visual Arts in the Islamic World* (with Richard Ettinghausen, 1988) and *Masterpieces from the Department of Islamic Art in the Metropolitan Museum of Art* (co-authored, 2011).

Qin Dashu 秦大樹 is Professor in the School of Archaeology and Museology at Peking University. He completed his PhD at Peking University and post-doctoral research at the Smithsonian Institution. His research interests focus on Song to Ming dynasties archaeology and ceramics archaeology. His publications include *The Arts of Stone and Fire: Chinese Ceramics* (1996),*The Cizhou Kiln Site at Guantai* (1997) and *The Archaeology of Song-Yuan-Ming Dynasties* (2004), *Complete Collection of Ceramic Art Unearthed in China* (16 volumes, acting chief editor, 2008).

Sally K. Church is Affiliated Researcher in Chinese Studies in the Faculty of Asian and Middle Eastern Studies, University of Cambridge. She completed her PhD in Chinese literature at Harvard University. Her research focuses especially on the maritime expeditions of Zheng He (1405–33), the history of Chinese ships during the Ming period and earlier and Chinese diplomatic history during the Ming. Her recent publications include *Zheng He and the Afro-Asian World* (co-edited with Chia Lin Sien, 2012), and articles on Ming ships and shipyards in Nanjing. She is an Associate Editor for the *Medieval History Journal*.

Sarah Schneewind is Associate Professor in the Department of History at the University of California, San Diego. She completed her PhD at Columbia University. Her publications include *Community Schools and the State in Ming China* (2006) and *A Tale of Two Melons: Emperor and Subject in Ming China* (2006). She has also edited a collection of essays by 21 scholars entitled *Long Live the Emperor! The Uses of the Ming Founder across Six Centuries of East Asian History* (2008). Her current project is on pre-mortem enshrinement. She has been President of the Society for Ming Studies.

Shih Ching-fei 施靜菲 is Associate Professor at the Graduate Institute of Art History, National Taiwan University. She was previously Assistant Curator in the Department of Antiquities at the National Palace Museum, Taipei. She completed her DPhil in Oriental Studies at the University of Oxford. Her research focuses on artistic exchanges between East Asia and Europe, and the history of decorative arts in East Asia. Shih's publications include *Radiant Luminance: Painted Enamelware from the Qing Court* (2012).

Tansen Sen is Professor in the Department of History at Baruch College, City University of New York. He completed his PhD at the University of Pennsylvania. He specialises in Asian history and religions and has special scholarly interests in Buddhism, India-China relations, Indian Ocean trade and Silk Road archeology. His publications include *Buddhism, Diplomacy, and Trade: The Realignment of Sino-Indian Relations, 600–1400* (2003) and *Traditional China in Asian and World History* (co-authored with Victor H. Mair, 2012).

Timothy Brook is Republic of China Chair at the Department of History and Institute of Asian Research at the University of British Columbia. He has published widely, especially on the social and cultural history of the Ming dynasty. His more recent books include *The Chinese State in Ming Society* (2005), *Vermeer's Hat: The Seventeenth Century and the Dawn of the Global World* (2008), *The Troubled Empire: China in the Yuan and Ming Dynasties* (2010) and *Mr Selden's Map of China: The Spice Trade, a Lost Chart and the South China Sea* (2014).

Yin Ji'nan 尹吉男 is Professor and Chair of the History of Art department, and Dean of the Humanities Faculty at the Central Academy of Fine Arts, Beijing. He is an art historian, art critic and expert of ancient Chinese painting and calligraphy. He has published books on contemporary art in China and has written on the calligraphy and paintings found in Wang Zhen's tomb and the concept of Gu Kaizhi in the late Ming dynasty.

Yu Hui 余輝 is Curator and Head of the Research Department at the Palace Museum, Beijing. His research focuses on Chinese calligraphy and painting and issues of connoisseurship. He has published widely on a range of topics, including a book focusing on the artistic accomplishments of the Zhao clan of the Song dynasty (2008), edited volumes on Yuan dynasty painting (2005) and paintings in the Anhui and Zhejiang provinces (2007).

Yuan Wenqing 院文清 is an archaeologist and Curator at Hubei Museum, China. He contributed to books on tombs of the Chu kingdom and Chu culture, and has published many articles. He has led important archaeological projects and was involved in the excavations of Prince Jing of Ying tomb of the Ming Dynasty in Zhongxiang of Hubei province in 2005. Prince Jing of Ying was the 24th son of the founder of Ming Dynasty, Zhu Yuanzhang.

Zhao Zhongnan 趙中男 is the Chief Sub-Editor of the *Palace Museum Journal* at the Palace Museum, Beijing. He studied Ming history at Peking University. He is the author of a biography of the Xuande emperor (2008) and is a contributor to a two-volume book on the decrees and regulations of the Ming court (2010).

Illustration Credits

Map (pp. viii–ix): © Trustees of the British Museum

Introduction (Craig Clunas)

0.1 Roku'on-ji Temple, Kyoto. Image: Wikimedia Commons
0.2 Taizo-in, Kyoto
0.3 Nezu Museum, Tokyo
0.4 Nezu Museum, Tokyo
0.5 Fujita Art Museum, Osaka
0.6 Tokyo National Museum
0.7 Tokyo National Museum

Chapter 1 (David M. Robinson)

1.1 © Trustees of the British Museum
1.2 The Institute of Oriental Manuscripts, Russian Academy of Sciences
1.3 The Palace Museum
1.4 © Trustees of the British Museum
1.5 © Trustees of the British Museum

Chapter 2 (Geoffrey Wade)

2.2a National Library of China
2.2b National Library of China
2.3 Xianying Temple, Changle, Fujian province
2.4 © Trustees of the British Museum
2.5a–d The Maritime Experiential Museum, Resorts World Sentosa Singapore
2.6a Wikimedia Commons photo by Victorcouto
2.6b Wikimedia Commons photo by Hadiyana
2.7 Institute for Research in Humanities, Kyoto University
2.8 National Museum of Colombo. Photo by Dominic Sansoni/ThreeBlindMen

Chapter 3 (Tansen Sen)

3.1 © Victoria and Albert Museum, London
3.2 © Trustees of the British Museum
3.3 © Trustees of the British Museum
3.4 Worcester Art Museum, Massachusetts, USA / Jerome Wheelock Fund / Bridgeman Images
3.5 © Trustees of the British Museum
3.6 The National Central Library
3.7 © Getty Images photographer: Karl Johaentges
3.8 The Palace Museum
3.9 National Library of China

Chapter 4 (Kenneth M. Swope)

4.1 The Capital Museum, Beijing
4.2 Photograph courtesy of Sun Laichen
4.3 Photograph courtesy of Sun Laichen
4.4 Photograph courtesy of Sun Laichen
4.5 Photograph courtesy of Sun Laichen

Chapter 5 (Jonathan Hay)

5.1 Courtesy of Jonathan Hay
5.2 NASA
5.3 Courtesy of Jonathan Hay
5.4 National Museum of China
5.5 Photograph by Diane Nelson
5.6 Photograph by Diane Nelson

5.7 Photograph © 2016 Museum of Fine Arts, Boston
5.9 Nanjing Museum
5.10 Courtesy of Jonathan Hay
5.11 © Fuyi | Dreamstime.com – Ming Tomb Photo

Chapter 6 (Yu Hui)
6.1 © Trustees of the British Museum
6.2 © Trustees of the British Museum
6.3 © Trustees of the British Museum
6.4 The Palace Museum
6.5 The Palace Museum
6.6 Anhui Museum Collection
6.7 Anhui Museum Collection
6.8 © 2015. Princeton University Art Museum/Art Resource NY/Scala, Florence
6.9 Guangdong Museum Collection
6.10 Freer Gallery of Art, Smithsonian Institution, Washington, D.C.
6.11 The National Art Museum of China
6.12 National Museum of China
6.13 Nanjing Museum
6.14 The Collection of National Palace Museum
6.15 The Collection of National Palace Museum
6.16 The Collection of National Palace Museum
6.17 Wikimedia Commons photograph by Sean Shih (時雨)
6.18 © Trustees of the British Museum
6.20 The Collection of National Palace Museum
6.21 The Palace Museum
6.22 The Royal Ontario Museum © ROM
6.23 The Royal Ontario Museum © ROM

Chapter 7 (Luk Yu-ping)
7.1 The Collection of National Palace Museum
7.2 Dingling Museum, Beijing
7.5 The Collection of National Palace Museum
7.6 The Collection of National Palace Museum
7.7 The Collection of National Palace Museum
7.8 Hubei Provincial Museum
7.9 The Collection of National Palace Museum
7.10 The Collection of National Palace Museum
7.11 The Collection of National Palace Museum
7.12 © Victoria and Albert Museum, London
7.13 © Trustees of the British Museum

Chapter 8 (Jessica Harrison-Hall)
8.1 National Gallery of Art, Washington, D.C.
8.2 Sir Percival David Foundation of Chinese Art. Photo © The Trustees of the British Museum
8.3 © The J. Paul Getty Museum, Digital image courtesy of the Getty's Open Content Program
8.4 Jingdezhen Institute of Ceramic Archaeology
8.5 Museum of Art and History, Geneva
8.6 ©2015. Photo Scala, Florence/bpk, Bildagentur fuer Kunst, Kultur und Geschichte, Berlin
8.7 The Cleveland Museum of Art
8.8 The Palace Museum
8.9 The Palace Museum
8.10 The Palace Museum
8.11 Private collection
8.12 Private collection
8.13 Private collection
8.14 Jingdezhen Institute of Ceramic Archaeology
8.15 National Museum of China
8.16 National Museum of China
8.17 © 2015. Image copyright The Metropolitan Museum of Art/Art Resource/Scala, Florence
8.18 © 2015. Image copyright The Metropolitan Museum of Art/Art Resource/Scala, Florence
8.19 Nanjing Museum
8.20 Shanxi Museum
8.21 Nanjing Shipyard Museum

Chapter 9 (Joseph S.C. Lam)
9.1 © Victoria and Albert Museum, London
9.4 Photograph courtesy of Joseph S.C. Lam

Chapter 11 (Yin Ji'nan)
11.1 © 2015. Image copyright The Metropolitan Museum of Art/Art Resource/Scala, Florence
11.2 Zhenjiang Museum Collection
11.3 Courtesy of the Library of Congress
11.4 The Cleveland Museum of Art

Chapter 12 (Zhao Zhongnan)
12.1 Tokyo National Museum
12.2 © Getty Images, photographer: Karl Johaentges
12.3 © Getty Images
12.4 SOAS Library
12.5 SOAS Library

Chapter 13 (Shih Ching-fei)
13.1 National Library of China
13.3a Leeum, Samsung Museum of Art
13.4 The Collection of National Palace Museum
13.5 © Baur Foundation, Museum of Far Eastern Art, Geneva. Photography by Marian Gérard
13.6 National Library of China
13.7 Sir Percival David Foundation of Chinese Art. Photo © The Trustees of the British Museum
13.8 The Palace Museum
13.9 The Palace Museum
13.10 Private collection
13.11 © Victoria and Albert Museum, London

Chapter 14 (Lina Lin)
14.1 The Collection of National Palace Museum
14.2 The Collection of National Palace Museum
14.3 Bibliothèque nationale de France
14.4a–c Tibet Museum
14.5a–b The Collection of National Palace Museum
14.6 The Palace Museum
14.7 The Collection of National Palace Museum
14.8a–e The Collection of National Palace Museum
14.9a–h National Museum of China
14.10 The Collection of National Palace Museum
14.11 The Collection of National Palace Museum

Chapter 15 (Maggie Chui Ki Wan)
15.1a The Palace Museum
15.2 Photo by Hao Qinjian, Hubei Provincial Museum

15.3 The Palace Museum
15.4 National Central Library
15.5a–b Photo courtesy of Hsieh Tsung-hui
15.6 Photo courtesy of Hsieh Tsung-hui
15.7 © The British Library Board
15.8 © The British Library Board
15.9 Herbert F. Johnson Museum of Art, Cornell University
15.10 White Cloud Monastery, Beijing
15.11a–b White Cloud Monastery, Beijing

Chapter 16 (Marsha Haufler)
16.1 The Palace Museum
16.2 Tibet Museum
16.3 Norbulingka Collection
16.4 Tōfuku-ji, Kyoto
16.6 The Collection of National Palace Museum
16.7 The Collection of National Palace Museum
16.8 Potala Palace

Chapter 17 (Karl Debreczeny)
17.1 Shanxi Museum
17.2 Photo © Musée Guimet, Paris, Dist. RMN-Grand Palais / Thierry Ollivier
17.3 Hubei Provincial Museum
17.5 University of California, Berkeley Art Museum and Pacific Film Archive
17.6 Fahai Monastery, Beijing
17.7 Fahai Monastery, Beijing
17.8 Photograph courtesy of Zhang Haidong, Xihai Metropolis Daily
17.9 Photograph courtesy of Karl Debreczeny
17.10 Photograph courtesy of Karl Debreczeny
17.11 Pilu Monastery, Hebei province
17.12 Photograph courtesy of Karl Debreczeny
17.13 Photograph courtesy of Karl Debreczeny
17.14 Qinghai Provincial Museum
17.15 Photo © Stéphane Piera / Musée Cernuschi / Roger-Viollet

Chapter 18 (Yuan Wenqing)
18.1 Photograph courtesy of Yu Le, Hubei Provincial Museum
18.2 Photograph courtesy of Hao Qinjian, Hubei Provincial Museum
18.3 Hubei Provincial Museum
18.4 Hubei Provincial Museum
18.5 Hubei Provincial Museum
18.6 Hubei Provincial Museum
18.7 Hubei Provincial Museum
18.8 Hubei Provincial Museum
18.9 Hubei Provincial Museum
18.10 Qichun Museum, Hubei province
18.11 Qichun Museum, Hubei province

Chapter 19 (Caroline R. Cartwright, Christina M. Duffy and Helen Wang)
19.1 © Trustees of the British Museum
19.2 © Trustees of the British Museum
19.3 Shanxi Museum
19.4 Shanghai Museum
19.5 Image Caroline Cartwright. © Trustees of the British Museum
19.6 Image Caroline Cartwright. © Trustees of the British Museum
19.7 Image Caroline Cartwright. © Trustees of the British Museum
19.8 Christina M. Duffy © The Trustees of the British Library
19.9 Christina M. Duffy © The Trustees of the British Library
19.10a–c Christina M. Duffy © The Trustees of the British Library

Chapter 20 (Clarence Eng)
20.1 SOAS Library
20.2a–b Photograph courtesy of Clarence Eng
20.3 Nanjing Municipal Museum
20.4 Nanjing Municipal Museum
20.5a Nanjing Municipal Museum
20.5b © 2015. Image copyright The Metropolitan Museum of Art/Art Resource/Scala, Florence
20.6a Sir Percival David Foundation of Chinese Art. Photo © The Trustees of the British Museum
20.6b © Trustees of the British Museum
20.7 Courtesy of Clarence Eng
20.8a Private collection
20.8b Jingdezhen Institute of Ceramic Archaeology
20.8c Jingdezhen Institute of Ceramic Archaeology
20.8d The Museum of Ceramic Specimens, Humanity College, Nanjing Art University
20.9 Courtesy of Clarence Eng
20.10a–b Photograph courtesy of Clarence Eng

Chapter 21 (Aurelia Campbell)
21.1 Photograph courtesy of Aurelia Campbell
21.2 Photograph courtesy of Aurelia Campbell
21.3 Photograph courtesy of Karl Debreczeny
21.6a Photograph courtesy of Aurelia Campbell
21.6b Photograph courtesy of Aurelia Campbell
21.6c Photograph courtesy of Aurelia Campbell
21.7 Photograph courtesy of Aurelia Campbell
21.8b Courtesy of Guo Daiheng
21.9b Photograph courtesy of Aurelia Campbell

Chapter 22 (Sally K. Church)
22.1 Artwork by Martin Brown
22.2 National Library of China
22.3 Nanjing Treasure Shipyard Relic Site Park
22.4 Photo courtesy of Sally K. Church
22.5 Photo courtesy of Zheng Yijun
22.6a–b Map data ©2016 Google
22.7 National Library of China
22.8a Artwork by Martin Brown
22.8b Nanjing Treasure Shipyard Relic Site Park
22.9 National Library of China
22.10 The Bodleian Libraries, The University of Oxford
22.11 National Library of China
22.12 Courtesy of Sally K. Church
22.13 Nanjing Municipal Museum
22.14 Artwork by Martin Brown

Chapter 24 (Lee Soomi)

24.1 © National Museum of Korea
24.2 © Royal Portrait Museum/ Photo © Jeonju National Museum
24.3 The Korean Central History Museum, Pyeongyang
24.4 Tenri Central Library
24.5 © National Museum of Korea
24.6 © National Museum of Korea
24.7 © National Museum of Korea
24.8 © National Museum of Korea
24.9 © National Museum of Korea

Chapter 25 (Sarah Schneewind)

25.1 Princeton University Library
25.2 The Bodleian Libraries, The University of Oxford
25.5 © Trustees of the British Museum

Chapter 26 (Priscilla Soucek)

26.1 Freer Gallery of Art, Smithsonian Institution, Washington, D.C.
26.2 © Calouste Gulbenkian Foundation, Lisbon Calouste Gulbenkian Museum
26.3 © The British Library Board
26.4 © Calouste Gulbenkian Foundation, Lisbon Calouste Gulbenkian Museum
26.5 The Bodleian Libraries, The University of Oxford
26.6 Photo: Imaging Department © President and Fellows of Harvard College
26.8a–b The Cleveland Museum of Art
26.9 © Detroit Institute of Arts, USA / Bridgeman Images
26.10 © Detroit Institute of Arts, USA / Bridgeman Images
26.11 © Royal Asiatic Society, London, UK/Bridgeman Images
26.12 © Royal Asiatic Society, London, UK/Bridgeman Images

Chapter 27 (Craig Clunas)

27.1 Wikimedia Commons photo by Andreas Praefcke
27.2 © Trustees of the British Museum
27.3 Hubei Provincial Museum
27.4 Hubei Provincial Museum
27.5 Hubei Provincial Museum
27.6 © Trustees of the British Museum
27.7 © 2015. Photo Scala, Florence – courtesy of the Ministero Beni e Att. Culturali
27.8 Hubei Provincial Museum
27.9 Hubei Provincial Museum
27.10 Hubei Provincial Museum
27.11 Hubei Provincial Museum
27.12 The Palace Museum

Chapter 28 (Qin Dashu)

28.1 Photo by Peking University Archaeological team in Kenya
28.2 Photo by Peking University Archaeological team in Kenya
28.3 Photo by Peking University Archaeological team in Kenya
28.4 Photo by Peking University Archaeological team in Kenya
28.4 Photo by Peking University Archaeological team in Kenya
28.5 Photo by Peking University Archaeological team in Kenya
28.6 Photo by Peking University Archaeological team in Kenya
28.7 Photo by Peking University Archaeological team in Kenya
28.8 Photo by Peking University Archaeological team in Kenya
28.9 Photo by Peking University Archaeological team in Kenya
28.10 Photo by Peking University Archaeological team in Kenya
28.11 Topkapı Palace Museum
28.12 Photo by Peking University Archaeological team in Kenya
28.13 Jingdezhen Institute of Ceramic Archaeology
28.14 Photo by Peking University Archaeological team in Kenya
28.15 Photo by Peking University Archaeological team in Kenya

Chapter 29 (Timothy Brook)

29.1 The Bodleian Libraries, The University of Oxford
29.2 National Library of China
29.3 The Bodleian Libraries, The University of Oxford
29.4 The Bodleian Libraries, The University of Oxford

Index

Note: page numbers in ***bold*** refer to captions.

Abdallah b. Ibrahim (r. 1434–46) 233
Abel-Rémusat, Jean-Pierre 219n.10
Admonitions of the Instructress to the Court Ladies (*Nüshi zhen tu* 女史箴图) (after Gu Kaizhi) 223–4, ***223***
Adoration of the Magi (Mantegna) 78, ***78***
The Adventures of the Eunuch... (*Sanbao taijian xiyang ji* 三寶太監西洋記) (Luo Maodeng) 198, ***198***
Ahmad al-Tīfāshi (1184–1253) 238
Ai, Empress 哀 (Tang dynasty) 114
Ailiu 隘留, Jianzhi province 18
Allah 23, 30
Allom, Thomas, Porcelain Pagoda 179, ***179***, 182, 185
altars
  Altar of Heaven and Earth (*Tianditan* 天地壇) (later Altar of Agriculture), Beijing 51, 54, ***54***, 55n.17
  Altar of Mountains and Rivers (*Shanchuantan* 山川壇) 51
  Altar of the Spirits of the Soil and the Five Grains (*Shejitan* 社稷壇) 51
    Shejitan front hall 社稷壇前殿 (1425) 51, 192
  Circular Mound Altar (*Huanqiu* 圜丘) 114, ***115***, 118
amber 32
ambergris 33
Amogha 148, 149
Amusement of Fishermen in a River Landscape (*Jiangshan yule tu* 江山漁樂圖) (Wu Wei) 60, ***60***
Amusements in the Four Seasons (*Siji shangwan tu* 四季賞玩圖) (anonymous) 82, ***82***, 83, ***83***
Amusements in the Xuande Emperor's Palace (*Zhu Zhanji xingle to* 朱瞻基行樂圖) (anonymous) ***81***
An Gyeon 安堅 (active *c.* 1440–70), *Dream Journey to the Peach Blossom Land* (*Mong-yudowondo* 夢遊桃源圖) 213, 214, ***214***
Angola, *padrão* ***22***
Anhui province 59, 104, 110, 181
Anige (1245–1306) 149, 153
animals
  auspicious 125, 129
  motifs 115, ***117***, 118, ***119***
  see also elephants; giraffes; horses
Anlu 安陸 (now Zhongxiang 鐘祥) 163, 164
The Annals of Ryukyu (*Liuqiu guo zhi lüe* 琉球國志略) (Zhou Huang) 204, ***204***
Annam (Annan; Đại Việt, now northern Vietnam)
  annexation 15, 16, 17–20, 25n.60, 37–45, 107, 186, 207
  tribute 126, 129
Anpyeong, Prince (1418–53) 213
Anthology of Brilliant Flowers (*Hwanghwa jip* 皇華集) (Ni Qian) 216
Anthology of Iskandar Sultan 230–1, ***231***
Arabia 31, 207, 256, 258
architecture 62, ***63***, 64, ***64***, 66, 67, 134, 181
  early Ming Court 189–96
  Shah-i Zindeh 229
  see also Da Baoensi; Qutansi; Changling
aromatics 18, 32, 243
Arugtai (d. 1434) 12
Ashikaga shoguns 4, 81
Ashikaga Yoshimitsu, portrait (anonymous) ***4***
Assam, India 16
Assembly of Artists and Scholars of Various Talents and Schools of Former Times (*Wanggu jiuliu baijia zhu shi yishu zhong* 往古九流百家諸士藝術眾) (anonymous) 85, ***85***
astronomy 87
auspicious signs, Yongle period 122–33, ***123***, ***124***, ***125***, ***126***, ***127***, ***128***, ***130***, ***131***, ***132***
Ava-Burma 17
Ayudhya 21

Babai 八百 (Lanna) 16, 17, 207
Badakhshan 240
Bai Juyi 白居易 (772–846) 100
Baiyi 百夷 (Möng Mao) 16, 207
Baiyun guan 白雲觀 (White Cloud Monastery) 124, 140, ***140***
Bakau shipwreck, guns 21, ***21***
Ban Gu 班固 (32–92) 221
Bantam, Java 256
Baogoi River, Great Battle of 125
Baoguangdian 寶光殿 (Hall of Blazing Jewel Light) *see* Qutansi
Baoningsi 寶寧寺 (Precious Peace Monastery) 152
Baysunghur b. Shah Rukh ***234***
Beijing 北京 41, 46–55, ***48***, 59, 75, 106, 107, 129, 134, 189
  Eight Views of Beijing (*Beijing bajing tu* 北京八景圖) ***50***, 55n.12, 129, ***130***, ***131***
  imperial palace 56–67, ***63***, 82, 106, 129, 183, 187, 195n.2
  maps ***49***, ***54***
  Mongol palace 153
  ritual sites 51, 52, 89
  Taimiao 太廟 (Imperial Ancestral Temple) 22, 51, 53, 113, 117, 144, ***192***, 193, ***193***
  water supply 48–50, 201
  see also Buddhism; Changling; Dadu; Forbidden City; named buildings; Zhu Bang
Beijing Association for the Study of Zheng He and Maritime Culture 201
Beiping 北平 (formerly Dadu; later Beijing) 47, 48, 144
Beiyou ji 北遊記 (*Journey to the North*) 141
Benaglio, Francesco (*c.* 1432–92), *Madonna and Child* 77–8, ***77***
Bengal 30, ***32***, 33, 36, 126
  maps ***29***
Bharat Kala Bhavan, Banaras 230
Bi 畢, Celestial Lord 135, 137, 139, 141
Bian Wenjin 邊文進 (*c.* 1356–*c.* 1428) 129, 132
  The Three Friends and a Hundred Birds (*Sanyou baiqin tu* 三友百禽圖) 132–3, ***132***
bird motifs 132–3, 228, 231
  see also pheasant; phoenix
Birthday Gathering in the Bamboo Garden (*Zhuyuan shouji tu* 竹園壽集圖) (Lü Wenying and Lü Ji) 99–100, 104
bodhisattvas 33, 35, 158, 160, ***160***
  Bodhisattva Guanyin ***168***, 169
Bong sa Joseon changhwa sigwon 奉使朝鮮倡和詩卷 ***215***, ***216***
Boni *see* Brunei
Book of the Five Relationships (*Wulun shu* 五倫書) 219–28, ***220***
Borneo 20, 247
Boxer Rebellion (1900–1) 171
bronze, ritual vessels 113, 114, 115, 117
Brunei (Boni) 20, 22, 23, 29
Buddha
  Buddha's Tooth 26–36
  statues 171
  stele in Sri Lanka 23, 30
Buddhism 34, 36, 92, 123, 125, 165, 166, 167, 168, 180, 240
  in Annam 18, 19
  early Ming court 143–51
  elements in royal tombs 165, 166, 167, 169
  in Korea 211
  and precious stones 238, 240
  sacred sites 30, 164
  temples 3, 51, 194
    see also named sites
  and Xuande emperor 85
  and Yongle emperor 35, 154
  see also Chan; Korean; Mongols; Tibet
Bunyashiri (d. 1412) 11, 12
bureaus 59, 207–9
  Bureau for Foreign Shipping (*Shibo si* 市舶司) 112
  Bureau of Painting (Dohwawon) 212
Burma 17, 21, 42

Calicut (*Guli* 古里, now Kozhikode) 23, 27–8, 29, 32, 239, 256, 258
calligraphy 3, 104, 126–7, ***127***, 129, 214
Cambodia 207
camphor 33
canals 49–50, 52, 107, 186, 201
  see also Grand Canal
Cang 蒼 of Annan (Annam) 39
Cão, Diogo ***22***
Celestial Worthy of the Primordial Beginning (Yuanshi tianzun 元始天尊) 137
ceramics ***78***, ***79***, ***80***, ***83***, ***84***, ***85***, ***88***, 232, ***232***, 233, ***233***, 235
  blue-and-white ***248***, 249, 251
  celadon 118, 249, 250
  discovered in Kenya 245–52
  Joseon *buncheon* wares 115, 117
  ritual vessels 113–21, ***116***, ***118***, ***119***, ***120***
  see also porcelain; named kilns; named types
Chabi, Yuan Empress (1227–81), wife of Qubilai Khan, *Official Portrait of* (anonymous) 71, ***72***
Champa 27, 30, 38, 43, 52, 207
Chams 42
Chan Buddhism 144, 145, 146, 147, 150
Chang'an 132
Changjing 173
Changle city, Fujian province ***20***, 35, 201, 240
Changling 長陵
  Mausoleum of the Yongle emperor and Empress Xu 48, 107, ***107***, 189
    Ling'endian 祾恩殿 (Hall of Eminent Favour) (1416) 189, ***189***, 190–5, ***192***, ***194***, ***195***
  Sacrificial Hall 52, ***53***
Changsha 92, 246, ***246***
Chaotiangong 朝天宮 (Palace in Homage to Heaven), Nanjing 123, 124
Chapters from the Liao Sea (*Liaohai pian* 遼海篇) 216
charcoal 52
Cheli 車里 (Chiang Hung) 17
Chen Boyou 陳伯友 (1601 *jinshi*) 66
Chen Cheng 陳誠 (d. after 1457) 243
Chen Deqing 陳得清 (act. 1438) 30
Chen Gui 陳珪 (d. 1415) 126
Chen Jingzong 陳敬宗 (1377–1459) 102, 103
Chen Tianping 陳天平 (Trần Thien Binh) (d. 1406) 17, 38
Chen Xian 132
Chen Xiang 陳享 (active 1427) 161
Chen Xun 陳循 (1385–1462) 101, 102, 103
Chen Zongyuan 陳宗淵 (b. 1370) 104
Chen Zuyi 陳祖義 (d. 1407) 22
Cheng Hao 程顥 (1032–85) 96
Cheng Kuan 程寬 (active *c.* 1400) 39
Cheng Yi 程頤 (1033–1107) 96
Chenghua 成化 emperor (Zhu Jianshen 朱見深) (r. 1465–87) 59, 164, 200
  ceramics 77, 247, 249, 251
  patron of arts ***81***, ***83***, 137, 141, 155
  voyages 108, 111–12
Chengtian 承天 prefecture 163
Chengtian Gate, 59, 62, 64, 66, 67
Chetty merchants 32, 33, 239
Chinggis Khan (Genghis Khan) (1162?–1227), and Chinggisids 1, 9, 10, 229, 230, 239

Chongguosi 崇國寺 (Honouring the Nation Monastery) 150n.11
Chouhai tubian 籌海圖編 (*Illustrated Compendium on Maritime Defence*) 254
Chu Pengling 初彭齡 (d. 1825) 100
Circular Mound Altar (*Huanqiu* 圜丘) *see* altars
Cizhou ware 248, 249
Clavijo, Ruy González de 229, 241
cloth, as official salary 111
clothing 5, 10, 28, 33, 39, 101, 146, 147, 149, 225, 237
cloud motif 62, 64, 66, 81, 123, 124, 125, 146–9, 183, 238
  'cloud collar' embroideries ***230***, 231
Cloud Terrace, Juyong Pass 居庸關 180
Cochin (*Kezhi* 柯枝, now Kochi) 23, 28, ***28***, 29, 32, 36, 239
coins 30, 171, 172, ***172***, 230, 240, 251, 252n.23
  bronze 165, 173
  copper 28, 33, 112, 117, 252n.23
  gold 78, 168
  silver 30, 168
  Timurid dynasty, 1393 11, ***12***
Collected Glosses on the Precious Book of the Jade Pivot... (*Jiutian yingyuan leisheng puhua tianzun yushu baojing jizhu* 九天應元雷聲普化天尊玉樞寶經集註) 137–8, ***139***
Collected Statutes of the Great Ming (*Da Ming huidian* 大明會典) 53, 69, 70, ***70***, 72, 73, 89, 114, ***115***, 118, 120n.12, 150, 243, 250
Collected Rites of the Ming Dynasty (*Da Ming jili* 大明集禮) 113, 115, 117, ***117***
Columbus, Christopher 197
Confucianism 12, 18, 113, 125, 219–28, 223
congratulational rituals 113
Contemplative (*Seon* 禪) school 211
Conti, Niccolò de' (1395–1469) 239
copper 28, 33, 43, 112, 117, 149, 252n.23
coral 32, 69, 70, 241
cotton 3, 33, 173
cowries 17, 33
crowns 149, 156, ***156***, 158, ***158***, 168, 231, 235, 241
  Empress' Dragon Crown 68–76, ***69***, ***70***, ***71***, ***73***, ***74***
  fengguan 鳳冠 (phoenix crown) 68, 72, 76, 168

Da Baoensi 大報恩寺 (Great Monastery of Filial Gratitude), Nanjing 35, 95, 109, 183
  Porcelain Pagoda 178–88, ***179***, ***180***, ***181***, ***182***, ***183***
da Gama, Vasco 36, 247
Da Longshan huguosi 大隆善護國寺 (Great Flourishing Goodness Protecting the State Monastery) 53, 145
Da Ming huidian 大明會典 (*Collected Statutes of the Great Ming*) 53, 69, 70, ***70***, 72, 73, 89, 114, ***115***, 118, 120n.12, 150, 243, 250
Da Ming jili 大明集禮 (*Collected Rites of the Ming Dynasty*) 113, 115, 117, ***117***
Da Ming lü 大明律 (*Great Ming Code*) 220
Da Ming men 大明門 (Gate of the Great Ming) 56
Da Tang xiyu ji 大唐西域記 (*Records of the Western Region [Visited During] the Great Tang Dynasty*) 34, ***34***
Da Xinglongsi 大興隆寺 (Great Prosperity Monastery) 145
  see also Qingshousi
Đa-bang City 18
Dade guan 大德觀 (Temple of Great Virtue) 139
Dadu 大都 (later Beiping; Beijing) 9, 47, 50, 51, 187
Dahou 大候 (now Inner Mongolia) 16, 17
Dai Jin 戴進 (1388–1462) 105
Đại Việt Sử Ky ToanThư 大越史記全書 19
Đại Việt/Đại Ngu *see* Annam
Dali 16
Dangtu, Taiping prefecture 181–2
Dangyang 當陽 164
Daning 大寧 88
Daoism 88, 123, 124, 134–41, 165, 166, 168, 194
Daoist Canon of the Zhengtong Reign (*Zhengtong Daozang* 正統道藏) *see* Ming Daoist Canon
Daoyan 道衍 (Yao Guangxiao 姚廣孝) (1335–1418) 35, 123, 124, 143–6, 150
  portraits ***143***, 146, ***146***, 150
De'an 德安 (now Anlu 安陸) 163
deforestation 49, 52, 54
Deng 鄧, Celestial Lord 135, 137, 139, ***139***, 141, ***141***
Deshin Shekpa, Fifth Karmapa of Tibet (1384–1415) 33, 125, 151n.60, 154, ***154***, 155, ***159***
Dingling 定陵 (Ding Mausoleum) 69
Ding ware 117, 246
Dongdadian 東大殿 (East Main Hall) *see* Foguangsi
Dongmentou 東門頭 182, ***251***
Dongxi yang kao 東西洋考 (*Study of the Eastern and Western Seas*) (Zhang Xie) 255, 256, 258
dragon motif 50, 68, 69, 70, 71, 72, 74, 228, 230, 231, 238
  see also thrones
drainage 3
drama 6, 87–93
Dream Journey to the Peach Blossom Land (*Mongyudowondo* 夢遊桃源圖) (An Gyeon) 213, ***214***
dress
  court 56, 69, 70, ***70***, 71, 72, 73, 74, 145, 159, 243
  see also clothing; headdresses
Dunhuang grottoes 187n.20
Duobao fota 多寶佛塔 (Buddhist Pagoda of Many Treasures) 164
Duren jing 度人經 (*Scripture on Salvation*) (1406) 137, ***137***
Dutch East India Company 79

E'xi 鄂西 163
Early Court Audience (*Zaochao tu* 早朝圖) (anonymous) 66, ***66***
Eastern Ocean (*Dongyang* 東洋) 20, 255
Eight Steeds of Taejo (*Taejo Paljundo* 太祖八駿圖) (anonymous) 214–15, ***214***
  poems about 215
Eight Views of Beijing (*Beijing bajing tu* 北京八景圖) (Wang Fu) ***50***, 55n.12, 129, ***130***, ***131***
Elegant Gathering in the Apricot Garden (*Xingyuan yaji tu* 杏園雅集圖) (anonymous, after Xie Huan) 4, 52, 84–5, ***84***, 99–105, ***100***, ***101***
elephants 4, 16, 42, 47, 52, 52–5, ***54***, 125, 180, 238
  war 18, 40, 41
  white 126, ***128***, 148
Enni Ben'en 圓爾辯圓 (1202–80) 145
Esen (r. 1438–53/4) 13
Esen-Tughal (d. 1431) 12, 13
eunuchs 4, 59, ***83***, 219
  court 5, 19, 40, 51, 59, 80, 82, 84, 85, 89, 95, 111, 112, 153, 156–7, 200
  envoys 18, 20, 25n.62, 26, 28, 30, 34, 40, 42, 125, 155, 161, 198, 216, 254
  maritime ventures 20, 21, 31, 198, 200, 204, 237, 256
  supervisors 51, 111, 112, 161, 238
  see also Zheng He
Extensive Records of the Four Barbarian [Regions] (*Siyi guangji* 四夷廣記) (Shen Maoshang) ***32***, 33

Fahaisi 法海寺 (Monastery of the Sea of the Law), Beijing 85, 156, ***156***, 157, 161, 192
Fanchang white ware, Anhui 246
Fang Xiaoru 方孝孺 (1357–1402) 104
Fangshan 房山 144
Fei Xin 費信 (*c.* 1385–*c.* 1436) 30, 32, 33, 20
Fengdongyan kiln 247, ***249***
fengguan 鳳冠 (phoenix crown) 68, 72, 76, 168

Fengtian jingnan ji 奉天靖難記 (*Record of Responding to Heaven and Pacifying the Troubles*) 95
Fengtiandian 奉天殿 (Hall for Worshipping Heaven) 56, 106, 161
Fengtianmen 奉天門 (Gate for Worshipping Heaven) 53, 56
Fengxi daoren 豐溪道人 (Master of Fengxi) 56
festivity rituals 113
Figures (*Renwu tu* 人物圖) (attributed to Zhu Bang) 60, ***60***
Firdawsi, Abu'l-Qasim Manur, *Shahnama* (*Book of Kings*) 79, ***80***, 232, ***232***, ***233***, ***234***, 235
firearms *see* guns
Firearms Division (*shenji ying* 神機營) 41
Fishermen in a River Gorge (*Xigu yufu* 溪谷漁父) (attributed to Zhu Bang) 56, ***58***, 60
'Five Phases' ('Five Virtues') (*wu xing* 五行) 241, 242
Five Rites (*wuli* 五禮) 113, ***116***
flower motifs 70, 71, 72, 132–3, 168
flower-and-bird paintings, auspicious symbols 129, 132–3
Foguangsi 佛光寺 (Monastery of Buddha Light) ***157***
  Dongdadian 東大殿 (East Main Hall) 191
Forbidden City 46–55, 106, ***106***, 134
  see also Chengtian Gate; Da Ming men; Fengtiandian; Fengtianmen; Qin'an dian; Taihedian; Taihemen; Wumen; Yongshougong Palace; Zhengyangmen
Fort Jesus, Mombasa 245, 246
Four Great Celestial Lords of the Thunder Gate (*Leimen sida tianjun* 雷門四大天君) *see* Bi; Gou; Liu; Pang
Four Great Celestial Lords of Thunderclap (*Leiting sida tianjun* 雷霆四大天君) *see* Deng; Tao; Xin; Zhang
Four Saints (*Sisheng* 四聖) 137
frankincense 32
Fujian province 3, 22, 104
  wares 248, 249
Fuliang 富良 River 18
funerals 65, 113, 144, 221
Furnishing Archives of the Qing Palace (*Qinggong chenshe dang'an* 清宮陳設檔案) 134

Gaeseong 212
Galle, Sri Lanka, stone stele 23, ***23***, 30, 33, 239
Ganyai 干崖 16, 17
Gao Gong 高拱, 219n.11
Gao Sixun 高司訓 99
Gaochang glossaries 207
Gaoliang 高粱 River 49
Gaoshang yuhuang benxing jijing 高上玉皇本行集經 (*Scripture of the Jade Emperor*) (1424) 135, 137, ***138***, 139
Gathering of Five who are Alike (*Wu tong hui tu* 五同會圖) 104
Gedi Ruins, Malindi 245, 248–51, ***248***, ***251***
gems *see* precious stones
Genghis Khan *see* Chinggis Khan
Ghazan Khan 240
giraffes 30, ***30***, 33, 36, 126, ***126***, 127, 129
glossaries 107–10
Goguryeo kingdom (37 BCE–668 CE) 212
gold
  colour sacred to the Mongols 241
    figure of Mārīcī ***169***
  figure of the Three Pure Ones ***169***
  gold belt set with gems ***239***
  gold phoenix pendant (*Yinzuoju* 銀作局) ***72***
  group of gold and gem-encrusted hairpins ***237***
  hat-top ornaments ***242***
  levies, tribute and trade 16, 17, 18, 20, 33, 71, 149, 219, 236, 238, 243
  mantra tablet ***167***
  pair of gold pillow ends ***237***
  pendant in the form of a pelican ***241***
  plaque of Mahākāla ***167***
  seed syllables ***167***
  statue of the Bodhisattva Guanyin ***168***, 169
  toothpick box with chain ***236***, 237
  vájra thunderbolts ***168***
  see also precious stones
Golden Writings on the Great Achievement of Deliverance of the Numinous Treasure of Highest Clarity (*Shangqing lingbao jidu dacheng jinshu* 上清靈寶濟度大成金書) (Zhou Side) (1433) 135, 139, 140
Goldsmith, Oliver 2
Gong Xiang 恭項 17
Gong Zhen 鞏珍 200, 201
Goryeo dynasty, Korea (918–1392) 12, 211, 212–13
Gou 苟, Celestial Lord 135, 137, 139, 141
Gourd and Catfish (*Hyōnen zu* 瓢鮎図) (Josetsu) 4, ***4***
grain transport 201
Grand Canal 49–50, 52, 107, 186
Great Ming Code (*Da Ming lü* 大明律) 220
'Great Ritual Controversy' (*Daliyi* 大禮議) 113, 115
Gu Kaizhi 顧愷之 (344–405), *Admonitions of the Instructress to the Court Ladies* (*Nüshi zhen tu* 女史箴图) 223–4, ***223***
Gu Zechang 顧澤長 (b. 1941) 92
Guan 關, Celestial Lord 135, 137, 139, 141
Guangdesi 廣德寺 (Monastery of Spreading Virtue) 164
Guangdong 18, 22, 249
  ware 248, 249
Guangxi 18, 39
Guanyin (bodhisattva) ***168***, 169
Gui Zongru 桂宗儒 103
Guizhou 貴州 province 18, 52, 108
Gujarat 33
guns and gunsmiths 18, 39–41, ***40***, ***41***, 42, 43
  Bakau shipwreck 21, ***21***
Guo Chun 郭純 (1370–1444) 104
Guo 郭氏, Lady (d. 1451) 164, 165–7
Gyeongbok Palace, Seoul 216

Hafiz (d. 1389) 230
Haichen 海澄 county 255
hairpins 168, ***237***, 238
Hall of Worthies (Jiphyeonjeon 集賢殿), Royal Academic Institute 213
Han dynasty (206 BCE–220 CE) 16, 27, 71, 74
Han Yong (1422–78) 225
Hangzhou 3, 27, 105, 255
Hanlin Academy (*Hanlin yuan* 翰林院) 98, 104, 126, 127, 129, 207, 216, 221
Hanlin ji 翰林記 (*Records of the Hanlin Academy*) 221
Hanyang 漢陽 163, 212
hat ornaments 153, ***242***, 243
Hazhi Mahamo Qilanni 哈只馬哈沒奇剌泥 31
He Liangjun 何良俊, *Siyouzhai hualun* 四友齋畫論 (*Theory of Painting from the Studio of the Four Friends*) 132
headdresses 68, 70, 71, 76, 148, 238
Heda, Willem Claesz (1594–1680), *Breakfast Still Life* 79, ***79***
Herat ***12***, 230, 231, 232, ***234***, 235, 243
Hindu traditions 180
Hồ dynasty 18, 40
Hồ Nguyen Trừng (Le Trừng), 19, 43
Hồ Quy Ly (*c.* 1335–*c.* 1407) 18, 19, 38, 40, 42
Hongjue Temple ***84***
Hongjuesi 宏覺寺 (Monastery of Vast Awakening) 85
Hongwu 洪武 emperor (Zhu Yuanzhang 朱元璋) (r. 1368–98) 7, 9, 10, 12, 17, 47, 68, 76, 81, 95, 113–21, 125, 145, 153, 224, 225
  ceramics 114, 117, 118, 119, 248

Da Baoen Monastery 178, 184
drama and music 89
Linggusi 靈谷寺 (Numinous Valley Monastery) 155
military actions and armies 15, 104, 163, 242
new palace in Nanjing 58
paper money 171, 172, ***172***, 173, 178
policies 3, 27, 31, 37, 74
princely enfeoffment 163
renovation of Tianxisi 天禧寺 (Monastery of Heavenly Blessings) 178
ritual regulations 69, 113, 114, 115
Hongxi 洪熙 emperor (Zhu Gaochi 朱高熾) (r. 1425) 74–5, 96, 97, 101, 104, 109–10, 122, 164
Hongzhi 弘治 emperor (Zhu Youtang 朱祐樘) (r. 1488–1505) 118, 139, 146
Hormuz, Persian Gulf 125, 203, 231, 240, 256, 257, 258
horses 11, 15, 17, 18, 30, 32, 33, 36, 42, 53, 209, 215, 224, 238, 241, 243
Horses and Grooms under Willow Trees (anonymous) 52, ***52***
Hou Xian 侯顯 (active 1403–27) 20, 30, 33, 35, 125, 155, 157, 243
Hu 胡, Empress (d. 1443) 76
hu 胡 10
Hu Guang 胡廣 (1369–1418) 96, 97, 103, 104, 123, 129
Hu Yan 胡儼 (1360–1443) 104, 123, 129
Hu Zongyun (active early 15th century) 胡宗蘊 104
Huai En 懷恩 (d. 1488) 112
Huang Huai 黃淮 (1367–1449) 95, 97, 104, 105, 123, 129
Huang Ming ji lüe 皇明紀略 (*Brief Records of the August Ming*) 58
Huang Ming xiangxu lu 皇明象胥錄 (*Record of the Interpreters of the August Ming*) (1629) 219n.14
Huang, Prince of Lu 魯荒王 (1370–89) 81
Huang Quan 黃筌 (*c.* 903–65) 132
Huang Zhong 黃中 (d. *c.* 1413) 38
Huang Zongxi 黃宗羲 (1610–95) 225
Huang Zuo 黄佐 (1490–1566) 98, 123, 221–2
Huangchao liqi tushi 皇朝禮器圖式 (*Illustrated Regulations for Ceremonial Paraphernalia of the Imperial Court*) 114, 120
Huangmei 黃梅 164
Huangzhou 黃州 163
Hubei province 72, 124, 136, 163–9, 237, 243
Huguang 湖廣 province 18, 102, 108, 163
Huiwujeong 喜雨亭 213
human sacrifice 164, 166
see also immolation
Hunan province 52, 163
Hunting by a Lake (*Hupan shelie tu* 湖畔射獵圖) *c.* 1426–35 243, ***243***
Huo Tao 霍韜 (1487–1540) 98
Hwanghwa jip 皇華集 (*Anthology of Brilliant Flowers*) (Ni Qian) 216
Hyejong, King (912–45; r. 943–5) 212
Hyoryeong, Prince (1369–1486) 213

Ibn al-Bannā 3
Ibrahim Sultan b. Shah Rukh (r. 1414–35) 230, 231–2, 232, 233
Icheon 213
Ilkhanid Mongols 228, 240
Illustrated Guide to the Three Bonds (*Samgang haengsildo* 三綱行實圖) 213, 219, 220, 221, ***221***, 222, 223
immolation 76
Immortal Lü (*Lü xian tu* 呂仙圖) (attributed to Zhu Bang) 60, ***61***
Imperial Academy 207
imperial kilns 117, 118, 119
Imperial Palace in Beijing (*Beijing gongcheng tu* 北京宮城圖) (anonymous) 62, ***63***, 65
Imperial Palace of the Ming Dynasty (*Mingdai gongdian tu* 明代宮殿圖) (anonymous) 62, ***63***, 64, ***64***, 65, ***65***
Indian Ocean
rim 26, 27, 239–51
sailing routes 253–8
Indonesia 20
Inspector of Days (*Zhiri* 值日) 134
Inspector of Hours (*Zhishi* 值時) 134
Inspector of Months (Zhiyue 值月) 134
Inspector of Years (*Zhinian* 值年) 134
Iran, Timurid 228–37
Isfahan 229
Ishakani, Coast province 250
Iskandar Sultan b. Umar Shaikh (r. 1404–14) 230, 231, ***231***

jade 73, 83, 89, 145, 146, 165, 167, 168, 240
cup 11, ***13***, 230
hairpins ***237***
hat-top ornaments ***242***, 243
jug ***230***
Jade Emperor (Yuhuang 玉皇) 134, 135, 137–9, ***138***
Jade Fascicles (*Tianhuang zhidao taiqing yuce* 天皇至道太清玉冊) 140
Jade Maiden (*yunü* 玉女) 136, 140
Jalayirid dynasty 228
Japan 4, 8, 15, 27, 29, 43, 81, 207
ceramics 245
paper 173
Sino-Japanese cultural exchange 143, 144, 145
stele 23
Jaunpur Sultanate ***29***, 30
Java 21, 23, 27, 30, 31, 33, 77, 207, 239, 256
Jegidoseol 祭器圖說 (*Illustrated Catalogue of Ritual Vessels*) 115
Jeong Yinji 鄭麟趾 (1396–1478) 215, 216, 217
Jeongneung 212
Jeonju 212
Jiajing 嘉靖 emperor (Zhu Houcong 朱厚熜) (1522–66) 66, 69, 98, 113, 164
Jian of Liao, Prince 遼簡王 *see* Zhu Zhi
Jian Yi 蹇義 (1364–1435) 97, 123
Jiang Ji 蔣驥 (1378–1430) 104–5
Jiang Zicheng 132
Jiangnan 3, 5, 6, 65, 148
Jiangsu province 56, 102, 104, 110, 172
Jiangxi province 3, 18, 102, 103, 104, 129
Jiangxia 江夏 school 56, 59, 60
Jiangyin 江陰 172, 173
Jianwen 建文 emperor (Zhu Yunwen 朱允炆) (r. 1399–1402) 94, 104, 122, 165, 184, 207
Jiaofangsi 教坊司 (Office of Entertainment Music) 89
Jiaozhi 交趾 18, 19, 25n.62, 40, 126, 238
Jiaxing Tripiṭaka (*Jiaxing zang* 嘉興藏) 34, ***34***
Jin dynasty (1115–1234) 27, 47, 172, 207
Jin Youzi 金幼孜 (1367–1431) 104, 105, 126, 129
Jin ping mei 金瓶梅 (*Plum in the Golden Vase*), 'Funeral of Li Pinger' 65, ***65***
Jinchi 金齒 16, 17
Jindian 金殿 (Golden Hall, Mount Wudang) 135, 164, ***165***
Jing of Ying, Prince 郢靖王 *see* Zhu Dong
Jingdezhen 77, 78, 82, 84, 117, 118, 182, 248, 249, 250
imperial kilns 72, 82, 117, 118, 182, ***184***, 248, ***251***
Jinghaisi 靜海寺 (Calm Sea Monastery) 201
stele ***200***
Jingtai 景泰 emperor (Zhu Qiyu 朱祁鈺) (r. 1450–6) 48, 111, 216
Jingxiang 荊湘 region 163
Jingzhou 荊州 163, 164
Jipgyeongjeon, Gyeongju 211
Jiphyeonjeon 集賢殿 (Hall of Worthies), Royal Academic Institute 213
Jiutian yingyuan leisheng puhua tianzun yushu baojing jizhu 九天應元雷聲普化天尊玉樞寶經集註 *(Collected Glosses on the Precious Book of the Jade Pivot...)* 137–8, ***139***
Jokhang Monastery, Lhasa 80

Joseon 朝鮮 dynasty, Korea (1392–1897) 11, 13, 126
  ceramics, ritual vessels 114, 115, ***116***, 117, 120
  cultural exchange with Ming China 4, 41, 99, 211–18, 219–20
  royal portraits 211–13
Joseon wangjo sillok 朝鮮王朝實錄 (*Veritable Records of the Joseon Dynasty*) 212, 213, 216, 222
Joseph of Cranganore 29, 33
Josetsu 如拙, *Gourd and Catfish* (*Hyōnen zu* 瓢鮎図) 4, ***4***
Journey to the North (*Beiyou ji* 北遊記) 141
Jubao, Mount 聚寶山 179, 180, 181, 182, 183, 186
Jubaomen 聚寶門 (Gate of Collected Treasures) (modern Zhonghuamen 中華門) 178
Jun ware 82
Junweonjeon 濬源殿 211
Jurchens 2, 10, 13, 49, 207, 219
  Jin dynasty (1115–1234) 51, 71, 172, 207
Juyong Pass 居庸關 (1345) 129, ***131***, 151n.45, 154, 155

Kagyü order imagery ***158***, 160
Kaifeng 開封 186
Kal Zangpa 158
Kan Duo 闞鐸 (1875–1934) ***63***, 65
Karmapas 153, 154, 155, 160
  Fifth *see* Deshin Shekpa
  Seventh *see* Zhengde emperor (Rinchen Palden)
Ke Qian 柯潛 (1423–73) 225
Kenkō Shōkei 賢江祥啓, *Mountain and River* 4, ***5***
Kenya, Ming ceramics 245–52
Keyili 可亦里 , ruler of Cochin 29
Khusraw wa Shirin ***229***
kingfisher feathers 18, 33, ***69***, 73
Kirkman, James 248
Kokan Shiren 151n.59
Kollam, Malabar coast 27
Korea 4, 12, 38, 43, 72, 211–18
  see also Joseon court
Kṣitigarbha 159
Kuai Fu 蒯福 (active 1368–98) 58
Kuai Xiang 蒯祥 (1398–1481) 56, 58–9, 62, 64, 65, 67
Kumbum Jampa Ling, Geluk monastery 157, 158
Kyushu, Japan 23

Laccadives 33
lacquer 18, 59, 108
  wares 73, ***75***, 80, 81, 85, 149, 166
Landscapes of Autumn and Winter (Sesshū Tōyō 雪舟等楊) ***6***
language 6–7, 12, 30, 46, 90, 96, 143, 206–10, 239
Lani 剌泥 31
Lantern Festival Celebrated in Emperor Xianzong (Chengua)'s Palace (*Xianzong yuanxiao xingle tu* 憲宗元宵行樂圖) 83, ***83***, 84
Laos ***38***
'Laud rutter' or *Dispatched on Favourable Wind* (*Shunfeng xiangsong* 順風相送) 253–4, ***253***, 255, 256, 257, 258
Lavagnoli Chapel, Verona 78
laws 5, 6, 75
  sumptuary 68, 69, 71, 72, 73, 74, 82
Lê dynasty (1428–1527) 42
Le Lợi (1385–1433) 19, 42
Ledu 樂都 county 157, 190, ***190***
legitimacy
  Beijing 51–2
  see also Yongle emperor
Leizu 雷祖 137
Li Bin 李彬 (d. 1422) 19
Li Dongyang 李東陽 (1447–1516) 99, 225
Li Jili 黎季犛 (Hồ Quy Ly) 38
Li Kui 李奎 (1389–1457) 225
Li Long 李隆 (active 1435) 110
Li Shimian 李時勉 (1374–1450) 101, 102, 105, 126
Li Shizhen 李時珍 (1518–93) 163
Li Tong 李童 (Li Fushan 李福善) (*c.* 1390–1453) 5, 85
Li Xian 李賢 (1408–67) 98
Li Zhaoxiang 李昭祥 (fl. 1537–53), *Longjiang Shipyard Treatise* (*Longjiang chuanchang zhi* 龍江船廠志) ***203***
Liang Fang 梁芳 (fl. 1470) 112
Liang Qichao, 'Our Motherland's Great Navigator Zheng He' (*Zuguo da hanghaijia Zheng He zhuan*) 祖國大航海家鄭和傳 7
Liao dynasty (907–1125) 27, 47, 51
Lijiang 16
Līlātilakam (Tamil text) 241
Ling'endian 祾恩殿 (Hall of Eminent Favour) *see* Changling
Linggusi 靈谷寺 (Numinous Valley Monastery) 125, 155, 186, ***186***
Lingquan, Mount 靈泉山 164
literature 5–6, 163
Liu 劉 Celestial Lord 135, 137, 139
Liu Chaozong 劉朝宗 (active early 15th century) 72, 103
Liu Daxia 劉大夏 (1436–1516) 108, ***108***, 111, 200
Liu Ji 劉基 (1311–75) 104
Liu Jiang 劉江 (fl. *c.* 1370) 225
Liu, Lady 劉氏 (d. 1560) 164, 168
Liu 劉, Song Empress (969–1033), wife of Emperor Zhenzong, *Official Portrait of* (anonymous) 70, ***71***
Liu Tingshi 劉庭式 (fl. *c.* 1078–85) 222–3
Liu Yan 劉儼 (1394–1457) 221, 226
Liu Yun 劉允 (active 1515) 155
Liujiagang, inscription 201
Liuqiu guo zhi lüe 琉球國志略 (*The Annals of Ryukyu*) (Zhou Huang) 204, ***204***
Liuzun tu 六尊圖 (Images of Six Vessels) 114, ***114***
Lizong 理宗 emperor (r. 1224–64) 146
Longchuan 隴川 Pacification Commission 17
Longguodian 隆國殿 (Hall of Enriching the State) *see* Qutansi
Longjiang chuanchang zhi 龍江船廠志 (*Longjiang Shipyard Treatise*) (Li Zhaoxiang) (fl. 1537–53) 108, 203, ***203***
Longqing 隆慶 emperor (Zhu Zaihou 朱載垕) (r. 1567–72) 249
Longquan ware 84, 118, 246, 247, ***247***, 248, 249–51, ***249***, ***250***
lu 籙 (Daoist register) 138
Lu Ban 魯班 (507–444 BCE) 59
Lu Hong 盧鴻 (active Tang dynasty) 62
Lu Rong 陸容 (1436–94) 125
Lu Zhen 呂震 (1365–1426) 123
Lü Dongbin 呂洞賓 60
Lü Ji 呂紀 (b. 1477), *Birthday Gathering in the Bamboo Garden* (*Zhuyuan shouji tu* 竹園壽集圖) (with Lü Wenying) 99–100, 104
Lü Wenying 呂文英 (1421–1505), *Birthday Gathering in the Bamboo Garden* (*Zhuyuan shouji tu* 竹園壽集圖) (with Lü Ji) 99–100, 104
Lü Yi 呂毅 (d. 1409) 38
Lü Yuan 呂原 (1418–62) 221
Luchuan 麓川 (Luchuan-Pingmian 麓川平緬) 16, 17
Lujiang 潞江 16, 17
Luling 盧陵, Jiangxi province 96
Luo Zhenyu 羅振玉 (1866–1940) 215
Luoyang 洛陽, Henan province 114
Luzon 20

Ma 馬, Marshal, Celestial Lord 135, 139, 141
Ma 馬, Empress (d. 1382) 76n.12, 125, 155, 184, 225, 236
Ma Huan 馬歡 (d. *c.* 1460) 28, 32, 33, 201, 236
  Yingyai shenglan 瀛涯勝覽 (*Overall Survey of the Ocean's Shores*) ***15***, 236, 239, 240, 243, 252n.9
Ma-na-re-jia-na-nai 麻那惹加那乃, King of Boni 22
Ma'bar, Coromandel coast 27
Madonna and Child (Francesco Benaglio) 77–8, ***77***
Mahākāla (Buddhist deity) 153, ***153***, 158, ***158***, 159, 167, ***167***

Mailapetam 29
Majapahit empire, Java 23
makara (*jing* 鯨 or *yu long* 魚龍) 50, ***50***
Malabar coast 26, 27, 28, 29, 32, 33, 36
Maldives 33
Malindi 126, 245, 247, 248
Mambrui ***247***, 250, ***250***, 251, ***251***
Mamluk Sultanate 8, 239
Manda Island 245
Mañjuśrī (bodhisattva) 33
Mantegna, Andrea, *Adoration of the Magi* 78, ***78***
Mao Kun 茅坤 (1512–1601) 202, 203, 254
Mao Qara 毛哈喇 (1394–1468) 225
Mao Ruizheng 茅瑞徵 (fl. 1597–1636) 219n.14
Mao Yuanyi 茅元儀 (1594–1640) 202, 254, 257
maps
  Beijing ***49***, ***54***
  Bengal-Jaunpur ***29***
  Mongol empire ***8***
  Nanjing ***295***
  southern expansion ***15***
  Southern India ***28***
  Sri Lanka ***31***
  Zheng He's voyages ***20***
Mārīcī (Buddhist deity) 35, ***35***, 156, ***156***
maritime trade 18, 21, 50, 106, 108, 111, 258
  commodities *see* trade
  Indian Ocean 26–36, 238, 245–52, 256
  restrictions 8, 27, 31, 247
Maritime Trade Supervisorates (*Shi bo ti ju si* 市舶提擧司) 18
mathematics
  Jiu zhang xiang zhu suan fa bi lei da quan 九章詳注算法比類大全 (*Complete Book on the Classification of the Mathematical Arts in Nine Sections*) (Wu Jing) 3
Maw Shans (Shan polities) 42
measures
  chi 尺 200, 203
  liao 料 201, 203
  zhang 丈 104, 197, 198, 199, 201
Meiyintang collection 77
Melaka (*Manlajia* 滿剌, now Malacca) 20–1, 22, 23, 28, 29, 33, 36, 207, 238
Mengding 孟定 16, 17
Menggen 孟艮 17
Mengyang 孟養 16, 17
Mianyang 沔陽 163
Miaozhian 妙智庵 (Marvellous Wisdom Hermitage) 144
Michele da Verona (1470–1536/1544) 78
military campaigns 35, 97, 107, 108, 109, 112
  Vietnam 37–45
military rituals 113
Ming Chengzu (1360–1424) *see* Yongle
Ming Daoist Canon (*Zhengtong Daozang*) (1445) 124, 135, 138, 140, ***140***, 141, ***141***
'Ming Gap', ceramic exports 247–8
Ming shi 明史 (*History of the Ming*) 21, 22, 23, 29, 40, 59, 67, 68, 75, 113, 122
  shipbuilding 197, 198, 199
Ming shilu 明實錄 (*Ming Veritable Records*) 4, 12, 21, 22, 28, 30, 31, 35, 59, 94, 95, 96, 97, 98, 124, 149, 200, 238
Ming Veritable Records see *Ming shilu*
Ministry of Works (*Gongbu* 工部) 20, 43, 59, 64, 65, 109, 110, 156, 189, 200, 250
Miracles of the Mass of Universal Salvation Conducted by the Fifth Karmapa for the Yongle Emperor (*Pudu Ming Taizu changjuan tu* 普渡明太祖長卷圖) 34, 36, 123, 124, 125, 125, 154–5
Mogok, ruby mines 238
money *see* coins, paper money
Möng Mao 17
Mong Mit 238
Mongols 1, 2, 8–13, 27, 41, 43, 47–9
  Buddhism 125, 152, 154, 263
  campaigns against 139, 184, 185, 186, 207, 216, 225, 242
  and Dadu/Beijing 47, 49, 52, 53
  empire 71, 113, 136, 153
    map ***8***
  and Iran 228, 229, 231
  and Ming culture 71, 74, 75, 83, 153, 155, 161, 207, 208, 209, 239, 241, 243
  see also Oirat Mongols 216
motifs *see* animals; bird; dragon; flower; pheasant; phoenix
Mountain and River (Kenkō Shōkei 賢江祥啓) 4, ***5***
Mu Sheng 沐晟 (1368–1439) 16, 17, 42
Mu Ying 沐英 (1345–92) 16, 250
Mubang 木邦 (Hsenwi/Theinni) 16, 17
Muhammad al-Sultani 233
Muhammad b. Tughluq 243
Muhammad Juki b. Shah Rukh ***234***, 235
Mu'in al-din Natanzi 230
Munjong, King (r. 1450–2) 213
Muromachi shogunate 23
Musho Tokushi 無初德始 (Ch. Wuchu Deshi, d. 1429) 145, 146
music 87–93, 124
musk 33
Muslims 29, 31, 33, 185, 231, 239

Nan cun chuo geng lu 南村輟耕錄 (Tao Zongyi) 239–40
Nan Dian 17
Nanchang 南昌, Jiangxi province 87, 140
Nanjing 南京
  annexation of Vietnam and transfer of artisans 18, 19, 25n.61, 38, 40, 43, 58, 104
  capital 47, 106, 109, 129, 132, 143, 145, 154, 189
  excavations 85, 108, 183, ***184***
    see also shipyard
  imperial workshops 237
  Muslim community 185
  palaces 58, 59, 195n.2
  ritual ceremonies 33, 35, 117, 123, 125
  shipyard 110, 199, 203, 204, ***205***
    Treasure Shipyard Relic Site Park ***199***, 201, 202, ***202***, 204
  silk ***27***, ***123***
  see also Da Baoensi; Linggusi;
Narsingha, King of 29
naval power 26, 27, 30, 31, 39, 43
navigation 27, 202, 247, 249, 251, 253–9
Nénying Monastery, Tsang province, Tibet 154
Neo-Confucianism 96, 210, 211, 214, 215, 217, 220, 222
Nepalese art 148, 149, 153
Ngô Sĩ Liên 19
Ni Qian 倪謙 (1415–79) 99, 215–17, 226
Ni Yue 倪岳 (1444–1501) 99
Night Banquet at Huiwujeong (*Huiwujeong yahyeondo* 喜雨亭夜宴圖) 213
Nine Elders of the Mountain of Fragrance (*Xiangshan jiulao tu* 香山九老圖) 100, ***102***, 103
Nizami ***229***, 230
Numinous Official Wang *see* Wang, Marshal

Ode to Ascending a Pavilion after Snow (*Xueji denglou fu* 雪霽登樓賦) (Ni Qian) 216
officials 5, 10, 13, 14, 19, 28, 31, 33, 35, 47, 49, 52, 59, 64, 94, 111
  civil and military 19, 95, 104, 110, 111

Confucian 27
court 5, 10, 11, 12, 16, 17, 19, 26, 27, 31, 32, 66, 74, 95, 96, 98
Korean 11
scholar 4, 88, 96, 97, 99–105
Vietnamese 40, 43
Oirat Mongols (Qalmaqs/Kalmyks) 10, 13, 216
'Orchard Factory' (Guoyuanchang 果園廠) 73–4, 75
Ouyang Xiu 歐陽修 (1007–72) 94, 95, 96, 241

Pacification Commissions (*Xuan fu si* 宣撫司) 17, 39, 42
Pacification Superintendency (*Xuan wei shi si* 宣慰使司) 16, 21, 22
padrão 22, ***22***
Palace and Gardens of the Ming Dynasty (*Mingdai gongyuan tu* 明代宮苑圖) (anonymous) ***53***, 62, ***63***
Palace of the Southern Rock (*Nangang gong*) (1494) 135
Palden Zangpo (Palden Tashi) 157, 159
Palembang 31
Pang 龎, Celestial Lord 135, 137, 139
Pangasinan 20
Panjaranātha Mahākāla ***153***, ***158***
paper money 17, 28, 32, 170–7, ***171***, ***172***, ***173***, ***176***
paper and paper-making 170, 173–7, ***174***, ***175***, 233, 234, 235
Parakramabahu VI (r. 1412–68) 239
parrots 30, 125
patricide 220
Pawo Tsuklak Trengwa (1504–66) 155
pearls 25n.62, 28, 32, 33, 68, 69, ***69***, 71, 72, 73, 239, 243
Peng Xianren 彭顯仁 103
pepper 2, 27, 28, 32, 33, 36, 111
Persia
language 23, 30, 125, 207, 208, 209, 239
literature 230, 234, 240
maritime trade 33, 251
paintings 79
Persian Gulf 26, 240, 256, 257, 258
Phakpa (Tibetan Imperial Preceptor) 153, ***153***, 154
pheasant motifs 70, 72, 76
Philippines 20, 255
phoenix motifs 68, 69, 70, 72, ***72***, 73, 74, 76, 124, 125, 129, 133, 168
Picking Lotuses (*Cailian tu* 采蓮圖) (attributed to Zhu Bang) 62, ***62***
pigeons 30
Pilusi 毗盧寺 (Vairocana Monastery) 159
Pipaji 琵琶記 (*The Lute*) 89
Pires, Tomé 33
Pleasure of the Moon along the Riverbank (*Imgang-wanwoldo* 臨江玩月圖) 213
Plum in the Golden Vase (*Jin ping mei* 金瓶梅), 'Funeral of Li Pinger' 65, ***65***
poetry 6, 87, 88, 89, 95, 96, 97, 99, 104, 211, 225
poetry exchanges 99, 213, 216, 217
Anthology of Brilliant Flowers (*Hwanghwa jip*) 216
Poem on Sweet Spring Water (*Yecheon si*) 213
Poems Shared by Envoys in Joseon (*Bongsa Joseon changhwa sigwan*) 215
Songs of Flying Dragons (*Yongbi'eocheonga*) 213, 215
Persian 232, 240
see also Bai Juyi; Daoyan; Han Yong; Ni Qian; Yang Shiqi; Yuan Hongdao; Zibo Zhenke
Polei 坡壘 18
Pollaiuolo, Antonio (1433–98) ***241***
Pollaiuolo, Piero (1443–96) ***241***
Polo, Marco 206
porcelain 33, 73, 110, 181–2
blue-and-white 33, 74, ***75***
ritual vessels 69, 70, 72, 73, 113–21, ***116***, ***118***, ***119***, ***120***
see also ceramics
Porcelain Pagoda (*Liuli ta* 琉璃塔) *see* Da Baoensi
portraits
Portrait Halls 211–12
Buddhist 142–50
Portrait of an Official in Front of the Beijing Imperial Palace (*Beijing gongcheng tu* 北京宮城圖) (anonymous) 56–67, ***57***, ***64***
Portrait of a Civil Official Awaiting Audience (*Shangchao wenguan xiang* 上朝文官像) (anonymous) 66, ***67***
see also named individuals
Portuguese 22, 33, 35, 36, 41, 43
Potala Palace, Lhasa 35, 148, ***148***, *149*
Precious Admonitions (*baoxun* 寶訓) 94
Precious Book of the Jade Pivot (*Yushu baojing* 玉樞寶經) 138
precious stones 25, 25n.62, 32, 33, 71, 236–44
gold belt set with gems ***239***
group of gold and gem-encrusted hairpins ***237***
hat-top ornaments ***242***
loose gems from tomb of Zhu Zhanji ***238***
pair of gold pillow ends 237, ***237***
pendant in the form of a pelican (Franco-Burgundian) ***241***
toothpick box with chain ***236***, 238
princely enfeoffment 163–4
putchuck (medicinal root) 32
Pyeongyang 212

Qara-qoto
document fragment 1382 9, ***9***
seal with 'Phag-spa inscription 9, ***9***
Qarshi, Transoxiana 230
qi yong tao pao 器用陶匏 ('employing vessels made of pottery and gourd') 117
Qian 錢, Empress (d. 1468), wife of Zhengtong Emperor, *Official Portrait of* (anonymous) 73, ***74***
Qian Xili 錢習禮 (1373–1461) 101, 102, 103, 221
Qianlong 乾隆 emperor (r. 1736–95) 114, 120
Qiantang 錢塘 city (modern Hanzhou) 105
Qianzi wen 千字文 (*Thousand Character Classic*) 180–1, ***181***
Qichun 蘄春 (formerly Qizhou) 164, 168, 169, ***169***
qilin (auspicious beast) 125, 126, ***126***, 127
see also giraffe
Qin Junchu 秦君初 (1385–1441) 219n.7
qin (musical instrument) 88, ***88***, 91, 92
Qin'an dian 欽安殿 (Hall of Imperial Peace) 134, 135, 141
statue of Zhenwu 136, ***136***
Qing dynasty (1644–1911) 42, 43, 74, 114, 155, 215
construction 190, 191, 194
Qingbai wares, Jingdezhen 249
Qinghai province 157, ***157***, ***159***, 190
Qingshousi 慶壽寺 (Celebrating Longevity Monastery) 144, 145
Qingshui 清水 River 49
Qingwei 清微 (Pure Tenuity) school 137
Qingwei shenlie bifa 清微神烈祕法) (*Secret Methods of Divine Fire of Pure Tenuity*) 138
Qiu Jun 邱濬 (1418–95) 225
Qiuwen 丘溫 18
Quanzhou 泉州 255
Qubilai Khan (1215–94; r. 1260–94) 9, 10, 27, 34, 153, ***153***, 154, 161, 206
paper money 172
Queen Mother of the West (Xiwangmu 西王母) 71, 75
quicksilver 33
Qur'an 234, ***234***, 235
Qutandian 瞿曇殿 (Gautama Hall) *see* Qutansi
Qutansi 瞿曇寺 (Gautama Monastery) (1392) 152, 157–61, ***157***
Baoguangdian 寶光殿 (Hall of Blazing Jewel Light) (1418) 159–60, ***159***
Longguodian 隆國殿 (Hall of Enriching the State) 161, 190, ***190***, 191, ***192***, 193, 194, ***195***

Qutandian 瞿曇殿 (Gautama Hall) (1392) 158, 158–9, 159
wall painting 159

Rakta Yamari 80
Raozhou 饒州 117
Rashid al-Din 240
Record of Imperial Prouncements of Three Reigns (*Sancho shengyu lu*) 三朝聖諭錄 (Yang Shiqi) 94–8
Record of Responding to Heaven and Pacifying the Troubles (*Fengtian jingnan ji* 奉天靖難記) 95
Records of the Western Regions [Visited During] the Great Tang Dynasty (*Da Tang xiyu ji* 大唐西域記) 34, ***34***
Red River delta 42, 80
reign marks, Yongle and Xuande eras 80–1
reliquary, Ming dynasty, Hongjue Temple ***84***, 85
Renzhidian 仁智殿 (Hall of Benevolent Wisdom) 59
Returning Home on a Moonlit Night (*Xiye guizhuang tu* 夕夜歸莊圖) (attributed to Zhu Bang) 62, ***62***
rice 5, 17, 49, 163
Rinchen Palden 領占班丹, Seventh Karmapa (1454–1506) *see* Zhengde emperor
Ritual Offering of the Golden Register (*Jinlu Jiao* 金籙醮) 139
ritual vessels 113–21, ***114***, ***116***, ***117***, ***118***, ***119***, ***120***
Rolpai Dorjé, Fourth Karmapa (Rol pa'i rdo rje; 1340–83) 153
Royal Confucian Academy (Seonggyun'gwan 成均館) 216, 217
Royal Portrait Halls 213
Ruan An 阮安 (d. 1453) 51
rubies 237, 238–9, 240, 241, 242, 243

Sa Shoujian 薩守堅 (fl. 1141–78?) 139
Sa'di (d. 1292) 230
Sacrifical Hall *see* Changling
Sacrifice to Sages (*shidian* 釋奠) 115
Saiyinchidahu 賽因赤荅忽 114
Śākya Yeshé (1354–1439) 35, 125, 143, ***144***, 147–8, 157, 158, 160
portraits 147–9, 150
Samarqand 12, 80, 207, 220, 230
Samgang haengsil 三綱行實圖 (*The Illustrated Guide to the Three Bonds*) 213, 219, 220, 221, ***221***, 222, 223, 224, 225
Samten Zangpo 159
Samudera (*Sumendala* 蘇門荅剌) 28, 32
Sanbao taijian xiyang ji 三寶太監西洋記 (*The Adventures of the Eunuch...*) (Luo Maodeng) 198, ***198***
Sancho shengyu lu 三朝聖諭錄 (*Record of Imperial Prouncements of Three Reigns*) (Yang Shiqi) 94–8
Sangyé Tashi (d. 1414) 157
Sanli tu 三禮圖 (*The Illustrated Catalogue of Three Ritual Classics*) 114
Sanli tu system 114, ***114***, 115, 117, 119
Santa Maria (ship) 197–8, ***197***
sappanwood 111
Śāriputra 實哩沙哩卜得囉/室利沙 (also known as Pandita 板的達 1335–1426) 34
Scholar Viewing a Waterfall (Shingei Gei'ami 真芸芸阿弥) 4, ***5***
A Scholars' Feast (*mKhas pa'i dga' ston*) (1545) 155
Scripture of the Jade Emperor (*Gaoshang yuhuang benxing jijing* 高上玉皇本行集經) (1424) 135, 137, ***138***, 139
Scripture on Salvation (*Duren jing* 度人經) (1406) 137, ***137***
Secret Methods of Divine Fire of Pure Tenuity (*Qingwei shenlie bifa* 清微神烈祕法) 138
Sejong 世宗, King (1397–1450; r. 1418–50) 115, 211, 211–15, 212, 219
Selden map of China 255–7, ***255***, ***256***, 258
Selling Fish in the Snowy River (*Xuejiang maiyu tu* 雪江賣魚圖) (attributed to Zhu Bang) 60, ***61***
Senglusi 僧錄司 157
Seo Geojeong 徐居正 (1420–88) 215
Seol Sun 偰循 (?–1435) 220
Seong Hyeon 成俔 (1439–1504) 217
Seong Sammun 成三問 (1418–56) 213, 215, 216
Seppings, Robert 197
Sera Monastery, Lhasa 125, 148, 151n.42, 157
Sesshū Tōyō 雪舟等楊
copy of 1491 self portrait ***5***
Landscapes of Autumn and Winter ***6***
splashed-ink style landscape 6
Sforza, Galeazzo Maria (1444–76), Duke of Milan, portrait (Pollaiuolo) 241, ***241***
Shad-i Mulk Agha mausoleum 229
Shah Rukh (1377–1447, r. 1407–47) 11, 228, 230, 231, 235
Shah-i Zindeh, Samarqand 229
Shahnama (*Book of Kings*) (Firdawsi) 79, ***80***, 232, ***232***, ***233***, ***234***, 235
Shan polities 42, 238
Shandong province 62, 81, 231
Shang Yi 尚義 161
Shanga, Pate Island 245, 250
Shangqing lingbao jidu dacheng jinshu 上清靈寶濟度大成金書 (*Golden Writings on the Great Achievement of Deliverance of the Numinous Treasure of Highest Clarity*) (Zhou Side) (1433) 135, 139, 140
Shanghai 85, 110, 201
Shanxi province ***33***, 48, 85, 100, 172, 187
ceramics 187
Shaoxi zhouxian shidianyi tu 紹熙州縣釋奠儀圖 (*Illustrated Shaoxi Confucius Worshipping Ceremony of Counties*) 114
Sharaf al-din-Ali Yazdi ***232***, 233
Shen Du 沈度 (1357–1434) 126, ***127***
Shen Maoshang 愼懋賞, *Extensive Records of the Four Barbarian [Regions]* (*Siyi guangji* 四夷廣記) ***32***, 33
Shenwumen 神武門 (Divine Military Gate) (1420) 192
Shenyueguan 神樂觀 (Imperial Music Office) 89, 123
shi 勢 (Beijing) 46–7, ***47***, 54–5
Shi Jinqing 施進卿 (d. 1423) 22
Shingei Gei'ami 真芸芸阿弥 (1431–85), *Scholar Viewing a Waterfall* 4, ***5***
ships and shipbuilding 20, 27, 106, 108, 109, 110, 112, 197–205, ***203***, ***204***, ***205***
replica of Zheng He's treasure ship 199, 201–2, 202
'Sutra spoken from on high ...' (*Taishang shuo tianfei jiuku lingying jing* 太上說天妃救苦靈應經) 203
Shiraz 229, 230, 231, 232, 233
Shirin Bika Aqa 229
Shiyan 十堰 163
Shizhou Guard (Shizhou wei junmin zhihui shisi 施州衛軍民指揮使司) 163
Si Jifa 思機發 (d. 1454) 17
Si Kenfa 思揹法 (active 1454) 17
Si Lunfa 思倫發 (d. 1399) 16, 17, 238
Si Renfa 思任發/Thonganbwa (fl. 1400–45) 17, 238
Sizhou 思州 18
Sichuan 16, 18, 52
silk 28, 108, 146, 147, 173, 222
damask 27
embroidery ***148***
garments 146, 212
paintings ***52***, ***53***, ***58***, ***60***, ***61***, ***62***, ***63***, 65, 66, 81, ***81***, ***82***, ***83***, ***84***, ***85***, ***100***, ***102***, ***123***, ***125***, ***126***, ***132***, ***140***, ***152***, ***214***, ***223***, ***243***
portraits ***4***, ***57***, ***67***, ***68***, ***71***, ***72***, ***73***, ***74***, ***143***, ***144***, ***145***, ***147***, ***212***
tapestry 147
textiles 3, 27, 28, 33, 149, 231
Vajrabhairava ***155***
Silk Road 13, ***13***, 252
Silla kingdom, Korea (54 BCE–935 CE) 72, 211–12
silver 33, 112, 243
monetisation 109, 111, 112, 251

Sima Guang 司馬光 (1019–86) 94, 95
Sima Xun 司馬恂 (?–1466) 215, 216
Sin Sukju 申叔舟 (1417–75) 213, 215, 216
Sip Song Chau Tai 16
Śiva (Brahmanical deity) 30
Siyi guan 四夷館 see Translator's College
Siyi guangji 四夷廣記 (*Extensive Records of the Four Barbarian [Regions]*) ***32***, 33
Siyouzhai hualun 四友齋畫論 (*Theory of Painting from the Studio of the Four Friends*) (He Liangjun) 132
Sonam Gyaltsen 159
Sonam Sherab 148, 149
Song dynasty (960–1279) 26, 27, 39, 68, 70, 74, 113, 134, 222, 242
  architectural construction 55n.19, 190, 191, 192
  consorts 68–9
  guan ware 117
  imperial dress 70, 72, 74
  portraits 146
  relationships 222, 224
Song Lian 宋濂 (1310–81) 104
Song Taizu 宋太祖 (r. 960–76) 119, 225, 226
Song Yun 宋允 (active 1439) 30
Songs of Flying Dragons (*Yongbi'eocheonga* 龍飛御天歌) ***213***
Southen India, map ***28***
Southern Zhili 南直隸 110
spices 2, 111, 112
spinels *see* rubies
'splashed-ink style landscape' (Sesshū Tōyō 雪舟等楊) 4, ***5***, ***6***
Sri Lanka 21, 23, ***23***, 30, 33, 239
  map ***31***
  Tooth Relic of the Buddha 31, 34–6, 155
stelae 19, 22, 23, 95, 124, 144, 157, 160, 161, 201
  Da Baoen Monastery 95, 184, 185
  Galle, Sri Lanka 23, ***23***, 30, 33, 239
  Jinghai Temple ***200***
  Melaka 22
Su Shi 蘇軾 (1037–1101) 104
Suganla in Samudera 21
Sulu 20, 238
Sumatra 21, 22, 23, 31, 255, 258
  Old Port (*Jiugang* 舊港) 21, 22
sumptuary laws 68, 69, 72, 73, 74
Sun 孫, Empress (d. 1462), wife of Xuande Emperor, *Official Portrait of* (anonymous) 73, ***74***, 75
'Sutra spoken from on high of the miraculous efficacy of Tianfei in salvation from distress' (*Taishang shuo tianfei jiuku lingyingjing* 太上說天妃救苦靈應經) 203
Suzhou 59, 64, 66, 143
  flooring bricks 183
  silk ***27***
Suzhou Alley (Suzhou hutong 蘇州胡同) 59, 65

Tabriz 228, 229, 240
Taejo, King 李成桂 (1335–1408; r, 1382–98) 211, 212, 212, 217
Taejo, King 王建 (877–943; r. 918–43) 212–13, ***213***
Taejong, King 太宗 (r. 1400–18) 11, 211, 213
Tai areas 3, 16
Tai Mao polity 16, 17
Taicang 201
Taihang 太行 Mountains 52, 54
Taihedian 太和殿 (Hall of Supreme Harmony) 56, 191
Taihemen 太和門 (Gate of Supreme Harmony) 56
Taihuiguan 太暉觀 (Abbey of Great Radiance), Jiangling 165
Taimiao 太廟 (Imperial Ancestral Temple) (1545), Beijing 22, 51, 53, 113, 117, 144, ***192***, 193, ***193***
Taiping 太平 18, 181
  uprising (1856) 178
Taishang shuo tianfei jiuku lingying jing 太上說天妃救苦靈應經 ('Sutra spoken from on high …') 203
talismans (*lingpai* 靈牌) 164
Tamerlane *see* Timūr
Tamil 23, ***23***, 30
  merchants 33
Tan Yuanchun 譚元春 (1586–1637) 163
Tang dynasty 100, 113, 114
  codes of law 5
  construction 191, 192
Tang Hanti 唐翰題 (1816–75) 215
Tang Taizong 唐太宗 (627–49) 94
Tang tongdian 225
Tanzhesi 潭柘寺 (Deep Pond and Wild Mulberry Monastery) 145, ***146***, 150n.23
Tao 陶, Celestial Lord 135, 137, 139, 141
Tao An 陶安 (1312?–68) 117
Tao Zongyi 陶宗儀 (*c.* 1316–*c.* 1402), *Nan cun chuo geng lu* 南村輟耕錄 239–40
taxes 18, 32, 42
temples 49, 50, 51, 52, 59, 145, 157, 158, 159, 161
  Buddhist 3, 51, 148, 149, 155, 156, 193, 194, 211
  Confucian 113, 114, 117
    Temple of Confucius, Qufu 62, ***64***
  Daoist 3, ***107***, 123, 140, 141, 190, 192, 194
    see also Wudang, Mount
  Temple of Heaven, Beijing ***50***, 51
  see also named monasteries and temples
Tengchong 騰衝 16, 17, 24n.11
textiles 3, 33, 73, 80, 231, 232, 233, 235
Textual (*Gyo* 教) school 211
thangka (silk embroidery) 147, 148, ***148***, 149, 155
Thánh-tông, emperor (r. 1460–97) 19
Three Friends and a Hundred Birds (*Sanyou baiqin tu* 三友百禽圖) (Bian Wenjin) 132–3, ***132***
thrones 122, 238, 240
  dragon 146, 149, 150
Thunder Division (*Leibu* 雷部) 135
Thunder Inspectorate (*Leiting dusi* 雷霆都司) 134
thunder marshals 134–41, ***135***
Tian Subprefecture 田州 18
Tianfei 天妃 (Celestial Spouse) 203, 240
Tianhuang zhidao taiqing yuce 天皇至道太清玉冊 (*Jade Fascicles…)* 140
Tianjiang miao 天將廟 (Temple of Heavenly General) 139
Tianjin (formerly Zhigu) 49
Tianpeng 天蓬 137
Tianping 陳天平 (Trần Thien Binh) (d. 1406) 17, 38
Tianqi period (1621–7) ***18***, ***202***, 249, 254
Tianshun 天順 emperor (Zhu Qizhen 朱祁鎮) (r. 1457–64) (formerly Zhengtong emperor) 48, 59, 76, 98, 111, 137
Tianxisi 天禧寺 (Monastery of Heavenly Blessings) 178, 184
  see also Da Baoensi
Tianyou 天猷 137
Tibet 34, 36, 92, 123, 125, 143–51, 152–62, 165–9, 180
  art 143, ***144***, 147–50, 152–62, 167–9
  Buddhism 125, 147–9, 152–62, 167–9
    see also Xuande emperor; Yongle emperor; Yuan dynasty
  dress 148
  gems 238, 240
  language 125, 207
  sacred sites 3, 51, 190, 194
    Gelug School 30, 147, 148, 149, 164
  and Xuande emperor 85
  and Yongle emperor 35, 125, 154

Tieguai Li 鐵拐李 60
Tieta 鐵塔 (Iron Pagoda), Youguosi 佑國寺 (Protecting the State Monastery) 186
tiles
  Da Baoensi Pagoda 179, 181, 182, 183, ***184***
  Shad-i Mulk 229
timber
  construction 108, 179, 186, 187, 191, 192, 196n.33
  shipbuilding 198, 199, 205n.12
Timūr (Tamerlane) 11, 12, 220, 228, 229, 230, 241
  receiving gifts from Egyptian ambassadors ***30***
Timurid dynasty 3, 11, 12, 79–80, 240–1
  coin 11, 12
  fashions, hat buttons 242, ***242***, 243
  Iran 228–37
Toghan-Timür (r. 1333–70) 9–10
tombs 59, 163–9, 229, 237–43
  Prince of Jing of Ying 荊憲王 and Lady Guo 郭 165–7, ***166***
  Prince Xian of Xiang 湘獻王 165
  Prince Zhao of Chu 楚昭王, Zhu Zhen 朱楨 164–5, ***165***
  Prince Zhuang of Liang 梁莊王, Zhu Zhanji 朱瞻垍 and Lady Wei 魏 167–8, ***167***, ***168***, ***236***, 237–43, ***237***
  Shah-i Zindeh 229
Tooth Relic of the Buddha, Kandy, Sri Lanka Kandy 31, 34–6, 155
Toqto'a-Buqa (r. 1433–52) 13
Traces of a Beast in a Pine Forest (*Songlin shouji tu* 松林獸迹圖)) (attributed to Zhu Bang) 60, ***61***
trade 27
  ceramics 77, 79, 246, 247, 251
  gems 71, 238, 239
  guns 40, 42, 43
  horses 209
  slaves 3
  see also tribute system
Tran dynasty 19, 38, 40, 42
Translators' College (*siyi guan* 四夷館)) 207, 208, 209, 210, 219n.12
transportation of goods 32, 49, 50
Treasure Shipyard, Nanjing ***199***, 200, 201, 201–2, 202, ***202***, 204
Treatise on Military Preparedness (*Wubei zhi* 武備志) 18, ***18***, 20, 202, ***202***, 254, ***254***, 257
Treaty of Nanjing 179
trees
  Beijing 47, 51, ***51***, 52, ***52***
  see also paper; timber
tribute system 16, 21, 22, 23, 27, 28, 30, 31, 37, 40, 43, 44, 77, 109, 236, 240
Tripiṭaka 34
Tsongkhapa (Tsong kha pa) (1357–1419) 33, 34, 35, 125, 147, 157, 158
Tsurphu (Tshur phu) Monastery 154
Tumu 土木 campaign (1449) 2, 15, 111, 216
Turfan 207
Turkan Agha (d. 1386) 229

'Udayana Buddha' 154
Uighurs 207, 220
Ulugh Beg (1394–1449) ***13***, 229–30
Ungwana 250, ***250***

Vairocana *Maṇḍala* 156, ***156***
Vajrabhairava ***148***, 149, ***155***
Veritable Records of the Joseon Dynasty (*Joseon wangjo sillok* 朝鮮王朝實錄) 212, 213, 216, 222
vermilion 33
Vietnam 16, 18, 19, 37–45, 80
  see also Annam; Đại Việt
The Visit (anonymous) 78, 79, ***79***

Walking Alone in Empty Mountains (*Kongshan duxing tu* 空山獨行圖) (attributed to Zhu Bang) 60, ***61***
Wan Dian 灣甸 16, 17
Wan 萬, Lady (1428–87) 112
Wang 王, Marshal, Celestial Lord, Numinous Official 135, 136, 137, 139, 140, 141, ***141***
Wang 王, Empress (1564–1620), crown 68–76, ***69***, ***70***, ***71***, ***73***, ***74***
Wang Fu 王紱 (1362–1416) 129
  Eight Views of Beijing (*Beijing bajing tu* 北京八景圖) ***50***, 55n.12, 129, ***130***, ***131***
Wang Guitong 王貴通 (active *c.* 1407) 20
Wang Ji 王驥 (1378–1460) 17
Wang Shu 王恕 (1416–1508) 225
Wang Shuqying 王叔英 (d. 1402) 104
Wang Ying 王英 (1376–1449) 101, 102, 103, 104, 105, 129
Wang Zhen 王振 (d. 1449) 95, 111
Wang Zhi 汪直 (1379–1462) 4, 101, 102, 103, 104, 105, 200
Wanli 萬曆 emperor (Zhu Yijun 朱翊鈞) (r. 1573–1620) 38, 66, 69, 141
'Water-Land' (*shuilu* 水陸) ritual paintings 152, ***156***
Wei, Lady 魏氏 (d. 1451) 72, 72, ***153***, 164, ***237***, ***238***, ***239***
  tomb ***241***
Wei Ji 魏驥 (1374–1471) 225
Wei Jiao 魏校 (1483–1543) 225
Weiyuan 威遠 17
Wen 溫, Marshal, Celestial Lord 135, 137, 139, 141
Weng Fanggang 翁方綱 (1733–1818) 100
Western Jin period (265–316) 74
Western Ocean (*Xiyang* 西洋) 20, 21, 39, 255
  voyages to 106–12
women 5, 69, 73, 75, 76, 82, ***82***, 219, 220, 224
  and music 88
  see also dress
Wu Jing 吳敬 (active 1450) 3
Wu, King of 吳王 (528–473 BCE) 58
Wu Kuan 吳寬 (1435–1504) 99–100
Wu, Lady 吳 (d. 1402), consort of the Jianwen emperor 165
Wu Wei 吳偉 (1459–1508) 59, 60, ***60***
  Amusement of Fishermen in a River Landscape (*Jiangshan yule tu* 江山漁樂圖) 60, ***60***
Wubei zhi 武備志 (*Treatise on Military Preparedness*) 18, ***18***, 20, 202, ***202***, 254, ***254***, 257
Wuchang 武昌 prefecture 163, 164
Wudang, Mount 武當山 ***107***, 108, 124, 136, 136–7, ***136***, 141, 163, 164, 193, 194
  see also Jindian; Zixiaodian; Zixiaogong
Wujing qishu 五經七書 (*Military Classics*) 43
Wulonggong 五龍宮 (Palace of the Five Dragons), Mount Wudang (1473) 135
Wulun shu 五倫書 (*Book of the Five Relationships*) 219–28, ***220***
Wumen 午門 (Meridian Gate) 56
Wushan school 吳山派 56
Wusong river 3
Wutai 五臺山, Mount 33, ***33***, 52, 125
Wutasi 五塔寺 (Mahābodhi temple, Beijing) 34, 35
Wuzhun Shifan 無準師範 (1177–1249) 145, ***145***, 146

Xia Liangsheng 夏良勝 (1480–1538) 225
Xia Yuanji 夏元吉 (1366–1430) 3, 109, ***109***, 110, 125, 126
Xian of Xiang, Prince 湘獻王 *see* Zhu Bo
Xiang Da 向達 (1900–66) 254
Xiang Zhong 項忠 (1421–1502) 111
Xiangshan 58, 59, 67
Xiangyang 襄陽 163, 164
Xianluo (modern Thailand) 238, 239
Xiawang 遐旺 22

Xie Huan 謝環 (1388–1452) 99–105
Elegant Gathering in the Apricot Garden 4, 52, 84–5, ***84***, 99–105, ***100***, ***101***
Nine Elders of the Mountain of Fragrance (*Xiangshan jiulao tu* 香山九老圖) (attributed) 100, ***102***, 103
Xie Jin 謝縉 (1369–1415) 97, 104, 105, 123, 129
Xie Zhaozhe 謝肇淛 (1567–1624) 127
Xin 辛, Celestial Lord 135, 137, 139, ***139***, 141
Xin'an 新安 (She 歙 county) 59
Xingguosi 興國寺 (Temple Revitalising the State) 51
Xinjiang 10, 12
Xiudingsi 修定寺, Anyang 188n.37
Xiuning 休寧 59
Xu 徐, Empress (1362–1407), wife of the Yongle emperor, *Official Portrait of* (anonymous) ***68***, 69, 70, 75, 125, 154, 184
Xu Da 徐達 (1332–85) 250
Xu Gao 徐杲 (16th century) 59
Painting of (*Xu Gao xiang* 徐杲像) (anonymous) 62–6, ***63***
Xu Hongqing 許鴻磬 66
Xu Jie 徐階 (1494–1574) 219n.11
Xu Jin 許進 (1437–1510) 100
Xu Lun 許論 (1487–1559) 100
Two Garden Gatherings (*Eryuan ji* 二園集) 99, ***102***
Xuande 宣德 emperor (Zhu Zhanji 朱瞻基) (r. 1426–35) 5, 75, 94, 95, 97, 101, 104, 110–11, 139, 219, 240
portraits 146, ***147***, 149
reign
artefacts 73–4, ***75***, 78, ***78***, 80, ***81***, ***83***, 146, ***148***, ***237***
maritime voyages 106, 110–11, 112, 237
mark 80, 81, 154
writing style 129
and Tibetan Buddhism 155, 159, 161
and *Wulun shu* 219, 220, 221, 225
see also Da Baoensi pagoda; Hu, Empress; Qutansi; Sun, Empress; *Veritable Records*
Xuanguang reign 9
Xuanhe bogu tu system 114, ***114***, 115, 117, ***117***
Xuanzang 玄奘 (602?–64) *Da Tang Xiyu ji* 大唐西域記 (*Records of the Western Regions [Visited During] the Great Tang Dynasty*) 34, ***34***
Xương Giang 42

Yaliekunaier 亞烈苦奈兒 or Aliekunaier 阿烈苦奈兒 ([Vira] Alakéswara or Alagakkonāra) 30–1
Yan, Mount 燕山 52
Yang Ding 楊鼎 (1410–85) 221
Yang 楊, Empress (1162–1232), wife of Emperor Ningzong, *Official Portrait of* (anonymous) 70, ***71***
Yang Pu 楊溥 (1372–1446) 95, 101, 102, 103, 105, 163
Yang Rong 楊榮 (1371–1440) 95, 100, 101, 102, 103, 104, 105, 109, 129
Yang Sanbao 楊三寶 (active early 15th century) 157
Yang Shiqi 楊士奇 (1365–1444) 10–11, 99–105, 109, 111, 129
Record of Imperial Pronoucements 94–8
Yang Yiqing 楊一清 (1454–1530) 98, 225
Yangtze River 3, 52, 148, 163, ***205***
Yao 堯 (sage-king) 224
Yao Canting 姚灿庭 (Qing dynasty) 59
Yao Guangxiao 姚廣孝 (1335–1418) *see* Daoyan
Yaozhou ware 117
Ya'qub ibn Hasan (known as Siraj al-Husayni al-Sultani) ***232***
Yazd, Iran 229
Ye Sheng 葉盛 (1420–74) 225
Ye Wang (Ye dbang) 'Prince of Yan 燕' *see* Yongle
Yebanaina 耶巴乃那 ([Parākramābahu] Apana?) 31
Yellow River 123, ***128***, 129
Yi Gyejeon 李季甸 (1404–59) 215
Yi Seonggye *see* Taejo
Yim Wonjun 任元濬 (1423–1500) 213
Yin 殷, Marshal, Celestial Lord 135, 137, 141
Yin Qing 尹慶 (active 1400–10) 28, 29
Yin Xiangbao 尹向寶 (fl. early 15th century) 123
Yongchang 永昌, Yunnan 16
Yongding 永定 River 48–9
Yongdingmen 永定門 (Externally Pacified Gate) 66
Yongjae chonghwa 慵齋叢話 (*Sayings from the Yong Studio*) 217
Yongle 永樂 (Zhu Di 朱棣) emperor (r. 1403–24) 2, 3, 6, 7, 15, 47–8, 69, 87, 144, 153, 224, 225
administration 102, 104, 110
artefacts 78, 80, ***80***, 83–4, 109, 160–1, ***160***, ***239***
auspicious signs 122–33
building works 47–8, 51, 107, 108, 136, 178, 184, 189–96, 201
ceramics 78, 80–3, 110, 118, 182, ***182***, 249–51, ***250***
Edict in Response to the Fengtian Hall Disaster (*Fengtian dian zai kuan xu zhao* 奉天殿災寬恤詔) 106
language glossaries 207–10
legitimacy 20, 23, 26, 28, 36, 37, 38, 39, 51–2, 81, 109, 122, 127, 154, 155, 184, 255
maritime voyages 50, 106, 108, 109, 112, 199, 237, 254–5
military campaigns
north 9–13, 107, 108, 186
south 15–25, 26–36, 37, 38, 45, 186
paintings 159
portraits 85, 96–7, 98, 122, 146, ***147***, 149
records 94–8, 109, 224–6
religion 123, 124, 125, 134, 136–7, 139, 140
Daoist 3, 163
Tibetan Buddhism 3, 34, 35, 136, 153–5, ***154***, 168
seal script 80, 81
usurpation 2, 6, 11, 15, 37, 47, 94, 109, 122, 127
see also Da Baoensi
Yongle beizang 永樂北藏 (Yongle Northern Tripitaka) 34
Yongle tongbao 永樂通寶 (Circulating treasure of the Yongle era) coin 251
Yongshougong 永壽宮 (Palace of Eternal Longevity) 66
Yongzheng 雍正 emperor (1723–35) 114
Youguosi 佑國寺 (Protecting the State Monastery), Tieta 鐵塔 (Iron Pagoda) 186
Yu 裕 Mausoleum of the Thirteen Ming Tombs (*Ming shisan ling* 明十三陵) 59
Yu Xuekui 余學夔 (1372–1444) 103
Yuan dynasty (1271–1368) 1, 3, 9–11, 13, 26, 27, 39, 41, 74, 75, 201, 238, 239
ceramics 85, 117, 187, 246, 247, 248, ***248***, 249
construction 47, 49, 50, 53, 191, 192, 193, 194
literature and music 6, 89, 90, 91
paper money 172, ***173***
portraits 71, 72, ***72***, 146, 149, 243
rituals and ritual vessels 114, 135, 136
Tibetan Buddhism 153, 154, 168, 180
Yuan Gong 袁珙 (1335–1410) 122
Yuan Hongdao 袁宏道 (1568–1610) 145, 163
Yuan Qi 袁琦 (act. 1427) 161
Yuan Zhongdao 袁中道 (1570–1623) 163
Yuan Zongdao 袁宗道 (1560–1600) 163
Yue ware, Shanga 246, ***247***
Yuegang 月港 (Moon Harbour) 255, 256
Yuhuchun vase, Gedi Ruin ***248***
Yunhuatai 蕓花臺 179
Yunnan 雲南 province 10, 15–16, 15–17, 18, 19, 22, 24n.3, 33, 39, 108, 207
Yuquan 玉泉 (Jade Spring) canal 49, ***50***
Yuquansi 玉泉寺 (Monastery of Jade Spring) 164

Yushu baojing 玉樞寶經 (*Precious Book of the Jade Pivot*) 138
Yuxugong 玉虛宮 (Palace of Jade Void) 124, 137
Yuzhengong 遇真宮 (Palace of Encountering the Perfected) 137, 192

Zafarnama (*Book of Victories*) (Sharaf al-din Ali Yazdi) 232, ***232***, 233
zaju 雜劇 dramas 6, 89
Zamorin 29
Zeng Qi 曾棨 (1372–1432) 10, 103, 104, 126, 127, ***127***, 129
Zhang 張 Celestial Lord 135, 137, 139, ***139***, 141, ***141***
Zhang Chang 章敞 103
Zhang 張, Empress (1379–1442), wife of the Hongxi emperor, *Official Portrait of* (anonymous) 72, ***73***, 74–5, 95, 101, 111
Zhang Fu 張輔 (1375–1449) 18, 39, 40, 41, 42, 44n.30
Zhang Juzheng 張居正 (1525–82) 163
Zhang Lu 張路 (1464–1538) 59
Zhang Maocheng 張懋丞 (1388–1447) 139
Zhang Ning 張寧 (1426–96) 99
Zhang Qian 張謙 (active 1408–20) 20, 22
Zhang Shicheng 張士誠 (1321–67) 104
Zhang Xie 張燮 *Dongxi yang kao* 東西洋考 (*Study of the Eastern and Western Seas*) 255, 258
Zhang Zai 張載 (1020–77) 96
Zhang Zhidong 張之洞 (1837–1909) 221
Zhang Zonglian 張宗璉 (1374–1427) 103
Zhangjiawan 張家灣 50
Zhangzhou 漳州 prefecture 255
Zhao 趙, Marshal, Celestial Lord 135, 137, 139, 141
Zhao of Chu, Prince 楚昭王 *see* Zhu Zhen
Zhe school (Zhepai 浙派) 56, 59, 62
Zhejiang province 3, 18, 20, 103, 104
Zhele Dian 者樂甸 16
Zheng Ci 鄭賜 (d. 1408) 96–7
Zheng He 鄭和 (1371–1433) 2, 6, 20, ***20***, 23, ***23***, 207
  Da Baoen Monastery project 185
  military action in Sri Lanka 34, 35
  statues, with his attendants ***20***
  voyages 15, 20–1, 22, 26, 28, 29, 31, 71, 110, 125–6, 186, 200, 202–3, 231, 247
    map ***20***
    navigational materials 202–3, 215, 253–9
    see also ships and shipbuilding
Zheng He hanghai tu 鄭和航海圖 (*Zheng He's Navigation Chart*) 202–3, 251
Zheng Wenlin 鄭文林 (fl. 1522–66) 59
Zhengde 正德 emperor (Zhu Haozhao 朱厚照 Rinchen Palden) (1506–21) 66, 98, 155, 251
Zhengtong 正統 emperor (Zhu Qizhen 朱祁鎮 (r. 1436–49) (later Tianshun emperor) 2, 3, 5, 6, 48, 73, 85, 95, 97, 98, 101, 111, 216, 221, 225
Zhengyangmen 正陽門 (Gate of the True Yang) 56
Zhenjuesi 真覺寺 (True Enlightennment Monastery) 151n.45
Zhenkang 鎮康 17
Zhenwu 真武 (Perfected Warrior) (Daoist deity) 124, 134, 136–7, ***136***, 139, ***140***
  as Ancestral Master (*Zushi* 祖師) 139
  Flag Holder (*zhiqi* 持旗) 136, 140
  with Five Dragon Kings 134, ***135***
  as Patriarch of Myriad Methods (*Wanfa jiaozhu* 萬法教主) 138
  Sword Holder (*pengjian* 捧劍) 136
Zhenzong 真宗 emperor (r. 997–1022) 70
Zhi An 芝庵 90
Zhigu 直沽 (Tianjin) 49
Zhihuasi 智化寺 (Transformation of Wisdom Monastery), Beijing 151n.45, 161, 180, 192
Zhong Sichen 鍾嗣成 (fl. 1320s) 90
Zhong Xing 鐘惺 (1574–1624) 163
Zhongyuan yinyun 中原音韵 (*Phonology of the Central Plains*) (Zhou Deqing) 90
Zhonggusi 鐘鼓司 (Music Office of the Inner Court) 89
Zhongli Quan 鐘離權 60
Zhongxiang 鐘祥 72, ***72***, 93, ***153***, 164, 165, 167, ***167***, ***168***, 237, ***237***, ***238***, ***239***, ***242***
Zhou Chen 周忱 (1381–1453) 103
Zhou Dunyi 周敦頤 (1017–73) 96
Zhou Huang 周煌, *The Annals of Ryukyu* (*Liuqiu guo zhi lüe* 琉球國志略) 204, ***204***
Zhou Jing 周經 (1440–1510) 99
Zhou Shu 周述 (d. 1439) 101, 102, 105
Zhou Side 周思得 (1359–1451) 139, 140
Zhouli 周禮 (*Rites of Zhou*) 70
Zhu Bang 朱邦 (active mid to late Ming dynasty) 56, 59–62, 64, 65, 66
  Figures (*Renwu tu* 人物圖) (attributed) 60, ***60***
  Fishermen in a River Gorge (*Xigu yufu* 人物圖) (attributed) 56, ***58***, 60
  Immortal Lü (*Lü xian tu* 呂仙圖) (attributed) 60, ***61***
  Imperial Palace of the Ming Dynasty (anonymous) ***63***, 64, 65, 66, 67
  Picking Lotuses (*Cailian tu* 采蓮圖) (attributed) 62, ***62***
  Returning Home on a Moonlit Night (*Xiye guizhuang tu* 夕夜歸莊圖) (attributed) 62, ***62***
  Selling Fish in the Snowy River (*Xuejiang maiyu tu* 雪江賣魚) (attributed) 60, ***61***
  Traces of a Beast in a Pine Forest (*Songlin shouji tu* 松林獸迹圖) (attributed) 60, ***61***
  Walking Alone in Empty Mountains (*Kongshan duxing tu* 空山獨行圖) (attributed) 60, ***61***
Zhu Bang zhi yin 朱邦之印 (seal of Zhu Bang) 56, ***58***
Zhu Bo 朱柏 (1371–99), Prince Xian of Xiang 湘獻王 164, 165
Zhu Changrun 朱常潤 (1594–1647), Prince of Hui 惠王 164
Zhu Chenhao 朱宸濠 (1469–1521), Prince of Ning 寧王 87–8
Zhu Di 朱棣 (1360–1424) *see* Yongle emperor
Zhu Dong 朱棟 (1388–1414), Prince Jing of Ying 郢靖王 164, 165
Zhu Gaochi 朱高熾 (1378–1425) *see* Hongxi emperor
Zhu Gaoxu 朱高煦 (1380–1426), Prince of Han 漢王 97
Zhu Gui 朱貴 (*c.* 1370–1420) 39
Zhu Houquan 朱厚烇 (d. 1553), Prince Duan of Jing 荊端王 168
Zhu Houxi 朱厚熙 (1500), Prince Huai of Yue 岳懷王 164
Zhu Jiyou 朱季友 (n.d.) 96
Zhu Neng 朱能 (1370–1406), Duke of Chengguo 成國公 38, 39
Zhu Qizhen 朱祁鎮 *see* Tianshun emperor; Zhengtong emperor
Zhu Quan 朱權 (1378–1448), Prince Xian of Ning (寧獻王) 87–93, 140
  Shenqi mipu 神奇秘譜 (*Wondrous and Secret Notation*) ***90***, 91, ***91***, 92
Zhu Shu 朱橚 (1361–1425) Prince of Zhou 周王 122–3
Zhu Xi 朱熹 (1130–1200) 96, 114, 115
Zhu Youdun 朱有燉 (1379–1439), Prince of Xian 6, 93
  Chengzhai yuefu 誠齋樂府 (*Lyrics of Chengzhai*) 6
  Chengzhai zaju 誠齋雜劇 (*Zaju Dramas of Chengzhai*) 6
Zhu Youlun 朱祐棆 (1478–1502), Prince Hui of Qi 岐惠王 164
Zhu Youyuan 朱祐杬 (1476–1519), Prince Xian of Xing 興獻王 164
Zhu Youzhi 朱祐榰 (1481–1545), Prince Ding of Shou 壽定王 164
Zhu Yuanzhang 朱元璋 (1328–98) *see* Hongwu emperor
Zhu Yunming 祝允明 (1461–1527), *Qianwen ji* 前聞記 (*Record of Things Heard*) (*c.* 1500) 201
Zhu Zaiyu, Prince 朱載堉 (1536–1611) 93, 225
Zhu Zaizhen 朱載圳 (1537–65), Prince Gong of Jing 景恭王 87–8, 164
Zhu Zhan'gang 朱瞻堈 (1406–53), Prince of Jing 荊憲王 164, 168
Zhu Zhanji 朱瞻基 (1398–1435) *see* Xuande emperor
Zhu Zhanji 朱瞻埈 (1411–41), Prince Zhuang of Liang 梁莊王 72, 72, 153, 153, 161n.6, 164, 237, 238
  tomb ***64***, 81, 82, 167, ***167***, 168, ***168***, 237–43, ***237***, ***238***, ***239***, ***241***

Zhu Zhanshan 朱瞻墡 (1406–78), Prince Xian of Xiang 襄憲王 164, 165
Zhu Zhen 朱楨 (1364–1424), Prince Zhao of Chu 楚昭王 164
Zhu Zhi 朱植 (1378–1424), Prince Jian of Liao 遼簡王 164
Zhu Zhifan 朱之蕃 (1564–?) 219n.14
Zhuang of Liang, Prince *see* Zhu Zhanji (1411–41)
Zhushan 珠山, imperial kilns ***78***, 183, ***251***
Zibo Zhenke 紫柏真可 (1543–1603) 145, 146
Zixiaodian 紫霄殿 (1412) (Hall of Purple Cloud) 189, 190, ***190***, 191, ***192***, 193, 194, ***195***
Zixiaogong 紫霄宮 (Palace of Purple Cloud) 124
Zongle 宗泐 (1318–91) 144, 145
zouyu 騶虞 (mystical beast) 122–3, ***123***
Zunlei tu 尊罍圖 (Images of Wine Vessels) ***114***, 117

Index compiled by Elizabeth Wiggans

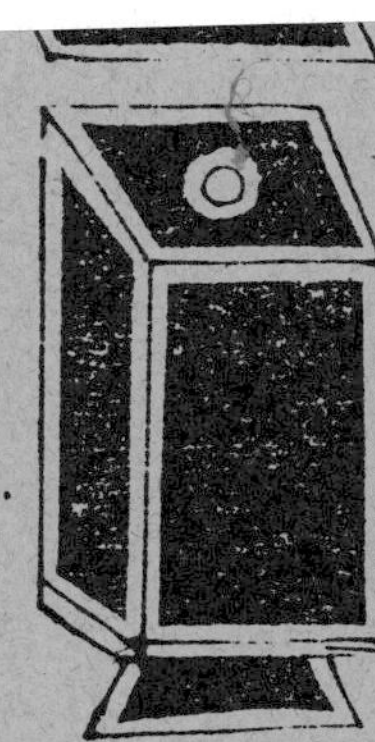

外方內圓曰簠漆赤中稻粱器

俎

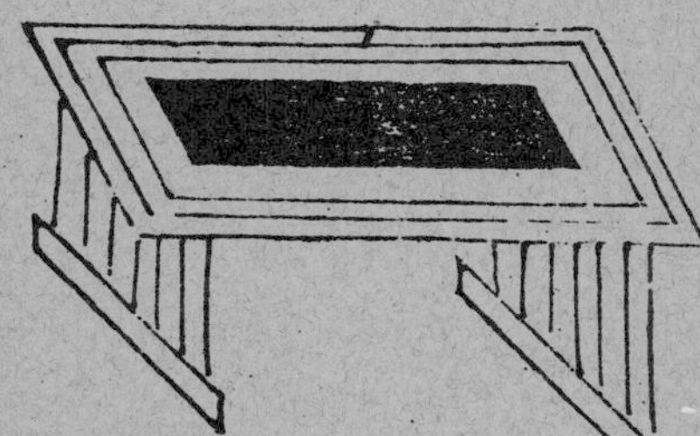

周制房俎漆兩端赤中央黑

爵　坫

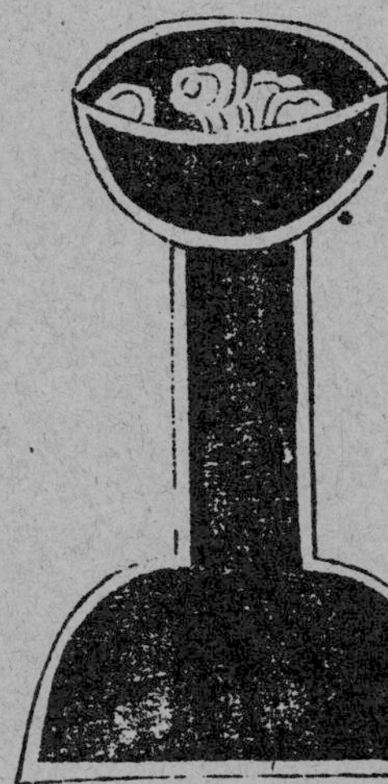

坫以致爵漆赤中畫赤雲氣亦隨爵爲飾

簋

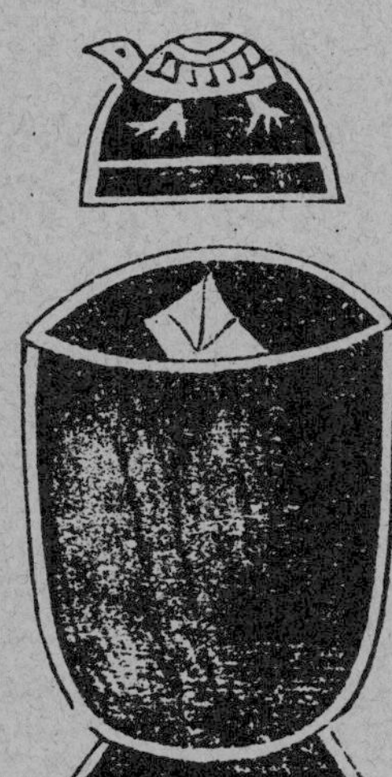

內方外圓曰簋足高二寸漆赤中盛黍稷

玉爵

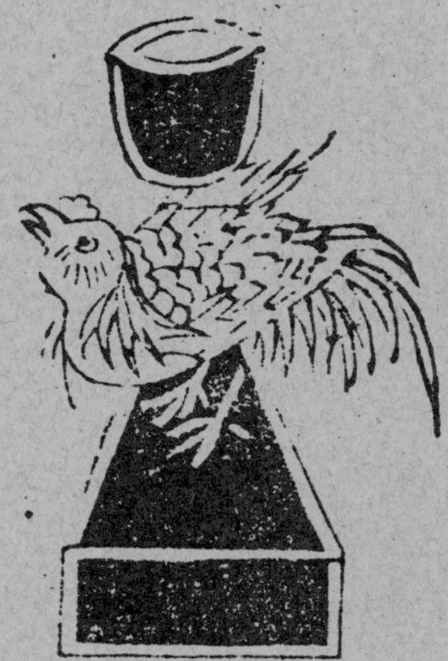

玉爵受一升口徑四寸底二寸上下徑二寸二分

罍

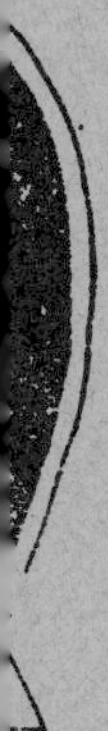

受一斛口徑

彝　舟

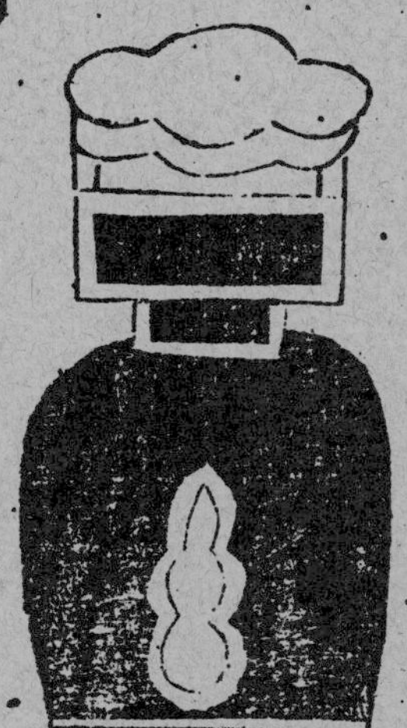

尊下臺君今承槃外漆朱中足隨舟刻畫

龍

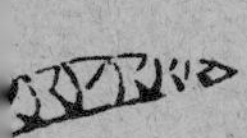

柄長二尺

GRAMMAIRE DE L'OBJET CHINOIS

ISBN : 2-85917-233-5

Michel Culas

Grammaire de l'objet chinois

les éditions de l'amateur

REMERCIEMENTS

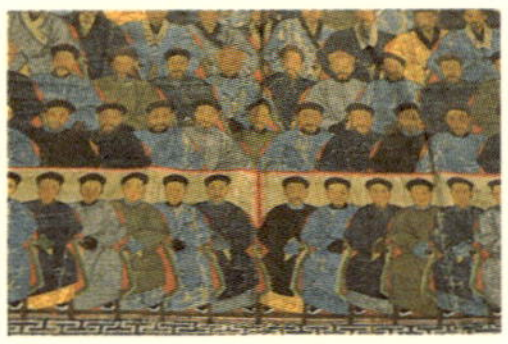

Ils vont tout particulièrement à

Madame TSUI Luoyi (Louise)
pour sa savante collaboration et son aide de tous les instants,

Monsieur XU Guanghua
pour les admirables calligraphies qui illustrent chacun des chapitres,

tous mes amis chinois qui ont apporté une contribution
à la connaissance de leur culture,

tous ceux qui ont bien voulu m'ouvrir leur bibliothèque
ou leur fonds documentaire,

Monsieur Christian LAMOUROUX,
Madame Claude LAMOUROUX
et
Madame Sandrine CHENIVESSE
pour leurs conseils éclairés,
la rigueur de leurs corrections
et leur bienveillance à l'égard de l'œuvre de leur élève,

mes amis de la société AIR FRANCE
pour leur indéfectible soutien

et enfin,
ceux ou celles qui m'ont encouragé à réaliser cet ouvrage.

à mes parents

N'est-il pas suffisant
pour constituer l'œuvre d'art
qu'une émotion se manifeste
à propos de l'objet ?

Michel Leiris

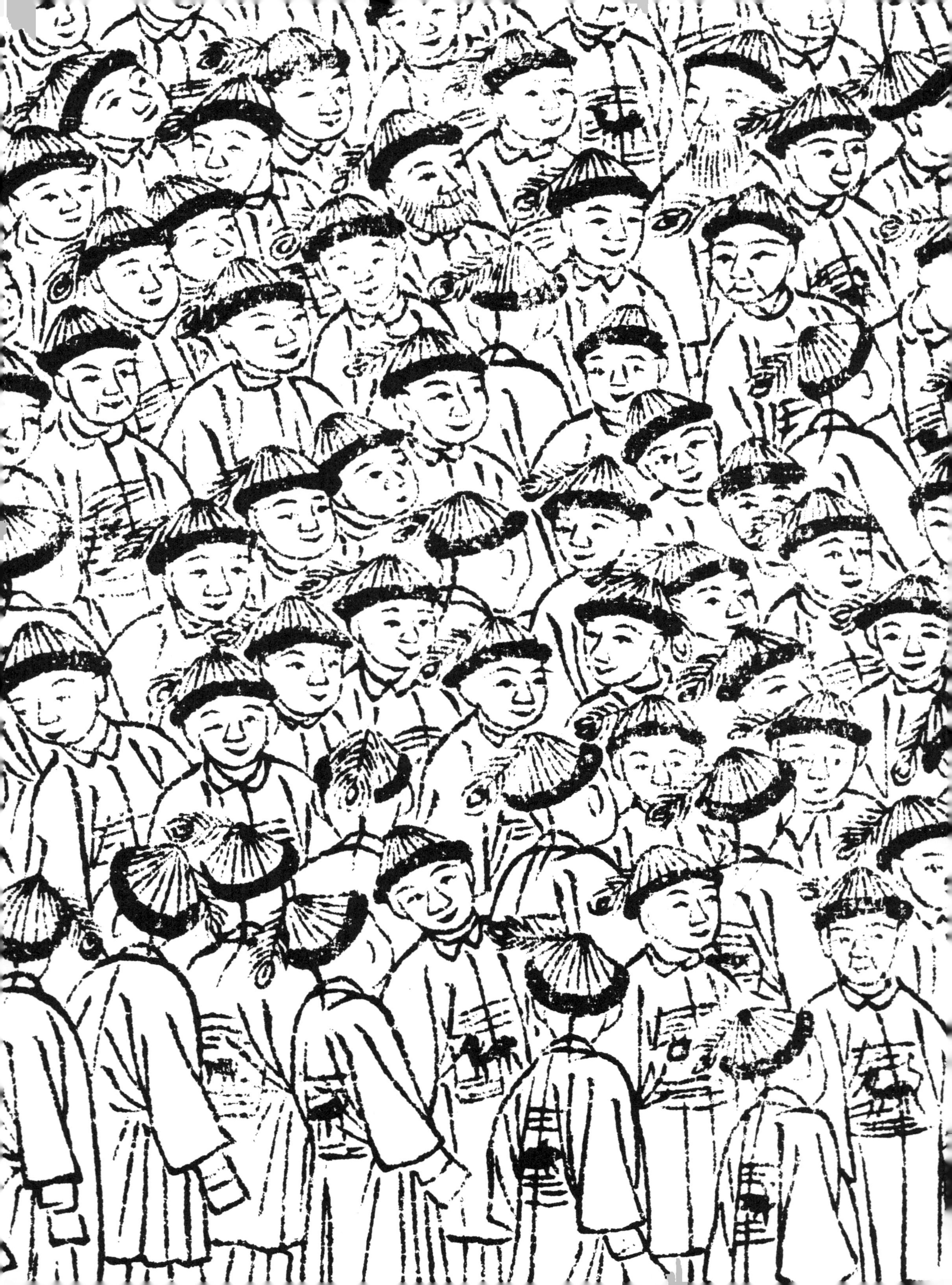

À la recherche du temps passé

回眸

hui mou, littéralement, « poser le regard en arrière ».

Il y a presque deux mille ans qu'ont eu lieu les premiers échanges entre la Chine et l'Occident avec l'arrivée des marchands chinois sur les rivages du Golfe Persique et le début du commerce de la soie avec les Romains. Il faudra toutefois attendre le XIIIe siècle pour que Marco Polo resté, selon ses dires, pendant seize années au service de l'empereur mongol Kubilay Khan, enflamme notre imagination avec son *Livre des Merveilles du Monde*. Celui-ci sera suivi de nombreuses autres relations de voyageurs qui raconteront les étranges et séduisantes productions de ce pays lointain et fermé. Marchands, voyageurs ou soldats ont ainsi rapporté de leurs voyages dans l'Empire du Milieu des « singularités » qui ont trouvé place dans les cabinets de curiosités. Les plus célèbres produits de la Chine sont certainement les « bleu-et-blanc » du XIVe siècle qui, exportés deux cents ans plus tard, donneront naissance, au XVIIIe siècle, aux fabuleux « cabinets de porcelaine ». Les « chinoiseries » s'emparent alors de l'Europe qui importe et produit des faïences, des porcelaines, des meubles et des tapisseries « façon de Chine ». À la période contemporaine, l'engouement pour l'art et la culture chinoise est resté vif peut-être à cause du long enfermement du pays à l'intérieur de ses frontières et des restrictions apportées à l'entrée des Européens (la première ambassade de France n'arrive à Pékin qu'en 1861). Le succès des grandes expositions contemporaines sur la Chine, la multiplication des galeries d'art asiatiques et des prestigieuses ventes aux enchères internationales témoignent de cet intérêt constant pour l'art chinois.

Pour leur part, les Chinois des classes aisées, les lettrés, les hauts fonctionnaires et certains empereurs éclairés ont composé depuis longtemps d'extraordinaires collections. Ils ont ainsi encouragé les artistes, favorisé l'ouverture d'ateliers et permis à l'art et à l'artisanat de se développer au gré des goûts, des modes, pour la seule passion de thésauriser de beaux objets. On peut citer, pour l'exemple, l'interminable inventaire réalisé lors du procès de Heshen, aristocrate mandchou, premier ministre et favori déchu du vieil empereur Qianlong (1736-1796). Il comprenait, entre autres pièces magnifiques, 2 390 flacons de tabac à priser d'une valeur inestimable faisant de cet infortuné fonctionnaire, condamné à se suicider, un des plus grands collectionneurs de son temps. Au cours de la période contemporaine, d'innombrables objets d'art ont été dispersés ou détruits par suite de l'instabilité

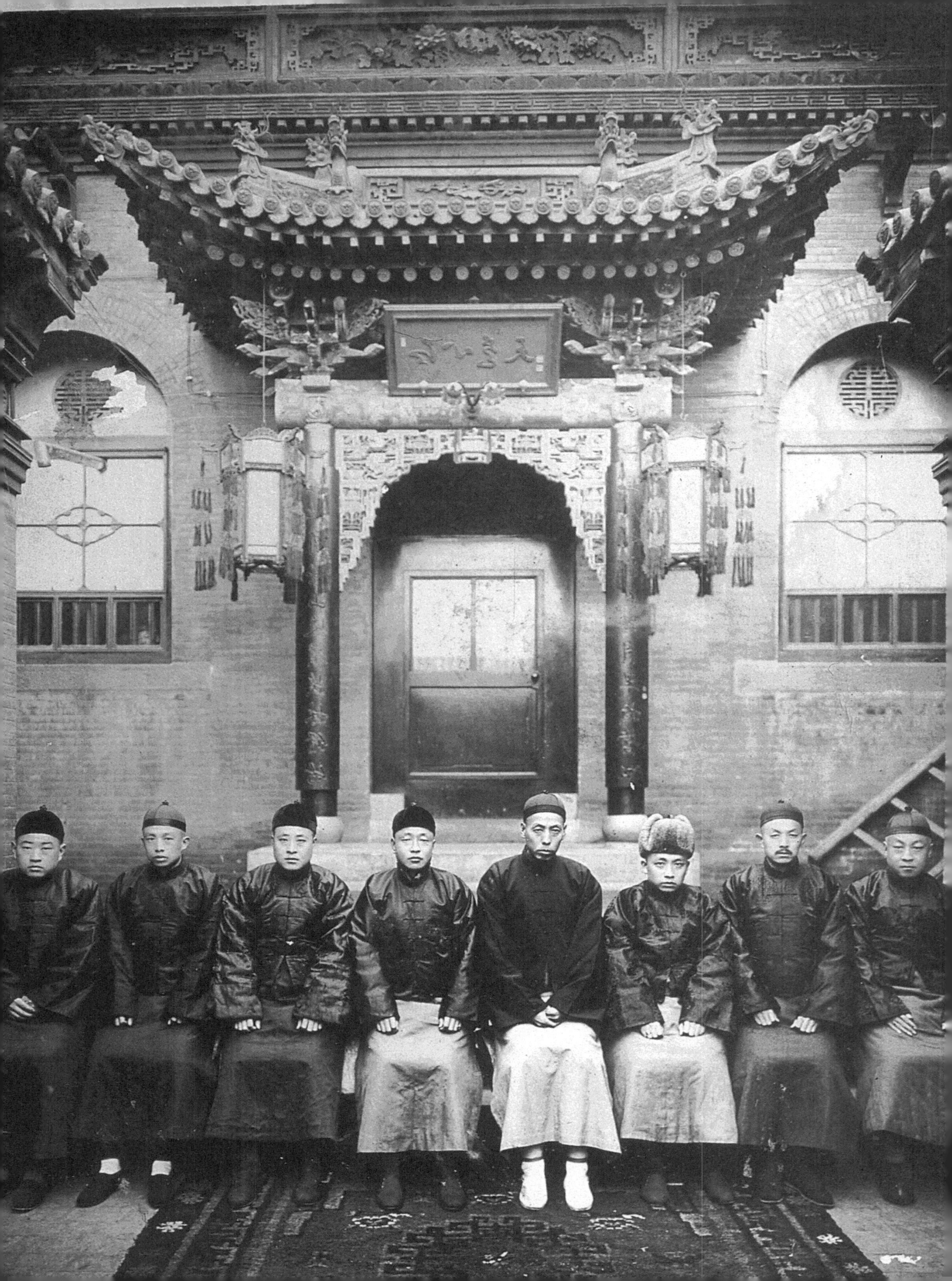

politique qu'a connue récemment la Chine, dès le XIXe siècle avec les guerres de l'opium, le sac de Pékin, la chute de la dynastie des Qing puis, au début du XXe siècle, avec la guerre civile entre nationalistes et communistes, le conflit sino-japonais et enfin la Révolution culturelle. Dans les années trente, d'importantes exportations d'antiquités ont alors lieu vers l'Europe et les États-Unis. De l'instauration de la République Populaire de Chine (1949) à la révolution des « Cent Fleurs » (1956), d'innombrables pièces confisquées aux « ennemis du peuple » et autres « droitiers » réapparaîtront encore lors de ventes publiques. Puis pendant trente ans, le marché de l'objet d'art chinois se tiendra hors des frontières de la République. Aujourd'hui, vingt ans après la disparition de Mao Zedong, et avec l'émergence d'une nouvelle bourgeoisie, on observe un regain d'intérêt des Chinois pour les objets anciens. L'amour pour les choses du passé qui distinguait autrefois le gentilhomme et une nouvelle aisance matérielle relancent le commerce des antiquités. Mais la Chine continentale n'a plus que des pièces de moindre importance à offrir, les grandes œuvres sont devenues très rares ; depuis une trentaine d'années, elles sont dans les musées ou chez de richissimes collectionneurs à l'étranger. Les petits « marchés libres » des grandes villes de tourisme sont néanmoins encore alimentés par les fouilles sauvages des paysans ou par des imitations manufacturées plus ou moins bien réussies. À défaut de réaliser de fabuleuses « affaires », chiner reste une agréable activité. Avec des ambitions modestes, l'amateur pourra se lancer dans la cohue des marchés de brocante ou explorer les rares échoppes d'antiquaires. Bousculé, trompé par des marchands cupides et bien souvent ignorants, il ne tirera satisfaction de sa quête et de ses acquisitions qu'au prix d'un apprentissage élémentaire des objets qui lui sont présentés.

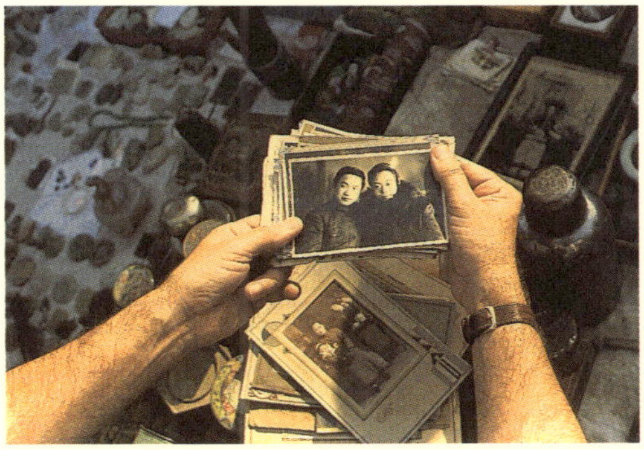

La *Grammaire de l'objet chinois* ne prétend pas rivaliser avec les livres spécialisés sur l'art de ce pays. C'est surtout un manuel d'initiation aux objets chinois, et donc à la civilisation matérielle et à la culture chinoise. Par comparaison avec les savantes études qui ont consacré de si belles pages aux « arts majeurs » (peinture, céramique et sculpture), notre propos s'est plutôt porté sur les « arts mineurs ». C'est donc de l'objet quotidien qu'il sera question plus que de l'œuvre d'art. Les pièces exceptionnelles sont de moins en moins accessibles ; en revanche, l'artisanat et l'art populaire, s'appuyant sur une forte tradition, se sont perpétués. C'est cette culture pérenne, celle qui a résisté aux guerres, à l'idéologie destructrice et aux nouvelles valeurs capitalistes actuelles que nous avons voulu raconter.

Page de gauche, photo souvenir d'un groupe d'amis prise le jour de la fête des Lanternes, le 21 février 1932.
Page suivante, Zhou Jianshen (1448-1487), encre et couleur, musée du Gugong, Pékin *(photo Liu Zhigang).*

La *Grammaire de l'objet chinois* est un ouvrage didactique qui tente d'expliquer simplement l'origine des objets, l'histoire de leur fabrication et leur usage au cours des cinq derniers siècles. La première partie *(Des symboles à comprendre)* est un lexique des innombrables symboles, emblèmes, attributs, analogies, qui fourmillent dans l'art décoratif sous forme de personnages mythiques, d'animaux, d'oiseaux, de fleurs ou d'objets et dont la signification est une énigme pour la plupart des étrangers à la Chine. La seconde partie *(Des techniques à apprendre)* traite des procédés de fabrication qui ont fait la renommée des artisans chinois. Enfin, dans la troisième partie *(Des objets à vivre),* grâce à des notes et des anecdotes, le lecteur pénétrera dans ce qui devait être la vie privée et la vie publique à l'ère des Ming (1368-1644) et des Qing (1644-1911). L'objet d'art et l'objet usuel sont indifféremment les points de départ de ces parcours-découverte. Certes, la vingtaine de chapitres retenus pour illustrer ce propos ne peut couvrir 630 années d'une histoire bouillonnante d'événements, pas plus qu'elle n'est en mesure de refléter l'extraordinaire production artistique ou artisanale des peuples qui composent la nation chinoise. Ces notes apportent tout au plus de brefs éclairages sur une Chine traditionnelle, celle qui avait encore une âme, celle qui a enchanté nos lectures et peuplé nos rêveries, celle que ces modestes objets peuvent encore faire resurgir... Comme le note un célèbre photographe qui l'observe depuis près d'un demi siècle à travers sa lentille, « la Chine tourne le dos à sa propre culture, perd son identité et ses valeurs morales. C'est la grande tristesse du voyageur qui aime la Chine chinoise et se retrouve à Chicago ».

La *Grammaire de l'objet chinois* s'adresse à un public cultivé mais non spécialiste qui manifeste un intérêt pour ce pays. Elle se veut une initiation, par l'objet, à cette étonnante culture qui devrait inciter bien des lecteurs à se plonger, ultérieurement, dans la lecture d'ouvrages plus spécialisés qui ont toute notre admiration.

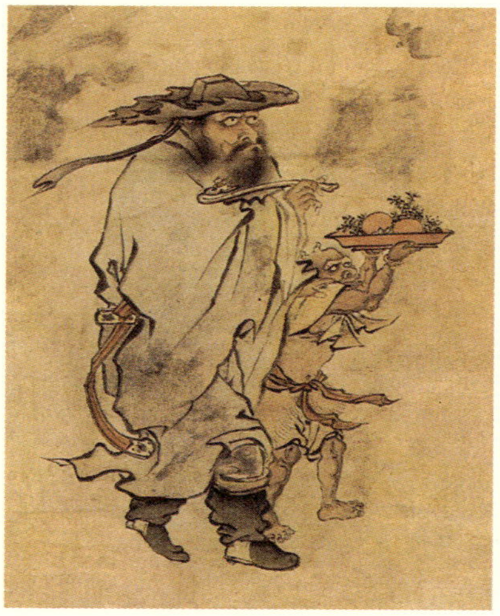

TABLE

À la recherche du temps passé 9

CHAPITRE 1

Des symboles à comprendre

Le symbole dans l'art décoratif 17
Le bestiaire des animaux à poil 25
Les animaux à plume 36
Les animaux à écaille 47
Les animaux à carapace : la tortue 54
Le langage des fleurs et des plantes 57
Les pierres à rêver 69
Le fabuleux panthéon des dieux et héros légendaires 77
La magie des chiffres et des nombres 89

CHAPITRE 2

Des techniques à apprendre

Les trésors du lettré 99
L'art du pinceau de fer 109
Le jade, pierre de toutes les passions ... 116
La porcelaine, une alchimie secrète 121
Marques, signatures et sceaux 129
La laque, vernis de Chine 135
L'émail et le cloisonné 139

CHAPITRE 3

Des objets à vivre

L'art du thé ... 145
Les cadenas de sortilèges ... 152
Les carrés de mandarins ... 156
Chanteurs et combattants en cage ... 164
Les chevaux de papier ... 173
Les cithares du vent ... 178
De curieux gardiens de toits ... 184
Le feu maîtrisé : lanternes et pétards ... 189
Les fleurs de tête ... 199
Les lunettes chinoises ... 207
Les miroirs de bronze ... 213
Oiseaux de cage et cages à oiseaux ... 219
Ombres, silhouettes et découpages ... 228
L'opium, pâte de félicité et de longévité ... 237
Le pékinois, chien-lion, chien bouddhique ... 243
Le vent et l'eau, les mystères de la géomancie ... 245

Annexes ... 253
- Dynastie des Ming ... 255
- Dynastie des Qing ... 255
- Chronologie comparative ... 256
- Marques de règne de la dynastie des Qing ... 258
- Calendrier lunaire et grégorien à l'époque des Yuan, des Ming et des Qing ... 259
- Carte de Chine ... 260

Bibliographie ... 263
Index ... 267

DES SYMBOLES À COMPRENDRE

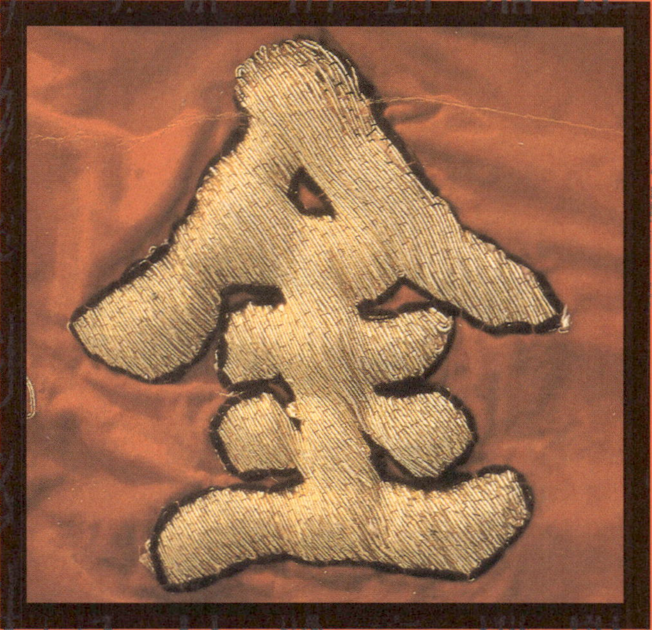

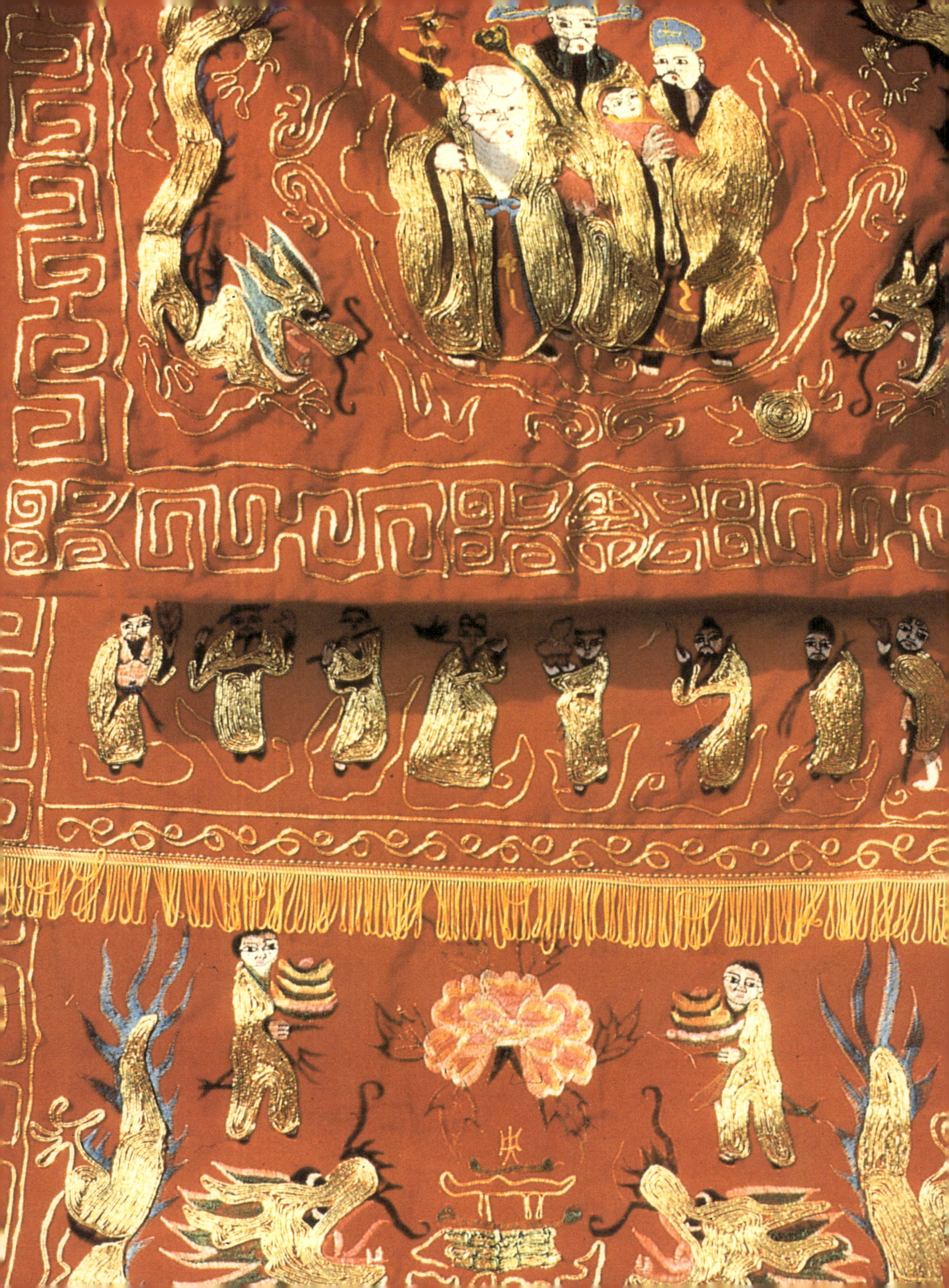

Le symbole dans l'art décoratif

C'est dans l'art décoratif que l'imaginaire des Chinois a trouvé un formidable terrain d'application : décors géométriques, décors floraux, animaliers ou à personnages des porcelaines peintes, motifs stylisés des tapis ou des broderies, innombrables bibelots et objets aux formes étranges, inscriptions indéchiffrables… Voilà autant d'images mystérieuses que, depuis près de trois siècles, nous cherchons à comprendre ou au mieux à expliquer. Ce déchiffrement passe par l'étude des symboles, des attributs, des emblèmes, des associations d'idées *(lianxiang)* et des analogies *(xieyinzi)* qui fourmillent dans l'art chinois.

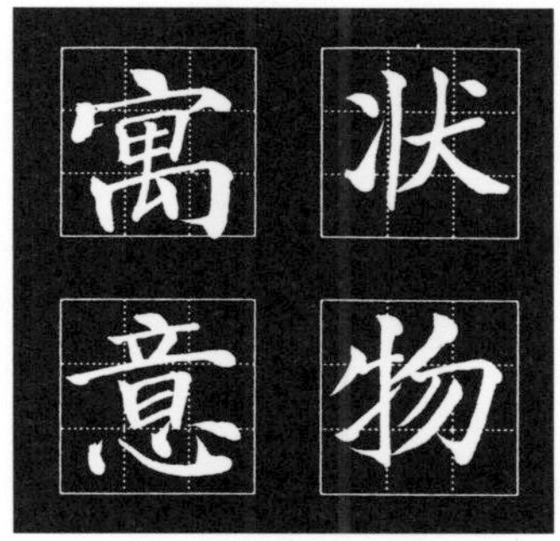

zhuang wu yuyi, littéralement, « décrire le sens caché de toutes choses ».

Selon la définiton du dictionnaire Robert, le « symbole est un objet ou un fait naturel de caractère imagé qui évoque, par sa forme ou sa nature, une association d'idées naturelle (dans un groupe social donné) avec quelque chose d'abstrait ou d'absent ».

Si nous prenons pour exemple la gourde (voir p. 61), symbole de longévité et d'immortalité maintes fois représenté dans l'iconographie, il faut remonter à la pratique des ermites qui utilisaient ce modeste récipient (calebasse) fait avec la plante *lapenaria vulgaris* de la famille des cucurbitacées, pour transporter les simples qu'ils ramassaient en vue d'en faire des remèdes. Adoptée comme enseigne par les apothicaires, on fabriqua aussi des flacons pharmaceutiques de porcelaine en forme de gourde car cet objet de bon augure ne pouvait que renforcer l'action du médicament. De petites gourdes taillées dans le bois de pêcher ou en papier découpé ont été des amulettes traditionnelles pour se protéger des maladies. L'un des Huit Immortels du panthéon taoïste, Li Tieguai, était toujours représenté en guenilles avec une béquille, portant une gourde d'où s'échappent des volutes de fumée. Pour sa part, le dieu de la Longévité, Shouxinglao, tenait un bâton noueux au bout duquel était liée une gourde, il était accompagné d'un cerf et d'une ou plusieurs chauve-souris voletant au-dessus de lui. Mazhashen, le dieu des sauterelles, tenait aussi une gourde fumante, symbole de son pouvoir sur les insectes destructeurs. Cette modeste plante est donc devenue un symbole, une « image de substitution » (Maurice-Louis Tournier), un signifiant pour une idée abstraite : dans le cas présent, la protection contre les maladies et l'assurance de l'immortalité.

Page de gauche, broderie de temple avec, en haut les « Trois Purs », au centre les « Huit Immortels » et en bas une paire de dragons.

Li Tieguai porte une gourde et une béquille ; ces deux objets sont ses attributs. Non seulement, ils servent à le distinguer des sept autres Immortels mais ils sont aussi le lien avec sa légende. En effet, Li Tieguai (ou « Li-béquille-de-fer ») était de son vivant un ascète qui avait reçu de Laozi en personne un enseignement profond. Il pouvait ainsi envoyer son âme hors de son corps au cours de voyages qui duraient plusieurs jours. Une fois, il recommanda à l'un de ses disciples de garder son corps pendant six jours et de le brûler le septième s'il n'était pas redescendu des cieux. Ne voyant pas revenir son maître à la date convenue, le disciple se débarrassa du corps. Quand l'âme de Li revint sur terre, elle n'eut pas d'autre solution que de se réincarner dans le seul corps disponible, celui d'un vieux mendiant laid et infirme qui venait de mourir de froid. Les volutes de fumée qui s'échappent de la gourde rappellent la séparation de l'âme et du corps, la béquille évoque le malheureux mendiant.

Quant à Shouxinglao, le bâton qu'il porte est l'attribut normal de la vieillesse mais c'est aussi une marque de dignité. Pour les taoïstes, il était même le « double » du personnage. Le cerf qui apparaît souvent en compagnie de Shouxinglao ou de l'Immortel Li Tieguai n'est toutefois pas leur compagnon exclusif, on le retrouve comme monture du dieu de la Richesse, Caishen. Ce n'est donc plus un attribut mais un emblème, car il traduit, à travers l'image de l'animal, une idée de longévité ou d'immortalité. Le cerf, en effet, était réputé vivre très vieux mais, selon la tradition, il était aussi le seul animal à trouver le champignon de l'immortalité (*lingzhi* ; voir p. 60). C'est d'ailleurs, à cause de cette réputation, que les jeunes bois de cerfs sont encore utilisés comme aphrodisiaque.

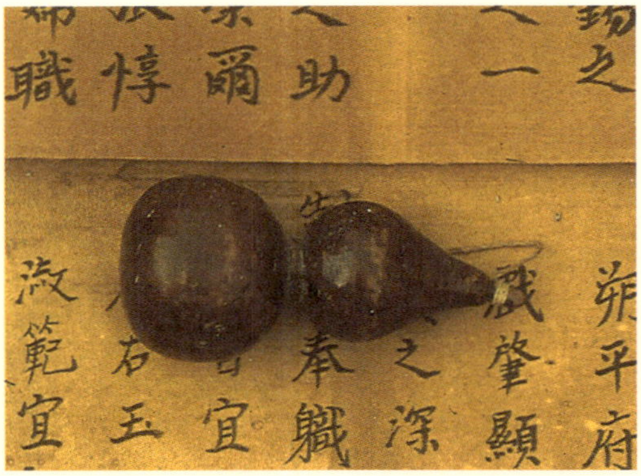

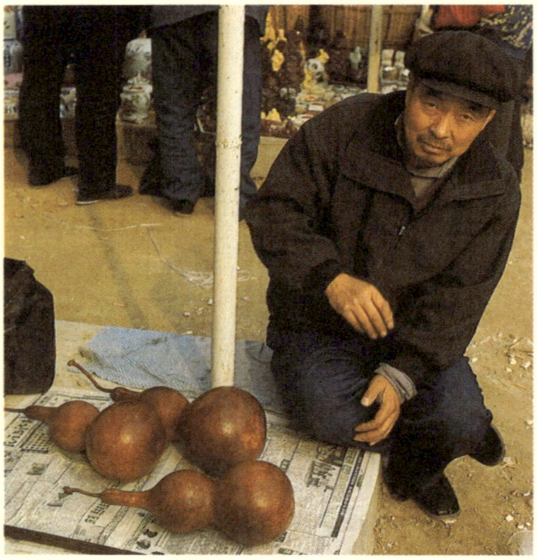

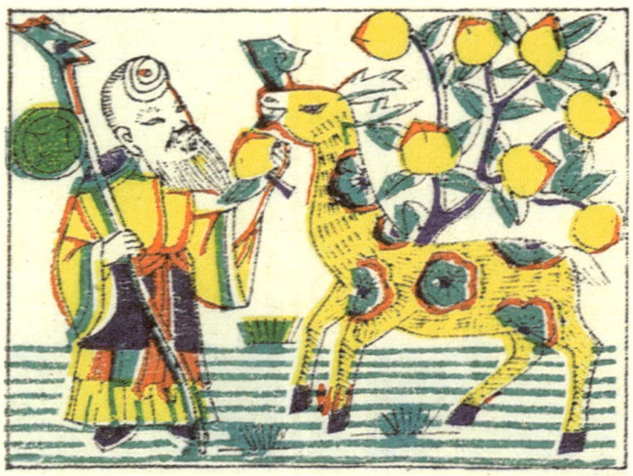

En haut, amulette en bois de pêcher en forme de gourde ; au centre, vendeur de calebasses ; en bas, Shouxinglao nourrissant son cerf de pêches (image du Jour de l'An, nianhua, de Weitian, Shandong).

En outre, la prononciation du mot « cerf » *(lu)* est semblable à celle de « bonheur, félicité, faveurs, salaire des fonctionnaires » *(lu)*. C'est ainsi que le cerf sur un cadeau était un vœu d'accéder à de hautes fonctions dans l'administration impériale. Ce cas d'homophonie, très fréquent dans la langue chinoise, permet une construction analogique, c'est-à-dire à l'emploi de mots ou d'expressions dont « le seul lien avec le signifiant est la ressemblance phonétique ». Il convient de rappeler ici que la langue chinoise est fondée sur une échelle de quatre tons. Pour le seul phonème *lu,* pris comme exemple, on trouve déjà une quarantaine d'homophones et quelques homographes… Seul l'usage, au fil des années, a déterminé dans la liste des homophones possibles celui qui répondait le mieux au jeu de l'analogie. Ce sont, en général, des mots ou expressions à caractère faste et auspicieux. La chauve-souris *(bianfu),* selon ces principes, est phonétiquement proche de « faveur céleste, bonheur, félicité, prospérité » *(fu)* et de ce fait est considérée comme l'emblème le plus évident du bonheur. Le soulier *(xie)* que l'on trouve souvent par paires, en amulette de bois ou d'argent a deux homophones prestigieux : « vivre en harmonie » mais aussi « unir ses forces, s'entraider ». C'est donc un présent à la symbolique très forte.

L'utilisation des « images de substitution » a été fréquente, leur choix s'est porté sur des symboles qui pouvaient déclencher des associations d'idées relativement simples : la grue et la tortue expriment la longévité ; la grenade, la cacahuète, le raisin et la jujube *(zaozi)*, à cause de leurs pépins ou noyau, sont associés à une nombreuse descendance et sont donc des motifs traditionnels pour les cadeaux de mariage, à cause de l'analogie avec *zi* (graine ou enfant)… Les symboles ont été utilisés soit seuls soit par groupes stéréotypés (ou associations emblématiques) que les artistes ont souvent repris dans leurs compositions. Le saule et l'hirondelle expriment la grâce, la douceur (féminine) et le printemps, le tigre dans les bambous est l'association de la force terrestre avec celle de la nature. La pêche, la grenade et la main du Bouddha (la bergamote ; voir p. 62) sont les trois fruits qui traditionnellement représentent les Trois Bonheurs : longévité, descendance nombreuse et richesse. Le pin, le bambou et le prunier sont désignés sous le nom de « Trois amis » parce qu'ils résistent à l'hiver. Des « associations » ont été faites entre animaux, oiseaux et plantes, résultat sans doute d'observations quotidiennes. Ainsi, les canards sont souvent mis en scène avec les nénuphars, les cailles avec le millet, les faisans avec les pivoines, la grue ou l'aigle avec le pin, le rat avec les raisins…

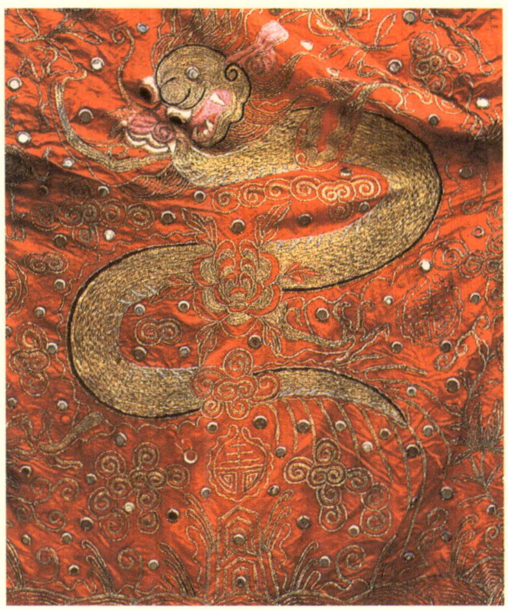

En haut, décor de chauve-souris, de pêches et de symboles taoïstes (boîte à courrier en laque du XIXe siècle) ; en bas, dragon brodé.

S'agissant des objets symboliques, il faut rechercher l'origine de leur signification dans les mythes et les religions. Ces objets sont le plus souvent connus sous

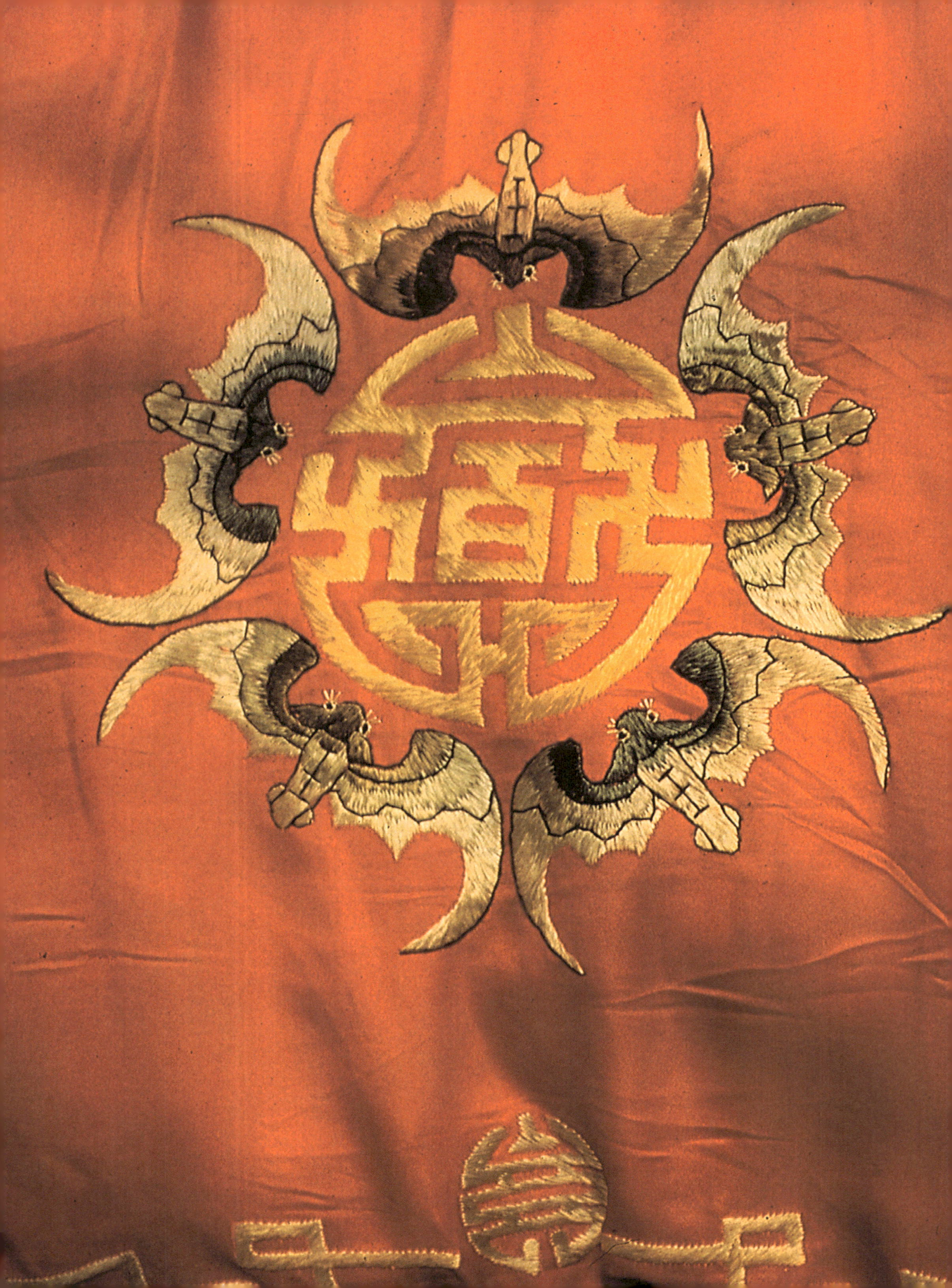

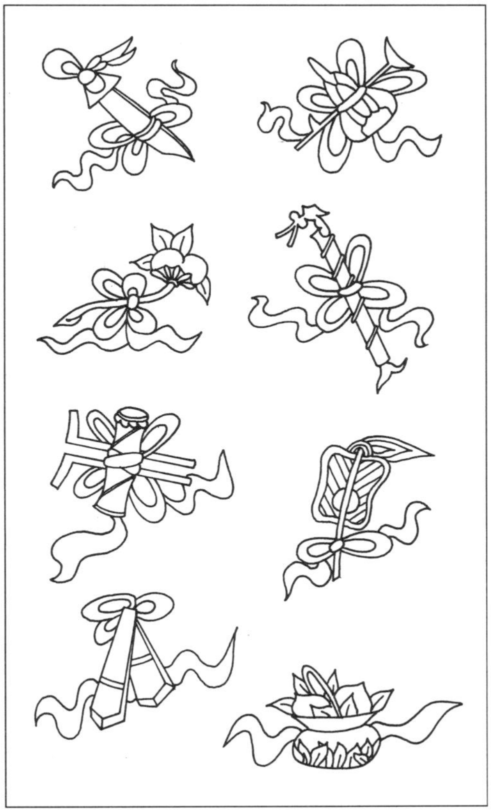

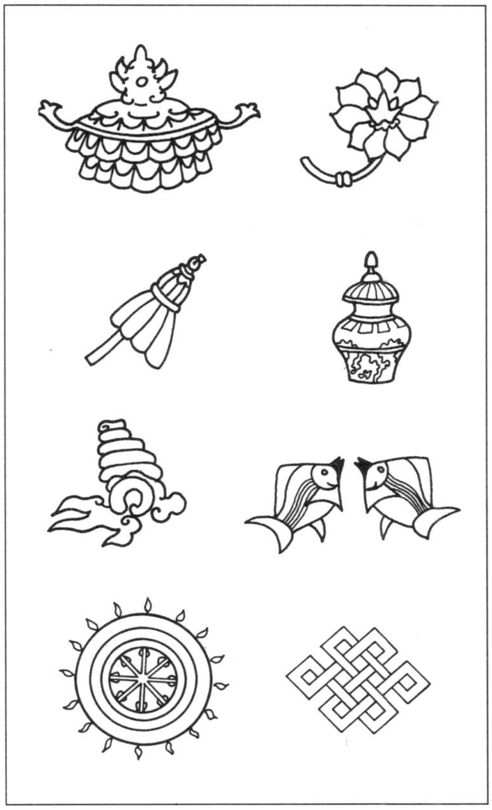

forme de « collections ». Les taoïstes ont constitué les « Huit immortels cachés » *(cang ba xian)*. Ce sont des attributs qui caractérisent les Immortels (voir p. 79) ; ils sont souvent utilisés sans leur propriétaire mais la référence est explicite pour les Chinois. On y trouve l'éventail en feuille de palmier, le tube de bambou, l'épée, les tablettes de cour (et non les castagnettes), la gourde et la béquille, la flûte, le panier de fleurs ou de fruits, la tige de lotus avec les graines ou la fleur.

Les bouddhistes ont emprunté au riche patrimoine de l'Inde les « Huit signes de bon augure » *(ba jixiang)* : le dais (symbole du pouvoir suprême et de la vraie doctrine), le parasol (protection contre le mal), la conque (voix du Bouddha prêchant), la roue (loi bouddhique), la fleur de lotus (perfection et pureté), le vase à couvercle (contient les trésors), les poissons géminés (liberté d'esprit et du corps), le nœud sans fin, nœud mystique ou « entrailles du Bouddha » (renaissance).

Les « Huit (objets) précieux » *(ba bao)* sont souvent confondus avec les symboles bouddhistes. On ne connaît pas très bien leur origine. Il s'agit d'une collection d'images auspicieuses très utilisée en décoration. La perle représente les énergies condensées du *yin* et du *yang* ; c'est le « joyau de l'omnipotence ». Le losange évidé (ou rhombe) est un instrument sacré, symbole de victoire. La pierre musicale (ou lithophone) évoque l'intégrité et la félicité. Les coupes en corne de rhinocéros protégeaient du poison ; elles sont deve-

Page de gauche, ronde de cinq chauve-souris marquées du caractère wang *(roi) autour du caractère* shou *(longévité) renforcé par deux svastika (bonheur) sur broderie.*
Ci-dessus à gauche, les « Huit Immortels cachés », à droite, les « Huit signes de bon augure ».

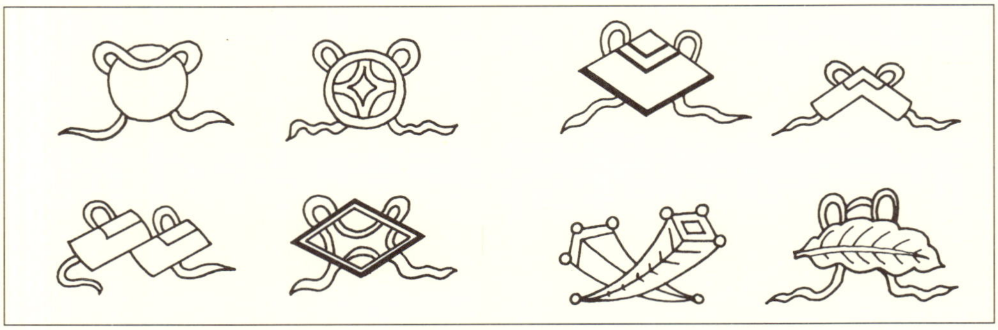

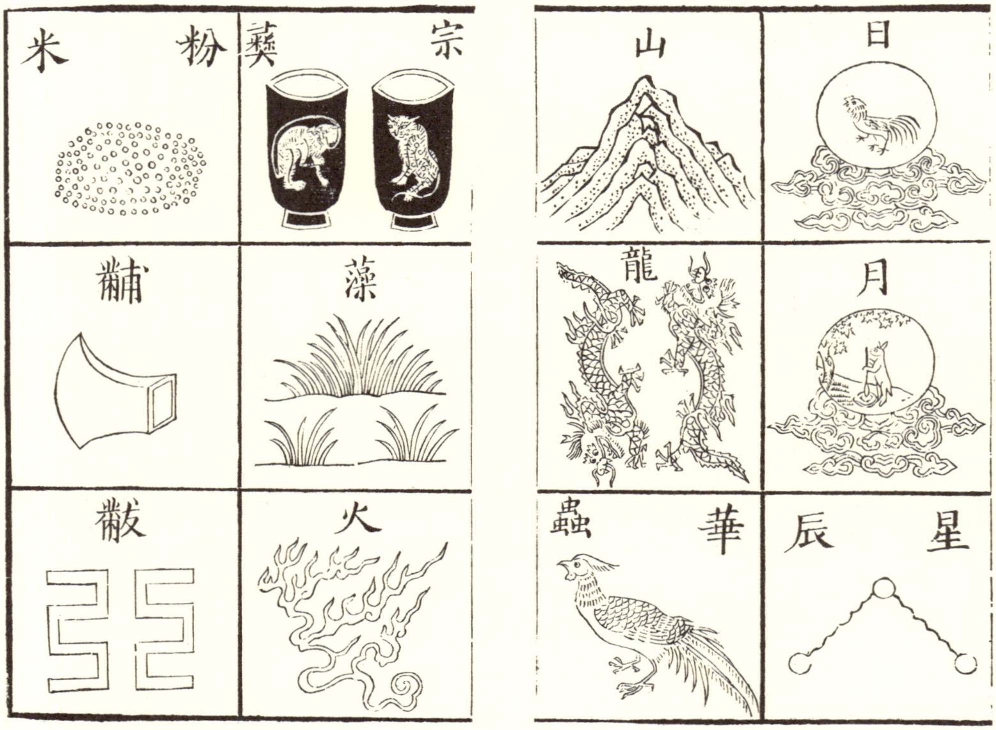

En haut, les « Huit précieux » ; en bas, les « Douze ornements impériaux ».

nues un symbole de bonheur. La sapèque se rattache à la richesse, c'est un porte-bonheur pour la réussite. Le losange plein est appelé en chinois « peinture » *(hua)* mais on ne connaît plus très bien sa signification. Les livres (allusion aux « Classiques ») n'étaient pas seulement l'expression de la culture mais avaient un véritable pouvoir talismanique. Enfin, la feuille d'armoise servant à repousser les maladies était un porte-bonheur.

Mais il existait encore bien d'autres collections d'objets commes les Quatre trésors du cabinet du lettré (voir p. 99), les Quatre divertissements élégants (le luth, le jeu d'échecs, les rouleaux de soie, les livres en fascicules) ou les Cent (objets) antiques *(bai gu)*. La plupart de ces objets-symboles étaient représentés enrubannés pour afficher leur caractère sacré et protecteur, toutes les divinités dans l'iconographie bouddhique portant des rubans.

Selon le *Livre de l'histoire (Shujing)*, l'un des cinq Classiques, une très vieille et énigmatique collection, celle des « Douze ornements » *(shier zhang)* daterait de l'époque des souverains légendaires (IIIe millénaire av. J.-C.). Ces symboles, le plus souvent brodés sur les vêtements impériaux, restèrent en usage jusqu'à l'époque Qing. Sur la partie supérieure de la robe figuraient le corbeau à trois pattes (emblème du soleil), le lièvre pilant la drogue de l'immortalité (la lune), une chaînette de ronds (représentation traditionnelle des constellations), les montagnes (résidence des dieux et des sages), le dragon impérial et le faisan ou phénix (symbole de bon gouvernement)). À la partie inférieure de la robe se trouvaient deux gobelets (vases rituels) ornés d'un singe et d'un tigre (habileté et fermeté du souverain), une plante aquatique (sagesse), des flammes (la vertu), des grains de riz ou de millet (nourriture indispensable), une hache (autorité, justice) et le caractère *ya* dont le sens reste obscur.

Il existe de nombreuses études sur la symbolique chinoise. Le dictionnaire étymologique des caractères, *Shuowen,* de Xu Shen (IIe siècle ap. J.-C.) et la célèbre encyclopédie illustrée des objets anciens, *Baigutu,* compilée par Wang Fu, archéologue et critique, détaillent les motifs décoratifs provenant des époques très anciennes (dynasties des Xia, Shang et Zhou). En effet, en ce temps-là, on préférait les motifs géométriques aux motifs décoratifs (animaux, plantes, objets). De nombreuses controverses entre érudits eurent lieu à propos de leur interprétation. Les dessins *(huawen)* que l'on retrouve plus fréquemment sur les bronzes, certaines porcelaines, les tissus brodés ou les tapis sont des figures stylisées (nuages, vagues, montagnes, flammèches), des frises (comme la grecque dénommée « tonnerre », *leiwen*) ou des dessins géométriques (carrés, ronds, croix svastika, « graines » ou « œufs de poisson »...).

Enfin, les ornemanistes chinois ont su tirer un grand parti de la beauté de la langue écrite pour en faire des motifs décoratifs mais aussi porteurs d'une charge symbolique. Les quatre caractères porte-bonheur les plus fréquents sont *fu* (bénédiction céleste), *lu* (richesse), *xi* (bonheur simple) ou *shuangxi* (double bonheur), *shou* (longévité). Ce dernier est celui qui a sans doute fait l'objet du plus grand nombre de variations. On peut citer à cet effet un vase de porcelaine bleu-et-blanc offert en 1705 à l'empereur Kangxi sur lequel figuraient « dix mille » versions différentes du caractère *shou,* souhaitant ainsi à son bénéficiaire « dix mille vies sans limite »... En contre-partie, l'empereur ne dédaignait pas prendre le pinceau pour tracer de son auguste main, à l'encre rouge, un de ces caractères de vœux qu'il faisait envoyer comme présent impérial.

À la manière des anciennes classifications chinoises et comme la plupart des auteurs du genre, le chapitre consacré aux symboles est établi sous forme de répertoires alphabétiques du monde animal, végétal, minéral et même divin. C'est dans les *Annales,* le *Livre des Rites* et surtout le *Classique des Montagnes et des Mers* que les premiers modèles ont apparu. S'il est relative-

Page suivante, le caractère shou *(couvercle de boîte en argent, XIXe siècle).*

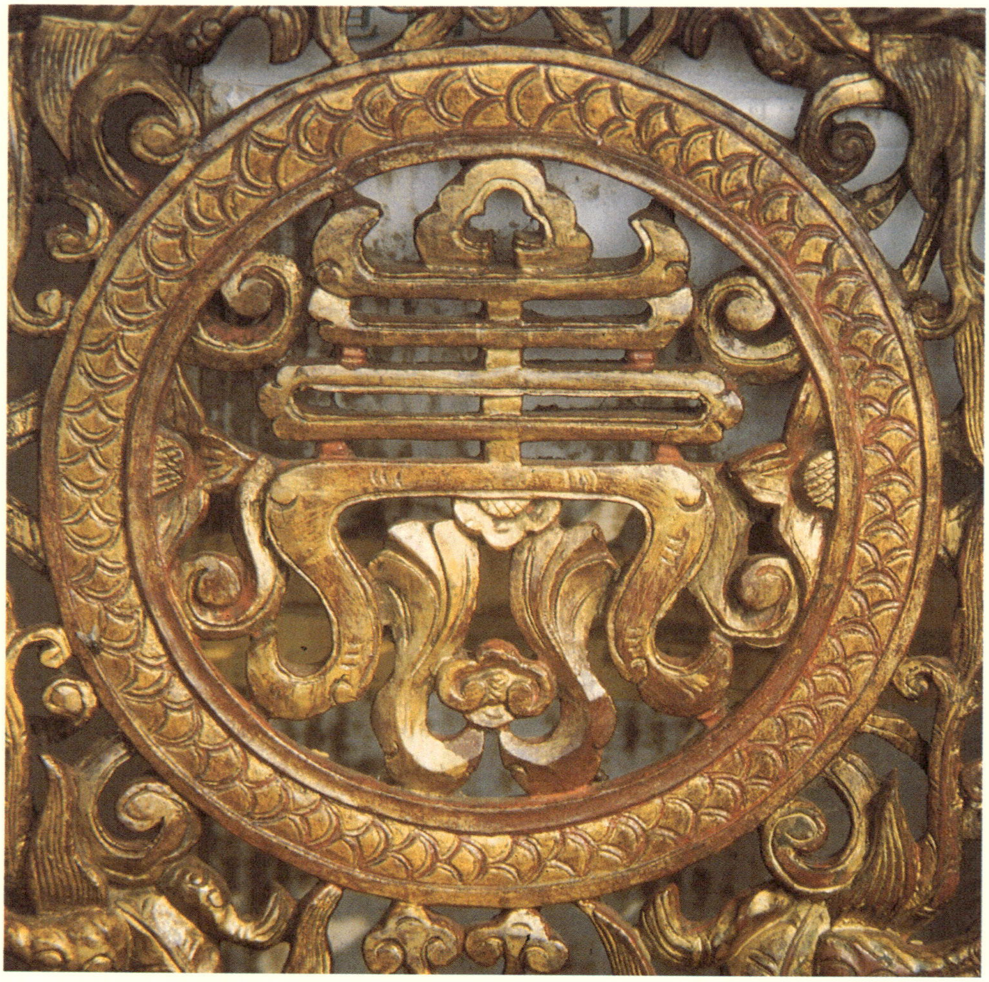

ment facile de présenter pour chacun d'eux les significations les plus communément admises colportées par la tradition, il est, en revanche, hasardeux de tenter d'expliquer leur origine. On peut ainsi dater l'apparition du *svastika* (croix gammée tournant vers la gauche) au moment de l'introduction du bouddhisme en Chine, c'est du *Livre des Mutations (Yijing)* que sont issus les trigrammes fondamentaux *(ba gua)* et c'est le *Classique des Montagnes et des Mers (Shan Hai Jing)* qui fait mention pour la première fois du bois de pêcher pour repousser les maléfices. En revanche, aucune source n'explique quand le saule est devenu « l'arbre de l'amour » et même de la luxure, et pourquoi le renard, par ses métamorphoses successives, devient un « immortel » à neuf queues…

C'est donc avec précaution que l'on s'aventurera dans ce monde complexe, riche et attrayant d'images encore maniées avec tant d'aisance par la plupart des Chinois cultivés et qui offrent un trésor inépuisable au peintre, au sculpteur ou au poète.

Le bestiaire des animaux à poil

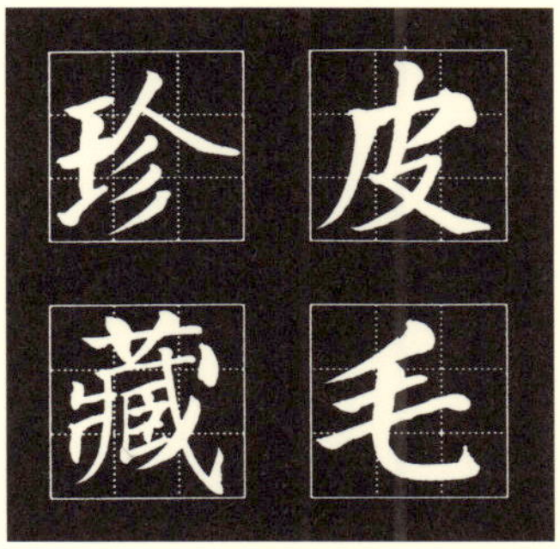

pimao zhencang, littéralement, « précieuses collections de fourrures ».

L'âne *(lü)*, le plus humble et l'un des moins estimés des animaux était peu fréquent dans la décoration. On le représentait toutefois comme la monture bien pratique de l'immortel Zhang Guolao qui le repliait comme une feuille de papier après usage et le rangeait dans le tube de bambou qu'il portait en bandoulière. Ce peu de respect pour l'âne a peut-être inspiré le dicton populaire : « quand il a fini de tourner la meule, on n'a plus qu'à le tuer » *(xiemo, shalü)*. Capable de parcourir mille lieues *(li)* en une journée avec cet animal fabuleux, l'Immortel avait la particularité de le chevaucher assis à l'envers.

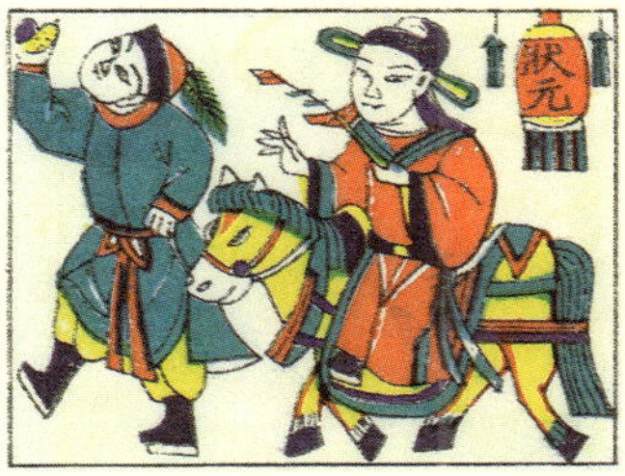

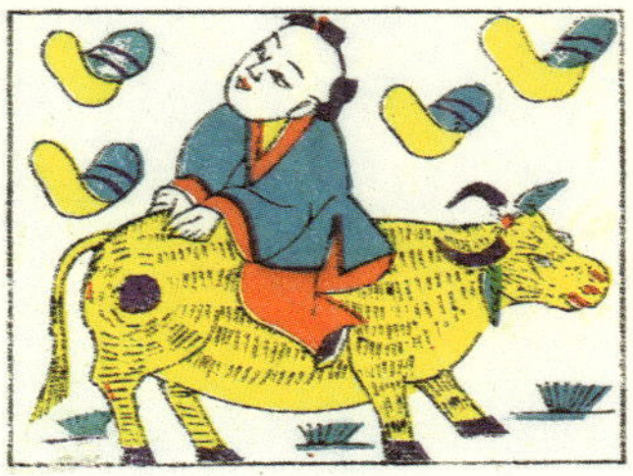

Le bœuf dans le nord et le buffle dans le sud *(niu)*, est un des thèmes souvent utilisés en peinture ou en poésie pour exprimer la bonté, le calme, la force paisible, la tolérance, la vie rurale. Celui de « l'enfant au buffle » est très connu : il exprime, à travers l'allégorie du berger qui reprend la maîtrise de son troupeau, l'une des grandes leçons de la philosophie *chan* (*zen* en japonais) : la victoire du faible sur le fort. Un autre thème célèbre est celui du vieux maître taoïste Laozi monté sur un buffle vert, quittant le royaume de Zhou parce qu'il ne supporte plus la corruption qui s'y est installée. Par superstition on attribuait à des statuettes de bronze représentant un buffle (animal lié à l'eau) le pouvoir d'empêcher les inondations et les effondrements et on les scellait dans les ponts ou les digues. Le bœuf servait aussi quelquefois de monture (à la place du cerf) au dieu de la Longévité, Shouxinglao. Symbole des travaux agricoles, un bœuf jaune participait aussi aux cérémonies annuelles du tracé des sillons par l'empereur, au temple du Ciel. Pour le rite de l'arrivée du printemps, on fabriquait un bœuf en terre qui représentait le froid. Au moment des offrandes, la statuette était alors brisée et ses morceaux répandus dans les champs pour marquer la fin de la mauvaise saison. Par ailleurs, le mythique Shennong, dieu de l'agriculture, était quelquefois représenté comme le Minotaure, avec une tête de

En haut, retour triomphal du candidat qui a réussi aux examens impériaux ; en bas, l'enfant au buffle entouré de monnaies d'argent en forme de cothurne (images populaires, bois gravés de Weitian).

taureau. Les idoles de papier, vénérées à la campagne, représentaient souvent le Roi-Bœuf auquel des sacrifices étaient offerts le premier jour du dixième mois lunaire.

Le cerf *(lu)* a joué un rôle important chez les peuples des steppes. Il avait une double symbolique : la longévité et la richesse. Au titre de la longévité, il était la monture traditionnelle de Shouxinglao, ou de Ma Gu, une taoïste vénérée comme la protectrice des vieilles gens, et même de l'Immortel Li Tieguai. À en croire les légendes, le cerf vivait très vieux ; à mille ans, sa fourrure devenait grise, cinq cents ans plus tard, elle était blanche comme la neige et quand ses cornes avaient noirci, il atteignait l'immortalité. Alors, le cerf ne se nourrissait plus que de *lingzhi* (l'amadouvier considéré comme champignon de l'immortalité). La jeune pousse de bois de cerf *(lurong),* à laquelle une légende bien vivace prête des vertus aphrodisiaques, est encore consommée de nos jours. On fit même des trônes en andouiller sous les Ming. Comme le caractère *lu* (cerf) pouvait aussi désigner, par homophonie, les émoluments des fonctionnaires, il évoquait la richesse. À ce titre, il était le compagnon du dieu de la Richesse. Mais ce fut aussi un symbole bouddhiste : le Bouddha prêchant son premier sermon dans un parc près de Bénarès est souvent représenté au milieu d'un troupeau de cerfs et de biches. Le cerf reste donc associé au bouddhisme.

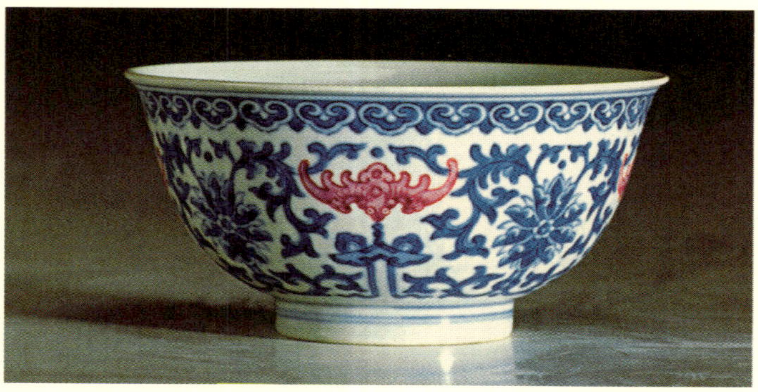

Le chat *(mao)* est un animal peu présent, sauf sur certaines images populaires. C'était une idole que les paysans vénéraient comme le protecteur de leurs récoltes de grains ou de cocons de vers à soie contre les rats des champs. Dans beaucoup de régions, on lui attribuait des pouvoirs magiques : indiquer l'heure (par la dilatation de ses pupilles), annoncer la pluie (en passant sa patte derrière la tête), voir les démons ou même se transformer en génie malfaisant (il fallait neuf esprits des morts pour faire un chat) et à ce titre, il était un peu craint, donc peu populaire. À cause du jeu de mots entre « octogénaire » ou « nonagénaire » *(mao)* et le « chat » *(mao),* ce dernier était un souhait de longévité et il figurait sur les cadeaux offerts aux personnes âgées.

La chauve-souris est sans doute le rébus le plus typique de la symbolique chinoise. Son nom *bianfu* est lié par homophonie à *bian* (« partout », « transformer ») et *fu* (« bonheur, richesse, abondance »). La chauve-souris figure donc dans toutes les formes possibles, de la plus figurative à la plus abstraite, sur un très grand nombre d'objets décoratifs. C'était, pour les taoïstes, un symbole de longévité car elle vit dans les grottes qui sont le passage vers le domaine des Immortels, se tient la tête en bas comme pour « nourrir le

Bol, porcelaine émaillée, règne de Qianlong (1736-1796) à motif de chauve-souris.

principe vital », un exercice taoïste connu de « fortification du cerveau », enfin, selon la légende elle se nourrirait de stalactites. Réputée pour ses vertus aphrodisiaques, la chauve-souris était utilisée dans certaines drogues, en particulier ses excréments brunâtres poétiquement appelés le « sable d'escarboucle » *(yemingsha)*. En groupe de trois, ces petits mamifères symbolisent les trois bonheurs : Bonheur, Richesse et Longévité. Par groupe de cinq, entourant le plus souvent le caractère stylisé de la longévité *(shou)*, elles expriment les cinq bonheurs auxquels aspire tout chinois : la Longévité, la Richesse, la Santé, la Vertu, la Mort naturelle. La chauve-souris est donc l'attribut habituel des divinités comme Shouxinglao ou de Zhong Kui, le féroce chasseur de démons.

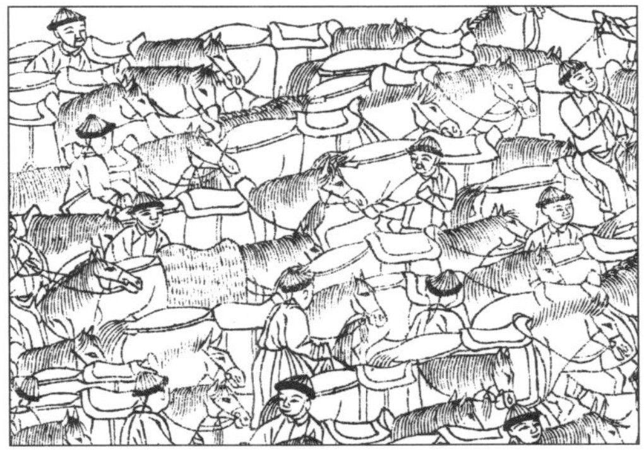

Le cheval *(ma)*, emblème de sagesse, d'endurance et de vitesse, comme dans beaucoup d'autres civilisations, était la monture de personnages importants (empereurs, généraux ou Immortels). Les légendes anciennes le font naître de l'eau ; dans celle des « Huit chevaux du roi Mu », ces extraordinaires animaux parcoururent des milliers de *li* en un temps record pour conduire leur maître vers la Reine Mère d'Occident (voir p. 86). On a depuis immortalisé ces fabuleux coursiers, chacun dans une pose différente, soit en peinture soit dans la porcelaine, le jade ou l'ivoire. Nombreux sont les artistes que le cheval a inspirés. Parmi les précurseurs, on peut citer Xie Taowei dès le IVe siècle, Han Kan, Cao Pa sous les Tang et Chao Mengfu sous les Yuan. Les poteries vernissées « trois couleurs » *(san cai)* de l'époque Tang restent un bel hommage des artisans à ce noble animal, symbole du *yang*. Un culte particulier était réservé au Roi-Cheval *(ma wang)* qui figurait sur les papiers fétiches avec le Roi-Bœuf. Le cheval était aussi associé à la promotion. En effet, celui qui venait de réussir aux examens impériaux se dépêchait d'en avertir sa famille par un courrier à cheval. Ainsi est né le proverbe : *ma dao, sheng gong* (« quand le cheval arrive, le succès est obtenu »). Son image est donc fréquemment liée aux lettrés et aux études. Les répétiteurs qui préparaient les candidats aux examens impériaux étaient d'ailleurs surnommés « chevaux » et leurs salles d'études « écuries »...

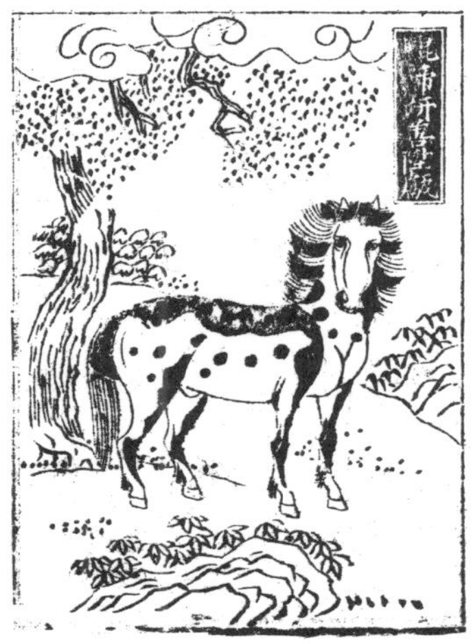

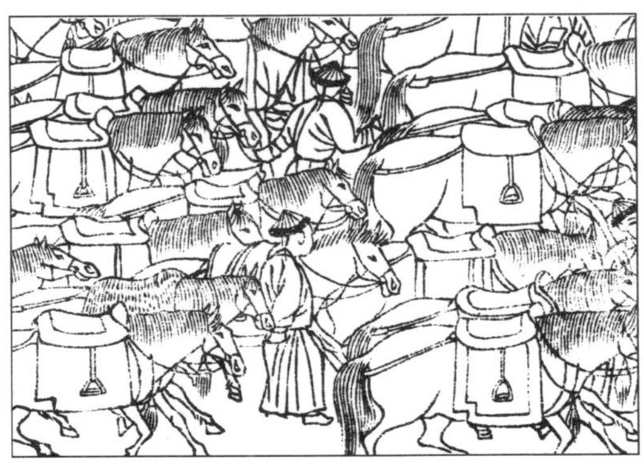

En haut et en bas, palefreniers conduisant des chevaux au fleuve (gravure extraite de Dondxijiangji*) ; au centre, cheval pommelé (gravure du dictionnaire* Ying Songchao huitu erya, *période Song).*

Le chien *(gou)* est d'un symbolisme ambivalent. Domestiqué depuis l'âge néolithique, gardien vigilant des hommes et des défunts, on trouva dans les tombes anciennes des statues vernissées de molosses ou mastiffs du Tibet dressés sur leurs pattes. Le chien pouvait être le compagnon des Immortels. Un des très anciens mythes se rapporte au « Chien Céleste » qui dévorait les astres, d'où l'expression lors des éclipses : « le Chien Céleste a mordu la lune » *(tiangou yao yueliang)*. Plus tard, on lui attribua la réputation de dévorer les enfants. De nombreuses images, vénérées par les femmes, montrent l'Immortel Zhang mettant en fuite le Chien Céleste en tirant des flèches de bois de pêcher dans sa direction. Pendant longtemps enfin, on utilisa comme offrandes des « chiens de paille » qui étaient piétinés puis brûlés pendant certaines cérémonies.

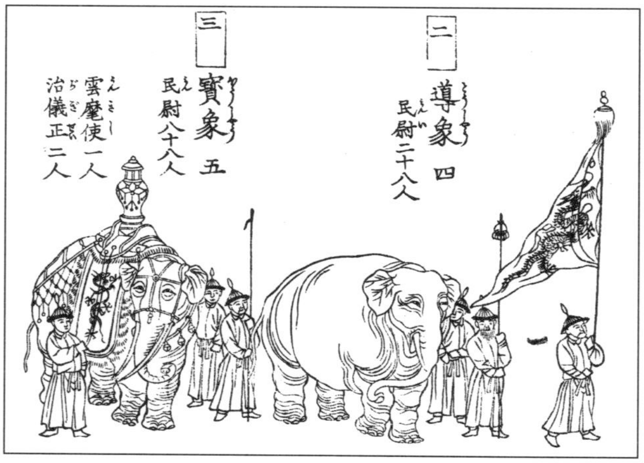

L'éléphant *(xiang)* a sans doute existé en Chine il y a bien longtemps dans le sud et le centre du pays. Il fut réintroduit en Chine parmi les cadeaux offerts à l'empereur par ses vassaux du sud, le Vietnam et la Birmanie. Des éléphants ont été décrits participant à certaines grandes cérémonies impériales dans la capitale et à quelques batailles héroïques. Toutefois son image reste étroitement associée au bouddhisme : un des disciples de Sâkyamuni était représenté par un éléphant blanc, symbole de bonté et de connaissance. L'éléphant était le symbole de la stabilité du pouvoir (sans doute par homophonie avec *taiping you xiang,* littéralement « présages de grande paix ». Il figurait à ce titre parmi les objets décoratifs proches du trône.

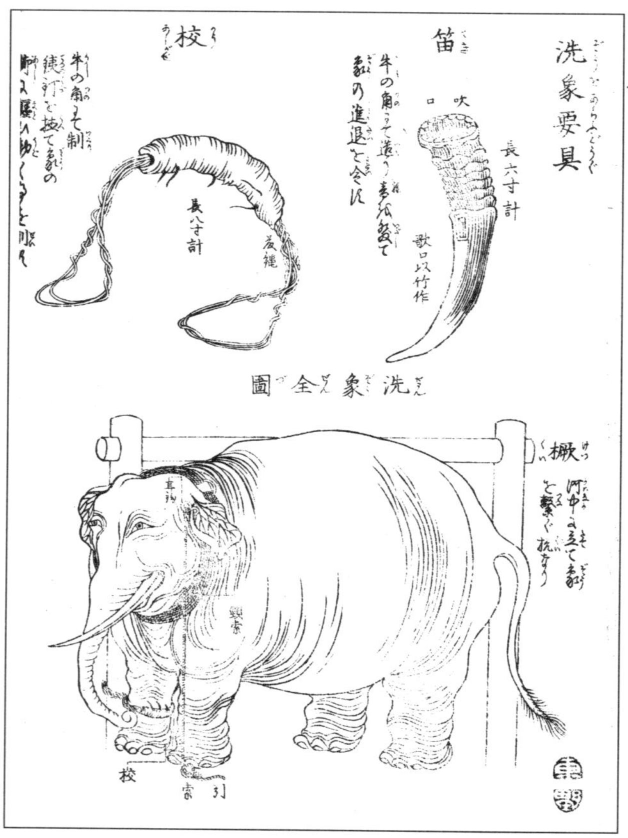

Le lièvre *(tuzi)* se retrouve dans de nombreuses légendes du monde entier associé à la lune. La tradition la plus ancienne viendrait de l'Inde : au Bouddha qui avait faim, le lièvre offrit sa chair et, en manière de récompense, le saint homme dessina son image sur la lune. Les Chinois ont hérité de cette vieille légende : quand il atteint l'âge de mille ans, le lièvre devient blanc (on le nomme alors « lièvre de jade », *yutu*), il habite dans la lune et on le voit, préparant dans un mortier, à l'ombre d'un figuier, le célèbre élixir d'immortalité. Les forgerons chinois recherchaient son fiel pour tremper leurs lames d'acier ou pour fabriquer des miroirs magiques. Le lièvre fournissait le meilleur poil pour les pinceaux, à condition de le prendre à l'automne, quand il était le plus doux…

En haut, l'ordonnancement d'une procession impériale ; en bas, page du manuel de soins pour le bain des éléphants (extrait de l'encyclopédie Tangtu mingsheng tuhui).

La licorne, dans la classification traditionnelle, était le troisième des « Quatre animaux divins » *(si ling)* et le souverain des « animaux à poil ». Tout en distinguant le mâle *(qi)* de la femelle *(lin),* on parlait d'une manière générale de *qilin.* C'était un animal mythique qui empruntait au cerf la forme de son corps, ses pattes et ses sabots, au dragon sa tête, les écailles de son dos, sa ou ses cornes et au lion sa crinière et sa queue en panache. Le son de sa voix était aussi harmonieux que « le son d'une cloche de monastère ». Animal particulièrement respectueux des autres, la licorne évitait de fouler l'herbe en se déplaçant, n'écrasait aucun insecte et ne se nourrissait pas de plantes vivantes. Avec sa corne, elle purifiait l'eau des sources et des rivières. Depuis on attribue à la corne des vertus d'antidote. Son intelligence particulière lui permettait de n'être jamais capturée et les animaux la reconnaissaient comme leur maître. Comme pour le phénix, ses rares apparitions sur terre annonçaient d'heureux présages. C'était notamment le signe d'un bon gouvernement ou d'une naissance prestigieuse. Une *qilin* aurait apporté à l'empereur Huangdi un livre des doctrines sacrées. Pour certains auteurs, la mère de Confucius aurait reçu avant la naissance de l'enfant la visite de cet extraordinaire messager, pour d'autres, elle aurait marché dans les pas invisibles d'une licorne. Le symbole de « la licorne à l'enfant » est traditionnel dans les images de Nouvel An, il exprime le souhait d'avoir des enfants doués. La licorne est symbole de succès scolaires.

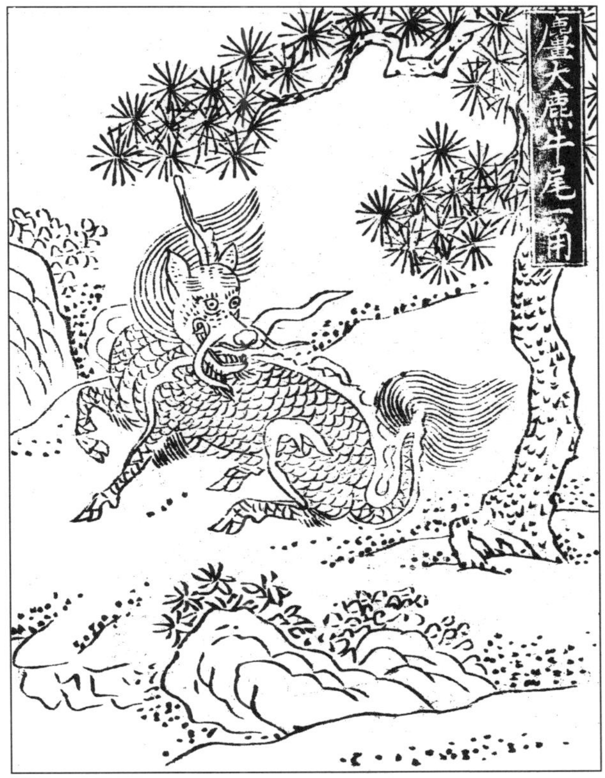

Le lion *(shizi)* est un motif très répandu dans tous les pays où le bouddhisme est présent. En effet, c'est avec l'introduction de cette religion en Chine qu'apparaît vers le IVe siècle l'image de cet animal encore inconnu. Il était la monture de Manjusri (*Wenshu* en chinois), un des dix-huit disciples de Sâkyamuni dont la principale fonction était de chasser l'ignorance. Le lion qui le portait acquit alors les qualités de son maître : sagesse et bravoure. À cet effet, on lui assigna la garde des portes de temples. Au XXe siècle encore, à l'occasion des cérémonies organisées pour appeler la pluie, dans la province du Shaanxi, sept petites filles procèdent trois fois par jour pendant une semaine au toilettage des petits lions de pierre qui gardent l'autel de la divinité. Les arts mineurs ont fait usage de ce motif dans une grande variété de matériaux (or, argent, bronze, porcelaine, pierre) et les artisans ont employé la tête de lion tenant un anneau dans sa gueule comme heurtoir de porte, poignée de tiroir, de

Licorne ou unicorne, qilin *(gravure du dictionnaire* Ying Songchao huitu erya*).*

vase et de flacon de tabac à priser. Inconnu en Chine, il faut attendre la dynastie des Song pour que quelques exemplaires vivants de lions parviennent dans les ménageries impériales. Avant cette date, les sculpteurs ont donc laissé aller leur imagination sur le sujet. Avec leurs yeux protubérants et féroces, une queue fournie, une crinière bouclée et quelquefois une corne sur le front, les lions de pierre *(shizi)* ou de bronze *(tongzi)* gardiens des édifices publics, ont sans doute eu pour modèle les chiens tibétains, connus sous le nom de « chiens-lions » *(shizi gou)* que les lamas avaient ramenés de leur pays d'origine. Devenu un animal légendaire qui écarte les génies malfaisants, il est souvent représenté (en sculpture tout au moins) par paire : le mâle, à l'est, jouant avec une balle, la femelle à l'ouest avec un lionceau sous sa patte. On disait que c'est par les pattes que la lionne allaitait son petit. Toucher ses pattes portait donc bonheur. Quant à la boule, elle aurait été, à l'origine un œuf de lion, et jouer avec le faisait éclore… Cet objet rond et sacré, quelquefois entouré de flammes, est semblable à celui que poursuit le dragon : c'est le « joyau de l'omnipotence », la « perle lumineuse », « l'essence de la vie » *(baozhu)*. Elle est souvent représentée comme une boule creuse décorée. C'est un symbole bouddhique de pureté qui figure parmi les « Huit Objets Précieux ». La première référence de lions de pierre gardant les entrées remonterait au IIe siècle av. J.-C. mais ce n'est que sous les Tang et les Song que leur usage se répandit, à telle enseigne que les empereurs durent réglementer précisément la taille et la matière de ces statues en fonction du rang de leur propriétaire.

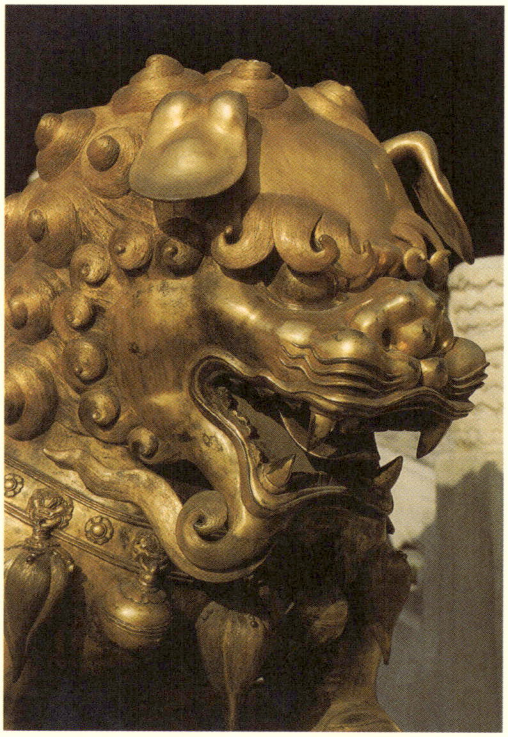

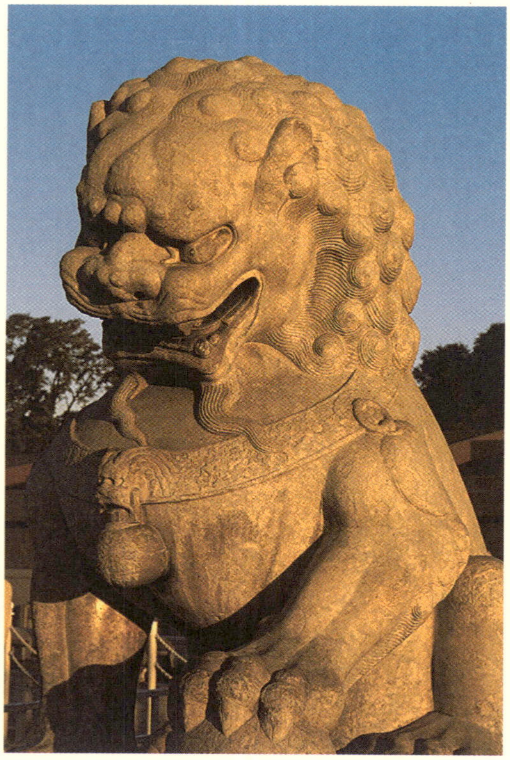

Le porc *(zhu)* et le sanglier *(yezhu)* : le premier a bien pauvre réputation, sa goinfrerie et son allure peu esthétique n'ont guère inspiré les peintres ou les poètes. Il est néanmoins resté symbole d'abondance, de prospérité et de réussite aux concours. C'est un motif traditionnel en papier découpé (voir p. 32) que l'on affiche sur les fenêtres pour une naissance. C'est aussi l'emblème de la grossièreté et de la luxure personnalisé dans *Le Voyage en Occident* par Zhubajie (littéralement, « le Cochon aux Huit Péchés »). Le sanglier est devenu l'emblème du courage et de la réussite et a souvent figuré sur les armoiries ou les oriflammes des militaires.

Le rat *(shu)*: ses qualités d'intelligence lui ont valu la première place du cycle zodiacal chinois. Ses aptitudes à découvrir et à s'approprier le bien d'autrui en ont fait un symbole de prospérité mais aussi de cupidité. La présence d'un gros rat dans un magasin était tout de même signe de richesse, on l'appelait le « rat précieux » *(jin shu)* et à ce titre personne ne devait lui faire de mal. Le rat des champs était d'ailleurs vénéré comme le Jeune Dieu des Greniers avec le hérisson car ces animaux prévoyants font des provisions pour l'hiver. Le 10e jour de la 1re lune était la nuit du « mariage des rats » au cours de laquelle on leur laissait de minuscules offrandes sur le sol. Associé à l'idée de fécondité, le thème folklorique du « Rat qui marie sa fille » est souvent repris sur les estampes populaires et les papiers découpés. À une époque plus récente, son image s'est ternie et depuis les fameuses campagnes de dératisation lancées par le président Mao (1950), il est toujours perçu dans les villes comme un animal nuisible.

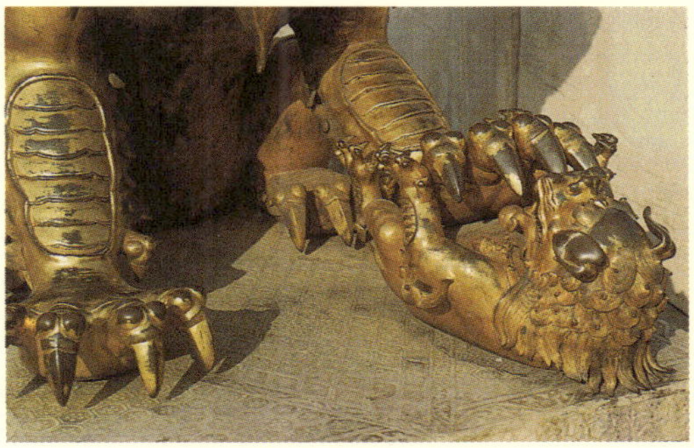

Le renard *(hu)* était connu comme un animal capable de vivre très vieux parce qu'il habitait dans des terriers d'où il tirait une énergie régénératrice. On lui attribuait aussi des métamorphoses en démon: après cinquante ans, transformé en femme ou à cent ans en belle jeune fille, il ensorcelait les hommes par ses tours de magie. Arrivé à mille ans d'âge, il devenait alors le « Renard éternel » et on le reconnaissait à ses neuf queues *(jiuwei hu)*. Les renards étaient aussi considérés comme les esprits des morts car ils faisaient leur trou près des tombes. Imprévisibles dans leurs réactions vis-à-vis des humains, il fallait donc se concilier leurs bonnes grâces en leur offrant des sacrifices sur de petits autels placés au bord des chemins.

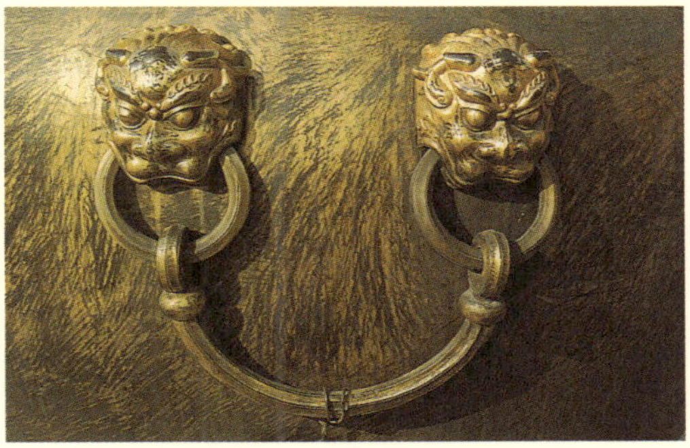

Le rhinocéros *(xiniu)* qui existait jusqu'au XVIe siècle dans le Yunnan, apparaît rarement comme élément décoratif. Sa corne, en revanche, est citée parmi les Huit précieux. On racontait qu'elle avait le pouvoir de détecter les poisons, aussi, dès le IVe siècle av. J.-C., faisait-on des coupes pour boire et pour manger dans cette matière. C'est à Zhangzhou (Fujian) où l'on sculptait déjà l'ivoire que l'on fabriquait des objets décoratifs, des breloques et des boucles de ceinture, tous considérés comme des talismans sans doute à cause de l'homophonie avec *xi* (joie, bonheur). Considérée encore comme un antidote, la poudre de corne de rhinocéros est classée dans la pharmacopée chinoise comme médicament pour l'estomac, le foie et le cœur.

Page de gauche, en haut, lion de bronze, mâle (Cité Interdite), en bas, lion de pierre, mâle; ci-dessus, en haut, détail de la patte de lionne sur son lionceau, en bas, anneaux d'un chaudron de bronze destiné à recueillir l'eau pour éteindre les incendies.

Le singe *(hou)* symbole d'agilité, d'agitation, de ruse et d'intelligence, est devenu, sans doute sous l'influence des croyances tibétaines ou des légendes

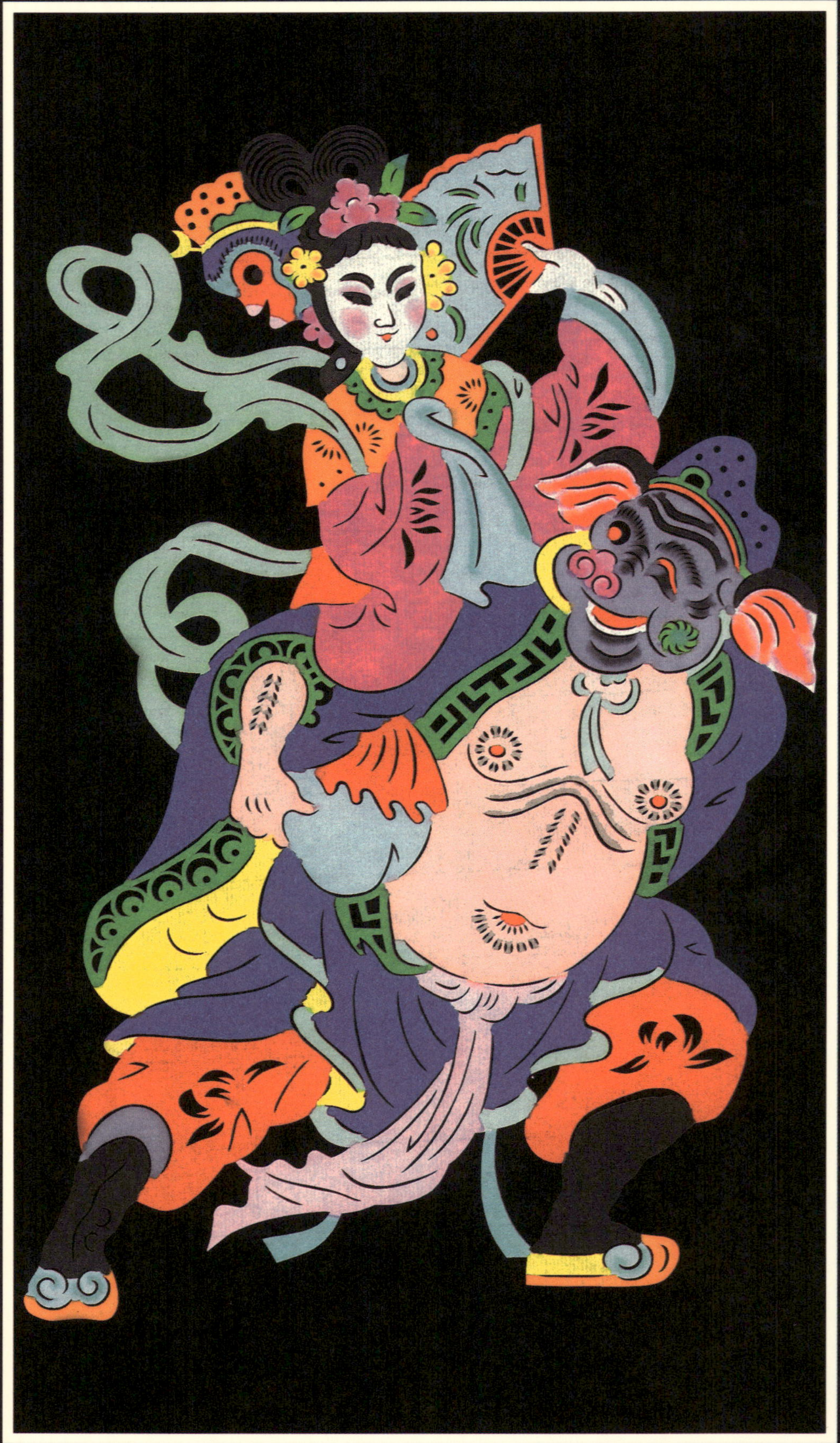

Le «Cochon aux Huit péchés», un des personnages du **Voyage en Occident** *(papier découpé).*

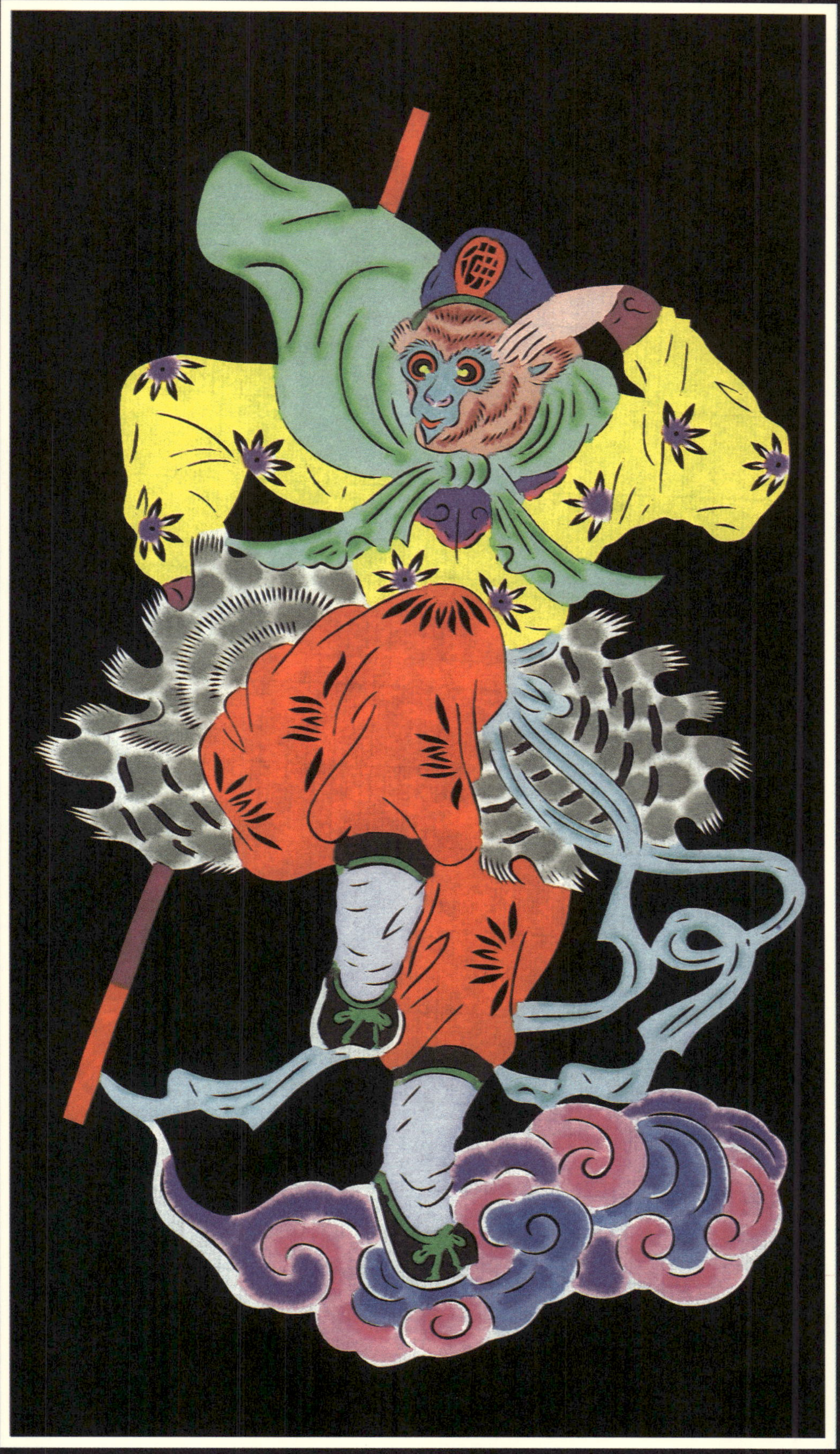

Le singe Sun Wukong, un des héros du* Voyage en Occident *(papier découpé).

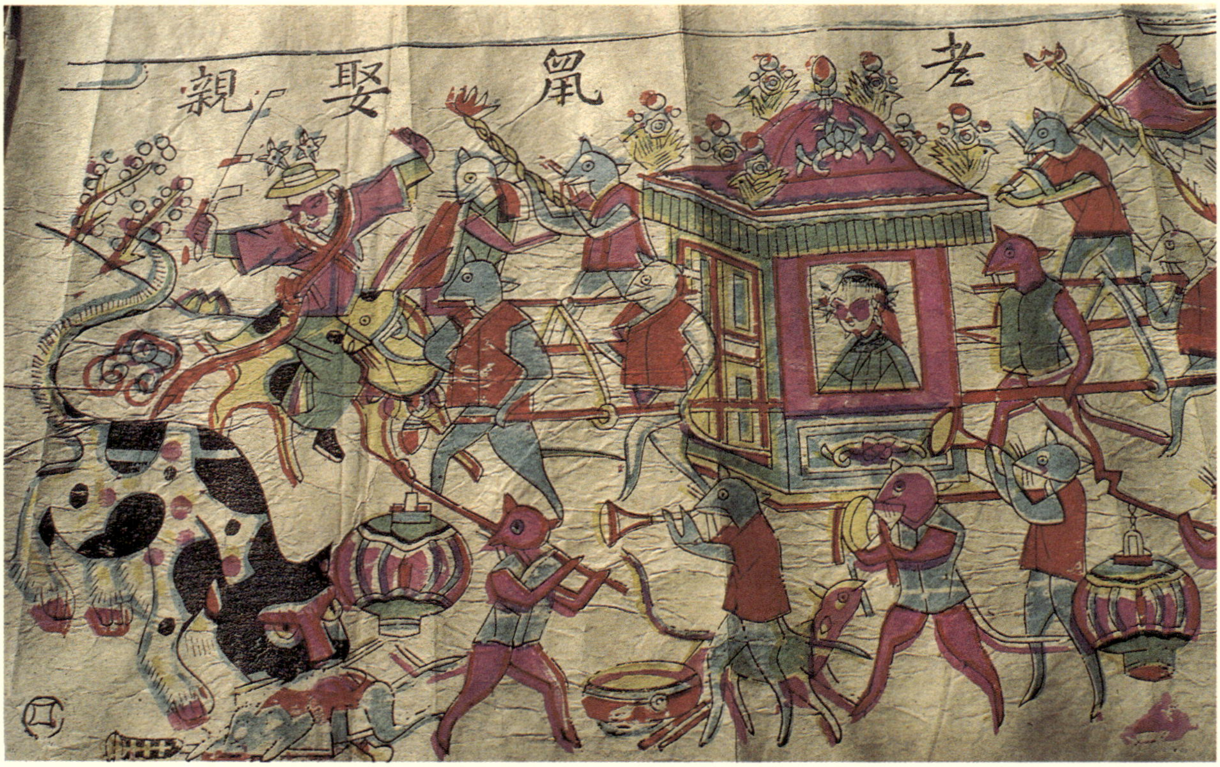

indiennes, une divinité que l'on pouvait implorer pour lui demander du secours. Les taoïstes et les bouddhistes lui ont consacré des autels. Le singe chinois est en réalité un sage qui cache son jeu sous une apparence ridicule. Sous le nom de Sun Wukong, il est un des héros principal d'un roman du XVIe siècle, *Le Voyage en Occident (Xiyouji)* qui relate les aventures du moine Xuanzang parti en Inde de 629 à 645 à la recherche des écritures sacrées, accompagné d'animaux aux pouvoirs surnaturels. Le thème de ce singe fabuleux a été repris au théâtre, dans les peintures ou les papiers découpés. Il participe à des voyages extraordinaires, des métamorphoses et des combats contre les démons. L'homophone de son nom *(sun)* signifie singe, macaque et *wukong* est une expression bouddhiste traduisible par « absence et vide ».

Le tigre *(hu)* symbolise la puissance et la férocité. C'est un animal chasseur, il est donc l'emblème des soldats qui revêtaient un costume jaune à rayures pour aller au combat. Il figurait sur leurs armes, leurs uniformes (officier de 4e classe), sur les bannières des armées en marche (tigre blanc à l'ouest, tigre noir au nord). Ce n'est qu'à l'âge de cinq cents ans, dit la légende, qu'il devenait blanc. Au Yunnan il est considéré comme un ancêtre tout comme chez les populations himalayennes. Les « cinq tigres » *(wu hu),* les gardiens des quatre points cardinaux et du centre, était le nom attribué à de valeureux soldats. Les zébrures de son pelage dessinent sur son front le caractère « roi » *(wang)* et le désignent comme le roi des animaux à fourrure des montagnes. Il était la monture de divinités, chasseurs de démons ou d'Immortels et

Ci-dessus, le « mariage de la fille du Rat », image populaire (collection Wang Shucun) ; page de droite, tigre portant au front la marque royale wang (talisman populaire, collection Wang Shucun).

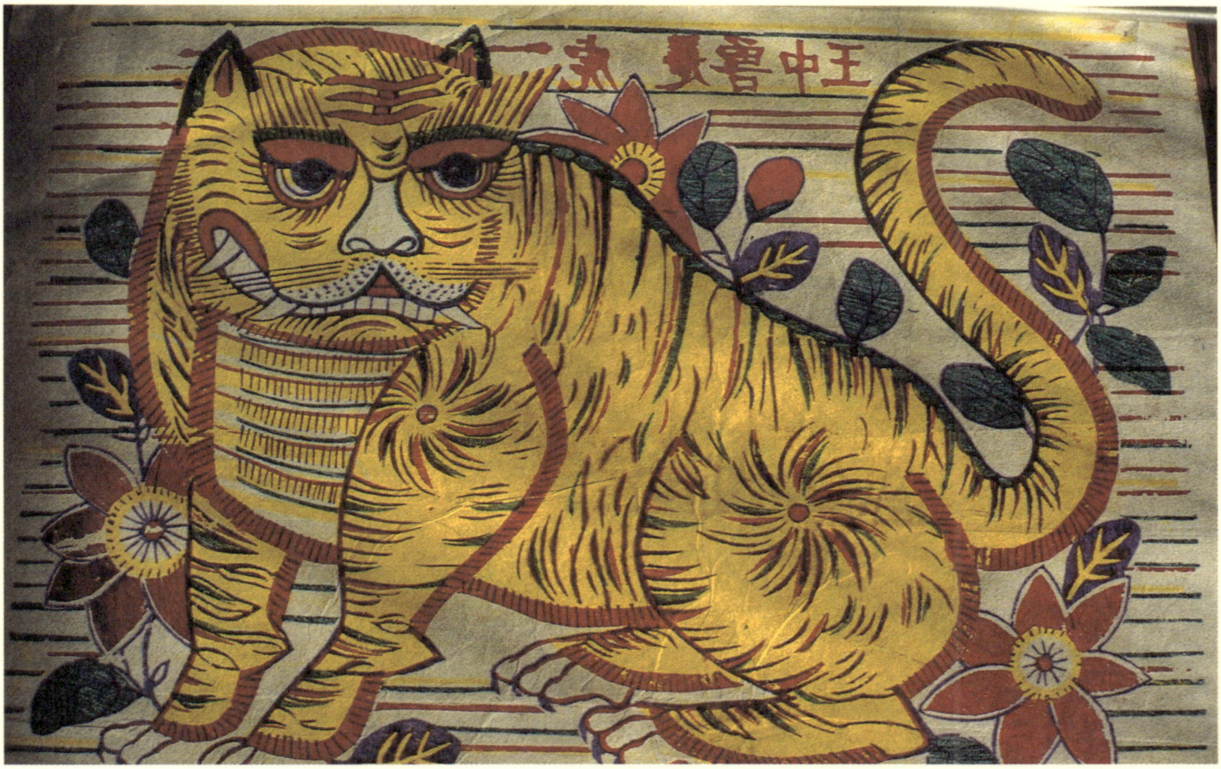

vénéré même dans les tripots où il était l'une des montures du Dieu de la richesse avec des vases remplis de pièces d'or. Pour attirer la chance, on collait même son effigie sous les tables de jeux. Le tigre était aussi un puissant démonifuge, on le représentait souvent sur les estampes populaires écrasant les Cinq (animaux) venimeux. On en faisait encore des guirlandes de tissu découpé qui étaient accrochées dans le dos des enfants. Pour certaines fêtes, ceux-ci revêtaient des bonnets en forme de tête de tigre, des costumes à larges rayures et même des pantoufles à son image. Sa fête, qui avait lieu au printemps donnait l'occasion, dans le sud, d'accrocher des tigres de bambou et de papier coloré dans la maison. Les amulettes faites de peau, de griffes, de poils ou de dents de tigre étaient portées pour lutter contre les peurs, les maladies ou le feu. La pharmacopée chinoise fait encore usage des os de tigre pilés en poudre et de sa graisse pour certains onguents, en dépit des réglementations pour protéger cette espèce en danger.

Il n'est pas rare de trouver sur certains objets de bronze très anciens (deuxième millénaire) les masques du *taotie* (personnage mythique grimaçant) qui rappellent plutôt une tête de tigre stylisée ou éventuellement de dragon.

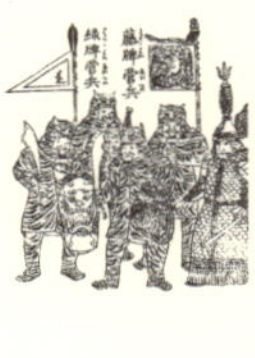

Les animaux à plume

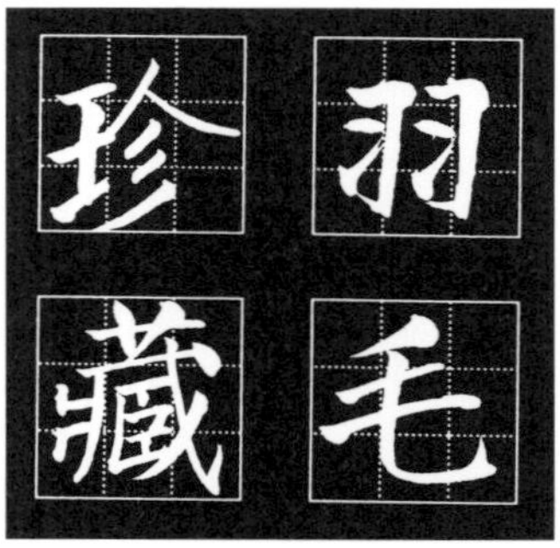

yumao zhencang, littéralement, « précieuses collection de plumes ».

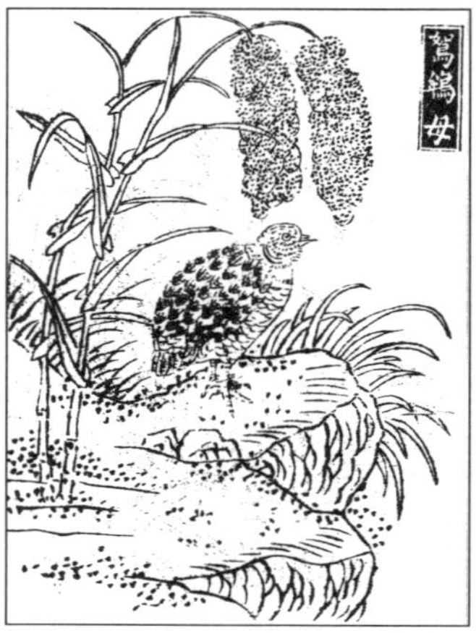

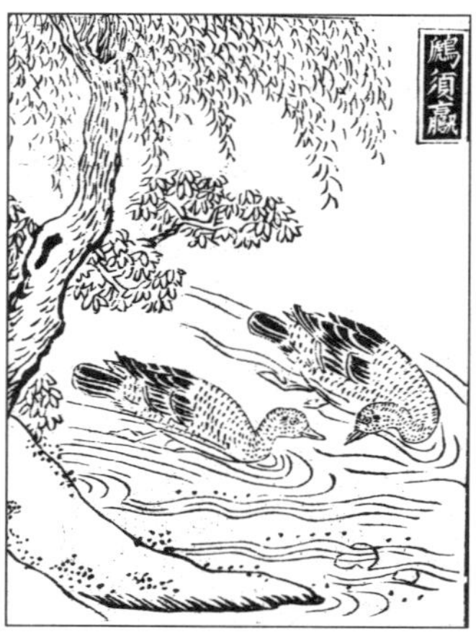

En haut, caille, en bas, canards sous un saule (gravures extraites du dictionnaire Ying Songchao huitu erya*).*

L'aigle *(aquila chrysaetus daphanae),* le milan, le faucon sont communément désignés en Chine sous le nom générique de *ying.* Ils sont symboles de courage (*ying* est homophone de « bravoure et talent éminent »). L'aigle est souvent représenté solitaire sur un pin ou sur un rocher. À l'époque féodale, il figurait comme un totem sur les bannières de certains chefs et il est resté, avec le faucon, un motif traditionnel pour les cerfs-volants. Selon Marco Polo, les Mongols pratiquaient déjà la chasse au faucon et Kubilay Khan utilisait par milliers des oiseaux de proie dans ses expéditions. Les empereurs Kangxi et Qianlong aimaient entraîner leurs soldats dans des chasses d'automne près de leur résidence d'été (Jehol) au delà de la Grande Muraille. L'aigle était enfin considéré comme chasseur de démons ; on caressait le visage des enfants avec ses plumes pour les protéger des maladies, en particulier de la variole.

La caille *(coturnix communis)* personnifie la tendresse, le mariage heureux. On lui attribuait volontiers des qualités de pugnacité car elle était, comme les coqs ou les grillons, engagée dans des combats où les paris allaient bon train. Toutefois, son plumage tacheté semblable à un habit en loques en faisait aussi un symbole de pauvreté et de modestie. Son nom *(anchun)* évoque la paix *(an).* Selon les croyances de la Chine ancienne, on disait qu'elle réapparaissait à la belle saison après s'être transformée l'hiver en mulot. Compte tenu de toutes ces vertus, les œufs de caille étaient utilisés en médecine traditionnelle pour calmer les nerfs et enrayer les hémorragies.

Le canard *(anas domestica),* et surtout le canard mandarin *(anas galericulata),* représentaient l'union et la fidélité conjugale. En effet, ils étaient toujours représentés nageant deux par deux, l'un contre l'autre. Le canard tire sans doute son nom chinois de son cri rauque *(ya).* Le canard mandarin *(yuan yang)* doit son titre à un plumage particulièrement coloré. C'est un motif très fréquent que l'on retrouve dans les papiers découpés et les images populaires. On le peint souvent avec une tige de lotus *(lian)* enroulée autour du cou, car *lian* est homophone de «joindre, unir». Des tableaux ou des sculptures de canards étaient souvent placés dans les chambres nuptiales. À l'époque des Qing, on était friand de publications romanesques à l'eau de rose que l'on appelait ironiquement la «littérature canards mandarins et papillons». La chair du canard et la langue, auxquelles on prête d'innombrables qualités curatives, étaient souvent recommandées pour traiter les déficiences sexuelles.

La colombe ou la tourterelle *(streptopelia chinensis chinensis)* et le pigeon (famille des *columbæ*) sont en Chine des symboles de longue vie. Ils ornaient les cadeaux faits aux vieillards, on disait que la chair de la colombe *(banqiu)* était un puissant stimulant et facilitait la digestion. Il fallait aussi manger des œufs de pigeon pour se prémunir contre la variole. Connus pour leurs mœurs amoureuses, ces oiseaux étaient associés à la fidélité conjugale, à la loyauté, à l'honnêteté et à la piété filiale. La «déesse donneuse d'enfants» (Sonzi Niangniang) portait une colombe dans sa coiffe. L'extraordinaire endurance du pigeon *(ge)* et son intelligence en ont fait des messagers fidèles dans l'ancien temps. Sans doute, est-ce pour effrayer les oiseaux de proie que les marchands prirent l'habitude d'attacher de petits sifflets dans les plumes des pigeons voyageurs. Cette tradition se poursuit encore et ce sont de véritables concerts que donnent leurs propriétaires, certains jours de fête, pour le seul plaisir de l'ouïe.

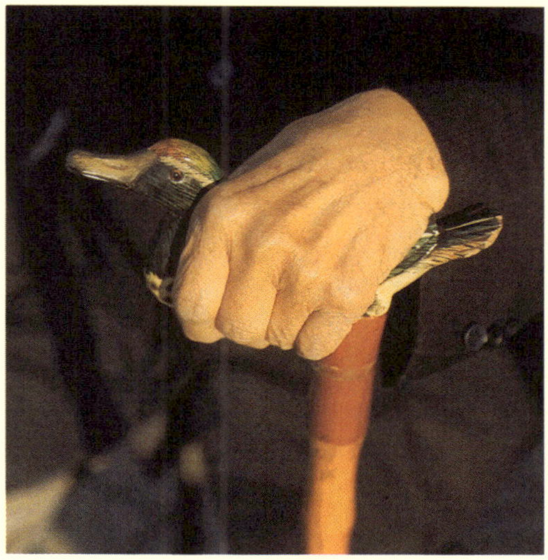

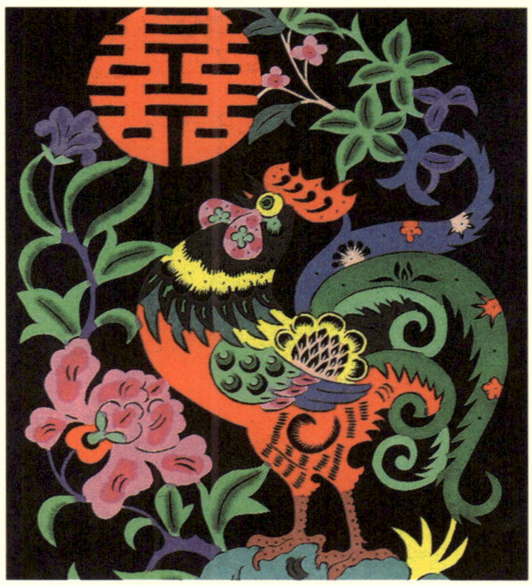

Le coq *(gallus domesticus)* existe en Chine depuis au moins 1400 av. J.-C. Son nom *(ji)*, homophone de l'expression «pratiquer la divination», et surtout du qualificatif «heureux, bon augure», en fait un animal important de l'astrologie et de la nécromancie. Symbole du *yang* (chaleur et vie), le premier réveillé, il chasse par son chant les mauvais esprits de la nuit. Les Chinois l'appelaient d'ailleurs «l'oiseau divin aux cinq talents»: sa crête était l'expression de l'esprit littéraire, ses ergots le désignaient comme un guerrier, il était courageux au combat (les combats de coqs existent depuis cinq cents ans), attentionné avec les siens, fiable pour annoncer l'heure (et même les crues). Les œufs marqués de signes sur la coquille, puis bouillis, servaient à la divination, tout comme les bâtonnets

En haut, poignée de canne en forme de canard, en bas, coq symbolique (papier découpé).

d'os de poulet. Pour se protéger des épidémies ou des incendies, on faisait le sacrifice d'un coq, rouge ou blanc, et on accrochait sa tête au toit ou à la porte. Ce rituel a peu à peu été remplacé par des papiers découpés que l'on colle sur les vitres ou des images fétiches sur les murs. On sacrifiait aussi un coq pour s'assurer d'une bonne récolte. Enfin, lors des funérailles, un coq blanc était déposé sur le cercueil pour éloigner les mauvais esprits. Lors des mariages, on plaçait deux petites effigies de coq en sucre sur l'autel des ancêtres. Principal ennemi des « cinq venimeux », on le nommait le « petit roi des serpents ». Moins populaire qu'au Japon où il était vénéré par les prêtres shintoïstes, le coq en Chine est souvent représenté avec des pivoines, des papillons et des arbres en fleurs.

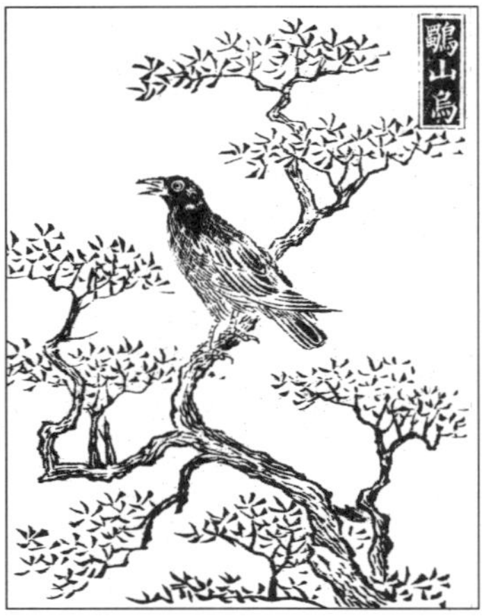

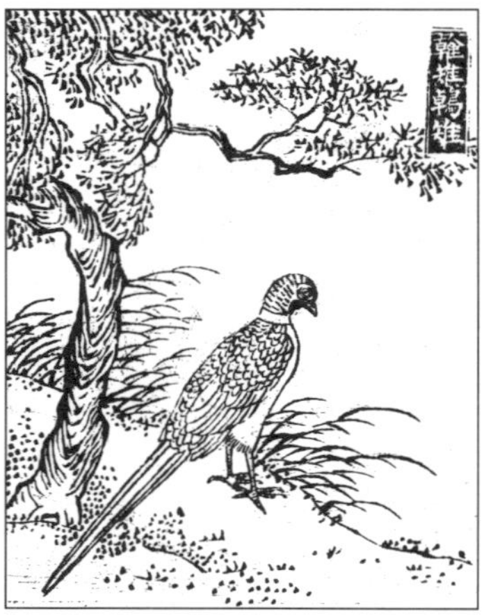

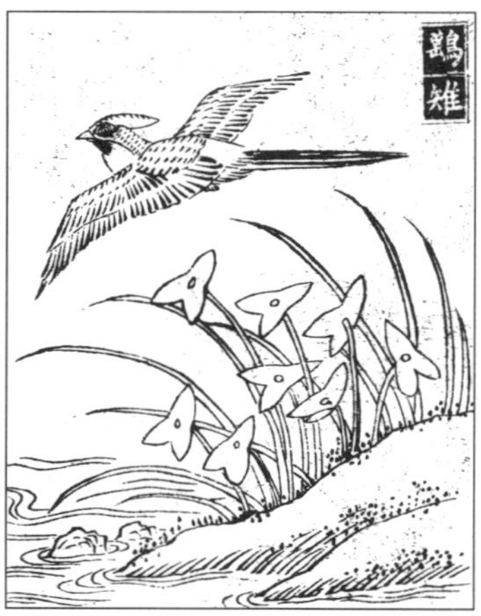

De haut en bas, corbeau et faisans (gravures extraites du dictionnaire Ying Songchao huitu erya*).*

Le corbeau (*corvus*) tire sans doute son nom *(wuya)* du croassement qui est homophone de « mordre » et « malicieux ». Il était donc perçu comme un animal de mauvais présage, surtout à la fin de la nuit où il annonçait une mort. Mais il existait aussi un dicton qui ajoutait : « voix rauque mais bon cœur ». Un corbeau venant du sud dans l'après-midi annonçait un cadeau ou un visiteur ; en soirée, c'était la pluie et le vent. On racontait qu'ayant atteint l'âge adulte, le corbeau retournait nourrir ses vieux parents, d'où le vieux dicton : *wuya fan bu.* En Chine, il était intimement lié au soleil, comme le dit un ancien poème : « l'esprit du soleil est dans un corbeau à trois pattes ». Le chiffre trois est emblème de *yang,* dont le soleil est l'essence suprême. Le corbeau à trois pattes, nommé aussi *yangwu* (« corbeau de la lumière » ou « corbeau rouge ») fut le symbole héraldique de la dynastie des Zhou (1100 av. J.C.). L'intelligence de cet oiseau était connue, aussi lui attribuait-on des pouvoirs magiques et les devins l'utilisèrent tout comme les charlatans qui proposaient des potions de cervelle de corbeau pour atteindre un grand âge ou d'œil de corbeau pour améliorer la vue… Un proverbe rappelant les origines modestes d'un personnage devenu célèbre disait que « dans un nid de corbeau était né un phénix » *(ya chao sheng feng).* En peinture, le corbeau est souvent représenté (en noir) à côté du héron (blanc) dans la tradition d'opposition du *yin* et du *yang.*

Le faisan (famille des *phasianidae*) comprend de nombreuses variétés en Chine. Son nom *(zhi)* contient le radical de la flèche car son vol peut être comparé à la trajectoire d'une flèche. C'est un animal à double symbolique : par son cri, il annonce le tonnerre qui est le prélude aux pluies du printemps, c'est l'éveil du *yang* ; quant à sa danse nuptiale, elle a inspiré les fêtes du printemps où, comme les faisanes, les jeunes filles appelaient les jeunes gens à des danses rituelles. L'usage des longues plumes de sa queue s'est d'ailleurs perpétué au théâtre où les immenses plumes (jusqu'à deux mètres de long) du « faisan de Reeves » ou « faisan vénéré » font partie de la coiffe traditionnelle des acteurs interprétant les rôles de guerriers ou d'aventuriers. À la cour des Ming, dans les carrés brodés des robes de cérémonie, apparaissaient le « faisan doré » *(chrysolophus pictus)* pour désigner les hauts fonctionnaires de 2e classe, et le «faisan argenté» *(gennaeus nychtemerus)* pour ceux de la 5e classe. Le « faisan Argus » a sans nul doute été le prototype du mythique phénix. Le faisan fait partie du groupe des « animaux fleuris » décrits par les commentateurs de l'époque Song. Il figura sur les robes d'apparat des impératrices. L'éventail de cérémonie ou *flabellum (zhangshan),* insigne de l'impératrice porté dans les cortèges, était fait de plumes de faisan ou de paon.

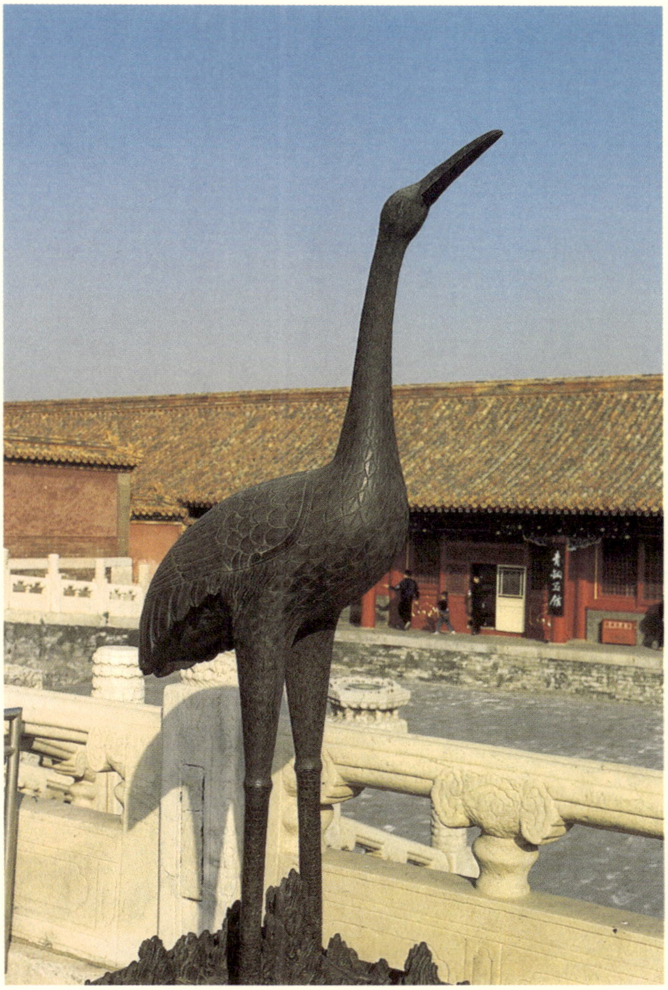

La grue (*megalornis japonensis* ou grue de Mandchourie) était à la fois la monture habituelle des Immortels et un symbole de longue vie. Elle était donc représentée en jaune, tenant dans son bec le champignon *lingzhi*, ou perchée sur un pin (lui-même symbole d'immortalité). Il était bienséant, en s'adressant à un vieillard, de lui souhaiter une « longévité de grue » *(he shou).* La littérature abonde d'histoires de sages, d'empereurs, de lettrés qui se plaisaient en sa compagnie ou même qui se transformaient en cet extraordinaire oiseau. À l'âge de six cents ans, la grue ne se nourrissait plus que d'eau et, à mille ans, son plumage blanc devenait tout noir. Par ailleurs, son nom chinois est homophone de *he* qui signifie « concorde, harmonie, paix ». C'était donc un motif très fréquent des artistes peintres ou des brodeuses. Les vieillards affectionnaient particulièrement les vêtements porteurs de ce symbole. Dans certaines cérémonies funéraires anciennes, on plaçait sur le cercueil une grue aux ailes déployées pour conduire l'âme du défunt vers le paradis des Immortels. Son image était tellement précieuse qu'elle fut l'emblème arboré sur les robes officielles des mandarins civils de première classe pendant plusieurs siècles.

Grue en bronze (Cité Interdite).

Le hibou (famille des *strigidæ*) est appelé en chinois « le rapace à tête de chat » *(maotouying)* ou « le chat de la nuit » *(yemaozi)* et, dans la langue du Hebei, d'une manière plus explicite : « l'oiseau qui vous emporte rapidement » *(kuaikangniao)*. Cet oiseau nocturne, comme en Europe, est annonciateur de mort. Son cri strident faisait même dire aux vieilles femmes que « l'on entend creuser les tombes ». On lui attribuait aussi la détestable réputation de dévorer ses parents. Un enfant né le 5e jour du 5e mois lunaire, c'est-à-dire le jour du hibou, avait de fortes chances de tuer son père compte tenu des mœurs parricides attribuées à cet oiseau de nuit. Autant de critères suffisants pour en faire un animal redouté et donc pourchassé pendant des années. Après le supplice, les têtes des condamnés étaient en général exposées au public sur un pal, on les appelait « têtes de hiboux ». Faut-il voir dans cette expression populaire le peu de cas que l'on faisait de ces pauvres rapaces ? Comme il apparaissait à l'été, à l'époque des orages, le hibou fut identifié à la foudre et aux forgerons, maîtres du feu. C'était, croyait-on, à cette période que l'on fabriquait les meilleures épées et les miroirs magiques.

L'hirondelle (*hirundo rustica guturalis ; yan*) aurait donné son nom à Pékin qui s'appelait autrefois Yanjing (la « capitale aux hirondelles ») tant elles étaient nombreuses à nicher sous les toits des maisons et des bâtiments publics, à moins que ce soit une évocation de la capitale de l'ancien royaume de Yan, l'un des Royaumes Combattants. On se réjouissait de voir les hirondelles construire un nid sous le toit de la maison. Dans la langue populaire, « les hirondelles viennent offrir leurs félicitations » *(yan he)* était une formule utilisée lors de l'inauguration d'une maison. Leur arrivée en mars et leur départ en septembre correspondant aux équinoxes, elles étaient souvent associées au printemps, aux rites du mariage ou des fiançailles. De nombreuses légendes chinoises attribuaient aux œufs d'hirondelle des pouvoirs de fécondité, comme dans la Grèce antique. Les taoïstes expliquaient la disparition saisonnière de cet oiseau migrateur par des métamorphoses. On disait qu'elle se réfugiait dans l'eau où elle devenait un coquillage puis revenait avec le retour du soleil. De nombreuses peintures la montrent d'ailleurs rasant l'eau près des saules pleureurs. Les nids de salanganes ou hirondelles de mer *(yanwo)*, en soupe, sont encore très recherchés pour leurs vertus fortifiantes et stimulantes.

Le loriot *(oriolus chinensis indicus)* avec son corps jaune et ses ailes rayées de noir, est un oiseau connu pour son chant, en particulier au moment où les mûriers donnent leurs fruits. Il était associé aux fêtes anciennes du printemps et il est devenu symbole d'amitié et d'amour. Son nom chinois *(huangying)* pourrait être l'onomatopée de son chant : *ying ying*… À cause de ses qualités musicales, il figurait sur la livrée des musiciens impériaux à l'époque Qing.

Page de droite, loriot (broderie sur soie à fils d'or, insigne des mandarins de 8e classe puis, sous les Qing, des musiciens de la cour).

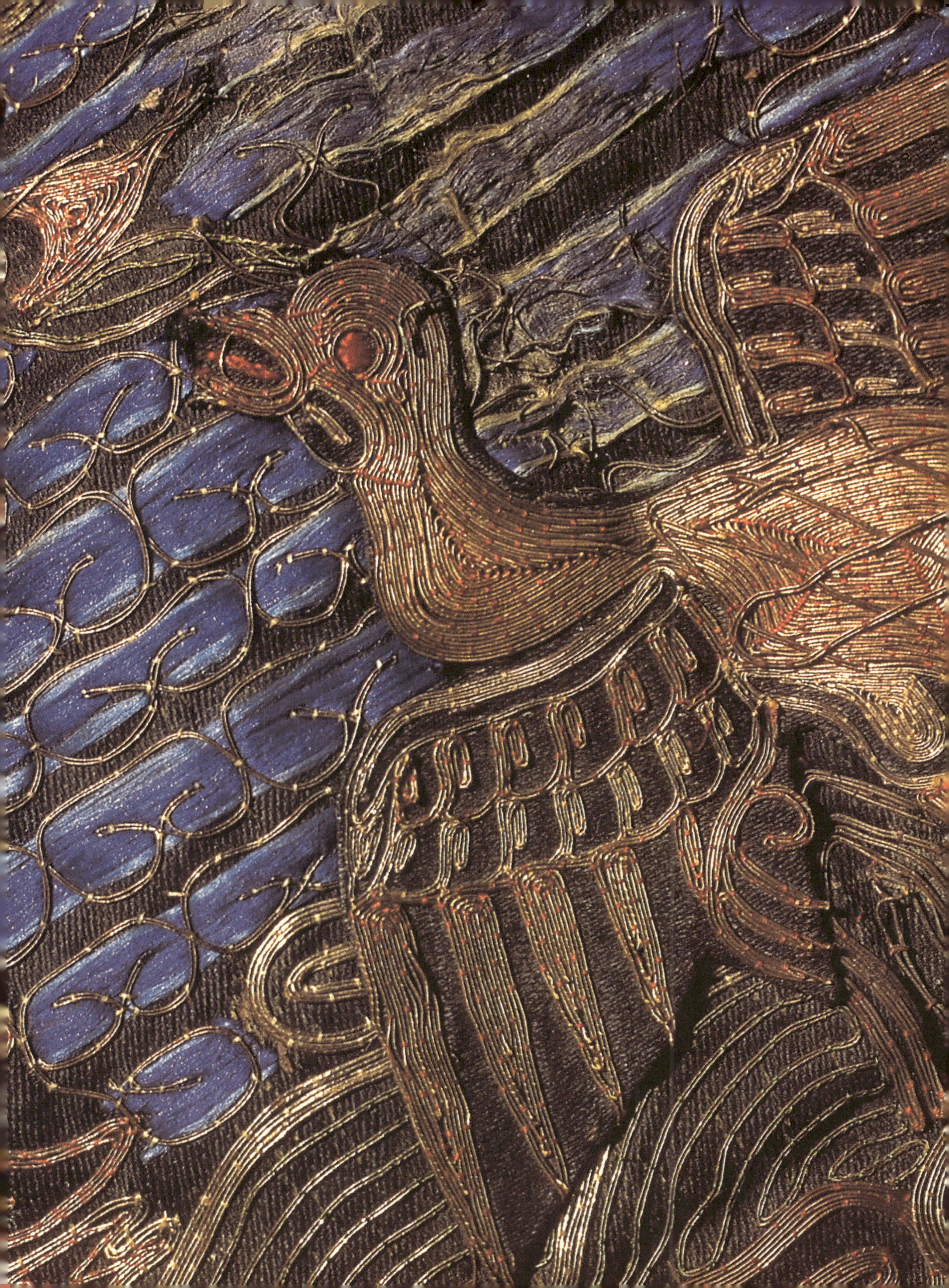

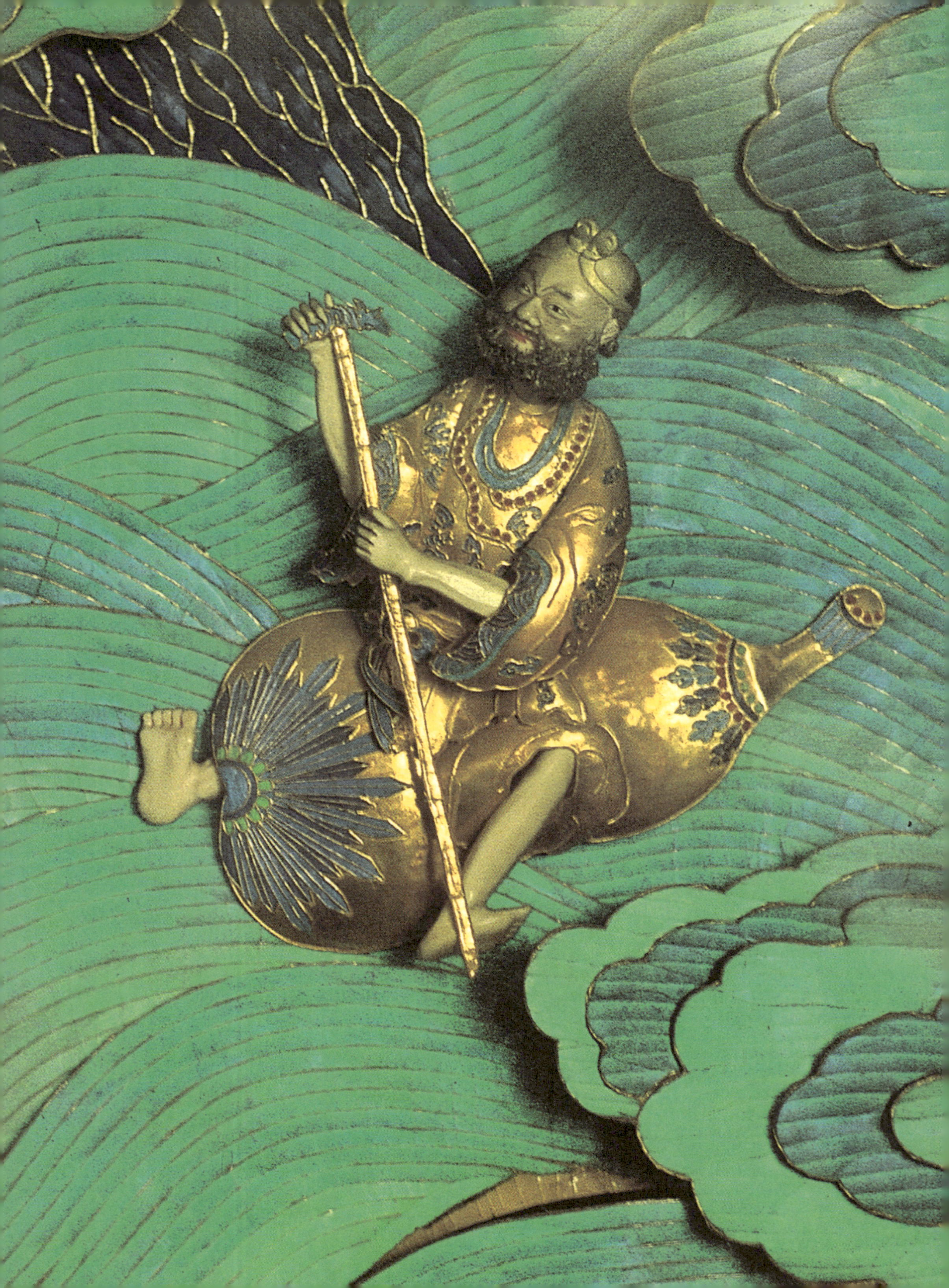

Le martin-pêcheur *(alcedo atthis bengalensis)*, parce qu'il vole en couple, est un symbole de fidélité, de bonheur conjugal ou de beauté naturelle. La tradition en fait un oiseau vain car il passe son temps, dit-on, à se regarder dans le miroir de l'eau. Appelé en chinois « l'oiseau bleu-vert » *(cui niao)*, ses plumes servent depuis des siècles à la fabrication de broches et d'épingles pour la décoration des cheveux et des coiffes de cérémonie, en particulier dans le sud. La célèbre concubine de l'empereur Xuanzong (VIIIe siècle), Yang Guifei, aurait possédé un char décoré de plumes de martin-pêcheur.

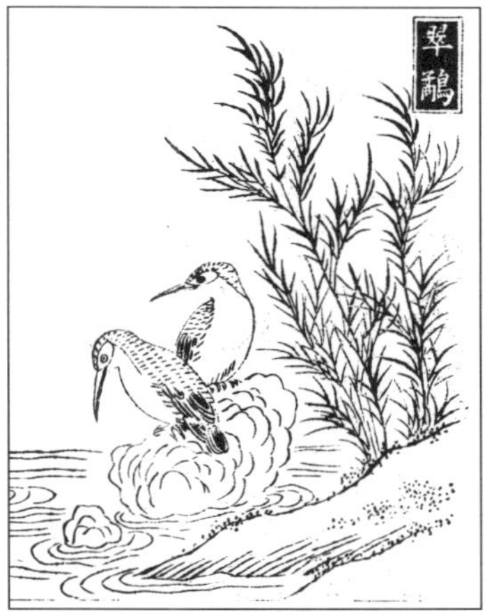

Le moineau *(passer montanus montanus)* est connu pour ses mœurs tapageuses et sensuelles ; aussi la pharmacopée chinoise fait-elle grand usage de sa chair et de ses œufs comme aphrodisiaque pour les hommes et pour soigner la stérilité des femmes. Élevés dans des cages près des temples ou dans les maisons, on avait l'habitude de libérer des moineaux lors des fêtes pour se ménager des faveurs célestes ; cette scène est souvent traitée en peinture. Le nom chinois du moineau signifie « oiseau de chanvre » *(maque)* et c'est aussi le nom donné au célèbre jeu de dominos, connu sous le nom de *mahjong*, que l'on appelait en France dès le XVIIIe siècle le « jeu du moineau ».

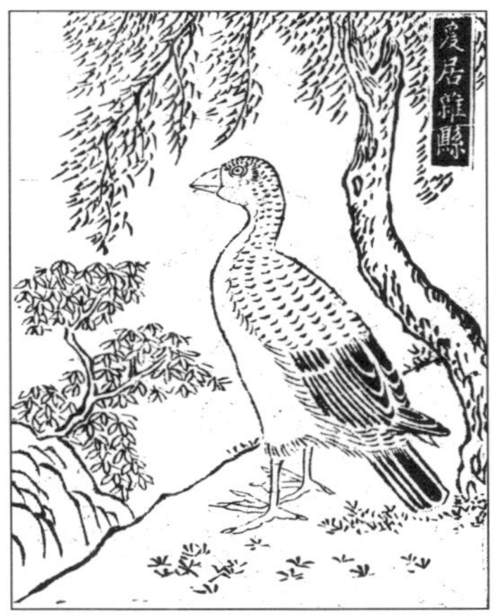

L'oie, figure de la littérature ou de la peinture, ne fait pratiquement référence qu'à l'oie sauvage *(anser fabalis)*. Symbole du *yang* – car dans ses migrations vers le sud elle recherchait le soleil –, elle était considérée comme un messager de bonnes nouvelles. Par allusion, pour désigner la correspondance, on parlait « d'échanges d'oies » *(yanbo)*. On utilisait les plumes d'oie comme cadeau symbolique, une vieille expression dit toujours : « envoyer une plume de mille lieux est un cadeau léger mais signe d'une solide amitié » *(« qian li song e mao, li qing qingyi zhong »)*. L'oie blanche servit aussi à exprimer la sincérité et la paix, en particulier pour les demandes en mariage. De nos jours, des oies aux plumes teintées de rouge sont encore offertes entre familles. Dans l'iconographie traditionnelle, une paire d'oies en vol est symbole de mariage et de bonheur. Les mouvements migratoires des oies sauvages qui se réfugient régulièrement au sud du fleuve Yangzi Jiang ont beaucoup inspiré les écrivains, qui font ainsi allusion au déchirement de ceux qui sont séparés de leur foyer.

Page de gauche, la traversée du fleuve Jaune sur une outre, détail d'un cloisonné en plumes de martin-pêcheur bleu-vert (Cité Interdite, fin du XVIIIe siècle) ; ci-dessus, martin-pêcheur et oie (gravures extraites du dictionnaire Ying Songchao huitu erya*).*

Le paon *(pavo)*, est connu sous le nom d'« oiseau de Confucius » *(kongqiao)* par homophonie avec son nom propre *kongque*. Esprit du feu, il fut considéré de tout temps comme le symbole de la beauté, de la dignité et de l'immortalité. Il fut sans doute un des modèles pour le mythique phénix. Les légendes évoquent souvent sa danse quand il entend de la musique ou quand il attaque les serpents. On attribuait même aux paonnes de coupables relations avec ces reptiles. La beauté de ses plumes était, selon les croyances, une transmutation des venins qu'il absorbait, ce qui faisait dire que son sang et sa bile ne devaient pas être consommés. Il est souvent représenté sur un rocher ou perché sur de hauts arbres. Originaires de l'Inde, les premiers paons furent offerts à la cour par des souverains voisins et leurs plumes étaient très recherchées pour les éventails de cérémonie ou les décorations de chapeau. Elles étaient en fait attribuées par l'empereur pour services rendus aussi bien aux mandarins civils que militaires. Selon l'importance des honneurs, les plumes se classaient en « motif floral », « couleur verte », ou « à un, deux ou trois ocelles ». Une vieille légende raconte comment une jeune princesse qui consacrait ses journées à broder des paons trouva un époux. Le père de la jeune fille avait promis d'accorder sa main à l'archer qui serait capable de loger, en courant, deux flèches dans les yeux du paon de l'ouvrage qu'elle brodait. Le vainqueur fut celui qui, plus tard, fonda la dynastie des Tang. Depuis, on appelle, d'une manière allusive, le gendre agréé par la famille : « l'homme de la broderie aux paons ».

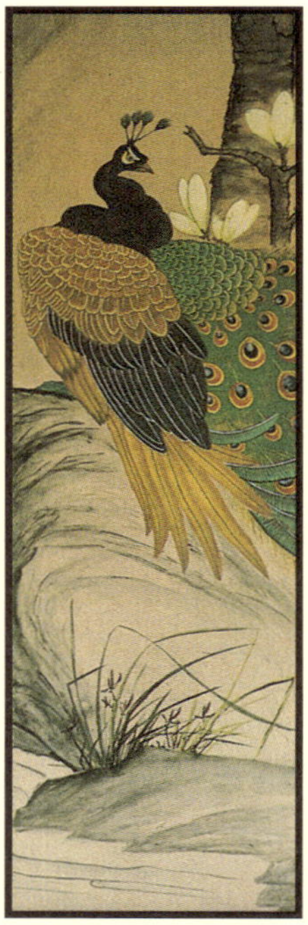

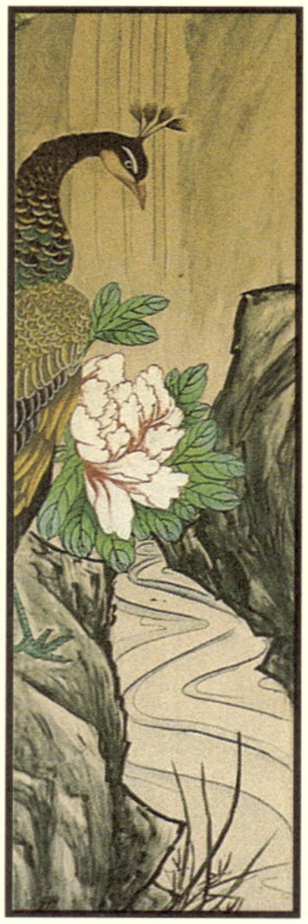

Ci-dessus, paons (détails d'un paravent du Palais d'Été à Pékin) ; page de droite, bols en céladon à motif de phénix (règne de Daoguang, 1821-1850).

Le phénix occupe la deuxième place parmi les quatre animaux mythologiques *(si ling)* qui sont traditionnellement, le dragon, le phénix, la licorne et la tortue. Il était considéré comme le chef des 360 espèces d'oiseaux répertoriées. Son nom *(feng huang)* est composé du nom du mâle *(feng)* qui est le symbole de félicité et de paix, et du nom de la femelle *(huang)* qui symbolise la féminité et tout ce qui se rapportait à l'impératrice, par opposition au dragon impérial. Le nom composé exprime donc le caractère indissociable d'union heureuse et, à ce titre, les robes et les coiffes de mariées font grand usage de ce symbole. Certains auteurs pensent que ce sont le paon et le faisan Argus qui ont inspiré les écrivains et les poètes dans la description de cet animal composite. C'est un oiseau du sud, qui correspond à l'été, donc au feu, et le rouge est une de ses couleurs principales (les taoïstes l'appellent d'ailleurs « l'oiseau de cinabre », *danniao*). Tout en combinant la grâce et la beauté de la plupart des oiseaux, il possédait des attributs spécifiques : une tête de faisan, une crête de coq, un bec de moineau, un cou de tortue à la base duquel se trouvent des plumes en forme de flammes, un corps de cigogne et une queue de paon. Sa queue est composée comme une flûte de pan et son chant comprend cinq notes. À sa maturité (trois ans), son plumage était de cinq couleurs : bleu-vert, jaune, rouge, blanc et noir qui symbolisent les cinq vertus cardinales : la droiture, l'honnêteté, la justice, la fidélité et la bienveillance. À ce sujet, respectueux des autres, le phénix ne se nourrissait pas d'insectes, ne mangeait que des graines de bambou et se désaltérait dans les sources sacrées. Il ne se perchait que sur un arbre rare appelé *wutong* dans lequel les botanistes ont voulu reconnaître tantôt le *sterculia platanifolia*, tantôt le *dryandra cordifolia* (dont les graines sont utilisées dans les «gâteaux de lune» du festival d'automne), ou enfin le *pauwlonia* (un grand arbre ornemental à fleurs mauves odorantes et à grandes feuilles). Ses rares apparitions sur terre, qui annonçaient la paix dans le royaume (donc un bon gouvernement), ou d'heureux présages comme des naissances extraordinaires, ont donné lieu à d'innombrables légendes. La première remonte à l'avènement du célèbre Empereur Jaune, Huangdi, qui reçut la visite d'un phénix venu le féliciter. Tout aussi célèbre fut cette autre apparition à l'occasion de la naissance de Confucius. La dernière remonterait au XIVe siècle et annoncerait l'avènement de la dynastie des Ming. Selon les auteurs classiques, il y aurait encore cinq sortes d'oiseaux extraordinaires semblables au phénix mais servant de messagers aux divinités. Les plus fréquemment représentés dans l'iconographie sont les messagers de la Reine Mère d'Occident qui convoquait de hauts personnages à son lointain palais de Jade des monts Kunlun en leur envoyant des oiseaux aux ailes bleues (*luan* ou *yuan*).

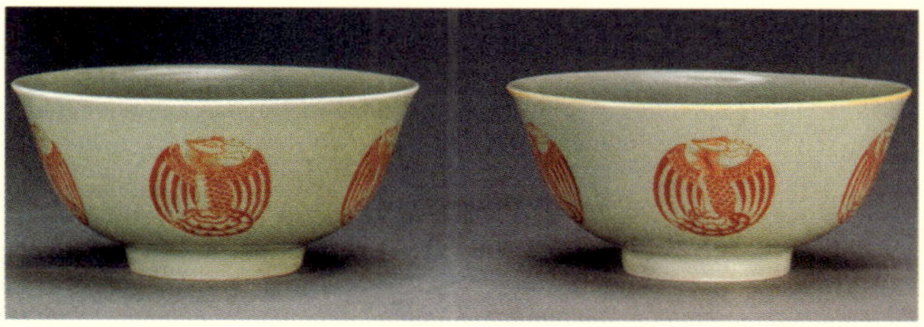

La pie *(pica pica sericea)* est considérée comme un oiseau de bon augure et son nom chinois est *xique* (« oiseau de la joie »). Son jacassement était un heureux présage d'une visite proche ou de réussite. Deux pies volant ensemble exprimaient la joie double du mariage et cinq pies représentaient les Cinq bonheurs (comme les chauve-souris). La légende du *Bouvier et de la Tisserande* raconte comment les pies, venues de tous les coins du monde à l'appel du bienveillant phénix, ont construit un pont sur la Voie Lactée pour permettre aux deux amants séparés de se retrouver le soir du 7e jour de la 7e lune. Depuis cette date, tous les étés, on célèbre cette fête *(qixi)* en regardant le ciel pour y voir briller l'étoile du Bouvier et celle de la Tisserande. Est-ce pour cette raison que les magiciens utilisaient la cervelle de pie comme puissant philtre d'amour ? Mais la pie, décidément associée aux histoires d'amour, est aussi réputée connaître les infidélités conjugales. Comme elle aime collectionner les objets brillants et les morceaux de miroir, on croyait qu'elle pouvait voir comment se comportaient les époux séparés. C'est donc un motif très fréquent en peinture, ou dans les papiers découpés, associé aux vœux de bonheur conjugal et de joie.

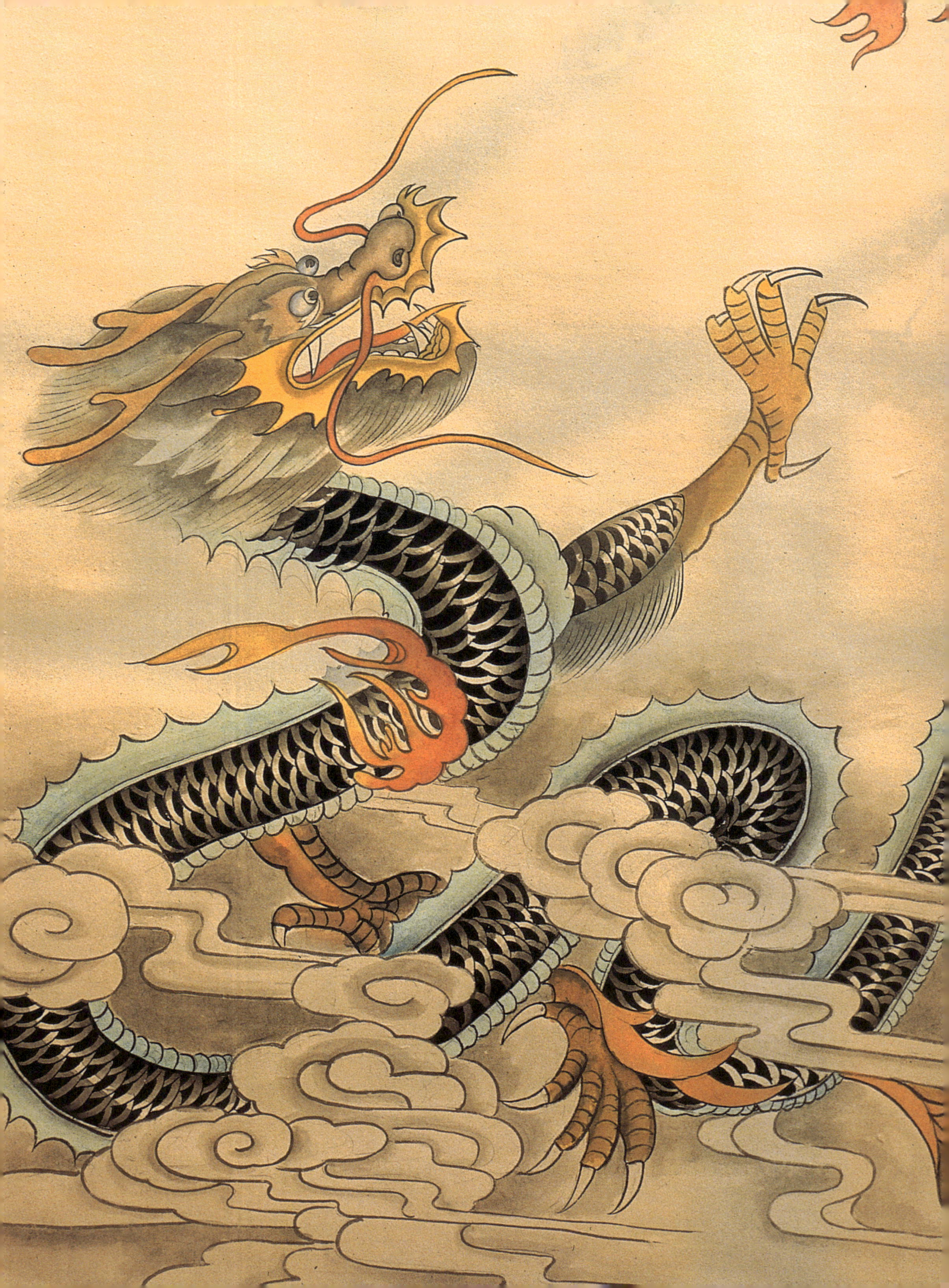

Les animaux à écaille

鱗甲珍藏

linjia zhencang, littéralement, « précieuses collections d'écailles et carapaces ».

Le dragon : selon le dictionnaire *Shuowen,* c'était le chef des 369 espèces de reptiles à écaille. Il fut sans doute le motif le plus représenté dans l'art asiatique. Ses origines en Chine pourraient remonter à quatre mille ans. Certains auteurs en font déjà l'emblème de la dynastie mythique des Xia (2000 av. J.-C.). En fait, le thème du dragon sera utilisé sans discontinuité de l'époque Han (206 av. J.-C.) jusqu'à la chute de la dynastie des Qing (1912) où il figurait encore sur le drapeau officiel… Fuxi, le premier héros légendaire de la Chine, apparaît déjà avec sa sœur Nuwa sur des bas-reliefs de l'époque Han avec un corps de serpent. Il aurait tué un dragon avec la peau duquel il fit un tambour que l'on entendait très loin. On prête de même à l'Empereur Jaune un dragon domestiqué qui utilisait son pouvoir sur l'eau dont il était issu pour aider son maître dans ses entreprises. Les mythes ont été nombreux : il servait de monture aux personnages importants à leur mort ou, comme flambeau, éclairait le sombre empire des morts. L'imagination a créé pour la représentation de cet animal de nombreuses variantes. Les dragons se classaient ainsi en trois catégories : les dragons célestes (*long* ou *tianlong*) qui étaient les plus puissants, les dragons aquatiques *(li)* qui n'avaient pas de cornes et dont l'environnement était l'eau des rivières ou des mers, et enfin les dragons des grottes et des cavernes *(jiao)* qui habitaient dans des endroits humides comme les marais. Génies de la force et de la bonté, de la protection et de la vigilance, les dragons étaient dotés du pouvoir de se rendre invisibles. *Long* était l'archétype du dragon chinois, sa morphologie a fait l'objet de descriptions variées et quelquefois contradictoires : une tête de chameau avec des cornes de cerf, des oreilles de bœuf, des yeux de lièvre surmontés de sourcils en broussaille, une longue barbe

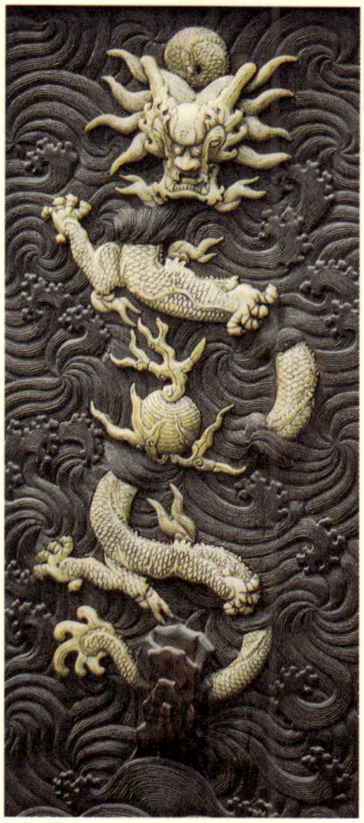

Ci-dessus, dragon dans les flots (ivoire et bois sculpté).

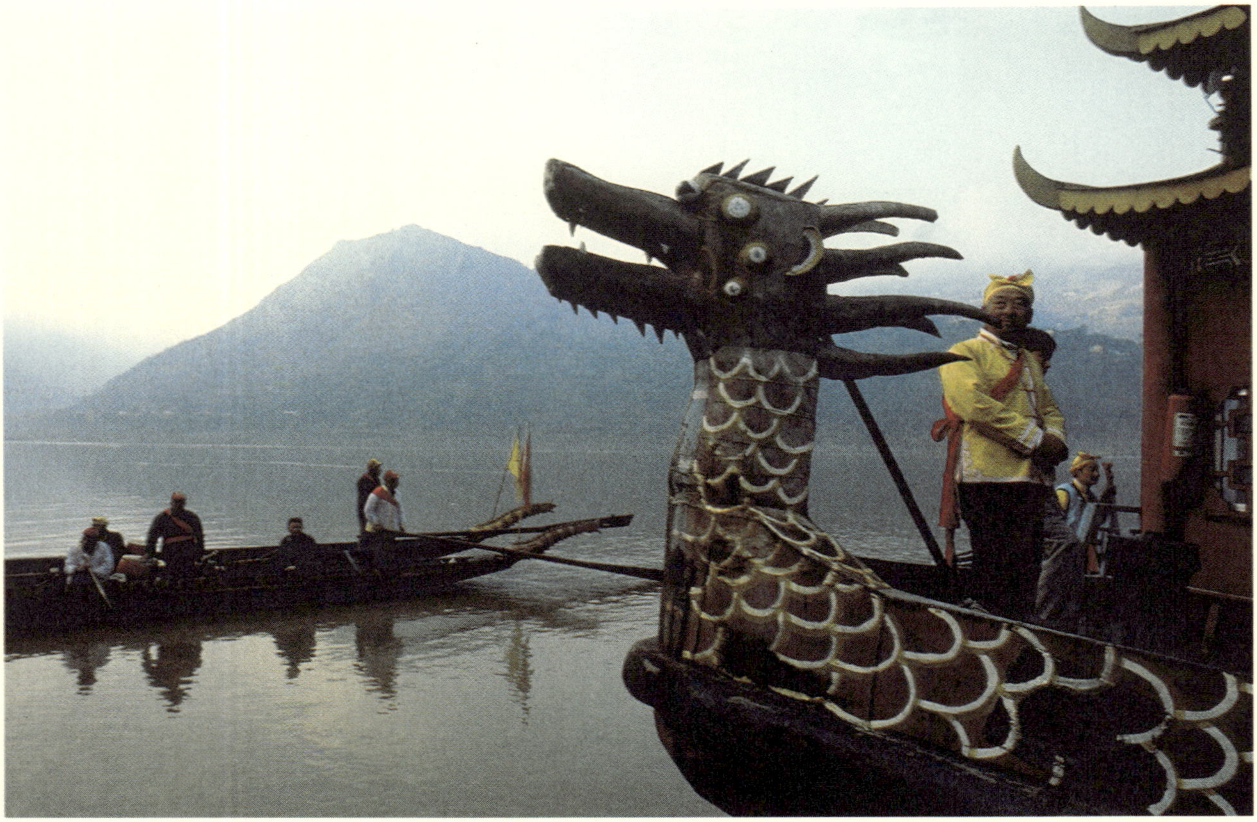

effilochée, des défenses, un corps de reptile recouvert d'écailles de poisson et une épine dorsale surmontée d'ailerons pointus se terminant par des piques, une queue de serpent, quatre pattes de tigre se prolongeant par des griffes de faucon et, pour compléter cette effrayante description, des appendices en forme de flammes jaillissant des épaules et des hanches. Son corps portait quatre-vingt une écailles (9 x 9, symbole bénéfique *yang*). Ses griffes étaient au nombre de quatre pour les dragons ordinaires (donc dans les attributs de personnages de moindre importance) et de cinq pour tout ce qui concernait les dragons impériaux. Le dragon était souvent représenté jouant avec la « perle » *(zhu)*, symbole de puissance et de gloire. Cet objet rond a donné lieu à de nombreuses hypothèses ; certaines l'associent à la lune, d'autres au roulement du tonnerre, à l'œuf, au joyau de l'omnipotence ou à la « perle qui brille dans la nuit » que H.-A. Giles décrit comme « l'escarboucle » (rubis). Tout autour du dragon figuraient toujours des nuages stylisés et des flammes. Il exhalait de sa bouche un nuage qui pouvait se transformer en eau ou en feu.

La Chine se révéla être un pays riche en dinosaures fossiles (appelés ici *konglong,* les « féroces dragons ») et on comprend qu'il a été aisé de mêler la réalité avec l'imaginaire. La poudre d'os de dinosaure ou « os de dragon » *(long gu)* est entrée dans la pharmacopée chinoise pour soigner l'hypertension, les

Bateau-dragon (Chine méridionale).

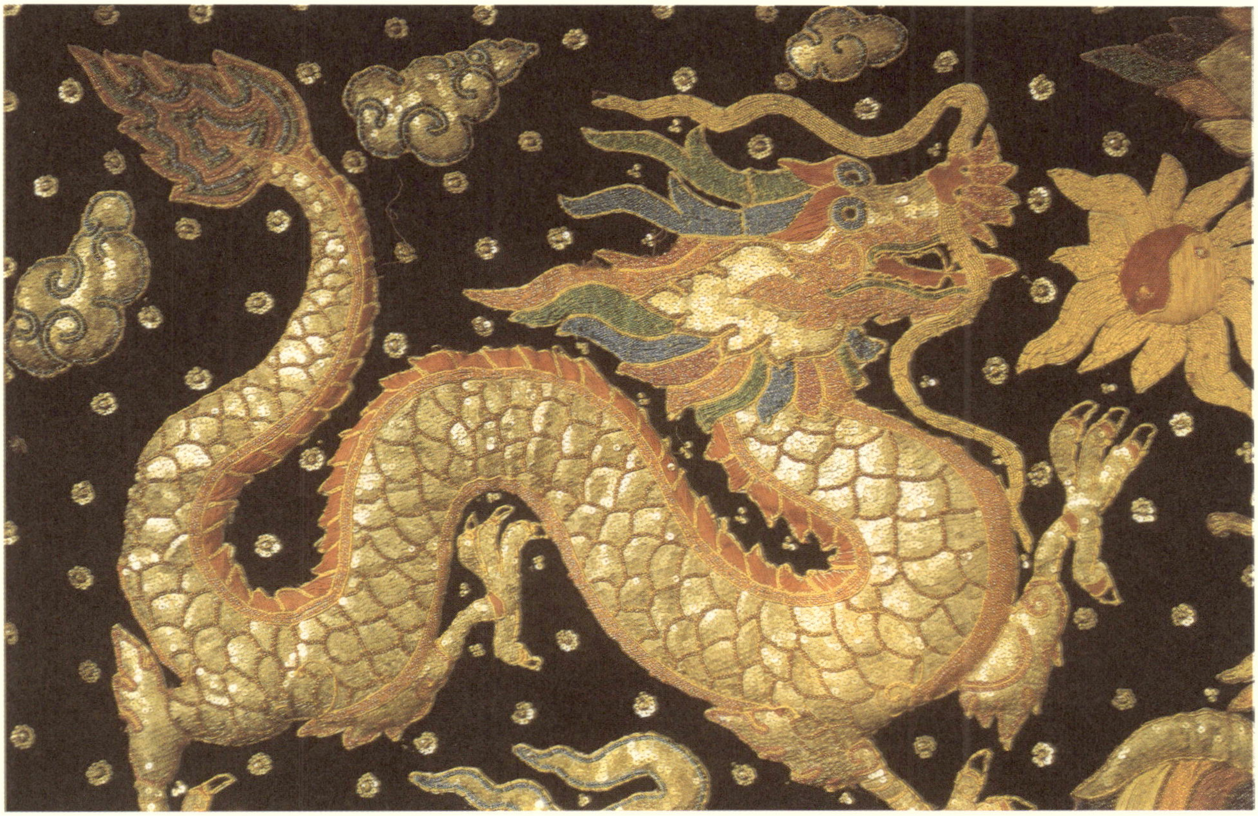

insomnies, les peurs et les diarrhées ; les œufs de dinosaures chinois connurent un certain succès avec la mode lancée par *Jurassic Park*. Les importantes variations sur le dragon ont donné naissance à une classification par couleurs qui parut sous les Song et qui définissait leur caractère : dragon bleu ou vert, compatissant ; dragon rouge, joie ; dragon jaune, accueillant favorablement les vœux ; dragon blanc, vertueux et pur ; dragon noir, mystérieux. On lui attribuait le pouvoir de produire de l'or en soufflant sur la terre. Le dragon de couleur jaune fut traditionnellement attribué à l'empereur et l'association avec ce personnage fut si forte depuis sa première représentation qu'on prit l'habitude de faire allusion à la contenance solennelle du souverain par « la figure de dragon », à son trône par « le siège du dragon » et à ses colères par « le renversement des écailles ». Quand il entrait dans son palais, l'empereur assis dans son palanquin passait au-dessus d'une énorme pierre de marbre sculptée en forme de mer où s'ébattait un ou plusieurs dragons taillés dans la masse. La première peinture de dragon est attribuée à Zhuge Liang et depuis, de nombreuses histoires ont couru sur ces artistes qui n'osaient peindre les yeux de leurs dragons de peur de les voir s'envoler. Né de l'imaginaire des hommes, le dragon asiatique a occupé une bonne place dans les broderies, sur les porcelaines, en frise murale ou en sculpture, en moulage vernissé sur les murs de protection des

Dragon jouant avec la perle zhu (broderie d'inspiration taoïste).

entrées de palais, tout comme dans ses neuf avatars sur les cloches, au bas des stèles, sur les poutres de temples ou sur les gardes de sabres.

Deux grandes fêtes populaires mettent encore en scène le dragon. La première, le 2e jour de la 2e Lune, a lieu au printemps : « le dragon relève la tête. » À ce moment, pour marquer la fin de son hibernation, il provoque le tonnerre et la pluie. La seconde est la fête des « bateaux-dragons », le 5e jour de la 5e Lune. Au cours de cette fête de l'été a lieu une course de pirogues en forme de dragons dans les régions du sud et de la côte. Pour mimer les combats de dragons, les équipages de chaque bateau (environ une cinquantaine de rameurs) poussent des clameurs sauvages. Curieusement, cette fête de l'eau sert aussi à honorer la mémoire du poète Qu Yuan (343-290 av. J.-C.) qui, à l'époque des Royaumes Combattants se noya dans la rivière Miluo (Hunan) parce qu'il n'avait plus la faveur de son souverain. Depuis, des offrandes aux esprits des noyés sont faites sous forme de petits paquets de sucreries que l'on place sur un radeau avec une bougie ; ainsi, le *zongzi* en forme de triangle, de cône ou de trapèze était à l'origine un gâteau de riz glutineux roulé dans des feuilles de roseaux ; maintenant il est fourré de jujubes, de sucre, de marrons, de noix de cannelle et de parfum d'anis.

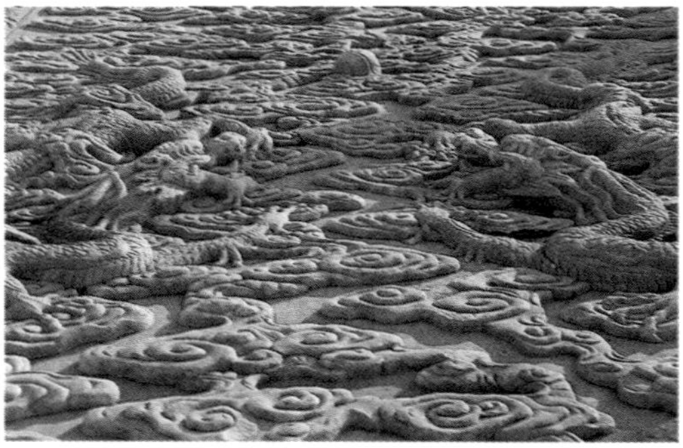

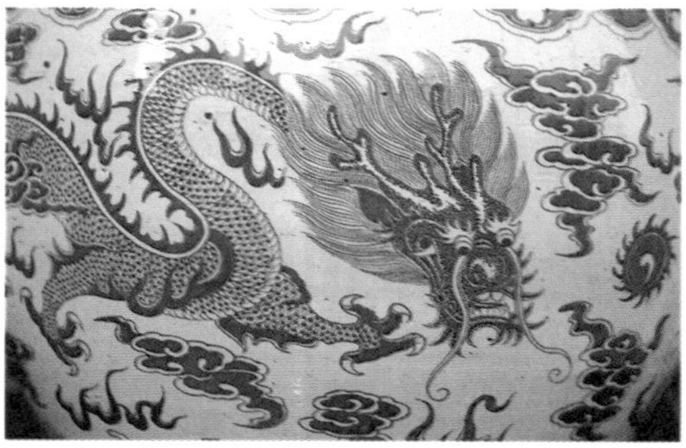

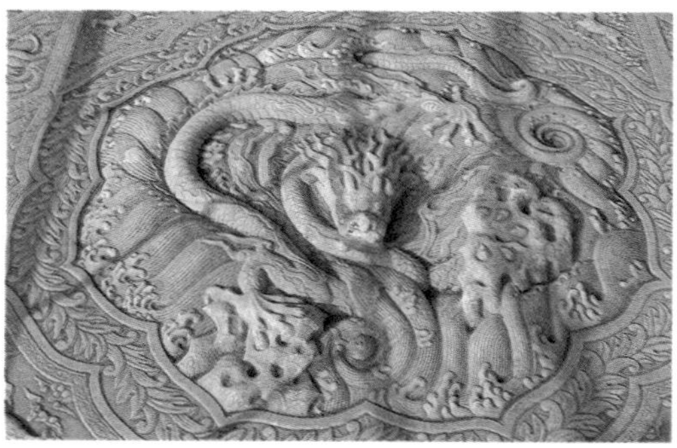

Le crapaud *(laihama)*, curieusement classé parmi les animaux à écaille, appartient au groupe des Cinq venimeux ; la grenouille *(wa)*, elle, serait née d'œufs tombés du ciel avec la rosée. Tous deux appartiennent au monde de l'eau et on retrouve des représentations de grenouilles sur le côté des « tambours de pluie », appelés ainsi parce que leur sonorité rappelle le tonnerre ou l'orage. Ces instruments de bronze servaient à appeler la pluie dans les civilisations du Sud-Est asiatique. Les légendes racontent que le crapaud fabuleux Chan Chu qui vivait dans la lune l'avalait au moment des éclipses ; c'est de ce nom que l'on désigne les taches noires sur cet astre.

Le crapaud est peut-être aussi l'incarnation de l'épouse de Hou Yi, l'archer héroïque qui avait reçu de la Reine Mère d'Occident une pilule d'immortalité en récompense de ses services. Son épouse Chang'E l'avala et fut immédiatement transformée en crapaud et envoyée dans la lune. Une autre légende beaucoup plus matérielle évoque le crapaud de Liu Hai. Ce magicien taoïste avait décidé d'assainir des marais pestilentiels dans lesquels

En haut et en bas, dragons (dalles d'escalier des palais impériaux) ; au milieu, décor de dragon sur porcelaine bleu-et-blanc (copie de Ming).

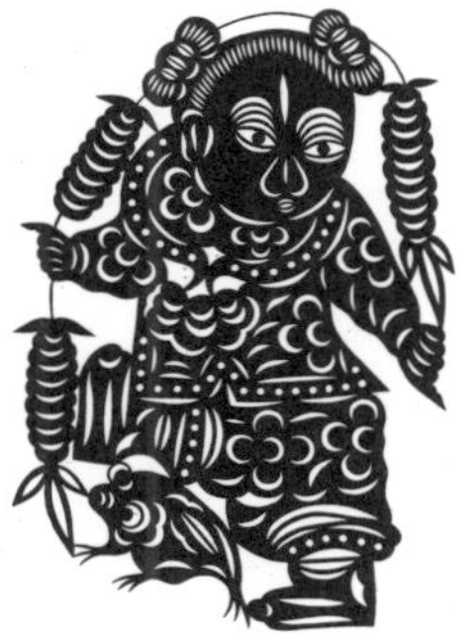

vivait un énorme crapaud à trois pattes. Impossible à attraper, celui-ci se laissa cependant tenter par des sapèques d'or mises au bout d'un fil. Depuis mille ans, on ne représente plus Liu Hai qu'avec des ligatures de sapèques et son étrange compagnon batracien à trois pattes, une pièce dans la bouche. Devenu une sorte de dieu de la Richesse, Liu Hai est particulièrement vénéré par la corporation des marchands qui affichent des estampes à son effigie dans leurs magasins. Les légendes sur la longévité du crapaud-buffle ont conduit les médecins traditionnels à recueillir des verrues de l'animal un suc utilisé dans des pilules pour le cœur.

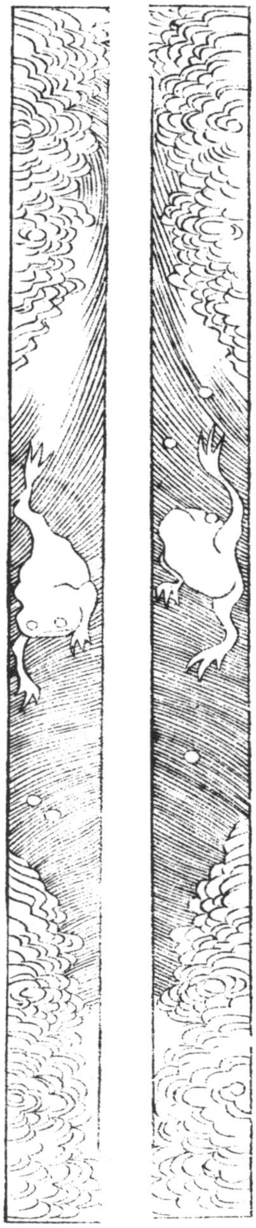

Le poisson *(yu),* par homophonie avec « abondant », « superflu », est un symbole de richesse. Le légendaire Fuxi, qui apprit à son peuple la pêche, lui aurait donné son nom. Sans doute parce que le poisson a une grande facilité de reproduction, il est devenu aussi symbole de vie et de fécondité. Il figure parmi les Huit symboles bouddhistes et exprimerait la liberté d'esprit et du corps de l'adepte. Les taoïstes ont repris cette symbolique et, à l'occasion de certaines fêtes, on libère dans le bassin de chaque temple des poissons rouges, des tortues et des carpes pour gagner des indulgences. Dans certains temples, on peut voir de gros grelots de bois destinés à rythmer les chants lors des cérémonies. Ils portent le nom de « tête de poisson » *(yutou)* parce que, dit-on, le moine Xuanzang, lors de son voyage en Occident ne dut la vie qu'à un énorme poisson dont il garda la tête après avoir assouvi sa faim. Elle lui servit à rythmer sa marche pendant le reste de son pèlerinage. Une autre interprétation est que, comme le poisson qui ne ferme pas les yeux, l'adepte doit consacrer ses jours et ses nuits à l'étude sacrée. Représentés depuis la période archaïque, les meilleures peintures de poissons datent cependant de l'époque Song (Xe-XIIe siècle).

La carpe *(liyu)* avec ses écailles puissantes était considérée comme un guerrier ayant revêtu une cuirasse. Elle était vénérée car on lui attribuait (ou peut-être s'agit-il de l'esturgeon du fleuve Jaune) le courage et la persévérance de nager à contre-courant jusqu'aux « Portes du dragon » (Longmen) et de se transformer en dragon. C'est à cet endroit, près de Luoyang, dans la province du Hunan, que le légendaire Yu-le-Grand parvint à dompter les eaux du fleuve Jaune.

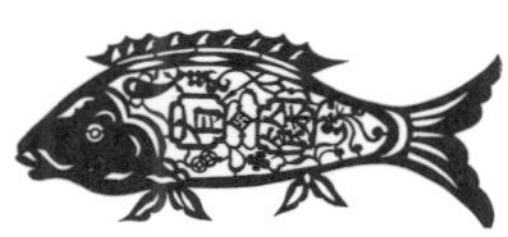

Depuis, la carpe est devenue le symbole de succès aux examens (on dit d'un candidat heureux qu'il est « poisson transformé en dragon et qu'il a franchi les portes du dragon »). La carpe est associée aux plaisirs de la pêche, une des activités divertissantes des lettrés. On élève des carpes depuis plus de deux mille ans en Chine et, sous les Tang, on classait la queue de carpe parmi les Huit mets les plus exquis *(bazhen)* avec la langue de canard, la laitance de poisson, les lèvres de singe, la mœlle de bœuf, la patte d'ours, la bosse de chameau et la queue de cerf. On raconte qu'à la naissance de Confucius, l'empereur du royaume de Lu offrit à son père une carpe, qui alors prénomma son fils Kong Li du nom du poisson *(li)*. La carpe fait partie aussi des traditions populaires et elle est associée à toutes les fêtes de famille dans le nord de la Chine. Pendue à la porte de la maison par un fil rouge, c'est un porte-bonheur du Nouvel An. Lors du mariage, le marié offre à son épouse une paire de carpes, symbole d'une grande descendance. Pour la fête des « bateaux-dragons », il est de coutume de fabriquer dans les provinces du Shandong et du Shaanxi des carpes en mie de pain qui sont alors offertes aux anciens comme souhait de bonheur.

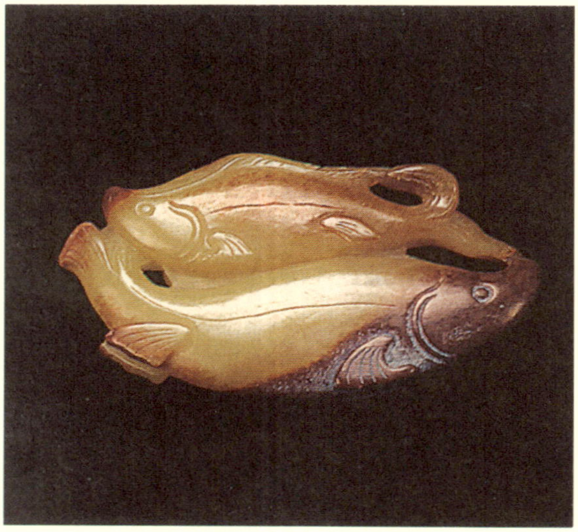

Le serpent *(she)* est l'emblème de la ruse et du mal, de la méchanceté sournoise. Comme le dragon, c'est un gardien de « trésors » et le fait de vivre dans l'obscurité et près de l'eau le relie à la mort. Il est annonciateur d'enfants femelles (serpents blancs et gris), c'est son aspect *yin*. Mais il est aussi *yang* et incarne la sécheresse. La peau de serpent était symbole de richesse. Représentation bouddhique par excellence (le naja protecteur), il est devenu en Chine le Roi-serpent. En application des principes du bouddhisme, on gagnait de nombreux mérites à relâcher des serpents en liberté. Malgré cela, la cuisine du sud continue d'offrir du serpent au menu et aussi de la bile de serpent mélangée à de l'alcool comme fortifiant. En médecine traditionnelle, la chair de serpent sert à guérir les rhumatismes et l'arthrite.

Poissons géminés (pendant de jade, dynastie des Ming, 1368-1644). Page de droite, quatre des « Cinq venimeux » (gravure extraite du dictionnaire Ying Songchao huitu erya*).*

Les Cinq Venimeux *(wu du)* sont inclassables et forment une collection à part qui comprend le serpent, le lézard (ou l'araignée), le scorpion, le crapaud et le mille-pattes. Ils apparaissaient lors de la saison chaude qui apportait les épidémies. On essayait donc, le 5e jour de la 5e lune, de combattre avec la magie ces mauvaises influences. Des papiers magiques portant le *taiji* taoïste (le « Faîte suprême ») avec les trigrammes accompagnés des représentations des venimeux) étaient accrochés dans la maison. On utilisait aussi la repré-

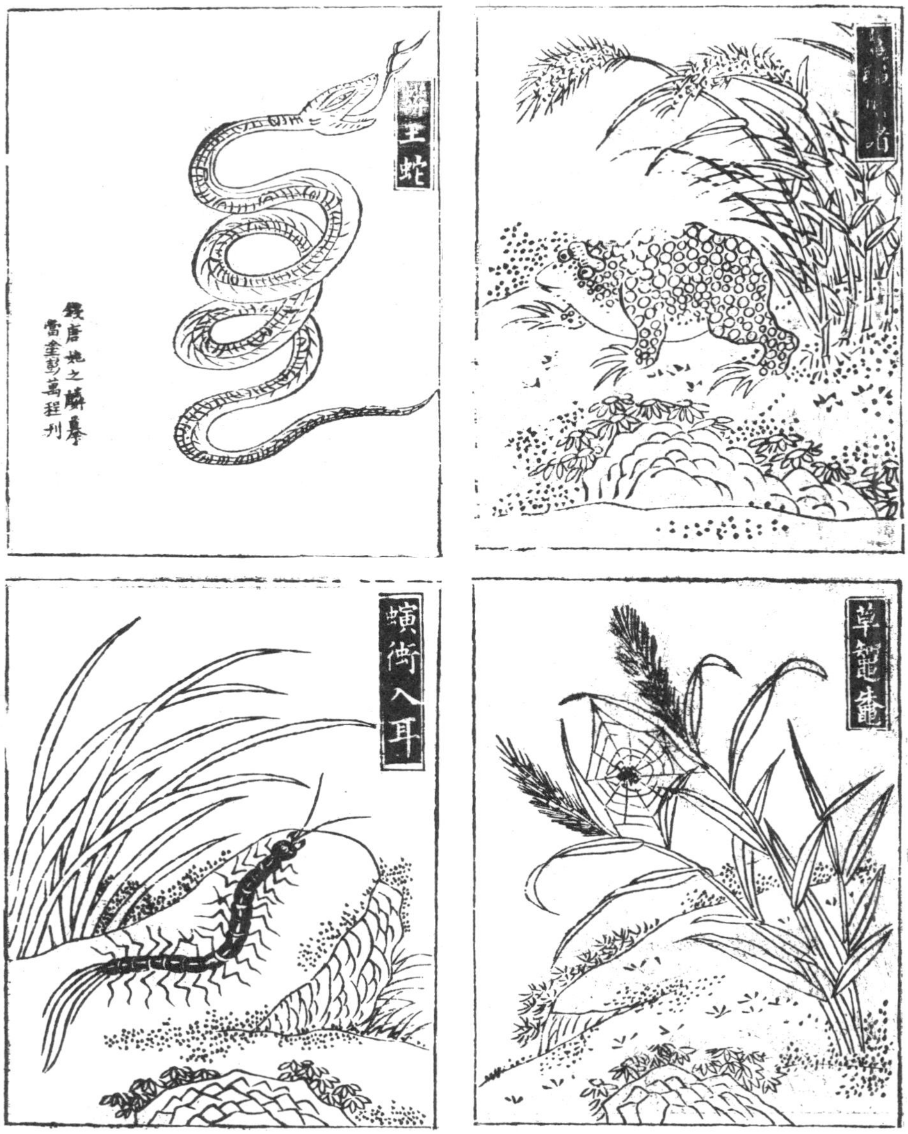

sentation du tigre ou du coq, tous deux fiers ennemis de ces fléaux, à moins que l'on n'ait recours au redoutable Zhong Kui. Pour ne rien laisser au hasard en ces temps difficiles, on fabriquait encore des talismans de tissu représentant les venimeux, qui étaient ensuite cousus sur les vêtements d'enfant comme amulettes. Les pharmaciens préparaient enfin à partir des Cinq venimeux de puissantes décoctions destinées à guérir le tétanos, les convulsions, l'asthme et les infections.

Les animaux à carapace : la tortue

龟甲珍藏

guijia zhencang, littéralement, « précieuses collections d'écailles de tortue ».

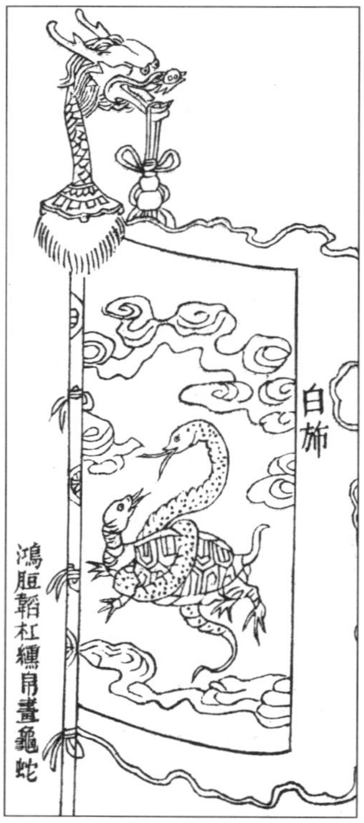

Bannière figurant, selon la légende, une tortue emprisonnée dans les anneaux d'un serpent.

La tortue est un symbole très ancien en Chine, utilisé depuis près de 4000 ans. C'est le quatrième des animaux fabuleux *(si ling)*. Comme eux, sa morphologie est composite : on la décrit souvent avec des oreilles apparentes, des flammes aux épaules et une longue queue couverte de poils. Ce long manteau d'algues et d'herbes qui reste accroché à sa carapace quand elle nage dans les marécages l'a d'ailleurs fait surnommer par les Chinois le « messager en habit vert » ; cette traîne végétale ressemble au manteau de pailles que portaient les paysans chinois ou japonais. La tortue est indifféremment associée à l'eau comme à la terre et il est fait peu de différence entre la tortue de rivière, de mer ou de terre.

Dans le mythe de la création du monde, le monstre Gong Gong ayant ébranlé la voûte céleste à la suite d'un combat, le Ciel commença de basculer et le Fleuve céleste menaça de joindre ses eaux à celles des fleuves de la terre. Pour éviter cette grande catastrophe, Nuwa, épouse et sœur du premier héros légendaire Fuxi, répara la voûte céleste en coupant les pattes d'une grande tortue de mer (*ao,* nom mythologique) et en les plaçant sous les quatre piliers. Depuis cet exploit, la tortue servait traditionnellement à consolider les fondations de ponts et de digues. Dans une autre légende, cinq grandes tortues reçurent pour mission de fixer les îles à la dérive de la mythique mer de l'Est où se trouvaient les monts des Immortels.

C'est sans doute en référence à ces légendes que l'on croyait que la tortue pouvait porter des charges très lourdes pendant des temps immémoriaux sans se nourrir ni respirer... Près de nombreux mausolées, dans des temples taoïstes ou dans des parcs publics, on peut ainsi voir d'énormes stèles *(shigui tuo bei)* posées sur le dos d'une tortue. Les plus précieuses de ces pierres gravées sont d'ailleurs abritées sous un petit pavillon spécialement construit à cet effet. Au sommet de la stèle se trouve un animal fabuleux qui ressemble à un dragon (en fait, c'est un de ses neuf fils que l'on nomme *chi*). Toutes les stèles sur lesquelles figurent une inscription impériale portent à la base une tortue ; ce sont les « stèles d'achèvement divin et de vertus sacrées ». Certaines ne portent aucun texte, ce sont les « stèles sans mots » que le premier empereur des Ming voulut ainsi pour rompre avec la tradition des louanges excessives. La tortue est en général sculptée la tête levée, le regard au loin et, sur le sol, autour d'elle, figurent les vagues de la mer et de nombreux animaux marins. En fait, en dépit de l'étonnante ressemblance, il ne s'agit pas d'une tortue *(gui)* mais plutôt d'un animal fabuleux *(bixi)*. Sa force extraordinaire fut utilisée par le légendaire Yu pour dompter les flots du Déluge puis, une fois ses travaux terminés, *bixi* fut transformé en porte-stèle. Dans la Cité Interdite et dans certains temples se trouvent aussi des tortues de bronze à tête de dragon *(ao heng)*. Ce sont les « tortues du succès » que pouvait chevaucher le candidat reçu premier aux examens impériaux. On disait de lui qu'il « était le seul à se tenir sur la tête de la tortue » *(duzhan aotou)*. De nos jours, il n'est pas rare de voir d'ambitieux jeunes hommes se faire photographier devant ces tortues porte-bonheur.

Mais la tortue était aussi un symbole de longévité, on la disait capable d'atteindre plusieurs centaines d'années (les légendes chinoises parlent de 3 000 ans) grâce à sa carapace qui la rendait invulnérable. Parce qu'elle pouvait rester sous la terre sans boire ni manger et qu'elle empêchait le bois de pourrir, on raconte que les fondations du Temple du Ciel (Tiantan) reposeraient sur quatre tortues. Les dictons populaires faisaient d'ailleurs allusion à cette étrange particularité : « une petite tortue de mille ans c'est une grande tortue de dix mille ans » *(qian nian wangba, wan nian gui)*. De nombreuses histoires circulent sur des tortues repêchées portant sur leur dos des inscriptions très anciennes. En Chine comme au Japon, des « cérémonies de libération des choses vivantes » avaient lieu dans les temples pour gagner des indulgences ; on relâchait les tortues après avoir fait un trou dans leur carapace. Une des expressions pour « longévité » est l'association des noms de deux animaux réputés immortels : la tortue et la grue *(guihe)*.

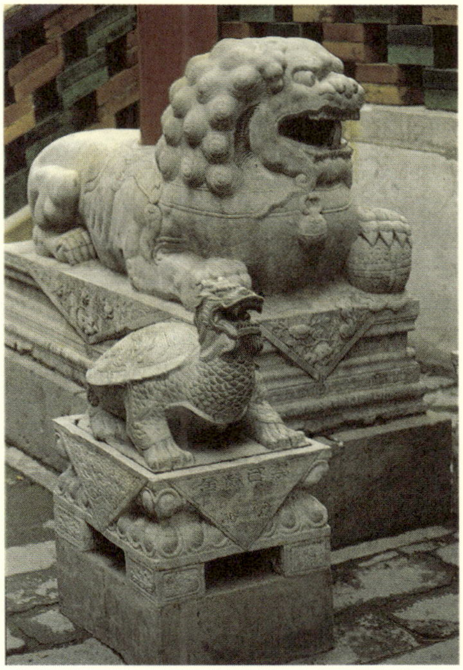

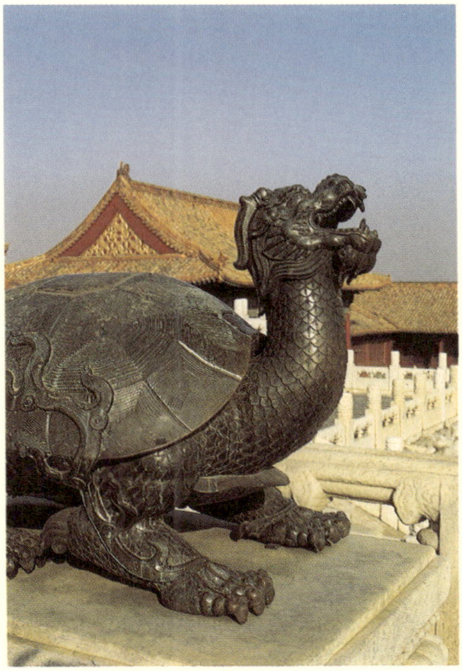

En haut, tortue de pierre à tête de dragon et lion de pierre (temple des Lamas) ; en bas, tortue de bronze à tête de dragon (Cité Interdite).

Dès 1500 av. J.-C., à l'époque des Shang et plus tard sous les Zhou, on pratiqua la chéloniomancie (les tortues sont des reptiles appartenant à l'ordre des chéloniens), une méthode de divination par examen des craquelures faites par le feu sur des carapaces de tortues. Ces signes étaient les réponses apportées par les divinités aux questions qui leur étaient posées par l'intermédiaire du prêtre. Pendant des années, les oracles ont donc utilisé ces signes artificiellement créés et ceux qui apparaissaient naturellement dans les écailles. On raconte que ce sont les dessins de la carapace d'une immense tortue d'eau sortant du fleuve qui auraient suggéré à Fu Xi le système des trigrammes.

Selon les traditions anciennes, le dôme de la carapace figurait la voûte céleste et la plaque inférieure, la terre : la tortue était donc une représentation parfaite de l'univers et, à ce titre, c'était le plus précieux des cadeaux cérémoniels.

Elle était utilisée en astrologie taoïste pour symboliser les « esprits » des quatre directions *(si fang)*. Sous le nom de « sombre guerrier », la tortue était l'emblème du Nord et de l'hiver, le dragon bleu-vert était le symbole de l'Est et du printemps, le tigre blanc celui de l'Ouest et de l'automne, l'oiseau rouge celui du Sud et de l'été. La tortue figurait aussi sur des bannières emprisonnée dans les anneaux d'un serpent. Les légendes racontent que la tortue, après avoir défié le Bouddha, se sauva à la nage. Le saint homme lui lança alors un cheveu qui se transforma aussitôt en un serpent qui l'enserra. Cette double image est peut-être liée au caractère *yin* (féminin) de la tortue et *yang* (masculin) du serpent, leur combinaison représentant la procréation. L'expression populaire « œuf de tortue » (*wangbadan*, « enfant né de père inconnu, bâtard ») est une formidable insulte couramment employée.

Parce que Confucius avait déclaré que, sous peine de les oublier, elle était obligée de porter gravée sur son dos les « Huit interdictions » (ne pas tuer, voler, commettre d'actes impurs, mentir, boire de l'alcool, se parfumer ou se parer, faire usage de sièges larges, pécher par gourmandise), la tortue fut alors considérée comme un animal irresponsable. Depuis, on attribue à celui qui oublie ces huit principes *(wang ba)* le qualificatif injurieux de salaud *(wangba)*. En dépit de ces désagréables avatars, la tortue reste souvent employée comme motif décoratif. C'est aussi une amulette fréquemment portée pour le caractère de longévité qu'elle exprime.

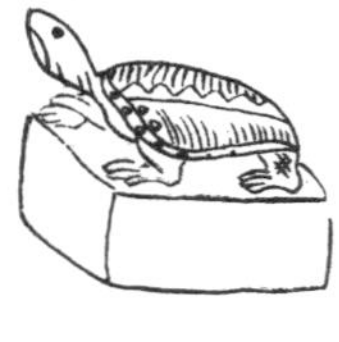

Le langage des fleurs et des plantes

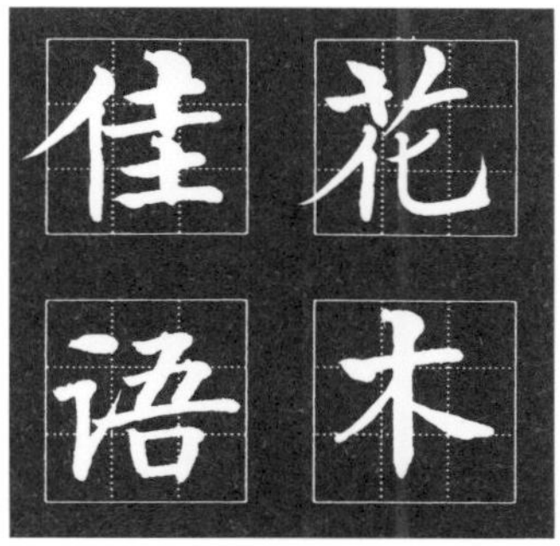

huamu jiayu, littéralement, « le beau langage des fleurs et des plantes ».

L'abricot *(xingzi)* était pour les femmes chinoises le symbole de la beauté et plus particulièrement son amande (ou noyau) considérée comme la forme idéale des yeux. En outre, en souvenir de Confucius qui enseignait ses disciples sur la « Terrasse des Abricotiers » à Qufu, la fleur de cet arbre est restée symbole des examens impériaux qui avaient lieu au printemps. On parle aussi de la « forêt des abricotiers » *(xinglin),* une allusion à ce médecin de l'époque des Trois Royaumes qui plantait un arbre à chaque guérison. *Xing* c'est aussi « heureuse fortune, chance ».

L'achillée (*shicao,* littéralement « l'herbe des devins ») est une plante aux feuilles très découpées, de la famille des composées, dont une des espèces est le mille-feuilles. Depuis la plus haute antiquité chinoise, elle servait à la divination. Comme une de ses racines pouvait produire « cent » (beaucoup de) tiges, les devins, après avoir coupé quarante neuf brins, les répartissaient en deux tas, représentant respectivement la terre et le ciel, puis procédaient à de nouvelles divisions en nombres pairs et impairs permettant de constituer les soixante-quatre hexagrammes. L'achilléomancie fut une des pratiques divinatoires qui fut utilisée, dans le temps, après l'ostéomancie (observation des craquelures sur les os de bovidés ou de cervidés) et la chéloniomancie (étude des carapaces de tortue). La lecture des trigrammes ou des hexagrammes, l'observation du vol des oiseaux et des mouvements de l'araignée complétaient ces techniques divinatoires très anciennes.

L'armoise (*artemisia vulgaris, aiye* ou *haozi*) appartient à un groupe de plantes sauvages aromatiques représentées par des espèces comme l'absinthe, le génépi ou l'estragon. C'est sans doute à cause de ses caractéristiques odoriférantes que cette plante était brûlée comme offrande, et pour éloigner les mauvais esprits lors des mariages ou des accouchements. L'armoise, appelée aussi « herbe brûlante » est utilisée dans la médecine traditionnelle chinoise et japonaise pour traiter par moxibustion *(jiu)* les saignements de nez, les rhumatismes ou les douleurs internes. Roulées en petits cônes, boulettes ou bâtonnets *(aijuan),* les feuilles d'armoise sont brûlées au-dessus de la peau. La feuille d'armoise figure dans la collection des Huit Précieux comme symbole de protection contre les maladies.

Page suivante, détail d'une peinture à l'encre sur papier ; les nœuds du bambou sont symboles de l'intégrité.

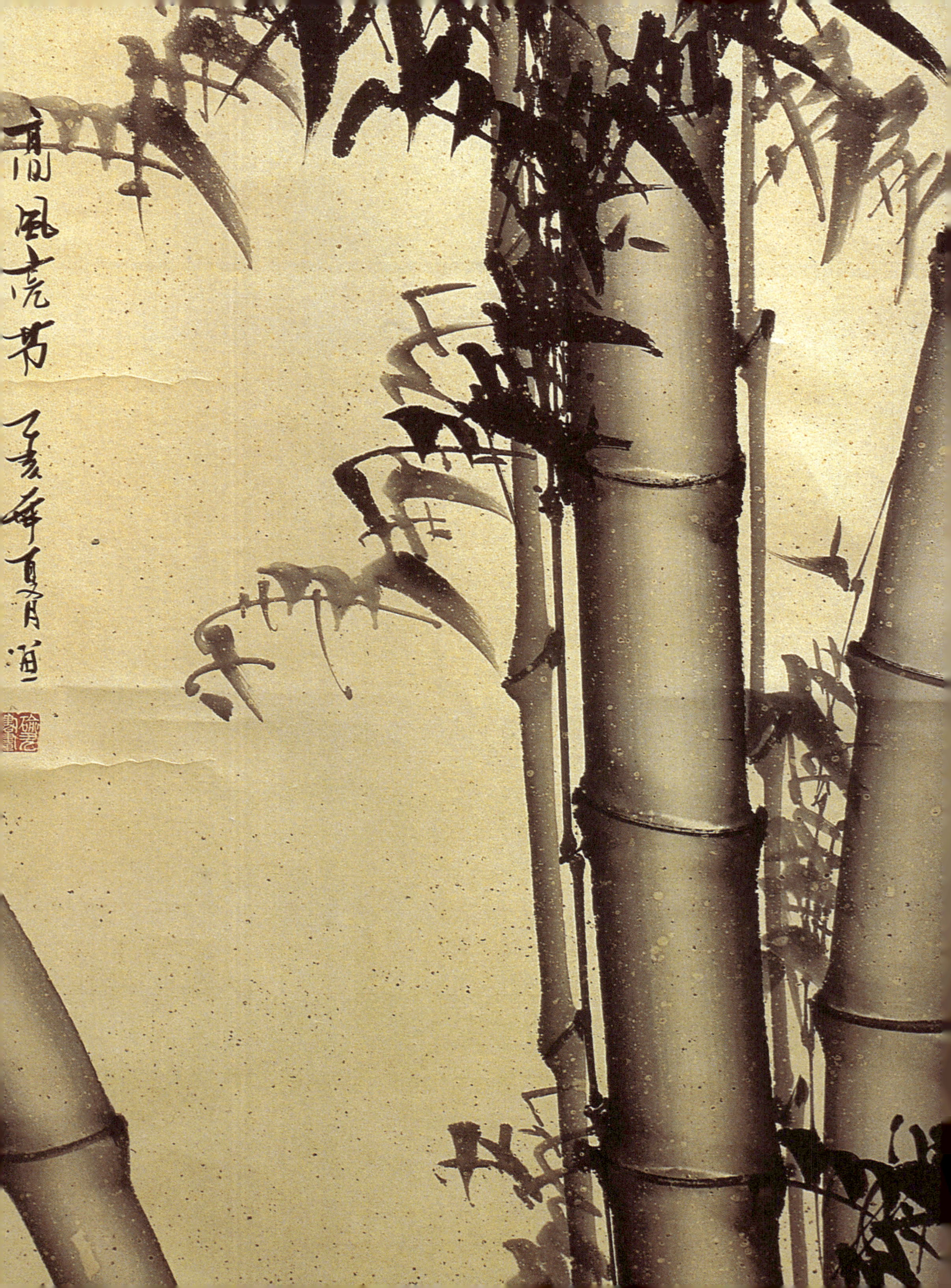
清風亮節
丁亥年夏月

L'azalée *(dujuan)* dont les fleurs rouges apparaissent au printemps est symboliquement liée au coucou qui se met à chanter à cette période : on désigne d'ailleurs la fleur et l'oiseau par le même nom. La tradition raconte que le coucou qui s'était époumoné à chanter toute la nuit avait taché de son sang les fleurs blanches de l'azalée.

Le bambou (*bambusa arundinacea, zhuzi*) est sans doute la plante la plus utilisée par tous les peuples d'Asie et donc la plus vénérée. Son emploi est très fréquent dans la construction, pour les objets de la vie quotidienne, les arts, la nourriture (pousses de bambou) et la médecine (décoction de feuilles et de racines, sève). Le jus de bambou au goût amer *(zhuli)* soignait de la fièvre et était réputé permettre d'atteindre l'immortalité... Le bambou est souvent représenté avec le pin et le prunier (les « Trois amis qui ne craignent pas l'hiver »). Ce symbole confucéen est celui de la constance et de l'amitié indéfectible. C'est aussi celui de la longévité car le bambou est résistant et il reste toujours vert. Il trouve donc sa place à côté du pin où se plaisent à se percher la grue et l'aigle, symboles d'immortalité. D'ailleurs, les légendes racontent que les phénix ne se nourrissaient que de graines de bambou et ne se posaient que sur l'arbre *wutong*. Quand on brûle du bambou, il explose avec un bruit sec ; c'est ainsi qu'il a donné son nom au pétard (*baozhu*, « bambou qui éclate ») dont il est l'ancêtre avant l'invention de la poudre. Une histoire raconte comment un fils désespéré de ne pouvoir nourrir sa mère en hiver pleura sur une touffe de bambou qui, réchauffée par ces pleurs, se mit à pousser... Le symbole préféré des adeptes de Confucius est aussi utilisé par les ascètes taoïstes qui portent un bambou à neuf nœuds comme canne.

Le bananier (*musa sapientum, bajiaoshu*) pousse dans les régions du sud ; il est moins connu en peinture pour son fruit, la banane plantain, que pour la forme de ses feuilles qui servaient de parasol, de parapluie ou d'éventail. Selon la légende de l'étudiant pauvre qui ne pouvait acheter de papier, la feuille de plantain lui servit de support pour ses écritures ; elle est devenue l'emblème de l'autodidacte.

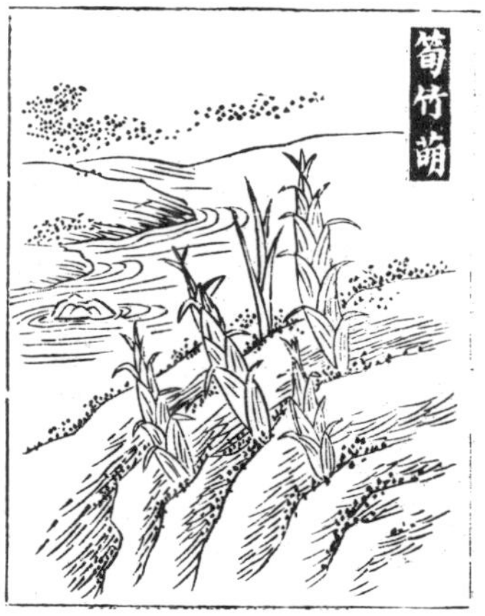

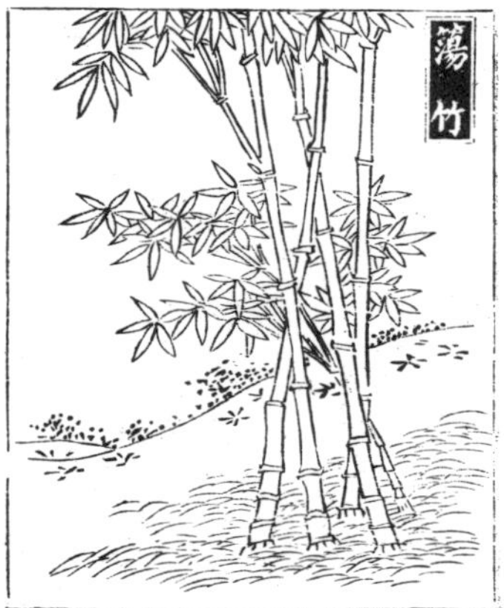

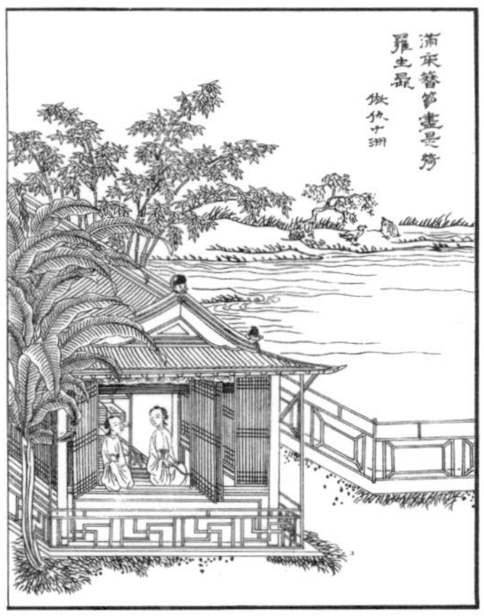

En haut et au centre, pousses de bambou et bosquet de bambous ; en bas, la maison au bananier (Dong Xieyuan, Dongxijiangji).

Le banian (*ficus religiosa, putishu*) est plus connu sous le nom « d'arbre des pagodes » ou « arbre de Bo » (abréviation de *bodhidruma*, « l'arbre de l'Intelligence »). C'est sous cet énorme figuier aux racines adventives que le Bouddha atteignit l'illumination après sept années d'ascèse. Cet arbre à la symbolique importante était planté dans toutes les cours des temples et des monastères. Il fut sans doute introduit de l'Inde en Chine au Ier siècle.

Le camélia *(shanchahua)* et le narcisse *(shuixian)* sont les fleurs qui symbolisent l'hiver car toutes deux résistent au froid du nord de la Chine et annoncent l'arrivée du printemps. Le narcisse est un cadeau traditionnel au Nouvel An chinois. Avec la neige blanche, les fleurs de camélia rouges, blanches ou violettes ont inspiré les poètes. Les feuilles de cette plante sont utilisées en tisane (le camélia appartient à la famille des théacées et son nom chinois est *shancha,* « thé de montagne »). Avec ses fleurs on prépare des médicaments.

Le cerisier (*prunus tomentosa* ou *mume, yingtaoshu*) est l'emblème même de la beauté féminine, des « jeunes filles en fleurs » représentées par les peintres des Han mais surtout des Tang, sous la forme de branches fleuries. Le célèbre poète de l'époque Tang, Bai Juyi (772-846), auteur du *Chant de l'éternel regret,* comparant les lèvres de sa concubine à la cerise, donna naissance à une expression classique, les « petites lèvres vermeilles » qui trouve place dans la liste des canons de la beauté chinoise : « sourcils en feuille de saule, yeux en noyau d'abricot, bouche de petite taille et rouge comme la cerise » *(liuye mei, xinghu yan, yingtao xiao kou, yi diandian).*

Le champignon de l'immortalité ou amadouvier (*polyporus lucidus, lingzhi*) est fréquemment utilisé comme symbole de longévité et de bonheur. On le représente dans les mains des Immortels ou de Laozi, dans la bouche du cerf et même entre ses cornes… Il pousse sur les troncs des arbres feuillus, prend une couleur acajou en séchant et devient ligneux tout en gardant sa forme une fois cueilli. Comme il se conserve longtemps, les légendes d'immortalité se sont développées à son sujet. La mythologie taoïste raconte qu'il n'apparaissait que lors de règnes exceptionnels. Mais on ramassait aussi des agarics pour fabriquer des remèdes et la truffe *(fuling)* était un cadeau de prix pour la cuisine impériale. Elle entrait aussi dans la pharmacopée traditionnelle et la fabrication de cosmétiques. Selon H. A. Giles, *(Chinese English Dictionnary),* le « sceptre de mandarin » *(ruyi),* étrange objet décoratif ou bâton de commandement en forme de volute à pommeau, aurait emprunté sa forme au champignon *lingzhi.* Avec le temps, il a perdu sa fonction première pour devenir un symbole de souhait de réussite (par homophonie avec l'expression *ruyi,* « comme vous le souhaitez, à votre gré »). C'était, à l'époque impériale un cadeau très apprécié que l'on échangeait entre gens aisés qui en faisaient fabriquer dans des matières aussi précieuses que le jade, l'or ou l'argent.

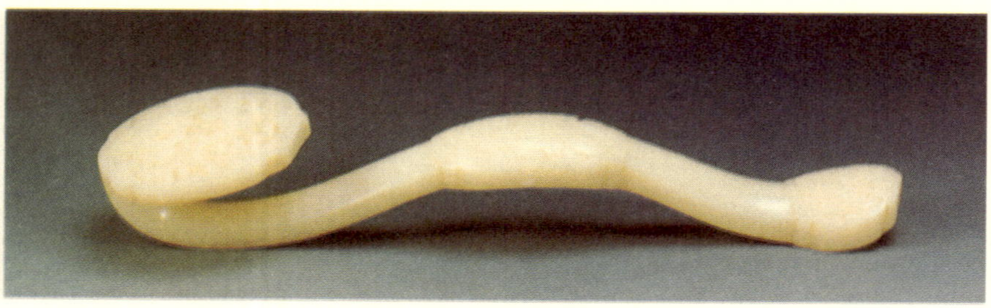

Sceptre ruyi, *jade blanc, dynastie des Qing (XIXe siècle).*

Le chinomanthe odorant *(lamei)* est une plante typiquement chinoise qui fleurit en hiver. Comme «elle goûte en premier le printemps», elle est symbole de renouveau. Ses petites fleurs ont la couleur jaune de cire d'abeille. Elle sert essentiellement de décoration.

Le chrysanthème (*chrysanthemum indicum, juhua*) est cultivé depuis presque 3000 ans, et il est connu pour ses qualités médicinales. On en faisait un thé en infusant ses pétales dans du vin chaud. C'est la fleur de l'automne, qui se célèbre le 9e jour de la 9e lune (fête de Chongyang). À cette occasion, on sortait en groupe pour une excursion dans les collines, on tressait des couronnes de feuilles d'oranger, on buvait du vin de chrysanthème en se livrant à des exercices poétiques. Mais le chrysanthème était aussi associé à la solitude et à une retraite paisible. Le poète Tao Yuanming (372-427) refusa les honneurs qui lui étaient offerts pour se consacrer aux arts et à la culture de ces fleurs. Parce que le nom du chrysanthème *(ju)* était phonétiquement proche du mot « longtemps » *(jiu)* il a été associé à la longévité et à la chance *(ji)*.

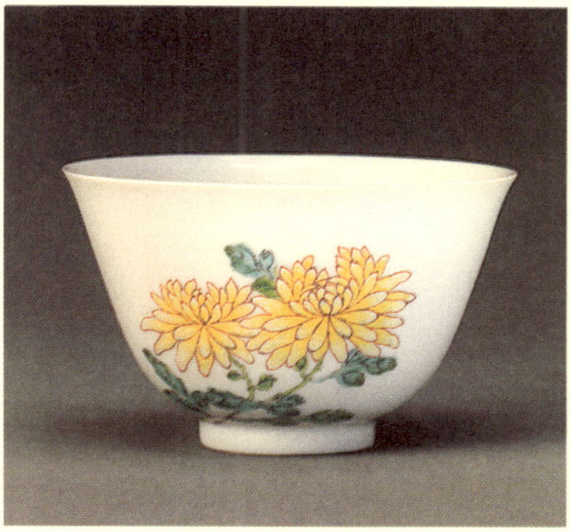

La gourde (*lapenaria vulgaris, hulu*), plante grimpante de la famille des cucurbitacées, produit un fruit qui fut longtemps utilisé comme récipient à haute valeur symbolique. Les renflements de la calebasse étaient comparés par les taoïstes à l'intérieur d'une grotte miniature, résidence des Immortels. C'est dans ce récipient que les Immortels plaçaient aussi les herbes médicinales qu'ils ramassaient dans la campagne. La gourde est donc devenue tout naturellement l'enseigne des pharmaciens. Elle est l'attribut de l'Immortel Li Tieguai qui « se retirait dans sa gourde pour dormir », et figure aussi accrochée au bâton de pèlerin de Shouxinglao, le dieu de la Longévité. Cette forme à double renflement est donc devenue un symbole traditionnel pour se protéger des maladies. Ceci explique la fréquence de ce thème en peinture, en sculpture et en céramique. On en fit même des empreintes de sceaux pour apposer sur les calligraphies. Comme amulette, elle était taillée en bois de pêcher et portée au poignet ou autour du cou.

La grenade (*punica grantata, shiliu*) est venue du Moyen-Orient probablement au IIe siècle av. J.-C. et fut cultivée pour sa fleur et son fruit. À cause de leurs nombreuses graines ou de leurs pépins, un certain nombre de fruits comme la grenade, la cacahuète, le melon, la courge ou le lotus font partie des cadeaux de mariage exprimant des souhaits d'une grande descendance. À l'origine, on offrait de vrais fruits, puis on prit l'habitude d'offrir des figurations de ces fruits sous forme de peintures, porcelaines, ou bibelots de

Coupe en porcelaine, décor de chrysanthèmes, règne de Yongzheng (1723-1735).

bois taillé. La grenade est souvent représentée, en peinture notamment, au sein d'une triade porte-bonheur associant la pêche et la bergamote (*citrus medica* ou *sarcodactilis*). Ce fruit est communément appelé en Chine la « main de Bouddha » *(foshougan)* car il a une forme multidigitée. Il symbolise la protection divine et la richesse à cause du geste de la main qui prend l'argent. Mais on peut aussi y voir une homophonie avec les caractères traditionnels de bonheur *(fu)* et d'éternité *(shou)*. Les trois fruits forment donc, en association avec la chauve-souris, un signifiant classique de vœux de bonheur que l'on retrouve surtout peints sur la porcelaine.

L'hémérocalle *(xuan)*, fleur jaune de la famille des lys, est aussi appelée « belle-d'un-jour » car sa floraison, qui a lieu en été, est très éphémère. On conseillait aux femmes de porter à la ceinture de l'hémérocalle fauve pour avoir un fils. La plante était connue pour ses propriétés calmantes et diurétiques. Une fois séchées, on peut consommer les fleurs *(huanghuacai)* mais fraîches, elles sont un violent poison.

Le jasmin (*moli* ou *suxing*) est originaire de Perse et ses petites fleurs odorantes qui ne s'ouvrent que le soir étaient appréciées déjà depuis l'époque des Han. C'est sous les Song que sa culture se répandit : on en mit en pot dans tous les palais. De cette même époque date l'utilisation du jasmin pour parfumer certains thés verts ou noirs. Le thé au jasmin *(molihua cha)* dont la meilleure fleur pousse dans la province du Fujian, est fort, il est bu pour combattre le goût prononcé des fruits de mer ou du mouton. Sous les Ming fut fabriquée la crème de jasmin qui deviendra un cosmétique populaire, faisant de cette petite fleur blanche le symbole de la féminité et de la douceur. Pour la décoration des cheveux, des fleurs de jasmin étaient aussi piquées sur les bandeaux que portaient les femmes en certaines occasions. On en faisait dans le sud de petits bouquets en boule, portés à la boutonnière des robes longues du soir.

Le kaki (*diospyros kaki, shizi*) est le fruit du plaqueminier. Les fruits charnus de couleur jaune-orange ne sont mûrs qu'après les premiers froids. Leur couleur éclatante a inspiré les artistes qui en ont fait un emblème de la joie. C'est un motif très répandu en peinture (en général avec des singes qui en sont friands). Homophone de *shi* (« affaires, situation, emploi »), c'est un souhait de succès.

Le lotus ou nénuphar lotus (*lian* ou *he*) regroupe sous ce nom plusieurs espèces de nymphéacées, dont le célèbre « lotus sacré » *(bailian)*. De couleur blanche, celui-ci est le symbole de la pureté et de la perfection. « Il pousse dans la boue, mais n'est pas souillé, il se baigne dans l'onde, mais il n'est pas provocant. » Tout comme les enseignements du Bouddha, les fruits du lotus sont mûrs quand les fleurs s'épanouissent. La littérature n'a pas été avare de compliments pour cette belle plante ornementale dont la symbolique est

Page de droite, bouton, fleur épanouie et graines de lotus : le passé, le présent et le futur (symbolique bouddhique).

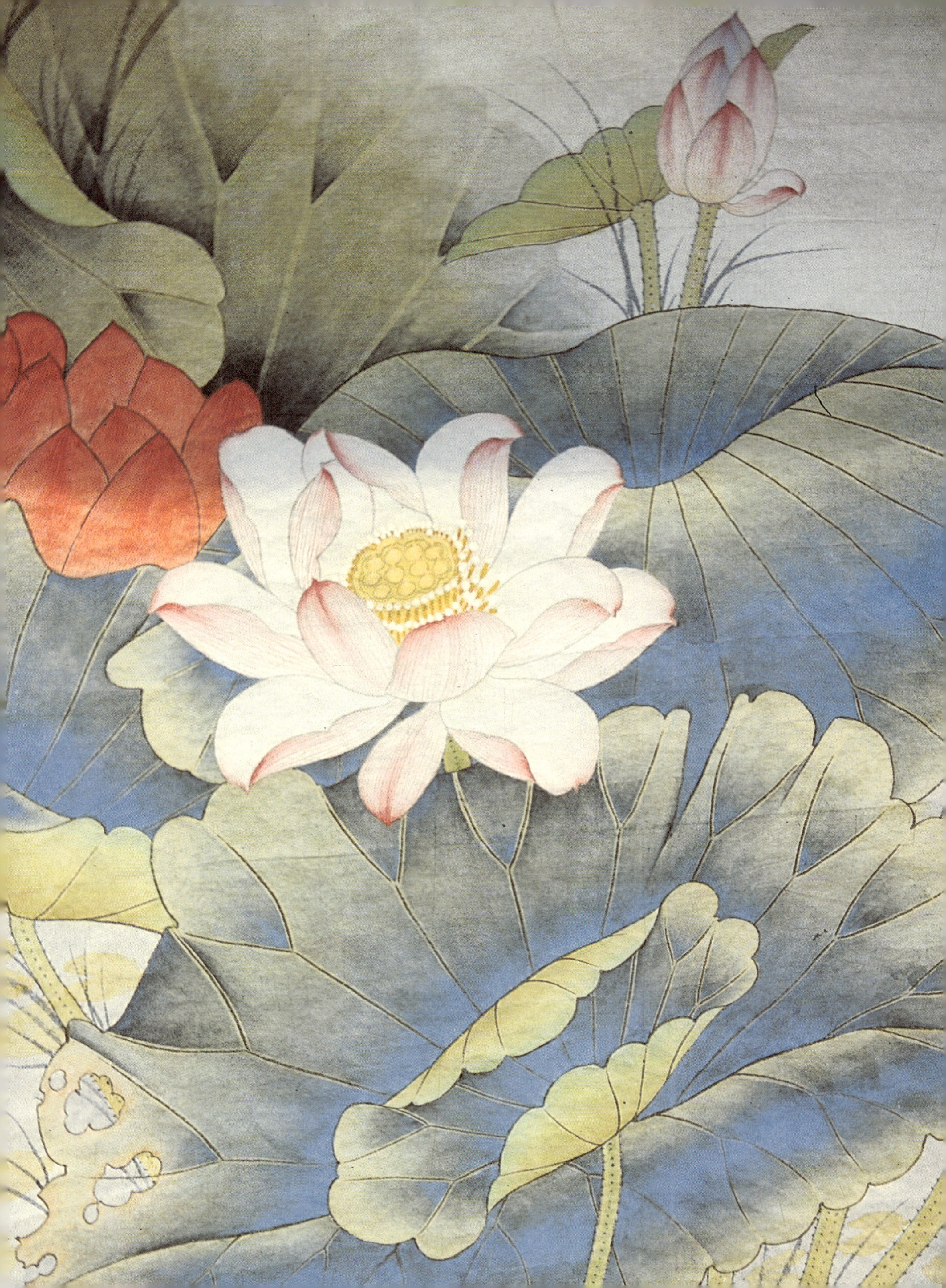

riche. Pour les bouddhistes, le lotus figure parmi les Huit Précieux. La Roue de la Loi serait même une représentation stylisée de la fleur de lotus (voir p. 21). Dans l'art bouddhique, elle sert de siège ou de piédestal aux divinités qui tiennent aussi à la main un bouton de lotus. C'est le cas de la déesse de la miséricorde Guanyin, version chinoise féminisée d'Avalokiteçvara. Pour les taoïstes, l'Immortelle He Xiangu porte sur l'épaule une énorme fleur de lotus, symbole de pureté, ou une tige avec les graines, emblème de fécondité. Les très nombreux noms littéraires donnés au lotus permettent plusieurs analogies: *lian* peut aussi s'entendre comme « unir, enchaîner ou aimer passionnément », *he* c'est aussi « l'union, l'harmonie » et *lianzi* (la graine) c'est « réussir aux examens ». L'expression « les lotus d'or » *(jinlian)* ou par jeu de mot « les serpes d'or » *(jinlian),* allusion à leur forme, désignait les pieds bandés des femmes d'autrefois. Un poème décrit les « lys d'or » poussant dans l'empreinte des pied de Pan Fei, une danseuse fameuse qui serait à l'origine de la mode des pieds bandés. Le lotus est la plante dont on utilise la racine, la tige, la fleur, et la graine. Sa cueillette était l'objet de réunions traditionnelles et de cérémonies dans les jardins publics ou des palais. L'impératrice Tseu Hi (Cixi) qui pourtant craignait l'eau n'hésitait pas à se faire photographier dans sa barque impériale au milieu d'un champ de nénuphars, déguisée en Guanyin.

Le magnolia (*mulanhua* ou *yulan,* « fleur de jade ») s'appelle aussi « la fleur qui accueille le printemps » et fleurit avant que n'apparaissent les feuilles. Pour sa beauté et son parfum, elle est l'emblème de la beauté féminine. C'est parce qu'elle porte le même nom qu'une héroïne de l'époque des Jin (Hua Mulan), qui combattit pendant douze années à la place de son père sans que l'on ne devine son identité, que cette fleur symbolise la modestie.

Le mûrier *(sangshu)* est un arbre du centre et du sud de la Chine, en particulier le « mûrier blanc » *(morus alba)* qui fournit les feuilles pour l'élevage du ver à soie, une des richesses de ces régions. Il est donc l'emblème du confort à la maison et du « sol natal » *(sangzi)*. En effet, le mûrier et le catalpa *(qiumu)* étaient deux arbres que l'on plantait traditionnellement près des maisons d'habitation, le premier pour la culture du ver à soie, le second parce qu'on en tirait du bois dur pour les cercueils. Hélas, le mot *sang* étant homophone de « deuil, mort », on devait veiller à ne pas planter les mûriers trop près des portes ou des fenêtres pour ne pas attirer le malheur sur la famille. C'était aussi une branche de mûrier que tenait le fils à l'enterrement de sa mère. Au demeurant, dans le nord de la Chine, le mûrier n'est jamais planté dans la cour de maison car on dit qu' il porte malheur…

Le narcisse est appelé « le génie des eaux » *(shuixian)* car on trouvait cette plante près des marais. C'est une des fleurs d'hiver préférées des Chinois qui cultivent son bulbe dans une porcelaine remplie d'eau et de galets. La fleur est offerte comme cadeau à la Fête du Printemps. On faisait en sorte qu'elle fleurisse à temps, c'était alors signe de bonheur pour toute l'année. Le narcisse est le symbole de la pureté et de l'indépendance.

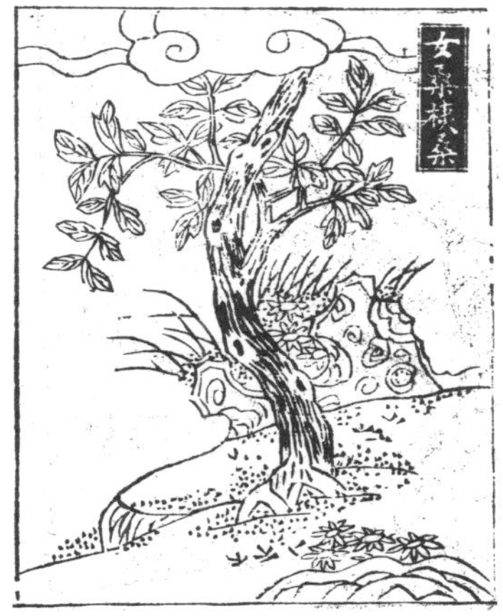

L'orchidée *(lan)* dont la culture remonte à la plus haute antiquité compte près de mille espèces en Chine (en particulier dans la province du Yunnan). Elles sont maintenant cultivées comme fleurs ornementales mais il semble, selon les textes anciens, que les orchidées sauvages avaient autrefois un pouvoir purificatoire d'une part (utilisées lors de cérémonies de l'eau) et d'autre part le pouvoir magique d'écarter les maladies. Classée parmi les « Quatre fleurs nobles », elle est symbole de pureté et, sous les Ming, on lui accorda le titre d'« homme intègre » *(junzi)*. Le célèbre traité de peinture, le *Jardin gros comme un grain de moutarde,* expliquait comment faire une reproduction parfaite de feuille d'orchidée d'un seul coup de pinceau. C'est bien entendu un motif très fréquent de l'art décoratif sur porcelaine pour exprimer la beauté, le parfum, le raffinement, l'amour et même une grande descendance.

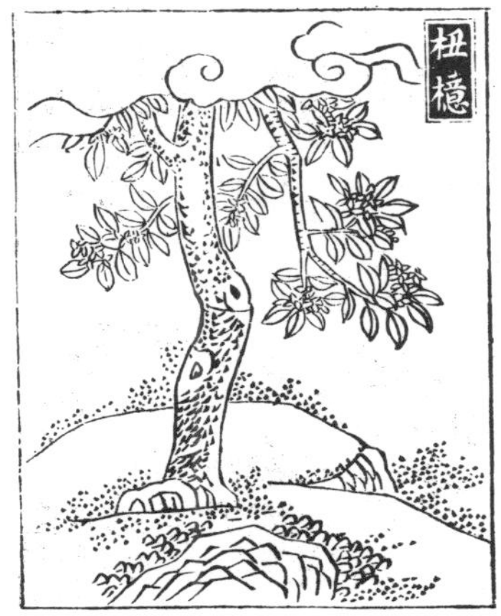

Le pêcher (*amygdalus persica, taoshu*), serait originaire de Chine où depuis longtemps on lui attribuait des pouvoirs magiques pour repousser le mal. Très tôt des talismans *(taofu)* furent faits dans ce bois ; on les suspendait de chaque côté de la porte. Ils se transformèrent en planchettes porteuses d'inscriptions puis, plus tard, en sentences parallèles de papier que l'on renouvelait au Nouvel An. Les taoïstes gravaient des sceaux dans du bois de pêcher pour apposer leur marque sur les papiers talismans. La résine du pêcher mélangée à de la cendre de mûrier servait de laque à cheveux. On raconte que, pour conjurer le mauvais sort, des noyaux de pêche étaient enterrés dans les fondations des maisons nouvelles. Par ailleurs, sa dureté fit de ce bois le matériau privilégié pour la fabrication des peignes. Les pêchers en fleurs ont inspiré les peintres qui les représentent souvent avec le prunier. Mais c'est surtout le fruit, la pêche, à laquelle est attachée toute une symbolique. C'est d'abord l'emblème du printemps, donc de l'union, car on attendait la fin de l'hiver pour célébrer les mariages, mais surtout c'est le fruit de l'immortalité. Selon la tradition, le pêcher des dieux poussait dans les jardins de la Reine Mère d'Occident et ne produisait de fruits que tous les trois mille ans ; ils étaient alors consommés par les Immortels au cours d'un banquet rituel.

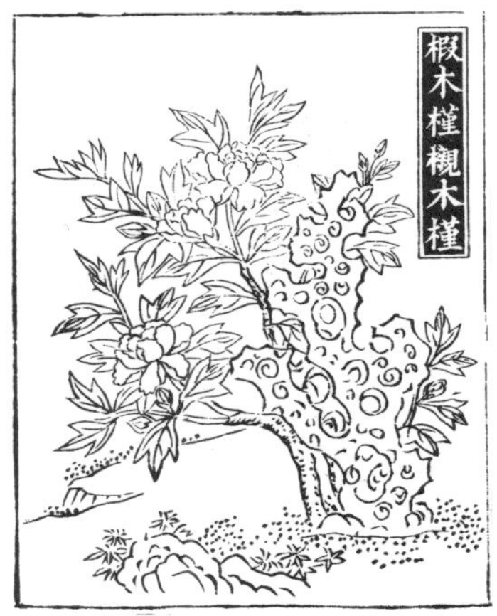

De haut en bas, mûrier, pêcher et buisson de pivoines dans une rocaille (gravures extraites du dictionnaire Ying Songchao huitu erya*).*

Selon le roman de Wu Cheng'en *(Le Voyage en Occident)*, cette fête aurait été perturbée par le singe Sun Wukong qui vola les pêches sacrées. Le dieu de la Longévité, Shouxinglao, est souvent représenté aussi naissant d'une énorme pêche sous le regard de chérubins.

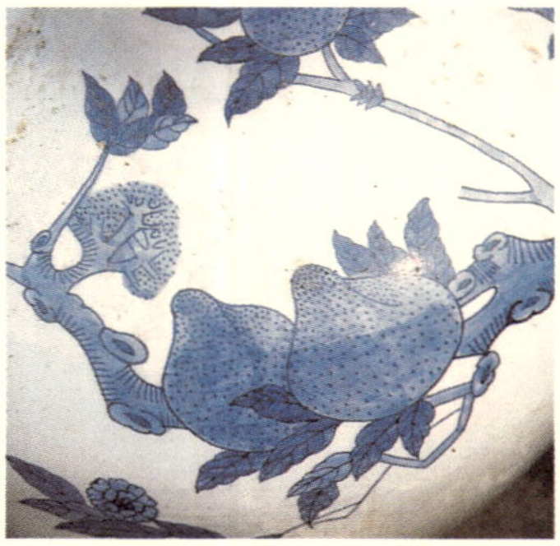

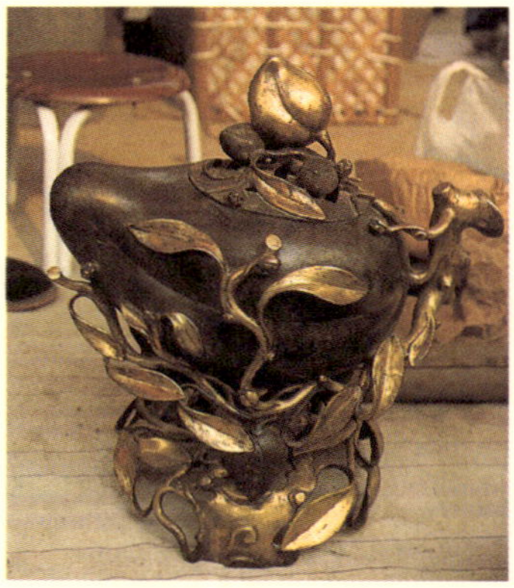

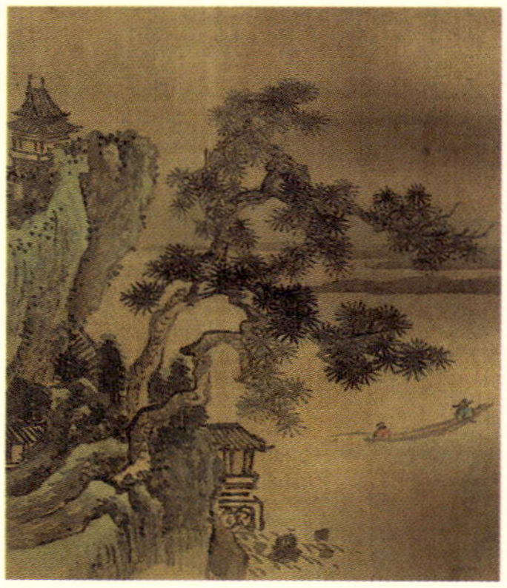

Le pin *(song)* est souvent confondu par les Chinois avec le sapin et le cyprès qui ont la propriété de ne pas perdre leur feuillage. C'est ce qui avait frappé les anciens et le qualifia pour être l'emblème de la longévité. Toutefois, dans certaines régions, le pin est redouté car il est souvent planté près des sépultures et donc associé à la mort. Les paysages miniatures, si prisés par les lettrés chinois et japonais, sont souvent composés d'espèces de pin que l'on peut soumettre à de nombreux traitements. Comme le pin pousse dans des terrains rocheux, les Chinois y voyaient là « l'essence de la pierre » confirmant son caractère d'immortalité. La propagande communiste s'empara d'ailleurs de cette image pour en faire le symbole de la résistance et de l'indomptabilité.

La pivoine (*pæonia arboria, mudan*), originaire du centre et de l'ouest de la Chine, était déjà cultivée sous les Tang. L'empereur Gao Zong en aurait lancé la mode et l'impératrice Wu Zetian en aurait développé la culture à Luoyang. L'engouement devint de plus en plus grand sous les Song puis sous les Ming. Déclarée « beauté nationale et parfum céleste », c'est une fleur du printemps très appréciée pour ses grosses fleurs décoratives de couleur rose clair ou rouge. Elle était un symbole de richesse, de réussite sociale (d'où ses surnoms « fleur des riches », « fleur des rois », « reine de toutes les fleurs »). La représentation d'un papillon *(die)* sur une pivoine évoque un souhait de « richesse jusqu'à 70 ans » (*die*, littéralement, « septuagénaire »). La pivoine exprimait la beauté féminine sous toutes ses formes (blanche : jeune femme pure ; rouge : courtisane). Cette fleur fut très fréquemment utilisée en peinture, seul ou associé avec des oiseaux (faisan et phénix) ou avec d'autres fleurs comme l'hibiscus, le chrysanthème, le lotus.

Le poirier (*pyrus sinensis, lishu*) abritait le duc de Shao, (1053 av. J.-C.), lorsqu'il rendait la justice, tout comme notre bon roi saint Louis sous son chêne... De cette époque date la comparaison du poirier à la justice équitable. Le poirier est un arbre qui peut vivre plus de trois cents ans, il symbolise donc aussi la longévité. On évoque fréquemment le Parc des Poiriers qui est le nom de la première école d'art dramatique ouverte à Xi'an au IXe siècle. Mais il est aussi homophone de « quitter, se séparer » ; on s'abstenait donc d'offrir des poires à des jeunes mariés !

En haut, porcelaine à décor de branche de pêcher ; au centre, brûle-parfum taoïste en forme de pêche (bronze et cuivre, XIXe siècle) ; en bas, pins accrochés à des rochers (peinture sur soie, XVIIIe siècle). Page de droite, pivoine (peinture sur papier).

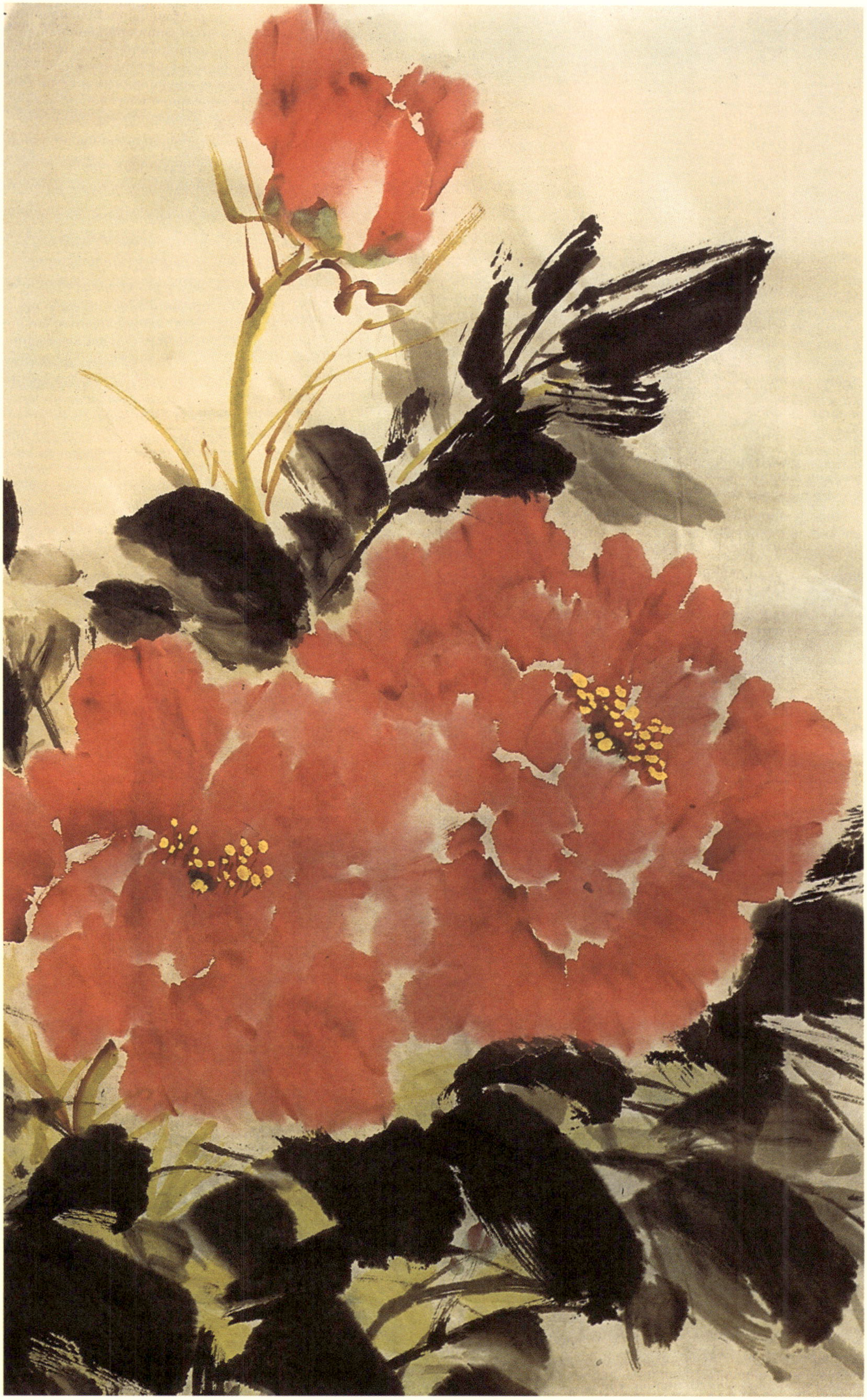

Le pommier *(pingguoshu)* est un motif traditionnel des peintres car ses fleurs blanches et roses représentent la beauté féminine. La pomme *(pingguo),* qui se trouve être homophone de « vivre en paix, paisible » *(ping),* est utilisée dans de nombreuses locutions.

Le prunier (*prunus, lishu* ou *mei*) est l'arbre de l'hiver qui annonce l'arrivée du printemps. C'est un motif classique des vases *meiping* que l'on offrait à l'occasion du Nouvel An chinois : des fleurs et des branches de prunier étaient peintes en blanc sur un fond bleu réticulé qui exprimait la glace en train de se rompre. On disait que le prunier vivait longtemps et pouvait produire en dépit de son grand âge de nombreux fruits et des fleurs ; c'est donc un symbole de longévité renforcé par son homophonie avec l'adverbe *mei* (« toujours, souvent, continuellement »). La légende dit aussi que Confucius serait né sous un prunier, d'où son nom, Li Er. La fleur de prunier *(meihua),* blanche aux cinq pétales, stylisée en décoration, devint avant 1949 l'emblème national représentant les cinq races de la Chine. L'étoile rouge à cinq branches remplaça à l'avènement de la République populaire cette fleur qui figure encore sur le drapeau de Taiwan.

Le saule (*populus, liushu*) était l'arbre du printemps et de l'eau, une expression populaire faisait d'ailleurs allusion au « vert de son feuillage et au rouge des fleurs » *(liu lü, hua hong)* qui caractérisent cette saison. C'est aussi à l'arrondi gracieux de ses feuilles que l'on comparait des sourcils bien dessinés (*liu mei,* « sourcils de saule »). En dépit de ces qualités, on se gardait bien d'en planter près des maisons car il avait la fâcheuse réputation de favoriser les mœurs galantes (*fengliu,* littéralement, « le vent et le saule »). On disait que la nuit il se transformait en belle femme qui accostait les voyageurs pour les ensorceler. Comme pour le bois de pêcher, le bois de saule était démonifuge, on l'utilisait pour la fabrication d'amulettes. Des cure-dents faits dans ce bois étaient censés guérir les maux de dents. Lors de la Fête des Morts (Qingming, « fête de la pureté et de la clarté »), on balayait les sépultures avec des branches de saule et on tressait des couronnes d'osier pour se garantir un peu de longévité. Les feuilles de saule préservaient des morsures des Cinq venimeux. La décoction de bouton de saule était utilisée en médecine. Dans la tradition bouddhiste, il était l'attribut de la déesse Guanyin qui se servait d'un bouquet de feuilles de saule pour asperger de l'eau sacrée. Les peintres ont, bien entendu, fait usage de toute cette mythologie et un saule pleureur est très souvent présent dans les paysages des peintures traditionnelles.

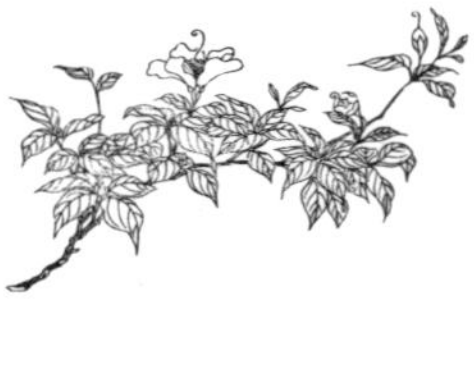

Les pierres à rêver

梦石

mengshi, littéralement, « pierres de rêve ».

« L'eau qui tombe goutte à goutte, à la longue perce la pierre » *(di shui chuan shi).* Symbole de la dureté, la « pierre » *(shi)* était l'emblème de l'immuabilité, de l'éternité, de l'honnêteté. Pendant des milliers d'années, les pierres ont fait l'objet d'un véritable culte en Chine. Toutefois, de cette passion pour les pierres, il ne reste dans la Chine contemporaine que de rares vestiges... Quelques lettrés-collectionneurs ouvrent encore de temps à autre leur collection à des amis et échangent dans la plus grande confidentialité de précieux spécimens minéralogiques. Les architectes-paysagistes continuent toutefois de dresser des rochers dans les jardins publics ou devant les bâtiments officiels, mais ces « fausses montagnes » cimentées n'ont plus rien à voir avec les exquises réalisations de leurs prédécesseurs. En revanche, les stèles sont encore l'objet d'une vénération particulière, car elles sont le support inaltérable d'œuvres écrites de la plus haute valeur : les « forêts de pierre » ou forêts de stèles, vieilles de plus de mille ans, restent encore des références, même pour les calligraphes contemporains.

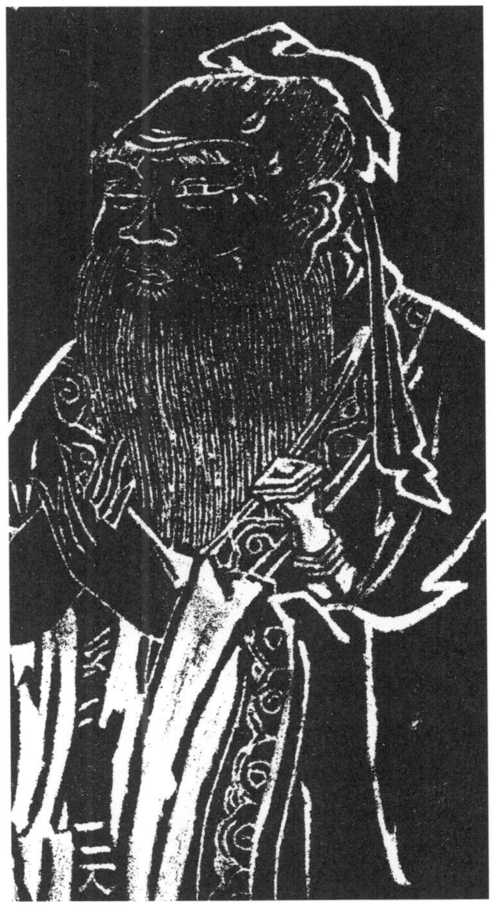

À l'époque des dynasties légendaires, on raconte que Yu-le-Grand, le fondateur des Xia (2000 av. J.-C.), serait né d'une pierre, tout comme son fils qu'il fallut arracher aux entrailles de la mère d'un coup d'épée. C'est aussi en exécutant une danse sacrée sur des pierres que ce même Yu aurait mis fin aux inondations qui ravageaient son pays... Autre héros légendaire, Nüwa, sœur et épouse de Fuxi, aurait réparé l'un des piliers soutenant le ciel et donné ainsi naissance à la parabole populaire « réparer le ciel » (*Nüwa bu tian* : « rétablir une situation »). Sous les Zhou, il était déjà fait mention des pierres précieuses. C'est sous les Song que se développeront les échanges, les produits de luxe comme les pierres rares en Chine : la cornaline, l'agate, l'ambre, étaient payés en minerais d'or, d'argent ou d'étain et en monnaie de cuivre. Dans les légendes anciennes, des pierres précieuses comme le lapis-lazuli servaient de nourriture aux génies qui entouraient la Reine Mère d'Occident vivant dans son fabuleux palais des monts Kunlun, où poussait notamment l'Arbre de Jade. On y trouvait aussi ces extraordinaires lithophones *(qing),* dont certains en

Estampage d'une stèle, détail, « Confucius allant enseigner », portrait par Wu Daozi, dynastie des Tang (618-907 ap. J.-C.).

jaspe vert *(biyu)*, taillés en forme d'équerre, donnaient un son inégalé. La pierre musicale qui figure ainsi dans la collection des Huit Objets Précieux bouddhistes était le symbole de la pureté et l'intégrité. Pour les cérémonies, on les utilisait seuls ou sous forme de carillons suspendus à un cadre de bois.

C'est sans doute sous l'influence des taoïstes qui vénéraient les montagnes comme séjour des Immortels que les jardins de rocailles se développèrent. Mais c'est vraiment sous les Song (du Xe au XIIe siècle), que la vogue des paysages en miniature se répandit. Le *Jardin gros comme un grain de moutarde,* (1679-1701), s'attarde en de nombreux chapitres à la description de ces « paysages en pot » (*penjing* ou *bonsaï* en japonais) que l'on qualifia aussi de « poésie sans mot et de peinture sculptée ». Ces œuvres se rangeaient dans deux genres : des compositions de montagnes miniatures, en pierre naturelle ou travaillée, que l'on complétait avec de minuscules éléments de céramique (personnages, ponts, pagodes, bateaux). L'ensemble reposait sur un bac rempli d'eau. Certaines pierres ayant la particularité d'absorber l'eau se couvraient peu à peu de mousse ou de végétation naine. Comme en témoignent les traités sur la peinture et le paysage de Gu Kaizhi (époque Jin), la montagne et l'eau étaient depuis le IIIe siècle ap. J-C. des motifs traditionnels de la peinture chinoise, l'homme y apparaissant tout petit comme un élément infime de l'univers. Comme le *yin* et le *yang,* les deux éléments naturels de ces compositions traditionnelles s'opposent et se complètent : l'eau descend et la montagne monte, l'eau est l'expression même du mouvement, du fugitif, la pierre celle de l'immobilité et de la permanence. La contemplation de ces paysages faisait partie de l'état d'esprit des lettrés qui trouvaient dans ces petites merveilles la sérénité et l'inspiration. L'expression « monts et cours d'eau » *(shanshui)* est d'ailleurs devenue le mot désignant la peinture de paysage. Presque mille ans plus tard, l'Europe s'extasiera devant les « jardins de rocaille » chinois ou japonais qu'elle placera à profusion dans ses « folies ». Les arbres nains (pins, cyprès, ormes, bambous) ou des racines composaient la deuxième catégorie de ces décorations. La patience et l'ingéniosité des jardiniers chinois firent des merveilles, non seulement pour sélectionner des espèces, mais pour créer des formes extraordinaires. L'un des plus grands connaisseurs du XVIe siècle, Du Long, a théorisé sur l'importance de la forme, de la couleur de ces plantations mais aussi sur leur environnement.

C'est sous les Song que parut le premier *Catalogue des pierres de la forêt des nuages (Yunlin shibu)* attribué à Du Wan, peut-être le descendant d'un des plus célèbres poètes chinois de la dynastie des Tang, Du Fu (712-770). L'ouvrage classait les pierres selon les appellations données par les artistes : elles étaient décrites comme des « pics » ou des « creux », des « assoiffées »… Sous les Ming, l'appréciation des pierres se fit plus rationnelle, selon les

Page de droite, paysage avec décor de montagne peint sur soie (règne de Jiajing, dynastie des Ming, 1534).

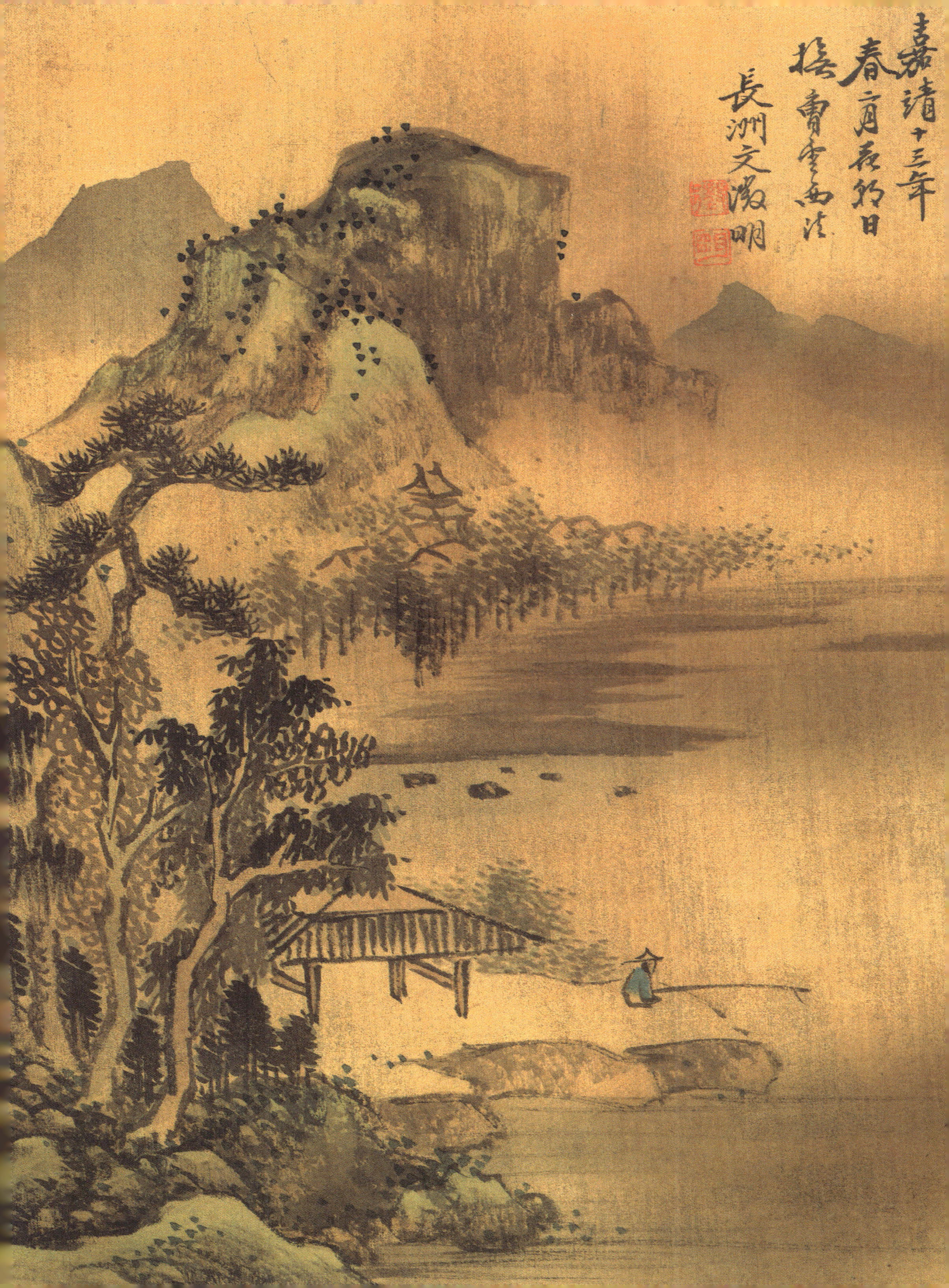
嘉靖十三年
春二月花朝日
摹曹雲西法
長洲文徵明

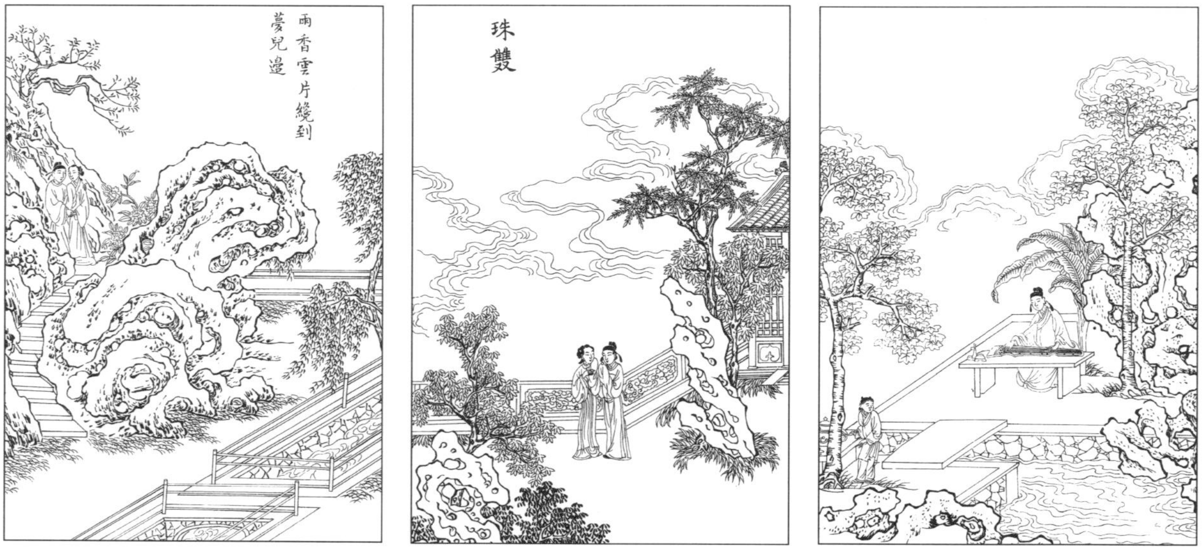

« Quatre vertus », elles étaient classées en minces *(shou),* plissées *(zhou),* poreuses *(tou)* ou translucides *(touguang).*

Traditionnellement, les pierres se rangent, pour les experts, dans les catégories suivantes.

Les « pierres paysages » *(jingshi)* étaient d'extraordinaires reproductions en miniature de montagnes aux pics découpés et aux vallées profondes, évoquant les Cinq montagnes sacrées de Chine. Montés sur des socles de bois précieux en palissandre ou bois de rose, spécialement ajustés à leur forme. Ces « paysages » à trois ou cinq monts étaient souvent utilisés par les lettrés comme pose-pinceaux.

Les pierres multicolores *(caishi),* appelées aussi « fleurs de pluie » *(yuhuashi),* tiraient leur nom des nombreuses légendes qui les faisaient tomber du ciel sous forme de graines se transformant en fleurs à l'arrivée au sol. Ce sont en fait de simples galets d'agate ou de cornaline (ceux de la région de Nankin sont célèbres), aux couleurs vives, quelquefois translucides et polis pour être agréables dans le creux de la main. Les mélanges de couleurs créent d'une manière naturelle d'étonnants motifs que l'on rehausse en les trempant dans l'eau. Ces galets sont souvent employés dans les aquariums pour poissons ou tortues.

Les « pierres de rêve » *(mengshi)* étaient des plaques montées dans un cadre de bois sur socle et utilisées comme écran de table ou même de *kang* (le lit de briques chauffées de la Chine du Nord). Les veine du marbre de Dali (Yunnan), suggèrent d'imaginaires paysages aux cimes embrumées comme les monts Huangshan et même des silhouettes de personnages.

De gauche à droite, gigantesque pierre de Taihu, rencontre dans un jardin de rocaille, lettré jouant du luth à l'abri d'un bananier sous le regard d'un domestique préparant le thé (d'après le Dongxijiangji).

Les « pierres *chan* » *(chanshi)* étaient particulièrement recherchées des bouddhistes qui, dans le secret de leur retraite, s'adonnaient à la méditation *chan* (*zen* en japonais) en contemplant leurs couleurs et leurs formes étranges.

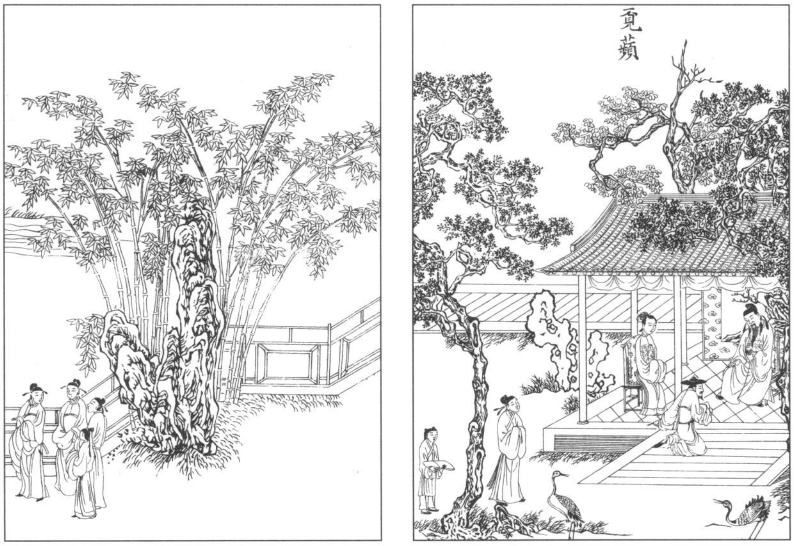

Les « pierres ressemblantes » *(leishi)* étaient collectionnées pour les formes de personnages, d'animaux, de ponts et même de caractères d'écriture qu'elles évoquaient…

Les fossiles *(huashi),* plus rares, charmaient par le mystère de leur ancienneté et par l'originalité des sujets. Animaux, poissons, coquillages, fougères incrustées revêtaient un aspect légendaire qui les rendaient encore plus précieux. C'est dans cette catégorie qu'entrent les œufs de dinosaures dont de si nombreux exemplaires sont exhumés chaque jour en Chine. Les stalactites et les stalagmites sont aussi particulièrement appréciées, non seulement pour leurs formes étonnantes ou leur couleur laiteuse, mais parce que ces concrétions proviennent de grottes, résidence des Immortels dans la tradition taoïste.

Les « pierres cristallines » *(jingshi),* très nombreuses dans le sous-sol de la Chine, tout autant pour leur diversité que pour leur valeur marchande, jouèrent un grand rôle dans les accessoires du costume. Dès la période féodale, certains dignitaires arboraient sur leurs vêtements des plaques de rang en métal précieux, incrustées de pierres semi-précieuses *(baoshi)* comme l'améthyste, la turquoise ou le saphir… Plus tard sous les Ming et sous les Qing, les chapeaux de mandarin s'orneront d'un « bouton » dont la matière et la couleur variaient avec le rang. L'étiquette prévoyait même la nature et la couleur des pierres des pendants que l'on portait à la ceinture *(peiyu)* – jade blanc ou vert – ou des « pierres de saison » (vert ou bleu au printemps, rouge l'été…).

Mais parmi toutes ces merveilles de la nature, ce sont pourtant de bien modestes calcaires qui durent leur popularité à la forme étrange de leurs cavités *(guaishi).* D'énormes blocs arrachés aux carrières de Suzhou étaient volontairement abandonnés pendant des années sur les rives du lac Tai (Taihu) où les vagues, le vent et la pluie leur sculptaient des formes déchiquetées et insolites. D'autres, de la même province du Jiangsu, étaient

De gauche à droite, réunion de lettrés devant un « bosquet de bambous » (nom attribué à un groupe d'artistes), grues devant un pavillon d'audience, pierre de Taihu en forme de chataigne d'eau décorant une terrasse (d'après le Dongxijiangji).

connues sous le nom de « pierres aux formes curieuses de Yangzhou » *(Yangzhou guaishi)*. Placés dans un jardin, ces rochers évoquaient pour les taoïstes un monde de grottes et de montagnes où s'abritaient les Immortels. C'est par ces nombreuses cavités, disaient-ils, que circulaient les « souffles vitaux » *(qi)*. Les jardins de Suzhou ou de Shanghaï, le palais du Prince Gong, les parcs Zhongshan, Beihai et le Palais d'été à Pékin offrent d'intéressants exemples de ces rocs percés. Des pierres de Taihu de taille plus modeste, montées sur un socle de bois, servaient aussi bien à la décoration qu'à la méditation posées sur des consoles à l'intérieur des riches demeures. Certaines avaient, en plus, la qualité d'avoir une belle sonorité comme celles de Lingbi, dans la province de l'Anhui.

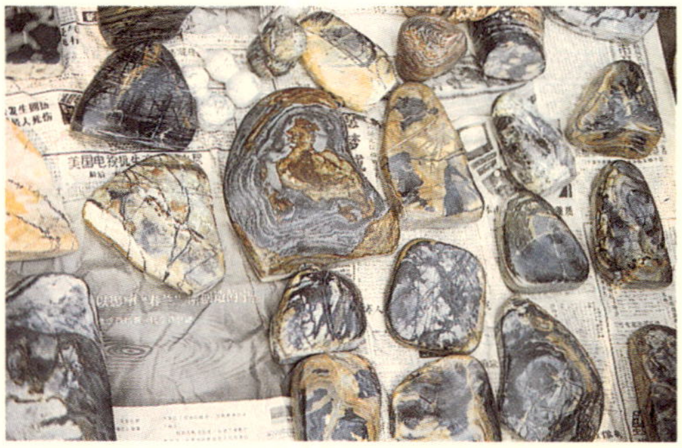

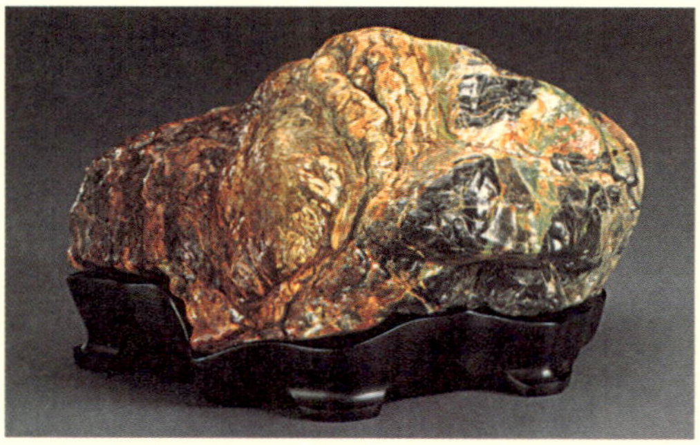

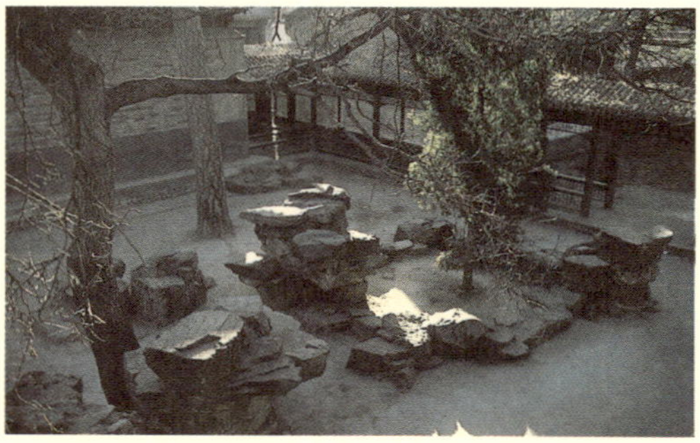

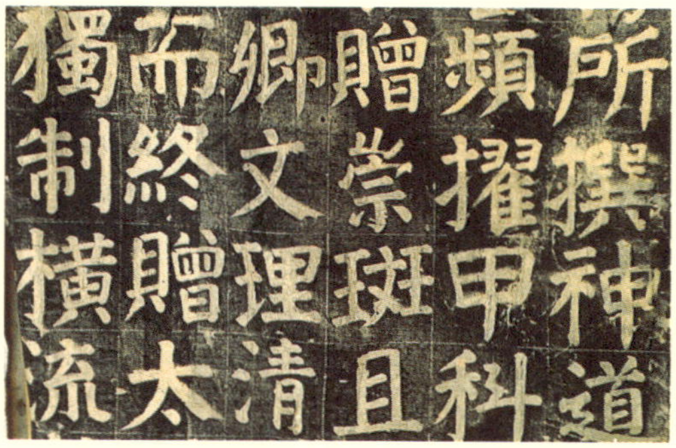

De haut en bas, pierres multicolores, pierre avec veinage de cinq couleurs, jardin de rocaille dans la résidence d'été des empereurs à Chengde, estampage d'une stèle.

Subsistance d'un rite très ancien, les pierres levées furent toujours considérées, en Chine comme au Vietnam, comme l'habitation de génies protecteurs auxquels un culte était rendu. De nombreux rochers sont devenus des lieux sacrés et portent à cet effet d'énormes inscriptions gravées et colorées en rouge. Le plus souvent, il s'agit d'un caractère unique (*Fo,* « Bouddha ») et dont « le signe écrit tient lieu de la représentation de la divinité ». Certains temples furent même construits sur ces lieux consacrés. Une des montagnes les plus sacrées de Chine, le Taishan (province du Shandong), fournissait des pierres réputées pour éloigner les mauvais esprits, on les appelait « celles qui résistent » *(biyaoshi)*, elles étaient placées le long des chemins où rôdent toujours les esprits malins.

La coutume de graver les pierres en Chine date du Ve siècle av. J.-C., à l'époque des Royaumes Combattants, et se fit d'abord sur des « tambours de pierre » *(shigu)*. Ce sont les premiers exemples d'écriture « grand sceau ». Les inscriptions sur stèle *(beiwen)*, ou plus communément les « livres de pierre » *(shishu)*, datent du IIe siècle ap. J.-C. C'est sous les Han que les Treize Classiques furent gravés dans ces pierres et appelés les Classiques de pierre *(shijing)*. Dès l'époque Tang, les 650 252 caractères des Classiques furent pour les lettrés les seules références autorisées que l'on pouvait copier sans risque d'erreur. La « forêt de stèles » *(beilin)* de X'ian, qui contient environ 1 700 spécimens, est une extraordinaire bibliothèque classique sur l'histoire et la littérature couvrant plus de mille années. L'estampage de ces stèles en vue de composer des recueils destinés à l'étude et au recopiage a été à l'origine de l'imprimerie en Chine.

L'empereur Huizong (1100-1125) de la dynastie des Song se signala par son goût de la poésie, de la calligraphie, de la peinture et sa passion immodérée des pierres. Il les faisait quérir à grands frais au Shanxi ou au Jiangsu, d'où elles étaient transportées à Kaifeng (province du Henan) par voie fluviale. Puis elles étaient gravées et installées sur le site d'une montagne artificielle qu'il avait fait spécialement aménager près de son palais. Les géomanciens lui avaient assuré la naissance d'un fils après la construction de ce fabuleux jardin de rochers, et leur prédiction se révéla juste. L'histoire ne lui laissa toutefois guère le temps de profiter de ses trésors lapidaires. Kaifeng fut prise par des armées ennemies et l'empereur fut emmené en captivité avec son fils. Mi Fu (1051-1107), poète de renom, calligraphe, peintre et grand collectionneur, était qualifié d'excentrique par ses contemporains car il accordait à ses pierres une considération étonnante ; il s'adressait à elles après avoir revêtu ses plus beaux atours en les parant de noms familiers. Les « Huit Excentriques de Yangzhou » *(Yangzhou ba gua)* furent huit peintres célèbres de l'époque Qing, qui formèrent un groupe dissident des peintres académiques. L'un d'entre eux, Zheng Banqiao, n'hésitait pas à peindre la délicate orchidée ou le traditionnel bambou en compagnie de ces pierres aux formes étranges et rugueuses.

Depuis que la cour impériale chinoise offrit vers le VIe siècle à l'empereur du Japon un premier cadeau de « pierres fantastiques », l'amour des Japonais pour ces ornements de la maison et des jardins ne s'altéra pas au fil des siècles. Appelées au Japon « pierres d'eau » *(suiseki),* sans doute en référence au bac dans lequel on les plaçait, elles donnaient du caractère aux paysages miniatures *(bonsai).* Ceux-ci connurent une grande vogue au Japon jusqu'au XIIIe siècle. Puis, sous l'influence des philosophes zen, on se mit à préférer des décors plus dépouillés pour éviter la distraction pendant la méditation. De cette recherche naquit un grand art, sobre et raffiné, pour lequel les Japonais sont passés maîtres au détriment des Chinois qui avaient pourtant été les premiers à introduire les pierres dans la décoration d'intérieur et d'extérieur.

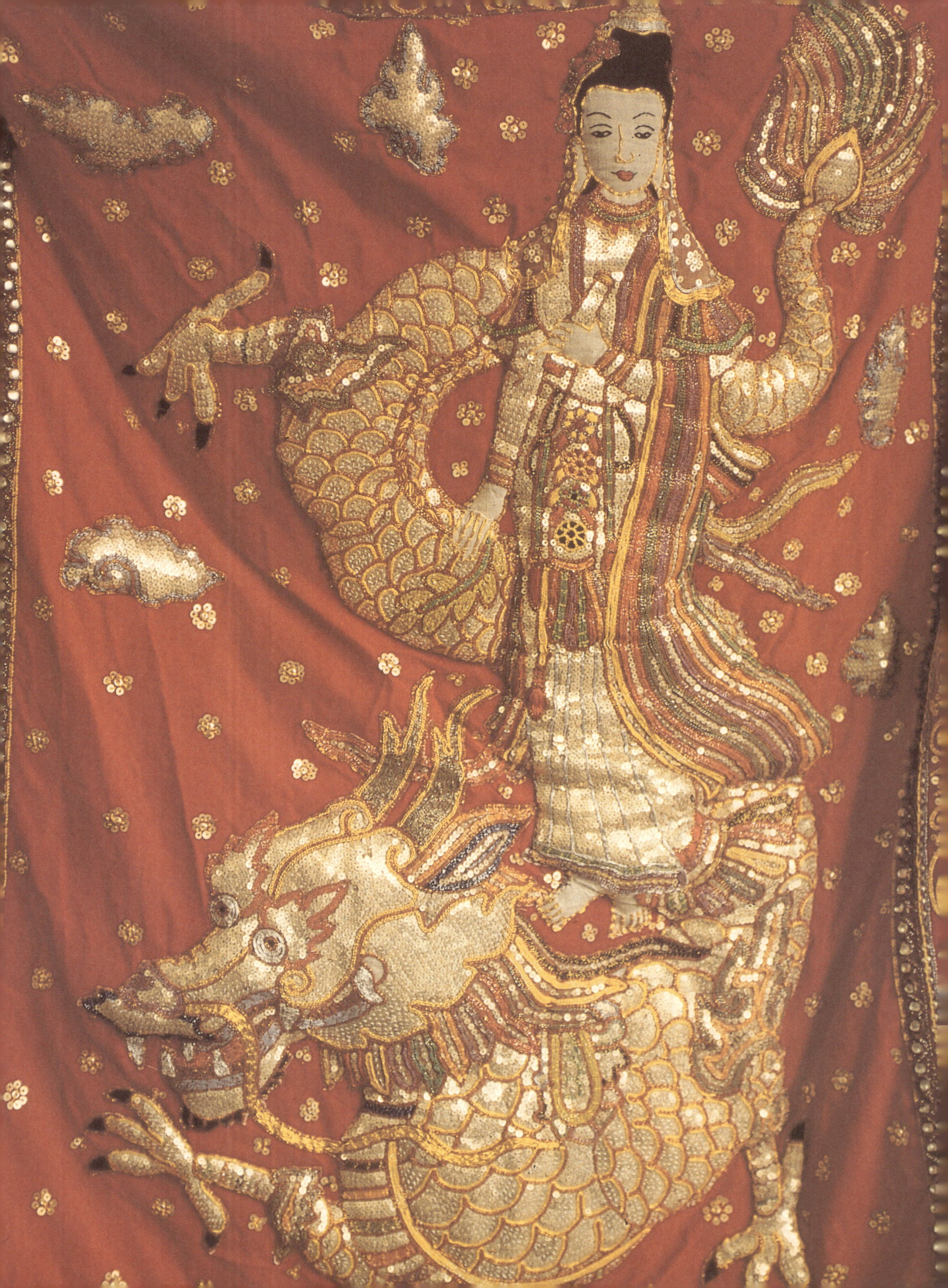

Le fabuleux panthéon des dieux et héros légendaires

偶像

ou xiang, littéralement, « représentation des dieux : idoles ».

Selon le mythe le plus connu, l'origine du monde résulterait d'un chaos qui aurait donné naissance à deux divinités fondatrices du ciel et de la terre. Pour les uns, l'ancêtre des hommes aurait été Pangu, et pour d'autres, Fuxi et Nüwa, frères et sœurs incestueux, souvent représentés avec des corps de serpents entrelacés. Ils marquent l'âge pastoral des dynasties légendaires. Parmi les grands ancêtres figure encore Shennong (ou Yandi) qui sera vénéré jusqu'à nos jours comme le dieu de l'agriculture. Puis viendra Huangdi, l'empereur Jaune (*ca* 2697-2599 av. J.-C.), le plus connu des cinq souverains, il devint le père de la culture chinoise auquel fut attribué non seulement l'unification de la Chine mais l'élevage du ver à soie et le tissage de la soie, l'invention de l'écriture, de la musique et de la médecine. Lui succèderont ensuite des rois mythiques comme Yao (*ca* 2357-2258 av. J.-C.), connu pour sa modestie, puis Shun (*ca* 2257-2208) avant que Yu-le-Grand ne fonde la dynastie des Xia (*ca* 2207-1766 av. J.-C.) à la période de l'âge de Bronze. Pendant son règne, racontent les légendes, des travaux colossaux auraient été entrepris pour se protéger des inondations qui ravageaient le royaume. Ce n'est qu'avec la dynastie des Shang (*ca* 1500-1000 av. J.-C.) fondée par Tang-le-Victorieux que commenceront les temps historiques.

Les astres et les étoiles, les esprits des fleuves et des montagnes, le tonnerre et la pluie, certains animaux aux formes étranges et même des plantes liées à la mythologie furent personnifiés. Comme les hommes, ces dieux ou esprits avaient un caractère, des sentiments, vivaient en famille et avaient des besoins en vêtement, nourriture, respect. Puis, à une période plus récente (sous les Tang, VIIe au Xe siècle) apparut le culte de personnages qui, ayant réellement vécu, étaient devenus célèbres par leurs exploits ou leur conduite exemplaire. Après la reconnaissance populaire, ils devaient attendre la canonisation (en général, prononcée par les empereurs) qui leur accordaient des titres comme à des hauts fonctionnaires investis d'une mission bien précise. On les installa comme dans le royaume terrestre dans une hiérarchie et les offrandes qui leur étaient offertes suivaient une étiquette rigoureuse. Confucius attendra 1910 avant d'être admis comme divinité de première classe. Guanyu, actuellement reconnu comme dieu de la Guerre, ne recevra le titre d'empereur qu'en 1594 ap. J.-C., soit 1 800 ans après sa mort. Le dieu du Foyer n'appartenait qu'à la troisième classe.

Page de gauche, broderie, déesse chevauchant un dragon.

Chaque religion ou philosophie laissa sa marque dans la religion populaire qui naquit avec l'empire. Le taoïsme (VIIIe av. J.-C.) se consacra à la recherche du bonheur et de l'immortalité. En un étrange amalgame, les esprits, la nature, les morts et les saints étaient honorés. Selon les sectes, on se livra à des pratiques magiques, à la méditation ou à l'alchimie. Le confucianisme (VIe siècle av. J.-C.) avait encouragé le « culte des ancêtres », celui des héros qui ont protégé l'État et des saints patrons de corporations. Le bouddhisme (IIIe siècle av. J.-C.) apporta une philosophie particulièrement prisée des lettrés, l'école de méditation *chan* (*dhyâna* en sanscrit, *zen* en japonais).

Ces « êtres doués de puissance surnaturelle », comme les désigne Henri Maspéro, portaient des titres différents selon les pouvoirs qui leur étaient conférés et selon leur origine. C'est avec une certaine amertume que le père jésuite Henri Doré écrivait en 1910 dans l'introduction de son œuvre monumentale *Recherche sur les superstitions en Chine* : « on rend un culte à une foule d'hommes, d'esprits ou même d'étoiles ; le règne minéral, végétal, animal, reçoivent de l'encens, seul Celui qui le mérite, en est privé. »

L'inventaire qui suit, loin de se vouloir exhaustif, présente les plus colorés de ces mythes issus d'un ancien culte des ancêtres qui aurait aggloméré des éléments venus des Trois enseignements dont les représentants sont les Trois précieux *(san bao)* : Laozi, Confucius et Bouddha. Désignées ici sous leur nom chinois, ces divinités sont tantôt des vénérables célestes *(tianzun)* ou des immortels *(xian)*, des empereurs ou des impératrices (*di* ou *hou*), des rois *(wang)* ou des saints *(shen)*, des déesses *(niangniang)*, des pères *(ye)* ou des mères *(mu)*. Bien sûr, n'ont pas été cités tous les innombrables saints patrons de corporations aussi folkloriques qu'utiles comme les entremetteuses, les marchands de bougies, de vin, de perruques, de lunettes, diseurs de bonne aventure et devins, vanniers, fondeurs, papetiers, savetiers, marchandes de fard et même tenanciers de maisons closes... Voici donc les plus connus de ceux dont on voulait s'attirer les bonnes grâces par des offrandes de nourriture, d'encens, de vêtements, de papier-monnaie ou de fêtes (spectacles de marionnettes ou de théâtre d'ombres chinoises, processions, danses).

Amitofo ou Mitofo, (transcription du sanscrit *Amitabha* ou *Amida*) était le Bouddha de la Lumière Infinie régnant sur le paradis de l'Ouest dont le sol était couvert d'or et d'argent, les fleurs et les fruits faits de pierres précieuses et les arbres possédaient des feuilles de jade.

Ba xian, les Huit Immortels étaient les protecteurs du Taoïsme. Après bon nombre d'aventures dans leur vie de mortels, ils parvinrent à ce statut particulier et étaient souvent représentés comme des vieillards heureux voyageant ou s'adonnant aux plaisirs de la table. Ils ne faisaient pas véritablement l'objet d'un culte mais étaient souvent sollicités comme protecteurs. On les reconnaît à leurs attributs stéréotypés :

– Li Hanzhong porte un éventail avec lequel il peut ressusciter les morts ;

– Lü Dongbin a un grand sabre, allusion aux exploits qu'il accomplit avant de quitter le monde des vivants. Il est le plus important des Huit Immortels, protégeant des maladies et des démons ;

– Zhang Guolao, magicien, assis à l'envers sur son âne pliable comme un simple papier, porte un mystérieux tube en bambou avec deux baguettes *(yügu)* ;

– Lan Caihe, éternel vagabond, joueur de flûte, est le patron des musiciens ;

– Han Xiangzi, avec son panier de fleurs ou de pêches, est le patron des jardiniers ;

– Cao Guojiu est en costume de cour avec une tablette de dignitaire rappelant ses origines, il fut le frère d'une impératrice de l'époque Song avant de devenir moine ;

– He Xiangu, est la seule femme du groupe, elle tient sur l'épaule une énorme fleur de lotus et aurait vécu dans les montagnes comme nonne ;

– Li Tieguai ou Tieguai Li est un mendiant qui s'appuie sur une béquille de fer et tient une gourde. Il est le patron des pharmaciens.

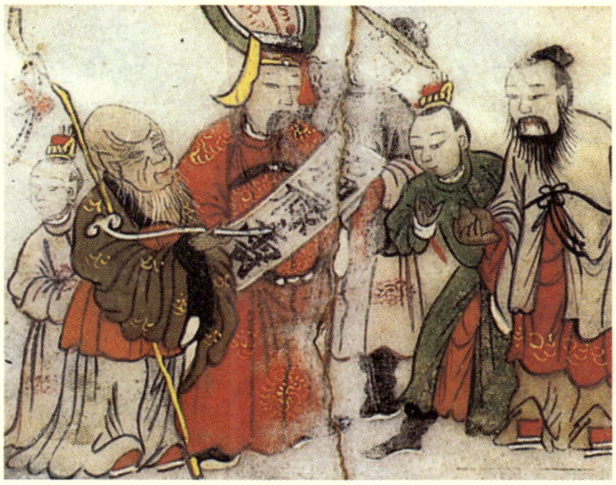

Caishen ou Caisheye, le dieu de la Richesse, était extrêmement populaire et figurait sous forme d'estampe populaire dans toutes les familles. Il était souvent représenté par un duo : un dieu civil de la Richesse et un dieu militaire. Les attributs traditionnels du dieu de la Richesse sont l'arbre à sapèques, les lingots d'argent et d'or en forme de cothurne *(yuanbao),* les coffres remplis de trésors et des enfants heureux qui ramassent les fruits de cet arbre qu'il suffit de secouer pour faire tomber de l'or *(yaoqianshu).*

Chang E ou Heng E, était la belle épouse du héros Hou Yi-l'Archer qui, en récompense de ses faits d'armes (abattre neuf des dix soleils, exterminer des monstres), reçut de la Reine Mère d'Occident (Xiwangmu) la drogue de l'immortalité. Sa femme en avala la moitié et n'ayant pu atteindre les cieux, parvint jusqu'à la lune où elle demeure depuis cette tentative pour devenir une immortelle. On l'appelle improprement la « déesse de la Lune ».

Chenghuang, le génie protecteur de la ville (littéralement, « des murailles et des fossés »), était imploré pour que la paix règne, que les récoltes soient bonnes et que la peste soit évitée. Chaque ville en possédait un en particulier, dès l'époque Tang, et il recevait des titres différents en fonction de ses mérites.

Le dieu de la Richesse accompagné de Shouxinglao (peinture sur marbre, écran de table, XIXe siècle). Page suivante, Bouddha (sculpture sur bois, XVIIIe siècle) et boîte de temple à compartiment, appelée « horloge à encens » ; ces boîtes permettaient de calculer le temps entre les offices religieux.

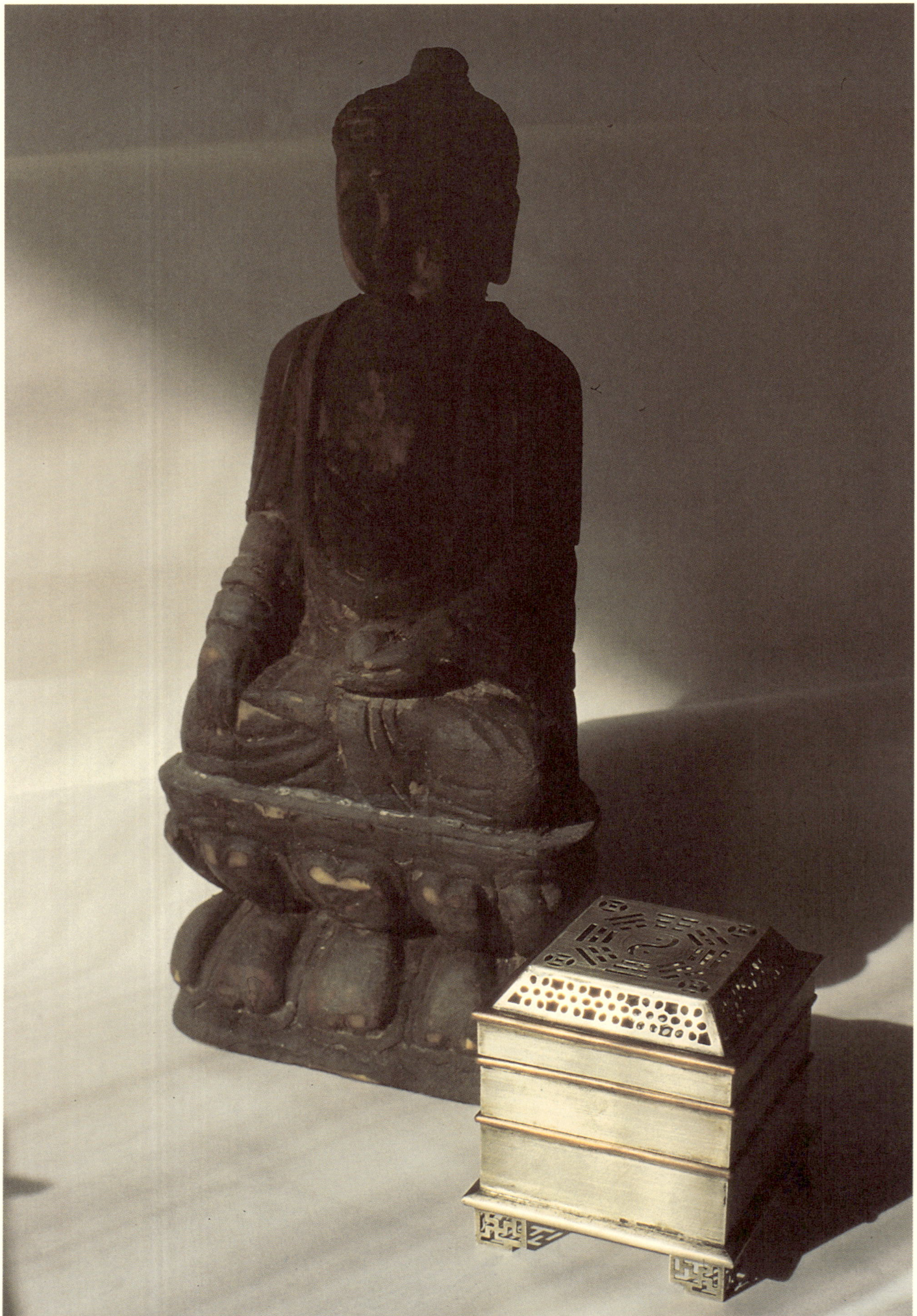

Chuanggong, le seigneur du Lit était une petite divinité protectrice avec son épouse, à laquelle il convenait de rendre hommage, à la fin de l'année ou après la Fête des Lanternes, pour s'attirer ses bonnes grâces en vue de la conception d'enfants et de la paix du ménage.

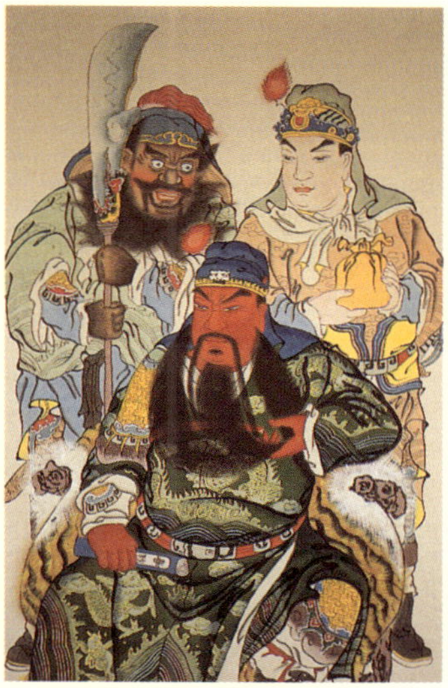

Dianmu, était la Mère des Éclairs qu'elle produisait à l'aide de deux miroirs. Selon les régions, elle était considérée comme l'épouse de Leigong, le Dieu du Tonnerre.

Dizang, (littéralement le « trésor de la terre ») est l'interprétation chinoise du nom sanscrit *kshitigarbha,* le bodhisattva qui jugeait les âmes et les délivrait des enfers. On le reconnaît à sa tenue de moine bouddhique avec, dans une main un long bâton et dans l'autre la Perle qui illumine le monde des Ténèbres.

Erlang (littéralement le « deuxième dieu »), de son vrai nom Yang Tian, connu pour chasser les démons grâce au Chien Céleste *(tiangou),* faisait partie de la cour de l'empereur de Jade dont il était le premier collaborateur.

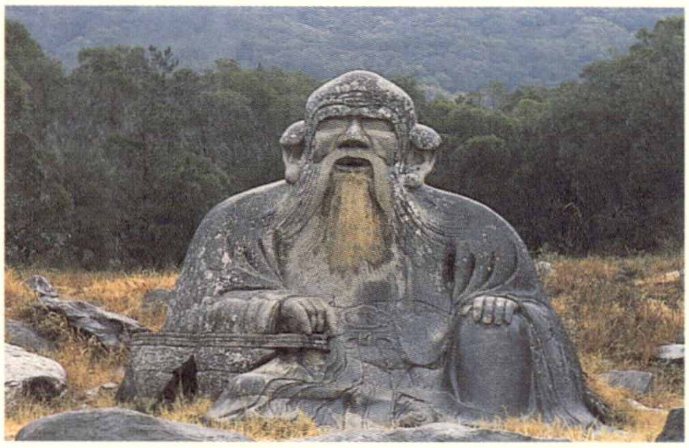

Fo ou Foye (abréviation en chinois de *Fo To,* transcription du sanscrit *Buddha*), c'est Gautama Siddhârta, fondateur du bouddhisme, appelé Sâkyamuni, celui qui a atteint l'éveil *(bodhi).* C'est vers le milieu du Ier siècle ap. J.-C. que cette religion fut introduite en Chine par l'Asie centrale.

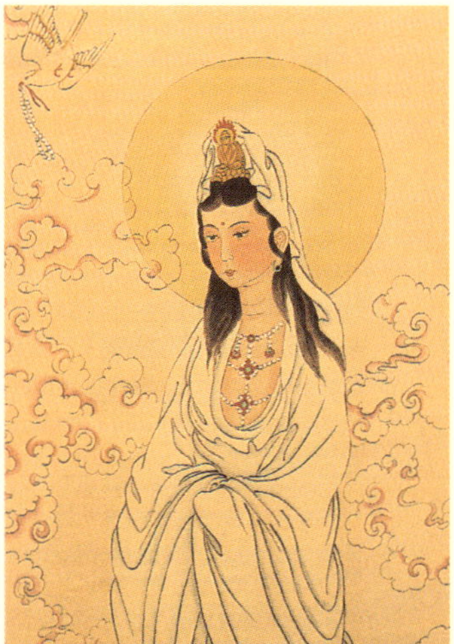

Guan était à l'origine un général du nom de Guan Yu de l'époque des Trois Royaumes (IIIe siècle ap. J.-C.) dont la vie héroïque lui valut une vénération qui se transforma en véritable culte depuis les Song. Il devint le protecteur officiel de l'État, symbole de loyauté et de justice, et fut canonisé en 1594 comme empereur sous le nom de Guandi (ou Guansheng Dijun). Ce *wuren* (« homme de puissance »), un géant avec un visage pourpre et une très longue barbe, revêtu d'une armure se tenant soit debout avec une hallebarde, soit assis lisant un des Classiques, était aussi reconnu comme le dieu des lettrés et des marchands.

Guanyin ou Guanshiyin est le nom chinois du bodhisattva Avalokiteçvara. Il a pris, depuis l'époque Tang, une forme féminine et portait une longue robe blanche en tenant une fleur de lotus, symbole de pureté, et quelquefois un enfant au bras, d'où son autre appellation : la « donneuse d'enfants » (Songzi Guanyin ou Songzi niangniang). Issue du bouddhisme indien depuis le VIIIe siècle ap. J.-C., cette divinité est devenue dans la religion populaire un des personnages les plus vénérés. En

De haut en bas, Guan Yu (peinture sur papier), sage taoïste (statue colossale taillée dans un rocher à Qingyuanshan, Fujian, Xe siècle ap. J.-C.), Guanyin (peinture sur soie).

effet, on s'adresse aussi à elle pour exaucer d'autres souhaits car elle est devenue la déesse de la Miséricorde, « celle qui écoute ». Guanyin était souvent représentée sur des images populaires, en peinture ou sur des statuettes de porcelaine blanc de Chine ou de bois doré à la feuille.

Kongzi ou Kongfuzi (transcrit en latin sous le nom de Confucius), était appelé par ses disciples, Maître Kong. Il était souvent représenté dans un costume impérial, assis sur un trône. Né en 551 av. J.-C., il mourut en 479 av. J.-C. et fut élevé à Qufu (province du Shandong, dans l'ancien royaume de Lu). Il fut l'auteur d'œuvres magistrales *(Le Livre des Odes, Le Livre des Documents, Les Printemps et Automnes, Le Livre des Mutations...).* Son culte commença au lendemain de sa mort et il avait lieu dans les temples de la Littérature (*wenmiao* ou *kongmiao*).

Laozi (littéralement le « Vieil Enfant ») ou Lao Dan (le « Vieillard aux Longues Oreilles »), celui que ses disciples ont appelé le « Vieux Maître », fut le fondateur du taoïsme. On n'est sûr ni de son lieu ni de sa date de naissance. On lui a attribué le *Daodejing,* le *Livre de la Voie et de la Vertu.* Son nom de famille fut sans doute Li Er. Selon la légende, sa mère l'aurait porté dans son sein pendant quatre-vingt-une années ; aussi naquit-il avec les cheveux blancs. Au VIIe siècle ap. J.-C., on lui conféra le titre de « Premier Ancêtre » et un culte lui fut dédié dans plusieurs temples.

Leigong, le dieu du Tonnerre, était peut-être à l'origine un hibou dont il a conservé la laideur. On le représentait avec un maillet et des tambours.

Liu, général du XIIe siècle ap. J.-C., fut divinisé comme protecteur des récoltes. Il est souvent représenté armé de son sabre pourfendant des nuages de sauterelles.

Longwang, était le Roi-Dragon qui commandait à plusieurs dizaines de dragons frères, souvent confondus avec les grandes tortues marines *(ao).* C'était une divinité faiseuse de pluie qui, en s'élevant jusqu'au ciel et en marchant sur les nuages, faisait pleuvoir.

Lu Ban ou Gongshu Ban, parce qu'il sut fabriquer un cerf-volant de bois en forme de milan puis inventa la scie, le rabot, le cadenas et la charrue, devint le saint patron des menuisiers, des charpentiers, des forgerons et même des potiers. Chaque corporation avait d'ailleurs son saint : Mengtian pour les fabricants de pinceaux, Cai Lun pour les artisans du papier, Sun Bin pour les chausseurs ; même les voleurs avaient adopté Song Jiang, un rebelle héros du Shandong au XIIe siècle ap. J.-C...

Luohan ou alohan, au nombre de dix-huit ou de cinq cents, étaient des disciples (*arhat* en sanscrit) dont la mission fixée par le Bouddha était de protéger la religion et de l'enseigner aux hommes. Ces saints hommes, habillés comme des moines ou des ermites, sont placés dans les salles latérales des temples.

Page de droite, statuette de bois représentant l'un des « Quatre rois du Ciel » (Tianwang, voir p. 86).

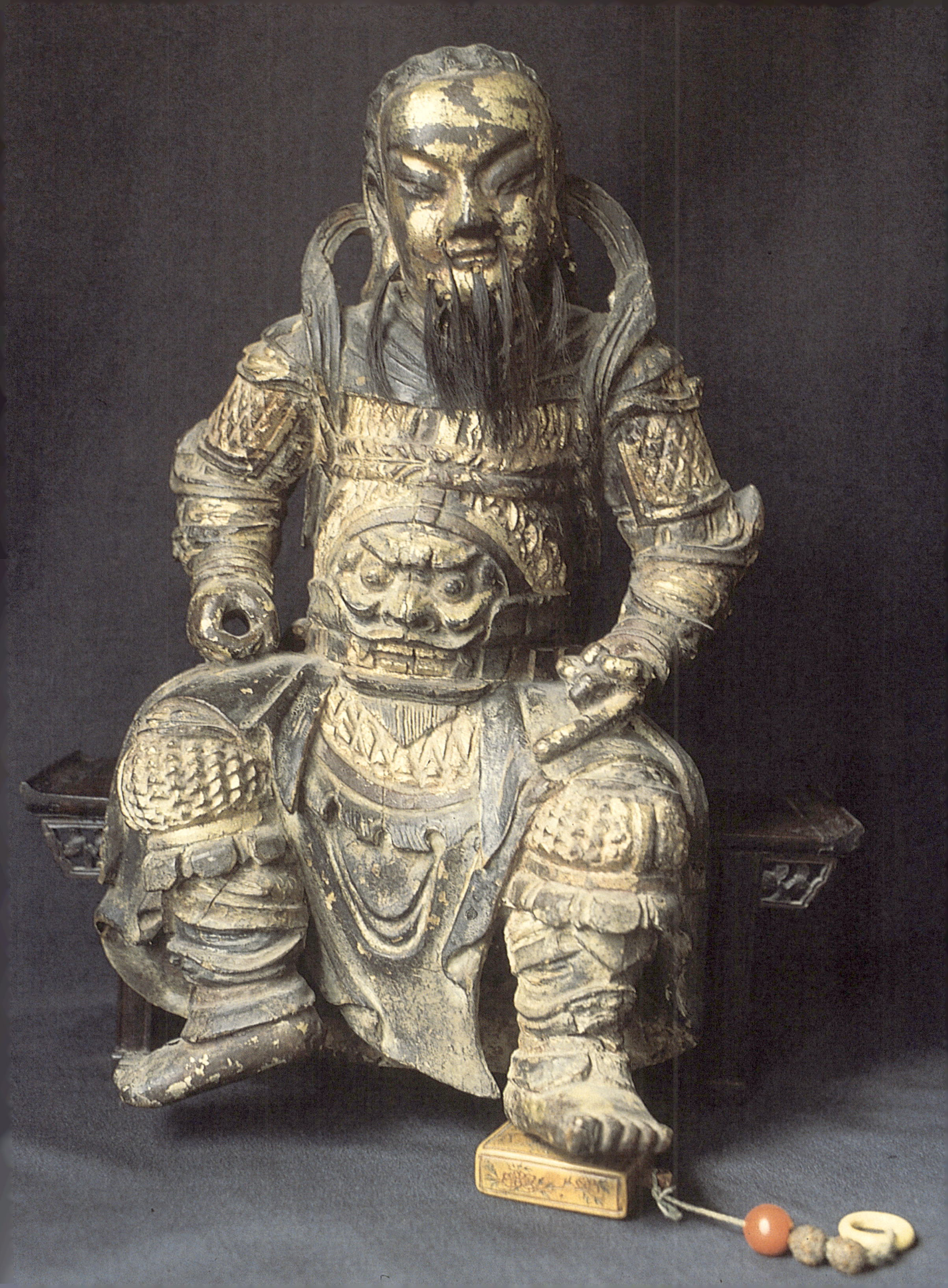

Mazhashen, le dieu très ancien que l'on implorait dans les campagnes pour se protéger des invasions de sauterelles, était représenté avec une tête et des pattes d'oiseau.

Mile (Maitreya en sanscrit), le Bouddha du Futur, attendu comme un messie, apparaît comme un moine joufflu, rieur, pansu, à demi-nu, tenant à la main un chapelet et souvent entouré d'enfants. Il était le saint patron des bijoutiers. L'expression *«poussah»* vient du chinois *pusa,* une abréviation de *putisato* (transcription du sanscrit *bodhisattva*) et désigne les statuettes en porcelaine peinte de ces divinités grasses et hilares, si populaires au début du siècle en Europe sous le nom de «magot».

Niuwang, le Roi-Bœuf, était un des principaux dieux de l'élevage avec Zhuling, le dieu des porcheries. Les divinités du monde agricole étaient très nombreuses.

Qin Shubao et Hu Jingde ont remplacé les anciens dieux des Portes *(menshen),* Shen Tu et Yulei, comme protecteurs des issues. Ils portent quelquefois le nom de Qinqiong (reconnaissable à son visage blanc) et Jingde (à la face rouge). Autrefois, on suspendait l'effigie de ces féroces généraux taillée dans des planchettes de bois de pêcher puis, dès le XIIe siècle ap. J.-C., on prit l'habitude d'apposer sur les battants des portes extérieures les images imprimées de ces guerriers munis d'une hallebarde et d'une épée et porteurs de longues barbes pour effrayer les mauvais esprits.

Sanxing sont les trois divinités appelées les «Trois Étoiles» et représentées sous la forme d'une triade: le dieu du Bonheur *(Fuxing),* le dieu de la Richesse et des Honneurs *(Luxing)* et le dieu de la Longévité *(Shouxing).* Ce dernier, connu aussi sous le nom de Shou Lao, est reconnaissable à différents attributs de l'immortalité (chauve-souris, cerf, champignon *lingzhi,* bâton et gourde, pin et surtout la pêche de l'immortalité).

Saoqingniang, la «Dame qui balaye le Ciel», était une divinité de moindre importance très ancienne qui se trouvait néanmoins souvent invoquée par les femmes. Elle avait non seulement pour fonction de balayer les nuages mais aussi d'apporter la pluie.

Sun Simiao, fut un paysan de la province du Shaanxi (VIe siècle ap. J.-C.) qui consacra sa longue vie à récolter les simples, préparer des médicaments et soigner ses contemporains. Quelques cures miraculeuses lui valurent d'être élevé au rang d'immortel et de se voir décerner le titre de roi de la Médecine *(yaowang).*

Page de droite, deux représentations traditionnelles de Zhong Kui, le pourfendeur de démons et, au centre, Shouxinglao portant une énorme pêche, symbole d'immortalité (peintures sur papier).

Taiyue dadi, dieu du Taishan (une des cinq montagnes sacrées de Chine dans la province du Shandong), était aussi connu sous le nom d'«Empereur du pic de l'Est». Il était considéré comme le régent de l'empereur de Jade et, à ce titre, présidait à la tenue des registres des naissances et des morts. Sa fille, la «dame du Taishan» (Taishan niangniang ou Nainai niangniang) était une

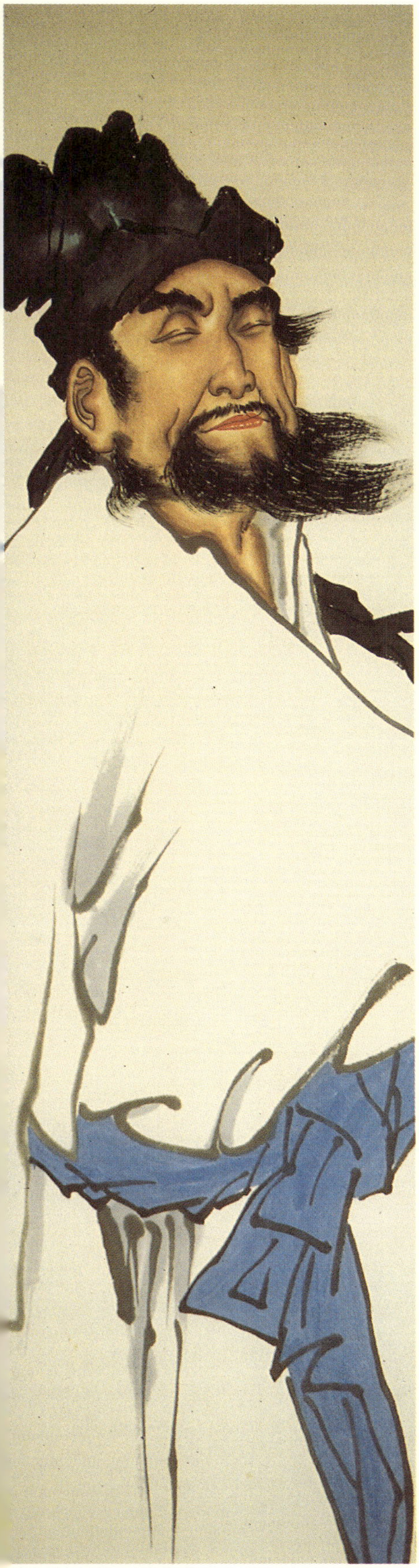

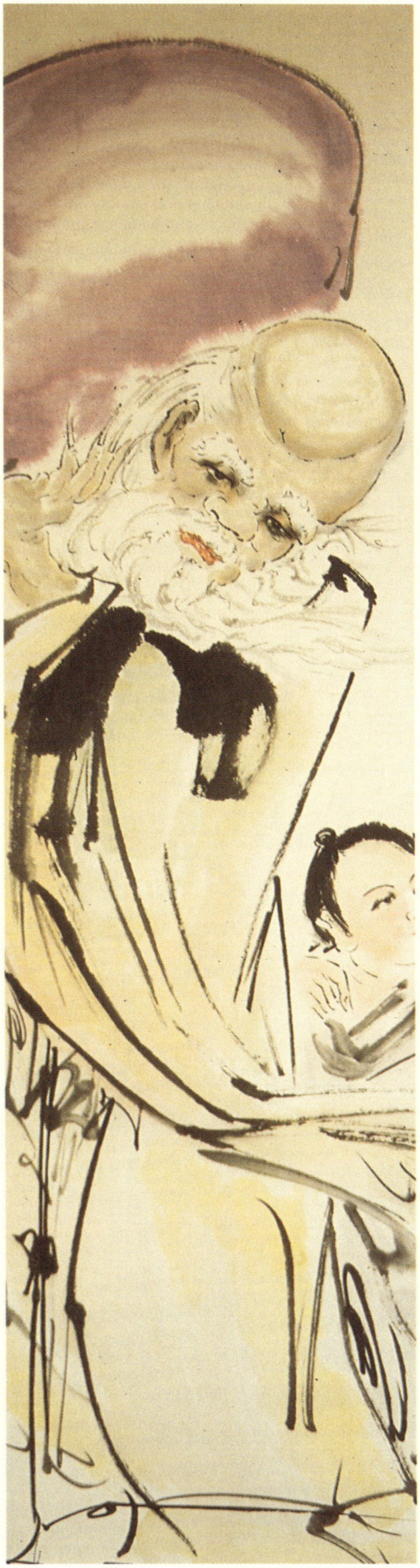

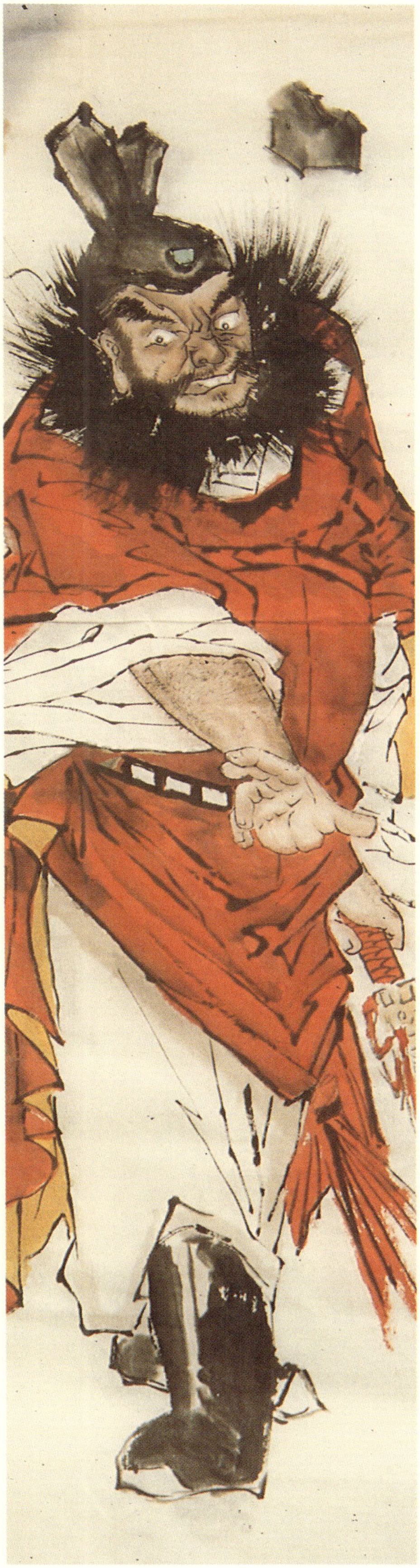

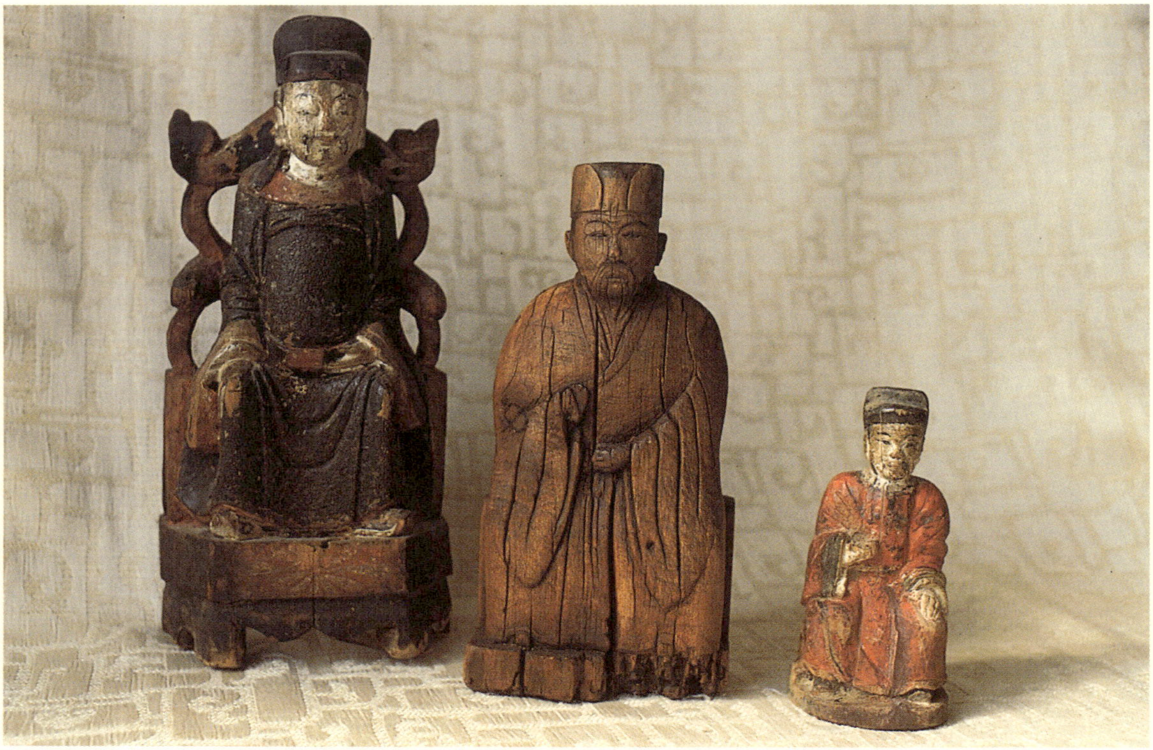

Trois divinités avec, à gauche, Wenchang en costume de lettré (sculptures populaires sur bois).

des protectrices des femmes et des enfants. Elle est souvent accompagnée de deux assistantes dont la « Donneuse d'enfants », Songzi niangniang, qui tient un bébé dans ses bras.

Tianhou, l'impératrice du Ciel, est plus connue sous le nom populaire de Mazu, sainte-mère du Ciel. Elle était la protectrice des pêcheurs et des marins. Ce fut une pieuse bouddhiste qui vécut au Xᵉ siècle dans la province du Fujian. C'est une des divinités les plus vénérées à Taïwan. On la représente assise sur des nuages ou sur des flots, vêtue d'un costume d'apparat avec un bonnet officiel.

Tianwang, les Quatre rois du Ciel, sont de gigantesques guerriers que l'on trouve à l'entrée des temples dont ils sont les gardiens. Ils ne font pas l'objet d'un culte (en sanscrit, *lokapala*). Le dieu noir, muni d'un serpent, surveille le Nord, le dieu rouge avec une ombrelle surveille le Sud, le dieu bleu avec un instrument de musique surveille l'Est et le dieu blanc avec une épée garde l'Ouest.

Wenchang, dieu de la Littérature, portait un costume de mandarin et tenait un sceptre *ruyi*. C'est ce dieu que l'on implorait pour une réussite aux examens.

Xiwangmu, la Reine Mère d'Occident, l'un des plus anciens personnages mythiques décrit dans le *Classique des Montagnes et des Mers,* régnait sur les monts Kunlun, résidence des Immortels. Protectrice des épidémies, elle était divinité de la longévité. C'est dans son extraordinaire jardin que poussaient les pêches de l'immortalité *(pantao)* dont se nourrissaient Immortels et

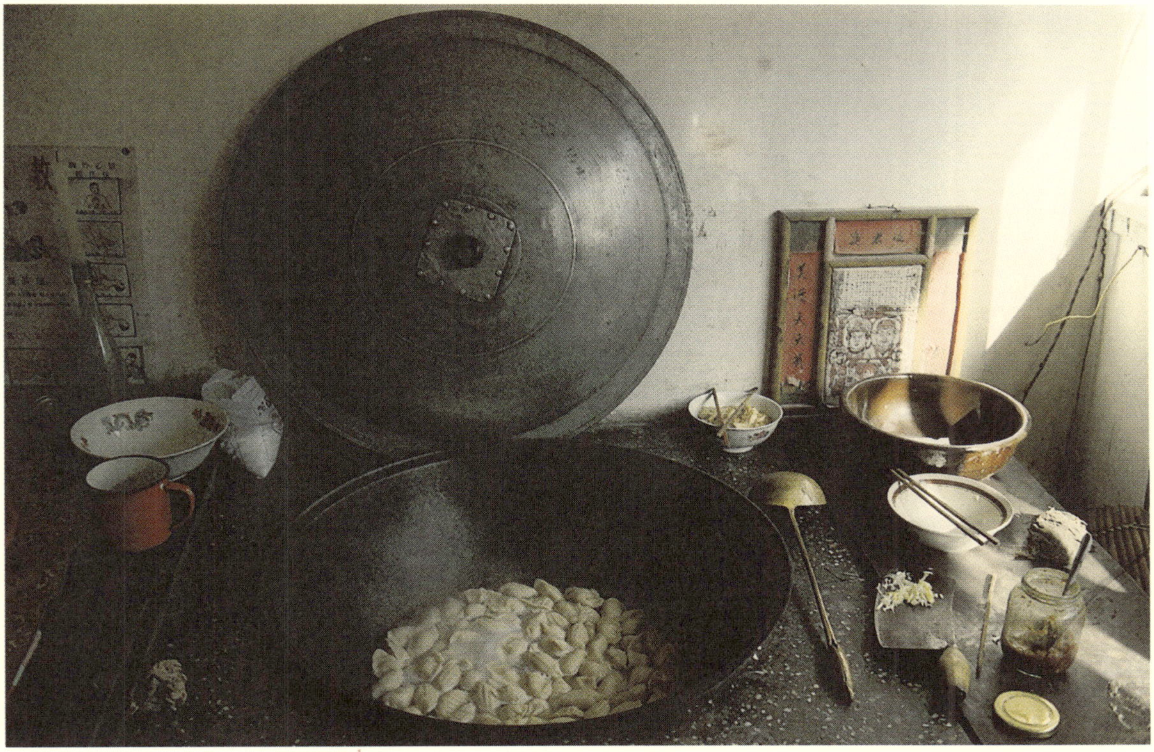

Immortelles à l'occasion de somptueux banquets. Elle est reconnaissable à sa coiffe à aigrette et aux oiseaux bleus sacrés ou aux paons qui l'entourent.

Yanlo ou Yanwang (du sanscrit *Yama*) était le nom donné au roi des dix Enfers dans lesquels étaient plongées les âmes des condamnés où les attendaient des supplices raffinés, chauds et froids.

Yuhuang ou Laotianye était le dieu suprême, souverain de toutes les divinités, connu sous le nom d'empereur de Jade (Yuhuang dadi) ou Père Céleste (Laotianye). Il était en général représenté assis sur un trône entouré de ses courtisans, vêtu d'une longue robe d'apparat et de la coiffe impériale formée d'une planchette de laquelle tombent des pendeloques de perles. Dans ses mains croisées, il tenait une tablette de jade ou d'ivoire, insigne de son pouvoir *(gui)*. Il portait une barbiche, de longues moustaches et des favoris.

Zaojun ou Zaoshen ou encore Zaowangye, le dieu du Foyer, était en général imprimé sur une estampe, collée au dessus du fourneau et des offrandes lui étaient faites toute l'année. Le vingt-quatrième jour du douzième mois, la famille lui offrait un repas important avant son départ en mission vers l'empereur de Jade. Parmi les cadeaux figuraient de nombreuses sucreries destinées à lui « coller les lèvres » *(maiyatang)* pour éviter que le rapport qu'il était censé faire sur le comportement de la famille au cours de l'année ne soit trop défavorable. L'effigie était ensuite brûlée et remplacée par une image neuve au moment du Nouvel An, son retour était alors salué par un concert de pétards et de nouvelles offrandes.

Le dieu du Foyer affiché à droite sur le mur de la cuisine d'une maison rurale dans le Shanxi. Page suivante, l'empereur de Jade, divinité souveraine du panthéon taoïste, entouré de sa cour (gravure extraite de Gao Shang Yu Huang Benjingjijing, *XIXe siècle).*

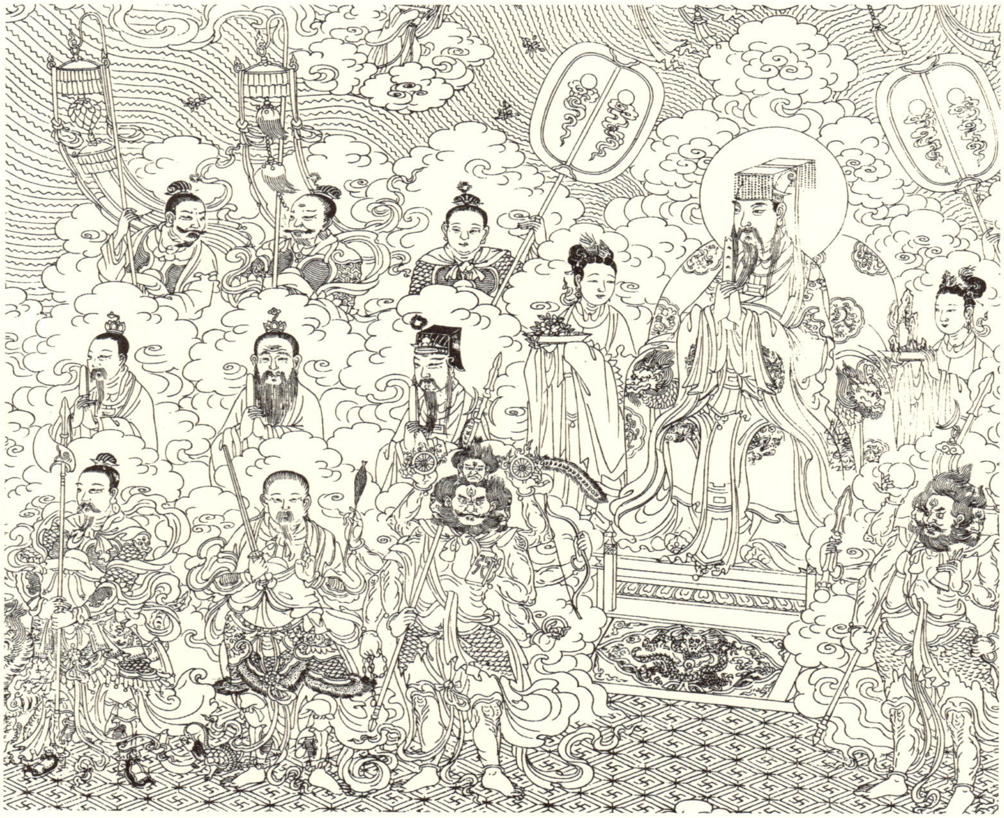

Zhang ou Zhangxian (l'immortel Zhang) était la divinité à laquelle on s'adressait pour avoir des garçons. On le représentait comme un guerrier tirant des flèches dans le ciel en direction du Chien céleste (Tiangou) qui cherche à dévorer les enfants.

Zhong Kui, le chasseur de diables, figurait sur de nombreuses estampes populaires dans l'attitude d'un terrifiant guerrier, à la barbe et aux moustaches ébouriffées, revêtu d'une robe rouge de lettré et portant une seule botte, menaçant d'une épée ou d'une lance de curieux démons en forme de petits hommes verts nus. Selon la légende, il s'agirait de l'âme d'un étudiant reçu aux examens impériaux et auquel le titre fut cependant refusé. Désespéré de tant d'injustice, Zhong Kui se suicida mais fut récompensé par les dieux qui le désignèrent comme pourfendeur de démons, une de ses spécialités étant de leur arracher les yeux. Les artistes prenant quelques libertés avec le sujet le décrivent souvent servi par des gnomes ou pris d'un lourd sommeil après force libations. Ce personnage mythique connut une grande popularité depuis les Song. Sous les Ming et sous les Qing, des romanciers, des peintres célèbres et des auteurs dramatiques l'immortalisèrent comme un véritable dieu protecteur contre les mauvais esprits.

La magie des chiffres et des nombres

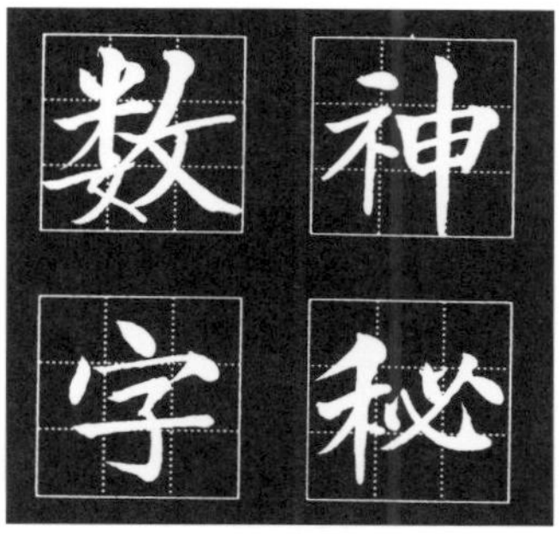

shenmi shuzi, littéralement, « le mystère des nombres et des chiffres ».

La Chine est le premier pays au monde à avoir employé la numération décimale qui apparut avec l'écriture pictographique, c'est-à-dire celle des inscriptions sur os d'animaux, sur les écailles de tortue et sur les bronzes de la dynastie des Shang. Ce système permit donc aux calculateurs chinois de l'ancien temps de représenter des nombres et d'effectuer des calculs, soit à l'aide de « fiches » (ou jonchets, jetons, *suanchou*), soit avec le boulier-compteur ou abaque, dénommé en Chine « plateau à calcul » *(suanpan)*. *L'Histoire des Han* (Ier siècle ap. J.-C.) fait mention, par exemple, de ces jonchets servant au calcul mais aussi à la divination. Selon cet ouvrage, ils mesuraient une dizaine de centimètres. À l'origine en bambou, ils furent aussi fabriqués en bois, en fer, en os de poulet, en ivoire ou en jade. Suivant qu'on les plaçait en position verticale ou horizontale, on pouvait exprimer les unités, les dizaines, les centaines… jusqu'aux millions. Puis on les colora en rouge et noir pour distinguer les nombres positifs des nombres négatifs dans des opérations plus complexes. Dès le IIIe siècle ap. J.-C., les *Notes sur l'Art des nombres* de Xu Yue font mention pour la première fois de boules pour représenter des nombres en fonction de leur couleur et de leur position mais il faudra attendre la dynastie des Song, au Xe siècle pour que l'usage du boulier (ou plateau à boules, *qiupan*) se généralise. C'est seulement sous les Ming que l'abaque fut exporté au Japon. Les boutiquiers chinois qui continuent d'utiliser cet instrument avec peut-être une plus grande dextérité que les calculatrices électroniques sont très superstitieux à l'égard de leur outil de travail. Quand le magasin ouvre, il est coutume de secouer violemment le boulier pour en chasser les démons qui auraient pu s'y loger pendant la nuit et il n'est pas recommandé de l'employer trop tôt le matin, cela porte malheur…

Un peuple avec une tradition arithmétique aussi ancienne ne pouvait que se passionner pour la symbolique des nombres et leur interprétation. Pour les Chinois comme pour beaucoup d'autres peuples, « les nombres, qui ne servent apparemment qu'à compter, ont offert un support d'élection aux élaborations symboliques. Ils expriment non seulement des quantités mais des idées et des forces » (J. Chevalier, A. Gheerbrant). Il est facile d'observer cette propension des Chinois à manier depuis longtemps les concepts numériques, à les employer dans des expressions populaires, à se complaire dans des « classifications », « inventaires » ou « collections » dont la plus familière aux occidentaux est sans doute celle des « Douze animaux ». Initialement créés pour désigner les heures de la journée chinoise (par exemple, l'heure du rat, de 23 heures à 1 heure du matin ; l'heure du bœuf, de 1 heure à 3 heures...), ces animaux emblématiques du zodiaque chinois servaient à désigner les années. Le *Livre des mutations* (*Yijing* ou *Zhouyi*), un des Cinq Classiques, dont l'origine remonte aux périodes légendaires, utilisait déjà des concepts arithmétiques tels que les deux polarités (le *yin* et le *yang*), les huit trigrammes, les soixante-quatre hexagrammes pour représenter toutes les situations des êtres au cours des mutations de l'univers.

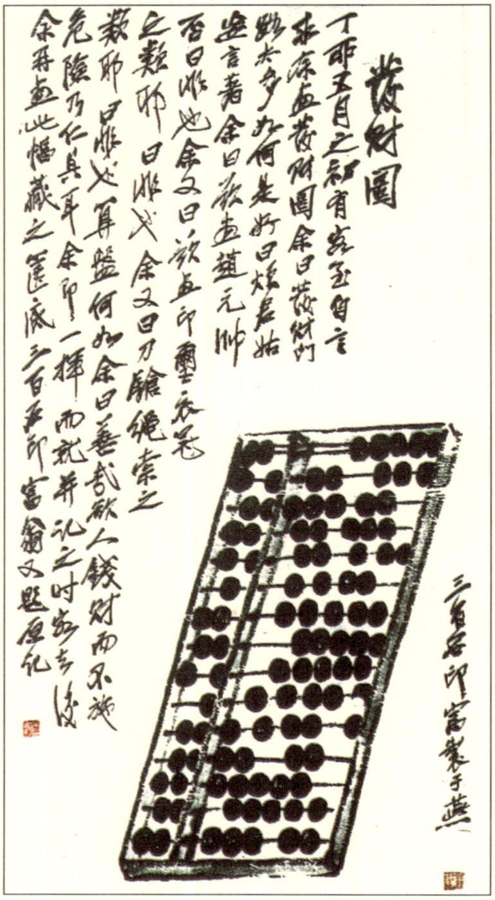

Dans la numérologie chinoise, le nombre trois *(san)* était le nombre parfait, fondamental, à partir duquel, selon le *Livre de la Voie et de la Vertu (Daodejing),* tous les êtres vivants furent créés. La cosmogonie taoïste se résumait à cette formule lapidaire : « Le Dao produit le Un, le Un produit les Deux, les Deux produisent les Trois, des Trois naissent les Dix mille (l'humanité) ». Les fondateurs mythiques Fuxi, Shennong et Huangdi étaient trois, tout comme il y eut les Trois doctrines (le confucianisme, le taoïsme et le bouddhisme) et aussi pour les bouddhistes, les Trois Mondes (le monde du désir, le monde matériel et le monde sans formes), les Trois Astres et les Trois Royaumes (Shu, Wei et Wu) qui se partagèrent la Chine de 220 à 280 ap. J.-C. Non sans fierté, les Chinois citent encore leurs Trois Inventions (*san da faming* ; la poudre, la boussole et l'imprimerie) et Sun Yat-Sen inventait, au début du siècle, les Trois Principes du Peuple (le nationalisme, la démocratie et le socialisme). On parlait des Trois Familles, celle du père, de la mère et de l'épouse ; en poésie les « lotus d'or de trois pouces » *(san cun jin lian)* désignaient les petits pieds bandés des femmes. Mais « trois » pouvait être aussi l'expression du pluriel ou de la multiplicité. Dans la langue écrite, il est fait quelquefois usage de ce système répétitif : *sen* (« serré, sombre ») s'écrit avec les trois caractères identiques du bois (sombre comme dans une forêt), *pin* (apprécier, juger) s'écrit avec trois bouches, et *jing* (« brillant, étincelant ») est fait de trois soleils, quant à *xin* (« richesse »), elle est naturellement exprimée par trois coffres ou cassettes.

Abaque ou boulier chinois (1927, peinture de Qi Baishi).

On pourrait multiplier les exemples pour montrer la charge symbolique de certains nombres. Ainsi le « quatre » *(si)* qui donna lieu à quelques belles classifications – les Quatre Bonheurs, les Quatre Grands, les Quatre Vertus, les Quatre Livres, les Quatre (enfants) heureux, les Quatre Trésors du cabinet du lettré – n'est toujours pas très populaire. Les superstitieux, et ils sont nombreux en Chine, redoutent de l'employer, car il est homophone de « mourir, la mort » *(si)*. Pour les joueurs, c'est le chiffre de la malchance. On note que les acheteurs ou les locataires des immeubles nouvellement construits ne veulent pas du 4e étage et que certains promoteurs ont même supprimé le chiffre 4 sur les boutons de l'ascenseur (tout comme dans nos hôtels, on n'attribue plus de chambre au n° 13). Après avoir tenté de supprimer les Quatre vieilleries *(sijiu)*, les révolutionnaires maoïstes continuèrent néanmoins d'utiliser des slogans tout aussi symétriques comme les Quatre nouvelles idées *(xin si xiang)*. Et dans les années 1980, Deng Xiaoping lança son programme de réforme sur le thème des Quatre modernisations…

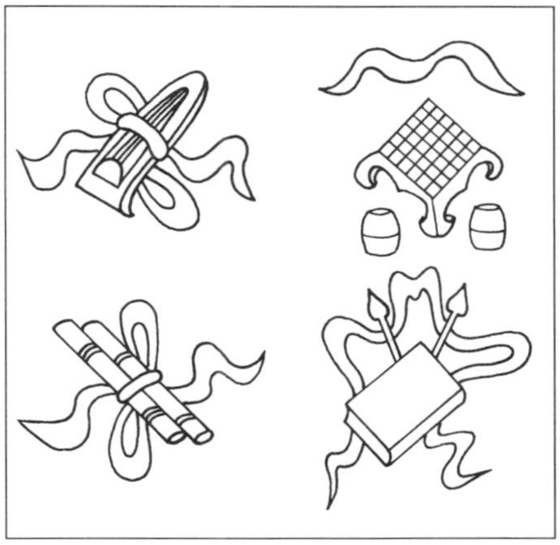

En revanche, le nombre cinq *(wu)*, comme en témoigne l'inventaire suivant, était autrefois fréquemment employé. On citait volontiers :

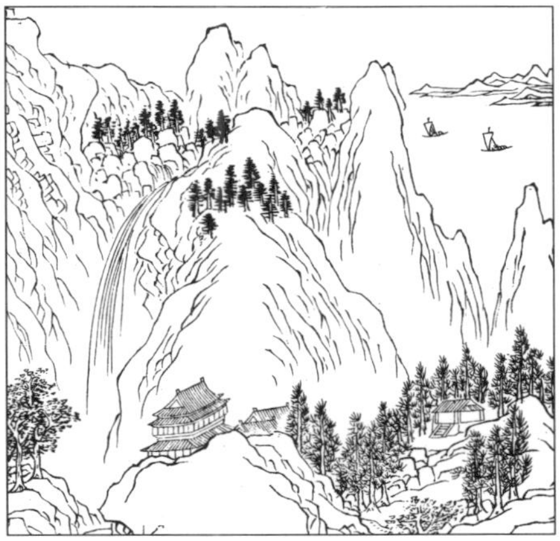

– les Cinq animaux domestiques : le bœuf, le mouton, le porc, la poule et le chien ;
– les Cinq bonheurs : la longévité, la richesse, la santé, la vertu et la mort paisible. Ils sont symbolisés par une ronde de cinq chauves-souris ou de cinq pies ;
– les Cinq catégories fondamentales d'animaux : à poil, à plume, à écaille, à carapace et sans poil (l'homme) ;
– les Cinq couleurs : le bleu-vert (associé au bois), le jaune (à la terre), le rouge (au feu et au soleil), le blanc (au métal) et le noir (à l'eau) ;
– les Cinq éléments : le bois (la vie, la féminité, la créativité), la terre (la stabilité, l'endurance), le métal (l'homme, la compétition, le commerce), l'eau (les transports, les voyages), le feu (l'énergie, l'intelligence) ;
– les Cinq montagnes sacrées : Taishan (dans la province du Shandong), Hengshan (Shanxi), Songshan (Henan), Hengshan (Hunan) et Huashan (Shaanxi) ;
– les Cinq Classiques, ou les livres les plus anciens sur lesquels est établi le confucianisme : le *Livre des Mutations (Yijing)*, le *Livre des Odes (Shijing)*, le *Livre de l'Histoire (Shujing)*, le *Livre des Rites (Liji)*, et la *Chronique des Printemps et Automnes (Chunqiu)* ;

En haut, les « Quatre attributs du lettré » (le luth, le damier, les rouleaux de peinture ou de calligraphie, les livres) ; en bas, l'une des « Cinq montagnes sacrées » (gravure extraite de Ming Shan Sheng Gai Di*).*

– les Cinq épices : le poivre, la coriandre, le clou de girofle, la cannelle, le gingembre ;
– les Cinq céréales : le riz, le millet, le millet glutineux, le blé, le haricot ;
– les Cinq métaux : l'or, l'argent, le cuivre, le fer, l'étain ;
– les Cinq organes des sens : les yeux, les oreilles, le nez, la bouche, le cœur (ou la peau) ;
– les Cinq planètes : Vénus, Jupiter, Mercure, Mars et Saturne ;
– les Cinq points cardinaux, dans l'ordre chinois d'énumération : l'Est, l'Ouest, le Sud, le Nord et le Centre ;
– les Cinq préceptes (ou interdits du bouddhisme) : tuer, voler, se livrer à la débauche, mentir, boire de l'alcool ;
– les Cinq nationalités de la Chine : les Chinois (de souche *han*), les Mandchous, les Mongols, les Musulmans et les Tibétains ;
– les Cinq relations immuables : prince-sujet, père-fils, aîné-cadet, mari-femme, amis ;
– les Cinq saveurs sur lesquelles est fondée la cuisine chinoise : l'amer, le doux, l'acide, l'âcre et le salé ;
– les Cinq souillures (bouddhisme) : les guerres et les calamités, les hérésies, les passions violentes, les faiblesses, les vies courtes ;
– les Cinq animaux venimeux : le scorpion, le serpent, le mille-pattes, le lézard et le crapaud ;
– les Cinq viscères de la médecine chinoise : le cœur, le foie, l'estomac (ou la rate), les poumons et les reins ; ils sont en étroite liaison avec les Cinq éléments : au cœur correspond le feu, au foie le bois, à l'estomac la terre, aux poumons le métal et aux reins l'eau…

Mais depuis 1982, date à laquelle s'amorce l'ère des réformes et de la libéralisation, le nombre « cinq » est tombé en désuétude. En effet, les nouvelles générations supportent moins bien les privations ou les interdits et dans leur inconscient, le 5 *(wu)* est trop lié par homophonie à *wu* (« il n'y a pas, pas de, sans ») dont le signifié est éminemment négatif. C'est donc le nombre « six » *(liu)* qui va bénéficier de toutes leurs faveurs car *liu,* c'est aussi « couler rapidement, glisser » ; comme le dit une expression récemment créée, *liu liu da shun* (« aller comme sur des roulettes, vivre "cool" »). Il est donc devenu habituel de choisir des jours fastes comme le 6, le 16 ou le 26 du mois pour entreprendre un voyage ou se lancer dans une entreprise difficile.

Selon Sima Qian, l'auteur des *Mémoires historiques,* les nombres *yang* atteignent leur perfection à « sept » *(qi).* C'est sous le nom des Sept apparitions *(qi xiang)* que l'on désignait en Inde et en Chine les motifs dessinés sur l'empreinte du pied que le Bouddha aurait laissées sur un rocher avant d'entrer au Nirvana. Ces dessins imprimés dans la pierre représentaient des emblèmes dont une partie figure dans la collection des Huit symboles. Ce sont le svastika, les poissons géminés, la masse de diamant, la conque marine, le vase, la roue de la loi, la couronne de Brahma... C'était aussi avec sept fois sept (soit 49) baguettes d'achillée que l'on pratiquait dans les temps anciens la divination. Enfin, tous les sept jours, du 7e au 49e jour du décès, la tradition prévoyait, une cérémonie funéraire.

Le nombre « huit » *(ba)* se prononce en cantonais *fa* (« prospère ») et, écrit en chiffres arabes ressemble alors au caractère *xi* (« joie, bonheur »). Voilà peut-être pourquoi le 8, le 88 ou le 888 sont si fréquents comme symboles de bonheur simple, double ou triple. Ce sont sans doute les Huit trigrammes *(ba gua)* qui ont le plus intrigué les occidentaux. Tirées du *Livre des Mutations* et attribuées à Fuxi, ces lignes géométriques seraient nées des craquelures observées sur les os ou les carapaces de tortues lors de pratiques divinatoires. C'est encore autour de ce même nombre « huit » qu'ont été constituées les collections emblématiques connues sous le nom des Huit trésors ou Huit précieux (*ba bao*; voir p. 21).

Dans la Chine ancienne les nombres impairs étaient masculins *(yang)* et le « neuf » *(jiu)* représentait le plus haut et le plus complet symbole masculin. Ce nombre exceptionnel fut l'attribut de l'empereur et apparut, seul ou en multiple, dans tout ce qui touchait à son univers. Autrefois, le *mingtang* (palais lumineux) était la représentation de l'univers en carré de neuf cases, il était symbolisé par le palais impérial. Les portes monumentales de ces palais, traditionnellement de couleur rouge, comprenaient neuf rangées de clous dorés, horizontalement et verticalement, soit quatre-vingt une pointes au total. De nombreux palais étaient composés de neuf cours carrées, et la surface au sol du palais Impérial de Pékin serait de 9 900 baies (une ancienne unité de mesure). Deux murs-écrans *(yingbi)* de la Cité Interdite sont décorés de neuf dragons. Le temple du Ciel à Pékin où l'empereur se rendait deux fois par an pour les sacrifices, est un exemple parfait d'application du nombre neuf, en particulier dans le dallage. On se souviendra enfin que le salut à l'empereur comportait neuf prosternations *(koutou)* et qu'une étiquette concernant le grand service de la table impériale prévoyait 108 plats (12 x 9) pour l'empereur et l'impératrice douairière, seulement 96 pour l'impératrice et 64 pour les concubines de première classe.

Un vieil adage populaire déclarait : « après le neuf on revient au un » *(jiujiu guiyi)*. Le « dix » *(shi)* était donc, dans la mentalité ancienne, une étape ultime au delà de laquelle il ne pouvait y avoir de développement, d'avenir, d'espoir, ce qui expliquerait son emploi peu fréquent. Les Dix troncs célestes *(shi gan)* assemblés deux par deux, servaient à désigner les directions, les saisons, les planètes, les couleurs, les saveurs, les vertus. Combinés avec les Douze rameaux terrestres *(shier zhi)*, ils formaient les soixante éléments du cycle sexagésimal dans le calendrier lunaire traditionnel et désignaient les années, les mois et les jours. Le *Livre des Rites* faisait aussi état des Douze ornements de l'empereur (voir p. 22).

On ne saurait clore cette longue pérégrination dans le monde des nombres et des chiffres sans s'arrêter à cent *(bai)*. À l'époque de Mao, le slogan qui promettait « la révolution des Cent fleurs » gagna une sinistre renommée car il servit à déclencher une vague de purges sans précédent parmi les intellectuels. On parlait autrefois des Cent (objets) antiques *(bai gu),* une collection d'objets symboliques, des Cent Enfants *(bai zi),* des Cent Animaux *(bai shou)*... car le terme « cent » dans un emploi plus général signifiait « nombreux, une foule, toutes sortes de, tous » pour exprimer une entité. C'est dans ce sens que l'on parlera aussi des « Cent noms » *(baixing)* pour désigner le peuple, les gens ordinaires ou que l'on évoquera le très célèbre *Livre des Cent Noms de familles (baijiaxing)*. C'est une compilation datant de l'époque des Song comprenant en fait les 430 patronymes les plus courants de Chine. Son apprentissage par cœur est un des exercices obligatoires auquel sont encore soumis tous les écoliers chinois : c'est la première expression de leur identité. Le mot « cent » est manifestement populaire car les dictons qui y font référence sont nombreux (par exemple, « voir une seule fois vaut mieux qu'entendre dire cent fois »).

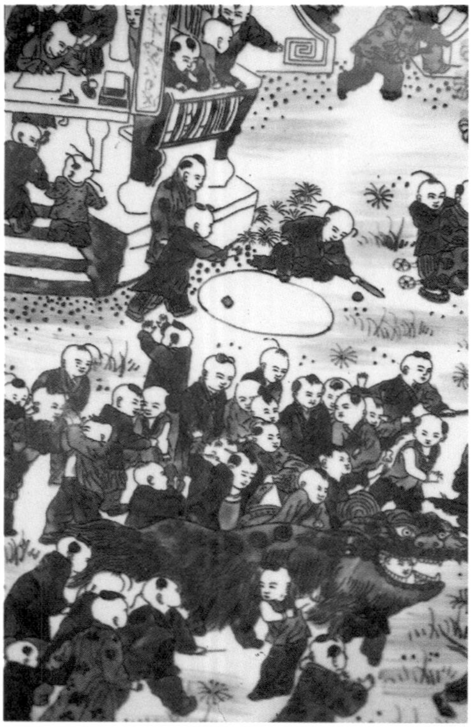

Le nombre 10 000 s'écrit avec le caractère *wan* ; son usage est fréquent dans les souhaits de bonheur, de longévité et, en décoration, sa représentation est le svastika (croix à branches coudées), tiré de la tradition indienne. On retrouvera cet étrange motif géométrique d'origine bouddhique (inversé par les nazis) sur des statues ou des vases rituels, sur les poutres de certains bâtiments sacrés et surtout tissé ou brodé. En décoration, cette croix se trouve souvent intégrée dans le caractère « longévité » *(shou)* auquel il sert de multiplicateur (*wan sui,* « dix mille années de longévité »). De nombreuses expressions utilisent ce nombre infini : « dix mille bonheurs » *(wan fu)* qui s'applique aussi à l'Ave Maria des chrétiens *(wan fu Mariya),* « dix mille lieues » *(wan li)*... Ainsi, la Grande muraille de Chine est appelée la « Muraille des Dix Mille lieues » *(wan li changcheng)* alors qu'elle ne mesurerait que 12 700 *li,* l'empereur portait le titre de « Seigneur de dix mille ans... »

Les « Cent Enfants », motif traditionnel en peinture (porcelaine bleu-et-blanc). Page de droite, porte de palais cloutée avec heurtoir à tête de lion (XIXe siècle).

À l'époque contemporaine, les nombres ont conservé une place importante dans la langue. Au delà des collections traditionnellement utilisées, il existait des expressions familières toutes faites à partir des nombres. Parler d'un « deux cent cinquante » *(erbaiwu),* au nord de la Chine, c'était évoquer un

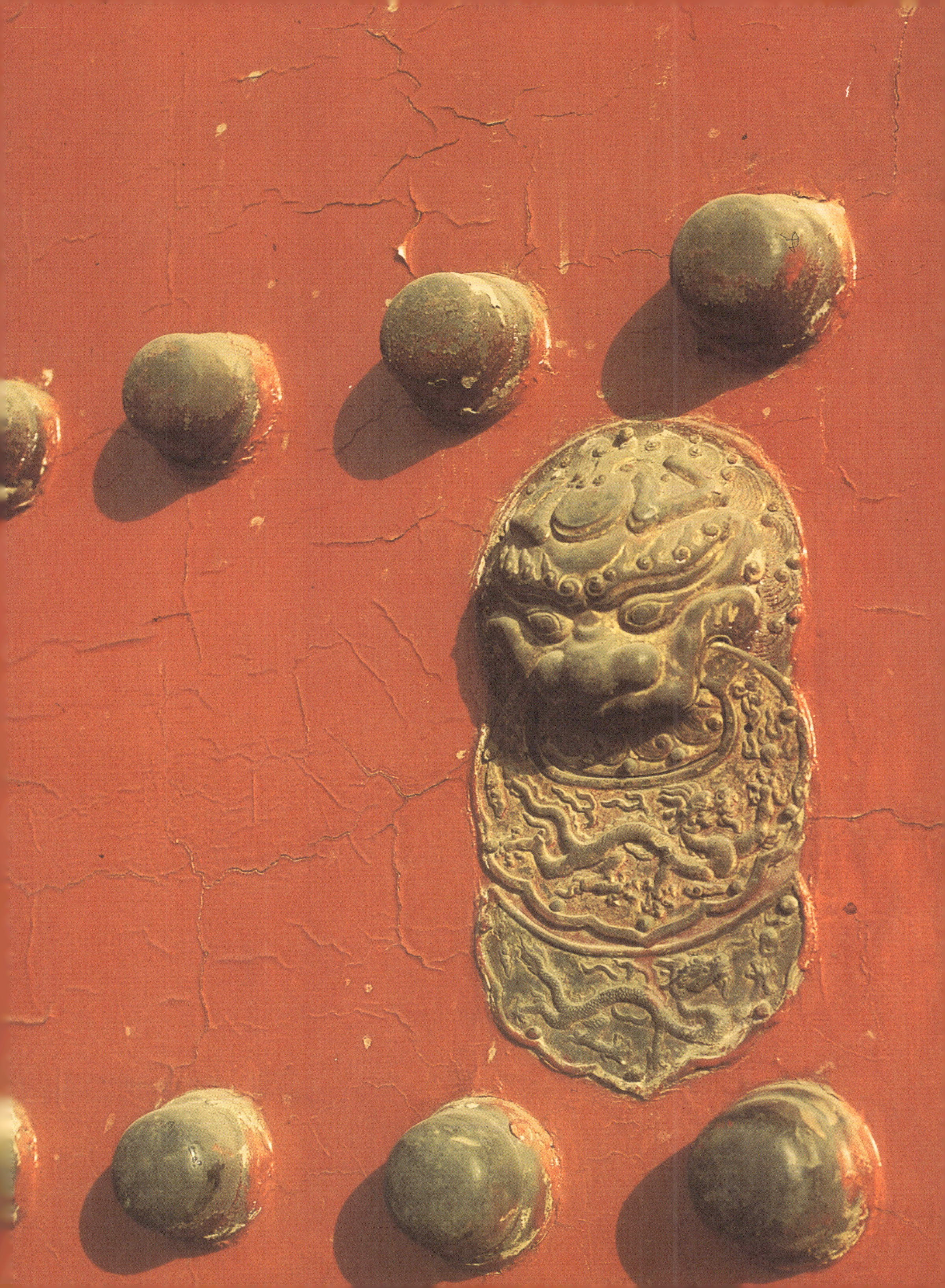

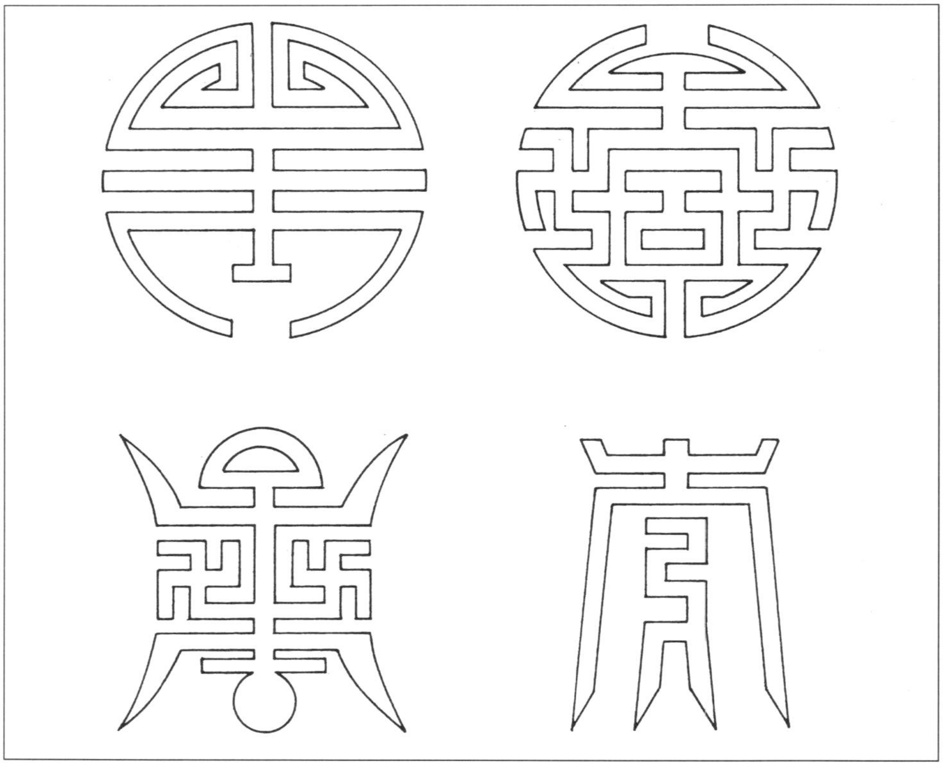

Variations décoratives du caractère « longévité » (shou) avec le svastika indien qui est un emblème du bonheur (un des signes sur le corps du Bouddha) mais aussi l'écriture stylisée du chiffre « dix mille ». Page de droite, la fabrication du papier (peinture sur soie).

sot, un niais, un nigaud ; dans le sud, on l'appelait « un deux et demi » sans doute parce qu'on entendait par là que l'intéressé ne disposait que de la moitié de ses facultés. Il n'était pas rare, dans certaines familles d'attribuer un numéro d'ordre aux enfants en fonction de leur âge. « Deux-huit » *(erba)* désignait une jeune fille de seize ans. Bien entendu, la propagande, la politique ou la publicité ont puisé dans cet extraordinaire thesaurus de signifiants que forment les nombres. De nos jours, « 101 » est le symbole bien connu d'une lotion capillaire, « 999 » celui d'un médicament miracle, « 505 » celui d'une ceinture d'herbes réputée pour soigner la circulation sanguine, « 863 » est le nom d'un plan national de développement (lancé en mars 1986), « 211 » celui d'un plan concernant l'enseignement supérieur et « 8.1 » est une référence historique connue de tous (c'est la date de la fondation de l'Armée Rouge, le 1er août 1927).

La numérologie et les croyances qui s'y rattachent ont encore de beaux jours en Chine comme en témoignent les émeutes que déclenche la mise aux enchères de numéros porte-bonheur de téléphone ou l'inimaginable trafic des numéros de plaques d'immatriculation des véhicules privés.

DES TECHNIQUES À APPRENDRE

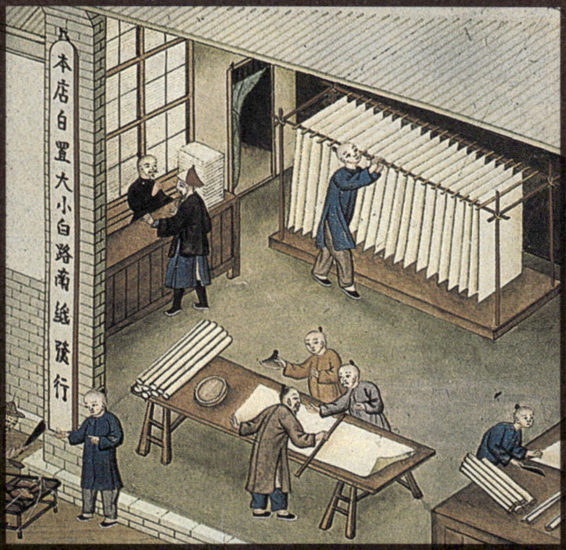

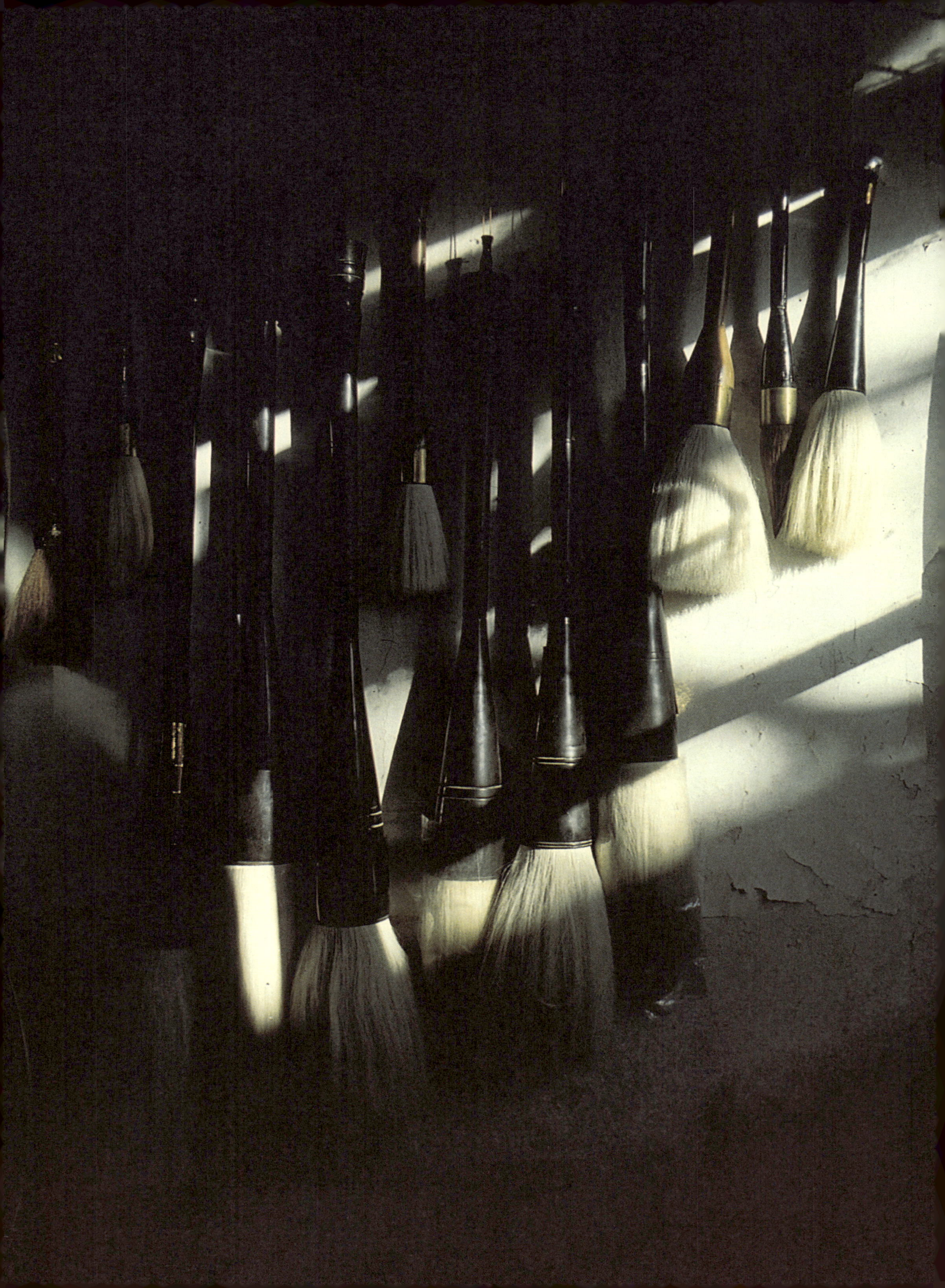

Les trésors du cabinet du lettré

L'art de la calligraphie est classé par les Chinois dans les Beaux-Arts au même titre que la peinture, appelée « la peinture lettrée » *(shifuhua),* la poésie et la musique. Depuis près de deux mille ans, les outils du calligraphe et ceux du peintre sont les mêmes ; ils ont peu évolué et font toujours l'objet d'une considération particulière. Si sous les Tang, la calligraphie parvint à sa plus grande perfection, plus tard sous les Song, les Yuan et les Qing, des générations de lettrés se firent connaître tant pour leur maîtrise des cinq styles de calligraphie que pour l'art du paysage et plus rarement du portrait. Le célèbre Mi Fu ou Mi Fei (1051-1107), peintre, poète, calligraphe, professeur, expert et collectionneur d'objets d'art, auteur de l'*Histoire de la Peinture (Huashi),* de l'*Histoire de la Calligraphie (Shushi)* et du *Traité de l'Encrier (Yanshi),* nous a donné de précieuses informations sur les « armes du lettré ». On les appelle traditionnellement les Quatre Trésors du cabinet du lettré *(wenfang si bao)* ; ce sont le pinceau, l'encre, l'encrier et le papier.

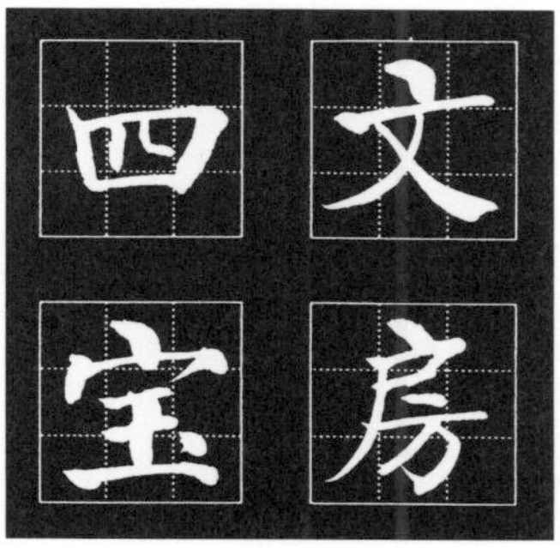

wenfang sibao, littéralement, « les quatre trésors du cabinet du lettré ».

Le *pinceau*

On ne sait pas exactement à quand remonte l'invention du pinceau. Elle est attribuée à un général de l'empereur Qin Shihuang. Meng Tian (mort en 210 av. J.-C.) passe pour être l'inventeur d'un instrument composé d'un manche en bois auquel on attachait une touffe de poils de cerf entourée de fins poils de laine de mouton ; en réalité cette découverte remonterait déjà au néolithique car des fragments de poteries de cette époque ont été retrouvés avec des traces de pinceau. Depuis cette période, les fabricants eurent à cœur de répondre aux exigences de leurs clients qui souhaitaient tout à la fois des pinceaux souples et durs. Pour cela, des poils d'animaux divers étaient insérés dans des manches creux (bambou, laque, ivoire, écaille de tortue, porcelaine et même métal précieux). La touffe était faite de plusieurs couches concentriques de poils formant un cœur *(xin),* un ventre *(fu)* et un manteau *(bei),* chaque partie étant fixée par un fil de soie. Quand le pinceau était appliqué sur la pierre à encre, la touffe s'ouvrait comme un éventail, se remplissait par capillarité et se refermait en conservant l'encre entre les couches. La quantité de liquide qui se déposait sur le

Page de gauche, brosses et pinceaux chinois.

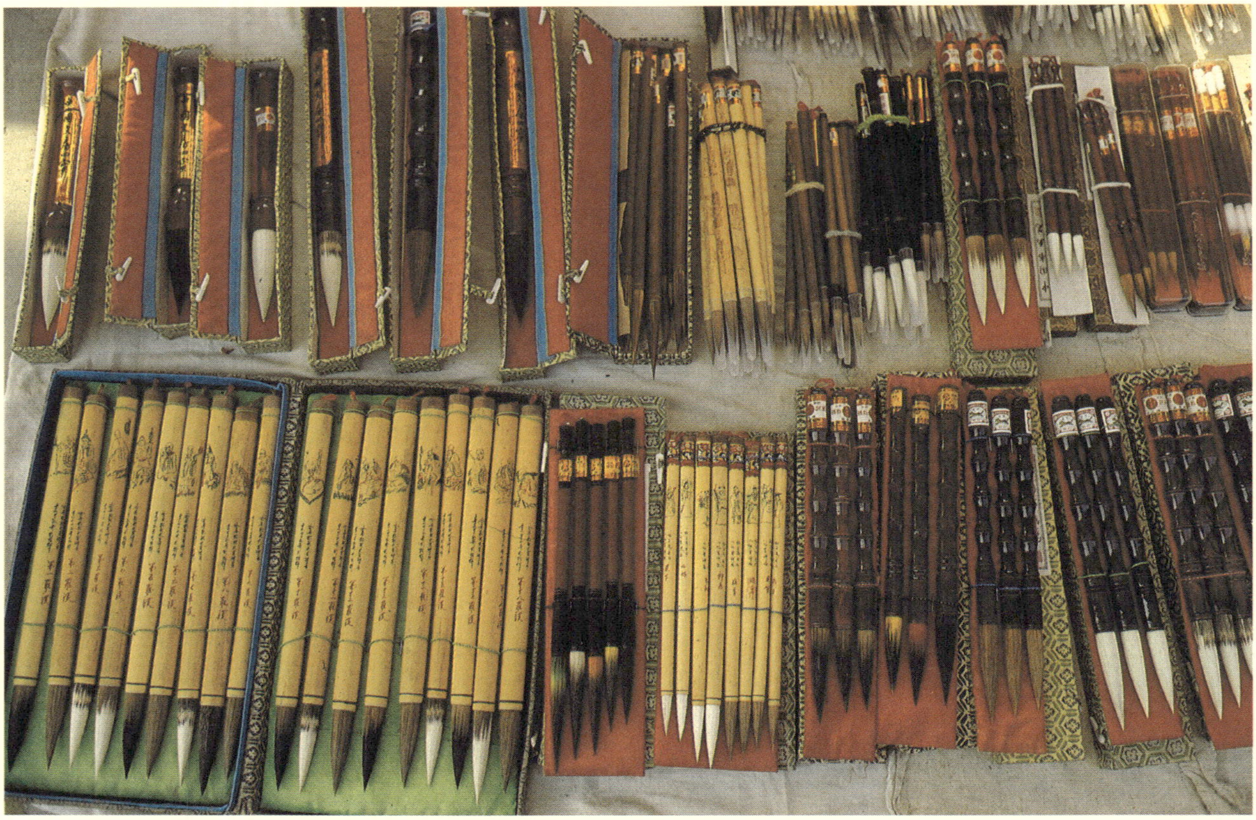

papier était alors proportionnelle à la pression de la main du calligraphe. Il a toujours existé une grande variété de pinceaux, du plus fin au plus large (certaines brosses larges pour la peinture atteignent quinze centimètres de diamètre). Les pinceaux se classent selon leur fonction, pour la calligraphie *(maobi)* ou pour la peinture *(huabi),* mais en fait ils portent des noms poétiques qui définissent plus précisément leur usage. Ainsi, le « Grand-Nuage-Blanc » *(dabaiyun)* est-il utilisé pour la peinture des paysages. Le « Nervure-de-Feuille » *(yejing)* est réservé à la peinture délicate des oiseaux et des fleurs. « L'Orchidée-Bambou » *(lanzhu),* comme son nom l'indique, ne sert qu'à ce type de peinture. Des inscriptions figurent sur les manches ; elles indiquent la nature du pinceau, le nom du fabricant ou transcrivent quelquefois un petit poème ou une dédicace. La qualité du pinceau dépend des poils utilisés. Les plus appréciés pour les petits caractères, parce que les plus durs, proviennent de la queue de la belette, de la martre ou du putois (tous trois de la famille des mustélidés). Il s'agirait plutôt de la belette *(huangshulang),* mais les Chinois les appellent pinceaux de « poil de loup ». Beaucoup plus flexibles sont les pinceaux en « poil de chèvre » *(yanghao)* de couleur blanche, recherchés par les peintres. Les traités anciens mentionnent encore des pinceaux en poil de cerf, de renard, de barbe de rat, de tigre, de loup, de singe, de loutre, de porc, et même de cheveux

Pinceaux pour calligraphie.

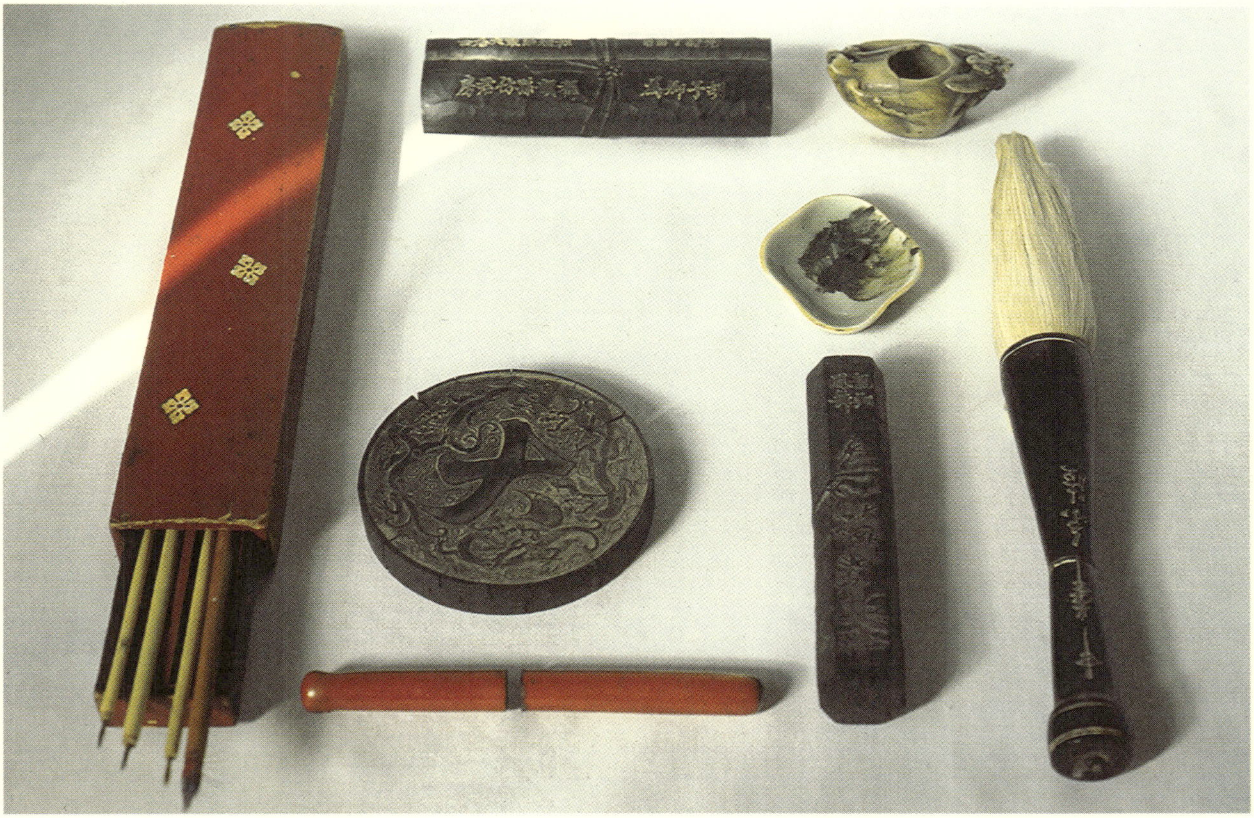

d'enfants… Su Dongpo (1036-1101), poète et calligraphe de la période Song, utilisait, dit-on, des moustaches de souris. On se servit aussi de plumes d'oie, de canard, de paon… Il existe enfin une troisième catégorie de pinceaux, les « poils mélangés » *(jianhao)*, caractérisés par leur souplesse et leur tenue : le « Grand-Nuage-Blanc » est ainsi fait de poil de martre, de chèvre et de chat sauvage. On trouve aussi dans cette catégorie des « poils de lièvre mélangés à ceux de chèvre » *(ziyanghao)*.

Les pinceaux étaient l'objet de soins particuliers. Pour une bonne conservation, il fallait les rincer soigneusement. On pouvait les laisser s'égoutter dans de charmants petits godets à trous, lisser les poils puis les faire sécher la tête en bas accrochés à des chevalets (*bijia* ou *bigua*). Une fois secs, on les rangeait dans des pots de bois précieux ou de céramique, des plumiers pour les plus fins ou même des sacs contenant des morceaux de camphre pour éloigner les insectes. Il fallait enduire souvent les poils du milieu de cire pour obtenir une pointe plus souple qui devait répondre à quatre critères : être ronde, pointue, ordonnée et ferme.

Les *encres*

D'après la tradition, l'invention de l'encre remonterait au IIIe siècle de notre ère, toutefois des inscriptions découvertes à Anyang, la dernière capitale de l'empire des Shang (1500-1100 av. J.-C.), paraissent

Nécessaire du peintre-calligraphe : pinceau large, bâtons d'encre, godets à eau, plumier de bois laqué.

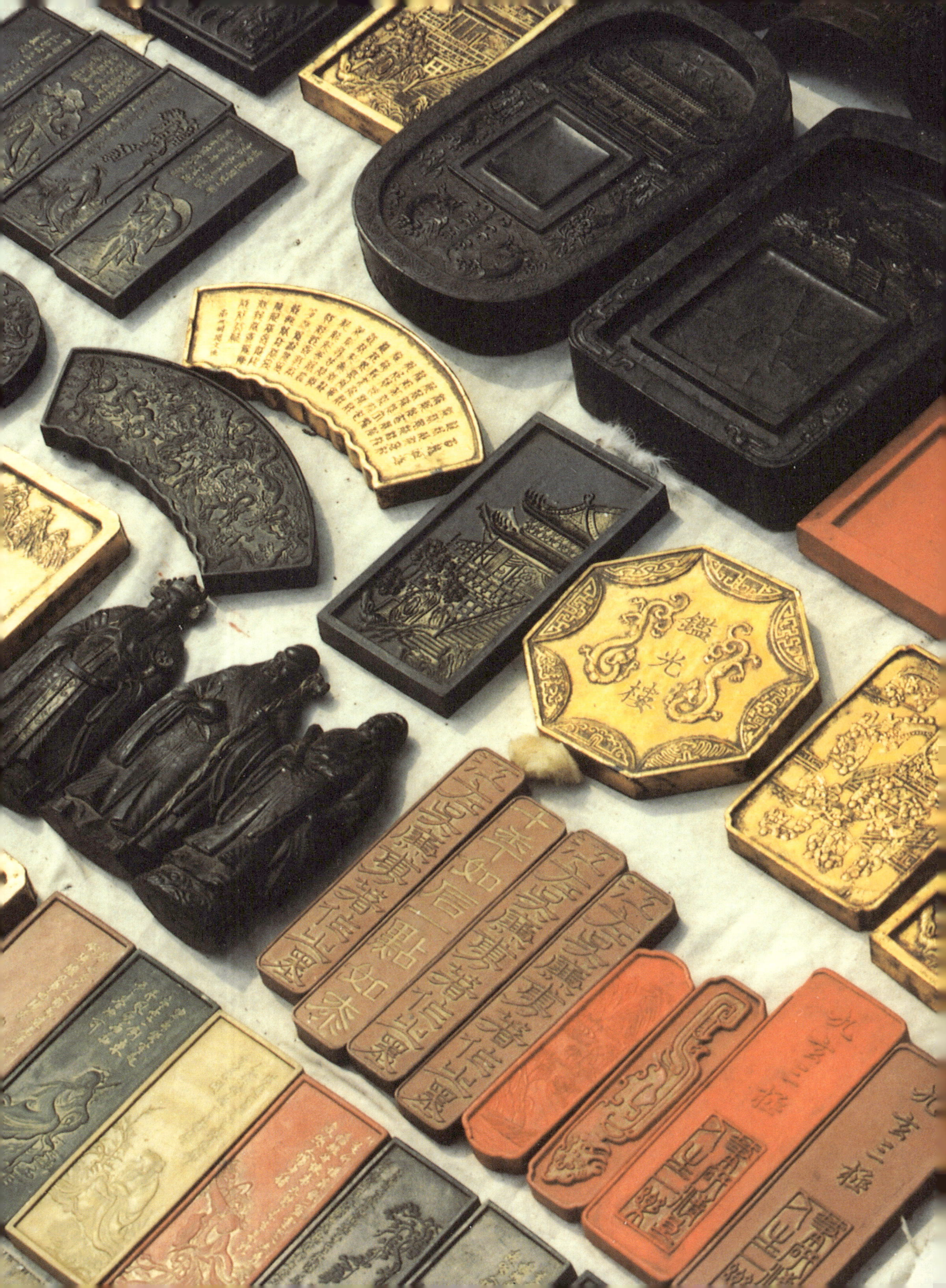
鑑光樓

avoir été tracées au cinabre (sulfure de mercure). Cette encre rouge fut utilisée par les prêtres taoïstes pour leurs écrits ; elle servit aussi à certains édits impériaux avant d'être communément employée sous forme de pâte à sceller. Curieusement, alors qu'il est connu pour sa toxicité, le cinabre correspondait, chez les taoïstes, à un élixir d'immortalité et il était absorbé non sans quelques conséquences catastrophiques. Selon le *Classique de l'Encre* (XIIe siècle), les Chinois auraient d'abord utilisé un vernis fait de la sève de l'arbre à laque auquel on ajoutait un pigment (sulfure de fer) pour obtenir une couleur noire. Ce fut sans doute la première « encre de Chine » *(mozhi)*. Difficile à produire, ce vernis ne fut utilisé que pour des ouvrages de grande valeur comme les textes religieux, qui étaient écrits avec un stylet (ou calame). Certains textes comportent même des inclusions d'or dans l'encre. Avec l'invention du papier, la laque, trop épaisse, fut délaissée au profit de l'encre. Les lettrés et surtout les peintres préféraient fabriquer la leur selon des recettes très personnelles.

Les procédés de fabrication ont varié ; il semble qu'il ait existé une encre provenant de poudre de charbon appelée *shimo* (« encre de pierre »). Dès le VIe siècle apparut le procédé dit « noir de fumée » *(songyan)*. On brûlait du pin, la suie ainsi obtenue était mélangée avec de la colle animale (gelée de cerf, de poisson ou de bœuf), plus tard on utilisa des huiles végétales *(youyan)* : l'huile d'aleurite ou d'abrasin, de colza ou de sésame. Le noir de fumée recueilli sur un entonnoir était alors mélangé à la colle, à laquelle on ajoutait du musc, du bornéol (un alcool de camphrier), des épices, des herbes médicinales. La pâte ainsi obtenue était mise dans des moules de formes variées : petits blocs en forme d'animaux ou de cloches, bâtonnets cylindriques, parallélépipèdiques ou ronds. Ils pouvaient être peints et même laqués. On recommandait de les enduire d'eau sucrée pour éviter qu'ils ne s'effritent en vieillissant. Sous les Song, on fabriqua des encres de couleur par l'adjonction de poudre de perle, de jade, de corne de rhinocéros. Ces colorants furent remplacés plus tard par des pigments naturels (l'indigo pour le bleu, le plomb pour le blanc, le cinabre pour le rouge et la malachite pour le vert). Dans un catalogue du XVIIe siècle figurent des bâtonnets décorés de motifs chrétiens qui auraient été dessinés par le célèbre jésuite italien Matteo Ricci. Les bâtons d'encre *(mokuai)* les plus réputés venaient de Huizhou dans la province de l'Anhui dont les forêts de sapins étaient célèbres. Les lettrés étaient particulièrement exigeants sur les qualités de l'encre ; elle devait avoir une fluidité particulière, une odeur et même une certaine sonorité quand on frottait le bâton d'encre sur la pierre. Certains de ces bâtonnets pouvaient atteindre des prix extraordinaires pour leur ancienneté ou leur appartenance à un propriétaire célèbre. Jugés trop précieux pour être utilisés, ils étaient alors échangés ou conservés comme de véritables objets d'art.

Page de gauche, bâtons d'encre et pierres à encre.

Les encriers

Les traités sur l'encrier, outre celui de Mi Fu déjà cité, ont été très nombreux en Chine comme au Japon. On distinguait les encriers *(mohe)* destinés à contenir l'encre liquide (*moshui* ou *mozhi*) – que l'on appelle en Occident « l'encre de Chine » – et les pierres à encre sur lesquelles s'effectuait la fabrication de l'encre par frottement d'un bâtonnet d'encre solidifiée. Cette encre liquide n'était bonne que pour le pinceau ou l'impression sur planches de bois, en revanche elle ne convenait pas pour l'imprimerie par caractères métalliques ; on en fit une plus pâteuse du nom de *moyu.*

Les encriers (ou boîtes à encre) ont été fabriqués dans tous les matériaux possibles, en pierre, en terre cuite, en porcelaine, en verre, en fer, en laiton et même en bois. Ceux destinés au transport avaient un couvercle. Ils étaient remplis de bourre de soie *(simian)* imprégnée d'encre liquide. Moins pittoresques que les pierres, ils sont moins recherchés des amateurs.

Les pierres à encre *(yan)* sont de fait des pierres plates comprenant toujours à la partie supérieure (ou « tête ») une cavité (*yanchi* ou *shuichi*) poétiquement appelée « le puits d'or » et, à la partie inférieure un espace légèrement creux de forme variable, dénommé « la mare » *(mochi),* que l'on humecte avec un récipient verseur ou une petite cuillère. C'est sur cette surface humidifiée que l'on frotte le bâton d'encre en tournant. Coquetterie de lettré, au lieu de pierres, Mi Fu se servait de tuiles ou de briques vernissées, vieilles de mille ans (de l'époque Han) provenant des temples de Anyang. On connaît la passion des *wenren* (les lettrés) pour les choses antiques. D'autres ont utilisé des coquilles d'huître, de l'os plat ou du bambou. Les pierres à encre de forme rectangulaire ont été les plus fréquentes mais il en a existé de forme très baroque. On les classait traditionnellement en huit catégories : en forme de hache, de carré, de tablette de jade, de rectangle, de trapèze d'après le caractère « vent » *(feng),* de nuage et de lune, d'octogone et enfin des pierres à bordure gravée. Les plus fréquentes étaient en schiste allant du brun au noir avec des teintes grises ou vertes ; elles se différenciaient des grès rouges de Yixing, certaines ont même été taillées dans le jade. Sous les Ming, la mode fut aux pierres à encre de céramique, avec ou sans couvercle, et dont l'intérieur n'était pas vernissé pour permettre un meilleur frottement du bâtonnet d'encre. Les pierres de la province de Canton, connues depuis les Tang sous le nom de *duanyan* parce qu'elles venaient de la région de Duanxi, étaient réputées « aussi dures que le jade ». D'autres, en provenance du Henan, dénommées « soie rouge », étaient très recherchées pour leur aspect soyeux. Mais celles des provinces du Shandong, du Jiangxi et du Gansu (pierres de la rivière Taohe) étaient aussi renommées.

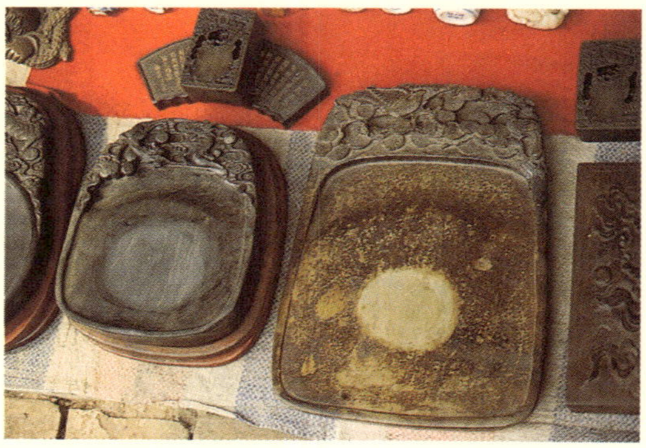

Pierres à encre de Duanxi (province de Canton).

Parce que les pierres, parmi les Quatre Trésors, étaient pour les lettrés leur compagne la plus fidèle dans le temps (elles ne s'usaient pas comme l'encre ou le pinceau), ils entretenaient avec elles une relation particulière en leur attribuant des petits noms familiers, en leur dédiant des poèmes, en célébrant devant des connaisseurs leurs qualités et en les emportant, même cassées, dans la tombe. Il existait tout un vocabulaire pour décrire leur comportement ; on disait d'une pierre qu'elle était « lente » ou « rapide » (à produire de l'encre), « glissante » ou « fatiguée », trop « absorbante » ou « repoussant l'encre », et surtout « à belle sonorité »... Certaines, trop précieuses pour être utilisées, figuraient dans la collection comme un objet d'art. Une place de choix leur était réservée sur la table de travail, bien en apparence car elle indiquait non seulement le statut d'homme de culture du propriétaire, mais aussi ses goûts pour les belles choses. Les pierres étaient généralement encastrées dans des étuis de bois taillés à leur forme ou dans de riches coffrets contenant les autres « trésors ». C'est encore de nos jours un cadeau très apprécié des connaisseurs. La plupart de ces encriers anciens furent taillés dans des pierres mais il y en eut aussi en laque, en grès, en fer, en argent et en porcelaine blanche à décor bleu dès le Xe siècle.

Le *papier*

Le choix du papier était important pour le rôle qu'il jouait comme support de l'œuvre. Mi Fu, dans son *Histoire de l'art,* cite une dizaine de types de papier fabriqués avec du chanvre, du bambou, de l'écorce de mûrier, du bois de santal et de la paille de riz. Le bon papier devait avoir la particularité d'être pur, blanc, résistant, d'une texture fine et de bien vieillir. Il semblerait que le premier papier obtenu ait contenu même de la bourre de soie (ce qui expliquerait le radical « soie » dans l'idéogramme « papier », *zhî*). En effet, lors du dévidage des cocons, des déchets de soie se déposent en une mince pellicule, donnant ainsi une sorte de papier. Un rapport de 1843 adressé au ministère français de l'Agriculture recensait une cinquantaine de types de papier fabriqués à cette époque en Chine. On y relevait le résistant *jinbanzhi,* fabriqué avec du coton et réservé aux édits impériaux ou aux grandes œuvres peintes car la taille des feuilles (trois mètres) était importante. Le papier de thé *(chazhi)* était fabriqué avec du bambou et servait à faire des bandes à coller sur les caisses de thé (d'où sans doute son nom), des enveloppes, des emballages, des cerfs-volants et même des étuis de cartouches. Le papier de paille *(caozhi),* peu résistant, servait pour les écritures courantes et pour calquer car il était assez transparent. Chaque région avait sa spécialité. Dans le Sichuan, on le fabriquait à partir du chanvre *(ma),* dans le Fujian avec du bambou *(zhu),* dans le Zhejiang avec de la paille de riz *(daocao),* dans le Jiangsu à partir de cocons de ver à soie *(canjian)* et enfin dans le Hebei avec du mûrier *(sangshu).*

L'invention du papier remonterait au IIe siècle ap. J.-C., probablement dans la province de l'Anhui à Xuancheng (d'où le nom chinois *xuan* pour ce que nous appelons « papier à dessin » ou « papier de Chine »). Son invention est attribuée à Cai Lun (*ca* 61-121), chef des eunuques qui eut une mort tragique après quarante-six ans au service de quatre empereurs. Nommé intendant général des ateliers du palais, il avait fait procéder à de nombreuses expériences avant de parvenir à un résultat acceptable, c'est-à-dire un papier non fibreux, peu absorbant pour l'encre et ne se désagrégeant pas. Il est probable que Cai Lun utilisa l'écorce de certains arbres comme le mûrier ou le chanvre. La matière première (écorce d'arbre, vieux chiffons, filets de pêche, déchets de soie, de lin...) était immergée pour la ramollir, puis bouillie et broyée en pâte. On trempait ensuite un fin tamis dans la cuve et une fine pellicule se déposait sur les lamelles du tamis que l'on mettait à sécher à l'air libre pour obtenir des feuilles. Pour faire face aux besoins grandissants de l'administration, mais aussi à de nombreux autres usages domestiques (papier pour lanternes, pour fenêtres, pour fleurs artificielles), il fallut augmenter la production. Avec la découverte de l'impression sur planches, cette production devint quasi industrielle. Selon ce que rapporte l'écrivain Su Dongpo (1036-1101), le papier fabriqué avec du bambou et le papier de paille de riz n'existent que depuis le IVe siècle. Le « papier de riz » aurait été fabriqué, entre autres, avec la mœlle de l'*aralia papyrifera,* qui se nomme *tongcao*.

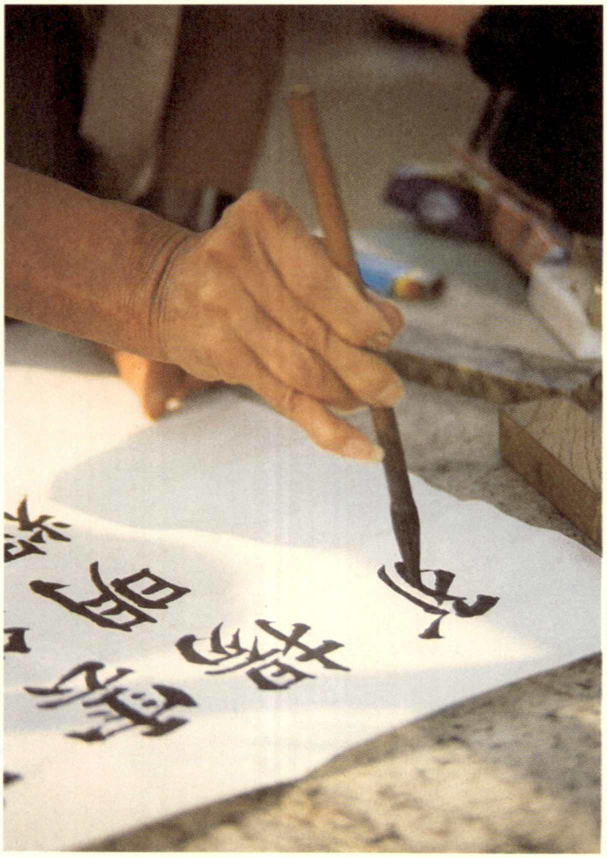

Calligraphe au travail.

Les autres accessoires du lettré

Les peintres et les calligraphes aimaient s'entourer dans leur cabinet de travail d'un grand nombre d'autres petits objets qui avaient une valeur pratique ou esthétique. Parmi les plus utilisés figuraient les verseurs ou goutte-à-goutte (*dilou, diping* ou *diguan*) à bec avec lesquels on humectait la pierre selon l'épaisseur requise de l'encre. On en fit de charmants en forme de minuscules théières, d'animaux ou de personnages en céramique, en porcelaine bleu-et-blanc, en céladon, en blanc de chine, en terre de Yixing ou creusés dans des pierres tendres (pierre à savon). Il en exista aussi en jade mais ils sont rares. À côté des verseurs, il y avait un très grand nombre de petits pots, en général de forme bulbeuse, dans lesquels on puisait de l'eau avec la petite cuillère, à moins qu'ils ne servent aussi de rince-pinceaux *(bixi)*. Ces récipients eurent toutes les formes : « cage à poules» *(jizhaozun),* godets, «soulier» *(xie).* Celui-ci était apprécié des lettrés car *xie* est homophone d'«harmonie, entente». Les «appuis-bras» *(zhijia)* en forme de tuile faîtière sur lesquels l'artiste pouvait reposer le poignet ou l'avant-bras permettaient de travailler sans tacher l'œuvre en cours. Faits dans le bois de bambou, en ivoire ou en porcelaine, ils étaient surtout utilisés pour les travaux délicats. Des presse-papiers de céramique, de laiton ou de bois qui devaient être à l'origine, comme leur nom *yashi* l'indique, des galets, servaient à maintenir le papier bien tendu sur la table de travail. Les peintures ou plutôt les pigments étaient mélangés dans des palettes ou dans des coupelles qui pouvaient s'emboîter les unes dans les autres. Elles étaient de la même forme que les boîtes à fard et à cosmétique. Mais la pièce maîtresse du cabinet du lettré restait sans doute le pot à pinceaux (*bitong* ou *bicha*) dont les matériaux les plus recherchés étaient le bois de rose ou l'acajou ; on en fit aussi en bambou, en ivoire ou en jade, en céramique figurant parfois des scènes mais portant le plus souvent des inscriptions. Ces pots étaient en général cylindriques et leur beauté résidait dans la sobriété. Homophone de «continuité» *(tong),* le pot faisait donc référence à la longévité. Les lettrés pouvaient y ranger leurs pinceaux la tête en l'air ou les suspendre à un petit portique (*bijia* ou *bigua*) s'ils n'en n'avaient pas l'usage immédiatement. Les pose-pinceaux *(bige)* étaient reconnaissables à leur forme de pics montagneux. La forme la plus traditionnelle était celle des Cinq Montagnes sacrées de Chine, dont le nombre s'est traditionnellement réduit à trois pics. C'est dans les plumiers *(bihe)* que l'on rangeait les pinceaux fins ou les calames. Ces belles boîtes arrivèrent du Moyen-Orient et furent populaires au XVe siècle. On en trouvait en porcelaine et en laque. Les sceaux *(duzhang)* portant le nom du propriétaire, la boîte à encre *(yinshaihe)* dans laquelle se trouvait la pâte rouge (cinabre) à sceller, faisaient partie des accessoires indispensables.

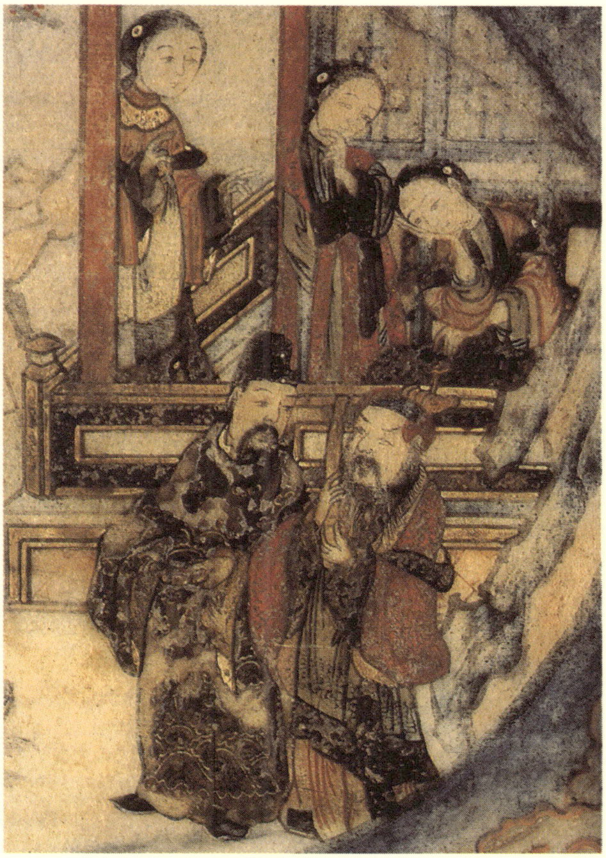

Mais, à côté de ces accessoires techniques, figuraient aussi d'étranges objets qui créaient une atmosphère propice à la méditation et à la contemplation. Pour cacher le désordre d'une table de travail, pour empêcher les courants d'air qui éparpillent les papiers et protéger des influences malfaisantes, les lettrés installaient des écrans, sorte de petits paravents *(taiping).* C'étaient des cadres montés sur un socle de bois qui contenaient une plaque de marbre veiné ou

Détail d'un écran de table, une «réunion de gens distingués» (peinture sur marbre, époque Ming).

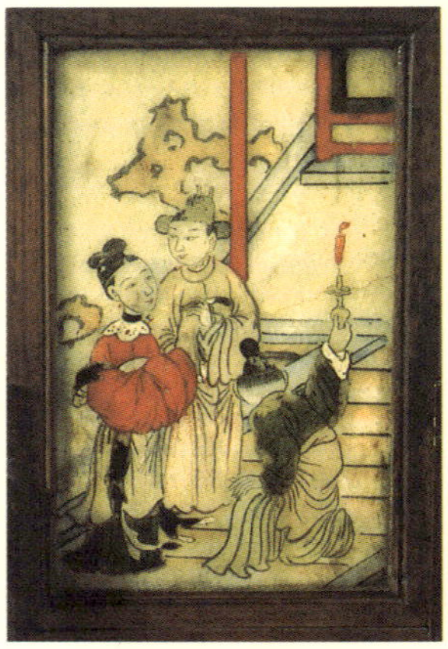
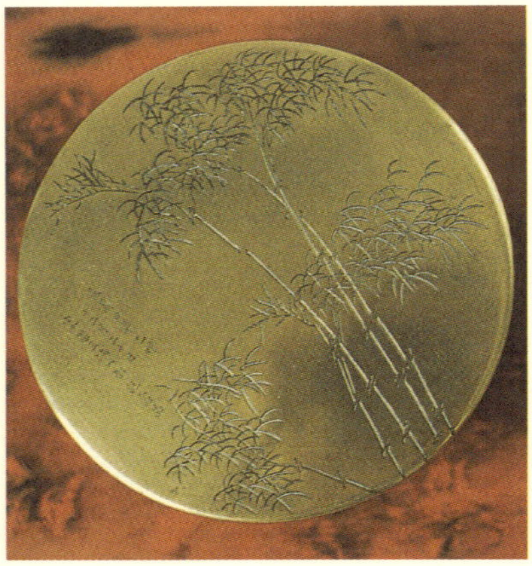
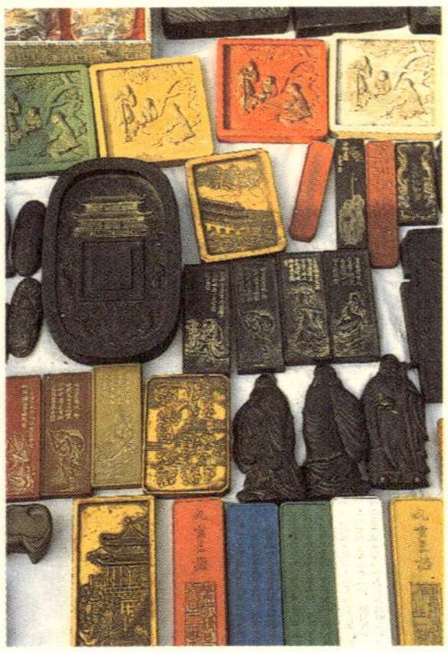

une peinture avec un petit poème au verso. Des fleurs ou des branches fleuries dans un beau vase, un paysage miniature, une statuette de jade ou d'ivoire ancien, un fragment de rocher ou une racine aux formes étranges apportaient une touche supplémentaire qui égayait le cabinet de travail tout comme la présence de grillons, d'oiseaux et même de minuscules singes (pas plus gros qu'une souris) que l'on appelait justement « singe-encre » ou « singe-pinceaux » *(bihou)*.

Tous ces objets fabriqués dans des matières nobles portaient souvent, peints ou gravés, les attributs des gens de lettres. On y voyait, par exemple, les Quatre Trésors qui symbolisaient les « délassements élégants » : le luth, les rouleaux de calligraphie enrubannés, les livres avec les pinceaux et l'échiquier ou le damier. Très souvent, les Huit Précieux, emblèmes favoris des lettrés et des fonctionnaires, ornaient aussi les objets dont ils aimaient s'entourer. La vie de ces privilégiés n'était pas faite que de retraite studieuse et de méditation solitaire. Des « réunions de gens distingués » *(yaji)* avaient lieu entre amis au cours desquelles ceux-ci partageaient des mets fins, des thés rares et du vin, en compagnie de musiciennes *(ji)* ou de poétesses renommées. Les jeux littéraires (palindromes, devinettes, rébus) assortis de gages étaient très prisés. Le « jeu de l'encens », par exemple, consistait à deviner la nature des différents parfums que l'on brûlait à cette occasion dans des cassolettes. On adorait aussi se retrouver dans des pavillons *(liubeiting)* dont le sol était creusé d'un petit ruisseau aux nombreux méandres. Le jeu consistait à faire flotter des coupes remplies de vin ; le gage *(fajiu)* était de les boire quand elle s'arrêtait à la hauteur du convive et de se soumettre aux décisions du meneur de jeu. C'était peut-être la survivance d'un vieux rite de célébration du printemps au bord de l'eau.

En haut à gauche, écran de table ; au centre, boîte à encre de cinabre ; à droite, bâtons d'encre de différentes couleurs.

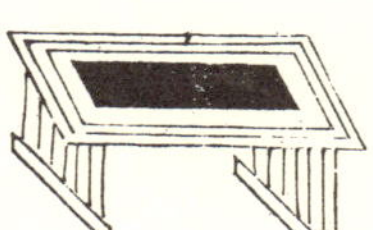

L'art du pinceau de fer

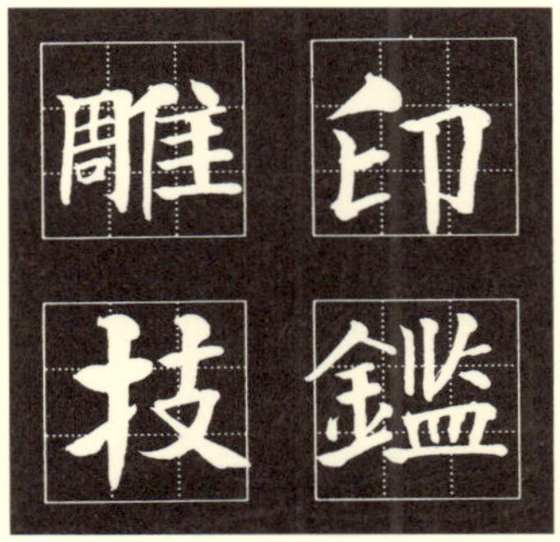

kedao yishu, littéralement, « l'art de la gouge ».

On appelle « pinceau de fer » *(tiebi),* les outils comme le burin, le ciseau ou la gouge qui servent à graver des sceaux *(yinzhang)* dans les pierres relativement tendres et qui se manient avec autant de dextérité que s'ils étaient des pinceaux à poils… Pour les lettrés, passionnés par cette technique, la gravure de sceaux était aussi importante que la peinture, la calligraphie ou la poésie. Une œuvre ne pouvait d'ailleurs atteindre l'excellence que si elle comprenait un beau texte (le « colophon », texte manuscrit écrit sur le côté d'une peinture ou d'une calligraphie, indiquant en général, le nom de l'artiste, le nom de son studio et la date de réalisation) accompagné d'un cachet de qualité par lequel l'artiste signait cette œuvre. Cette marque « n'était d'ailleurs pas placée au hasard ; elle avait pour but de corriger l'équilibre de la composition ou d'attirer l'attention. Au fil des années apparaissaient ainsi, sur les pièces de valeur, les sceaux privés des différents propriétaires ; marques d'appréciation ou preuves d'authenticité, elles rendent ces documents encore plus célèbres.

De nombreux spécialistes s'accordent maintenant sur le fait que les premières gravures de sceaux pourraient remonter à l'époque des Qin (221-207 av. J.-C.). Les empereurs faisaient graver un sceau d'État *(xi),* en jade, en sept exemplaires, pour commémorer l'établissement de l'empire et pour marquer leur accession au trône. Celui sur lequel figurait la mention « sceau privé du Fils du Ciel » était porté par l'empereur sur son costume d'apparat comme une marque d'autorité. On désignait alors par *yin* tous les autres sceaux ou cachets réservés aux dignitaires qui, à l'origine, étaient faits en bronze, en corne ou en pierre. Ils servirent d'abord à marquer la propriété ou l'autorité conférée puis à attester la validité de documents, devenant ainsi une sorte de signature. Cette pratique s'est prolongée jusqu'à nos jours et il n'est pas rare de voir des personnalités littéraires, scientifiques ou politiques signer au pinceau et apposer leur sceau à l'encre rouge. La période des Han de l'est (25-220) fut, sans nul doute, l'âge d'or de la

Ci-dessus, sceau officiel de l'empereur Daoguang, dynastie des Qing (1820-1850).

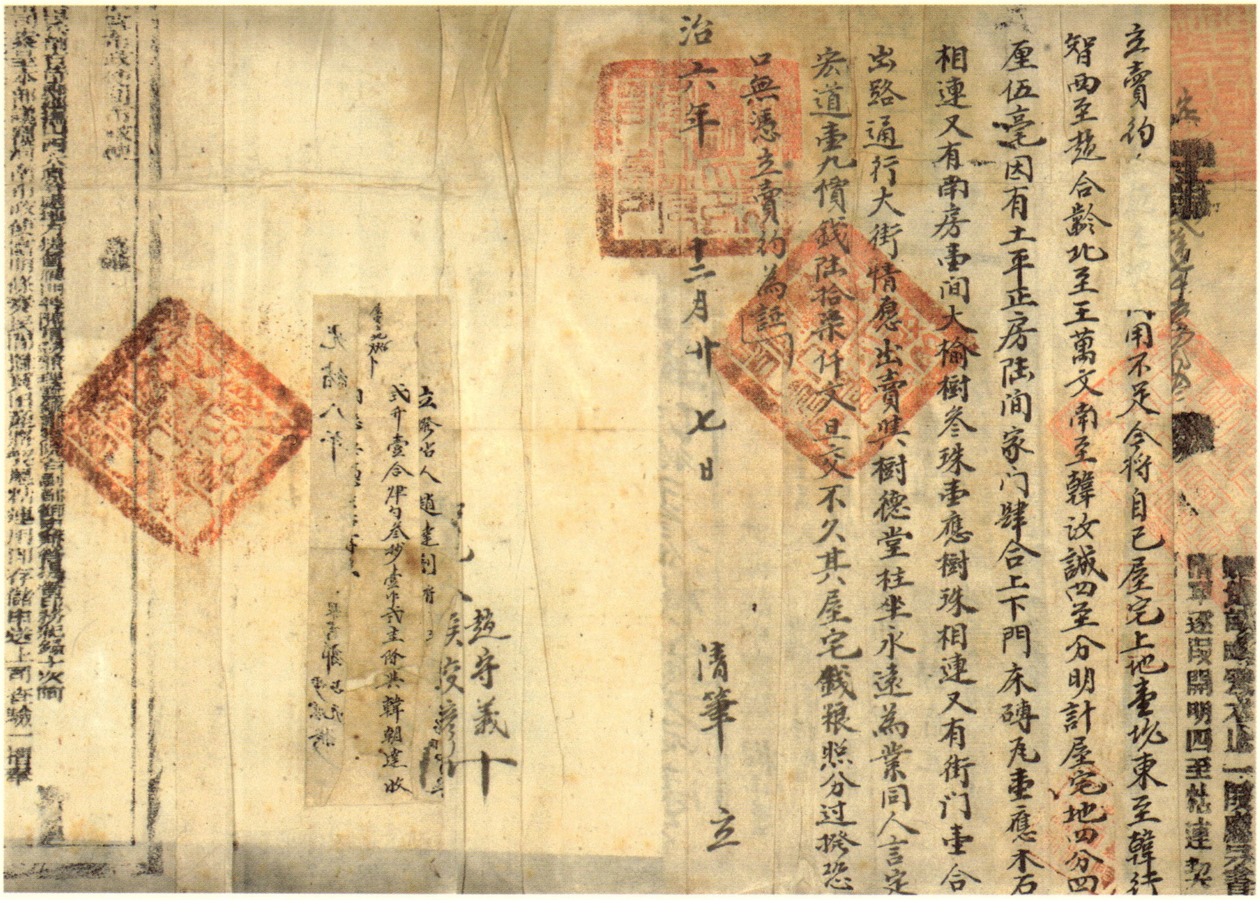

gravure de sceaux. Le sceau impérial se transmit successivement de génération en génération jusqu'à l'époque troublée des Jin (265-316), où il fut perdu dans de mystérieuses circonstances. À cette époque, le sceau portait sur le dessus un bouton (à l'effigie d'un tigre pour celui de l'empereur) dans lequel passait une tresse de soie de cinq couleurs, principalement jaune, la couleur impériale. Une réglementation très stricte fixait la couleur des rubans et la matière dans laquelle les sceaux des hauts personnages devaient être fabriqués (or, argent). Le sceau de Zhenfei (concubine de l'empereur Guangxu, 1875-1908), de 6,8 kg d'or massif, était en forme de tortue et portait un texte en mandchou et en chinois. Il fut l'objet de plusieurs tentatives de vol… Les premiers caractères furent gravés dans une graphie appelée *zhuan* qui donna son nom à un style d'écriture officielle sigillaire (dite « grand sceau » ou « petit sceau ») ; ce type de gravure s'appela *zhuanke.* Avec la fin des Han, l'art de la gravure périclita. Alors qu'il était de règle de ne graver que le nom, le surnom, le nom de plume ou le statut du propriétaire, bientôt apparurent des « sceaux de fantaisie ». Ils portaient des fragments de poésie, des formules philosophiques, des devises et des sentences. Sous les Tang, l'art de la gravure faillit disparaître. Cent ans plus

Ci-dessus et page de droite, sceaux officiels à l'encre rouge sur des actes de propriété (règne de Tongzhi, 1862-1875).

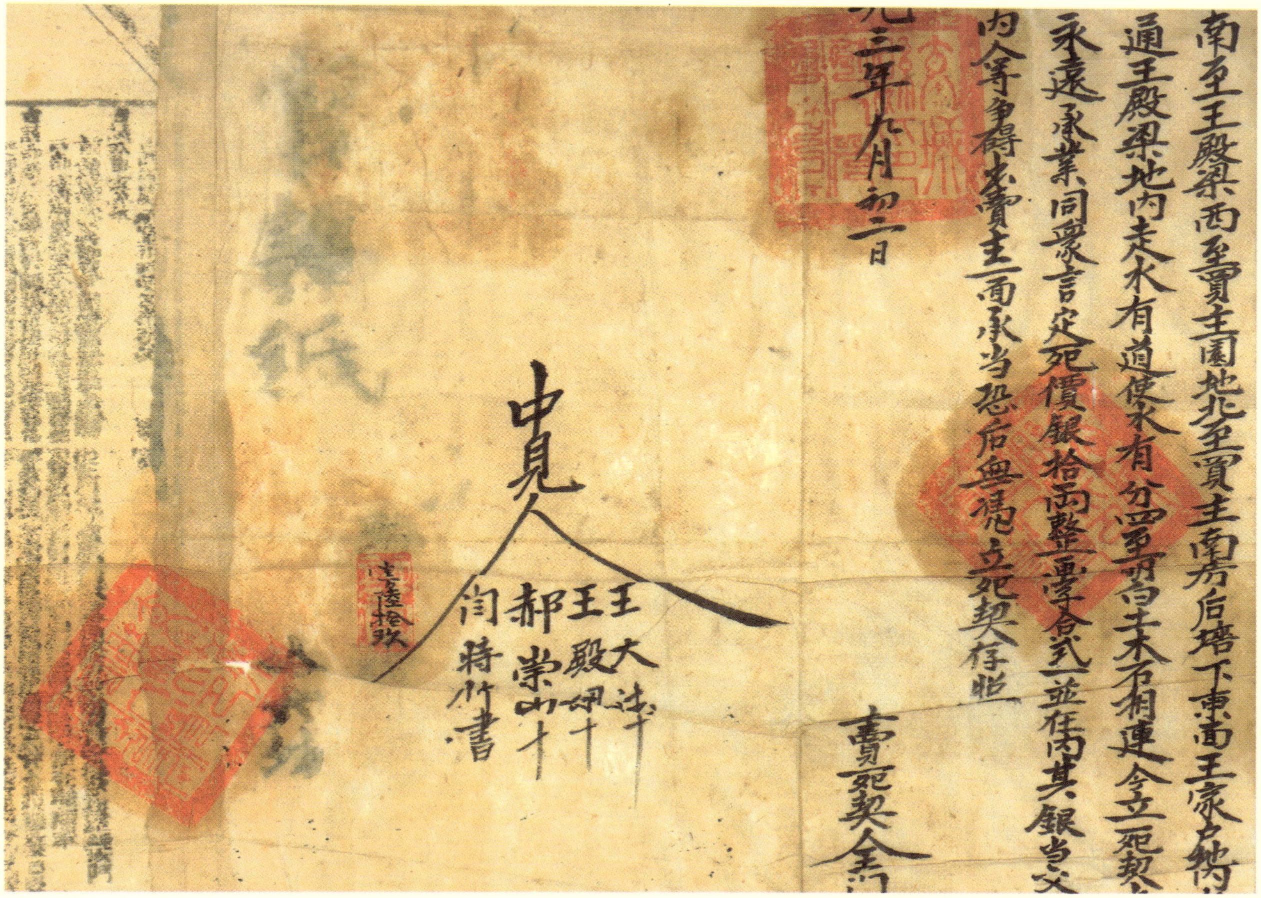

tard, sous les Song, le classicisme de l'époque Han fut de nouveau à la mode, on commença d'extraordinaires collections et un catalogue d'estampages de sceaux anciens *(Xuanhe yinpu)* fut même publié. Il devint l'ouvrage de référence pour les amateurs. Comme on le faisait à la bibliothèque impériale, les propriétaires commencèrent à marquer aussi leurs livres avec un cachet. Ces ex-libris donnèrent alors naissance aux « sceaux privés » *(tushu)*. Vers le XIIIe siècle, les peintres et les calligraphes prirent l'habitude d'apposer un sceau sur leurs œuvres. Ce n'est véritablement que vers la fin du XVe siècle que l'art de la gravure de sceaux connut une renaissance sous l'impulsion d'un groupe de lettrés de Suzhou, la romantique ville des canaux de la province du Jiangsu. Chantée par les poètes (« au ciel, il y a le paradis, sur terre, il y a Hangzhou et Suzhou »), la « Venise de l'Ouest » allait connaître la gloire avec l'industrie de la soie et la présence de nombreux lettrés. Parmi ceux-ci, Wen Peng et He (Ho) Chen fondèrent une école. Sous les Qing, apparut l'école du Zhejiang créée par Ding Jing (1697-1768) qui prôna le retour au classicisme et donna naissance au groupe des Huit de Hangzhou ; puis vinrent l'école de l'Anhui (d'où était originaire le célèbre He Chen), l'école Teng et l'école du Fujian. Sous la présidence de

À gauche, images miniatures gravées ; à droite, empreintes de sceaux en relief et en réserve (d'après le Manuel d'initiation à la gravure des sceaux *de Kong Yubai, 1935).*

Wu Changshi s'établit enfin, en 1903, à Hangzhou, la Société d'Épigraphie du Pont Xilin (Xilinyinshe) qui, avec son musée lapidaire, devint la véritable académie de l'art de la gravure sur pierre comme sur bois.

À l'exemple de la calligraphie, la gravure de sceaux s'appréciait aussi bien pour la forme de chaque caractère que pour la composition générale de ceux-ci et l'habile occupation de l'espace limité que représente la section inférieure du sceau. On tailla même des sceaux à deux, quatre ou cinq faces ; ils avaient l'inconvénient de tacher les doigts ; ces œuvres sont devenues rares. Un bon sceau devait être fait selon les « normes de gravure » *(daofa)* qui imposaient un maniement particulier du burin (en taille double, inversée, volante...) et ces techniques devaient bien sûr se refléter dans l'œuvre finale. Pour la réalisation et l'appréciation d'une belle œuvre, de nombreux critères entraient en ligne de compte : les « Six lois » (vivacité, tradition, équilibre...), les « Six (principes) essentiels » (distinction, naïveté, plénitude, force...), les « Six mérites » (élégance et gaucherie, force et délicatesse, rythme et vide, force et faiblesse, douceur et dureté...), et le classement final en « Trois genres » distinguait le divin, l'exquis et le capable. Deux méthodes du travail de la pierre était en usage : la taille en relief *(yang wen),* et la taille en creux, ou en réserve *(yin wen),* cette dernière étant la plus ancienne. À l'époque Han, on se contentait d'inciser la pierre. Plus tard, il s'établit une sorte de règle qui fit que la gravure en creux était

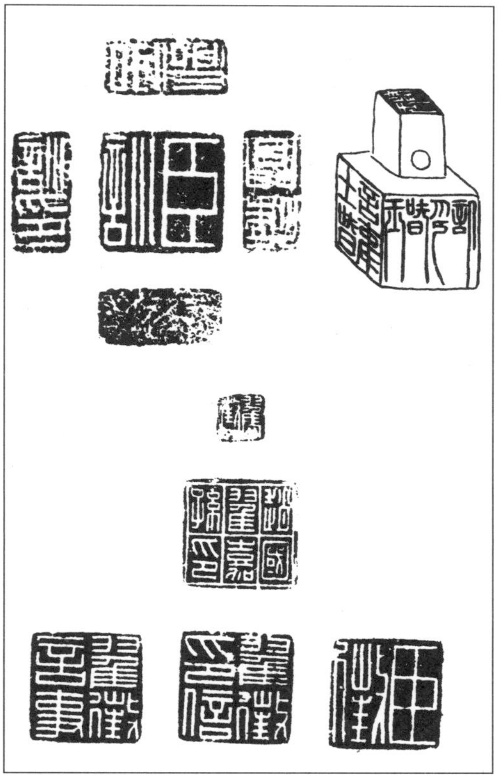

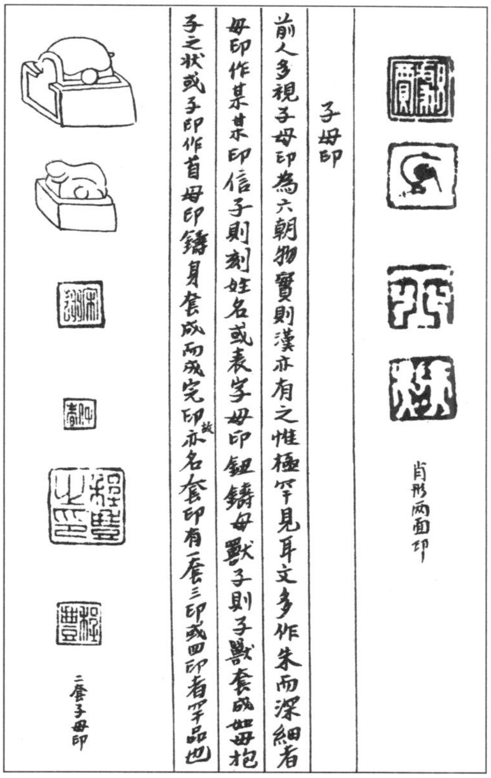

réservée à l'usage officiel alors que la gravure en relief était l'apanage des littéraires et des poètes. Mais un bon sceau ne pouvait être complet sans une inscription latérale *(biankuan)*. Sur le côté de la pierre, considérée comme une stèle en miniature, l'artiste gravait son nom et éventuellement celui du bénéficiaire. Alors que la composition du texte de la base d'un sceau devait être préalablement préparée par décalque ou peinture au pinceau des caractères inversés, l'inscription latérale était taillée directement avec toute la force et l'agilité du burin donnant tout son sens à son appellation traditionnelle : le « pinceau de fer ».

La gravure d'images miniatures sur sceau *(xiaoxingyin)* est un art directement issu de la technique précédente, il est très proche des « intailles » (de l'italien *intaglio*, « entaille ») de l'antiquité gréco-romaine. On y découvre des personnages sacrés, des héros combattants, des danseurs, des animaux ou des bêtes imaginaires. Depuis l'époque Han, cette élégante technique fut très prisée des esthètes qui s'échangeaient des pièces rares. Toute une symbolique se rattachait au choix du motif à apposer sur le papier (animaux du zodiaque, animaux votifs).

Les sceaux actuels se divisent en sceaux de bureau et sceaux portatifs. Ces derniers sont des bâtonnets de section carrée, ronde ou ovale, certains pas plus gros qu'un stylo. En revanche, les sceaux d'autrefois, à usage officiel, étaient plus massifs, plus larges avec une poignée décorée d'un animal

À gauche, un sceau à cinq faces ; à droite, sceau gigogne en bronze à motif de tortue (d'après le Manuel d'initiation à la gravure des sceaux *de Kong Yubai, 1935).*

accroupi ou couché (dragon, tortue, tigre, bélier). On appelait *zimuyin* (sceau « enfant dans la mère ») des sceaux gigognes, s'encastrant les uns dans les autres, dont la tortue fut un des motifs les plus fréquents.

En matière de pierres pour tailler les sceaux, les empereurs se réservaient le jade. Dès l'époque des Han, on utilisa aussi des pierres tendres comme la « pierre de savon » (ou stéatite), une roche opaque ou translucide, riche en talc et aux coloris ambrés. La pierre « sang-de-poulet » *(jixueshi)* ou « sanguine » (héliotrope ou jaspe) était particulièremernt appréciée pour son veinage rouge rehaussé de vert et de jaune. On en trouvait dans les provinces du Zhejiang et du Fujian (Shoushan). Mais on fit aussi des sceaux dans le cristal, l'agate, l'ivoire, le verre moulé puis incisé, le bronze, l'or, l'argent, le bois de buis, la racine de prunier et de bambou, la corne et même la porcelaine. L'empereur Qianlong, grand amateur du genre, possédait des centaines de sceaux en tous genres dont un impressionnant sceau d'ivoire carré, et il prenait plaisir à apposer abusivement son visa (*Qianlong qianshang,* « inspecté par Qianlong ») sur les œuvres de qualité. De la tombe de Liu Wu, un prince de la période des Han, les archéologues de la province du Jiangsu viennent récemment d'exhumer pas moins de deux cents sceaux de grande qualité. C'est dire l'importance qu'occupait le sceau comme symbole d'autorité ; sa perte entraînait d'ailleurs pour le fonctionnaire sa mise à pied.

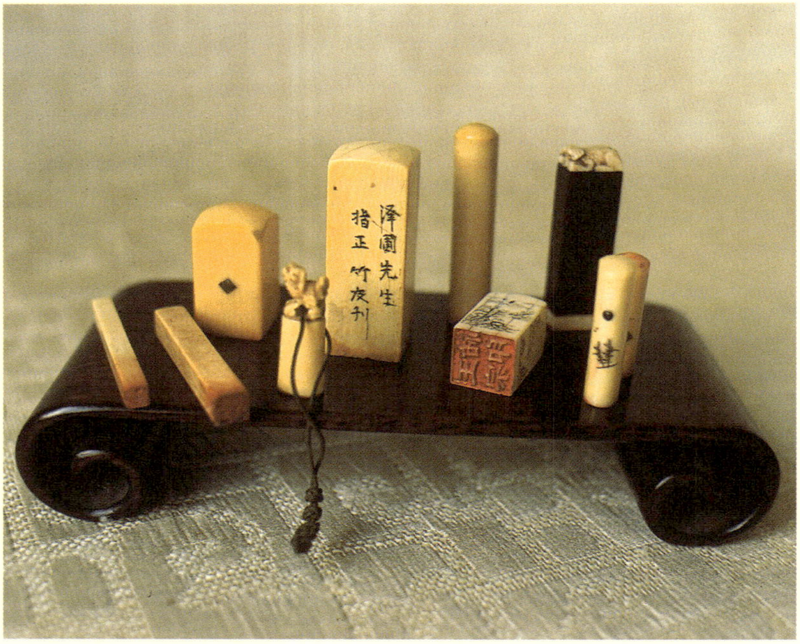

L'avènement du papier entraîna simultanément la fabrication d'une pâte pour encrer les sceaux *(yinni).* Avant cette date, sous les Han, les pièces officielles étaient authentifiées par des cachets imprimés dans une argile brune, semblables à nos modernes scellés judiciaires. La pâte à sceau (ou « pâte des huit trésors », *babao yinni*), de couleur vermillon, fut fabriquée avec divers ingrédients comme du cinabre (sulfure naturel de mercure), de la perle, du corail, des fibres d'armoise ou de coton, des pigments naturels et de l'huile de castor ou de végétaux. Les pâtes de qualité pouvaient même contenir des poudres précieuses comme l'or et le rubis et être parfumées au musc. Cette pâte, qui ne coulait pas en été ni ne gelait en hiver, pouvait être utilisée pendant de très nombreuses années. Sa composition exacte reste toujours un secret jalousement gardé par quelques vieilles familles de fabricants comme une formule d'alchimie. Son extraordinaire longévité, alliée au fait

Collection de sceaux privés en ivoire (XIXe et début de siècle). Page de droite, en haut à gauche, sceau en pierre de Shoushan, œuvre du peintre Qi Baishi (1863-1957) qui fut aussi un grand graveur de sceaux ; en haut à droite, paire de sceaux en pierre de Qingtian ; en bas, paire de sceaux en pierre de Shoushan.

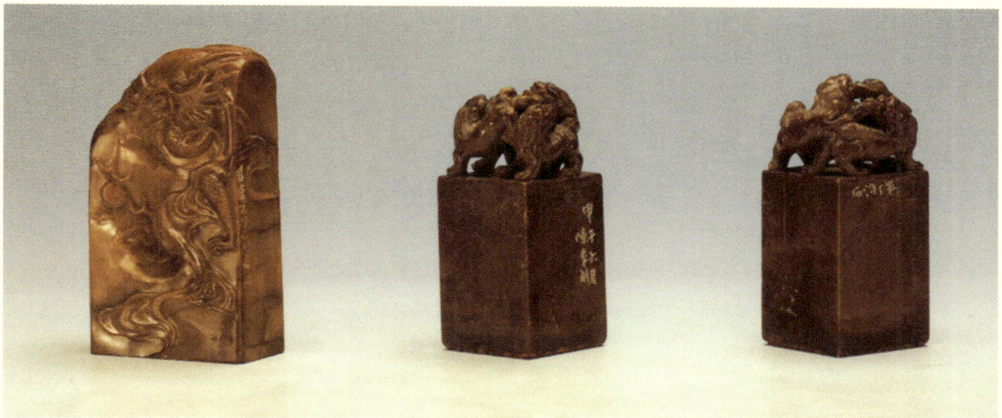

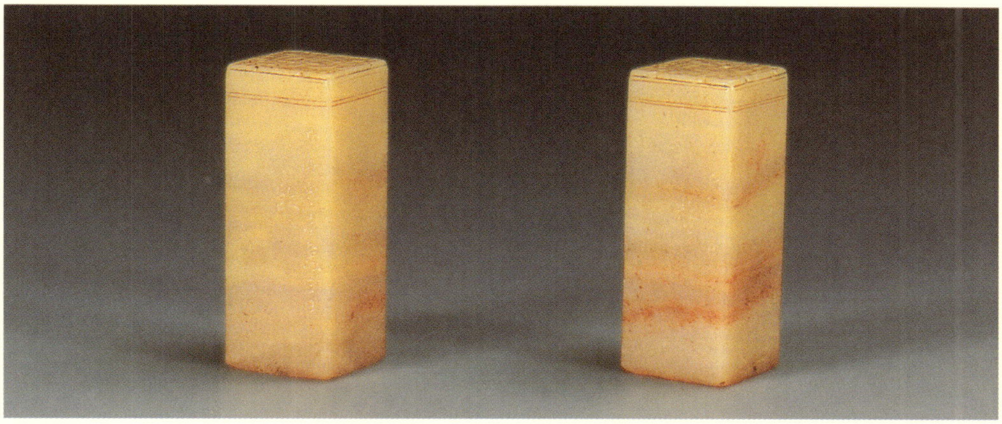

qu'elle imprégnait tous les documents d'importance, lui conféra un caractère magique ; les cachets de documents anciens étaient souvent découpés et récupérés par les gens du peuple comme amulette contre le mauvais sort ou même utilisés comme pansement directement sur les plaies… La plupart des boîtes à cinabre étaient rondes ou carrées, à couvercle, en porcelaine généralement décorée de délicats motifs peints, en terre cuite et surtout en métal incisé (bronze, laiton, maillechort).

L'époque des voyages a vu l'apparition d'étuis destinés à garder ou transporter les sceaux pour la plupart fabriqués dans des matériaux fragiles (pierre tendre, cristal, ivoire). Les plus connus sont de minuscules plumiers à couvercle, en bois, en corne, en métal, ou des coffrets gainés de cuir ou de serpent avec fermoir. Ceux-ci comprennent un logement pour le sceau (taillé à la mesure et capitonné de soie ou de feutre rouge) et un évidement pour le tampon encreur rempli de pâte rouge.

Le jade, pierre de toutes les passions

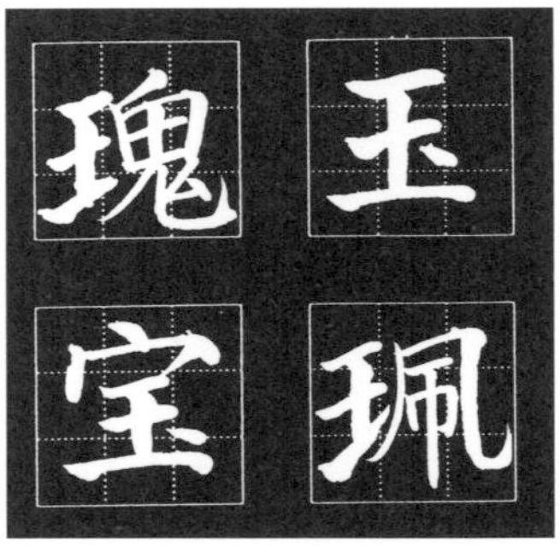

yupei guibao, littéralement, « le jade, pierre précieuse ».

« Doux et brillant, il apparaît aux hommes comme la bienveillance ; fin, compact et résistant, il est l'intelligence ; anguleux mais non pas acéré, il est coupant comme la droiture ; en grains, l'un en dessous de l'autre, c'est l'humilité ; clair et sonore, il est comme une note de musique ; avec des défauts qui ne cachent pas la beauté, il est la loyauté ; avec son rayonnement intérieur, il est l'expression de la bonne foi ; aussi brillant qu'un arc en ciel, il est le ciel ; exquis et mystérieux, provenant des collines et des rivières, il est l'expression de la terre ; insigne de rang, il indique la vertu ; apprécié de tous, il montre le chemin de la vérité et du devoir. » C'est en ces termes que dans les *Mémoires sur les rites (Liji),* on attribua à Confucius la description des multiples qualités du jade, symbole d'excellence.

Les Aztèques du Mexique, 1500 av. J.-C., l'utilisaient déjà et le considéraient comme plus précieux que l'or. Les conquistadores espagnols le rapportèrent en Europe et lui donnèrent un nom : la « pierre des reins ». Du néolithique chinois (environ 3000 av. J.-C.) sont parvenus des ornements de jade, des haches, des lames. Sous les Shang (1500-1100 av. J.-C.), ce sont des plaquettes de rang et des armes d'apparat et surtout des disques perforés *(bi)* qui caractériseront le jade archaïque. Puis viendront, sous les Zhou, les mystérieux *cong,* ces tubes encastrés dans des blocs carrés, qui furent peut-être des objets rituels ou des instruments d'astronomie. À l'époque des Royaumes Combattants (475-221 av. J.-C.) apparaissent de nombreux objets utilitaires en jade (anneaux d'archers, boîtes, plaques à coudre sur les vêtements, fibules, agrafes de ceinture, pendentifs). Sous les Han, les créations atteignirent une finition inégalée grâce à l'usage de poudres abrasives (sable de quartz). Le jade servit donc comme offrande aux diverses divinités ; il fut ensuite utilisé dans certaines cérémonies et les tablettes de jade *(gui)* étaient alors distribuées par l'empereur aux princes, comme insigne de pouvoir, puis à ses ambassadeurs pour les accréditer.

Depuis ces temps reculés, les Chinois ont toujours voulu posséder du jade ou en porter sur eux, non seulement par superstition (on lui attribuait le pouvoir d'allonger la vie) mais pour indiquer leur statut dans la société car il était réservé aux nobles. De nos jours, même chez les gens de modeste condition, cette pierre mythique continue d'exercer la plus grande fascination. En effet, les croyances les plus folles ont circulé depuis des siècles sur les extraordinaires propriétés du jade que l'on absorbait en poudre fine, en granulés mélangé à du riz ou du millet ou avec de l'eau de rosée. Ces recettes rappellent curieusement les pratiques taoïstes sur les « drogues à base de pierres ». L'alchimie, sans doute la plus ancienne du monde, née du taoïsme et pratiquée cinq siècles avant les Arabes, ne cherchait pas tant à fabriquer de l'or qu'à trouver la matière qui conférerait l'immortalité. Le réalgar et l'orpiment, tous deux des sulfures naturels d'arsenic (l'un rouge l'autre jaune vif), appelés les « graines d'or » car on les trouvait souvent dans des dépôts aurifères, jouèrent un rôle important dans l'alchimie. Ils étaient censés transformer le cuivre en or mais aussi, absorbés à petites doses, ils devenaient des élixirs de longue vie. Ces pratiques, du VIIIe au IXe siècle ap. J.-C., s'adressaient à d'autres minéraux comme le cinabre (sulfure naturel de mercure), le soufre, le mica, le quartz, l'alun, le « lait de stalactite » (le calcaire) et même les perles ou les coquillages écrasés (ainsi, la poudre de coquilles d'huîtres pilées est encore utilisée comme somnifère). Toutes ces « drogues d'immortalité », composées souvent à partir de poisons violents comme le « jus de plomb noir » (du graphite), donnèrent lieu bien entendu à des accidents fatals. K. Schipper nous indique qu'il y eut à l'époque médiévale une drogue qui connut aussi une très grande vogue parmi les nobles et les lettrés... Il s'agissait de la « poudre aux cinq pierres ». Pour sa part, le jade (en particulier celui appelé *qiong,* qui était rouge vermillon comme le cinabre) bénéficia de la même réputation « d'élixir d'immortalité » : il calmait les douleurs, assurait l'invisibilité et permettait même de voler pour rejoindre le royaume des Immortels. Les bracelets de jade, outre leur fonction décorative, sont toujours recherchés pour le massage qu'ils procurent au poignet sur des points bien précis qu'on utilise en acupuncture. De plus, le jade, avait-on observé, conservait les tissus humains après la mort. Un auteur du IVe siècle ap. J.-C. écrivait à ce sujet : « si l'on place de l'or ou du jade dans les neuf ouvertures du corps, alors il ne se

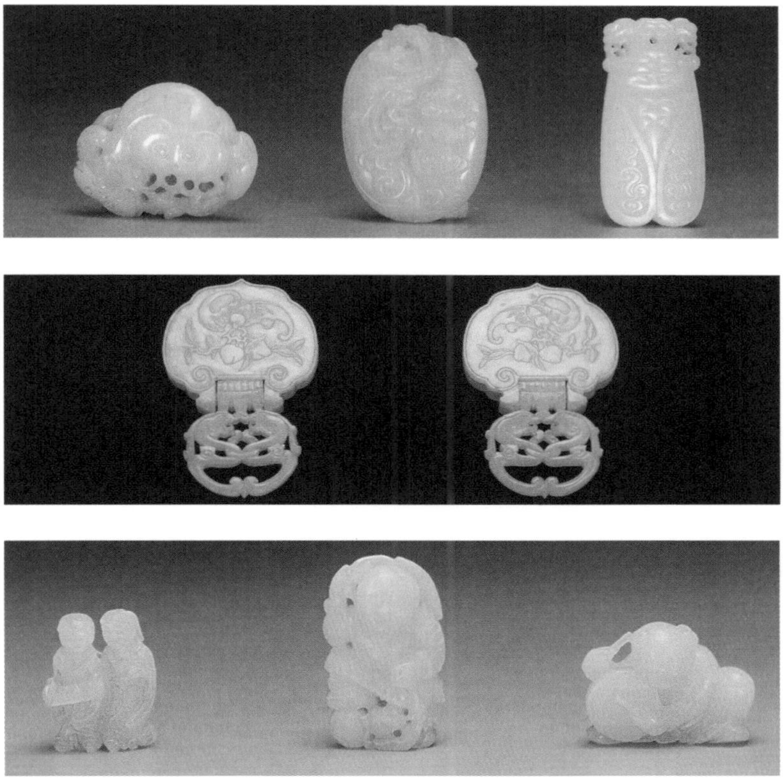

Petits objets sculptés de jade blanc (dynastie des Qing, XVIIIe siècle). En haut, trois pendants (poisson, fruit et cigale) ; au centre, une paire de boucles de ceintures à motifs de chauve-souris et pêche ; en bas, motif de Hehe (jumeaux, symbole de la bonne entente), motif à l'enfant et motif de Liu Hai.

décomposera point». Dans les rites funéraires qui étaient pratiqués dès la période des Zhou, l'embaumement n'était pas connu mais, en revanche, on garnissait la bouche du défunt de riz non cuit et on obturait ses orifices naturels de morceaux taillés de jade blanc *(baozhu)*. La cigale que l'on plaçait sur la langue avait été choisie pour l'aspect symbolique de résurrection (en référence à ses métamorphoses), des poissons étaient placés sur les yeux. Des tuniques mortuaires composées de deux mille plaquettes de jade retenues par de minces fils d'or *(jinlü yuyi)* ont d'ailleurs été retrouvées dans des sépultures impériales de l'époque Han (206 av. J.-C.-24 ap. J.-C).

Le mot «jade» dérive de l'espagnol des découvreurs du Nouveau Monde (*piedra de ijada,* «pierre de côté»), sans doute parce que l'on calmait les douleurs en appuyant un morceau de jade sur les reins. Mais la ressemblance des galets de jade avec le rein est peut-être l'autre raison d'avoir nommé ainsi l'une des deux variétés de jade, la néphrite (du grec *nephros,* rein et du latin, *lapis nephriticus,* pierre de reins). En effet, la dénomination «jade» recouvre deux minéraux différents: la néphrite et la jadéite, alors que le mot chinois *yu* ne tient pas compte de cette distinction et qualifie bien d'autres minéraux comme le quartz cristallin de «jade d'eau» ou la topaze de «jade jaune». Le mot «jade» est d'ailleurs associé dans la langue populaire à tout ce qui est précieux et pourra être employé pour d'autres matériaux. Le caractère chinois représente symboliquement trois éléments reliés par un cordon et rappelle les pendentifs que toute personne de qualité arborait à la ceinture. Confucius lui-même ne dédaignait pas porter sur lui ce symbole de vertu.

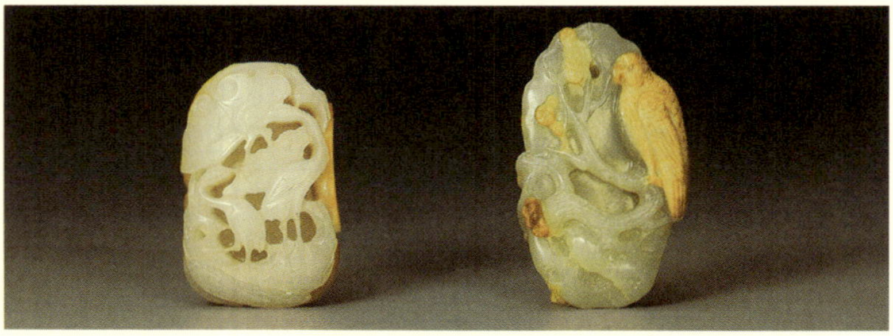

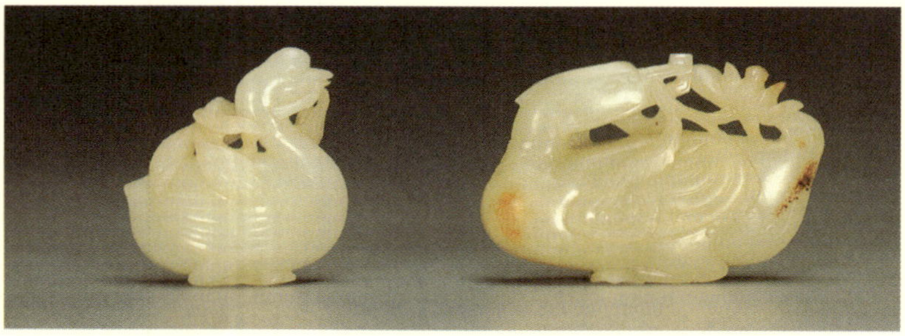

Quatre pendants de jade blanc à motif d'oiseaux: grue, aigle, oie et canard mandarin (dynastie des Qing, XVIIIe siècle).

Néphrite et jadéite sont des roches métamorphiques très semblabes que seuls des tests de dureté peuvent différencier. La jadéite, un pyroxène, a la même dureté que le cristal de roche (6,5 à 7 sur l'échelle de Mohs) alors que la néphrite, de la famille des amphiboles, un silicate de fer et de magnésium, est plus tendre (5,5 à 6,5), plus légère et d'une valeur commerciale moindre. Depuis près de deux mille ans, la néphrite a été extraite du lit des rivières de la région de Khotan (dans le Turkestan chinois) ou de mines au pied des monts Kunlun où les anciennes légendes plaçaient la résidence des

Immortels. On y décrivait des paysages paradisiaques avec des arbres aux feuilles et fruits de jade. Pour la seule année 1760, sous le règne de Qianlong, la région de Khotan livra deux tonnes de jade brut aux ateliers du Palais. La néphrite se retrouve aussi un peu partout dans le monde, en Nouvelle-Zélande, sur le continent américain, en Europe, en Sibérie, à Taïwan, au Japon et en Corée (où on la travaille depuis bien avant l'Âge du Bronze). En revanche, la jadéite, dont les anciens Chinois utilisaient la dureté pour faire des armes et des ustensiles mais aussi des objets rituels et des bijoux, n'a jamais été une pierre chinoise ; elle provenait essentiellement de Birmanie, à travers la province du Yunnan. Le jade peut avoir de nombreuses couleurs : bleu-vert, indigo, vert, lavande, rouge cinabre ou rouge sang, jaune, ou blanc pur mais la plus rare des espèces reste la « graisse de mouton à points rouges » et les plus recherchées, la « mousse prise dans la neige fondante » (un vert pomme noyé dans un blanc laiteux) ou le « vert épinard » parsemé d'inclusions d'or... Certaines pièces qui ont séjourné longtemps dans les tombeaux ont subi des décompositions chimiques et portent des couleurs étonnantes ; les Chinois les nomment « jades des Han » sans pour autant que ces pièces datent véritablement de l'époque Han (206 av. J.-C. - 220 ap. J.-C.). En vue de leur donner cet aspect archaïque, au XVIIIe siècle notamment, on n'hésita pas à les chauffer (à environ 600°) pour qu'ils s'altèrent et prennent la couleur très appréciée « d'os de poulet » ou « graisse de mouton ». On sait que les Chinois font des copies de jade ancien depuis près de deux mille ans.

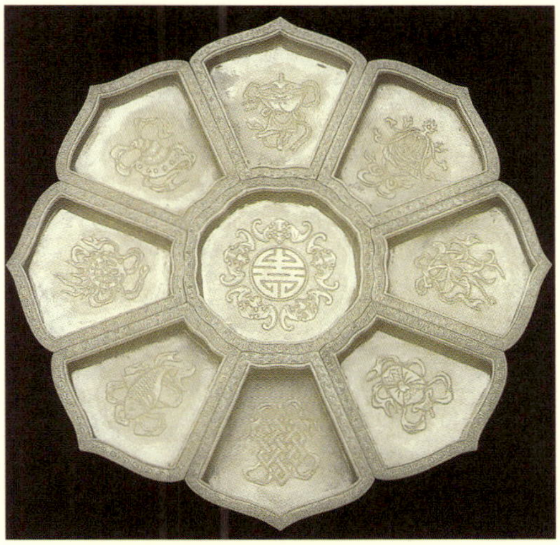

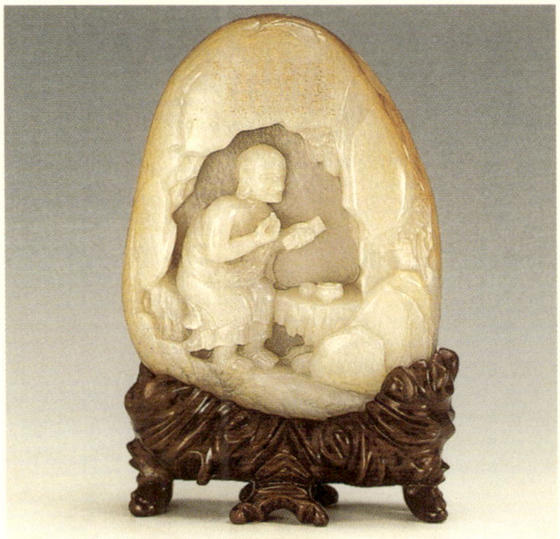

Mais les artisans chinois ont utilisé plus d'une centaine d'autres pierres qu'ils ont aussi appelées « jade », parce qu'elles étaient moins difficiles à tailler, donc moins chères et d'un commerce plus aisé. On y trouve la bowénite (« nouveau jade » ou « jade de Suzhou »), la calcédoine très utilisée pour les bijoux dans la plus haute Antiquité méditerranéenne (rouge-brun : la cornaline ; brune : la sardoine ; verte : la chrysoprase ; noire : l'onyx), la serpentine (à la couleur vert foncé) et même l'agate que l'on teintait en vert pour la faire ressembler à la jadéite. Enfin, la pierre de savon (ou stéatite) de couleur verte, tendre et rayable, mais qui est néanmoins parfois présentée comme du jade par des marchands peu scrupuleux.

En haut, présentoir à huit lobes en jade gravé des « Huit (objets) précieux » bouddhistes (dynastie des Qing, XVIIIe siècle) ; en bas, galet de jade sculpté en forme de grotte abritant un ermite (règne de Qianlong, 1736-1796).

La taille du jade en Chine date du deuxième millénaire av. J.-C. On fit usage d'outils de bambou, de pierre, puis progressivement de bronze et de fer. La découpe des blocs reste cependant un mystère, en l'absence de documents précis sur le sujet. Tout au plus, sait-on qu'au XIIe siècle on sciait les pierres avec des fils métalliques sur lesquels on versait un liquide contenant des abrasifs minéraux (sable de quartz ou de grenat). Par sa structure plus tendre, la néphrite permettait la technique dite de *qiaodiao* (« sculpture ingénieuse ») ou « taille de Suzhou », qui consistait à utiliser les variations de couleur, la gangue ou même les défauts de la pierre pour créer un motif décoratif. La jadéite, plus dure, donnait après la taille un fini lustré, brillant et translucide, avec une légère touche huileuse.

Les principaux objets d'art qui furent tirés de ces pierres avaient un caractère décoratif et utilitaire (vases, coupes, brûle-parfum, anneaux d'archer, sceaux, pose-pinceaux, boîtes à encre, écrans de table, éventails, boucles d'oreilles, peignes, cadenas magiques et carillons...). Ils ont remplacé les armes et les objets mythologiques ou rituels de l'époque préhistorique. L'empereur Qianlong (1736-1795), qui était connu pour son goût des beaux-arts, s'intéressa passionnément aux jades dont il encouragea la collection et la fabrication. Il engagea les artistes à retourner au style archaïque dont il admirait le dépouillement et signa même un édit interdisant la taille excessive du jade pour ne rien perdre de cette précieuse matière. Bien qu'il appréciait au plus haut point le travail des tailleurs de jade de Suzhou et de Yangzhou, plus d'une centaine d'artistes travaillaient au palais Impérial vers 1769. C'est sous son règne, en 1781, que fut livré un énorme bloc de jade qui prit six années à être sculpté. Ce chef-d'œuvre, qui se trouve dans le pavillon de la Joie et de la Longévité de la Cité Interdite, mesurant 2,24 mètres de haut et d'un poids de 5 350 kilogrammes, reprend le célèbre thème mythologique de « Yu-le-Grand domptant les flots ».

« Il y a un prix pour l'or, le jade, lui, n'a pas de prix. » Ce proverbe chinois résume bien la profonde considération que l'on a toujours accordé à cette pierre qui pendant des siècles fut acheminée du lointain Xinjiang vers Pékin ou Suzhou pour se transformer, entre les mains d'habiles artisans, en objets décoratifs ou en amulettes auxquels on attachait tant d'importance qu'on les emportait dans la tombe. « Un jade cassé vaut encore mieux qu'une tuile intacte » *(ning wei yu sui, wu wei wa quan)* !

La porcelaine, une alchimie secrète

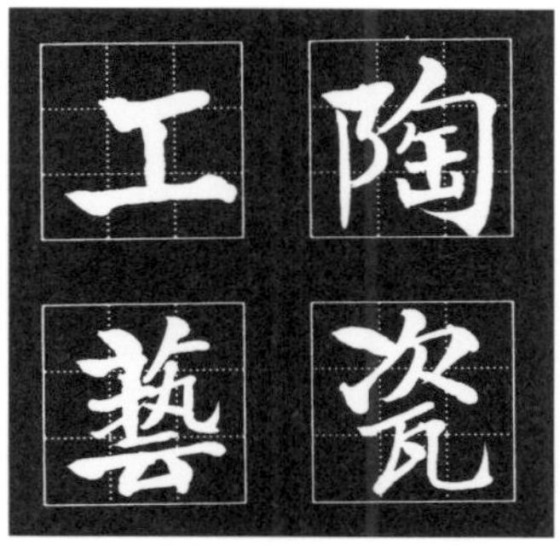

taoci gongyi, littéralement, « l'art de fabriquer la poterie et la porcelaine ».

« Le séjour que je fais de temps en temps à Kim te tchim (Jingdezhen) pour les besoins spirituels de mes néophytes, m'a donné lieu de m'instruire de la manière dont s'y fait cette belle porcelaine qui est si estimée, & qu'on transporte dans toutes les parties du monde. » Ainsi écrivait le R. P. d'Entrecolles, missionnaire de la Compagnie de Jésus en 1712, sur cette petite ville de la province du Jiangxi qui allait devenir, dès le XIIe siècle, sous les Song du Sud, un des plus grands centres manufacturiers de la porcelaine de Chine. En plusieurs lettres (1712 et 1722), le missionnaire français raconta comment s'effectuait la fabrication de cette étrange matière dans les « trois mille fourneaux d'où s'échappaient continuellement des tourbillons de flammes et de fumées »... De ces « édifiants » récits devait naître en France, la porcelaine vers 1725.

La porcelaine de Chine est composée de kaolin (une argile fine appelée « poussière de Gaoling ») et de petuntse (*baitunzi,* une roche cristalline). Tous deux sont les produits de la décomposition du feldspath (minéral contenant du silicium et de l'aluminium). Indissociables, les Chinois les nomment « les os et la chair » de la porcelaine, ils forment un composé ; d'une part, le kaolin, très plastique, résistant au feu qui devient blanc à la cuisson, d'autre part le petuntse qui fond et forme un liant. Après cuisson aux environs de 1 280 degrés, apparaît alors un corps de couleur blanche, cristallin, sonore, dur et cassant que les Portugais ont appelé « porcellana » d'après les coquillages cauris qui ressemblent à des petits cochons. Marco Polo aurait été le premier à utiliser le mot de « porcelaine » ; plus tard, les Anglais appelèrent « china » les céramiques translucides ou les grès porcelaineux. Pour les Chinois, le seul test de différenciation est celui de la sonorité.

La préparation de la porcelaine comprenait des phases complexes dont la première était le lavage des kaolins bruts pour séparer les cristaux de quartz, de feldspath et le mica de l'argile. Les morceaux de petuntse étaient réduits en poussière puis jetés dans l'eau. La pâte ainsi obtenue était débitée en briquettes. C'est en mélangeant le kaolin et le petuntse dans de l'eau et après un pétrissage important que l'on obtenait enfin une pâte prête à être moulée ou tournée sur le tour du potier. La glaçure (ou couverte) était faite des meilleures pièces de petuntse écrasé auquel on rajoutait de la chaux et des cendres de végétaux comme la fougère ainsi que les éventuels colorants. Ce travail long et fastidieux était souvent confié à des handicapés ou des aveugles. Le mélange liquide était alors appliqué à la pièce d'argile crue soit en l'immergeant soit en le versant sur l'objet. L'absence de couverte sous le pied de certaines pièces permet ainsi une datation.

Les pièces étaient ensuite rangées dans des caissons d'argile dont le fond était saupoudré de sable et de kaolin pour éviter des adhérences. Plus tard on inventera des systèmes de petits supports, les pernettes, qui ne laissaient pratiquement pas de marques. La forme des fours et leur technologie a grandement varié. Initialement larges d'environ deux mètres, on parvint à faire fonctionner des fours longs de 80 mètres qui pouvaient cuire près de 10 000 pièces en une seule fournée. Certains villages de céramistes s'étendaient ainsi sur cinq à dix kilomètres. La cuisson commençait, en général, à petit feu pendant les premières vingt quatre heures puis se continuait par un grand feu. Elle était surveillée par des orifices. On ne défournait que trois à cinq jours après l'arrêt du feu.

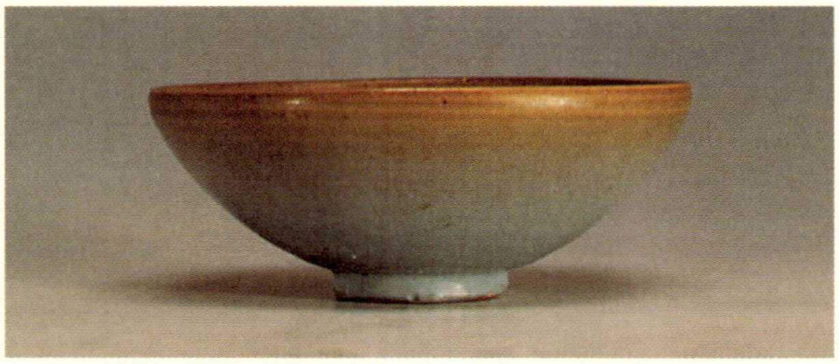

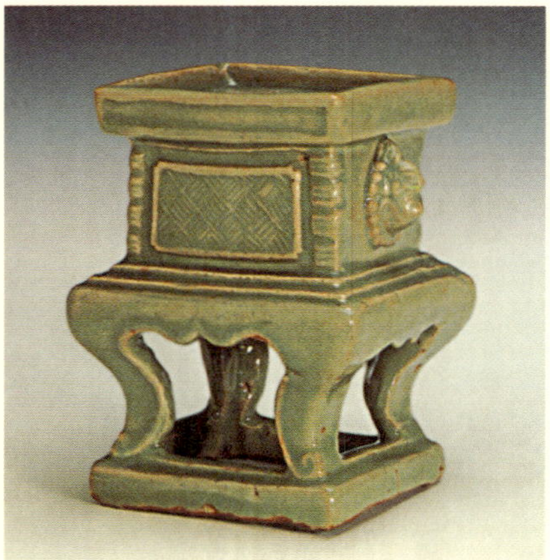

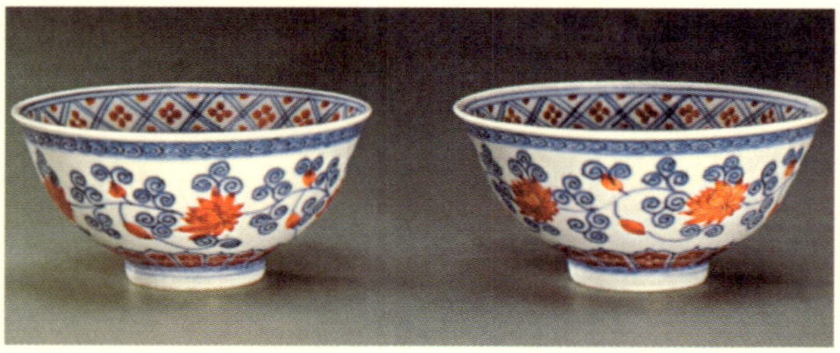

En haut, bol, dynastie Song (960-1279) ; au milieu, céladon, encensoir, dynastie Ming (1368-1644) ; en bas, bols, époque Qianlong (1736-1795).

Les matières colorantes pour les teintes monochromes ou les décors étaient des oxydes métalliques qui résistaient à une chaleur élevée. L'oxyde de cobalt donnait les bleus, l'oxyde de cuivre faisait du vert allant jusqu'à la teinte turquoise, l'oxyde de manganèse offrait une gamme du violet au noir, il fallait de l'oxyde d'antimoine pour obtenir des jaunes, l'oxyde de fer très calciné allait du brun au rouge, mais un autre rouge pouvait être obtenu avec de l'oxyde de cuivre, et le carmin avec des sels d'or, le blanc enfin était obtenu par l'acide arsénique, quant au rose il était fait avec de l'acide arsénieux et du chlorure d'or. Ces oxydes étaient incorporés au mélange de la couverte avant d'aller au four. Au fil des siècles, le savoir alchimique des céramistes chinois se développa, des porcelaines primitives des Song et des Yuan aux porcelaines polychromes à décor Qianlong, le génie des artisans trouva non seulement une extraordinaire gamme de coloris mais réussit quelques tours de force techniques comme les « coquille d'œuf » de l'époque Yongzhen ou les « craquelés » *(guan)* de l'époque Song.

Selon la tradition la plus répandue, l'invention de la poterie remonterait au légendaire Shennong qui s'adonnait à l'agriculture et fabriquait des poteries ou à son successeur Shun (Yu Shun ou Di Shun) qui aurait exercé le métier de potier avant de monter sur le trône (2257-2208 av. J.-C.). Quant à la porcelaine, une des inventions typiquement chinoises, on se perd en conjonctures sur la date de son origine : soit à l'époque des Trois Royaumes (IIIe siècle ap. J.-C.) ou sous les Zhou (Xe siècle av. J.-C.) et même les Shang (XVIe au XIIe siècle av. J.-C.), comme l'attestent les protoporcelaines (coupes à vin) qui apparurent avec le développement de la vigne. Ce sont des porcelaines à glaçure relativement épaisse, d'un vert clair. (Le mot « céladon » fut donné en Europe à ce type de porcelaine vert pâle par référence à la couleur du costume de Céladon, l'un des héros du roman pastoral *L'Astrée* d'Honoré d'Urfé, 1607-1628).

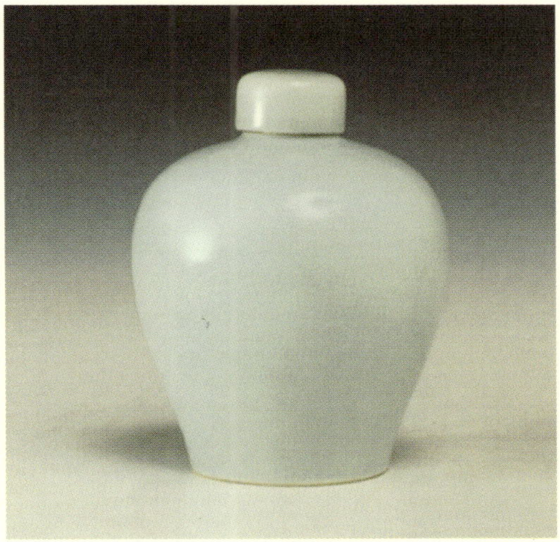

À la fin des Han, il existait donc deux techniques qui connaîtront des développements parallèles : la poterie *(tao),* terre cuite entre 750 et 990°, et la porcelaine *(ci),* obtenue par une cuisson de 1 150 à 1 450°.

Du IIIe siècle au VIe siècle, en dépit des guerres qui ravagèrent les états, les céladons connurent un grand développement. La porcelaine noire fut inventée sous les Jin de l'Est et les couleurs des céladons de cette époque vont du vert olivâtre au brun. De grands pots funéraires surmontés de maisons et de figurines *(gucangguan)* font leur apparition. Les dynasties du Nord verront encore une autre invention d'importance : la porcelaine blanche qui peu à peu remplacera le céladon. Elle fut obtenue par une amélioration de l'argile et une réduction du fer.

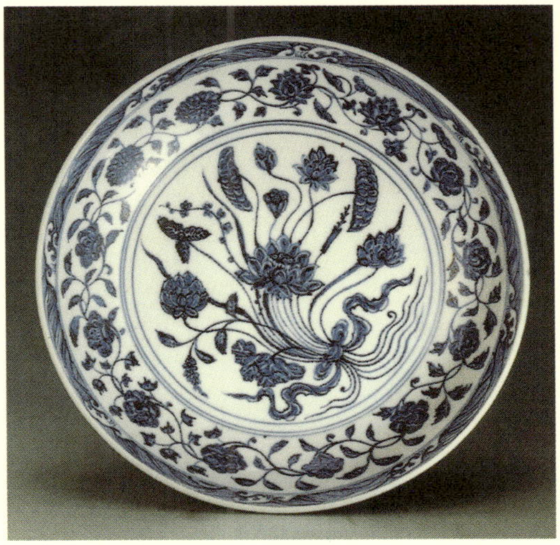

Du VIe au Xe siècle, sous les Sui et les Tang, c'est l'âge florissant de la céramique chinoise. Il correspond à un développement économique important et une période de prospérité. La production augmentant, la porcelaine remplace peu à peu les bronzes, les laques et les poteries employés dans la vie de tous les jours. La porcelaine sert alors à faire des vases, des pots, des jarres, des boîtes, des bols, des vases à vin, des brûle-parfum, des chandeliers, des crachoirs, des oreillers, des tambourins, des échiquiers et de nombreux petits objets miniatures comme mobilier funéraire. Les céladons de cette période portent le nom de l'emplacement géographique des fours *(yao).* Les Yueyao de la province du Zhejiang se caractérisaient par leur finesse, leur luminosité turquoise et surtout leur sonorité ; à ce titre, ils étaient utilisés comme instruments musicaux. Très prisés pour le vin ou le thé, ils connurent une grande vogue parmi les lettrés qui, lors de « rassemblements élégants », faisaient flotter leurs

En haut, céladon, règne de Yongzheng (1723-1735), dynastie des Qing ; en bas, plat, porcelaine bleu-et-blanc, règne de Xuande, Ming (1426-1435).

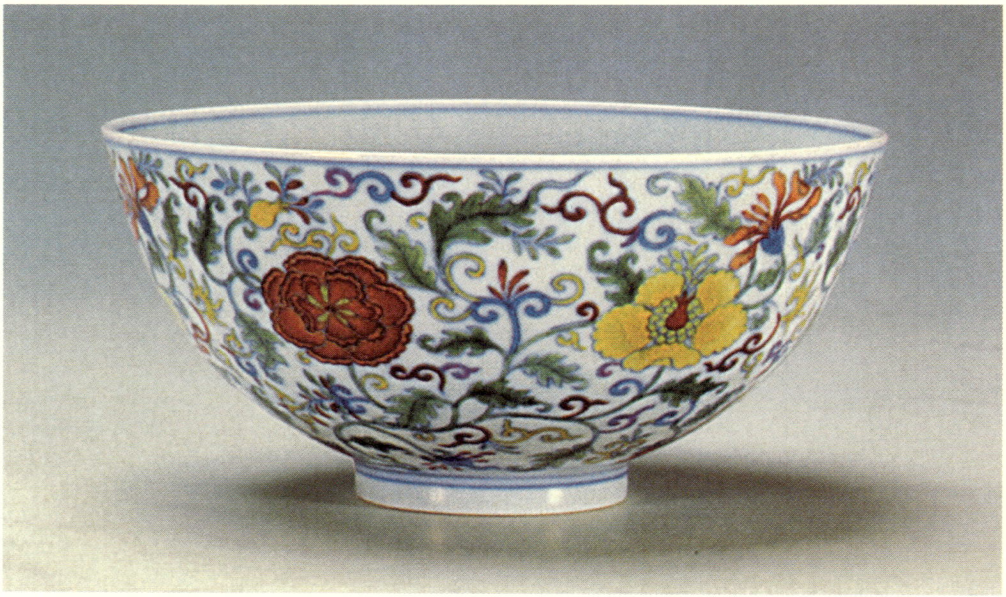

coupes dans les ruisseaux… Les Dingzhou du Shaanxi furent fabriqués en porcelaine blanche. Les Wuzhou du Zhejiang avaient des couleurs allant du vert émeraude au vert clair. L'auteur du *Traité sur le thé,* Lu Yun, vantait les porcelaines vertes Yuezhou du Hunan, parce qu'elles « rehaussaient la couleur du thé ». Les porcelaines des fours Shouzhou de l'Anhui produisaient des pièces d'un vert-jaune tandis que les Hongzhou étaient connus pour leur vert émeraude appelé « carapace de crabe » *(xieke).* Les Xingyao du Hebei étaient « blanches comme l'argent et la neige ». Mais le succès des artistes Tang est surtout dû aux céramiques « trois couleurs » *(sancai).* Les plus anciennes datent du VIIe siècle et représentent des musiciens, des danseurs à cheval, des chevaux (l'empereur Xuanzong avait une passion pour cet animal), des chameliers avec leurs animaux, mais aussi des gardiens féroces aux formes mi-humaines mi-animales, tous étant des objets funéraires que l'on plaçait dans les tombes des dignitaires. Pour obtenir ces fameuses coulures brunes, vertes et jaunes, les artisans utilisaient des oxydes métalliques. Les pièces étaient cuites une seconde fois, à 900°, avec une couverte polychrome, l'effet d'émail étant obtenu par des ajouts de silicate de plomb.

À l'époque des Cinq dynasties et des Song (907-1127), les céladons se diversifient. Les Dingyao du Hebei sont des porcelaines blanches d'une légère teinte ivoirée, serties d'une bague à l'embouchure pour en cacher le rebord non verni. Les fours Yaozhou du Shaanxi produisaient des pièces d'un vert bleuté avec un décor en relief obtenu par une légère incision. Les Ruyao du Henan, fabriqués au XIIe siècle, se distinguaient par une couverte épaisse, d'un bleu turquoise, légèrement craquelé. Ces porcelaines étaient réservées à l'usage impérial, tout comme celles des *guanyao* (fours d'État ou fours impériaux) qui se spécialisèrent dans les bleu-vert (*feicui,* « couleur de mar-

Bol, porcelaine émaillée (doucai), règne de Yongzheng (1723-1735), dynastie des Qing.

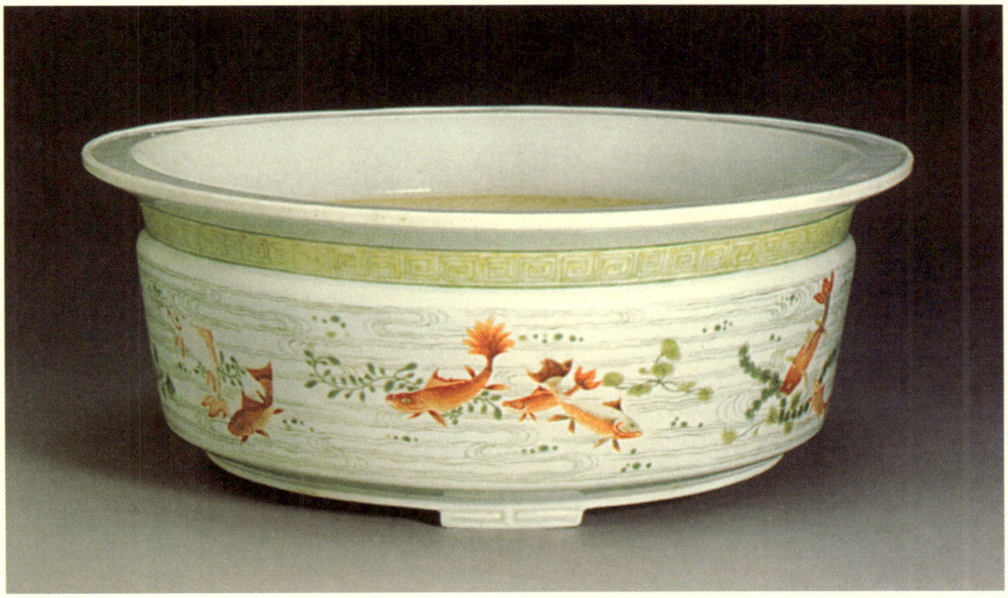

tin-pêcheur ») avec des craquelures affirmées légèrement violettes. Pas moins de cent cinquante manufactures du type Longquan ont été dénombrées dans le Zhejiang. Les Junyao du Henan sont reconnaissables à leur forme de vase largement ouvert. Initialement faits pour contenir l'eau lustrale pour les temples, l'empereur Huizong s'en servit comme cache-pots dans son palais. Leur couleur, peu commune, était lie-de-vin tacheté de bleu. Dans le même genre, les porcelaines noires, Jianyao, se signalent par un fond pourpre enduit d'un vernis noir qui donne un effet de stries argentées et leur valut le surnom de « poils de lièvre ». Au XIIIe siècle, un artiste japonais vint s'initier aux secrets de la potereie du Fujian et en rapporta le procédé dans son pays où il porte le nom de *temmoku*. Les fours de Cizhou, dans le Hebei, sont connus pour leurs productions de couleur blanche, jaune ou tabac à motifs peints en brun-noir. Ils perpétuent la tradition des potiers Tang en offrant des thèmes animés (poissons, dragons, cerfs, lapins ou personnages) qui apparaissent le plus souvent sur des oreillers de porcelaine. Les *qingbai* (blanc-vert pâle) du XIIe siècle, d'une exceptionnelle minceur, furent comparés au jade à cause de l'extraordinaire blancheur de la glaçure.

Les artisans de l'époque Yuan (1276-1368) vont créer deux genres qui feront la célébrité de l'art du feu en Chine : les bleu-et-blanc *(qinghua)* et les porcelaines à motifs rouges sous couverte *(youlihong)*. Les premiers sont des porcelaines à motifs bleus sous glaçure blanche. L'innovation fut de fixer le colorant pour éviter qu'il coule comme pour les poteries Tang. On utilisa alors un kaolin poreux sur lequel on peignait avec un oxyde de cobalt importé d'Iran (le « bleu musulman »), puis on recouvrait la pièce d'un vernis transparent, légèrement laiteux, avant cuisson à haute température. Ces grands vases bleus et blancs, à thèmes historiques et motifs floraux, furent

Pot à fleurs, porcelaine à décor yangcai (famille rose), règne de Yongzheng (1723-1735), dynastie des Qing.

fabriqués par les ateliers du sud de la Chine en grandes quantités pour les pays d'Orient. Ils ont été ramenés en Europe par les Croisés et considérés comme très précieux. Saladin, premier sultan des Ayyubides, en possédait en Égypte et en Syrie de nombreux exemplaires dont l'un d'eux fut offert au doge de Venise. Marco Polo qui aurait séjourné à la cour de Kubilay (1275-1292) ramena à Venise un brûle-parfum. La porcelaine à glaçure rouge existait depuis les Song, les artisans de l'époque Yuan parvinrent à mettre au point la technique des motifs rouges sous couverte en utilisant le rouge de cuivre. Mais par suite d'une cuisson insuffisante, les rouges n'apparaissaient pas d'une manière stable. Il faudra attendre les Ming pour voir cette technique totalement maîtrisée.

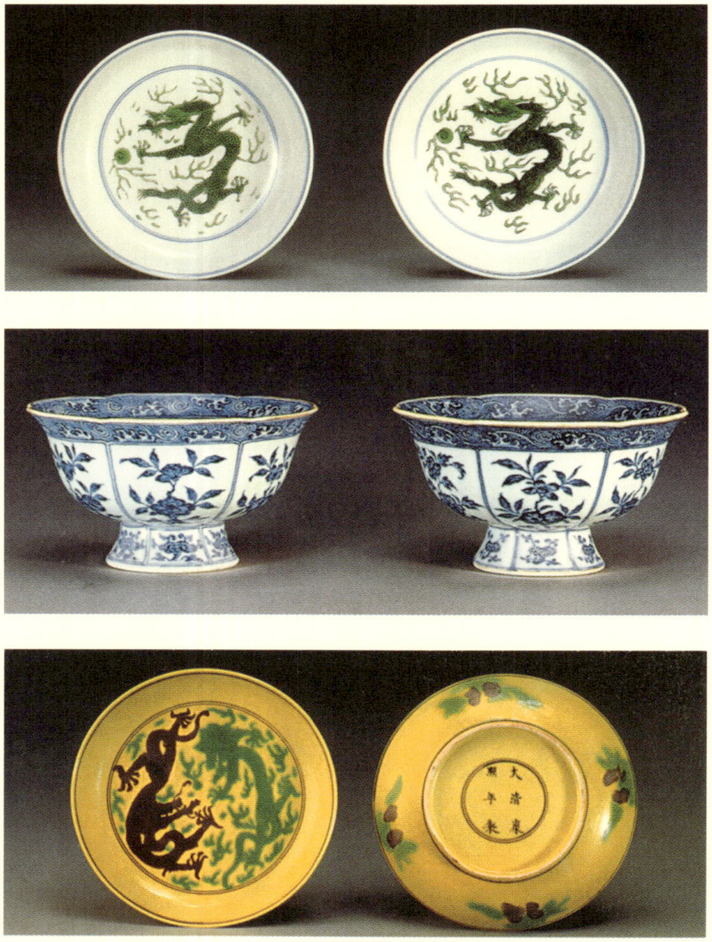

De haut en bas, plats, porcelaine à décor de dragon vert, marque de règne de Qianlong (1736-1795) ; coupes à pied, porcelaine bleu-et-blanc, marque de règne de Yongzheng (1723-1735) ; plats, porcelaine à fond jaune et motifs de dragon vert et aubergine, marque de règne de Kangxi (1662-1722).

Sous la dynastie des Ming (1368-1644), les potiers perfectionnèrent leur outillage et leurs procédés de fabrication : ils purent ainsi augmenter la production et en accroître la qualité. Les échanges commerciaux avec l'étranger se multipliaient et les porcelaines faisaient partie des articles les plus demandés. C'est sous les Ming que les porcelaines blanches furent les plus réussies. Les fours Dehua donnèrent leur nom à la célèbre porcelaine *baijian* (« blanc de Chine » ou « blanc de Fujian ») caractérisée par un émail doux, translucide et d'une blancheur d'ivoire. C'est dans cette matière que furent fabriquées d'innombrables statues de Guanyin, la déesse de la Miséricorde. Dès le XIVe siècle, la ville de Jingdezhen devint alors le plus grand centre porcelainier. Les bleu-et-blanc des époques Yongle et Xuande ont été les plus réussis grâce à l'emploi du bleu musulman. Ils seront exportés vers l'Europe au XVIe siècle. Les pièces à glaçure rouge (en chinois « rouge rubis ») – que l'on appela en Europe moins poétiquement des « sang-de-bœuf » *(niuxue)* – étaient colorées par un émail au cuivre. Sous l'empereur Chenghua (1465-1488) avait été mis au point un nouveau procédé : les décors à émaux, une combinaison de couleurs sur et sous couverte, appelée *doucai* (littéralement, les « couleurs qui rivalisent ») parce qu'elles étaient juxtaposées. Les couleurs employées pour les « trois couleurs» *(sancai)* étaient le vert de cuivre, le jaune pâle et le rouge tiré de l'oxyde de manganèse. Des décors polychromes, appelés «cinq couleurs» *(wucai)* furent créés plus tard pendant les règnes de Jiajing et de Wanli.

Les pièces de la «famille verte» *(susancai)* sont représentatives de la fin du XVe et du XVIe siècle à tel point que l'on pensa désigner les porcelaines Ming sous ce nom générique. Les premières années de la période des Qing (1644-1796), sous les empereurs Kangxi, Yongzheng et Qianlong, doivent être considérées comme l'âge d'or de la production chinoise. La porcelaine polychrome de Kangxi est caractérisée par un émail vert lumineux et translucide. Avec Yongzheng apparaissent des porcelaines raffinées et précieuses qui feront la gloire de la Chine du Nord pour leur finesse: les «coquilles-d'œuf». C'est sous Qianlong (1736-1796) qu'apparaît la porcelaine dite de la «famille rose» *(fencai,* couleurs en poudre ou *yangcai,* couleurs venues de l'étranger, en allusion à la découverte de A. Cassius, un Hollandais qui importera en 1725 en Chine sa technique de précipité obtenu à partir d'un sel d'or). La «pourpre de Cassius» (ou carmin d'or) mélangée au blanc opaque de l'acide arsénique donnait des teintes de rose plus ou moins dégradées. Ces nouveaux émaux utilisèrent les motifs de fleurs, d'oiseaux ou d'insectes qui, peints avec une grande minutie, se caractérisaient par la douceur des couleurs et l'impression de relief. C'est encore à cette période que de nombreuses innovations techniques eurent lieu: les températures furent de mieux en mieux maîtrisées ainsi que les procédés de glaçure et d'émail. Le «bleu poudré» ou «bleu soufflé» était obtenu par du cobalt en poudre délayé dans l'eau puis soufflé en pluie fine sur la pâte crue au moyen d'un chalumeau de bambou recouvert d'une gaze. Lors de la cuisson, il se formait alors des grains uniformes de bleu profond à la surface de la pièce. Des émaux orangés sur fond blanc furent utilisés avec des motifs décoratifs floraux pour donner un bel effet de dentelle. Les porcelaines émaillées de la période des Qinq seront classées en 1862 par Jacquemart en «familles» verte, rose et noire. Cette dernière connaîtra un immense succès chez les collectionneurs européens. Les monochromes continuèrent toutefois d'être fabriqués dans une gamme très étendue de coloris: rouge haricot, aubergine, vert carapace de crabe ou vert de pomme, jaune anguille, rouille de fer...

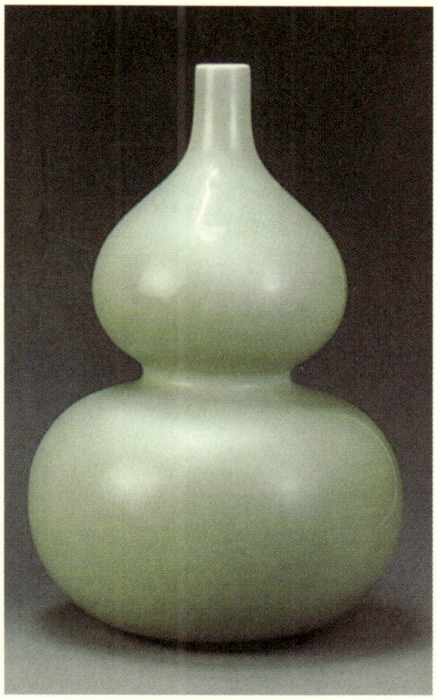

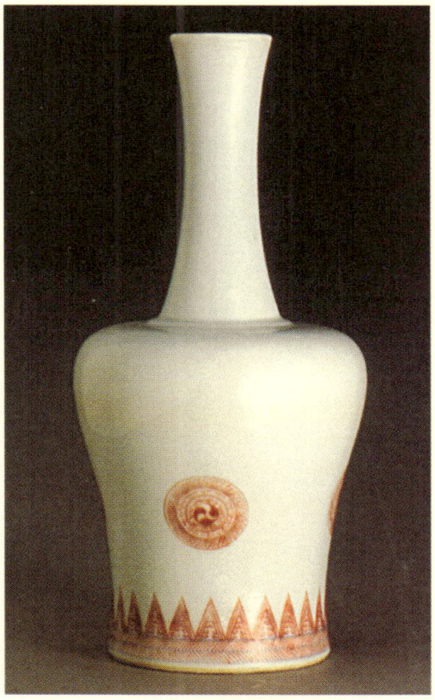

En haut, vase, céladon, marque de règne de Qianlong (1736-1795); en bas, vase, porcelaine à décor rouge, marque de règne de Kangxi (1662-1722).

Pour répondre aux importantes commandes de l'étranger, les artistes chinois s'inspirèrent des techniques décoratives européennes. Les porcelaines *falangcai* (de *falang*: français, émaux d'Europe) étaient fabriquées dans les fours d'État de Jingdezhen puis acheminées à Pékin où des artistes chinois et étrangers invités à la Cour (le « Studio des vœux exaucés ») les décoraient de la manière la plus réaliste, empruntant leurs thèmes aussi bien au répertoire européen que chinois. Les motifs traditionnels (les bambous, les fleurs de prunier, les orchidées, les montagnes) voisinaient avec des personnages occidentaux dans un étrange répertoire. Ces œuvres étaient strictement réservées pour l'usage impérial.

C'est en 1699 que l'empereur Kangxi consentit à ouvrir le port de Canton au commerce avec les étrangers. La Compagnie anglaise des Indes, en 1715, puis la Compagnie hollandaise, en 1729, furent autorisées à fonder des comptoirs. La Compagnie des Indes Orientales (hollandaise) transportait vers l'Europe des pièces que les grandes familles européennes faisaient fabriquer en Chine sur commande. On envoyait aux artisans des croquis annotés ou des modèles en bois pour des assiettes, des plats, des potiches, des garnitures de cheminées mais aussi des salières, des beurriers, des plats à barbe et même des manches de couteaux… La petite histoire raconte que des pièces furent retournées en Europe avec les annotations de la commande fidèlement recopiées sur la porcelaine… Les tasses destinées à l'Europe, désormais équipées d'une anse, répondent à la nouvelle mode de boire du thé et des services complets furent commandés. Alors que le goût pour le chocolat et le café se répand, on fait exécuter en Chine des tasses hautes et des chocolatières pansues. Même la poterie de grès rouge non verni de Yixing sera exportée puis copiée en Europe devant le succès qu'elle rencontra comme récipient pour le thé auquel elle donnait un meilleur goût.

À l'époque des empereurs Jiaqing (1796-1821) et Daoguang (1820-1850), la porcelaine chinoise perd de sa qualité, la concurrence de l'Europe et du Japon est grande et la Chine connaît des problèmes internes. Les célèbres manufactures de Jingdezheng seront quasiment abandonnées sous Guangxu (1875-1908) et il ne subsista à peine que cent dix fours privés.

L'artisanat trouvera toutefois un nouveau souffle
avec les techniques récentes : les émaux
cloisonnés et le verre.

Marques, signatures et sceaux

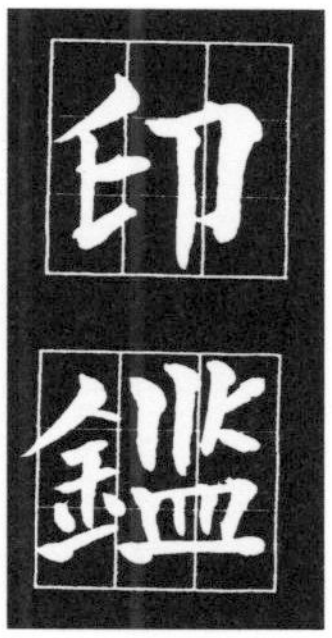

yinjian, littéralement, « vérifier les sceaux ».

Les marchands peu scrupuleux ont tendance à utiliser les marques qui figurent à la base des objets faits en Chine comme une garantie de leur origine et de leur ancienneté, ils jouent sur le fait que les caractères ou les symboles qui y sont apposés ne peuvent être compris par des profanes. En effet, le déchiffrement d'une marque n'apporte qu'une information toute relative sur l'origine et la datation de l'objet ; il faut la compléter par une analyse du style et de la forme, des couleurs, des thèmes décoratifs de la matière, de ses défauts, de l'usure de l'émail… Autant d'éléments qui demandent des connaissances minimales que seuls la lecture d'ouvrages spécialisés et la pratique des objets pourront apporter.

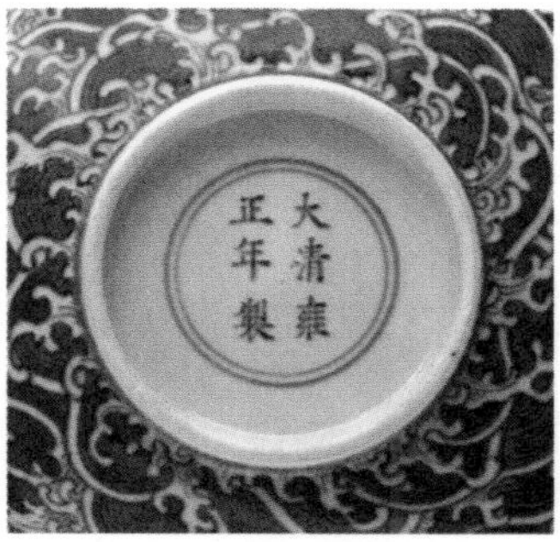

Marques de règne en six caractères : « fabriqué sous le règne de Yongzheng de la dynastie des Qing » (1723-1735).

Les artisans chinois ont de tout temps pratiqué l'art de la copie ; certains auteurs voient là l'expression consciente (ou inconsciente) de l'admiration qu'ils ont toujours portée aux choses du passé. On sait maintenant que pour leur donner plus de valeurs, certaines fabriques impériales n'ont pas hésité à produire des pièces antidatées. Par exemple, les noms des empereurs Xuande (1426-1436), Chenghua (1465-1488) ou Jiajing (1522-1567), contemporains de notre roi François Ier, apparaissaient fréquemment sur des porcelaines fabriquées à l'époque Kangxi, contemporain de Louis XIV ! Dans son étude sur les poteries chinoises de l'époque Han, B. Laufer écrivait déjà en 1909 que « ces copies sont faites par des Chinois pour des Chinois car il y a un marché pour ces objets dans le pays ».

Avec l'avènement de la mode des « chinoiseries » et parce que les productions de l'époque des Ming étaient particulièrement recherchées, les marques de cette époque seront contrefaites en Europe et au Japon. Ces porcelaines furent toutefois de qualité inférieure et les signatures facilement détectables. Au Japon, puis même en Chine, les « bleu-et-blanc » et les « sang-de-bœuf » connaîtront d'innombrables imitations. L'engouement pour la porcelaine chinoise est tel que ces pratiques continuent de nos jours avec presque le même succès.

Les *Lettres édifiantes et curieuses* du jésuite François-Xavier Dentrecolles (1664-1741) sont les premiers documents fournissant, en français, des informations sur la fabrication de la porcelaine chinoise et en particulier celle de Jingdezhen (province du Jiangxi), la « ville aux trois mille fours », où un four impérial existait depuis le XIVe siècle. En revanche, les productions destinées à l'usage des moins fortunés étaient réalisées dans des fours privés dont on a retrouvé des traces dans de nombreuses provinces, notamment le Zhejiang, le Fujian, le Hebei, le Shaanxi… Ces manufactures privées qui produisaient des objets de moindre qualité, souvent non signés, permirent d'alimenter un marché en pleine croissance car les fours impériaux ne parvenaient pas à satisfaire tous les besoins en porcelaine, matière qui était devenue à la mode.

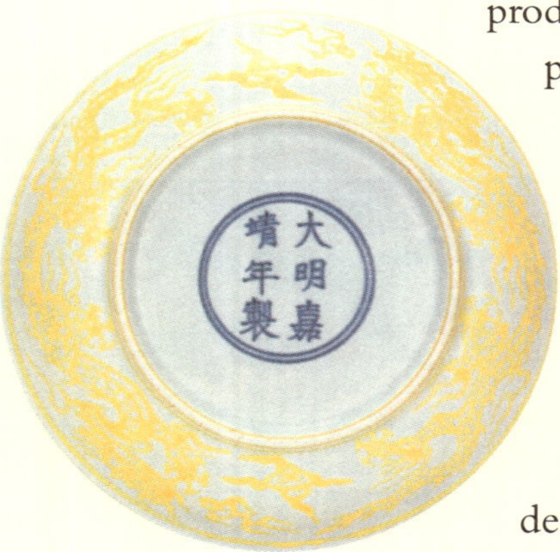

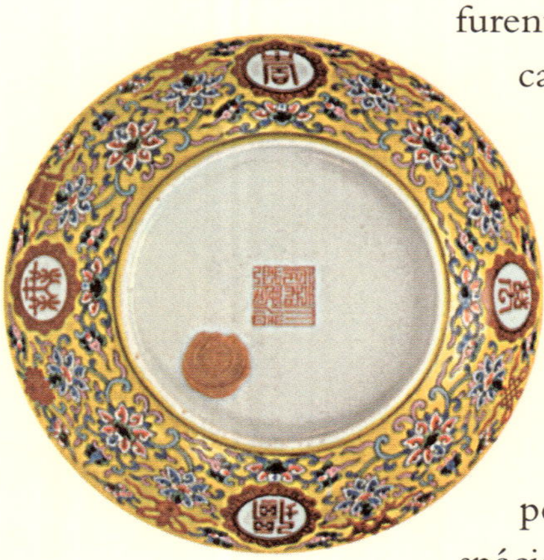

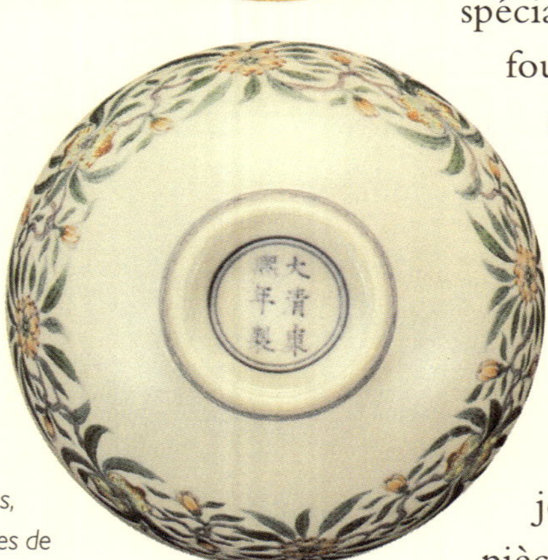

De haut en bas, marques de règne de Jiajing, 1521-1566, dynastie des Ming; cachet de Jiaqing, 1796-1820, dynastie des Qing; marques de règne de Kangxi, 1662-1723, dynastie des Qing.

Bien que la pratique en fut antérieure, c'est sous les Ming, en particulier sous le règne de Xuande (1425-1435), que se généralisèrent les marques à la base des pièces, peintes à la main ou imprimées sous forme d'un sceau, plus rarement incisées dans la pâte avant cuisson. Sur les pièces Ming, ce sont des caractères peints sous couverte en bleu (au grand feu) qui furent les plus fréquents. On préféra l'écriture régulière *(kaishu)* aux caractères des sceaux *(zhuanshu)*. Les marques furent quelque fois entourées d'un double cercle ou inscrites dans un carré ou un rectangle. Au XVIIIe siècle, on fit usage de couleurs émaillées et même de couleur d'or. En 1526, sous le règne de Jiajing (1521-1566), les marques furent interdites et ne réapparurent que cent ans plus tard, sous les Qing. Une belle calligraphie restait un critère de qualité car ce travail était généralement effectué par quelques artistes sélectionnés pour leur belle écriture et qui travaillaient pour un département spécial des manufactures impériales *(zaobanshu)*. Les productions des fours impériaux au XVe siècle n'étant encore pas très élevées, on a pratiquement pu identifier le style de chacun des calligraphes qui signaient les œuvres à cette époque. Certaines périodes connaîtront même des pièces issues des fours impériaux sans marques ; il pouvait s'agir d'un oubli des peintres ou encore, pour une certaine période (sous Kangxi par exemple), on interdisait d'inscrire le nom sacré de l'empereur de peur qu'il soit profané si des débris de vaisselle étaient jetés aux ordures… Ceci expliquerait le nombre important de pièces de cette période ne portant plus que les deux cercles sans inscription à l'intérieur avec des « marques de fantaisie » ou des noms d'empereurs antérieurs comme Xuande ou Chenghua.

À partir du règne de Qianlong (1736-1795), on prit l'habitude de remplacer les caractères tracés à la main en deux colonnes par des marques en cachet de couleur bleue et quelquefois rouge imprimé dans la pâte avant glaçure dans une réserve d'un fond bleu vert.

Les « marques » se classent en cinq catégories : les marques de règne, les marques de fabrique, les inscriptions votives, les marques d'appréciation, les marques symboliques.

Les marques de règne

Elles apparaissent en quatre ou six caractères dont deux représentent le nom de l'empereur, en fait son nom de règne (ou d'ère : *nianhao*). Car l'empereur possédait de nombreux autres noms : un nom privé *(ming)* qu'il était interdit d'employer, un nom honorifique *(zunhao),* un nom posthume (*shi* ou *shihao*), un nom de temple *(miaohao)* qui figurait sur les tablettes funéraires et qui deviendra une sorte de nom dynastique. Ainsi, l'impératrice douairière Xiaoqin (1835-1908) qui portait le nom (mandchou) de Nala était appelée Yulan (magnolia) et reçut, entre autres, le nom honorifique de Cixi (compassion-bénédiction céleste) ce qui n'empêcha pas son entourage de la surnommer irrespectueusement : « vieux bouddha » *(laofoye).* C'est à partir du IIe siècle av. J.-C. sous l'empereur Wendi qu'avait commencé l'usage des *nianhao.* Cette coutume se maintiendra jusqu'à la fin des Qing (1912). Les noms de règne étaient choisis par l'empereur comme d'heureux présages et servaient à compter les années (on parlait de la troisième année de Qianlong, soit 1739). Certains empereurs changèrent de *nianhao* plusieurs fois au cours de leur règne (ainsi l'impératrice Wu, ou Wuzetian, en adopta seize de 684 à 704). Les Ming et les Qing, en revanche, n'en utilisèrent qu'un seul et ils passèrent dans l'histoire sous ce nom de règne et non sous leur nom dynastique (voir p. 258). Pour la dernière dynastie des Qing, les souverains avaient aussi un nom mandchou mais sur les objets (porcelaine, bronze, verre, métal) ne figuraient que les marques du nom chinois.

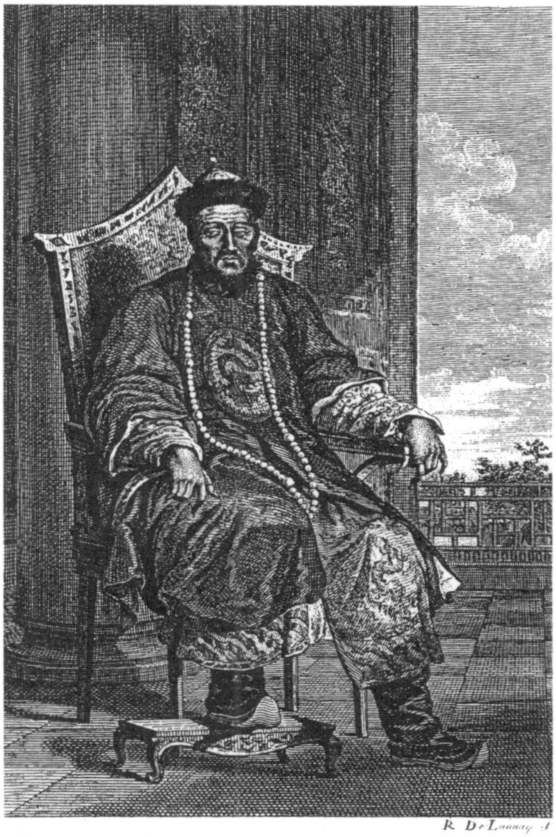

乾 隆 大 皇 帝
Tchien Lung Ta Whang Tee
Tchien Lung Le Grand Empereur

Pour les inscriptions sur les pièces produites dans les manufactures impériales, de la période allant du XIVe au XXe siècle, on observera les six caractères groupés en deux colonnes. Leur déchiffrement s'effectue de haut en bas en commençant par la colonne de droite :

大清康
熙年製

- le premier caractère est invariable (*da* ou *tai*, « grand ») ;
- le second varie selon les dynasties (Ming ou Qing) ;
- le troisième et le quatrième forment le nom de règne *(nianhao)* ;
- le cinquième est invariable (*nian*, « année ») ;
- le sixième est invariable (*zuo* ou *zhi*, « fait, fabriqué »).

En se référant à l'inscription ci-dessus, on obtient alors le texte suivant : *da qing yongzheng nian zhi* = fabriqué (pendant le règne de) Yongzheng de la grande dynastie des Qing, (soit entre 1723 et 1736). D'autres mentions pouvaient apparaître, en particulier l'expression *yu* (« fabriqué dans les manufactures impériales » ou « fait sur ordre de l'empereur »). Quelquefois, l'inscription ne comportait que quatre caractères, le verbe « faire » *(zhi)* et le mot « année » *(nian)* étaient omis, l'ordre de lecture restant le même.

Comment lire un sceau ?

A. Taille normale.
B. Taille agrandie.
C. Version éclatée pour lecture avec :
1 et 2 : dynastie des Qing.
3 et 4 : nom de règne
5 et 6 : année de fabrication.
(Fait sous le règne de Qianlong de la grande dynastie des Qing).

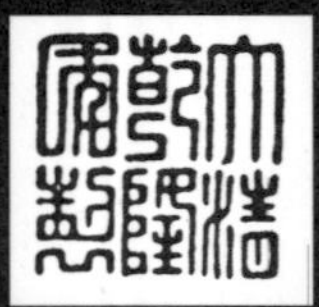
A

B

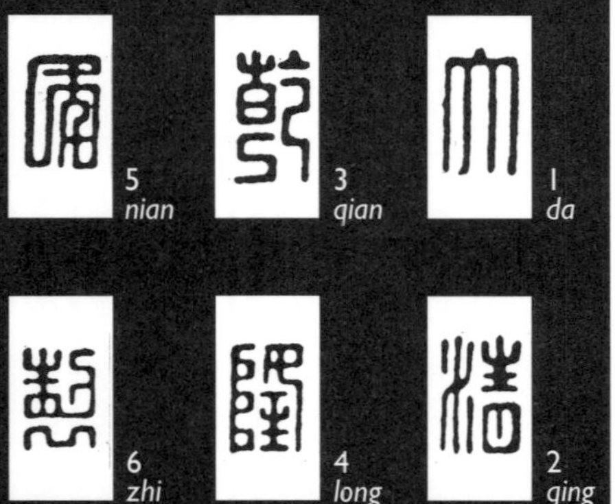

C

Dans quelques cas, les potiers dataient leurs pièces par un sytème plus traditionnel de désignation des années, le cycle sexagésimal du calendrier lunaire dont la première année serait 2697 av. J.-C. Depuis la dynastie des Zhou (1100-770 av. J.-C.), les Chinois utilisent les appellations des Dix Troncs Célestes et des Douze Rameaux Terrestres pour désigner les années. Ainsi la première année du cycle récurrent de soixante années est-elle designée sous le nom de *jia-zi* (ou année du Rat). Font alors partie de cette série, les années 1204, 1264, 1324, 1444, 1504, 1564, 1624, 1684, 1744, 1804, 1864 (voir p. 258) On pouvait trouver, par exemple, sur deux colonnes et en huit caractères, la marque suivante : *da ming chenghua yuan nian yi-you* = « fabriqué pendant la première année du règne de Chenghua de la grande dynastie des Ming à la période yi-you ». La lecture de la table de correspondance fait alors apparaître la 22e année du cycle sexagésimal, soit l'année (grégorienne) 1465, comme la seule qui convienne au règne de Chenghua. Les pièces provenant de manufactures privées n'étaient, bien entendu, pas marquées avec autant de précision.

La lecture des cachets (de couleur rouge ou bleue) est rendue difficile même pour des épigraphistes chinois, car les caractères du sceau sont écrits dans un style archaïque. Le principe de lecture en est presque le même, sauf que les six caractères sont répartis en trois colonnes et forment un carré, avec ou sans bordure. Inutile de préciser que les imitations de ces sceaux ont été nombreuses depuis leur apparition au XVIIIe siècle ; celles réalisées en Europe par des artisans qui n'avaient aucune connaissance de la langue chinoise sont aisément reconnaissables à leur maladresse.

Les marques de fabrique ou d'artisan On en trouve encore un grand nombre pendant la période Qing portant la mention *tang* (grande salle, hall) ou *ting* (pavillon), *zhai* (atelier, bureau de travail), *fang* (chambre ou maison), mais il est difficile de localiser les lieux de production à partir de ces indications. Écrites dans un style poétique et allusif – « fait dans le pavillon des brillantes couleurs, fait dans la retraite des multiples rocs, fait dans l'atelier du jade merveilleux » –, ces inscriptions sont insuffisantes pour déterminer avec précision le nom et le lieu des ateliers privés, des manufactures impériales ou des artistes eux-mêmes. Paul Pelliot, dans ses *Notes sur l'histoire de la céramique chinoise* (1923), rapporte à ce sujet que le caractère *zhi* (fabriqué, fait) ajoute à la confusion car il peut, selon lui, tout aussi bien indiquer un lieu de fabrication (« fait à »), le nom ou le surnom de l'artiste (« fabriqué par ») ou celui de son destinataire (« fabriqué pour »). On raconte même que sous les Qing, certains marchands de porcelaine, soucieux de publicité, faisaient apposer en termes fleuris sur chaque pièce le nom de leur commerce ou une lettre pour les identifier. Si les noms de potiers n'apparaissaient jamais sur la porcelaine issue des ateliers impériaux, à cause du trop grand nombre d'intervenants, en revanche, les artisans des fabriques privées n'hésitaient pas à faire figurer leur nom ou surnom (nom d'artiste), surtout quand ils réalisaient l'œuvre tout seuls.

Les inscriptions votives Elles avaient pour fonction de véhiculer des messages de souhaits pour l'acquéreur ou de rappeler la fonction de l'objet (en particulier pour les pièces à usage religieux). À côté des vœux traditionnels exprimés par un seul caractère – « qui attire la bénédiction céleste » *(fu),* souhaite la « richesse » *(lu),* un bonheur « simple ou

Sceaux des empereurs de la dynastie des Qing (1644-1912)

(d'après B. C. Stevens, Les Tabatières chinoises)

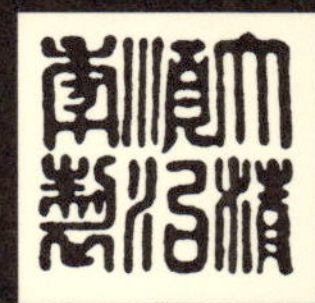

Shunzhi 1644-1661

Daoguang 1821-1850

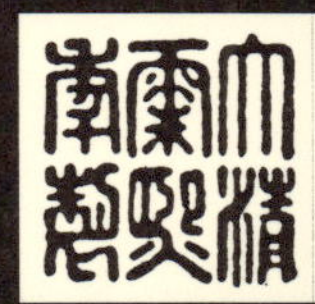

Kangxi 1662-1722

Xianfeng 1851-1861

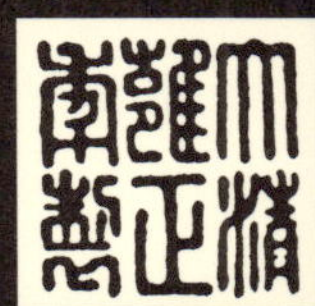

Yongzheng 1723-1735

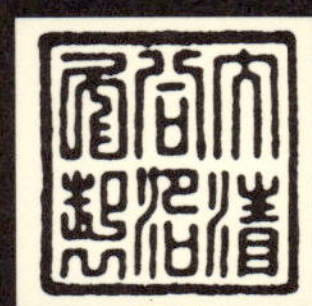

Tongzhi 1862-1873

Qianlong 1736-1795

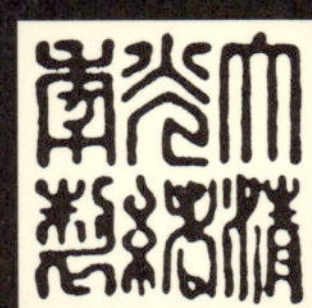

Guangxu 1874-1907

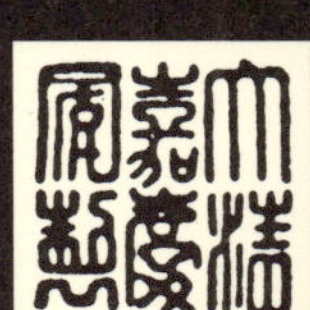

Jiaqing 1796-1820

Xuantong 1908-1912

double » (*xi* ou *shuangxi*), la « longévité » *(shou),* la « pureté » *(qing),* ou évoque « le dragon » *(long)* –, on trouvait de courtes dédicaces comme « très grande chance » ou « nombreuses années sans fin », « puissiez-vous rester éternellement jeune » (*yong bao chang chun* ou *chang ming fu gui*), « que la richesse et les honneurs soient toujours avec vous » *(fu gui chang chun).* La langue chinoise permettait un nombre infini d'énoncés de même qu'elle autorisait des images avec le jeu des analogies.

L*es marques d'appréciation*

C'est l'artiste qui portait un jugement sur son œuvre, en exprimant ainsi sa satisfaction et en recommandant cet objet de qualité à l'admiration de tous les éventuels clients. Comme le disait Confucius, « la vertu est semblable au jade » ; c'est donc le caractère *yu* désignant cette pierre, appréciée par tous les Chinois comme la plus précieuse, qui figurait dans des formules du type connues. On avait le choix entre « beau comme le jade », « précieux objet de jade », « trésor extraordinaire et distingué de jade », « joyau parmi les précieuses vaisselles de jade »... On y trouvait aussi des mentions particulières comme « ancien » *(gu)* ou « noble, éminent, distingué » *(gui).* Sur la plupart des théières de la période Qing, une inscription près du couvercle, en accompagnement de l'illustration, commentait la qualité de la peinture ou de la porcelaine elle-même.

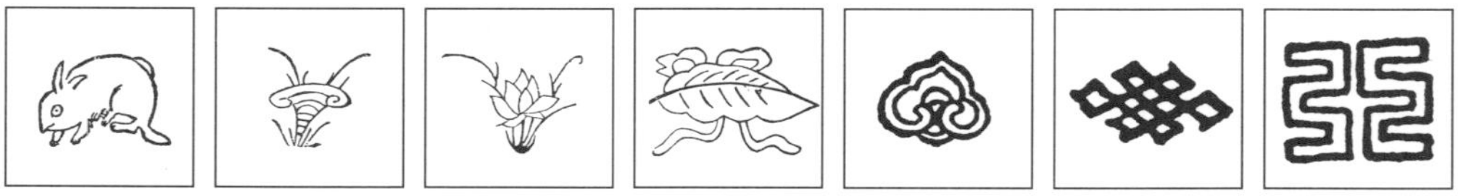

L*es marques symboliques*

Pour remplacer les *nianhao* interdits à certaines périodes, les artistes ont puisé dans l'énorme inventaire de motifs décoratifs que sont les emblèmes bouddhistes ou taoïstes pour apporter, par ces vignettes, une note plus symbolique à leur œuvre. La « perle » se retrouvait sur des pièces destinées aux hommes de lettres, « la pierre sonore » ou le « nœud sans fin » pour les religieux et les objets liturgiques, la « feuille d'armoise » avait des vertus curatives, le « lièvre » et le « champignon » souhaitaient l'immortalité, la « hache » était l'expression du pouvoir... On trouvait aussi des caractères stylisés : *shou* (longévité), le nœud bouddhiste ou une représentation du trépied sacré de bronze ou du sceptre *ruyi.*

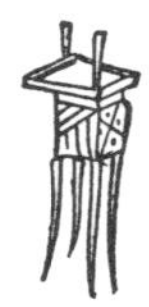

La laque, vernis de Chine

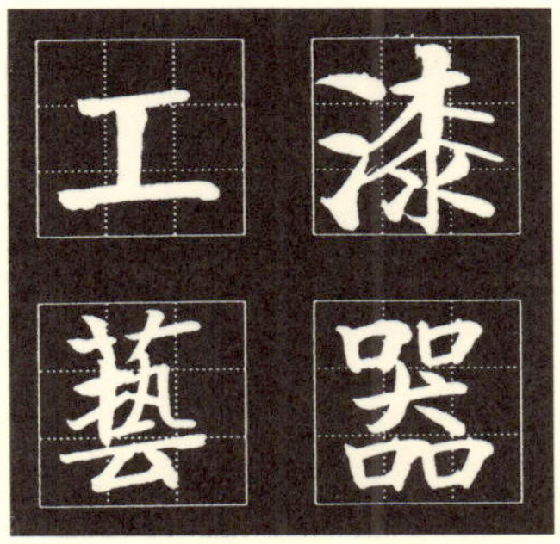

qiqi gongyi, littéralement, « l'art de la laque ».

La laque *(qi)* est la sève de l'arbre *rhus vernicifera* (appelé en Chine *qishu* et au Japon *urushi*). Originaire des provinces du sud et du centre de la Chine, on le trouve aussi en Corée, au Japon (d'où l'autre nom de la laque, « vernis du japon ») et dans de nombreux autres pays de l'Asie du Sud-Est. En Chine, il est cultivé dans les provinces du Zhejiang, du Fujian, du Guangxi, du Hunan, du Hubei et du Sichuan. On considère qu'il donne la meilleure qualité de laque après sa dixième année. La récolte se fait en pratiquant une incision dans l'écorce ; la sève est recueillie dans des godets (autrefois on utilisait les coquilles de moules de rivière). Dangereuse à manipuler ou à respirer, elle causait des abcès et de graves affections respiratoires. On tentait de combattre ces intoxications en donnant à manger aux ouvriers de la chair de crabe.

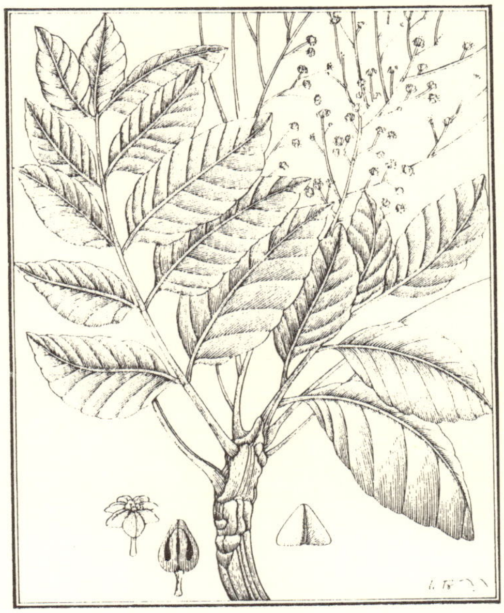

La laque se compose de 5 % de gomme, 2 % d'albumine, 23 % d'eau et 70 % d'un hydrocarbure appelé « urushiol ». On sépare les impuretés de la laque par filtrage à travers une toile, puis on la débarrasse de son excédent d'eau par une lente ébullition. À ce stade, d'un blanc laiteux elle devient incolore et légèrement ambrée. Il faut alors la conserver dans des récipients hermétiques à l'abri de l'air ou de la lumière, faute de quoi elle vire au gris, puis au noir. Pour la colorer avant usage, on ajoute des substances comme le noir de fumée ou l'oxyde de fer en vue d'obtenir le noir, du cinabre ou du sang de porc pour le vermillon, de l'orpiment (sulfure d'arsenic) pour le jaune et, enfin, de l'indigo (extrait de l'indigotier) pour le bleu.

L'objet à laquer est en général fait d'une base (ou support) sur laquelle sont appliquées des couches de laque. Le mot masculin (« un laque ») désigne maintenant un objet fait en laque ; on l'appelait au XVIIIe siècle un « laqué ». Pour obtenir un très beau laque *(qiqi),* on racontait qu'il ne fallait pas moins de deux cents applications. En réalité, la moyenne s'établit entre une dizaine et une cinquantaine de couches. La laque s'applique, comme un vernis, avec

L'arbre à laque (rhus vernicifera) *de la famille des térébinthacées.*

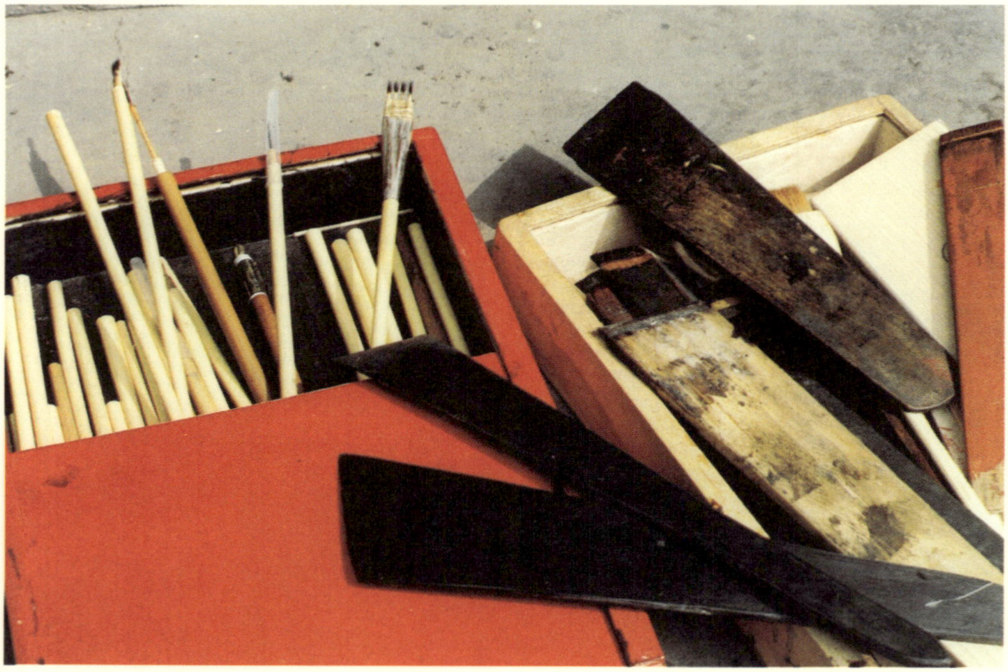

une spatule ou un pinceau de poils doux sur les supports les plus divers : laiton, étain, or et argent, porcelaine, cuir, vannerie, bambou et, surtout, bois de pin et toile de chanvre. Le séchage de chaque couche s'effectue dans une sorte de chaudière dont l'atmosphère est saturée d'humidité. C'est dans ces conditions qu'a lieu la polymérisation de l'urushiol qui produit le durcissement de la laque. On obtient alors des surfaces lisses par polissage au charbon de bois pour les couches préliminaires, puis à la cendre de corne de daim pour les autres. Le produit obtenu est brillant, dur mais cassant, résistant toutefois à l'eau, aux températures élevées et même à l'acide. Il est alors prêt à être peint, sculpté, gravé, incrusté.

Le plus ancien laque de Chine (un bol) a été retrouvé dans la province du Zhejiang et remonterait à 4000 ou 5000 av. J.-C. Un des plus célèbres traités sur la laque chinoise, le *Xiushulu (Recueil de décoration),* écrit par Huang Cheng à la fin du XVIe siècle sous les Ming, servit de base aux classifications qui distinguent une dizaine de types de laques : les monochromes, transparentes, marbrées ou peintes, à reliefs sculptés, ajourées, incisées, en intaille ou incrustées d'objets précieux…

À l'époque légendaire, il aurait existé une vaisselle de bois laqué incolore. Sous les Zhou apparut une vaisselle noire et rouge et surtout à l'époque des Royaumes Combattants (475-221 av. J.-C.) ; on utilisa alors la laque dans les mêmes couleurs pour des boîtes à fard, pour des coupes, des instruments de musique, des harnais de chevaux, des chars, des bateaux, des arcs et même des boucliers. Dans des chambres funéraires, on retrouva les premiers piliers laqués.

Brosses, pinceaux et spatules de bois ou de corne pour l'application de la laque.

Sous les Han (206 av. J.-C. - 220 ap. J.-C.), les accessoires de toilette et les cercueils montrent une évolution dans les formes et les couleurs. Les supports n'étaient plus faits en bois mais en couches superposées de toile trempée et appliquée sur un moule, en cuir ou en bambou léger. La toile, après durcissement, était décollée du moule dont elle avait pris la forme ; cette technique est connue sous le nom de « laque sèche ». Dans diverses provinces apparaissent des ateliers officiels *(gongguan).*

Les laques de l'époque Tang (618-907) sont notamment connues par la fabuleuse collection d'un empereur japonais, grand admirateur de cet art, qui en possédait trois mille pièces. Elles se caractérisent par de nouveaux pigments *(mituohui),* des incrustations *(pingtuo)* de nacre, d'écaille de tortue, d'or et d'argent, particulièrement sur les instruments de musique comme les cithares à sept cordes. Le cuir laqué est utilisé pour les fourreaux de sabre. C'est à cette époque que fut aussi réalisée pour l'impératrice Wu Zetian une colossale statue en laque sur toile de chanvre de trois cents mètres de haut.

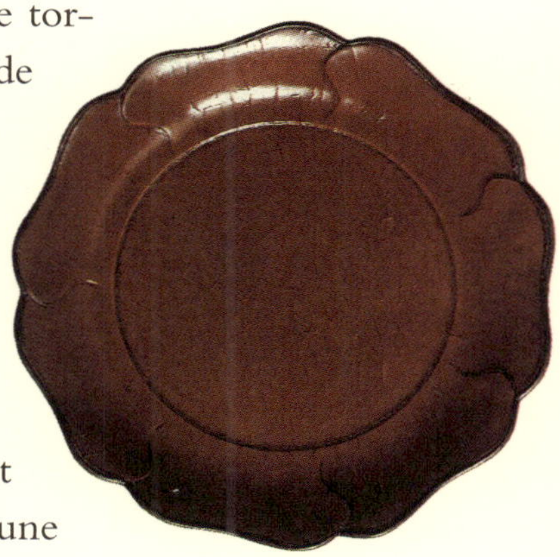

Sous les Song (960-1279), la production des régions du Hubei et du Zheijiang connaît un grand développement ; ce sont les monochromes (noir ou rouge) sans décor. Puis, grâce à une nouvelle technique d'incision, on dora les motifs en creux à la poudre ou à la feuille. Le renouveau religieux qui a marqué cette période encouragea la création d'innombrables statues (Bouddha, Guanyin) en bois ou laque sèche.

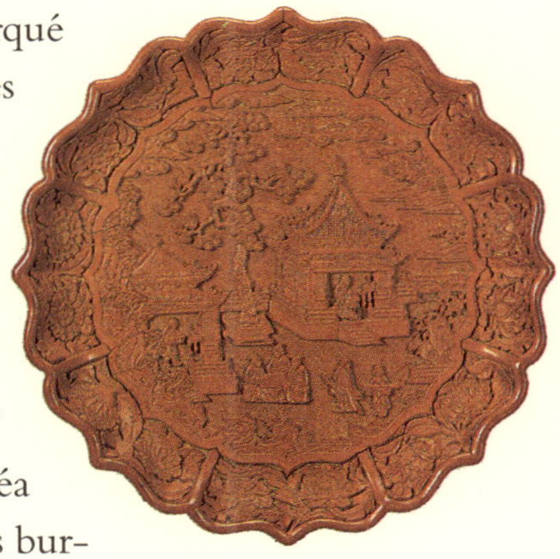

La laque rouge sculptée *(tihong),* réalisée à partir d'une cinquantaine de couches, communément appelée « laque de Pékin » ou « laque de cinabre », existait depuis les Tang, mais elle ne se développa que sous les Yuan (1271-1368). Ce sont des plateaux, des boîtes rondes et des pots à motif floral qui furent le plus fréquemment fabriqués. Mais on créa aussi des laques incrustées de nacre *(luotian)* appelées laques burgautées (de « burgau », un gros coquillage). La gravure en profondeur ou les incisions d'or sont aussi caractéristiques de l'art de cette époque.

C'est sous les Ming qu'on observe la plus grande variété de laques. Au XVe siècle, de nombreux échanges ont désormais lieu avec le Japon qui est déjà célèbre pour sa laque transparente que les Chinois ne parviendront jamais à imiter. L'empereur Yongle (1402-1424) confie à Zhang Degang, fils d'un maître laqueur, la direction de la manufacture Guoyuan dont les trois cents ouvriers se consacrent dans des conditions de travail difficiles à la fabrication d'œuvres d'art pour la cour. Ils produiront, entre autres, en laque de Pékin, de nombreuses pièces de mobilier qui ne seront jamais exportées. Reprenant la

En haut, plat en forme de fleur à sept pétales, laque rouge sur bois (dynastie des Song, 960-1127) ; en bas, plat sculpté et laqué.

technique de *qiangjin* (incisions d'or) des Song, les artisans l'appliquent principalement aux coffres, à des bassins et à des sièges. Ces laques incisées et colorées s'appellent en français des « laques cuir ».

Sous les Qing (1644-1912), le mobilier laqué connut un formidable développement grâce à la technique du *kehui* ou « coromandel » (appelé aussi par les Anglais « travail de Bantam »). Il devint très en vogue en Europe au XVIIe et au XVIIIe siècle. Recherchés pour leur taille impressionnante et la beauté des décors, ces paravents à dix ou douze feuilles servaient de cloisons amovibles dans les immenses salons anglais. Ils étaient faits dans des panneaux de pin tendre ajustés avec des chevilles. Ce luxueux mobilier tire son nom de la côte de Coromandel (Inde orientale) d'où il était expédié par mer ; en fait, il venait principalement, par voie fluviale, de la province chinoise centrale du Henan. La technique consistait à graver jusque dans l'apprêt un décor en champlevé sur un fond de laque noire. Les couleurs allaient du blanc à l'aubergine en passant par le bleu, le vert, le jaune et le rouge. C'est encore à cette période qu'apparut la « laque de Canton », une technique de décoration de meubles utilisant des motifs peints à la feuille d'or ou à la poudre *(miaojin)* sur fond de laque noire. Certains sont modelés en relief *(tuicai)* puis dorés. C'est à Yangzhou (Jiangsu) que naquit enfin la laque aux « cent trésors incrustés » *(baibaoqian)* dans laquelle on encastrait des pièces de jade, de malachite, de lapis-lazuli, de turquoise, d'agate, de corail, d'ambre, d'ivoire, de nacre et même de corne de rhinocéros.

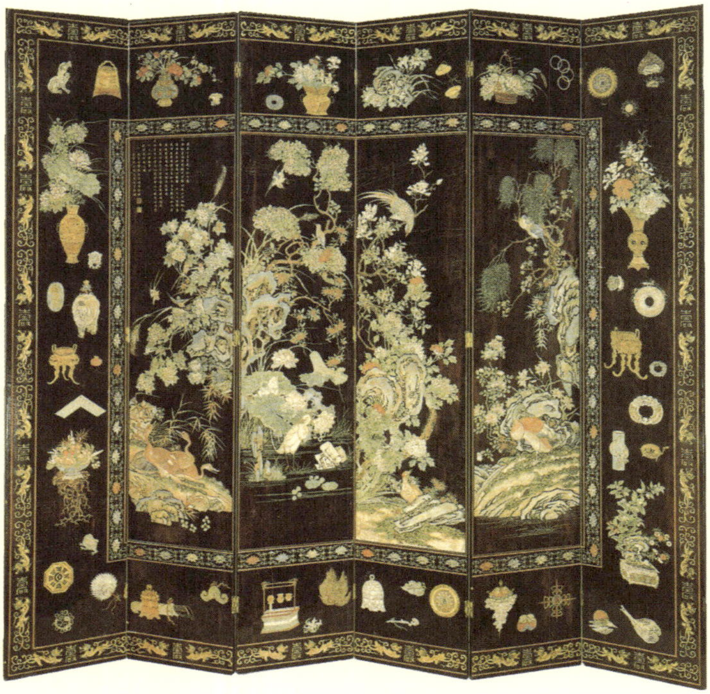

Paravent sculpté à six feuilles en laque de Coromandel (règne de Kangxi, 1662-1723) représentant les quatre saisons.

Il semble que les laques de qualité disparurent peu après la mort de Qianlong (1795), grand amateur de cet art. Les ateliers impériaux subsistèrent cependant jusqu'en 1866, date à laquelle ils furent détruits au cours de la révolte des Taiping. Bien entendu, des ateliers de laqueurs existent encore mais leurs productions sont sans commune mesure avec ce qui fit la gloire des artisans chinois des siècles passés.

L'émail et le cloisonné

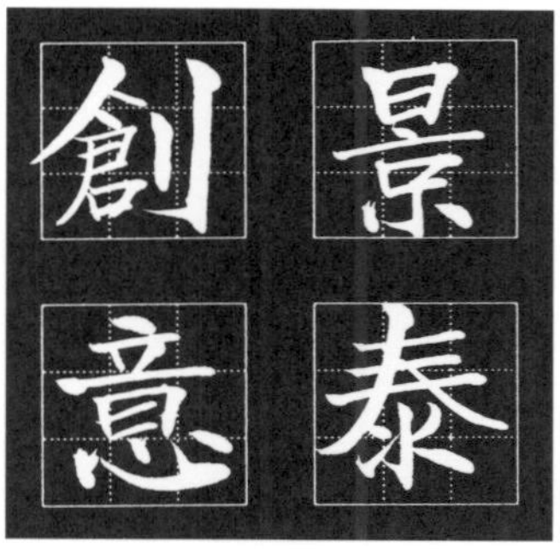

jingtai chuangyi, littéralement, « l'invention de Jingtai = l'émail cloisonné ».

Les émaux chinois se rangent dans plusieurs catégories techniquement distinctes : les émaux cloisonnés, les émaux champlevés et les émaux peints. La langue populaire les nomme indistinctement *jingtailan* ou « bleu de Jingtai », en référence au court règne de cet empereur de la dynastie des Ming (1449-1457) au cours duquel cet art nouveau apparut. En effet, deux couleurs fondamentales étaient alors utilisées : le bleu turquoise et le bleu lapis-lazuli. Tous les experts s'accordent à reconnaître que l'art de l'émaillage parvint en Chine sans doute vers XIVe siècle, en provenance de l'Occident et de l'Orient. Le *Traité des principaux critères concernant les objets anciens* rédigé au début des Ming (1387) qualifie ainsi l'émail de « porcelaine étrangère » *(yangci),* « d'objet cuit au four provenant d'Asie centrale », et même « d'émail des Francs » ou des « Byzantins » (*falan, falang, folang* ou *folin*). Toutes les suppositions concernant ces dernières dénominations, ont été faites à propos d'un certain Guillaume Boucher (ou Buchier), orfèvre à Paris, qui se trouvait, dès 1242, avec son fils à la cour mongole des Yuan, entouré d'une cinquantaine d'ouvriers. Avait-il eu connaissance des techniques de l'émail que les artisans de Constantinople maîtrisaient si bien depuis trois siècles, et les avait-t-il fait connaître aux artisans chinois qui auraient alors donné son nom à ce procédé ? L'envoyé du roi Saint-Louis, Guillaume de Rubroek (1253) fait mention de sa présence mais ne s'étend pas sur le sujet... En l'absence de certitudes historiques, on retiendra donc que cet art a probablement été introduit en Chine, au XIVe siècle, par des marchands ou des artisans ambulants (européens, arméniens, arabes, persans, chrétiens nestoriens, juifs...) venus de gré ou de force à la cour de Xi'an. Les Chinois parlaient d'ailleurs de ces émaux comme de « produits du pays des diables étrangers » *(guigouyao).*

Les émaux ne pouvaient, bien entendu, que séduire les Mongols par leurs couleurs vives et leur caractère inaltérable. Ce goût des couleurs émaillées se prolongera sous les Ming avec autant de bonheur que pour les porcelaines. Il faut toutefois attendre le règne de Xuande (1425-1435) pour trouver des pièces émaillées portant son *nianhao.* Sous l'empereur Jingtai (1449-1457), les cloisonnés « auraient gagné une telle réputation » que les manufactures de l'époque Qianlong (soit plus de trois cents ans plus tard), continueront d'apposer le *nianhao* de cet obscur empereur des Ming pour leur donner plus de valeur sans que l'on puisse en expliquer les raisons. On sait maintenant que les mentions portées à leur pied pouvaient être rajoutées à l'émail à des dates différentes de celle de la fabrication de l'objet. Ceci permit d'antidater de très nombreuses pièces, le procédé s'appliquera aussi aux porcelaines. À cette date, ce sont des brûle-parfums, des vases, des boîtes et des chandeliers qui seront fabriqués pour les palais impériaux. Sous les Qing, bon nombre de ces objets seront offerts aussi aux temples bouddhistes ou lamaïstes. La production de cloisonnés sera particulièrement importante sous les règnes de Kangxi (1662-1722), Yongzheng (1723-1735) et surtout Qianlong (1736-1795). Dès 1680, près d'une trentaine d'ateliers d'émaillage fonctionne, à Pékin, pour le service de la fabrication des objets destinés à l'empereur Zuobanju. Lors du sac du palais Yuanmingyuan (1860) et surtout après l'intervention des armées étrangères lors des « 55 jours de Pékin » (1900), un nombre considérable de pièces émaillées fera partie du butin pris par les soldats, déclenchant en Europe un engouement particulier pour le cloisonné au début du siècle.

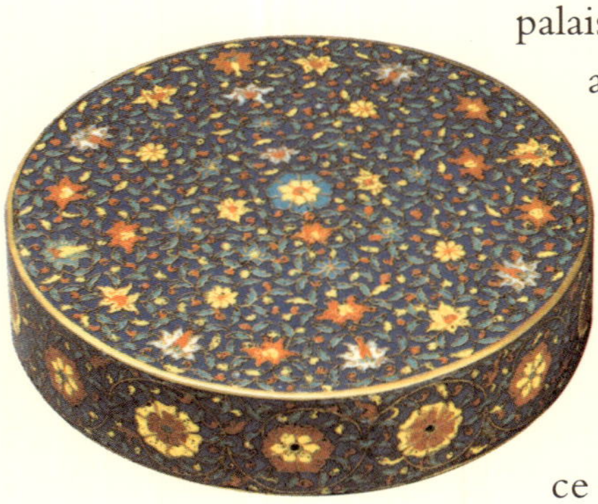

L'appellation « cloisonné » s'adresse à des émaux dont les motifs décoratifs sont séparés par de minces cloisons verticales qui retiennent la matière vitrifiée. La première étape de ce long processus de réalisation concerne la mise en forme de la pièce. Bien que l'on puisse appliquer de l'émail sur de l'or, de l'argent, du bronze, de la céramique, de l'argile et même du verre, ce sont le cuivre et le laiton qui ont formé la base la plus fréquente pour l'émaillage. Toute la production chinoise du XVIIIe siècle a fait usage du cuivre rouge *(tong)* alors que sous les Ming, au XVIIe siècle on se servit du laiton (*huangtong* ou cuivre jaune, un alliage de cuivre et de zinc). Dans un deuxième temps, l'artisan procédait au tracé des motifs décoratifs au pinceau et à l'encre ou s'il était un expert confirmé, appliquait directement sur la pièce de fines lamelles de cuivre, d'or ou d'argent mises en forme qu'il maintenait par une sorte de colle à base de laque. Ces cloisons déterminaient des alvéoles dans lesquelles l'émail allait prendre place. Les minces parois étaient ensuite soudées à la pièce avec du plomb ou de la poussière d'argent. La troisième étape concernait l'émail proprement dit. Cette pâte vitreuse devait avoir un point de fusion assez bas pour ne pas déformer ou fondre le réseau de cloisons métalliques installées sur l'objet. L'émail, un mélange de sable siliceux, de potasse, de soude et d'oxydes métalliques (plomb), donnait, après cuisson, une pâte presque transparente, de couleur bleuâtre ou verdâtre. Écrasé en poudre, humidifié, coloré par divers ingrédients, il était déposé dans les alvéoles puis subissait une première cuisson

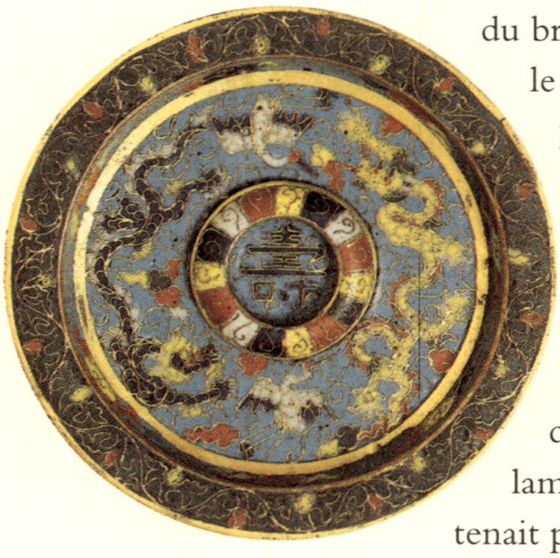

En haut, boîte en émail cloisonné (dynastie des Ming, milieu du XVe siècle) ; en bas, soucoupe en émail cloisonné (règne de Jiajing, dynastie des Ming, 1521-1566).

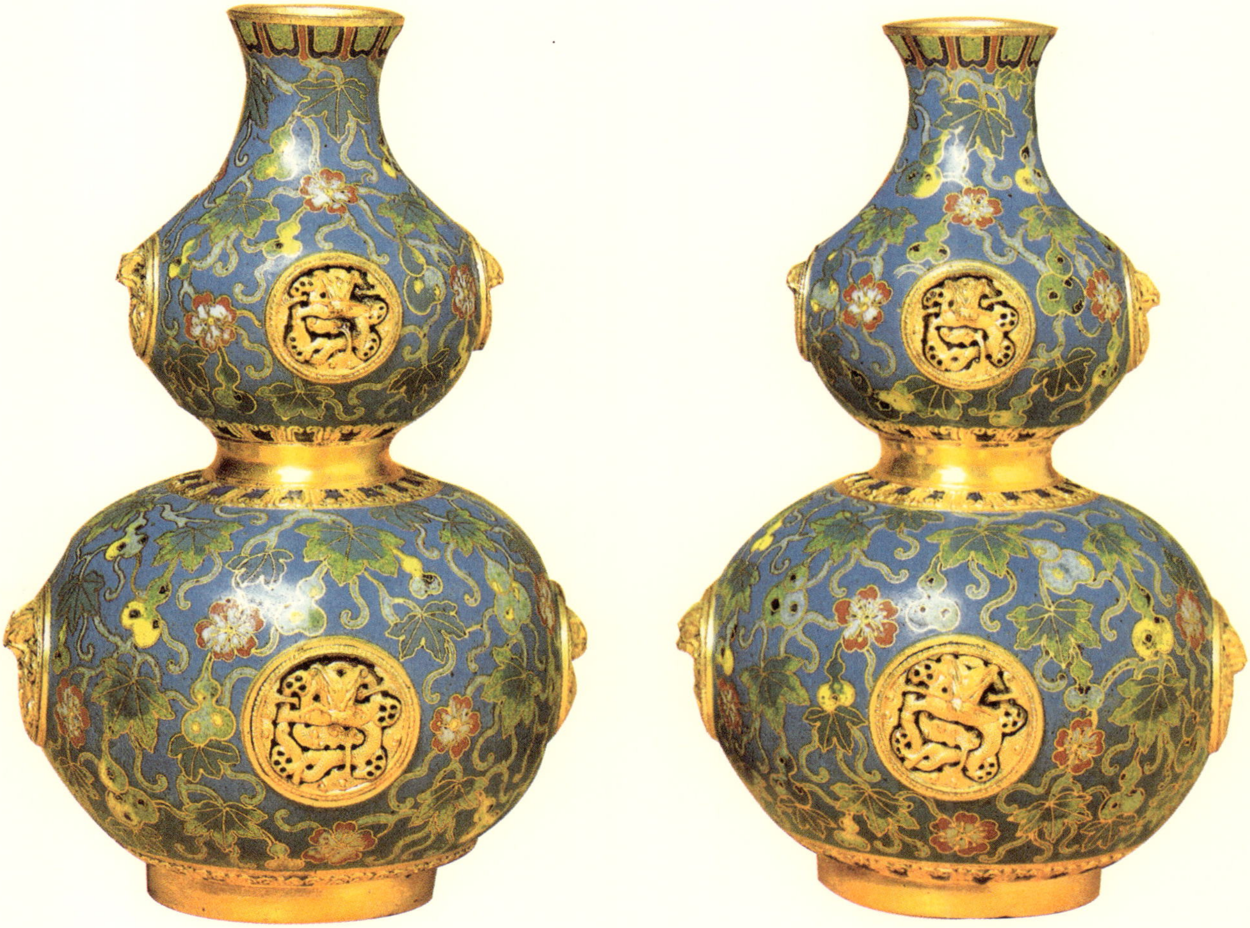

qui le faisait adhérer en se rétractant légèrement. Les temps de cuisson étaient variables, de plus, pour chaque couche, il fallait repasser la pièce au feu pour bien remplir les interstices ou supprimer les aspérités. Le polissage représentait la quatrième phase, la finition des pièces rondes comme les vases ou les plats s'effectuant sur un tour où les pièces étaient frottées à la pierre ponce ou à la cendre de charbon de bois dans les ateliers situés dans le quartier de Qianmen à Pékin. Alors seulement, la pièce était prête pour la dorure qui s'appliquait dans un bain contenant une solution d'or venant se fixer sur toutes les parties apparentes de cuivre. L'épaisseur de la dorure a varié en fonction des goûts et des époques.

Le champlevé était un autre procédé de cloisonnement, l'artisan ménageait des alvéoles dans la base de cuivre avec des outils à creuser pour y couler la pâte d'émail qui se trouvait alors encastrée dans le métal et non plus à sa surface, elle pouvait même apparaître en léger relief. Dès l'époque Han, les Chinois incrustaient du verre, de la turquoise, de l'or et de l'argent sur du bronze selon cette technique de champlevé (bijoux, parures, vases rituels).

Paire de vases en forme de gourde, cloisonné turquoise et bronze.

Le repoussé est le troisième procédé utilisé en émaillage, il pouvait se combiner avec les autres. Dans ce cas, les alvéoles étaient martelées en relief, puis recouvertes d'émail et passées au four.

Les émaux peints portent quelquefois les appellations d'« émaux de Canton » ou « émaux de Pékin ». Ils apparurent dans ces deux centres entre 1700 et 1720. Seule la dorure et l'épaisseur distinguaient les objets de la meilleure qualité réalisés à la capitale. Leur technique était très semblable à celle des émaux de Limoges ou de Battersea, en Angleterre, et certaines pièces montrent une importante influence européenne. Les premiers émaux (des montres émaillées et des boîtes de tabac à priser) furent rapportés par les missionnaires français qui les firent ensuite copier par des artisans chinois, au milieu du règne de l'empereur Kangxi (1662-1722). Son règne étant marqué par un renouveau artistique, de nombreuses manufactures d'horlogerie et d'émaux se créèrent. Un jésuite, le R. P. Jean-Baptiste Gravereau, fut même envoyé à Pékin pour enseigner l'art de l'émaillerie. L'empereur Yongzheng (1723-1735) continuera d'accorder son parrainage à cet art nouveau ainsi que son successeur Qianlong (1736-1795). C'est de cette période que datent les pièces les plus connues. Les couleurs qui caractérisent cette production sont toujours tendres ; on dénombre beaucoup de « famille rose ». Avec le développement des échanges avec l'étranger, les artisans de Canton se mirent à produire des pièces destinées à l'exportation. Les motifs étaient peints dans le goût européen. On y trouvait parfois des armoiries ; les sujets et les décors, pour répondre à cette mode d'exotisme, étaient souvent persans, siamois ou hindous mais manifestement traités par des artistes chinois. Une bonne partie de la production des « émaux de Pékin » fut destinée à l'usage de l'empereur qui s'en servit comme cadeaux à des hôtes prestigieux. Les émaux peints, contrairement aux cloisonnés, ne furent pas produits en grande quantité. Comme pour les porcelaines, ces émaux portaient, à la base, la marque des empereurs ; celles de Qianlong ou de Yongzheng sont particulièrement recherchées des amateurs. À la fin du règne de ce dernier, en 1795, cet art délicat disparaîtra pour faire place à des copies industrielles qui ne sont que pacotille en comparaison des admirables miniatures du XVIIIe siècle.

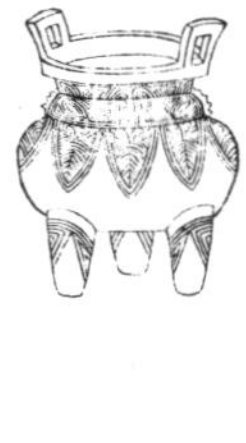

DES OBJETS À VIVRE

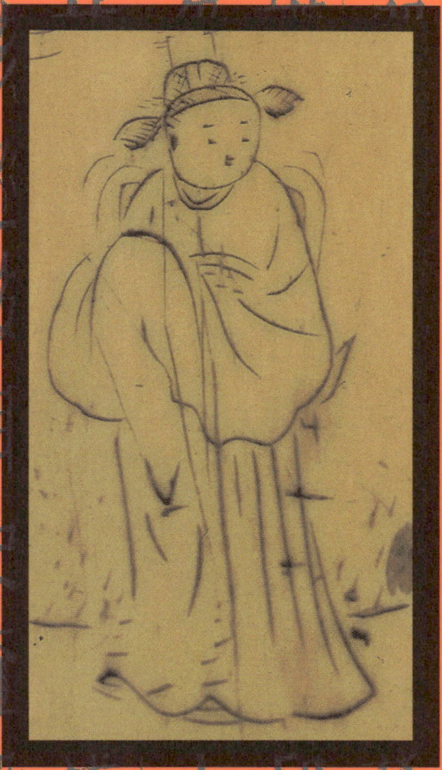

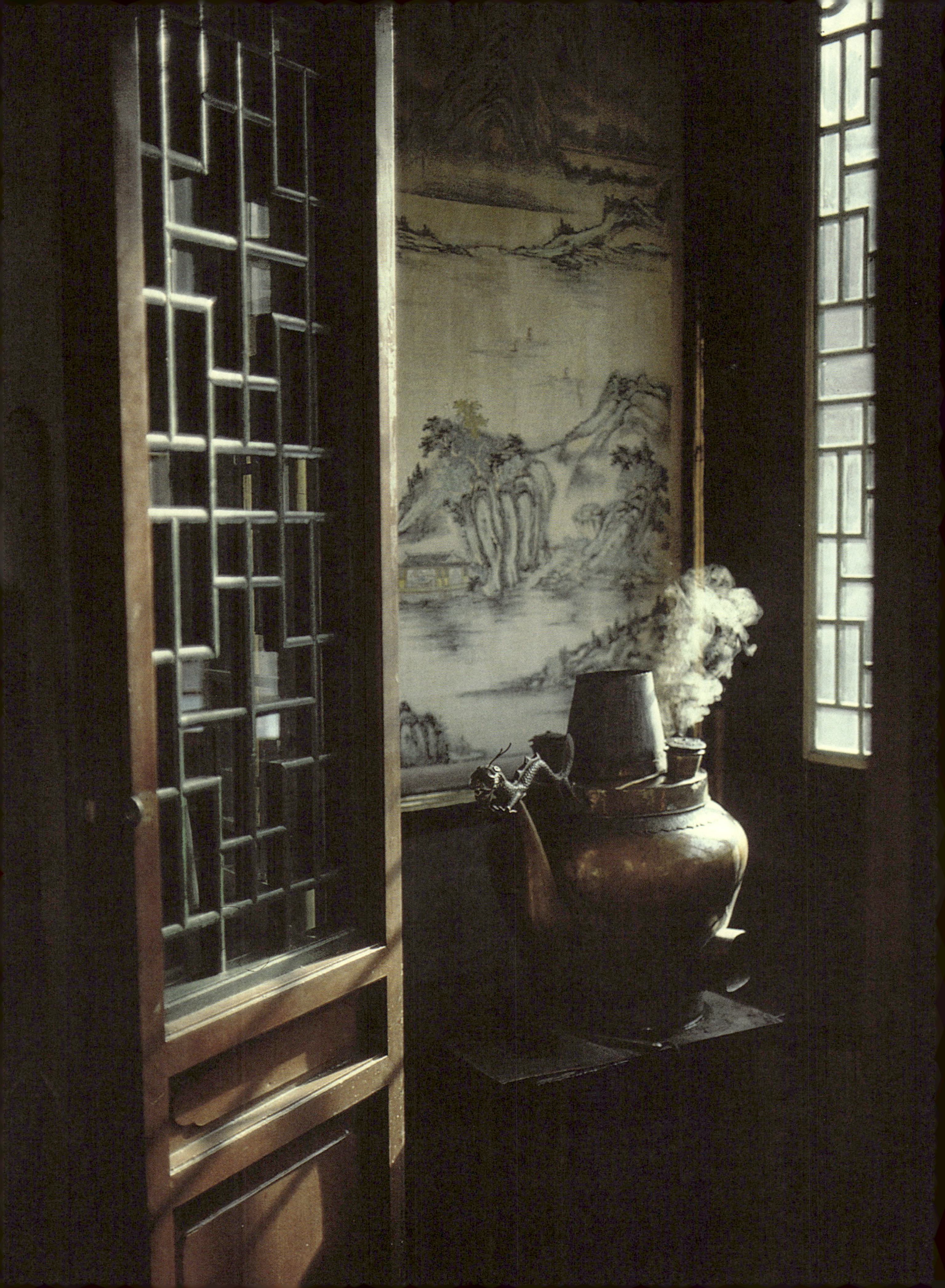

L'art du thé

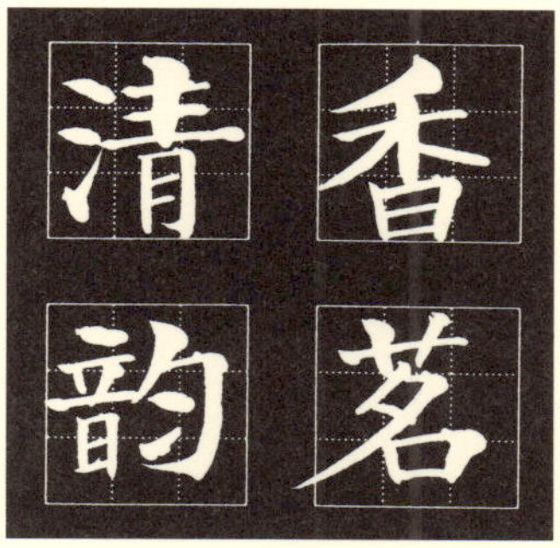

xiang ming qing yun, littéralement, « thés parfumés et rimes limpides ».

Classé pourtant parmi les Sept nécessités *(qi jian shi)* avec les combustibles, le riz, l'huile, le sel, la sauce de soja et le vinaigre, le thé n'a jamais été célébré en Chine avec la même ferveur qu'au Japon avec leur célèbre *chanoyu.* Il existait toutefois en Chine un rituel d'accueil, *gongfu* (littéralement « thé préparé avec une application particulière »), pratiqué dans les provinces du Fujian et de Canton où l'on servait d'habitude le thé *wulong* dans des théières faites en terre de Yixing. La Révolution Culturelle s'attachera, dans le cadre de l'élimination des « Quatre Vieilleries », à supprimer la cérémonie du *gongfu,* jugée bourgeoise et décadente. L'offrande d'une tasse de thé, en Chine, reste un geste de pure politesse et de respect à l'égard du visiteur. Pendant les périodes difficiles qu'a connues la Chine depuis le milieu du XIXe siècle, le thé étant une denrée de luxe, on prit l'habitude de le remplacer par un bol de *kaishui* (littéralement « eau bouillie »).

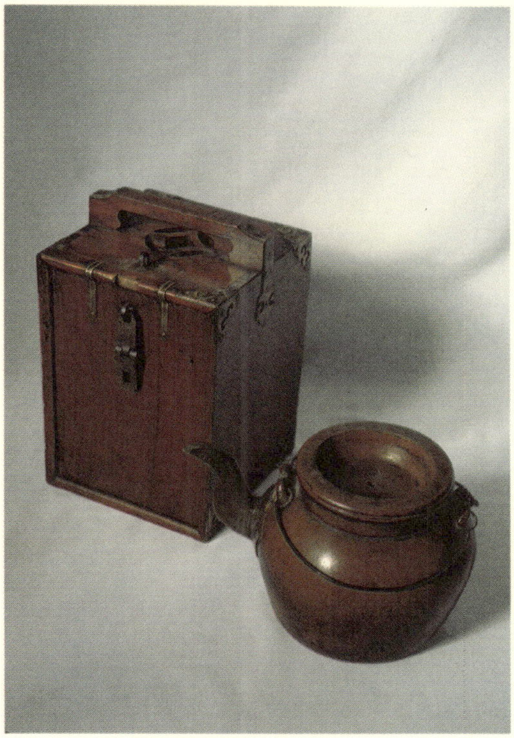

Le premier *Traité du thé (Chajing),* paru en 780 ap. J.-C., décrit un véritable art du thé qui existait à l'époque ; il donne un inventaire détaillé des variétés, disserte savamment sur l'eau à utiliser et, avec un raffinement rare, décrit un choix d'ustensiles pour faire et boire le thé. Ainsi l'eau – de source si possible – devait bouillir jusqu'à ce que les bulles « atteignent la grosseur des yeux d'une langouste », mais pas au-delà. Son auteur, Lu Yu (733-804), un enfant trouvé originaire du Hunan, consacra vingt ans de sa vie à la rédaction des dix volumes de ce *Classique* qui devait lancer la mode du thé à l'époque Tang (618-907) puis la prolonger sous les Song (960-1127). Un expert de cette dernière période, Cai Xiang, intendant des thés de la province du Fujian, puis gouverneur, complétera par son œuvre magistrale, les *Annales du thé (Chalu),* la connaissance de cette plante et ses applications. À cette date, les villes de Kaifeng (capitale des Song du Nord) et de Hangzhou (capitale des Song du Sud) devinrent de grands centres de commerce du thé. L'empereur Huizong (1100-1125) qui recevait de ses sujets un tribut de feuilles de thé, fut aussi l'auteur d'un *Traité détaillé du thé (Daguan chalun)* qui parut en 1107.

Page de gauche, intérieur d'une maison de thé ; ci-dessus, théière en argile de Yixing et son coffret de transport.

La découverte de la plante est attribuée à Shennong, le légendaire. La première « offrande du thé », selon les légendes taoïstes, aurait eu lieu quand Laozi (VIe siècle av. J.-C.), sur le point de quitter le monde des mortels, traversa le col qui mène vers les monts Kunlun et y fut accueilli par Yin Xi, le gardien des lieux auquel le Maître dicta les « Cinq mille mots » (le *Livre de la Voie et de la Vertu, Daodejing*). Pour les bouddhistes, le thé aurait été ramené de l'Inde, notamment de l'Assam, en 520 ap. J.-C. par un moine indien, Bodhidarma (nom chinois : Tamo, transcription du sanscrit, *dharma,* « la loi »). On lui attribue la fondation de l'École *Chan* (en japonais, *zen*). Le brahmane aux yeux bleus, selon la tradition, se serait endormi pendant une séance de méditation. Pour se punir, il se serait coupé les paupières et les aurait jetées ; elles auraient pris racine et donné le premier plant de théier... Le thé devint ainsi la « plante de l'éveil » et les moines continuent de l'utiliser dans les temples pour maintenir leur concentration pendant les interminables offices. Dès le XVIe siècle, les missionnaires européens décrivaient les effets de la caféine (non encore révélée) sur l'organisme qui « contribuait à la longévité des Chinois et les exemptait de maladies graves ». En 1625, un grand débat sur les mérites et les dangers du thé s'engagea en Hollande, puis en France sous le règne du roi Louis XIV. La querelle s'arrêta quand le tout puissant Mazarin, qui en consommait, lui accorda son appui.

C'est vers le IXe siècle que le thé parvint au Japon, par des moines bouddhistes qui le ramenèrent de Chine. Les Japonais copièrent les pratiques qui étaient alors en vigueur sous les Tang et développèrent un rituel rigoureux toujours en usage alors qu'il n'existe plus en Chine. En 1610, les Hollandais ramenèrent en Europe dans leurs bateaux, la première cargaison de thé en provenance de Java. En quelques années, la mode de boire du thé, supplantant celle du café, se répandit dans la bonne société hollandaise puis, dix ans plus tard, en Angleterre, mais avec moins de succès, en France et en Allemagne. On y ajoutait, comme en Chine autrefois, du safran, du gingembre, de la muscade et même du sel. Le nom chinois *(cha)* est quelquefois remplacé par *ming* pour désigner un thé de qualité (de jeunes pousses). En Europe, son appellation a varié en fonction des premiers échanges. Les Hollandais qui commerçaient avec les marins de la province du Fujian l'appelèrent *te* ; c'est sous diverses orthographes que ce nom sera adopté par la plupart des langues européennes (thé, *tea, thee, te...*) alors que les Portugais qui avaient des relations avec Macao et Canton ont retenu le *cha* du mandarin, suivis par les Japonais, les Indiens, les Arabes et les Russes. C'est vers 1618 que le premier thé apporté par des caravanes de chameaux, à travers la Mongolie et la Sibérie, parvint à Moscou. La Compagnie (anglaise) des Indes Orientales ouvrit son premier négoce de thé à Canton en 1684 ; ce produit était à l'époque plus demandé que les porcelaines ou les soieries. Au XVIIIe siècle, les maisons et les «jardins» de thé devinrent de véritables institutions en Angleterre et la contrebande se développa car les taxes sur ce produit étaient élevées. Les importations de thé atteignirent un tel niveau que le gouvernement anglais chercha par la vente illicite d'opium indien aux Chinois à équilibrer sa balance des paiements, entraînant ce pays dans la première guerre de l'Opium (1839-1840). Les feuilles de thé fraîchement traitées, devant séjourner le moins longtemps possible à l'air humide sous peine de pourrir, on chercha par tous les moyens à raccourcir les délais d'acheminement. La rivalité entre armateurs, capitaines britanniques et américains pour le transport des caisses de thé dans les délais les plus rapides donna naissance à l'épopée des clippers, ces voiliers à fine carène qui, entre 1845 et 1871, ralliaient l'Europe par le cap de Bonne Espérance en moins de trois mois.

La plante appartient au genre *camelia* (en chinois *cha*) et le savant suédois Charles de Linné la classa dès 1753 sous le nom de *thea sinensis* (thé chinois). Il ignorait, à l'époque, que le thé vert et le thé noir provenaient de la même plante mais résultaient d'un traitement différent, ce qu'un botaniste écossais, Robert Fortune put révéler en 1848 après avoir séjourné en Chine, déguisé en indigène. Les Chinois ayant pris conscience de la valeur de cette plante exceptionnelle s'efforcèrent dès le XVIIe siècle de maintenir un secret absolu sur leurs techniques de production et de traitement du thé. Les meilleurs thés poussent en altitude et la période de récolte s'effectue entre avril et octobre. Les premières feuilles sont les plus recherchées, elles sont ramassées selon la technique dite de « deux feuilles, un bourgeon », quand les feuilles ne sont pas encore complètement dépliées ; on les appelle alors « cueillies juste avant la pluie ». Il faut deux kilogrammes de feuilles vertes pour obtenir cinq cents grammes de thé.

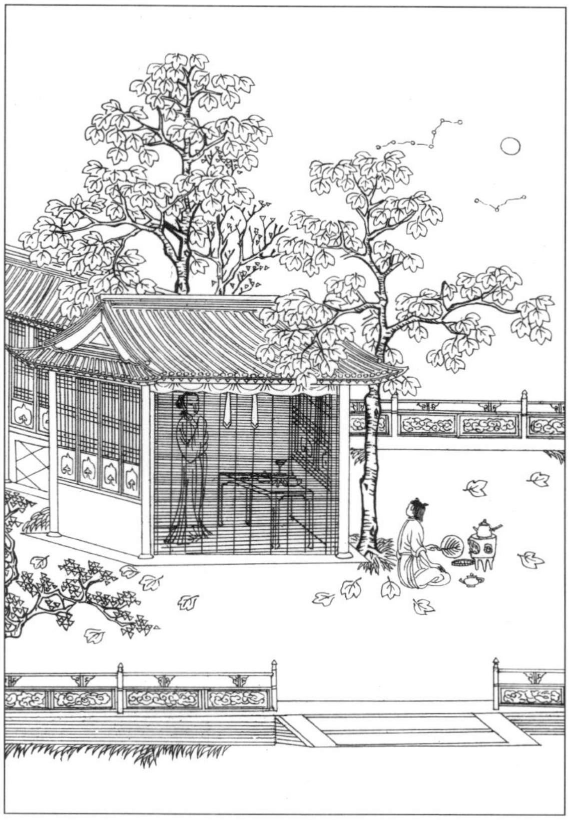

On classe traditionnellement les thés chinois en trois catégories : les thés verts, les thés noirs et les thés parfumés. Le thé vert *(lücha)* est celui qui est le plus fréquemment consommé par les Chinois. Les feuilles sont torréfiées ou passées à la vapeur puis roulées et séchées. Les thés verts de Chine sont, en général, commercialisés sous le nom de leur province d'origine (par exemple, thé du Fujian) ou d'une appellation due à leur forme ou à une légende locale. Parmi les plus fameux, on trouve le Longjing (« Puits du

Servante préparant le thé dans l'attente d'une visite (gravure extraite de Dongxijiangji).

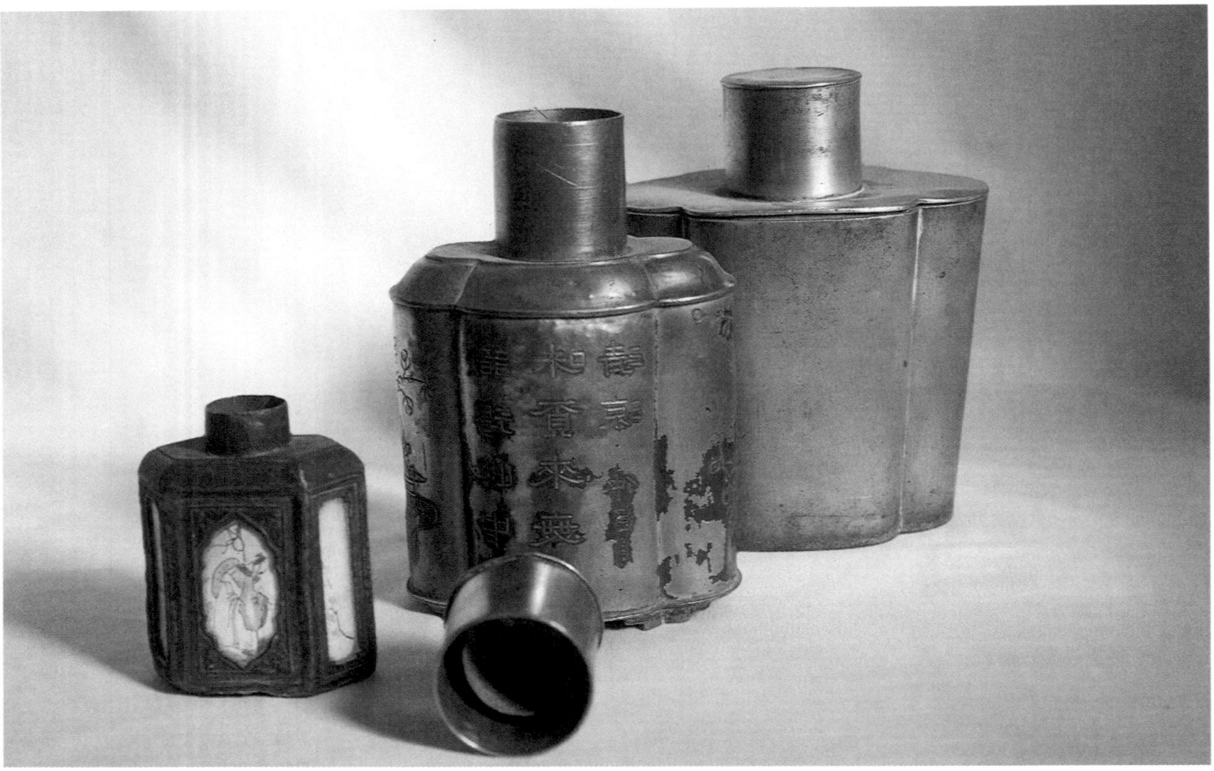

Dragon »), célèbre pour la qualité de ses eaux et qui ne comprend pas moins de seize variétés, le Huangshan maofeng (« Pointes de cheveux des Monts Jaunes »), le Biluochun (« Escargot de Printemps »), le Putuo Focha (« le thé des bouddhistes du mont Putuo »), le Lu'an guapian (« la graine de melon de Lu'an »). Le « Poudre à canon » (*zhucha,* littéralement « thé en perles »), de la région de Hangzhou, produit une infusion au goût prononcé et tenace. Il fut l'un des premiers thés à être exporté. Presque toutes ces variétés sont originaires du Zhejiang ou de l'Anhui.

Le thé noir (*hongcha,* en chinois « thé rouge ») est le résultat d'un traitement plus élaboré qui, après la cueillette, comprend le roulage, la longue fermentation dans des récipients de bambou au cours de laquelle les feuilles deviennent rouges, la torréfaction à grand feu puis le séchage, le tri et enfin le mélange. La plupart de ces opérations étant assurées manuellement, les ouvriers des « fermes de thé » *(chazhuang)* se reconnaissaient aux brûlures de leurs mains. Les thés noirs, pratiquement réservés à l'exportation, sont souvent des mélanges d'une vingtaine d'autres variétés. Les plus connus des thés noirs sont le Qihong de la province de l'Anhui, le Dianhong du Yunnan, le Suhong du Jiangsu, le Chuanhong du Sichuan et le Huhong du Hunan.

Le thé Wulong ou Oolong, produit dans les montagnes Wuyi du Fujian, se différencie du thé noir car il n'a subi qu'une demi fermentation. Une des variétés les plus populaires se nomme la « Déesse de fer » *(tieguanyin)* parce qu'elle est « séduisante » comme une fée *guanyin* et forte comme le fer. Dans

Boîtes à thé (caddies) *dont l'une en étain, laquée et gravée, fabriquée à Swatow (XIXe siècle).*

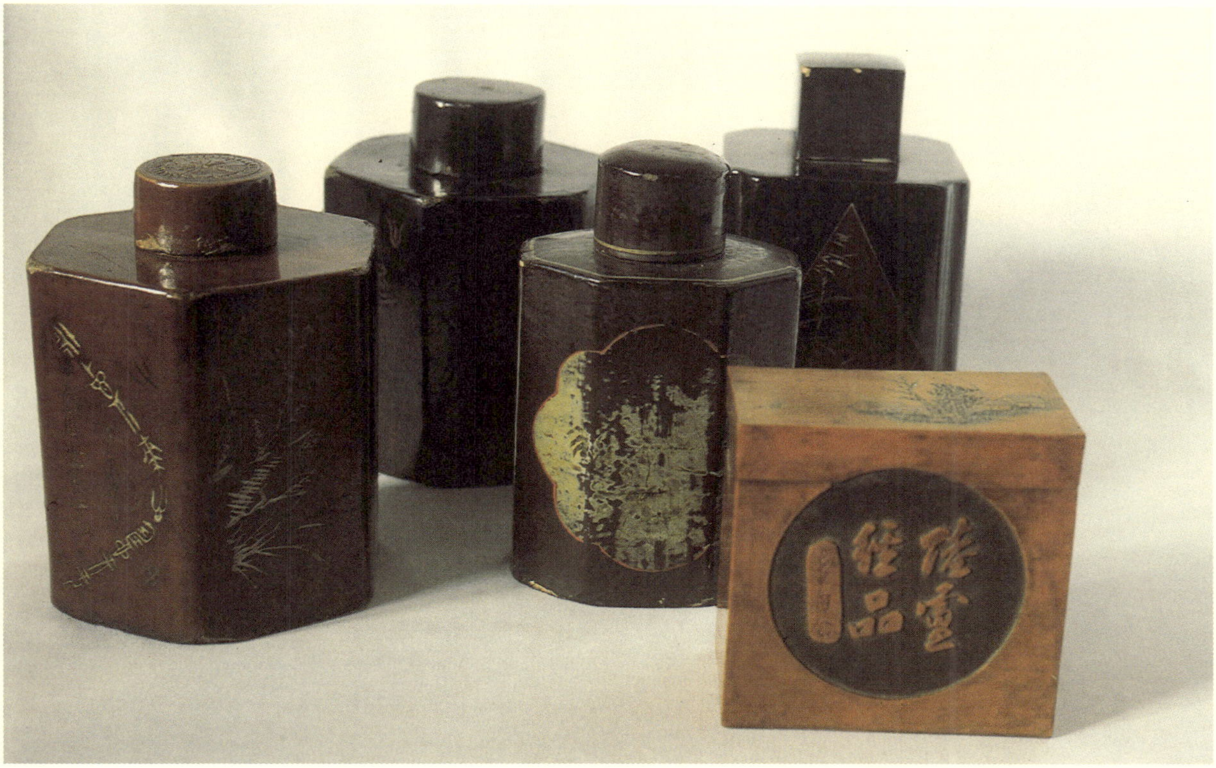

cette catégorie se range aussi le fameux thé de Pu'er, originaire des montagnes du Yunnan, qui pourrait avoir pour ancêtre la variété sauvage à grandes feuilles *(daye)* connue en Chine depuis près de deux mille ans. Il est réputé soigner les maux d'estomac et d'intestin, et est vendu pressé en forme de bol *(tuocha),* de pain *(bingcha)* ou de boule *(tuancha).* Les thés de plantes médicinales *(yaocha)* étaient en usage depuis les Yuan (1271-1368) et l'impératrice douairière Ci Xi (1834-1908) avait de nombreuses recettes personnelles pour les maux de gorge, les étourdissements et les fièvres. Pour qu'il conserve toutes ses qualités, on le torréfiait sur une plaque métallique avant de le transférer dans la théière pour infuser.

Les thés parfumés (*huacha,* « thé de fleurs ») sont souvent des thés verts auxquels sont mêlées des fleurs (oranger, jasmin, magnolia, rose, orchidée, gardénia). Le thé de litchi, originaire de Canton, était le favori de l'empereur Xuanzong (923-926 ap. J.-C.) et de sa concubine Yang guifei. Les paysans pauvres ont pris l'habitude de préparer des « thés » à partir de feuilles de saule ou de peuplier. Le Hunan est la principale province productrice de thé olifère (ou thé à huile, *camelia oleosa*). L'huile *(chaziyou)* obtenue après broyage des graines de thé est utilisée en cuisine malgré son goût amer.

L'usage de plus en plus répandu du thé en Chine développa au fil des années les ustensiles nécessaires à sa conservation, à sa préparation puis à sa dégustation. Sous les Tang, on mettait à infuser les feuilles de thé dans un pot en y ajoutant du gingembre, de la datte, de la menthe, des pelures d'orange,

Boîtes à thé en laque peinte et gravée (Chine du Sud) et boîte carrée en bois de camphre.

de l'oignon ou du poireau et même du sel. Le thé était alors servi dans de petites coupes *(chawan)* de céladon transparent ou de porcelaine blanche. On pouvait aussi utiliser des feuilles de thé qui avaient été hachées, torréfiées puis réduites en poudre *(chayemo)*. Sous les Song, on prit l'habitude de fouetter le thé : de l'eau bouillante était versée sur la poudre de thé et l'ensemble était ensuite battu avec un instrument de bambou pour obtenir une boisson plus épaisse. On le buvait alors dans des bols de couleur noire aux parois épaisses. La théière *(chahu)* naquit avec le besoin de laisser infuser les feuilles (XVIe siècle) et les plus appréciés de ces récipients furent les terres cuites de Yixing (province du Jiangsu) connues en Europe sous le nom de *boccaros*. Située sur les bords du lac Taihu, la petite ville de Yixing était connue depuis plus de deux mille ans pour ses poteries, en particulier les grès. Les légendes racontent que ce sont des moines taoïstes vivant dans les grottes près du village de Dingshu qui auraient découvert cette fine argile aux trois couleurs : pourpre (*zisha*, « sable pourpre »), brun-violet *(zusha)* ou jaune clair *(banshanlu)*. L'habitude de boire directement au bec de minuscules théières *(taoguan)* vint sans doute du Nord de la Chine et de l'Ouest (Shanxi et Mongolie). Ces petites théières figuraient souvent sur le plateau des accessoires du fumeur d'opium qui pouvait ainsi boire en position couchée. Sous les Ming, des bols, des théières de porcelaine décorées avec plateau assorti apparurent et sous les Qing fut inventé un ensemble appelé *zhong* qui comprenait le bol avec un couvercle et la soucoupe. Depuis que Lu Yu écrivit le *Classique du thé* (VIIIe siècle), il existait une grande controverse entre spécialistes sur la matière dont devaient être faits les récipients pour infuser le thé et conserver les feuilles. Dès le XIIIe siècle, l'étain (en alliage avec le plomb) était utilisé pour fabriquer des infusoirs, des boîtes à thé *(chayeguan)* mais aussi des verseuses à vin. L'usage des ces récipients se prolongea jusqu'au XIXe siècle, avant que l'on ne découvre la toxicité de ces métaux quand ils sont en contact avec de l'eau très chaude ou du tanin. Le seul avantage reconnu des boîtes à thé en étain (en anglais *caddies*) était d'être hermétiques, assurant une bonne conservation de l'arôme. Au XVIIe siècle, les Chinois inventèrent un bouchon à double paroi que l'on garnissait de papier absorbant. Certaines de ces boîtes furent quelque fois doublées à l'intérieur d'une paroi de céramique. Le thé continua d'être conservé dans de grandes jarres hermé-

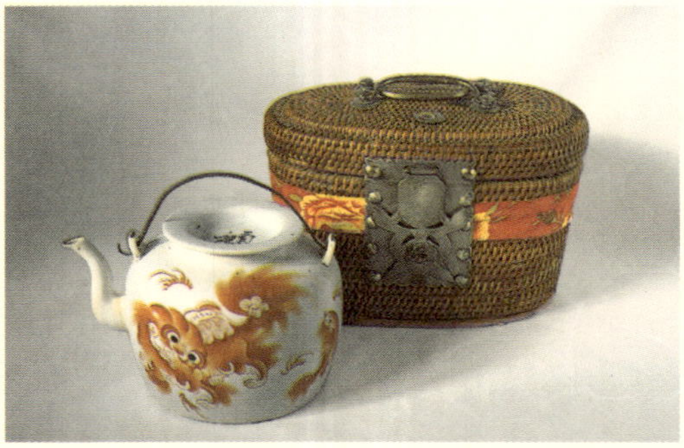

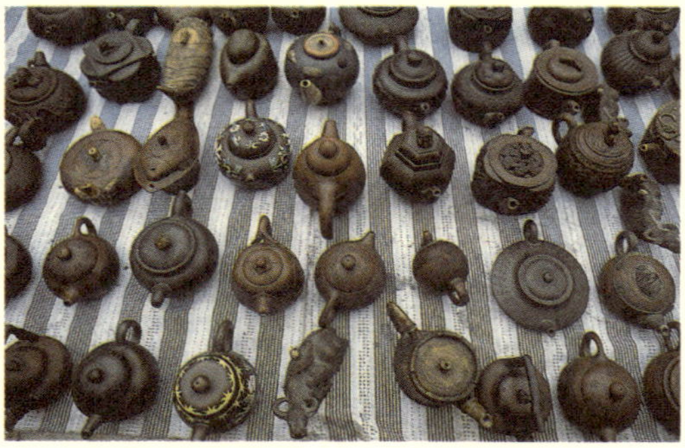

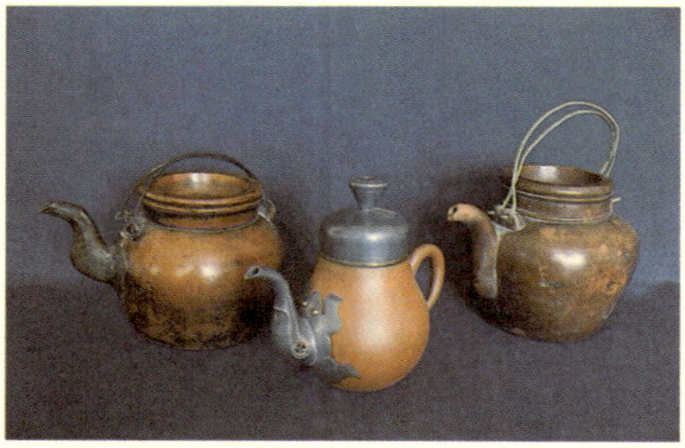

En haut, théière en porcelaine blanche décorée d'un chien de Fo avec son panier de transport (XIXe siècle) ; au centre et en bas, théières en terre de Yixing. Page de droite, intérieur d'une maison de thé à la campagne ; sur la table, des zhong en porcelaine blanche.

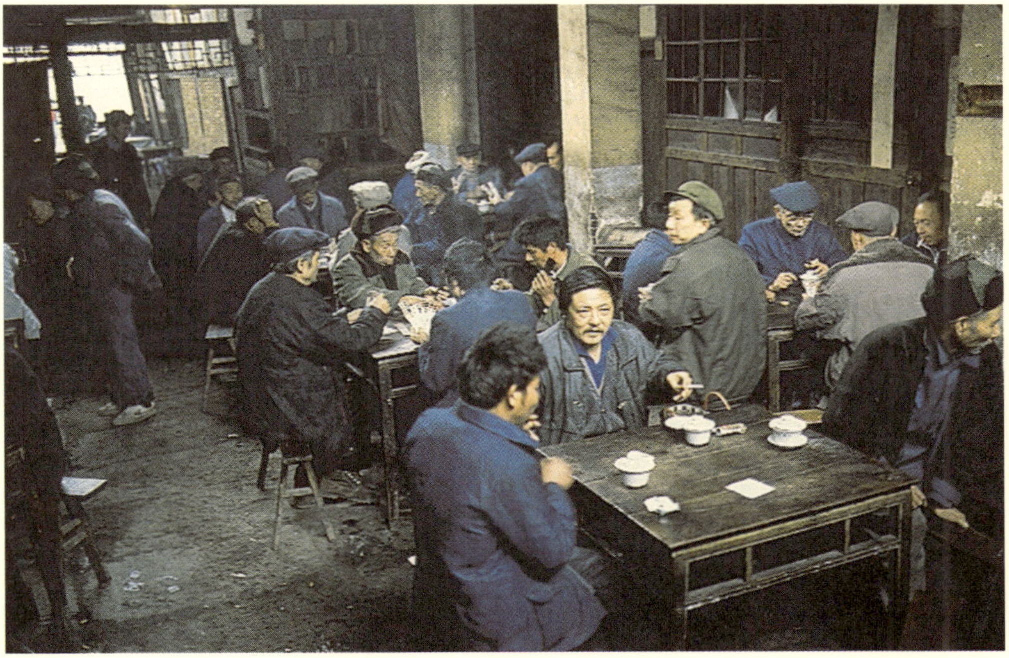

tiques, mais on fabriqua aussi des récipients plus commodes, rectangulaires, carrés ou à pans, en céramique décorée, en bois de camphrier (dont l'odeur éloigne les insectes) ou en étain gravé et même laqué. Ils contenaient aproximativement une livre de thé mais pour les thés rares, il existait des boîtes d'une capacité d'une once (environ 30 grammes) que l'on offrait comme un précieux cadeau. Dès le XVIIIe siècle, la ville de Swatow (l'ancien nom de la ville de Shantou, province de Canton) était connue pour les ateliers où se fabriquaient ces « caddies » d'étain *(xiguan)*. C'est de cette ville aussi que partiront, au XIXe siècle, sur les clippers, des milliers de coolies à destination des grands chantiers du chemin de fer de l'Amérique ou des mines d'argent du Pérou. Le commerce du thé a été à l'origine de l'invention en Chine du papier monnaie. En effet, au IXe siècle, les marchands, après avoir livré leurs ballots, reçurent en échange une reconnaissance de dette payable dans leur province. Ce fut le début du billet de banque (*feiqian,* littéralement « monnaie volante »).

Les « maisons de thé » *(chaguan)*, immortalisées par le roman de Lao She (1899-1966), fermées plus d'une dizaine d'années pendant la Révolution Culturelle, sont redevenues le point de rencontre des retraités, le lieu où les nouvelles s'échangent, où les tables de jeux s'organisent. D'astucieux entrepreneurs ont fait en sorte, dans les grandes villes, de redonner à ces vénérables institutions leur rôle d'antan en réhabilitant d'anciens bâtiments.

Les cadenas de sortilèges et autres amulettes

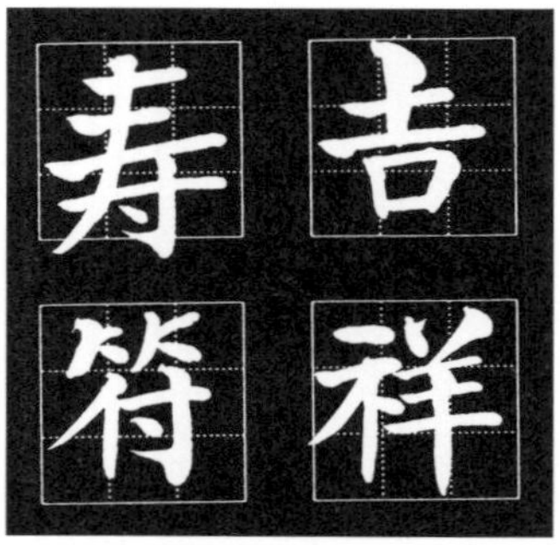

ji xiang shou fu, littéralement, « talismans pour une longue et heureuse vie ».

On connaît tout l'attachement des Chinois pour les procédés destinés à conjurer le mauvais sort. Lors des moments importants de la vie de nombreuses amulettes *(fu, hufu, hushenfu)* étaient utilisées soit pour éloigner les mauvais esprits, soit pour se ménager la protection des divinités, soit pour guérir des maladies, soit enfin, d'une manière générale, comme porte-bonheur *(jixiangfu)*. Ces talismans étaient en général portés suspendus à un cordon, une chaîne ou cousus sur un vêtement. D'autres, fabriqués sous forme de pilules ou de poudres, devaient être avalés. Certains papiers porteurs d'inscriptions magiques étaient réduits en cendres puis avalés mêlés à un liquide *(shaohuitunfu)*.

Parmi les talismans les plus fréquents, se trouve le « cadenas de sortilèges ». Utilisé lors des mariages, cet objet de la vie courante, un cadenas de bronze ou de laiton *(suo)* au corps parallélépipédique ou cylindrique qui ouvre avec une longue clé plate, revêtait alors une signification particulière. Offert au jeune couple sur un meuble peint ou laqué rouge avec le caractère « double bonheur » *(shuangxi)*, il était le souhait d'une vie conjugale heureuse et sans faille, à cause du rébus *suo* (garder lié, uni, enchaîné).

Aux enfants, c'étaient des cadenas à la fonction plus complexe qui leur étaient offerts, celle de les « enchaîner à une longue vie » en les protégeant des influences malfaisantes, d'où leur nom « cadenas de longue vie » *(changmingsuo)*. Comme ils étaient destinés à des enfants en bas âge, ils étaient réalisés dans des matériaux légers et de forme simplifiée ne rappelant plus que d'une manière lointaine le cadenas d'origine. Fines plaques de poitrine, ou boîtes creuses, les « cadenas de longue vie » ressemblent à des bijoux et n'ont ni mécanisme ni clé. Les orfèvres les décoraient en utilisant la technique de gravure par incision ou repoussé en relief, comme on le fit longtemps en Europe pour les hochets de bébés. L'endroit et l'envers portaient presque toujours des inscriptions auspicieuses avec les caractères du bonheur et de la longévité, complétés par d'aimables formules comme « longue vie sans interruption » *(mingchang)* ou « cent familles lui garantissent une longue vie » *(bai jia bao sui)*. Pour les filles, les dédicaces étaient plus poétiques : « elle ressemble à la fleur et a les vertus du jade » *(ru hua si yu)*. Comme toujours en la matière, les inscriptions s'accompagnaient de motifs décoratifs dont la signification symbolique était aisément perceptible pour la plupart des Chinois. Par exemple, la pomme de pin ou la grappe de raisin, comme tous les fruits à graines, souhaitent une grande descendance. Le rat ou l'écureuil sont connus pour leur prolificité, le poisson est un symbole de richesse. Les cadenas fabriqués dans des matières comme l'argent, l'ivoire ou l'os, le jade et même le bois (de pêcher) étaient portés autour du cou. On en trouve aussi en émail ou en cloisonné. Ils portaient souvent des pendeloques garnies de fleurs ou de clochettes (*lingzi* ; ces dernières avaient notamment pour fonction, selon H. Doré, « d'effrayer les esprits malveillants »). Les plus communs des cadenas sont en *baitong* (ou *packfung*), un alliage de cuivre, de nickel et de zinc appelé aussi maillechort imitant l'argent par la couleur et le poids. Certains antiquaires offrent encore des cadenas d'ivoire très ancien, faits dans « l'ivoire fossile de Sibérie » (défenses de mammouth ou dents de morse).

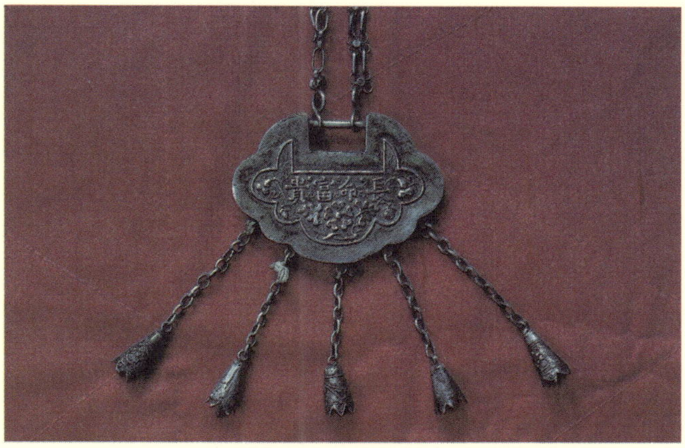

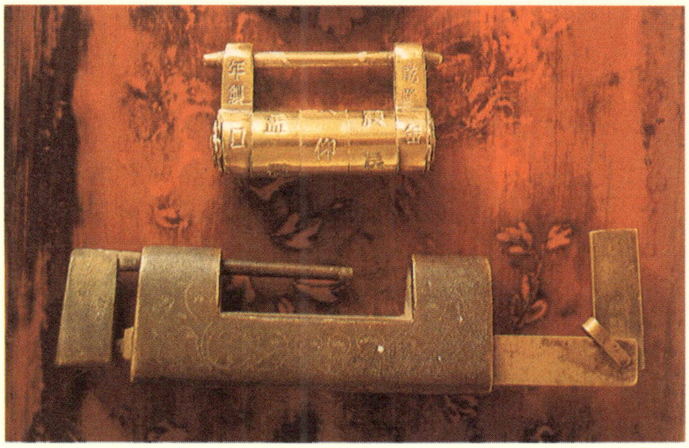

Dans certaines familles, il était transmis de génération en génération. Si l'on n'était pas très fortuné, on faisait la tournée de la famille et des amis proches pour réunir la somme requise, d'où leur nom de « cadenas des cent familles » *(baijiasuo)*. La tradition voulait que ni la mère, ni le bébé ne reçoivent de visites pendant le premier mois, car ils ne devaient pas être mis en contact avec le monde extérieur où rôdent les mauvais esprits. Un rideau de soie rouge (ou à défaut un ruban) était même placé devant la porte de leur chambre pour en interdire l'entrée aux démons assoiffés de sang. Trente jours après la naissance *(manyue,* littéralement, « le mois écoulé ») avait donc lieu une grande fête à laquelle participaient parents et amis. C'était, selon M. Granet *(Civilisation chinoise)* « le moment où l'enfant peut être présenté à son père. C'est le moment où l'on observe ses premiers gestes, où l'on commente le son de sa voix et ses premiers cris mais surtout où l'on décèle les marques d'un signe funeste ». La présentation des vœux et des cadeaux, et notamment l'offrande du « cadenas » (qui devait être donné dans un morceau de soie rouge ou dans une boîte tapissée de rouge), s'effectuait à l'occasion de cette cérémonie. En règle générale, les garçons recevaient un cadenas plus grand et plus décoré que les filles. Curieusement, en cas de maladie, on enlevait momentanément le cadenas, sans

En haut, « cadenas de sortilèges » ; en bas, cadenas traditionnels chinois.

doute parce que le talisman n'ayant pu faire son office, il convenait de ne pas exiger l'impossible du sort. Lors du premier anniversaire de la naissance *(zhousui)* avait lieu une étrange cérémonie qui consistait à déposer devant l'enfant un certain nombre d'objets. Celui qu'il choisissait indiquait alors ses goûts et donc sa future carrière. En règle générale, le « cadenas de longue vie » n'était plus porté par les garçons après l'âge de quinze ans.

Les femmes adultes n'hésitaient pas à porter aussi ce type de bijou-talisman qu'on appelait « cadenas-tour de cou » *(jinquansuo)*. Des motifs d'oiseaux décoraient le cadenas et le collier était souvent en argent.

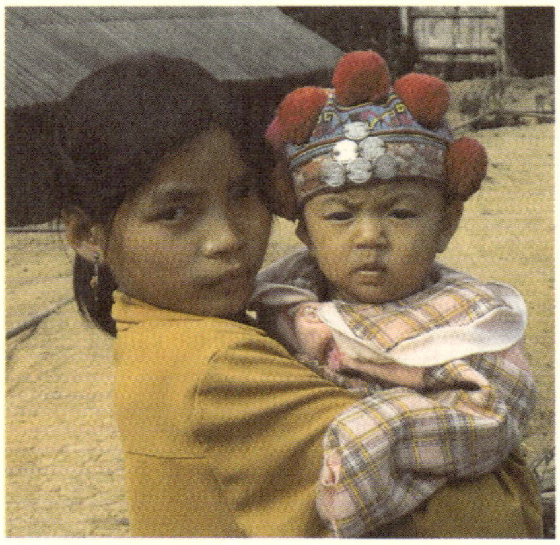

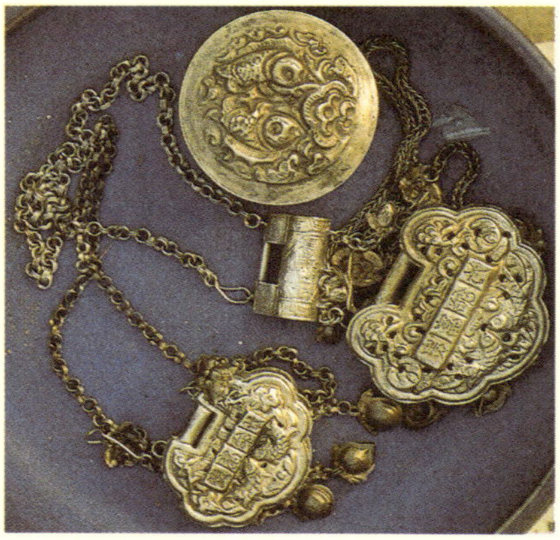

D'autres étranges talismans étaient portés par les enfants. Pour attirer leur protection, les orfèvres réalisaient de petites figurines (les Huit Immortels, le Bouddha, Shouxinglao...) en métal repoussé (argent, maillechort ou cuivre émaillé) qui étaient cousues sur des bonnets ou des bandeaux. De la même manière, des pièces de monnaie étrangères d'argent décorent de nos jours les coiffes d'enfants. Des sapèques (pièces de monnaie à orifice carré) enfilées sur un fil rouge et portées autour du cou, étaient aussi un talisman fréquent. Dans certaines régions, on suspendait aussi un bijou d'argent ou de métal argenté en forme de patte de coq qui lui « conférait ainsi le pouvoir de trouver sa nourriture en toutes circonstances ». Comme le coq lui-même, cette amulette avait le pouvoir de protéger des maladies, des épidémies et notamment des « Cinq animaux venimeux ». La griffe de tigre *(huzhua)* était un remède contre les peurs et la porter sur soi permettait d'acquérir les vertus du tigre (courage, protection contre les maladies et les accidents). On mettait ainsi des colliers de noyaux de pêches sculptés aux chevilles des enfants pour les empêcher d'être enlevés par les mauvais esprits ou de tomber malade. La pêche étant le fruit de l'immortalité, les berceaux d'enfants étaient faits en bois de pêcher. On trouve d'ailleurs encore bon nombre d'amulettes à porter autour du cou, qui ne sont que de simples petits cylindres de bois de pêcher *(taofu)*, sculptés et percés de deux trous pour y passer un cordon. Il y avait aussi des plaques *(bazifu)* à accrocher au cou, qui portaient les « caractères cycliques » ou trigrammes (*ba gua*) de l'horoscope du bébé. On leur attribuait un rôle important de porte-bonheur. Cette croyance était d'ailleurs tellement forte que même pour une fille abandonnée, on prenait la sage précaution de les inscrire sur ses vêtements en vue d'éviter qu'elle ne soit mariée plus tard à un homme dont le signe ne soit pas compatible ! Dans certaines régions, on composait un petit écheveau en allant demander rituellement à chaque

En haut, mère et enfant portant une coiffe ornée de pièces d'argent (Chine méridionale) ; en bas, « cadenas de sortilèges ».

membre de la famille et aux voisins un brin de laine ou de soie pour faire le « pompon des cent familles ». Cousu sur les vêtements, il témoignait que son porteur bénéficierait toute sa vie durant de nombreuses protections. Un pendant d'oreille *(erhuan)* était quelquefois mis à un petit garçon pour le faire passer pour une petite fille sans importance aux yeux des démons toujours avides de s'emparer des garçons, considérés comme une meilleure proie. Il en était de même pour le « collier de chien » *(gouquan),* qui avait aussi pour fonction de tromper les mauvais esprits sur leur propriétaire auquel on donnait même un « surnom d'animal » *(xuming).* L'expression familière « tête de chien » *(goutou, gouzi)* pour les garçons découle sans doute de cette pratique. C'est vers un an que l'on faisait porter aux enfants d'étranges « bonnets d'animaux » (tigre, chien ou lion) assortis à des pantoufles du même genre. Croyant voir là un animal peu digne de leur convoitise, les démons ne les inquiéteraient pas. Pour renforcer cette ruse, on pouvait aussi avoir recours au « talisman de poil de chien » *(goumaofu),* qui était fait de poil de chien et d'une mèche de cheveux du bébé. Il fallait le porter cousu dans la doublure du vêtement. Cette amulette servait surtout à dérouter le trop célèbre Chien céleste, réputé pour enlever les enfants afin de prendre leur âme. Toutes ces précautions étaient encore plus particulièrement recommandées pour les natifs du signe du chien, qui avaient alors toutes les chances de mourir en bas-âge. Curieuse coutume enfin, pour le fils aîné d'une famille (le plus précieux des enfants), il était sage de lui faire porter au poignet jusqu'à la puberté un bracelet d'argent contenant de vieux clous de cercueil particulièrement efficaces contre les mauvais esprits. On assurait aussi une meilleure protection des enfants contre les « Cinq animaux venimeux » en cousant sur les vêtements des reproductions de ces animaux nuisibles...

Il faudrait enfin, sans être encore véritablement exhaustif sur le sujet, faire mention des «talismans écrits» *(yinfu).* Ces bandelettes de papier jaune sur lesquelles étaient écrites par les prêtres des formules cabalistiques à l'encre rouge étaient savamment repliés et enfin cousus sur les vêtements des enfants. Un traité spécialisé a recensé plus d'un millier de ces formules s'accompagnant d'étranges dessins que seuls des initiés pouvaient déchiffrer, et qui étaient surtout à l'usage des adultes. Les taoïstes et les bouddhistes eurent souvent recours à ce type d'amulettes dans leur rituel d'exorcisation. Il n'est pas rare de trouver dans la niche encastrée dans le dos des statues des divinités de semblables documents qui sont soit des charmes protecteurs soit des suppliques.

Les carrés de mandarins

錦袍图案

jinpao tuan, littéralement, « motifs sur vêtements de brocard ».

Dans son étude *The Costume of China, Picturesque Representations of the Dress and Manners of the Chinese* (1805), William Alexander décrit, illustrations à l'appui, les attributs des dignitaires chinois : « Tous les fonctionnaires, civils et militaires, du rang le plus élevé au moins élevé, ont été appelés par les écrivains portugais "mandarins" (du verbe *mandar,* "commander"). Et ce nom, bien qu'impropre, a été conservé depuis. L'emblème d'un oiseau brodé sur un carré porté sur la poitrine indiquait que c'était un fonctionnaire civil. Les militaires portaient un emblème d'animal... Le degré du rang était, par ailleurs, indiqué par une petite boule sur le haut du chapeau... Par faveur impériale, on pouvait se voir attribuer une, deux ou trois plumes de paon attachées au chapeau... Tous les fonctionnaires civils ou militaires portaient aussi autour du cou des colliers de corail, d'agate ou de verre coloré... »

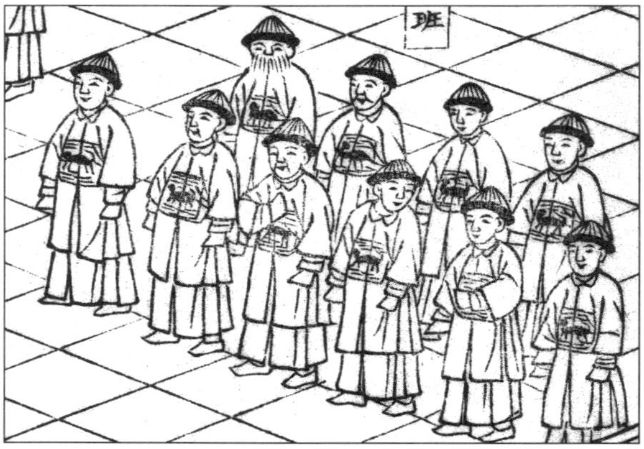

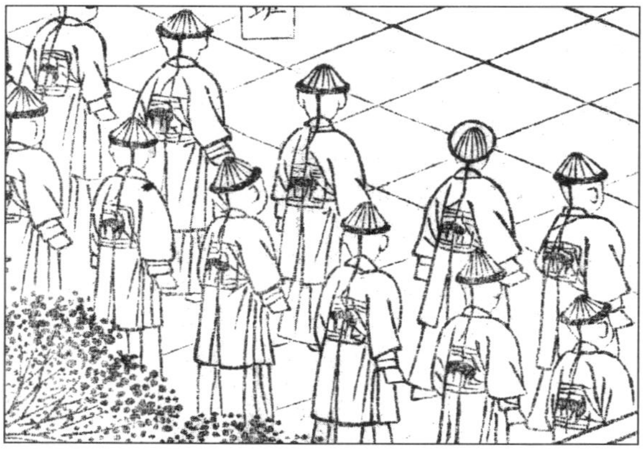

Mandarins en costume de cérémonie (gravure extraite de Tangtu mingsheng tuhui).

Avant que les « carrés » et les « boutons » de mandarin ne soient utilisés pour indiquer le rang d'une personne, seules les boucles de ceinture, incrustées de pierres précieuses, et les chapeaux à pointes permettaient d'identifier leur porteur comme une personne importante dans la hiérarchie du début de l'époque des Ming (1368). Sous les Yuan (1271-1368) toutefois, les nobles portaient déjà, sur la poitrine et dans le dos de leurs robes d'apparat, des broderies ornementales (fleurs, animaux ou oiseaux). Il faut toutefois attendre 1391 pour qu'une instruction fasse mention du « carré de mandarin » (*buzi* ou *xiubu*). Large, sans bordure et de forme presque trapézoïdale (sans doute pour ne pas être cachée par les bras), la pièce était tissée ou brodée directement sur le tissu et coupée dans son milieu pour permettre le boutonnage du devant de la robe. Au moment où les Mandchous prennent le pouvoir (1644) et donnent naissance à la dynastie des Qing, ils ne représentent que deux pour cent de la population totale mais imposent leur costume et leurs coutumes à la population chinoise. Les marques de rang de l'époque précédente sont toutefois conservées et, à quelques variations minimes près, resteront en usage jusqu'en 1911. À cette date, qui marque la fin de l'époque impériale, la robe et la veste courte seront encore portées mais les carrés auront disparu en même temps que la pratique des pieds bandés pour les femmes, interdite par la nouvelle République, et qui en fait disparut vers 1930.

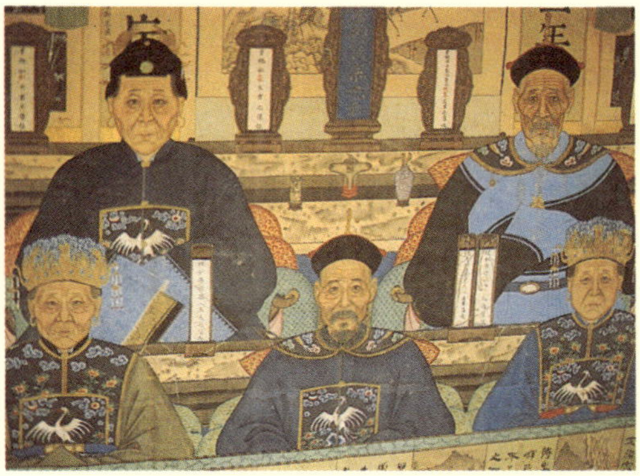

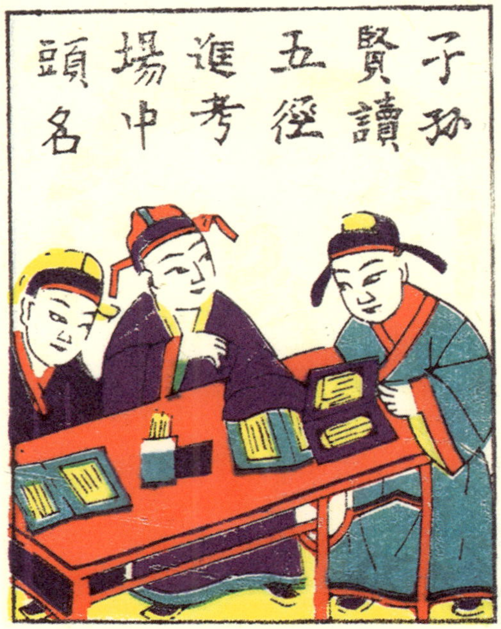

Des variations, dans la taille comme dans la composition, ont eu lieu au cours des différents règnes ; sous Kangxi (1662) par exemple, les carrés deviennent plus petits et les compositions sont chargées. Le disque solaire est introduit dès le XVIIe siècle. Sous Qianlong, en 1766, paraît le *Guide illustré des accessoires cérémoniaux de la dynastie Qing (huangchao liqi tushi)*. À cette période, les carrés sont débarrassés de leur décoration exubérante. En 1843, en vue de générer des revenus, le gouvernement mit en vente les charges mandarinales, entraînant une augmentation de la demande de ces insignes de rang. La production des carrés devint alors quasi industrielle. On préparait à l'avance des décors sur lesquels le motif principal souhaité était appliqué en dernière minute. Cette technique permet actuellement une datation de ces broderies. En 1898, apparut la dernière réforme du jeune empereur Guangxu en vue de simplifier ces marques honorifiques. Elles conservèrent toutefois les motifs d'inspiration bouddhique que les Chinois avaient adoptés. On attribue à Cao Cao, chef militaire et poète (155-220), l'introduction d'un système de promotion fondé sur neuf grades *(jiupin)*.

Dès 1585, l'encyclopédie *Sancai tuhui* présentait pour la première fois des modèles de marques de rang correspondant au grade des fonctionnaires civils *(wenguan)* et militaires *(wuguan)*. Aux premiers les oiseaux, symboles du raffinement des lettrés et d'une bureaucratie céleste, aux seconds des animaux sauvages, emblèmes de leur charge martiale. Compte tenu de la

En haut, portrait d'ancêtres en costume d'apparat et tablettes des ancêtres (peinture sur toile, XVIIIe siècle) ; en bas, groupe d'enfants se préparant aux examens et portant des chapeaux de lettrés (estampe populaire).

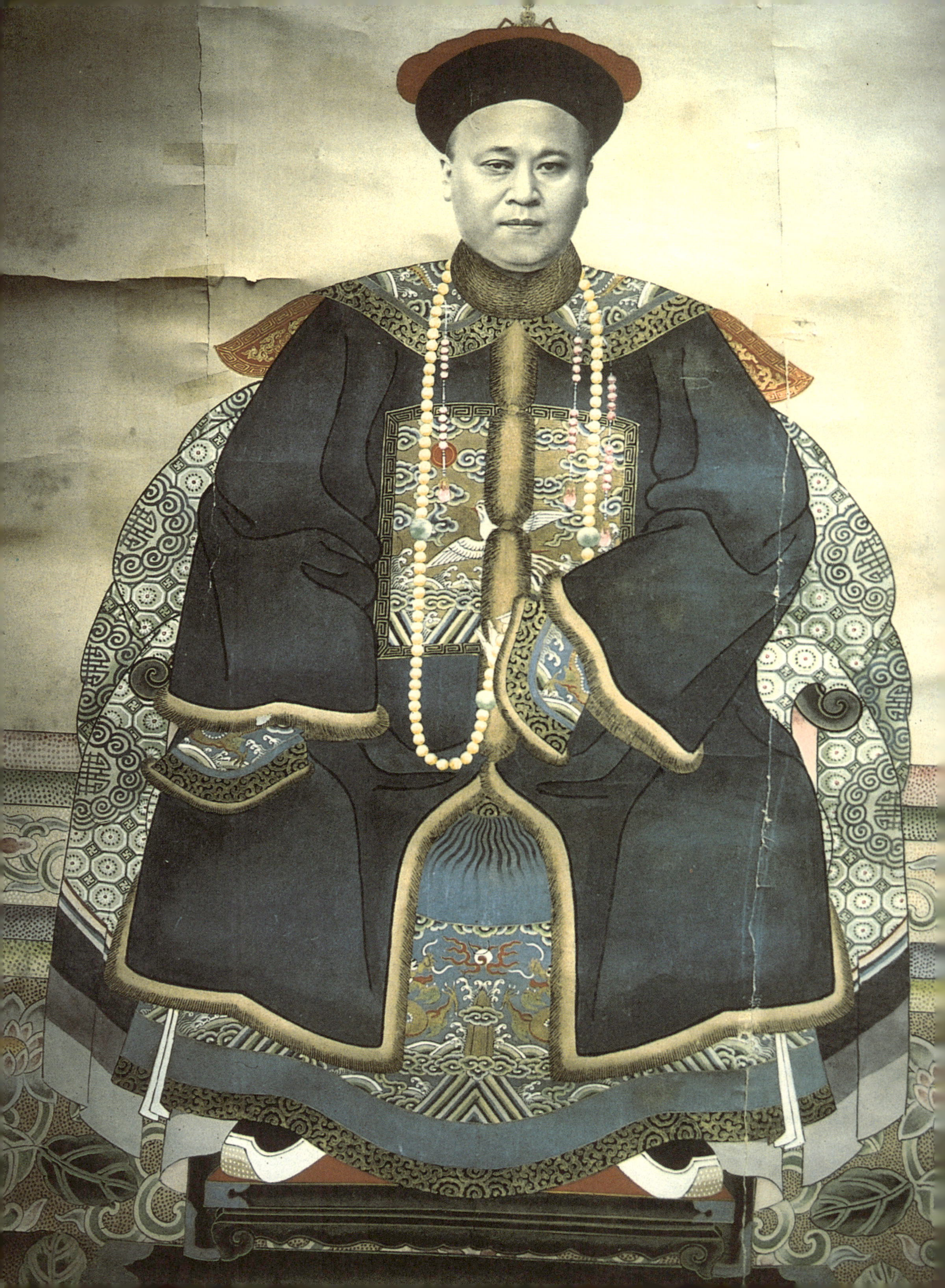

difficulté des examens impériaux, les emplois civils étaient plus appréciés que les carrières militaires, dont la plus grande partie s'exerçait hors de la capitale, loin de la cour. D'ailleurs, la place d'honneur (à gauche) était réservée aux mandarins civils alors que les militaires s'asseyaient ou circulaient protocolairement à droite.

Au sein des deux ordres, il y avait neuf grades qui se subdivisaient en fonctionnaires supérieurs et fonctionnaires subalternes ; leur nombre total avoisinait les 200 000 personnes. En général, les mandarins de première classe exerçaient à l'administration centrale. En province, le gouverneur qui représentait l'empereur appartenait à la 1re classe, le gouverneur adjoint et le superintendant des finances appartenaient à la deuxième classe, les juges provinciaux et le collecteur des impôts à la troisième classe, l'intendant, le collecteur des grains et le préfet à la quatrième classe, le sous-préfet et les juges de district à la cinquième classe, le sous-préfet adjoint à la sixième classe, les juges de rang inférieur à la septième et huitième classe, les inspecteurs de police à la neuvième classe.

Depuis les Ming, les emblèmes des marques de rang se répartirent comme suit :

Grade	Fonctionnaires civils	Fonctionnaires militaires
1re classe	Grue blanche *xianhe*	Lion, *shizi* 1662 : Licorne, *qilin*
2e classe	Faisan doré *jinji*	Lion *shizi*
3e classe	Paon *kongque*	Léopard *feizhoubao*
4e classe	Oie sauvage *dayan*	le tigre *hu*
5e classe	Faisan argenté *baixian*	Ours noir *xiongpi*
6e classe	Aigrette *luci*	Panthère *bao*
7e classe	Canard mandarin *xichi = yuanyang*	Ours tacheté *xiong*
8e classe	Loriot *huangli*	Rhinocéros *xiniu*
9e classe	Oiseau de paradis *lianque*	Cheval blanc de mer *haima*

Page de gauche, portrait de mandarin.

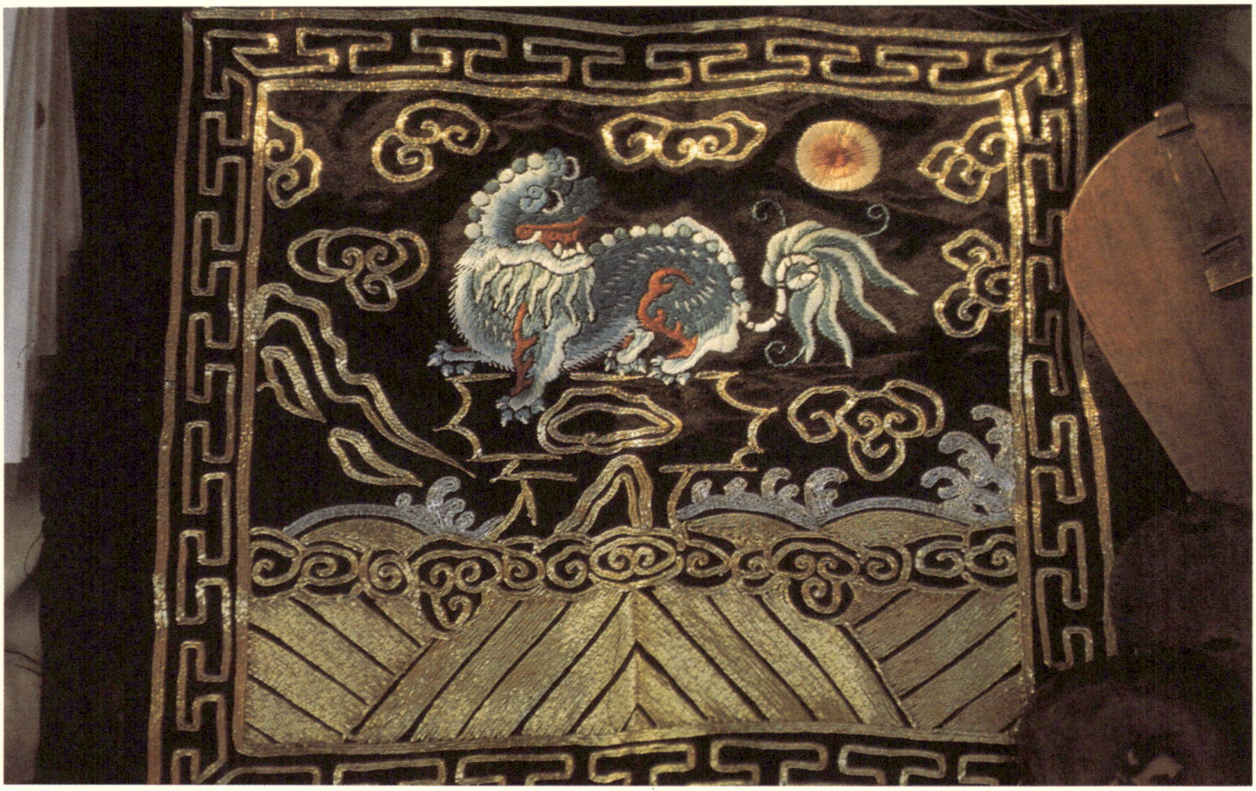

C'est dans le *Guide illustré* de 1766 qu'apparaît la classification des vêtements des nobles Qing : les habits de cour *(chaofu)* pour les grandes occasions, les habits semi officiels *(jifu)* comprenant les « robes au dragon » et les habits non officiels *(changfu)*. Les célèbres « robes au dragon » se divisaient en *long pao* – robes à neuf dragons à cinq griffes, réservées à l'empereur et à sa famille – et en *mangpao* – robes à neuf, huit ou cinq dragons à quatre griffes pour les autres personnalités de la cour. Les vêtement de l'empereur, de l'impératrice, du prince héritier étaient de couleur jaune (clair, abricot ou or), alors que ceux des autres nobles étaient colorés de bleu, de brun ou de noir. Le « lion blanc à corne » *(xiezhai)* ornait l'uniforme des censeurs impériaux chargés de la justice car cet animal mythique pouvait juger du bien et du mal. En récompense d'actes méritoires, on pouvait recevoir de l'empereur des marques de faveur sous la forme de « dragons à cornes » *(douniu)* ou de « dragons-poissons *(feiyu)*.

La composition des carrés *(buzi)* répondait à des règles précises. Au centre, se trouvait le sujet principal (oiseau ou animal) dans un décor comprenant un rocher au milieu des vagues de la mer, un ciel rempli de nuages stylisés et un disque solaire de couleur rouge (parfois brodé de grains de corail) vers lequel regardait le sujet. Il faut, sans doute, voir là le regard du fonctionnaire vers son empereur. Le port des insignes pour les femmes des hauts

Carré de mandarin (broderie d'argent et d'or, dynastie des Qing, XIXe siècle).

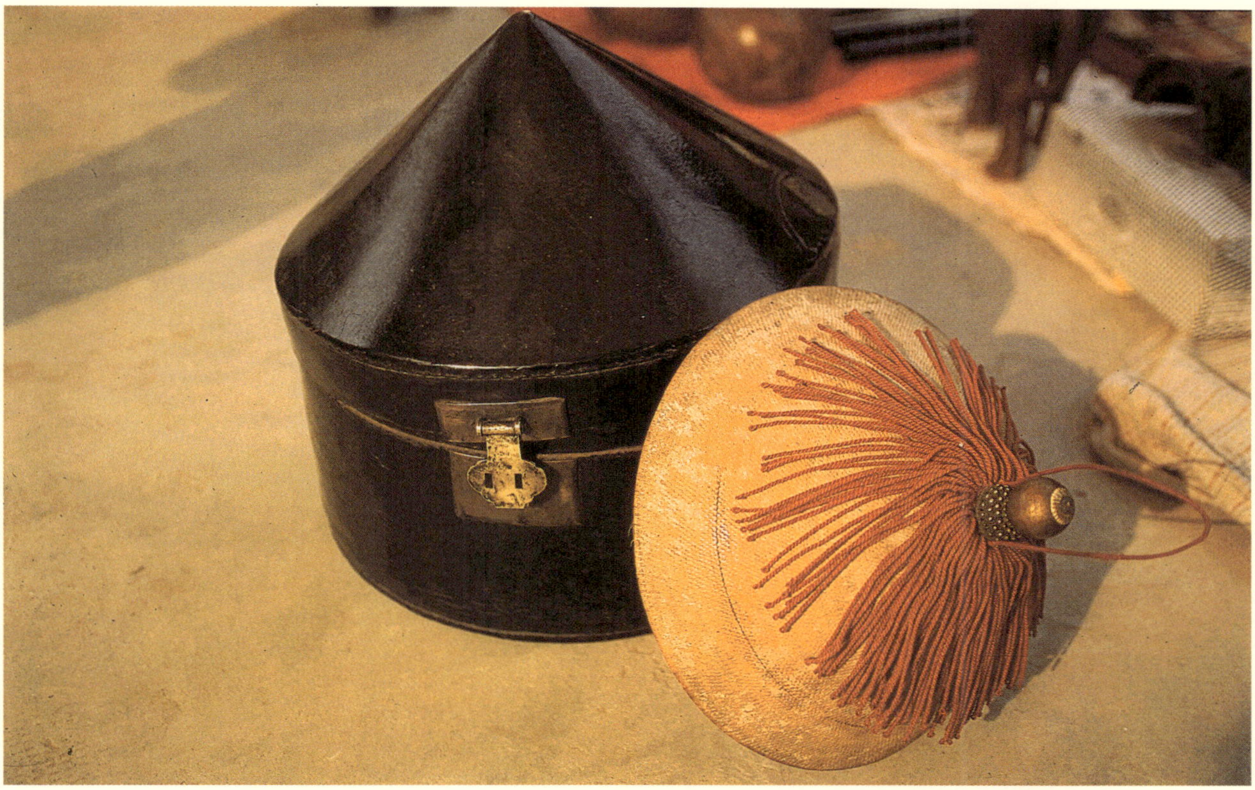

fonctionnaires ou les filles non mariées avait la même rigueur. Le protocole vestimentaire du milieu du XVIIIe siècle précisait qu'elles devaient porter des insignes symétriques à ceux de leurs époux, ou père, de telle sorte qu'assises à leur gauche, les regards des sujets des broderies convergent. Au fil des ans, les artistes introduisirent dans leurs broderies des motifs supplémentaires de décoration : des arbres (pins ou poiriers), des fleurs (pivoines), des montagnes aux formes étranges, et surtout de nombreux emblèmes taoïstes ou bouddhistes (chauve-souris, perle, nœud sans fin, fleur de lotus...). Les variations d'un carré à l'autre pouvaient être importantes. La plupart des artisans brodeurs n'avaient sans doute jamais vu un lion ou un ours de leur vie. Il en résulta des créations très imaginatives. Certains mandarins de rang inférieur, qui ne souhaitaient pas faire apparaître leur rang, ne se plaignaient pas du manque de réalisme des emblèmes et de nombreux abus eurent lieu. Les empereurs eurent à réprimer ces usurpations de titre qui avaient surtout lieu en province. Alors que sous les Ming les « carrés » étaient en général tissés à même la robe (technique *kesi* : brocart ou brochage de soie, d'argent ou d'or), sous les Qing, les carrés brodés, montés sur une doublure de soie, étaient cousus sur la veste trois-quarts bleu foncé *(bufu)*.

Des carrés qui n'avaient plus de caractère officiel furent encore utilisés jusqu'au début du siècle, ornés de motifs floraux (pivoines, chrysanthèmes) ; ils étaient offerts à la famille ou aux amis comme cadeaux. Par ailleurs,

Chapeau de fonctionnaire et son coffret de cuir (dynastie des Qing, XIXe siècle).

soucieux de récompenser certains vieux serviteurs qu'il ne pouvait anoblir, l'empereur offrait des carrés avec la mention en larges caractères « conféré par grâce impériale » *(huang'en qin zi)*. Les prêtres taoïstes portaient aussi des carrés sur le devant et dans le dos de leur robe avec des motifs religieux, essentiellement l'emblème du « faîte suprême ».

Parmi les accessoires que comprenait le costume de mandarin figurait en bonne place le couvre-chef. Un personnage important n'était jamais tête nue, sauf dans ses appartements privés, et encore portait-il une petite calotte. Les règles imposaient un changement de chapeau et de vêtements selon les saisons, qui faisait l'objet d'une annonce dans le *Journal Officiel*. Ainsi, dès le huitième mois du calendrier lunaire, on portait un petit chapeau de satin noir au bord retourné (quelquefois bordé de fourrure ou de velours noir) et dont le dessus était décoré de franges rouges. Certains de ces chapeaux portaient même de fausses tresses de soie ou de cheveux quand leur propriétaire était chauve. (En effet, quand les Mandchous prirent le pouvoir en 1644, ils imposèrent aux Chinois le port de la natte). En été, on mettait un chapeau de paille conique (pour les fonctionnaires des classes inférieures) ou de fines lamelles de bambou (pour les fonctionnaires plus importants) recouvert de franges rouges de soie, de poils de cheval ou de chèvre colorés. Ces chapeaux relativement coûteux portaient le nom de leur propriétaire à l'intérieur et étaient conservés dans de luxueuses boîtes à chapeau en cuir tapissées de soie rouge.

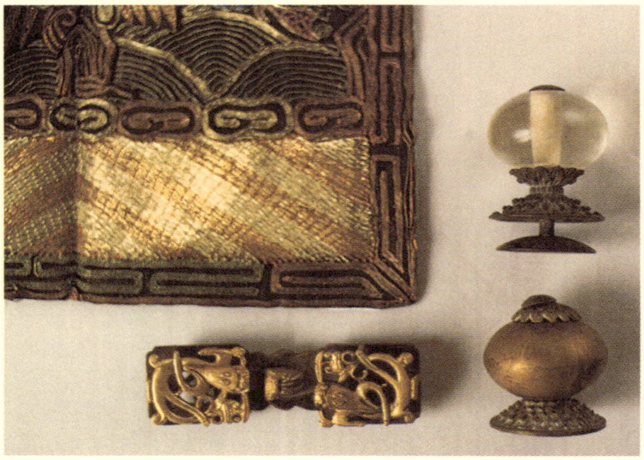

Tous ces chapeaux de cérémonie portaient au sommet un dispositif pour adapter un bijou qui désignait le rang de son propriétaire. Il était identique pour les militaires et pour les civils. C'était une petite boule vissée sur un socle de métal doré. Instaurés en 1727 par l'empereur Yongzheng, ces insignes de chapeau *(ding)* appelés en Europe « boutons de mandarin », n'étaient arborés que lors des cérémonies officielles. De 1730 à 1911, ils se classaient ainsi : le corail ou le verre rouge opaque pour la 1re classe, le même avec le caractère *shou* pour la 2e classe, le saphir ou le verre bleu transparent pour la 3e classe, le lapis-lazuli ou le verre bleu opaque pour la 4e classe, le cristal ou le verre transparent pour la 5e classe, la « pierre de lune » (adulaire) ou le verre blanc pour la 6e classe, le métal doré plein pour la 7e classe, le même avec le caractère *shou* pour la 8e classe, le métal doré avec deux caractères *shou* pour la 9e classe.

Divers boutons de mandarin, de 5e classe (cristal), de 8e classe (métal doré), plaquettes-boucles de ceinture (XIXe siècle).

Par ailleurs, de la 1re à la 5e classe, les fonctionnaires pouvaient fixer à leur coiffe de une à trois plumes de paon *(huayu)*, qui étaient accordées par faveur impériale aux fonctionnaires méritants. Le nombre d'ocelles (yeux de la plume) correspondait à l'importance des honneurs. Leur attribution comme leur retrait étaient soigneusement consignés dans un recueil biographique, véritable *Who's who* avant l'heure. Quant aux fonctionnaires de moindre rang, ils devaient se contenter des plumes bleu-noir de corbeau *(lanyu)*. Tous ces fragiles accessoires honorifiques étaient d'ailleurs conservés dans de magnifiques plumiers laqués.

Il était encore prévu par le protocole, pour les fonctionnaires des cinq premières classes, le port d'un collier d'apparat, improprement appelé « collier de mandarin » *(chaozhu)* composé de 108 grains de jade, de corail, d'ivoire ou de perles, terminé par un pendentif en forme de gourde. Celui-ci, placé dans le dos, servait de contrepoids au reste du collier. Inspiré du rosaire des moines bouddhistes que le Dalai Lama offrit à l'empereur Shunzhi en 1643, le collier comprenait quatre grosses boules dénommées « têtes de Bouddha » *(fotou)* qui étaient placés tous les 27 grains. Les perles d'eau douce étaient aussi très prisées par les Mandchous qui les appelaient « perles de l'Orient » *(dongzhu)* car elles venaient de la Mandchourie, exclusivement de la rivière Songhua (province du Heilongjiang).

Alors que les carrés de mandarin allaient disparaître dans les convulsions de la fin de la dynastie des Qing (1912), leur usage se prolongea à l'extérieur des frontières de la Chine. Dès le XVe siècle, la Corée avait emprunté les modèles chinois, elle les transforma au XIXe siècle. En Indochine, le royaume d'Annam adopta en 1744 pour ses hauts fonctionnaires la mode des Qing, qui se prolongea jusqu'au début du siècle.

Les marques de dignité qui avaient été arborées avec arrogance pendant plus de cinq cents ans par l'aristocratie et l'administration chinoise vont désigner leurs propriétaires à la vindicte populaire quand se déclencha la révolution de 1911. Beaucoup de ces petits chefs-d'œuvre, en particulier les insignes militaires, disparurent dans les pillages et les bouleversements sociaux que connut alors le pays. La tradition du « carré » sera toutefois préservée par les « portraits d'ancêtres » que l'on commandait à l'occasion d'anniversaires ou de mariages. Avant l'avènement de la photographie, ils étaient réalisés par des artistes-peintres qui proposaient à la famille de choisir dans les catalogues de stéréotypes ce qui lui semblait être le plus ressemblant au défunt. Quand la photographie parvint en Chine, les artistes n'eurent qu'à placer les têtes photographiées au-dessus de costumes peints à l'avance avec le plus grand détail, en fonction du rang social annoncé. De nombreuses peintures généalogiques ont été réalisées au début du siècle et elles ont perpétué, dans ce style un peu figé des photographies d'autrefois, le souvenir ces extraordinaires broderies qui étaient le reflet d'une société parfaitement hiérarchisée.

Chanteurs et combattants en cage

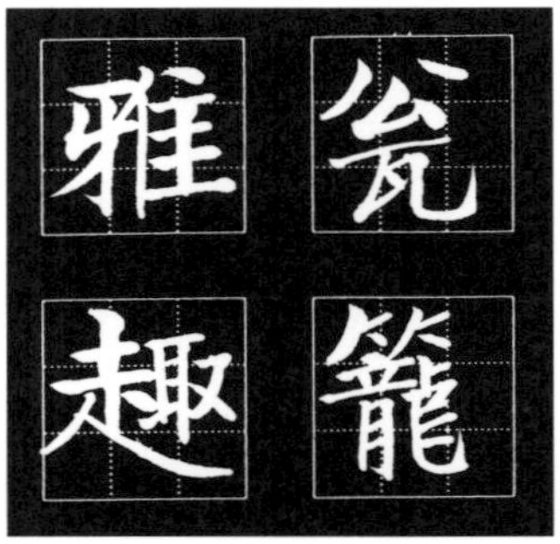

wong long yaqu, littéralement, « plaisirs distingués des pots et des cages à grillons ».

Les Chinois ont toujours manifesté un intérêt particulier pour l'infiniment petit ; très tôt ils se sont passionnés pour les insectes – grillons, criquets, cigales, mantes religieuses, libellules, papillons... – qui figurent en bonne place dans la poésie, la sculpture, la peinture et même la médecine. On citera à cet effet le célèbre manuel du XVIIe siècle, le *Jardin grand comme un grain de moutarde,* qui décrit chacun des insectes de manière détaillée. Comme les fleurs, ils ont été dotés de qualités, d'une symbolique. Il n'est donc pas étonnant que ce soit à ce peuple que revienne le mérite d'avoir inventé la soie, mieux que quiconque il a su se pencher avec tant d'attention sur le modeste ver à soie... Tous ces insectes ont donné lieu à d'admirables miniatures, à de merveilleux bibelots qui étaient échangés comme de précieux cadeaux.

Un vieil adage chinois place pourtant les insectes en première position parmi les « quatre calamités » de l'agriculture (insectes, givre, inondation et sécheresse ; *chong, shuang, shui, han*). Le mille-pattes et le scorpion se rangeaient aussi parmi les « Cinq venimeux » dont il fallait se protéger par des sacrifices. Présents sur la terre depuis 225 millions d'années, les grillons font l'objet de la part des Chinois d'un amour très particulier pour leur chant. Selon Carol Hammond *(The Courtly Crickets),* la « culture » du criquet s'est développée historiquement en trois phases. Dans l'antiquité, les grillons étaient appréciés pour leur chant, dans une seconde période, sous les Tang (618-906), ils furent mis en cage et trouvèrent place dans les maisons où l'on appréciait leur compagnie (cette mode gagna le Japon dès le VIIIe siècle), puis du Xe au XIIIe siècle, se développa chez les Chinois un engouement particulier pour les combats de grillons qui n'a pas cessé.

La sauterelle jaune ou verte *(mazha),* appartient, comme le criquet, à l'ordre des orthoptères mais le criquet n'a pas de tarière ; ils sont connus pour leurs ravages des cultures. Des sacrifices étaient offerts au génie protecteur des récoltes *(mazhashen)* contre les invasions de criquets pèlerins, tout comme se développa le mythe du féroce général Liou qui, sabre au poing, dispersait des nuages de ces insectes malfaisants... En Chine, le criquet vert dénommé *guoguor,* est vendu pour son chant particulièrement strident dans des cages de fibres tressées en boules ajourées. Elles sont accrochées ensemble par les colporteurs qui se promènent avec ces charmants « arbres sonores ».

Les appellations du grillon, en revanche, sont beaucoup plus nombreuses, variées et poétiques. Le grillon des champs se nomme *xishuai* et le grillon de combat *doushuai* ou *douxishuai,* mais dans la langue de Pékin on utilise cette admirable onomatopée de *ququr.* Toutefois, un insecte aussi populaire ne pouvait se contenter d'un seul nom. On parlait de « celui qui active le tissage » *(chuzhi)* parce que son chant stridulant rappelle celui d'un métier à tisser ou d'une machine *(chuji).* La langue littéraire a eu d'admirables images pour le célébrer selon sa forme (*youhulu,* « gourde luisante » ; *jinbaoda,* « pagode d'or »), et pour son cricri (*jinzhong,* « clochette d'or » ; *maling,* « cheval à sonnette » ; *qingling,* « chenille musicale »). On l'a même qualifié à tort, de « libellule céleste » *(tianling),* de « chien de terre » *(tugou)* ou de « rat de pierre » *(shishu).*

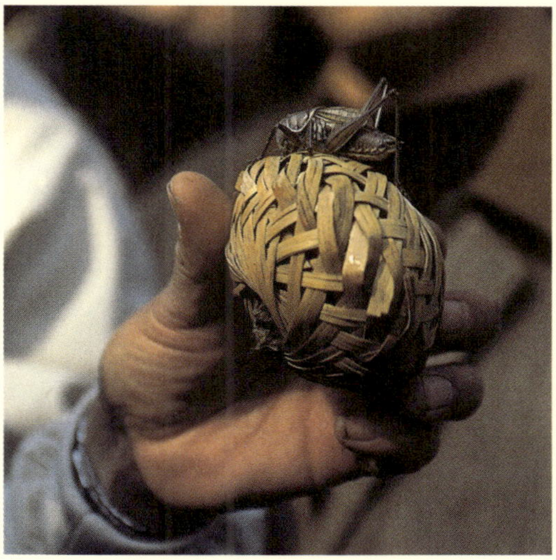

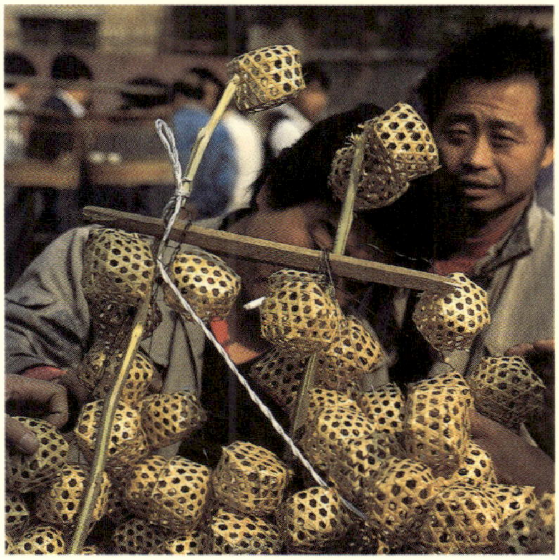

Les grillons appartiennent à la famille des *gryllidæ* (du latin *gryllidus*). À en croire les spécialistes chinois, on compterait pas moins de soixante espèces de combattants, de forme et couleur différentes. La femelle est reconnaissable à sa tarière (organe qui lui permet de déposer ses œufs dans la terre). Seuls les grillons, les criquets et les cigales mâles chantent. Les jeunes et les femelles ne produisent aucun son. En Chine, les grillons les plus connus sont :

– *gryllus mitratus Burmeister,* de couleur noir foncé, on le trouve dans la région de Pékin et de Suzhou, réputé comme combattant et chanteur, mais sans valeur pour les gens du Shandong qui le donnent à manger à leurs oiseaux...

– *homeogryllus japonicus Haan,* est connu sous le nom de « clochette d'or » ;

– *gryllus testaceus Walker* (ou grillon du sud), jaune brun foncé, est plus grand que le précédent ;

– *teleogryllus infernalis Saussure* se trouve dans la province du Gansu et se caractérise par des pattes noires et des mandibules rougeâtres ;

– *loxoblemmus doenitzi Stein,* grillon à tête plate (ou « tête de grand cercueil » en raison de la forme de sa tête), est de couleur brun foncé à noir ;

– *loxoblemmus arietulus Saussure,* grillon à « tête de petit cercueil » *(xiao guantou)* est plus petit et de couleur uniformément noire ;

– *scapsipedes aspersus Walker* ou grillon à longues mâchoires *(changge xishuai)* se caractérise par sa petite taille et sa voix très aigue ;

– *scapsipedes micado Saussure* est connu pour son caractère agressif.

En haut, criquet noir sur sa cage de fibres tressées (guoguor) *; en bas, un « arbre sonore » de cages à criquets.*

Les provinces du Nord les plus réputées pour leurs combattants sont le Shandong et le Hebei, dans le Sud, c'est la région de Shanghai, le Jiangsu, le Zhejiang, l'Anhui et la région de Canton.

Certes la vie de ces insectes qui semble suivre dans leurs métamorphoses les trois âges de la vie ne pouvait qu'intriguer, mais c'est surtout leur chant particulièrement joyeux qui a charmé les Chinois. Selon le *Livre des Odes,* les grillons qui sont nés à l'été, « vivent à découvert pendant la septième lune, se rapprochent des maisons à la huitième, chantent devant la porte à la neuvième, et se cachent sous le lit à la dixième... »

Dès le VIIIe siècle, sous la dynastie des Tang, des gravures montrent des concubines alanguies qui ont placé des grillons dans des cages dorées près de leur oreiller pour tromper leur ennui. Cette mode se répandit très vite dans toutes les classes de la société et les artisans créèrent de ravissantes cages et boîtes à grillons dans toutes les matières. C'est sous les Song du sud, à l'époque de l'empereur Lizong (1224 -1264), que fut écrit le premier traité sur les grillons par Jia Setao, un de ses ministres. Ce lettré qui s'intéressa à tous les domaines de l'art possédait dans sa riche demeure de Hangzhou de merveilleuses antiquités et une extraordinaire collection de grillons. Il serait l'auteur du *Zujijing,* un des ouvrages encyclopédiques les plus connus sur les mœurs, l'élevage, le dressage et les soins à prodiguer aux grillons. Un complément à cette étrange encyclopédie par Liu Tong paraîtra sous les Ming. La légende attribue d'ailleurs à sa passion excessive pour les grillons la fin tragique du ministre qui, banni par l'empereur, fut condamné à mort pour avoir négligé les affaires de l'État. Les anecdotes concernant l'impératrice douairière Tseu Hi *(Cixi)* font mention de son talent pour imiter leur chant afin de les attirer sur elle. Les méthodes de capture de ces insectes étaient nombreuses et variaient selon les régions ; la chasse se faisait en général de nuit. Dans le nord de la Chine, on plaçait une chandelle allumée devant leur trou. Attirés par la lumière, ils sautaient dans une boîte-piège placée à cet effet près de la bougie. Dans le sud, on mettait des braises rougeoyantes dans un petit récipient, on versait de l'eau dans leurs trous ou on les appâtait avec des fruits mûrs. Les chasseurs de grillons étaient munis de petits paniers tressés en forme de nasse.

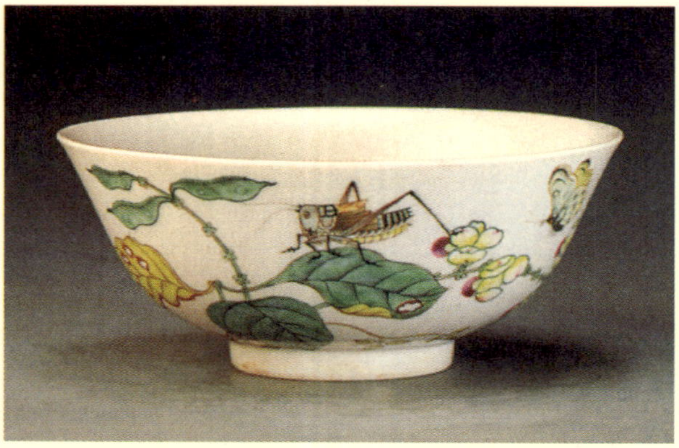

Seuls des personnages influents pouvaient posséder des « écuries » de grillons, car cela demandait du personnel et un outillage délicat. La tradition de l'élevage des grillons est encore bien vivace de nos aujourd'hui parmi les gens du peuple et il est toujours possible de trouver tous les accessoires dans les différents marchés aux oiseaux où une section leur est toujours consacrée.

Motif de criquet peint sur un bol de porcelaine blanche (XVIIe siècle).

Les boîtes à grillons *(hulu)* les plus répandues et les plus anciennes étaient faites dans la gourde *(lapenaria vulgaris)*. Ce fruit de la famille des cucurbitacées est placé très tôt dans un moule de plâtre portant des motifs intérieurs. En poussant, le fruit épouse très exactement la forme du moule et, après séchage, donne un étui de forme oblongue décoré en relief. L'intérieur est tapissé d'une matière blanchâtre, semblable au plâtre, pour rendre l'habitat plus confortable. Son couvercle est souvent fait d'ivoire, de bois précieux ou de jade finement ajouré pour laisser passer l'air. Ces récipients étaient autrefois portés dans une poche de poitrine pour les réchauffer au contact du corps, ou suspendus à la ceinture par une lanière. Ils pouvaient aussi être fabriqués dans d'autres matières plus nobles comme l'ivoire ou la corne. De nos jours, pour le transport en hiver du précieux occupant, la boîte est quelquefois entourée d'un filet de laine amoureusement tricoté par son propriétaire.

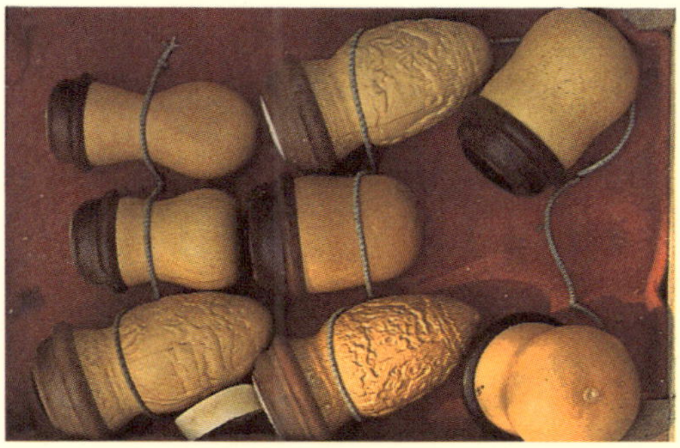

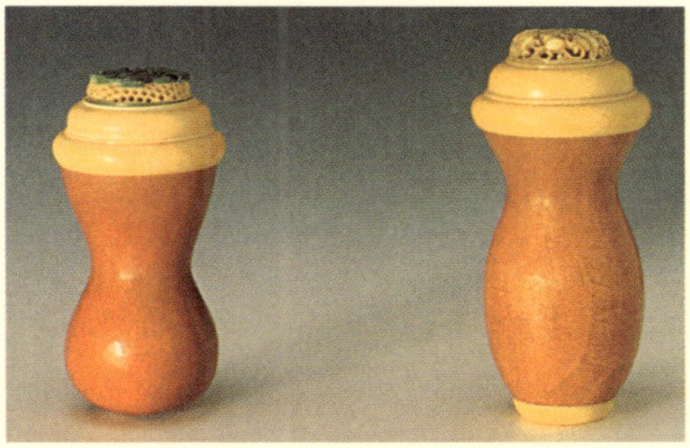

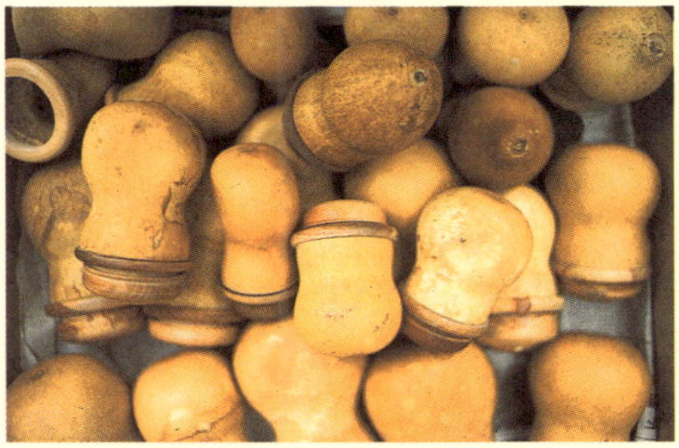

Il existait aussi des boîtes à grillons de porcelaine cylindriques ou en forme de losange avec un couvercle percé de trous. Ces pièces pour intérieurs aristocratiques furent produites, sous les Qing, en porcelaine blanc de Chine ou avec des motifs floraux ou animaliers.

Les pots à grillons généralement cylindriques, avec un couvercle, sont en terre cuite rouge, noire ou grise, rarement en porcelaine. Appelés *ququguan,* ils servent à élever les insectes et à les transporter. Le sol du récipient est, en général, sablé ; les parois extérieures sont richement décorées de moulages de scènes mythologiques.

Les cages pour grillons ou criquets sont construites sur le principe des cages à oiseaux, mais elles se caractérisent par la finesse du travail. Elles possèdent une petite porte à potence qui coulisse du haut vers le bas. Le toit de la cage porte souvent quatre caractères : *ge you suo le* (littéralement, « chacun a sa raison de se réjouir »). Ces cages qui mesurent de 5 à 10 cm de haut sont de forme hexagonale, cylindrique ou cubique ; elles sont en ivoire, en argent ou en bois de bambou laqué.

À côté de ces accessoires destinés au transport ou à l'élevage, on trouvera encore sur les marchés d'étonnants petits « échangeurs » pour grillons de combats *(guolong)*. Ce sont de petits tunnels d'argile grise – une couleur qui n'effraie pas les insectes – utilisés comme chambre de rencontre *(guo-*

Boîtes à grillon en gourde évidée ; au milieu, boîte avec couvercle d'ivoire ajouré (XVIIIe siècle).

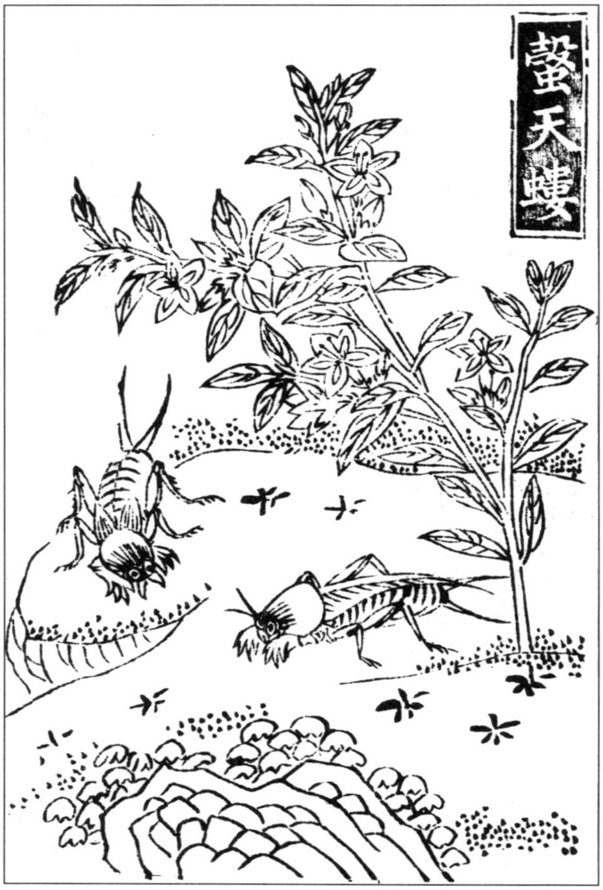

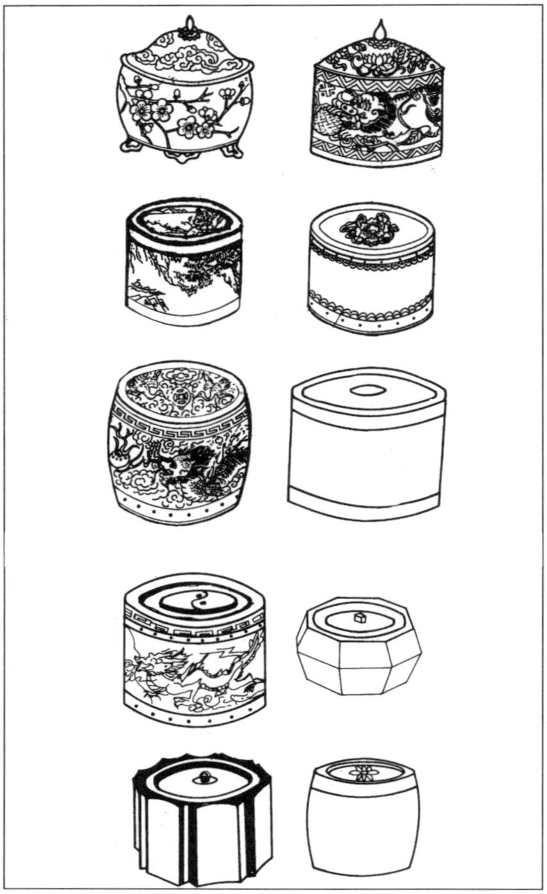

long). Parce qu'ils sont sensibles à la trop grande lumière et au bruit, c'est une véritable « chambre nuptiale » qu'on offre au mâle et à la femelle à la saison des amours sous la forme de cette étrange boîte à couvercle et à deux entrées arquée pour suivre la courbure du pot. Il y a aussi des pinces pour leur présenter de la nourriture et de minuscules pelles pour déposer les aliments dans les plats, autant d'instruments ingénieux pour dispenser des soins attentionnés à ces délicats insectes. Une vaisselle de porcelaine décorée et forcément lilliputienne leur était réservée. On y déposait d'infimes doses de nourriture : du riz jaune mélangé à du concombre, des marrons, des haricots préalablement mastiqués mélangés avec du poisson (de la perche de préférence), des insectes et des larves.

La passion des Chinois pour les grillons s'expliquerait aussi par le fait que nombreuses espèces sont naturellement aptes au combat. Leurs propriétaires s'engageaient dans des paris effrénés lors de rencontres d'extérieur (jardins, places publiques ou marchés) ou d'intérieur (maisons de thé) lors des « amusements d'automne ». Les grandes manches des robes chinoises traditionnelles du début du siècle des hommes permettaient de fixer à l'abri des regards curieux, par attouchements des doigts, le montant des paris. L'encyclopédie traitant de la préparation des combattants explique

À gauche, grillons (extrait du dictionnaire Ying Songchao huitu erya*) ; à droite, évolution des formes de boîtes à grillons en argile ou porcelaine, de la dynastie des Song aux Qing.*

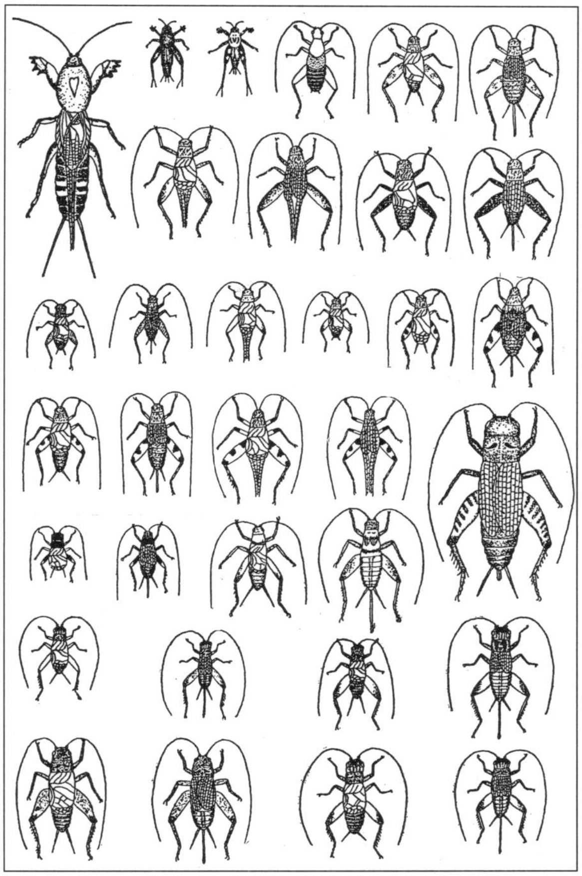

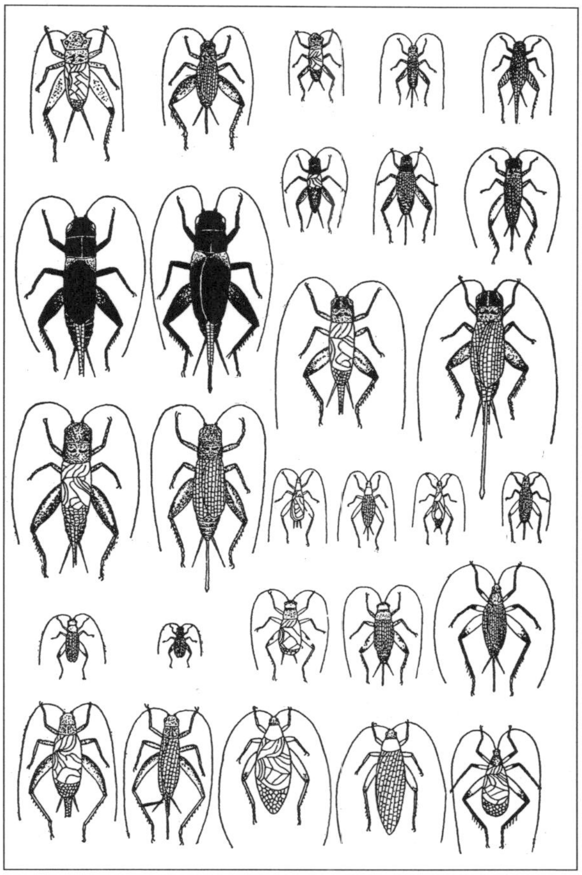

comment les mettre au régime, comment leur donner plus d'agressivité en les nourrissant de moustiques gavés de sang, comment soigner leurs blessures en les baignant dans du thé, comment les guérir d'un coup de froid avec une goutte d'urine d'enfant… Le miel et les moustiques étaient réservés aux combattants. Les règles concernant l'élevage selon les saisons étaient bien précises, tout comme le régime alimentaire. Il fallait surveiller sans cesse leur santé et, avant le combat, séparer les mâles des femelles pour qu'ils gardent leurs forces. La sélection de bons combattants est affaire d'expérience. Les meilleurs se distinguent par un chant strident, une grosse tête et un cou fort, de longues pattes, un corps et un dos massifs. Rien n'est trop beau pour celui qui, vainqueur du championnat, se voit qualifié du titre de «grand maréchal» et a droit à sa mort à des obsèques officielles. On raconte qu'un des héros eut même droit à un petit cercueil en argent. S'il avait été vainqueur plusieurs fois, il s'échangeait alors à des prix astronomiques après avoir rapporté à son maître les honneurs et la fortune.

De nos jours, ces joutes sont toujours pratiquées vers le 15 août, au moment du festival de la Lune, à l'écart des marchés d'oiseaux, dans des parcs ou des cours retirées, même si les paris sont officiellement interdits. Les ren-

Planches des soixante espèces de grillons combattants (d'après Yin Ch'i Hsu, Crickets in China*).*

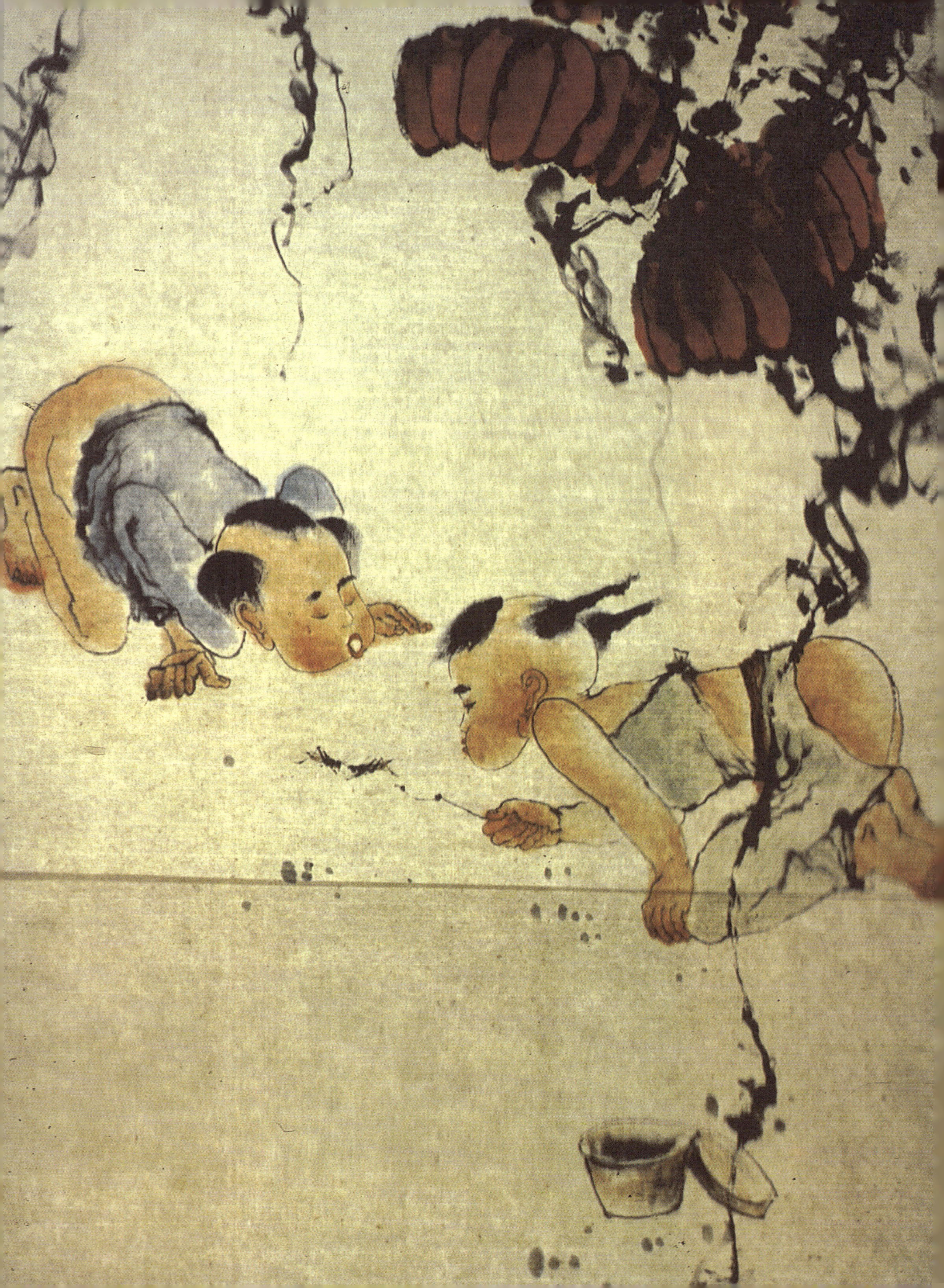

contres se font la plupart du temps dans des « arènes » de terre cuite ou de poterie émaillée *(ququpan)* : une sorte de coupe d'une vingtaine de centimètres de diamètre et à la paroi rentrante. Semblables aux boxeurs ou aux lutteurs, les grillons ne peuvent combattre que dans leur catégorie, en fonction de leur poids (lourd, moyen, léger). Avant l'épreuve, ils sont quelquefois marqués d'une touche de couleur pour les reconnaître. Pour le pesage, il existe d'admirables balances miniatures à fléau vendues dans un ravissant coffret. Afin de mettre en condition leur combattant, les propriétaires se servent de fins pinceaux faits d'herbes sèches spécialement sélectionnées *(xishuaicao)* ou de poils de cheval, de chèvre, de porc, de lièvre, ou de moustaches de rat et même de mille-pattes séché, avec lesquels ils caressent la queue, les jambes, les mâchoires et les antennes. Le grillon réagit immédiatement en montrant les crocs et en écartant les antennes, manifestant ainsi ses aptitudes au combat. Les manches de ces « baguettes à exciter » *(dougun)* sont taillés dans l'ivoire, dans un bois rare ou un fin bambou. Instruments fragiles, elles étaient transportées dans des étuis *(caotong)* de bambou, de loupe de bois ou d'ivoire de fort grand prix. Les combats s'achèvent rarement par la mort, tout au plus par de graves blessures causées par les morsures que s'infligent les belligérants en utilisant des prises dans lesquelles les spécialistes croient retrouver le célèbre *kongfu* (une vingtaine d'entre elles auraient été répertoriées).

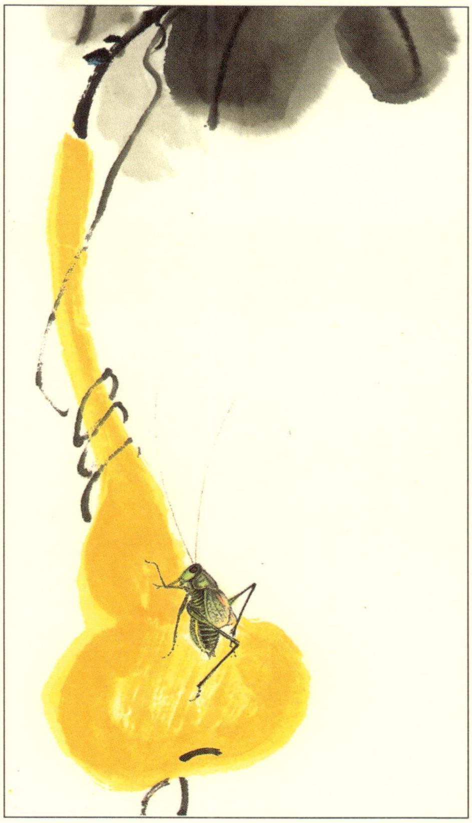

Page de gauche, enfants de la campagne engagés dans un combat de grillons (peinture anonyme, XVIIe siècle) ; ci-dessus, grillon et gourde (peinture sur papier à l'encre et couleurs) ; page suivante, cages en bois et boîte à grillon de poche, vaisselle et baguette (dougun). Au second plan, épingle à cheveux décorée d'un grillon en cloisonné de plumes bleues et, derrière, cigale en terre cuite.

Les combats de grillons sont toujours très populaires ; les règles ont peu varié et l'enthousiasme des parieurs n'a pas faibli. En revanche, l'habitat de ces insectes s'est modernisé. D'ingénieux artisans fabriquent maintenant en laiton ou en bois précieux décoré de marqueterie de petites « résidences » à deux ou trois places, avec vitres, panneaux grillagés, portes coulissantes et mangeoires. Certaines de ces boîtes sont galbées pour prendre place l'hiver dans une poche de chemise. La chaleur du corps humain se propageant à la boîte incite alors le locataire à chanter au grand ravissement de son propriétaire. Certes, originaux par leur conception et leur décoration, touchants d'ingéniosité, ces étuis de transport n'ont toutefois plus le charme des boîtes ou des cages d'antan.

Le quartier des marchands de grillons est toujours un endroit plein d'intérêt où l'on ressent bien la passion que portent les amateurs à ces minuscules insectes dont ils font un commerce très actif. Les étals offrent ainsi à l'ache-

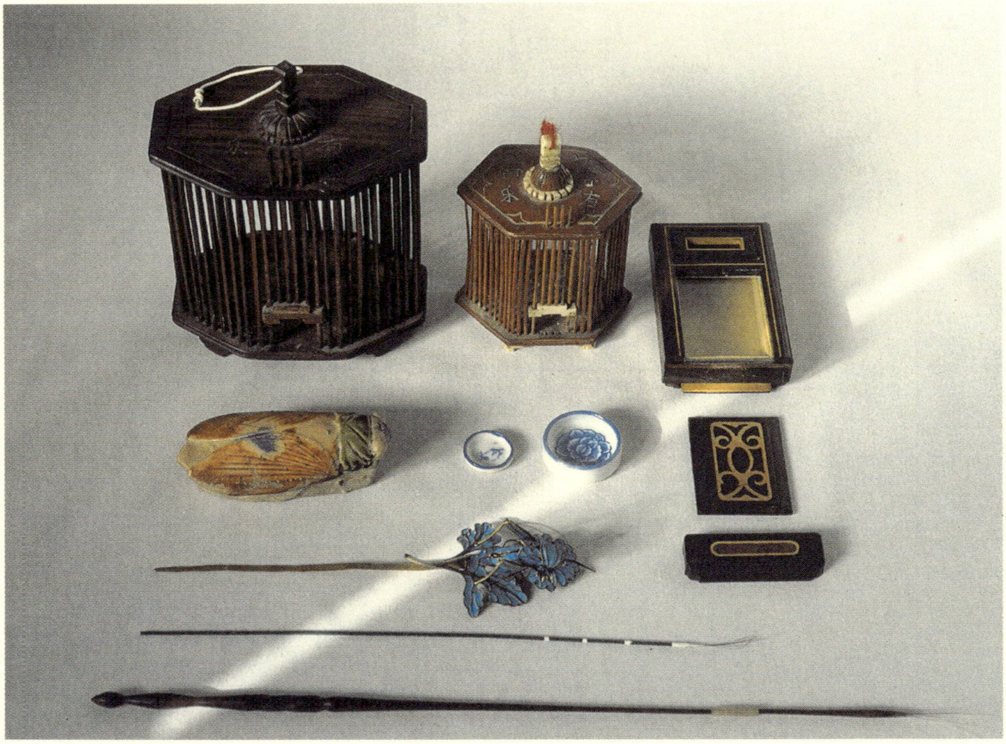

teur des rangées interminables de petites boîtes vitrées ou de fioles où sont classés les insectes d'espèces diverses comme les grillons, les sauterelles, les criquets, les lucioles, les araignées (que l'on engage aussi dans des combats)… Leur prix varie selon les qualités annoncées, il peut atteindre des sommes rondelettes.

Munis de filets de soie coniques, nobles et bourgeois n'hésitaient pas à se divertir en organisant des chasses aux grillons ou aux criquets dans les jardins de leurs résidences. On les mettait ensuite dans des cages accrochées dans les arbres ou dans les fourrés pour le plaisir des oreilles avant de libérer, à la tombée de la nuit, des vers luisants et des lucioles pour le plaisir des yeux.

Connu aussi au Japon sous les noms « d'insecte-cloche » *(suzumushi)* ou « criquet du pin » *(matsumushi),* le grillon, plus que tout autre insecte, a connu et connaît encore une faveur particulière auprès du public car il a su capter le cœur de l'homme par ses talents inégalés. Pour s'en convaincre, il n'est que de relever le grand nombre de références faites tout au long de l'histoire, par les poètes et les peintres chinois dont un des maîtres contemporains de la peinture traditionnelle, Qi Baishi (1854-1957).

Les chevaux de papier

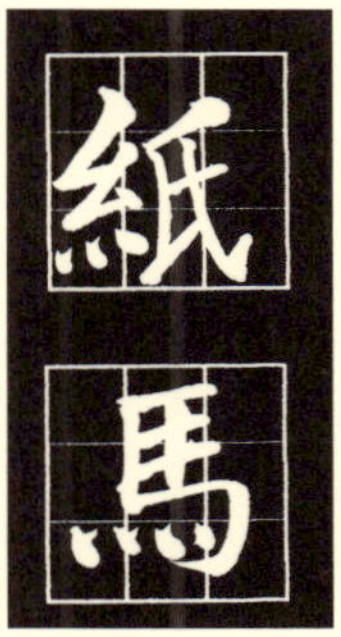

zhima, littéralement, « chevaux de papier ».

L'invention du papier, attribuée aux Chinois, date de l'époque des Han de l'Est (IIe siècle). L'impression de textes à l'aide d'une planche de bois gravé (xylographie) semble avoir été réalisée pour la première fois entre 175 et 183 ap. J.-C., à Luoyang, l'ancienne capitale. En revanche, la reproduction de dessins par le même procédé (xylogravure) pourrait avoir débuté vers le VIe siècle.

Selon le sinologue français Paul Pelliot, c'est dans l'invention du sceau qu'il faut rechercher l'origine de ces deux techniques d'impression. En effet, avec le développement du bouddhisme en Chine, on commença d'imprimer avec des blocs de bois, notamment dans la région occidentale du Yangzi Jiang (Fleuve Bleu), sur du papier ou de l'étoffe, des formules magiques, puis plus tard des textes et enfin des illustrations. Cette tradition est d'ailleurs toujours utilisée dans certains temples où les pèlerins font apposer des marques sacrées, contre paiement d'une obole, sur des morceaux d'étoffe ou des sacs de tissu de couleur jaune. De ces expériences destinées à répandre la foi naîtra l'imprimerie. Plus tard, les besoins des lettrés pour se procurer les *Classiques* (œuvres de Confucius) qui étaient gravés sur pierre, créèrent une demande d'impression sur bois en vue d'une plus grande diffusion. Le premier modèle de livre semble avoir été réalisé au Xe siècle, par Feng Tao, que les Chinois considèrent comme le père de l'imprimerie ; il s'agit des *Impressions du Collège Impérial*. On utilisa la xylogravure pour reproduire les images du Bouddha, sensiblement à la même époque ; le *Soutra du Diamant,* qui date de 868, est la première estampe à caractère religieux connue. Bien sûr, ces documents étaient réalisés en nombre limité, pour une certaine classe – les religieux et les lettrés – et sont donc rares. La relative prospérité du pays sous les Tang et sous les Song (XIe siècle) entraîna le développement de l'imprimerie d'images, le plus souvent à caractère religieux. C'est de cette période, dit le *Dongjing menghua lu* que date la coutume d'afficher sur les portes des images de bon augure. La fête du Printemps était non seulement l'occasion de coller ou d'offrir des images à thème mais aussi de placer de part et d'autre de la

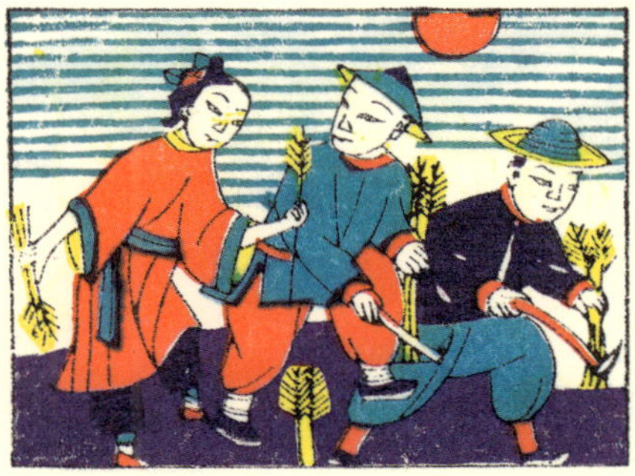

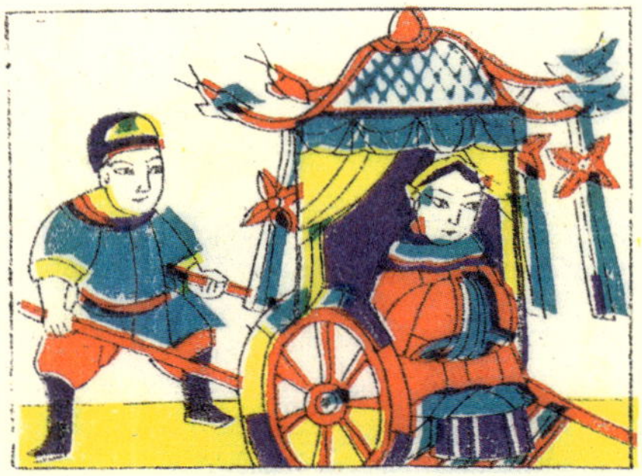

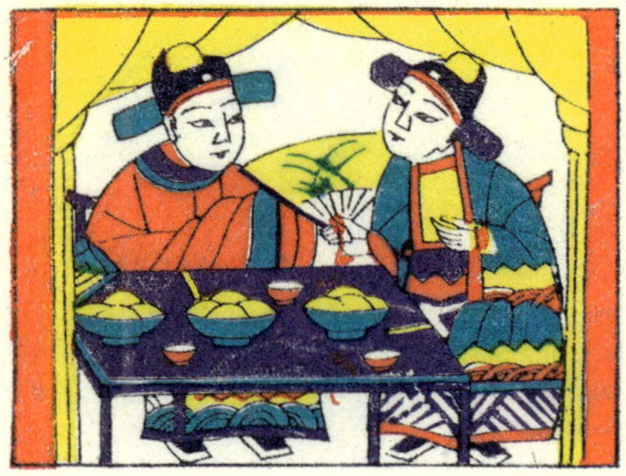

Gravures populaires de la province du Shandong : la récolte du riz, voyage en chaise à porteur, banquet de lettrés.

porte et sur le linteau des bandes de papier rouge portant des inscription auspicieuses (*tianxing* ou *hangpi*).

À l'origine, ces bandelettes étaient des planchettes de bois de pêcher *(duiping)* sur lesquelles étaient gravées ou peintes des inscriptions talismaniques. C'est vers le Xe siècle qu'on les remplaça par les bandes de papier. Ces paires de sentences *(duilian)* qui célèbrent souvent d'une manière symétrique et poétique le changement de saison, appellent sur les occupants de la maison de nombreuses félicités.

Les fêtes traditionnelles furent aussi l'occasion d'imprimer pour le grand public des estampes populaires colorées, appelées « chevaux sur papier » *(zhima)* ou « chevaux carapaçonnés » *(jiama),* sans doute parce que les premières représentaient des divinités à cheval. (Mais *zhima* ne désigne pas que des affichettes, c'étaient aussi des personnages, des animaux, des maisons ou des véhicules faits en papier collés sur une armature de bambou et destinés à être brûlés comme offrandes). Les images produites en centaines de millions d'exemplaires en Chine depuis 900 ans, ont fait la gloire de villages entiers qui occupaient des milliers de paysans-imprimeurs et coloristes. Elles étaient si populaires que la famille impériale ne dédaignait pas d'en faire acheter pour son usage privé. Chaque centre avait un style propre et les plus renommés se trouvaient à Weifang, Yanggu dans la province du Shandong, Taohuawu près de Suzhou, Mianzhu dans le Sichuan, Wuqiang et Yangliuqing au Hebei et Foshan dans le Guangdong, Liqiang, Dali et Baoshan dans le Yunnan. Ces estampes étaient en fait produites pour tous les moments importants de la vie (naissance, voyage, funérailles, mariage, examens) mais plus particulièrement pour la grande Fête du Printemps. Elles ne s'appelleront «images du Nouvel An» (*xinnianhua* ou *nianhua*) qu'en 1949 ; avant on parlait des « peintures du Nouvel An ». On reste surpris de la qualité de certaines de ces estampes, due à la finesse du travail du dessinateur puis de l'habileté du graveur sur bois. En revanche, le coloriage réalisé par les femmes et les jeunes filles était souvent assez grossier et criard car il fallait produire très rapidement et en grand nombre ces œuvres éphémères

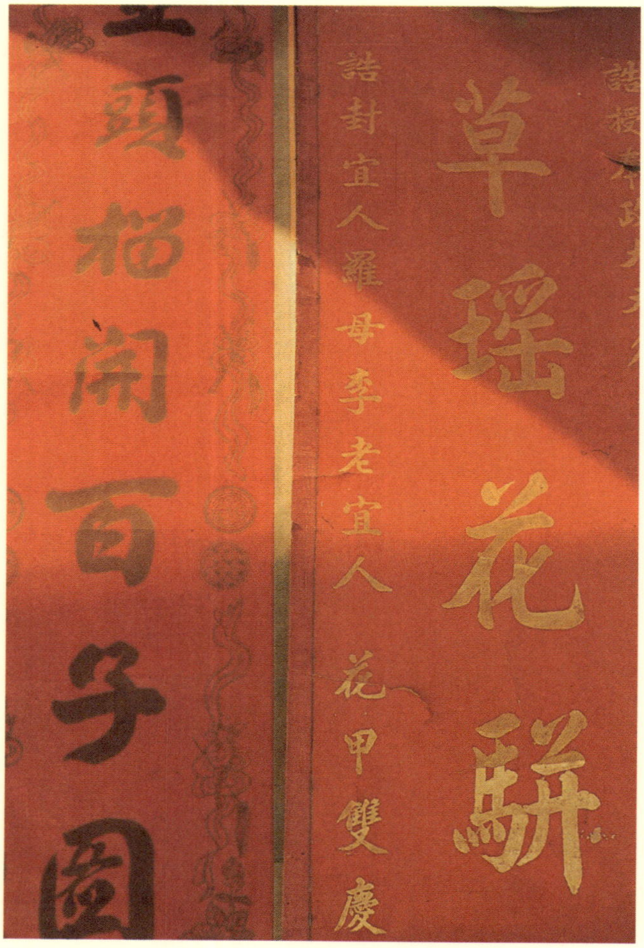

Une paire de sentences parallèles en papier (duilian).

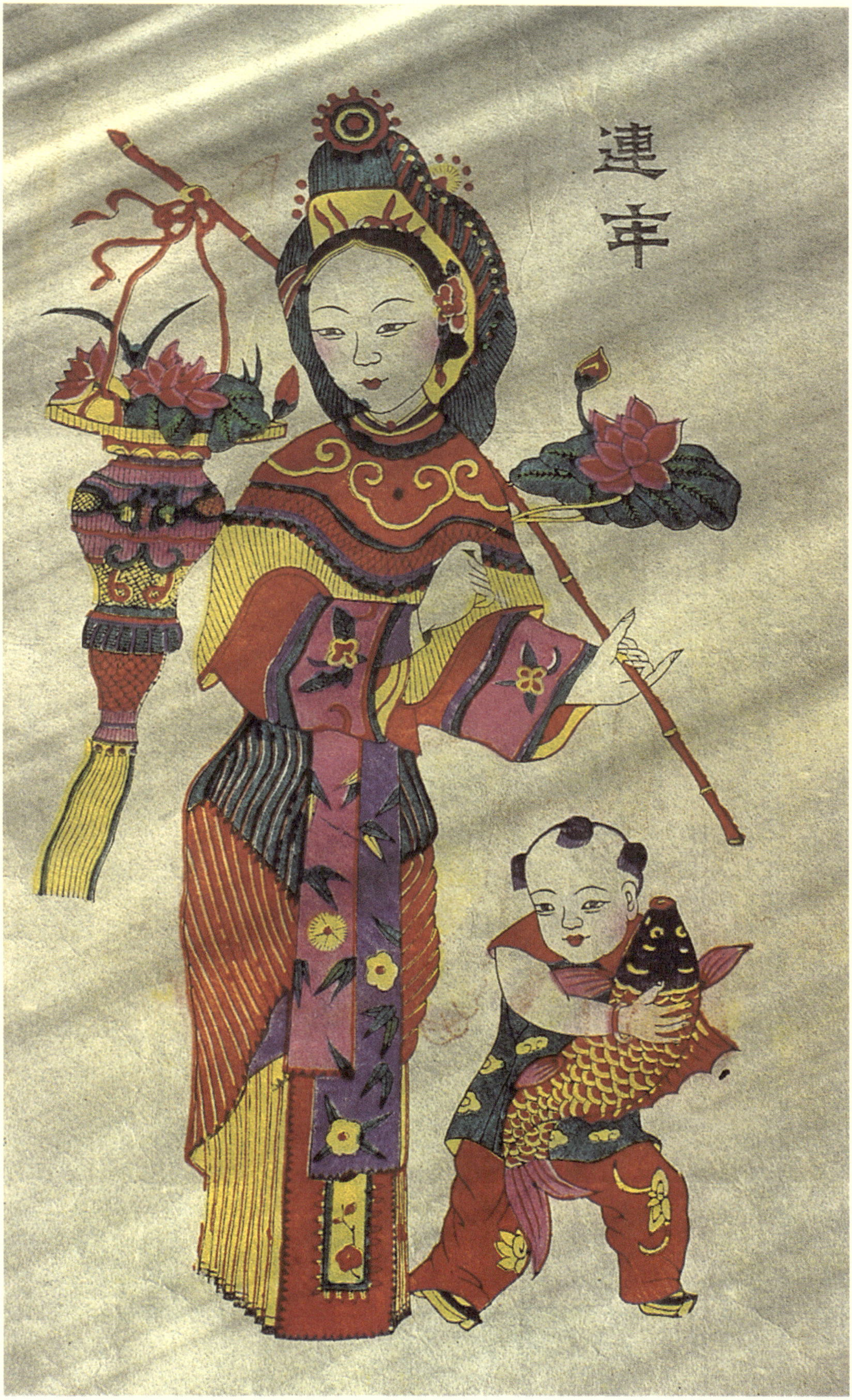

L'immortelle He Xiangu avec son lotus (image populaire).

puisqu'elles devaient être renouvelées chaque année. Les estampes pouvaient être imprimées en noir, rouge ou en couleurs. Il y avait des couleurs fortes (rouge, noir et violet) et des couleurs tendres (rouge, rose, jaune et vert).

Les spécialistes les classent en au moins une cinquantaine de catégories différentes. Les plus simples étaient de format carré et ne portaient, par exemple, qu'un caractère : *chun* (printemps) ou *fu* (bonheur). Curieusement, ce dernier, placé « à l'envers », dispense le bonheur dans tous les sens. Des images plus grandes pouvaient aussi être collées sous forme de pendants sur les battants de portes, sur les fenêtres (« les dieux gardiens de portes », *menshen* ou le « garçon et la fille joufflus », *dapang xiaozi, dapang yatou*). D'autres enfin étaient porteuses d'un souhait. La licorne *(qilin)* était toujours bienvenue dans les familles car elle apportait des enfants doués qui réussiraient aux examens impériaux. Liu Hai avec ses ligatures de sapèque et son crapeau à trois pattes tout comme le dieu de la Richesse étaient souvent invoqués par les pauvres gens. Zhongkui avec son air terrifiant ou les trigrammes entourant le « faîte suprême » exorcisaient les démons.

La Chine étant un pays essentiellement rural, les divinités de l'agriculture furent pendant longtemps les plus invoquées. À côté de Shennong, figuraient le Roi-bœuf, le Roi-cheval, le dieu des Eaux, le dieu de la Grêle, le dieu des Étables, la déesse Sauterelle, la déesse ver à soie, le dieu des plantations...

Mais dans les villes se développèrent aussi des cultes aux saints patrons des corporations *(shenren)*, tels que Confucius pour les enseignants, Gong Shuban (ou Lu Ban), pour les charpentiers, inventeur des outils de menuisier, Meng Tian pour les fabricants de pinceaux, Mei Fu pour les teinturiers. L'un des Immortels, Lü Dongbin, aurait été l'inventeur de l'encre, il était donc le patron des fabricants de bâtons d'encre. Shao Kang était célébré par les artisans de la distillerie, alors que Gao Liang, ce soldat qui rendit aux Pékinois l'eau que la Déesse de l'eau leur avait prise, était le patron des porteurs d'eau.

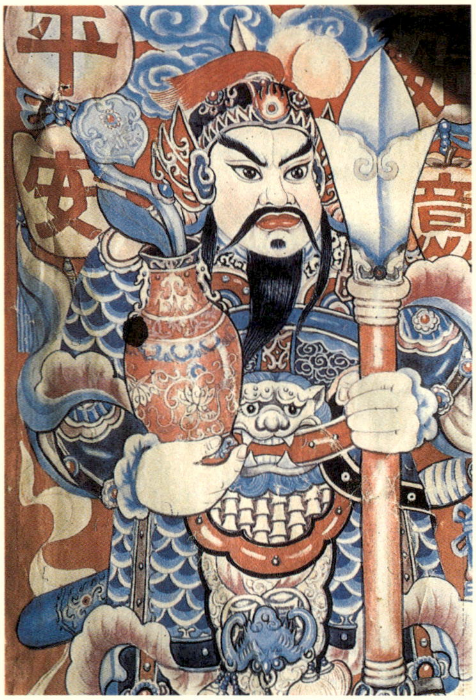

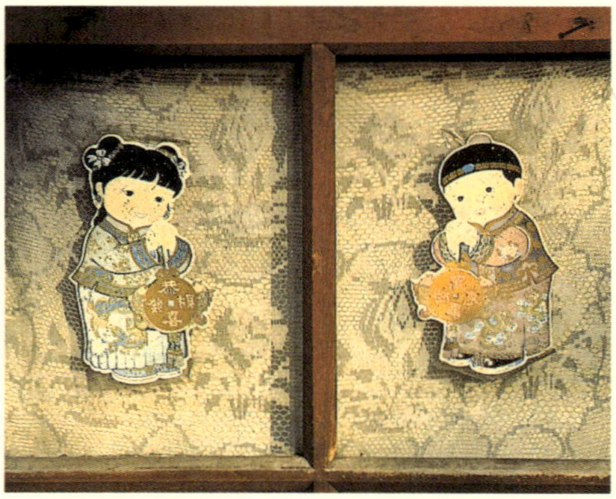

En haut, Guanyu, protecteur de l'État (image populaire) ; en bas, paire de papiers peints représentant les enfants qui souhaitent le Nouvel An.

Pour la décoration des intérieurs des maisons, au moment des fêtes où l'on recevait beaucoup, on achetait aussi des estampes représentant des scènes de la vie de tous les jours, comme la fête du Nouvel An en famille, à la

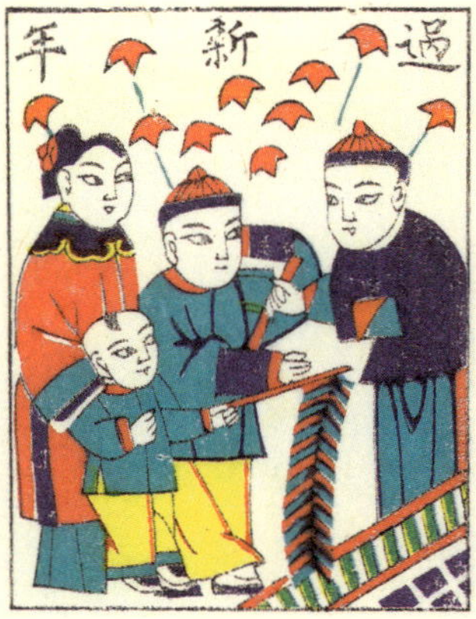

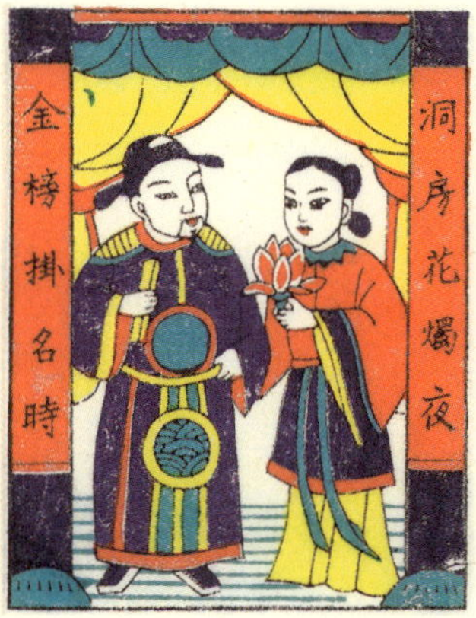

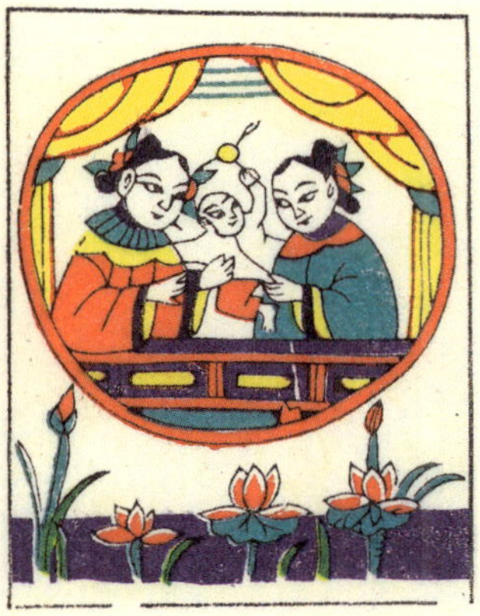

ville ou au village, les travaux des champs, des paysages de neige, les jeux d'extérieur au printemps. S'adressant enfin à un public cultivé et d'un goût plus sûr, les ateliers produisaient aussi les *hua duizi,* des « peintures » tirées d'œuvres littéraires célèbres comme le *Roman des Trois Royaumes,* le *Pèlerinage vers l'Ouest,* d'opéras connus comme le *Serpent blanc* ou d'histoires populaires comme celle du *Mariage de la fille du Rat.*

Les calendriers publicitaires, qui connurent une si grande vogue à Shanghaï et à Hong-Kong pendant l'entre-deux-guerres, bénéficiaient des progrès de l'imprimerie en couleurs. Ils ne furent, en fait, que le prolongement de cet art populaire qui existait dans le Sichuan depuis le IXe siècle, où l'on imprimait déjà des almanachs destinés à régler la vie quotidienne. À côté des jeunes beautés évoluant dans des intérieurs Modern Style ou Art Déco (pour vanter les mérites d'une crème de beauté ou d'une marque de cigarettes) subsistèrent les thèmes traditionnels d'antan. Bien moins répandues pendant la période contemporaine qu'au XIXe siècle qui fut leur âge d'or, certaines estampes furent néanmoins encore réalisées pendant la guerre entre nationalistes et communistes (1927), et lors de la résistance à l'occupant japonais (1931). Dans le souci de « balayer les Quatre Vieilleries » (idées, culture, coutumes et mœurs), la Révolution Culturelle condamnera cet art populaire, entraînant la disparition irrémédiable des *zhima,* ces populaires « chevaux de papier » qui avaient enchanté tant de générations tout comme nos naïves images d'Épinal.

Gravures populaires du Shandong : à gauche, parents remettant aux enfants des « enveloppes rouges » à l'occasion du Nouvel An sur un décor de yuanbao, au centre, échange de vœux entre mari et femme, à droite, trois générations sous le même toit.

Les cithares du vent

凌空紙鳶

ling kong zhiyuan, littéralement, « milan de papier dans l'espace ».

« Cithares du vent », c'est ainsi qu'en chinois, on appelle les cerfs-volants *(fengzheng)*, sans doute parce que, pour ajouter au plaisir des yeux, on les équipe de toutes sortes d'ingénieux instruments à vent (sifflets, cordes vibrantes) et même de tambourins. Avec la vitesse du vent, ils produisent des sons harmonieux que les Chinois n'hésitent pas à comparer à la musique d'un orchestre... Cette technique s'applique d'ailleurs aux pigeons, aux ailes desquels on accroche aussi de petits sifflets de bambou. Distraction courante des enfants et des adultes depuis des siècles en Asie, le cerf-volant occupe une place particulière en Chine qui en revendique l'invention. Légendes et récits épiques se mêlent pour donner à cet ingénieux objet volant ses lettres de noblesse.

Au VIIIe siècle av. J.-C., à l'époque des « Printemps et Automnes », il aurait été créé à des fins purement militaires. Mozi aurait consacré trois années de sa vie à la fabrication d'un cerf-volant de bois en forme d'oiseau qui ne vola qu'un seul jour. Depuis cette époque, c'est dans l'ancien royaume de Qi, l'actuelle province du Shandong, patrie de cet inventeur, que la tradition place le lieu de naissance des premiers cerfs-volants chinois. Au IIIe siècle av. J.-C., le général Han Xin fit fabriquer un cerf-volant de papier (plus probablement en soie), en forme de milan, pour évaluer la distance le séparant d'une place forte qu'il voulait investir. Après avoir mesuré la longueur de la corde, il fit creuser un tunnel souterrain d'une longueur égale et ses soldats purent ainsi pénétrer dans la citadelle. Plus tard, dans la province de Shandong, un menuisier, du nom de Gong Shuban (ou Lu Ban), aurait même inventé un cerf-volant en cuir sur lequel aurait pris place un observateur. Muni d'une flûte, il jouait des airs mélancoliques au-dessus de l'armée ennemie. Ce stratagème avait pour but de briser le moral des soldats dont le chef se noya de désespoir. Au VIe siècle, près de Nankin, le général Hou Jing qui assiégeait l'empereur Wu, intercepta un message d'appel au secours porté par un cerf-volant en le faisant abattre par ses archers. L'empereur Wenxuan (550-559), connu pour sa cruauté, avait même inventé un jeu qu'il nommait « libérer les animaux captifs » ; il faisait précipiter du haut d'une falaise des condamnés attachés à un cerf-volant. Rares furent ceux qui survécurent à ces terribles expériences qui préfiguraient les premiers essais d'aile volante. Les Chinois pensent aussi que le prototype d'hélicoptère conçu par Léonard de Vinci n'était en fait

Page de droite, en haut et en bas, différents modèles d'« hirondelles de Pékin » ; au centre, un cerf-volant « mille-pattes à tête de dragon » dans le ciel de la place Tian An Men.

qu'une copie de leur « libellule de bambou », connue depuis des siècles, et dont les ailes étaient actionnées par le mouvement d'un fil torsadé.

Après la découverte de la poudre à canon, des essais furent faits à partir du Xᵉ siècle pour équiper des cerfs-volants d'explosifs que l'on envoyait au-dessus des armées ennemies. La mise à feu était assurée par des anneaux d'encens incandescent qui brûlaient lentement comme une mèche. Le nom de « corbeau du feu céleste » *(tianhuowu)* fut ainsi attribué à cette étrange nouvelle arme qui fut en usage jusque sous les Ming.

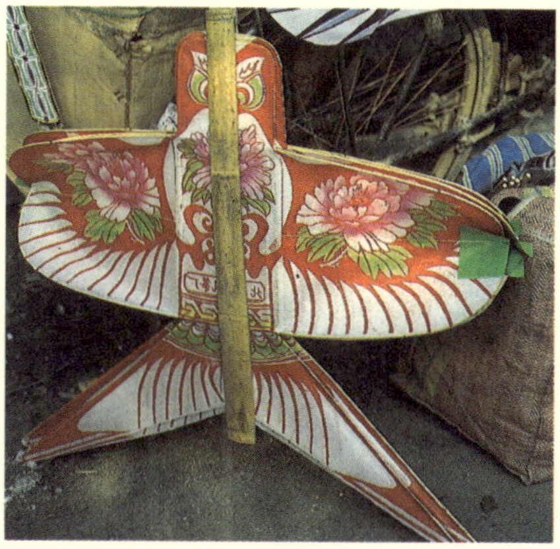

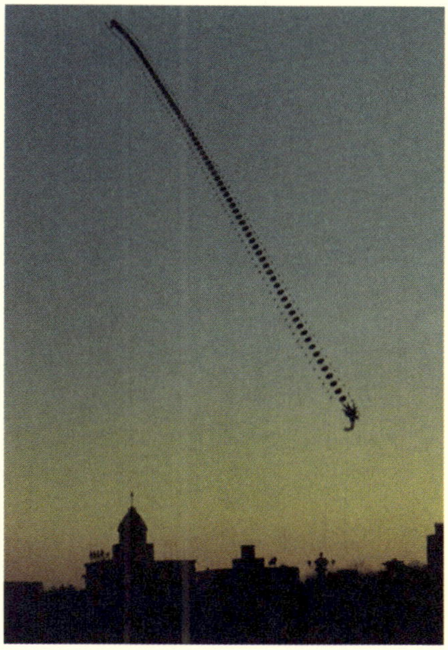

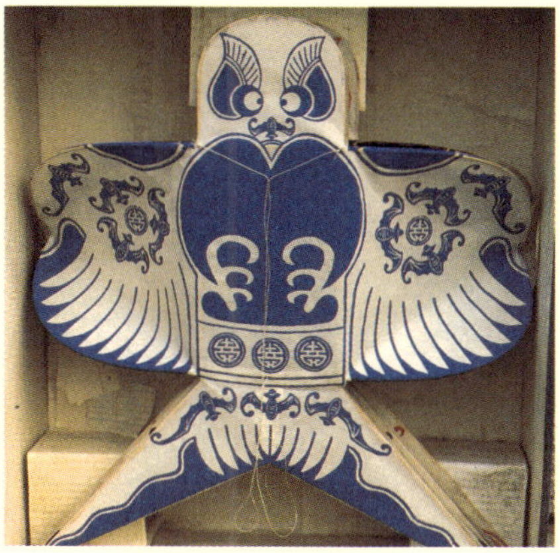

C'est au moment où la fabrication du papier commença à se développer (IIᵉ siècle ap. J.-C.) que les premiers cerfs-volants de divertissement apparurent. Sous les Tang, l'empire connaissant une véritable ère de prospérité, les cerfs-volants devinrent accessibles à tout le monde. Une scène célèbre, *Les cent enfants s'amusant au printemps,* peinte par Su Hanchen à l'époque Song, témoigne de la popularité de ces jeux pratiqués par toutes les classes sociales. De nombreux poèmes ou des romans, comme *Le Rêve dans le pavillon rouge,* font référence à cette mode à l'époque des Qing. Pour son anniversaire, l'impératrice Tseu Hi (Cixi) commanda au célèbre fabricant Wei de Tianjin un cerf-volant sur le thème de la déesse de la Longévité chevauchant la Grue. Ces objets de luxe étaient alors confiés à des experts que l'on engageait pour les faire voler dans les meilleures conditions. Les compétitions portaient sur la hauteur et sur les évolutions acrobatiques mais il y avait aussi des combats de cerfs-volants dont la mode était venue de l'Inde. Le principe de ces joutes était de cisailler le fil du cerf-volant de ses adversaires ; pour cela, ces fins cordages étaient trempés dans du verre pilé, ce qui les rendait très coupants. Les courtisans, les riches bourgeois, les eunuques et les acteurs célèbres se passionnaient pour ces compétitions et accordaient leur parrainage à des équipes dont les vainqueurs étaient primés. Les lettrés qui venaient juste de subir les difficiles épreuves des examens impériaux faisaient voler un cerf-volant pour évaluer leurs chances de réussite. La résistance à l'invasion japonaise (1931-1945) utilisa même les cerfs-volants pour appeler à la révolte contre l'occupant.

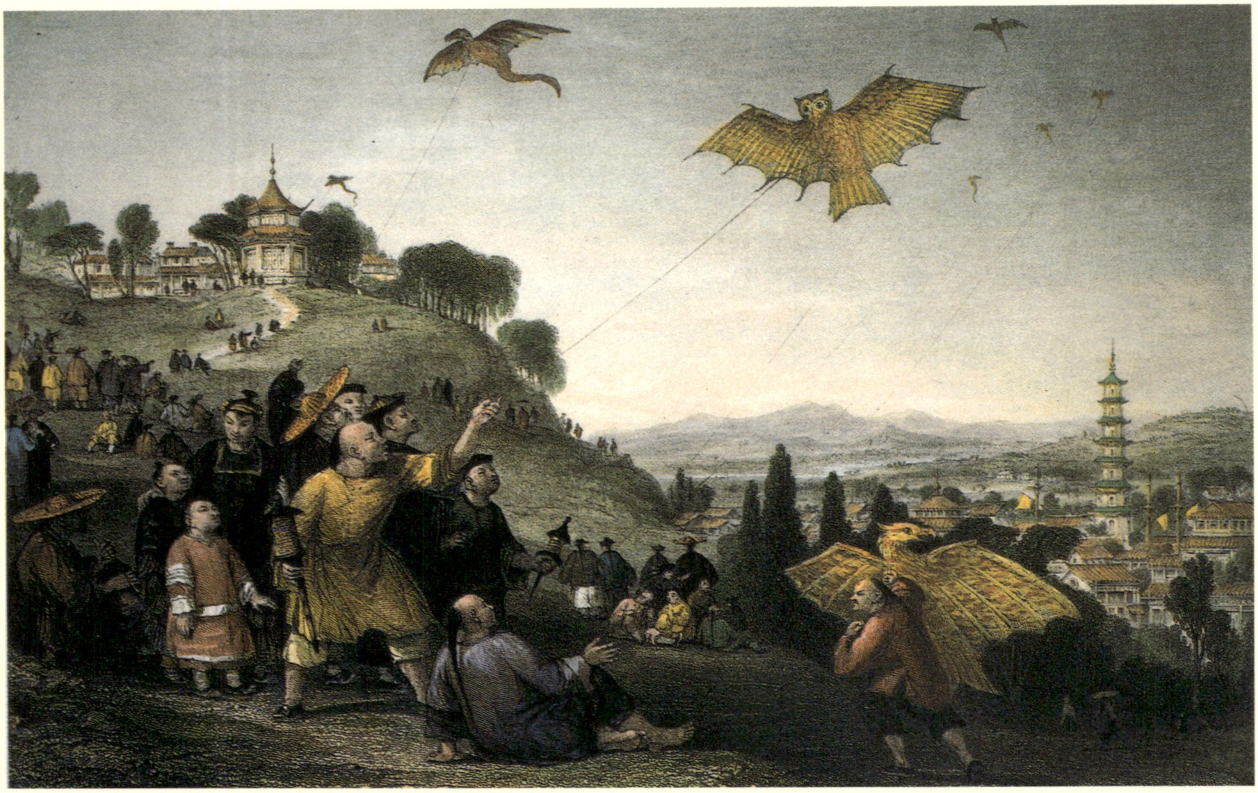

De nos jours, l'engouement reste très vif parmi ces amateurs qui se réunissent sur la place Tian An Men, au printemps ou à l'automne, ou qui se rendent au très réputé festival de Weifang, dans la province occidentale du Shandong. Créé en 1984, il réunit chaque année les meilleurs spécialistes chinois et étrangers. Déjà, en 1914, à l'occasion de la foire internationale en l'honneur de l'ouverture du canal de Panama, un artisan de Tianjin se voyait décerner une médaille d'or.

Une fête populaire chinoise est particulièrement associée au jeu du cerf-volant. Vers le 5 avril, la fête de la Pureté et de la Clarté (Qingming), aussi connue sous le nom de Fête des morts ou du Repas froid, est l'occasion pour toute la famille de se rendre sur la tombe des ancêtres pour y faire des sacrifices. Cette cérémonie, qui remonte à plus de deux mille ans, est prétexte à un pique-nique à la campagne. Tous les jeux d'extérieur sont alors pratiqués : balançoire, ballon, combats de coqs, cerfs-volants. En cette saison, c'est le printemps et il souffle toujours un petit vent propice à ce divertissement. La tradition veut qu'en route les femmes tressent des couronnes de branches de saule pour s'assurer de l'immortalité. Comme le dit le proverbe, « si elle ne se pare pas de rameaux de saule, le jour de Qingming, la jeune fille vieillira »…

La fête des cerfs-volants le 9e jour de la 9e lune (d'après une gravure de Chinese Empire Illustrated *de Th. Allom et G.N. Wright, 1859).*

On attribuait au cerf-volant des propriétés magiques. Pour Maurice-Louis Tournier, il figurerait l'esprit des défunts qui s'envole, rattaché au monde des

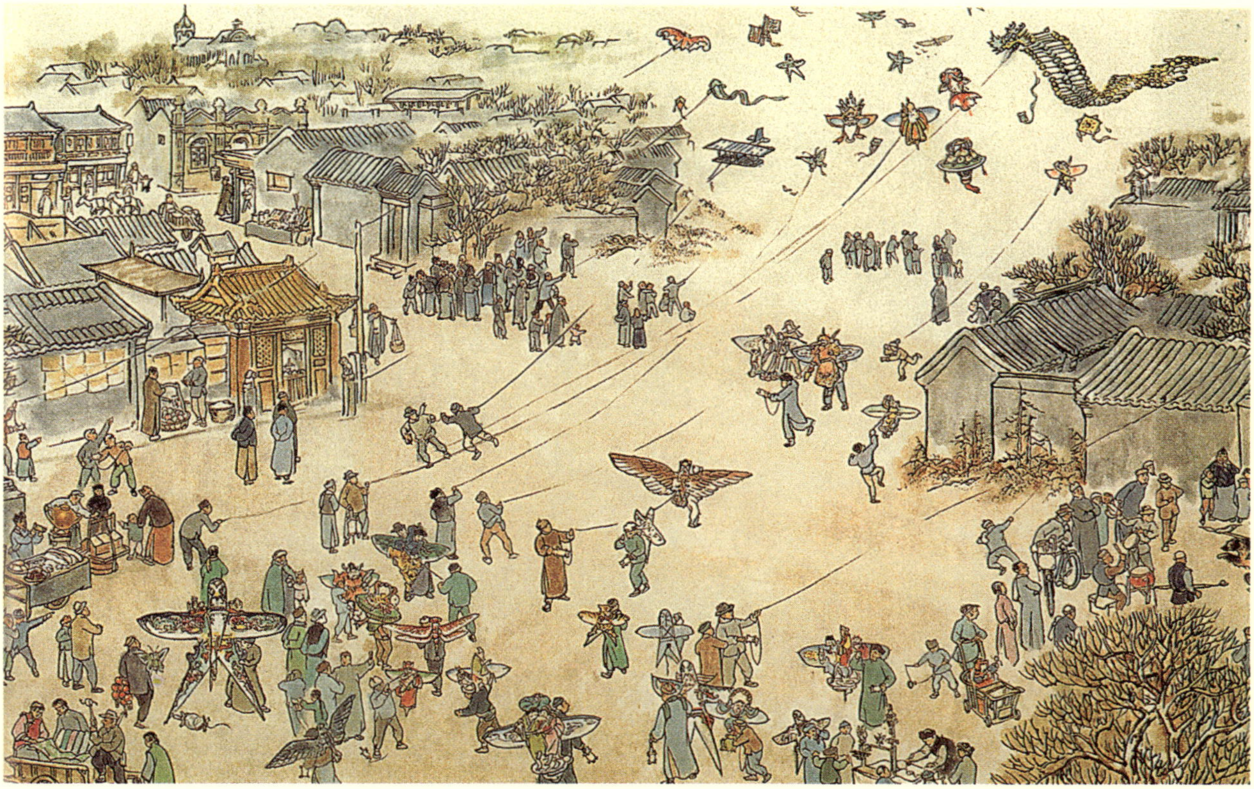

vivants par un fil ténu. On coupait donc la corde en certaines occasions et le cerf-volant emportait ailleurs, pensait-on, les mauvais esprits. Certaines de ces réunions se déroulant sur les collines avoisinant des villes, il n'était pas rare que l'un d'entre eux retombe sur le toit d'une maison. Pour conjurer ce mauvais sort, il fallait s'en saisir au plus vite et le brûler. Au Vietnam, on leur accordait une fonction protectrice ; les cerfs-volants à sifflet avaient le pouvoir de protéger des mauvais esprits et en particulier des épidémies. P. Huard et M. Durand racontent que « pour rendre cette thérapeutique efficace, on chargeait le sifflet de disperser dans l'air du sulfure d'arsenic en poudre ».

Faut-il alors associer le cerf-volant au rhombe (du grec *rhombos*), ce losange de bois plein ou évidé que l'on faisait tournoyer au bout d'un fil et qui produisait un ronflement interprété comme la voix des ancêtres ? Connu de nombreuses autres civilisations, le rhombe était utilisé dans l'antiquité grecque pour des rituels initiatiques, notamment lors d'orgies sexuelles, où il exprimait la force virile fécondante. En Chine, on le retrouve dans la collection des Huit Objets Précieux ; il est symbole de victoire et de prospérité collective. Au fil des ans, le rhombe comme le cerf-volant vont perdre leur caractère sacré pour n'être plus qu'un jeu pour enfants comme la toupie ou le yo-yo. Toutefois, on continue, par tradition ou superstition, à leur attribuer des vertus pédagogiques ou même curatives. Les anciens manuels d'éducation recommandaient la pratique de ce sport qui développait chez

La fête des cerfs-volants le jour de Qingming (illustration de Wang Daguang, A Round Glancing of Old Beijing, *d. r.).*

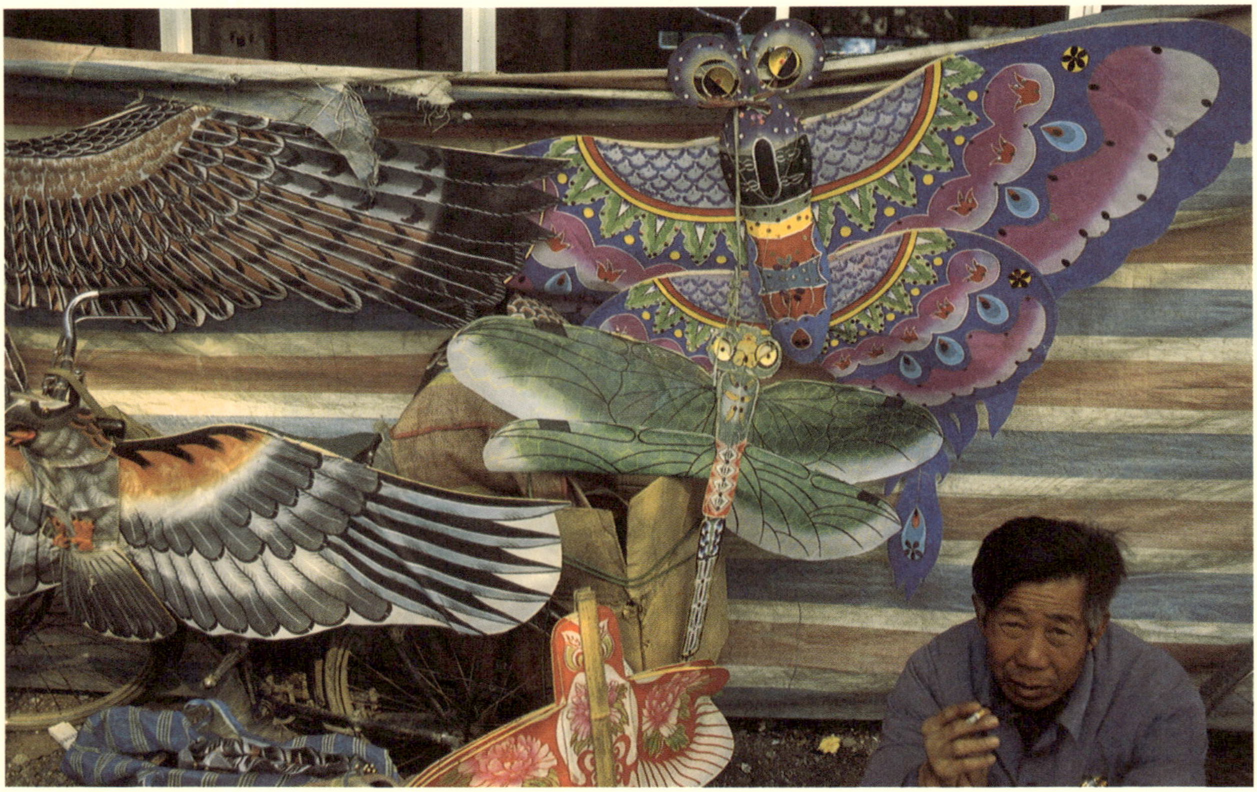

l'enfant la force, l'habileté, la concentration, le jugement. Le savant Li Shi, dans son *Histoire perpétuelle des sciences naturelles* de la période Song, notait que l'enfant qui suit son cerf-volant des yeux, la bouche ouverte, exhale ainsi les mauvaises humeurs… D'autres n'hésitaient pas à affirmer que ce sport renforçait la vue, protégeait des maladies vasculaires, de l'hypertension et même des maladies mentales.

La grande variété des cerfs-volants produits dans toutes les régions a conduit les experts à rechercher des critères de classification par le style, la structure, l'utilisation, la forme ou le volume. Les modèles les plus simples ont la forme de carrés, de losanges ou d'octogones. Ils sont plats (on les appelle des « plaques », *paizi*) et ont une queue de rubans. À cause de leur vol maladroit, on les nomme familièrement dans le sud, des « balourds », des « simplets » (*erbaiwu,* littéralement des « 250 »). La seconde catégorie comprend des cerfs-volants à la structure renforcée. Sur le papier tendu sont soigneusement peints des personnages mythologiques ou historiques : Zhong Kui, le pourfendeur des démons, la déesse Ma Gu, le singe Sun Wukong… des animaux, des poissons rouges, des fleurs, des caractères auspicieux (double bonheur, longévité). Les classiques « hirondelles » (*yaoer,* littéralement, « objet volant fait main ») de Pékin et de Tianjin, de couleur bleue, noire ou rouge, sont en fait des représentations abstraites d'un oiseau décoré lui-même de symboles de bon augure (chrysanthème, chauve-souris). Les

Ci-dessus et page de droite, cerfs-volants populaires (yaoer).

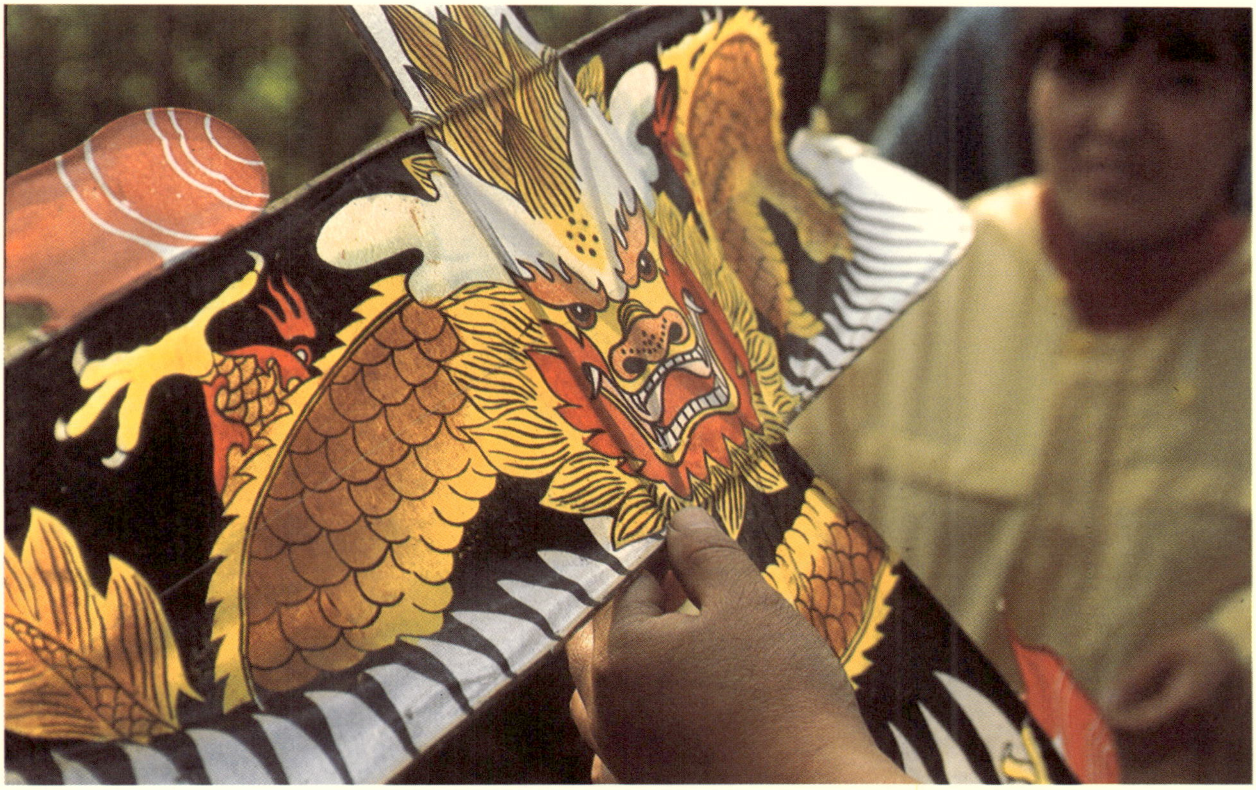

cerfs-volants à ailes souples représentent la troisième catégorie ; d'excellente tenue, ornés de motifs d'un grand réalisme (aigle, milan, papillon, cigale, libellule, mante), ils sont particulièrement intéressants à suivre dans leurs évolutions. C'est dans la quatrième catégorie que se rangent les cerfs-volants aux formes défiant les lois de la pesanteur, car ce sont des volumes creux en forme de cylindre ou d'octogone. On y trouve des vases à fleurs, des paniers de fleurs, des cages à oiseaux, des lanternes de palais, et même des aquariums… D'immenses groupes plus complexes comme le « Mille-pattes à tête de dragon », le « Vol d'hirondelles », les « Huit Immortels traversant la mer » ou les « Sept beautés célestes descendant sur terre », nécessitent un nombre impressionnant de manipulateurs à cause de leur grande taille (jusqu'à 200 mètres de longueur). Le génie des artisans d'autrefois et d'aujourd'hui ne s'est pas arrêté à l'esthétique. D'habiles dispositifs placés sur les cerfs-volants permettent de faire de la musique (orgues, sifflets de roseaux, de bambous ou tambourins), d'autres portent des boîtes à fumée, à confettis réfléchissant les rayons du soleil ou à poudre explosive. D'étonnants cerfs-volants miniatures ont aussi été produits : les mini-hirondelles de Pékin ou de Weifang, les cigales n'ont que quelques centimètres de long et tiennent dans une boîte d'allumettes, tout comme le mini mille-pattes, ils peuvent tous voler mais demandent autant de dextérité que les grands modèles.

De curieux gardiens de toits

文兽

wenshou, littéralement, « les animaux d'ornement ».

Alors que l'architecture occidentale a toujours accordé une certaine importance aux façades, ce sont les toitures qui, en Chine, ont reçu toute l'attention des constructeurs et des décorateurs. Les toits des édifices importants (résidences impériales ou princières, temples, bibliothèques) se caractérisent non seulement par leur forme élancée que les Chinois nomment « toits volants » *(feiyuan),* une allusion au vol du phénix, mais aussi par les couleurs vives de la charpente, au savant entrecroisement et surtout par l'éclat des tuiles vernissées (*liuliwa,* littéralement « tuiles au vernis qui coule »). Fabriquées en argile et cuites au four pour les durcir, les tuiles et les ornements de toit étaient recouverts d'une glaçure à base de silice rendue fusible à grand feu par l'introduction de potasse et de soude. À l'origine, seules quatre couleurs étaient produites : jaune, vert, bleu et noir.

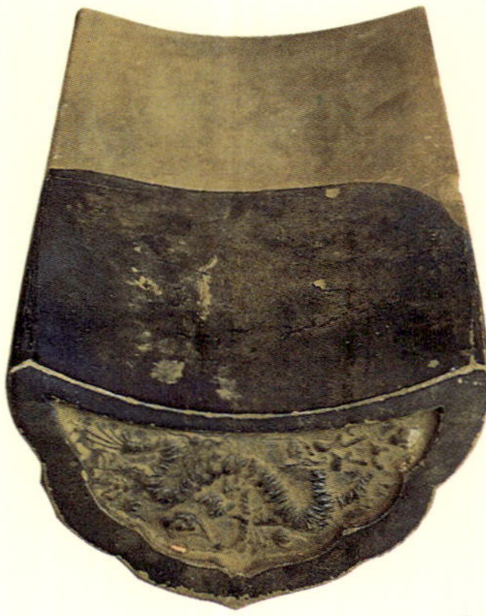

Tuile vernissée bleue de l'époque Ming.

Dès le IIe millénaire av. J.-C., de petits objets vernissés apparurent, mais ce n'est que sous les Sui et surtout les Tang que la production de tuiles et de briques vernissées se généralisa. La « Pagode de fer » de Kaifeng construite en 1049 est un premier exemple d'architecture de ce type. La construction de la célèbre pagode du temple de Bao'en (Nankin) construite entre 1412 et 1428 nécessita 100 000 ouvriers et une soixantaine de fours à tuiles à Jubao. Bien plus tard, le frère Attiret, peintre jésuite, raconte dans une correspondance de 1743 comment l'empereur Kangxi, lorsqu'il atteignit la 48e année de son règne, fit cadeau à son fils Yongzhen du fameux *Jardin de la clarté parfaite* (Yuanmingyuan). On y voyait, entre autres merveilles architecturales, des toits de couleur jaune, rouge, bleu ou aubergine ainsi que des parements de murs émaillés aux couleurs encore plus chatoyantes (bleu turquoise, bleu marine, jaune d'or ou vert d'eau). La couleur jaune fut uniformément réservée aux bâtiments impériaux. Toutefois pour certains personnages aussi légendaires que Confucius ou Guanyu, on construisit aussi des temples de cette couleur. Le jaune était, dans la classification traditionnelle, la couleur de la terre et du Centre (donc de l'empereur, celui qui occupe cette position). Le vert était réservé aux princes du sang. La bibliothèque impériale de la Cité interdite (Wenyuange) se caractérise, en revanche, par un toit de tuiles noires et vertes. Le noir est

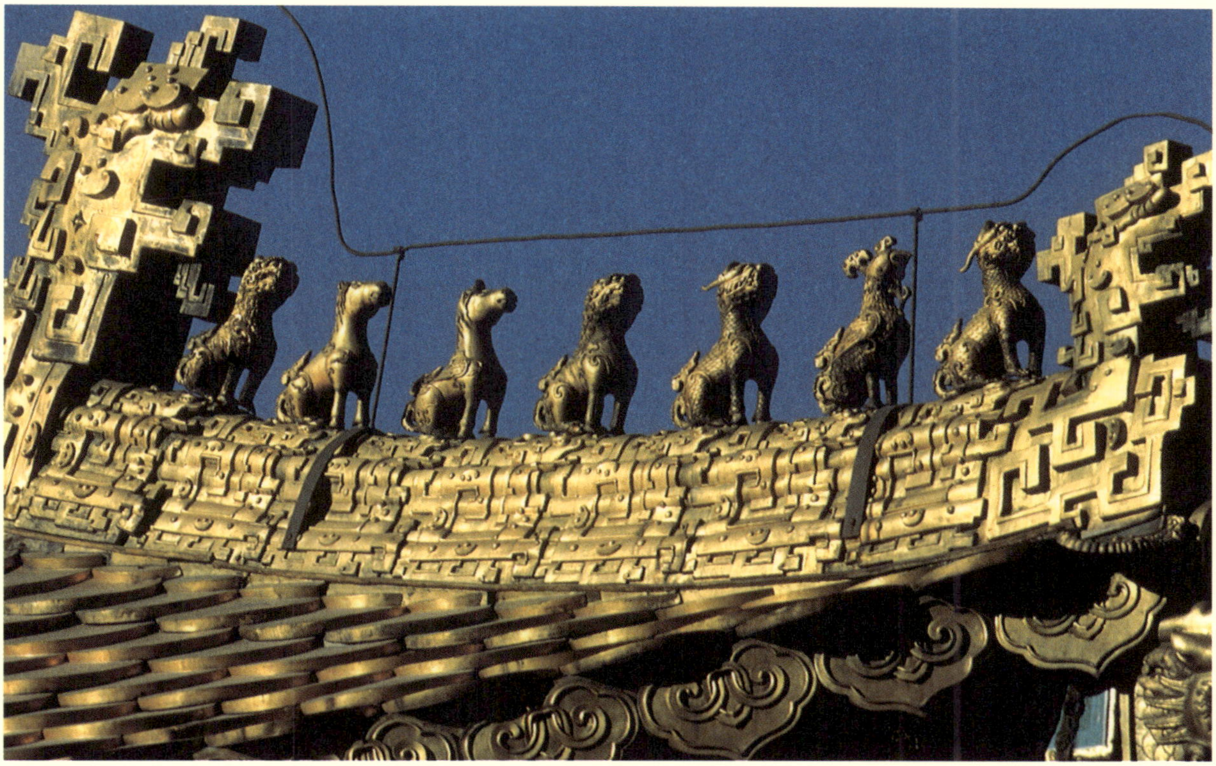

l'une des cinq couleurs qui correspond à l'élément « eau ». Comme ce bâtiment était destiné à renfermer de précieux papiers et que les accidents par le feu étaient fréquents, un toit de couleur noire était une bonne assurance contre l'incendie. Le temple du Ciel (Tiantan) est connu pour ses magnifiques tuiles bleues couleur de ciel et pour son dôme.

Les tuiles de bordure avaient pour rôle de retenir la toiture et de protéger des intempéries l'extrémité des poutres en bois. On en distingue deux types : les tuiles semi-cylindrique, décoratives *(wadang),* se terminant par un disque et les tuiles gouttières de forme incurvée *(dishui)* qui dessinent une délicate frise vernissée entre chaque rangée. Les premières ont fait l'objet, dès 1721, d'une description du lettré chinois Lin Dong qui a étudié les tuiles d'anciens palais de l'époque Han. Son intérêt portait notamment sur les motifs moulés que l'on pouvait lire de la rue en passant sous le toit. De nombreux relevés (réalisés par estampage) montrent des souhaits en caractères archaïques (« que vos années se prolongent, mille et mille années sans fin, vie éternelle »), des motifs d'oiseaux, des têtes de tigre ou de lion et des faces grimaçantes *(taotie)* dont le masque terrifiant protégeait des esprits malfaisants. Dans *Chinese Pottery of the Han Dynasty,* Laufer note que l'intérêt des Chinois pour tout ce qui relève de l'antiquité les a conduits à collectionner avec passion ces fragments de tuiles prises sur les toits anciens et même à utiliser certaines d'entre elles comme pierres à encre. Pour empêcher l'argile de s'imbiber d'encre, on la rendait imper-

Détail du toit du temple Putuozongsheng à Chengde (1767).

méable en la vernissant. C'est tout particulièrement à l'époque de Qianlong que les lettrés se livrèrent à ces curieux détournements archéologiques. Le célèbre peintre Mi Fu (1051-1107) de l'époque Song avait déjà eu, sept cents ans auparavant, cette idée originale en récupérant les tuiles d'une pagode construite dans la province du Henan par le fameux général et poète, Cao Cao, héros du *Roman des Trois Royaumes*.

Certes les tuiles présentent un intérêt esthétique, mais les collectionneurs recherchent aussi les ornements des toitures que l'on nomme en chinois *wenshou* (littéralement, « animaux d'ornement »), *xianrenzoushou* (« animaux qui se suivent en marchant ») ou *kuilongzi* (« chimères »). Ce sont des moulages zoomorphes (plus rarement anthropomorphiques) de céramique qui ornent le faîte, les arêtes et les bordures des toitures. Ils ont à la fois une fonction symbolique et une fonction technique. Certains remontent au IIe siècle av. J.-C., si l'on en croit les inscriptions gravées à l'intérieur.

Les décorations de faîte se limitent souvent à une pièce, une formidable tête de dragon ou plutôt l'un de ses neuf fils *(chiwen)* à chaque extrémité du faîtage (celle du hall de l'Harmonie suprême, dans la Cité Interdite, mesure 3,4 m de hauteur et pèse 3,6 tonnes). Ces deux énormes faïences composées d'une douzaine de pièces de couleur jaune brun avaient pour fonction, à cause de leur aspect terrifiant, de protéger le bâtiment et ses occupants en effrayant les mauvais esprits ; on les appelait d'ailleurs « les bêtes qui dévorent le faîte » *(tunjishou)*. Autrefois, la toiture des édifices était surtout en bois et les incendies causés par la foudre étaient nombreux. Comme on ne pouvait encore expliquer ces phénomènes naturels, on chercha à les conjurer en plaçant à chaque extrémité du faîte un hibou. Cet oiseau nocturne, lié à la mort, avait aussi la réputation d'arriver avec les orages des solstices et de protéger de la foudre. On le célébrait le 5e jour de la 5e Lune. Sous les Ming, le hibou disparut et fut remplacé par des « queues de poisson » qui, sous les Qing, firent alors place à la tête de *chiwen*. Du hibou, il ne subsiste aujourd'hui que la « queue de hibou ». Dressée vers le ciel, cette pièce de céramique, reconnaissable à la forme des plumes, est destinée à masquer la cheville qui joint les poutres du toit et à empêcher l'écoulement de l'eau sur les bois de la charpente. Elle sert symboliquement de paratonnerre *(bileisheng)*. On doublait les précautions en collant sur les bois de charpente de nombreux charmes ignifugeants.

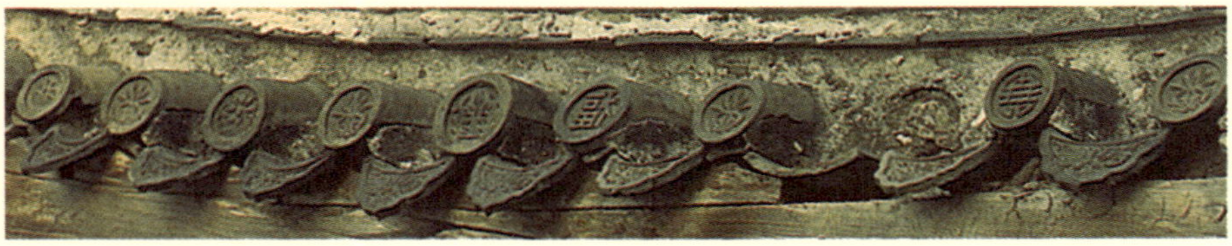

Tuiles de bordure de toit.

Les figurines d'arête de toit *(wenshou)* sont en général en nombre impair et variable selon le rang du personnage qui est abrité dans le bâtiment et son statut. Le toit des pavillons où travaillait et logeait l'empereur en comptait neuf et quelquefois même une dizaine, ceux des appartements privés de l'impératrice n'en avaient que sept, ceux des concubines cinq et d'autres constructions de moindre importance n'avaient droit qu'à une figurine. Ces animaux de faïence jaune, réels ou mythiques, de 15 à 40 cm de haut, moulés en ronde bosse, forment un amusant cortège qui semble sortir de la gueule du dragon. La procession est ouverte par un personnage chevauchant un coq. Il ne s'agit pas, comme on l'a souvent avancé, de l'empereur en personne mais d'un saint taoïste dont la vertu vient renforcer le caractère symbolique du coq. Depuis longtemps, au jour de l'an, on appliquait des images de coq (avec une crête rouge) sur les portes pour se protéger des épidémies, des malheurs et des désastres (*ji,* « coq » est homophone de *ji,* « bon augure, chanceux »). Le reste de la procession peut être composé des animaux suivants : dragon, phénix, lion, cheval de mer, cheval ailé, dragon-poisson *(yayu),* oiseau de proie *(suanni),* animal mythologique à corne *(xiezhi),* dragon à cornes *(douniu)* et, éventuellement, un autre animal mythique *(xingshi).* Ces figurines avaient une fonction technique précise ; c'étaient des caches pour les chevilles d'assemblage. Sous les Ming, les figurines de certains toits étaient de véritables œuvres d'art de céramique : cavaliers à cheval sabre au clair (on y a vu le dieu de la guerre), carpes jaillissant de l'onde, prêtes à se transformer en dragons, statues de dieux tutélaires… Le temple de Longhua à Shanghai reste un bon exemple de ces étonnants « personnages de toits ». À Chengde, le temple Xumi Fushou érigé pour le 70e anniversaire de Qianlong porte d'énormes dragons métalliques ondulant sur les quatre arêtes.

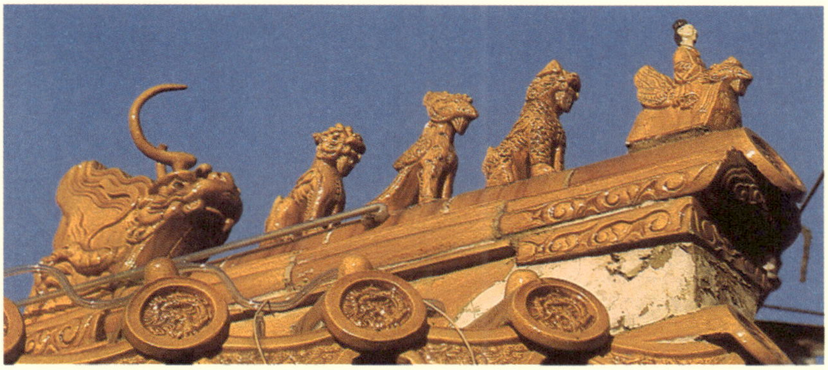

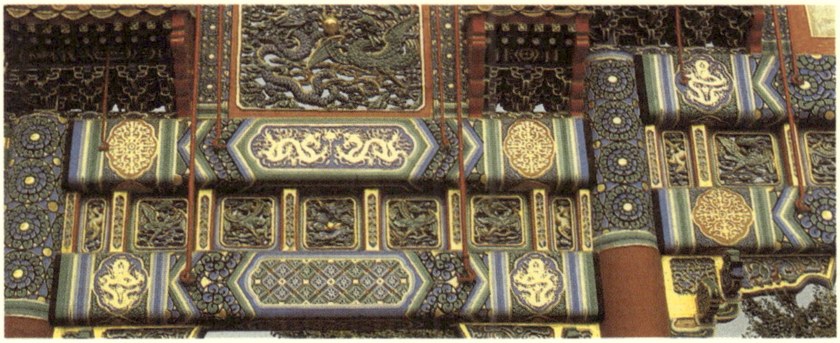

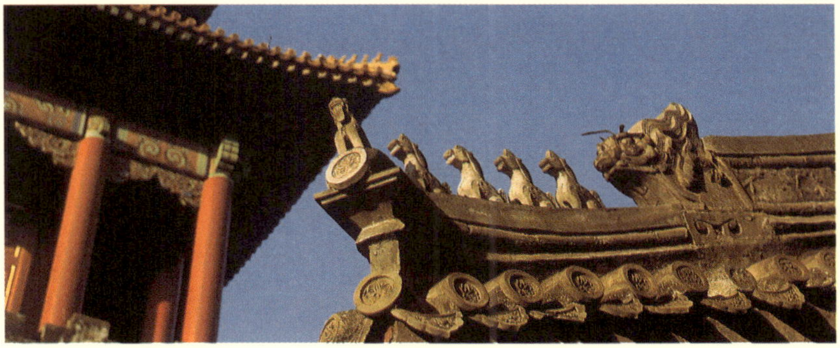

Gardiens de toits au Temple des Lamas (Pékin, 1732). Page suivante, détails de toiture et, au centre, le « joyau de faîte » (Pékin, Cité Interdite).

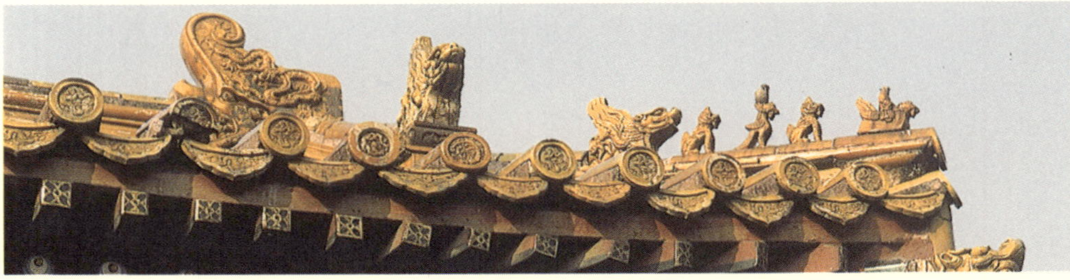

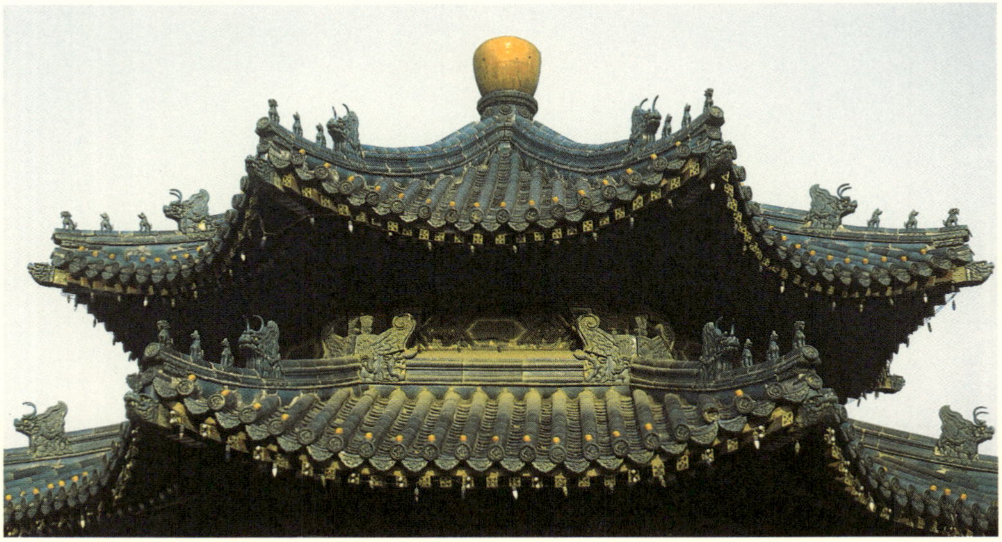

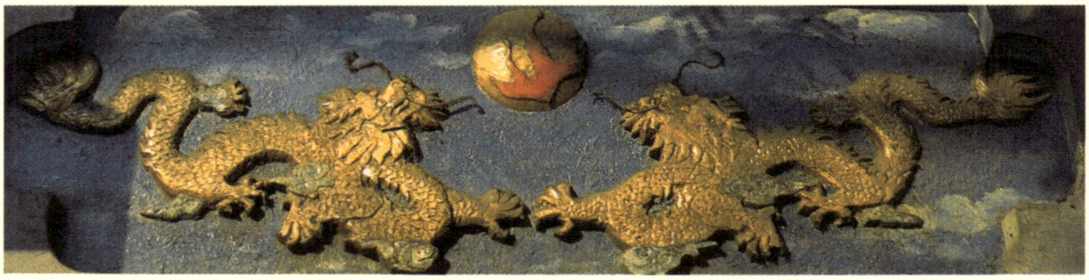

La description des ornements de toits serait incomplète si l'on ne faisait pas mention du « joyau de faîte » *(baoding)* qui surmontait les toits de certains pavillons ou pagodes. Ces énormes faïences, en forme de vase renversé, de forme ovoïde étaient comparables au « bouton de mandarin » *(ding)* qui ornait le haut du chapeau des hauts fonctionnaires. Elles avaient pour rôle d'isoler le sommet de la construction de la foudre et de l'eau et de maintenir assemblées les poutres. Certains bâtiments de la Cité Interdite (palais de l'Harmonie Parfaite, le palais de l'Union), parce qu'ils servaient à des cérémonies solennelles ou abritaient des salles d'audience, portaient au sommet de leur toit ce type d'ornement rehaussé à la feuille d'or.

Le feu maîtrisé : poudre, pétards et lanternes

灯籠
爆竹

denglong baozhu, littéralement, « lanternes-cages et pétards ».

Le caractère chinois du mot « feu » *(huo)* s'écrit avec un pictogramme composé d'une flamme montante et d'étincelles de part et d'autre. Selon le *Livre des mutations,* le feu correspond au sud, à la couleur rouge, à l'été et au cœur. Il est le symbole des passions, de l'esprit, du caractère et de la connaissance mais aussi purificateur et démonifuge. La lumière et le feu qui sont *yang* repoussent les forces de l'obscurité qui sont *yin.* Les légendes racontent que c'est avec des pétards, des lanternes, des feux d'artifice et des papiers de couleur rouge que l'on repoussa un monstre cornu du nom de Nian qui descendait des cieux, à la fin de chaque hiver, pour chercher son tribut de vies humaines. Depuis cette époque, on célèbre chaque année au nouvel an la disparition de cet animal fabuleux par une grande débauche de bruit et de lumière. De nombreuses expressions populaires désignent ce moment d'exorcisation : on parle de « brûler l'année » *(shao nian),* le mot « année » se disant d'ailleurs *nian.* Dans les légendes chinoises, c'est avec le feu que l'homme se protégeait des bêtes sauvages, des démons-renards (ou renardes) et des revenants que l'on rencontrait, la nuit, près des sépultures. Le *Calendrier des coutumes des Qi et des Zhou* (VIe siècle) conseillait, au premier mois de l'année, d'allumer des torches de roseaux et d'éclairer les puits et les grottes, là où les esprits malins auraient pu trouver refuge.

Bien avant que les Chinois ne découvrent la poudre, il y a peut-être deux mille ans, ils avaient l'habitude, dès le lever du soleil, au premier jour du premier mois de l'année, de jeter dans le feu des bambous bien secs qui explosaient en brûlant, pour chasser les mauvais esprits de la nuit. Les pétards tireront plus tard leur nom de cette coutume ; on les appellera *baozhu* (littéralement, les « bambous qui éclatent »). Un lettré de l'époque Song, Wang Anshi, dans son poème *Jour de l'An,* évoquait cette coutume : « Une année s'achève au claquement des pétards » *(baozhu shengzhong, yi sui chu).*

Selon un traité attribué à Zheng Yin, la poudre explosive aurait été découverte accidentellement vers le IIIe siècle ap. J.-C., probablement par des alchimistes taoïstes, en mélangeant du soufre au salpêtre (*xiaoshi,* nitrate de potassium) et à de la poussière de charbon de bois. On continua d'utiliser les bambous en les remplissant de ce mélange détonant, ils s'appelèrent alors les tubes explosifs *(baozhang).* Les flèches incendiaires *(huojian)* étaient connues, par contre, dès le Ier siècle avec d'autres stratagèmes guerriers comme les « abricots de feu » (littéralement, les « oiseaux-abricots », *xingque*) qui consistaient en un récipient (ou un fruit creux) rempli de mélange incendiaire (poudre ou armoise), attaché autour du cou ou à la patte d'infortunés oiseaux *(huoqin)* que l'on lâchait à proximité des toits de bois de la ville à détruire. Cette même ruse de guerre s'appliquait aux « bêtes incendiaires » (chevaux, bœufs) rendus furieux par un récipient en feu fixé à leur tête ou à leur queue et que l'on poussait vers l'ennemi. Au Xe siècle, la poudre (*huoyao,* littéralement « drogue de feu ») servait de mèche lente dans un lanceur de flammes, formé d'un tube de bambou *(feitian huotong)* ; au XIe siècle elle était utilisée pour des bombes et des grenades jetées à l'aide d'une baliste *(paoche)*. Mais ce n'est que bien plus tard, au XIIIe siècle, sous les Yuan, que l'on commença de faire usage des « bombes-tonnerre » *(pilipao)* aux effets destructeurs sur les portes et les remparts par l'augmentation de la teneur en nitrate ou des mines anti-personnel qui projetaient toutes sortes de projectiles métalliques. Les Chinois avaient presque trois siècles d'avance sur l'Europe en matière de poudre à canon et pourtant les premières bombardes chinoises *(gunchetu)* et les mousquets *(huoqiang)* n'apparurent qu'en 1290.

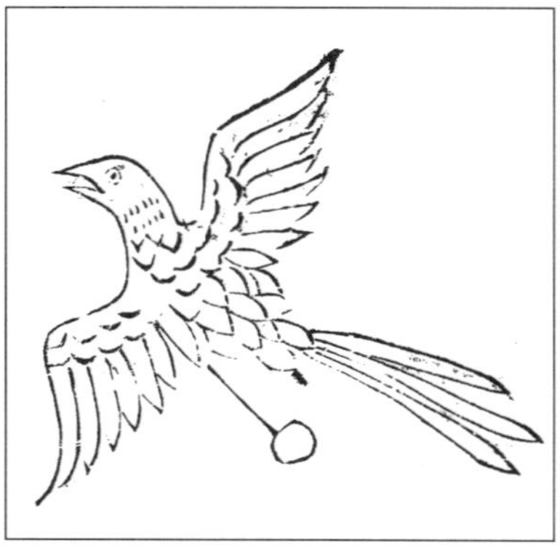

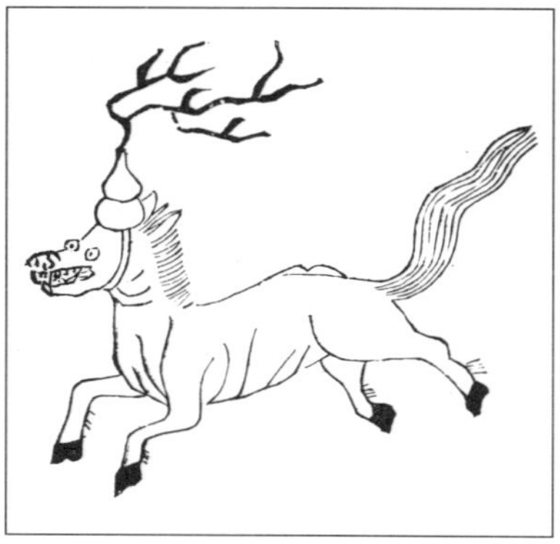

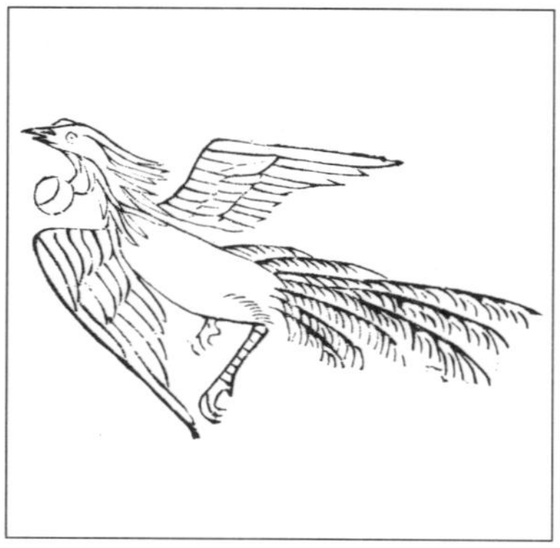

En haut et en bas, les oiseaux incendiaires ou « abricots de feu », au centre, un cheval incendiaire (gravures extraites de Wubei zhijuan).

Pour un usage plus pacifique, presque toutes les provinces produisaient des pétards, les plus connus venant du Hebei, du Jiangxi, du Fujian, du Guangdong, étaient vendus dans la capitale comme produits régionaux par les négociants de thé de ces lointaines provinces. Les États-Unis, avant-guerre, achetaient d'ailleurs leurs feux d'artifice pour le célébration du 4 juillet aux fabricants chinois réputés pour leur ingéniosité. La nuit du Nouvel An n'était pas le seul moment de l'année marqué par d'assourdissantes explosions pour « réveiller le Yang du printemps », on célébrait aussi bruyamment l'ouverture de magasins, les mariages, les funérailles, certains anniversaires et même le départ d'une personnalité locale promue à d'autres fonctions. Dans les provinces du Sud, à la saison chaude, on faisait aussi exploser des pétards pour prévenir les épidémies de choléra. Toutes ces cérémonies s'accompagnaient en général du claquement sonore des cymbales, de coups de gong et de battements de tambour.

Chaque région avait sa spécialité de pétard. Un des plus anciens modèles était connu sous le nom de « tonnerre de chanvre » *(maleizi)* car on serrait la poudre noire dans de la toile de chanvre. Plus spectaculaire, le « doublé » (*ertijiao* ou *shuangxiang*) consistait en un pétard chargé de poudre sur deux

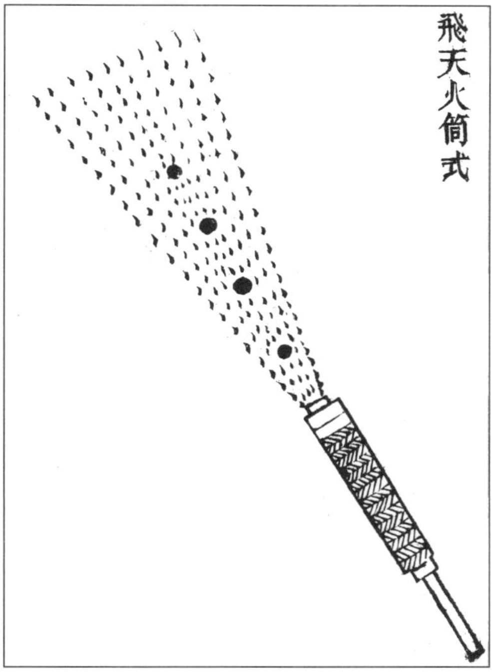

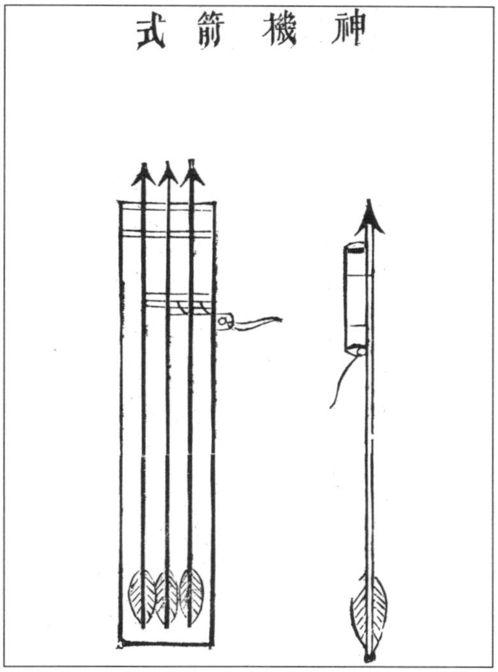

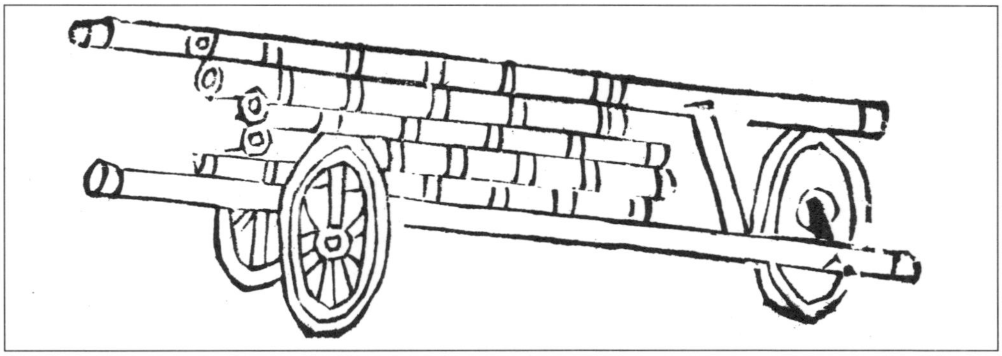

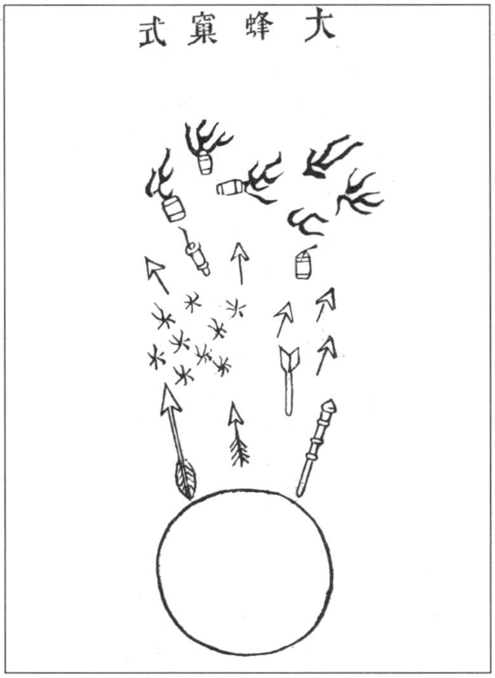

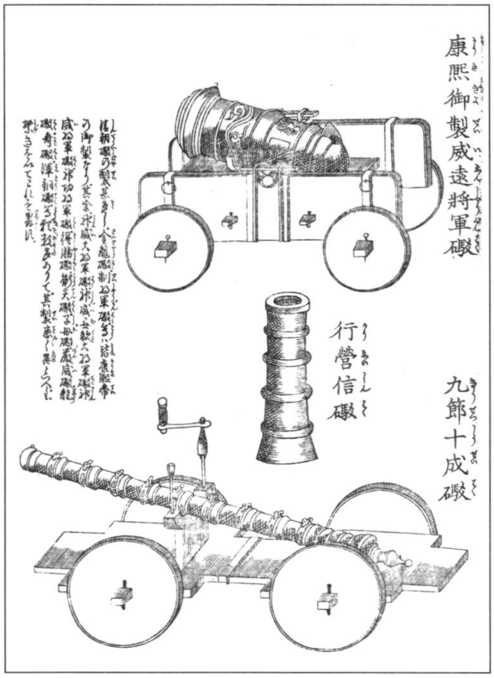

Matériel militaire (XIIIe au XVe siècle) : en haut à gauche et au centre, tubes explosifs, en haut à droite, flèches incendiaires (« corbeaux à feu »), en bas à gauche, mine explosant, en bas à droite, bombarde et couleuvrine (gravures extraites de Wubei zhijuan).

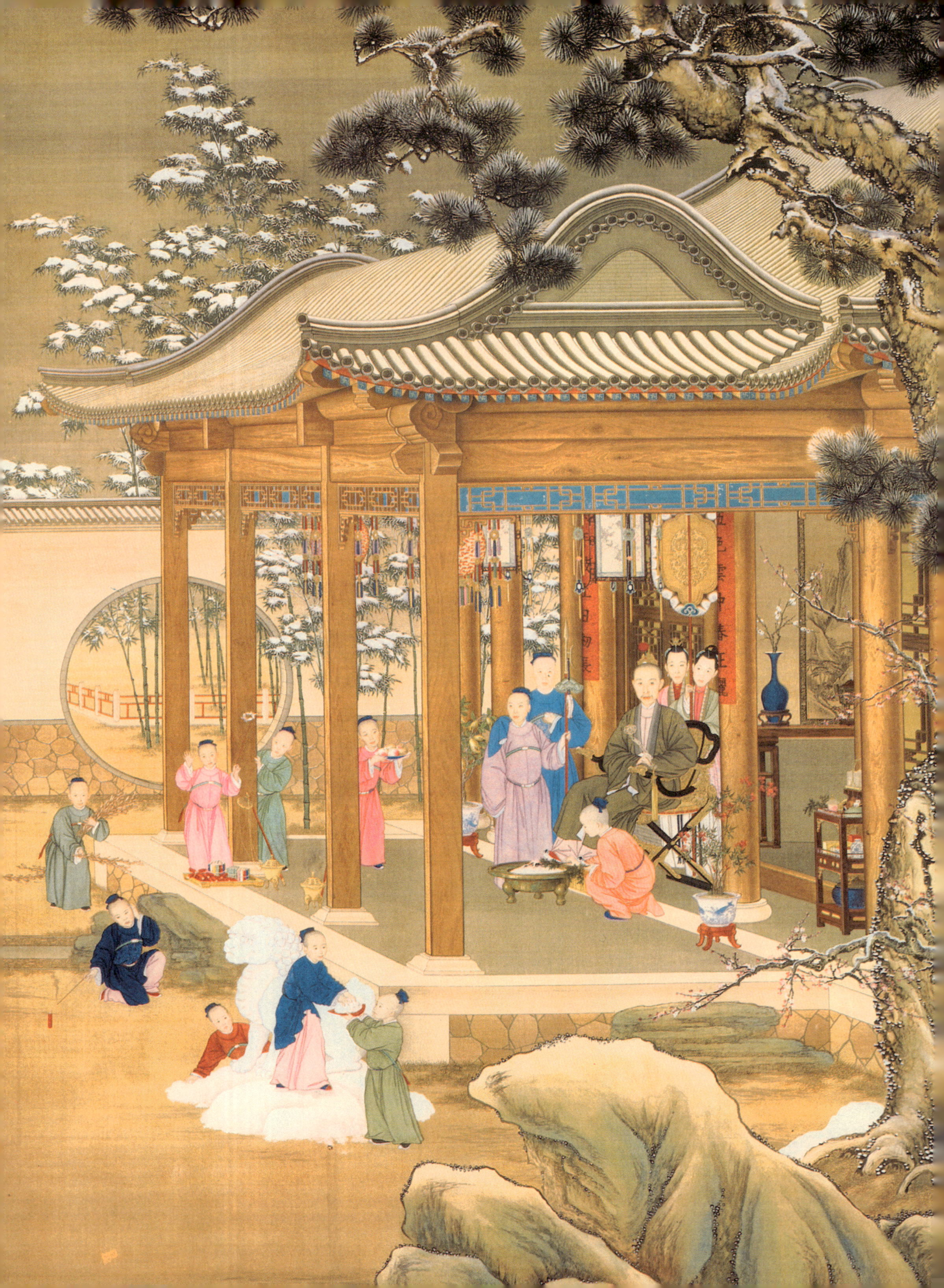

étages qui s'élevait jusqu'à une certaine hauteur puis explosait en deux fois. Parmi les pétards les plus populaires, on trouvait aussi les « tresses de pétards » *(bianpao)* qui se tenaient au bout d'une canne ou accrochées à un clou. Elles brûlaient dans un infernal bruit de mitraille soit devant l'entrée des maisons soit à l'intérieur de la cuisine, devant l'effigie du dieu de la Richesse ou celle du génie du Foyer, avant son départ de fin d'année. On disait alors qu'on « changeait le feu » *(huan huo)*. Selon les croyances, ce dieu faisait, chaque année, un rapport au ciel sur le comportement de la famille. Les offrandes qui lui étaient faites (encens, gâteaux et pétards) avaient pour but de se ménager ses faveurs. Les enfants et les adolescents étaient bien sûr les plus acharnés dans ces jeux devenus si dangereux que les autorités durent prendre en 1994 un arrêté interdisant les pétards dans la plupart des grandes villes de Chine. Les habitants de la capitale prirent alors l'habitude de se rendre au Jour de l'An dans les villages avoisinants pour sacrifier à la tradition qui voulait que plus on dépensait d'argent en pétards plus on avait de bonheur dans l'année à venir…

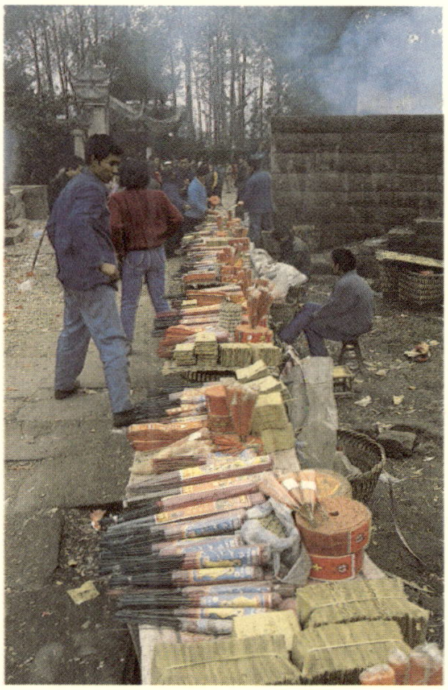

Les pétards avaient donc un caractère rituel et furent toujours associés aux fêtes religieuses ou aux grands événements. En revanche, les feux d'artifice n'étaient faits que pour l'amusement. Traditionnellement, on les classe en deux catégories : ceux qui produisent des flammes *(deng)* et ceux qui produisent des pluies d'étincelles *(huohua, huoxing)*. Le traditionnel « huit-coins » *(bajiaozi)* pouvait s'élever jusqu'à vingt mètres en l'air et le plus connu des feux d'artifice chinois, « la boîte aux fleurs » *(huahezi)*, était une énorme machine explosive montée sur échafaudage, contenant de savants dispositifs qui éclataient en l'air en lançant des fleurs lumineuses, des grappes en feu et des lanternes colorées grâce à des mélanges chimiques de manganèse et de magnésium. Les Chinois ont aussi inventé des fusées appelées *cihua* (« fleurs qui s'élèvent dans le ciel ») qui atteignaient des hauteurs spectaculaires et qui furent utilisées dès le XIIIe siècle dans l'art militaire sous le nom de « corbeaux à feu » *(huoya)* parce qu'on leur ajoutait des ailes. Les enfants qui ne voulaient pas être en reste de la fête se procuraient des pétards spécialement faits pour eux, des bâtonnets de poudre noire qui brûlaient en lançant des étincelles (*didijin*, « gouttelettes d'or ») ou des petits pétards attachés ensemble qui tournoyaient en explosant. Ceux-là portaient la poétique appellation de « pivoines enfilées sur un fil » *(xianchuan mudan)* ; citons aussi les longs rouleaux de carton que l'on tenait pointés vers le ciel et qui, dans un grand bruit de canon *(paoda shuangdeng)*, lâchaient deux boules de feu rouge et verte, et enfin les fusées

Page de gauche, enfants d'une riche famille allumant des pétards pour célébrer le Nouvel An (collection du Palais Impérial). Ci-dessus, étalage d'un marchand de pétards au Nouvel An chinois à Baoding (Sichuan).

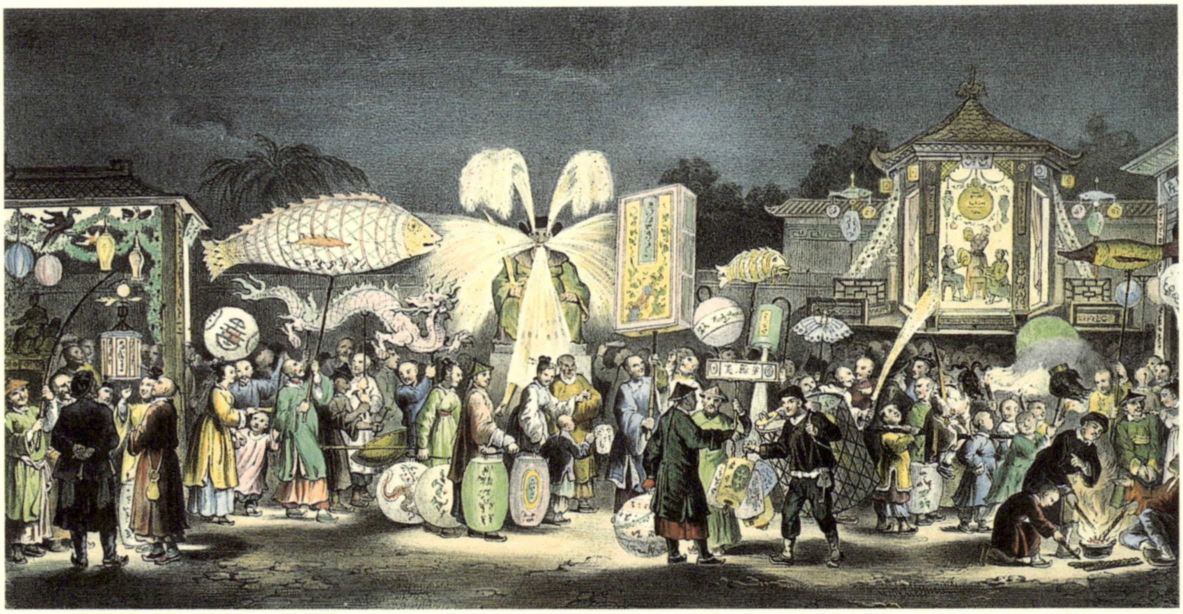

(huojian) qui montaient dans le ciel dans un sifflement strident pour exploser en une pluie savante d'étincelles. Utilisé depuis le XIIe siècle à la cour comme dans le peuple, par les enfants et les femmes, le « rat de terre » (*dilaoshu* ou *zuandihaozi,* littéralement, celui qui s'introduit dans les trous) était, à l'origine, un petit tube bourré d'un mélange pauvre en nitrate qui brûlait en se déplaçant à même le sol très rapidement, dans tous les sens.

La fête des Lanternes *(Dengjie)* est célébrée la nuit du 15 de la 1re lune – d'où son nom *Yuanxiaojie* (« la nuit du premier mois »). Elle marque la fin du festival du Printemps et le retour au travail. Pendant plusieurs soirs, les rues et les maisons sont illuminées par d'innombrables lanternes et, en dépit du froid encore vif dans le Nord, tout le monde sort dans les rues pour les admirer.

L'origine de cette fête nocturne est incertaine, elle remonterait au sacrifice que l'on offrait, à l'époque des Royaumes Combattants (475-221 av. J.-C.), à l'empereur de l'Est, celui qui préside aux naissances et à la vie. Pour d'autres, les âmes des morts venues en visite sur terre devant retourner ce soir-là dans leur domaine, il fallait éclairer leur chemin. Avec l'invention du papier, les lanternes en papier, moins chères, remplacèrent petit à petit les lanternes en soie. Pour la fête, le traditionnel couvre-feu en vigueur dans toutes les villes chinoises était levé afin que le peuple puisse venir voir les lanternes. En ce temps-là, les illuminations étaient rares, cette fête devint vite populaire. C'est vers le VIe siècle qu'on prit l'habitude d'accrocher des lanternes aux bâtiments publics. Sous les Tang, l'empereur Xuanzong (712-756) fit dresser devant le palais à Chang'an un portique où il fit accrocher plusieurs milliers de lanternes, objet d'admiration de tous. Sous les Song, cette coutume

Fête des Lanternes (gravure du XIXe siècle).

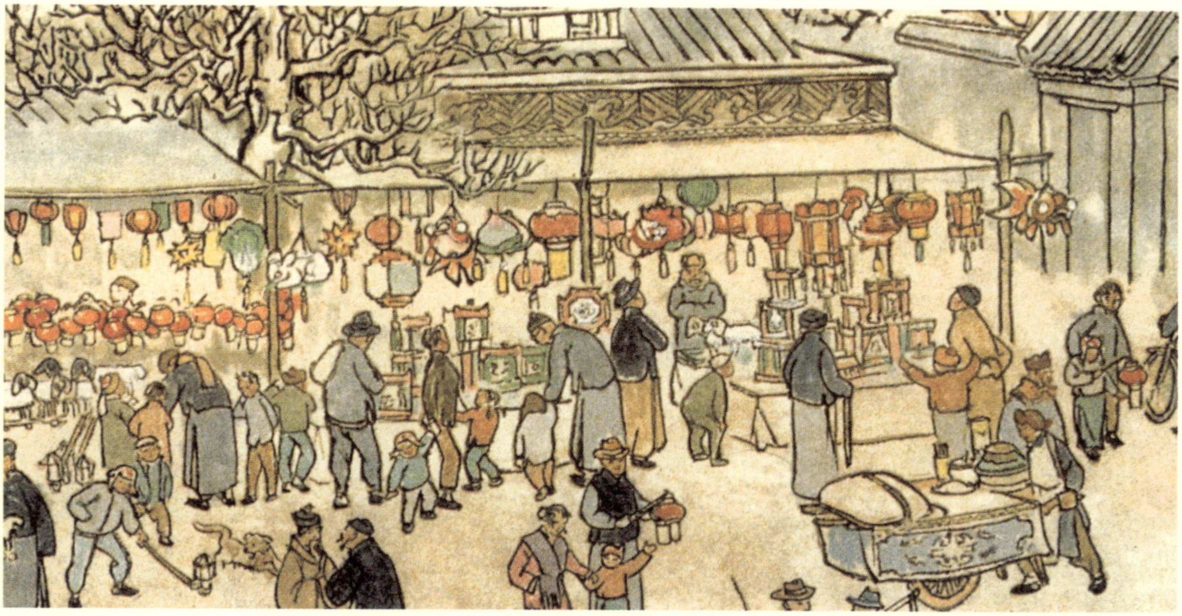

persista et de nouveaux modèles de lanternes apparurent, appelés *caideng* (lanternes multicolores) ; elles portaient de nombreuses décorations (paysages, personnages, fleurs, montagnes, pagodes). Sous les Ming et sous les Qing, les trois jours traditionnellement fériés se transformèrent en une dizaine de jours au cours desquels on pouvait assister à des spectacles, des feux d'artifices, des jeux d'échasses, des chants et des danses. Mais aussi on jouait à déchiffrer les énigmes *(dengmi),* inscrites sur les lanternes sous forme de jeux de mots ou de rébus. C'était un moment important pour les femmes qui n'avaient pratiquement jamais l'occasion de sortir. En dépit des escortes de servantes qui les accompagnaient dans cette sortie unique, les jeunes femmes parvenaient à rencontrer leur soupirant avec lequel elles échangeaient de menus cadeaux. De nombreuses histoires circulaient cette nuit-là ; on disait qu'il fallait absolument sortir de chez soi si l'on voulait éviter de tomber malade pendant le reste de l'année. De même, les femmes qui voulaient un garçon devaient aller discrètement caresser les clous qui ornaient les portes impériales. Toutes ces croyances causaient de grands mouvements de foule devant le Palais impérial qui devenait alors, pour cette nuit-là, un lieu où les promeneurs achetaient des *yuanxiao* (ou *tangyuan*) ; ces boulettes de riz glutineux fourrées au sucre, à la cannelle, aux jujubes ou aux azerolles, au sésame, aux prunes sèches ou aux haricots rouges, sont symboles d'harmonie et d'union de la vie familiale.

Les lanternes chinoises doivent leur originalité tant à leur forme qu'à leur décoration. Les lanternes de procession que l'on portait au bout d'une hampe étaient faites, comme les lampions (ou lanternes vénitiennes), de papier huilé plissé rarement décoré, ou de papier collé sur une armature de fin

Marchands de lanternes au début du siècle (illustration de Wang Daguang, A Round Glancing of Old Beijing, *d. r.).*

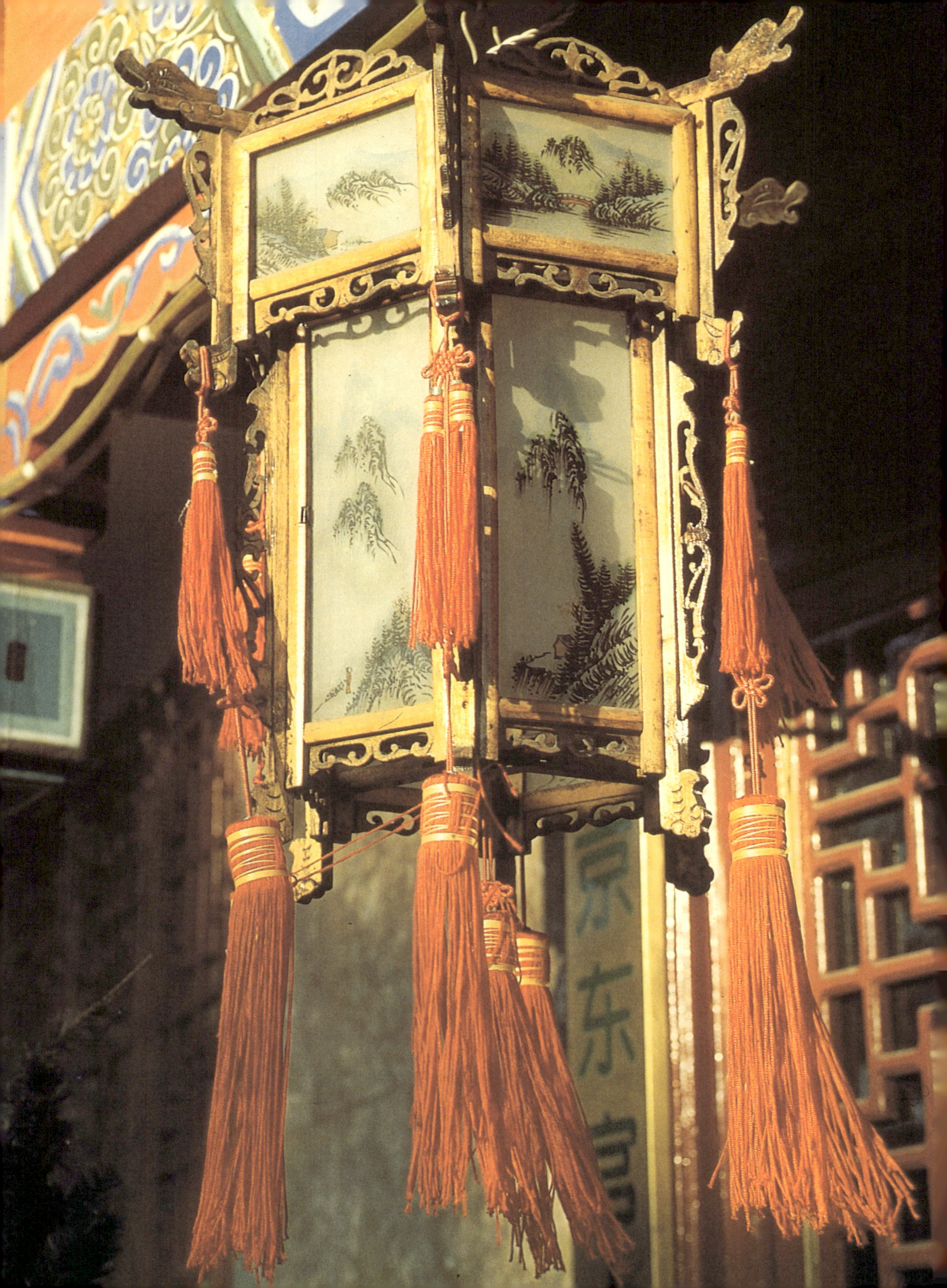
京东

grillage à l'intérieur de laquelle se plaçait une chandelle. En 1841, les autorités de Hong Kong rendirent leur usage obligatoire pour chaque individu se déplaçant de nuit, de même que, pour des raisons de sécurité, on imposait depuis le début du siècle d'éclairer le porche des maisons.

Les lanternes d'extérieur des maisons ou des bâtiments publics, exposées aux intempéries (appelées, *qishifengdeng,* « celles qui s'insurgent contre le vent ») sont les plus connues. Elles étaient en soie rouge imperméabilisée à la colle de poisson, montées sur une grosse armature métallique de forme sphérique se terminant par des pompons de soie jaune. À la fin du XIVe siècle, les Chinois se révoltèrent contre la dynastie régnante mongole des Yuan et parvinrent à chasser le dernier empereur. Comme l'appel à la révolte contre l'envahisseur avait commencé le jour de la pleine lune, juste au moment de la célébration de la fête de la Mi-Automne, chacun mit un point d'honneur à montrer son opposition à l'occupant en accrochant, selon la coutume chinoise, des lanternes aux fenêtres et aux porches des maisons. Le balcon historique de la porte de Tian An Men d'où fut proclamée la République, le 1er octobre 1949, par Mao Zedong, portait aussi une série de lanternes rouges monumentales anciennes. L'une d'entre elles, d'un poids de 250 kg, fut mise aux enchères en 1994 et achetée par un particulier à un prix fabuleux. Même les ministères rivalisaient d'ingéniosité et s'engageaient dans de véritables concours de lanternes ce jour-là. Avec l'avènement de l'électricité, cette charmante coutume qui durait depuis tant de siècles, disparut en 1883. Pour la fête des esprits, en juillet, des lanternes en forme de lotus portant une bougie sont mises à flotter sur l'eau.

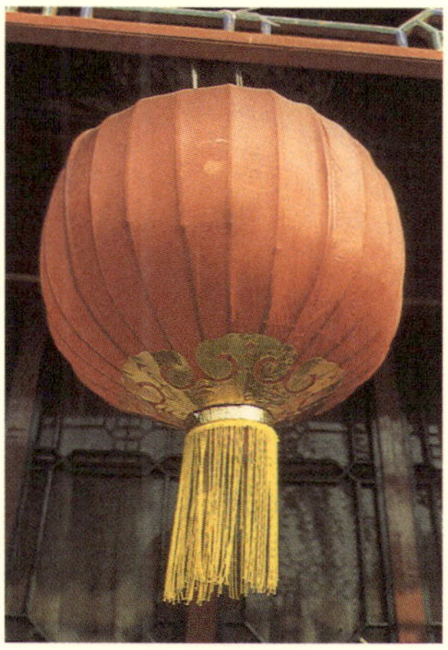

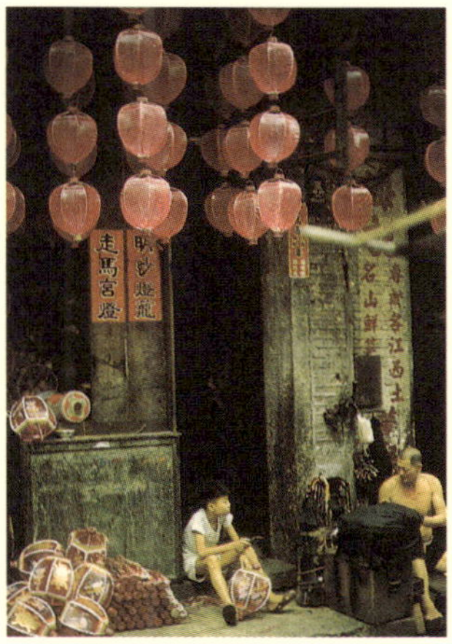

Les lanternes de table étaient faites de quatre pans en verre translucide ou décoré de motifs peints et quelquefois de découpages en papier huilé ou en soie claire. Les montants de bois ou de métal pouvaient se replier et on allumait à l'intérieur une bougie ou une lampe à huile (de sésame). Dans des intérieurs bourgeois, sous les Qing en particulier, elles étaient montées sur un pied de bois rare. Il y avait aussi des lampadaires *(dengtai)* qui portaient des lanternes en forme de pastèque *(xiguadeng).* Les grosses lanternes d'escorte que l'on posait à chaque arrêt, rondes, en papier huilé translucide monté sur bambou, étaient suspendues à un trépied de bois. Les lanternes de mariage portaient le caractère « double bonheur » inscrit en rouge ou bleu, sur celles utilisées pour les funérailles figurait, en noir, le nom du défunt. Quant aux multiples lanternes de fantaisie dont certaines gigantesques, elles pouvaient être cubiques, octogo-

Page de gauche, lanterne décorative d'intérieur à six pans (XIXe siècle). Ci-dessus, lanterne ronde traditionnelle d'extérieur en soie rouge ; en bas, échoppe d'un fabricant à Hong Kong.

nales, en losange, sphériques, en forme de personnages célèbres ou d'animaux. On fabriqua ainsi des « lanternes-dragons » de cent mètres de long, utilisées lors de processions dans les provinces côtières du Sud, des « lanternes-lapin » pour évoquer le « lapin de jade » qui habite dans la lune et fabrique l'élixir d'immortalité, des « lanternes-silhouettes » comme celle de la belle Chang E qui devint immortelle après avoir bu la potion d'immortalité de son mari, l'archer Hou Yi, et trouva refuge dans la lune. L'imagination des fabricants fut infinie ; ils créèrent, dès l'époque Tang, des lanternes tournantes *(zoumadeng)* actionnées par l'air chaud de la mèche ; on y voyait ainsi défiler d'admirables scènes d'intérieur ou des paysages peints ou de papier découpé ; il y eut enfin des lanternes de papier que l'on pouvait rouler comme une boule lumineuse sans que la flamme ne s'éteigne… Les fabricants les plus réputés se trouvaient encore, au début du siècle à Tianjin et pour vanter la qualité d'un produit, on n'hésitait pas à le qualifier de « lanterne de Tianjin » *(weideng).* Comme en Amérique, pour la fête de Halloween, les pêcheurs pauvres du Sud, creusaient des navets dans lesquels ils plaçaient une chandelle et les apportaient en offrande au temple. Ce sont les « lanternes de pêcheurs » *(yudeng).* Depuis trente ans, les autorités ont créé dans la ville de Harbin un festival au cours duquel sont présentées des sculptures sur glace et en particulier, les « lanternes de glace » *(bingdeng),* une tradition typique du nord de la Chine. La fête de la Mi-Automne (le 15e jour de la 8e lune) est l'occasion de célébrer la lune qui, cette nuit-là, est la plus brillante et la plus ronde. On déguste le *yuebing* (ou « gâteau de lune ») fourré aux jujubes ; on admire les feux d'artifice et on fait flotter sur les rivières, les lacs et les étangs des lanternes en forme de lotus.

Au début du siècle, il existait encore des automates que l'on appelait improprement des « lanternes à sable » *(shadeng)* car le mécanisme qui animait les personnages était assuré par un sablier. Après avoir renversé la lanterne, on l'accrochait au mur et les enfants pouvaient admirer les petits sujets animés. Ce jouet très astucieux était en fait inspiré d'un automate très célèbre du monde grec (Ier siècle), le théâtre de marionnettes de Héron d'Alexandrie…

Les lanternes ont ainsi joué un rôle important dans la vie sociale et religieuse en Chine, symboles de joie et de vie, elles ont encore une place de choix dans toutes les célébrations importantes : la fête du Printemps (ou Nouvel An chinois), la fête des Lanternes, la fête de la Mi-Automne et la fête des « Sept Sœurs »… Mais les artisans de lanternes traditionnelles sont hélas de moins en moins nombreux car les lanternes en plastique, éclairées et animées par des piles électriques, ont maintenant la faveur d'une clientèle plus tournée vers la technologie moderne que vers la tradition.

Les fleurs de tête

妆扮青云

zhuangban qingyun, littéralement, « décorations pour nuages noirs ».

Contrairement aux femmes mandchoues qui portaient des coiffes aux formes élaborées, les femmes d'origine Han prirent l'habitude de confectionner des chignons qu'elles décoraient de bijoux, de plumes, de perles ou de colifichets. Ces joyaux étaient à la fois une marque de leur statut social et un faire-valoir de leur beauté. Pour les rendre plus attirantes, les joailliers eurent recours à des trésors d'imagination.

Les peintures murales de Dunhuang et les nombreuses poteries de la Chine des Tang (618-907) nous offrent d'extraordinaires exemples de coiffes et surtout de chignons de femmes. Classées en chignon haut, descendant ou plat, ces œuvres d'art nécessitaient l'utilisation de rubans de soie sur lesquels on torsadait les mèches et de postiches destinés à donner du volume et de la hauteur. Ces coiffures audacieuses, réservées aux femmes de qualité, portaient des noms poétiques comme le « chignon du bonheur », le « cygne effarouché », la « double épée » ou l'« éventail du paon »… Dans les cheveux, on piquait donc des épingles de taille et de forme différentes, appelées « fleurs de tête » *(touhua)* ou « bijoux de tête » *(toushi, touzan)*. Ces épingles qui n'étaient portées que par les femmes ayant atteint leur majorité servaient à garder les cheveux en place en mettant une note étincelante dans la masse sombre des cheveux poétiquement dénommée les « nuages noirs ». En effet, alors que pour les garçons la cérémonie de remise du bonnet viril *(jiguan)* avait lieu à vingt ans, c'est à l'âge de quinze ans que l'on remettait aux filles « l'épingle à cheveux » *(jiji)* symbole de sa nouvelle vie d'adulte. Les parures de cheveux peuvent se classer, selon leur forme, en trois catégories :

– les « épingles à chignon », plates, longues d'une dizaine de centimètres (semblables à un marque-pages de livre), servaient à retenir le chignon qui, dans certaines régions de la côte, pouvait être monumental. Faites d'une seule pièce en or, ivoire, écaille mais le plus souvent en argent simple, niellé ou émaillé, ces épingles se terminent par un petit rouleau ou un motif en

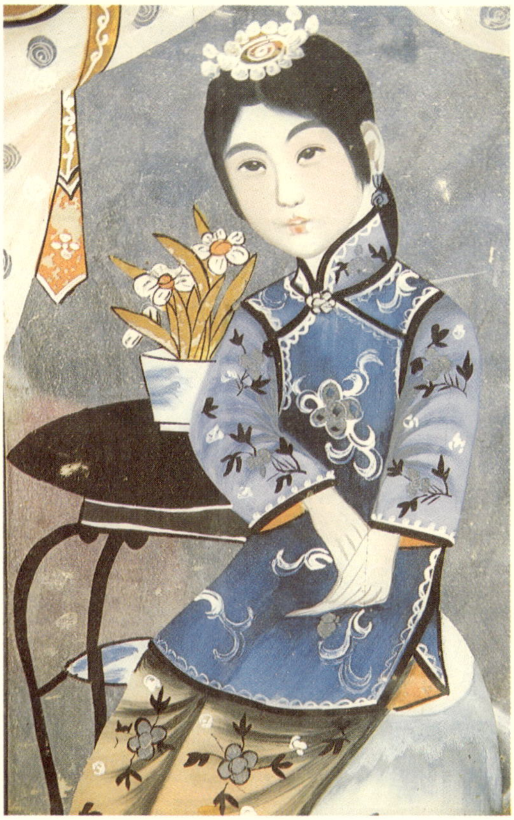

Portrait de femme (peinture sur miroir, dynastie des Qing, XIXe siècle).

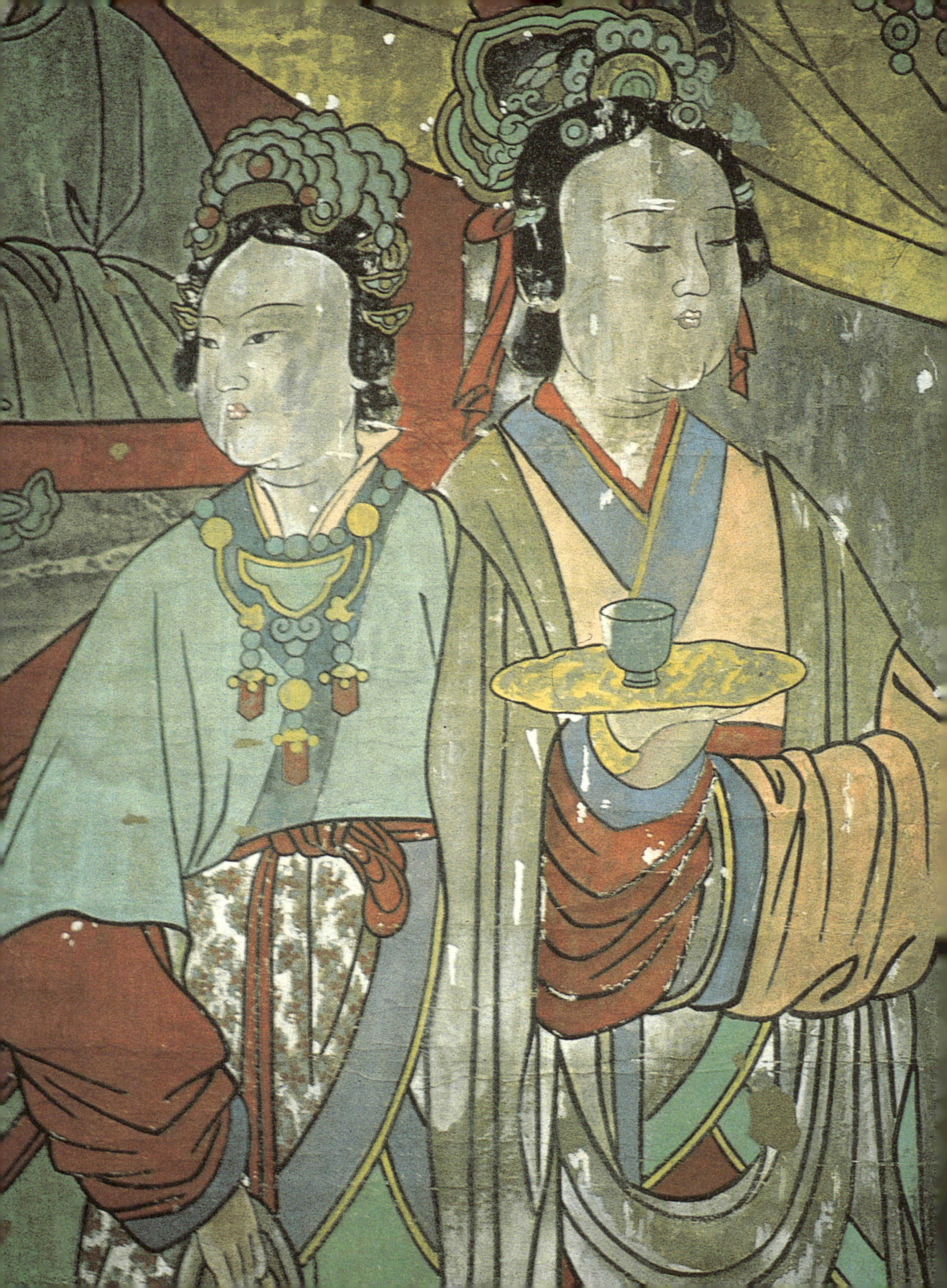

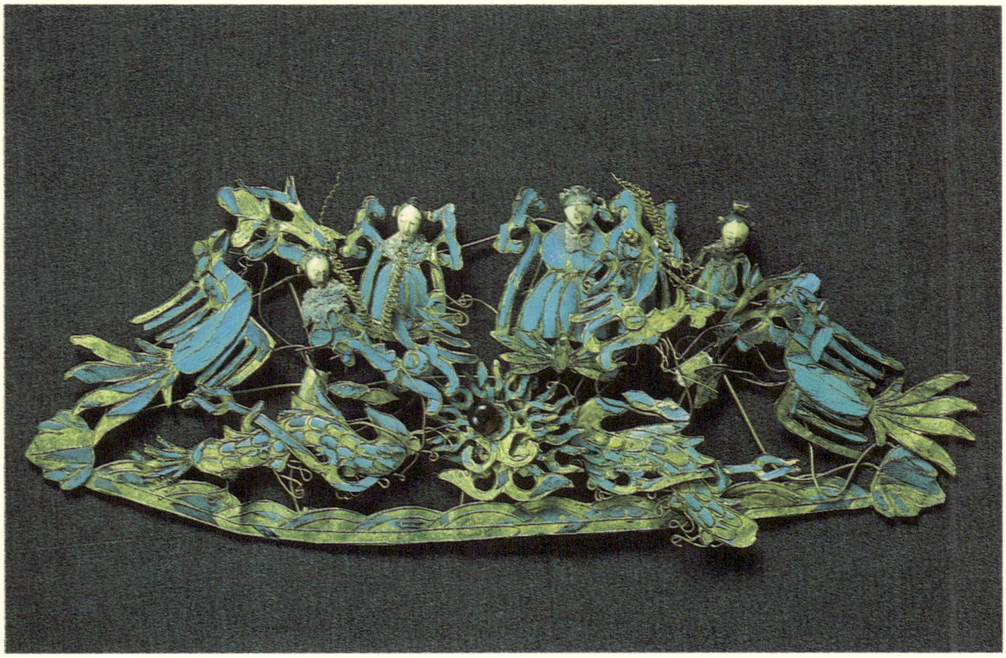

palmettes. Le plat de la pièce est décoré de fines ciselures et porte quelquefois, au dos, le poinçon de l'orfèvre ;

– les « épingles à cheveux » *(facha, faqia)* que l'on piquait et qui pouvaient être simples ou doubles, en général en or ou en argent. Les doubles, appelées « épingles de vieille femme » *(lao taitaide facha),* désignaient dans la langue populaire une personne qui traite des affaires en deux endroits à la fois. En effet, ces petites fourches pouvaient servir à d'autres usages, comme curedents, grattoir, pinces… Les épingles simples se terminent par un cabochon de jade (d'où leur nom, *yuzan*), corail, pierre précieuse ou filigrane. Alors que les épingles longues étaient en vogue sous les Tang, ces objets prirent plus de volume sous les Song. À la fin de la période des Qing, l'orfèvrerie se caractérisa par l'exubérance des motifs, l'incrustation de pierres semi-précieuses comme la malachite, le grenat, le lapis-lazuli, la turquoise…

Bon nombre de ces épingles étaient décorées avec des incrustations de plumes de martin-pêcheur ; on les appelait les « ornements en métal bleu-vert » *(cuidian).* Le martin-pêcheur que l'on peut trouver en Chine (*Alcyon smyrnensis* ou *Alcedo Atthis Bengalensis*) est un oiseau des rivières de couleur bleu-vert *(cui)* dont les petites plumes servent depuis longtemps à la confection de parures féminines. (Le bouillon de viande de martin-pêcheur est utilisé par les charlatans pour éliminer les arêtes de poisson de la gorge.) Déjà bien avant la dynastie des Ming, on parlait de cette technique décorative qui s'apparente au cloisonné utilisée aussi bien pour des bijoux que pour la décoration de tableaux ou de paravents. Certains pensent qu'on

Page de gauche, femmes nobles portant un diadème de plumes (peinture murale, période Yuan, 1324). Ci-dessus, diadème de métal doré décoré de plumes de martin-pêcheur à motifs de phénix, de paons et de personnages féminins à tête d'ivoire (coiffe d'opéra, XIXe siècle).

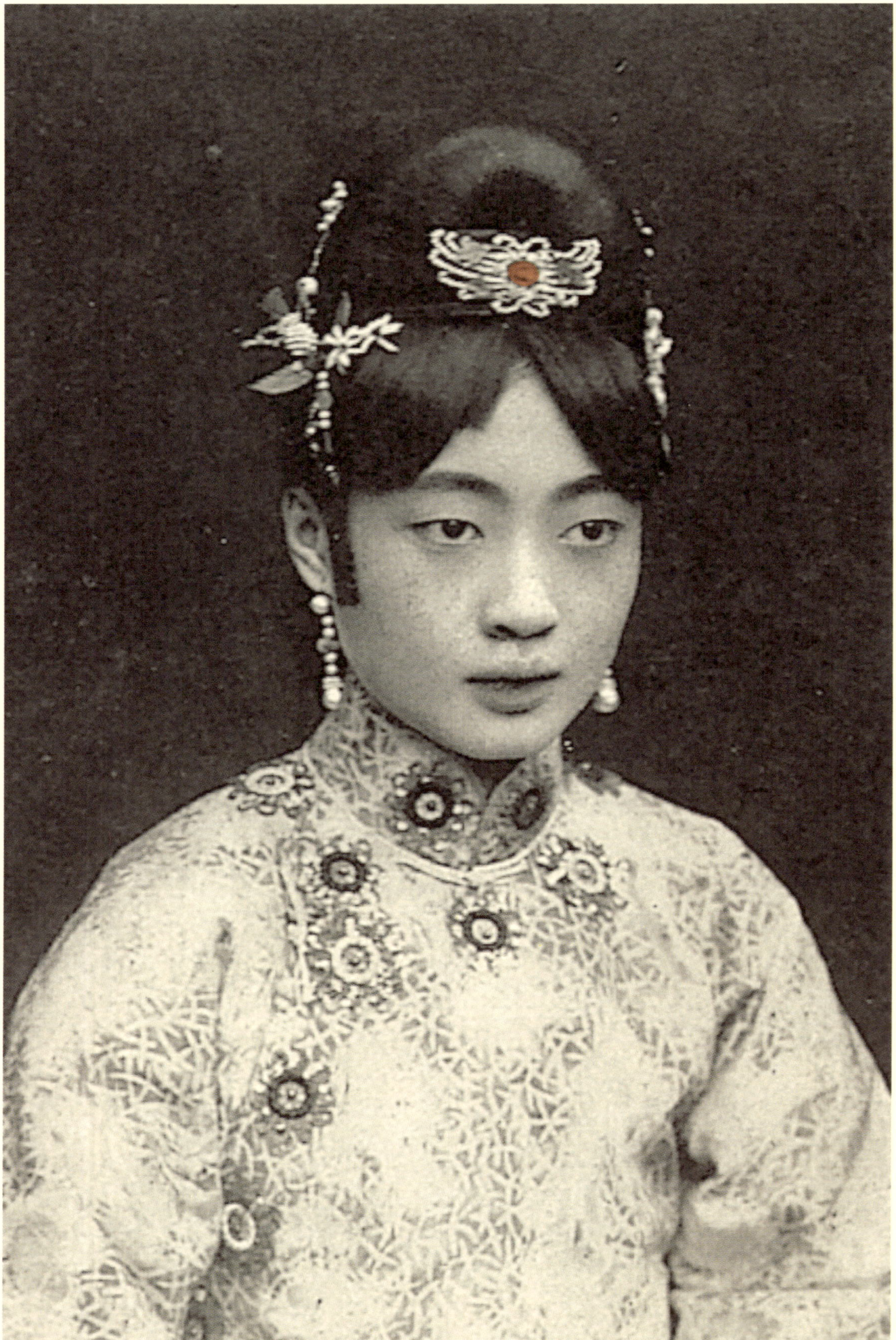

trempait d'abord les plumes dans un bain colorant pour obtenir d'une manière uniforme la célèbre teinte turquoise irisée, d'autres disent qu'on les utilisait directement. Les plumes étaient découpées sur une plaque de corne puis collées sur des montures d'argent, de métal argenté ou de carton bouilli en forme de fleurs, d'animaux ou de poissons au dos desquelles était fixée une longue épingle. De nos jours, ces délicats et fragiles bijoux sont devenus rares, ceux que l'on trouve encore sont fabriqués pour les costumes de l'Opéra de Pékin et reprennent les formes des bijoux autrefois réservés à l'aristocratie. La rareté du martin-pêcheur, dont l'habitat naturel se trouve dans les provinces de la Chine méridionale riches en lacs et rivières, limita la production de ces bijoux aux ateliers de Canton et de Pékin. La fameuse concubine Yang Guifei de l'époque Tang, possédait une robe d'apparat faite de ces précieuses plumes ainsi qu'un char couvert de ces ornements rares. À l'époque contemporaine, on remplaça les plumes trop fragiles par de la soie bleue imitant les rémiges de l'oiseau ;

– les diadèmes, appelés « coiffes de phénix » *(fengguan, fenggao, huangguan)*, sont formés d'un entrelacs de fils métalliques, monté sur une coiffe *(tianze)* ou un bandeau, sur lesquels on fixait des motifs décoratifs traditionnels (fleurs, papillons, phénix, dragons) ou de petits sujets à tête d'ivoire peints (les Huit Immortels). Dès l'époque Tang, il existait des diadèmes portant de fins tubes dans lesquels on pouvait insérer de longues épingles flexibles. L'ensemble était complété de fils souples torsadés « aussi fins que les moustaches d'une crevette ». Toutes ces pendeloques formaient un halo qui oscillait gracieusement à chaque mouvement de la tête. Les élégantes avaient remis à la mode la technique du *buyao* (oscillations) pratiquée dès le IVe siècle par les femmes Murong, une minorité ethnique nomade du nord de la Chine. Comme le montrent les portraits peints de l'époque Qing, les diadèmes pouvaient aussi se prolonger par un rideau de perles tombant du front.

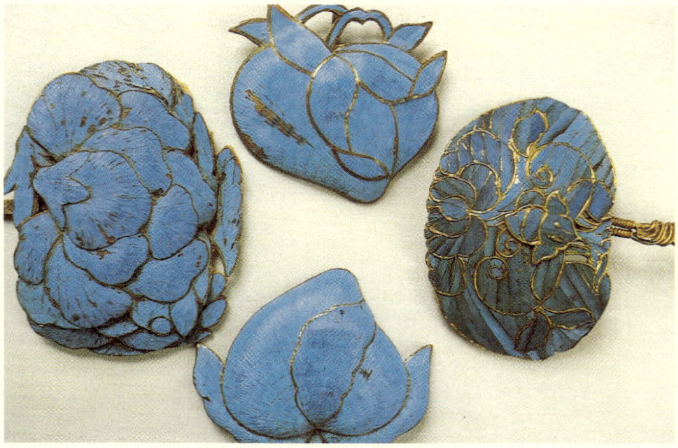

De nos jours, ces nombreuses décorations ont disparu, en particulier les pendeloques longues d'une trentaine de centimètres qu'arboraient les femmes mandchoues sous les Qing. Selon les usages, le port de chignons élaborés et de parures était réservé aux femmes ayant atteint la majorité et appartenant aux classes supérieures de la société. D'extraordinaires diadèmes et coiffes se portaient à la cour pour certaines cérémonies ou à l'occasion des mariages. Une exposition de pièces exceptionnelles de la Cité Interdite a montré la « coiffe de phénix » de l'impératrice Xiaodan (période Ming),

Page de gauche, portrait photographique de Wang Rong qui épousera en 1922 le dernier empereur des Qing, Xuantong (ou Pu Yi). Ci-dessus, cabochons d'épingles à cheveux faits en cloisonné de plumes de martin-pêcheur de couleur bleu-turquoise, motif floral, période Qing.

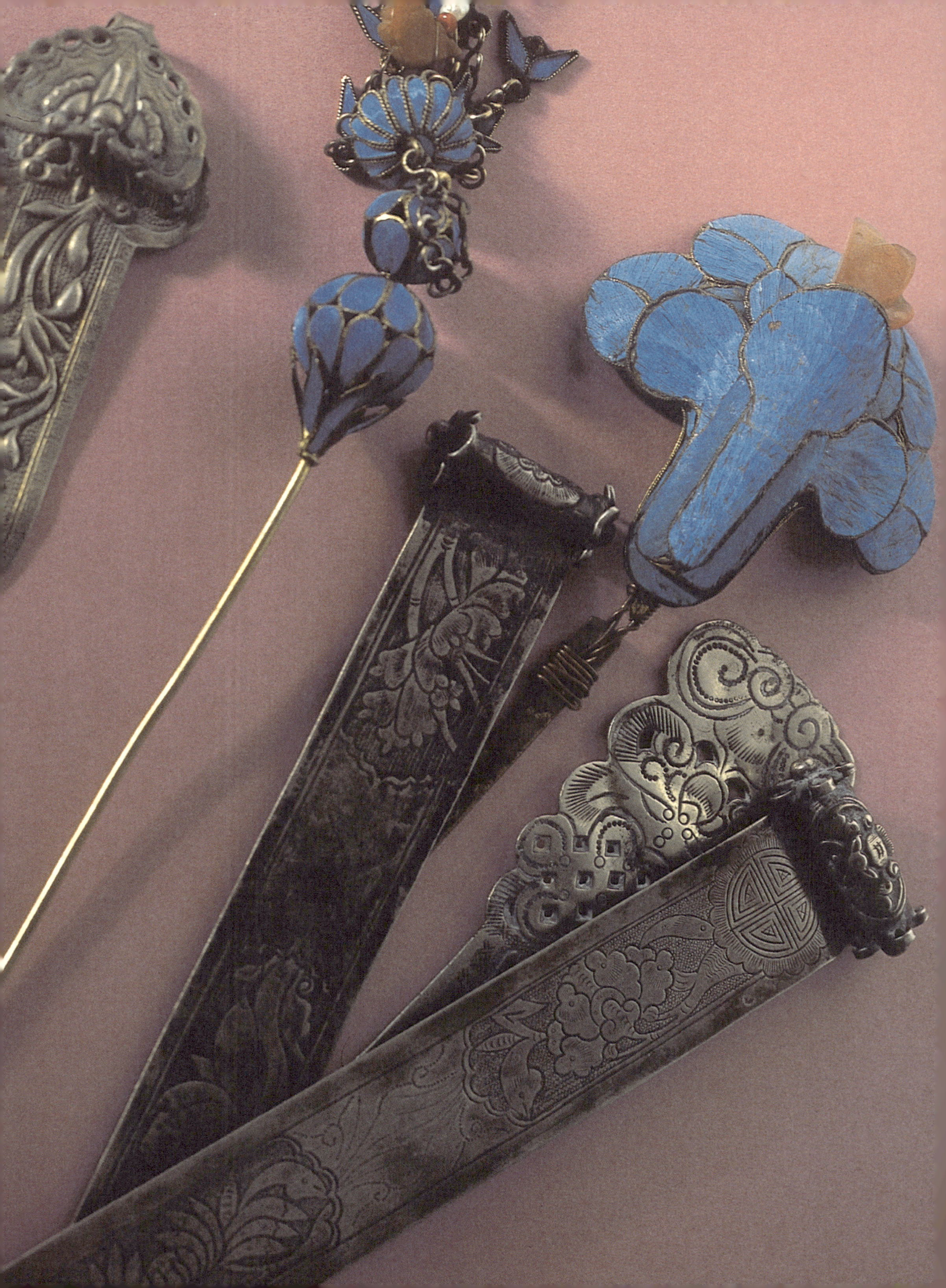

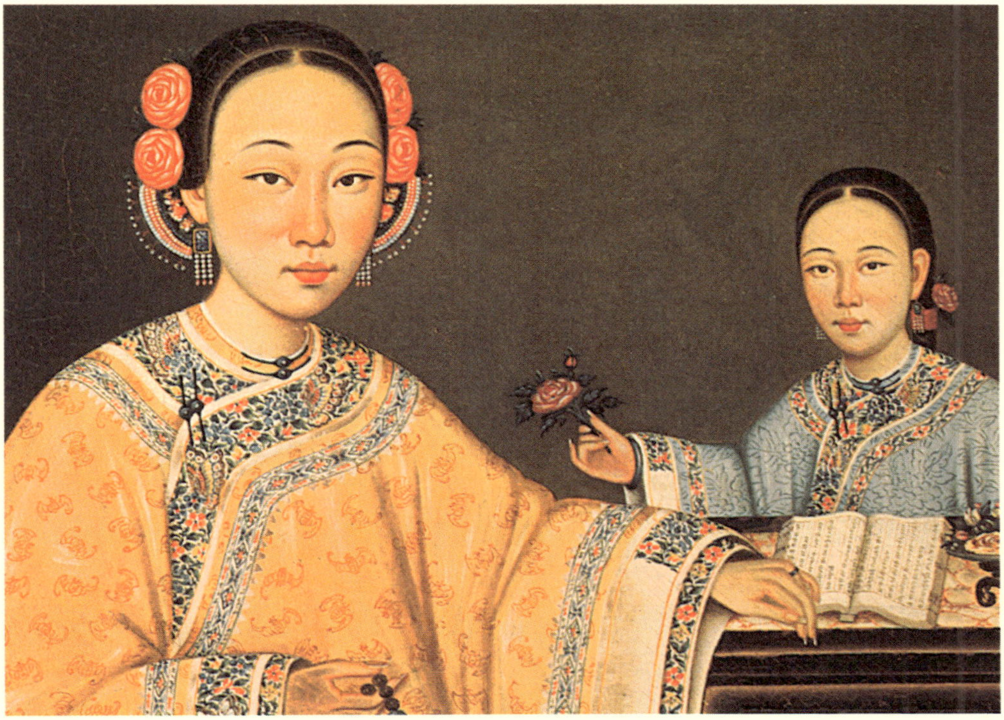

retrouvée intacte dans sa tombe. Le joyau comprenait un millier de perles fines en pendeloques ou montées avec une bonne centaine de pierres précieuses (rubis, saphirs, topazes). Six dragons de filigranes d'or surmontant trois phénix en plumes de martin-pêcheur, complétaient cet extraordinaire ensemble. Peu de temps après la chute de l'empire (1911), les révolutionnaires commencèrent à montrer une certaine réprobation à l'égard du luxe déployé lors des mariages. On n'osa plus alors afficher tant de fortune sur la tête des mariées qui portèrent dorénavant des bandeaux de fleurs naturelles. Michel Beurdeley note, à ce sujet, que « les moins fortunées de ces élégantes devaient se contenter de garnir leur coiffe de petites fleurs naturelles ou de petits insectes aux ailes irisées ("insectes de jade"). Ces bestioles, qui avaient la réputation de s'accoupler dans les corolles des fleurs, étaient capturées à la saison de leurs amours, ce qui donnait plus de prix à leur parure ».

Les mariées d'aujourd'hui continuent ainsi de piquer dans leur chignon un bouquet de petites fleurs rouges artificielles montées sur de longues tiges flexibles. Un adage populaire ne dit-il pas : « voilà venu le temps de monter dans le palanquin (de mariage), aussi faut-il piquer les fleurs » *(xian shang jiao, xian cha hua)* ?

Page de gauche, différentes épingles à cheveux ; ci-dessus, portrait d'une femme noble portant une coiffure typiquement chinoise du début du XIXe siècle (peinture de Zhang Litian, Macao, détail).

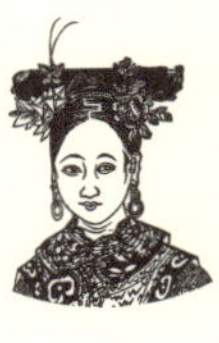

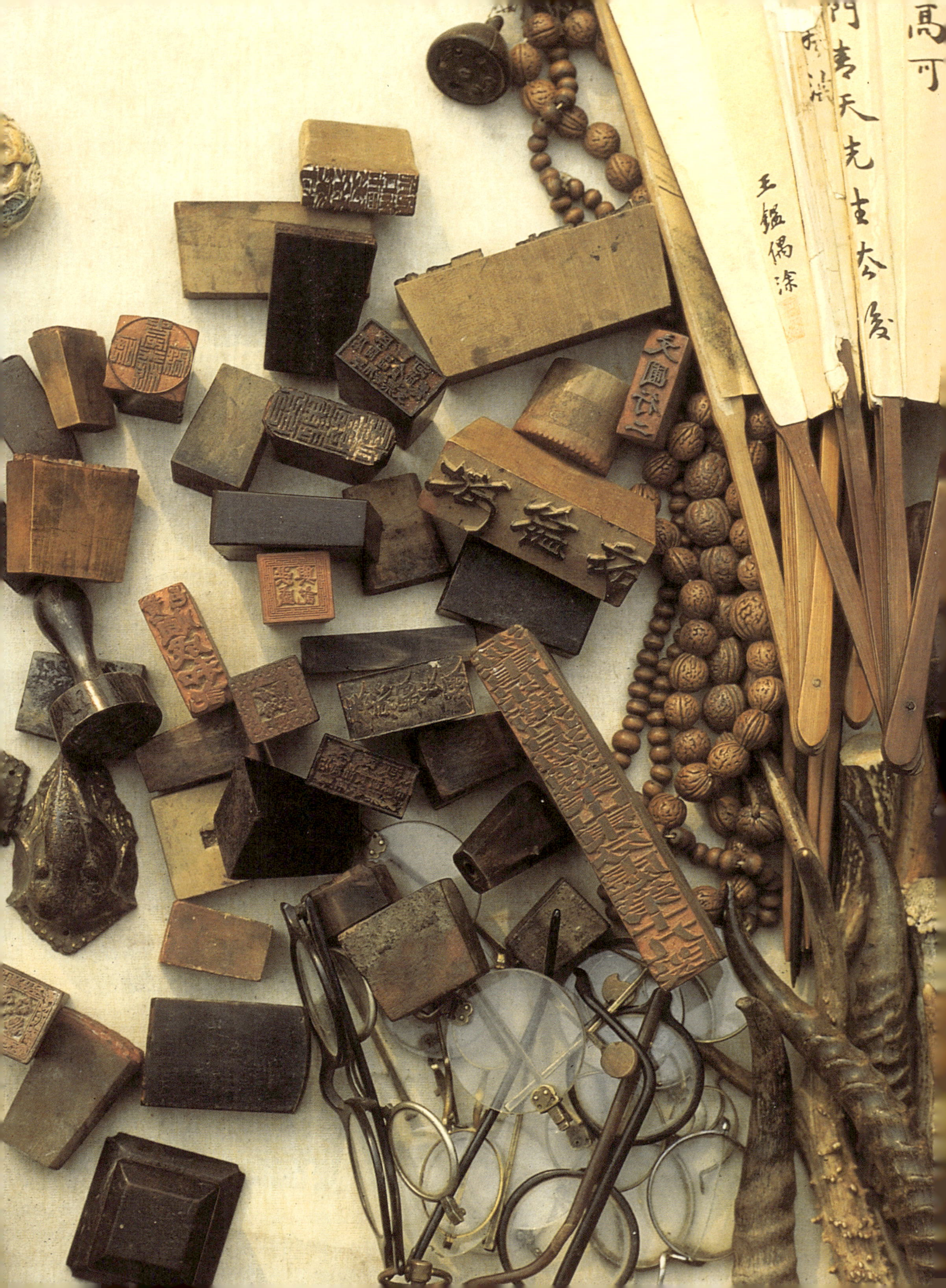

Les lunettes chinoises

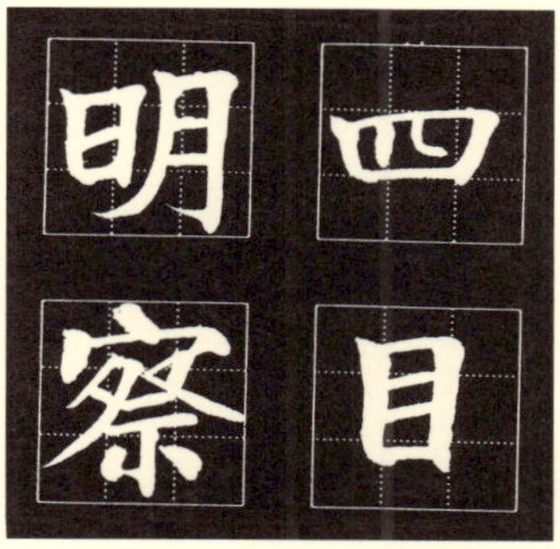

simu mingcha, littéralement, « quatre yeux pour bien voir ».

« Découvrir le vrai visage du mont Lu » *(Lushan zhen mian mu…),* tel était le souhait le plus cher de tout Chinois qui souhaitait, une fois dans sa vie, se rendre dans la province du Jiangxi pour tenter d'apercevoir, à l'œil nu, cette montagne mythique enfouie dans les brumes et les nuages qui fut l'objet d'une admiration particulière de générations d'ermites, d'artistes ou de touristes…

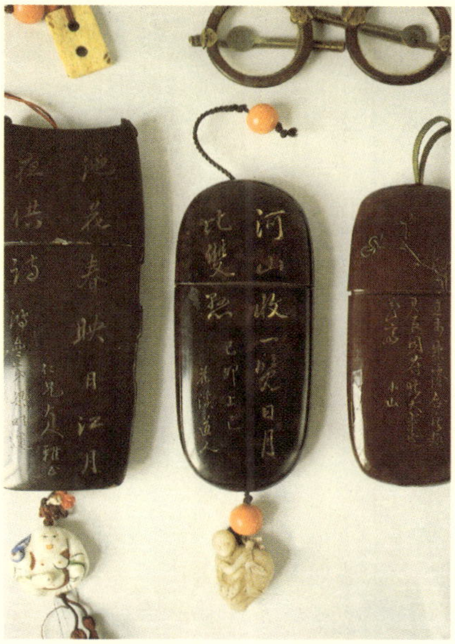

L'invention des lunettes en Occident, qui remonte au XIIIe siècle, est attribuée soit au moine florentin Alessandro di Spina, soit à l'un des plus grands savants du Moyen Âge, l'anglais Roger Bacon (1220-1292), l'auteur de l'*Opus Maius,* dans lequel il étudiait le phénomène des lentilles. Les premières lunettes furent des lentilles correctrices enchâssées dans des montures conçues pour être posées sur le nez. Destinées à ceux qui ne pouvaient voir des objets proches, elles avaient pour fonction de corriger la presbytie. Les premiers verres furent fabriqués dans une gemme, fine, transparente, appelée béryl, qui a donné son nom à « besicles » (ou « bésicles »). Le béryl, constitué de silicate naturel d'aluminium et de béryllium, est en fait le terme générique d'un groupe de pierres précieuses aux couleurs différentes ; la morganite est un béryl rose, l'héliodore est jaune, l'émeraude, très recherchée, est de couleur verte, l'aigue-marine est bleu-clair. On croit que les premiers béryls venaient de l'île de Ceylan, de la presqu'île de Malacca ou de Java. Dès le IIe siècle av. J.-C., les échanges des Chinois avec les contrées de l'ouest (Turkestan, Bactriane, Inde) sont attestés et il est probable que les caravanes de la Route de la Soie ont ramené en Chine des pierres semi-précieuses, comme le béryl ou le quartz, originaires de ces régions. Le quartz concassé entrera d'ailleurs dans la fabrication du verre et des vernis pour porcelaines. Les qualités du quartz étaient connues depuis la haute antiquité mésopotamienne ; on a retrouvé à Ninive une lentille convexe destinée à allumer des feux sacrés datant du IXe siècle av. J.-C. Au Ve siècle,

Ci-dessus, paire de lunettes cerclées de corne et étuis de bois laqués et gravés (XIXe siècle).

Alexandrie est le plus grand centre exportateur d'objets en verre. Ce n'est que vers le VIIe siècle seulement que des lentilles semblables parviendront en Chine par l'Inde. On les appellera alors les « gemmes à feu » *(huozhu)* et elles seront utilisées en médecine, notamment pour la moxibustion (*moxa* est le nom japonais de l'armoise).

Il faudra ainsi attendre le XIVe siècle et la dynastie mongole des Yuan pour qu'apparaissent en Chine les premières lunettes de vue. Les références les plus anciennes se trouvent dans deux collections de l'époque Ming. Selon ces auteurs, les lunettes faisaient partie d'un « tribut payé par des étrangers » à la province du Gansu (un des points de passage obligé des caravanes) ; selon d'autres sources, elles faisaient partie d'un accord entre marchands chinois et « marchands venus de l'ouest pour acheter de bons chevaux »... Dans un autre ouvrage, il est aussi fait référence à un inspecteur de l'instruction publique *(duxue)* de la province de Canton qui possédait déjà « une paire de lunettes apportées par un bateau de Malacca ». Déjà, sous les Song (960-1279), on avait parlé de juges qui avaient utilisé un morceau de cristal ou de quartz *(shuijing)* comme loupe pour déchiffrer, à la lumière du soleil, un document nécessaire à leur enquête. À cette époque, on ne savait pas encore très bien fabriquer ces lentilles grossissantes. Sous la dynastie des Ming, un siècle plus tard, les lunettes restaient un luxe réservé aux seuls membres de la famille impériale et à quelques riches marchands. C'est dans la région de Canton que l'on commença à fabriquer des lunettes dans du « quartz » et l'on disait qu'elles étaient meilleures que les lunettes qui venaient de l'étranger.

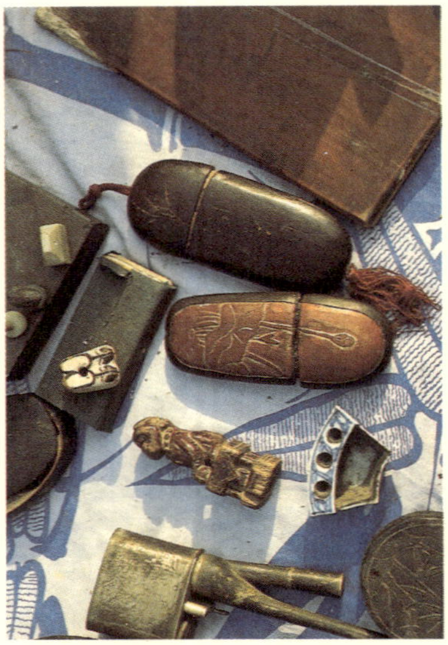

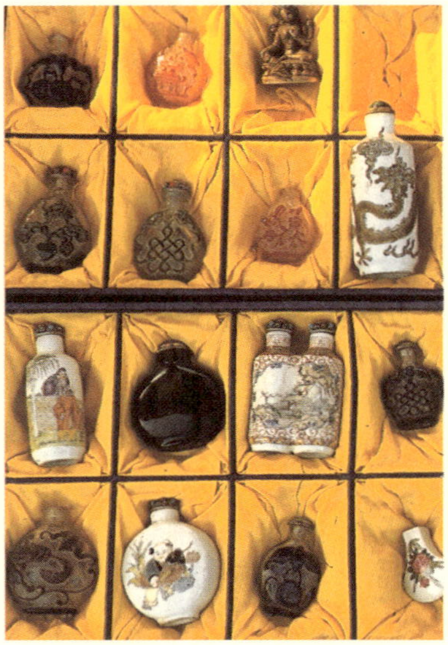

En haut, étuis à lunettes chinois sur un étal de brocanteur ; en bas, flacons pour tabac à priser (yanbihu) en porcelaine et verre de Pékin.

Des controverses ont eu lieu au sujet du nom que les Chinois donnèrent aux lunettes. Berthold Laufer (*Zur Geshichte der Brille,* 1907) cite Zhao Xigu, un membre de la famille impériale à l'époque des Song, qui parle des « *aitai* au moyen desquelles les vieilles gens peuvent lire des écritures fines, et qui proviennent d'Asie centrale... Elles ressemblent à deux grosses pièces de monnaie et leur couleur est celle du mica ». Il a depuis été démontré que *aitai* n'était pas un mot chinois mais un terme utilisé par les caravaniers. C'était probablement une translittération de l'arabe *uwainat* (lunettes). Curieusement, un auteur très ancien, Liu An (mort au IIe siècle av. J.-C.) faisait déjà référence à des « yeux d'or » *(jinmu)*... S'agit-il d'une invention tombée dans l'oubli ? Aucune allusion n'apparaîtra plus jamais sur le sujet dans les ouvrages ultérieurs. C'est donc au début du XVIe siècle qu'apparut le terme de « verres ou lentilles pour les yeux » *(yanjing)*, qui continue d'être utilisé de nos jours.

S'agissant du verre, il est probable qu'il était connu en Chine depuis l'Âge du Fer. On a retrouvé des agrafes de vêtements de l'époque des Royaumes Combattants portant déjà des incrustations en pâte de verre. Au Ve siècle av. J.-C., les marchands de la Route de la Soie rapportèrent non seulement du Moyen-Orient des objets en verre, mais certainement des secrets de fabrication. Un four aurait existé dès 140 av. J.-C. dans la province du Shanxi. Mais ce n'est qu'avec l'arrivée des Jésuites au XVIIe siècle que le verre fut véritablement « réintroduit » en Chine. Jusqu'à cette date, aucun besoin pour ce matériau ne s'était fait sentir tant l'usage de la porcelaine était répandu. Il existait toutefois depuis le XVe siècle une verrerie fondée par l'empereur Yongle qui aurait donné son nom à une venelle du vieux Pékin, Liulichangjie, mais l'on ne sait si elle fabriquait du verre ou des tuiles. Les Chinois nommaient le verre transparent, *boli* et le verre opaque ou l'émail pour les tuiles vernissées, *liuli*. Ce mot a même été utilisé autrefois pour désigner le quartz. Le jésuite Matteo Ricci, qui arriva à Pékin en 1601, raconte que les verres vénitiens exerçaient sur les Chinois une grande fascination. Le verre était considéré comme une matière précieuse à cause de sa rareté. C'est en 1680 que fut créée dans la Cité Interdite, sur ordre de Kangxi, la première manufacture impériale de verre dont la direction fut confiée à un jésuite allemand, Kilian Stumpf. Celui-ci fera la célébrité du fameux « verre de Pékin ».

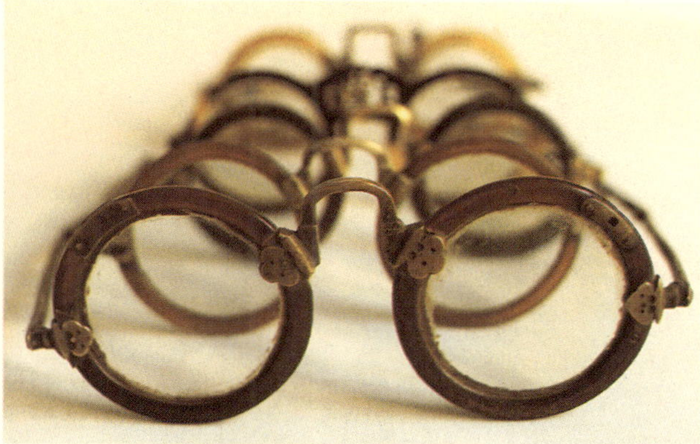

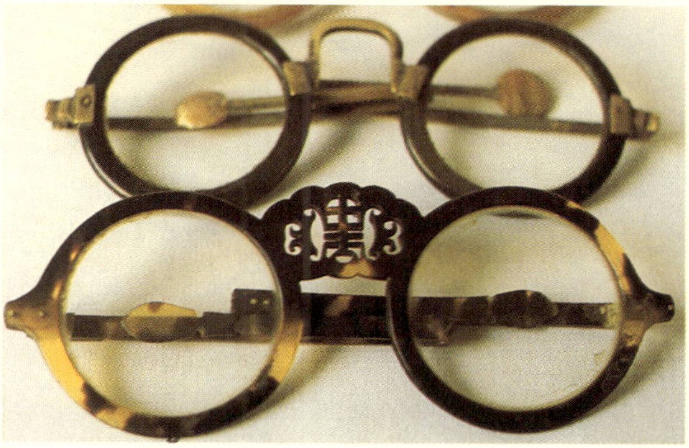

Sous les Qing, il existait donc plusieurs centres de fabrication du verre. Dans la capitale, outre la verrerie impériale, on dénombrait des ateliers privés comme celui des Jésuites français, actif dès 1696. En province, à Canton et Boshan (province du Shandong), on produisait du verre brut qui était ensuite retravaillé à la capitale. C'est de cette période que date la fabrication de verres de lunettes et de lentilles pour télescopes d'astronomie. Plus facile à travailler, le verre remplaça les gemmes pour les lunettes.

Comme en Europe, les lunettes chinoises connurent les mêmes difficultés à tenir sur le nez de leurs propriétaires. On imagina d'abord des systèmes à ressort (selon le principe de nos pince-nez ou lorgnons), puis on adopta un système de fils qui faisaient le tour des oreilles. Enfin, on plaça au bout des

Lunettes chinoises (fin XIXe - début XXe siècle) en écaille avec, en bas, motif décoratif shou.

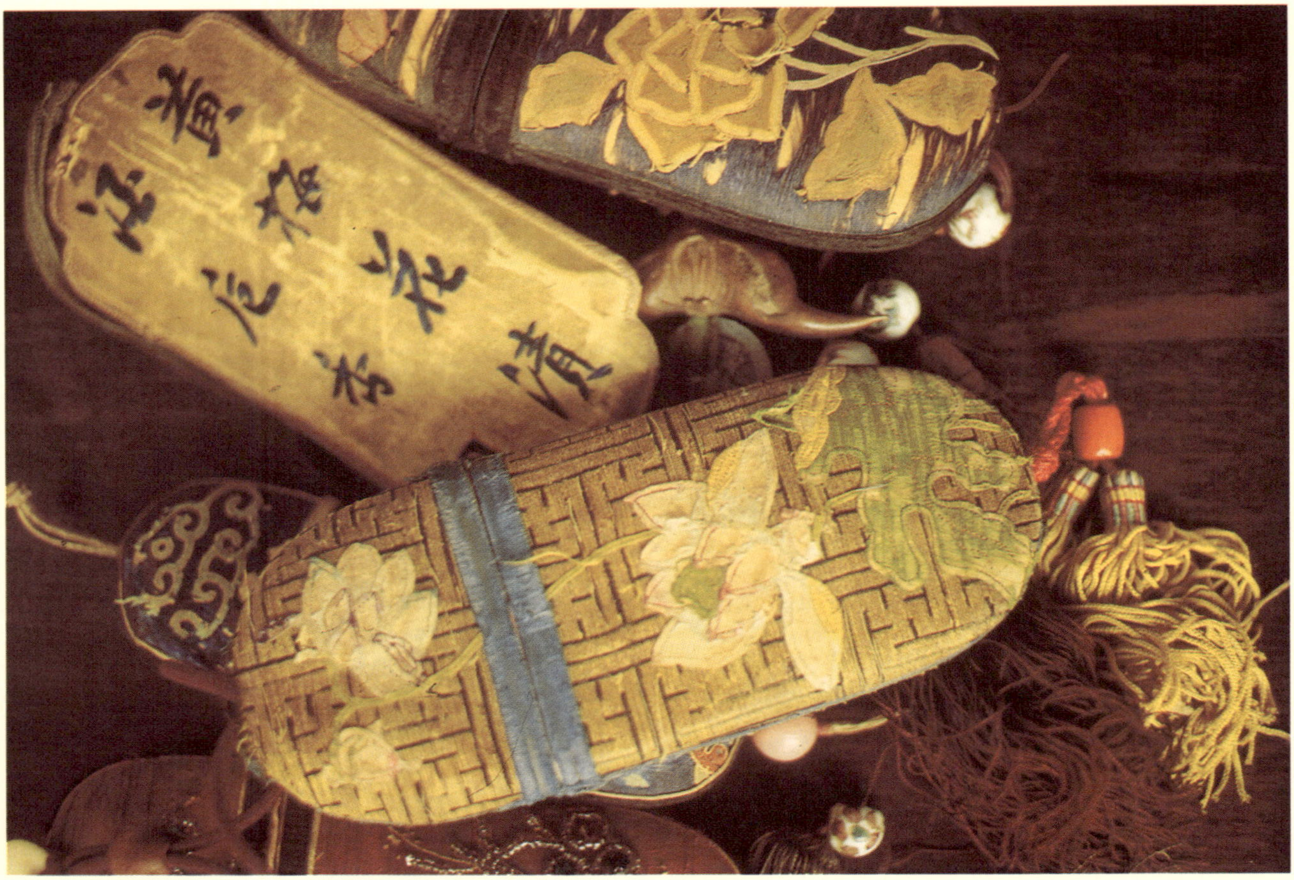

Étuis à lunettes de femme en soie brodée (XIXe siècle).

deux cordons qui passaient sur les oreilles de petits contrepoids pour maintenir un équilibre qui restait néanmoins précaire. Vers le milieu du XVIIIe siècle apparurent les montures à branches en métal (*baitong,* laiton, argent) et plus tard en écaille. Les lunettes de cette époque se caractérisent par des branches articulées à mi-longueur, se terminant par une pastille de corne, d'écaille ou du même métal pour éviter le frottement des branches sur la peau. Les verres de forme ronde et larges (5 à 6 cm de diamètre) n'avaient encore pas de cerclage mais étaient maintenus à la monture par de minuscules chevilles métalliques. Leur taille diminua et on fit aussi des verres de forme ovale. L'usage de plus en plus fréquent des lunettes entraîna la protection des verres par un cerclage de corne, d'écaille de tortue ou de métal portant de discrètes décorations prisées par les lettrés (caractères *shou* ou *wan*). Des lunettes à monture de « fil d'or » *(jinsitui)* furent fabriquées pour les nantis et, dès le début du siècle, il était de bon ton d'afficher son statut d'homme cultivé *(xuewenren)* en arborant à la poche du veston une paire de lunettes et un stylo. Usés par d'interminables heures de lecture des minuscules caractères chinois, les vénérables lettrés avaient en effet besoin de verres grossissants, mais ce sont les dandys des années vingt qui lancèrent le port de verres neutres *(pingguangjing)* comme signe de statut social. À peine

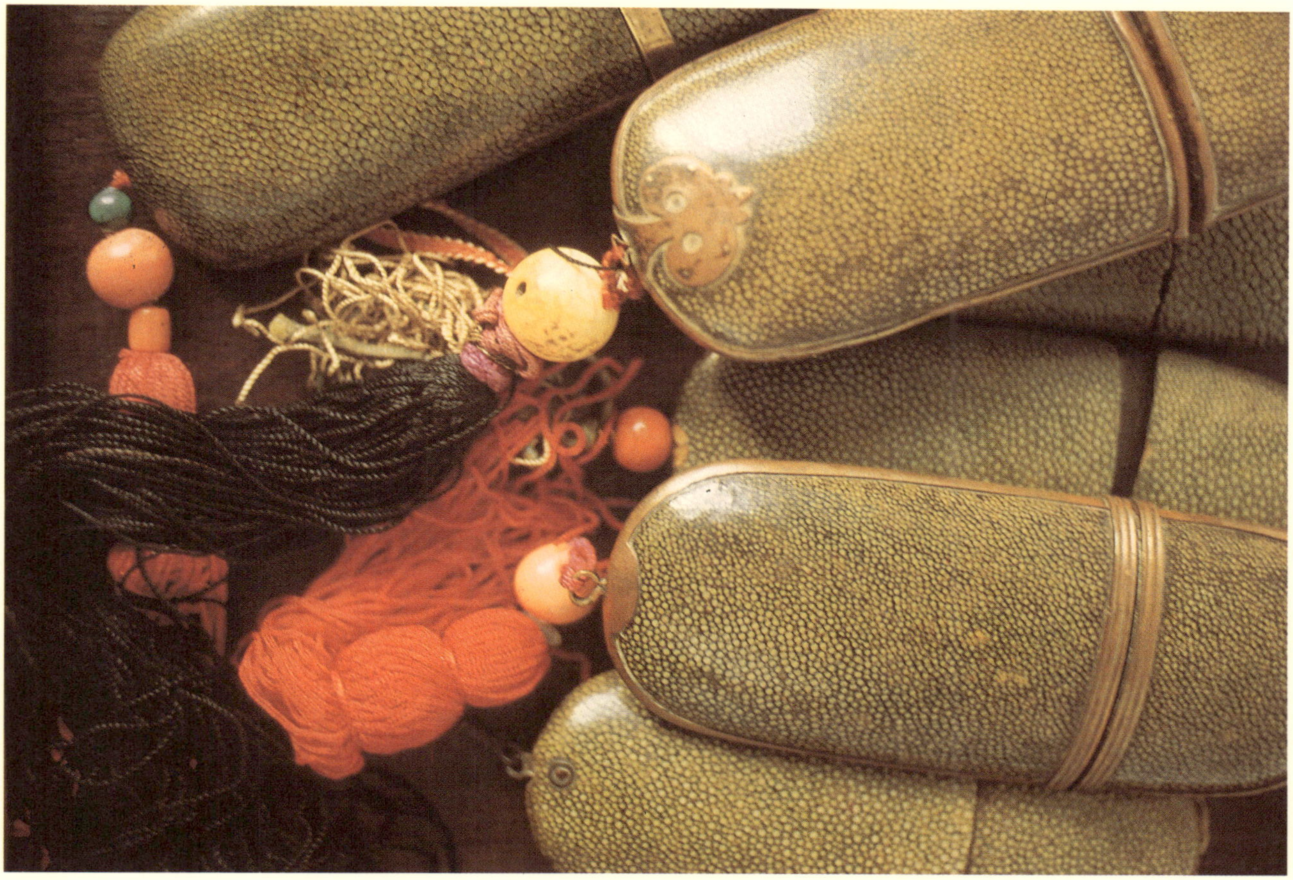

plus tard, la mode des verres colorés venue d'Europe fut reprise en Chine pour les lunettes de soleil. Jusqu'à une période très récente, elles restent un luxe et de nos jours, on peut voir les paysans nouvellement enrichis les arborer fièrement avec leur étiquette d'origine encore collée sur le verre...

La fragilité de ces accessoires entraîna bien entendu la création d'étuis pour leur transport. Les robes des Mandchous ou des Hans ne comportant pas de poches, tous les accessoires qu'un homme de qualité devait porter étaient suspendus à sa ceinture *(chaodai)*. Selon les circonstances, on pouvait y mettre y une bourse en forme de besace *(dalian)*, une blague à tabac, un étui de montre, une blague à parfum en soie, un porte-couteau avec baguettes, un étui à éventail, un petit nécessaire de toilette, une boîte à cartes de visites, des pendeloques et, éventuellement, un étui à lunettes à moins qu'il ne soit accroché à un bouton sur le devant de la jaquette. Ces étuis furent fabriqués en différentes matières : tissu (soie brodée en général pour les femmes), bois laqué, gravé de poèmes, de dédicaces ou de motifs décoratifs, carton laqué. Toutefois, les plus répandus furent faits en peau de poisson teintée vert. Le procédé d'application de ces peaux de raie sur un support était connu au Japon sous le nom de *same* depuis le VIIIe siècle et il se transmettra jusqu'au XVIIIe siècle. On gainait les manches de sabres et de

Étuis à lunettes en galuchat (peau de raie ou de squale laquée).

poignards afin d'obtenir une meilleure adhérence de l'arme à la main. À cet effet, les artisans employaient la peau de la raie *(dasyatis sephen)*, caractérisée par ses gros grains dorsaux, ou celle de la roussette et du chien de mer aux grains plus petits et moins réguliers. Les peaux rugueuses de ces poissons étaient connues en Europe depuis le XVIe siècle et utilisées comme abrasif par les ébénistes. À partir de 1757, quand les Anglais furent autorisés à commercer en Chine, et pendant plus d'un siècle, c'est à Canton, où la main-d'œuvre était habile et peu chère, que d'entreprenants commerçants firent recouvrir selon cette technique de nombreux étuis à lunettes, des manches de cannes et des boîtes. On les rapporta en Europe sous le nom de *shagreen* (sans doute par analogie au « chagrin », un cuir grenu et plissé de mouton ou de cheval utilisé en reliure). La peau de poisson, souple comme un tissu, était collée sur un bâti de bois puis polie jusqu'à ce que n'apparaisse plus que la forme ronde et régulière des granulations arasées, elle était ensuite teintée en vert, marron ou laissée naturelle et enfin laquée.

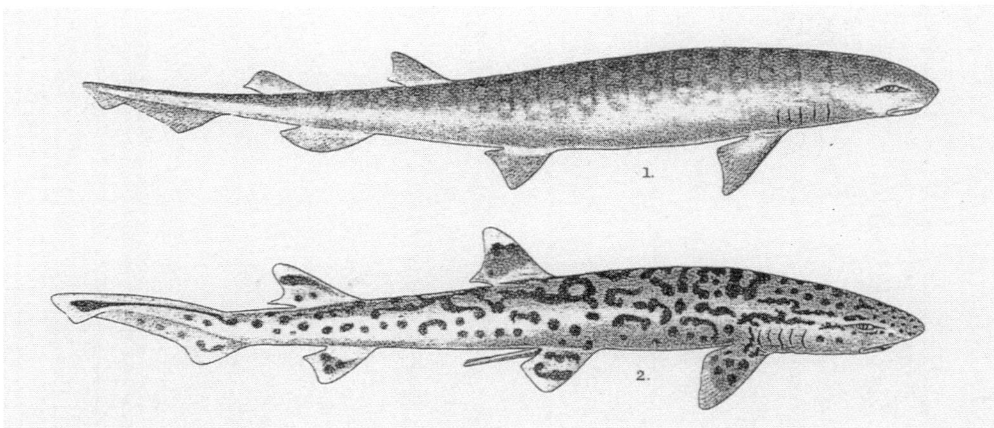

À la même période (1750) à Paris, Jean-Claude Galluchat, artisan-gainier, proposait à ses contemporains de nombreux objets (jumelles de théâtre, lunettes d'astronomie, étuis à ciseaux, manches de couteaux, tabatières, nécessaire de toilette) habillés selon la même technique. Sa renommée fut si grande que c'est désormais sous le nom de « galuchat » que l'on désigne cet étrange cuir ocellé de couleur vert foncé, connu en Chine comme de la « peau de requin » *(shayu pi)*. La fragilité de ces laques amena toutefois les artisans à les renforcer par des cerclages de cuivre. Tous les étuis possédaient un lacet qui passait à travers le couvercle et était décoré de pompons, de franges, de petites pendeloques de pierre, d'ivoire et même de billes de porcelaine peinte.

Les miroirs de bronze

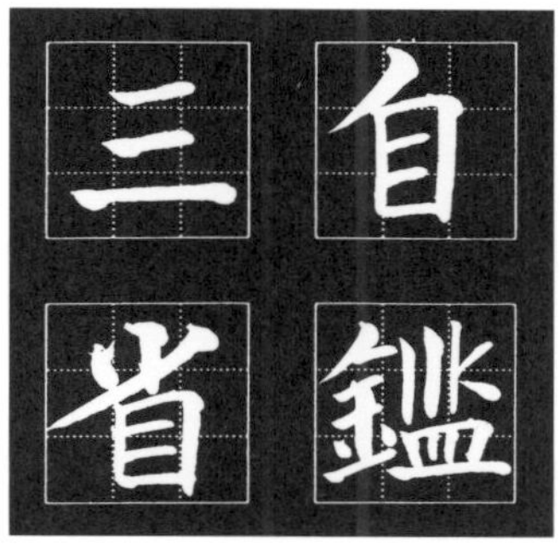

zijian sanxing, littéralement, « s'examiner trois fois avant de porter un jugement sur soi ».

« Brillant comme un miroir » *(mingjing),* c'est par cette métaphore que l'on désigne en chinois quelqu'un de perspicace… Car le miroir est bien en Asie symbole de sagesse et de connaissance, il reflète la vérité. Dès la plus haute antiquité, il lui était attribué le pouvoir de « voir à l'intérieur » des individus, de renvoyer l'image de la véritable apparence des êtres et des choses. Le premier empereur de Chine, Qin Shi Huang, aurait possédé cette sorte de miroir avec lequel il sondait les âmes et les cœurs de ceux qui l'approchaient. Au début de l'ère chrétienne, les taoïstes possédaient ces sortes de miroirs avec, au dos, une représentation gravée de l'univers. Les Chinois ont ainsi de nombreuses expressions relatives au pouvoir de cet objet : « Le miroir reflète l'image de l'homme et l'observation du passé le présent » *(mingjing keyi chaxing, wang gu keyi zhi jin).*

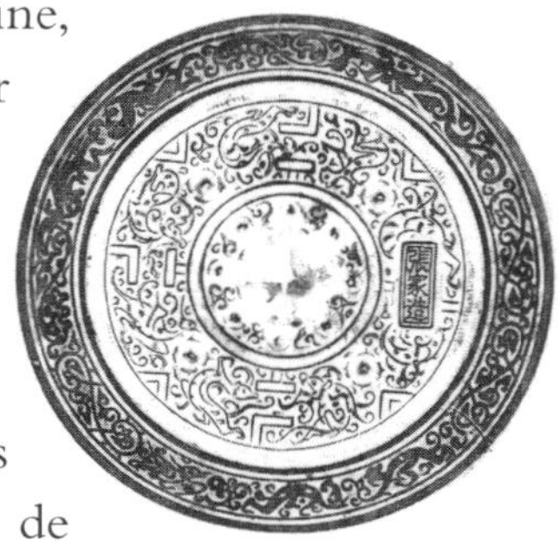

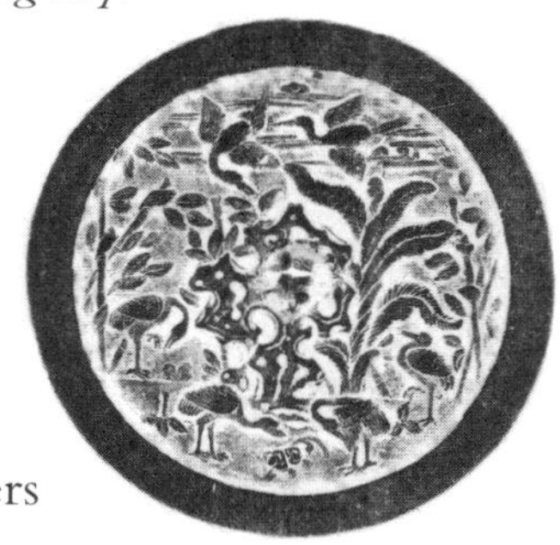

Comme le racontent les légendes, les femmes d'autrefois n'avaient pour se mirer que la surface des mares ou celle des jarres. Les miroirs de bronze seraient apparus dès le Xe siècle av. J.-C. sous les Zhou ; ils resteront en usage jusqu'à la découverte de la miroiterie, c'est-à-dire vers le XVIIe siècle. Les premiers avaient sans doute un caractère sacré, les derniers ne seront plus que des objets décoratifs ou d'un usage courant. Des découvertes archéologiques récentes ont cependant permis de retrouver en très bon état des pochettes circulaires en soie brodée, munies d'une bretelle, destinées au transport des miroirs ; elles datent du IIIe siècle av. J.-C. Ces sacs à miroir ont été retrouvés dans des tombes à côté de nécessaires de toilette et de cosmétiques.

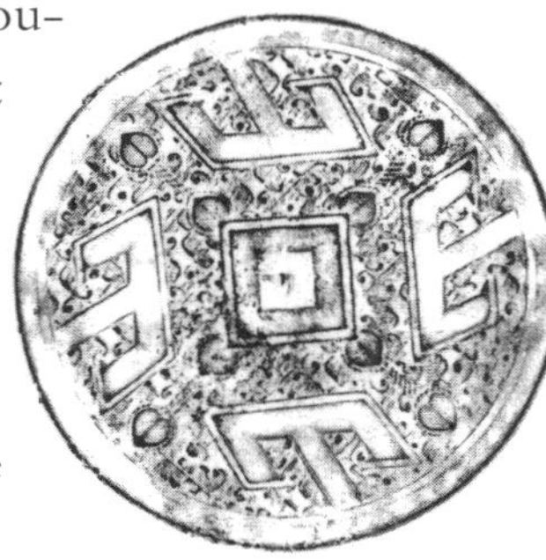

Collection d'estampages de miroirs de bronze anciens *par Shanshi Sanliang (on remarquera, en bas, le miroir à motif en T* (ou shan, *« montagne »).*

Les miroirs *(jing)* étaient donc des disques de bronze dont une des faces légèrement convexe, était polie de façon à refléter les images ou la lumière. Le revers portait des motifs décoratifs gravés ou en relief avec au centre, un bouton percé d'un trou pour y passer une cordelette. Au début, ils n'avaient encore pas de manche et devaient être tenus à la main ou posés sur un socle en demi-lune dont les plus spectaculaires datent de l'époque Song. Des miroirs du Ve ap. J.-C. siècle ont été découverts dans des tombes du Hubei. La pierre de couleur bleue ou verte dont ils étaient faits proviendrait de carrières des provinces méridionales (Hunan, Zhejiang et Yunnan). Certains auteurs (Hirth, *Chinese metallic mirrors*) pensent que c'étaient des miroirs de jade, mais ce n'est pas prouvé…

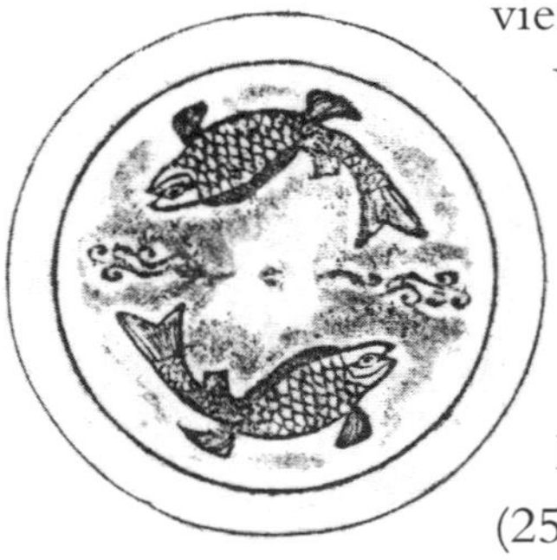

« Après les Qin, il n'y a plus rien d'ancien » *(Qin hou wu gu),* annonce une célèbre formule et pourtant la période la plus fameuse des miroirs de bronze est bien celle de la dynastie des Han (206 av. J.-C. - 24 ap. J.-C.). En effet, à partir des Han de l'Est (25-220), pour tous les objets de bronze, c'est une période de déclin sauf pour les miroirs. Ils se caractérisent par des décorations géométriques et une certaine simplicité, certains sont peints. Sous les Tang, des influences étrangères apportent des nouveautés, les motifs abstraits font place au réalisme et au mouvement. De cette époque, datent des innovations techniques comme les incrustations de nacre et de feuille d'or ou d'argent. Sous les Song enfin, on se mit à fabriquer des copies archaïsantes, ce fut la fin de productions originales. Au XVIIe siècle, la maîtrise de la technique de l'argenture et de l'étamage des glaces remplacera alors le travail des bronziers qui se sera maintenu pendant plus de deux mille cinq cents ans… Les miroirs de bronze anciens sont des pièces de collection particulièrement recherchées.

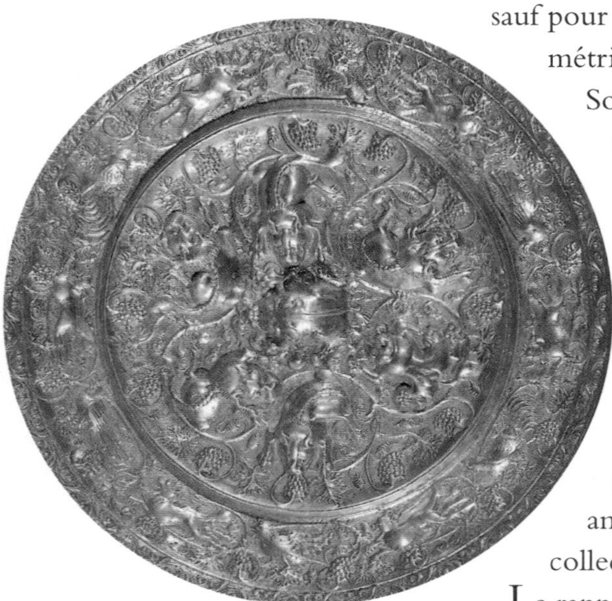

Le rapport entre le poids et la taille permet d'évaluer l'ancienneté des miroirs. Sous les Zhou, ils sont petits, ceux de la période Qin sont fins et fragiles, ceux des Han sont plus épais. En revanche, ces derniers se caractérisent par un alliage de qualité. Ils étaient faits avec les « bons bronzes » *(shantong)* qui contenaient, disait-on, de l'or provenant du Jiangsu. Au fil des siècles, la teneur des alliages a varié (de 70 % à 79 % de cuivre, de 13 % à 23 % d'étain, des traces de fer, de plomb et d'argent). L'éclat de la face réfléchissante a souvent été un critère de qualité. Il est facile de voir à l'usure de cette partie si le miroir était utilisé pour un usage quotidien ou pour toute autre fonction car dès qu'un miroir de toilette se ternissait, on l'apportait à des artisans spécialisés (*mojingde,* les polisseurs), qui lui faisaient subir un nouveau ponçage. Certains avaient une couleur très particulière, semblable à un émail noir *(heichigu)* qui fit leur réputation ;

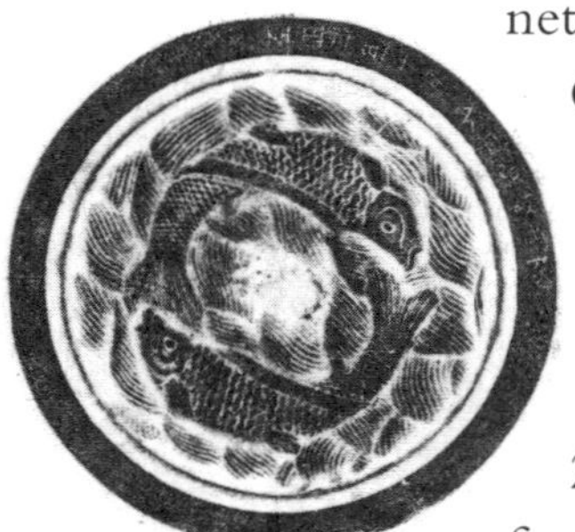

En haut et en bas, miroirs à motifs de poisson ; au centre, miroir de bronze à décor de lions et de vigne (dynastie des Tang, 618-907).

cette patine était en fait due à la nature de l'alliage et non à l'entretien dont il aurait été l'objet. D'autres, dont la teneur en étain était forte, formaient les « bronzes blancs » et les Chinois les désignaient comme « revêtus d'une couche de vif-argent » *(shuiyin pian)*. Les meilleurs, affirmait-on, devaient être fondus au solstice d'hiver : le forgeron devenait alors alchimiste.

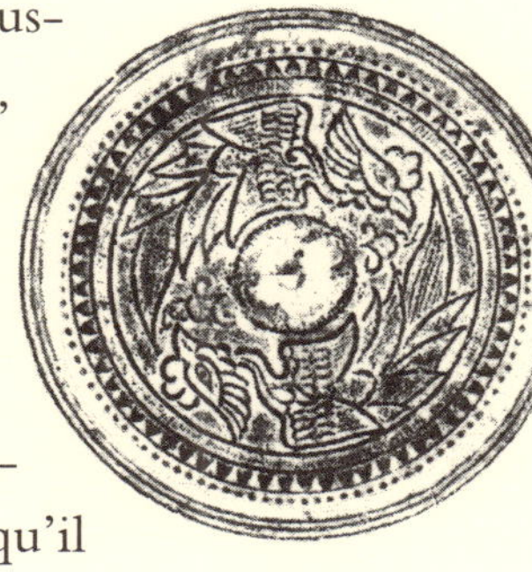

Les tailles ont varié aussi selon les époques. On connaît de minuscules miroirs de l'époque Tang de 2,5 cm de diamètre mais, dans leur majorité, ils mesuraient de 10 à 12 cm de diamètre. Dans le *Recueil des articles de métal et de pierre (Jinshisou),* il est même fait mention d'un grand miroir de 42 cm de diamètre. En 1980, dans le Shandong, on a découvert le plus grand miroir de l'époque Han, de forme rectangulaire et d'une taille rare (115 x 57,7 cm). On raconte aussi qu'il existait une étrange « collection de douze miroirs » qui aurait appartenu à un empereur des Zhou. Ils avaient la particularité d'être d'une taille différente pour chaque mois de l'année (de 2,5 cm pour janvier à 30 cm pour décembre).

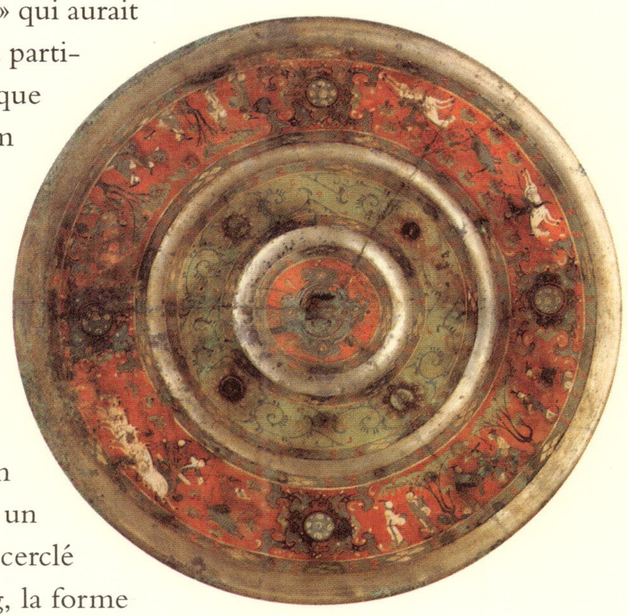

Avant l'apparition des manches sous les Tang, tous les miroirs avaient au revers un bouton généralement en forme de mamelon *(ju)* – parfois remplacé par des animaux stylisés (tortues, grenouilles) – qui était percé pour y passer une cordelette. On ne connaît qu'un très rare exemple de miroir à trois boutons. Un spécimen de l'époque des Royaumes Combattants portait un bouton central fait de lazulite (minéral bleu) cerclé d'un anneau de jade. Jusqu'à la période des Tang, la forme générale du miroir sera ronde, mais il exista des formes baroques (carrées, en demie lune ou polylobées) . Pour la décoration des bordures, les artisans s'inspirèrent de la forme particulière de la châtaigne d'eau (ou macre, *linghua*), car elle ressemble à la chauve-souris, animal de bon augure. Répétés huit fois, les lobes rappelaient les « cols de nuages » *(yunjian)* des vêtements de cour ou de mariage. Les décors du revers ont été nombreux et variés, ils prennent place harmonieusement sur le socle autour du bouton central, soit sous forme de dessins géométriques, soit avec des motifs animaliers (phénix, paons, chevaux célestes, dragons, papillons) soit des motifs floraux. Au début, les décorations trouvent place dans des bandes concentriques. Pour les époques plus récentes, les compositions se répartissent sur tout l'espace du socle. À

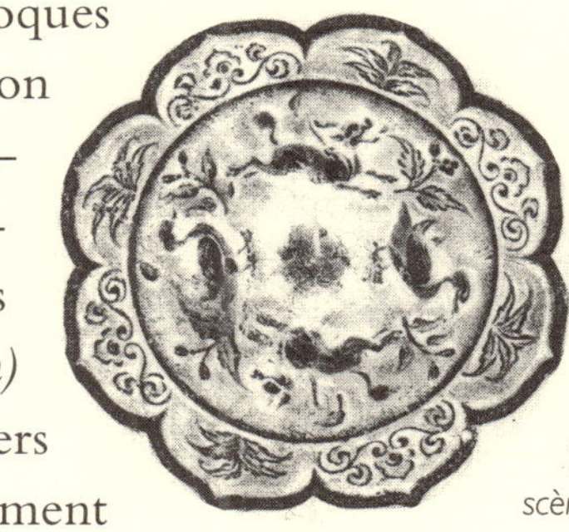

Au milieu, un des très rares miroirs de bronze peint avec des scènes de chasse (archers, conducteurs de char), période des Han de l'Ouest (206 av. J.-C. - 24 ap. J.-C.) ; en bas, miroir de forme polylobée à motifs de canards mandarins, de chiens et de décors floraux.

l'époque des Royaumes Combattants (Ve au IIIe siècle av. J.-C.), puis sous les Qin, les miroirs sont très fins et cassants. Ils ont une très belle surface réfléchissante et les motifs du revers les plus fréquents sont des spirales, des arcs de cercle, des dragons, des oiseaux et des fleurs, des scènes de chasse. Un motif bien particulier en frise, en forme de lettre (T, L ou V), va caractériser les pièces de cette époque. Sous les Han, les miroirs sont plus épais et les décors plus fournis (animaux fantastiques et génies, oiseaux stylisés aux ailes ouvertes), mais ils se différencient des précédents car ils portent désormais sur une des bandes des inscriptions souvent écrites en caractères archaïques. On y trouve la date et le mois de fabrication auxquels se rajoutent des textes d'inspiration très littéraire (poèmes, louanges, dédicaces). Dans beaucoup de cas, il s'agit des traditionnels vœux de bonheur, longévité, grande descendance et réussite sociale. Sous les Six dynasties du Sud (317-420), Su Relan, une dame de la bonne société, lança la mode de jeux littéraires, les « palindromes » (*huiwen,* littéralement, « caractères qui se lisent dans tous les sens »). Un caractère pris dans une colonne servait à construire des phrases qui pouvaient être lues verticalement, horizontalement ou en oblique... Sur d'autres, certains fabricants, soucieux de se démarquer des fabriques impériales, faisaient figurer leur nom qui devint une forme de publicité. On vit ainsi apparaître les noms des grandes familles de bronziers et les études chinoises ont souvent recours à ces noms célèbres pour classer les miroirs.

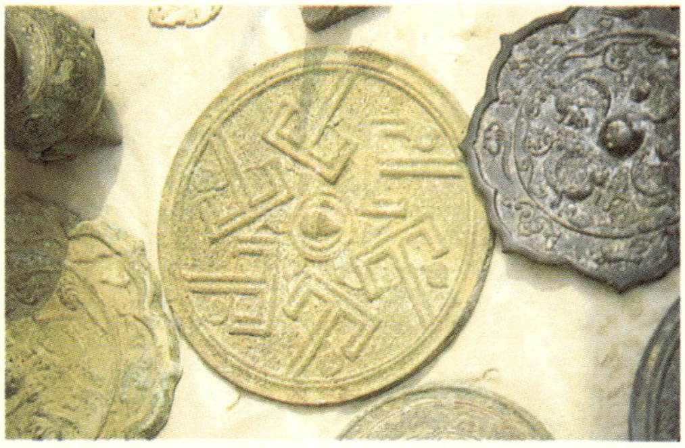

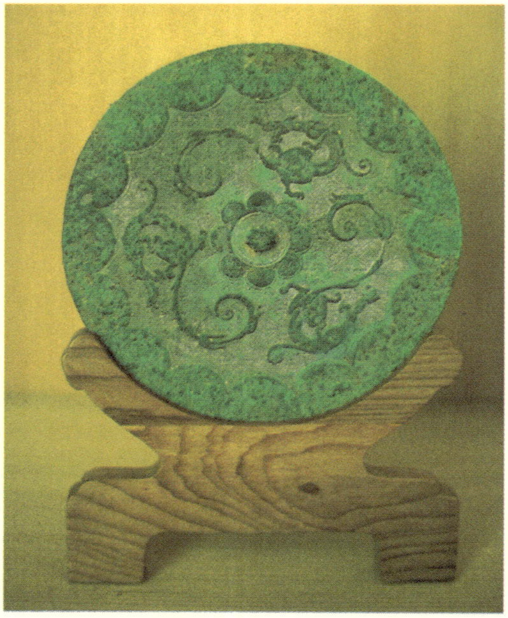

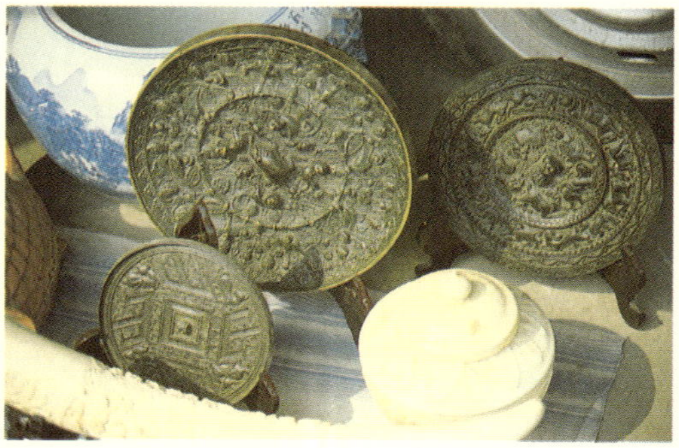

En haut et en bas, copies contemporaines de miroirs anciens ; au centre, miroir et socle (musée d'histoire de Chine, Pékin).

Il est certain que les premiers miroirs furent fabriqués à d'autres fins qu'un simple usage domestique. Les uns servaient à concentrer les rayons du soleil sur des matériaux combustibles (comme la feuille d'armoise pour la moxibustion, une forme de cautérisation de la peau recommandée en particulier pour les morsures de rat ou des piqûres venimeuses). De petit format, utilisés comme briquet *(sui),* ils étaient alors portés à la ceinture. D'autres, portant des messages et des vœux de félicité, étaient échangés comme cadeaux. Selon certains récits épiques, les guerriers se rendaient au combat avec un miroir sur la poitrine pour se protéger du malheur, la jeune mariée en portait aussi un sur son cœur quand elle passait le pas de la porte de sa nouvelle demeure. Au cours de la cérémonie du mariage, on lui renvoyait d'ailleurs les rayons bénéfiques du soleil à l'aide de petits miroirs. Les ermites taoïstes en avaient toujours un marqué de trigrammes accroché sur leur havresac quand ils s'aventuraient dans des lieux désolés où rôdaient les génies malfaisants. Enfin, les géomanciens conseillaient d'accrocher des miroirs au-dessus des portes, sous les toits, dans les chambres à coucher, pour révéler les influences néfastes et les repousser. Cela s'appliquait ainsi aux habitations situées dans l'environnement de « mauvais lieux » (dépôts de charbons, lieux de mort violente, marchands de cercueils...). On espérait aussi guérir les fous en les faisant se regarder dans un miroir, car on pensait qu'ils étaient habités par des démons. Ceux-ci, effrayés par leur propre image, retourneraient à leurs enfers. Cette croyance, entretenue par le *fengshui* (p. 245), est restée bien présente dans l'inconscient des Chinois qui aujourd'hui encore font placer des glaces réfléchissantes dans les endroits « stratégiques » de leur demeure, en particulier face à la porte d'entrée (et même sur les vitres de leur voiture). À partir des Han, on se servit des miroirs lors de cérémonies funéraires ; ils étaient posés sur la poitrine des morts dans leur tombe pour les protéger lors de leur dernier voyage et ils furent appelés, comme ceux des guerriers, les « miroirs protecteurs du cœur » *(huxinjing).*

Le miroir, devenu un attribut féminin, était toutefois considéré par les Chinois comme un élément aussi bien *yin* que *yang* : sa forme ronde exprimait le ciel (et le soleil), les formes carrées, la terre. Le miroir octogonal des géomanciens, complété par les trigrammes, symbolisait l'harmonie et la perfection. Dans le cas de la disparition d'un époux ou de séparation du couple, on parlait de « miroir brisé ». De nombreuses légendes racontent comment l'époux emportait un morceau de miroir ayant la propriété de se transformer en une pie qui venait lui raconter les éventuelles infidélités de son épouse...

On a attribué enfin le nom de miroirs « magiques » ou « transparents » à quelques rares miroirs de bronze classiques qui, éclairés par le soleil, avaient la faculté de réfléchir le motif gravé au revers, alors qu'apparemment rien ne figurait sur la surface réfléchissante. Cette énigme technique a longtemps intrigué les scientifiques jusqu'à ce que l'on puisse observer par grossissement que les gravures du revers, après de nombreux polissages, réapparaissaient de l'autre côté sous forme de traces invisibles à l'œil nu.

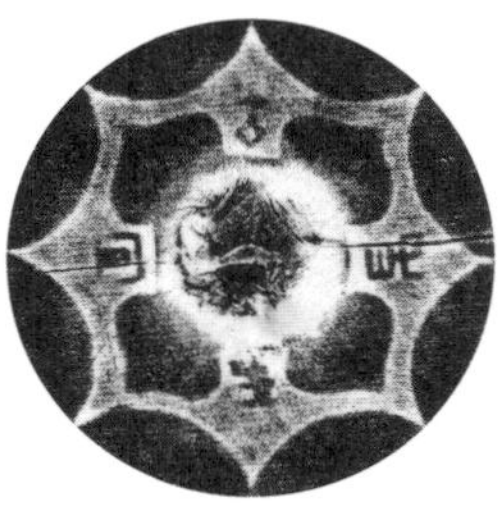

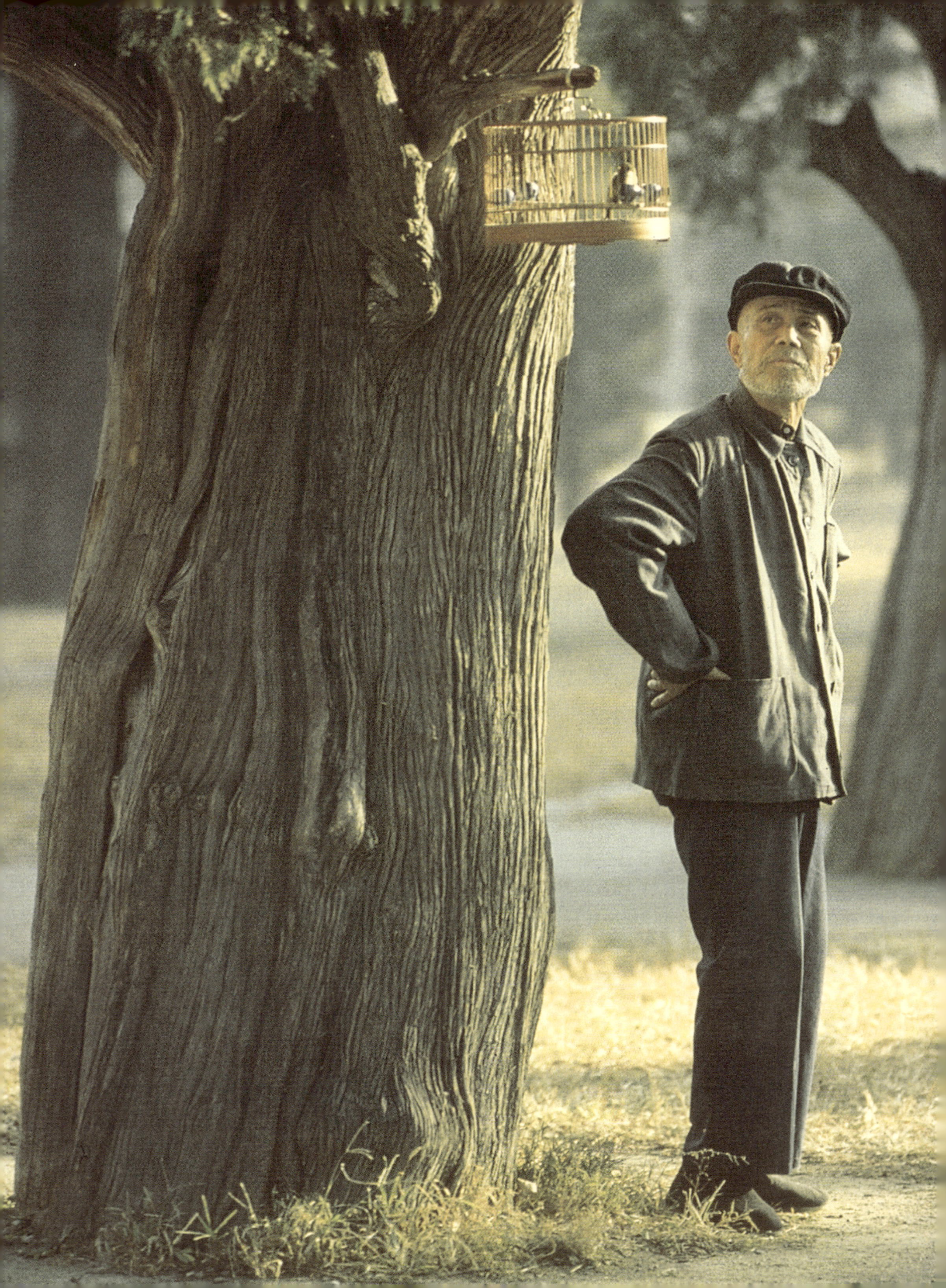

Oiseaux de cage et cages à oiseaux

关鎖
清音

guansuo qingyin, littéralement, « mélodies de la captivité ».

« Si tu m'aimes, alors tu aimes aussi mes oiseaux » *(ai wu, ji niao)* ; ce proverbe résume sans doute d'une façon lapidaire cet amour traditionnel des oiseaux qui s'est curieusement maintenu en Chine jusqu'à l'époque actuelle. Pour le vérifier, il n'est que de se promener tôt le matin pour observer les amateurs d'oiseaux qui se dirigent vers le jardin public, à pied, une ou deux cages à la main, à vélo ou en triporteur, leur chargement amoureusement ficelé. Autrefois, les maisons de thé restaient un lieu propice pour ces rassemblements d'hommes unis par la même passion (G. W. Lannom parle d'une véritable « sous-culture » des éleveurs d'oiseaux). Là, au cours de longues palabres, on comparait les acquisitions nouvelles dont on vantait les mérites ; des concours de chants étaient d'ailleurs organisés, on échangeait des recettes, on s'engageait même dans des paris effrénés lors de combats de mésanges ou de cailles. Pour attirer leur clientèle, les tenanciers mettaient à la disposition des oiseleurs des salles de soins où l'on trouvait nourriture et accessoires et, bien sûr, un jardin ombreux pour y suspendre les précieuses cages. De nos jours, les maisons de thé sont plus rares mais les parcs publics accueillent désormais ces grands-pères affairés. Le but principal de leur activité est certainement l'amusement et la fierté de posséder un oiseau pour son joli plumage, son chant mélodieux ou ses imitations de la parole humaine, mais aussi pour certains, son aptitude à combattre ou à faire des tours.

Sur le millier d'espèces répertoriées en Chine, les oiseaux de cage n'en représentent que vingt-sept, dont quatorze seulement sont des chanteurs. Les oiseaux de cage préférés des Chinois se trouvent surtout dans l'ordre des passereaux et des psittacidés.

Le canari (*serinus canaria, furong*), très populaire parce que facile à élever, est un très bon chanteur et il sert souvent de modèle pour d'autres oiseaux en cours de dressage. On voile la cage des « élèves » avec une housse pour les obliger à écouter, et on les rapproche de celle du « maître » qui donne alors sa leçon en plein air.

Le gros-bec à queue noire (*eophonia magnirostra, lazui*) a un bec conique puissant, gris et jaune. On peut lui apprendre à faire de nombreux tours comme saisir des graines au vol *(chi feishi)*, attraper une ou deux petites

Page de gauche, *« l'homme aux oiseaux »* (niaoren).

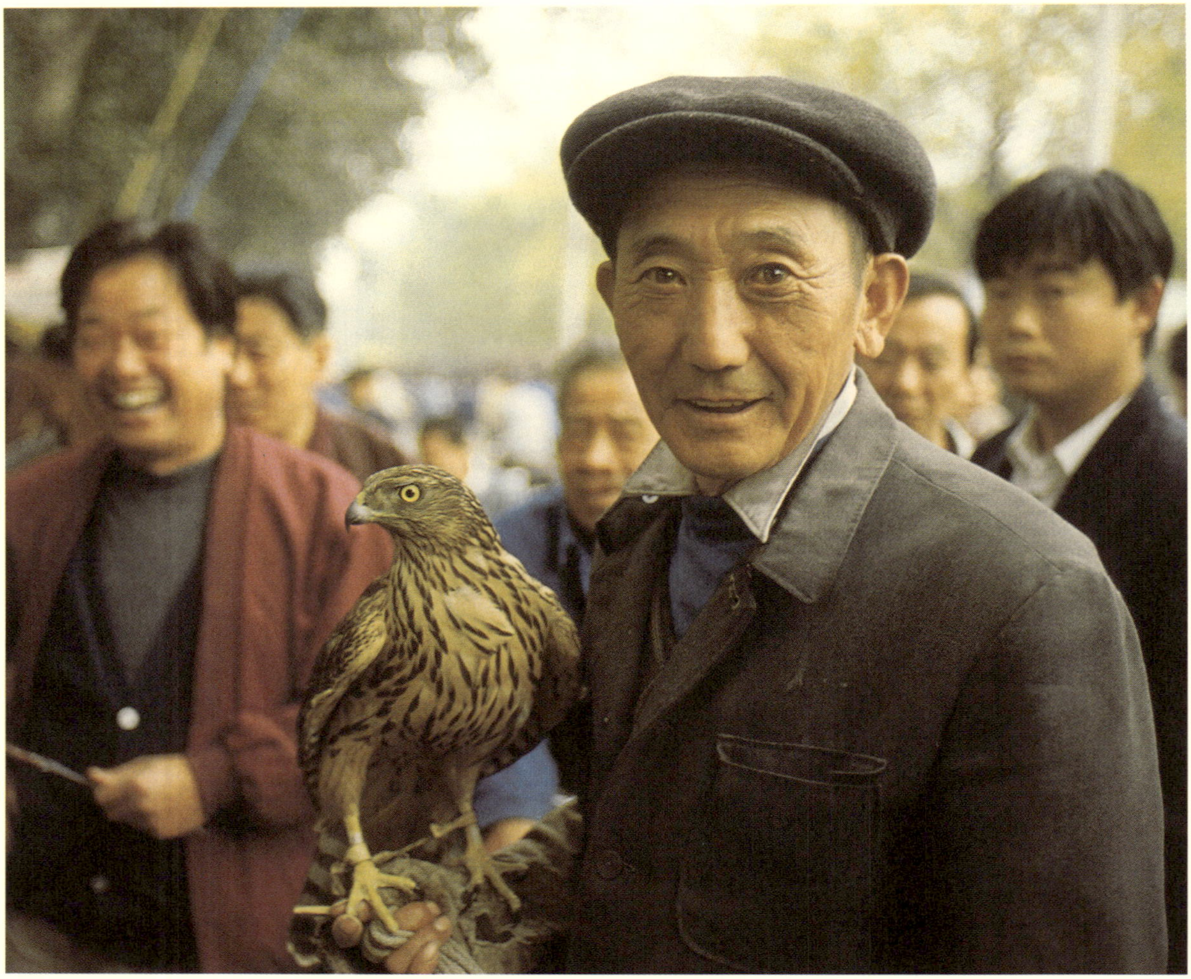

boules en vol *(da tanzi),* ou rapporter d'une certaine distance un billet ou un morceau de papier. À l'époque impériale, ces oiseaux étaient très recherchés des eunuques. Comme ils s'apprivoisent facilement, on peut encore en voir attachés par une patte sur une canne, ou même en liberté jouant avec leur maître.

Le moineau de Java (*munia oryzivora, wenniao*), « l'oiseau qui a des connaissances », a une tête noire, des joues et des oreilles blanches. Il était souvent dressé par les diseurs de bonne aventure à désigner en sautillant une carte dans un jeu étalé, avant de réintégrer sa cage, une fois récompensé.

L'alouette de Mongolie (*melanocorypha mongolica, bailing,* littéralement « les cent merveilles » ou *gaotianzi,* « celle qui informe le ciel ») est un oiseau de couleur brune avec des pattes rouges. Elle est très recherché car c'est un remarquable chanteur qui, de plus, imite bien les autres oiseaux et peut vivre une vingtaine d'années.

La mésange de Webb (*suthora webbiana, huangtou,* littéralement « tête jaune »), est aussi connue sous le nom de « combattant » à cause de son agressivité. La seule vue d'un congénère la précipite vers les barreaux ; aussi sa cage est-

Fauconnier avec son élève (Chine occidentale).

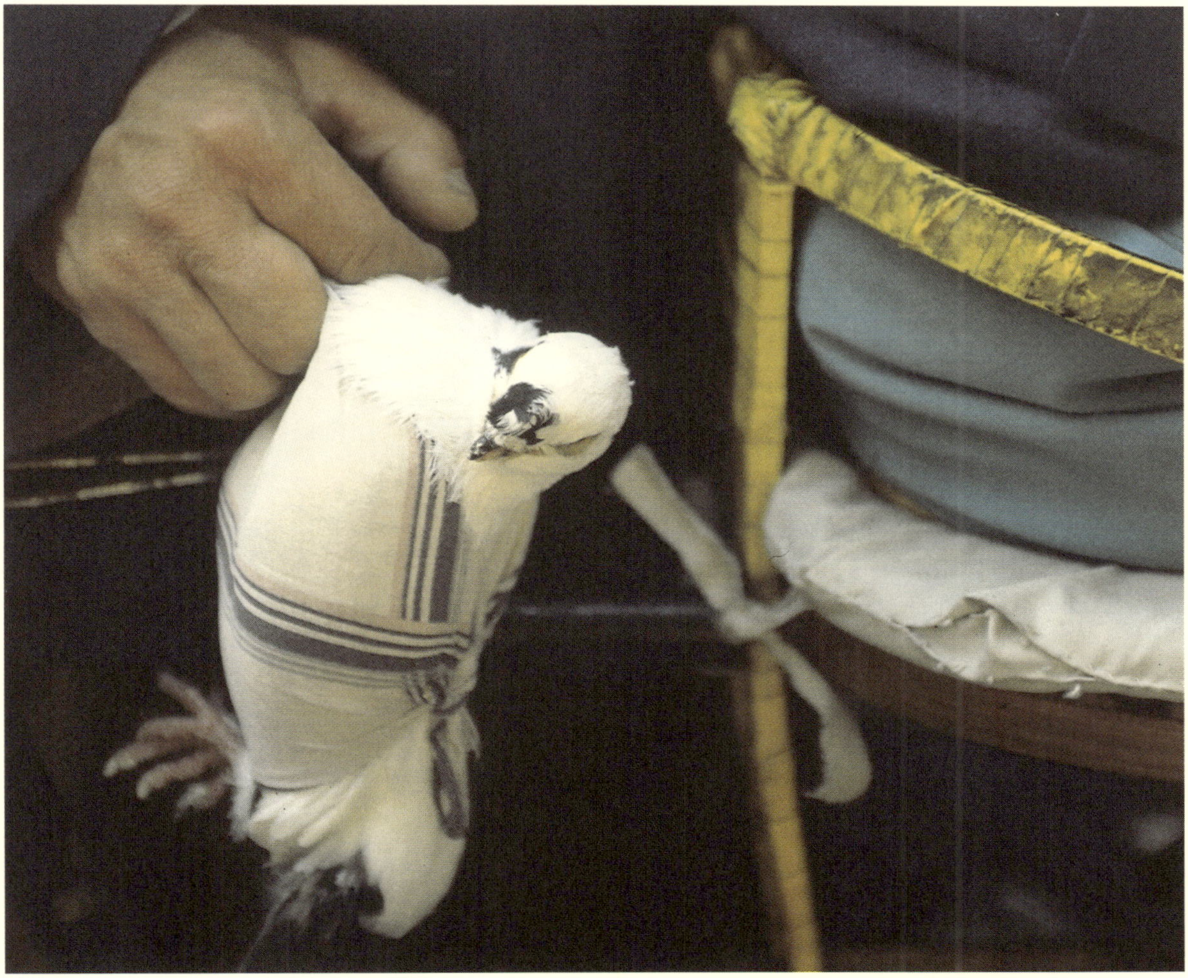

elle souvent recouverte d'une housse. Le prix de ces oiseaux est très élevé car on mise des sommes importantes sur ces combattants particuliers. Aucun d'entre eux ne meurt, seul le vaincu s'enfuit en poussant des cris perçants. Traumatisé par cet échec, il n'acceptera plus la compétition avant quelque temps. À l'entraînement, les propriétaires se contentent de rapprocher les cages pour exciter les protagonistes. Ces mêmes techniques s'appliquent à la caille (*coturnix communis, anchun*) qui est élevée dans les provinces du Nord.

Le gorge-bleu (*cyanosylvia, landianke*) se caractérise par un menton et une gorge d'un bleu brillant. Il est originaire de la province du Shandong mais on le trouve aussi à Pékin et Tianjin. Il possède un chant très doux de jour comme de nuit. Le rouge-gorge (*calliope calliope, hongdianke*), avec une gorge et des joues vermillon bordées de noir, est aussi un excellent chanteur, mais ils sont tous deux fragiles et difficiles à élever.

Le rossignol chinois (*trochlopteron canorum, huamei*) fut de loin, en Chine, l'oiseau préféré de toutes les classes sociales, des boutiquiers aux empereurs ; il est d'ailleurs cité dans de nombreux contes et légendes et souvent repré-

Transport d'un pigeon voyageur dans un foulard.

senté en peinture. C'est un des meilleurs chanteurs, il commence à chanter clairement dès l'âge de trois ans et il peut même imiter le chien et la poule. Lorsqu'il chante, il serre fortement son perchoir ; aussi, tous les propriétaires soucieux d'éviter l'ankylose de leurs oiseaux balancent, lors de la promenade, leur cage d'avant en arrière d'un mouvement régulier en marchant. Dans les provinces du sud, le rossignol est aussi élevé pour les combats.

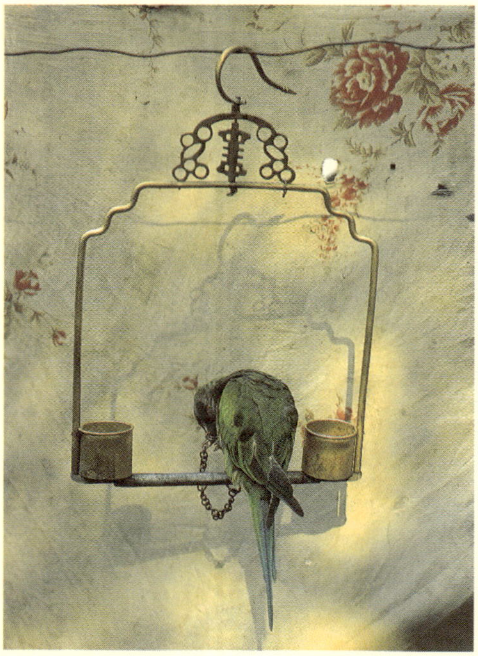

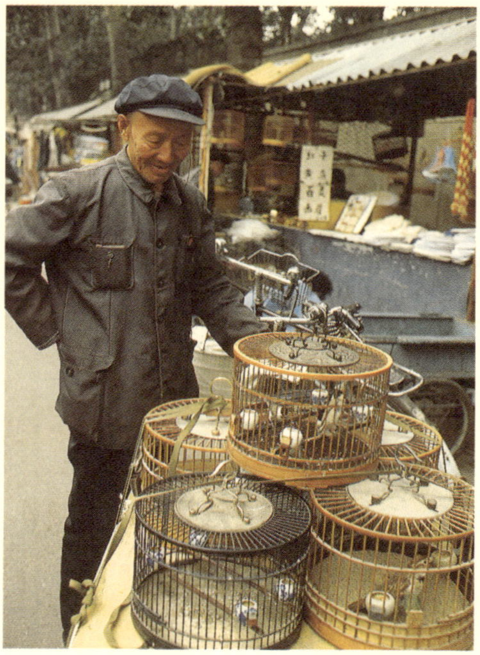

En haut, perroquet sur son perchoir ; en bas, marchand d'oiseaux.

Le merle mandarin ou mainate (*eulabes intermedia, liaoge* ou *jiuguanniao,* littéralement « oiseau des mandarins de neuvième rang ») est un gros oiseau dont toutes les plumes sont noires à reflet violet. Le bec, les yeux et les pattes sont d'un jaune vif. Originaire de Malaisie et d'Inde, il est très prisé car c'est un bon linguiste, on peut lui apprendre des mots ou des bribes de phrases. Son chant est gai, fait de trilles roulées. Certains affirment qu'il imitera d'autant mieux la parole si on lui a taillé la langue, d'autres se livrent avec un petit bâtonnet fourchu à des massages de langue pour développer ses aptitudes.

Le bec fin ou œil d'argent (*zosterops simplex, xiuyan,* littéralement « œil brodé ») a, en effet, un cercle blanc autour des yeux. Il est capturé surtout dans les provinces du sud pour son chant doux et agréable et peut, de plus, imiter celui d'autres oiseaux. C'est à cause de ces qualités qu'il était prisé des lettrés. Ils le gardaient dans une petite cage sur leur table de travail.

Parmi les psittacidés, la perruche (*melopsittacus, jiaofeng,* « phénix charmant »), qui vivait autrefois, à l'état naturel, dans les grottes de l'ouest de la Chine, était l'oiseau de compagnie des femmes qui aimaient son joli plumage. Les perroquets *(yingwu),* appelés « oiseaux sacrés » sans doute à cause de leur talent d'imitateur, étaient aussi très aimés pour leurs couleurs vives. Ils furent introduits des pays du Sud-Est asiatique en Chine. Les eunuques faisaient croire aux femmes dont ils avaient la garde que les perroquets leur rapportaient tout ce qui se disait dans leurs appartements. On cite volontiers le cas d'un perroquet vermillon qui était capable de réciter le *Soutra du Diamant* quand il entendait tinter la cloche de son monastère. Le cacatoès, (*cacatua galerita, xuejiniang,* littéralement « demoiselle au costume de neige ») aux plumes entièrement blanches était relativement rare en Chine. L'un d'entre eux, à l'époque des Tang, est bien connu pour avoir appartenu à la célèbre concubine, Yang Guifei qui partagea pendant près de vingt ans la vie de l'empereur Xuanzong (712-756). Elle possédait notamment une extraordinaire robe de plumes avec laquelle elle exécutait des danses lascives. Son perroquet était particulièrement dressé à disperser les pièces du jeu de dominos sur un signe de sa maîtresse quand l'empereur perdait... Ces louables ruses ne purent empêcher la tragique fin de cette femme d'une beauté exceptionnelle qui fut condamnée par l'empereur à se pendre lors de la prise de la capitale Xi'an par les rebelles.

À cause de leur vie dans les airs, les oiseaux ont toujours symbolisé pour l'homme « les états supérieurs de l'être ». Ainsi dans la littérature mythologique chinoise, les messagers célestes qui sont au service de la Reine Mère d'Occident sont des oiseaux bleus se nourrissant de pierres précieuses. Dans la plupart des civilisations, l'oiseau est l'auxiliaire des dieux. Libérer des oiseaux de leur cage est alors une action de grâce que l'on fait dans certains temples au moment des fêtes. Pour célébrer la naissance de l'empereur Tongzhi en 1862, l'impératrice douairière signa un édit impérial ordonnant de libérer tous les oiseaux en cage de toute la Chine. La mode de l'élevage des oiseaux était apparue avec la dynastie mongole des Yuan. Mais l'oiseau était déjà bien présent dans l'art décoratif dès l'âge du bronze (1600 av. J.-C.). Sous les Tang et surtout les Song, les peintures et la poésie associèrent d'une manière stéréotypée oiseaux et fleurs : le canard avec le lotus, la caille avec le millet, l'hirondelle avec le saule, la grue avec le pin. L'engouement pour les oiseaux ne cessa pas avec les Qing, car l'impératrice douairière Tseu Hi (Cixi) aimait s'entourer de cages ou de peintures d'oiseaux. On lui prêtait même un pouvoir particulier de fascination sur les oiseaux échappés qu'elle ramenait à leur cage quand toutes les tentatives de son entourage s'étaient avérées vaines. Vers 1860 arriva à Pékin un missionnaire, le père Armand David, qui, par ses connaissances en histoire naturelle, se distingua lors de ses nombreux voyages d'études. Il découvrit de nouvelles espèces animales, parmi lesquelles une dizaine d'oiseaux qui portent dorénavant son nom : un hibou, des passereaux, un faisan... Certains spécimens rares furent expédiés au Muséum de Paris. Le père David fonda à Pékin un muséum d'histoire naturelle où l'on trouvait notamment huit cents oiseaux et près de huit mille insectes et papillons. Cette extraordinaire collection, qui commençait d'être connue à la Cour, attira l'attention de l'impératrice qui vint la visiter

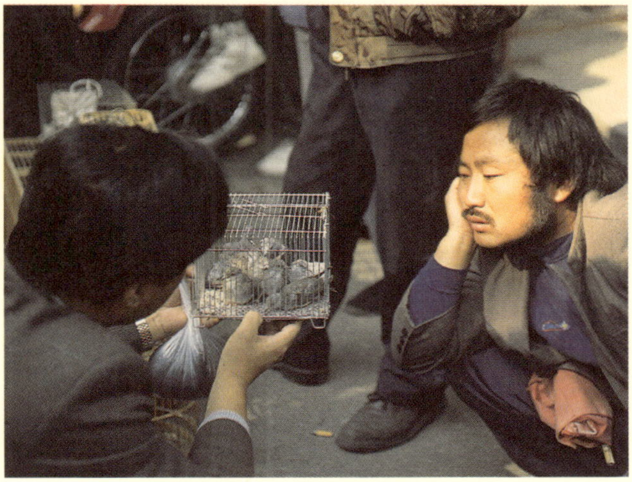

Scène de marché aux oiseaux : acheteur en contemplation.

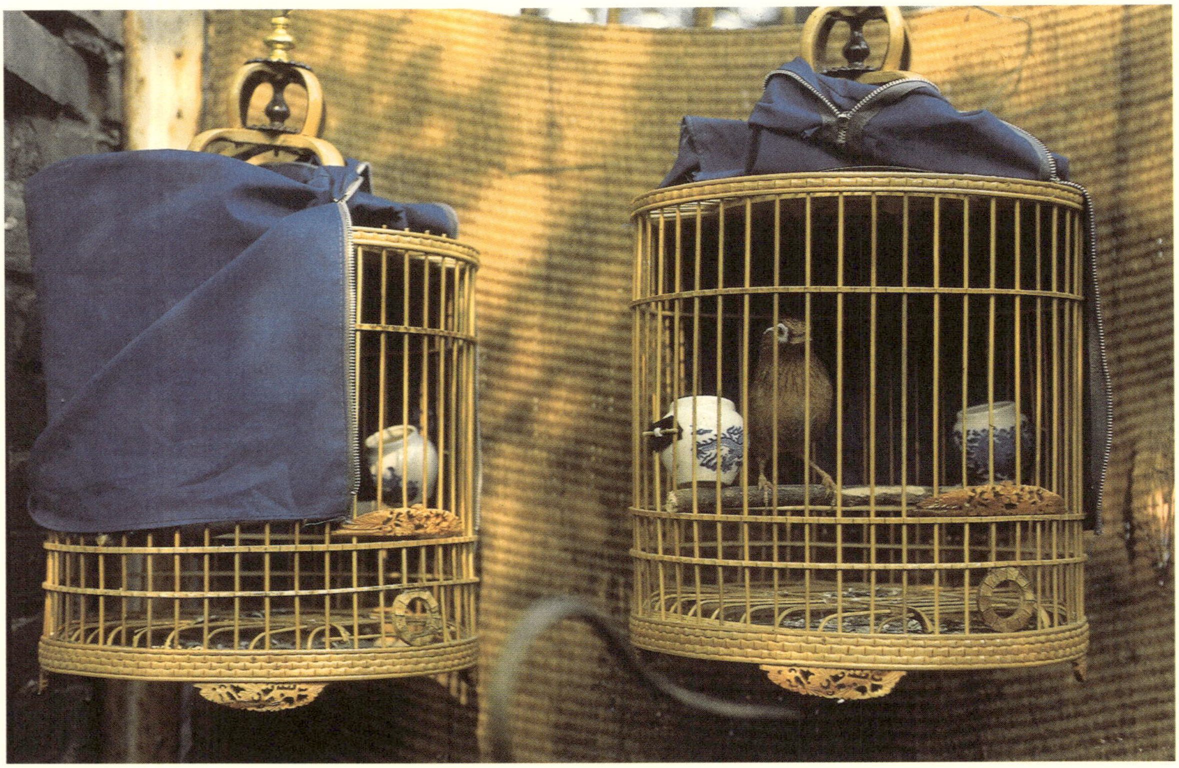

incognito. En 1885, au moment de la rétrocession des biens des Jésuites, une clause stipula que la collection serait offerte à l'impératrice.

Le musée d'art asiatique de San Francisco abrite une cage de bronze à couvercle avec des incrustations de malachite datant du Ve siècle av. J.-C. Depuis cette période, les artisans ne cesseront d'imaginer pour leurs clients des cages raffinées et ingénieuses. Les légendes se rapportant aux cages d'or, d'argent, d'ivoire ou de laque des empereurs sont nombreuses. Pour le voyage, certains mandarins n'hésitaient pas à emmener leur compagnon favori et firent fabriquer d'admirables coffrets pour cages à oiseaux dans des bois précieux. Néanmoins, ce sont les cages en bambou, de la meilleure qualité (le bambou céleste, *tianzhu*), ou en chêne des Indes, qui furent les plus fréquentes. Le bambou est particulièrement utilisé car il est abondant en Chine, résistant, et a la réputation de maintenir les oiseaux en bonne santé. L'architecture des cages a peu évolué au fil des ans, on continue de fabriquer des cages de forme cubique, de petite taille (20 cm), destinées aux petits oiseaux comme la mésange. Les cages à alouettes sont plus hautes (50 cm), elles ont un dôme et comportent un perchoir en forme de petite table ronde posée sur le plancher. C'est une des rares cages à avoir un fond plein car on y met du sable tamisé mélangé à de la poussière d'argile dans lequel l'alouette aime tout particulièrement s'ébrouer. Les cages pour rossignols sont en forme de poire. Enfin, les rouges-gorges ou les becs-fins sont gardés dans des cages plus petites de forme cylindrique (I5 cm de

Ci-dessus et page de droite, cages à rossignol avec leur housse de tissu bleu.

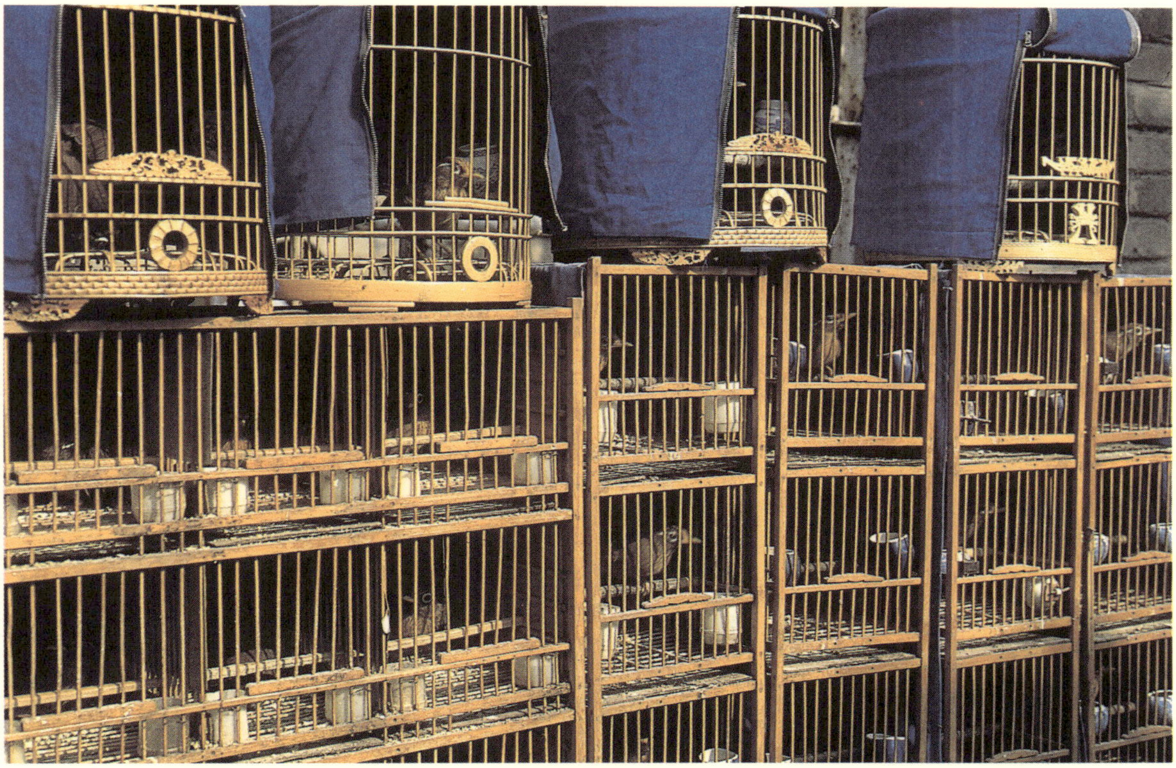

hauteur). On connaît de ravissantes cages d'apparat du XVIIIe siècle en laque décorée réservées aux cailles de combat. Mais des formes baroques ont aussi existé, en particulier une étrange forme en éventail, emblème d'un rang social élevé.

Mais c'est surtout pour les accessoires de cages que s'est exercé le talent des artisans. L'anatomie de ces cages, la plupart démontables, compte une bonne vingtaine de pièces ; elles varient selon son prix, les goûts de l'amateur ou l'amour qu'il porte à son protégé. Le crochet (*longzigou* ou *guagou*) qui surmonte toutes les cages chinoises est un chef-d'œuvre de ferronnerie. Fabriqué en argent, en bronze ou en maillechort *(baitong)*, il est un des plus importants éléments décoratifs de la cage. La forme du crochet s'inspire d'un long cou de cygne, il sert à accrocher la cage dans les branches d'arbre. On a noté, sous les Qing, que certaines cages étaient décorées, sous le crochet, d'une boule de couleur identique au bouton de rang que les mandarins arboraient à leur chapeau. Fantaisie ou protocole, on ne sait trop ce qui amena ces dignitaires à marquer même leurs cages. Les formes les plus variées (oblongues, cylindriques, piriformes) ont été adoptées pour les godets à grain ou à eau *(shiguan)*. On en trouvait en porcelaine, en ivoire sculpté, en bois et en cuivre. Comme toutes les céramiques, ces miniatures étaient finement peintes de motifs traditionnels et de fleurs. Certaines de ces œuvres d'art minuscules étaient même signées à la base. Tous ces petits récipients se fixent par un système de tenon placé entre les barreaux. Les

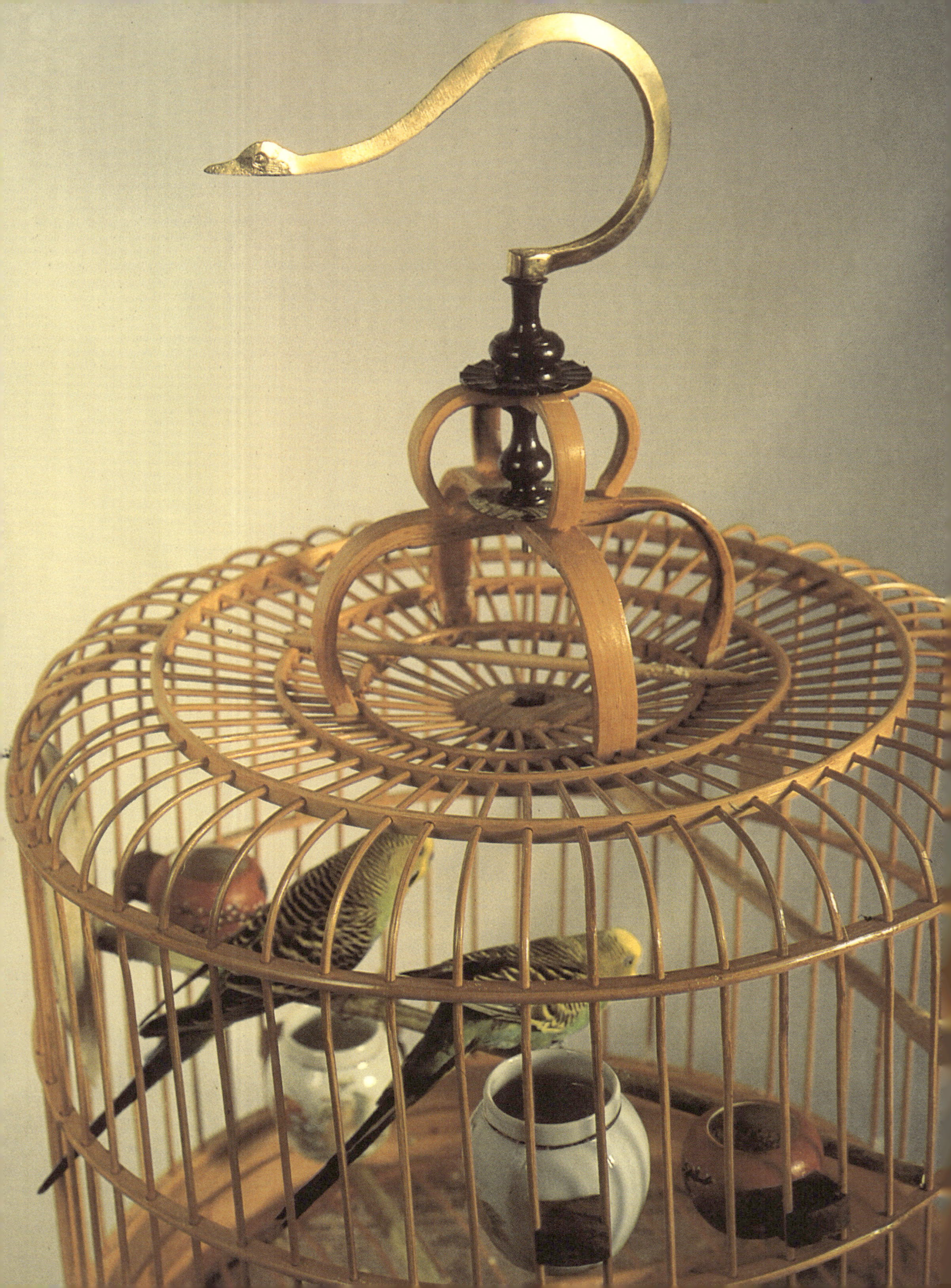

perchoirs ont fait l'objet de nombreuses recherches ; certains portent des embouts d'ivoire, d'autres des sculptures ou de savantes moulures. Les bois employés sont très variés : des bambous lisses, des branches rugueuses et noueuses, des pièces de bois de santal ou d'ébène, tous réputés bons pour la santé des oiseaux encagés.

En matière de nourriture et d'entretien de leurs oiseaux, les propriétaires ont un savoir millénaire. Si l'on donne des fruits mûrs, il faut prévoir de fixer entre les barreaux une double pique *(niaoshichazi),* en bois ou en ivoire pour ne pas blesser l'oiseau. C'est dans des coupelles rondes *(shiwan)* que se placent les larves d'insectes ou les farines cuites. Les « becs durs » sont des oiseaux faciles à entretenir car ils se nourrissent de graines (millet, colza, lin, riz). En revanche, les « becs mous » demandent une nourriture spécialement préparée et difficile à conserver. C'est là qu'intervient toute la sollicitude de l'éleveur ; au canari, par exemple, il donnera des graines, des feuilles de légumes et un mélange d'œuf et de millet ; au rossignol, il faudra préparer des œufs, du riz, des morceaux de bœuf et des larves ; quant au régime de l'alouette de Mongolie, il sera fait d'araignées, de vers, de criquets vivants éventrés, de cigales et de farine de pois vert... Tout bon propriétaire doit aussi posséder des pinces effilées *(weishicha)* qui permettent de donner la becquée de larves ou d' insectes vivants. Pour les sorties, si l'oiseau est bien dressé, on le promène sur un perchoir. C'est alors qu'il faut prévoir encore de petites gourdes pour le faire boire et un système de chaînette pour l'empêcher de s'envoler. Le spectacle d'un « gros-bec » qui rapporte un petit billet de banque à son maître puis rejoint son perchoir, est toujours suivi avec bonheur par les badauds.

Le monde secret des amateurs d'oiseaux a ses règles, son histoire, son vocabulaire. Il n'est pas facile à pénétrer car, cette étrange confrérie qui, tous les matins, tient son rituel à l'écart de l'agitation frénétique des grandes villes, reste repliée sur elle-même. Dans une mise en scène du célèbre Liu Zhaohua, l'auteur dramatique Guo Shixing a tenu le public pékinois en haleine avec son extraordinaire pièce *Niaoren* (littéralement « les hommes à oiseaux » ou « les hommes-oiseaux »). Ce fut l'occasion de raconter avec humour et truculence, par rossignols interposés, les défis qui opposent les gens de Tianjin, la rivale, à ceux de la capitale.

Page de gauche, détail d'une cage chinoise avec crochet en col de cygne.

Ombres chinoises, silhouettes et découpages

chuanghua jianying, littéralement, « fleurs de fenêtre et silhouettes découpées ».

窗花
剪影

Le papier découpé *(jianzhi)* est un art associé à la plupart des fêtes en Chine. Cette technique date pourtant de plus de 1 500 ans, et les Chinois y sont toujours attachés car elle exige peu de moyens et offre une très grande variété de thèmes d'inspiration. Les découpages de papier rouge destinés à mettre une note de gaieté dans les foyers sont très proches des spectacles d'ombres chinoises *(piyingxi)*, ce sont en quelque sorte les précurseurs de la « lanterne magique » et plus tard du cinéma.

L'origine des papiers découpés est encore incertaine ; il faut écouter les légendes qui racontent comment Shao Weng, un célèbre prêtre taoïste de l'empereur Wu, pris de pitié devant la douleur de son maître qui venait de perdre sa concubine, projetait sur une tenture, par un habile système d'éclairage, la silhouette de la bien-aimée Li… L'histoire ne précise pas s'il s'agissait d'un papier découpé ou d'une marionnette. Selon une autre légende, Zhang Guolao, un autre mage du VIIIe siècle, qui deviendra par la suite un Immortel, possédait une monture magique qu'il repliait après usage et rangeait dans sa poche comme un simple papier découpé. Du mythe à la réalité il n'y a qu'un pas : la coutume voulait, en effet, que l'on munisse le voyageur de l'époque de viatiques de toutes sortes avant d'affronter un grand voyage. Des papiers découpés portant des motifs porte-bonheur, des amulettes destinées à repousser le mal (en forme de tigre ou de dragon, des Cinq venimeux…), figuraient parmi les cadeaux que l'on offrait au départ.

Si l'on ne peut situer avec précision la naissance des papiers découpés, l'archéologie a toutefois mis au jour, datant de la période des Shang (XVIe au XIIe siècle av. J.-C.), des découpages en feuilles d'or ou d'argent utilisés comme motifs décoratifs rituels. À l'époque Song, des découpages de soie et de feuille d'or (motifs géométriques, figures humaines ou arrangements floraux) étaient échangés au nouvel an comme cadeaux de qualité. Peut-être que les découpages de papier furent réservés à ceux qui ne pouvaient s'offrir de la soie ou de l'or, donnant ainsi naissance à un art qui perdurera. Les premiers découpages de papier pourraient se situer vers la fin des Han de l'Ouest (206 av. J.-C.-24 ap. J.-C.). Cinq papiers découpés ont été découverts dans la province occidentale du Xinjiang, parfaitement conservés

Page de droite, papiers découpés et peints à la main.

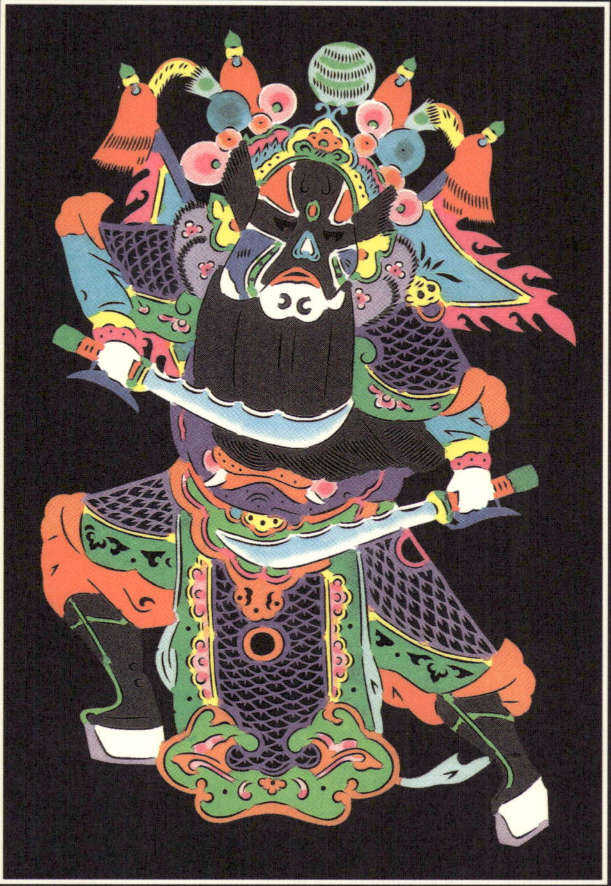

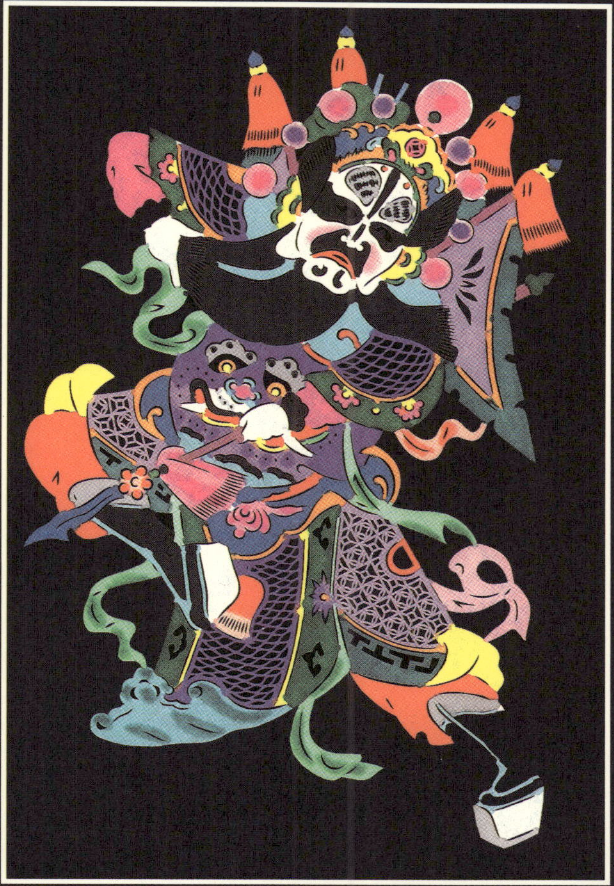

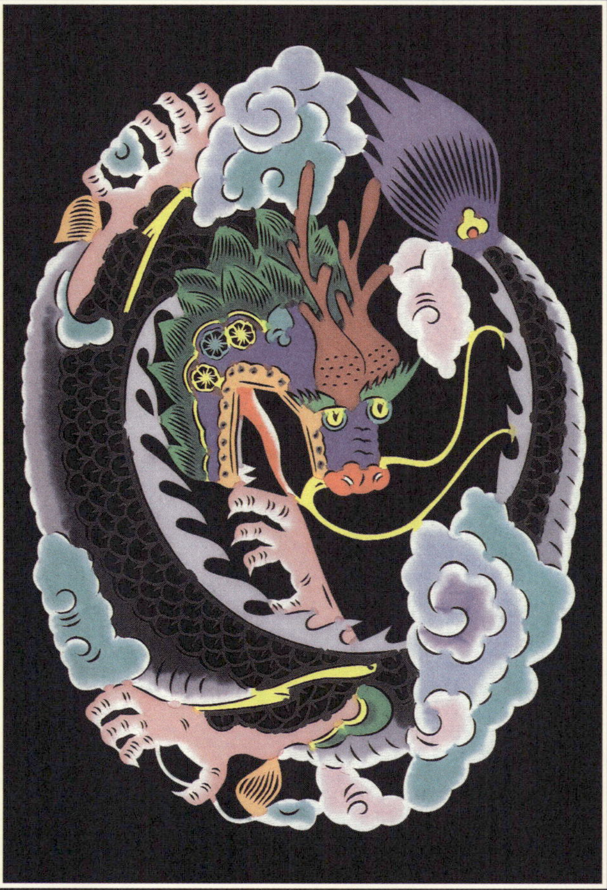

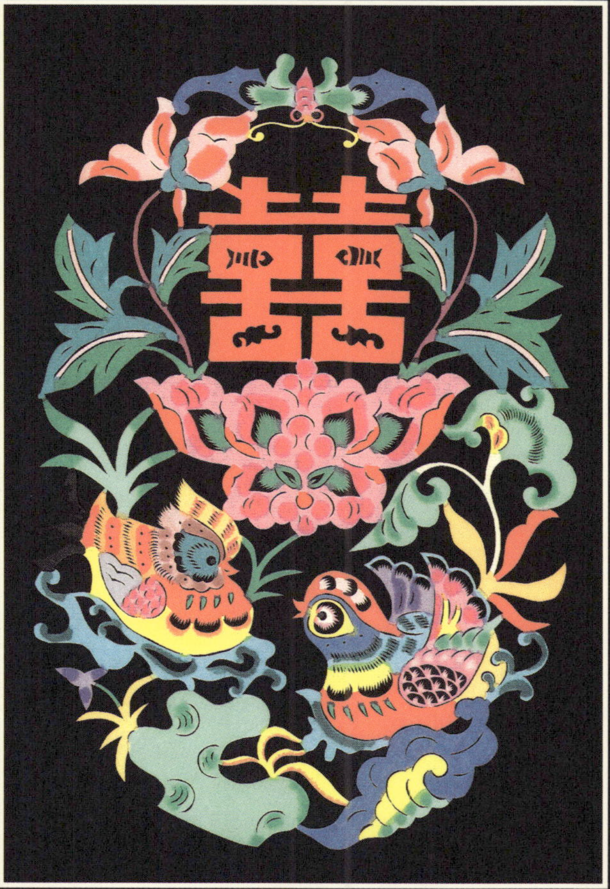
囍

grâce à la sécheresse du climat de cette province désertique. Ce sont des rondes de chevaux, de singes ou des rosaces de fleurs. Trouvés à côté d'objets funéraires, ces documents vieux de 1 700 ans pourraient représenter des miroirs. Sous les Song, leur usage s'était déjà largement répandu : on décorait les cadeaux, les fenêtres, les lanternes et on les utilisait pour l'impression sur textile, selon la technique du batik. Des coupes issues des fours de Jizhou, dans la province du Jianxi, portent des motifs de couleur brun-rouge qui ne sont pas peints mais silhouettés sur la porcelaine avant cuisson. Une industrie du papier découpé se créa donc dans les villes donnant naissance à des artistes professionnels alors que dans les campagnes subsistait un artisanat traditionnel animé par des paysans.

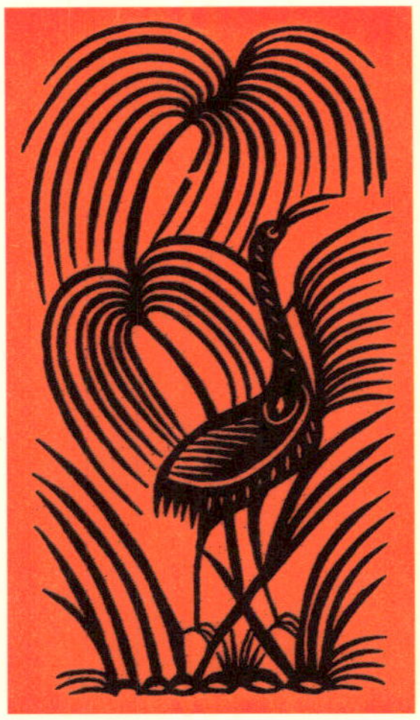

Les papiers découpés se classaient en trois catégories selon l'usage auquel on les destinait. Les plus communs étaient ceux qui servaient à la décoration pour égayer les maisons : on collait des motifs sur les portes, les fenêtres, les murs, les plafonds de papier, les jarres de riz et même le *kang*… Les fenêtres d'autrefois étant recouvertes de papier huilé, la tradition voulait qu'on en change au nouvel an lors des grands nettoyages de la fête du Printemps. C'était alors l'occasion d'apposer de nouvelles décorations, appelées dans le nord de la Chine « fleurs de fenêtre » ou « fleurs de murs ». Pour donner plus de vie à ces images, d'ingénieux systèmes d'accrochage avaient même été inventés pour que ces papiers puissent vibrer au moindre courant d'air. De la même façon, on inventa sous les Ming des lanternes à double paroi de gaze entre lesquelles les légers découpages montaient ou descendaient au gré de l'air chaud produit par la mèche. Ce même tour de magie fut appliqué à des éventails qui faisaient apparaître, par transparence au soleil, de mystérieuses formes se mouvant entre les deux fines parois.

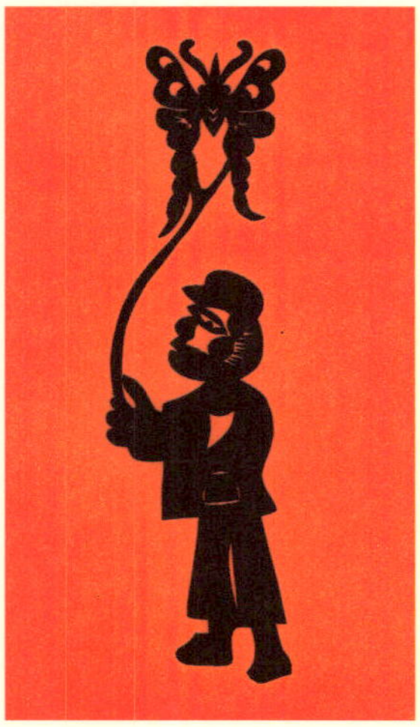

Puis venaient les décorations à caractère plus symbolique, celles qui figuraient sur des cadeaux ou les cartes de vœux pour les mariages, les naissances, les anniversaires ou le nouvel an. On utilisait alors le répertoire classique des caractères et des images porteurs de message de bon augure (bonheur, longévité, richesse et pêche, gourde, lotus, poulet, phénix, grillon, tête de cochon, poisson, dragon, grenouille…). Lors des visites traditionnelles de vœux, il était de bon ton d'apporter des pâtisseries (*longfengbing*, les « gâteaux dragon-phénix ») ou des nouilles dont les emballages étaient décorées de papiers découpés. Pour les grandes occasions, on mettait aux chandelles et aux brûle-parfums une collerette de papier découpé. Au cours de la fête du « Double Neuf » (*Chongyang,* fête de l'automne), jour de sortie à la campagne de toute la famille, les enfants jouaient avec des fanions de papier découpé. Dans les temples, il se vendait des charmes en papier découpé destinés à protéger les enfants des maladies. Lors des funérailles, les objets qui devaient accompagner le mort dans son dernier voyage et qu'on brûlait au cours d'une cérémonie, étaient aussi faits de papiers découpés mais de couleur blanche ou argent, la couleur du deuil autrefois.

Les femmes de la campagne faisaient grand usage des papiers découpés comme patrons pour leurs broderies *(tajianzhi).* Les vêtements des femmes et des enfants des minorités du sud et de l'ouest de la Chine comportent d'innombrables motifs brodés sur les manches, les coiffes, les sacs, les bavoirs d'enfants, les coussins et les pantoufles. De véritables marchés aux papiers-calques découpés se tiennent dans certaines provinces chinoises où les femmes des minorités ethniques, spécialistes de broderie, viennent s'approvisionner.

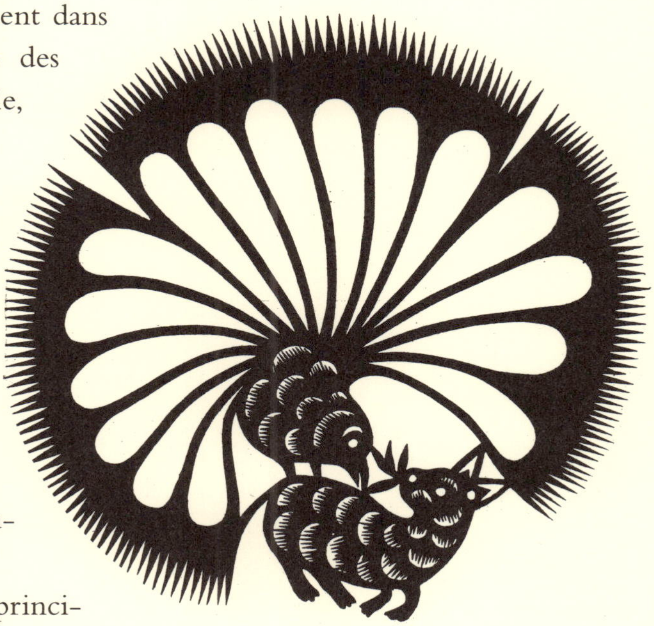

Comme pour les estampes populaires, le nombre et la variété des papiers découpés, est infini. En effet, d'une région à l'autre, chaque école avait son style. Dans le Sud, à Foshan ou Chaozhou, les productions étaient « plus raffinées et plus ingénieuses », avec des références littéraires plus fréquentes (thèmes de romans, d'opéras célèbres ou de légendes) ; dans le Nord, les motifs allégoriques étaient « simples et vigoureux » (animal, fleur, caractère, personnage).

Le découpage s'effectuait selon deux techniques principales. La première, sans doute celle qui fut utilisée aux périodes anciennes, consistait, après pliages successifs, à découper avec des ciseaux des silhouettes simples pour obtenir des rondes, des guirlandes et des rosaces d'une seule pièce. L'autre procédé utilisait un couteau fait d'une fine lame très tranchante montée dans un manche. Avec un peu de métier, l'artisan pouvait tailler jusqu'à une dizaine de feuilles à la fois et réaliser des motifs très élaborés à partir d'un patron. Ce modèle pouvait être décalqué, par la technique du pochoir, en le plaçant au-dessus d'une mèche fumeuse de chandelle. L'autre méthode, proche de l'estampage, consistait à frotter le papier recouvrant le patron avec une cire teintée au noir de fumée.

Les variétés de papier se sont limitées au *maobianzhi* (papier à écrire, relativement épais fabriqué avec du jeune bambou) et au *xuanzhi* (papier fin dit « de Chine », ou papier à dessin). Le papier d'argent ou d'or n'était utilisé

Ci-dessus et page de gauche, papiers découpés.

que dans le Sud sur des fonds de couleurs vives. Les dessins étaient travaillés soit en positif (les découpages sont comme les lignes d'un dessin) soit en négatif (le dessin n'apparaît que dans les blancs). Pour ajouter au raffinement, certains artistes n'ont pas hésité à utiliser les trous d'épingle qui donnaient un effet de délicates dentelles au découpage.

S'agissant des couleurs, la plupart des papiers découpés ont été réalisés dans les couleurs primaires : rouge, rose, vert, bleu ou jaune. Dans quelques cas, des papiers de couleurs différentes ont été mêlés créant un effet plutôt criard. En utilisant du papier relativement absorbant, les artistes coloraient aussi à la main les découpages avec des pigments rendus fluides dans l'alcool qui s'étalaient dans un halo. Ces images aux couleurs vives et aux motifs simplistes ne sont pas sans rappeler les imprimés *(zhima)* de nouvel an.

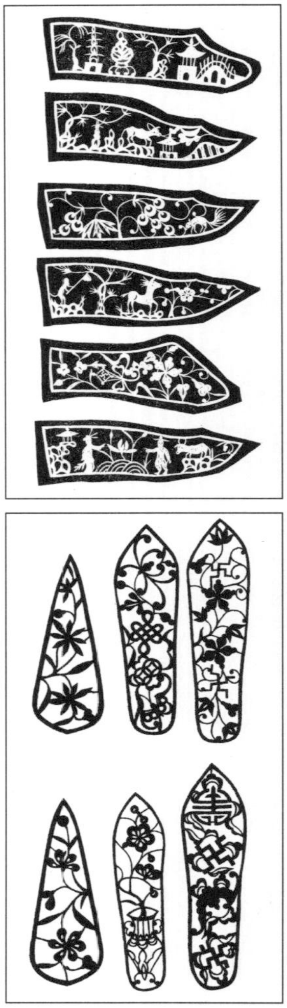

Découpages de papier (en positif et en négatif) servant comme patron pour des broderies de pantoufles (côté et semelle). Page de droite, marionnettes (ombres chinoises).

Le théâtre d'ombres chinoises est appelé en Chine *piyingxi* (littéralement, « théâtre des ombres de cuir »). Cet art est très proche du découpage auquel il emprunte ses origines et certains de ses procédés. Depuis plus de mille ans, c'est par ces ingénieuses projections qui relevaient de la magie que l'on racontait les mythes, les épopées, les légendes populaires et même l'histoire contemporaine au public naïf et bon enfant des campagnes et des bourgades perdues dans les montagnes des lointaines provinces. Environ trois fois dans l'année, lors de la célébration du nouvel an et après les récoltes d'été ou d'automne, les troupes se produisaient, le soir, dans les villages, sur les places publiques, devant les temples ou quelquefois dans une maison de thé. L'arrivée des artistes était un moment de réjouissance générale pour tous les villageois qui contribuaient collectivement aux frais de la représentation. Aux époques où les divertissements étaient rares, le passage d'une troupe de théâtre (quatre à six acteurs et quelques musiciens) était un évènement d'importance pour grands et petits. Les femmes, en général interdites de sortie, étaient exceptionnellement autorisées à assister au spectacle qui n'était pas jugé inconvenant car une toile les séparait des acteurs…

Les légendes qui se rapportent à l'origine du théâtre d'ombres sont nombreuses. L'une d'elles est celle de la servante qui, ne parvenant pas à calmer le bébé impérial dont elle avait la garde, eut recours aux ombres mouvantes des branches d'arbres sur les fenêtres de papier du palais. Devant l'intérêt manifesté par l'enfant, l'astucieuse servante fit des découpages de feuilles qu'elle animait derrière la fenêtre à la grande joie de son royal spectateur. Originaire du Moyen-Orient, c'est à la période Tang (VIIe au Xe siècle) que parvint, sans doute de la Perse, cet art nouveau des « ombres de cuir ». En Inde, elles avaient servi à diffuser le bouddhisme et leur utilisation avait un caractère sacré. En Chine, le rôle religieux de ces silhouettes fut important, il mettait en scène tout un panthéon. L'image projetée était pour les spectateurs le dieu même, les spectateurs éprouvaient une véritable peur à leur apparition sur l'écran ; aussi les représentations théâtrales étaient-elles précédées de séances d'exorcisation de l'aire de jeu. Guanyin, la forme sinisée d'Avalokiteçvara, devenue la déesse de la Miséricorde, est une des premières figures du théâtre d'ombres, elle devint d'ailleurs la patronne des marionnettistes. La légende lui attribue l'origine du découpage de petits personnages dans des feuilles de bambou. Pour marquer tout le respect dû à cette sainte venue du bouddhisme, son effigie de cuir était toujours rangée sur le haut de la malle aux accessoires. C'est véritablement sous les Song (960-1127), et en particulier sous le règne de Renzong, que des spectacles de théâtre d'ombres furent donnés dans les villes à l'occasion des fêtes. Plus tard, sous les Yuan, avec l'introduction du bouddhisme lamaïque dans les régions du nord et de l'ouest de la Chine, de nombreuses troupes de théâtre se créèrent à Xi'an et à Tangshan (province du Hebei). Au XIIIe siècle, sous les Yuan, le théâtre d'ombres était un des spectacles préférés de l'empereur mongol et de ses soldats. Il suivit d'ailleurs les armées et se retrouva ainsi exporté à l'ouest et au sud de la Chine. Sous les Ming, les prêtres bouddhistes s'en servaient encore pour prêcher les soutras et il ne devint un divertissement populaire dans le Nord que vers le XVe siècle. Sous la dynastie des Qing, la période la plus florissante du théâtre d'ombres se situe à l'époque de Kangxi ; on comptait plusieurs dizaines de troupes dans la capitale. Les voyageurs (et les Jésuites) auraient ramené en France en 1767, puis en Angleterre en 1776, des marionnettes de carton et de cuir qui furent montrées sous le nom d'« ombres chinoises » et connurent un grand succès. Toutefois, au XIXe siècle, l'impact de ces spectacles était tel en Chine qu'il lui valut d'être interdit en plusieurs occasions par les autorités, à cause de son caractère subversif. Quand la critique du pouvoir était trop forte, les montreurs d'images étaient jetés en prison et leur spectacle interdit.

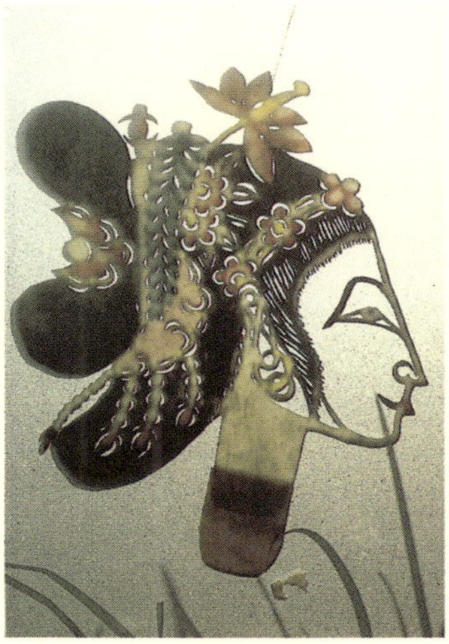

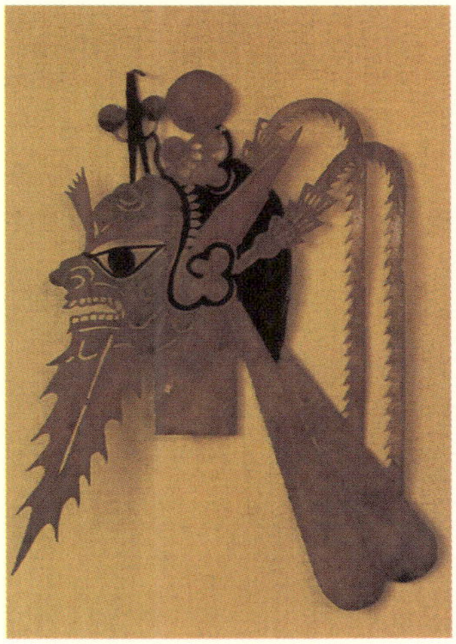

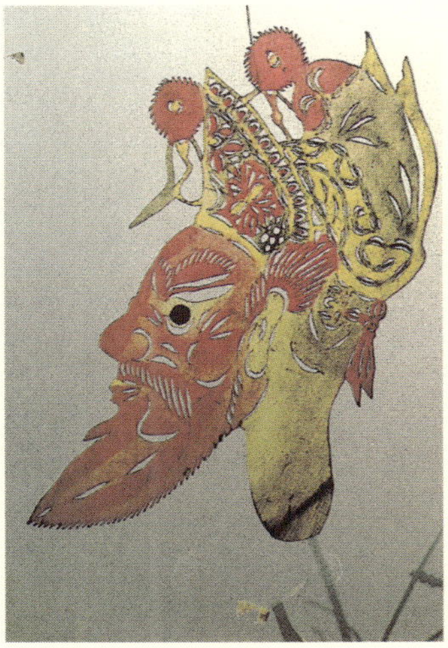

À l'origine, le rideau de scène derrière lequel évoluaient les marionnettes de cuir, était fait de papier blanc ; il sera bientôt remplacé par une fine toile enduite d'amidon. Cet écran était éclairé de l'arrière par des lampes à huile à mèche qui ne diffusaient pas une bonne lumière. Au début du siècle, elles furent remplacées par des lampes à gaz et enfin des ampoules électriques qui présentaient l'avantage de fournir un éclairage uniforme où l'on ne voyait plus l'ombre des tiges des marionnettes.

Les personnages, traditionnellement classés en cinq catégories, étaient relativement stéréotypés. On les identifiait par leur tête (toujours vue de profil et volontairement grossie) :

– le vieil homme digne *(laosheng),* reconnaissable à son chapeau de lettré ou de fonctionnaire, portant une longue barbe et des moustaches, et *xiao sheng,* le jeune homme aux délicats sourcils ;
– la femme *(dan)* aux coiffes multiples et variées (chignons, tresses, fleurs, diadèmes…) qui pouvait être, suivant les rôles, la « séduisante » (*yaodan* ou *huadan*), la « sorcière » *(caisangdan),* la « vieille » *(laodan)* ou la « guerrière » *(daomadan)* ;
– le soldat *(jing)* à la mine féroce et bariolée comme à l'opéra de Pékin, en noir (*tiechen,* « face de fer », symbole de justice et de détermination), en rouge (*hongliande,* honnêteté et fidélité à l'empereur) ;
– le traître *(mi)* au visage plâtré (*jianchen,* face blanche) ;
– le bouffon *(zhou)* au visage hilare et grotesque, souvent vu de trois quarts.

Initialement découpées dans du carton blanc, les marionnettes (*piying,* « silhouettes de peau ») furent faites, plus tard, dans du cuir de vache, de buffle, de cheval ou d'âne. Après tannage et grattages successifs, on obtenait une peau fine et translucide. C'est à partir d'un patron que l'artisan gravait alors son dessin sur la peau avec une aiguille avant de la découper à l'aide de scalpels au-dessus d'une plaque de cire ou de bois. La découpe, comme pour le papier, pouvait être « en relief » ou « en creux » selon l'effet recherché. Les visages auquel il convenait de donner de l'expression et de la transparence étaient découpés selon le premier procédé ; pour les vêtements, les décors ou les animaux, on préférait le second qui donnait de la profondeur et du volume. Après le découpage des pièces de cuir, celles-ci subissaient différents traitements de coloration. Les couleurs criardes apparaissaient mieux sur l'écran par transparence. Elles étaient soit trempées dans des bains soit peintes à la main puis vernies. Enfin, toutes les pièces étaient assemblées entre elles par des fils. La taille des silhouettes variait selon les régions entre 25 et 60 centimètres.

Page de droite, marionnettes posées au sol avec, pour chacune, les manches en bambou qui permettent au manipulateur d'animer la tête et les bras.

Sauf pour les éléments de décor qui étaient appuyés contre la toile ou certains animaux qui n'étaient pas articulés, toutes les autres marionnettes avaient

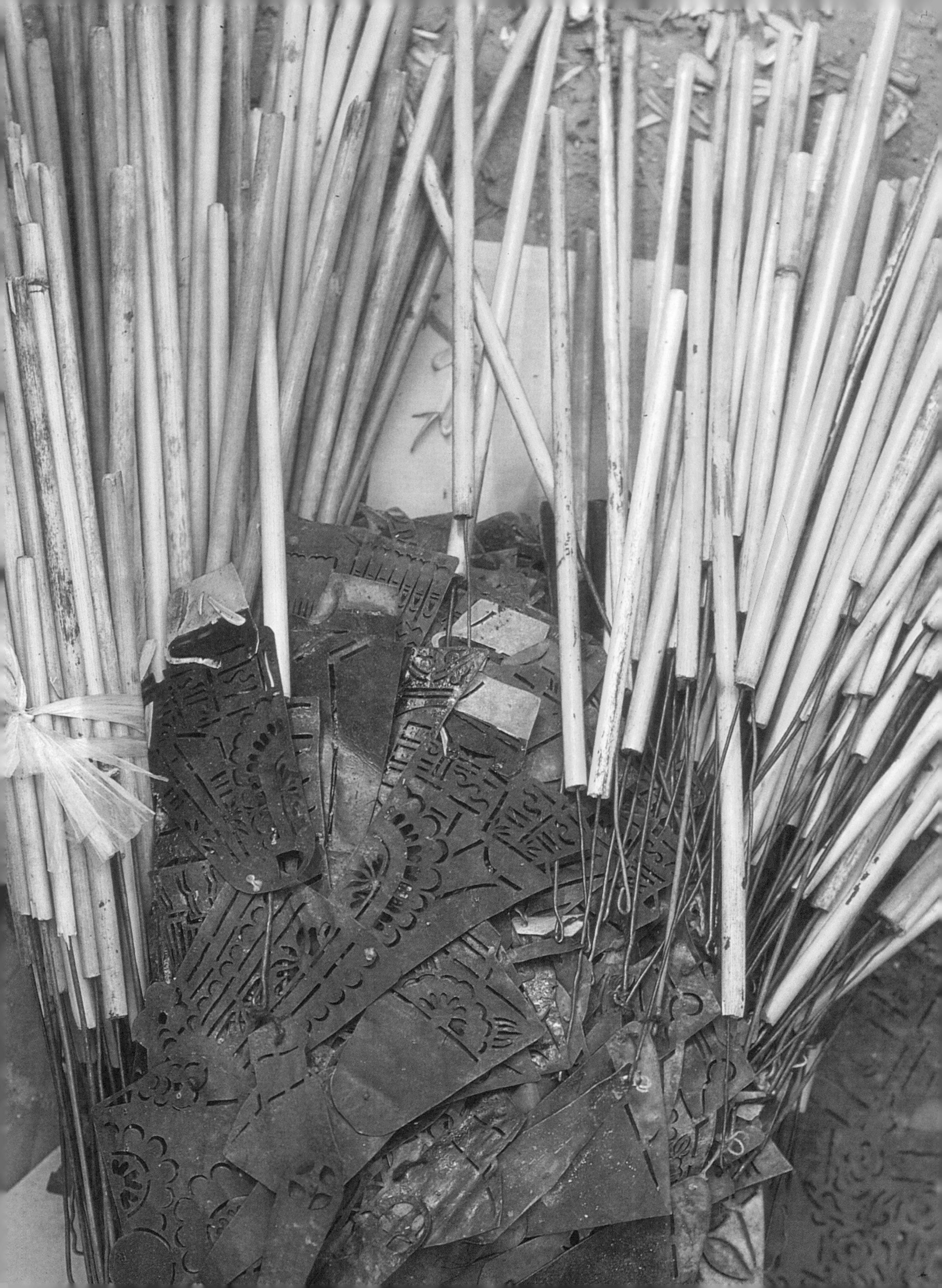

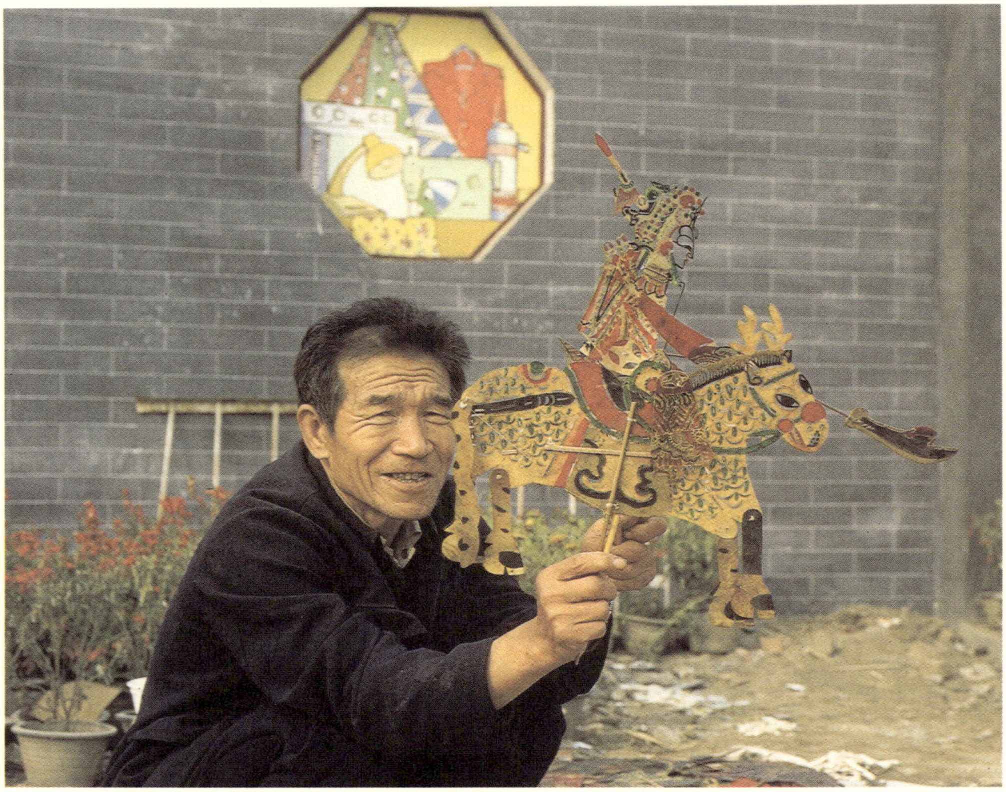

trois manches en bambou qui permettaient aux manipulateurs de faire bouger la tête et les deux bras. Les jambes étaient fixées au corps de telle sorte que, par un mouvement sec du poignet, elles donnaient l'illusion du mouvement. Le marionnettiste, qui jouait de trois à quatre silhouettes à la fois, devait avoir aussi des talents d'acteur et de chanteur. Dans le cas de pièces avec de nombreux personnages, les musiciens venaient prêter main-forte aux acteurs dans la manipulation des silhouettes, en particulier quand les spectacles étaient longs. Lors de festivals, les représentations pouvaient durer ainsi plusieurs nuits consécutives.

Le répertoire variait en fonction des écoles. Celles du Nord, de l'Ouest et de Pékin étaient plus célèbres que celles du Sud. L'impératrice Tseu Hsi (Cixi) fit venir en plusieurs occasions des troupes à l'intérieur de la Cité Interdite car elle était friande de ces spectacles où l'épique, le merveilleux se mêlaient au drame (les classiques du répertoire restaient le *Voyage en Occident*, le *Serpent Blanc*, les *Huit Immortels célèbrent l'anniversaire de la Mère du Ciel*...). Dans les provinces du Sud, la tradition du théâtre d'ombres était aussi forte, le répertoire, datant de l'époque Yuan, était fondé sur les *nanxi* (pièces dramatiques du Sud) qui se jouaient avec des marionnettes en carton, d'une facture moins élaborée.

Ci-dessus, vendeur de marionnettes de cuir.

L'opium, pâte de félicité et de longévité

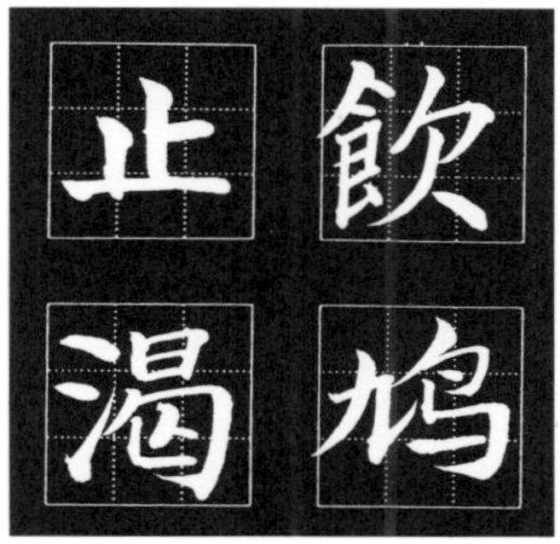

yinjiu zhike, littéralement, « boire du poison pour étancher la soif ».

Le pavot *(papaver somniferum)* était connu dans l'antiquité grecque sous le nom de *opion,* les Arabes le nommaient *afyun* et les Persans *apyun* sans doute en référerence à un nom de lieu en Turquie d'où la plante serait originaire. On l'appelle en chinois *yapian* (ou *yingsu,* « jarre de millet », à cause de la forme arrondie de sa capsule) et ce nom figurait déjà dans le classique de la pharmacopée chinoise, le *Bencao Gangmu* (1552-1578).

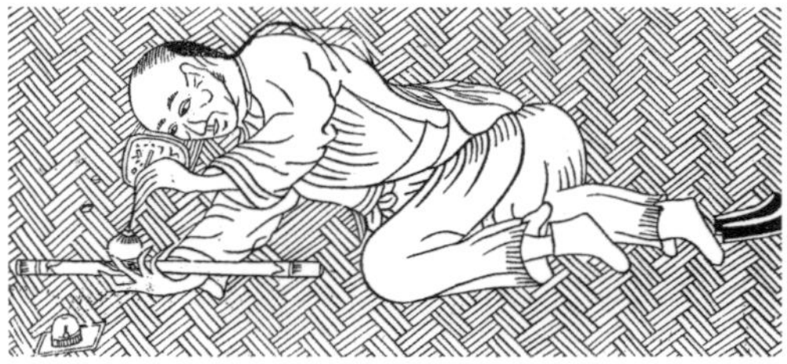

C'est probablement sous la dynastie des Tang (618-907) que les Chinois découvrirent le pavot et l'opium rapportés par les caravaniers d'Asie centrale, d'Arabie ou de Turquie. Dès le VIIIe siècle, la plante était cultivée dans les provinces du Sud (Yunnan, Sichuan) et de l'Ouest (Gansu) pour ses vertus médicinales. Consommé en soupe ou en pilules, l'opium a une action sédative, hypnotique, antispasmodique, astringente et analgésique, il était donc indiqué contre la toux chronique, la diarrhée, les maux d'estomac et l'asthme.

Au début du XVIIe siècle, on prit l'habitude de le fumer comme le tabac *(yan)* et on le dénommait *dayan* pour les différencier. Au XVIIIe, son usage se répandit en Chine et bien que produit localement, on continua à lui préférer l'opium d'origine indienne. On le désignait comme la « pâte de félicité et de longévité » *(fushougao)*. Mais il reçut aussi des appellations moins aimables comme la « boue des étrangers » ou la « boue noire » *(hei tu)*. Dès 1729, les autorités chinoises avaient réagi en prenant un premier édit interdisant sa consommation mais il faudra attendre plus de deux cents ans pour que l'usage de cette drogue se perde. En effet, sous couvert d'exportation en Chine de textiles du Yorkshire dont elle avait le monopole depuis 1785, l'Angleterre, par l'intermédiaire de sa toute puissante Compagnie des Indes Orientales, avait lancé le commerce illicite de l'opium en provenance du Bengale. En 1850, les entrées d'opium en Chine étaient estimées à 6 250 tonnes. C'est en voulant mettre fin à cette situation grave que le gouverneur des provinces du Sud, Lin Zexu, fit jeter à la mer 20 291 caisses d'opium indien, déclenchant ainsi la première guerre de l'opium entre les Anglais et les Chinois (1838-1842). Elle se termina par le traité de Nankin

Fumeur d'opium d'après A. Favier, Peking, 1902.

ouvrant, dans un premier temps, cinq ports de l'Empire aux étrangers avant l'apparition des concessions. Le vicaire apostolique de Pékin, Mgr Alphonse Favier écrivait en 1902 : « les maisons d'opium sont ouvertes partout, le riche fume chez lui, le pauvre n'importe où, les autres fumeurs remplissent ces officines d'empoisonnement où on est servi par des femmes qui préparent les pipes. C'est comme le jeu, une passion dont on guérit difficilement… On rencontre de malheureux jeunes gens pâles, d'une maigreur effrayante, qui meurent saturés d'opium, sur la voie publique. »

Pour obtenir la pâte *(yangao)*, il faut extraire le suc blanchâtre et gluant en incisant la capsule du pavot. Ce liquide se transforme peu à peu en une pâte brunâtre dont on conserve l'élasticité pour la mettre en forme de « pains » ronds (d'environ un kilo et demi) en les enveloppant dans des feuilles de pavot. Une fois sec, l'opium a une consistance dure et cassante, il est noir comme du goudron et marque toutes les surfaces avec lesquelles il a été en contact (fourneau de pipe, aiguille, lampe). Ces pains se conservaient pendant près de dix années. Leur transport s'effectuait à l'époque dans des coffres de bois de manguier d'un poids standard de soixante kilogrammes. Avant de le consommer, il fallait reconstituer l'opium dans de l'eau bouillante et laisser le liquide imbiber la pâte. Alors on pouvait la façonner en boulettes qu'il fallait conserver dans des boîtes étanches.

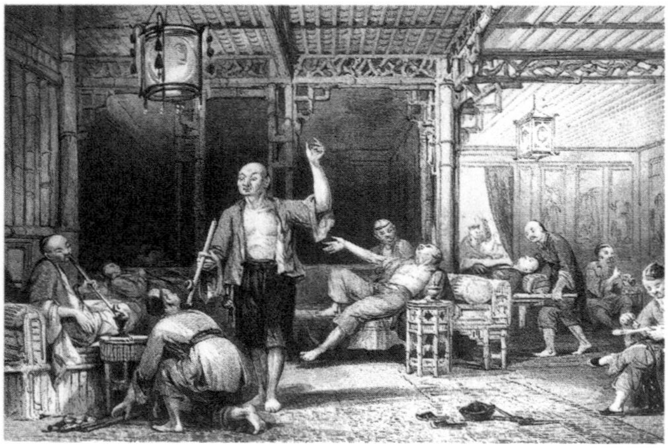

Les accessoires du fumeur *(yanju)* ont pratiquement disparu lors de la répression lancée par les autorités de la Jeune République en 1949 et ensuite pendant la Révolution culturelle. Des mesures particulièrement sévères furent prises à l'égard des opiomanes *(yangui)* qui avaient fait les beaux jours des fumeries. Il fut plus difficile d'empêcher l'usage de l'opium à domicile, surtout dans les milieux aisés ou dans les lointaines campagnes du Sud-Ouest. Le nécessaire du fumeur ne comportait pas moins d'une demi douzaine d'articles, en général réunis sur un plateau. Dans les fumeries, ces accessoires étaient fournis contre paiement, avec une place sur une couche, une théière et les services d'une préposée pour la confection des boulettes.

Ci-dessus, intérieur d'une fumerie d'opium (d'après The Chinese Empire *de T. Allom et N.G. Wright, 1859). Page de droite, gravure de morale représentant un vertueux jeune homme tentant de dissuader un de ses camarades de fumer de l'opium (affiche, 1930).*

La pipe à opium (*yandou* ou dans la langue populaire, *yanqiang,* « fusil à opium ») était d'une taille variant entre dix et cinquante centimètres de longueur. Elle avait un embout en matière noble (jade ou ivoire) pour être agréable aux lèvres. Le tuyau, fait d'un tube de bambou fermé à un bout, portait pour les pipes de valeur, des décorations d'argent, d'écaille de tortue, d'ivoire, de pierres semi-précieuses, de jade ou de nacre. Le fourneau de la

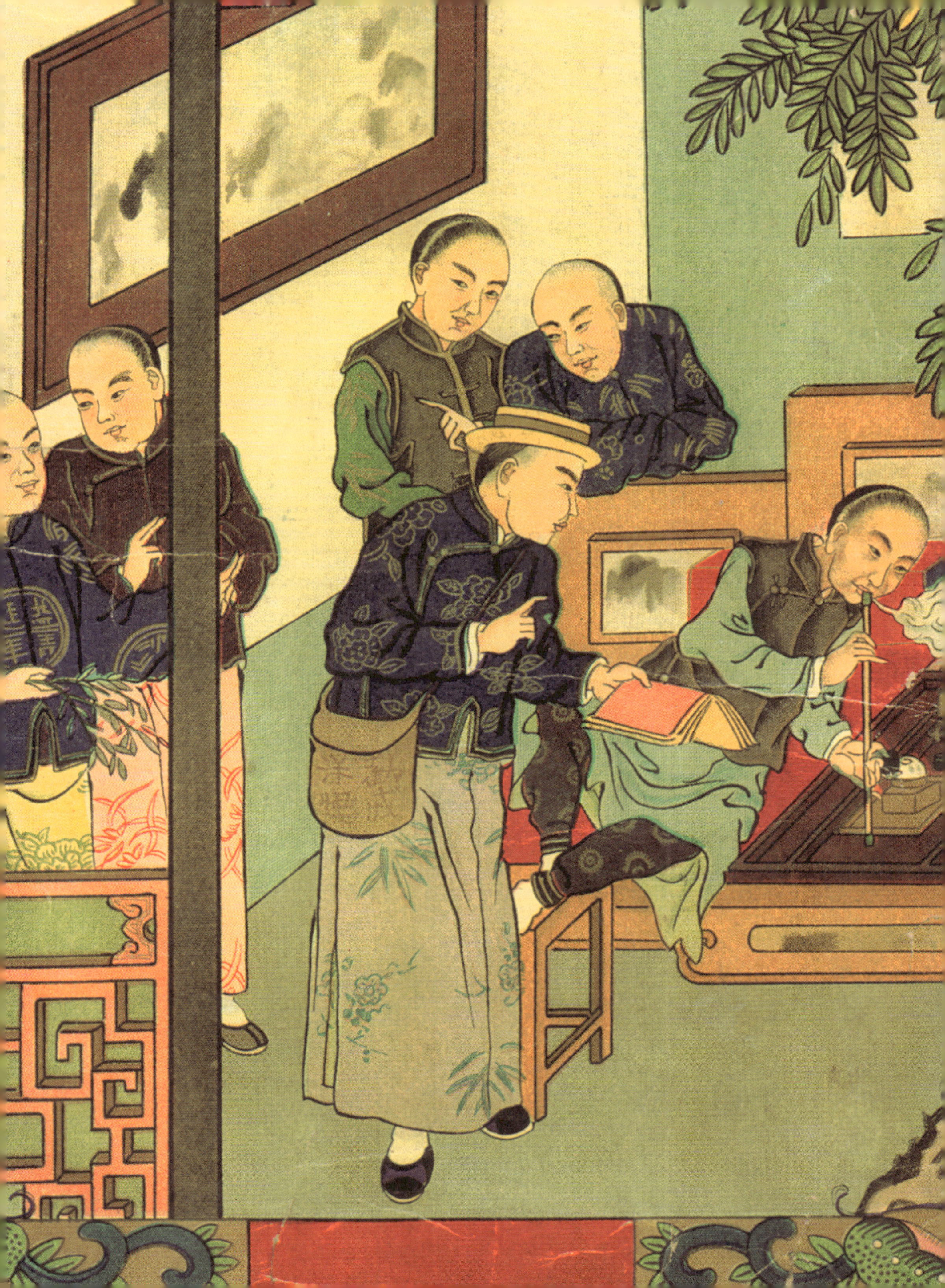
勸戒洋煙

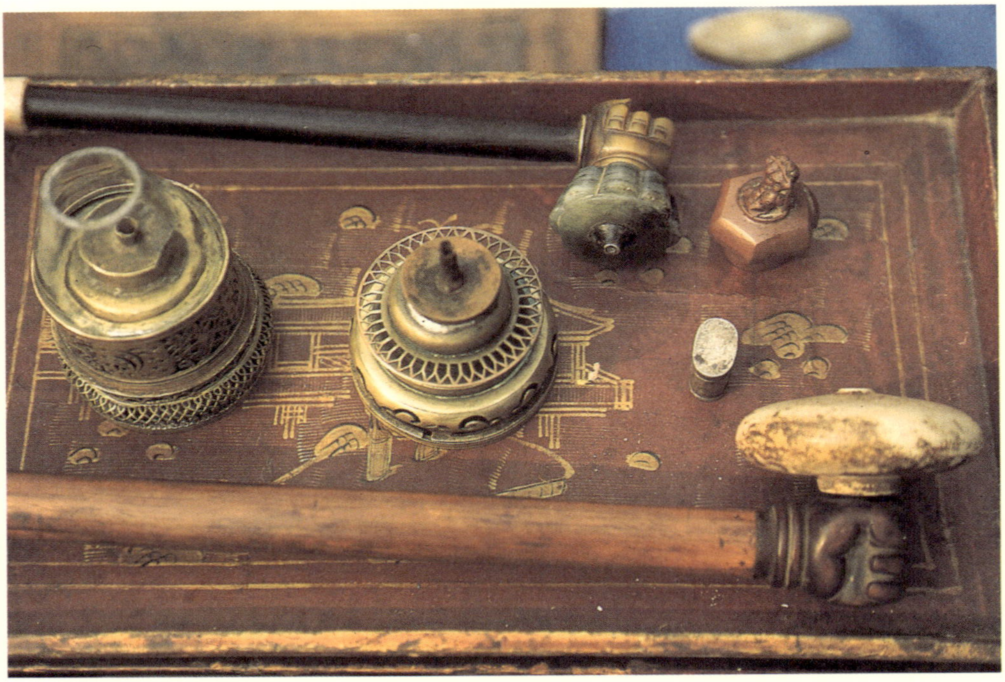

pipe s'encastrait dans le tuyau grâce à un collier de cuivre, d'étain ou d'argent rendu hermétique par un petit morceau de tissu. La forme des fourneaux variait selon les régions ou les modes. Ils pouvaient être sphériques, cylindriques, octogonaux, en forme de champignon, de toupie ou d'animaux et même de personnages. Les plus communs étaient fabriqués dans une argile rouge foncée *(yixing)* ou noire, résistante au feu, sans décoration particulière. À la partie inférieure, on pouvait lire les marques de fabricants imprimées dans la terre cuite. D'autres étaient en porcelaine avec des motifs peints ou des inscriptions, en céladon, en argent, en cloisonné et même en ivoire. Le foyer dans lequel est déposé la boulette en fusion consiste en un évidement au centre du fourneau. Dans certains intérieurs bourgeois, les collections de fourneaux de pipe étaient alignées sur des étagères de bois laqué, incrustées de nacre ou de céramique et percées d'un évidement pour y encastrer le fourneau. En général, l'opiomane utilisait souvent le même tuyau auquel il adaptait un fourneau différent selon ses goûts du moment. Les fourneaux sont en soi des pièces décoratives pour collectionneurs.

La lampe à opium *(yandeng)* était une petite lampe à pétrole (certaines minuscules) dont le réservoir était encastré dans un socle rond ou octogonal en cuivre ajouré, décoré de motifs auspicieux, en verre ou en métal cloisonné. Le verre de lampe, de forme bulbeuse, épais pour résister à la chaleur et largement ouvert sur le haut, empêchait la mèche de fumer en maintenant la flamme verticale.

Ci-dessus et page de droite, le nécessaire du fumeur d'opium (oreiller et bas-flanc, pipes, lampes, boîtes...).

L'aiguille *(yanqianzi)* en forme de spatule permettait de façonner la boulette et de la présenter à la flamme pour amorcer la combustion. À ce moment, elle

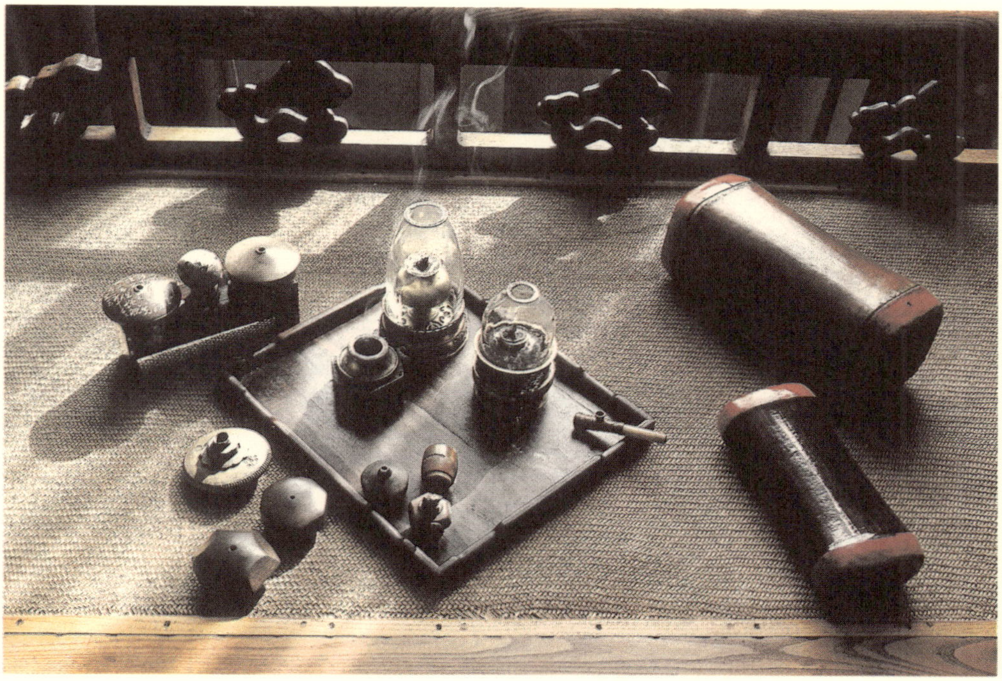

se mettait à grésiller et à changer de couleur (du noir au doré), il se dégageait une odeur âcre très caractéristique. En roulant l'aiguille entre les doigts, on déposait alors la boulette sur l'orifice du foyer, répétant plusieurs fois cette opération pour s'assurer d'une bonne combustion de la drogue. Une fois la boulette posée sur le fourneau, le fumeur pouvait enfin aspirer profondément et la boulette se consumait lentement.

L'oreiller *(zhentou)* permettait de tenir la pipe à la hauteur de la lampe sans avoir à changer de position. Les oreillers traditionnels sont des blocs parallélépipédiques d'osier tressé, de céramique creuse et ventilée, ou de cuir laqué.

Les boîtes à opium (*yanhu* ou *chuyanguan*) servaient de réserve pour la maison ou le voyage. Certains opiomanes consommaient jusqu'à vingt boulettes par jour de la grosseur d'un petit pois. On ne connaît pas exactement l'origine de ces boîtes ; pour certains c'étaient des boîtes à pilules médicinales, pour d'autres les inscriptions que l'on y relève (« frais parfum et bon goût, pure comme de l'eau, à utiliser souvent pour prolonger sa vie »...) ne font pas mystère de leur fonction. De forme ovale, cylindrique ou rectangulaire, ces boîtes d'une taille variant de deux à cinq centimètres, devaient être avant tout étanches, le couvercle était donc ajusté avec précision. Certaines possédaient même une deuxième enveloppe coulissante. S'adressant à des clients de toutes les classes sociales, les artisans ont donc fabriqué ces récipients dans des matières très variées : en ivoire, argent niellé, jade, laiton, cloisonné, émail, corne, écaille, os, mais le plus souvent en maillechort *(baitong)*, qui par sa couleur ressemble à l'argent. Des vœux ou des motifs traditionnels (chauve-souris, caractères Bonheur et Longévité) ainsi que de

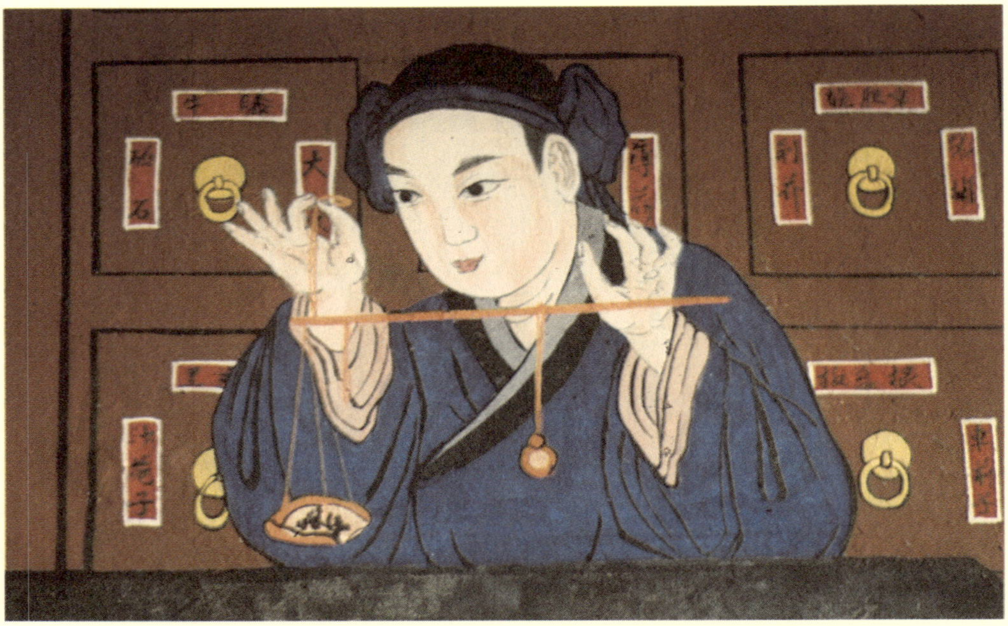

courts poèmes étaient gravés sur les parois ou le couvercle. Suivant la taille et la décoration, on peut reconnaître les boîtes destinées aux hommes (plus sobres) et celles faites pour les dames.

Construites sur le principe de la balance romaine *(gancheng),* les balances à opium servaient aussi à la pesée de petites quantités de produits précieux comme la poudre d'or ou d'argent, les médicaments. Pour le transport, elles étaient rangées dans des étuis en forme de boîte à violon. Ces balances comprennent trois éléments reliés entre eux par des fils : le fléau formé d'une aiguille d'ivoire portant des graduations, un plateau de cuivre et un contrepoids. Parlant de ces balances, un vieux dicton chinois rappelle que « le fléau ne doit pas être séparé du contrepoids » *(chenggan bu li chengtuo),* allusion à l'épouse chinoise qui maintient l'équilibre du ménage par son dévouement et sa sagesse.

La consommation non médicale de l'opium, généralisée en Chine à partir du XVIIIe siècle, se répandra dans tous les pays comptant une forte communauté chinoise. Les fumeries connaîtront même des clients européens et dans certains cercles intellectuels du début du siècle on trouvait des opiomanes célèbres. En 1909, les États-Unis adoptèrent une loi pour interdire l'importation de l'opium et en limiter l'usage au seul domaine médical. Curieusement, ni le Japon ni la Corée ne virent se développer ce vice en dépit de leur proximité géographique de la Chine.

Apothicaire faisant usage d'une balance (peinture du temple de la Cloche d'or à Wutaishan, Shanxi).

Le pékinois, chien-lion, chien bouddhique

寵物

chongwu, littéralement, « animaux favoris ».

Ce chien de la race des carlins (caractérisés par leur museau aplati) fut particulièrement recherché de l'aristocratie de tous les temps, sans doute parce que sa morphologie rappelait celle du lion, animal intimement associé à Bouddha dont il était l'une des montures. Le pékinois est souvent confondu avec ces gardiens des entrées, dont il est la représentation miniaturisée. Le « chien-lion » est aussi appelé « chien bouddhique », « chien de Fo ou Fu » (abréviation de Fo To, « le Bouddha »). Au XVIIe siècle, particulièrement à la période Kangxi, on fabriquait des paires de chiens de Fo, assis sur leurs pattes de derrière et montés sur un socle, en biscuit bleu turquoise ou en trois couleurs ; ces porcelaines devinrent très populaires au XIXe siècle en Europe.

Les prêtres lamas avaient ramené du Tibet les célèbres chiens blancs de Lhassa, qui ne furent guère appréciés par les Chinois car le blanc est associé au deuil. Les pékinois, qui, en dépit de leur nom sont probablement aussi d'origine tibétaine sont appelés d'une manière populaire *bagou* (« le chien qui se traîne à terre »). On en signale déjà sous les Zhou en provenance des provinces occidentales. Ils se rangent en deux catégories : ceux à poil ras et ceux à long poil dénommés justement les « chiens-lions » *(shizigou)* à cause de leur crinière. De couleur blanc et noir ou fauve, c'est cette dernière race qui était la plus prisée des amateurs. Ils n'hésitaient pas à les qualifier de « pékinois-soie-d'or » *(jinsipa)*. Ceux-ci seront d'ailleurs immortalisés par les décorateurs de la porcelaine de l'époque Qing sous les traits des célèbres chiens au pelage orangé. Un animal de trois couleurs était appelé par les spécialistes « carapace de tortue », un chien noir à pattes blanches « nuages noirs sur la neige », il était présage d'enfants mâles sur de nombreuses générations. Un traité prévoyait ainsi : « Si un homme élève un chien noir à oreilles blanches, il deviendra riche et noble, s'il produit un chien blanc à tête jaune, sa famille prospérera. Un chien jaune à queue blanche assure des réussites officielles. Un chien blanc à tête noire ajoute la richesse à la chance… »

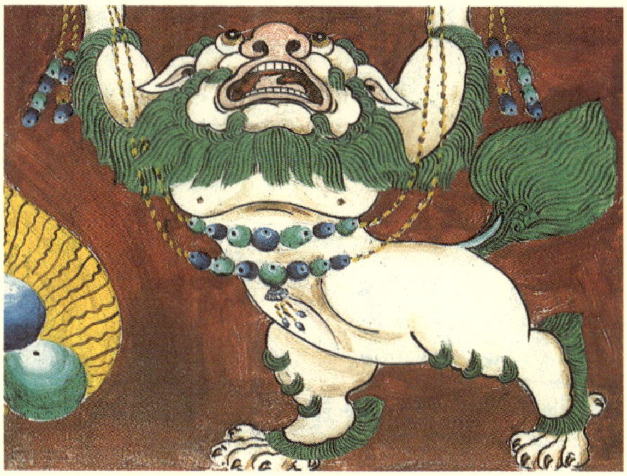

Un chien-lion (peinture murale du monastère lamaïque de Wusutuzhao, Mongolie, XVIIe siècle).

Les amateurs jugeaient d'ailleurs les qualités de ces petits chiens sur bien d'autres critères. La tête devait être plutôt rectangulaire et massive, semblable à celle du lion. À cet effet, les chiots étaient enfermés très tôt dans des cages exiguës d'où ne dépassait que leur tête. Les yeux devaient être protubérants et écartés comme ceux des poissons chinois. Certains appréciaient des yeux couleur « châtaigne d'eau » (*ling,* la macre), d'autres préféraient de grands « yeux de léopard » ou des *siyan* (les « quatre yeux », bordés de cercles). Pour obtenir un museau court, large et écrasé, on opérait ou on le massait à intervalles fréquents depuis le plus jeune âge. Certains clouaient un morceau de peau de porc sur une planchette et ils le donnaient à lécher à l'animal chaque fois qu'il avait faim. Une belle bouche devait être arrondie, la mâchoire inférieure en léger retrait, façon « bouche de tortue » *(guizui).* La langue devait être suffisamment longue pour dépasser légèrement et retomber à droite ou à gauche (mais pas au milieu car elle rappelait alors celle des pendus). Les éleveurs qui, jusqu'à une époque récente tenaient leurs quartiers près du Temple de Confucius à Pékin, non loin du célèbre Temple des Lamas, n'hésitaient pas à tirer souvent sur la langue de leurs chiots pour obtenir un résultat apprécié. La fameuse « queue de lion » en panache fut obtenue aussi par de nombreuses mutilations dont eurent à souffrir ces chiens. Les peintres sur porcelaine n'ont pas manqué de reproduire toutes ces particularités morphologiques sur des vases, des plats, des assiettes, et des boîtes à grillons.

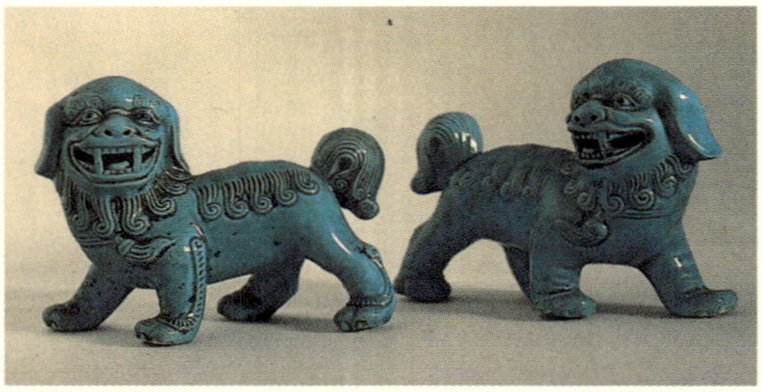

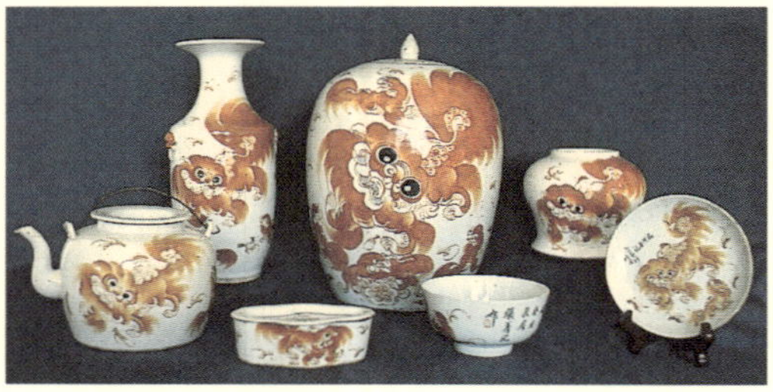

Passés maîtres dans les croisements depuis plus d'un millénaire, les Chinois sont parvenus à créer un chien de compagnie très recherché. Petit de taille, on le portait en hiver dans les larges manches des robes traditionnelles, véritable chaufferette pour élégantes. Le pékinois était, par ailleurs, connu pour son intelligence et son heureux caractère ; on lui apprenait à faire des tours : conduire un cheval par les rênes, précéder son maître avec une bougie allumée dans la gueule, apporter une pipe ou une blague à tabac...

Une encyclopédie raconte que, sous les Tang, un couple de pékinois venant d'Asie centrale ou même de Constantinople (Fulin), aurait été offert à l'empereur Gao Zu (618-626). Plusieurs empereurs s'entouraient de ces chiens élevés par les eunuques. Écartés par les Ming qui préférèrent les chats, les « chiens de palais » revinrent à la mode sous les Mandchous (période Qing), descendants de chasseurs et d'éleveurs. L'impératrice douairière Tseu Hsi (Ci Xi) en possédait près d'une centaine, elle fut accompagnée lors de ses funérailles en 1908 par son pékinois préféré, « Pivoine », qui en réalité ne fut jamais enterré avec sa maîtresse mais immédiatement revendu à un prix astronomique par un eunuque peu respectueux du rituel.

En haut, paire de chiens de Fo (biscuits de couleur turquoise) ; en bas, porcelaine blanche à motif de chien de Fo, (période Qing, XIXe siècle).

Le vent et l'eau, les mystères de la géomancie

風水

fengshui, littéralement, « vents et cours d'eau ».

Fengshui (« vents et cours d'eau ») est le terme que Guo Pu (276-324), originaire du Shanxi, donna à cette pratique dont l'objectif était de mettre l'homme en harmonie avec son environnement naturel. Alors que l'astrologie étudie l'influence des planètes sur les hommes, la géomancie cherche à déterminer les influences positives ou négatives d'un lieu. Le temps mesuré par le calendrier et l'orientation définie par la boussole doivent être en accord et c'est cet équilibre que le *fengshui* se propose de rechercher.

Le monde était composé selon les croyances anciennes de cinq éléments : le bois, le feu, la terre, le métal et l'eau et leur interaction pouvait être pour les hommes source de bonheur (ordre productif : bois-feu-terre-métal-eau) ou de malheur (ordre destructif : bois-terre-eau-feu-métal). On raconte ainsi que les incendies qui ravagèrent plusieurs fois le hall de l'Harmonie Suprême dans la Cité Interdite étaient dus au mauvais choix du nom (Tai Hedian) qui contient les éléments du feu *(tai)* et de l'eau *(he)* dans un ordre « destructif ». Bien avant que l'on découvre le magnétisme de la terre, les anciens traités chinois parlaient de « courants » souterrains invisibles qui se classaient en « souffles » bénéfiques *(qi),* au parcours sinueux, et en flux néfastes *(sha),* qui se propageaient en ligne droite sous formes de « flèches magiques ». La géomancie est donc l'art d'accentuer et de concentrer les souffles bénéfiques. Les lieux humides, creux, plats ou en ligne droite (torrents rapides, failles de montagne, ligne de chemin de fer ou lignes téléphoniques…) sont favorables aux *sha.* Selon le *Classique de la Construction,* la disposition idéale d'une résidence demandait d'avoir une montagne dans le dos pour se protéger des influences néfastes du Nord (Tortue noire), de l'eau courante à l'Est (Dragon vert), un chemin à l'Ouest (Tigre blanc) et une exposition au Sud, vers le soleil (Oiseau rouge). À défaut d'eau courante, dans les villes, une petite pièce d'eau en forme de demi-lune pouvait être placée sur le versant sud pour assurer le dégagement recommandé. On la trouve devant la plupart des bâtiments officiels.

La géomancie s'appliquait et continue de s'appliquer partiellement de nos jours au choix concernant le site d'une ville, d'une résidence, d'une sépulture ou d'un lieu de travail. Elle déterminait des sites favorables appelés « cavernes du dragon » *(longxue).* Mais cette science intervenait aussi dans d'autres domaines comme la stratégie militaire et il était recommandé de consulter les experts avant d'entreprendre de longs voyages ou d'importantes négociations. Au Ve siècle av. J.-C., la fondation des villes ou l'établissement des résidences impériales se pliaient déjà aux règles de l'orientation sans qu'elles aient été encore formalisées. Le Palais Impérial de Pékin (construit vingt siècles plus tard) et la vieille ville sont des applications de ces principes de planification. Dans la Cité Interdite, au Sud (élément du feu et de l'autorité) se trouvaient les bâtiments à usage administratif, au Nord (élément de l'eau et de la préservation) les résidences, à l'Est (élément du bois, printemps, voyages) ce qui relevait de l'administration civile, alors qu'à l'Ouest (élément du métal, automne) se regroupaient les activités de justice et de l'armée. Un peu plus loin, à l'Est, se trouvaient le temple de Confucius et le Collège impérial ; les futurs mandarins qui avaient réussi aux examens provinciaux arrivaient en ville par la porte de la Littérature Suprême, située aussi à l'Est, alors que les troupes partant en campagne quittaient la ville par la porte des Prouesses Universelles située à l'Ouest. La colline du Charbon fut élevée au nord de la Cité Interdite pour arrêter les mauvaises influences venant de cette direction. L'influence du *fengshui* se retrouvait aussi dans la dimension des bâtiments. On sait que les nombres pairs sont *yang* et les nombres impairs *yin*. Ainsi les pavillons de la Cour extérieure *(yang)* étaient plus grands que ceux de la Cour intérieure *(yin)* ; le palais de la Pureté Céleste où se trouvaient les appartements de l'empereur fut donc construit aussi grand que le palais de l'Harmonie Suprême. Et le palais de l'Union, situé entre le palais de la Paix Céleste *(yang)* et le palais de la Tranquillité Terrestre *(yin)*, symbolisa la synthèse de ces deux polarités.

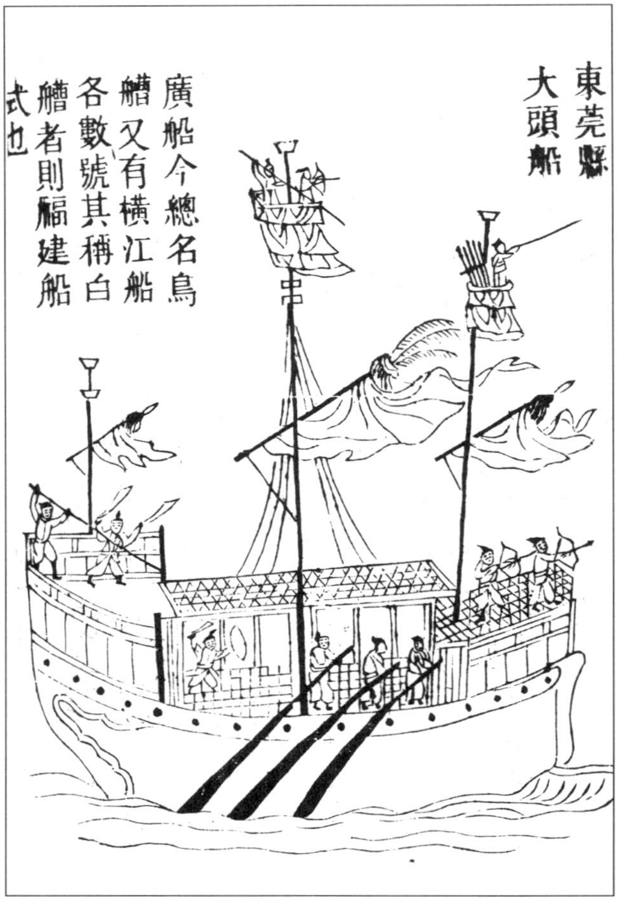

Grâce à l'invention de la boussole, les Chinois lancent dès le XVe siècle des expéditions commerciales en Asie et en Afrique. Page de droite, les « cavernes du dragon », extraits d'un manuel de fengshui du XVIIIe siècle qui analyse « les vrais, les faux dragons » et les « tigres » (collines ou montagnes aux parois abruptes ou en pente douce et la circulation des eaux…).

On faisait mention du *fengshui* (vents et cours d'eau) au IIIe siècle dans les traités sur l'inhumation ; sous les Han, on parle de *kanyu* (le ciel et la terre). Il faut attendre le IXe siècle pour que paraisse un ouvrage compilé par un lettré de la province du Guangxi, terre d'élection des géomanciens et des magiciens. À l'école des « Formes » du Sud, succédera plus tard l'école de la « Boussole » (ou compas géomantique). Les savants du nord de la Chine, soucieux d'introduire plus de rigueur dans cet art, utilisèrent désormais la

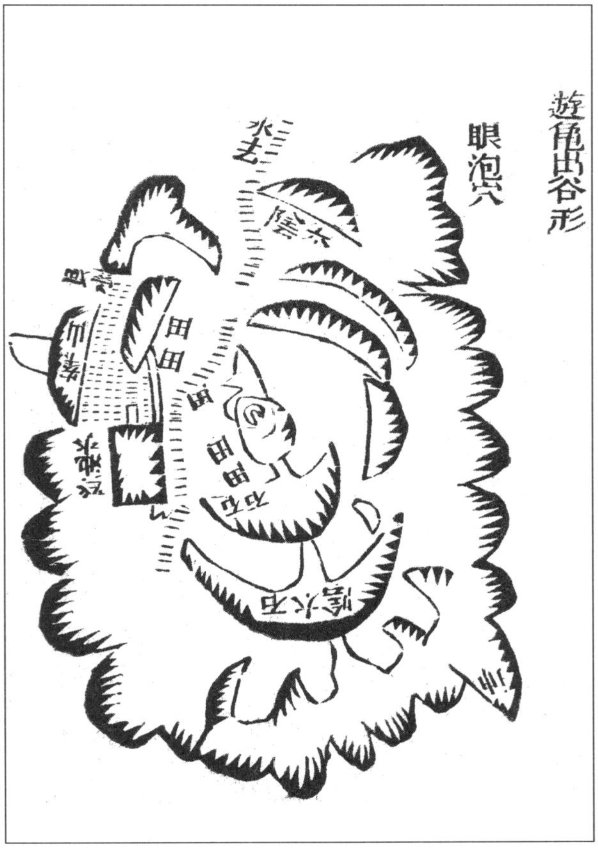
遊龜出谷形
眼泡穴

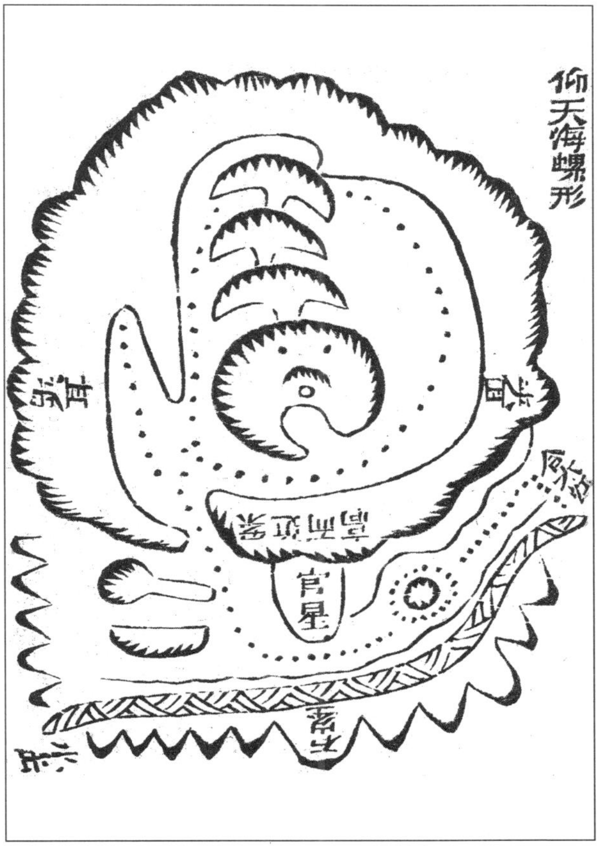
仰天海螺形

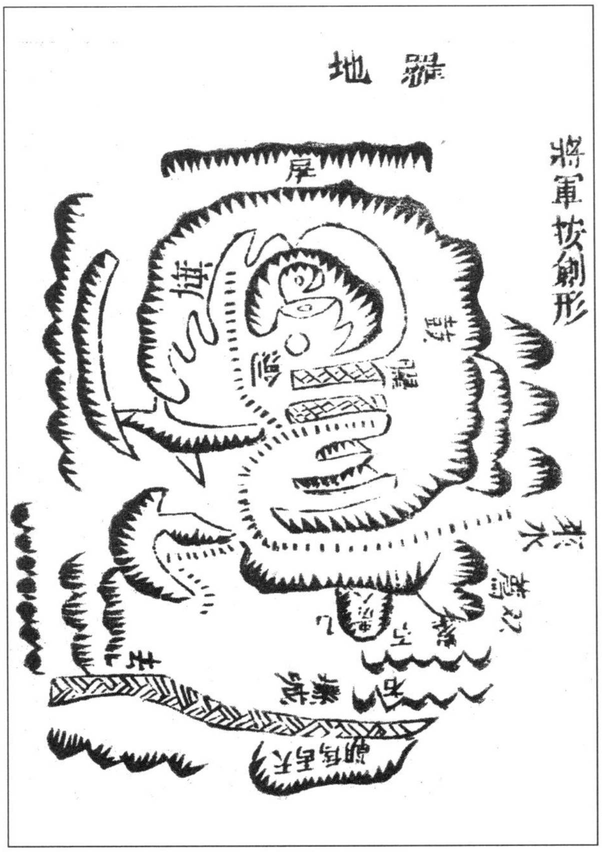
將軍按劍形

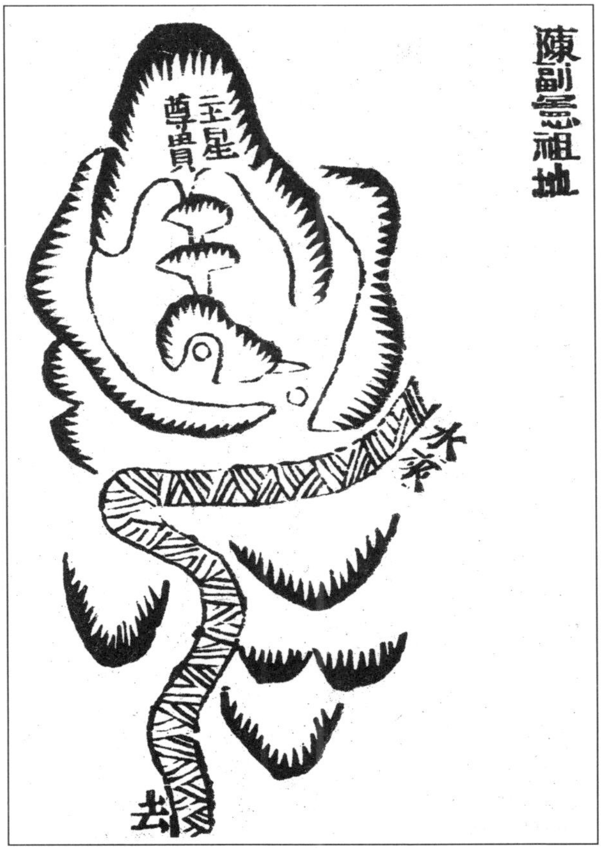

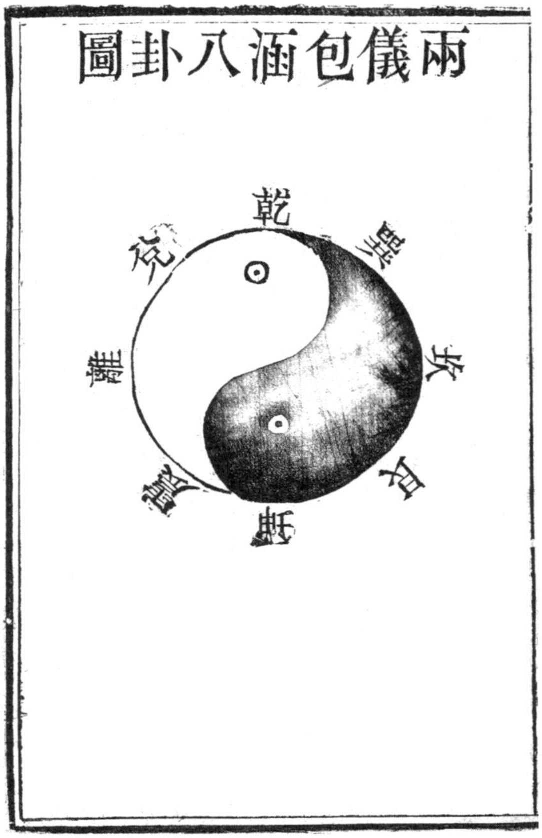

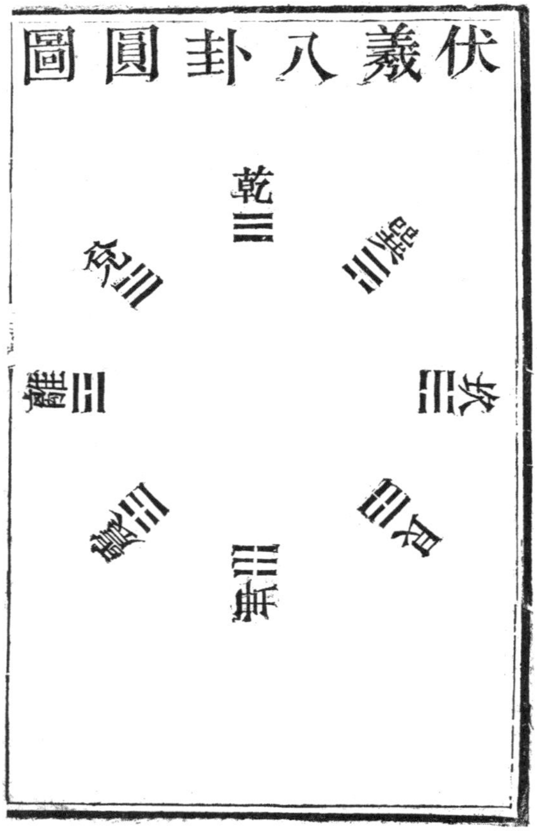

boussole, le calendrier, l'astrologie, les calculs mathématiques. Amalgame d'observations de bon sens (ainsi, se mettre à l'abri d'une élévation protège du vent froid du Nord), de règles esthétiques et écologiques ainsi que de philosophie mystique, la géomancie va s'ériger au rang d'une science respectée pendant près d'un millénaire. À la proclamation de la République (1949), les nouveaux maîtres tentent de déraciner les croyances du passé mais rencontrent de vives réactions de la part des populations rurales. Ainsi, lors de la pose du réseau de chemins de fer, vital pour le développement de la jeune république, les ouvriers se heurtent à la résistance des paysans qui voient dans ces travaux colossaux un bouleversement de leur environnement traditionnel (percements de tunnels, déplacements de sépultures). Comble de malheur, le mot « rail » *(tiegui)* est homophone de « démon, génie malfaisant » *(gui)*. Il fallut l'intervention de la troupe pour garder les chantiers qui étaient sabotés la nuit. Les urbanistes et les architectes des nouvelles générations, même s'ils ne veulent pas l'admettre, tiennent encore compte de ces superstitions, surtout à Hong Kong, dans le sud de la Chine et de plus en plus à Pékin. Avant la pose de la première pierre, certains font encore appel à un géomancien et il n'est pas rare de relever dans une publicité de promoteur que sa réalisation « bénéficie d'un bon *fengshui* » !

Dès le Ier siècle, les Chinois auraient découvert l'aimant artificiel et utilisaient, dit-on, des « cuillères » aimantées, des « chariots » porteurs de statues, qui indiquaient le Sud *(zhinan che)*. Toutefois, ce n'est qu'au XIe siècle, dans l'encyclopédie de Shen Kuo *(Mengxibitan)* que l'on put lire comment fabriquer une aiguille qui s'orientait vers le sud *(zhinan zhen)* en la frottant sur la pierre-aimant *(cishi)*. Vers le XIIe siècle, le principe de la déclinaison magnétique fut adapté à la navigation et l'amiral Zheng He put ainsi conduire sept expéditions en haute mer entre 1405 et 1433 avec ce compas dont l'invention est attribuée aux Chinois.

Les maîtres de géomancie, appelés aussi « maîtres du sort » (*fengshui xiansheng, fengjia* ou *shusheng*), tiraient leur savoir du *Livre des Mutations (Yijing)* ; ils interprétaient en particulier les figures étranges du *Yijing* qui sont les huit trigrammes *(ba gua)* ou les soixante-quatre hexagrammes. C'est à Fuxi, l'un des cinq empereurs mythiques (les « Rois sages ») que la légende attribue l'invention de ces lignes pleines *(yang)* et interrompues *(yin)* créées à partir d'animaux tout aussi mythiques (cheval, tortue ou dragon) sortis du fleuve Jaune... Depuis l'antiquité, ces étranges lignes servent à exprimer toutes les situations auxquelles sont confrontés les êtres. Rangés autour du « faîte suprême » *(taiji)*, les *ba gua* servent à la divination mais ils ont aussi une

TABLEAU DES HUIT TRIGRAMMES PAR CATÉGORIE ET PAR ANALOGIE

nom	figure	nature	action	animal	famille	organe	orientation	saison
Qian	☰	ciel	être dynamique	cheval	père	tête	sud	été
Kun	☷	terre	être réceptif	vache	mère	ventre	nord	hiver
Zhen	☳	tonnerre	éclater	dragon	fils aîné	pied	nord-est	hiver-printemps
Xun	☴	vent	pénétrer	coq	fille aînée	jambe	sud-est	printemps-été
Kan	☵	eau (lune)	tomber dedans	cochon	fils cadet	oreille	ouest	automne
Li	☲	feu (soleil)	s'attacher dessus	faisan	fille cadette	œil	est	printemps
Gen	☶	montagne	arrêter	chien	fils benjamin	main	nord-ouest	automne-hiver
Dui	☱	lac	plaire	mouton	fille benjamine	bouche	sud-ouest	été-automne

D'après Wang Dongliang, *Les Signes et les mutations*, 1995.

fonction talismanique. Ces maîtres pratiquaient aussi la médecine traditionnelle, le *qigong*, l'astrologie et la divination. À cet effet, ils utilisaient une boussole (*luopan* ou *luojing*). La boussole de géomancie, légèrement différente du compas de marine, était encastrée d'une manière artisanale dans un disque de bois dont la taille varie de 4 à 30 cm. Les premières *luopan* ont été faites en bois de poirier, en argile, en laque ou en cloisonné. Celles qui sont fabriquées actuellement dans le sud de la Chine ne sont que des disques de bois blanc sur lesquels est collée une feuille de carton imprimée. La boussole, « espace céleste », indique toujours la direction du sud (direction du soleil, de la chaleur, de la vie) ; elle se distingue du reste du

Page de gauche, en haut, le « faîte suprême » ou « limite suprême » : c'est l'état initial avant la formation du cosmos, unité et dualité en même temps, d'où le yin (terre) et le yang (ciel) ; en bas, tableau des huit trigrammes : selon l'ordre de Fu Xi, qian (sud) est en haut alors que kun (nord) est en bas.

plateau, « plaque terrestre » *(dipan)*, qui porte des inscriptions, des graduations, voire le dessin des trigrammes et quelquefois celui des animaux du zodiaque chinois. L'ensemble est complété par deux fils rouges qui se croisent à angle droit au centre de la boussole et servent de repères. Certaines boussoles sont de forme rectangulaire et comportent des cadrans solaires sur des planchettes amovibles réglables selon les saisons, d'autres plus élaborées pouvaient même servir à faire des visées astronomiques. Les plateaux des boussoles présentent des variations de taille et de modèle selon leur ancienneté. Ils peuvent porter de cinq à quinze espaces concentriques dans lesquels apparaisent les « Huit trigrammes » *(ba gua),* les deux Polarités (*yin* et *yang*), les soixante-quatre hexagrammes, les vingt-huit constellations, les « douze rameaux terrestres » *(shierzhi)* qui servent à la désignation des heures, quelquefois symbolisés par les douze animaux du zodiaque chinois, les « dix troncs célestes » *(shigan),* les cinq planètes et les cinq éléments qui leur correspondent, les douze points de la boussole, les vingt-quatre quinzaines solaires et les 365 degrés... Tous ces éléments étaient alors combinés par le maître pour étudier l'influence mutuelle des différentes orientations, des dates du calendrier, des éléments.

La géomancie s'appliquant aussi aux mesures, les maçons, les charpentiers et les géomanciens d'autrefois utilisaient une règle de bois verni plate et graduée. Longue de 43 cm et large de 5 cm environ, cette pièce de bois ressemblait aux instruments de mesure des bâtisseurs de cathédrales qui, au Moyen Âge, fondaient leurs calculs sur le fameux « nombre d'or ». La règle chinoise de géomancie *(guachi)* portait huit sections correspondant aux huit trigrammes et indiquait en noir les mesures favorables et en rouge les mesures défavorables. Elle pouvait se lire verticalement et horizontalement. Chacune des huit sections avait une appellation précise : 1. sauveur des hommes ; 2. châtiment du ciel ; 3. désastre ; 4. bienfaits célestes ; 5. honneurs et argent ; 6. veuve et orphelin ; 7. le ciel retire son aide ; 8. honneurs et promotion. Il appartenait donc aux artisans de respecter ces « nombres magiques » pour attirer toutes les félicités sur leurs réalisations et éviter les catastrophes.

On mesure donc l'importance que les géomanciens pouvaient avoir dans la société, car le *fengshui* s'adressait, en fait, à un grand nombre d'activités humaines. Seul le maître de géomancie pouvait, grâce à son savoir des choses surnaturelles, déceler les influences néfastes et y trouver des remèdes : les « murs-écrans » *(yingbi)* que l'on trouve devant toutes les entrées avaient ainsi pour but d'empêcher la progression en ligne droite des génies malfaisants ; on recommandait de placer, pour la même raison, des miroirs face à l'entrée et d'éviter les portes en alignement ou de longs corridors rectilignes qui favorisent la circulation des mauvais esprits. Il

Page de droite, boussole de géomancie traditionnelle (bois verni, Ø 16 cm) et, au fond, règle de géomancien.

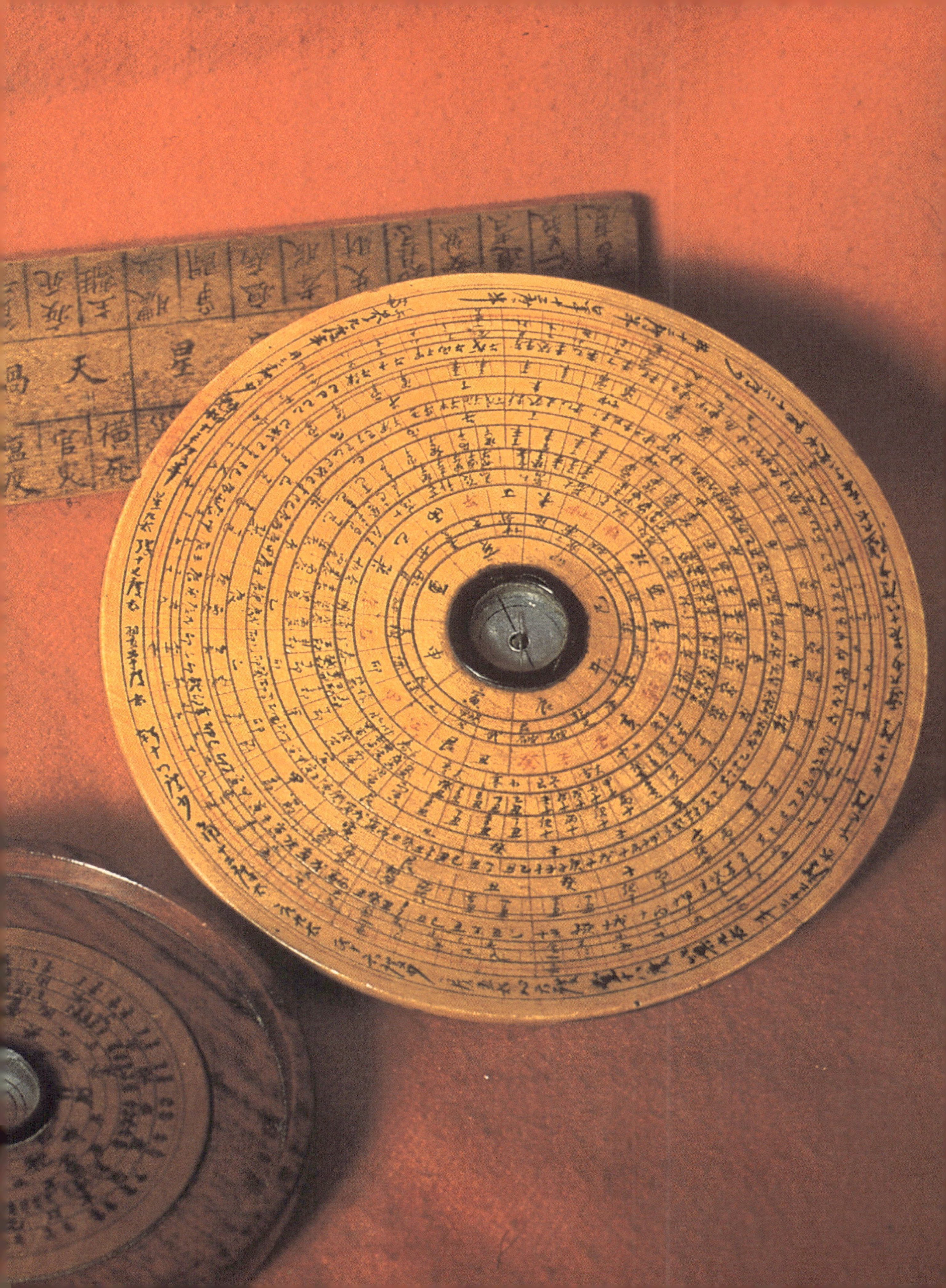

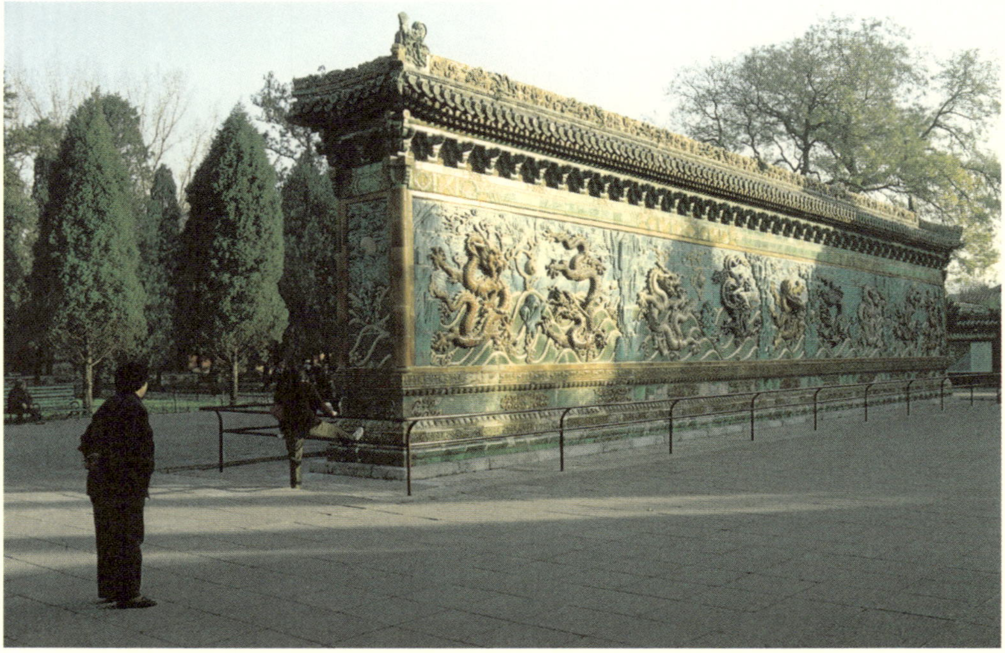

était important d'avoir des boules de cristal (qui dispersent les excès de *qi*), des cloches ou des clochettes (liées au vent et à l'air), des fleurs et des plantes (qui apportent beauté et vitalité) et des aquariums (symbole d'eau dans la maison, ils sont l'expression de la prospérité et du bonheur). La répartition des pièces en fonction de l'horoscope de chaque membre de la famille, la couleur des murs de chaque pièce en fonction de leur orientation et de leur destination, l'orientation et la décoration des jardins, étaient autant de détails que l'expert réglait minutieusement pour donner une « bonne atmosphère ».

Certes depuis cinquante ans, le *fengshui* semblait avoir disparu dans les villes, mais on note actuellement une recrudescence de comportements superstitieux et de religiosité. À l'étranger, sa pratique s'est étendue à tous les pays qui ont accueilli d'importantes communautés chinoises (Asie du Sud-Est, Vietnam, Corée) où elle reste bien vivace.

Ci-dessus, le « Mur aux Neuf Dragons » situé dans le parc du Lac du Nord (Beihai) érigé en 1417 sous les Ming pour protéger des mauvais esprits l'entrée d'un temple (tuiles vernissées, longueur : 27 mètres).

ANNEXES

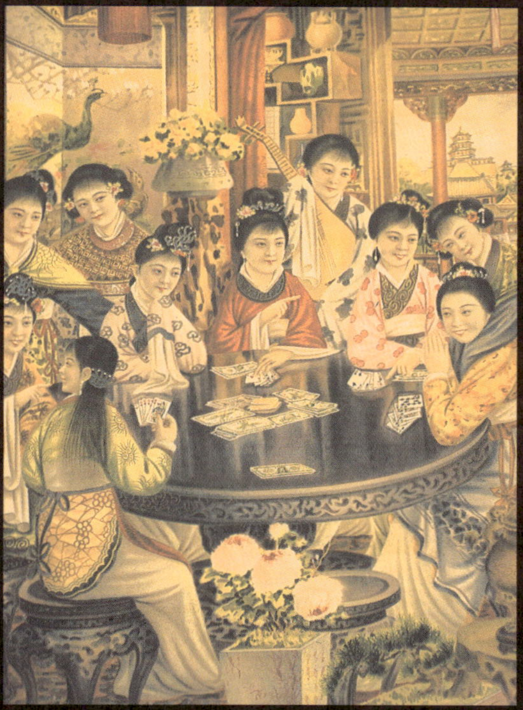

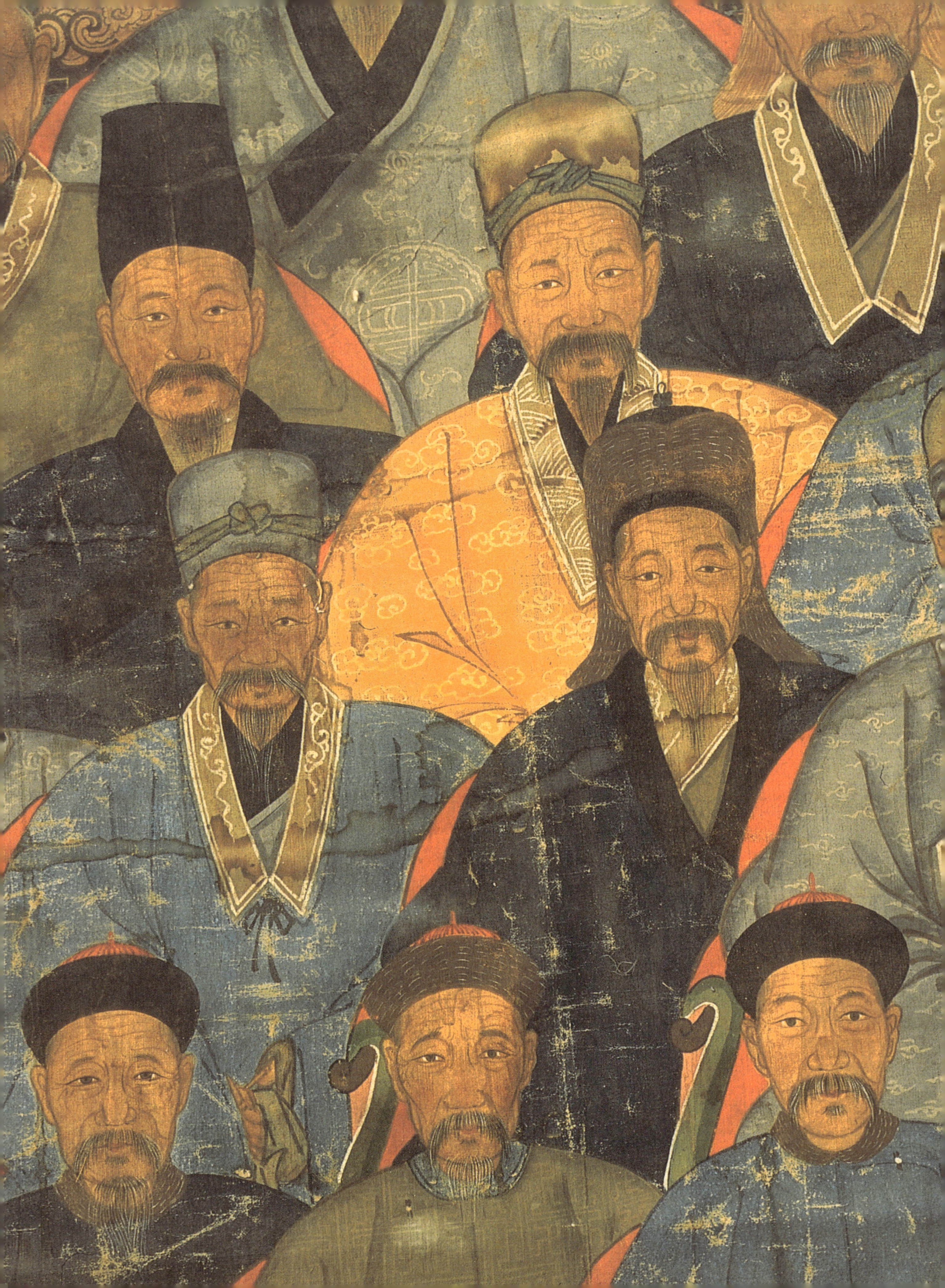

I. Dynastie des Ming

(1368-1644)

(17 empereurs, capitale : Nankin, 1368-1409, puis Pékin, 1409-1644)

Nom dynastique	Années de règne	Nom d'ère *(nianhao)*	Années de *nianhao*
Taizu	1368-1398	Hongwu	1368-1399
Huidi	1398-1402	Jianwen	1399-1403
Chengzu	1402-1424	Yongle	1403-1425
Renzong	1424-1425	Hongxi	1425-1426
Xuanzong	1425-1435	Xuande	1426-1436
Yingzong	1435-détrôné en 1449	Zhengtong	1436-1450
Daizong	1449-1457	Jingtai	1450-1457
Yingzong	1457-1464	Tianshun	1457-1465
Xianzong	1464-1487	Chenghua	1465-1488
Xionzong	1487-1505	Hongzhi	1488-1506
Wuzong	1505-1521	Zhengde	1506-1522
Shizong	1521-1566	Jiajing	1522-1567
Muzong	1566-1572	Longqinq	1567-1573
Shenzong	1572-1619	Wanli	1573-1620
Guangzong	1620	Taichang	1620-1621
Xizong	1620-1627	Tianqi	1621-1628
Zhuangliedi	1627-1643	Chongzhen	1628-1644

II. Dynastie des Qing

(1644-1912)

(10 empereurs ; capitale : Pékin)

Nom dynastique	Années de règne	Nom d'ère *(nianhao)*	Année de *nianhao*	Nom posthume
Shizu	1644-1661	Shunzhi	1644-1662	Zhang Huangdi
Shengzu	1662-1722	Kangxi	1662-1723	Ren Huangdi
Shizhong	1723-1735	Yongzheng	1723-1736	Xian Huangdi
Gaozong	1736-1795	Qianlong	1736-1796	Chun Huangdi
Renzong	1796-1820	Jiaqing	1796-1821	Rui Huangdi
Xuanzong	1821-1850	Daoguang	1821-1851	Cheng Huangdi
Wenzong[1]	1851-1861	Xianfeng	1851-1862	Xian Huangdi
Muzong	1862-1874	Tongzhi	1862-1875	Yi Huangdi
Dezong	1875-1908	Guangxu	1875-1909	Jing Huangdi
Xun Di	1908-1912	Xuantong[2]	1909-1912	Nom privé : Puyi[3]

1. *Son épouse Xiaoqin, Tseu Hsi ou Ci Xi, impératrice douairière, sera régente de 1875 à 1908.*

2. *L'empereur Xuantong, âgé de six ans, n'abdiquera que le 12 février 1912 mais la République sera officiellement proclamée à Nankin le 1er janvier 1912 avec pour président Sun Yatsen (ou Sun Wen), remplacé quarante jours plus tard par le général Yuan Shikai qui meurt en 1916 sans avoir pu rétablir la monarchie.*

3. *Aisingioro Puyi se marie à dix-sept ans, en 1922, avec Wan Rong, mais deux ans après, ils sont chassés de la Cité Interdite de Pékin et se réfugient à Tianjin avec l'aide des Japonais. En 1932, Puyi est installé comme empereur fantoche du Mantchoukuo (Mandchourie) qui restera sous la domination japonaise jusqu'à la date de sa libération par les troupes soviétiques. Puyi abdiquera pour la seconde fois le 15 août 1945.*

III. Chronologie comparative

DATES	CHINE	CIVILISATION	FRANCE
5000-2000 av. J.-C.		Âge néolithique, culture de Yangshao, culture de Longshan.	
2205-1767 av. J.-C.	Dynastie des Xia fondée par le légendaire Yu-le-Grand		
1766-1122 av. J.-C.	Dynastie des Shang (ou Yin)	1600 âge du bronze. Inscription sur des os d'animaux et écailles de tortues. Invention du pinceau. Connaissance du calendrier.	
1100-770 av. J.-C.	Dynastie des Zhou de l'Ouest (capitale Xi'an)		
770-475 av. J.-C.	Époque des Printemps et Automnes (Zhou de l'Est)	700 : Laozi fonde le taoïsme 560 : Sâkyamuni fonde le bouddhisme 551-478 : Confucius.	
475-221 av. J.-C.	Époque des Royaumes Combattants (Zhou de l'Est)	400 : âge du fer. Découverte de l'aimant.	
221-207 av. J.-C.	Dynastie des Qin (unification de l'Empire)	Qin Shihuang brûle les livres, construit la Muraille, normalise l'écriture et fait enfouir une armée d'argile à Xi'an.	
206 av. J.-C. – 24 ap. J.-C.	Dynastie des Han de l'Ouest	Découverte de la porcelaine. Échanges avec l'Asie centrale. Examens administratifs.	
25-220	Dynastie des Han de l'Est	Papier, sismographe, magnétisme (char et cuillère aimantés).	Gaule romaine (58-51 av. J.-C.)
220-280	Les Trois Royaumes (Wei, Wu et Shu)		
265-316	Dynastie des Jin		
316-580	Les Seize Royaumes du Nord et les Cinq Dynasties du Sud		Mérovingiens (428-743) : Clovis (487)
581-618	Dynastie des Sui	Découverte de la poudre explosive.	
618-907	Empire des Tang	Route de la soie rétablie. Commerce et industrie prospères. Arts et poésie. Papier monnaie en usage. Gravure sur pierre des Classiques.	Carolingiens : Charlemagne (768-814)
907-960	Les Cinq Dynasties et Dix Royaumes		
960-1127	Dynastie des Song du Nord	Céramiques céladons. Caractères d'imprimerie mobiles.	Capétiens (987-1328)
1126-1234	Dynastie des Jin	Boussoles. Premier aménagement du Palais d'Été à Pékin.	Philippe Auguste (1180-1223)
1127-1279	Dynastie des Song du Sud	Guillaume de Rubroek, envoyé par saint Louis, rencontre le Grand Khan en 1254.	Louis IX (saint Louis)
1271-1368	Dynastie (mongole) des Yuan	Céramiques bleues et rouges. Marco Polo aurait séjourné en Chine (1275-1292).	Philippe le Bel Philippe VI Jean le Bon

DATES	CHINE	CIVILISATION	FRANCE
1368-1644	Dynastie (chinoise) des Ming	La Chine ferme ses frontières. Pékin devient la capitale. Grande Muraille restaurée et prolongée. Construction du palais d'Été. Renouveau social, économique et culturel jusqu'en 1521. Macao cédé aux Portugais. 1583 : arrivée des Hollandais et des Jésuites. 1637 : arrivée des Anglais.	Charles V Louis XI François Ier Henri III, Henri IV Louis XIII
1644-1912	Dynastie (mandchoue) des Qing	1683 : conquête de Formose. 1720 : les Chinois au Tibet. 1757 : Canton seul port de commerce autorisé pour les étrangers. 1793 : ambassade de Lord Mac Cartney. 1839 : première Guerre de l'opium ; rébellion des Taïping. 1860 : sac du palais d'Été par une expédition anglo-française. 1883 : guerre avec la France qui établit un protectorat au Tonkin et Annam. 1900 : révolte des Boxers et intervention internationale. 1912 : proclamation de la République par Sun Yat Sen (Sun Wen ou Sun Zhongshan) à Nankin.	Louis XIV Louis XV Louis XVI Louis-Philippe Napoléon III Troisième République
1912-1949	La République en danger : guerres civiles et guerres sino-japonaise	1912 : abdication du dernier empereur des Qing, Xuantong (Puyi) ; adoption du calendrier grégorien. 1915 : Sun Yat Sen cède le pouvoir au maréchal Yuan Shikai qui se fait proclamer empereur. 175 000 ouvriers chinois sont envoyés en France au titre de l'effort de guerre. 1925 : Tchang Kaïchek (Jiang Jieshi) prend la direction du Guomindang. 1934-1935 : « Longue marche » dirigée par Mao Tsé Toung (Mao Zedong, 1893-1976). 1er octobre 1949 : Mao proclame la République Populaire de Chine et Tchang Kaïchek trouve refuge à Taiwan.	Première Guerre mondiale Deuxième Guerre mondiale Président Vincent Auriol

IV. Marques de règne de la dynastie des Qing

(1644-1912)

大清順治年製
Shunzhi
1644-1661

大清康熙年製
Kangxi
1662-1722

大清雍正年製
Yongzheng
1723-1735

大清乾隆年製
Qianlong
1736-1795

嘉慶年製
Jiaqing
1796-1820

大清道光年製
Daoguang
1821-1850

大清咸豐年製
Xianfeng
1851-1861

大清同治年製
Tongzhi
1862-1874

大清光緒年製
Guangxu
1875-1908

宣統年製
Xuantong
(Pu Yi)
1908-1912

洪憲年製
Hong Xian, nom adopté par le général Yuan Shikai qui se fait proclamer empereur en 1915 et ne règnera qu'une année.

v. Calendrier lunaire et grégorien à l'époque des Yuan, des Ming et des Qing

Année	Nom chinois	Animal symbole	Années correspondantes du calendrier grégorien											
1	jia-zi	rat	1204	1264	1324	1384	1444	1504	1564	1624	1684	1744	1804	1864
2	yi-chou	bœuf	1205	1265	1325	1385	1445	1505	1565	1625	1685	1745	1805	1865
3	ping-yin	tigre	1206	1266	1326	1386	1446	1506	1566	1626	1686	1746	1806	1866
4	ding-mao	lièvre	1207	1267	1327	1387	1447	1507	1567	1627	1687	1747	1807	1867
5	wu-chen	dragon	1208	1268	1328	1388	1448	1508	1568	1628	1688	1748	1808	1868
6	ji-si	serpent	1209	1269	1329	1389	1449	1509	1569	1629	1689	1749	1809	1869
7	geng-wu	cheval	1210	1270	1330	1390	1450	1510	1570	1630	1690	1750	1810	1870
8	xin-wei	chèvre	1211	1271	1331	1391	1451	1511	1571	1631	1691	1751	1811	1871
9	ren-shen	singe	1212	1272	1332	1392	1452	1512	1572	1632	1692	1752	1812	1872
10	kui-you	coq	1213	1273	1333	1393	1453	1513	1573	1633	1693	1753	1813	1873
11	jia-xu	chien	1214	1274	1334	1394	1454	1514	1574	1634	1694	1754	1814	1874
12	yi-hai	sanglier	1215	1275	1335	1395	1455	1515	1575	1635	1695	1755	1815	1875
13	ping-zi	rat	1216	1276	1336	1396	1456	1516	1576	1636	1696	1756	1816	1876
14	ding-chou	bœuf	1217	1277	1337	1397	1457	1517	1577	1637	1697	1757	1817	1877
15	wu-yin	tigre	1218	1278	1338	1398	1458	1518	1578	1638	1698	1758	1818	1878
16	ji-mao	lièvre	1219	1279	1339	1399	1459	1519	1579	1639	1699	1759	1819	1879
17	geng-shen	dragon	1220	1280	1340	1400	1460	1520	1580	1640	1700	1760	1820	1880
18	xin-si	serpent	1221	1281	1341	1401	1461	1521	1581	1641	1701	1761	1821	1881
19	ren-wu	cheval	1222	1282	1342	1402	1462	1522	1582	1642	1702	1762	1822	1882
20	kui-wei	chèvre	1223	1283	1343	1403	1463	1523	1583	1643	1703	1763	1823	1883
21	jia-shen	singe	1224	1284	1344	1404	1464	1524	1584	1644	1704	1764	1824	1884
22	yi-you	coq	1225	1285	1345	1405	1465	1525	1585	1645	1705	1765	1825	1885
23	ping-xu	chien	1226	1286	1346	1406	1466	1526	1586	1646	1706	1766	1826	1886
24	ding-hai	sanglier	1227	1287	1347	1407	1467	1527	1587	1647	1707	1767	1827	1887
25	wu-zi	rat	1228	1288	1348	1408	1468	1528	1588	1648	1708	1768	1828	1888
26	ji-chou	bœuf	1229	1289	1349	1409	1469	1529	1589	1649	1709	1769	1829	1889
27	geng-yi	tigre	1230	1290	1350	1410	1470	1530	1590	1650	1710	1770	1830	1890
28	xin-mao	lièvre	1231	1291	1351	1411	1471	1531	1591	1651	1711	1771	1831	1891
29	ren-chen	dragon	1232	1292	1352	1412	1472	1532	1592	1652	1712	1772	1832	1892
30	kui-zi	serpent	1233	1293	1353	1413	1473	1533	1593	1653	1713	1773	1833	1893
31	jia-wu	cheval	1234	1294	1354	1414	1474	1534	1594	1654	1714	1774	1834	1894
32	yi-wei	chèvre	1235	1295	1355	1415	1475	1535	1595	1655	1715	1775	1835	1895
33	ping-shen	singe	1236	1296	1356	1416	1476	1536	1596	1656	1716	1776	1836	1896
34	ding-yu	coq	1237	1297	1357	1417	1477	1537	1597	1657	1717	1777	1837	1897
35	wu-xu	chien	1238	1298	1358	1418	1478	1538	1598	1658	1718	1778	1838	1898
36	ji-hai	sanglier	1239	1299	1359	1419	1479	1539	1599	1659	1719	1779	1839	1899
37	geng-zi	rat	1240	1300	1360	1420	1480	1540	1600	1660	1720	1780	1840	1900
38	xin-chou	bœuf	1241	1301	1361	1421	1481	1541	1601	1661	1721	1781	1841	1901
39	ren-yin	tigre	1242	1302	1362	1422	1482	1542	1602	1662	1722	1782	1842	1902
40	kui-mao	lièvre	1243	1303	1363	1423	1483	1543	1603	1663	1723	1783	1843	1903
41	jia-chen	dragon	1244	1304	1364	1424	1484	1544	1604	1664	1724	1784	1844	1904
42	yi-si	serpent	1245	1305	1365	1425	1485	1545	1605	1665	1725	1785	1845	1905
43	ping-wu	cheval	1246	1306	1366	1426	1486	1546	1606	1666	1726	1786	1846	1906
44	ding-wei	chèvre	1247	1307	1367	1427	1487	1547	1607	1667	1727	1787	1847	1907
45	wu-shen	singe	1248	1308	1368	1428	1488	1548	1608	1668	1728	1788	1848	1908
46	ji-you	coq	1249	1309	1369	1429	1489	1549	1609	1669	1729	1789	1849	1909
47	geng-xu	chien	1250	1310	1370	1430	1490	1550	1610	1670	1730	1790	1850	1910
48	xin-hai	sanglier	1251	1311	1371	1431	1491	1551	1611	1671	1731	1791	1851	1911
49	ren-zi	rat	1252	1312	1372	1432	1492	1552	1612	1672	1732	1792	1852	1912
50	kui-chou	bœuf	1253	1313	1373	1433	1493	1553	1613	1673	1733	1793	1853	1913
51	jia-yin	tigre	1254	1314	1374	1434	1494	1554	1614	1674	1734	1794	1854	1914
52	yi-mao	lièvre	1255	1315	1375	1435	1495	1555	1615	1675	1735	1795	1855	1915
53	ping-chen	dragon	1256	1316	1376	1436	1496	1556	1616	1676	1736	1796	1856	1916
54	ding-si	serpent	1257	1317	1377	1437	1497	1557	1617	1677	1737	1797	1857	1917
55	wu-wu	cheval	1258	1318	1378	1438	1498	1558	1618	1678	1738	1798	1858	1918
56	ji-wei	chèvre	1259	1319	1379	1439	1499	1559	1619	1679	1739	1799	1859	1919
57	geng-shen	singe	1260	1320	1380	1440	1500	1560	1620	1680	1740	1800	1860	1920
58	xin-yu	coq	1261	1321	1381	1441	1501	1561	1621	1681	1741	1801	1861	1921
59	ren-xu	chien	1262	1322	1382	1442	1502	1562	1622	1682	1742	1802	1862	1922
60	kui-hai	sanglier	1263	1323	1383	1443	1503	1563	1623	1683	1743	1803	1863	1923

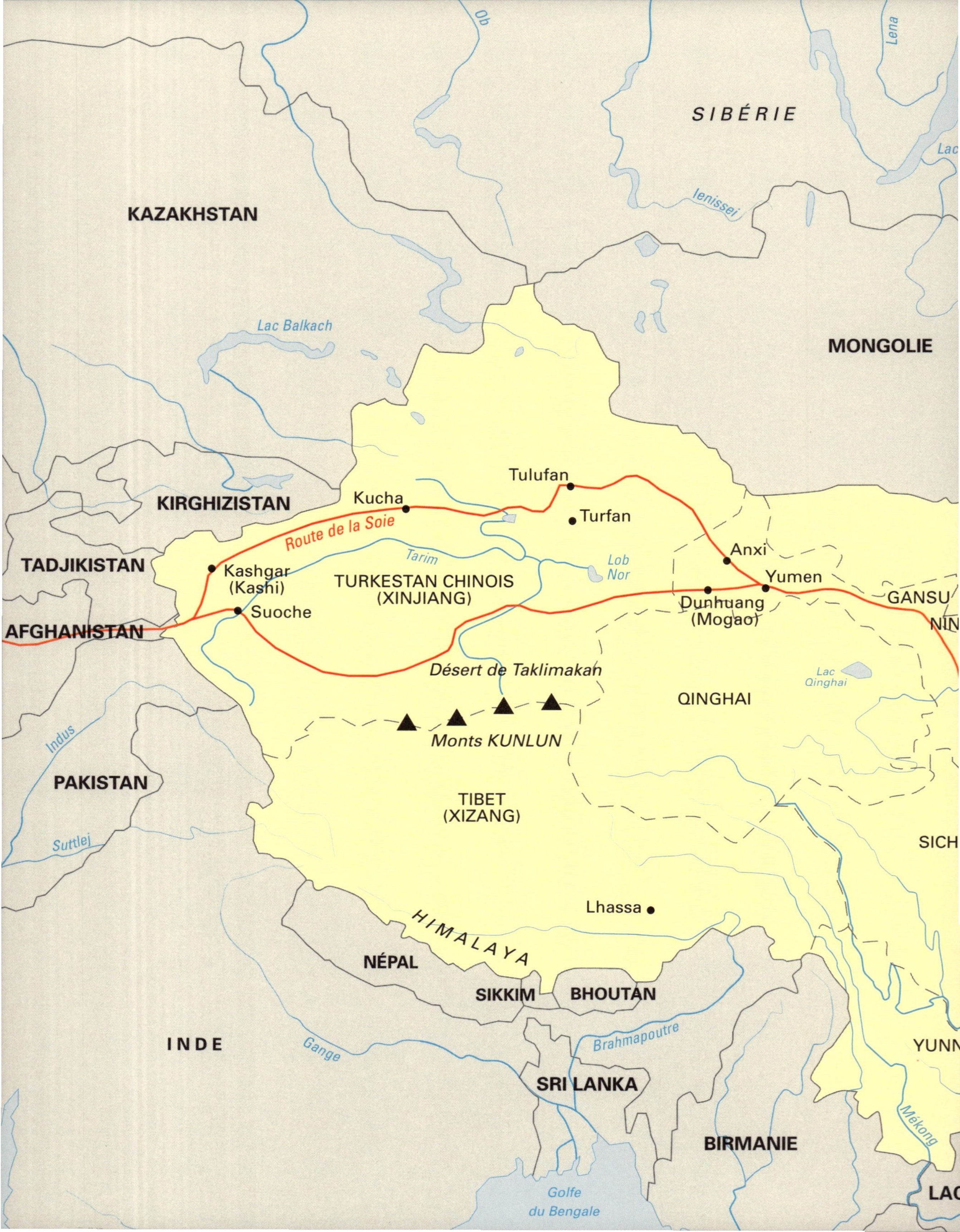

Ob
Lena
SIBÉRIE
KAZAKHSTAN
Ienissei
MONGOLIE
Lac Balkach
Tulufan
Kucha
KIRGHIZISTAN
Turfan
Route de la Soie
TADJIKISTAN
Tarim
Anxi
Lob Nor
Kashgar (Kashi)
TURKESTAN CHINOIS (XINJIANG)
Yumen
Suoche
Dunhuang (Mogao)
GANSU
AFGHANISTAN
Désert de Taklimakan
Lac Qinghai
QINGHAI
Indus
Monts KUNLUN
PAKISTAN
TIBET (XIZANG)
Suttlej
Lhassa
HIMALAYA
NÉPAL
SIKKIM
BHOUTAN
INDE
Gange
Brahmapoutre
SRI LANKA
Mékong
BIRMANIE
Golfe du Bengale

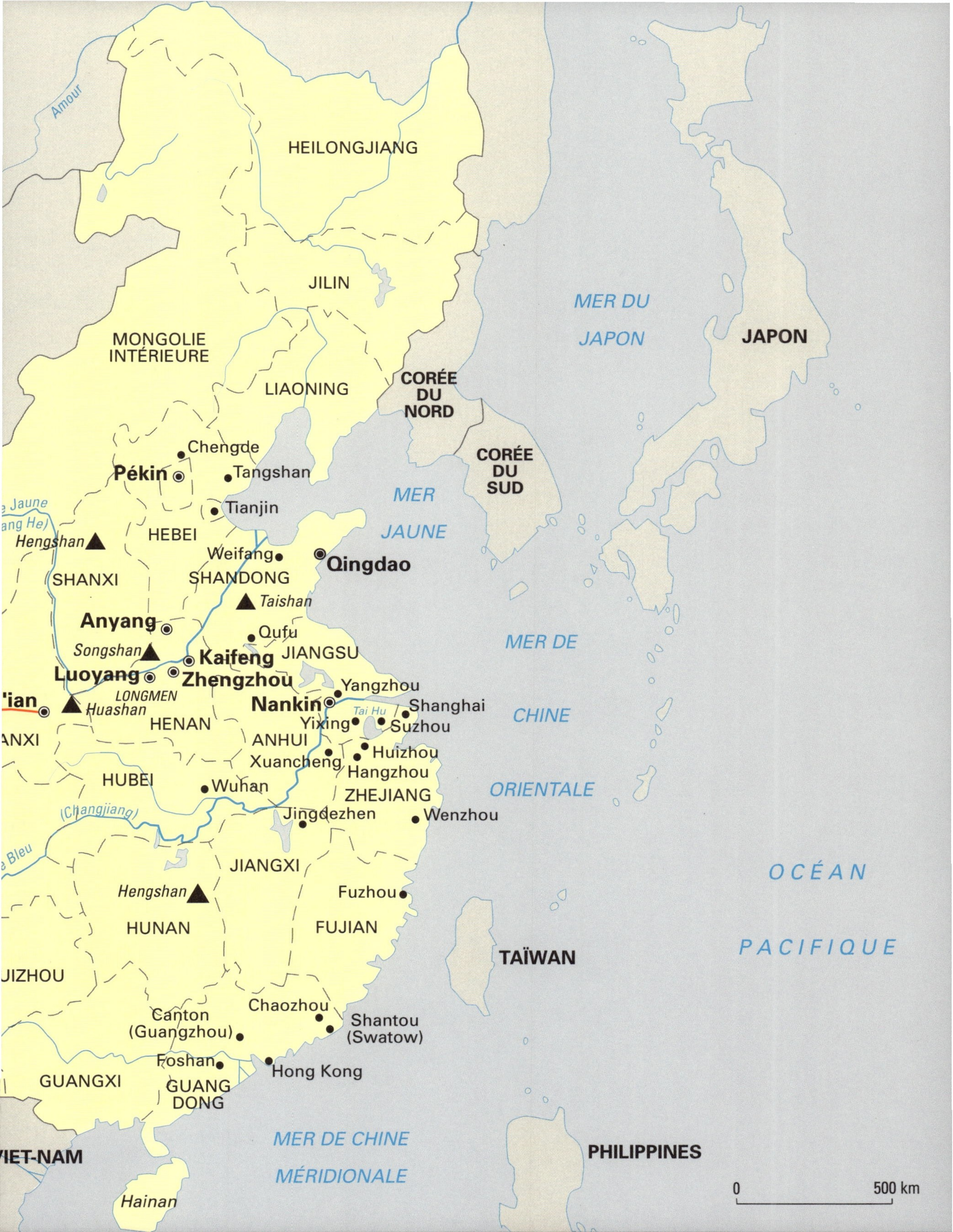

Amour
HEILONGJIANG
JILIN
MONGOLIE INTÉRIEURE
LIAONING
CORÉE DU NORD
CORÉE DU SUD
MER DU JAPON
JAPON
Chengde
Pékin
Tangshan
Tianjin
HEBEI
Hengshan
Weifang
Qingdao
SHANXI
SHANDONG
Taishan
MER JAUNE
Anyang
Qufu
Songshan
Kaifeng
JIANGSU
MER DE CHINE ORIENTALE
Luoyang
Zhengzhou
LONGMEN
Huashan
Yangzhou
Nankin
Tai Hu
Shanghai
Yixing
Suzhou
HENAN
ANHUI
Xuancheng
Huizhou
Hangzhou
HUBEI
Wuhan
ZHEJIANG
(Changjiang)
Jingdezhen
Wenzhou
JIANGXI
Hengshan
Fuzhou
HUNAN
FUJIAN
OCÉAN PACIFIQUE
TAÏWAN
Chaozhou
Canton (Guangzhou)
Shantou (Swatow)
Foshan
Hong Kong
GUANGXI
GUANG DONG
MER DE CHINE MÉRIDIONALE
PHILIPPINES
Hainan
0
500 km

天地悠久日月并
用報神貺表孝情
神之来于風泠泠
紉光吐納陰陽精
祛袄蕩札民物亨

Bibliographie

ALLANE, Lee, *Chinese Rugs : a Buyer's Guide,* Thames and Hudson, 1993.

ALLOM, Thomas, *The Chinese Empire Illustrated,* J. Nicholson, Hong Kong, 1988.

ARMERO, Carlos, *Antiques Pipes,* Madrid, 1989.

BALL, Katherine, M., *Decorative Motives of Oriental Art,* Dodd, Mead and Company, New York, 1927.

BALLOT, M.-J., *Les Laques d'Extrême-Orient : Chine et Japon,* G. Vanoest, Paris et Bruxelles, 1927.

BEURDELEY, Michel, *L'Amateur chinois : des Han au XXe siècle,* Bibliothèque des Arts, Paris, 1966.

BILLETER, Jean-François, *L'Art chinois de l'écriture,* Éditions d'art A. Skira, Genève, 1989.

BRANKSTON, A. D., *Early Ming Wares of Chingtechen,* Henri Vetch, Peking, 1938.

BURTON, W., HOBSON, R. L., *Pottery Marks,* London, 1928.

BUSSAGLI, Mario, *Bronzi Cinesi,* C. C. & C. T'ai Tchong, 1965.

CAMMANN, Schuyler, V. R., « Notes on the Development of the Mandarin Square », 1942, « The Development of Mandarin Square », 1944, « Chinese Mandarin Squares : Brief Catalogue of the Letcher Collection », 1953, « Old Chinese Mandarin Squares », 1954, « Old Chinese Badges of Rank, in The University Museum Bulletin », 1954, University of Pennsylvania, Philadelphia.

CARL, A. Katharine, *With the Empress Dowager of China,* Société française de Librairie et d'édition, Tientsin, 1926.

DE CAUNES, Lison, PERFETTINI, Jean, *Galuchat,* éditions de l'Amateur, Paris 1994.

CHAVANNES, T., *Les Mémoires historiques de Sse-ma-Tien,* Leroux, Paris, 1967 (rééd.).

CHEN, Congzhou, *On Chinese Gardens,* Tongji University Press, Shanghaï, 1984.

CHENG, Manchao, *The Origin of Chinese Deities,* Foreign Language Press, Beijing, 1995.

CHEVALIER, Jean, GHEERBRANT, Alain, *Dictionnaire des symboles,* Robert Laffont-Jupiter, Paris, 1969.

CHOW, K., KRAMER, I., *All the Tea in China,* China Books & Periodicals Inc., San Francisco, 1990.

COLLECTIF, *Dictionnaire archélogique des techniques,* Éditions de l'Accueil, Paris, 1963.

COLLECTIF, *China's Rare Stones,* Shanghaï Chinese Classics Publishing House, 1994.

COLLECTIF, catalogue de l'exposition « La Cité interdite, vie publique et privée des empereurs de Chine », musée du Petit-Palais, Paris Musées, Paris, 1996.

COMENTALE, Christophe, « Les collections d'images populaires de Wang Shucun », in *Arts & Métiers du Livre,* n° 200, 1996.

COMENTALE, Christophe, « L'imagerie du Nouvel An chinois et sa symbolique », in *Bulletin du Vieux Papier,* 1988.

COTTERELL, Arthur, *La Chine des empereurs,* Gallimard, Paris, 1996.

COUVREUR, F.-S., *Mémoires sur les bienséances et les cérémonies,* Les Belles-Lettres, Paris, 1951 (rééd.).

COVELLO, T. Vincent, « The Japanese Art of Stone Appreciation », in *Arts of Asia,* janv.-fév. 1995.

DAUTRESME, François, catalogue de l'exposition « Chine, art de vivre et art de survivre », Fondation J. Miro, Barcelone, 1995.

DE GROOT, J. J. M., *The Religious System of China,* vol. VI, livre II. *Les Fêtes annuellement célébrées à Emoui (Amoy),* Annales du musée Guimet, vol. XI et XII, E. Leroux, Paris.

DICKINSON, Gary, WRIGGLESWORTH, Linda, *Imperial Wardrobe,* Bamboo Publishing, London, 1991.

DOOLITTLE, *Social Life of the Chinese.*

DORE, Henri, P. (S.-J.), *Recherches sur les superstitions en Chine,* 2e partie, « Le Panthéon chinois », Imprimerie de la mission catholique à l'orphelinat de T'ou-Se-We, Shanghaï, 1918.

EBERHARDT, Wolfram, *Lexikon Chinesischer Symbole,* Diederichs, Düsseldorf, 1983.

FAVIER, Alphonse (Mgr), *Péking : histoire et description,* Desclée de Brouwer et Cie, Paris et Lille, 1902.

FRANKEL, J. Eith, « The Scholar's Rock », in *Arts of Asia,* sept.-oct. 1995, Hong Kong.

GARNIER, Édouard, *Histoire de la céramique,* Éditions Alfred Mame et fils, Tours, 1882.

GARRETT, Valery, M., *Chinese Clothing, an Illustrated Guide,* Oxford University Press, Hong Kong, 1994.

GARRETT, Valery, M., *Mandarin Squares, Mandarins and their Insignia,* Oxford University Press, Hong Kong, 1990.

GERNET, J., *Le Monde chinois,* Armand Colin, Paris, 1972.

GOETTE, J., « Jade and Man in Life and Death », in *Tian H'sia,* Pékin, 1936.

GRANET, Marcel, *La Civilisation chinoise, la vie publique et la vie privée,* La Renaissance du Livre, Paris, 1929.

GUIDES BLEUS, *Chine,* Éditions Hachette, Paris, 1989.

GUO, Bonan, *Petit Traité de calligraphie chinoise,* Éditions en langues étrangères, Beijing, 1995.

Historic Chinese Architecture, Tsinghua University Press, Beijing, 1985 (rééd. 1990).

HOBSON, R. L., *The Wares of the Ming Dynasty,* Benn Brothers, Londres, 1923. *The Later Ceramic Wares of China,* Ernest Benn, Ltd, Londres, 1925.

HONEY, William, Bowyer, *The Ceramic Art of China and other Countries of the Far-East,* Faber and Faber Ltd, London, 1944.

INSTITUT RICCI, *Dictionnaire français de la langue chinoise,* Kuangchi Presse, Taipei, Taïwan, 1990.

JENYNS, R. Soame, WATSON, William, *Arts de la Chine : or, argent, bronzes, émaux, laques, bois,* Office du livre, Fribourg et Société française du livre, Paris, 1963.

LANNOM, W. Gloria, « Chinese Birdcages : a New Study Based on the Donegan Collection », in *Arts of Asia,* sept.-oct. 1989.

LAUFER, Berthold, *Chinese Pottery of the Han Dynasty,* E. J. Brill Ltd, Leiden, 1909.

Jade, a Study in Chinese Archaelogy and Religion, Field Museum of Natural History Publications 154, Chicago, 1912.

LIAO, Jingdan (sous la direction de), *5 000 Ans d'art chinois, arts artisanaux : les bronzes* (tome 2), Éditions Vander-Chine, Bruxelles, 1989.

LIU, Jilin, *Chinese Shadow Puppet Plays,* Morning Glory Publishers, Beijing, 1988.

LIU, Zhen, *China Kites,* Shandong Science and Technology Press, Jinan, 1994.

LI, Zhiyan, CHENG, Wen, *La Céramique ,chinoise,* Éditions en langues étrangères, Beijing, 1984.

LOWE, H. Y., *The Adventures of Wu, the Life Cycle of a Peking Man,* The Peking Chronicle Press, Pekin, 1941.

LYNN, J. C. H., *Social Life of the Chinese (in Peking),* China Booksellers Ltd, Peking-Tientsin, 1928.

MOSER, M., MOSER Y. W. C, *Foreigners within the Gates, the Legations at Peking,* Oxford University Press, Hong Kong, 1993.

NEEDHAM, Joseph, *Dialogue des civilisations Chine-Occident : pour une histoire œcuménique des sciences,* Éditions de la Découverte, Paris, 1991.

PAGANI, Catherine, « Late Qing Dynasty Opium Boxes », in *Arts of Asia,* mai-juin 1991, Hong Kong.

PIMPANNEAU, Jacques, *Chine, culture et tradition,* éditions Philippe Picquier, 1988.

QI, Xing, *Les Fêtes traditionnelles chinoises,* Éditions en langues étrangères, Pékin, 1987.

RAPAPORT, Benjamin, *A Complete Guide to Collecting Antique Pipes,* Exton, Pensylvania, 1979.
« The Chinese Opium Pipe : the Art and Beauty of an Evil Custom », in *Arts of Asia,* mars-avr. 1995, Hong Kong.

READ, Bernard, E., *Chinese Materia Medica : Avian Drugs,* Peking natural history bulletin, 1932.

REID, Daniel, P., *Chinese Herbal Medicine,* CFW Publications, Hong Kong, 1987.

SCARBOROUGH, W (Rev.), *A Collection of Chinese Proverbs,* Revised by ALLAN W. C. (Rev.), Prebyterian Mission Press, Shanghaï, 1926.

SCHAFER, Edwaerd, H., *The Golden Peaches of Samarkand,* University of California Press, Berkeley and Los Angeles, 1963.

SCHIPPER, Kristofer, *Le Corps taoïste,* Fayard, Paris, 1982.

SCOTT, J. M., *The White Poppy : History of Opium,* London, 1969.

SHUNYUAN, Jiang et collectif, *Behing the Veil of the Forbidden City,* Panda Books, Chinese Litterature Press, Beijing, 1996.

STANDFORD MUSEUM OF ART, *Opium Pipes, Prints and Paraphernalia,* Standford, California, 1979.

STRONG, Hilda Arthur, *Chinese Arts and Crafts,* Henri Vetch Publisher, the French Bookstore, Peiping, 1933.

SWALLOW, R. W., *Ancient Chinese Bronze Mirrors,* Henri Vetch, Peiping, 1937.

THORP, Robert L., catalogue de l'exposition « Imperial Arts of China », Son of Heaven Press, Seattle, 1988.

TOURNIER, Maurice-Louis, *L'Imaginaire et la symbolique dans la Chine ancienne,* L'Harmattan, Paris, 1991.

TRANS, O. C. S., *Ming and Ch'ing Porcelains : the* nianhao *and Period Identification,* 1935-1936.

THE T.T. Tsui Gallery of Chinese Art, *Chinese Art and Design,* Victoria and Albert Museum, 1991.

VAN GULIK, R. H., *Mi Fu on Ink-Stones,* Henri Vetch, Peking, 1938.

VITOLS, Astrid, *Dictionnaire des lunettes,* Éditions Bonneton, Paris.

WALTERS, Derek, *Feng Shui : Perfect Placing for your Happiness and Prosperity,* Asiapac, Singapour, 1988.

WANG, Dongliang, *Les Signes et les mutations,* L'Asiathèque, 1995.

WANG, Shucun, *Le Papier fétiche : le culte des dieux à travers les estampes folkloriques,* Éditions du Nouveau Monde, Beijing, 1991.

WILLIAMS, C. A. S., *Outlines of Chinese Symbolism and Art Motives,* Ch. E. Tuttle Company, Rutland (Vermont) et Tokyo, 1941 (5e éd., 1981).

WOU, Tchen-Fou, *Chine : l'estampe,* éditions Philippe Picquier, 1990.

YANG, Boda, « Jade emperor Chien Lung's collection in the Palace Museum, Peking », in *Arts of Asia,* mars-avr. 1992, Hong Kong.

ZHANG, Daoyi, *The Art of Chinese Papercuts,* Foreign Languages Press, Beijing, 1989.

Index thématique et index des noms propres

Abaque, 89
Abricot, 57
Achillée, 57
Administration impériale, 159
Amitofo, 78
Amulette, charme, talisman, 35, 152
Aigle, 19, 36
Âne, 25, 79
Anhui, 103, 106, 111, 123, 148
Annales, 23
Anyang, 101, 104
Araignée, 57
Arbre miniature, 70
Arbre *wutong*, 44
Armoise, 57
Attiret, Jean-Denis, 184
Avalokiteçvara, 64, 81

Bacon, Roger, 207
Bai Juyi, 60
Bambou, 19, 58, 59, 189
Bananier, 59
Banian, 59
Beihai, 75, 252
Bijoux, 199
Birmanie, 28, 119
Bœuf, 75
Boucher, Guillaume, 139
Bouddha, 28, 56, 59, 62, 75, 78, 80, 82, 154
Bouddhisme, 28, 34, 63, 64, 81
Boussole, 246
Bouvier et Tisserande, 45
Buffle, 75

Cacahuète, 19
Cadenas, 152
Cage, 164, 167, 224
Caille, 19, 36
Cai Lun, 106
Caishen, 18, 35, 51, 79, 193
Calebasse, voir Gourde
Camélia, 60
Canard, 60
Canton *(Guangzhou)*, 104, 145, 208
Cao Cao, 186
Cao Guojiu, 79
Carpe, 51
Carré de mandarin, 156
Cassius, A., 127
Catalogue des pierres de la forêt des nuages, 70
Catalpa, 64
Céladon, 123
Cent animaux, 94
Cent enfants, 94
Cent objets antiques, 22, 94
Cerf, 17, 18, 26
Cerf-volant, 36, 178
Cerisier, 60
Chan Chun, 50
Champignon de l'immortalité, 18, 26, 60
Chang E ou *Heng E*, 50, 79, 195
Chapeau, 162
Chat, 26
Chauve-souris, 17, 19, 26, 27
Chéloniomancie, 57
Chenghua, 130
Chenghuang, 79
Cheval, 27
Chien, 27, 30
Chien céleste, 28, 88
Chien pékinois, chien de *Fo*, 50, 243
Chinomanthe, 61
Chronique des Printemps et Automnes, 91
Chrysanthème, 61, 66
Chuanggong, 81
Cinq Classiques, 91
Cinq bonheurs, 27
Cinq couleurs, 127
Cinq venimeux, 35, 38, 52, 68, 154
Classique des Montagnes et des Mers, 23, 24, 86
Classique de l'encre, 103
Classique de pierre, 74
Cloisonné, 139
Coiffure, 199
Collier de mandarin, 163
Colombe, 36
Compagnie (anglaise) des Indes, 128, 146, 237
Compagnie (hollandaise) des Indes, 128
Confucius, 29, 45, 56, 59, 68, 77, 78, 82, 116, 118
Conque, 21
Coq, 36, 53
Constantinople, 244
Corbeau, 23, 38
Corée, 119
Corne, 21, 31
Coromandel, 137, 138
Coucou, 59
Crapaud, 50
Criquet, 164

Dais, 21
Dali, 72
Daoguang, 45, 128
David, Armand, 223
Deng Xiaoping, 91
Dianmu, 81
Dictionnaire *Shuowen, Jiezi*, 23, 47
Dictionnaire *Ying Songchao Huiti erya*, 27
Dieux, 25, 27, 36
Dinosaure, 48, 49
Dix troncs célestes, 93
Dizang, 81

Doré, Henri, 78
Douze ornements, 22, 94
Douze rameaux terrestres, 132
Dragon, 35, 46, 47
Du Fu, 70
Du Long, 70
Dunhuang, 199
Dynastie des Han, 47, 60, 75, 104, 109, 110, 112, 116, 118, 137, 214, 215, 228
Dynastie des Jin, 110, 123
Dynastie des Ming, 12, 39, 45, 62, 66, 70, 71, 88, 89, 104, 126, 129, 137, 139, 140, 156, 187
Dynastie des Qin, 109
Dynastie des Qing, 11, 12, 36, 40, 47, 88, 137, 139, 201, 233
Dynastie des Shang, 23, 56, 77, 101, 116, 123, 228
Dynastie des Song, 30, 51, 66, 69, 70, 75, 89, 101, 122, 168, 173, 228, 233
Dynastie des Sui, 123
Dynastie des Tang, 30, 44, 60, 77, 79, 110, 123, 137, 173, 199, 214
Dynastie des Xia, 23, 47, 69, 77
Dynastie des Yuan, 122, 125, 156, 200, 233
Dynastie des Zhou, 23, 38, 56, 69, 118, 123, 135, 215, 243

École *chan,* (japonais, *zen*), 72, 78, 146
Écriture sigillaire, 130
Éléphant, 28
Émail, 139
Encyclopédie *Bai gu tu,* 23
Encyclopédie *Sancai tuhui,* 157
Encyclopédie *Tangtu mingsheng tuhui,* 28
Encyclopédie *Zhujijing,* 166
Entrecolles, François-Xavier d'-, 121, 129
Épée, 21, 79
Erlang, 81
Estampage, 75
Éventail, 21, 79

Faisan, 19, 38, 66
Faîte suprême, limite suprême, 52
Feu d'artifice, 193
Figurine de toit, 184
Flacon de tabac à priser, 9, 30
Flammes, 22, 48
Feuve Bleu ou Yangzi Jiang ou Yang Tsé *(Changjiang),* 43
Fleuve Jaune *(Huang He),* 42, 51
Flûte, 21, 79
Fo, Foye, 81
Frise « tonnerre », 23
Fujian, 31, 62, 77, 81, 105, 111, 114, 130, 135, 145
Fuxi, 47, 54, 56, 69, 90, 248

Galuchat, 210, 212
Galluchat, Jean-Claude, 212
Gansu, 104
Gao Zong, 66
Gao Zu, 244
Gâteau, 50
Géomancie, 217, 245
Gong Gong, 54 ,
Gourde, 17, 21, 66, 79, 167
Grande Muraille, 36, 94
Gravereau, Jean-Baptiste, 142
Grenade, 19, 61
Grèce, 40
Grenouille, 50
Grillon, 36, 164
Grotesque *(taotie),* 35
Grue, 19, 39
Gu Kaizhi, 70
Guan ou *Guanyu* ou *Guandi,* 77, 81, 176
Guangxi, 246
Gangxu, 110, 128
Guanyin, 64, 68, 81, 82, 233
Guerre de l'opium, 147, 237
Guide illustré des accessoires cérémoniaux des Qing, 157

Hache, 23
Hangzhou, 111, 145
Han Xiangzi, 79
He Xiangu, 64, 79, 175
Hebei, 40, 105, 123, 125, 130, 166
Hémérocalle, 62
Henan, 104, 125
Heng E, voir *Chang E*
Heshen, 9
Hexagrammes, 57
Hibou, 40
Hirondelle, 19
Histoire des Han, 89
Hollande, 146
Hou Yi, 50, 79, 195
Hu Jingde, 84
Hua Mulan, 64
Huangdi, 45, 47, 77, 90
Hubei, 135
Huit excentriques, 75
Huit immortels, 17, 21, 61, 74, 78, 154
Huit immortels cachés (taoïstes), 31
Huit interdictions (bouddhistes), 56
Huit mets exquis, 52
Huit objets précieux, 21, 30, 31, 51, 64, 69, 93
Huit signes de bon augure, 51
Huit trigrammes, 24, 57, 93
Huizong, 75, 145
Hunan, 50, 52, 123, 135, 149

Image populaire, 173
Impressions du Collège Impérial, 173
Inde, 44, 60, 179, 208, 237
Inscriptions sur stèle, 74

Jade, jadédite, 116
Japon, 104, 119, 129, 135, 137, 172, 179
Jardin de la Clarté parfaite, 184
Jardin gros comme un grain de moutarde, 65, 70, 164
Jasmin, 62
Jehol (Chengde), 187
Jiajing, 127
Jiangsu, 73, 75, 114, 166
Jiangxi, 104
Jingdezheng, 121

Joyau de faîte, 188
Jujube, 19
Jumeaux *Hehe,* 117

Kaifeng, 75, 145, 184
Kaki, 62
Kangxi, 23, 132, 157, 209
Kaolin, 121
Khotan (Turkestan), 119
Kubilai Khan, 29, 36, 126

Lanterne, 194
Lan Caihe, 79
Laozi ou *Lao Dan,* 18, 78, 82
Laque, 135
Leigong, 81, 82
Li Er, 68
Li Hanzhong, 79
Li Tieguai, 17, 26, 79
Licorne, unicorne, 29
Lièvre, 28
Lion, 29, 95
Lithophone ou phonolithe, 21, 69
Liu (général), 82
Liu Hai, 51, 117, 176
Liulichang, 209
Livre des Cents Familles, 94
Livre de l'Histoire, 22, 91
Livre des Mutations, 24, 82, 90, 91
Livre des Odes, 82, 91
Livre des Rites, 23, 91, 116
Livre de la Voie et de la Vertu, 82, 90, 146
Longwang, 82
Loriot, 40
Losange, 21, 22
Lotus, nénuphar lotus, 19, 21, 36, 61, 62, 64, 66, 79
Lu Ban ou *Gongshu Ban,* 82
Lü Dongbin, 79
Lu Yu, 145
Lunettes et étuis à lunettes, 207
Luoyang, 51, 66
Lushan, 207
Luth, 22

Macao, 146, 204
Macre, 215
Maillechort ou *packfung,* 153, 210
Main de Bouddha (bergamote), 62
Magnolia, 64
Mahjong ou majong, 43
Ma Gu, 26, 182
Malacca, 208
Mandarin, 156
Manjusri, 29
Manufactures impériales, 130
Mao Tsé Toung *(Mao Zedong),* 11, 31, 197
Marques, 129
Marques de règne, 132
Martin-pêcheur, 43, 201
Mazhashen, 17, 84
Melon, 61
Meng Tian, 99
Mi fu ou *Mi Fei,* 75, 99, 186
Mile, 84
Millet, 19, 23
Miroir de bronze, 213
Moineau, 43
Mongolie, 150
Monts Kunlun, 45, 69, 86
Motifs décoratifs *(huawen),* 23
Moxibustion (du japonais *moxa*), 57
Mu, 27
Mûrier, 64

Nankin *(Nanjing),* 72, 184
Narcisse, 60, 64
Nénuphar lotus, 19, 21, 36, 61, 62, 64, 66, 79
Néphrite, 116
Niuwang, 84
Nœud sans fin, 21
Numérologie, 89
Nüwa, 47, 54, 69, 77

Objets symboliques, 19
Oie, 43
Oiseaux, 44, 190
Oiseaux de cage, 219
Opium, 237
Orchidée, 65
Ostéomancie, 57

Pan Fei, 64
Pangu, 77
Panier de fleurs, 21, 79
Paon, 43
Papier, 97, 105
Papier découpé, 228
Papier monnaie, 151
Papillon, 66
Parasol, 21
Pêche, pêcher, 61, 65, 85, 86, 154
Pelliot, Paul, 133, 173
Perle, 21, 48, 163
Pétard, 189
Phénix, 43-45, 66
Pie, 45
Pierre, 69, 72, 73
Pigeon, 36
Pin, 19, 36, 66
Pinceau, 98
Pinceau de fer, 109
Pivoine, 19, 65-67
Poirier, 66
Poisson, 51
Poissons géminés, 21
Polo, Marco, 9, 36, 121, 126
Pommier, 68
Porc, sanglier, 30
Porcelaine, 121
Portes du dragon, 51
Portrait d'ancêtres, 157
Poudre, 189
Prunier, 68

Qianlong, 9, 114, 119, 127, 131, 138, 142, 157
Qi Baishi, 115, 172
Qin Shubao, 84
Qingming, 68, 180
Quatre divertissements élégants, 108
Quatre trésors du lettré, 22, 99
Qufu, 57 , 82
Qu Yuan, 50

Raisin, 19
Rat, 31
Reine Mère d'Occident, *(Xiwangmu),* 24, 45, 50, 65, 79, 223
Renard, 24, 31

Réunion de gens distingués, 108
Révolution des « Cent fleurs », 11, 94
Révolution culturelle, 11
Rhinocéros, 31
Rhombe, 21, 181
Ricci, Matteo, 103, 209
Romains, 9
Roue, 21
Route de la Soie, 207
Royaumes Combattants, 40, 50, 75, 116, 136, 194, 209
Royaume de Zhou, 25
Rubroek, Guillaume de, 139

Sac de Pékin, 11, 140
Saint *luohan*, 82
Sâkyamuni, 28, 29
Saladin, 126
Sang-de-bœuf, 126
Saoqingniang, 84
Sapèque, 22
Saule, 68
Sceau, 109
Sceptre *ruyi*, 60, 86
Sentences parallèles, 174
Serpent, 52
Shaanxi, 29, 52, 84, 123, 130
Shandong, 52, 74, 104, 177, 180
Shanxi, 75, 150
Shanghai, 74, 166, 187
Shennong, 25, 77, 90, 122, 146
Shouxinglao ou *Shoulao*, 17, 18, 25, 66, 79, 85, 154
Shoushan, 114
Shun, 77, 122
Sibérie, 119
Sichuan, 105, 135
Sima Qian, 92
Singe, 23, 31
Société d'épigraphie du Pont Xilin, 112
Songzi, 81
Soutra du Diamant, 173, 222
Spina, Alessandro di -, 207
Stèle, 55, 69
Stumpf, Kilian, 209
Su Dongpo, 101, 106
Suzhou, 73, 74, 111, 119
Sun Wukong, 33, 66, 182
Svastika, 20, 94, 96
Swatow (Shantou), 151
Symboles, 17

Tablettes de cour, 21, 79
Taishan, 74, 84
Taïwan, 68, 86, 119
Taiyue dadi, 84
Tambour de bronze ou de pluie, 50
Tang-le-Victorieux, 77
Tao Yuanming, 61
Taoïsme, taoïste, 18, 21, 27, 34, 40, 44, 51, 56, 59-61, 65, 66, 69, 78, 117, 155, 213, 228
Temple des Lamas, 244
Temple du Ciel, Pékin, 25, 55, 185
Thé, 62, 145
Thé olifère ou thé à l'huile, 149
Théâtre d'ombres chinoises, 232
Tianhu ou *Mazu*, 86
Tianwang, 86
Tigre, 23, 34, 53
Tortue, 19, 54, 82
Tortue mythique, 55
Tortue porte-stèle, 55
Traité du thé, 145
Trois amis, 19, 59
Trois bonheurs, 19, 27
Trois couleurs, 126
Trois étoiles, 84
Trois inventions, 90
Trois Royaumes, 90, 123
Ts'eu Hi *(Cixi)*, 64, 131, 149, 179, 223, 236
Tube de bambou, 21, 25, 79
Tuiles, 185

Vase, 21
Verre, 209
Vêtements, 23, 160
Vietnam, 28, 181
Voyage en Occident, 30, 32, 34, 66

Weifang, 180
Wenchang, 86
Wu Zetian, 66, 131

Xi'an ou *Chang'An*, 66, 74, 233
Xiwangmu, voir Reine Mère d'Occident
Xu Chen, 23
Xuanzang, 34, 51
Xuantong (Pu Yi), 202
Xuanzong, 43, 123, 149, 194, 223

Yanjing, 40
Yang guifei, 43, 149, 223
Yanlo, 87
Yangzhou, 74, 75, 119
Yao, 77
Yixing, 104, 106, 145, 150
Yongzheng, 122, 127, 142
Yu-le-Grand, 52, 69, 77
Yuhuang, 87
Yunnan, 31, 34, 65, 72

Zaojun ou *Zaoshen* (dieu du Foyer), 87, 193
Zhang (immortel), 28, 88
Zhang Guolao, 25, 79
Zejiang, 105, 111, 114, 123, 130, 148, 166
Zheng Banqiao, 75
Zheng He, 246
Zhong Kui, 27, 53, 85, 88, 176
Zhuge Liang, 49

CRÉDITS PHOTOGRAPHIQUES

Photographie de couverture et de 4e de couverture par Patrizzia Bonanzinga. Calligraphies en ouverture de chaque chapitre par Xu Guanghua.

—

MARIT E. NIEUWLAND
Photographies pages 6 (peinture, assemblée de notables), 10, 11, 15, 16, 18 en haut et au milieu, 19 en bas, 20, 24, 30 en haut et en bas, 31 en haut et en bas, 34, 35, 37 en haut, 39, 41, 46, 48, 49, 50 en haut et en bas, 55 en haut et en bas, 58, 63, 66 au milieu, 74 en haut et en bas, 76, 79, 80, 81 en haut et en bas, 83, 86, 95, 100, 101, 104, 105, 106, 107 à gauche, au milieu et à droite, 114, 143, 148, 149, 150 en haut, 150 en bas, 153 en haut, 154 en bas, 157 en haut, 160, 161, 162, 165 en haut et en bas, 167 en haut et en bas, 172, 175, 176 en haut et en bas, 179 en haut et en bas, 182, 183, 184, 186, 187 en haut, au milieu et en bas, 188 en haut, au milieu et en bas, 196, 197 en haut, 199, 203, 204, 206, 207, 208 en haut et en bas, 209 en haut et en bas, 210, 211, 216 en haut et en bas, 220, 221, 222 en haut et en bas, 223, 224, 225, 226, 235, 236, 240, 244 en haut et en bas, 251, 253, 254.

MICHEL CULAS
Photographies pages 19 en haut, 47, 50 au milieu, 66 en haut, 85 à gauche, au milieu et à droite, 94, 102, 110, 111, 136, 145, 150 au milieu, 239.

AGENCE RAPHO, ROLAND MICHAUD
Photographies pages 42, 44, 74 (3e en partant du haut), 81 au milieu, 87, 90, 97, 144, 151, 153 en bas, 158, 170, 180, 185, 193, 194, 197 en bas, 200, 201, 216 au milieu, 219, 233 en haut et en bas, 237, 238, 241, 242, 243, 252.

PATRIZZIA BONANZINGA
Photographies pages 98, 154 en haut, 179 au milieu, 233 au milieu, 262.

CHINA GUARDIAN, BEIJING, CHINA
Photographies pages 26, 45, 52, 60, 61, 115 à 127, 130 au milieu, 166, 167 au milieu (d. r.).

Page 12, photographie de Liu Zhigang, © musée du Gugong, Pékin ; page 74 (seconde en partant du haut), photographie galerie Blue Moon Jade, États-Unis ; pages 129, 130 en haut et en bas, 137 en bas, photographies d'après Arts of Asia *; pages 137 en haut, 215 au milieu, Eskenazi, Londres ; pages 138, 140 en bas, URS Frech, Zurich ; pages 140 en haut, 141, Spink, Londres ; page 193, coll. du Palais Impérial ; page 205, Horstmann & Godfrey, Hong Kong, page 214 au milieu, galerie Samuk, San Francisco.*

—

Les reproductions en noir et blanc, les images populaires, les papiers découpés... ont été réalisés d'après des documents fournis par l'auteur. La carte de Chine pages 260-261 a été réalisée par Éditerra, Paris, XIIIe.

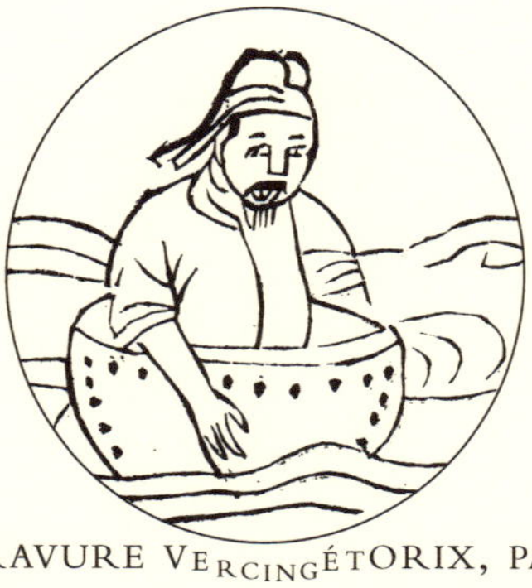

PHOTOGRAVURE VERCINGÉTORIX, PARIS XIVe
ACHEVÉ D'IMPRIMER EN AVRIL 1997
SUR LES PRESSES DE L'IMPRIMERIE
CANALE, TURIN, SUR
DU CENTAURE
IVOIRE

洗

寸後旁一寸

勺

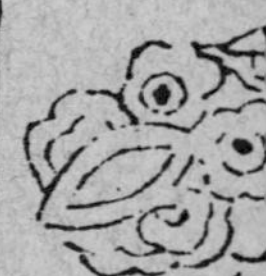

升爲龍頭

豆

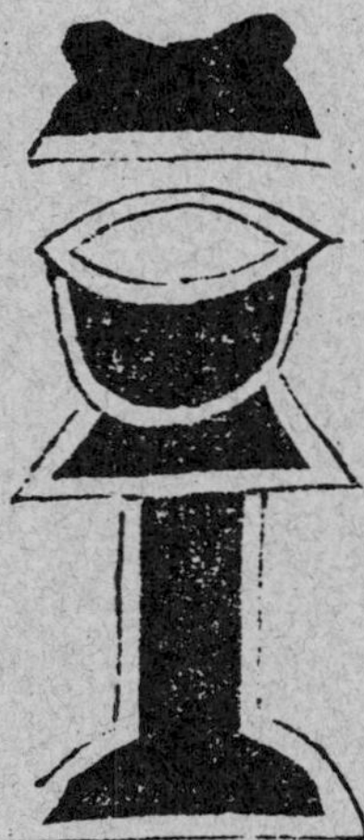

豆高尺二
寸漆赤中
畫飾不同

洗

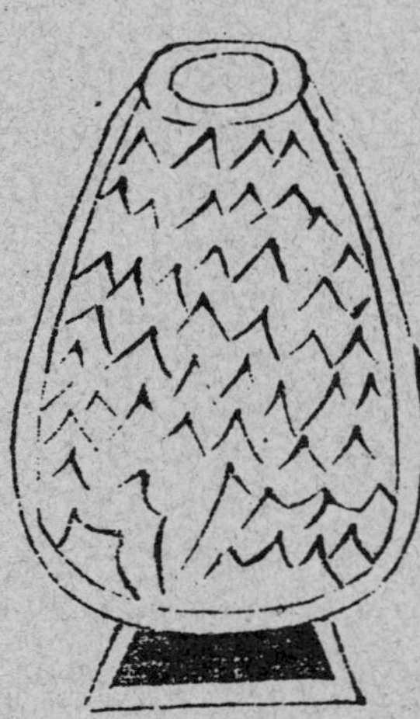

洗高三尺口
徑一尺五寸
足徑三尺

壺

酒壺受一
斛口徑尺
足高二寸
徑尺反爵
著壺漆赤
中有畫飾

罋

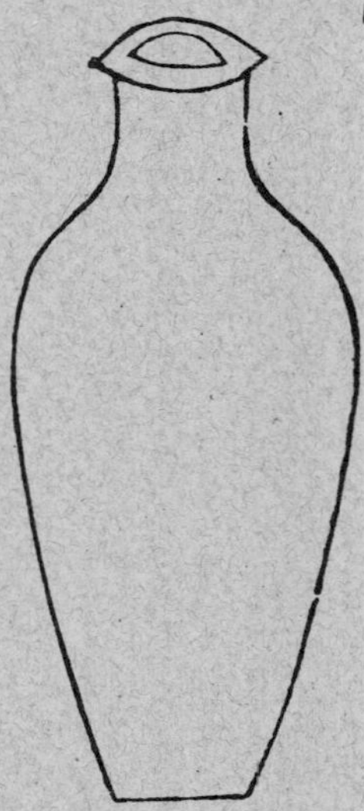

罋盛醯醢
高一尺受
三斗醯人
云王舉供
醯五十罋
醢五十罋

筐

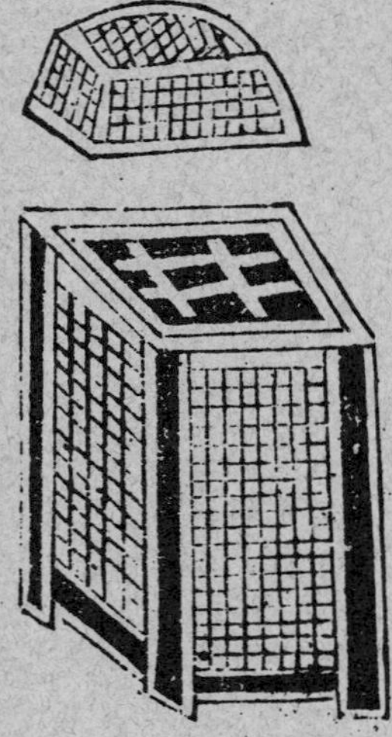

筐以竹爲之
長三尺廣一
尺深六寸足
高三寸

筥

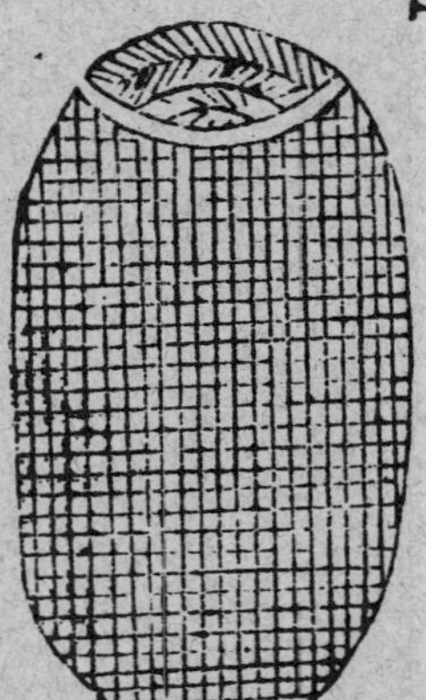

圓曰筥受
半斛主君
致饔餼於
賓與大夫
上介皆以
筥盛米